The Oxford History
of New Zealand
Second Edition

The Oxford History of New Zealand

Second Edition

Edited by

Geoffrey W. Rice

First edition edited by
W. H. Oliver with B. R. Williams

Auckland

OXFORD UNIVERSITY PRESS

Melbourne   Oxford   New York

OXFORD UNIVERSITY PRESS

Oxford   New York
Athens   Auckland   Bangkok   Bombay
Calcutta   Cape Town   Dar es Salaam   Delhi
Florence   Hong Kong   Istanbul   Karachi
Kuala Lumpur   Madras   Madrid   Melbourne
Mexico City   Nairobi   Paris   Port Moresby
Singapore   Taipei   Toronto
and associated companies in
Berlin   Ibadan

Oxford is a trade mark of Oxford University Press

National Library of New Zealand
Cataloguing-in-Publication data

The Oxford history of New Zealand. 2nd ed. / edited by Geoffrey W.
Rice. Auckland, N.Z. : Oxford University Press, 1992.
    1 v.
    First ed. / edited by W. H. Oliver; with B. R. Williams, Oxford:
Clarendon Press; Wellington [N.Z.] : Oxford University Press, 1981.
    Includes bibliographical references and index.
    ISBN 0–19–558257–8
    1. New Zealand—History. I. Rice, Geoffrey. II. Oliver, W. H.
(William Hosking), 1925– III. Williams, B. R. (Bridget R.)
    993

Cover designed by Nikolas Andrew
Typeset in Bembo by Egan-Reid Ltd
Printed through Bookpac Production Services, Singapore
Published by Oxford University Press
540 Great South Road, Greenlane
Auckland 5, New Zealand

Contents

Part One: Beginnings

Part Two: Growth and Conflict

Part Three: A Time of Transition

Part Four: Precarious Maturity

TABLES

MAPS

GRAPHS

Preface to the Second Edition

Since its publication in 1981, *The Oxford History of New Zealand* has become the standard textbook for undergraduate courses in New Zealand history in the universities, and though it was not originally intended for schools it is also widely used in senior history classes. It is now regarded as an indispensable reference work for anyone embarking upon research into New Zealand's past.

This revised and expanded second edition retains much of the first edition's content, but with some significant additions and updating. It is not 'The *New* Oxford History of New Zealand': that task awaits a younger generation of historians, and a different editor. Readers should recognize this edition as the same tree a decade on, still vigorous and handsome, with new fruits and foliage on several of the old branches, but with a cluster of entirely new branches and an extended rootstock.

Why do publishers embark on revised editions of standard textbooks? One obvious commercial reason, that of keeping abreast of competitors in the marketplace, does not really apply in this case, for there is (as yet) no comparable rival textbook. Sometimes a new edition is necessary to amend defects or omissions in the first edition, but the primary motive is surely to keep the work up to date with the latest scholarship in the field, and to cover more recent developments. As with most human endeavours, a mixture of motives prompted this revision. One contributor expressed surprise that a new edition should be contemplated so soon after the first, but most contributors shared the publisher's concern that some sections were already becoming outdated, and that the rapid pace of economic and social change in New Zealand during the 1980s demanded an extension of coverage.

Bill Oliver and Bridget Williams formed a remarkable partnership as editor and publisher of the first edition, and though both have gone on to greater things, they are entitled to look back with some satisfaction on 'this risky venture' which has become such a landmark in New Zealand historiography. Their hard work is still recognized on the title page. Editing this revised and expanded second edition has been a much easier task than theirs, but not without its own difficulties and frustrations. It has certainly taken far longer than any of us anticipated. The decision to invite a new editor who was not one of the original contributors was intended to avoid dissension, but it did not please one or two contributors, who may also have harboured doubts about the new editor's credentials as a latecomer to research in New Zealand social history. The proof of the pudding, as always, is in the eating, but critics should be aware that this revision has proceeded under a number of practical constraints, and the end result is not quite what was originally envisaged. As with politics, publishing is also the art of the possible.

All reviewers found something to criticize about the first edition, from simple factual errors (which were remarkably few) to more profound disagreements over approach and methodology. (The most significant group of reviews appeared in *The New Zealand Journal of History*, vol. 16, no. 1, April 1982, pp. 68-76.) Most contributors have taken this opportunity to make changes where they seemed warranted. Yet it is unlikely that any academic reviewer will approve of this revised edition, which is the outcome of a number of compromises between aims and circumstances. For some, the second edition will simply add more scope for criticism to the faults of the first. In such a large collaborative work as this it is inevitable that there will be some unevenness between chapters produced by different minds with different styles, but there is now an obvious imbalance which is the result of deliberate editorial policy: Part IV has been greatly expanded, with what some reviewers may see as excessive attention to the decade of the 1980s. This is because we believe that this turbulent decade is the one which most general readers will be most anxious to understand. As one contributor notes, using a geological or meteorological analogy, New Zealand society has just experienced a 'once in fifty or a hundred years' cataclysm. Historians are apt to be cautious creatures, preferring the dust to settle on recent events before venturing their carefully considered judgements, and the next decade will almost certainly alter our view of the 1980s, but we thought it essential that the new edition be as up to date as possible in its coverage, and provide an account of important recent events.

Some critics of the first edition complained that the chapters were too long to read comfortably at a single sitting. Students who have grown up in the era of videos and the personal computer revolution sometimes complain that they find the *Oxford History* 'heavy going', or 'too academic'. They may be relieved to find that most of the new chapters are significantly shorter than those of the first edition. The new editor also favoured the introduction of sub-headings, to make the work more convenient and accessible for students, but when it was pointed out how much this would add to the cost and length of a book which was already very large and about to be expanded by six new chapters, this idea had to be abandoned. The *Oxford History* remains, therefore, a challenging work which makes heavy demands of its readers. But for the student asking serious questions about our past, it offers a wealth of information and an abundance of analysis and explanation. The statistical tables have been updated by Gary Hawke, and students should note that Graph 5 has been corrected: the first edition omitted to show any exports to Australia in 1881 and 1891. Map 2 showing Māori tribal locations has also been refined with the help of maps used by the Waitangi Tribunal.

All of the first edition contributors were invited to revise and update their chapters, and only a few declined, citing other commitments or personal circumstances. Some of these, however, later produced revisions when it became apparent that the project could not meet its original 1990 deadline. Sadly, others who had promised extensive revisions then found that altered circumstances prevented their involvement. It was no easy task to keep such a large team of busy academic historians in harness over several years: illness, sabbatical leave, conference papers, and the demands of other publishers kept getting in the way, requiring further extensions of deadlines. This is an appropriate place to pay tribute to the patience of those contributors who revised promptly, and then had to wait for all the other pieces of the jigsaw puzzle to slot into place. It is also an appropriate place to recognize the skills and determination of Oxford University Press's New Zealand publisher, Anne French, to whom much credit is due for bringing this revision finally to press.

By far the most significant development in New Zealand historiography since 1981 has been the remarkable expansion of writing on Māori history, which will be evident from a comparison of the bibliographies of the first and present editions. Partly this was the product of a decade which some observers have called a 'Māori Renaissance'; but increased public interest in race relations was also fuelled in part by anxiety over the outcome of claims before the Waitangi Tribunal, after its jurisdiction had been extended back to 1840. Whatever the reasons for their popularity, academic historians were pleasantly surprised to see some of their sober scholarly works become best-sellers during the 1980s. James Belich's *The New Zealand Wars and the Victorian Interpretation of Racial Conflict* (1986) and Claudia Orange's *The Treaty of Waitangi* (1987) were both prize-winning books which remained on the non-fiction best-seller lists for many months. Indeed, publishers were quick to see a market for books about the Treaty and the Tribunal, causing some authors to joke (half-seriously) about the extraordinary demands of this 'Waitangi industry'. With so much about the Treaty appearing in print, the necessity to include it in this second edition tended to diminish, especially as a higher priority had already been given to covering the momentous changes of the 1980s. Thus there is not as much as some readers might expect to find in this edition about the Treaty of Waitangi, or the variously named New Zealand Wars/Māori Wars/Land Wars of the 1860s. They tended to fall between chapters in the first edition, and regrettably still do so, as the contributors most directly concerned were among those unable to revise for this edition.

Much new scholarship in Māori history has been generated by the work of the Waitangi Tribunal: evidence in support of the Ngāi Tahu claim, for example, fills several metres of library shelf space. The 1980s also saw a new generation of Māori graduates emerging from the universities, often with theses or research essays based on tribal histories or oral sources. Unfortunately, not many of these were historians, and most were recruited by government departments anxious to improve their bicultural awareness, so few have continued with postgraduate research. There are still scarcely any Māori graduates with doctorates in Māori history. Much of the recent work on Māori tribal history remains as yet unpublished, and is by its very nature highly complex and localized.

It was thought desirable from the outset of this revision to include new chapters on Māori history, if possible by Māori contributors, but the search for new writers proved long and difficult. All of the most suitable scholars were too heavily committed to existing projects. Ironically, one who agreed to contribute an introductory chapter explaining the concepts and canons of Māori history had to withdraw at a late stage because of the urgent demands of a claim being heard by the Waitangi Tribunal. By then, another contributor on the Māori side had also withdrawn. Fortunately, Ranginui Walker delivered his new chapter on Māori people since 1950 very promptly. That still left an unsatisfactory imbalance in the first half of the book, but at this point, despite heavy personal and professional obligations, Ann Parsonson agreed to replace her original chapter, 'The Pursuit of Mana', with an entirely new chapter which would reflect some of the new evidence and perspectives engendered by theses, tribal histories, and claims before the Waitangi Tribunal. Her chapter should be required reading for any New Zealanders who still profess puzzlement at the depth of Māori feeling about loss of lands or fisheries.

With the exception of Ann Parsonson's new chapter, no radical changes have been made to the first two parts of the book, apart from occasional new paragraphs incorporating recent work, and updated notes and bibliographies. Most of the chapters in Part III have weathered the last decade remarkably well, and only minor changes will be noticed here, apart from the new sections which Erik Olssen and Peter Gibbons have added to their chapters. One common criticism of the first edition was its virtual neglect of external relations. Contributors were encouraged to incorporate this theme where possible, but not all did so, and there was no connected summary standing alone for easy reference. This gap has been filled by David McIntyre's two new chapters, the first of which now concludes Part III.

One of the most controversial new books to appear on nineteenth century New Zealand history during the 1980s was Miles Fairburn's *The Ideal Society and its Enemies* (1989), which explicitly challenged the interpretations offered by several of the contributors to the *The Oxford History of New Zealand*. This revision offered an obvious opportunity for them to respond to Fairburn's criticisms, but not all were in a position to make further revisions at this late stage and it was finally decided to leave these chapters as they were, rather than bewilder students who had not already read Fairburn. (A special issue of *The New Zealand Journal of History*, vol. 25, no. 1, October 1991, was devoted to discussion of Fairburn's book.)

Part IV has been significantly altered and expanded, with the addition of no fewer than five new chapters. Gary Hawke has greatly expanded his chapter, to cover the 1980s, and its changed balance is reflected in the new title. Alan McRobie picks up from the end of Robert Chapman's largely unaltered chapter to narrate political developments from 1972 to 1991, while the editor has added an account of social policy to Graeme Dunstall's chapter on the social pattern. Ranginui Walker discusses Māori people since 1950, and David McIntyre's second chapter describes external relations into the 1980s. Bill Oliver's chapter remains unaltered, because his work as general editor for the first volume of the *Dictionary of New Zealand Biography* prevented him from conducting any detailed research on cultural developments in the 1980s; instead, Peter Simpson has contributed a new chapter which surveys contemporary New Zealand literature and the visual arts.

New Zealand's 1990 celebrations of the sesquicentennial of the signing of the Treaty of Waitangi spawned a plethora of local and general histories of New Zealand, many of which were lavishly illustrated with hitherto little-known paintings and photographs. Some of the illustrated general histories were excellent and stimulating (in which we must of course include *The Oxford Illustrated History of New Zealand*, edited by Keith Sinclair), but others, written primarily for general or school markets, were less satisfactory. Undergraduate students may need to be reminded that illustrated histories are simply not in the same league as *The Oxford History of New Zealand.*. However instructive and up to date they may seem, they cannot hope to match the level of detail and scholarly analysis of the present volume. Time alone will tell, but it may be some while before an equally authoritative and comprehensive textbook of New Zealand history appears; unless of course some unexpected upheaval in New Zealand historiography demands an entirely new 'root and branch' revision. Even then, it should not surprise anyone to find that some of the panels, if not the timbers of the new edifice, have been milled from the stout branches of this edition.

Geoffrey W. Rice
October 1992

Introduction to the First Edition

New Zealand has had many general histories; they have appeared regularly over the past century, and the writing of history goes back to the beginning of British colonization. For the last twenty years, readers have depended upon books which were shaped by the condition of thinking and research in the 1950s. Since then, the self-awareness of New Zealanders has been deepened by a rapid pace of social change, a quickening of intellectual activity, and a pervasive sense of concern. All this has brought about a sharp increase in the quality and quantity of social investigation, including historical enquiry. Some of this research has been brought to a steadily growing audience by a few energetic publishers and by *The New Zealand Journal of History*. Nevertheless, much remains unpublished, especially the results of postgraduate study. This book provides an up-to-date report on the state of New Zealand historical research: it distils what has been achieved; it reveals the considerable lacunae that remain.

The Oxford History of New Zealand brings together, in a book designed as a unified history of the country, the work of several writers, drawn from the body of researchers who have transformed the discipline over the last two decades. As such, it does not attempt to present a single personal vision of the New Zealand past; however, the great advantage of a 'work by several hands' lies in its ability to call upon the special capacities of a range of writers. The book's unity derives from its initial design, from its structure, and from contact and co-operation between contributors as they wrote.

The structure combines a broad chronological shape with a detailed thematic analysis. Each of the four parts covers a period; within the three later parts, each period is explored through a series of themes. Part I, 'Beginnings', covers the longest period of time, but one for which neither the amount nor the nature of the material permits (in a general work) a thematic approach. Its two chapters end about 1840. Part II, 'Growth and Conflict', covers the next half-century; Part III, 'A Time of Transition', starts in the 1890s; Part IV, 'Precarious Maturity', opens with the Second World War and closes with the 1970s. These periods identify significant turning points; the beginnings of British colonization in the 1840s; the new directions exemplified by Liberal reconstruction in the 1890s; the social impact of the Second World War; the signs of the end of an era which appeared in the 1970s. But while such divisions are useful, they do not deny the underlying continuity in New Zealand's history.

A thematic organization within the parts cannot preclude the appearance of an event, a character, or a movement in more than one place. Political, economic, social, and cultural history, Māori and Pākehā history, intersect. Such major matters as colonization, wars, economic development, land settlement, industrial conflict, class and stratification, party organization, social welfare, government policy recur from chapter to chapter. The reader is presented with many viewpoints and encouraged to explore a variety of interpretations. Often discussions of the one topic are widely separated; the index should be used to bring them together.

In its basic character, this book is a social history. The analysis of social systems, of the relationship of classes and groups, of stratification, mobility, consensus, and conflict, is to be found here, as well as social history of a more qualitative kind, chiefly devoted to taste, leisure, culture, and habits of social interaction. But in addition a broader principle pervades the book: the principle that a society reveals itself in those activities commonly classified as political, economic, technological, intellectual, and artistic. Politics, in this light, expresses social aspirations, conflicts, and accommodations; economic events reveal the condition of a society as they shape its development; technology extends the goals of a society but imposes its own limitations; ideas and art articulate the preoccupations, the fears, and the hopes that otherwise remain obscurely expressed.

In a social history of New Zealand, the development of Māori society and race relations must figure prominently. Māori history and interaction between the two major ethnic communities are treated distinctly in Parts II and III — roughly, over the period extending from British annexation to the onset of Māori urbanization and the enforced proximity of Māori and Pākehā. In Parts I and IV Māori history and race relations are integrated into a general account of each period. From Cook's discovery in 1769 to colonization in the 1840s, the two groups lived together, harmoniously for the most part, in a country inhabited largely by Māori tribes. Since the 1940s they have again been in close contact, under radically different circumstances, in a society predominantly Pākehā, in a capitalist economy, as neighbours in the towns and cities of a highly urbanized society.

Histories are shaped by the times in which they are written. Just as a deeper interest in Māori history indicates the current resurgence of Māori in New Zealand life, so the emphasis placed upon the total life of a society is characteristic of the decade just completed, a decade marked by social diversity, anxiety, and enquiry. At its close, no one could have written New Zealand's history with the collectivist optimism of William Pember Reeves, the individualist assurance of J. B. Condliffe, or the radical expectancy of J. C. Beaglehole. They wrote general histories which can now be seen to express something of the years in which they lived. *The Oxford History*, in its turn, shows something of the mood, the tone, and the style of an inwardly turned decade, a time of introspection and of questioning about the course of social change, and of impatience with traditional answers.

This shift of interest has led to a reduction in the attention paid to external affairs — an aspect of New Zealand life that has been thoroughly explored elsewhere. There is more here on industrial than international relations, and more on welfare at home than warfare abroad. The presence of powerful friends and enemies is not neglected, but the question of 'New

Zealand in the world' is treated more broadly. There is a constant awareness of the context of New Zealand history, and of the way in which an understanding of related societies may define its character. Further, the influences that have helped to form New Zealand are seen to be economic, social, and cultural as well as political. Development is an interchange between these complex pressures and the locality. Earlier general surveys, often commissioned by a publisher in another country, paid more heed to the influences that flowed in upon New Zealand and less to the shapes that were forged in their new habitat.

These new shapes have never been so evident, nor developed with so much assurance, as they have in post-war New Zealand. By the 1970s, intellectual confidence had grown beyond the problems of dependence and identity to a more profitable curiosity about the nature of society, its activities, its achievements, its failures, and its inadequacies. Attention has turned towards basic social questions — to the evolution of both Māori and Pākehā society, their unity and their separateness; to the position of women and the role of the family; to the self-awareness of groups and the conflict of opinion; to the growth of literature, scholarship, and the arts. The same spirit has been at work in other disciplines — archaeology, anthropology, sociology, geography, demography — and, perhaps especially, among novelists, painters, poets, composers, and journalists. Today, historians are more than ever aware that they belong to a community of people who have looked to the past for answers to the questions suggested by the present. This book is the result not simply of the awakening of academic history, but of a much more widespread quickening of a society's historical sense.

W. H. Oliver
February 1981

ACKNOWLEDGEMENTS

The following provided various forms of practical assistance without which the book could not have been completed: Peter Alcock, Graham Bagnall (and his library), William Broughton, Jennifer Butcher, Glenis Foster, Margaretha Gee, Michael Hoare, Ilse Jacoby, Hugh Kawharu, Lucy Marsden, Heather Read, Margaret Tennant.

While many libraries were used by contributors in the course of their work, thanks are due specifically to Alexander Turnbull Library, Auckland Institute and Museum, Auckland Public Library, Hocken Library (University of Otago), National Archives, the Bett Collection of the Nelson Provincial Museum, and Taranaki Museum for permission to quote from material in their possession.

W. H. O.

The cover illustration was taken from a 1937 painting 'Lyttelton From the Bridle Path' by Sydney Lough Thompson, which is in the collection of the Robert McDougall Art Gallery, Christchurch. It is here reproduced with the permission of the gallery and the copyright holder, Mme Annette Thompson, Concarneau, France.

Maps were drawn by the staff of the Cartography Laboratory, Massey University, with the exception of the Māori tribal maps, which were prepared in the Department of Geography, University of Canterbury. Tables 1–4 were derived from the doctoral thesis of Campbell Gibson. We are particularly indebted to Gary Hawke for the graphs and the new Statistical Appendix.

Apart from the acknowledgements made by individual contributors, the editor is grateful for advice and assistance received from Judith Binney, Linda Bryder, Jim Gardner, Peter Gibbons, Lindsay Head, Hugh Kawharu, Michael King, David McIntyre, Bill Oliver, Erik Olssen, Tipene O'Regan, Ann Parsonson, Eric Pawson, Judy Robertson, Pauline Wedlake, and John Wilson.

Simon Cauchi prepared the index, and the enormous task of copy-editing was entrusted to Anne Russell. As the whole book had to be reset, a great deal of checking and re-checking was required. The general editor takes full responsibility for any surviving errors.

G. W. R.

Notes

MĀORI USAGE

Many Māori words and phrases have become part of everyday New Zealand speech, and in this book the convention has been extended to the use, as primary terms, of Māori words and phrases to identify major activities, ideas, and institutions.

Translations of Māori terms are given sparingly in parenthesis in the text; more frequently-used words are listed in the glossary on p. 586. Readers should note, however, that the meanings of many words and phrases in Māori depend upon their context, and that the English translations given here are not always exact, nor the only possible meanings for a given word.

The Māori plural does not add the letter s. Unlike the first edition of this book, the second edition employs the Māori plural for Māori and Pākehā throughout. This was part of a policy which aimed at including macrons (the mark denoting a long vowel) for all Māori words. Tribal names have all received macrons. Māori personal names presented more difficulties. Though agreed pronunciations for many names have been established by the Māori Language Commission, and some now appear in print (for example, in the Māori language volumes of *The Dictionary of New Zealand Biography*), not all could be verified in time for this edition, and the decision was made at a late stage to retain macrons only for tribal names, but not to use them for personal or place names. The result is a regrettable lack of consistency, and falls far short of the ideal, but reflects a stage in the modern development of the language's written form which is not yet complete.

Māori personal names have been indexed under the first word of their traditional form (for example, Te Kani Te Ua) or under the last word where the form appears to be anglicized (for example, Tamihana, Wiremu).

MEASUREMENT

Units of distance, weight, area, and money are given in the form that arises from the sources. Many imperial forms of measurement are conventional terms, such as the 'forty-acre' block; others defy comparison with metric equivalents. Where two forms of measurement are in use, as in comparisons between archaeological evidence and contemporary observations, equivalents are given in parenthesis.

REFERENCES

When a numbered reference indicates an item listed in the bibliography, on the first occasion the author's name and the title are given in full and on subsequent occurrences only the author's last name and a short title. When a reference does not occur in the bibliography, full particulars are given on the first occurrence, and an abbreviated form is used subsequently. With manuscript and archival references, the location is stated only on the first occurrence. With official papers, especially those published in the *Appendices to the Journals of the House of Representatives,* the title is not given unless it is in itself of some significance. Statistical information derived directly from the *Official Yearbooks* and the *Censuses* is not usually referenced. In many instances, a paragraph of the text combines quotations and information from a number of sources; these are normally listed sequentially in a reference to the paragraph as a whole. In other cases a series of paragraphs is derived from a wide range of sources; this is noted in the relevant reference. Often the references list sources which will give further information and discussion; this does not necessarily imply that the writers thus cited support the opinions expressed in the text.

SELECT BIBLIOGRAPHIES

Taken together, the bibliographies do not constitute a comprehensive bibliography of New Zealand history. No such work yet exists. There is a great deal of historical material in the *New Zealand National Bibliography to the Year 1960* (ed. A. G. Bagnall, 1969), in the annual *Index to New Zealand Periodicals* (1940–) which also includes an annual bibliography of books for the years 1961 to 1965, and in the annual *New Zealand National Bibliography* (1966–). To go beyond these aids, the reader should consult the reference staff of the larger libraries.

Each of the bibliographies relates to a specific chapter, and is intended to provide a guide to further reading. Duplicate entries have been kept to a minimum, therefore the bibliographies should be used in conjunction with each other, especially in the case of closely related chapters. The entries are of three kinds: books, articles from journals and symposia, and unpublished theses, dissertations, and research essays. A variety of titles exists for this third category: here 'thesis' is used to designate a work submitted for a Master's or a Doctor's degree, and 'research essay' to describe one presented as part of a Bachelor's degree, (and, in a few cases, as a part of a Master's degree less weighty than a thesis). Further bibliographical information is available in the references, which include a full description of items not included in the bibliographies — first, books, articles, theses, and essays not of central importance to a specific chapter; secondly, many official publications, especially the *New Zealand Parliamentary Debates* and the *Appendices to the Journals of the House of Representatives*; thirdly, manuscript and archival material; and fourthly, unpublished sources (such as research papers) not generally available in libraries or through the library interloan service. Many early accounts of life in New Zealand, and many earlier standard historical works, have become available in facsimile editions. When these are listed, publication details relating to the reprint follow those of the edition used.

STATISTICS

The statistical information given in this book is, to a considerable extent, derived from the series of censuses beginning in 1851, and held at regular quinquennial intervals since 1881 (with the exception of the years 1931 and 1941). The nature of that information, especially of a demographic kind, is shaped by the values and interests of contemporary statisticians. Until 1926 information on the Māori population was collected and presented in a different and less informative manner from that on the 'European' population. As Māori were not included in the 'standard' (or 'European') population, the convention has developed of analysing the New Zealand population in the nineteenth and early twentieth centuries under two major categories, 'European' and 'Māori'. Both groups contain unknowable numbers of people of mixed descent. Further, the population conventionally designated 'European' includes a small number of Asians, notably Chinese, and other groups. Their numbers cannot consistently be taken into account; they are not, however, large enough to affect the overall accuracy of the information given. The demographic information in Chapters 5 and 10 thus relates to the 'European' (that is, non-Māori) population. The separate Māori sections of the censuses are used in Chapters 6 and 11. For the period since the Second World War, Chapter 17 reflects the altered habits of the statisticians in presenting information which relates primarily to the total population, and where relevant to its 'Māori' component.

TABLES, MAPS, AND GRAPHS

The graphs and maps (except one) are to be used in connection with many parts of the book, and are collected together on pp. 588-604. The tables, like the maps and graphs, are numbered consecutively, but are included in the chapters to which they refer.

The maps serve a location function only: for further information the reader should turn to *A Descriptive Atlas of New Zealand* (ed. A. H. McClintock, 1959), to the *New Zealand Atlas* (ed. I. McL. Wards, 1976), and to *New Zealand in Maps* (ed. Grant Anderson, 1977). Regrettably, there is as yet no historical atlas of New Zealand. Nor is there a general collection of New Zealand historical statistics. However, a large number of tables is printed in M. F. Lloyd Prichard, *An Economic History of New Zealand to 1939* (1970).

Log graphs such as Graphs 1 and 7 are designed to indicate rates of growth. In a log graph, a rise from 6 to 9 and from 9 to 13 ½, being an increase by 50 per cent in each case, will be shown as equal vertical movements. A constant rate of growth therefore appears on a log graph as a straight line, the slope of the line increasing with the rate of growth. This can be seen in the keys to Graph 1 and Graph 7 and the graphs should be read with the keys rather than by the numbers on the vertical axis.

PART I

Beginnings

CHAPTER 1

The Polynesian Foundation

Janet M. Davidson

The discoverers and first colonists of New Zealand were Polynesian people. Their voyages in the southern and eastern Pacific were among the last of a long series of explorations originating far to the west and eventually reaching some of the most remote and isolated islands of the globe. In New Zealand, these voyagers found a land unlike any their ancestors had known in the tropical Pacific — far larger than the small islands of central Polynesia, temperate rather than tropical, and diverse in the range of environments it offered to human pioneers. The study of Māori society before AD 1769 is largely the study of the adaptation of a group of Polynesians to this new land in which they found themselves.

This society had much in common with other Polynesian societies. The people lived by hunting and fishing, gardening, and the gathering of plant foods. Social organization was based on kinship. Rank depended on descent from significant ancestors, usually but not always in the male line, and the tracing of genealogies was very important. Like other Polynesians, the Māori people were aggressive and war-like; the prowess of the warrior was admired and valued. Concepts such as mana and tapu which pervaded Māori life were also known throughout Polynesia.

Yet the New Zealand society developed its own variations on the basic Polynesian themes. Gardening practice and techniques of hunting and fishing were considerably modified in response to the colder climate. Settlement patterns and other aspects of culture changed as a result of the shift from small islands with limited resources to large islands with more varied resources. The isolation of New Zealand fostered new fashions in artefacts and art styles.

The size of the country and its diversity meant that the society also showed marked diversity from region to region throughout prehistory. This was particularly true of the economy, but other aspects of Māori life were also affected. Thus contemporary communities in the northern North Island and southern South Island were probably less alike than were communities living in one area 500 years apart.

In discussing the society of pre-European New Zealand, several lines of evidence can be brought together. For the earlier periods, archaeology provides the main source of information. This in turn draws on the results of other scientific disciplines to reconstruct the environmental setting of prehistoric life, to determine the age of former occupation sites, to identify the sources of prehistoric tools, and to describe the people themselves. Understanding of the more recent prehistoric past is greatly enriched by Maori oral tradition and the writings and drawings of the earliest European visitors. Each kind of evidence has its limitations as well as its strengths. From all of these, and in particular from archaeology, a picture of life in pre-European New Zealand may be drawn.

The first settlers of New Zealand came from somewhere in Eastern Polynesia — the region that includes the Society Islands, Cook Islands, and Marquesas. These islands had probably themselves been colonized from the west — from Samoa and Tonga. The more remote origins of the Polynesians are more difficult to establish with certainty, but modern excavations and the use of radiocarbon dating now suggest that people possibly ancestral to Polynesians may have reached the western Pacific about 3,500 years ago, much earlier than had previously been supposed.

These people made a form of pottery with a distinctive decoration, known as Lapita. The name has been extended to the associated culture and sometimes to the people themselves. Sites where Lapita pottery users lived have been found scattered throughout Melanesia, from Mussau north of New Guinea to the Ile des Pins at the southern tip of New Caledonia, and in a number of places in Fiji, Samoa, and Tonga.[1] The sites seem to reflect an eastward movement of people whose maritime technology was sufficiently developed to enable them to cross the gap to Fiji and become the first human colonizers of the central Pacific archipelagos.

The racial affiliations of the people who made and used Lapita pottery in the western Pacific are uncertain. The people using Lapita pottery in the eastern part of Fiji in the first millennium BC, however, were physically similar to modern Polynesians. These early settlers of the central Pacific brought with them from the west their skill at building ocean-going canoes and making voyages into the unknown. Their economy was probably not unlike that of tropical Polynesians of historic times, based on cultivation of South-East Asian root and tree crops, pig farming, fishing, and hunting. Over a period of several centuries, in the Tonga–Samoa region, the distinctive features shared by all Polynesian languages evolved. Certain new styles of artefact appeared, such as forms of stone adzes that were later carried further east and eventually to New Zealand. Pottery-making, however, declined, and had disappeared from Polynesia before the settlement of New Zealand. Many of the features of Polynesian kinship and social organization probably also developed during the first millennium BC.[2] Here, in a region that now sends migrants directly to New Zealand, the foundations of Māori society were already being laid.

From Tonga and Samoa, people sailed further east to the heart of the Polynesian triangle — the area that encompasses the Cook, Society, and Marquesas Islands. At present, radiocarbon dates suggest that this movement took place in the last centuries of the BC era. However, students of

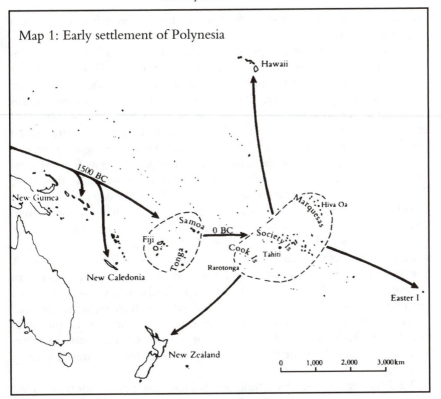

Map 1: Early settlement of Polynesia

Polynesian voyaging have argued that people would have been unlikely to pause for very long in the central Pacific and that the Cook and Society Islands may have been discovered as much as 3,000 years ago. In either case, it was from this region that the most isolated parts of Polynesia — New Zealand, Hawaii, and Easter Island — were eventually settled.[3]

No aspect of the Māori and Polynesian past has caught the imagination more than the ability of these people to voyage across the Pacific. Controversy has raged about the nature of and reasons for such voyages. Some have credited the Polynesians with the ability to make two-way voyages between the most far-flung parts of the Pacific; others have attributed almost all Polynesian colonization to the accidental voyages of parties blown off shore. There can be little doubt that time and again Polynesians set out into the unknown to find new land; only thus could the plants and animals on which they depended have been transported throughout Polynesia. Recently it has been shown that the west to east movement could have been the result of a deliberate strategy of sailing into the prevailing winds, knowing that it would be easy to run for home if no new land was found. Oral traditions offer one explanation for such expeditions — the desire of the vanquished and oppressed to find a better way of life. The quest for adventure and the search for new resources were probably also important motives. Many accidental voyages also took place, and numerous examples were documented during the early European period. At that time, two-way voyages of up to about 500 km were a regular occurrence.[4]

Neither the date nor the place of the first landing in New Zealand is known. First settlement has often been set at about AD 800 on the basis of evidence of a widespread population by about AD 1200 and a few earlier radiocarbon dates. Recently, there has been renewed discussion of this issue, but as yet no general agreement has been reached. The possibility of much earlier settlement of the Cook and Society Islands raises the related possibility of earlier discovery of New Zealand. However, rigorous review of all available radiocarbon dates from New Zealand suggests that many of the earlier dates may be unreliable. Some authorities now argue, therefore, that first settlement may have been around AD 1100 or even later.[5]

Whether there was a single colonization, several, or many is not known. Oral traditions tell of numerous voyages from Hawaiki, but although some of these may describe arrivals in New Zealand from the tropical Pacific, some probably refer to migratory voyages within New Zealand waters.[6] A few may even relate to distantly remembered voyages taking place in Polynesia before the colonization of New Zealand. By the fourteenth century the material culture in New Zealand was showing some regional variation, but this may represent either early diversification of the same founding culture within the country or several colonizations of New Zealand at about the same time by people with related but already slightly different cultures.

The culture of the first New Zealanders has been variously called Archaic (more specifically, the Archaic Phase of New Zealand Eastern Polynesian Culture) or New Zealand Eastern Polynesian. These terms, although unwieldy, are preferable to Moa-hunter with its economic connotations (in some parts of the country people who used New Zealand Eastern Polynesian artefacts seldom or never saw a live moa), and the older 'tribal' names such as Moriori and Maruiwi, with their long discredited assumptions of racial difference. The Eastern Polynesian affinities of the material culture of these people are quite clear,[7] and the Polynesian physical characteristics are patently evident in their bones.

Whatever the details of their arrival, it seems reasonably clear that these people came in one or more groups from the same general area of Eastern Polynesia — those islands long supposed to be the traditional Hawaiki — and that thereafter few or no continuing influences were felt from anywhere in the Pacific. The subsequent development of Māori culture was to be the development in isolation of one variant of Polynesian culture.

The land in which these early Māori found themselves inevitably helped to shape the society of its new inhabitants. A vast and varied country, extending for more than 1,500 km from north to south, New Zealand offered a range of habitats to the incoming Polynesians. If the first people arrived in search of a new land, bringing with them plants from their homeland, and expecting to make landfall at another island similar to Rarotonga, Tahiti, or Hiva Oa, they must have faced many problems in establishing themselves in their new land. The climate in much of the South Island, for instance, prevented them from growing any of their crops. Everywhere, however, they found an abundance of wildlife — sea mammals and birds, particularly large flightless birds, previously undisturbed by mammalian predators.

If the land made an impact on society, the immigrants too made their mark upon the land. The arrival of man with his attendant dogs and rats and his weapon of fire set in train a series of changes that greatly altered the landscape in many parts of the country. Accidental fires and activities such as the clearing of bush for gardens gradually removed parts of the forest and sometimes started processes of erosion that led to such barren and altered landscapes as the North Cape peninsula in the farthest north or the barren coastal platform and active shingle fans in Palliser Bay at the other end of the North Island. In areas such as the Auckland isthmus, long and densely inhabited, bush was replaced by fern and scrub after centuries of Polynesian occupation. But these changes were additional to those wrought by natural events, and the effects of the two cannot always be disentangled. Natural fires swept over the eastern South Island before the arrival of man, converting forest to grassland; volcanic eruptions devastated the central North Island; and changes in climate subtly affected vegetation patterns in many areas. The chain of events may be seen in the central North Island, where parts that were stripped of forest and wildlife after the eruptions in the first centuries AD appear to have been reforested and recolonized by moas and other birds, only to be reduced again to a patchwork of fern-covered clearings by the progressive nibbling of Māori fires.[8]

Any adverse changes in climate, however slight, during the last 1,000 years or so would have had some impact on the Polynesian way of life in New Zealand. Evidence from various sources suggests that during the early period of Polynesian settlement the climate was probably similar to that of recent years. There may have been a brief deterioration beginning about the middle of the fifteenth century followed by a recovery. Between about 1600 and 1850 there was a cooler interval, probably corresponding to the European 'Little Ice Age'.[9] These variations were relatively minor but would still have been significant for Polynesian gardening, particularly towards the southern limits of kūmara cultivation. The kūmara, being essentially a tropical plant, could be grown only with difficulty under New Zealand conditions. Sea-faring and fishing would also have suffered from any deterioration in climate. Cooler temperatures probably brought an increase in storminess, and there would have been fewer days in the year when canoes could put to sea or people could forage in shallow water. Fishing and shell-fish gathering would thus be limited, and so would long-distance communications between different parts of New Zealand.[10]

If there was change in land and climate during pre-European times, the people themselves changed little. Although some regional variation can be detected among prehistoric New Zealanders, they were at all periods relatively homogeneous when compared to other human groups. A strong and robust people, they were taller than most other pre-industrial populations. The men averaged 170 cm or more in height, and the women 160 cm. Their size impressed early European observers, who found them 'a strong raw boned well made Active people rather above than under the common size especialy the men', and reported: 'The men are the size of the larger Europæns, Stout, Clean Limnd and active, fleshy but never fat. . . . vigorous, nimble and at the same time Clever in all their excersizes.'[11]

People in pre-European New Zealand were likely to die relatively young. An average adult age at death of thirty years has been suggested, although this differed from one community to another. At the burial ground of Wairau Bar in Marlborough, in use between the twelfth and fourteenth centuries, the average adult age at death was twenty-eight, whereas that of the people in Palliser Bay in the same period was thirty-eight. An average life-span of about thirty was also typical of other parts of the Pacific during pre-European times. Old age was reached at forty, and few lived beyond their fifties. A kaumātua would be thirty-five rather than sixty-five, while the healthy 'old people' observed by early European visitors would be in their forties rather than their seventies. These figures have many social implications: few people would survive long enough to become grandparents, and the extended family and frequent adoptions would ensure that children were cared for when their parents died. A person over the age of thirty-five or forty would be likely to become a burden on younger relatives, being no longer able to participate fully in the active life of the community, and requiring special food preparation. None the less, some people did survive for many years as dependants, and presumably were well cared for. The average number of children born to each woman was probably only three, suggesting that children were spaced at three- or four-yearly intervals. Infant mortality has been estimated at between 15 and 30 per cent, in which case life expectancy at birth would have been between 19 and 24 years.[12]

The people were free of acute infectious diseases before the coming of Europeans and also lacked one of the great scourges of the tropical Pacific — yaws. The existence of other diseases is more difficult to determine. Although leprosy was reported in the nineteenth century, no evidence of it has yet been found among the prehistoric people. Internal parasites, so often the companions of man, will doubtless eventually be identified by the study of coprolites or the fossilized faeces which are sometimes preserved in archaeological deposits. Arthritis and spinal degeneration were prevalent, indeed almost normal over the age of twenty-five.

The study of bones and teeth reveals much about health and nutrition, and about the practices of the society. Harris lines, observed in limb bones by X-ray, indicate periods of illness or malnutrition during youth. These are relatively uncommon in pre-European New Zealanders, although a higher incidence may be found in the later populations of some regions. Fractures and dislocations occurred, but were always uncommon. There is hardly any evidence of the so-called parrying fracture of the forearm, or of violence increasing over the years. These last findings suggest that the use of hand-to-hand weapons such as taiaha (a double-ended wooden weapon) may have been largely ceremonial and that the increased use of fortifications in later times may not have been accompanied by more mortality and injury resulting from violence.

Early New Zealanders suffered frequently from painful backs. These were probably the consequence of a very active life, excessive hard work, and the carrying of burdens. Modifications to the muscular attachments of the shoulder girdle suggest too that canoe paddling was a usual activity. Men and women alike probably participated in this during the earliest period, but there is some evidence that it was more restricted to men in some regions in later times.

The other great problems were dental: periodontal disease, heavy tooth wear, abscessing, and tooth loss are all evident. A survey of dental conditions has suggested that before about AD 1500 people had a softer diet, resulting in less tooth wear, and more periodontal disease, and that later populations suffered from extreme tooth wear, abscessing, and tooth loss. This generalization, however, is challenged by the fact that the early inhabitants of Palliser Bay display far more severe tooth wear than their contemporaries at Wairau Bar.[13] Such differences are more likely to be the result of varying social and economic conditions throughout the country than of conditions changing over the years.

The initial adaptations of Polynesian people to New Zealand are reflected in archaeological sites throughout the country. Despite the regional variation that these reveal, a reliable picture of early Polynesian life in New Zealand may be gained from an examination of one example. In the twelfth to fourteenth centuries AD people were living scattered in small villages along the coast of Palliser Bay, at the southern tip of the North Island; their way of life, which was typically Polynesian, is not remembered in oral tradition or described in written records, but it has been reconstructed in some detail from archaeological evidence.[14]

The villages or hamlets of the Palliser Bay people were to be found on the coast, at river mouths. These settlements were almost certainly permanent, and near them were gardens in which the inhabitants devoted much effort to growing kūmara. They also fished and gathered shell-fish, and hunted birds in the nearby forest and on the coast. Probably each group regarded the immediate hinterland, and particularly the river valley behind its settlement, as its own territory. The exact social organization of the Palliser Bay people cannot be determined, but it is likely that their communities were kin-based, following a Polynesian pattern that foreshadowed the whānau and hapū of later times. Their houses included substantial rectangular dwellings with porches, similar to the nineteenth-century wharepuni, although in an early example the door was to the left of the centre looking out rather than to the right. Food was cooked in earth ovens, probably under rough shelters, and the settlements also contained a variety of fences and racks, presumably for the storage and drying of food. According to another Polynesian custom, the dead were buried in shallow graves on the fringes of the settlements.

These people had only recently moved into the area, probably from further north, and initially they maintained contact with kin groups to the north as well as developing contacts with other groups already established at the top of the South Island. Trade with the south is suggested by the traces of moa found in these settlements. The rubbish dumps are remarkable for the general absence of moa bones: only a few were found, and some were from species only known in the South Island. The small amount of moa enjoyed by these people was probably all obtained by trade, perhaps in exchange for garden produce. The range of contacts they had with people in other parts of New Zealand is also indicated by the variety of raw materials for tools found in the Palliser Bay sites — obsidian from the Coromandel Peninsula, Mayor Island, and the central North Island, silcrete and nephrite (greenstone) from Central Otago and the West Coast of the South Island, and numerous other rocks from the southern North Island and northern South Island.

The early Palliser Bay sites show the strongly Polynesian nature of the settlement pattern and its mixed economy, based partly on horticulture and partly on the hunting and fishing of a wide variety of species. Where conditions permitted, horticulture was to continue as the basis of the Māori economic system throughout prehistory. The emphasis on kūmara is shared with Hawaii and Easter Island, although the specialized storage techniques, necessitated by a colder climate, were unique to New Zealand. Just as the Pākehā settlers struggled to reproduce their northern hemisphere way of life in the remote antipodes, so the Polynesian settlers struggled to reproduce in a colder climate the way of life they knew in their tropical homeland. The early inhabitants of Palliser Bay seem initially to have been remarkably successful in achieving this aim, although eventually their own activities brought changes to the landscape that together with deteriorating climate rendered the area almost uninhabitable.[15]

A more general description of pre-European society draws on other lines of evidence besides archaeology. Written accounts of life in New Zealand as first observed by literate Europeans offer a rich picture of the end point of the isolated development of Polynesian culture in New Zealand, full of detail that archaeology can never provide. James Cook's first expedition explored New Zealand in 1769 and 1770. His journals, and the writings of men who came with him on this and subsequent voyages, especially Joseph Banks, Sydney Parkinson, the Forsters, and William Monkhouse, contain much valuable information, as do those of the early French explorers. However, these accounts have their limitations: the observations were sometimes severely restricted in scope and the observers had their own biases. Naturally the record grew fuller as more Europeans came to New Zealand and stayed longer, becoming more familiar with Māori and their culture. But Māori society did not, of course, remain unaffected by this contact with Europeans, and the further an observation is from 1769, the less likely it is to apply to pre-European New Zealand.[16]

Māori oral traditions also throw light on the more recent prehistoric past. These deal with the deeds of important ancestors and are usually a charter for the situation existing at the time they are recorded. In particular, they support claims to land and status, and set out past alliances that are deemed to be of present importance. They are invariably the traditions of victors rather than of vanquished, and are essentially local or regional, describing the charter of local communities or at best tribal groups. In no way do they provide a universal account of New Zealand prehistory held by all Māori at the point of contact with Europeans, even though certain simplistic versions promulgated by European scholars in the late nineteenth and early twentieth centuries have now gained wide popular acceptance.[17]

The gathering of evidence and its interpretation poses particular problems for all aspects of pre-European society, but among the most difficult to document is the social and political organization of the Māori people. Some features of social and political groupings in 1769 can be sketched from European accounts, but little specific can be said about earlier periods.

On their first voyage in 1769–70 Cook and his companions made estimates of population size in various communities they encountered. The sizes of communities clearly varied considerably: the largest pā seen in 1769 was estimated to have 500 houses, while the smallest had only three. Groups of people were described as consisting of six, fifteen to twenty, thirty, forty or fifty, sixty, a hundred, up to six hundred, and other estimates in between.[18] Reliable estimates of community size in earlier periods are few. By assessing the number of people able to be supported by the stone-walled gardens at Palliser Bay, average community size there was estimated as thirty-three, with the major settlements ranging from twelve to fifty people. The total population of eastern Palliser Bay was assessed on this basis as 319 if all the garden complexes were in use from the earliest period, or 225 if only certain of the major complexes were in use during the first two centuries. These figures are of the same order as those for the eighteenth century and comparable examples can be found in other parts of Polynesia. Other approaches have used numbers of living terraces and storage pits, and volume of storage to estimate populations of individual sites and regions.[19] Calculating the size of the total population for any period in prehistory is more difficult. Estimates of the late prehistoric population have ranged from less than 100,000 to more than 500,000. A figure of around 100,000 seems probable.[20]

Calculations by the 1769 visitors about the number of warriors in individual canoes, about the canoes mustered at one place, and about the numbers of people, houses, and 'chiefs' at places visited also provide some grounds for conclusions about social gatherings. Māori at this time apparently lived in small independent communities, each under its own authority but perhaps loosely linked in alliances with related groups, and possibly also under threat from enemies in adjoining regions. No observers mention the tribal groupings that were to be important in the nineteenth century, but information about these would be difficult if not impossible for the first transient Europeans to obtain. The opinion (formed by both Cook and Banks) that people over a vast area of the North Island were subject to a single ruler named Teratu appears to have been mistaken.[21]

Local community patterns were observed to vary in 1769–70. On the East Coast, people seemed to be living in a state of 'profound peace', although occasional ruined fortifications suggested that this had not always been the case. At Anaura Bay groups of fifteen to twenty people were living in hamlets of two to four houses, each with its own latrine and rubbish dump. Two 'chiefs' appeared to have authority over about sixty people. Estimates of the area under cultivation varied from 100 acres to 150–200 acres, which seemed a lot in view of the relatively small population. However, recent archaeological research has suggested that Anaura Bay may not have been typical of this part of the East Coast. Much of the population was concentrated in the Uawa Valley, which was not seen by the explorers. In the Bay of Plenty, gardens were extensive, but people were living in fortifications, clearly prepared for war. These fortified settlements were described as towns, and estimates of their size ranged up to 500 dwellings in one large pā. At Mercury Bay on the Coromandel Peninsula, the population of Wharetaewa pā was estimated at 100 men, women, and children — about the same number as the scattered population of Anaura Bay. In the Bay of Islands and Queen Charlotte Sound, 'towns' were again described. Two different units of social organization seem to be implied: an extended family group of perhaps between ten and thirty people, headed by a senior male, and a larger unit, combining several smaller groups, which might muster up to 150 fighting men. In the open settlement pattern observed on the East Coast, the smaller units were more obvious, each occupying its own hamlet. In areas where fortifications predominated, larger units were more prevalent, although internal subdivisions within pā, such as were described for Wharetaewa, were probably the domain of the smaller groups. Individual small families were also seen. A particularly friendly family comprising 'a man, his wife, two Sons; an old Woman and a younger who acted as servants' occupied 'a single house pleasantly situated' on the hills on the south side of Anaura Bay.[22]

Variations in settlement pattern similar to those described by Cook and his companions existed also in regions for which there are no early European accounts. On the Auckland off-shore islands, small hamlets were far more numerous than fortified pā during the latter part of the prehistoric period. People here apparently spent much of their life peacefully in small hamlets, but had a fortification in the vicinity which they could rebuild and retreat to, should the need arise.[23] In parts of Northland and Taranaki, however, and in the Bay of Plenty and the Bay of Islands, pā were numerous, suggesting that conditions encountered in 1769 had probably existed for some time.

Ethnological reconstructions of traditional Māori life describe three units of social organization: whānau (extended family), hapū (sub-tribe), and iwi (tribe). Membership of these groups was based on kinship and particularly

12

on descent from a common ancestor, usually in the male line. The system developed over time. After several generations a large whānau, now containing several subdivisions, might become a hapū. Eventually a large hapū could come to be considered a tribe. There was also the waka, a loose grouping of tribes whose members believed that they were descended from ancestors who had travelled on the same migratory canoe.[24] This generalized account of Māori social organization tends to obscure the complexities of the system and the extremes of regional variation, and caution must be exercised in imposing modern beliefs about the nature of hapū or whānau on prehistoric social units. There can be no doubt, however, that Māori society was organized according to a particular type of kinship system firmly rooted in the remote past, which was found also in other parts of Polynesia.[25]

Anthropologists use the term ramage organization to describe this kind of Polynesian social system. The term likens the growing, changing social unit with its branches and sub-branches to a branching tree. Some branches grow and develop and produce new branches which in turn grow and develop, but some wither and die. The relationship between more remote branches becomes symbolic rather than effective and eventually may be forgotten. The image is apt for Māori society with its uneven growth of branches, shifting balance of power, variable size of hapū, and changing alliances. Oral traditions describe the origins of hapū and indicate the antiquity of the system without giving precise details of size and structure of the units involved. Concern with descent and ancestors was always of prime importance; indeed, in 1770 some of the inhabitants of Queen Charlotte Sound, in discussion with Tupaia, the Tahitian aboard the *Endeavour,* 'discoursed with him about their antiquity and Legends of their ancestors'.[26]

The significance of tribal groupings and the larger confederations of tribes and canoe areas to pre–European Māori is difficult if not impossible to assess. In everyday life, the hapū was probably the biggest significant unit. Hapū might own property such as the great canoes and huge seine nets seen in 1769, could build 'towns', and probably formed the normal fighting units in warfare. However, remembrance of common descent from a more remote ancestor could provide the basis for alliances, and must have been symbolically important even in pre-European times to have become important recently. The existence of large fortifications such as those on the Auckland volcanic cones and of small, tightly defended 'ring ditch' pā in several parts of the North Island has led to the suggestion that at one time Māori social organization was capable of developing into larger and more cohesive units which subsequently broke down into smaller groups. But in some regions both very large sites and numerous smaller ones were occupied during the same period, the population segmenting into smaller units and occupying smaller pā in times of relative peace, when they squabbled amongst themselves, and congregating in a few larger sites in response to a major threat from outside the region. This occurred in the Tauranga region in the nineteenth century, and the apparent contemporaneity of large and small pā at earlier periods suggests that similar patterns could have occurred in the past. Oral traditions about the Auckland area tell of a similar pattern of fluctuating community size and shifting alliances amongst the people who lived on the volcanic cones.[27]

The internal structure of these groups is equally difficult to reconstruct. The early European explorers thought they saw evidence of social status varying from 'chiefs' to 'servants', but their observations are hard to interpret. Authority often appeared to reside in 'old men' who wore fine cloaks, carried distinctive weapons, sometimes of greenstone, and had extensive tattoo. Whether these men were heads of extended families or of larger groups or both is unclear. Age was not the only qualification for high status, however, for in Queen Charlotte Sound was encountered a 'most agreeable Indian family' consisting of '17 people; the head of it was a pretty child of about 10 years old who they told us was the owner of the land about where we wooded'.[28] The Europeans were also told that women and children from Mercury Bay had been taken as slaves by raiders from the north. Many of the 'servants' they saw during their travels, however, may simply have been junior members of a kinship group rather than captured slaves.

More concrete reflections of social life, such as dwellings and the layout of settlements, can be described more precisely. The houses of 1769–70 did not greatly impress the European visitors:

Their houses are certainly the most inartificialy made of any thing among them, scarce equal to a European dog kennel and resembling one in the door at least, which is barely high and wide enough to admit a man crawling upon all fours. They are seldom more than 16 or 18 feet long, 8 or 10 broad and five or 6 high from the ridge pole to the Ground and built with a sloping roof like our Europæn houses. The materials of both walls and roof is dry grass or hay and very tightly it is put together, so that nescessarily they must be very warm. Some are lind with bark of trees on the inside, and many have either over the door or fixd somewhere in the house a peice of Plank coverd with their carving, which they seem to value much as we do a picture, placing it always as conspicuously as possible. All these houses have the door at one end and near it is generaly a square hole which serves for a window or probably in winter time more for a chimney, for then they light a fire in the middle of the house. At the same end where this door and window are placed the side walls and roof project, generaly 18 inches or 2 feet beyond the end wall, making a kind of Porch in which are benches where the people of the house often set.[29]

An early house excavated at Moikau, Palliser Bay, shows that the rectangular house with porch and internal hearth was present very early in New Zealand, although no exact parallel is yet known elsewhere in Polynesia. Later examples from Palliser Bay and elsewhere document its persistence through to the nineteenth-century wharepuni and ultimately to the meeting-houses that are still being built in the second half of the twentieth century.[30] Continuity in house design tends to imply continuity in many aspects of social life, and indeed in fundamental attitudes about personal space and personal interaction. Thus in the Māori house the spaces allotted to males and females, hosts and guests, and people of high and low status are clearly defined and relate to the overall plan and the position of the door. Such aspects of modern Māori society probably derive from the earliest periods of settlement in New Zealand.

Although the carved meeting-house is now popularly considered the focal point of any Māori settlement, there is little evidence for the pre-European existence of the meeting-house as it is now known. Only one exceptional house was seen in 1769–70, despite the number of settlements visited. This was an unfinished house with carved side planks of fine workmanship at Tolaga Bay on the East Coast. It was '30 feet in length' (9 m). One large house 15 m long and another 11.6 m long have been uncovered in excavations in Northland and Hawke's Bay, but most archaeological examples of houses are in the range described in 1769–70. The largest houses have been interpreted as the dwellings of chiefs and the meeting-house proper is seen as a nineteenth-century development.[31]

Early European descriptions suggest that 'houses' varied from substantial dwellings to the flimsiest of shelters. Archaeological excavations have revealed traces of a similar range of structures. In some areas there seem to have been several distinct kinds of building, the functions of which are not always clear. In the southern South Island round houses and huts may have been preferred.[32] None the less, there was continuity in the most substantial form of house over a long period.

Settlements, however, exhibit a bewildering variety of size and shape. The nature of a settlement depends on the subsistence pattern, the climate, and the social and political situation at the time. The early occupants of Palliser Bay probably lived in permanent settlements but went occasionally into the bush or to other parts of the coast to exploit particular resources. This was also the case in later times throughout much of the country. Horticultural communities needed a settlement close to their gardens, but even the people of the southern and western South Island, who spent much of the year moving from one seasonal resource to another, had their winter base villages to which they returned. A single group of people might during one year occupy several sites in which they could leave very different archaeological evidence, depending on the activities carried out at each place. Moreover, one community might live together in a village at certain times but divide into smaller family units occupying smaller settlements at other times.[33] This obviously affects attempts to estimate community or population sizes from the size and distribution of archaeological sites. The duration of occupation at any one site is also difficult to estimate, and a particular group of archaeological sites may represent long-term occupation of individual sites by several different communities, or frequent moves of one highly mobile group. Mobility was a pronounced factor of Māori life in the late eighteenth century and there is little reason to suppose that this was a new development.

At the close of the pre-European period Māori society differed markedly from most other Eastern Polynesian societies in one respect — the absence in New Zealand of massive religious edifices, and the organization required

15

to construct, maintain, and use them. Māori religion left little material trace. The marae of New Zealand, which are essentially open spaces in settlements, are more closely related to the marae of Western Polynesia, which served both as secular meeting grounds and as the venue for religious festivals, than to the more strictly religious marae of the Society and Cook Islands. The simple and insignificant tūāhu or shrine of New Zealand is a poor relation of the ahu of Easter Island or the ahu incorporated in a Tahitian marae. The absence of religious structures is a strong argument for the lack of recent contact between central Eastern Polynesia and New Zealand, for the elaboration of the marae–ahu system appears to be a relatively late development.[34]

Values and beliefs in pre-European Māori society have to be extrapolated from the subsequent records of ethnologists, for neither archaeology nor the earliest European accounts throw much light on them. Concepts of tapu and mana undoubtedly pervaded prehistoric New Zealand society, since they are Polynesian rather than strictly Māori concepts, but their exact manifestations in early Māori society remain largely unknown. Extrapolation is a difficult and indeed dangerous exercise, for Māori concepts and values have continued to change in the last 200 years, just as they developed initially from those brought by the first migrants from Polynesia.[35]

Archaeology has, however, provided a few examples of ritual. During the sixteenth century a number of apparently tapu objects, particularly head-combs, hair-cuttings, and the tools used for hair-cutting, were carefully deposited in a special place in a swamp in the western Bay of Plenty. Concern with the sacredness of the head would thus appear to be of some antiquity. The placing of obsidian flakes in a rock pool from which a stream had been carefully diverted by an artificial channel may reflect a related ritual. Other instances include the burial of a dog jaw carefully placed beside the main post of a sixteenth-century house in Palliser Bay and the deliberate destruction of a stone adze by flaking it into a grave in Palliser Bay. These few instances are a poor reflection of the nature of Māori ritual and belief.[36]

It is through burial practices that archaeology can contribute significantly to the understanding of ritual. Early burials in New Zealand appear mostly to have been in, or perhaps on the fringes of, settlements, in simple shallow graves. Although the most famous early burials, those at Wairau Bar, reveal a preference for burying people in an extended position, graves at Wairau and at other early sites also include examples of people buried in crouched and flexed positions. There were also some disarticulated remains that had apparently been first buried elsewhere, or perhaps exposed for the removal of the flesh.[37] All these practices are known elsewhere in Polynesia and probably were brought to New Zealand by the first migrants. As elsewhere in Polynesia, a variety of burial customs seems to have been practised in different parts of the country during the first centuries of occupation. In later times secondary burial or disposal of disarticulated remains became more common in New Zealand, and in early European times the body was often first buried or exposed, the bones cleaned, and then finally disposed of, frequently in a cave.[38] The custom of primary burial, usually in a crouched position, in or near settlements, still persisted, however, in some regions in the eighteenth century. At no time was there any one universal burial practice. Two main customs — primary burial and secondary disposition of previously cleaned bones — were practised throughout prehistory, although as time went on the dead were increasingly segregated from the living, perhaps in conjunction with the development and elaboration of the concept of tapu.

Grave goods were sometimes placed with the dead. In early times, both men and women might have objects placed with them in their individual graves, although the offerings might range from the abundance of objects in the richer graves at Wairau to the poorer ones at Palliser Bay. At both places there were also graves without any offerings.[39] In later times, grave goods were often placed in the repositories such as caves in which the bones of numerous individuals were placed, but they are seldom found with primary burials.

Only one aspect of the death ritual — the shedding of blood in mourning — was observed in 1770: 'then 5 or 6 women set down together and cut and scarified their legs, thighs, Arms and faces some with shells and others with peices of jasper. . . . This was done on account of their husbands having been lately kill'd and devoured by their enimies.'[40] A lament expresses the mourner's feeling:

> Give me the obsidian blade, that I might cut myself
> Let me cut deeply my skin that is close to the friend
> Powdered now with red ochre from Parahaki
> Here is my blood. . . .[41]

Concern with the ancestors, and with death, like other Māori ritual and belief, is illuminated more by oral tradition and poetry, than by tangible vestiges of the past. Occasionally, however, an artefact will reveal the significance of these themes to the pre-European Māori. Ancestors were often depicted in wood-carving, and the importance of carvings in the houses of the living was noted in 1769. In several places, particularly in the northern North Island, elaborately carved wooden chests were placed in burial caves.[42] These are impressive carvings, even when taken out of context; in their original setting, among the bones of the ancestors of the hapū that used the caves, they convey more eloquently than words the awesome power of tapu, and the supreme significance of ancestors and death.

The ways in which individual communities interacted with each other are fundamental to the study of New Zealand prehistory. New ideas can be spread either by peaceful interaction and the exchange of commodities and ideas, or by conquest and warfare. Conquest and migration have until recently been seen as the principal vehicles of cultural change. Modi-

17

fications taking place in one region would subsequently spread by the expansion of the inhabitants of that region at the expense of the less fortunate. It now seems likely, however, that there was a series of changes, particularly in artefact styles, in several places. While some new ideas could have been spread by warfare and invasion, many were undoubtedly spread by more peaceful means.

The extent to which early inhabitants were in at least indirect contact with people the length and breadth of the land has already been indicated in the early communities at Palliser Bay. It is clear also that by this period stone was exchanged in many other places. Obsidian, which occurs naturally only in some parts of the northern half of the North Island, has been discovered in early sites throughout the country. One site in Northland has been shown to have not merely obsidian from Mayor Island in the Bay of Plenty, but basalt (for adzes) and siliceous sinter (for drill points and cutting tools) from the Coromandel Peninsula. Stone adzes of Coromandel basalt and Nelson–D'Urville Island argillite were also widely distributed. Only the durable items that were exchanged during this period can be documented, but if ethnographic and traditional accounts of later periods are any indication, a variety of foodstuffs and items such as clothing and canoes might also have been part of the communication system.[43]

It is sometimes argued that the exchange systems of early times may have broken down later, with an increase in warfare leading to greater isolation. The use of products from the early adze factories does appear to have declined, but it was replaced by the use of greenstone, while the movement of obsidian continued undiminished, even if the exact routes by which it travelled may have changed. In 1769, despite the extent of warfare in some areas, greenstone was widely distributed and there was little sign of any breakdown in communications. Moreover, the Māori to whom Cook talked through his Tahitian interpreter exhibited a considerable knowledge of the country's geography, and the news of Cook's own presence in New Zealand waters preceded him with amazing rapidity. Two men who came aboard the *Endeavour* between Bream Head and Cape Brett in Northland said they had heard of her presence on the coast — news they could only have got from Coromandel or Thames.[44] And news of the existence of iron and its miraculous properties travelled south from Hawke's Bay or across Cook Strait, for people off Palliser Bay asked for nails:

. . . they were no sooner on board than they asked for nails: but when nails were given them they asked Tupia what they were which was plain that they had never seen any before, yet they not only knowed how to ask for them but knowed what use to apply them to. . . .[45]

Communications between eighteenth-century communities were clearly extensive, even though warfare was widespread in society at that time.

Fighting of one kind or another was probably a feature of pre-European life from the very beginning of the country's occupation. The idea that the early people were peaceful and succumbed to the superior military capacity of later arrivals is improbable. Warfare was almost universal in Polynesia and fortifications were widespread. Competition for status and authority, the desire for mana, hunger for revenge, and the wish to be the victor rather than the vanquished are motives that were probably brought to New Zealand by the first settlers. Although there is as yet no evidence of fortifications in the earliest times, personal violence against individuals is shown in the early burials in Palliser Bay. An absence of weapons in early sites cannot be taken to indicate an absence of warfare, since so many Polynesian weapons were of wood. The discovery of wooden and whalebone patu (short striking-clubs) identical to the later Māori patu in an early site on Huahine in the Society Islands suggests that even the concept of this typically late Māori weapon may have been brought to New Zealand by the earliest settlers.[46]

Violence and weapons, then, were part of the Polynesian heritage. However, the intense elaboration of fortifications, the pā Māori, distinguishes eighteenth-century Māori society from contemporary Eastern Polynesian societies. More than 6,000 fortifications have been recorded in New Zealand. Their date and origin are still uncertain, as only a tiny proportion have been investigated by archaeologists. However, present evidence suggests a sudden appearance of pā in a number of different regions in the fifteenth or sixteenth centuries.[47] This change in patterns of warfare must have spread rapidly through most of the country, fitting the Māori proverb that 'war is a devouring fire kindled by a spark'. Eighteenth-century observers, however, impressed by the pā they saw, felt that warfare must be an ancient custom in New Zealand:

. . . this people must have long and frequent wars, and must have been long accustom'd to it otherwise they never would have invented such strong holds as these, the errecting of which must cost them immence labour considering the tools they have to work with which are only made of wood & stone.[48]

Many reasons have been advanced for the development of pā warfare. A Māori proverb explains succinctly: 'for women and land men die'. The former cause has been largely ignored, but several variants of the latter have been suggested, including competition for horticultural land and competition for cleared land, although it has also been argued that there was more than enough land for all.[49] Undoubtedly the building of pā was related to the desire to protect food supplies — always an early casualty in Polynesian warfare — but competition for land may not have provided the only or indeed the most important motivation for war. In other parts of Polynesia status and competition rather than land were reasons for fighting. A glance at New Zealand in 1769 suggests a similar pattern. The largest gardens were seen on the East Coast, where the people who cultivated them were not at that time involved in war. The poorest and most oppressed North Island people, however, at Mercury Bay, had been defeated in war by people who had apparently not driven them from their lands, but were feared as likely to reappear and wreak further havoc at any time. Warfare was most intense and cannibalism most evident in Queen Charlotte Sound, an area capable of supporting Māori horticulture, at least marginally, but not doing so in 1770.

Tribal migration is often linked with warfare in New Zealand: the victors move into the lands of the vanquished and the vanquished move on. This is unusual in Polynesia, where warfare for conquest rarely occurred. After 1769 tribal migrations certainly took place in New Zealand as a result of fighting. Oral traditions relate that they also occurred earlier, and some interpretations of New Zealand prehistory have been based on the concept of migrating tribes from the north introducing horticulture and other new ideas to the south. Close study of archaeological materials does not, however, suggest northern sources for many southern traits. One instance, the migration of the Ngāi Tahu from the Wairarapa to the South Island, also indicates that if such a movement took place only a few people may have been involved. That some migration took place in pre-European times seems indisputable from the evidence of oral tradition. It also appears, however, that in many areas continuity of settlement was maintained by the same people over long periods. Whether migration was the principal vehicle for the spread of new traits remains open to question.[50]

Food is fundamental to all human societies, and changes in methods of obtaining food underlie most theories of economic change in Māori society. Until recently the economy of pre-European New Zealand has been seen in two phases. The first was a non-horticultural phase, when the early settlers throughout the country lived by hunting, fishing, and gathering, and particularly by hunting the moa and other now extinct birds. It has been suggested that at this time most of the population was in the South Island.[51] The second phase followed the introduction of the kūmara, probably brought by a new wave of immigrants from tropical Polynesia. Kūmara horticulture allowed more people to settle in the North Island, an area supposedly not favoured earlier because of a shortage of moas and other game. As moa hunting declined, dependence on horticulture increased, and the South Island gradually became a refuge for those vanquished in the wars of the north.

It now appears, however, that long before the end of moa hunting in some regions, horticultural communities were established even in marginal areas such as Palliser Bay and that Polynesian settlers endeavoured from the beginning to reproduce a tropical Polynesian style of economy wherever the climate permitted. The ideal subsistence base of early New Zealand was thus kūmara horticulture supplemented by fishing, hunting, and plant gathering, but variations were considerable. Horticulture was impossible in the southern South Island, where the early middens give a picture of a hunting economy, heavily dependent on seal, fish, moa, and other birds. In those parts of the North Island that attracted a large population, such as the Auckland area, hunting and birding declined rapidly, and the protein component of the diet came largely from fishing and shellfish gathering. Māori culture in the late eighteenth century as in the twelfth embraced economies as different as those of the horticultural north and the hunting and gathering economies more common in the south. No one form of subsistence can be regarded as typical: the Poutini Ngāi Tahu of the West Coast of the South Island, for instance, who were the principal exploiters of the greenstone resources providing some of the best known Māori artefacts, were as 'typical' as their more numerous northern compatriots.[52]

Although the basic forms of economic activity remained much the same throughout prehistory, time brought some changes. Moa hunting declined, and the moa and several other species of bird were eventually exterminated. Sea lions rapidly retreated from much of the coast and fur seals were killed in such large numbers that many of their colonies were wiped out.[53] Other birds, particularly seabirds, were probably also reduced in numbers from their first abundance. They still appeared numerous to the European explorers, however, and were being eaten by Māori in the eighteenth century.

Unlike hunting, fishing remained an important part of the economy in all coastal regions. Techniques were modified — moa bone fish-hooks were replaced by hooks of other materials as moa bone became harder to obtain; styles of fish-hooks changed; and in some areas net fishing probably gained in popularity over angling. But fishing was a major activity in coastal communities throughout the prehistoric period, and the kinds of fish caught may have varied more from region to region than they did within any one region over the centuries. Archaeological sites of all ages on the east coast between North Cape and the Bay of Plenty, for instance, produce large quantities of snapper bones but exhibit a variety of fish-hook types at different periods. Fishing was also important in inland regions, but less is known of techniques for inland fishing.[54]

The effort devoted to horticulture can be seen in both the stone-walled gardens of the early Palliser Bay people[55] and the eighteenth-century gardens observed by the European visitors. These made a strong impression:

The ground is compleatly cleared of all weeds — the mold broke with as much care as that of our best gardens. The Sweet potatoes are set in distinct little molehills which are ranged in some in straight lines, in others in quincunx. In one Plott I observed these hillocks, at their base, surrounded with dried grass. The Arum is planted in little circular concaves, exactly in the manner our Gard'ners plant Melons as Mr.—— informs me. The Yams are planted in like manner with the sweet potatoes: these Cultivated spots are enclosed with a perfectly close pailing of reeds about twenty inches high.[56]

The principal development in horticulture was not the introduction of the kūmara (now believed to have been present very early) but the elaboration of storage techniques, particularly the sunken 'cellars' and underground pits which are such a feature of the archaeological landscape.[57] In the tropical Pacific the kūmara is a perennial plant which can be propagated by the direct transfer of growing vines. It is highly susceptible to frost. The first

Polynesian settlers, in adapting it to New Zealand conditions, made 'one of the greater agricultural achievements of Oceania'.[58] They discovered that, by lifting the crop in autumn and storing it in pits under relatively constant humidity and temperature, tubers could be retained for winter consumption and also as seed tubers for planting out the following spring. Only a few shallow pits were found in the Palliser Bay settlements, and most of the crop may have been stored in baskets in houses. Large storage pits were probably developed further north and their use then spread gradually throughout the horticultural region. A distinctive regional variant known as the raised–rim pit, found in eastern regions from the Bay of Plenty to the southern limits of horticulture in Canterbury, reached Palliser Bay at a much later date.[59]

Certain other Polynesian cultivated plants, including taro, yam, gourd, and paper mulberry, were recorded in New Zealand in the eighteenth century. Of these only the gourd was widely and successfully grown, although taro was probably important in a few areas. Yams and paper mulberry were marginal under the climatic conditions of the eighteenth century. The yam, however, could have been quite important in northern regions under the slightly milder conditions prevailing some centuries earlier. In addition to cultivated plants, wild plants of several kinds were exploited for food as well as fibre. The large sweet root of the cabbage tree was an important food source for many South Island people throughout the prehistoric period. The root of the bracken fern was a major food in many areas in 1769, although evidence of its use in earlier periods is poor.[60] The eighteenth–century explorers indeed regarded the fern–root as the country's staple food, but so little use was made of it in some areas that it cannot properly be regarded as a universal staple. Even in regions where fern–root was a major part of the day-to-day diet, the people who ate it probably considered themselves kūmara horticulturalists and invested more effort in their gardens than they did in the gathering and processing of fern–root. The concept of a single staple food cannot be readily applied to New Zealand at any period.

Artefacts made and used by people long ago provide some of the most tangible links with the past. In New Zealand, they provide valuable clues to the origins of Māori settlement, and illustrate the adaptations and regional differentiations of Māori society. Although early New Zealand adzes, fish-hooks, and ornaments have strong affinities with those of Eastern Polynesia, those described and collected in 1769–70 and on subsequent voyages appear at first glance so different that additional outside influences have been invoked to explain the changes.[61] However, closer examination suggests an underlying continuity in many kinds of artefact, and it seems that fashions may simply have changed at different times and in different places, and the new styles spread gradually through the country. The discovery and use of raw materials such as greenstone and some hard, dense, North Island rocks, and the lack of some traditional Polynesian materials such as pearl shell, must inevitably have brought some alterations in style, while others were just changes in fashion such as all societies experience.

Stone adzes were used for all kinds of woodworking — from the manufacture of canoes and the dressing of house timbers to the intricate carving of small wooden objects. The elegant and varied stone adzes of the early period, which show most clearly the relationships with tropical Eastern Polynesia, had by the eighteenth century been replaced by plainer tools made from other types of stone. Analysis of several adze forms has shown that two major types, characteristic of early and late periods, are functionally quite different implements. It has been suggested that the early adze forms were used mainly for shaping and trimming connected with maritime activities such as canoe building. The later implements, however, are more suited to rapid chopping and splitting of wood — activities related to the clearing of forest or the building of wooden defences on pā sites.[62]

The distinctive early kinds of adzes were mostly made at a few quarry sites — one on the Coromandel Peninsula serving much of the northern part of the country, a series in the Nelson–D'Urville Island region whose products reached all parts of the country in small numbers, and another in Southland. Smaller manufacturing centres existed in Auckland and Taranaki and others undoubtedly remain to be discovered.[63] In the South Island, greenstone was soon exploited, but only came into its own in later periods. The greenstone adze, highly prized for its hardness, was valued as an item of exchange throughout the North Island, but in the South Island, closer to the sources and with a much smaller population, it became the standard tool. Little is known of the manufacture and distribution of the later North Island adzes. Technology as well as style seems to have changed, or rather, emphasis shifted from one of two technologies used in different regions in the early period to a preference for the other in the later period. Regional variation in techniques can also be seen in the stone flake industries — the making of small tools such as hand-held knives from obsidian, various cherts or flints, and silcrete. In the southern half of the South Island, during the early period, large and distinctive prismatic blades were made by a special technique, which required considerable skill in stone working, but this technique was apparently never fashionable in the North Island.[64]

Fish-hooks included both trolling lures and bait hooks made for different kinds of fish, but forms varied from region to region and changed over time. The early relationships with Eastern Polynesia are obvious in both kinds of fish-hook, which were initially adapted to New Zealand conditions and copied in new raw materials. In the northern half of the North Island the Polynesian forms lasted in some areas until AD 1500 and even later in the case of trolling lures, but had largely been superseded by early European times. The southern South Island was an area of innovation and elaboration of fish-hooks and more variety in form has been recorded there than elsewhere. In general, changes in fishing gear were towards greater elaboration of forms and the addition of barbs and notched decoration.[65]

The differences between Eastern Polynesian and eighteenth-century Māori ornament forms and between early forms of necklace and later single pendants obscure the underlying continuity in ornaments. But the presence in European accounts and collections of necklaces and of a number of forms also in use much earlier, such as strung ornaments of bird-bone beads and others of dentalium (tusk shell) segments, confirm continuity.[66] The most striking early ornaments are the 'reels' and whale tooth pendant units which formed the necklaces of the people who were buried in the burial ground at Wairau Bar. These were also in vogue in other parts of the country and continued in use as late as AD 1500 in areas such as the Coromandel Peninsula.[67] They had, however, disappeared by the end of the eighteenth century. Greenstone ornaments first appeared in the South Island well before 1500, in the form of simple straight or pebble-like pendants. The more elaborate forms such as hei tiki, a neck ornament in the form of a stylized human figure, have seldom been found in excavations, but historical accounts make it quite clear that they were widely distributed in the late eighteenth century.

Tattooing chisels made of bone have been found in some of the earliest known archaeological sites in New Zealand, and it seems certain that this distinctive type of personal adornment was known to the first settlers, although the designs cannot be reconstructed with any precision. By 1769 there was striking regional variation in tattooing, both in the part of the body to which it was applied and in the designs themselves. In the Bay of Islands, for example, men were tattooed on their buttocks and thighs and the rare male facial tattoo patterns were different from the spirals observed elsewhere.[68]

Māori clothing was described in some detail in 1769. Men often went almost naked: 'About their Waists was tied a belt from which hung a string which was tied round the preputium and in this seemd to consist most or all of their decency in that particular. . . .' The women, however, 'round their waists instead of a belt . . . constantly wore a girdle of many platted strings made of the leaves of a very fragrant Grass; into this were tuckd the leaves of some sweet scented plant fresh gatherd.'[69] Both sexes wore rough rectangular flax garments of the rain-cape kind; these could be worn around the shoulders or around the waist, and a complete dress included both. Important men wore fine flax cloaks ornamented with dog skin, tāniko borders, or rarely with feathers of the decorative black thrums characteristic of the korowai.[70] No women were seen wearing such fine cloaks and it appeared that 'the Women contrary to the custom of the Sex in general seemd to affect dress rather less than the men.'[71] Māori clothing has continued to change since 1769, but its development up to 1769 remains largely a matter of speculation. The lack of archaeological evidence obscures one of the best examples of Polynesian adaptation to new materials and colder conditions — the change from bark cloth and the use of other tropical plants to a mastery of flax working.[72]

In the field of art, always important in Māori culture, only a few water-logged wooden artefacts yet provide a hint of the development of carving styles. However, modern archaeological techniques are uncovering more evidence. Wooden artefacts have been found recently in swamps in the Bay of Plenty, the Waikato, and Taranaki, and some have been dated. Material from Waitore in South Taranaki and a number of isolated and undated swamp carvings emphasize Eastern Polynesian relationships. The Waitore material shows that decorative notching, known elsewhere in Eastern Polynesia, and a crude double spiral motif were in use in South Taranaki by the early fifteenth century AD.[73]

In 1769, prehistory was 'caught alive' in New Zealand.[74] Cook and his companions described a group of Polynesians whose society and culture had been developing in isolation since the original colonization. Classic Māori culture (the term used to describe Māori culture at this time) was unique to New Zealand but clearly Polynesian in origin. Māori culture was to continue developing and changing under the stimulus of European contact after 1769, in ways that were often vigorous and exciting, but it was no longer Classic Māori culture in that it was no longer the result of Polynesian achievement in isolation.

The Classic Māori culture of archaeologists and ethnologists has been defined primarily in terms of material culture and is characterized by the objects familiar in museums — ornate wood-carvings on houses, canoes, and many smaller things; decorative carving on many utilitarian objects; a profusion of wooden and stone weapons and utensils; greenstone tools and ornaments; sophisticated flax garments and cloaks ornamented with dog skin or coloured tāniko borders. The Classic Māori is personified as a tattooed warrior wrapped in a flax cloak, wearing a greenstone ornament, and carrying a weapon of some kind, standing near a canoe with elaborately carved prow and stern pieces, or a house ornamented with a carved lintel or barge boards. In his clothing, his ornaments, and the nature of his house and its decoration, he differs from any other Polynesian, yet he himself and his language reveal his relationship to other Polynesians. In other important respects, less apparent to the casual observer, such as his family and community organization, he also reflects his Polynesian origin.

This man is not precisely fixed in space — he is a generalized New Zealander. The lifestyle of the Classic Māori would depend considerably on the region, as it had for his predecessors. The design of his tattoo and the part of the body to which it was applied, the nature of the carving on his house and canoe, and perhaps his ornaments and weapons would vary depending on which part of the country he lived in. Even his language would vary — regional dialects were apparently well developed.[75] Most of all, his way of obtaining food would depend on where he lived. His weapon might be carried in genuine expectation of sudden attack, or it might be a symbol of his status and authority.

All of these variations and others were noted by observers in 1769–70. On parts of the East Coast, people were living in small hamlets near extensive gardens. In the Bay of Islands, pā were occupied but so were hamlets; cultivations were extensive. In Mercury Bay people were impoverished and obviously lived in fear of further attack, while in Queen Charlotte Sound not only was warfare highly developed, but cannibalism was also sufficiently prevalent to provoke the comment that the people appeared to 'live intirely upon fish, dogs and Enemies'.[76]

In places not visited by the early explorers archaeology provides a basis for reconstruction. On Motutapu Island near Auckland, eighteenth-century inhabitants spent much of their time living in hamlets on the ridges behind the sheltered beaches where they kept their canoes. They had numerous gardens, and after several centuries of human life on the island there was hardly any forest left. The landscape was one of rolling ridges of fern and scrub with frequent clearings and neat gardens. The diet consisted largely of kūmara and fern-root, fish and shell-fish, although wild plants and occasionally a dog, rat, or seabird added variety. These people were fortunate in the outcrops of good stone for tool manufacture on the island, and many of the men were tool makers. They were obliged to import obsidian, however, which they obtained from several sources. Both men and women were adept at handling canoes, and the relatively calm waters of the Hauraki Gulf provided their principal highway. They still buried their dead in shallow graves in their settlements, although they may sometimes have taken up the bones and hidden them in caves on nearby Rangitoto Island. Periodically, their life was altered by outbreaks of war. At such times they abandoned their hamlets and retreated to one of several fortified headlands around the island. Had they been observed in 1769, they might well have been living in one of these 'towns'. Only a few years earlier, however, their lifestyle might have resembled that on the East Coast much more closely. This way of life differed from that practised on Motutapu Island several centuries previously only in the relative lack of birds and complete absence of seals in the diet, and in the outbreaks of warfare, during which the population retreated to fortifications. The island itself had altered considerably in appearance from the virgin forested place discovered by the first settlers, but was still abundantly capable of supporting Māori life.[77]

Other areas were not so fortunate. The uncertain relationship between people and their environment is illustrated in the fate of the prosperous twelfth- to fourteenth-century communities of Palliser Bay. There occupation gradually rendered the land and the coast less suitable for habitation. People struggled to maintain their way of life, although increased pressure and hardship are reflected in the appearance of fortifications, and the concealment of burial places and food storage pits up the river valleys. Eventually, perhaps in the seventeenth century, faced with deteriorating climate as well as increasingly barren conditions, they were compelled to abandon the area. The canoe that Cook encountered off Cape Palliser in 1770, whose crew asked for nails, probably belonged to the Ngāti Kahungunu people who lived in the main Wairarapa Valley and visited the coast only temporarily to fish.[78] Thus the fate of settlers in different parts of the country varied and no uniform sequence of development or decline can be described.

Māori society in 1769 was rich and diverse. Many cultural features, traditions, and beliefs were shared by most or all New Zealanders but the way of life differed both economically and socio-politically from region to region. What further developments might have taken place can never be known, for the isolation of Māori society, apparently unaffected by Tasman's brief visit in 1642, was about to be shattered completely.

CHAPTER 2

New Zealand before Annexation

J. M. R. Owens

In the late eighteenth century the area coming to be known as New Zealand had a Polynesian culture with distinct regional variations. During the next fifty years it was to feel the pressure of successive groups of Europeans, all of whom brought different kinds of influence: the explorers, mostly in the late eighteenth century; the sealers, whalers, and traders from the 1790s onwards; the missionaries, present from 1814 but effective only from the mid-1820s; and finally the more permanent settlers who began arriving in numbers in the late 1830s. These groups added to the variety of social developments not only because they differed in their nature and purpose but also because they were scattered around the country and thus overlaid the existing regional variations with new forms of difference.

Few Europeans at the time, however, appreciated the diversity of New Zealand: such Māori as they encountered were taken as typical, particular localities were taken as all New Zealand. The dominant picture was based on observations at the Bay of Islands, where Europeans had arrived early and visited in some numbers. As 1840 approached and the British Government was making its decision to annex New Zealand, the proponents of annexation found in places such as the Bay of Islands some evidence of the 'anarchy and depopulation' that they claimed existed throughout the country as a result of the European presence. This was the main argument for annexation, produced by officials, missionaries, and merchants alike. But in other areas the 'fatal impact' of Europeans on the Māori population was much less obvious. In some the Polynesian culture of the late eighteenth century remained almost unchanged in the middle of the nineteenth; in others Māori society accommodated many of the new demands brought by Europeans and adapted to meet them. This process was optimistically thought of by some early Europeans as the first steps in the civilization of the Māori people.

This type of modification and a basic continuity were more common features of Māori culture in the period than its destruction under the impact of contact with Europeans. Between 1769, when Māori met the first British explorer, and 1840, when some chiefs signed the Treaty of Waitangi with representatives of the British Government, all the country's inhabitants were to be affected, directly or indirectly, by the presence of Europeans, and the changes that took place in all aspects of their life — intellectual, social, and economic — were significant. But there was also a fundamental continuity: the cultural framework of New Zealand in 1840 was still essentially Polynesian; all European residents absorbed Māori values to some extent; most Europeans were incorporated, however loosely, into a tribal structure; and the basic social divisions were tribal, not the European divisions of race, class, or sect. The history of these years is of tribal societies interacting with each other and with Europeans: societies still traditional but undergoing major cultural change.

Within the three islands that make up the country, the term 'New Zealand' was meaningless before 1840. The European world, however, learned to use it after 1642, when Abel Tasman visited the country (although the name he wrote in his journal was Staten Landt).[1] Tasman's instructions, drawn up by the Dutch East India Company at Batavia, foreshadowed two features that marked the European approach to New Zealand. First, they made a clear distinction between savage and civilized races. If he met the latter, the Dutch explorer was to give them more attention than wild barbarians and he was to parley with the 'magistrates'; but with savages he was to use extreme caution, 'since experience has taught in all parts of the world that barbarian men are nowise to be trusted'. Secondly, trade was to be the basis of any relationship with local peoples. Even the savages were to be won over with kindness, in order to learn 'whether there is anything to be got or effected'.[2]

With the British explorer James Cook, who first arrived in 1769, European knowledge became more precise. In six and a half months he mapped much of the coast, establishing an outline of the country. Accompanying Cook on his three voyages were a number of scientists and artists, among them Joseph Banks, Daniel Solander, J. R. and George Forster, Sydney Parkinson, William Hodges, and John Webber, who left an invaluable record in their accumulation of writings, drawings, and natural history exhibits. Cook, like Tasman, received advice on the treatment of native peoples. But the Earl of Morton, President of the Royal Society, was responsive to the new eighteenth-century sensibility about the 'noble savage', and less concerned with guarding against 'savage violence' than with checking bloodshed by the European visitors. This, he said, would be 'a crime of the highest nature:— They are human creatures, the work of the same omnipotent Author, equally under his care with the most polished European. . . . No European Nation has a right to occupy any part of their country, or settle among them without their voluntary consent.'[3]

Cook respected such advice. Occasions of violence brought pangs of conscience, and he took pains to demonstrate his weapons in ways that would minimize casualties. Observing the Māori were a 'brave open warlike people and voide of treachery', 'certainly in a state of civilization', and executing their arts 'with great judgement and unwearied patience', he raised issues and expressed opinions that were to typify the European response to the Māori for many generations.[4] He was convinced they needed central government. 'Living thus dispers'd in small parties knowing no head but the chief of the family or tribe whose authority may be very little, subjects them to many inconveniences a well regulated society united under one head or any other form of government are not subject to. . . .'[5] He also looked ahead to the possibility of 'fixing a colony', either on the river Thames or the Bay of Islands, arguing that the divisions among the local people would render it easy to settle among them. At Mercury Bay in the north and at Queen Charlotte Sound in the south, Cook went through the ceremony of claiming parts of New Zealand though he never sought to 'take possession' of the whole country.[6]

During Cook's first visit, he passed at sea the French explorer, Jean de Surville, without seeing him. De Surville visited Doubtless Bay and then continued his voyage. Three years later, another French explorer, Marion du Fresne visited the Bay of Islands and, after a series of blunders, was killed by the local tribe. His second-in-command, Julien Crozet, massacred some two hundred and fifty Māori in retaliation. Crozet's attitude was shown in his comment 'that there is amongst all the animals of the creation none more ferocious and dangerous for human beings than the primitive and savage man. . . .' Before leaving, he took possession in the French King's name 'of the Island of New Zealand, which . . . Marion had called *France Australe*. . . .'[7]

The visits of the explorers brought the early New Zealanders an awareness of a wider world, experience of new weapons and the use of iron, and, on a limited scale, new crops and diseases, but these first contacts were not of great significance. As the eighteenth century progressed, traders gradually took the place of the explorers; they were to dominate the European presence in New Zealand until the late 1830s, when the population of more permanent European settlers reached noticeable proportions.[8] Traders and settlers were alike in their susceptibility to the world-wide economy — to fluctuations in demand and investment opportunities and to variations in government policies overseas — but the trading period also showed many features that distinguished it from the society that was to follow. Early relationships between Māori and European were usually of mutual convenience and economic benefit, the preservation of which was likely to regulate behaviour. Apart from the few missionaries amongst the Europeans, nobody consciously sought to alter values or customs. The fact that the European population was almost entirely male brought considerable flexibility to the normal pattern of European family life. Since one of the parties was transient, natural resources were plundered freely, but there was also little conflict between Māori and European over land. Māori rather than European influence predominated, but within a context of mutual dependence. For Māori, trade in muskets was often a matter of survival; for Europeans, Māori food was usually essential. Violent conflict between the races erupted occasionally, but such incidents were rare within the total amount of social interaction. Politically, economically, and militarily, the two peoples resident in New Zealand in the late eighteenth and early nineteenth centuries were in need of each other, and a spirit of tolerance and respect generally prevailed.

The exploitation of a few basic resources noted by Cook and his party — whales, seals, timber, New Zealand flax (*Phormium tenax*), and some agricultural products — provided the basis for trade before 1840. Commerce with New Zealand opened in the 1790s, in the wake of the founding of the New South Wales penal settlement. The very first instructions to its Governor contained a reference to the economic possibilities of New Zealand flax. But New Zealand was not just an Australian frontier: British traders were to be found in New Zealand waters from the beginning; Americans were more active in some areas; and French enterprise was at times vigorous. International rivalry was one reason why resources were often over-exploited.

The traders' first contacts were tentative. Lieutenant-Governor King of Norfolk Island had two northern Māori kidnapped in 1793 in the hope that they could explain the working of flax. Deep-sea whaling began in 1791–92 when the whaler *William and Ann* tested the prospects off the New Zealand coast. The first sealer was the *Britannia*, which left a gang at Dusky Sound in 1792. These men collected 4,500 sealskins for the Chinese market and began to build a vessel. In 1794–95 the *Fancy* spent three months at the Thames cutting spars for the Indian navy and collecting flax. It was followed by the *Hunter*, which took spars to China in 1798, and the *Plumier* and *Royal Admiral* in 1801. Although the East India Company's monopoly over commerce in the South Pacific for a while inhibited trade, by 1802 Governor King wrote that whaling off the New Zealand coast was now established.[9]

Most of the sealing ships came from Sydney, Hobart, the United States, or Britain. The Americans in particular played a major role and outlasted their colonial and British rivals. They were present in New Zealand waters from 1797, and an American sealer, O. F. Smith, has been credited with the discovery of Foveaux Strait in 1804. They had 'reckless efficiency' in the work, one vessel entering Sydney in 1806 with a cargo of 60,000 sealskins. Their activity was one of the arguments for whittling away the monopoly of the East India Company.[10]

Although seals were found, and doubtless hunted, as far north as Cook Strait, the sealing gangs usually operated in the far south, from Dusky Sound around to the Otago coast. The period of greatest activity was from 1803 to 1810, in Foveaux Strait; the discovery of the sub-antarctic Campbell and Macquarie Islands in 1810 then led sealers to concentrate on this area; thereafter the industry declined, although it revived somewhat in the 1820s and 1830s. But sealing was no longer profitable on its own and became a supplement to shore whaling and to trade in other commodities, such as potatoes and pork, flax and timber.

The long-term benefits brought to the New Zealand economy by sealing are doubtful, but it was attractive in the early years because the capital investment required was relatively small.[11] At a time when little else offered, sealing provided possibilities for large profits. As Sir Joseph Banks commented in 1806, the animals were there for the killing, as easily as men 'kill hogs in a pen with mallets'.[12] International demand also encouraged sealing: skins from the fur seal were exported to China, America, or England to be used in the making of felt hats; oil from the elephant seal was also a valuable although sometimes neglected commodity. But felt hats went out of fashion, and demand for other sealing products dropped: the rise and fall of sealing underlined the fact that New Zealand was already caught in the world economy.

Whaling in New Zealand was of two distinct kinds: deep-sea whaling in pursuit of the cachalot or sperm whale, valued for its blubber and the spermaceti oil used in lubrication and lighting; and shore or bay whaling, the hunting of the black right whale, sought both for 'black' oil and for whalebone, used principally in women's corsets. Deep-sea whaling was only significant to New Zealand because from the 1790s the whalers called in, mainly at the Bay of Islands, for refreshment, women, and occasional trading. Some Māori served on whalers and travelled the world. Large numbers of these short-term visitors could have more impact on local communities than some of the long-term settlers such as the missionaries.

Deep-sea whaling, unlike sealing, needed a good deal of capital; the backing was mainly American and British, although a significant number of French vessels and some from Portugal arrived in the later 1830s. The Australians engaged in deep-sea whaling only from the 1820s, and then usually in combination with British firms. This form of whaling reached its peak in the 1830s, and in 1839 there were, on one estimate, eighty American whaleships in New Zealand.[13] By the late 1830s, however, British and New South Wales whalers had begun to decline in numbers, partly because of over-fishing but also because of a depression and 'changes in investment opportunities and expected returns'.[14] Although some sperm whaling continued in the New Zealand region until the 1870s, foreign whalers ceased to come after 1840: this resource, like others in New Zealand, had been over-exploited by the early traders; customs duties were also imposed after annexation; and other whaling grounds were opening up.

The ancient method of hunting known as bay whaling began to be used in Van Diemen's Land (Tasmania) in 1805, but was not practised in New Zealand until the late 1820s. Sharing many features with sealing, it appears to have been developed because sealing declined. More capital, however, was required, and most of this finance was provided by the merchants of Sydney and Hobart. But the Australians did not monopolize shore whaling. From 1834 on, Americans were frequently to be found, mainly in the Kapiti coast area; the French too exploited grounds off Banks Peninsula after 1836, usually operating from anchored vessels rather than shore stations; and the occasional Portuguese, German, or Dutch ship was to be seen. The different nationalities sometimes clashed but more often there was advantage in co-operation. This was also the case in relationships between Māori and whalers.

The earliest whaling stations were those of John Guard at Te Awaiti in Tory Channel, and Bunn and Company's station at Preservation Inlet.

Other notable stations were Cloudy Bay (Archibald Mossman), Banks Peninsula, Otago (the Weller brothers), Waikouaiti (Johnny Jones), and the Kapiti coast area. There were also a few further north, in Hawke's Bay, Mahia, and Taranaki. These bay whaling stations were often established settlements, involving more men and more money than the early camps set up by whalers. Johnny Jones, for instance, claimed in 1839 that he had seven whaling stations in New Zealand, employing 280 men and involving a yearly outlay of £15,000. The Wellers' settlement on the Otago Peninsula, which flourished between 1831 and 1840, had at its peak about 120 men in about eighty cottages, probably the biggest European settlement at that time apart from Kororareka in the Bay of Islands.[15] Because it was a seasonal occupation and also one with diminishing returns, bay whaling often led to farming, or was run in combination with general trade, particularly in flax but also in potatoes, timber, fish, and, for a while, dried Māori heads. Bay whaling stations often became originating points of permanent European settlement.

The life of the bay whalers was a strange mixture: idleness alternating with back-breaking toil and danger; self-indulgence mixed with iron discipline and an orderly routine. Visitors praised their Māori wives and the neatness and cleanliness of their homes. Yet in many a whaling station the 'drinking season' would last for months and the smell of arrack rum was said to infect the air to a great distance. A whaling station normally included houses, storehouses, boatsheds, and cookhouse, scaffolding and tackle for cutting the blubber off the whale, and large iron vats for boiling out the oil. A variety of dogs, pigs, goats, fowls, and pigeons was likely to be seen; children on one occasion were described as playing on the oily beach and having generally 'the large and fine eye and the dark glossy hair' of their mothers, but sometimes flaxen hair and blue eyes from their fathers. The whalers spoke a slang intelligible only to themselves and went by nicknames such as 'Geordie Bolts', 'Flash Bill', 'Fat Jackson', and 'Black Peter'. Their boats, twenty to thirty feet long, clinker built and sharp at both ends, were remarkably seaworthy and were frequently adopted by Māori in preference to canoes.[16]

The whales were killed in the months of May to October, when the females came in shore to give birth. The whalers would kill the calf and thus trap the mother which would not desert her young. This 'unprofitable and cruel proceeding' inevitably destroyed its own livelihood, like sealing before it.[17] But, as with sealing, there were additional reasons for the industry's decline — economic depression, better alternative investment opportunities, the use of cheaper vegetable oil in place of whale oil, British tariffs, and the annexation of New Zealand. Most bay whaling stations had closed down by the 1850s, though some Māori boat crews continued shore whaling into the 1930s.

Flax had been regarded as an important commodity ever since Cook and Banks had pointed out that this indigenous plant, growing freely throughout New Zealand, could be used for its fibre, particularly in ropes and cordage. Successive governors of New South Wales, from Governor

King onwards, took steps to foster the trade, and leading figures in the commercial world such as Simeon Lord and the Rev. Samuel Marsden sought to exploit it. Many schemes for European settlement put forward in Australia or Britain based their dreams on the conviction that New Zealand flax was an economic staple. Some of these projects were put into effect, with varying success.

In the early 1820s the New South Wales Government sent several vessels in an attempt to foster the flax trade. Although apparently unsuccessful, these visits were followed by a boom in the exporting of flax, possibly because the decline in sealing led to a search for alternative investments. In 1827 Thomas Raine and David Ramsay, together with Gordon Browne, established a base at Horeke in the Hokianga to gather flax and timber. During the next few years Sydney and Hobart merchants placed agents all around New Zealand to trade with tribes for flax. These traders, with the shore whalers, were the first European settlers of any consequence for the Māori, apart from missionaries. Many, such as Captain J. R. Kent who traded with the Waikato Māori or Philip Tapsell who lived among the Arawa at Maketu near Tauranga, had a significant impact on the surrounding tribes, mainly because they exchanged muskets for flax and because for a while Māori were prepared to make any sacrifices to gain the weapons they needed.

The value of flax exports reached a peak in 1831.[18] Thereafter it dropped sharply, showing some recovery in 1834, 1836, and 1839. Although the overseas market for flax had contracted, a failure to maintain the quality of dressed flax appears to have been the main reason for the decline. All attempts to find a satisfactory mechanical process for scraping flax had failed; the laborious methods of Māori women, working with the aid of a mussell shell, provided an excellent product, but these could not be transformed into methods of mass production.

Throughout this period, visiting vessels bound for all parts of the world also loaded timber to supplement their cargoes. The British navy had a particular interest and from time to time sent its own vessels in search of timber. The navy ships *Dromedary* and *Coromandel* visited the Bay of Islands, Whangaroa, and Thames in 1820, and in the 1830s HMS *Buffalo* called. In 1820 the colonial schooner *Prince Regent* successfully crossed the bar to the Hokianga river. Thereafter the Hokianga was opened to trading contacts, particularly with Sydney and Hobart. A new phase to the timber trade began when Raine, Ramsay, and Browne set up a shipyard at Horeke. Here the 40-ton schooner *Enterprise*, the 140-ton brigantine *New Zealander*, and the barque *Sir George Murray*, of nearly 400 tons, were built.[19]

The partners were soon bankrupt. Thomas McDonnell, who for a while was Additional British Resident, took over the establishment. The Hokianga harbour soon had a number of European sawyers scattered up its various inlets. The Māori of the Hokianga became deeply involved in the timber trade. As a Wesleyan missionary, Nathaniel Turner, put it: 'They pull and haul and sweat like Horses', dragging the timber out of the bush.[20] Gradually timber mills opened elsewhere. Gordon Browne, who became a leading figure in the trade, operated with Ranulph Dacre at Mahurangi in the Hauraki Gulf and at Mercury Bay. An American, William Webster, also milled timber on an ambitious scale in the Coromandel area. In the Bay of Islands, Gilbert Mair and James Reddy Clendon were leading timber merchants.

By 1833 the value of timber exports to New South Wales had exceeded that of flax and in 1840 reached its highest figure, £12,197. By then 'some hundreds' of Europeans and many Māori in different parts of the country were involved. The exploitation of timber was as ruthless as that of other resources. The German naturalist and surgeon, Ernst Dieffenbach, who lived in New Zealand from 1839 to 1841, expressed concern at the 'melancholy scene of waste and destruction'. The industry was equally destructive in its impact on Māori health in the Hokianga.[21]

All this activity helped to foster agriculture. From the 1800s Māori had been trading in pork and potatoes; by the late 1830s they were exporting considerable quantities of barley, oats, peas, maize, and wheat to New South Wales. This diversification was due partly to missionary influence. Samuel Marsden introduced horses and cattle in 1814; the first plough was used by a missionary at Kerikeri in May 1820; and a demonstration farm was set up at the Waimate mission station in 1831. Wesleyan missionaries grew crops and ran cattle until 1827 at Whangaroa, and later in the Hokianga. But bay whalers and timber merchants also had crops and ran stock, including cattle, sheep, and goats. In 1833 John Bell settled on Mana Island with 10 head of cattle and 102 sheep, and began to raise crops, including tobacco. A few years later there were 200 sheep on the island in very good condition together with 30 cattle and some horses; more cattle were reported on Kapiti Island. In November 1839 Captain W. B. Rhodes established at Akaroa the first cattle station in the South Island.

Innovations in Māori agriculture went hand in hand with European enterprise, sometimes following a European example, sometimes demonstrating a potential that Europeans were later to follow. Some innovations were accepted more readily than others: the potato, for example, spread rapidly. There was always a ready sale for this staple food among Europeans and its cultivation came easily to a people accustomed to growing kūmara, taro, and yam. But vegetables such as cabbage did not receive the same care. Wheat and maize, introduced by the earliest explorers and cultivated by the Bay of Islands chiefs Ruatara and Hongi in the first decade of the century, did not come into their own until the late 1830s. 'New Zealand is becoming a perfect granary for New South Wales', wrote the *Sydney Gazette* on 12 May 1836. For years Māori had remained indifferent to missionary efforts to encourage wheat farming: perhaps the missionaries' methods were at fault or the threat of raids by other tribes was too strong a deterrent, but there is no simple explanation for the sudden interest in wheat growing in the 1830s. Although the market for wheat had certainly expanded, a similar increase in the demand for dairy produce among ships visiting the Bay of Islands did not lead to the growth of dairy farming in that area. And although the Māori were not accustomed to cultivating crops such as wheat, nor did they have a tradition of caring for stock; the Kaikohe chief David Taiwhanga none the less successfully ran cattle and sold butter to the Bay of Islands merchants. The acceptance or rejection of innovations in agriculture was apparently more a matter of individual circumstance than general rule.[22]

Contact with the traders inevitably brought change to Māori society: their presence alone stimulated economic activity, and they brought with them new ways, tools, and techniques. More conscious in their efforts to introduce change were the missionaries. In many respects these men were not markedly different from traders — at least, the so-called respectable traders. Following a policy of 'civilization first', the Church Missionary Society began by sending men with technical skills and encouraged them to engage in trade. When more emphasis was placed on preaching and teaching in the 1820s, the mission station was still noted for its substantial buildings and its trade goods, always a source of great mana and profit to associated tribes, and technical skills were taught. But the missionaries differed from most other Europeans in that they did not normally cohabit with Māori women, and they sought to change rather than be absorbed in Māori social life. The mission station was commonly conceived as an island of civilization in a heathen world, setting an alternative pattern of life. Yet missionaries have been credited with more influence than they exerted and blamed for more harm than they caused.

Before 1840 there were three missionary groups, the Anglicans, represented by the Church Missionary Society, the Wesleyans, and the Roman Catholics. The CMS began at Rangihoua in the Bay of Islands in 1814 as a result of the lobbying of the Rev. Samuel Marsden, the New South Wales chaplain. Its members were Thomas Kendall, schoolmaster and Justice of the Peace, William Hall, a carpenter, and John King, a shoemaker. Their intended protector, the chief Ruatara, was dying, and Marsden sailed away leaving the three families and some unmarried men in a temporary, draughty, leaky home divided into partitions. It was hardly surprising that they achieved little beyond surviving. In 1823 the Rev. Henry Williams arrived to begin a mission at Paihia on the southern side of the Bay and was joined by his brother William in 1826. An ex-naval officer, narrow but courageous and determined, Henry Williams soon commanded respect. William Williams contributed much, especially through his skill with the Māori language. More CMS missionaries arrived: Robert Maunsell, another linguist, William Colenso, the printer and Māori scholar, George Clarke, later to be Chief Protector of Aborigines, and men such as A. N. Browne, Octavius Hadfield, and Richard Taylor, all of whom were to prove notable figures as the century advanced. In 1831 the missionary farm was established at Waimate, and after 1834 new missions were established, northwards at Kaitaia and Whangaroa, to the south at Thames, Manukau, Waikato, Matamata, Rotorua, Tauranga, and Poverty Bay. For the most part the CMS kept to the eastern side of the North Island, but in 1839 Hadfield was placed at Otaki and Waikanae.

The Wesleyan Missionary Society had fewer men, usually only about three or four in the country at any one time. Principal among them were Samuel Leigh, who initiated the mission, Nathaniel Turner, William White, John Hobbs, James Stack (later with the CMS), John Whiteley, William Woon, and James Wallis. The Wesleyan mission at Whangaroa lasted from 1823 to 1827 when it was attacked and sacked. They re-established themselves at Mangungu in the Hokianga and in the later 1830s set up further stations at Pakanae in the Hokianga, at Tangiteroria, inland from Whangarei, and at Kawhia and Whaingaroa (Raglan). The Roman Catholic Marist Mission, under Bishop Pompallier, began in the Hokianga in 1838, later shifting to Kororareka. By 1841 he reported that he had baptized about a thousand Māori.

The impact of the missionaries was at first slight. Taken together they were few in number, and their activities were limited in scope. Large parts of the country remained untouched by missionary influence. Among Ngāpuhi of the Bay of Islands, where they were most active in the early years, the results of their efforts were not readily apparent until the late 1820s. This greater success coincided with a period of considerable social upheaval.[23] After a succession of victorious raids to the south, Ngāpuhi began to suffer defeat as southern tribes acquired muskets. A number of notable chiefs, such as Hongi, Pomare I, and also Muriwai of the Hokianga, had recently died. European influence was increasing, and this was the time when smoking and alcohol became popular in the area. The growing response to missionary endeavour during this period is probably not coincidental. There is, however, only one other instance suggesting that social breakdown was the major reason for accepting Christianity. A study of the South Island in the 1840s and 1850s argues that Christianity, when it came, was a 'plug to fill a gaping need'. Against the case possibly made by these two instances, a series of studies of other areas have indicated that missionaries, or Māori evangelists, often made their impact before European influence had brought major change to a community. The response in such areas can probably be ascribed at least in part to the improvement in missionary resources and techniques. More money was being spent on missions, better-trained men of stronger character had arrived, more emphasis was being placed on preaching and teaching; knowledge of the language had grown; and, from 1827 onwards, translations of the Bible, Prayer Book, and hymns had been made. The realization that their language could be conveyed in printed form created much excitement amongst the Māori. Those who had learnt to read and write passed on the skills to others, and in the process conveyed much of the missionary message. In this respect the Ngāpuhi raids eventually and unexpectedly helped the expansion of Christianity. Their captives from southern tribes came under the influence of the missionaries, were freed, and returned home. Far from losing all mana as slaves, they enjoyed prestige as having been at the centre of the new influences. One such was Taumata of Ngāti Porou on the East Coast, who had a testament reputed to ward off bullets and who would begin his unorthodox teaching with: 'I have come from Keri Keri and from Paihia, and I have seen Williams of the four eyes.'[24]

The social situations in which Māori responded to the teaching of the missionaries made some difference to their success, but they were the context not the main cause. More significant in explaining missionary achievement at this point is the improvement in their methods. But an interchange of ideas does not take place in a social vacuum, and the variety of ways in which Māori came to respond to missionary teaching was the result partly of the interplay of Christian and Māori ideas and partly of the social problems for which religious solutions appeared relevant. Social context did not provide the initial impetus for conversion but it helped to determine, as time went on, what beliefs were acceptable. Māori responses to Christianity ranged from rejection to total acceptance. Sometimes only one facet of missionary teaching, such as medicine or the idea of the Sabbath as a day of rest, was accepted. Sometimes cult movements produced a new blend of Māori and Christian ideas. Among those who formally accepted missionary teaching there was every variety of belief and practice. There were also those who simply used traditional or Christian ideas or practices as they seemed appropriate. But, whatever the response, the fact that there was suddenly something for Māori to respond to was surely the consequence of more effective missionary communication.

Among the different responses, the religious movement associated with Papahurihia, who became known as Te Atua Wera, was particularly interesting. First reported in the Bay of Islands in July 1833, and later in the Hokianga, it began in the same period and area as the first Māori baptisms. Missionaries reported its teachings in a garbled form, but the movement clearly blended their own message with traditional Māori religion. The missionary Sabbath was kept but now observed on a Saturday; heaven and hell were retained in a revised form that excluded the missionaries from heaven; there was a European flag and flagpole but the additional symbolism of trees was distinctively Māori; evening services were held, but worshippers conversed with spirits in the traditional style; the god Nakahi was clearly derived from the serpent of the Book of Genesis but related also to the Māori ngārara or lizard spirit form; baptism was practised but Te Atua Wera's methods were generally those of a tohunga. The teaching reflected the oddities of missionary belief along with orthodox Christianity: followers of the cult were known as Hūrai, or Jews, in line with a common missionary belief that Māori were descendants of the lost tribes of Israel; millenarian aspects of the cult probably owed much to the faith some missionaries had in an imminent second coming. The cult persisted into the twentieth century, was influential in Hone Heke's rebellion of the early 1840s, and may have foreshadowed the Hauhau movement of the 1860s. The cult can be explained as anti-missionary, as an 'adjustment cult' (a religious reaction to a time of troubles), or as a matter of inter-tribal politics (the reaction of one tribe, the Hikutu, to the fact that its rivals had taken up Christianity).[25]

Originating as it did in the area of longest missionary activity,

Papahurihia's cult was a good example of missionary unexpected impact. In general, the missionaries had an effect quite other than they intended. Humanitarian effort in a new culture often had untoward and sometimes disastrous ramifications. Blankets were provided instead of muskets with the best of intentions, but if they were worn in the manner of traditional Māori clothing, they had bad effects on health; a hatchet was both a useful tool and a murderous weapon. Discouraging polygamy put more economic strain on women and removed a source of chiefly prestige; the ending of cannibalism left a serious gap in diet. Missionaries, of course, were too few to control the effects of their activities. They were, indeed, most influential where they could exert least control, through the printed word of Māori evangelists. It is perhaps the greatest irony that the main function of the missionaries was to prepare Māori for a secular world.

Putting the Māori language into printed form was undoubtedly one of the missionaries' achievements, but even this was not unambiguous in its consequences. In so far as it helped preserve the Māori language it was a triumph, but for the missionaries themselves a temporary triumph: briefly religious writings were able to dominate the exciting new medium. Eventually literacy was to be a great cultural step forward, but before 1840 it was of limited value. It could not unlock the literature and the technology of Europe, nor did it encourage the methods of abstraction, analysis, and comparison made available through a wide range of written materials. It was not the basis of a new approach to law and government and treaty making — as the lack of effective negotiation over the Treaty of Waitangi was to show. Literacy was for the Māori of this period a frustrated revolution, an example of the limitations of missionary impact.[26]

Exploration, a commercial presence, and missionary activity in the early years of European occupation brought to New Zealand a range of social consequences from the minimal to the profound. But the developments of this period were not solely the result of external influences: beside the potentially cataclysmic effect of Europeans on Māori society must be set the adaptation of existing social conditions to meet new demands, and an underlying continuity in many social forms throughout the period.

In many respects the Europeans who came to explore, trade, and settle brought radical change to New Zealand. Māori society moved from the age of stone to the age of iron; suddenly it was involved, if erratically, in the diverse cultures of the world. New crops, such as the potato which had so transformed Europe, made their appearance. The clock and the book arrived, the first signs of an existence regulated by exact measurement of space and time, and by the literate transmission and clarification of mental processes. New religious ideas came, offering alternative ideas of social relationship and human purpose. Alcohol was introduced, new ways of war, and new diseases. By the 1830s areas such as the Hokianga and Bay of Islands had moved from a barter system to a money economy.[27] Over a few decades Māori were participants in a series of developments which other cultures had taken centuries to absorb.

But, formidable as these changes were, they took place within a Māori framework of values representing continuity with pre-European Māori ways rather than innovation. The ability of Māori tribes to withstand powerful cultural pressures from outside lay partly in the nature of their social structure and controls. Māori kinship groupings were equipped to survive stress, and even disasters such as war and famine, at the local level. All kin groups interlocked: the whānau, or extended family of three or four generations, led out into the hapū which could number several hundred members, and so into the iwi, or tribe, even to the waka, or group of tribes.[28] These social groups, though based on descent, were capable of constant change and re-grouping.

External pressures were also limited in their effect because they were extremely uneven. Economic contacts were essentially local, although their effects spread out in wider circles. The degree of exposure to the European world thus varied greatly: one area, such as the Bay of Islands, was subjected to a disastrous pace of change while other areas, such as the interior of the North Island, enjoyed the gentle stimulus of useful innovation. Regional variation had always been a feature of New Zealand; now a new dimension was added — the distinction between areas of direct and indirect contact.

Where there was direct contact with Europeans, this could vary in intensity. Europeans were present in the Bay of Islands almost continuously from the time of Cook's first visit. The area appeared frequently in descriptions and reports, and it is often taken as typical. But Māori–European contact here was unlike that in any other area. Europeans (sometimes the same ones) were also present in the far south of the South Island for the same lengthy period; but there were fewer missionaries, the climate and resources were very different, and so too were the southern Māori. Traders entered the Thames and Coromandel areas to get timber from the 1790s onwards, but they had less impact there than Europeans did in the Bay of Islands.

Māori in other areas such as Cook Strait and the Hokianga first knew of Europeans at second-hand. These areas too differed one from another. Wesleyan missionary teaching preceded Anglican in the Hokianga; its Europeans were mainly in the timber trade; and it was strongly influenced by the Bay of Islands, both in inter-tribal relationships and the consequences of European contact. Europeans in the Cook Strait area were mainly bay whalers and flax traders; the Māori people of the area, recently arrived from further north, were deeply involved in warfare under their warrior chief Te Rauparaha, who gave a distinctive twist to relationships with the Europeans.

The majority of the Māori population — including tribes such as Tūhoe, Waikato, Ngāti Porou, and Ngāti Kahungunu — lived in areas where contact was usually indirect.[29] Little is known about such districts. These Māori communities might have an isolated Pākehā-Māori (a European living as a Māori) in them, or have visits from the occasional trader or missionary; shipping might call from time to time; or they might never see a European. Again no area was typical, but, generally speaking, people who had little or no direct contact with Europeans absorbed few of their practices, and learned of them through other Māori. They might be attacked by a neighbouring group with European muskets, or receive from them new artefacts, crops, weapons, religious ideas, literacy, or disease. While sudden or drastic change could occur, the more usual characteristic of these areas was innovation at a controlled rate. Continuity was more readily preserved than in areas of direct contact.

Differences between areas can lead to very different conclusions about the extent and significance of European impact by 1840: there is evidence both of the transforming power of European innovations and of the stability and continuity of Māori life. Each conclusion is true: European innovation had more power in areas of direct contact, and Māori society exhibited more continuity in areas of indirect contact. But neither generalization is wholly true of either kind of area.

Contemporary accounts by Europeans frequently contained a third view of developments in New Zealand early in the nineteenth century, one that is conveniently termed the 'fatal impact' theory. Especially in the 1830s, they depicted the country as devastated by European contact. In a typical missionary report Samuel Marsden wrote: 'no laws, judges, nor magistrates; so that Satan maintains his dominion without molestation.' A similar, if less eloquent view was taken by some two hundred British settlers who petitioned their monarch in 1837 about the lack of order in the land. But the most influential document was a despatch of 16 June 1837 from James Busby, the British Resident, in which he wrote of 'the accumulating evils of permanent anarchy' and of depopulation 'going on, till district after district has become void of its inhabitants. . . .'[30] These are unusual words to use of a country whose exports were booming, which continued to attract and hold traders and settlers and their families, and in which no missionary had yet suffered serious harm. But the alarmist reports persisted, and gained no little credibility in Britain.

Busby's despatch taken as a whole reveals that the picture of anarchy and depopulation in New Zealand was presented in order to persuade the Colonial Office to accept a complicated scheme of government in New Zealand — one that would enhance Busby's own role. The scheme was ignored, but the disorder alleged in New Zealand was taken seriously and helped to convince the British Government that it must intervene more actively in the running of the country. Ever since, it has been part of the humanitarian justification for British rule. The 'fatal impact' theory had more to do with British interests than the state of New Zealand society at the time.

None of these reports was a piece of impartial social analysis. Busby's despatch was a deliberate attempt to manipulate his masters by playing on their preconceptions and their sense of responsibility for the consequences of the British presence. Any references to the state of Māori society or of lawlessness in the white community in Colonial Office papers of the time 'were invariably underlined for further consideration'.[31] Although the convict colony of New South Wales was living evidence of the inadequacy of social controls in Britain, it was confidently believed that the British machinery of central government, legislation, and law enforcement offered the best means of preventing anarchy. The failure of attempts to control society from outside only fed the view that New Zealand was anarchical. Disorder was assumed to be the same in any culture and the Māori, as Busby wrote in his despatch, were children in need of protection.

Most of the external pressure for the institution of British order in these islands emanated from New South Wales, where successive governors, responding to agitation by missionaries or merchants, passed a series of 'Government and General Orders'. Most of these attempted to regulate the conduct of British subjects towards Māori. Governor Macquarie also, with dubious legality, appointed two missionaries as Justices of the Peace in New Zealand, Thomas Kendall in 1814 and the Rev. John Butler in 1819.[32]

The British Government was less concerned. Passing its first legislation relating to New Zealand in 1817, in response to CMS outrage about European atrocities, the British Government emphasized that the country was 'not within His Majesty's Dominions'.[33] Subsequent legislation in 1823 and 1828 made provision for offences to be tried in New South Wales. The most notable case was that of Edward Doyle, executed in 1837 for robbery with an attempt to murder in the Bay of Islands. More serious was the action of Captain Stewart of the brig *Elizabeth* who in return for a supply of flax transported Te Rauparaha to Akaroa to take vengeance against a tribal enemy. The legal process in this instance proved ineffective.

This and a scandal over trade in dried Māori heads, against which Governor Darling of New South Wales issued a Proclamation, precipitated the appointment of a British Resident. There were also at this time fears about French intentions to annex New Zealand, and in 1831 thirteen Bay of Islands and Hokianga chiefs appealed, at the instigation of the CMS, to the British King for protection. The new Resident, James Busby, reached New Zealand in 1833. He has generally been portrayed as a figure of fun and his inability to influence affairs has reinforced the picture of 'New Zealand anarchy'. Henry Williams of the CMS generally exercised the 'moral suasion' expected of Busby. He and other missionaries continued to be more effective than the Resident even on those occasions when Busby had the backing of British naval vessels. Williams had the advantage of a strong character; but he stood too for religious sanctions, which had always been able to influence Māori behaviour. The concepts of authority on which Busby relied for respect were alien.

But if Busby was largely irrelevant as a force for order, he was of some use in his other task, assisting the commercial relations of Britain and her colonies with New Zealand. He also achieved a number of other objectives, some of which had considerable symbolic significance. In October 1837, for example, Busby convened a gathering of thirty-four northern chiefs at Waitangi where they declared their country to be an independent state, though at the same time requesting the British King to continue as their parent and protector. Later the names of seventeen other notable chiefs, such as Te Hapuku of Hawke's Bay and Te Wherowhero of Waikato, were added. Ostensibly this move was a response to an announcement by an eccentric of French descent, Baron Charles de Thierry, that he intended to become 'sovereign chief of New Zealand'. In fact, Busby was again pursuing his own career by setting up a legislative body to circumvent his rival in the Hokianga, Thomas McDonnell, the Additional British Resident, who was acting as an independent authority. The New South Wales Governor, Bourke, saw through Busby and ridiculed the proceedings. The plan to meet annually at Waitangi to frame laws and exact justice came to nothing. But the British Government, which had recognized a national flag organized by Busby in 1834, formally accepted its role as parent and protector. This had little effect in New Zealand, but it was to complicate the later annexation of the country.[34]

The British navy had always influenced New Zealand affairs. In 1826 the Admiralty ordered that the ship stationed at New South Wales should occasionally inspect the coasts of New Zealand. Thereafter the navy visited regularly. Usually it carried out its task with tact and skill; it settled many disputes and acted as a general, if rather uncertain, deterrent against violence towards British subjects. But on the one occasion when HMS *Alligator* and troops of the 50th Regiment took significant action against Taranaki Māori in 1834, an inadequate interpreter and the indiscipline of the troops made the operation brutal and unjust. The French navy played a similar role, not only making a number of voyages of exploration but also showing the flag in support of its whaling fleet and its nationals, such as de Thierry and Bishop Pompallier. When the crew of the French whaler *Jean Bart* were killed by the inhabitants of the Chatham Islands, severe reprisals were inflicted by the French corvette, *L'Heroine*. Despite its considerable commercial commitment, the United States did not make a practice of sending naval vessels; but from 1839 onwards it maintained its own consular representative in the Bay of Islands, the English merchant Clendon.[35]

All of these efforts by other governments to influence behaviour in New Zealand had limited results. In contrast to Pacific islands such as Hawaii, Tahiti, or Tonga, the years of European contact did not lead to centralized government, despite the comments of Cook, the urgings of Marsden, and the efforts of Busby. This failure to impose order must have appeared particularly tragic to the European observer who saw the consequences of fighting between groups of Māori and noted the widespread use of European weapons. It was easy for a European to conclude that Māori warfare was anarchic and uncontrolled; that it had no constructive social role; that the supply of European weapons had caused much of the fighting; and that such apparent mass slaughter, unchecked, would be the destruction of the Māori people. But all these conclusions were false or exaggerated.

The main campaigns of the early nineteenth century can be briefly summarized, although there is relatively little information about warfare in the years around the turn of the century. Muskets were being used in localized warfare around the Bay of Islands in the 1800s, and in that region pā, or fortifications such as Waimate and Okuratope, had by 1814 been adapted to musket warfare.[36] Muskets gave greater protection against ambush, and enabled expeditions to go further afield. In 1818 there were two expectations that clearly demonstrated the offensive advantages of the new weapon: Hongi Hika and Te Morenga, Ngāpuhi chiefs of the Bay of Islands, led war-parties against the Ngāti Porou people near the East Cape, causing great slaughter and bringing back numbers of prisoners.

The following year, Ngāpuhi of the Hokianga, under the chiefs Patuone, Tamati Waka Nene, and Moetara led an extended expedition. Joined by southern tribes such as Ngāti Toa of the Kawhia area under Te Rauparaha, they ranged through Taranaki, Wanganui, the future Port Nicholson, and the Wairarapa. This expedition is said to have given Te Rauparaha the idea that his people could settle in the Kapiti coast area where they would have greater security against attack by the Waikato people and Ngāti Maniapoto, and better access to European trade.

Hongi's visit to London in 1820–21 in company with the CMS missionary, Thomas Kendall, augmented the Ngāpuhi supply of arms. On his return, Hongi embarked on a series of expeditions down the east coast and into the central North Island. In 1821 he attacked Ngāti Maru of the Thames district, and Ngāti Paoa of the Auckland area. In 1822 he attacked the Waikato tribe led by Te Wherowhero, the future Māori King, Potatau I, inflicting great casualties. The next year he attacked the Arawa people at Rotorua. At the battle of Te Ika-a-ranga-nui in 1825 he avenged a defeat at Moremonui in 1807 by Ngāti Whātua of the Kaipara and Tamaki areas. Wounded in a minor skirmish in the Hokianga in 1827, he died in March 1828.

After this there were fewer Ngāpuhi raids, but Te Rauparaha, joined in the Kapiti area by some of Ngāti Raukawa from north of Lake Taupo and by Ngāti Awa from Taranaki, was in constant conflict with the Muaupoko people of Horowhenua, with Ngāti Ira from the area to be known as Wellington, and with Ngāti Kahungunu of Wairarapa. In the years following his first attack in 1828, he was engaged in campaigns against the South Island tribe, Ngāi Tahu, seizing one of their chiefs, Tamaiharanui, with the help of Captain Stewart and the *Elizabeth*, and eventually capturing their powerful pā at Kaiapohia. However, Te Rauparaha suffered severe defeat at the hands of the southern Ngāi Tahu chiefs Tuhawaiki ('Bloody Jack') and Taiaroa in 1831, and in subsequent years they held their own against him.

Conflict erupted also in other parts of the North Island: the Waikato and Ngāti Maniapoto under Te Wherowhero moved not only against the Ngāti Toa in the Kawhia area, but also against the Taranaki peoples in the 1830s; Te Waharoa, chief of the Ngāti Hauā tribe of Waikato, led expeditions against Ngāti Raukawa in the Waikato area, Ngāti Maru in the Thames area, and some of the Arawa people in the area of Maketu. Further south there was a drawn out struggle in the 1820s between the joint forces of

Ngāti Raukawa and Ngāti Tūwharetoa against Ngāti Kahungunu, who managed to hold their position in Hawke's Bay.[37]

Estimates of casualties incurred in these wars have varied between 20,000 and 80,000.[38] As there are no figures for pre-European deaths from war, there is no statistical basis for comparison with the past. Massive slaughter certainly occurred on a number of occasions, particularly during the campaigns of Hongi and Te Rauparaha, but such episodes were confined to specific incidents. When the European traveller encountered a depopulated area, it might as much be the result of a raid for slaves, of voluntary migration to a safer area, or simply migration for economic reasons. It has been estimated that some 30,000 Māori moved to different areas because of warfare and this was subsequently to cause endless complications over land rights. But there was nothing new in warfare causing migration and resettlement.

This fighting between Māori groups also had political implications. For the European, Māori warfare seemed a breakdown of order, an aberration rather than part of a social system. It did not lead to results that would seem to a European constructive, such as the creation of larger political units. Māori warfare was, however, subject to the constraints of established custom. There were alternatives to war, such as the taua muru, a plundering expedition whose actions were accepted by the victim because they followed accepted rules; there were also recognized procedures for peacemaking, such as teretere (diplomatic missions), the efforts of high ranking chiefs who acted as peacemakers, the practices of feasting and gift giving, the exchange of hostages, and inter-tribal marriage.[39] Such procedures made it possible to redress wrongs, settle differences, and maintain order between otherwise independent tribes and sub-tribes. Warfare, in short, was not only subject to strict controls; it was in itself often an effective control on social behaviour.

The causes of the fighting were complex. Europeans were often misled when Māori cited a desire for utu — revenge for past wrongs which threatened the mana of the tribe or its chief — as the reason for a campaign. The importance of mana was not simply symbolic, as it generally accompanied security and well-being. But economic pressures were also a major reason for fighting, and these were exacerbated by the arrival of the Europeans. Battles were fought to control access to popular anchorages such as Kororareka, Whangaroa, Maketu, Tauranga, or those in Cook Strait, and to obtain slaves to serve European needs. Ngāpuhi needed slaves for prostitution or to grow crops in the Bay of Islands; Te Rauparaha needed them to scrape flax to trade for muskets in the Cook Strait area. Thus through war he obtained the weapons of war. War enabled chiefs to enhance their own mana and persuaded their people to tolerate the economic effort and social upheaval that came with the Europeans. War facilitated innovation and quickened the pace of change; destructive and creative, it was often a response, not to muskets only, but to the total European presence.

Whether fighting between Māori increased with the arrival of the

Europeans it is impossible to say. Certainly much of the conflict had little to do with Europeans, but, equally, all European activity connected with warfare in some way. The musket itself was not crucial: it was not very accurate, especially when poorly serviced. Initially it demoralized the enemy and thereby facilitated killing with traditional weapons; but soon new methods of pā construction and new tactics of keeping a distance and taking shelter meant not only that muskets were ineffective, but also that the more lethal close combat was prevented. The Bay of Islands trader Joel Polack described a battle there in which he said there were almost 20,000 rounds of ball cartridge expended daily by perhaps 3,000 Māori: 'The Loss was but a Cipher.' Both Polack and the missionaries agreed that once muskets had been supplied to most Māori there were fewer casualties and the impetus to fight declined, since the balance of strength was more even.[40] By the 1830s the worst of the fighting was over as far as the north was concerned; and although in the next decade conflict with settlers and the Government sometimes stimulated renewed conflict, tribes in the central and southern areas were also generally at peace with each other.

The missionaries' claims to have brought peace to the Māori were exaggerated; the equalization of arms and increasing economic opportunity also played a part. This decline in warfare was welcomed by humanitarian observers, yet its effects were not immediately beneficial. Māori fighting had operated under strict controls, and it provided a competitive zest for life. It tested and strengthened the leadership, acted as a motivation to economic effort, or as a control over social behaviour. For a while the social consequences of ending war may have been as bad as those of warfare itself, but the full effects of this were not to be felt until after 1840.

Order within and between Māori tribes was of course not maintained by fighting alone. Belief in the daily influence of the spirit world exerted another form of control by threatening automatic punishment for any infraction of recognized rules and prohibitions. Most stringent of these was the concept of tapu which placed a person or object under a religious or sacred restriction. Social obligations to one's kin were practically as powerful as the checks of the spirit world, which was in effect an extension of the kin–group. Mana was a special tapu that resided in certain leaders. But it was an elusive quality. Those who possessed mana would not necessarily command obedience. Marsden commented on his first visit to New Zealand that Māori 'are all either chiefs or, in a certain degree, slaves', and the early traveller Edward Shortland was later to write of 'democracy, limited by a certain amount of patriarchal influence'.[41] But the European phraseology of the period is misleading: many of the missionaries interpreted the disorder they discerned simply in terms of the child–rearing practices of the day. Yet Māori commonly had a highly developed sense of correct procedures in social relationships. This derived from a respect for the proper balance in all social situations that had to be restored if disturbed. By such beliefs was order maintained in Māori society.

When Europeans settled among the Māori they accepted these controls in varying degrees. At one extreme, the Pākehā-Māori appeared to merge into Māori life completely; at the other, most missionaries and some 'respectable traders' seemed to live a completely separate European existence. They would not escape, however, some influence from their neighbours: they might condemn and break tapu, but they often became concerned about their own mana and they were likely to be under tribal protection. The Pākehā-Māori in contrast rejected much of his European background: he usually married a Māori, accepted kin-group obligations, took part in warfare, as in the case of the whalers Dicky Barrett and John Love who helped Taranaki Māori defend Ngamotu against Waikato attacks in 1832, and sometimes cannibalism, as in the case of John Marmon. Along with the explorers, they were the true pioneers of race relations, establishing the conditions under which Europeans could be accepted and absorbed. As early as 1801 Europeans were reported as having lived among the Māori of the Thames area for a couple of years; and in the next few years there were a number of reports of Europeans living in the Bay of Islands, the most notable being George Bruce. Accounts of their way of life were left by a number of these men — by Frederick Maning of the Hokianga, by John Rutherford, who was probably in the Bay of Islands, by John Marmon of the Hokianga, and Barnet Burns or George White, a flax trader in Poverty Bay.[42]

Where Europeans were sufficiently numerous to protect themselves, as in the Bay of Islands, the Hokianga, Cook Strait, and parts of the South Island, they often acted as a separate tribe with a recognized leader, taking group responsibility for individual action, accepting, initiating, or resisting a taua muru in relation to their neighbours. In 1835, for example, a Māori attack on a Hokianga sawyer and his wife led to the so-called 'battle of the pork', in which some forty or fifty English, led by the Rev. William White (sometimes referred to as the 'Piratical Parson') and a Mr Russell, a merchant, slaughtered some 150 pigs and burned the houses of the offending tribe.

Europeans also experimented with forms of association they were accustomed to. Busby used an informal jury to hear evidence against a Hokianga Māori slave held responsible for murdering a European, Henry Biddle. The accused was then shot by a Māori executioner. Also in the Hokianga, a kind of jury met to hear and record the lurid allegations of sexual misconduct made against the missionary William White. Temperance associations were formed in the Bay of Islands and in the Hokianga. At Paihia in 1839 an attempt was made to found the Victoria Paternal Institution for the offspring of English fathers by New Zealand mothers. A more controversial attempt at settler self-rule was the Kororareka Association formed in 1838. It required its members to arm themselves with 'a good musket and bayonet, a brace of pistols, a cutlass, and at least thirty rounds of ball cartridge. . . .'[43] Punishments included tarring and feathering with three coats and drumming the victim off the beach, horse-whipping, or fining. The Association was denounced as lynch law; yet one observer commented that Kororareka was in 1840 one of the most orderly places in the world, where crimes of robbery and housebreaking were unknown and commercial bills were duly honoured.[44]

In this period two concepts of order, Māori and European, were meeting. Māori behaviour was determined by concepts of the sacred, directed mainly at the survival and well-being of the group. Concern for individual property and protection was less developed than in the more secular, literate European society; the missionaries' obsession with individual sin and its punishment struck few answering chords amongst the Māori. Māori reactions were designed rather to obtain compensation for injury than to inflict, in the European manner, 'salutary chastisement on the guilty person'.[45] The process of living together inevitably brought modifications for both sides. Māori sometimes looked to missionaries and to the Bible for guidance, and they began to take note of institutions such as the jury. Europeans absorbed some of the concern for equity which underlay Māori practices and learned to take direct action according to accepted rules in a local situation, rather than looking to a central authority. Trade operated as a powerful sanction, both Māori and European accepting limitations on behaviour in order that the economic relationship, desirable to both, might continue. Sexual relationships often also prevented conflict: experienced captains knew that if Māori women were on board ship the vessel was less likely to be attacked; individual Europeans who married Māori women knew that thereby they gained the protection of their wives' tribes. Perhaps surprisingly, sexual jealously was rarely a cause for Māori–European strife.

New Zealand society in the early nineteenth century thus had its controls, and though often crude and violent, they were effective. Māori and European ways had yet to blend, but they had begun to influence each other and new situations brought new solutions. The main characteristic of the New Zealand scene was local responsibility for local conduct. As one prospective settler put it, 'necessity will teach men . . . to maintain a government suited to their own wants and requirements.'[46] It would be hard to prove there was more 'anarchy' than in British society. Captain FitzRoy, questioned before a parliamentary committee about his visit to the Bay of Islands, agreed with the proposition that Kororareka was 'extremely immoral and addicted to low Vices', but, asked if it was any worse than British seaport towns, replied 'Certainly not; it is in much the same Kind of State.'[47]

Busby in his June 1837 despatch also claimed that New Zealand would soon be 'destitute of a single aboriginal inhabitant'.[48] The prediction was foolish, but it too touched a nerve in colonial policy. This was a period when aboriginal depopulation was a recurrent theme in British social thought, expressed in reports of the House of Commons Committee on Aborigines and in the publications of the newly formed Aborigines Protection Society. To think of aboriginal people was to think of depopulation, and it was a major issue in the public debate over New

Zealand between missionary bodies and those representing would-be settlers, such as the New Zealand Association.

The case for depopulation is not clear. The most reliable estimate of the Māori population at the end of the period is Dieffenbach's; his figure, published in 1843, was 114,850. But in 1769 Cook's party had calculated that the population was 100,000: either they significantly under-estimated, or the population had remained relatively stable.[49] Contemporary reports, from officials such as Busby, from the missionaries, or from the occasional visitor, commented frequently on the depopulation of 'the natives', but most of their observations were confined to their own locality, usually an area of major European contact. Often the number of deaths referred to was surprisingly small, and not all observers agreed that the population was decreasing. Those who did report depopulation did not do so consistently; after mid-1839, too late to influence decisions by the British Government about annexation, missionaries began reporting better health among the Māori.[50] The case for depopulation was often based on accounts of warfare, but while the fighting of the early nineteenth century sometimes caused considerable casualties, these were limited to particular occasions, and so allowed a degree of replacement. Also, the worst of warfare was over by the 1830s. Disease too must have taken its toll, but although many new diseases such as dysentery, venereal disease, tuberculosis, influenza, whooping cough, and measles were introduced, diseases such as yellow fever, typhus, bubonic plague, cholera, malaria, and smallpox, which decimated populations in other parts of the world, were absent from New Zealand.[51] Evidence of mortality is certainly available, but population size is also affected by the capacity to replace the adult population. This in turn is determined by the proportion of the population of child-bearing age and the ability to survive pregnancy, infancy, and childhood; the effects of polygamy, abortion, and infanticide are also relevant. Little is known about these factors in the early period of European contact.[52]

Different regions offer different evidence of depopulation. In the Bay of Islands and the Hokianga, the Māori population almost certainly did decline. But Dieffenbach, when he attempted his enumeration, stressed the separation of Māori tribes and the large number of Māori in the interior. There is also considerable evidence that at this time areas of indirect contact were maintaining or even at times increasing their population. It is likely too that areas of only marginal contact — Cook Strait, for example — suffered less than areas such as the Hokianga. These surmises are complicated by the mobility of the Māori population at this period but it seems likely that there was a correlation between the number of Europeans in an area and the amount of Māori depopulation. Social disruption such as the Europeans brought was more likely to cause depopulation than war or disease.[53]

Clearly, if Cook and Dieffenbach were both reasonably accurate, the population remained relatively stable. The possibility must be considered, however, that Cook seriously under-estimated the population in 1769. Archaeological examination of the estimated 6,000 pre-European fortified sites could confirm that the number of people was greater than Cook said. The most recent studies, however, substantially confirm the estimate of Cook's expedition. As '*at least* half the population lived in districts unknown to him', there could be room for error, but analyses of Cook's estimates elsewhere in the Pacific suggest that he tended to over-estimate populations. Any under-estimation in New Zealand thus could have been counter-balanced.[54]

At particular times and in particular places, numbers of people died as a result of disease, war or social upheaval; but whether the total population declined between 1769 and 1840 is open to question. If 'anarchy' was a misleading term and if depopulation cannot be established, the impact of the Europeans was probably not as 'fatal' as contemporaries believed. The situation was to change when Europeans began to settle in more significant numbers, which they had begun to do even before the Treaty of Waitangi was signed.

Underlying the increase in European settlement was the fact that disease favoured the European. While Māori were vulnerable to diseases which came with the European, immigrant settlers found New Zealand an exceptionally healthy place to live. As the decade of the 1830s drew to a close, the flow of immigrants from New South Wales, through areas such as the Bay of Islands, the Hokianga, and the Coromandel, grew rapidly. In 1830–31 there were between 300 and 330 Europeans in New Zealand: by the end of the decade there were thought to be some 2,000.[55] The biggest increase came in 1839 when it was known that the country was shortly to be annexed, though the flow of migration across the Tasman was under way before the New Zealand Association began exerting pressure in England and before it was certain in New South Wales that the British Government would act. The import–export trade of New Zealand had more than doubled in the 1830s.[56] In New South Wales a series of droughts, labour shortage, a fall in the price of wool, and, finally, at the beginning of 1839, the raising of the minimum price of Crown lands to 12*s*. an acre from 5*s*., led the *Sydney Gazette* to conclude: 'it is to New Zealand that the tide of Australian emigration will unquestionably flow.'[57]

This development, coupled with reports of 'anarchy and depopulation', rendered British annexation inevitable. Fears of French or American intervention, actively canvassed in New South Wales and by the New Zealand Association in Britain, do not appear to have played much part in the calculations of British officials. The New Zealand Association (soon to become the Company), manipulated by Edward Gibbon Wakefield, was to be commonly regarded as 'the principal author of the annexation of New Zealand'.[58] But far from patriotically defending a future jewel of the Empire, the Company rushed out the ship *Tory* in May 1839 because they had learned that the British Government intended to pre-empt the sale of land in New Zealand, thus removing the possibility of profit for the Company. They were following Wakefield's advice: 'Possess yourselves of the soil and you are secure.'[59]

The Company's main contribution in fact was to force the British Government and its representative, Captain William Hobson, to act too fast. He arrived in the Bay of Islands on 29 January 1840 and immediately announced himself as Lieutenant-Governor, under the authority of the Government of New South Wales. He began issuing Proclamations to British subjects and summoned the chiefs of the area to a meeting at Waitangi on 5 February. On the basis of instructions given to him by Lord Normanby, the Secretary of State at the Colonial Office,[60] the text of a treaty was drawn up by Hobson and his staff with some assistance from James Busby. It was quickly translated into Māori by Henry Williams and his son Edward.

The Treaty of Waitangi has been described as 'hastily and inexpertly drawn up, ambiguous and contradictory in content, chaotic in its execution'.[61] Hobson was a sick man, under pressure from the actions of land-sharks and the New Zealand Company in the Cook Strait area. He was legally untrained and had no legal adviser. He was surrounded by manipulators and self-seekers: all his advisers had land or wanted it; the Protestant missionaries were at odds with the Catholics; many settlers, British or American, did not want British rule. The Māori chiefs made eloquent speeches; but all the evidence suggests they were not concerned with closely analysing the clauses of the Treaty. With an eye always on tribal rivalries, they talked about whether Hobson should stay, about the land they had lost, about their chiefly mana.[62] The following day the Treaty was signed almost unanimously, even by those most vehement in opposition.

Ever since, the Treaty has presented problems, not only in the interpretation of the text, but also in deciding which of a number of versions in English and Māori is the authoritative text. The text signed by chiefs at Waitangi is in Māori; but later signatures at Waikato Heads were attached to a copy in English, and this version has sometimes been more convenient for Māori purposes. But this subsequent emphasis on the written text is somewhat anachronistic. Māori literacy in 1840 was limited and the Māori were not acquainted with the legal and literary traditions of Europe that would have enabled them to negotiate the Treaty. A full day's oratory resulted in little or no alteration to the text when it was inscribed on parchment for signing.

The text in English cannot easily be reconciled with the text in Māori. There are three articles. In the English version, the first clause says that the chiefs cede their sovereignty to the English Queen. The Māori version, literally translated, uses the word governorship, 'kawanatanga', for sovereignty. It is doubtful whether the words were understood in the same sense. The second article promised the chiefs and tribes, in the English version, 'full exclusive and undisturbed possession of their Lands and Estates Forests Fisheries and other properties'; the Māori version, more vaguely, spoke of 'the entire chieftainship of their lands, their villages, and all their property'. The more controversial aspect of the clause dealt with 'pre-emption'. The English version stated simply that the chiefs yielded to the

Queen 'the exclusive right of Preemption' over lands they wished to alienate. The confusion of the Māori text indicates some difficulty in translation. Had the Māori agreed they could only sell land to the Crown; or had they merely agreed that the Crown should have first offer? Had they in fact understood the clause in either sense? A later, anonymous statement, which appears to have been made by Henry Williams, said that the Māori were told the Queen could have first offer, after which they could sell to whomever they pleased.[63] Colenso's account, based on notes made at the time, casts doubt on this. The third clause, less controversial, promised the Māori the rights and privileges of British subjects.[64] It ignored the fact that British subjects were not normally subject to a pre-emption clause; and wisely it made no mention of the obligations of British subjects. Whitehall policy, as evident in Hobson's instructions, changed a good deal before it reached its final form in the Māori texts of the Treaty. In comparing the English with the Māori text it becomes apparent that Henry Williams was not simply trying to translate, but rather to re-write the Treaty into a form that would be acceptable to the Māori. The blunders of Hobson and his band of do-it-yourself diplomats can more properly be attributed to haste and inexperience than to deliberate deception.

Hobson was to add to the confusion when on 21 May 1840 he proclaimed sovereignty over the whole of New Zealand. Signatures were still being collected for the Treaty; a number of chiefs in fact refused to sign. But news came that the New Zealand Company settlers at Port Nicholson had formed themselves into a government, enacted laws, and appointed magistrates. Hobson, as he put it, 'yielded to the emergency of the case' and claimed the southern islands on the grounds of discovery and the North Island on the grounds of cession. These proclamations later received royal approval and were published in the *London Gazette*. Such proceedings left plenty of scope for argument over when and how Britain acquired sovereignty over New Zealand, by cession, proclamation, or occupation.

The point was interesting but not of immediate significance. The central government which Cook and Marsden and Busby had thought so desirable had come at last. The reasons behind its formation are of course complex. Although the country was annexed largely because of increased British migration, the prospect of annexation had in itself fostered migration. The humanitarian justification for annexation, the idea that New Zealand was sliding into uncontrollable warfare, anarchy, and depopulation, was grossly exaggerated: the migration from New South Wales of the late 1830s would not have occurred if men had not been confident enough to risk families and property in New Zealand conditions. The persistence of the image of chaotic New Zealand can only be explained by the two ideologies that lie behind much New Zealand history: the condemnation of European expansion, which tends to emphasize any evidence of consequent evil, and the justification of imperial expansion, by which British rule is imposed in order to rescue indigenous peoples. However, in 1840, the only threat from which New Zealand needed to be rescued was the threat of uncontrolled British migration.

The achievements of the pre-1840 period, in economic development, race relations, social controls, and in the search for a socially relevant religious outlook, were considerable. In the absence of annexation and massive European immigration, this synthesis of a 'new people' would have been much more Polynesian than European. Tribal divisions would have continued to be important, with emphasis on the small-scale community and the pressures of unwritten custom rather than the controls and legislation of central government. Divisions, based in the European manner on race, class, and sect would have had little meaning.

For the most part it is a road not followed: these were 'the good old times' that the Pākehā-Māori, Frederick Maning, longed for in old age. In remoter areas, 'Old New Zealand' continued for generations. Even today it survives in memory and sometimes surfaces in the way of life of dissenting groups, in reactions to authority, in informal social attitudes and relationships, in leisure pursuits. Because it is not dead but replaced and not disproved, the social world of the pre-1840s left its legacy as an alternative tradition in New Zealand.

PART II

Growth and Conflict

CHAPTER 3

A Colonial Economy

W. J. Gardner

The basic feature of nineteenth-century New Zealand as a European-style economy was its dependence on the United Kingdom.[1] The chief agents of the colony's expansion were immigrants, capital, and technology from Great Britain; British sea power kept open the world's longest colonial trade routes; the main objective of New Zealand entrepreneurs was to find and exploit staple products of value to British importers. Among British settlement colonies none had closer trading ties with the United Kingdom, though New Zealand provided only a minor element in British trade. Within this primary economic relationship, a strong secondary influence was exerted by the eastern Australian colonies, from which a pastoral economy was derived. In its early colonial years New Zealand traded through Australian ports and to a great extent reflected Australian business trends. This trading tie later declined, until Australia came to appear as strong competitor rather than entrepôt and market.

Within this British–Australasian context, the economic progress achieved by nineteenth-century New Zealand was in the long term quite rapid, given the colony's small size and remoteness. Though lacking a sustained gold boom such as gave long-term strength to the Australian and South African economies, New Zealand possessed the advantages of reliable climate and pasture, and these were turned into a valuable staple export, wool. In the short term the colony experienced, like all new countries, periods of stagnation and depression. This instability reflected its dependence on the British economy,[2] which from the middle 1870s was wilting under the pressure of heavy international competition.

New Zealand's prosperity was often doubly at risk: its single staple was almost entirely sold in one overseas market. The problems of a largely pre-industrial economy so closely linked to its metropolitan centre waited on solutions found in Britain itself. How could New Zealand advance into multi-staple exporting? In the early 1880s, British technology began to provide the answer in refrigeration. How could a debt-ridden colony pay its way into long-term expansion? New Zealand's first major economic take-off followed the rise of British prices in the mid-1890s.

Alongside the theme of dependence must be set that of growing, if limited, self-reliance. New Zealand farmers showed themselves able to compete in any accessible market for pastoral products. Though its urban industries were slow in developing, the economy supported a steadily growing population at a reasonable standard of living in contemporary terms. Its prospects were usually sound enough to keep immigration buoyant. New Zealanders were always ready to claim credit for their progress and to blame British politicians, bankers, and shipowners for their troubles. These condemnations were often less than half-truths: New Zealand exhibited its share of the mismanagement, both public and private, associated with the exploitation of new European colonies.

The annexation of New Zealand in 1840 was not merely an act of British economic imperialism. The Colonial Office took up the question in the late 1830s not as an economic proposition but as a way of coping with distant but awkward social problems.[3] These islands were to be swept under the Imperial carpet with a minimum of effort and expense. Captain William Hobson was to be despatched to negotiate some kind of treaty of cession with the Māori. He was then empowered to proclaim himself Lieutenant-Governor over the ceded territory, which was to be initially attached to New South Wales. Yet as the proposal was being shaped in 1839, economic questions crept in. Lord Normanby, the Colonial Secretary in that year, could not escape a political obligation to show that the outlay would yield a satisfactory return. To justify annexation on economic grounds, the arguments of the New South Wales lobby in London and of the Wakefield group (however mutually incompatible) were distilled into the final draft of Captain Hobson's instructions. The former regarded New Zealand as a promising preserve for Sydney speculators; the latter coveted these islands as 'the fittest country in the world for colonization'.[4] A document largely taken up with the evil consequences of British settlement now contained proposals for emigration to New Zealand. Yet the economic implications of British policy were not explained at the signing of the Treaty of Waitangi in February 1840. Indeed, the Colonial Office did not work them out sufficiently for its own purposes. In general, it appears that the British Government hoped to stabilize race relationships and land dealings under the Governor's control, and then to embark on a secondary phase of expansion.

Under the Treaty a pre-emptive right over all Māori land was conceded to the colonial Government. Pre-1840 purchases by Europeans were in consequence declared void. They were to remain so unless investigated and validated in terms of Government policy and Māori rights as set out in the Treaty. Only the best claims survived this process, and even these were reduced in area. In principle, a sale of Māori land could only be initiated by a tribe offering to the Government, through its chief, a block regarded as surplus to tribal requirements. Māori customary land titles were accepted and were not to be the subject of European investigation. The Governor, however, did not intend to offer economic prices, arguing that 'civilization' under British rule constituted the real payment. Hobson anticipated a buoyant land revenue from sales to European settlers at greatly enhanced prices, the money to be used to bring a continual flow of British immigrants to New Zealand. In the early 1840s the colonial Government made attempts to observe the principles of Waitangi, but a decade later they were being steadily eroded. Government agents, under strong pressure from European settlers, were using or fomenting tribal discord in order to promote land purchases. From the outset British expectations of economic growth in the colony were based on Māori land, easily and cheaply bought and appreciating in British hands, whether public or private.

New Zealand was proclaimed a separate Crown Colony in 1841. The Colonial Office accepted responsibility for New Zealand on the usual principle that its government should be self-supporting. It was not to become (like South Australia) that greatest of all evils — a charge on the British taxpayer. Hobson's administration was given initial but limited finance from the New South Wales land fund. Thereafter, Hobson was expected to pay his way, out of land sales and customs. But the Māori soon saw through the Government's claim of benevolent monopoly. They wanted fair market prices for land they chose to offer. Hobson's nominal prices attracted fewer and fewer sellers. After a brief flurry of speculation in Auckland town sections, he also ran out of buyers. Equally obnoxious to the Māori was the British customs house. It drove away foreign traders and raised the price of imported goods.

From 1840 to 1845 the British administration in New Zealand was usually in heavy debt and at times insolvent. Yet it was able to survive these first critical years largely on Māori goodwill and economic assistance. In spite of disillusionment and racial friction, Māori continued to provide Europeans with food; they were still prepared to sell some land, surplus to their new farming requirements; as eager purchasers of tobacco, liquor, and other dutiable items, they contributed most of the customs revenue, if indirectly. Even so, Hobson and his successor, FitzRoy, could not be expected to sustain government without substantial financial aid from Britain. But the Colonial Office required that the colony was to be set up 'on the cheap'.[5] Under this impossible regime, FitzRoy, Governor from 1843 to 1845, finally ran out of currency as well as revenue, and his administration was deeply in debt by the latter year. It was his misfortune to work out the full absurdity of the 'self-supporting' principle — at the expense of his own career and to the benefit of his successor, George Grey.

The Government's policy of standing between European and Māori, however weakly it was implemented, was an intolerable hindrance to the New Zealand Company, whose calculations depended on virtually free land for settlement. Formed as a joint-stock venture by London capitalists in 1838, the Company proposed to obliterate the raffish free-for-all of 'Old New Zealand' with a 'New Old England', established according to Edward Gibbon Wakefield's principles of systematic colonization. A proper balance would be achieved between land, capital, and labour in the colony, through the mechanism of the 'sufficient price'. Land purchasing would be restricted to capitalists by setting a relatively high uniform figure; the proceeds would be used to bring labourers to the colony; the labour shortages and dispersion of settlement common to new colonies would be prevented. The Company's announced economic objective was to establish 'concentrated' agricultural settlements, on the model of the best English corn counties. Its overriding aim was to exploit the expected value of town sections in the port-capital of each settlement, especially the first. The directors made a shrewd but mistaken calculation that Wellington would become the colony's first capital.[6]

A lottery in London offered speculators a chance to buy unseen and unsurveyed town sections. Professedly rural in spirit, the Company was thoroughly urban in fact. It was, indeed, more interested in absentee investors' cash than in the skills of emigrant farmers. In none of the Company's settlements — Wellington (1840), Wanganui (1840), New Plymouth (1841), and Nelson (1842) — were the extent and quality of cropping land known beforehand. Would-be farmers kicked their heels in New Zealand, awaiting the long-delayed survey and a ballot with only a few modest rural prizes. In any case their chances were more than halved by the cards of absentees included in the ballot for rural sections. These absentees, vital to the Company's finances, were a major cause of the stagnation of settlement. They failed to fulfil their function as employers of labour; they caused dispersion by holding unused rural sections; their absence discouraged neighbouring farmers from fencing and draining.

Relations between the British Government and the New Zealand Company in the early 1840s demonstrated the failure of both to stand by their declared principles, and showed the weakness of humanitarianism in the face of commercial interests. Late in the year of Waitangi, the Company, though a bitter opponent of the Treaty, was accepted by the Government as official promoter of colonization in New Zealand. For its part, the Company was over-eager for quick, easy returns and almost criminally ignorant of conditions in the colony. Its agents rushed into dishonest and defective land purchasing from Māori, while emigrants were prematurely despatched from England. There was poetic justice in the fact that, when a political path was cleared for the Company in 1840, its commercial prospects had been irrevocably damaged by bad management.

The Company's preparations to receive its settlers in New Zealand were a mockery of promises made in London. Early in 1840 the first 1,000 Wellington settlers were dumped on the Petone beach between sea, swamps, and bush, with little or no shelter for themselves and their goods, and no ground of their own on which to settle.[7] A fundamental feature of Wakefield's plan was the swift establishment of a large nucleus. It would enjoy both 'instant civilization' and an instant internal market. In the six years after the despatch of the *Tory*, the Company landed nearly 9,000 settlers in New Zealand; but what might have made one undersized Wakefield nucleus was scattered between four little settlements, each struggling to survive.

Far from developing with the tidiness planned by Wakefield, Wellington and its successors exhibited much of the Australian crudeness he abhorred. In the initial stages the settlers found what shelter they could, cursed the

Company, lived off their capital, indulged in speculation, and survived mainly on food bought from the Māori. By the time country sections became available, most settlers were running out of cash and had to knuckle down to subsistence farming on what land they could clear. Some with more capital and more perception saw the value of grazing cattle. The emigrant labourers fared worst. They found employment in the first rush of building and road-making. As the Company's funds quickly dried up, its agents were compelled to dishonour promises of work and rations. Workers' families went hungry, some to the point of near starvation. In defiance of Wakefield's principles, labourers had to be put on land of their own. Either the Company drove them out to bush sections or they were given vacant land to cultivate. It took several years for this farming to provide even a basic living.[8]

Government expenditure was crucial to the development of the infant colonial economy, although revenue sometimes dwindled alarmingly. Hobson's choice of Auckland as his capital was made for political reasons, but it was in effect the most important economic decision he took. Most government money in the early 1840s was spent in the capital. Official positions and contracts were the lifeblood of the town, and public expenditure gave rise to private trafficking in urban sections. Wellington speculators were enraged that the most lucrative land-jobbing in the colony was snatched from them by Hobson's rather tattered retinue of officials and by hardened land-sharks from Sydney. Wellington was fighting painfully for a farming hinterland; Auckland seemed to have no need of one. By 1845 it had eclipsed Russell as the centre of the growing waterborne trade of the north.[9] Its harbour was in an unrivalled position to receive produce from the large surrounding Māori population. In the mid-1840s Wellington supported seven times the number of European farmers established in Auckland, where Māori agriculture flourished until blighted by war.

With the arrival of Captain George Grey as Governor of the colony in November 1845, some of the financial and economic problems hampering European settlement could be solved. Grey's successes — both apparent and real — were based on the Colonial Office's decision to abandon the self-supporting principle in New Zealand government. With large grants from London, Grey was able to liquidate FitzRoy's debts and (by 1850) almost balance colonial finance.[10] These grants ended in 1854, the year the General Assembly met, signifying a new start in finance as well as politics.

In the late 1840s and early 1850s the chief benefit of Grey's regime to Europeans was that he had the funds to launch into large-scale purchasing of Māori land. To this both Grey and his chief purchasing officer, Donald McLean, brought considerable skill and cunning. By shrewd, hard bargaining they had by 1853 bought 32 million acres for £50,000 and laid the foundations of a dominant European economy.[11] In the hinterland of the New Zealand Company settlements, great tracts were purchased in advance of need. When the North Island conflict over land sharpened again in the late 1850s, European population and resources had grown to a level of safe superiority. There could then be no long-term prospect of two different economies co-existing, given the European will and power to probe all exploitable areas. The Governor was also assisted by an outstanding piece of good fortune. Internecine warfare and the raids of Te Rauparaha had reduced the number and morale of South Island Māori: their ability to resist Grey's land purchase officers was broken in advance. The south quickly became, at derisory cost, an area of flourishing European development outside the sphere of effective Māori resistance.

Rescued by the British Government from bankruptcy in 1847, the New Zealand Company did little more thereafter than cut its financial losses. Its speculative profit-making had proved a serious handicap in the enterprise of founding settlements. Wakefield, with some new associates, had meanwhile been moving towards more fruitful plans for socially homogeneous settlements. They would be less likely to be plagued by absentee owners and labour troubles. Two new South Island settlements, Otago (1848) and Canterbury (1850), were formed, principally under the aegis of the Company, by the Otago and Canterbury Associations. In the early plans Otago was to be a concentrated community of Scottish farmers — without a 'Wakefield' gentry.[12] As the scheme worked out, the 350 founding immigrants formed too small and too diverse a group to make a 'New Scotland' of this type. Though the survey of sections was completed in advance, the nature of the site prevented rapid progress in agriculture. As a smallholders' settlement Otago was not much better off than early Nelson. However, Otago contained a larger proportion of farmers, and the province was soon to benefit from the demand for agricultural products created by the Australian gold-rushes of the 1850s.

The Canterbury settlement represented the best in social and economic planning that Wakefield and his colleagues could offer after a decade of experience.[13] The Canterbury 'Pilgrims' of 1850–52 formed a group of over 3,500. They were the nearest approximation to a 'Wakefield' colonial nucleus in both homogeneity and numbers. For a few years they also formed the nearest approach to a concentrated agricultural community. But the settlement's immediate prosperity owed more to fortunate circumstances than to planning. By 1849 every competent judge knew that the colony's future lay in pastoralism, but the Canterbury Association held obsolete views on the value of colonial agriculture and made only minor concessions to pastoralists. Canterbury settlers were lucky, however, in their choice of site; their advance agent, Joseph Thomas, procured for them some of the best pastoral land in the country — the Canterbury Plains. The Canterbury Association's chief practical achievement was to provide a swiftly assembled base for a rapidly expanding pastoral economy.

The growth of pastoralism towards the end of the 1840s changed both the geography and the economics of settlement. The open plains and downs of the east coast of the two islands were soon to become the heartland of the colony's economy. New Zealand sheep-grazing was an offshoot of an established Australian industry, but not a simple extension of the Australian pastoral frontier. The first wave of New Zealand squatters were Wellington colonists with capital. They saw that inexperience and legal prohibition had been no barrier to sheep-grazing in the Australian outback, and would not be in New Zealand. They did their own exploring, bargained with Māori chiefs for illegal leases, and shipped Merinos from Australia. In 1844 they drove their first flocks by difficult and devious routes out from Port Nicholson to the Wairarapa.[14] A few years later these pioneers — C. R. Bidwill, Frederick Weld, Charles Clifford, and others — were being deferred to as experts in a highly profitable field. A little later there was a similar movement from Nelson into the Wairau valley. By 1852 this was the colony's chief pastoral area, grazing about 100,000 sheep. From the Wairau surplus, much of Canterbury was quickly and cheaply stocked in the early 1850s by overland droving. In turn, Otago received its share of locally bred sheep from the same source.

Sheep came across the Tasman in thousands in the 1840s, but few sheepmen came with them. For Australian squatters, New Zealand was at this stage simply a useful place for the disposal of surplus stock. By about 1850 a number of them, wearied by prolonged drought, were aroused by reports of greener South Island pastures. Several enterprising spirits sailed for Lyttelton in 1851 with sheep for sale, intending also to spy out the land. J. R. Godley, then in charge of the new Canterbury settlement, quickly realized that they must be offered cheap grazing leases virtually on Australian terms, if Canterbury was to hold them and their money. He found ways of circumventing the Canterbury Association's narrow pasturage regulations, and set Canterbury on the way to quick pastoral growth.

Grey did not like or understand pastoralism — especially in the hands of his chief political opponents. He professed to be founding an economy of 'small landed proprietors',[15] but markets in New Zealand could not sustain an expanding yeomanry. The only independent essay in smallholding was made, with his encouragement, at Masterton and Greytown in 1853–54. These villages developed very slowly, mainly as service centres for pastoral Wairarapa. Meanwhile, during Grey's regime, squatters had been establishing themselves with illegal Māori leases or with makeshift leases from the New Zealand Company. When at last in 1851 Grey made general regulations for the grazing of Crown Land, all he could do was to extend to the colony the system of fourteen-year pastoral leases which had been incorporated into Imperial policy in 1847 after a victorious campaign by New South Wales squatters. It seems that Grey nevertheless hoped to contain runholders' ambitions by firm use of the regulations, but the squatters found ways of circumventing his over-stretched administration. Grey's writ hardly ran over pastoral New Zealand. Only established runholders or wealthy new applicants could put up the requisite stock. The former had no difficulty in retaining their runs under distant or lax commissioners, and could use pastoral land for about a farthing an acre. Two years later, in a last-minute bid to leave his mark on the New Zealand economy, Grey sought his own means to help small farmers (who could not buy sheep) to buy land. Under his land regulations of 1853, Grey reduced the price of rural land per acre from £1 to 10s. or 5s., according to certified quality.[16] But cheaper land could not alone make for stronger smallholding. On the contrary, pastoralists, in the absence of special restrictions, now had the means of defending their runs by selective freeholding against all but wealthy speculators. A further group of Australian runholders was attracted to New Zealand, making purchases of unprecedented size under Grey's regulations. Whatever Grey's subsequent justifications and denunciations, the effect of his laws in the 1850s was to compound the economic and political power of runholders.

The 'pastoral age' in New Zealand spanned the 1850s and 1860s.[17] During these years the colony's basic economic unit was an efficiently managed sheep-run of 10,000 acres or more. Some men established themselves on runs by grazing investors' sheep on 'terms', taking a proportion of wool and lambs in payment. By the mid-1860s shrewd leaseholders had used their credit with merchant or bank, their growing capital, and their pre-emptive rights to freehold all or the strategic part of their runs, achieving for themselves security of tenure. George Rutherford of Leslie Hills purchased his whole run of 29,000 acres for £10,000 between 1859 and 1864.[18] In 1860, he shore 4,600 sheep; in 1869, 19,000. During these years he imported Australian Merino rams, improved drafting yards, and, from 1863, erected wire fences. The use of boundary keepers living in solitary huts had been generally eliminated by 1870. Runholders continued to graze their hardy Merinos (the almost universal South Island breed) on native tussock, rough areas being burnt off annually to produce new growth. Drought, flood, and snow (especially the storm of 1867) provided seasonal hazards for stock, but generally the New Zealand climate was, with pasture, the runholders' great natural asset. A serious drawback for pastoralists was the contagious sheep disease 'scab' imported from Australia; this spread vigorously in a damper environment and was endemic in many pastoral districts during the 1860s. On rising or stable prices these trials could be endured, and the cob or slab huts of the 1850s gave way to the comfortable homesteads of the 1860s. By that time a station such as Leslie Hills formed a settled community of about a score: family, shepherds, and station-hands. There was an invasion of at least as many again for the shearing in November–December, the climax of the pastoral year.

Regionalism dominated the economic development of the 1850s and 1860s. The 'Compact of 1856' recognized the fundamentally regional nature of the economy by establishing a quasi-federal framework of public finance under which each province was to take charge of its waste lands and land revenue, thus ensuring that development would be in the hands of provincial governments.[19] The latter were also to be heavily subsidized from colonial customs revenue. It was agreed that the central government would undertake minimal functions in co-ordination. Auckland was relieved of responsibility for the New Zealand Company debt; North Island provinces received a large grant for Māori land purchases. As most saleable Crown land lay south of Cook Strait, these short-term concessions to the North Island were a good bargain for the South, where farming forged ahead. From this financial basis, most provinces launched into extensive public works, which were mostly financed by overseas loans. Within a few years these constructions had generally failed to generate the anticipated returns. Regional development was mostly at a standstill by the mid-1860s. The provincial economies were severely depressed by the late 1860s, and in 1867 the colonial Government passed an Act terminating provincial powers of raising loans. The next round of major development would be mounted on colonial finance, bringing with it the associated question of colonial control.

The economic development of the North Island in the 1860s was bound up with war and the expenses of war. Racial conflict raised two incompatible, possibly insoluble, questions: was the dominance of a European economy inevitable? Was it possible to strike a just balance between European and Māori economic interests? If inevitability tempered by injustice is an apt summary of the wars, they are to be seen from the common European perspective as temporary set-back leading to long-term advantage. Though humanitarians and some frontier farmers recoiled from war as too high a price to pay for expansion, the general body of colonists considered it a necessary condition of breaking what they saw as economic deadlock. The wars themselves were a source of gain for many Europeans. A reluctant but compromised British Government provided troops to fight, and paid them. Supplying Imperial troops, whose numbers rose to over 11,000 in 1864, became a major economic activity, especially in Auckland.

Military victory and Auckland's expansion were organically linked in the confiscation policies of 1863–65. Grey, as Governor for the second time (1861–66), made limited proposals for punishing Māori 'rebels' by taking some of their land. Two Auckland businessmen in the Ministry of 1863–64, Frederick Whitaker and Thomas Russell, seized upon Grey's proposals and inflated them into massive confiscation on an economic rather than a punitive basis.[20] They calculated that Auckland would find the farming hinterland it now needed by selection of the best Waikato lands virtually as a prize of war. A British loan of £3 million would float necessary development, and the main 'peace weapon' would be a screen of military settlements in the Waikato. The scheme would be self-supporting and Auckland land speculators would be the chief beneficiaries. These devices for extending European settlement had very meagre results. Where war had failed, uneasy peace and private purchasing (legalized in 1865) had greater success. Auckland speculators, notably Thomas Morrin and J. C. Firth, acquired huge tracts of the Waikato by unscrupulously exploiting both European law and Māori disarray and poverty.

Meanwhile the South Island was experiencing the greatest economic growth shown in New Zealand in the nineteenth century. Gold had already transformed California and Victoria; its impact on New Zealand in the 1860s and early 1870s was less spectacular and more regionally confined. In 1861 an ex-miner with both Californian and Victorian experience set out to test for himself reports of gold-bearing country in Otago. On an evening in May of that year Gabriel Read made his celebrated discovery at Blue Spur, Tuapeka. The Otago rushes that followed formed initially an Australasian episode: the great majority of diggers were from Victoria; their demand for supplies was met mainly by imports from Melbourne. The longer-term beneficiaries were Dunedin and the banks. Otago's capital emerged from the early 1860s as the colony's largest town and its chief commercial centre. Out of the growing need for transport and for more sophisticated mining equipment Dunedin soon took the first steps towards heavy industry. Gold-miners rarely got the price they wanted; agents sometimes misjudged the quality of gold and the considerable cost of converting it into bank assets. Nevertheless, goldfield banking was good business and 'the total direct profits' in gold-buying were 'considerable' for at least one bank.[21]

The steep decline in production after 1863 caused a rapid exodus of miners from Otago. From a maximum of over 10,000 in 1864 their numbers dropped to fewer than 6,000 in 1867. Many who remained were employed by the new mining companies. Others tried to change to farming and joined in radical agitation for the subdivision of agricultural land.[22] Otago pastoralists who had set up before the gold-rushes were able to fend off this threat. The established urban and rural interests generally survived unscathed, and many businesses were greatly strengthened by the custom miners brought, however little their proprietors liked miners.

Miners and miners' needs dominated the new goldfields on the West Coast, where the first rush occurred in 1865.[23] Here, more than in Otago, miners' requirements were other men's profits in a remote region of dense bush, dangerous rivers, and poor harbours. The main supply base was again Melbourne. By the time sea-borne goods had crossed the hazardous Hokitika bar, they were priced beyond the reach of many miners. Stock driven from Canterbury over the ranges usually fetched comparable prices — though drovers sometimes found on arrival that demand had decamped with the miners. Mostly by ship-board immigration from Australia, West Coast population was raised to a peak of 29,000 in 1867. Hokitika enjoyed a brief eminence at this time as the colony's leading place of export and as its chief port of call.

In the period 1857–70 the official return of gold exported from New Zealand was 5.54 million ounces, of which Otago and Southland had contributed 49 per cent, and Westland and south-east Nelson 41.5 per cent.[24] The West Coast's output did not rise to the height of Otago's, but neither did it fall so fast. The alluvial and beach leads were still workable on a smaller scale by individual and small groups after the great rushes. However, especially at Ross and Reefton where expensive equipment was needed, mining companies took over. Using a wide variety of methods, Westland retained its lead into the 1890s. From the mid-1880s dredging in the Clutha river revived Otago production, and the colony's annual export of gold exceeded £1 million in 1891, for the first time since 1882,[25] but this was gold won at far greater cost than in the 1860s.

One of the landmarks in New Zealand's history was the foundation of the Bank of New Zealand.[26] The advent of responsible government in 1856 was a sign of the colony's political autonomy; the nearest parallel in commerce was the BNZ's establishment five years later. There had been very limited scope for bankers in the scattered and struggling settlements of the 1840s. The first bank to gain a permanent place in New Zealand was the Union Bank of Australia (UBA). As official bank to the New Zealand Company, it opened its first branch in Wellington in 1840. Private business was small and the Union Bank relied greatly on the colonial Government's account. The Union Bank was set back in 1847 when Grey, acting under instructions from the Colonial Office, established a Colonial Bank of Issue. The Bank was a state institution with sole right of note issue, and Grey gave it government business. Growing commercial interests were hostile to this monopoly, and in 1856 the General Assembly closed the Bank. The way was now open for full-scale competition between private banks.

At the beginning of the 1860s some perceptive Australian bankers saw that pastoralism was bound to take off in New Zealand as it had in Australia.[27] The Bank of New South Wales, which had unrivalled experience in financing sheep-runs, set up in New Zealand in 1861. With the Bank of New South Wales and the Union Bank poised to dominate the colony's banking, it appeared that commercial credit policies would now be controlled in Sydney and Melbourne. Yet at the same time Thomas Russell, an enterprising — indeed ruthless — young Auckland solicitor, was planning to wrest the initiative in New Zealand banking from the Australians. Russell rightly calculated that he must give his scheme the appearance of a New Zealand union in the face of Australian aggression. As an Auckland member of the House of Representatives, he was able to exploit the General Assembly (which met in Auckland) in its character as a convention of commercial notables. During the 1861 session he assembled a private inter-provincial group of members in support of a 'Bank of New Zealand', to be floated in Auckland. The name itself was a manifesto and the Bank's prospectus a call to New Zealand nationalism — in commerce.[28]

A New Zealand Bank Act was quickly passed and the Government's account was handed over, though there was some subsequent hard bargaining. Promotional tours in southern provinces widened the new bank's regional support. By this time the Otago gold-rush was in full swing, and attempts were made to grasp the lead in colonial banking for the colony's chief commercial centre. But neither the Bank of Otago (1863–74) nor the Colonial Bank of New Zealand (1874–95) succeeded; both remained strictly regional banks, and the latter was in deep trouble by 1893. Russell had made the miss for Dunedin businessmen as good as a mile: Auckland had gained a colonial as distinct from a provincial advantage. In the meantime the BNZ had risen to clear supremacy. By 1865 its advances exceeded those of the Union Bank and the Bank of New South Wales together. Russell quickly gained recognition as the colony's leading financier, although his career was to suffer in the late 1880s.

Commerce in nineteenth-century New Zealand was 'British–Australian' in ideas and procedures. Sydney and Melbourne had worked out ways of adapting British practices to Australian needs, and New Zealand took over these innovations. Many Australians were appointed to high positions in New Zealand banking and exerted considerable influence in the country's commercial history. The three 'Australian' banks (which included from 1864 the Bank of Australasia) played a major part in providing capital for New Zealand development. Their joint share in advances is illustrated by the following figures: 1865, 47 per cent; 1870, 42 per cent; 1875, 35 per cent.[29]

As the New Zealand economy developed both greater momentum and greater instability, the Australian connection was condemned as a major source of the colony's troubles. The Australian banks were accused of withdrawing funds in crisis with a sole regard for Australian profit, not New Zealand need. The more mundane truth appears to be that banks in New Zealand with Australian connections offered higher rates of interest based on the prospects of investment in Australia. This policy attracted large amounts on fixed deposit. The money was then transferred via the banks' London accounts to Australia.[30] If Australian banks took money out of New Zealand, they did so in company with the BNZ, which also later transferred funds to bolster its tottering Australian branches. After about 1870 trade and commercial connections with Britain grew at the expense of Australia. A sign of this trend was the foundation of the National Bank of New Zealand which was floated in London in 1872. This bank set up in the colony by way of a take-over of the Bank of Otago in 1874.

Banks in New Zealand operated the branch system, already used in Australia and appropriate to the regionalized structure of the colony's commerce. It was the branch manager who had to decide on requests for credit, largely on his local knowledge. The cumulative effect of his day-to-day decisions (multiplied up and down the colony) might negate the general policy of his bank and seriously embarrass his superiors. Every bank had trouble in controlling bank managers. They were, or became, in greater or lesser degree associated with some local interests; they sometimes made private investments at odds with their position; they were often appointed for their family or business connections, in the absence of set professional standards.

Up until the 1870s the banks generally dealt in short-term loans, and left the demand for longer-term risk capital to be met by or through other agents, chief of whom were the general merchants in the provincial centres. These firms were able to acquire a wide range of business in importing, retailing, land-speculation, and money-lending at high rates of interest. There were eleven large multi-purpose firms in Auckland in 1865.[31] Their owners formed an 'inner circle' which dominated the province's commerce. There were similar merchants in Dunedin, Christchurch, and Wellington but they did not form such cohesive groups. It was from the ranks of the merchants that many of the leaders of the next phase in New Zealand commerce were drawn. Among them may be singled out John

Logan Campbell of Auckland and J. M. Ritchie of Dunedin. Even before the gold-rushes the colony was beginning to acquire more sophisticated and specialized commercial institutions. The New Zealand Insurance Company, floated in Auckland in 1859, was the first. The Joint Stock Companies' Act passed in 1860 opened the way for these larger and riskier ventures. Goldmining promotions were allowed even greater latitude under a mining companies Act of 1865.

The joint-stock companies with most influence in nineteenth-century New Zealand (apart from the banks), were in the field of mortgage finance. The 'rush to be rich' grew much along Australian lines and gave prominence to the mortgage as the main financial instrument of private development. Even the soundest capitalist sometimes needed large sums to purchase land, stock, or equipment, or simply to maintain liquidity. For instance, in 1874 the UBA held a mortgage over G. H. Moore's 201,000 acre Glenmark run to secure a massive overdraft of £81,000. The bank was not concerned: it estimated Glenmark's security value at £200,000. In the earlier period the banks did not offer mortgages directly. The Australian formula, adopted in New Zealand, was 'to interpose a merchant' between the banks and the borrower, the merchant taking most of the risk. In the 1860s, however, demand for long-term credit grew with gold and wool prosperity, compelling Australian banks to engage in mortgage business on their own behalf. These developments, though not strictly within the banks' chartered powers, were not seriously challenged in the courts. They gained full commercial acceptance and were confirmed in legislation.

New Zealand money-lenders could not meet all these demands, but by this time British capitalists were beginning to consider New Zealand as a field of investment comparable with the Australian colonies, particularly in wool and gold. To channel their funds to the colony they used mortgage companies formed in Great Britain with New Zealand initiative or strong participation. The leading company, the New Zealand Loan and Mercantile Agency, was also the first. It was set up in London in 1865 by directors of the BNZ, to which it was closely linked. Nineteen major incorporations of this kind survived in 1890. Most of them, though legally British, operated as 'New Zealand companies domiciled in New Zealand'.[32] They competed with the Australian banks which did their own mortgage business, with some independent 'merchant' companies of the old type, and with a strong Anglo-Australian firm, Dalgety and Company. The other banks were also in the field from 1873. With so many money-lenders in such an unregulated and competitive field, it was not hard to predict that borrowers would be tempted to over-commit themselves.

The most lucrative business in the 1860s and the 1870s was in expanding pastoralism and its financing. During the 1860s the colony had two staples: gold and wool with, more briefly, a possible third — the supplying of British troops. By the middle 1870s wool was the only staple; the output of gold had fallen to a secondary level. For better or for worse, most of the New Zealand economy was on the sheep's back. Between 1861 and 1870 the number of sheep rose three and a half times; the weight of wool exported was up fivefold. The runholder thus became the leading figure in the New Zealand economy. Pastoralists were never again to be so dominant as they were in the 1860s. Canterbury runholders and run-holding partners at any one time during the decade probably numbered fewer than 1,000, yet no other rural group in nineteenth-century New Zealand matched them in economic and political influence (though the influence of their money-lenders and bankers, notably Joseph Palmer of the Union Bank of Australia, must not be overlooked). It has been well said that in Canterbury 'sheep were politics and politics were sheep'.[33] The later 1860s put great strain upon the majority of runholders, who were heavily in debt. Of a sample of 100 Canterbury sheep-runs in this period, up to about 70 were apparently sold or mortgaged to the owners' disadvantage.[34] In addition, speculators increasingly competed to purchase the best unbought areas of runs, holding the owner of the lease to ransom and sometimes seriously hindering his management.

In 1869–70 New Zealand was suffering a new, unwelcome experience: its first period of substantial economic growth had collapsed into depression. Goldmining was in decline, but every alternative to gold seemed less promising. The Thames rush of 1867–68 briefly revived hopes, then turned into a speculators' rather than a diggers' affair. Such stimulus as it produced in the economy was confined to Auckland. The staples of the 1860s had lifted the New Zealand economy high above the level of the 1850s. Colonists had taken the new pace of development for granted, anticipating its continuance with excessive borrowing and importing. Yet in the later 1860s the increased investment in mining equipment failed to check the fall in gold output; the expected returns on money sunk in the purchase of land and stock were largely wiped out by declining wool prices; the British Government was glad to extricate its last troops in 1870, even at the cost of writing off New Zealand's considerable war debt. By 1868 government borrowing by both general and provincial governments had exhausted the colony's credit on the London money market.

During the late 1860s and early 1870s New Zealand was passing through a stage of transition. The pioneering phase was over, and the colony had to enter a secondary phase of consolidation; the individualism of the frontier had to be supplemented by collective action on a new scale. New Zealanders, who took private enterprise to be the natural economic order, were compelled to look to the state as the only agency with the financial power to lift the colony out of its stagnation. Current capital stock and infrastructure were insufficient for growth, and New Zealand turned again to Britain as a generator of colonial development. Indeed, New Zealand entered into a more truly colonial relationship after 1870. On the other side of the world, British businessmen and investors were, for reasons of their own, looking afresh at British dependencies.[35] It was a good time for New Zealanders to reappraise economic ties with the United Kingdom.

No politician was better placed and prepared to exploit this situation than Julius Vogel, Colonial Treasurer in the Fox Ministry from June 1869.

As strident Otago advocate he had demanded freedom for the wealthiest province to move forward at its own pace. Now, as colonial politician, he used New Zealand's collective credit to promote the whole colony's progress — and his own career. A mercurial businessman turned politician, Julius Vogel remained essentially the Victorian goldfield speculator of his youth. In the later 1860s he developed forward-looking ideas (some of them fantastic) in an Imperial economy in which the interests of Great Britain and its colonies would be complementary; colonial prosperity would be based on British loan capital. He regarded rapid growth, in 'leaps and bounds', as the mark and condition of a healthy society. This pace was to be sustained over a decade, a span of planning far longer than colonists were accustomed to. Established landholders would benefit most from his policies, but Vogel believed in the natural identity of interests between masters and men. The promise of good wages and quick acquisition of property gave Vogel's prescription much of the character of a 'working man's paradise'.[36] Although private enterprise was the intended beneficiary of state action, Vogel introduced New Zealanders to the extended use of state power. His policy resulted in the provision of a large public infrastructure in transport, communications, and other services.

Vogel expected that the expenditure of government loans would cause a rise in aggregate private demand. With increasing business in many fields would come further private investment in capital stock. The general effect would be an increase in colonial income. Events in the 1870s followed a very different course. Vogel's optimistic plans for the repayment of loan interest and capital out of general revenue and special reserves dissolved in the face of financial and political pressures. The first round of borrowing in 1871–74 appeared to be providing the colony with virtually free railways and roads. By its very success it stifled counsels of caution. Instead of the proposed £10 million over ten years at an average 5½ per cent, about £20 million were borrowed up to 1880, at generally higher rates of interest. In the same period about £9.5 million were absorbed in interest payment and sinking funds. In the later 1870s government borrowing was used to stimulate the sagging economy, which could not support the load of debt unaided, especially in view of falling export prices. In attempting to get itself out of debt, the colony got further into debt.

Throughout the decade there was close informal partnership between the Government and the banks in maintaining a substantial flow of British capital to New Zealand, the aim being to ensure that public development paralleled private. Even if this co-operation did not achieve its full objectives, it illustrated the dual character of the colony's 'business politicians', as Fox (indirectly) dubbed himself and his colleagues in 1870.[37] They moved easily between dealing with public and private affairs (including their own), regarding the two as readily compatible, and commercial contacts as part of a politician's necessary equipment.

Vogel hoped to create an aggregated colonial market which would supersede the provincial economies, chiefly through the construction of railways. He gave priority to trunk lines with prospects of heavy traffic, but he was soon under political pressure to approve lines through undeveloped country, allegedly to stimulate the spread of settlement. The public railways map of 1880 showed 1,288 miles of open track, 1,143 miles having been added since 1873. This disjointed, incomplete skeleton reflected the unequal struggle between regional interests of the 1870s. Most lines (including the one trunk railway) were in the richest provinces, Otago and Canterbury; the North Island's share was eight unconnected fragments. Railways promoted employment in their construction and to a lesser degree on the farmland they served. Their building and equipment accounted for over 45 per cent of gross public capital formation in the period 1873–80.[38] Railway workshops formed New Zealand's largest industrial undertakings.

The roads and bridges constructed during the 1870s had a greater effect than the inter-provincial railways in improving regional communications. Perhaps more than one-third of all public expenditure in the decade 1871–81 was in this field.[39] The number of horses in the colony doubled at the same time to 162,000. Horse-drawn vehicles continued to be the mainstay of New Zealand transport to the end of the century and beyond. The construction of many widely scattered harbours, most of them very expensive undertakings, also illustrated the regional nature of transport — and of politics.

The main effect of the investment boom was felt in the countryside. The level of bank advances rose by £8.2 million between 1870 and 1878, and this credit was reinforced by private funds (especially British) invested in other ways: the greater part of this money was channelled into land purchase, especially in the later 1870s. The rush to buy was stimulated by Atkinson's Land Act of 1877 which gave runholders only until 1880 to exercise their pre-emptive rights. The price of land was also gathering upward momentum under the pressure of renewed loan expenditure and there was misplaced optimism, especially in Canterbury, about the price of wool and wheat. In South Auckland, syndicates and individuals bought up huge tracts of land in advance of settlement.[40] Canterbury was the province most affected. In the final frenzy of 1878 the level of land values there rose more than twofold. All this speculation ignored two hard realities: agricultural and pastoral prices were falling and gold production was not responding to massive investment in mining. More than anything else, the failure of gold to recover destroyed Vogel's hopes.

As befitted a decade of consolidation, the 1870s formed the colony's first great period of residential, business, and public building. Land purchase continued, but when farm-product prices declined investment tended to shift away from agricultural and pastoral development. The increased population had to be housed, however cheaply. Expenditure on housing accounted for nearly half the gross private capital formation in the mid-1870s, whereas investment in farming did not reach one-third of this total in the same period.[41] The investment boom was directed more to the internal economy than to exporting activities. From his experience of Melbourne, Vogel (who was essentially an urban politician) grasped that a substantial manufacturing sector was a sign of economic maturity in a colony. He did not have much room for manoeuvre. New Zealand, as a predominantly rural country linked to free-trade Britain, followed New South Wales rather than Victoria on the fiscal issue: its low tariffs were revenue-producing and not protective. There was, however, significant growth in the 1870s in industries that gained some special advantage of distance and/or raw material as a result of their location in the colony. The industrial labour force rose from 10,000 in 1871 to 15,500 in 1881. If 'handicraft' is included in the latter figure, it is increased to 28,500 or 15 per cent of the total labour force.[42] New Zealand's Gross Domestic Product (GDP) per head sharply increased between 1871 and 1878, an indication that immigrants were being absorbed with reasonable success, at least while loan expenditure continued to sustain employment.[43] Yet wages began to fall in the later 1870s and urban unemployment became ominously common.

The most important regional development of the decade was the opening of the Great Bush which lay across the hinterlands of Wellington, Taranaki, and Hawke's Bay.[44] The horizons of mid-nineteenth-century New Zealanders were too much limited to goldfields, grasslands, and urban streets. It was an 'Australian' outlook and with it went fear of the bush. Some new injection of European peasant attitudes was provided by the 3,500 Scandinavian immigrants recruited by the colonial Government and established in 'special settlements' in the 1870s. They made an historical contribution far in excess of their numbers. They pioneered the felling of the Seventy Mile Bush which stretched from Masterton to Norsewood and beyond. These axemen turned farmers showed what cleared bush could be for small men with little capital — if they and their wives and families could survive the long years of mixed labouring and subsistence agriculture. Bush farming made little progress while it was mainly confined to cropping, but from the 1880s dairying enabled settlers to make better use of their hard-won sections. New Zealand's vigorous immigration policy encouraged a revival of private British ventures in colonization. In the wake of the first Scandinavians in the Manawatu, an English corporation bought a large block around Feilding and settled 1,600 immigrants on it in 1874–77. A larger Irish settlement was established in the Bay of Plenty in 1875–84, over 4,000 immigrants setting up on small farms. Other 'special settlements' organized by the Government made little headway.

Successful development would have been measured in the minds of most contemporary New Zealanders by the achievement of the 'working man's paradise': the growth of property-owning in which navvies and agricultural labourers would become yeomen, or at least independent smallholders. Vogelite policies returned an equivocal result. In the period 1874–86 the number of smallholdings grew by 54 per cent, but holdings above 320 acres increased by 93 per cent. Far from being a 'yeoman's paradise', New Zealand smallholding supported mainly subsistence farmers. Vogel and his successors were severely handicapped in their settlement policies. They had no means of checking property prices, and (until 1877) had no direct control over the sale and settlement of Crown land.[45]

New Zealand's internal development consolidated rather than decreased its links with the United Kingdom. The mortgagor colony was now obliged to increase its export to Britain substantially in order to keep ahead of its repayment of debts to British money-lenders; meanwhile export prices were dropping. The performance of New Zealand exporters in the 1870s is creditable, given such unfavourable external circumstances and massive immigration. The colony's terms of trade rose significantly from the 1871 figure, the lowest after the gold-rushes, but were still short of parity by 1881.[46] The value of exports in the latter year was 15 per cent above the return of 1881, but exports per head had dropped by 38 per cent. This seems a rather limited return in export earnings to set against £20 million of public borrowing, about one-third as much private borrowing, and an increase in European population of 91 per cent. The colony's dependence on its sheep farmers was striking, though this was less than in the pre-gold period. Wool in 1880 produced over half the value of exports, as against only three-eighths in 1870. The increase more than made up for the decline of gold. In addition, colonial woollen manufacturing had made substantial strides since its beginnings at Mosgiel in 1871.

Loud criticism was levelled against Vogel and 'Vogelism' at the end of the decade but this outcry was often little but hypocrisy. Many of his detractors had taken up the investment boom eagerly and for their private profit had pushed it well beyond the limit of the colony's resources. Grey denounced Vogel as the corrupter of New Zealand politics, but his own Ministry contained Vogelites as open-handed as Vogel himself, particularly James Macandrew, who carried borrowing for public works to its climax in the £5 million loan approved in 1879. Vogel knew he had to base his planning on inter-regional consensus, yet this system laid his schemes open to dismemberment by diverse regional interests, which called the tune in the politics of development. The main achievement of the decade, and Vogel's chief justification, was the near twofold increase in non-Māori population to 490,000 at the 1881 census. This figure did not nearly amount to the Victorian scale of internal market at which Vogel had aimed, especially as the provincial nature of the economy had not been much eroded. By 1880 the operation of Vogelite policies had substantially enlarged New Zealand society without correspondingly strengthening the economy. After the good times of the 1870s there would be hardship and unemployment for the added population. Nevertheless, a social and economic threshold had been passed and Vogel's policies would be shown to be justifiable in the long term.

By the late 1870s the New Zealand economy was saturated with debt, but an unreal property boom still held most monetary problems in uneasy suspension. Towards the end of 1878 a Scottish crisis suddenly exposed the serious and latent weakness of the New Zealand economy. The City of Glasgow Bank collapsed in October. Though the Bank's basic problems were in Glasgow, it was widely recognized as a principal agent in placing

Scottish investments in New Zealand, notably in the New Zealand and Australian Land Company. This conspicuous association dragged down the colony's credit in Britain.

In the following month, the speculative boom in New Zealand also collapsed. The banks, which had positively encouraged gambling in land values, now reacted with a severe credit squeeze (generally sparing, however, larger customers). 'The rotten eggs that have been broken were of the smaller size.'[47] This unfeeling comment by a banking journal ignored the misery growing in the countryside and, to an even greater extent, in the towns. The Grey Government came perilously near failing to meet its British interest payments in mid-1879, and compelled the BNZ to help tide it over the crisis. In turn the BNZ reduced its advances (including discounts) by over £1 million, and thereby damaged its reputation as a 'native bank'.

The aftermath of the crisis of 1878–79 was a severe downswing which went on into 1880 without any sign of recovery. A long period of stagnation or near-stagnation followed in many parts of the economy, lasting until 1895. These years, known in the past as 'the Long Depression',[48] were characterized by: low wages, unemployment, and poverty; low prices for primary exports which inhibited the progress and diversification of farming; the failure of secondary industries to keep pace with urban population growth; the heavy and unrelieved burden of debt-repayment which clogged both public and private development; the loss of people to still-prospering Australia; the contrast with economic upswing after 1895. These features do not meet the currently accepted criterion for the existence of depression: a fall in real income.[49] Colonial income between 1870 and 1918, calculated from monetary data, indicates that by this criterion these years exhibited 'little more than stagnation'. This estimate of annual GDP shows a moderate growth over the period, from £24.2 million in 1879 to £31.2 million in 1895. But this growth rate was less than one-fifth of the rate for the whole period 1870–1918. In seven of the seventeen years from 1879 to 1895 the estimated GDP shows decline, the greatest being in 1879 (-9.3 per cent). These figures tend to give statistical support to the traditional view, though this confirmation must co-exist with facts of growth, however slow, and with significant variations in economic performance during the period.

New Zealand's predicament in the 1880s reflected partly its dependence on the depressed British economy, partly its own crippling indebtedness, and partly the shape of the society emerging from the 1870s. The colony now had too many people for a pastoral economy and too few for a balanced pastoral–industrial economy. The result was tension between what may be called the trading and domestic sectors. The first, comprising mainly graziers, their financial backers, and importers, wanted wool landed in Britain as cheaply as possible and British goods similarly landed in New Zealand. Many of them considered that less efficient or surplus labourers would have to accept their fate in under-employment or unemployment. Urban wage-earners and manufacturers thought in terms of self-sufficiency, stable internal markets and employment, and industrial protection. This dichotomy did not become acute until the later 1880s, but it expressed itself earlier in rural–urban tensions. Sectional pressures were to a great extent neutralized in the continued competition between regional economies. The colony's search for new economic options in the 1880s took place against an unpromising social and political background.

There were short-term business cycles within the period 1879–95, with brief periods that were hailed as the beginning of better times. But the basic economic movement affecting New Zealand was the continued downward course of British prices, interest, and wages from the mid-1870s. This dominant trend affected holders of fixed assets and debtors;[50] perhaps a half of them could not find continuing means of maintaining liquidity for themselves. The land values of the 1870s could not be adjusted to realistic levels since most purchases had been made with borrowed money. The price of land was for many linked to the price of debt, and a great proportion of private assets in New Zealand became frozen or partly frozen in the hands of their nominal owners. Banks and land companies in a similar predicament were eventually forced to find means of writing off their debts at the expense of shareholders. The bankruptcy rate ran at its highest nineteenth-century level in the period 1879–88, accounting for 3,238 cases.

The power of government loans to offset downward movements in the private sector was being steadily eroded. Circumstances had deteriorated in the 1880s: export prices were lower and the total cost of servicing debt higher. The problem of finding money to meet public creditors now took unwelcome prominence in politics. In most of the years 1881–88 the actual amount of new public loan money (though still medium to large) fell below the current interest payments and the cumulative figures were in heavily unfavourable balance by 1890. Public borrowing had become counter-productive, and at last, in 1887–88, politically unacceptable. In 1888 Sir Harry Atkinson, the Premier and Colonial Treasurer, gained approval for a final loan, on the understanding that the Government would not appear again on the London money market until 1892. John Ballance, the Opposition leader who was to succeed Atkinson in office, was even more firmly committed to 'self-reliance' and non-borrowing. Debt statistics show that a reversal of Vogelite policies was overdue, given the extended failure of the colony to pay interest out of revenue. Between 1871 and 1890 the total overseas central government debt rose by £31.9 million, and in the latter year made with local government debts a total of £40 million. Interest amounting to £26.8 million (a small part of which arose from pre-1871 loans) had been paid on central government loans.[51]

The failure of the City of Glasgow Bank did not dry up all British sources of private funds, though a large amount of British money left New Zealand in 1881–82. This was partly balanced by continued inflow, estimated at £2.3 million, during the period 1881–85.[52] Thomas Russell, now domiciled in London, was apparently able to persuade many English investors to dissociate Auckland from Scottish 'meddling and muddling' in

Otago. After 1885, when the Auckland boom also collapsed, there was an increasing outflow of private capital, to which must be added interest on earlier loans. From 1880 to that year there was a total net loss of private overseas capital approaching £8 million.[53]

New Zealand's financial situation from about 1885 was therefore gloomy, and the problems of maintaining external liquidity were great. The colony's reputation abroad sank visibly, especially by contrast with the continued boom in Australia, where New Zealand was dubbed 'the ugly duckling of the Australasian group'.[54] During the mid–1880s, some British financial journals were expressing fears that the New Zealand Government was about to default. Such misgivings were sharpened by J. A. Froude's *Oceana* (1885), which clearly suggested that some New Zealanders faced this prospect without compunction. In 1888 colonists generally blamed grasping British money-lenders for most of the colony's ills. The Governor, Sir William Jervois, privately expressed a different view:

British statesmen may perhaps look forward to the day when the Australasian Colonies will form independent States, and hope that it may not be far distant. Separation would be a simple method of settling all difficulties, were England merely a suzerain and not also a mortgagee — But when we consider the enormous sums owed . . . to British capitalists, I apprehend that Great Britain cannot relax her hold on these Colonies. . . .[55]

If New Zealand was over-committed to Britain the reverse was also true, with the usual consequences for the lending country: Britain had the liveliest interest in the solvency of the colony, and would later respond readily to signs of improvement.

In spite of the general stagnation within the domestic sector, the exporting sector and the operation of the colony's banking system had improved the external balance by 1895. A turning point was reached in 1886 when exports crept ahead of imports for the first time (with the exception of 1880) since 1872. Thereafter, New Zealand's balance of trade remained favourable, and increasingly so into the 1890s. The colony's trading banks gave increasing priority to building up their London funds, thus assisting the growth of New Zealand trade with the United Kingdom. The net result was a substantial increase in New Zealand's external liquidity, at the cost of internal credit. Over the whole period 1880–95, London assets available to meet overseas debts increased by over £5 million.[56]

Within New Zealand itself, there were important structural changes. The 1880s saw the twilight of the old provincialism that had governed internal economics since the 1840s, the consolidation of a colonial economy, and the first phase in the shift from south to north. The decline of gold and wheat and falling prices for wool eroded the self-sufficiency of Canterbury and Otago. While these two provinces suffered the severest setback in the general colonial depression in the early 1880s, Auckland's apparent immunity in the same period was the last great sign of the old economic provincialism. Auckland had a range of products — timber, quartz gold, and kāuri gum — that were largely marketed in Australia and less affected by British prices, but the centre of the province's boom in the 1880s was Auckland city itself. It was British (and probably South Island) investment that promoted extraordinary speculation in urban and suburban property. The tendency for British capital to find its way into 'non-traded' commodities (especially residential building and city amenities), rather than into industries producing 'traded' goods, had been amply demonstrated in Australia.[57] Melbourne's great building explosion had its minor New Zealand parallel in Auckland. The close connection between the city's 'limited circle' of promoters and an influential group of London financiers gave it a unique advantage, which was both created and exploited by Russell.[58] In 1882 dealing in land and buildings increased at a hectic pace, only to collapse completely in 1885. From 1886 depression was general in New Zealand and economic provincialism of the old kind was practically dead.

With the power of the New Zealand Government to stimulate the economy severely reduced, the colony's dependence on British demand was all the more clearly revealed. The most fortunate individuals in New Zealand were established farmers on economic holdings. For them, the British market was sustained at a level that permitted survival, growth, and even prosperity, according to the efficiency and solvency of the individual producer. The fall in export prices was accompanied by a fall in the costs of imports, labour, and shipping, and this worked in favour of the colony's balance of trade. The margin between costs and returns was still narrow but by no means insignificant for pastoralists with large flocks. Many great station homesteads were built at low cost in what were supposed to be bedrock depression years, on cheques from wool and frozen meat.[59] It has been estimated that the minimum economic flock in the 1880s was between 3,000 and 4,000, grazed on 1,000 acres; sheep farming below this level was in some degree subsistence farming. In 1886 only 2 per cent of the adult male population was permanently employed in sheep farming.[60] Though pastoralism also depended on seasonal labour, wages were low and rural unionism almost non-existent, in contrast to the huge Australian shearers' unions.

From the mid-1870s many runholders and large farmers were induced to consider wheat-cropping as a means of offsetting poorer wool returns. Wheat prices were stable, or declined less; the prospects of exporting to Britain and Australia seemed reasonably bright; cropping costs eased as wages fell. Canterbury and Otago, the chief grain provinces, saw the advent of the so-called 'bonanza' wheat farming, mostly in huge paddocks on runholders' land. There were memorable scenes: hundreds of horses tethered in a ploughing camp; two dozen of the newly introduced mechanical reapers cutting a crop in echelon, followed by a hundred harvesters; the first wave of power-driven farming in New Zealand exemplified by a traction engine linked to a wooden threshing mill. Production rose to a peak in 1883 when wheat exports passed £1 million, but prices fell quickly and stronger competitors left little of the international market to New Zealand. However, wheat-cropping remained an important secondary aspect of New Zealand farming, especially in periods of Australian drought.

In these years 'second generation' runholders and other farmers were being forced to face the results of three decades of rural exploitation: the depletion of native pastures by over-stocking, fire, and erosion; the spread of noxious weeds; the unchecked depredations of rabbits. Yet in the last two decades of the century the colonial total of sheep rose by over a half, while the cattle figure doubled. The rapid decline of much native pasture was more than offset by the development of pastures sown in English grasses, particularly on former tussock plains and in cleared forest put under the plough.[61] By 1895 the colony's greatest farming resource was 8.8 million acres of sown pasture, though problems of maintaining quality were already serious.

The colony's hopes were raised from time to time by short-term prospects for other products, notably the depletables. Nineteenth-century New Zealand was 'a world built of wood', and its great forests, especially of kāuri, were ruthlessly exploited for both domestic and overseas markets.[62] From the mid-1870s to the mid-1880s the timber industry was the colony's largest manufacturing enterprise, highly mechanized and highly speculative, especially in Auckland. That province's large export trade in kāuri timber was erratic and sometimes unprofitable in the face of Australian and American competition. Digging for kāuri gum was a poor man's industry, mainly in North Auckland. It was second to gold in export value among the colony's depletable resources, but also faced erratic prices and the competition of substitutes. The mining of bituminous coal in Buller and Westland in the wake of gold was a boost to the colony's industries, railways, and shipping. From the mid-1880s coal was exported from West-port and Greymouth in some quantity, but Australian competition was again severe. The principal user, the Union Steam Ship Company, gained control of most West Coast coal companies and hence of the industry.

Writing a decade later, William Pember Reeves claimed that 'half the great estates were for sale', but he did not dwell on the other half.[63] Among Reeves's heavily mortgaged runholders there were of course many failures, and the over-generous BNZ was forced by 1888 to take over £4.3 million of frozen assets, most of them rural properties. The more efficient or less debt-burdened runholders were in fact making annual profits of £3,000 and better, their mortgages were usually routine devices for maintaining short-term liquidity, and they were regarded as first-class risks by banks and loan companies.[64] It was among these pastoralists and their financial backers that the most promising economic development of the 1880s was initiated. They eagerly awaited the outcome of the first Australian shipments of frozen meat to Britain in 1880. The wasteful processes of boiling down carcases for tallow and of tinning mutton for export had not proved economic in the 1870s. Australian success in refrigeration was quickly followed up in New Zealand, but the organization of a trial shipment took time. W. S. Davidson, the able general manager of the Glasgow-based New Zealand and Australian Land Company, quickly sized up the potential benefits to his company of refrigeration. While the first refrigerating companies were being formed in the colony to build freezing works, he stole a march by fitting out the ship *Dunedin* in Glasgow. Using company stock and capital and the *Dunedin*'s freezing equipment, Davidson himself with Thomas Brydone, his local superintendent, sent the first shipment from Port Chalmers in February 1882. The *Dunedin*'s cargo struck a favourable market in London and sold at 6d. to 7½d. a pound, well above colonial prices. This first triumph was, however, soon offset by some less fortunate voyages.[65]

During the 1880s the frozen meat trade was based on the flocks of big runholders, such as John Grigg of Longbeach. Few others could supply the large drafts of sheep of dependable quality which the freezing works and the market required. The standard of carcases shipped was greatly improved by 'the colonial half-bred', a dual-purpose wool and mutton sheep, which was a cross between Merino ewes and Lincoln rams. Such sheep were the basis of 'prime Canterbury' mutton which had an outstanding reputation in Britain by the 1890s. This breeding process was carried further by James Little and by Davidson, working independently along the same lines from the later 1860s. By inbreeding half-bred sheep, Little produced by 1890 the Corriedale sheep, well suited to New Zealand's drier pastures.

The meat trade required (in depressed times) fairly large amounts of capital, good standards of hygiene and storage, swift cheap transport, controlled marketing — and a growing market. Suffering from grievous deficiencies on all these counts (and others), the industry progressed slowly and somewhat unsteadily in its first decade. By 1892 there were twenty-one freezing works in New Zealand, but they were not working to capacity. The lower prices of 1885–88 discouraged many producers, and ships sometimes departed half empty. In return, ship-owners for some time refused to lower freights, which were the heaviest charge on profits. The whole system depended on the growing capacity of the British working class to afford cheap colonial meat on rising real wages. In 1891 frozen meat ousted gold as the colony's second export and its earnings passed the £1 million mark.

Few economies have been so dependent on mercantile marine for their growth as New Zealand, yet this country has had only a minor voice in the control of these services. A major exception was the Union Steam Ship Company, formed in Dunedin in 1875. This line played a leading part in Australasian inter-colonial trade during the 1880s and 1890s. Trade to the United Kingdom was dominated in the 1860s and early 1870s by two British firms, Shaw Savill and the Albion Line, which amalgamated in 1882. The New Zealand Shipping Company was formed in Christchurch in 1873 to challenge their monopoly. However, all these lines later jointly resisted the lowering of freight rates for many years. The cost of shipping frozen meat did not fall from its 1882 level of 2¼d. per pound to 1d. until 1891, but was down to a ½d. by 1897.

The moderate success of the industry towards 1890 emphasized the difference between the exporting sector and other parts of the New

Zealand economy. The colony's principal occupation was small farming but at this stage its contribution to economic growth was minimal. In 1891 there were 20,015 holdings of 1–50 acres, a great proportion of which probably yielded only a bare self-sufficiency in food. Every penny of outside earnings would be needed to keep the family in minimum decency. Farms up to 320 acres would yield a better return with the whole family's labour and some cash return on produce. A slight fall in wheat prices might spell a wasted season to many such Canterbury farmers. Hovering on the threshold of economic farming in 1891 were the owners of the 2,600 flocks of between 500 and 2,000 sheep. Very few of them could produce sheep for freezing, and their wool probably fetched prices well below the run-holders' average. However, many such farmers with skill and luck might achieve a comfortable living in the better seasons.[66] A major socio-economic resource of this period was the absorptive capacity of the countryside. As wage-earning declined, subsistence farming took up more and more of the excess labour force. It was a hard life but not a brutalizing one, contrasting markedly with the rural slum existence in Victoria which produced and protected Ned Kelly. The spread of small farming after 1900 had its roots deep in the subsistence farming before 1890, in that many rural families had long since come to terms with their environment without losing hope.

The 1880s are traditionally regarded as the decade of runholders and 'land monopoly'. Much of the best land was indeed gathered in the hands of a few, by such devices as 'spotting', 'grid-ironing', and 'dummying' in these years, as it was in the formative years of many other new countries. The accumulation of large holdings was worse in Australia, but New Zealand was a smaller country more suitable for close subdivision. Its 'land monopoly' was more visible to the land-hungry, and 'land for the people' a more realistic aim in politics. In 1882, 32 per cent of the area in holdings (consisting of runs above 10,000 acres) was held by less than 1 per cent of registered owners. The latter, including companies, numbered 247. By 1892 the situation was little altered: there were 337 owners in the same category and in about the same proportion. Canterbury, the classic squatter country, was the most tied up in large estates, and therefore the most land-hungry. But Canterbury was not New Zealand, and there was more close settlement in other parts of the country. From the late 1870s there was much private subdivision. Parliament passed a series of Acts designed to open up Crown land (especially in the North Island) to men of small means. These measures varied in success, but they served to keep open a rural frontier in some parts of New Zealand. The general trend was to smaller areas and lower rentals, but even these adjustments were not enough. Many state leaseholders fell into arrears, and revaluation in 1889 was necessary to bring rentals down nearer the realities of subsistence farming on poorer Crown land. Though a drift to North Island bush sections eased some of the 'land hunger' in Otago and Canterbury, the sight of great areas of under-used pasture aroused growing support for 'bursting up the big estates' in the south.

More important than South Island slogans in 'putting the small man on the land' was the steady growth of dairying in the North Island. Rising town population from the mid–1870s enabled more dairy farmers to set up within reach of urban markets. Anxious to raise the industry to more economic levels, the Hall Government in 1881 offered a bonus for large quantities of butter or cheese produced 'on the American principle', that is, by a factory collecting and processing the milk of a dairying district. Again Davidson saw an opportunity for his company. The New Zealand and Australian Land Company was anxious to subdivide a Southland property and Davidson decided to attract buyers by demonstrating its dairying potential. The company erected a factory at Edendale in 1882 and was soon able to claim the government bonus. This example was quickly followed elsewhere, mainly by private companies, there being few co-operative factories before 1890. Dairy exporting grew very slowly during the 1880s, except in Taranaki, which in 1891 was sending away more butter than the rest of New Zealand. Banks were reluctant to help small farmers in the new industry 'because of the "perishable nature of the product" '. They generally failed to adopt 'an adventurous policy' on assisting the refrigerated trade.[67]

Achieving a uniform and palatable product was beyond the unaided efforts of under-capitalized farms which were little above the subsistence level. Dairying was the first industry to benefit fully from government assistance and supervision. Set back by poorer prices in 1889–90, dairy farmers were more willing to accept inspection of their product — though not yet of their cowsheds. Two Acts (1892 and 1894) inaugurated higher standards for export produce by means of government inspection, grading, and cool stores. The Babcock test of butterfat content, which enabled factories to pay on quality of milk, also helped to improve standards.

The growth of subsistence farming in the countryside was matched in the 1880s by the limited expansion of urban industries. Regional divisions helped to prevent the rise of a New Zealand Melbourne, though the success of that city was always an alluring example. The buoyant 1870s had seen the development of a range of servicing, food, and clothing industries, and even more important was the increase in saw milling and building, notably in Auckland. After the crisis of 1878–79 there was a mildly favourable conjunction of circumstances for greater investment in factories. Some investors were withdrawing their money from depressed farming and looked toward non-farm production. Labour had never been cheaper or more readily available in New Zealand, and there was a significant proportion of experienced industrial workers among recent immigrants. Vogelite policies had fostered the growth of the internal market. Some New Zealand materials, such as hides, were now so cheap that a small range of British imports was made dearer in comparison by shipping costs. The first half of the 1880s, therefore, saw 'remarkable industrial growth' in New Zealand terms, generally in the sphere of light industry.[68] The industrial labour force (including workers in 'handicrafts') grew to 39,000 in 1886, an increase of 36.8 per cent over the 1881 figure.[69] On a low-cost, low-wage (and probably low-profit) basis New Zealand manufacturers achieved limited exporting, but not for long in the face of sharpened Australian and British competition. By 1888 internal markets were threatened, and a fitful campaign for protection was taken up vigorously, with trade-union support. Atkinson, by preference a free-trader and a farmer in outlook, nevertheless realized that secondary industry was now essential to the colonial economy. He decided on a compromise: key industries would be given sufficient protection to enable them to maintain their existing place in the colony's internal market. He alienated his free-trade supporters, but with Opposition votes carried a 20 per cent tariff on machinery, metal-work, clothing, and footwear. Atkinson thus took the protection issue out of the centre of politics. The Act of 1888 had a second purpose: to reassure British money-lenders that New Zealand would tax itself sufficiently (through customs) to provide interest payments on public loans.

Industrial growth continued in the later 1880s, but at a slower pace. By 1891 the four main categories of factory employment were: clothing and textiles (including footwear), 32 per cent; building materials, 19 per cent; food, drink, and tobacco, 18 per cent; metals, machinery, and carriages, 13 per cent. New Zealand's lack of resources for heavy industry was clearly reflected in these figures.[70] As shipping costs fell, there was increased overseas competition. Further protection was politically out of the question and employers cut costs by employing women, girls, and boys. The Sweating Commission of 1890 revealed how far New Zealand had reverted from hopes of a 'working man's paradise' to the industrial miseries of the old world. Trade unionism made limited and uneven progress until the late 1880s. Craft unions were primarily benefit societies. The two small Trades and Labour Congresses of 1885 and 1886 failed to achieve lasting results in colonial organization, and reflected the precarious state of urban industry. Shearing and transport unions, which grew mainly or substantially out of New Zealand's rural industry, were on a firmer base, and had allies in mining unions. Several such groups developed Australian links, had Australian names in their titles, and developed Australian aims on wages and conditions. The successful Seamen's Union strike of 1887, led by J. A. Millar, was a local landmark. The world-wide growth of the 'New Unionism' of unskilled workers in the late 1880s achieved a spectacular response in New Zealand, especially following the London Dockers' Strike of 1889. A Maritime Council was formed by the more militant unions under Millar's leadership, and union membership rose to an estimated 63,000 later in 1890. New Zealand labour appeared to have come together in an unprecedented colonial combination, reaching across old provincial boundaries.

Farming and commercial leaders were alarmed by what seemed to many of them a sudden, unprovoked aggression against the rights of property. In August 1890 the Maritime Council decided that Australasian solidarity was basic to its principles and to its survival. An Australian maritime strike was extended to cover New Zealand ports, and soon became something approaching a general New Zealand strike. No specific local union grievances were involved; the council saw its action as both a defence of the principles of unionism, and as a pre-emptive strike against hostile capitalism. On the contrary, conservative interests claimed that New Zealand was being overturned for an alien quarrel. Each side fastened a 'thesis of plot' on the activities of its opponents. New Zealand society was not prepared for the bitterness of its first head-on clash between capital and labour.

The outcome of the Maritime Strike in New Zealand was determined by long-standing economic and social realities rather than by the short-term success of a new movement. Interprovincial links were still too weak to sustain the necessary solidarity; after a decade of depression, unemployed workers readily took the place of strikers; government and law were weighted towards the employers. In any case, any challenge (real or supposed) to property in New Zealand was bound to encounter insuperable barriers in a fundamentally conservative society. The Maritime Council's support, though of a new order in New Zealand industry, was still only a minority of the labour force. Again, only a minority of that support was actively involved in the strike, which revealed the weakness of urban labour in a predominantly rural country, dependent on exporting. Between 1891 and 1896 the colony's industries stagnated and may have slightly declined in some sectors. It is calculated that the proportion of industrial workers to the total labour force fell.[71] Shipping rates were cut further, and British imports were able to compete with some local products on better terms. Whatever markets New Zealand manufacturers had across the Tasman (so named in 1891) were damaged by the disastrous Australian bank crisis of 1892–93. Both the colony's factories and trade unions were at a low ebb.

Another aspect of the depression years was the 'exodus' to Australia, which also weakened unionism. Winter unemployment in 'most major towns' varied from about 6 per cent to 12 per cent of their work-force. The Australian boom continued until at least 1889, and cheap fares across the Tasman encouraged workers to end their frustrations by leaving New Zealand. In the period 1885–91 more than 20,000 people emigrated, mainly to Australia.[72] Atkinson put the best face he could on these losses, which in fact reduced New Zealand's labour surplus, but the 'exodus' was a blow to confidence in the colony's economy. Some businessmen and farmers believed that New Zealand's best economic future was as part of an Australasian economy diversifying behind its own tariff barriers, which would operate against Britain. The facts of trans-Tasman trade were against them. By 1895 Australia was taking only 12 per cent of the colony's exports; in contrast, Britain was receiving 83 per cent. For the majority of New Zealanders, federation with Australia did not make economic or political sense in the face of the expanding British market.

By about 1890 it was clear that the future of New Zealand industry was limited: the land was again seen as the colony's best sphere of expansion. John Ballance came into office in 1891 on a platform of taxing the unimproved value of land, his avowed aim being to encourage the subdivision of large estates. Even at this gloomy stage New Zealand's economic future was clear: the colony's best profit lay in expansion as John Bull's remote farm. Though Liberal land legislation was still not reaching its full effect, the total of occupied holdings rose from 45,000 in 1891 to 61,000 in 1898, an impressive increase of 30 per cent. The fall in average size of holdings between these years was at twice the rate it had been for the whole decade 1881–91.[73] Nevertheless, for efficient runholders not needing to sell, the mid-1890s were even more encouraging than for small farmers. 'The twilight of the estates' was for men such as Duncan Rutherford of Leslie Hills prolonged glowingly into the new century.[74]

The most spectacular and dangerous episode of the Depression was the near collapse of the BNZ in 1894. It was the cornerstone of the colony's banking system, normally paying a dividend of 15 per cent. There were often times when the directors surpassed the colonial Cabinet in their power over the New Zealand economy. The BNZ took a leading part in financing the investment boom of the 1870s, and recklessly carried this policy forward into the 1880s. Its advances reached a record level of £10.5 million in 1885, amounting to two-thirds of all bank advances in New Zealand. Most of this money was tied up in grossly over-valued pastoral and business properties. The momentum of two optimistic decades had carried the BNZ beyond the bounds of common sense and even beyond the elastic limits of colonial banking practice. Worse still, confidence in the Bank was almost confidence in the colony and the directors resorted to dubious practices to defend the Bank, even at the expense of its shareholders.

The startled colony was not prepared for the unthinkable; in 1887 the BNZ announced that it would pay no dividend. The truth could no longer be concealed. In 1888 a committee of shareholders exposed the mutual indulgences of the Bank's inner circle, and their association with the New Zealand Loan and Mercantile Agency and its imprudent speculations. In efforts to restore the Bank's position, £800,000 of its capital was written off and its frozen assets passed to the BNZ Estates Company. This latter manoeuvre produced little relief. A final blow was the 1892–93 banking crisis in Australia which played havoc with BNZ investments there.

On 25 June 1894, J. G. Ward, the Colonial Treasurer, was confidentially informed that the BNZ faced bankruptcy, from which only government aid could save it. There were Liberal back-benchers to whom the BNZ was the greatest bastion of the colony's privileged classes, but the Premier, R. J. Seddon, and Ward grasped the realities: Bank, Government, and the colony's credit were inextricably linked. On 29 June a Bill was rushed through Parliament in a night giving a state guarantee for a new share issue of £2 million. In return, the Bank's affairs were to be investigated by a parliamentary committee and the Government took power to appoint the BNZ's president and auditor. The BNZ remained the bank holding the Government account, and its role as trading bank was unchanged. Its financial position was improved by the acquisition (with Government approval) of the tottering Colonial Bank in 1895. A crisis had been averted without any kind of monetary revolution. The investigation proved abortive, as there were no legal means of compelling the Bank to break confidentiality. It was in the circumstances hard to identify the guilty men or even to define what guilt was. The most culpable directors had merely carried to excess practices which were the stock-in-trade of Australasian banking. The main benefit of the crisis was that the state now possessed unchallenged primacy in New Zealand public finance and could introduce monetary policies with more consideration for their social benefit, without being hindered by an overmighty private corporation too well (if indirectly) represented in politics.

The years 1893–95 formed a watershed in colonial finance. As the Bank was slipping from its old eminence, the Seddon Government was feeling its way cautiously in policies that were bound to make state activity both wider and more expensive. Seddon strenuously denied that he was abandoning Ballance's 'self-reliance' policy of 1890, and indeed his first mildly expansive measures were made possible by the improved finances left by Atkinson. In addition, the New Zealand Government was gaining in reputation in London, mainly by contrast with the Australian colonies and with the South American states, whose credit had been shaken by the Baring crisis of 1890. The New Zealand Government's improved standing even survived the BNZ's bungling and the accompanying manipulations by which the London-based New Zealand Loan and Mercantile Agency survived its own crisis in 1893. These near-dishonest transactions destroyed whatever reputation New Zealand companies still possessed in Britain.[75]

The Government's revived credit would soon be needed. Public works expenditure was increasing and more unemployed were being absorbed into Seddon's co-operative labour scheme. Closer settlement and financial assistance to farmers had been set in train, and the civil service was beginning to expand in response to new administrative needs both in land and labour affairs. The parallels with 1869–70 were close, but this time the politics of expansion were more measured and better organized. The climax was J. G. Ward's unexpected visit to London in 1895: to the amazement of New Zealanders (and Australians as well) he gained a £1.5 million loan at the astonishingly low rate of 3 per cent. Ward received a royal welcome on his return to Wellington:

> You come in winter's dreary reign,
> And summer fills our hearts again.[76]

The Liberal Government had committed New Zealand to a new round of borrowing for development — in depression. By coincidence, prices began to rise in Great Britain and hence in New Zealand within the year. Well might William Pember Reeves, the defeated champion of self-reliance in the Ministry, have stuck to *The Fortunate Isles* for the title of his first book about New Zealand. Seddon's was certainly a fortunate Ministry. The 'interaction of geographical, technical and economic factors, many of them originating in other parts of the globe' would carry the Liberal Government forward to 1900 and beyond, just as similar but contrary elements had frustrated many of their predecessors in the nineteenth century.[77]

CHAPTER 4

The Politics of Settlement

Raewyn Dalziel

One day in September 1839 a party of directors of the New Zealand Company and their friends boarded the *Mercury* and travelled down the Thames to farewell the Company's first three emigrant ships, the *Oriental, Aurora,* and *Adelaide,* from Gravesend. Their trip had another, even more important, purpose. This was to get the emigrants' agreement to a code of law that would govern them until, and if, the British Government took control of New Zealand. George Frederick Young, the principal director present, went on board each ship in turn and read out the code. It was greeted by cheers from the emigrants and signed by all the men present. In signing they agreed that a committee should be established to make rules for the new settlement, to appoint officers, and to levy rates and duties; that they would muster and drill as was necessary for the security of the community; that they would accept, in civil matters, the authority of an umpire; and that they would submit to punishment for offences as if they had been committed in England. The first emigrants to Wellington willingly entrusted their government and political future to the men chosen to lead their settlement.[1] Their action illustrates two persistent features of settlement politics: the need for local self-government and the natural political dominance of a colonial élite.

The constitution of the New Zealand Company settlers, as the British Government hastened to point out, was illegal.[2] In the previous month, August 1839, instructions had been issued to Captain William Hobson to annex part of New Zealand and establish British rule.[3] Shortly after the emigrant ships arrived at Port Nicholson the first signatures were put to the Treaty of Waitangi and by 21 May 1840 the whole country was under British sovereignty. Initially New Zealand was a dependancy of New South Wales, a method of control that simplified annexation.[4] In November 1840 it became a separate colony, and Hobson, promoted from Lieutenant-Governor to Governor, set up the Crown Colony system of government. Under this system the Governor, appointed by the Crown in Great Britain and receiving his instructions from the Secretary of State for the Colonies, governed with the assistance of two councils. The Executive Council, made up of the three senior officials — the Colonial Secretary, the

Treasurer, and the Attorney-General — was to initiate and administer policy; the Legislative Council, made up of the same three people strengthened by the addition of three Justices of the Peace, was to pass Ordinances for the government of the colony.[5]

The first Governors of the colony under this system faced four major tasks: establishing an effective administration; founding a stable financial system; protecting and promoting the welfare of the Māori according to British policy; and looking after the interests of British settlers. They worked in conditions of considerable difficulty. The Governor was instructed to protect the interest of the Māori people and yet to promote those of the European settlers. He was the servant of the Crown, implementing the broad lines of British policy; but his first-hand knowledge of the colony meant that his superiors in London frequently had to defer to his judgement and await the outcome of his action. Many settlers resented the apparent extent of the Governor's responsibility and condemned his decisions. The Executive and Legislative Councils in practice met infrequently and had little power; the Governor usually made the decisions and ran the colony, using the Councils as he wished. Frustrated by the lack of settler representation in government, the settlers vented their hostility on the Governor.

During the period of Crown Colony government, 1840–52, New Zealand was governed successively by two naval officers, Hobson and Captain Robert FitzRoy, and an army officer, Captain (later Sir) George Grey. It fell to Hobson to set up the colonial administration. He made most of his appointments from the navy and, on Colonial Office instructions, from officials in Sydney. Willoughby Shortland, a naval officer, became Colonial Secretary; George Cooper, from the Treasury at Sydney, became Treasurer and Collector of Customs; Felton Mathew, a Sydney surveyor, became the Acting Surveyor-General. Like many men who found their way to New Zealand in the days of early settlement, these officials were opportunists and adventurers. According to Mathew, Cooper viewed his new position as the 'tide in our affairs, which is sure to lead on to fortune' and Mathew himself made up his mind 'to buy as much land as I can possibly find money to pay for, and if that do not prove a fortune to me in four or five years I am much mistaken'.[6] Fortunately in 1842 two talented and conscientious officials, William Swainson and William Martin, were sent out by the Colonial Office as Attorney-General and Chief Justice.

Most of Hobson's officials resided in Auckland, the site he chose in 1840 as the seat of government. Outside of Auckland the administration was hopelessly inadequate. Nelson's main official, Henry Thompson, held the posts of Police Magistrate, Postmaster, Protector of Aborigines, and Registrar of Deeds. He had scarcely any staff and few funds, and was less influential than the resident agent of the New Zealand Company.[7] The administrative 'neglect' of the southern settlements became a constant complaint of the settlers (although it must have also allowed them a certain freedom). Hobson did not, however, have the resources to establish a more extensive administration.

Hobson's difficulties with the settlers were both numerous and various. In the south they objected to his decision to site the capital on the Waitemata harbour instead of Port Nicholson. Landowners reviled him for offering high wages to workmen on government buildings, thus drawing away some of the southern labour force. The New Zealand Company representatives clashed with him over the site of the 'second colony', eventually founded at Nelson, and over his Māori policy. They considered that the Native Protectorate Department, set up by Hobson under the ex-missionary George Clarke, placed the Government firmly on the side of the Māori and against the European settlers. They criticized Hobson's Councils as 'toadying', ineffectual, non-representative bodies. In the north, at the Bay of Islands and in Auckland, a steady stream of criticism of the Governor appeared in the local newspapers. The editor of Auckland's *Southern Cross*, Dr S. M. D. Martin, was particularly virulent about Hobson, his officials, and his policies. Martin and William Brown, a leading merchant, led an opposition group called the 'Radicals', who held meetings at a place they termed the 'Senate'. Their aims were cheap land, direct land purchase from the Māori, reduced customs duties, and changes in Hobson's Māori policy.[8] Hobson was pushed into an obstinate resistance to the settlers and was wearied by the constant battles. Seriously ill from March 1840, he died in office in September 1842.

The conflict between the settlers and the Government continued under Shortland, who acted as Administrator until December 1843, and under the new Governor, FitzRoy. Shortland, a vain, attitudinizing man who was even more disliked than Hobson, let the Government drift into administrative chaos and legislative inertia. FitzRoy found on arrival a bankrupt Government, an administrative mess, and a growing problem of race relations. His resources for remedying the situation were meagre, and he received little sympathy from the settlers, who regarded his appointment (suggested by representatives of the Church Missionary Society in London) as favouring Māori interests. Despite his proven capacity as a naval officer and his distinction as a man of science, the problems of the colony and his own suspicious and neurotic personality made his governorship a political disaster.

FitzRoy tackled the financial problems of the colony by an issue of debentures that were later authorized as legal tender. This was merely a temporary expedient. The colony continued in a state of acute financial trouble — government contractors were unpaid, revenue declined, and the growing difficulties of the New Zealand Company in London brought severe economic and social distress. Lacking the funds to buy land from the Māori, FitzRoy decided to stimulate the economy by waiving the Crown right of pre-emption and by substituting a tax of 10s. an acre on all land sold. Although Europeans could now purchase land directly from the Māori, few did until the tax was reduced to 1d. an acre in October 1844.

Criticism from settlers continued, and FitzRoy tried to combat it by increasing their participation in government. An early experiment in democratic government had been made before his arrival when the Wellington settlers elected a municipal corporation in October 1842. To the settlers' disappointment, the Ordinance under which the election was held was disallowed by the Colonial Office and the corporation had to be disbanded.[9] As an alternative to elected assemblies, FitzRoy appointed a few of the leading settlers to his Legislative Council. He retained control, however, by manipulating the Council through the official members. The settlers would never again regard governor-appointed Councils as an acceptable means of participating in government. Later, when FitzRoy tried to make up for the lack of local government in the south by appointing Mathew Richmond, a government official, as Superintendent of the 'Southern Division', they complained at the cost, at the choice of Richmond, and at the imposition of control.

FitzRoy clashed with the settlers finally and definitively over his handling of Māori affairs. The Māori people were becoming increasingly aware of the meaning of annexation and European settlement; close contact between the two races produced antagonism and trouble in the far north and around Cook Strait. Lacking troops and trying to carry out the policy of Waitangi, FitzRoy dealt with resistance by a policy of 'moral suasion' and appeasement. The settlers saw this as cowardice. Their leaders vociferously demanded that FitzRoy be recalled, and were supported by the friends of the New Zealand Company and the Colonial Reformers in the British Parliament. The Colonial office had to give in. The luckless FitzRoy departed in 1845, following widespread celebrations in the Cook Strait settlements.

Although settler discontent with Government dominated politics at this time, other hostilities were readily apparent. In the southern settlements land purchasers opposed the New Zealand Company representatives because the Company failed to carry out proper surveys and secure the purchasers in their land. Working men, encouraged to emigrate by promises of minimum weekly wages and full employment, held demonstrations and strikes when these promises were unfulfilled. Throughout the country attitudes to the Māori divided the colonists — the 'philo-Māoris' such as William Martin and William Swainson being in conflict with the hardliners such as Alfred Domett, the Nelson settler, journalist, and politician. European settlers were opposed to the form of government and to the policies of the Governor; sections of Māori society were opposed to the very rule and settlement of the Europeans.

The Colonial Office hoped that the man appointed to succeed FitzRoy, George Grey, could resolve these conflicts. As Governor of South Australia he had already nursed a colony out of bankruptcy and been active in aboriginal welfare. He was given more money, more soldiers, and an almost free hand to set the new colony aright.[10] Clever, purposeful, and a man of vision, Grey was also dominant, wilful, and unscrupulous, and he resisted any interference in carrying out his policies. He had three major objectives in New Zealand — the restoration of financial solvency, the reformation of the administration, and the pacification and Europeanization of the Māori. The settlers figured little in these plans: Grey governed best when he was in sole command.

Autocratic rule, however, produced conflict with a growing section of the European settlers. The New Zealand Company settlements, and later the settlements of Otago and Canterbury, were led by a number of well-educated, politically aware gentry and middle-class families who, had they stayed in Great Britain, might well have been active in local and even national politics. They wanted self-government and were not content to stand by passively while government and policy-making was carried on by others. Together with some of the settlers in Auckland they kept up a steady campaign of agitation against 'despotism' and 'irresponsible' government.

The Colonial Office, too, expected that in time the settlers would be entrusted with their own government, as the 1839 instructions to Hobson had made clear. Several leading politicians spoke up in favour of self-government for New Zealand in debates in the British Parliament in 1845, and Wakefield and the friends of the New Zealand Company constantly lobbied in London for constitutional reform. The Colonial Office, however, and especially the Colonial Secretary from 1841 to 1845, Lord Stanley, were conscious that British commitment to Māori welfare meant that steps toward self-government must be taken cautiously. Only when W. E. Gladstone became Colonial Secretary in January 1846 did it become British policy to give New Zealand self-government as soon as possible.

The first New Zealand Constitution Act passed through the British Parliament in 1846. It provided for New Zealand to be divided into two provinces, New Ulster extending north of a line drawn east from the mouth of the Patea river, and New Munster covering the territory south. Government was based on elected municipal corporations, which had above them provincial Houses of Representatives, provincial Legislative Councils, and provincial Governors, and at the top a General Assembly and a Governor-in-Chief. The Act would have made New Zealand a much-governed country, but the settlers were delighted. Within a year of the Act arriving in the colony, however, it was suspended and self-government postponed for five years.

The settlers, somewhat unfairly, blamed Grey.[11] In discussions on self-government it had been understood that the Act should be brought into operation immediately in New Munster but delayed in New Ulster if relations between Europeans and Māori made this necessary. Absolute control in the north was essential for Grey's Māori policies, and he needed more time. Although clause 9 of the Act provided for self-government to be introduced into the two provinces at different times, the Colonial Secretary, relying on Grey's words that race relations were improving, instructed him to make both provinces self-governing at once. Grey protested vigorously, advising the British Government to suspend the constitution in the north and warning that there could otherwise be an armed uprising of the Māori.[12] The Colonial Secretary, Earl Grey, a man of quick reactions, seems to have felt that events in the colony had moved altogether too fast and an Act was passed suspending the entire constitution for five years.

The Suspending Act of 1848 gave the settlers a focus for their political activity. In Wellington and Nelson, Settlers' Constitutional Associations were formed to oppose Grey and to agitate for elected assemblies. These associations were the preserve of the wealthier, better-educated settlers, men like Isaac Featherston and William Fox in Wellington, Edward Stafford and David Monro in Nelson, who organized and spoke at public meetings, held reform dinners, and filled columns of the local press with their editorials and articles. They enlisted the support of the Colonial Reform Society in London and sent petitions, memorials, and missions to the British Government.[13] When the settlements of Otago and Canterbury were established in 1848 and 1850, new recruits were gained for the cause. In particular, J. R. Godley, one of the founders of Canterbury, led the southerners with a sophisticated understanding of constitutional processes and a powerful rhetoric. The settlers were not, however, in total agreement. Some of the more conservative felt that certain aspects of the agitation of the 'constitutionalists' — the demand for universal male suffrage and the secret ballot, for instance — would set the colony on the path to political chaos. They were prepared to accept a more leisurely move towards self-government to prevent this. In Auckland there was a political division between the anti-official group, which opposed Grey, and a pro-official group, which drew on the support of the military pensioners to support Grey and his policies.

The Suspending Act left New Zealand once again without any form of local government. In order to fill the vacuum and appease the southern settlers, Grey divided the colony into the two provinces proposed under the 1846 Act and despatched Edward Eyre, who had been sent out from England in anticipation of self-government, to Wellington as Lieutenant-Governor of New Munster. Then in November 1848, the Legislative Council passed an Ordinance for the establishment of provincial Legislative Councils, to be composed of a combination of officials and nominees. These Councils did not meet the demand for elected assemblies nor the insistence of the settlers for full self-government. In New Munster, a few men, such as Alfred Domett, agreed to serve, but in the main the Council was shunned and its members strongly attacked in the 'radical' newspapers. This southern Council disintegrated in 1850 when Grey and Eyre publicly clashed over whether or not it should meet, and two of the members resigned in protest. The Council for New Ulster never met.

The constitution that finally passed through the British Parliament in 1852 cannot be attributed to one hand, although it owed more to Grey than to any other individual. The form it should take had been widely discussed between 1848 and 1852. Grey, the Colonial Office staff, the Colonial Reformers, Edward Gibbon Wakefield, and the Constitutional Associations all contributed their proposals. A parliament based on the British model was taken for granted, although some more radical theorizers were prepared to accept an upper house only if it was a meeting place of a 'meritocracy' rather than a haven for the wealthy or the elderly. Because the European population was spread around the country in isolated communities with communications among them infrequent and difficult, effective local government was essential. There was a strong feeling for a democratic franchise. Grey in particular considered New Zealand a new society in which all men had a commitment to development and the preservation of social and political stability. Most of the politically articulate settlers also had liberal views on the vote.

The Constitution Act established a General Assembly with two chambers — an elected House of Representatives and a nominated Legislative Council — and divided the colony into six provinces, each governed by an elected Superintendent and an elected Provincial Council. The House of Representatives was to be elected every five years and to consist of between twenty-four and forty-two members. Every male over twenty-one who held a minimal amount of property was entitled to vote and if he held the requisite property in more than one electorate he could vote in each. The term for the Provincial Councils was four years and the voting qualifications the same as for the General Assembly. These Councils were prohibited from passing laws on a range of subjects including customs duties, currency, the court system, postal services, and marriage, and the Governor could veto provincial legislation. The Provincial Councils were subordinate to the General Assembly. New Zealand was to be a united colony, not a federation.

Settlers were given wide powers over internal affairs. Through these new institutions they could make their own laws, subject to certain reserve powers of the Colonial Office; they had control over land legislation and the sale of waste land; they could levy tariffs and duties on imports as long as these did not conflict with British trade treaties; there was an assumption (mistaken as it turned out) that they could alter the constitution. There were, however, some restrictions. Native policy remained in the hands of the Governor, and foreign policy in the hands of the British Government. The relations between the Governor, his Executive Council, and the General Assembly were left unclear. Nothing, indeed, was said about the Executive Council in the Act and this was to cause a major political conflict between 1854 and 1856. In 1857 a further Act was required to establish that the settlers could change the constitution.

Within six months of proclaiming the constitution, Grey had divided the country into electoral districts based on the numbers of voters in each district, prepared the rolls, and issued writs for the first elections. The settlers went to the polls over the months June to October 1853. Outside of Auckland, where strong political factions had already emerged, the seats for the General Assembly were not hotly contested. Few men had the time, the money, or the inclination to spend months in Auckland at a parliamentary session. Eighteen out of the thirty-seven members of the House of Representatives were elected unopposed and there were no contests in

Otago and only one in Wellington and Taranaki. Provincial elections aroused much greater interest. Provincial affairs intruded directly on the settlers' daily lives; settlers identified strongly with their own community — most had migrated to the 'colony' of Wellington, Nelson, New Plymouth, Otago, or to Canterbury, not to the 'colony' of New Zealand. The Provincial Councils became the forum for decisions on local development and finance, educational and immigration policy, and other matters of vital local importance. Indeed, the strong provincial feeling that already existed by 1853, together with the facts that the Provincial Councils met before the General Assembly and that Grey provided them with revenue, meant that the Provincial Councils seized the initiative in legislation and became a more powerful element in politics than the Colonial Office had intended.[14] The struggle over the powers and rights of the provincial governments was to continue for the next two decades.

When Grey left New Zealand at the end of 1853, the political situation was confused. It was for Colonel Wynyard, the Administrator and also the elected Superintendent of the Auckland province, to call the General Assembly together and to deal with the most urgent political issue — the establishment of responsible government. The Settlers' Constitutional Associations, or some of their members, had seen that elected assemblies in other colonies had little power unless the Governor was obliged to take the advice of ministers who enjoyed the support of the majority in the House of Representatives and were thus responsible to it. Yet the Constitution Act had been silent on the relationship between Parliament and the Ministry, and Sir George Grey had not envisaged the possibility of responsible government. Before Parliament met, Edward Gibbon Wakefield, who had migrated to Wellington the year before and who had had experience of a similar situation in Canada, worked assiduously among the elected members to make them aware of the issue and its implications.[15] Wynyard, on the advice of his Attorney-General, Swainson, was reluctant to introduce responsibility without the prior approval of the Colonial Office. When Parliament met in Auckland in May 1854 the House demanded a measure of responsible government. Wynyard responded by appointing a 'mixed ministry' of the three senior officials remaining from Grey's governorship, and three elected politicians, James FitzGerald, Henry Sewell, and Frederick Weld. This compromise did not last long. The elected members found it impossible to operate without full responsibility and resigned early in August. A period of extreme confusion, which Wakefield tried to manipulate to his own political advantage, followed and the session ended with the question unresolved. Wynyard was to give way only when an unequivocal despatch arrived from the Colonial Office in May 1855 instructing him to introduce responsibility. When Parliament met in 1856 Henry Sewell was called on to form the first responsible ministry.

The first sessions of Parliament showed that politics were a maze of competing and conflicting interests. There were no clear-cut political divisions, no sharp party lines until the late 1880s. Although the settlers brought to New Zealand sets of inherited and acquired political beliefs, there was little in the new environment that required voters and politicians to polarize into opposing ideological camps. The British party labels, 'Whig', 'Liberal', 'Conservative', 'Radical', had little applicability and were used in New Zealand largely as terms of abuse.[16] In Parliament Edward Stafford said that members could regard his Ministry as 'Radical Conservatives or Conservative Radicals', whichever they pleased.[17] The issues to be settled — the powers of the provinces, the distribution of revenue, relations with the Māori, the site of the capital — could not, for the most part, be determined by the principles of liberalism or conservatism. Land policy, or the competition between men with and men without capital to acquire land, might have divided members along liberal and conservative lines, but this issue was not sufficient to sustain a division into fixed political parties, and before the 1870s it was debated mainly in Provincial Councils. Ministries were formed not as a result of the voting at the polls nor usually because of their political programmes but as the result of parliamentarians coming together behind one leader on the basis of personal friendship, family or business relationship, national origins or religious affiliation, regional or local ties, or shared views on particular issues.

The elections were local affairs. Candidates for Provincial Councils or Parliament usually stood independently. They might make it known that they would support a particular leader or a particular policy in the House, but such statements of intent were not regarded as binding. Sometimes candidates in a town or province would band together in the hope of being returned in a bloc to win concessions for their community, but these alliances were fragile. Occasionally political associations, such as the Separatist Association in Otago in the early 1860s or the Political Reform Association in Auckland in 1869, appeared, but these were temporary and did not carry over into the wider political arena. Political leaders rarely tried to organize elections. Exceptions to this occurred in the early 1870s when Donald McLean acted as a sort of organizer for the Government and Julius Vogel, the Colonial Treasurer, made an election tour, and in 1879 when Sir George Grey stumped the country in an effort to get his followers returned.

An intending candidate would usually be requisitioned in the local newspapers. The requisition was got up by the candidate or a small committee of his friends. This committee would organize a canvass of voters and could offer rewards such as credit, payment of doctor's fees, or government contracts in return for support of their candidate. The candidate might also address public meetings. On the day of nominations the candidates appeared and addressed the voters. After a show of hands the electoral officer would declare a winner. Defeated candidates would commonly demand a poll and this would be held a few days later. The interval between the nomination and the poll could be used to great advantage — the polls often overturned the result of the show of hands.

Until 1870, when the secret ballot was introduced, polls were conducted openly. The voters wrote their own voting slip or signed a slip prepared by one of the candidates. There was no postal voting and few polling booths. Information on the state of the poll was released during the course of the day for some time, despite the fact that the practice had been made illegal in 1858. Candidates who found they were dragging behind were thus able to bring out reinforcements. Arthur Atkinson, a Taranaki politician, described the election for Omata in his diary in 1865:

The polling was very even at first 10 each, 15 each, till 1 o'clock when I was 5 ahead. This however did not last long & Gledhill [his opponent] led by 3 or 4 at 3.30. I was *one* ahead when Looney brought down Goodwin who had signed my requisition & promised to vote for me & Howell who had promised not to vote at all — & these two gave Gledhill a majority of 1. This made up the whole of their available resources & for half an hour the election was in suspense depending on the arrival or non arrival of two of my men from Tikorangi (Terrill & Gray) who had started with Free in the morning but whom he had left to come on by themselves when he got a horse — sent Free & then Pitcairn on horseback out to meet them & just *4 minutes* after the poll had closed in came Terrill leisurely trotting along. So Gledhill got in by one. . . .[18]

The elections were sometimes accompanied by great excitement and clamour. In New Plymouth in 1853 the supporters of William Halse for the superintendency organized a procession of people carrying blue flags and banners, and fifty of his women supporters turned out in blue dresses and stood on a stand draped with blue flags. Political banquets, broadsheets, slogans, and meetings all livened up elections, especially in the towns. Such a campaign could be expensive: William Brown was said to have spent £3,000 on his fight for the post of Superintendent of Auckland in 1853.[19]

In spite of occasional excitement, there was considerable apathy about elections and politics. A small group of active men were able to dominate the political scene with ease. The franchise and the electoral system prevented some groups from voting. The property qualification, although low, eliminated some, especially men living in boarding-houses or rural labourers' huts. Even after a purely residential qualification was introduced in 1879, itinerant rural workers, miners, and migrant urban dwellers could not establish the necessary term of residence and were disenfranchised.[20] But low levels of political participation are best explained by apathy, and perhaps by the lack of voting experience among many of the early working-class settlers. In 1858 a third of the men in the Wellington province who were entitled to vote did not register.[21] Edward Jollie noted this lack of interest during his election for Cheviot in 1859:

I was returned without opposition & without being present at the election, I made no speeches and no promises. Elections in those days were not considered of much consequence. Settlers had so much to occupy them in attending to their own affairs and were so widely scattered about, that but few electors & then only those in the immediate vicinity of the place of nomination cared to attend. In the towns there was often considerable excitement but generally more personal than political.[22]

Both before and after the electoral reforms of 1879 the proportion of eligible voters who exercised their right to vote was low. Regional studies prior to 1879 suggest that polls of under half the registered voters were common; in 1879, 53 per cent of enrolled voters went to the polls; in 1887, 64 per cent.[23] The increase in 1887 suggests a rising political interest, especially in towns and cities.

Apathy was not confined to the voters: frequently it proved difficult to find candidates to contest elections, especially elections for the General Assembly. When Julius Vogel was first elected to Parliament in 1863 he was nominated and seconded in his absence, at a meeting attended by only a handful of people. No other nominations were received and he was declared elected.[24] Politicians with a colony-wide reputation were rarely opposed, and uncontested elections remained common in the 1870s and 1880s.

The turnover of politicians in the House of Representatives was rapid. Over half the members of every Parliament elected before 1876 were sitting in the House for the first time. Resignations between sessions were common, reflecting geographical mobility and rapid changes of fortune and interest in colonial life. After 1879 the life of Parliament was shortened from five to three years and the number of resignations became fewer, but the number of inexperienced politicians in every Parliament remained high. This element of uncertainty in politics was only partially compensated for by the homogeneous composition of the House. The members usually shared the same social and economic background. They came from the colonial middle class, mainly being professional men, merchants, substantial farmers, and runholders. The plural vote, which lasted until 1889, gave property-holders an additional weight in the electorates. Few working men stood for or were elected to Provincial Councils or the General Assembly, although their socially mobile sons were more active and successful. There were some exceptions. An ex-Chartist, William Griffin, tried to organize the working man's vote in the 1853 Auckland Provincial Council elections. His one candidate, James Derrom, a carpenter, was successful. In Wellington, Joseph Masters, a brewer and cooper, led the Small Farm Association which aimed at making land available to working men. He won a seat on the Provincial Council but failed to get into Parliament. Perhaps the most successful of the working-men candidates was John Robinson of Nelson. Originally a wood and ivory turner in Birmingham, Robinson was Superintendent from 1856 to 1865.[25] Generally, however, it was not until the early 1890s that the working class and the lower middle class became aware of the power of the ballot box and began to use it.

The nominated Legislative Council was similar in composition to the elected House of Representatives. Men from the same social group were in this case appointed for life. The councillors tended to be older than the elected politicians (a gap that increased in the 1880s), and they were often slightly better educated. Politicians moved between the two chambers, active politicians going from the Council to the House and older, declining politicians being elevated into the Council. The Council's main work was in revising legislation, frequently on the wish of the Government. The two chambers were thus closely connected in personnel and function, although the Council was decidedly weaker.[26]

Politicians and governments were closely attuned to the wishes of the voters but, prior to the formation of political parties, ministries were only indirectly made and unmade as the result of elections. Cabinet-making was the prerogative of the parliamentarians. Every Parliament consisted of a number of factions and independent members who had to be courted before a leader had sufficient support to construct a ministry. From the first responsible ministry in 1856 until 1891 there were twenty-five ministries. Twelve of these lasted less than a year and seven less than three months. These figures may suggest cataclysmic upheavals, but in fact there was considerable stability and continuity in the administration. The short-lived ministries were either attempts by a faction leader to construct a ministry during a parliamentary session or changes of leadership within an essentially stable ministry. Thus in the 1856 session the southern members put Henry Sewell forward as their leader. He constructed a ministry with Francis Dillon Bell, H. J. Tancred, and the Auckland lawyer, Frederick Whitaker. As a result the Auckland 'Progress Party' members, who hated Whitaker, joined the Wellington 'provincialists' and three Otago members to defeat Sewell and bring William Fox into power. Fox's reign lasted until the Nelson members arrived in Auckland. His alliance then broke up and the Nelson Superintendent, Edward Stafford, became the Premier in the first stable ministry. A ministry formed by Fox in 1869 which remained in power until 1877, except for a brief period in 1872, experienced eight changes of leadership. Some ministries and ministers showed a high degree of persistence. Five ministries, each with one leader, remained in power for over three years. Stafford was Premier for over eight years between 1856–61 and 1866–69. Fox and Harry Atkinson both headed four ministries.

The ministers were drawn from a relatively small group of politicians. There was a core of able, experienced men who became, in certain combinations, the essential components of a ministry that was to last any length of time. Ministries were small, eight to ten members being the norm. When a leader was called on to form a Cabinet he had to take a number of factors into consideration. The different regions had to be adequately represented in the ministry; certain men had to fill certain jobs (from 1869 to 1876 Donald McLean, for instance, was the only man believed to be able to handle Māori affairs) and friends had to be rewarded. There also had to be at least one or two good administrators. As Stafford pointed out in 1868, ministers had to carry out a considerable amount of routine departmental work that would have been done by higher civil servants if the men of education and ability had been available.[27] All these matters had to be kept in mind if a ministry was to survive more than a brief time in office.

Once the question of responsibility was settled, the two main issues in politics in the 1850s and 1860s were relations with the Māori, and the respective powers and rights of the provincial and general governments. Most politicians put the interests of their own province or region before those of the colony. They differed principally as to whether the provinces were best served by strong central or strong provincial government. The representatives of the struggling Taranaki province were likely to see advantages for Taranaki in a strong central government; provincialists from the wealthier Otago province were to be found fighting for greater provincial autonomy and disentanglement from the problems of the north. These attitudes gave rise to two factions in the early Parliaments — the centralists and the provincialists, as they were known at the time. The centralists were led by Edward Stafford and Henry Sewell; the provincialists by William Fox and Isaac Featherston. Neither side, however, took extreme positions. The centralists did not want to abolish provincial governments; few provincialists advocated separatism. Nor did centralism and provincialism create mutually exclusive parties in the House. A politician might be centralist at one time and provincialist at another; centralists and provincialists could and did serve in the same governments; other issues, such as the conduct of the wars, the siting of the capital, or land settlement, could cut across the centralist–provincialist division.[28]

The provincial governments had become firmly established in 1853 and 1854. Before leaving New Zealand, Grey had issued financial circulars that gave them a large share of the land revenue from their own province and a part of the country's customs revenue. The provincial governments immediately took over control of key matters, including land administration, education, roading, hospitals, and immigration. The House of Representatives, absorbed in the struggle for responsible government, encouraged the provinces to gain further initiatives. In 1856 provincial control over land revenue and a share of the customs revenue was confirmed; in return the provinces accepted responsibility for colonization and development. The terms of this arrangement were to become a lasting source of discontent. The North Island provinces, especially Auckland and Taranaki, had little land to sell and were always short of funds. In the later 1860s, when settlers were allowed to purchase Māori land directly from its owners, the potential land resources of these provinces were reduced even further. Auckland seriously considered separation from the rest of the country; Taranaki put its trust in the central government. Within the provinces the distribution of revenue caused trouble. The central towns dominated. Little money reached the outlying districts, causing dissatisfaction and a desire for local autonomy. In 1858 Stafford sponsored a New Provinces Act that enabled settlers on the periphery to petition for separation from the mother province. Hawke's Bay, Marlborough, and Southland gained separate provincial status as a result. This, and the further localization of expenditure by the creation of local road boards, weakened the system of provincial government.

The success of the provincial governments depended on the effectiveness of their colonizing. This in turn depended on how much money they could get, either from internal revenue or by borrowing.

Constant arguments took place in the General Assembly over the provincial share of the revenue — arguments that grew more heated as the central government's military expenditure increased during the wars in the North Island and seemed to threaten provincial revenues. Borrowing also involved the central government, as the provinces had to obtain approval for their loans. This was given fairly readily in the late 1850s and early 1860s. Expansionist Superintendents such as William Moorhouse in Canterbury, James Macandrew in Otago, and Donald McLean in Hawke's Bay embarked on ambitious road, harbour, tunnelling, and immigration programmes. Other provinces, like war-torn Taranaki and revenue-starved Auckland, did not fare so well. The smaller, new provinces were soon in financial trouble. Even the larger, wealthier provinces, however, could not always carry out the works promised by their politicians. Frustrated ambitions on the provincial level led to acrimony in the General Assembly.

Personality played a large part in provincial, as it did in central, politics. Some of the best known and most popular men in the colony were elected to superintendencies. The old leader of Otago, William Cargill, ran his province until 1859; in Wellington the favourite Featherston won election after election despite the fact that he was frequently at loggerheads with his Council; in Otago, Macandrew, who was shown to be guilty of embezzlement and removed from his superintendency, returned to popularity only a few years later. As the majority of members of the House of Representatives before 1876 also served on Provincial Councils, political and personal conflicts were often transferred from the provinces to Parliament. Those who were 'out' in the province might well become 'centralist' in Parliament, seeing the central government as the means to influence local matters; a strong provincial leader in the Opposition could make things very awkward for the Government.

The relationship between the provincial governments and the central government was always difficult. The poorer provinces frequently had to appeal to central government for finance; both poor and wealthy provinces resented central government control or interference in their affairs. One of the worst incidents in inter-government relations occurred when the central government tried to prevent Macandrew, the Superintendent of Otago, from controlling the goldfields in 1867. Confrontations between representatives of the provincial and central government almost turned into brawls as each side struggled to uphold its rights. In the end the central government was bound to dominate. New Zealand was too small, its resources too limited, and the aspirations of the settlers too great for the provincial governments to prevail. Only a strong central government could carry out the policies of development required in all regions.

The struggle between provincial and central government over powers and revenue was often overshadowed in the 1860s by Māori affairs. When the colonists received self-government, the control of Māori affairs was withheld from them on the advice of Governor Thomas Gore Browne, who took over from Wynyard in 1855. It was widely held in England that native policy should remain in the hands of the Imperial authorities, and

Browne himself feared that if the settlers had control their policies would lead to war against the Māori. In practice control tended to be divided. Browne was advised and assisted by his Native Secretary, Donald McLean, who was an official, and later by the Native Minister, Christopher Richmond, who was a responsible minister. This situation arose because Browne relied on the General Assembly to vote funds for his native policy and because the Assembly had some powers of legislation that affected Māori interests.[29]

When fighting broke out in Taranaki, politicians became deeply divided over the questions of control and responsibility, which were linked to the command of the forces and payment for the war. Although Stafford had been in England during the events leading up to the war and was personally dismayed by the outbreak, he believed that war must be fought vigorously and brought to a speedy and successful conclusion. His followers became known as the 'war party'. William Fox became leader of the 'peace party'. In fact, Stafford and Fox had similar views: like almost all Englishmen they believed that European culture was superior and felt that the Māori people must become Europeanized.[30] Both thought the land should belong to men who would use it and they were prepared to fight for this belief. However, despite commitment to the war, few settlers or politicians wanted to divert valuable resources into waging war; in 1860 and 1861 their main concern was to pay as little of the cost as possible.

The conduct of the war brought an end to Stafford's long first premiership. A sound administrator, cautious and prudent in finance, Stafford had been the only man who could contain the friction caused by provincial and personal rivalries, but he lacked the political acumen and flair to remain in power in war-time. The war also ended Browne's governorship and brought Sir George Grey back to New Zealand. The Colonial Office hoped Grey would provide firm leadership and end the war quickly. Grey retained as much personal control over events as possible while trying to force successive governments to accept political and financial responsibility for the war. A series of ministries foundered on the handling of the war and the question of responsibility. Fox, Alfred Domett, and Frederick Whitaker went in and out of office arguing with Grey and Parliament over responsibility for native affairs. Finally, at the end of 1864, Frederick Weld, a prominent, highly respected Roman Catholic pastoralist, became Premier pledged to take over full responsibility for internal affairs. In return Grey agreed to confiscate sufficient rebel land for certain government needs, and to work for the shift of the seat of government from Auckland to Wellington.[31]

Thus the central government took on increased responsibility for Māori affairs, and with the end of the major phase of the war in 1864, Māori matters began to recede in national politics. The political instability of the early 1860s gave way to another lengthy Stafford rule. The decade was a time of some change in the structure and running of Parliament. In 1861 the number of members of the House of Representatives was increased to fifty-three; in 1866 it reached seventy-two. In 1868, as a temporary measure until Māori and Europeans could vote in the same constituencies, four Māori members were elected to Parliament to represent four newly created Māori electoral districts. In 1867 the debates in Parliament began to be officially recorded. Parliament, which had met in Wellington in 1862 because of fighting in the north, moved to Wellington in 1865, despite the efforts of Auckland politicians to retain the seat of government.

After 1865 politics were again concerned mainly with questions of provincial and local interest. Stafford came under some pressure from provincialists but managed to retain his position until 1869. His defeat then was brought about by panic among the Europeans at the activities of the Hauhau in Taranaki and the East Coast, by provincial hostility to central government policies for local development, and by economic recession. Gold-rushes in the 1860s had brought prosperity to Otago, the West Coast, and Thames, but the country's overall economic growth was slow and in the late 1860s stagnation set in. Prices for New Zealand exports were falling, the provinces had little money for development, businessmen were worried, and few new settlers were arriving. At the beginning of the 1869 session of Parliament there was a large majority opposed to the Government for a variety of reasons. With a push from Fox, as leader of the Opposition, the Government fell.

The Fox Government brought into power Donald McLean as Native Minister and Julius Vogel as Colonial Treasurer. McLean, a Hawke's Bay pastoralist with a great deal of experience and knowledge of Māori affairs, retained the portfolio of Native Minister until a month before his death in 1876. Vogel was an ambitious young politician who had come to Dunedin as a journalist during the gold-rushes. Through the 1860s his aggressive, assertive style of politics had made its mark on Otago provincial politics and national politics. His special interest was finance and he had already been Provincial Treasurer in Otago. He rapidly learnt how to dominate the Fox Ministry and, as the architect of a programme of immigration and public works financed largely by borrowed money, he created the context for the politics of the 1870s. In 1873 he became Premier.

Fox and his ministers were faced immediately with an apparent threat to settlers from Māori resistance leaders and the imminent withdrawal of the last British soldiers from New Zealand. McLean pursued a policy of containment while Francis Dillon Bell and Isaac Featherston went to England to plead with the Imperial Government to delay the withdrawal of troops. The intransigent attitude of the British Government to New Zealand on this occasion brought the first wave of anti-British sentiment in New Zealand. For the first time secession from the British Empire and union with the United States of America were discussed.[32] These views, expressed vigorously, if not too seriously, were to disappear as the threat of renewed war receded and as New Zealand tied the knot to Great Britain even more tightly with millions of borrowed pounds and with thousands of new British immigrants.

The course of politics in the 1870s was set when Vogel delivered the financial statement of 1870, a ten-year development programme of immigration and public works aimed at reviving the flagging economy.[33] Government-financed immigration and public works were not new but the scale of this plan was. Ten million pounds were to be spent over the next decade. Some politicians were appalled. James Richmond, for instance, thought that the scheme was reckless and imprudent; that it would saddle New Zealand with an impossible burden of debt repayments, increase taxation, and shift control of social and economic development from the committed colonist to the speculator and gambler.[34] Others, while agreeing that the colony needed some economic stimulus, would have preferred it to be applied more gently and by a different administration. These politicians tried to oust the Fox Government in the parliamentary session of 1872. Stafford returned to power but for only a month. An expansionist policy met the wishes of the electorate in the 1870s. Warnings of financial mismanagement and economic disaster were discounted in the hopes for economic growth and a new prosperity.

The major political issues of the 1870s were those of development. The first duty of the member of Parliament was to secure government expenditure in his electorate. This aspect of politics was not new; Frederick Weld had noted it in 1869:

Members come up to the General Assembly, not so much as members, as bands of provincial delegates . . . a Colonial Ministry does not so much stand or fall by its general policy — that may be excellent, but the question is — what are you going to give us to take home to our province? Hence all kinds of combinations, of 'logrolling', and political corruption. . . .[35]

After 1870, however, there was more to be gained from the central government as the dispenser of funds for development, concessions for business, positions, and patronage. Some of the older politicians claimed to be disgusted with the 'new' political climate but even they were not immune from its temptations. William Montgomery of Akaroa urged William Rolleston, the Superintendent of Canterbury and member for Avon, to secure some of the borrowed money for their province. 'Get us the Million', he wrote. 'We have a stomach for it. . . . We'll forgive anything but want of success.'[36] The scramble for roads, railways, bridges, and immigrants was on. The old, fluid structure of politics was well suited to this phase of rapid development and 'catching-up' after a decade of slow growth.

Under Vogel's policy the central government gradually assumed responsibility for colonization and development. It borrowed money for roads, railways, telegraph cables, and immigration. Discussions were held with the governments of the Australian colonies to establish mail steamer services to Great Britain via the United States. The Government entered spheres previously left to private enterprise, setting up the Government Life

Insurance Office and the Public Trust Office. The civil service expanded enormously. A few years before, when a Royal Commission inquired into the efficiency of the service, some 1,700 employees had served in a largely unorganized force in a few departments. By 1876–77, as the economy expanded and the Government established departments to administer immigration, public works, and education, the number of civil servants reached over 5,500 (excluding the 1,688 in the railways).[37] The New Zealand tradition of state involvement was firmly established.

The centralization of development operations spelled doom for the provincial governments. The provinces were now increasingly looked after by the central governments. Vogel had warned that when the 'iron horse' ran through the country the need for provincial government would no longer be evident. His 1870 budget had contained a veiled threat to the Provincial Councils that they must co-operate with him or run the risk of abolition. Most of the provincial governments had by now atrophied. Only in Otago was there much life left. Elsewhere, although provincial feelings ran high, confidence in provincial government was low. Support came mainly from a small group who hoped to find in provincialism a basis for uniting the opposition to Vogel; two old supporters of provincial government, Macandrew and the ex-Governor, Sir George Grey, added their weight to this group.

The opposition by provincialists in Parliament to certain Government policies finally put an end to the provincial governments. In 1873 Otago and Canterbury members thwarted a Government proposal to set aside provincial land as security for expenditure on railways; in 1874 Fitzherbert, the Superintendent of Wellington, led the opposition to a Government forest conservation scheme involving provincial land. Vogel, frustrated by these objections, convinced Parliament by August 1874 that the North Island provinces at least could be abolished. Over the next year, despite spirited resistance from Grey and Macandrew, it became clear that all the provincial governments could go. They were no longer carrying out their original functions; their existence was a source of bitter political conflicts; and the trend of the 1870s was towards a centrally directed country and economy. In 1875 Parliament agreed to total abolition of the provinces in the following year. In the election at the end of the year the candidates supporting a form of provincialism were successful only in Otago, Auckland city, and North Auckland. The Provincial Councils did not meet again. Instead, the country districts were divided into sixty-three counties, each with its own council responsible for making by-laws, constructing public works, subsidizing roads, and aiding charitable institutions, museums, and libraries. The county councils joined existing borough councils and road and harbour boards as the units of local government. Urban government was extended by the Municipal Corporations Act of 1876. The next year, when a national system of education was introduced, regional education boards were added: land boards followed. Thus the provincial governments gave way to a large number of bodies, many of which were later to be considered unnecessary and inefficient.

The Provincial Councils had gone, but much of the spirit of regionalism remained. For the rest of the 1870s, railway development and immigration continued at a good pace, despite signs that all was not well with the economy. Conflicts over development — the direction of the railway lines, the size of the loans, the share of each region, the most desirable immigrants — were mainly fought out in Parliament. Regional interests meant that there were few issues that could unite an opposition to the Government. After the short-lived attempt to topple the Fox Ministry in 1872, opposition was half-hearted. In September 1874 Harry Atkinson, previously an opponent, joined the Government as Minister of Crown Lands and Immigration. Atkinson was a Taranaki farmer, in favour of abolishing the provinces and of a rather cautious borrowing policy. His accession helped to reconcile the remaining opposition. The Ministry originally formed by Fox in 1869 ruled until Sir George Grey came to power in 1877, and became known as the 'Continuous Ministry' — 'a shifting combination or rather series of combinations amongst public men, by which the Cabinet was from time to time modified without being completely changed at any one moment'.[38]

A division of the politicians of the 1870s and the 1880s into the 'bold' borrowers and the 'cautious' borrowers ignores the complexities of politics in the period, but the distinction may be applied usefully to the economic policies of Vogel and Atkinson.[39] Throughout 1875 Vogel was in England representing the Government in loan negotiations and Atkinson became Colonial Treasurer. In 1876 when Vogel went to England, this time as Agent-General, the Government's permanent representative in London, Atkinson became Premier. Whereas Vogel's remedy for recession was to borrow largely and spend freely, Atkinson's policy was to limit borrowing, cut back on spending, and avoid increases in taxation. In 1877, alarmed by the size of the debt the country had incurred, Atkinson prescribed a 'political rest' — a remedy that was unpopular with a patient used to heady stimulants. In the parliamentary session of 1877 the political majority that McLean and Vogel had worked hard to retain began to fall away. The official leader of the Opposition was Grey but other opposition factions appeared, the most important being the 'Middle Party' led by William Montgomery, William Gisborne, William Larnach, and Henry Tancred.

The driving force of the 'Middle Party' came from the financial interests of some of its members.[40] This combination of political and financial interest was a feature of nineteenth-century politics. With so much power over land settlement, development, and the economy in the hands of the Government, business interests needed to be involved in politics. Questions were raised, for instance, on several occasions about overlapping interests in the railway development of the 1870s and 1880s. In 1876 a major row broke out in Parliament over the sale of the Piako swamp lands to a syndicate including Thomas Russell, a director of the Bank of New Zealand.[41] Russell had been a member of Parliament in the 1860s and was a strong and valuable supporter of the Government. The clearest example was the New Zealand Agricultural Company, a development company in which Larnach had a major interest and with which other politicians also had connections. In its efforts to sell rabbit-infested land in Southland the Company needed a Government sympathetic to the aspirations of land developers and saw its chance in the precarious position of the Atkinson Government. The machinations of the politicians interested in the Company played a crucial role in bringing down the Atkinson Government in 1877 and putting Grey into power. The later defection of the same politicians from Grey contributed to his defeat in Parliament in 1879. In 1884–87 the Company's interests were involved in the formation of the Stout–Vogel Ministry. This overlapping of financial and political interests was a cause for scandal in the nineteenth century but it can be seen as an inevitable and even constructive element in both politics and economic development. In the days before payment of members of Parliament and with a restricted pool of potential parliamentarians, some of the political talent necessarily resided in the country's businessmen and speculators. These men did not draw the distinction between their various interests too finely. On numerous occasions, too, private enterprise gained advantage from political contacts to carry out useful development schemes that would otherwise have been postponed for years.

The speculators floated Grey into power in 1877. As Premier he was not a great success. He had problems in getting legislation through the House; farmers and landowners were alienated by a land tax of a ½d. in the pound imposed on all estates worth more than £500; his policy of large-scale government purchases of Māori land created an active lobby of members of Parliament and others who were purchasing lands privately in competition with the Government. The main problem, however, was the economy. To continue with immigration and public works the Government continued borrowing. Those who wanted financial restraint were upset and, worse still, the loan money no longer satisfied the demands of the electorate. A loan authorized in 1879 was largely allocated before it was raised and could not be used to purchase political support. The defeat of Grey's Government by fourteen votes on a no-confidence motion in July 1879 surprised no one.

Parliament was dissolved and in the ensuing election Grey tried to convince the electorate that its choice was between Liberal and Conservative candidates. His rhetoric and the fact that Robert Stout and John Ballance, who both became prominent Liberals in the 1890s, had been his colleagues in office might suggest that the Grey Government was an early phase in the development of the Liberal Party in New Zealand.[42] Among Grey's followers there were certainly some politicians working towards a coherent liberal philosophy. Nevertheless, no clear-cut distinction between political ideologies had yet emerged; nor was there any organized 'party' structure. A detailed study of the 1879 election in Canterbury, where Grey campaigned, shows that the electors voted on the grounds of personality and local issues, not for ideologies.[43] The candidates in Canterbury whom Grey referred to as 'Conservatives' thought in much the same way as his own supporters. When John Hall, a leading member of the land-owning group Grey detested, became Premier in the year 1879, he carried through Parliament a series of electoral reforms, all of them obstructed by Grey.

Although the 1879 election was not an election between Conservatives and Liberals, in some electorates sectional interests were apparent. The land tax brought the rural interest together in places like Taranaki. Harry Atkinson, standing for Egmont, won more support from farmers and backblock settlers than ever before.[44] They had begun to see him as the champion of their interests against those of the town. In the Auckland area there was evidence of a rural–urban split which speculators in Māori lands used to their advantage.[45] The result of the election was very close. Grey and his supporters polled better than expected. When Parliament met, the next Government was not decided until four Auckland members defected from Grey to Hall who promised a number of concessions to Auckland and various parliamentary and electoral reforms.[46]

The Government that finally emerged in 1879 was definitely a rural-interest government. Of the ministers, Hall, Atkinson, William Rolleston, Richard Oliver, and John Bryce, were all farmers and Whitaker was a land speculator on a grand scale. Their rural interests were apparent in the substitution of a property tax (which would fall more heavily on urban property) for Grey's land tax, and in the 1881 country quota, a device to give rural areas a greater weight in elections than they would have had on a straight population basis.

Thoroughgoing conservatism had not, however, arrived, nor were urban interests ignored. The Government passed legislation reducing the parliamentary term from five to three years and giving a franchise based on length of residence rather than property. In 1882 Rolleston introduced a scheme for leasing Crown land rather than alienating it permanently — a nod in the direction of radical land policy and, on his part, an attempt to prevent class conflict from emerging in New Zealand.[47] Atkinson, who was concerned about the increase of poverty and the possibility of this leading to social conflict, advocated national insurance against sickness and old age. Some of his supporters began to view this 'radicalism' with distrust.[48]

The Hall Government, which survived an election in 1881, was re-shuffled twice and re-emerged under the leadership of Whitaker and Atkinson. These men had the misfortune to be in power in a time of economic difficulty. Loan money had largely been spent, some of it in anticipation of loans being floated; New Zealand had promised to stay off the London money market until 1882; prices for New Zealand exports were tumbling; land, bought at high prices in the 1870s, was a millstone around the necks of speculators; private investment was in decline. The Government had few answers. Retrenchment, increases in taxation, cuts in government expenditure, a wait-and-see attitude was all it could suggest. These policies were not popular, but the Opposition did not present a credible alternative. Grey still claimed to be leader of the Opposition despite diminishing support. In 1882 he finally had to concede the official leadership to William Montgomery, the leader of a faction of South Island members. The disagreement amongst the Opposition members helped to mitigate the effects of dissension within the Ministry itself. Government members disagreed particularly over the handling of affairs in Taranaki, where the Māori leader Te Whiti was encouraging passive resistance to Government attempts to open up confiscated land. Differences in Māori policy drove a wedge between Rolleston and Atkinson, and Bryce's later aggressive policy helped convince Hall he should resign from the premiership in 1882.[49]

The renewal of borrowing on a limited scale in 1882 did little to help the Government: the voters were becoming tired of reduced public works and financial restraint. The election of 1884 was the first in which a clear anti-Government vote was delivered. Atkinson did not wait for the usual no-confidence vote in Parliament but resigned the day after it met. It was the return of Vogel to New Zealand and to politics that had turned the tide against Atkinson. Vogel came back initially on private business. Once in New Zealand he found that the mood of the country was in favour of expansion — his sort of financial policy. In particular, several districts either wanted railways or government aid to complete privately constructed branch lines. The defection of members of Parliament committed to railway development had contributed to the defeat of the Government in the House in 1884. In Canterbury there was a well-organized movement, represented by the East and West Coast Railway League, agitating for a railway line to the West Coast and Nelson. In the Waikato and Otago railway companies were in trouble and were prepared to support a government that would help them.[50] Vogel, who had a personal interest in the welfare of the railway companies, spoke out for development. The demand for railways and the expectation that Vogel would hasten a return to prosperity were the crucial factors in the election, especially in Canterbury. Thirteen of the seventeen candidates elected in Canterbury declared for Vogel during the election campaign.

When Parliament met after the election the followers of Vogel and Montgomery together outnumbered Atkinson's followers by sixteen. Vogel, not anticipating that he would remain in New Zealand for long, and handicapped by illness, joined forces with Robert Stout to form the Stout–Vogel Ministry. The original Ministry contained three Canterbury representatives and did not win the favour of the House. The Aucklanders voted together to defeat it and then secured its reconstruction with a more balanced personnel.

The Stout–Vogel Government had a special appeal for speculators who saw it as a source of financial aid. A significant proportion of its legislation was aimed at rescuing speculative land and railway companies of the late 1870s and early 1880s.[51] More generally, its support came from a public eager for increased government spending and renewed economic development. Vogel, as Treasurer, found it difficult to fulfil these expectations. He began with cautious borrowing and proposals to continue public works. By 1887 he was faced with a fall in revenue, caused largely by a decline in the consumption of liquor, with difficulties in borrowing, and with the need to reduce government expenditure. The Opposition and the press were calling for retrenchment. Vogel's expansionist policies had failed. Public works and development were no longer available as a solution to political problems.

Although the Stout–Vogel Ministry cannot be noted for its economic achievements, it was enterprising and innovative in other respects. Following a policy begun in the 1870s, Stout and Vogel pressed for Great Britain to extend its sovereignty in the Pacific region. These politicians saw New Zealand as the centre of a thriving commercial empire in the South Pacific and chauvinistically wished to keep all foreign intruders out of the region.[52] At home, John Ballance, the Minister of Lands, pushed ahead with schemes for village settlements, making land available to men with little capital — a forerunner of later Liberal land policies. The 1885 Hospitals and Charitable Institutions Act put medical and welfare services on a firmer administrative and financial basis. In 1887 the Government introduced a Bill which enfranchised women on the same terms as men and enabled them to stand for Parliament. The Bill was not entirely unexpected. There had been earlier unsuccessful attempts to include the women's vote in general reform Bills. The Women's Christian Temperance Union, introduced into New Zealand in 1885, had appointed Kate Sheppard to organize a national campaign for the women's vote in February 1887. The Stout–Vogel Government had also passed in 1884 an Act to give married women rights over their own property. The franchise Bill of 1887 was, however, defeated by two votes in a surprise vote taken in committee after many Government supporters had left the House. The women of New Zealand were to wait for another six years before Parliament would enact a Bill giving them the vote.[53] Women's votes and small settlements could not save the Government. Plans to go ahead with the West Coast railway helped it survive the 1886 parliamentary session but by 1887 the economic situation had caused it to lose its majority in the House and, as it turned out, in the country as well.

The 1887 election has been seen as the first in which class interests emerged in an organized form and in which national issues took precedence over local and regional issues.[54] The main issue of the election was retrenchment. Property owners wanted retrenchment because they feared the alternative was higher taxation, which, together with low prices and a sluggish land market, could have ruined them. In several towns and rural areas, landowners and businessmen came together to form Reform Associations which demanded cuts in the education vote and the civil service, an end to borrowing, and reductions in the salaries of members of Parliament. This group also tended to favour free trade to give their products an advantage overseas and to keep down the prices of imports. Small farmers, however, did not want severe retrenchment — they still wanted public works and made a plea for 'fairer' taxation. In the cities, manufacturers, shopkeepers, some professional men, and working-class activists wanted some financial restraints but continued public works and protection of local industry to keep urban unemployment within acceptable limits. These groups also formed local associations, such as the Otago Protection League and the Canterbury Electors' Association, to press their views.

The Reform Associations may be regarded as incipient conservative associations. Their members had been forced by economic depression, by the threat of taxation, and by the emergence of some radical political demands into an organized defence of their interests. They opposed the Government. The associations calling for protective tariffs and continued spending can be seen as schools for future Liberals. One of these, the Canterbury Electors' Association, was led by William Pember Reeves. The Association supported the Stout–Vogel Government and its candidates, organizing a scrutiny of the rolls and a house-to-house canvass of Government supporters. Reeves and Westby Perceval stood as Government candidates with the backing of the Association. In Christchurch these tactics were successful, returning a full complement of supporters for the Government. Elsewhere, however, organization was limited or non-existent and the call for severe retrenchment was strong. The Government suffered heavy casualties. Stout lost his seat; Vogel was returned but his following had been so reduced that he was not called on to form a government. Atkinson once again became Premier. Even for Atkinson the construction of a ministry was difficult. The advocates of extreme retrenchment and free trade had hoped to get John Bryce as their leader and distrusted Atkinson. Bryce had lost his seat. Atkinson's Cabinet was a patched-up affair known as the 'Scarecrow Ministry'; it remained in power more on account of Opposition weakness than its own strength.

The next three years were years of continued low prices for New Zealand products, cuts in government expenditure, and disillusionment within the country. The main legislation passed by Atkinson was an 1888 Act levying tariffs on a wide range of imported goods. Several of Atkinson's rural, free-trade supporters left him as a result. The Act was passed with the help of a number of Opposition members including a group of younger urban politicians who were to become Liberals in the 1890s.

Atkinson had less success with other legislation. He tried unsuccessfully to introduce several labour reforms, including legislation to regulate the hours of shopworkers and an eight-hour day. A Bill to reform the Legislative Council was thrown out by the Council itself. Atkinson, a sick man frequently away from the House, had little control over Parliament. In 1889 John Ballance was elected leader of the 'liberal' Opposition, and Atkinson's supporters continued to vote with him mainly to keep Ballance out of power.

In 1890 there were many indications that the economic and social change of the 1880s would be reflected in more bitter political conflict than ever before. A commission set up to look into 'sweating' in New Zealand found that the use of this type of labour was widespread; legislation to improve working conditions was repeatedly thrown out of Parliament by the Legislative Council; strikes and industrial conflict broke out in a number of towns. In the election at the end of the year, although neither Government nor the Opposition was highly organized, the Opposition candidates presented an agreed policy of labour and land reform. This won them the overwhelming support of the urban working class, especially in the South Island. In the towns the interests of both candidates and voters had shifted decisively from local to national issues. In the rural areas the Government still had a majority but even there its following had been reduced. At the beginning of the 1891 session of Parliament the Liberals defeated Atkinson by seven votes.

In the early years of the 1890s recognizable parties emerged in New Zealand politics. The days of informality, of the 'floating' politician, of bargaining for the support of the uncommitted members were over. Personality and localism, the political factors most important in the settlement period, did not disappear but economic change, population growth, urbanization, and the increasing interest of labour in politics introduced new issues that could not be resolved within the old structure of politics. The old, informal, personalized style of consensus politics became outmoded in the 1890s. A more complex society demanded a different form of political organization.

CHAPTER 5

Settler Society

Jeanine Graham

I was walking down St Stephen's Avenue one day; I had been sent out on a message — who should stop and speak to me but Sir George Grey. It was in 1888, he walked quite a long way with me. He told me that New Zealand was going to be a great country and that everyone would have a chance to get on. I was 12 years old at the time and I have never forgotten it. I had no boots on at the time.

James Williamson wore no boots because he had none. The resources of the Parnell Orphans' Home did not extend to such luxuries for its 200 inhabitants, boys and girls from five to fourteen years old. On that walk down an Auckland avenue, the thin youngster was clad only in skimpy shorts and a cotton shirt. His diet consisted largely of 'bread and scrape'. Milk was '2 inches in the bottom of the can' and the rest filled up with water. The inside of a scavenged cabbage stalk was 'a real treat'. Orphaned at seven, he had grown up in an environment where conditions were more primitive and discipline more harsh than in a contemporary colonial gaol. Deprived by illness of much of the elementary education to which the 1877 Act entitled him, within a year he would be fending entirely for himself.[1] Yet it was fitting that the elder statesman should feel moved to share his vision of New Zealand's future with this ragged representative of colonial youth, for in many ways James Williamson epitomized a new phase in the country's development. The 1880s revealed some distressing shortcomings and inequalities in colonial society but that decade also marked the ending of a foundation era during which New Zealand's European population had grown, mostly through immigration, from 5,000 in 1841 to well over 600,000 in 1891. The 1886 census revealed that nearly 52 per cent of the population had been born in the colony. The future of the country would lie increasingly in the hands of these native-born, of whom James Williamson was a not untypical example.

The society in which he was growing had been fashioned during half a century of predominantly British immigration. People and possessions, attitudes and ideas — they formed a random and motley collection. Travellers through colonial New Zealand often found it difficult to grasp the essence of the new society evolving there. It was easier to write about the distinctive New Zealand landscape and to isolate particular points, such as an openness among the people, a proclivity for outdoor amusements, a high level of worker prosperity. Yet a strident originality was hardly to be expected: few European residents had come as an act of deliberate rejection of the society in which they had been raised. Rather, they wanted that very 'chance to get on' of which Grey had spoken. For those who succeeded, colonial New Zealand offered a more prosperous lifestyle than they would have enjoyed at home, but their values and attitudes still reflected the influence of their parent society. The first stage in evolving a distinctive New Zealand way of life was the immigrants' adaptation of a northern heritage to southern conditions. Only when that foundation was laid would the next generation develop its own form of an antipodean society.

The process of reconciliation between the imported and the indigenous was at its height during the first forty years of organized European settlement. Adaptability was the keynote as individual settlers and the society they were fashioning passed through stages of adjustment, establishment, and consolidation. Members of the Olson family came to Wellington in the 1850s as shoemakers: they soon found it more profitable to run a hotel in Lyttelton in the 1860s and settled happily as farmers in Taranaki in the 1880s. Seamstress Catherine Ralfe changed occupation and address several times as she experienced colonial life in Canterbury, Westland, and Wanganui before retiring with her equally itinerant widowed sister-in-law to Stratford.[2] Not all fared so well. The strain of reconciling the old with the new could become unbearable, particularly in the years of hardship in the first stages of settlement. Many immigrants left New Zealand, sometimes for another colony, more often for home.

Settler mobility was a notable feature of the adjustment and establishment years, though not all of the movement within the colony was voluntary. Earthquakes frightened many colonists away from Wellington in 1848; armed conflict in the North Island disrupted the lives of both settlers and their Māori opponents. Gold discoveries provoked a massive migration to the goldfields, and this was reversed once the most readily accessible supplies were worked out. The continuous stream of independent and organized immigration and the continued opening up of new areas of the country for settlement meant that the pattern of settler adaptation, establishment, and consolidation constantly recurred. Underlying this mobility was a sense of opportunity, if not in one part of the colony, then in another.

As colonial society entered a consolidation phase, that buoyant sense of optimism was vanishing. From the outset there had been efforts to attract both employers and employees but it had been rightly assumed that the working settler would make up with initiative and application what he lacked in financial resources. As time went on there seemed less chance of success unless one had 'big Capital'. The tone of the colony was also altering. Even in the 1850s there were recognizably 'new faces and mercenary ideas, different from those of the adventurers of the early days'. A new arrival in 1860 was distressed to find that money-making was the sole object of a colonial existence and that the colonists' conversations rarely turned upon any other subject.[3]

The colony-wide recession of the 1880s revealed that the much vaunted levelling process for which the colony was famed was now something of a myth. Social divisions did exist and they were based upon wealth. This truth was all the more distressing because it was so much at variance with the dream that had prompted so many immigrants to come. In the early years, when survival was the common objective, money was an asset second to health and a capacity for hard work. The distinctions that began to appear, usually within a decade of each settlement's establishment, had been localized. The granting of political powers to the colonists inadvertently exacerbated social differences. Only men of independent means could afford to take up political office. Since that independence was, in the majority of cases, derived from the possession of land, the association between landed wealth, political power, and social status grew. By the 1880s much popular rhetoric was directed against the 'landed gentry' and the 'governing classes'.

The colonial-born represented by the young James Williamson were thus part of a society that derived many of its features from its antipodean situation. These New Zealanders knew of their northern European origins only at second-hand. The bush, the mountains, and the clean air were part of their identity. So too was colonial class distinction, and with it, in the 1880s, a growing scrutiny of the society New Zealanders had come to regard as their own. From foundations laid in the decades of adaptation a distinctive colonial society had emerged.

Despite inter-colonial competition to attract settlers, especially during the middle years of the nineteenth century, New Zealand was never advertised as a haven for all comers. All efforts to promote settlement in the colony were based upon clearly defined policies of selection. In the 1840s the New Zealand Company sought respectful hard-working rural labourers and cultured men of capital as the two most desirable groups for the formation of an antipodean Arcadia. The Canterbury and Otago Associations added religious criteria as well. As provincial and then central government agencies, in the 1850s and 1870s respectively, took over the task of promoting New Zealand as a field for emigration, the selective approach persisted. Age, outlook, and occupation were not the only criteria. Chinese, Indian, and, to a lesser extent, Dalmatian settlers were to find that racial differences far outweighed any capacity to work. A restrictive immigration policy was not imposed until the 1880s but the declared objectives of the organized immigration schemes and the manner in which emigration agents interpreted those goals and distributed information about the country were effective forms of selection and exclusion.

Publicity handbooks were an important means of conveying appropriate impressions of the colony and its requirements. Writing in 1857, Charles Hursthouse had four categories of unfit emigrants: the 'Too-lates', the 'De Smythes', the 'Grumblers, or Dismal Dummies', and the 'Fast Gents'. The first had inadequate financial resources. 'The second, are the fastidiously genteel people of feeble intellect . . . who would prefer a crust and thin claret in the drawing-room, to roast beef and a pot of ale in the kitchen.' Then came the 'emigrant grumbler . . . the man or woman who grumbles *always* . . . the sun is too brilliant, the sky too blue, the trees too large, the meat too fat, the house not so large as the house they lived in when they kept three servants and visited a family who knew a baronet; *and they only wish they were back'*. Finally, the writer cautioned against sending 'ne'er-do-wells' to the colony. Government publications were equally blunt. One of the earliest *Year Books* stated quite simply that the colony did not want 'persons without *character'*.[4]

Reflecting the changing economic circumstances of the colony, the 1875 edition of the *Official Handbook of New Zealand* contained a judicious selection of letters from successful settlers, written to encourage others to come out under the nominated immigration scheme. Jesse W. was short and to the point. 'Dear Brother, — I hope you will make up your mind and come to New Zealand at once: it will be the best day's work you ever done. You will be sure of immediate employment at good wages when you land. Food is very cheap, and wages high: you will be able to save more every week here than you are earning where you are now. New Zealand is a fine and healthy country; no one can help but like it. Any man may do well that will work.' Charles McN., bootmaker, of Christchurch, had three reasons for nominating one of his English friends. 'First, we need good and steady men, such as you are, to assist in settling the country; second, your own prospects would be very much better than they are in England; and third, the prospects of your daughters would be increased a hundred-fold.'[5] Such letters made light of the difficulties in adjusting to a colonial existence.

In the same publication, each of the provinces competed with visions of an attractive new lifestyle. Canterbury thought it could offer to the 'industrious immigrant of the labouring class a certain prospect of employment, at good wages, for some time to come'. For the small farmer, too, there was no better area of New Zealand. Marlborough noted modestly that all kinds of labour were in demand 'but the classes most particularly required are ordinary farm labourers, carpenters, and mechanics, navvies, bush hands, shepherds, miners, and domestic female servants'. Shepherds were especially welcome if they brought their sheep dogs with them. Regional rivalry was demonstrated throughout. 'Of all the Provinces, Taranaki offers the greatest advantages to the petty capitalist or small farmer immigrant. Land inferior in quality to none in the Colony, and superior to most, is obtainable at a reasonable rate and within reasonable distance of a town . . . True, most of it is covered with forest, but this is rather an advantage than a drawback to the industrious small farmer settling down on his 50-acre section with the determination to make a home in the bush.' Mechanics would also readily find work; labourers of any class would never feel the 'pressure of want'. From Otago came the stern admonition that if a workman did not succeed and prosper, it would be his own fault.[6]

The intending emigrant's source of information influenced both his decision and his expectations. Those who corresponded with family or with reliable friends already in the colony were usually the best prepared for the life ahead. While their personal reaction to upheaval and re-establishment could not always be predicted, those who came as part of a chain migration were likely to settle more easily. As one young Northland farmer explained when trying to persuade his parents to allow his sister to emigrate: 'She should find as comfortable and pleasant a home as she could desire, her own freedom in all respects and I should be able to give that advice and assistance whenever she would require it that I feel myself able to do.'[7]

Amongst the wide range of individuals who did arrive, willingly or reluctantly, in New Zealand during the nineteenth century, three groups emerge. Pre-eminent were the British settlers who in 1886 totalled 40 per cent of the European population. Predominantly English, Scottish, and Irish, most were from labouring and lower-middle-class backgrounds, and many were small town and country dwellers. Second were the cultural minority groups, German and Scandinavian in particular, and some Asians and southern Europeans. The third group comprised those who came from other colonial societies. Many of the goldminers arriving in the 1860s, for example, came after periods in both Australia and America. Both they and the migrants who had preceded them across the Tasman during the pastoral boom of the 1850s were in search of fortunes and imbued with some of the contemporary antagonism towards the official regulation that appeared to restrict their initiative in the Australian colonies. In contrast to early North American settlement, however, a search for political or religious freedom was not a common cause for emigration to New Zealand.

Cultural homogeneity was therefore one of the hallmarks of colonial society. With it came a striking degree of intolerance towards non-European minorities and a strong sense of Anglo-Saxon superiority over coloured peoples. Moreover, despite efforts to attract men of culture and capital, and despite the aspirations of a few such immigrants, in composition and outlook colonial New Zealand was overwhelmingly a working settlers' society. Already evident in the 1850s, these traits were exacerbated by the high rate of labouring-class immigration during the next two decades. The lure of gold and state-sponsored immigration schemes contributed to the European population virtually trebling in size during the 1860s and nearly doubling again in the following ten years, with Otago, Canterbury, and Auckland provinces together absorbing the highest proportion of these increases. (See Table 1.)

However well prepared they believed themselves to be, the wrench of leaving their home country was far worse than emigrants anticipated. While few so enjoyed the voyage that they were anxious to repeat it, the experience was an important stage in the process of adaptation and adjustment. The enforced self-discipline and privation of shipboard life stood many a colonist in good stead during the first months of a primitive colonial existence. If, as was frequently the case in the early years, the entire ship's complement was destined for one area, then shipboard decisions, discussion, and alignments could shape much of the settlement's future

116

Table 1: Population (other than Māori) by provinces, 1851–91

	1851[1]		1861		1871		1881		1891	
	number	per cent	number	per cent	number	per cent	number	per cent	number	per cent
Auckland	9,430	35.3	24,420	24.7	62,335	24.3	99,451	20.3	133,178	21.3
Taranaki[2]	1,532	5.7	2,044	2.1	4,480	1.7	14,858	3.0	22,065	3.5
Wellington	6,409	24.0	12,566	12.7	24,001	9.4	61,371	12.5	97,725	15.6
Hawke's Bay[3]	–	–	2,611	2.6	6,059	2.4	17,367	3.5	28,506	4.5
North Island total	17,371	65.0	41,641	42.1	96,875	37.8	193,047	39.4	281,474	44.9
Nelson	4,287	16.1	9,952	10.1	22,501	8.8	26,075	5.3	34,770	5.5
Marlborough[4]	–	–	2,299	2.3	5,235	2.0	9,300	1.9	12,767	2.0
Westland[5]	–	–	–	–	15,357	6.0	15,010	3.1	15,887	2.5
Canterbury	3,273	12.3	16,090	16.2	46,934	18.3	112,424	22.9	128,663	20.5
Otago	1,776	6.6	27,163	27.4	60,722	23.7	107,481	21.9	116,088	18.5
Southland[6]	–	–	1,876	1.9	8,769	3.4	26,596	5.4	37,009	5.9
South Island total	9,336	35.0	57,380	57.9	159,518	62.2	296,886	60.6	345,184	55.1
NZ total	26,707		99,021		256,393		489,933		626,658	

1. Areas correspond closely to provinces formed in 1852
2. Name changed from New Plymouth, 1859
3. Separated from Wellington, 1858
4. Separated from Nelson, 1859
5. Separated from Canterbury,1868
6. Separated from Otago 1861, rejoined 1870

Source: Adapted from C. J. Gibson, 'A Demographic History of New Zealand', PhD thesis, University of California, Berkeley (1971), Tables 7, 8, 15, 16

development. The Nelson Literary and Scientific Institution, which soon had a membership of some eighty settlers and a library of over a thousand volumes, was founded during the passage of the *Whitby* in 1841. Attorney-General William Swainson and Chief Justice William Martin were reputed to have devised much of the colony's law code during their passage.[8] Above all, the social hierarchy on board ship served to provide new communities with their leaders. Those who travelled below decks developed their own group loyalties, but cabin-class immigrants were soon accorded, or soon assumed, the role of decision-makers. While many responded magnificently to the challenge, not all were ideally suited for the task.

Class distinction was fundamental to the Victorian social attitudes that were being imported. The division of the boat into cabin and steerage quarters prevented the mixing necessary for a modification of such views. Cabin-class passengers could write either disdainfully or sympathetically about the situation below decks but they did not question that a difference should exist. Forced by circumstances to tolerate their inequitable and unpleasant conditions, few steerage-class emigrants accepted or shared the upper-deck view that they were inferior beings. Dr A. C. Barker, surgeon superintendent on the *Charlotte Jane* bound for Canterbury in 1850, discovered to his surprise that a number of his 100 charges 'stoutly refused' to clean their quarters below decks, insisting that 'they hadn't been accustomed to scrub, etc'. Steerage passengers on a voyage to Otago complained vigorously about the night watch and cleaning duties. They objected even more strongly to their daily task of drawing fifty buckets of water from the hold: 'it is so disagreeable a job, wetting all your clothes and getting them iron rusted.'[9] The strength of character that had prompted these emigrants to embark for New Zealand was rarely perceived by the cabin-class passengers. The fierce pride with which working-class settlers regarded both themselves and their achievements in the colony was a source of amazement for many commentators.

Shipboard amusements also revealed social attitudes. The lengthiest debate on the *Lord Auckland* was occasioned by the question: 'Is the education of the working classes beneficial to the general interests of the community?' One young merchant had no difficulty in reaching his decision: 'I need scarcely say that as a good "Tory" I gave my opinion against education.' By a nine-to-four majority, the cabin-class passengers also decided that the colonization of New Zealand would benefit the aboriginal inhabitants. The vexed issue as to whether the intellectual endowments of the two sexes were naturally equal led eventually to a decision in the affirmative. The ship's newspaper, painstakingly copied in long-hand, could serve as the vehicle for advertisement, entertainment, and instruction. On discovering that there seemed to be some curious ideas afoot concerning race relations in the colony, Alfred Fell immediately prepared a salutary article for the *Lord Auckland Journal*. The *Maraval Jackdaw*, a well-illustrated and lively production, reveals that a good deal of trading took place during the *Maraval's* voyage in 1879. Poetry written exclusively for its pages was not of the highest quality but it well reflects the mixed emotions current near the journey's end:

> There are some here who wish fallow fortunes to better,
> Others a long-failing health to sustain;
> May the first be fulfilled to the uttermost letter,
> The latter a strong constitution regain. . . .

> Some may return to the land they were born in;
> Some where they go may remain good and true;
> Others may wish ere another year's dawning
> They had never forsaken the old for the new. . . .[10]

'I cannot say that we are disappointed in the country, though it is very different to what we had expected. . . .'[11] This typical reaction to colonial New Zealand often began before the immigrant had landed. Contrary winds could cause a ship to tack off shore for hours or even days before being able to enter harbour. Frequently boats called at a number of ports. Passengers thus had ample opportunity for viewing coastal scenery. Their response varied according to their aspirations. Intending farmers were the most doleful as they contemplated steep bush-clad hills or rugged terrain. The New Zealand landscape exerted a strong influence on the colonial communities and the society that grew up within it. Soil fertility affected farming; bush-cover limited land usage. Rivers provided a means of transport, but in flood they brought isolation, even death. Colonial regionalism was therefore geographic as well as social in origin. Each settlement claimed a superior environment, their rivalry disguising the fact that there were very few coastal areas of the colony where topographical features or climate were a deterrent to settlement.

Independent immigrants in the 1840s had six main centres to choose from but they were likely to stay in or close to the one where they disembarked. Such was the difficulty of communications that settlers moved little between communities during the first decade of colonization. In these years of relative isolation the essential character of each settlement was formed — a response to the new environment dictated by the range of backgrounds of the early inhabitants, by their possessions and customs, and, most of all, by the values which they held to be important and which they sought to re-establish. As the settlers came to know their new landscape and its resources an imported heritage found its colonial expression, through housing styles and gardens, farming methods and social gatherings, in churches, schools, and community services. When Governor Grey's wife first visited New Plymouth in February 1850, for example, she immediately felt herself to be in familiar surroundings. 'This is a lovely country', she confided to a South Australian correspondent, 'the finest agricultural country you can imagine with the nicest quietest, most simple, rural population you can imagine out of dear old England, & almost all of them from my own West Countree & it is a pleasure to hear the old Dorsetshire farmers speak of my dear father. We have too the friendliest church & some of the nicest schools in the Colony.' Southern representatives arriving in Auckland for the first session of the General Assembly were impressed by the countryside through which they rode: 'Stone fences & stone gate posts, hedges neat cottages, large fields of *the most* luxuriant grass — we were in a word all enchanted. Auckland itself is a very badly laid out town but not unlike an English sea side port. The scenery not equal to Wellington or the port of Nelson when the snowy range is clear but still beautiful. Many of the buildings infinitely better than anything we have in the South.'[12]

Economic and political circumstances also had a lasting effect on the nature and pace of a settlement's development. Auckland, with an excellent trading position, a good harbour, and a rapidly expanding population, was commercially the most lively of the early towns. Socially it was the most diverse. A strong military and official presence earned Auckland society a reputation for snobbishness and élitism. Yet alongside these dominant groups were the workers of Mechanics Bay, and the pioneer farmers of surrounding Onehunga and Howick, whose industry was already beginning to transform the landscape in an English image.[13] Lengthy disputes over land titles and consequent racial tension had a searing impact on Nelson, New Plymouth, and Wellington in their formative years. A foundation for later resentment was often laid at this time. Much of the criticism of the British Government's handling of native affairs came from Cook Strait settlers incensed at the lack of official reprisal for the Wairau affair; the continuing southern mistrust of Auckland's political influence began when Wellington was not selected as the site for the country's capital.

With the improvement of communications, the activities of explorers, the continuing influx of population, and the economic incentives provided by such commodities as wool, timber, and gold, settlement became more dispersed. Miners and timber millers sought wealth, or just employment, in Westland and on the Coromandel Peninsula during the 1860s. The towns that they established owed much of their character to the industry that had created them: the incessant rhythmic pounding of the quartz-crushing stamper batteries was the very voice and life of early Thames.

Strong though regional variation and regional loyalties were, new communities shared their essential features. Dunedin might build in stone and Wellington in wood, but both built banks, breweries, schools, shops, and hotels. No settlement was without its churches; few without a gaol. That the colony would be a Christian country, that the rule of law would prevail, and that New Zealand would owe allegiance to Great Britain were taken to be self-evident truths, and all found their expression in the developing society. And as an increasing proportion of the population began to live in urban areas, those common features came to be experienced more widely.

The lifestyle adopted by any settler in New Zealand depended upon the time and place of his or her arrival, on income and occupation, and most unpredictably of all, upon the immigrant's readiness and capacity for adjustment. Adaptation of the imported heritage appears to have been most rapid and most thorough in everyday matters. Dress and diet, housing styles and housekeeping methods, all soon reflected a distinctive colonial air. Attitudes and values were much slower to alter, the degree of adaptation depending upon a person's position in society. The higher up the social scale the less likely was significant change. Domestic service is a valuable indicator. The cost or scarcity of labour caused many a former mistress to become her own cook and housemaid; when the employment of domestic assistance became again possible, a maid and a cook were quickly acquired, usually amidst grumblings about the wages and working conditions demanded. The domestic servant who had married and found with her husband a new competence, confidence, and comfort in New Zealand, even a new social station, would never revert through choice to a position of servility and servitude. Ironically, the least successful adjustment was often amongst women whose social status had markedly improved in the colony. As one Bishop of Auckland remarked: 'There are doubtless servants and servants in the colonies as in England; but many of the employers of female servants in this country are new to the position, and do not know how to treat their subordinates. In many houses a "general servant" only is employed, and her drudgery is often great.'[14]

Colonial fashions were a recognizable combination of imported goods and values and local conditions. A list compiled in 1849 for the guidance of intending emigrants clearly showed that dress was an expression of social status. For the labouring man and his wife, the emphasis was on flannel, cotton, worsted, and fustian garments. The 'very full' recommendations for a gentleman ran to such items as seventy-two dress shirts and forty waistcoats. Despite the inclusion of some practical suggestions, the quantity and nature of the goods classified as essential led to false expectations. The consequences were predictable: chastised by a friendly neighbour for doing her housework in a silk dress, Mrs Flora MacDonald's simple answer was that she had no other.[15]

Once in the colony an immigrant could have difficulty in obtaining the desired type of clothing. When fire swept through a newly completed raupō whare in May 1841, Edwin Harris lost all of his surveyor's instruments, and his family saved only their lives. Since so few of their fellow Taranaki settlers had anything to spare, the young mother of three immediately began to collect the burnt articles. She made cloth shoes for the children and 'many little things sewed together came in useful until we could receive an outfit from England which arrived twelve months after'. The lesson of colonial adaptability was well learned. Some forty-eight years later, two of the Harris daughters, then living a life of genteel poverty in Nelson, earned themselves warm compliments for their fashionable appearance at a local ball. Their striking dresses were old garments re-made: a ninepenny packet of red dye and hours of patient sewing had transformed Ellen's old white silk while Frances' once familiar blue ball gown was unrecognizable with its black velveteen trimmings and artistic re-styling.[16] The importation of hand sewing-machines during the 1870s made such tasks for a colonial home seamstress much easier.

The need for clothes, footwear in particular, thus formed the basis of many a favour asked of correspondents at home. But although many settlers were dependent upon the tastes of these relatives and friends, fashion consciousness within the colony was maintained by new immigrants and by illustrated magazines. When the brothers Rust set up as drapers in Auckland in the early 1850s, they soon discovered that smallwear, cheap bonnets, and cheap, brightly coloured tartan shawls were in great demand. Three general instructions persisted throughout the brothers' advice to their Scottish suppliers: that goods should be inexpensive yet stylish, that they should be colourful, and that they should not be discarded stock. As one merchant was bluntly informed: 'We do not wish you to send another parcel, all OLD.'[17]

The brighter colour of clothing worn in the colony struck even those without a vested interest in the trade. Vicesimus Lush, first Anglican vicar at Howick, remarked that colours were gayer in the colony than at home. Arriving in Otago in 1849, Mary Homeyer was startled less by the colour than by the predominance of 'the Colonial Costum', a cotton, corduroy, and blue flannel garb which she conceded was useful for working conditions but still judged to be 'a most unbecoming dress'. This rough attire was common in the newly established settlement of Dunedin, where labouring work was still predominant. In Wellington more variation was apparent. There the people 'presented a much greater diversity of appearance than those of Otago, there were more grades, the merchants, and females, dress as at home, the military also made it look more lively, and there is less display of the blue Jersey'.[18]

With the blue gradually replaced by the coloured check shirt, this colonial garb became something of a uniform for outdoor workers, goldminers, farmhands, station-owners, and bush-fellers alike. Women's clothing, more affected by the dictates of fashion and propriety, was slower to adapt. Few gentlewomen displayed their ankles, despite the ubiquitous mud that plagued their every outdoor excursion after wet weather. Laundering clothes was a new task for many an immigrant's wife, yet collars were starched and multiple petticoats worn, even when there were no neighbours to notice. The colonial revolution in female attire began at the lower end of the social scale. When Blannie Lush, eldest daughter in the vicar's household, went out in her simple brown holland dress to interview a prospective domestic, the young lady in question 'came sailing into her "Mamma's parlour" prepared for a walk, decked out with feathers, flowers, flounces, ear-rings, gold chain, necklace and bracelets'. The would-be employer retreated rapidly, and the vicar noted gloomily that this was 'the style of "Helpers" we are fast coming to'.[19] While climate and the frequent shortage of supplies contributed to some of the adaptation in dress — it was soon acceptable practice for children to play barefoot, for example — former values were not necessarily discarded. Few settlers failed to distinguish between working days and Sunday and they dressed accordingly.

The food eaten by the early settlers changed radically as the circumstances of the colony altered. Real food shortages were experienced only in the first year or two of organized settlement, when the colonists felt themselves to be totally dependent upon imported supplies. As they benefited from the produce and example of the Māori agriculturalists and as they gained gardening skills appropriate to their new environment, the colonists' diet became healthier and more diverse. For earlier settlers such as Sarah Selwyn, pork was the basic fresh meat. With the advent of pastoralism came mutton, then beef. Flour, sugar, tea, salt beef, rice, and dried fruit were the staples of many European diets but in areas where those supplies were difficult to obtain, new resources were tried. The Caldwell family dined regularly on local fish and bird supplies; 'then at very low tides there were fine oysters on the bank and large mussels which as an article of diet are very good though few English people care for them'. Taranaki settlers soon developed a taste for the pear-like fruit and fleshy bracts of the kiekie while the kūmara, 'also delicious', was likened to a sweet chestnut. Vegetable gardens too were quickly established and not only by those accustomed to such activity. Within months of his arrival in the Wairarapa valley, the aristocratic Frederick Weld was writing proudly of his garden, then containing radishes, turnips, cabbages, young Scottish kale, potatoes, peas, carrots, beans, celery, parsley, watermelon, pumpkin, onions, and lettuce, together with sweet peas, sweet williams, and stocks. For settlers accustomed to clearly defined planting, growing, and harvesting periods, the rapidity and size of growth was 'perfectly amazing'. To Ellen Fox, a gentle Quaker slowly adjusting to life in a gold-town society, both growing and cooking the crop were new experiences. 'I planted 120 cabbages the other day and they have grown so fast that they are quite nice plants now. . . . Though things grow so fast here they are very tough, the cabbages are not tender after having been boiled for 2 hours. But I think it is partly that such a poor sort is cultivated that they are not good.'[20]

Housing styles also had to adapt to meet colonial conditions. Dwellings with verandahs, built with a northerly aspect, for instance, were more suited to the southern hemisphere than houses facing south. 'It is a true saying in reference to our houses of kāuri pine, "Where the sun enters not the doctor does." '[21] The calico shelters, raupō whare, and V-shaped huts so typical of the 1840s and early 1850s were erected from whatever material was available locally and designed so that a man could build one on his own. As the pioneer became more established, the original makeshift arrangement would be replaced by a small timber dwelling and only later by a more commodious house containing separate sleeping and living quarters. As the pioneering phase passed, housing styles gave a clearer indication of income and status. By the 1860s grand homesteads were appearing on some of the large estates, especially in the South Island. In Auckland, residential distinctions apparent in the 1840s were much more marked by the 1860s: workmen's wooden cottages stood in striking contrast to architect-commissioned mansions such as Highwic and Alberton.[22] Despite the enormous difference in scale and cost, there was one significant common feature: employer and employee alike lived in dwellings that stood as independent houses, surrounded by at least a little land. Rarely was that symbol of industrial oppression, the street of terraced houses, erected in these colonial communities. Early colonial homes were, however, often smaller than their English equivalent, probably because of the cost of labour and building materials. Many a settler had to store furniture and treasured possessions that would not fit into a first colonial home.

Local conditions could dictate the appearance of a whole settlement. After the damage of the 1848 earthquake in Wellington almost all buildings erected were wooden, a precaution that proved wise during the more severe tremors of 1855. Oamaru residents and public authorities alike made good use of the creamy white limestone nearby. Housing also reflected political and economic developments. 'To Let' signs were widespread in Auckland in 1864–65 following the decision to remove the seat of government to Wellington. The cost, quality, and availability of rental accommodation there altered accordingly, especially during the annual influx of politicians and their families. A new arrival endeavouring to find a home in Wellington in 1879, advertised and walked 'to every corner & available spot' of the capital, but still could hear of nothing for less than £75 a year '& that not even decent. 25/- per week is the lowest rent for a 5 roomed box with in almost every case a back yard 9ft. from the hill in which these houses are fitted in. All these wooden houses are about a foot from the ground, and the under part is open & affords a camping ground for the Rats & dirty rags broken tin pots & such like playthings. There are some villas but they are occupied by only those who can afford London west end rates. . . .'[23]

Although much of the domestic architecture exhibited a colonial air — particularly in the verandahed cottage and the more substantial bay villa — imported styles became increasingly evident in both public and domestic building as the temporary structures of the first two decades were replaced from the 1860s onwards. In scale and design, in the use of locally available materials and in methods of construction, the pioneering phase of public colonial architecture extended little beyond the 1870s.[24]

Food, clothing, shelter, and employment were the most immediate preoccupations of a colonist's existence, and with all four concerns the colony's women were closely involved. Recognizing the population imbalance that characterized colonial societies, Hursthouse had warned intending emigrants to New Zealand that an extra week spent in looking for a wife would be more advantageous than buying a patent plough or thoroughbred horse. William Morgan, extolling the virtues of country life in 1860, admitted: 'I certainly pity the unfortunate individual who lives in the bush all alone. What indeed is the bush without female society.' A 'good wife' had many functions to fulfil. Pioneer Nelson surveyor Samuel Stephens described the Hon. Mrs Constantine Dillon warmly as a 'notable specimen of what a settler's wife should be — giving her best energies cheerfully to the duties of her station, and supporting her husband well in his arduous undertaking — without damping his spirits by vain regrets at the change of situation, and the loss of friends and associations in her former English home'. When single men in the colony began to feel that they could support a wife, they realized that the lifestyle to which they were now economically and personally committed would have very little appeal for young ladies with whom they were formerly acquainted. As Robert Petch wrote from his 'first rate rough strong hut' in 1880: 'I fancy a girl from England wd be little good to me as a Colonial wife . . . for an English girl accustomed to society and flying round to parties towns etc, to come and settle as a squatter's wife out here I think it is rather out of the question.'[25] The selection of female immigrants in the 1870s helped to counteract the imbalance exacerbated by the gold-rushes (see Table 2), and by 1891 the position had further improved, although marriage and birth rates showed the impact of economic recession.

Table 2: Net external movement to New Zealand, 1858–90

Years	Males	Females	Total
1858–1860	12,082	8,749	20,831
1861–1865	63,285	29,884	93,169
1866–1870	11,167	9,369	20,536
1871–1875	46,501	35,445	81,946
1876–1880	31,870	22,917	54,787
1881–1885	15,958	13,001	28,959
1886–1890	–4,911	–3,791	–8,702

Source: Adapted from Gibson, 'Demographic History', Table 31

Life was physically and emotionally demanding for pioneer women. A country life brought its particular difficulties because of the size of meals to be prepared, the quantities of stores to be organized, the sheer volume of work to be done, often in the most basic conditions. Yet, thinking back on her years of isolation in the Aorere valley, Elizabeth Caldwell could comment: 'We greatly enjoyed the easy way of life then the fashion in New Zealand. Scarcely any furniture — people thought themselves quite comfortable with bare floors, a sofa or two, a table, a few boxes nicely covered with chintz. . . . It was far more pleasant in those days and folks were just as happy, whereas now, domestic servants are not to be had, and a large house fully furnished means actual slavery — unless indeed daughters are numerous.' For Adela Stewart, establishing with her husband at Athenree near Katikati a lifestyle more appropriate to the Ulster gentry at home, the extra burdens caused by an endless round of entertaining, including catering singlehanded for balls of more than a hundred, were largely self-imposed. Such a social pattern made few concessions to the hardship and limited facilities of a pioneer society.[26]

Unmarried women and working wives alike found greater employment opportunity in the towns. In 1891 most working women were still absorbed in domestic service (19,400), a category that included the supply of board and lodgings. The growth of colonial manufactories, health and educational services, and commercial enterprise was beginning to provide more jobs. Clothing, textile, and food processing industries employed 10,900; teaching and nursing fewer than 6,000. Shops and offices had less than 3,000 female wage-earners behind their counters. Marriage, the running of a home, and the raising of a family was still the more common employment for women. Few were openly critical of this situation: most women prided themselves on their role of colonial helpmeet.[27]

The quality of family life varied considerably during these years. The severe privation and limited medical care that were so often the characteristics of the adjustment phase took their toll on parent and child alike. While many women surmounted the challenge which the physically laborious nature of pioneering life provided, for the less robust the seemingly incessant childbearing at two-yearly intervals could severely tax both personal and financial resources. Although family size was reducing throughout the century, to an average of between three and four children by the end of the 1880s, childbirth was normally a time of anxiety. Newborn children were especially vulnerable, for not until late in the 1880s did the non-Māori infant mortality rate begin to fall below 100 per 1,000 live births. Maternal mortality was an ever-present fear since the death of a mother could often be the catalyst for the break-up of a family. Institutional care, or desertion, were sometimes the only alternatives perceived by a father who lacked a network of relatives in the colony.

Most children who survived the risks of early childhood were expected to work. That was their function. Yet they also found time to play and they were also loved. Youthful immigrants relished the opportunity to spend more time out of doors and exhibited a lively sense of adventure in their physical environment. Although life was often freer for boys than for girls, the emerging rhythm of colonial life came to provide for Saturday afternoon eeling expeditions and Sunday reading, for evening cricket on the roughly formed streets and marbles or 'jacks' (knuckle bones) as the season dictated. In the larger colonial families of the earlier years, such leisure time was precious and well-used. It was the younger siblings, the colonial-born, who benefited most from parental endeavours to provide an improved quality of life for the next generation. The labour of the older children was usually an essential part of the process of effecting that transformation.

Immigrants to New Zealand during the first decade or so of official settlement had the curious experience of arriving in a country where a strong religious presence was already established but where the first objective of that presence was ministry to the indigenous inhabitants, not to the incoming Europeans. Despite the indefatigable labours of individual clerics, such were the limited financial resources of the churches, the distribution of the population, and the difficulty of communications, that for much of the foundation era a significant proportion of the immigrant population did not have the benefit of regular formal worship conducted by ordained clergy. Instead, where worshipping communities gathered, especially in smaller or more isolated settlements, they depended heavily upon the leadership of their own lay members, with a high attendance and often a busy baptism schedule guaranteed whenever a member of the regular clergy could be present. Amongst the wide range of Christian creeds transplanted in the colony, Anglicans came to outnumber their Presbyterian and Catholic rivals on a basis of four to two to one, but the Church of England did not become the established church of New Zealand. Special privileges were not accorded to one denomination over another and local reaction was immediate whenever this principle of equality appeared to be under threat.

Bigotry, conflict, and sectarian strife were not unknown but in general there was a high level of religious tolerance amongst adherents of the major creeds. Followers of some of the newer sects, however, especially those of American origin which began to infiltrate the colony in the 1870s, could experience outright hostility. The sight of a Mormon preacher farewelling his Māori converts at Huntly station aroused an indignant reaction amongst observers on the waiting train.[28] Denominational strength showed regional variation, the consequence of population origins. Auckland gained a strong Irish Catholic contingent with the arrival of the Fencibles; Taranaki had its group of West Country Methodists. As for the rest of the country, the fiery Catholic Bishop of Dunedin declared: 'In Otago, it is Presbyterian Protestantism; in Canterbury, Anglican Protestantism; and in Wellington, Protestantism of any and every kind.'[29] The country had its share of atheists and agnostics, yet the weight of evidence suggests that the majority of immigrants came with the sense that their God was coming with them. Census returns in the last three decades of the century indicate that consistently less than 5 per cent of the European population declared that they had no religious affiliation, or objected to stating their views.

Adaptability was essential to religious practice in colonial New Zealand, for worshippers and clergy alike. Henry Harper preached in a Canterbury woolshed; early Thames ministers used the courthouse. Settlers removed from all possibility of attendance at formal worship had to adjust to a religious, though not a spiritual, isolation. Staunch Catholic Frederick Weld gave the matter a good deal of thought before deciding: 'But God can shower down His graces on the inhabitant of the wilderness as well as on him who is permitted daily to kneel at His holy altar. . . . and I am convinced that if God places a man in a position which deprives him of religious succour — and I feel sure that *it is* God who has placed *me* in *this* position He thereby binds Himself . . . to afford proportionate graces & assistance.' Children too received instruction: meal-time graces and regular Bible readings were common in many a colonial household, and in more remote areas, parents played an active part in bringing their children to faith. Sunday evenings in the Caldwell home were regularly spent with the parents giving their children Sunday lessons, 'called in Scotland

"Questions" ': 'I did not give them the Shorter Catechism as I consider its deep theological mysteries far beyond the understanding of a child'. Where Sunday Schools were accessible, they were usually well attended and enjoyed, especially on festive occasions. To the Thames annual Sunday Schools' Feast in January 1875 came 350 Anglican, 250 Wesleyan, 230 Presbyterian, 155 Baptist, 90 Methodist, and 50 Congregational children. The fare provided included 120lb of rich cake, 100 dozen buns, 100lb of bread, 25lb of lollies, 50lb of ham, 6lb of tea, 25lb of sugar, 10lb of butter, 6 gallons of milk, and a large quantity of peaches. Little was left for the birds.[30]

Religious bodies had extensive educational and welfare functions in all parts of the colony throughout the century, and particularly during the gold-rushes. Destitute or deserted wives turned to them for assistance. Many of the schools in gold towns were church-sponsored and the local clergy were usually active in organizing care for neglected children. The goldfield communities were in many ways more fortunate than other settlements in colonial New Zealand. All the major denominations thought it important to have a representative there, and such was the reputation of the miners that appointments to these centres tended to be men of considerable strength of character. The reputedly hard-bitten diggers seem to have expected the attention. It was with some indignation that Theophilus Cooper on the Thames field noted: 'We have thus had Wesleyans, Presbyterians, Catholics, Episcopalians; but where are the Independents and Baptists? Are they extinct in Auckland, or are they asleep? Why doesn't the Rev. Mr Cornford or the Rev. Warlow Davies come down and stir us up with their eloquence and zeal? Many are inquiring why.'

Throughout the colony, it was rare for adherents of the dissenter creeds to be able to share in worship with fellow believers. By 1891 there were still only some 300 Quakers in the country. Colony-wide too was the problem of financing the churches and charitable aid. Archdeacon Govett built St Mary's parsonage in New Plymouth at his own expense; only lucrative shares in the Caledonian Mine enabled Vicesimus Lush to build St George's parsonage and so provide a home for his wife and family in gold-town Thames.[31] Both on the goldfields and in the colony at large, much energy and effort was directed to the erection of church buildings but it was often years before a congregation could afford to replace a temporary structure with a more permanent and in their eyes more fitting place of worship.

The goldfields and country communities exhibited an openness of association and a freedom of worship not always found in the more settled centres. There the formalization of worship was steadily more noticeable, as was the increasing association of church-going with Victorian notions of respectability. Urban working-class settlers and the church as an institution grew further apart, a process that the belated abolition of pew rents did little to counter.[32] These trends, which reflected developments occurring in the churches at home, were brought to New Zealand by both lay and clerical immigrants. The distinction between the form and practice of religion was noted with distress by Mrs Barker after but a few months in the Anglican stronghold of Christchurch: 'It is really melancholy to see the different ways in which God's name and service is slighted in the World. On the ship there were only a very few who seemed to think anything beyond the form and here there is no care at all.' For William Runciman, a passenger on the *Hermione* during its voyage in 1881, differences over doctrines or forms of worship were less significant than the lack of commitment on the part of some who differed from him: 'Attendance is given to what we call the Heavenward Day, merely because it is correct so to do not because they have any Inward longing for that which is unseen. . . .'[33]

Christian faith and practice played a fundamental role in the shaping of colonial society. Consciously or unconsciously the greater proportion of the population acted according to what was essentially a Christian code. Charity may have been dispensed according to the degrading Victorian notions of the 'deserving' and 'non-deserving' poor, but it was the churches and their congregations who helped the needy in nineteenth-century New Zealand. Religious groups and committed individuals were quick, too, to be involved in crusades on social issues. The early growth of temperance movements in colonial New Zealand owed much to Christian initiative. The activities of the New Zealand Alliance and, in particular, of the Women's Christian Temperance Union, did much to foster and direct the growing public feeling in favour of prohibition during the 1880s. And pervasive in colonial society was the sense that faith was to be expressed more in deeds than in words — as the ready co-operation between pioneer settlers could so often testify.

When everyday needs were met and Sunday obligations fulfilled, there was still a little time in a colonial existence for some form of leisure and recreation. Again, indigenous and imported influences are clear. The climate encouraged outdoor recreation; functions necessary in a pioneering society became the basis of many sporting events. Shooting and wood-chopping competitions gave pioneers and axemen the chance to demonstrate the skills used daily in clearing the land. Regattas and races were less an imitation of English fixtures than an expression of the vital role played by boats and horses in colonial communications. Picnics were a popular form of colonial recreation, and a response to the problem of seeing friends in a widely dispersed community. While sports such as cricket, tennis, golf, and polo found their place in colonial society, far more popular were the pursuits that came to be associated with colonial occasions. Few anniversary days were celebrated without a regatta, a race day, team sports, or Caledonian games.

Indoor forms of recreation relied more upon imported resources. Many newspapers were printed in the colony but relatively few books or journals. For literary works, the population was almost entirely dependent upon overseas magazines, periodicals, papers, and books. Libraries, ranging from station collections to mechanics institutes and public lending libraries, were set up quickly throughout the country. The level of literacy was high, but the standard of reading taste was not. Although non-fictional accounts of colonial experience continued to find their British publishers, and there were faint signs that aspiring colonial poets were ceasing to depict the bush as woodland, this did not herald the anticipated development of a significant literary movement.[34] Local authors had to struggle with subject matter and public taste. As Sarah Selwyn commented: 'We had enough of the real thing, and wished for a different atmosphere from travels in the bush and settling, and sheepruns and squatting etc. etc. . . . .'[35] Literature, to be relaxing, needed to be escapist. Although there were settlers with impressive libraries and good reading taste and habits, the mass of the population in colonial New Zealand read for entertainment, not for instruction, and they read literature which was second-rate.[36]

The range of titles made available through the specially produced colonial editions included Dickens, Trollope, Thackeray, and Shakespeare, but much more popular with the majority of colonial readers were the authors whose works were often auctioned ingloriously in 'assorted lots'. W. S. Hayward was one such writer: a number of the Thames mines were named after his books or characters within them.[37] Reading preferences reflected the prevailing level of education and intellectual interest. For a predominantly working-settler population, the tiring nature of everyday employment was not conducive to the development of more stimulating and more discriminating reading tastes. Many sought instead the oblivion induced by drink. Hotels in colonial communities had some social function but their ready provision of liquor generally reinforced the social chaos resulting from a disturbingly high and widespread rate of alcohol consumption.

Musical and theatrical interests were similarly dependent upon an imported heritage, with musical repertoires often being influenced by what was available in Novello editions. Choral societies flourished and for every concert performance by amateur choristers, there were hundreds of informal gatherings where singing and piano playing provided hours of entertainment. The Scottish influence in New Zealand led to the proliferation of Highland pipe bands; the military presence of the 1840s and 1860s had its musical repercussions in the number of brass bands in the colony. Many a young colonial musician served his musical apprenticeship on the cornet or tuba. The middle and later years of the nineteenth century were the heyday of opera and large audiences eagerly awaited the travelling opera companies who regularly included New Zealand towns in their Australasian circuit. Theatre (or vaudeville) was less respectable than opera, but dramatic performances were popular. For local community occasions the full range of dramatic, musical, and artistic talents would be drawn upon. When the Harris sisters organized a tableau entertainment in Nelson in September 1889, their programme included readings, recitations, dramatic enactments, singing, dancing, and orchestral items, ranging from scenes of the Norman conquest to a chorus from the 'Ancient Mariner', and ending with 'God Save the Queen'.[38]

'Live' entertainment of this kind could be guaranteed an audience but the same could not be said for art exhibitions. While a certain artistic facility had been regarded as a sign of gentlemanly refinement in the early years of the colony, the level of artistic skill and interest declined as the century progressed. The early explorer-surveyor-artist group, represented by Augustus Earle, Charles Heaphy, and G. F. Angas, was replaced by the settler-artists, of whom J. C. Richmond, William Fox, John Gully, and C. D. Barraud were the most widely known. Working primarily as water-colourists, these men found in the New Zealand landscape their most constant source of inspiration. There were few professional painters. Even Gully did not paint full-time until his retirement from the Nelson Survey Office in 1878. The first art school was established in Otago in 1870; only in the 1880s did the other main centres follow suit.[39] Despite successful showings at the Melbourne Exhibition of 1880, the Wellington Exhibition of 1885, and the Indian and Colonial Exhibition in London in 1886, Emily Cumming Harris could attract few Wellingtonians to her exhibition in 1890. 'I am told the people have been so often taken in by worthless Exs that they cannot imagine mine to be realy good. Then Wirth's Circus & the elections keep people away. They go by thousands to the circus!'[40]

The problem was not one for the artist alone. More than forty years earlier, John Logan Campbell, in a mood of irritation with his life of 'eternal slavery' in the colony, had bemoaned the fate which left him no time to read of 'all the brilliant discoveries in arts and sciences that are being divulged at home'. He had come to the firm conclusion that emigration was 'only for clodhoppers *and* country bumpkins not for civilised beings'. Several decades later Arthur Clayden noted that: 'Colonists are impatient of men of leisure, and leisure is the cradle of literature and the condition of higher thought. The universal test of merit is success; the ideal colonist is one who yesterday had not the proverbial half-crown in his pocket, and today can write his name to a £50,000 cheque.' Time, he thought, would rectify the evils caused by this prevailing utilitarianism. 'As more and more cultured Englishmen find their way to the Colony, and as the conditions of life there become less arduous, the priceless blessings of leisure will come to be enjoyed.'[41]

Correct in his diagnosis, Clayden was wrong in his cure. Although conditions of life became less arduous, respect for cultural and intellectual pursuits did not increase. The legacy of early immigrants with a genuine love and appreciation of the arts and music was diminishing. As the immigrant proportion of the population decreased, the number of more cultured individuals declined alongside the increased working-settler intake. Economic wealth brought social positions in colonial society, but not a corresponding growth of patronage. The new leaders of colonial society generally lacked a cultural awareness. There were exceptions, such as the squatter who had started as a barely literate farmhand but who learned to read and to farm well: his own employees found a well-stocked library in their quarters.[42] Other employers regularly read to their workers. But the exceptions were not enough to counter the utilitarianism of which Clayden had spoken.

Colonial children were growing up with much of their parents' practical outlook. Educated parents may well have tried to inculcate an appreciation of the fruits of leisure in their children, but this was difficult, especially if the youngsters were actively involved in farm labour and tired in the evenings. Provision of education was at first very uneven. There were 'schools' on the emigrant ships, and in the infant settlements individuals set up their own private establishments, frequently in connection with the churches. When, in the 1850s, provincial governments were given responsibility for education, they discharged the task by subsidizing these private efforts. Nelson and Otago settlers showed the greatest commitment to the provision of education for their children through a combination of private and public enterprise. As early as 1858 Nelson abolished the fee-paying system in favour of an annual householder's levy of 20*s.* and 5*s.* per child. By contrast, Wellington provincial councillors voted in May 1874 for school fees of 5*s.* per child up to three per family to be paid on the first school day of every quarter.[43] Although there were often provisions for exemption in cases of extreme hardship, the variations in attendance indicated that many parents could not or would not afford the fees, which often came on top of the loss of a child's labour and income.

The 1877 Education Act replaced provincial variety with a colony-wide system of primary education. The churches, so prominent in the provincial systems, were excluded. The Catholic Church responded by setting up its own system; the others by attempting to implant Christian teaching in the state system. Regional disparity was reduced, but not eliminated. Conditions often remained cramped and unpleasant for pupils and teachers alike. Few schools had either the resources or the outlook to make education an enjoyable process. A curriculum stressing reading, writing, arithmetic, English grammar and composition, geography, history, elementary science, and drawing seemed irrelevant or unnecessary to many parents, especially to those who had 'got on' in the world with the barest minimum of schooling at home. Despite the compulsory attendance clause of the Act, truancy continued and was frequently sanctioned by the parents themselves. By 1891, four-fifths of the colony's 167,000 European children aged five to fifteen were receiving elementary education at one of the 1,255 public primary or the 281 private schools. As many girls as boys attended these schools. The colony's illiteracy rate had been further reduced, from 23 per cent in 1871 to 18 per cent twenty years later.[44] Some provision was made for deaf children at Sumner, near Christchurch, but blind children were sent to Australian schools until the opening of the Auckland Institute in 1890. Country children were seriously disadvantaged, particularly those in the more remote areas unless their families could afford boarding-school fees or a private tutor.

Secondary education remained the preserve of the wealthy until the end of the century. Another Act in 1877 provided state support for the few private secondary schools. They remained élitist. So too were the university colleges. Otago University (1869) and Canterbury College (1873) together formed the University of New Zealand, which was later to incorporate

Auckland University College (1883) and Victoria University College (1898). Derivative in appearance, structure, and teaching practices, these institutions were colonial in inspiration. Political aspiration, clerical enthusiasm, and goldfields revenue were the bases on which Dunedin's university was founded. Landed wealth enabled Canterbury to compete in the field of higher education. Unlike the Oxbridge colleges it outwardly resembled, Canterbury College would be open 'to all classes and denominations'. Women students were encouraged, and by the turn of the century the four university colleges were producing a high percentage of women graduates. John Macmillan Brown, the founding professor of Canterbury, foresaw that his institution must develop in a direction in keeping with the nature of colonial society. He sought to make of his university not a school for statesmen but a training ground of educated, public-minded citizens. In the colonial setting, Dickens took precedence over Cicero.[45]

Although agitators for education sometimes despaired of the parsimony and apathy displayed by fellow colonists, there existed nevertheless a high level of curiosity in the colony. Notice of scientific and literary lectures would arouse 'great expectations' of their speakers; sessions illustrated with lantern slides were a popular form of entertainment for all sections of the population. On the goldfields especially it was noted that any lectures had to be well prepared; one must give of one's best, as Harper soon discovered.[46] The establishment of museums and the steady growth of the scientific community were two of the great achievements of colonial society but the contribution of the New Zealand Institute (founded in 1867) under the inspired direction of James Hector went unnoticed and unheralded by many of the colony's leaders and educators. Given that New Zealand attracted many who were interested in the 'natural sciences' — botanists, zoologists, geologists, and anthropologists — it is curious that the local education system reflected so little of the surrounding countryside in its curriculum. The books and teaching materials belonged to the parent culture. Taught largely by colonists educated in the traditions of the old country, few colonial children grew up with a genuine appreciation of their own environment.

Ruminating over his experiences as a Westland parson, Henry Harper pondered the consequences of growing up in a country without obvious signs of an historical past. With nothing for the historical imagination to feed on, life would be 'intensely practical' and 'prosaic'. His generation of colonists still had their memories and their affections 'deeply rooted' in the home life they had left. In a few years their children would be 'Colonials, loyal, no doubt, to the idea of their old Mother Country, and to some extent interested in what they hear or read about it. But there must be, I fancy, much wanting.'[47] His distinction between colonist and colonial was important, for it was by this description that much of the development in the antipodean society came to be measured. The terms reflected the degree of adaptation of an imported heritage: they represented as much an attitude of mind as a country of origin. Many of the early cabin-class migrants were unashamedly colonists who never pretended that their permanent home would be in New Zealand. Others stayed but could never identify with the land in which they prospered. Unable themselves to regard the colony as home, they transmitted this attitude to their children and perpetuated a sentimentalized version of the British way of life. Typical of this was the lifestyle of the sheep-farming Ashburton gentry. In education, in social customs, in the architecture of their homes and in the furnishing of them, these colonists of the second and third generation were artificially English. It was a 'refined' lifestyle which, both in Canterbury and in its Hawke's Bay equivalent, set its closely-knit group of followers aside from the mainstream of colonial society and caused them to be the object of antagonism and envy.[48]

The very word colonial had come to conjure up a particular set of meanings, its connotations ranging from approval to disapproval, from fierce pride to diffident disclaimer. Standards of locally produced footwear might be apologetically colonial but personal achievements were a source of genuine pride. Manners and customs took on a distinctively colonial flavour. A New Zealand tradition of talking about mutual acquaintances was quickly established. When communications were difficult and travelling tedious, settlers appreciated the companionship and news of others which visitors brought. Similarly the openness and ease with which colonials met and talked struck new arrivals accustomed to greater formality and reserve. 'There is more abruptness about society here, even in the best; and, consequently, more liveliness.' Children were no exception. Ellen Fox had considerable difficulty in training her ten-year-old housemaid not to dip her fingers into the honey pot: 'Like all colonial children she is not very shy.'[49]

The freedom noted in manners and hospitality did not mean a lack of social distinction and division. The imported social hierarchy remained. In the early years there was enforced association, partly because of the need for mutual assistance and co-operation, partly because the communities were not large enough to sustain widespread or prolonged social exclusiveness. Mary Taylor noted of Wellington in 1851: 'Classes are forced to mix here, or there would be no society at all.' Accustomed to the military–official clique of Auckland society, Lady Grey enjoyed the New Plymouth ball held in her honour by local residents: 'It went off very well, and it was pleasing to see how the two classes mixed, without apparent condescension on the one hand or anything like forwardness on the other.' Social 'sets' persisted throughout the century, both in town and country society. Francis Dillon Bell wrote of Nelson: 'Of course, as in every place, the colonists are divided into "sets", but there is no set of exclusives. . . . At the same time the society here has never been, since 1846, what it was in the early days of the settlement. . . . [when] every man's house was open to the other, and a simple and frugal but cordial hospitality belonged to all.' Mrs Caldwell's considerable musical talent secured her entrée into one circle patronized by the provincial political associates of Edward Stafford and his wife. Those who by early arrival could claim 'Pilgrim' status gradually became a group apart, especially in Canterbury. Then there was the General Assembly and the social 'season' associated with the parliamentary session. For some politicians' wives, the pace could prove a little too hectic. 'This is a frightful place for calling, I have had nearly a hundred different visitors and still they come.' Political 'sets' were notoriously fickle, however, social position following closely developments in the House.[50]

From the outset distinctions of birth, education, income, and occupation were acknowledged. Yet there was little subservience, for working-class settlers grew rapidly in self-respect. Their staunch egalitarianism arose from their new-found pride, their prosperity, and their numbers. The outlook of these settlers shaped many of colonial society's attitudes, and with the extension of education and the vote they gradually became more influential. But rarely did the working settlers, on whose achievement so much of the colony's progress was based, provide the leaders of colonial society. Direction came instead from those who brought their status with them or, as time went on, from those who had acquired it through early possession of land or through accumulated wealth. As William Maskell had warned: 'You may meet a man at table who, by his conversation, you would imagine was some costermonger; he may be one of the richest men in the place, and, *therefore* one of the aristocracy.'[51] Prospects of land ownership had attracted many to the colony; money was the criterion against which their success could be measured. As long as access to these two assets remained open, entrée to colonial society and upward mobility within it were relatively unrestricted. By the 1880s the chances of acquiring either money or land were steadily diminishing, and only those already in possession seemed untouched by the economic and social distress then spreading through the colony.

'God made the country, man made the town', and William Morgan had no doubts as to his preferred location. A country life was free from the 'sights of drunkenness and vice', there was more time to read, one's evenings were not absorbed 'in going hither and thither' but one was almost invariably at home, enjoying the peace and company of wife and children.[52] The town–country distinction highlighted by Morgan as early as 1860 became more apparent as the century progressed. (See Tables 3 and 4.) At first the differences were not great. Both town and country dwellers suffered from shortages of supplies and inadequate services, but the problems were solved more speedily for the towns than for the country areas. In the 1840s and 1850s, for instance, a country child was just as likely to receive a good education at home as a town child attending a 'dame' school. By the 1870s, country parents were faced with a definite decision. For Ralph Pickmere and his wife, the choice was a matter of 'great anxiety': 'We cannot get the necessary high class education here, neither is there any society in our vicinity fit to form their manners. By leaving we lose the advantage of healthy rural life, and one great item, abundance of milk which in Auckland is 4d per quart now and 5d in the winter.'[53] Migration from country to town for the sake of educational and occupational opportunities had already begun. With the recession of the 1880s more settlers moved between provinces and between islands in search of employment. Country areas still had the greatest employment potential, with 88,000 men engaged in agriculture, pastoralism, or mining in 1891. In the same year, 59,000 males were involved in the industrial workforce, and 40,000 in commercial enterprises. Professional occupations accounted for 10,000 while 5,500 males fell into the domestic service category.

Table 3: Distribution of non-Māori population, 1861–91 (percentages)

	1861	1871	1881	1891
Urban	33.8	37.4	42.0	45.5
Rural	66.2	62.6	58.0	54.5

Urban area = place over 1,000 population

Source: Adapted from Gibson, 'Demographic History', Table 22

Table 4: Urbanization by size of urban area, 1861–91 (percentages)

Size of urban area   Percentage of non-Māori population in urban areas

Size of urban area	1861	1871	1881	1891
50,000+				8.2
25,000+			21.3	28.4
10,000+	10.6	19.9	25.5	28.4
5,000+	17.2	25.2	29.3	32.5
2,500+	28.4	28.9	35.5	39.0
1,000+	33.8	37.4	42.0	45.5

Source: Adapted from Gibson, 'Demographic History', Table 21

The 1880s threw into relief the level of hardship experienced by settlers, particularly in the towns, and accentuated the need for welfare provision. Charitable attitudes to the less fortunate in society had been imported from the parent culture, but all too often without the resources to sustain them. So many husbands were leaving Canterbury for the Australian goldfields in the early 1850s that James Edward FitzGerald thought fit to serve a magisterial warning: 'Wives can, in all cases, prevent their husbands from deserting them by applying to the magistrate. If they do not do so, they must take the consequences, and they have no right to expect anything from Charitable Aid, or any other sources, in case they should be reduced to distress.'[54] The growing towns contained large numbers of children categorized as 'destitute, neglected, and criminal'. The sins of the fathers were indeed visited upon the heads of their hapless offspring, who suffered all the consequences of middle-class righteousness and lack of imagination as provincial and eventually central government authorities moved reluctantly to assume a responsibility that private charity could not sustain. As the population aged, the number of unsupported elderly men, many of whom had never married, increased; the provision of care for the elderly was revealed to be sadly lacking in investigations conducted by Hospital Inspector G. W. Grabham in the early 1880s. Many of these pioneers had put themselves beyond the bonds of family care by their emigration from home and their mobility within the colony.[55]

Although Grey had recognized in 1846 that some government funds would be necessary to aid the casualties of colonial society, it was not until 1885, with the passage of the Hospitals and Charitable Institutions Act, that the beginning of a systematic provision for a health and welfare service throughout the colony was made. Hospitals had been set up in the first settlements but standards of care and of public health were low.[56] Lack of finance accounted for much of the slow progress. So too did a reluctance to acknowledge the existence of these problems, and an assumption that, in the field of welfare, voluntary charity would provide. In smaller communities, this belief was well founded. Thames miners funded their own hospital; the generosity of a few Okarito miners enabled the wife of a German gold-digger to be at his bedside in Hokitika when he died. Friendly societies practised the ideals of self-help and self-reliance that had become part of the colonial ethos. Imported with the immigrants of the 1840s, these organizations numbered 281 by 1884, and had 21,000 members.[57] Yet they excluded the poorer members of society, those who were migrant or were in irregular employment. Gradually church orphanages, 'refuges' for prostitutes, private and public industrial schools for uncontrolled children, and a patchy system of charitable aid administered largely through hospitals grew up.

None of these institutions was run on especially humane lines. Nor were prisons or mental asylums. Drunkenness, theft, assault, and vagrancy were the principal causes of imprisonment but, where no asylum existed, the mentally ill were also committed to gaol. Within the prisons, first offenders, hardened criminals, children, debtors, and lunatics were rarely separated. Only in 1880, with the appointment of Arthur Hume as Inspector of Prisons, did prison standards improve. But institutional reform could not attack the basic causes of crime, the most common of which was drink. It was years, too, before a pioneer society was prepared to devote adequate resources for the care of the mentally ill. The social stigma surrounding insanity was yet another manifestation of a Victorian attitude that accepted accident more readily than illness.[58] In spite of New Zealand's salubrious climate, disease still took its toll. Urban children were particularly susceptible to diphtheria, whooping cough, typhoid fever, and diarrhoeal diseases. Adults were better able to withstand the consequences of a deficient public health system but illness was by no means uncommon. Death from phthisis and cancer (520 and 195 respectively in 1890) together exceeded the numbers who died from accident (450) or suicide (64) in the same year.[59]

The hardship brought by the Depression was no novelty in the colony. Few even of the colonial-born had escaped an occasional lean time. For all their riches the gold-rushes had left a negative imprint; worse still had been the wars. But individual hardships had been localized, and the wars and gold-rushes had affected only certain areas of New Zealand and those at different times. Various communities had undergone their periods of strain and adjustment, but never all at once. The awareness that such setbacks were limited in time, scope, and region had enabled a sense of optimism to prevail. Now, during the 1880s, doubts grew to compete with hope, and colonial society came to reflect a sense of uncertainty as to its future.

The ideal of egalitarianism for which colonial society was famed was one of the first casualties of this new self-awareness. The social levelling of the early years was not the outcome of a commitment to any particular philosophy: it had arisen from the practical difficulties of pioneering and had diminished as soon as any settlement knew itself to be established. While inherited notions of class had not been challenged by a generation eager to prosper through emigration and opportunity, assertions of privilege were resented, particularly the association of social, economic, and political privilege with landed wealth. The possession of land in itself was an accepted common goal. Runholders acquiring seemingly vast estates had come in for local criticism but their position had not been seriously challenged while the prospect of land ownership still lay open to men of modest means. By the 1880s this was no longer the case. Land was increasingly difficult to buy; only the rich seemed able to live comfortably, and their lifestyle reeked of privilege to the working-class settlers. Growing imperceptibly at first but forcibly towards the end of the 1880s was a groundswell of reaction against the 'landed gentry' of the country and the 'capitalist' of the towns. Uncertainty turned to anger and a powerful popular desire to reform colonial society in an image in which privilege had no place.

This new tone began to pervade colonial rhetoric. Politicians were quick to capitalize on the growing mood of dissatisfaction. Oppression and privilege were popular catch-cries, but for many the commitment to change was genuine and widespread. Revelations of 'sweating', in Dunedin especially, added industrial exploitation to privilege and landed wealth as new evils in colonial society. The need for reform was urgent, and a new generation of politicians arose to meet it. One of the older generation, C. W. Richmond, surveyed the consequences:

Being, as we are, far ahead of both Europe and America in time we are bound to lead the world. We are going to have *Woman's Suffrage* (universal like men's), *Compulsory Conciliation* for making employers pay proper wages, *Prohibition* so that we may not let those wicked brewers go on *forcing* us to intoxicate ourselves. . . . Militant temperance . . . we have, thank heaven, already. Militant vegetarianism is in the background and coming we hope. It is quite settled that the rich people are to pay all the taxes and the poor people are to vote all the expenditure. Under this regime things will soon be righted. . . .

'Carpenters, boilermakers, printers, etc' would in future regulate all the country's affairs. Property and education now disqualified a man from forming a sound judgement on public matters. 'You see, I am fast getting rid of my Tory prejudices, and only wish that all these young people of ours had begun sooner with their reforms, as some of us will scarcely live to see the beneficent effects of Social Democracy.'[60] Richmond's disquiet was understandable. For four decades he and other members of that famous founder clan had distinguished themselves in private practice and in public service, working for the country they had grown to love. Fully aware of all the cultural and intellectual advantages of the society in which they had been raised, the Richmond and Atkinson families now identified totally with a country and a society which they had done so much to fashion. But the politicians and reformers of the 1890s would aggressively maintain that they were taking New Zealand in a 'new' direction, away from the inadequacies of the foundation era.

The new tone of politics was only one sign that the foundation era was at an end. A growing awareness of difference between colony and mother country was another. Visiting England in 1878 Jane Maria Atkinson confessed: 'I had almost forgotten what the disadvantages of this country were till I was here again. . . .' J. C. Richmond, a man for whom the old world still held so much, saw clearly the advantages of the new; that one could be 'a freer person — less wholly a cog of an automatic machine away from the overcrowding of Europe'. Changes within the colony, especially improved communications, had left their mark. In 1870 Bishop Cowie had travelled around his diocese on horseback and on foot; in the 1880s he had the train and the telephone at his disposal, even if there were only 500 subscribers on the Auckland exchange in 1887. Regionalism remained, but not isolation. Telegraph operator Roger Dansey was able to convey a graphic account of the Tarawera eruption in 1886 to the rest of New Zealand when the tremors had barely ceased. Colonial society had become more organized. Urbanization was a common experience; larrikinism a problem in all the main centres. The Boys' Brigade movement was widely welcomed as one means of dealing with the colony's youth. The crusade against that scourge, 'the demon drink', reached every settlement; the agitation for women's franchise was conducted throughout the colony.[61]

The introspection brought by depression in the 1880s forced colonist and colonial alike to examine the nature of New Zealand society and provided an atmosphere receptive to experiment and change. For the first four decades of organized European settlement much of the resolution of the imported and the indigenous had been unconscious and unnoticed. In the fifth decade, the atmosphere changed. Now that poverty and privilege had shown themselves to be present, it was time for a new phase to begin. There would be a conscious reaction against those aspects of the imported heritage that were inappropriate and hostile to a now cherished colonial ethos of open opportunity for all. Since the efforts of individuals had shown that it was impossible to protect that code, the state would have to safeguard it. Now too there would be a conscious assertion of distinctiveness as a colonial society built on foundations firmly laid. The assertion of a colonial identity had begun.

CHAPTER 6

Māori and Pākehā

M. P. K. Sorrenson

British sovereignty was proclaimed over New Zealand in 1840; fifty years later, with the extension of British law and administration to all but the most remote corners of the country, it had become an established fact. That year also marked the beginning of systematic European colonization. Within two decades the European population had passed that of the Māori, whose numbers were declining, and by 1890 the Europeans outnumbered Māori by fourteen to one. This change in the racial balance was the most important determinant in race relations. Europeans at first resided in New Zealand on Māori sufferance. But that situation was gradually reversed as Europeans established a number of coastal footholds, pushed into the interior by peaceful infiltration, and, when that failed, set up a barrier of armed might. When war became a last resort, it was welcomed as a final arbiter; a means of acquiring land and of commanding the men it sustained, of establishing a lasting settlement on European terms. By 1890 Pākehā dominated race relations in all but the most isolated areas of the North Island. But nowhere, except in parts of the South Island, were Māori inconsequential.

By 1840 some Māori had an inkling of the implications of British colonization. A few had travelled overseas, even to Britain itself, and were well aware of British wealth and power. In the debates over the Treaty of Waitangi some chiefs expressed doubts over their future if they signed, but the more prescient of them saw that it was impossible to turn back the British and necessary to come to terms with them. Thereafter, the chiefs had to make their own accommodations; often they did so with an eye to resolving long-standing tribal rivalries. Te Wharepouri and Te Puni of Āti Awa treated with Colonel William Wakefield of the New Zealand Company for Port Nicholson because they wanted protection against Ngāti Toa; Āti Awa exiles at Queen Charlotte Sound sold Wakefield land at Taranaki in the hope that they could return under his protection;[1] and Ngāti Whātua dealt with Hobson for land on the shores of the Waitemata because they wanted protection against Ngāpuhi. Everywhere Māori welcomed Europeans for the trading opportunities that would arise. Only later, indeed when it was too late, did they realize the consequences; in seeking an ally against their Māori enemies, they had found themselves a new enemy. And who would save them from the Pākehā? 'I thought you would have nine or ten [Pākehā]', Te Wharepouri told Jerningham Wakefield, 'I thought that I could get one placed at each *pa*, as a White man to barter with the people and keep us well supplied with arms and clothing; and that I should be able to keep these White men under my hand and regulate their trade myself!' But when he discovered that his own people were soon outnumbered by well-armed colonists who swarmed ashore from the Company's ships, Te Wharepouri was filled with a 'sudden panic'.[2] And so it was for others who had welcomed the Pākehā. For there was a difference between the few Pākehā who had earlier come to trade, and the many who now came to settle, to claim, occupy, and cultivate the land. They displayed an insatiable appetite, gave the land itself a commercial value, and used it as a means of speculation. Colonization became a tide that flowed but never ebbed.

The conflicts that resulted from European colonization had much in common with frontier conflicts in other colonies — but there were also some marked differences. While in Australia 'the Aboriginal was despised as a rural pest,' in New Zealand 'the Maori was respected as a warrior'.[3] The Māori were cultivators with a fixed abode, not hunters and gatherers who could be driven beyond the frontiers. New Zealand was too small for that. Māori were keen to participate in the economic and social life of the colony. By 1840 many of them had been 'converted' to Christianity; they had, in the view of contemporary observers, demonstrated a rare capacity for civilization.[4]

But it was not merely a matter of civilizing the Māori, turning them into brown-skinned Englishmen. For it was also assumed that the races could be 'amalgamated', a term which for some at least meant the mixture, by intermarriage, of the two races and ultimately the absorption of the Māori into a predominantly European population. From the beginning of contact with Cook's expeditions there had been sexual interaction, and this continued unabated whenever there were visits from explorers, whalers and sealers, and traders. Where Europeans became more permanently settled on shore, sexual liaisons developed into marriage, mostly by Māori custom but on a few occasions by Christian ceremonies performed by missionaries. One or two Pākehā-Māori, as these pioneers of inter-racial marriage became known, were to be found by 1840 at most ports, and in larger numbers at the Bay of Islands, the Hokianga, and the Cook Strait and South Island shore whaling establishments. Some of these settlements survived the decline of the whaling industry but after 1840 the Pākehā-Māori was to fade from the literature. According to one contemporary authority, the number of Pākehā-Māori declined from 150 in 1840 to 10 in 1853.[5]

Yet, although the term Pākehā-Māori had largely disappeared, sexual interaction and intermarriage continued. The extent of both is difficult to gauge since Victorians were not in the habit of discussing, let alone quantifying, their sexual behaviour. They were even less likely to admit to sexual relations with Māori, though occasionally newspaper correspondents lamented the extent of prostitution and the number of abandoned half-caste children.[6] Though none of the new settlements achieved the notoriety of Kororareka in its heyday, prostitution continued, especially at ports. There were sexual liaisons wherever European traders, mechanics, bushmen, and squatters moved into the interior. Some married their Māori mistresses, but most abandoned them when European women became available. A good many of the squatters who moved into the Wairarapa, Hawke's Bay, and Poverty Bay from the late 1840s had liaisons and sometimes marriages with local Māori women; these wives were commonly accepted in 'society'. In Waikato in the 1850s European traders and mechanics who tended Māori mills had Māori wives, but on the eve of the war most of them were sent out while their wives and children remained with their tribal kin.[7] Non-English Europeans were more welcome in Māori districts during the wars, and a number of them were married to Māori women. Frenchmen who had Māori wives included Emil Borell and Louis Bidois at Tauranga, and Louis Hetet, who was married to Te Rangi Tuatahi of Ngāti Maniapoto. The three of them founded well-known families which, moreover, have been Māori rather than European in their orientation. Jewish traders, particularly, were well received; the Māori saw their own plight as that of the Jews in the Old Testament, fleeing from oppression at the hands of the Egyptians. Two who had Māori wives were David Asher of Tauranga and Hyman Lewis of Otorohanga.

Such examples show that intermarriage was continuing after 1840. But the rates of intermarriage and miscegenation are not clear, for statistics on the total half-caste population were not kept until 1886. Nevertheless, intermarriage probably did not increase in proportion to the influx of colonists after 1840. For all his talk of amalgamating the races, Edward Gibbon Wakefield helped to promote sexual segregation, by trying to balance the sexes of immigrants.[8] The coming of the colonial women, whether as wives or servant girls soon destined for husbands, put a damper on liaisons and marriages with Māori women. New Zealand was to be no Portuguese colony. Also, most immigrants in the 1860s and 1870s settled in the South Island where there were few Māori. And even where inter-marriage occurred, it did not necessarily promote assimilation. It had been assumed that Māori wives of Pākehā would learn to keep house and bring up their children like Pākehā women; that the children would be fully Europeanized. This no doubt happened with some, but a considerable number of the Pākehā husbands and their children lived in a Māori rather than a European style, like the Pākehā-Māori before them.

Education was also expected to encourage assimilation. Indeed, it was assumed that children would be more easily assimilated than their parents, especially if they were segregated in boarding-schools. The missions had established Māori schools before 1840 and continued to be responsible for them afterwards, with the aid of government subsidies.[9] Initially, it was difficult to keep the children at school but from the beginning of the 1830s pupils — and their parents — displayed widespread enthusiasm for literacy. The demand for the printed word was insatiable; by 1845 about half of the adult Māori could read or write a little in their own language.[10] But this was the peak of achievement in mission-based Māori education. Its inadequacy was already becoming apparent. For the instruction was in Māori and confined to Christian tracts. These did little to equip the Māori to combat the colonizing movement that was threatening to engulf them; they needed to learn English.

In 1847 Governor Grey attempted to deal with this problem by passing an Education Ordinance which provided subsidies for mission schools, so long as the instruction was in English and the curriculum included industrial training. Several church boarding-schools were established to provide further education for the more promising pupils — and to draw them away from the Māori environment of the village day-schools. The schools included St Stephen's, established at Parnell in Auckland in 1846, and Te Aute, founded by Samuel Williams in Hawke's Bay in 1854. But with the coming of war in the 1860s many of the mission schools collapsed.

The waxing and waning of Māori enthusiasm for education was an integral part of their response to Christianity. Although the precise nature of the Māori conversion to Christianity has been much debated,[11] at least it can be said that by the early 1840s most Māori had become nominal Christians. They adhered more strictly to Christian obligations, like keeping the Sabbath, than their new Pākehā neighbours, and frequently assembled in large gatherings for worship. But missionary-taught Christianity provided Māori with only a limited means of dealing with European settlers and government; this is one reason for the fall-off in Māori interest in missions after 1845. The Māori had to discover the sources of the secular powers of the Europeans. Nevertheless, the Old Testament and the New provided new laws to replace the discredited customs of tapu and muru (plunder), and millennial inspiration for those who felt themselves oppressed. When Christianity failed to provide a covering for both races, then it had to provide for Māori alone, and Māori Christians went their own way. In times of tension Christianity becomes all things to all men.

The Protestant missionaries had at first opposed annexation, but when the influx of colonists made this inevitable, they accepted it and tried to protect Māori interests. Henry Williams and other missionaries helped to translate and negotiate the Treaty of Waitangi and to collect Māori signatures. After 1840 missionaries often defended Māori interests threatened by settler demands. George Clarke senior became the Chief Protector of Aborigines under the first two Governors, Hobson and FitzRoy, and several missionary sons were employed as sub-protectors and later as Native Department Officials. George Clarke junior actively defended Māori claims against those of the New Zealand Company. With the outbreak of war in 1860 several missionaries defended Wiremu Kingi's claim to the Waitara. But as the war intensified and spread, the missionaries fell silent or supported the European side, they had to withdraw from war-torn districts, and their missions collapsed.

This crisis in Christianity was but one aspect of the breakdown in race relations which culminated in war. By the late 1850s the races had also come into conflict over land, a conflict that grew as co-operation in the use of land gave way to competition for ownership.

Before 1840 there was a vigorous commerce between Māori and European. The New Zealand Company settlements and Auckland provided new opportunities for trade and Māori responded eagerly. Māori agriculture and commerce burgeoned, especially with the opening of export markets in agricultural produce to the Californian and Victorian goldfields. When Wiremu Kingi and his followers returned from Otaki to Waitara in 1848, they established large gardens, selling their produce to New Plymouth merchants. From large cultivations in Waikato, produce was transported by canoe down the Waikato river, hauled over the portage to Waiuku, canoed across the Manukau to Onehunga, and finally carried by porters into Auckland. Others shipped their produce to Auckland by schooners from the Hauraki Gulf, the Bay of Plenty, and even Poverty Bay.[12] All over the country Māori were taking advantage of the European market.

But the market did not last. There was a slump in the Victorian market in 1856 and after that Māori agricultural production fell off. By this time the New Zealand markets were being supplied increasingly by European farmers. Though the Māori had some advantages over European rivals — their communally organized labour was more efficient and cheaper — in the longer term the Europeans had the advantage. They held land in uncomplicated individual tenure, had access to credit, and were better able to make use of technical innovations. Europeans responded to the fall in agricultural prices by switching to pastoralism which required larger areas of land. Competition was now less in the produce of land and more in the land itself. Once land became a marketable commodity, Māori were ill-equipped to compete, more especially as the law was designed or manipulated to assist Europeans. Opportunities to deal in land offered Māori a new way to pay off old scores. Conflict and competition within Māori communities were ever-present in negotiations over the alienation of land to Europeans.

On becoming Governor in 1840, Hobson had to deal with two aspects of the land problem. He had to consider the pre-1840 land claims; and he had to initiate Crown purchases of Māori land, thus bringing into effect the pre-emptive clause of the Treaty of Waitangi. In February 1840 Hobson issued a proclamation prohibiting private European purchase of Māori land. In 1841 William Spain was appointed as commissioner to investigate the pre-1840 land claims.

Spain began his inquiry with the New Zealand Company claims — some 20 million acres covering nearly a third of New Zealand. They were based on Colonel William Wakefield's insubstantial negotiations in 1839 with Āti Awa at Port Nicholson, Queen Charlotte Sound, and New Plymouth, and Te Rauparaha of Ngāti Toa at Kapiti Island.[13] Aware of the fragile basis of their claims, Company officials obstructed Spain at every opportunity, hoping that their representatives in London would pressure the British Government into conceding a favourable settlement. In November 1840 the Colonial Secretary, Lord John Russell, offered the Company four acres for every pound spent on colonization. On the strength of this the Company claimed 1,300,000 acres. But Spain insisted on additional payments and awarded them much less: a mere 72,000 acres at Wellington and in the Hutt Valley; 40,000 acres at Wanganui; 150,000 acres at Nelson; and 60,000 acres at New Plymouth, only to have this reduced by FitzRoy to 3,500 acres with a right to purchase the remainder.[14] Attempts by the Company to occupy land, sometimes in advance of Spain's inquiries, provoked considerable Māori resistance.

The other pre-1840 land claims did not cause conflict between Māori and Europeans, though there was much bother and delay before most of them were settled, largely because Governor Grey had an unseemly row with some of the Church Missionary Society missionaries over their claims. Though the missionary claims were seldom excessive — most were for about 10,000 acres — and were undisputed by the Māori, Grey alleged, with typical hyperbole, that it would take 'a large expenditure of British blood and money' to put the missionaries in possession.[15] For all his bluster, Grey finalized very few of the land claims. Most were settled by a special commissioner, Francis Dillon Bell, between 1856 and 1862. But the Māori were left with one abiding grievance: surplus land that was not awarded to the European claimants was retained by the Crown, not returned to the original Māori owners. It was to be a hundred years before compensation was awarded.[16]

Though pre-1840 land claims caused much agitation in the early years of the colony, the question of further acquisition of Māori land was potentially of greater significance. While the Waitangi system of land purchase was upheld, Māori could halt the progress of colonization simply by refusing to sell. The New Zealand Company tried to whittle away the guarantes of the Treaty by arguing that Māori title to land did not extend beyond village sites and cultivations, and that the rest should be declared Crown land and made available for European settlement. This view was accepted by a select Committee of the House of Commons in 1844. Its report was received with consternation in New Zealand, especially at the Bay of Islands, where Māori were still smarting under the transfer of 'surplus' lands from the pre-1840 claims to the Crown, and where Heke's revolt was beginning. Grey, backed by Chief Justice Martin and Bishop Selwyn, refused to accept the Committee's interpretation. Māori title, they asserted, extended over all land, indeed over the whole of the country. This view prevailed and as a consequence the Treaty assumed central importance in Māori–European relations.[17]

Nevertheless, the pre-emptive clause of the Treaty did not last. So long as the Crown was able to purchase Māori land cheaply and in advance of the needs of settlement, there was little criticism of pre-emption. Hobson, having decided to establish his capital on the Waitemata, had no difficulty in buying land on the shore of that harbour. In October 1840, 3,000 acres were purchased along the foreshore from Hobson Bay to the Whau portage and inland to Mount Eden for goods and cash worth £281. Within nine months Hobson sold forty-four acres — the future commercial heart of Auckland — for £24,275.[18] But such whopping profits could not be sustained, the colony slipped into depression, and his successor, FitzRoy, had insufficient revenue to purchase Māori land for settlement. So the Auckland settlers got up an agitation for the abolition of pre-emption and in March 1844 FitzRoy gave way. However, the purchasers had to pay a tax of 10s. per acre on all land purchased from the Māori. There was a howl of complaint from the settlers, little land was purchased, and in October FitzRoy reduced the tax to a mere 1d. per acre. This at least satisfied the northern settlers and in a burst of speculation some 100,000 acres, mostly near Auckland, were purchased before Grey resumed pre-emption and instituted an inquiry which reduced the area claimed to about 20,000 acres.[19]

Grey and his able lieutenant in Māori administration, Donald McLean, set up an effective system of land purchase and obtained enough land to stem the settler demand for the abolition of pre-emption. The system required a measure of Māori approval. Once Māori offers to sell had been received, or solicited, a meeting was summoned at which all could assert their claims to the land. There was usually keen debate and sometimes the purchase had to be postponed until important opponents were bought off or conciliated. In the negotiations government agents laid great stress on the 'advantages' to Māori of selling, including the uses of ready cash, and the long-term benefits from European settlement, such as the enhanced value of retained Māori land. Once an agreement to purchase had been negotiated, a deposit was paid and the deeds signed. Then a final meeting was held at which additional payments were made, outstanding claimants paid off, the boundaries agreed and, as a final parting, a tangi was held for the land.[20] Where the rights of contending claimants and the susceptibilities of important chiefs were properly considered and the negotiations conducted in public debate on the marae, the purchases were seldom contested. But these were very difficult conditions to achieve and most purchases left a legacy of bitterness with some unsatisfied claimants.

The Crown purchases of Grey's first governorship opened the way for a considerable expansion of settlement. Purchases to the north of Auckland provided ample land for the 'Forty Acre' settlement scheme which the Auckland Provincial Council introduced in 1858. Other purchases to the south of Auckland provided land for a buffer of military settlements — at Onehunga, Otahuhu, Panmure, and Howick — across Auckland's exposed southern perimeter. These in turn became staging posts for an advance of settlement towards the fertile Waikato plain. Equally important were the purchases Grey initiated on the northern flanks of Wellington. These included the Turakina–Manawatu block of some 225,000 acres and several purchases in the Wairarapa and Hawke's Bay which, in due course, netted nearly 2 million acres for the Crown.[21] Nevertheless, Māori remained firmly in control of a broad belt of territory from Taranaki across the central

North Island to the Bay of Plenty and East Coast. In two vital areas of hinterland — Taranaki and Waikato — neither Grey nor his successor, Browne, was able to purchase much land.

But in the South Island Grey made some huge purchases, including the 3 million acre Wairau block in 1847, the 20 million acre Ngāi Tahu or Canterbury–Otago block in 1848, and the Murihiku and Waipounamu blocks in 1853. Grey had purchased most of the South Island for less than £15,000 plus promises, not carried out for many years, to set aside Māori reserves.[22] In the disposal of this Crown estate a huge profit was made, for the Otago settlers were charged £2 per acre, and the Canterbury settlers £3 per acre. But as colonization proceeded, the Māori population — never more than 2,000 — was quickly outnumbered, and maintained a precarious living on reserves, or as fringe-dwellers near the European settlements.

Where there was considerable opposition to land sales, the flaws in Grey's land purchase system were sharply revealed. Grey often averted trouble by not pressing purchases, but with a rapid increase in settler immigration in the later 1850s pressure to complete purchases became intense. Governor Browne lacked Grey's flair for dealing with Māori and left the business of land purchase to McLean and his aides. Now McLean began to deal in secret with a few collaborative chiefs and to rely on their signatures to deeds, rather than those of all claimants obtained at public assembly. Such dealings reactivated old disputes or provoked new ones, and some disputes flared into open warfare.

As Māori resistance to land sales increased in the 1850s, there was an attempt to enforce a pan-tribal veto or tapu on land sales. This move, which Europeans dubbed a land league, failed in Taranaki but it was stronger and eventually succeeded in Waikato. Here, as early as 1852, a meeting of tribes had placed a tapu over the sale of land south of the Mangatawhiri river, and this was largely effective. In 1858 the veteran Ngāti Mahuta chief, Potatau Te Wherowhero, was selected as the Māori King; chiefs and tribes owing allegiance to him put their land under his mana and accepted his veto of sales. The Māori were thus attempting to impose communal controls, exercised by a paramount chief or a king, to combat attempts by Europeans to purchase land from individuals.[23]

Land had become the focus of economic and political confrontation between the races. The central role of land in the wars between Māori and Pākehā has often been remarked; sometimes they have been called the Land Wars.[24] This is an exaggeration which imposes a monocausal explanation on a complex process of interaction that degenerated into war.[25] The rivalry that developed between the races was more than a naked contest for land, important though this was. It was also a contest for authority, for mana, for authority over the land and the men and women it sustained. Above all, there was the question of whose authority, whose law, was to prevail. Was the Queen's writ to run throughout the land, as the officials and colonists expected and as the first clause of the Treaty of Waitangi implied? Or were the chiefs, even a Māori King, to retain a local autonomy, their mana unimpaired, and their customs recognized in matters that were purely of Māori concern? Had not clause two of the Treaty granted them the tino rangatiratanga (the chieftainship) of their lands, places of abode, and other property — not mere possession but independent control over it, the substance and not merely the shadow? But it remained to be seen whether the Queen, her servants in New Zealand, and Parliament itself could make laws that would govern the land and the men it sustained. Europeans in New Zealand had no doubt that she and they could. In the fifty years that followed Waitangi sovereignty became a practical reality, as Māori and their land were brought under English civil and criminal law. The best of British justice was applied.

The very fact that the Treaty of Waitangi was negotiated was recognition of a Māori political capacity, though the British rather exaggerated chiefly political powers. Chiefs, forever jealous of their mana, had difficulty extending authority over their tribe; frequently they could not go beyond their hapū. Māori tribal assemblies were very democratic affairs and chiefs had to be adept at sensing and expressing a consensus. Europeans who treated with Māori had to learn how to handle the cut and thrust of debate on the marae, and to respect the mana of important chiefs. In dealing with Māori, diplomacy was as necessary as war.

War is often the failure of diplomacy, and this was true in New Zealand. In the early years of the colony it was hoped that a policy of 'moral suasion' would avert war. The Treaty of Waitangi was one expression of that policy. The Native Protectorate established by Hobson was another. The Chief Protector and his assistants were expected to protect Māori interests and welfare while also purchasing their lands and extending British law. On this last point there was some disagreement among Hobson's advisers. Clarke, the Chief Protector, was willing to postpone the full application of British law to purely Māori districts, whereas William Swainson, the Attorney-General, wanted English law to be applied throughout the country.[26] In theory Swainson's view prevailed, though in practice Māori law and custom remained in operation in some districts for years, since Hobson and his successors lacked the means to enforce British law.

Tacit recognition of the impotence of British law in Māori districts brought some concessions. FitzRoy's Native Exemption Ordinance of 1844 required magistrates to issue warrants for the arrest of Māori offenders through chiefs, and allowed offenders to avoid sentence by paying compensation to the aggrieved party, in effect an acceptance of the Māori principle of utu. The Ordinance was attacked by settlers as appeasement. In 1846 Grey replaced it by a Resident Magistrates Courts Ordinance which gave magistrates summary jurisdiction in disputes between Māori and Pākehā, but it required them to act with the concurrence of two Māori assessors in purely Māori cases. Compensation in lieu of sentence was continued. Clause 71 of the 1852 Constitution Act provided for the setting aside of Māori districts in which Māori law and custom were to prevail; but no such districts were ever proclaimed. However, the 1858 Native District

149

Regulation Act allowed local Māori councils (rūnanga), under a Pākehā chairman, to make bylaws on matters of local concern; and a Native Circuit Courts Act of the same year provided for the appointment of Circuit Court Judges, advised by Māori assessors and juries, to enforce the bylaws. Grey used the two Acts for the 'new institutions' he tried to establish in Māori districts when he returned to New Zealand in 1861; but they were a failure in districts already embroiled in the war, and notably in the territory of the Māori King where a rival rūnanga had been established to administer the King's laws.[27] Such autonomy was anathema to the settlers; thereafter every effort was made to bring the Māori — and their lands — within the jurisdiction of British law. Self-interest and humanitarian idealism could be neatly combined, as for instance in the Native Lands Acts (1862 and 1865), which abolished pre-emption and permitted settlers to purchase Māori lands; and the Native Rights Act (1865), which reiterated the third clause of the Treaty of Waitangi by which Māori were to be accorded the rights and privileges of British subjects. These included equality before the law; but it was a law that was being increasingly made in New Zealand by a settler Parliament. And once that law became a threat to the mana of the chiefs and the land of the people it could only be enforced at the cost of war.

In the 1840s there was some hope that the Governor and his officials could stand between the races and prevent war, but even then some individuals on both sides were unwilling to accept such arbitration. Proud chiefs were unwilling to subordinate their mana to that of a foreign governor. Settlers had little use for moral suasion, and looked to British arms to conquer and subordinate the Māori. But such a policy could not be easily applied in the early years of the colony when the well-armed and more numerous Māori were more likely to overwhelm the settlers.

The early 1840s were a time of testing. Though Māori were co-operative when the new settlements were established at Auckland and in the Cook Strait, they soon became apprehensive at the number of Europeans coming ashore. Numerous petty conflicts erupted at Wellington and New Plymouth when the survey and allocation of land to colonists disturbed Māori cultivations. Neither the Company officials nor the Māori paid much heed to the authority of a distant Governor at Auckland. The most serious conflict was at Wairau in 1843. Here, the Nelson officials of the Company, unable to get sufficient land at Nelson and unwilling to await Spain's adjudication of their claim to the Wairau, tried to seize it by *force majeure* from a defiant Te Rauparaha who denied ever having sold the land. After the Māori burnt a hut that the surveyors erected on the disputed land, an armed party headed by the Nelson magistrate, H. A. Thompson, and Captain Arthur Wakefield, went out to arrest Te Rauparaha on a charge of arson. The law was being distorted in the interests of the settlers. The Māori were determined to resist, were well armed, and had carefully selected their position. An attempt to arrest the chiefs erupted into fighting, and the Company force disintegrated under fire. Several of the European survivors who had surrendered were tomahawked by an enraged

Te Rangihaeata whose wife had been killed. Twenty-two Europeans, including Wakefield and Thompson, and about six Māori, were killed. The Māori had won this first trial of strength with the Pākehā.[28]

The Māori victory at Wairau threw all the Company settlements into a state of panic. FitzRoy held that the Europeans were at fault and took no action to avenge the dead settlers; being chronically short of troops, he had no alternative. All over the country Māori were stirred by Te Rauparaha's deed, and some, who had grievances against settlers or the Government, became more belligerent. Te Rauparaha returned to his settlement at Porirua and, although not directly involved in further fighting, was thought to have directed resistance, especially in the Hutt Valley where there were several skirmishes with settlers.

At the Bay of Islands, another chief, Hone Heke, was determined not to allow Te Rauparaha to have all the glory in fighting Pākehā. The fighting at Wairau and the Hutt Valley had been a direct consequence of land disputes; but Heke's war in the north was only indirectly related to land, and his quarrel was with the Governor rather than the settlers.[29] It was to a large extent an expression of disenchantment with the Treaty of Waitangi. Heke was one of the first chiefs to sign the Treaty at Waitangi, but he soon became dissatisfied with the way in which the Treaty was seen to be operating. The introduction of customs duties, and other government regulations, were held responsible for declining prosperity at the Bay of Islands, which was accentuated by the removal of the capital to Auckland. Disgruntled whalers and traders at the Bay, especially the Americans, blamed the Government and persuaded Heke that the flag, the symbol of the Queen's authority, was the source of the trouble. So Heke cut down the flagstaff at Kororareka in 1844. Thus began what seems in retrospect an amusing burlesque but which at the time was regarded by Europeans in authority with high seriousness. Heke's men cut down the flagstaff not once but three times. On the third occasion they sacked Kororareka after the European residents had taken to boats in panic. They gave the few troops that FitzRoy had despatched to the Bay a thorough pasting. By this time Heke's mana had risen and he had been joined by many of the Bay of Islands Ngāpuhi, including the important Kawakawa chief, Kawiti. FitzRoy temporized while waiting for more troops from Australia, but when the troops arrived they were repulsed at Puketutu and Ohaeawai and could not effect a decisive victory before FitzRoy was replaced by Grey.

Heke's rebellion was more than an action of a delinquent chief, keen to make a name for himself. Between Heke's second and third assault on the flagstaff, news arrived at the Bay of Islands of the recommendation of the British House of Commons Select Committee that all unoccupied Māori land should be declared waste and made available for settlement. This seemed to confirm all that disgruntled Europeans at the Bay had been saying: Māori lands were under threat, a threat that came from the Governor. Heke became a rebel with a cause; something of a Māori patriot. Nevertheless Heke was unable to weld the Ngāpuhi tribe into a united force. Some at the Bay of Islands stood out against him; so did the powerful and traditionally independent Hokianga section of the tribe, under the leadership of Tamati Waka Nene. FitzRoy and Grey exploited these divisions and got Nene and his people to fight against Heke and Kawiti. The Māori allies kept Heke at bay until the arrival of the main British forces, and provided the vital intelligence that enabled Grey to take Kawiti's strongly defended Ruapekapeka pā — seized on a Sunday morning while most of the defenders were outside of the ramparts. The war in the north was over and Grey made a lasting peace, cemented by his refusal to confiscate the land of the defeated.

Grey quelled resistance elsewhere by a combination of bold military action and devious stratagem.[30] He used troops to clear the Hutt Valley of Māori resistance. He had Te Rauparaha abducted in a dawn raid and kept him in gentlemanly detention, though without trial, until the aged chief's mana had been destroyed. Te Rangihaeata, entrenched in a pā overlooking the Horokiwi valley, was left alone; eventually he came down and made his peace. In 1846 Grey had one of the rebel chiefs, Matengi Te Wareaitu, hanged after a summary court martial. Finally, in 1847 there were several inconclusive skirmishes at Wanganui against the chief Te Mamaku. Grey's imperious actions earned him grudging respect from Māori allies and enemies, but they had also come to distrust him.

Within two years of his arrival Grey had brought about a *pax*; he now turned his talents to the peaceful arts of civilizing the Māori and amalgamating the races. Grey promoted Māori education through grants to mission schools, and established hospitals; he aided Māori agriculture and commerce with gifts of ploughs, mills, seed, and schooners; he appointed Resident Magistrates to bring the Māori within the scope of British law. In 1852 Grey asserted that the two races were 'insensibly forming one people'.[31] Though a measure of peace and prosperity had been achieved, the reality of race relations was far less impressive. A potentially explosive situation was building up from the very prosperity that Grey had helped to create. He had secured the perimeter settlements of the North Island, but their expansion into the Māori territory of the interior was fraught with danger. Grey could write effusively of the amalgamation of the races, but the settlers had little sympathy for the Māori, spoke disparagingly of them as 'niggers', and resented their occupation of land that they would neither fully cultivate nor release for settlement.[32]

Māori were becoming increasingly apprehensive at the long-term implications of European colonization. Chiefs who had been firm allies of the Government in the 1840s were in the 1850s to become opponents of land sales and in the 1860s were pushed into rebellion. The opposition had begun to develop before Grey's departure. During a final tour of the North Island in 1853, Grey came across a Māori deputation led by two of Archdeacon Hadfield's flock from Otaki, Tamihana Te Rauparaha and Matene Te Whiwhi. They were going around the Māori tribes calling for kotahitanga (unity) and the setting up of a Māori king. Grey regarded this as a harmless, idealistic exercise. But the sponsors were in earnest and they were meeting with a ready response. After Grey left the movement gathered momentum as a result of the growing pressure on Māori land and the need to resolve the consequential divisions and disputes within and between tribes. But there was a broader concern as well: a need for a code of law that would replace the declining force of tapu and take into account the changed social condition of the Māori people.

The Māori King movement was not so much an emulation of British monarchy but rather an attempt to stem the tide of European colonization by uniting the tribes into an anti-land-selling confederation.[33] Tribal confederations had operated in the past; the King movement, with its hard core in the Waikato–Maniapoto tribes, was a revival of the Tainui confederation which had attempted to resist the Ngāpuhi invasions in the 1820s. But it became more than this since it gained the allegiance, after the outbreak of the first Taranaki war, of such non-Tainui tribes as Āti Awa and Ngāti Ruanui. And it had the sympathy and sometimes the support of men and materials from a much wider fringe of tribes or hapū. It was an attempt to forge the tribes into a Māori nation — a nation within a nation. The King was to retain a distinct territory, starting at the Mangatawhiri river and leading back through Waikato into the interior, in which chiefs placed their tribal land under his mana as a guarantee against sale, and in which the King's law, exercised by his rūnanga, would prevail. Pākehā were not necessarily excluded, but they had to accept the King's authority and live on Māori sufferance, like the Pākehā-Māori before 1840. Idealists among the Kingites did not see the movement as rigidly exclusivist but rather as offering a form of co-existence: 'The King on his piece; the Queen on her piece, God over both; and Love binding them to each other.'[34]

To Europeans this was an awkward doctrine since it was pacific and based on Christian precepts that they themselves professed. It was also an affront to the Queen, and a denial of her sovereignty: neither could be taken lightly by a colonial governor. There could not be two rival sovereignties in New Zealand; nor could the King be allowed to impose his law on Pākehā or give sanctuary to Māori who had committed offences against Pākehā. The King was therefore more dangerous than a recalcitrant chief like Wiremu Kingi; and the invasion of the Waikato — 'the climactic event in New Zealand race relations'[35] — was ultimately more important than the seizure of Waitara.

Nevertheless, the wars of the 1860s began over the Waitara dispute and gradually escalated into a general conflagration, a New Zealand war. Waitara was typical of many locally based Māori disputes in which personal and intra-hapū rivalries were exacerbated by government attempts to buy land.[36] A feud over the Waitara had been running for some years and had erupted into fighting. The Europeans at New Plymouth had long been pressing the Governor to buy the Waitara, and to assert the law to prevent Māori from fighting one another.

In March 1859 Teira, to satisfy a private pique stemming from a quarrel over a woman, offered to sell part of the Waitara in defiance of Wiremu Kingi's opposition to the sale. Browne accepted Teira's offer and declared that he would not allow anyone to veto a sale of land unless he owned part of it. The 'investigation' of Teira's title failed to reveal that Kingi had a claim to the land (although he had a pā on it) so Browne decided to go ahead with the purchase and to impose martial law in the event of interference. Thus what had begun as a land dispute became a law and order issue. Browne regarded Kingi as an interfering bully who needed to be brought to heel. The Queen's sovereignty had been set at nought and needed to be asserted. When some of Kingi's supporters obstructed the surveyors, martial law was declared, troops sent to occupy the land, and fighting started when they attempted to take a pā. European involvement had turned Waitara from a Māori and specifically an Āti Awa dispute into an Anglo–Māori war. It quickly assumed more than local significance when the Ngāti Ruanui of South Taranaki and, more significant, some Waikato supporters of the King entered the fighting.

The engagements that followed in Taranaki established a pattern that was to continue for much of the war.[37] The Māori entrenched themselves in a carefully fortified pā. The British duly bombarded it with artillery, approached by sap, and finally assaulted with fixed bayonets. But frequently the Māori escaped before the final assault, only to fortify another pā and dare the British forces to attack again. Colonel Gold and his regulars became the butt of ridicule for their slow and inefficient prosecution of the campaign. But there were other sides to the war. Quite often regular troops or locally recruited militia were ambushed. Sometimes the Māori forces were brought to fight in the open — for instance, at Mahoetahi where a cocksure party from upper Waikato were badly mauled and suffered heavy casualties. Moreover, the fighting could not be confined to soldiers; the lives and property of civilians were soon being taken. Māori property was plundered by the troops and Māori plundered settler homesteads. The settlers took refuge in New Plymouth and their farms fell into the hands of the Māori. The military retained control of captured pā and a string of blockhouses, but conquest of the countryside and the defeat of the rebel Māori required a regular army.

In April 1861 a truce was arranged, largely through the mediation of the Ngāti Hauā chief, Wiremu Tamihana, on the promise of an investigation of the Waitara purchase. Hopes for peace were raised when Grey returned in place of Browne in September, formed a 'peace' ministry under William Fox, and began to establish civil institutions in Māori districts. He sent John Gorst to Te Awamutu as Civil Commissioner. But though he professed peace, Grey also prepared for war. With the build-up of British regiments, few doubted that war would long be postponed. To the King's supporters who tried to ascertain his intentions, Grey said that he would look on each chief as a king of his tribe. 'I shall have twenty Kings in New Zealand before long; and those Kings who work with me shall be wealthy kings. . . .'[38] Later he said that he would dig around the King until he fell.[39] More ominously, Grey used troops to cut a military road through the Hunua range to the Waikato river. In the Waikato he attempted to construct a courthouse at Kohekohe and to erect an industrial school at Te

Awamutu, both of which were suspected of having military uses.

Grey's handling of the Taranaki situation also created suspicion. In March 1863 he went to Taranaki and ordered the re-occupation of Tataraimaka, a block of Crown land that the Ngāti Ruanui had occupied as compensation for Waitara. Then he investigated the Waitara purchase and discovered what nearly everyone knew but few would admit, that it was unjust. Grey proposed to his reluctant ministers that it be returned to Kingi and the Āti Awa. But while the ministers dallied, the Māori treated the occupation of Tataraimaka as a resumption of war and, on the instruction of Rewi Maniapoto, ambushed a party of troops. A few days later the ministers announced their intention to return the Waitara. Nevertheless, Taranaki remained a side-show. As soon as the troops had achieved a substantial victory, Grey transferred most of them to Auckland to prepare for the invasion of Waikato.

By July 1863 General Cameron, the Crimea veteran now in command of the troops, had some 5,000 Imperial regulars and almost as many colonial militia poised for the advance. It remained for Grey to provide a pretext. He discovered a plot — in fact no more than vague rumours — that the Waikato Kingites were to attack Auckland. So Grey issued two Proclamations. The first, dated 9 July, called on all Māori living north of the Mangatawhiri to take an oath of allegiance to the Queen or retire beyond the river. The second Proclamation, dated 11 July, announced that it was necessary — to preserve law and order — to establish military posts beyond the river; any Māori who resisted were liable to have their land confiscated. But the Proclamation was not in fact issued until 14 July, two days after Cameron's troops had crossed the Mangatawhiri to begin the invasion of Waikato. It did not reach Waikato until after the fight at Koheroa on 17 July.[40]

In Waikato, as in Taranaki, the war assumed a twofold character. First, the Māori responded to Cameron's crossing of the Mangatawhiri by counter-attacking across a wide belt of partly settled country in South Auckland, killing a few settlers, forcing the rest to take refuge in blockhouses, and threatening Cameron's lines of communication. Settler militia, including an élite company of Forest Rangers, were used to combat the Māori in this form of guerilla warfare; later they carried the fight into Waikato itself. Secondly, there was the formal, set-piece warfare by which Cameron assaulted elaborately prepared Māori pā, remorselessly advancing by land and water into the Waikato. He took the strongly fortified pā at Meremere by landing troops in the rear and forcing the Māori to evacuate. At Rangiriri Cameron again tried but failed to land troops in the rear of the pā and had to rely on a frontal assault following a heavy artillery bombardment. Several assault parties were repulsed with heavy casualties — forty-one British troops were killed or died of wounds. In the night many of the Māori defenders escaped and the next day 183 survivors surrendered; thirty-six Māori dead were found in the pa.

The capture of Rangiriri opened the way into Waikato. Cameron swept forward to Ngaruawahia, the King's capital, which he took without a fight.

Some of the King party leaders, including Tamihana, were ready to surrender. Cameron wanted to negotiate but Grey prevaricated and his ministers demanded that the campaign be continued. A grandiose plan to confiscate land had been announced and the ministers were determined to prosecute the war into the fertile plains of the Waikato and Waipa. Cameron therefore continued a slow advance up the Waipa. The Māori supply village of Rangiaowhia was assaulted and put to fire, and many of the defenders perished. A Māori force, hastily assembled at Hairini, was dispersed by cavalry. Cameron by-passed the strongly entrenched pā at Paterangi and finally engaged the main Māori force at Orakau. Here, in the peach groves of a thriving agricultural settlement, in a hastily prepared pā, some three hundred Māori under the leadership of Rewi Maniapoto resisted three days of heavy bombardment. Cameron urged them to surrender but they refused with the immortal challenge: 'E hoa, ka whawhai tonu āhau ki a koe, āke, āke!' ('Friend, I shall fight against you for ever, for ever!').[41] Then, late in the day, when the British sap was on the edge of the pā, the defenders made a disciplined retreat and many escaped. The Waikato war was over. Cameron moved many of the troops to Tauranga where he was ordered to move against the Ngāi Te Rangi and their allies who were aiding the King. Here his troops were repulsed with heavy casualties at Gate Pa but soon afterwards avenged their defeat at Te Ranga where the Māori forces were caught in an unprepared position. It was the last major battle of the war.

The British regiments were gradually withdrawn — five went in 1865 and another four in 1866. The colonists, unwilling to pay the costs of the regulars, had to rely largely on their own resources. For the war was far from over; it had been a guerilla war, fought largely by colonial militia and Māori allies in remote country in southern Taranaki, the Wanganui river, the eastern Bay of Plenty, the East Coast, the Urewera, and Taupo. The rise of the Hauhau movement and the entry into the fighting of skilled, ruthless exponents of bush warfare like Titokowaru and Te Kooti gave the war a savage character that contrasted with the chivalry of the earlier campaigns. But the savagery was not one-sided, for Māori allies like Ropata Wahawaha gave no quarter (and kept no prisoners) and General Chute, Cameron's energetic successor, waged a ruthless scorched-earth campaign through southern Taranaki, 'killing, burning villages, destroying crops, looting, and occasionally shooting prisoners'.[42] Yet, for all this, it was the murder of the missionary Carl Sylvius Völkner at Opotiki and Te Kooti's massacre of thirty-three settlers and thirty-seven kūpapa ('friendly') Māori at Poverty Bay in 1868 that left the most enduring memories.[43] Once the war had entered this final guerilla stage, it proved very difficult to bring it to an end. Both Titokowaru and Te Kooti inflicted stunning defeats on the colonial forces before they were in turn defeated and put on the run.[44] Te Kooti took refuge in the King Country and was pardoned in 1883; Titokowaru eventually became a follower of the pacifist prophet, Te Whiti. Though the last engagement was fought in 1872 much of the North Island remained an armed camp for some years, with the Armed Constabulary garrisoned at frontier posts until it was disbanded in 1885. Many of the defeated Māori remained in arms until, one by one, they made their peace with the Pākehā.

The wars interrupted the amalgamation of the races that had been so confidently predicted. Casualties were substantial: according to James Cowan some 2,000 were killed on the Māori side, and about 560 British and 250 kūpapa, in wars between 1845 and 1872.[45] There was widespread destruction of property. On both sides personal tragedies brought bitterness. But there were also counter-balancing factors: on numerous occasions — at Rangiriri, Orakau, and Gate Pa in particular — both sides displayed courage and chivalry of the highest order, and in the end a warm comradeship between victor and vanquished. Māori 'generals' and British officers developed a considerable respect for one another. Moreover, the wars did not become race wars. There were a few Europeans who actively supported the Māori — the deserter, Kimble Bent, for instance — and many more who gave them verbal support. The former Chief Justice, Sir William Martin, Bishop Selwyn, and several of his missionaries supported Kingi's claims to Waitara.[46] But such critics were largely silent at the Waikato invasion. Some like John Morgan in the Waikato and Völkner at Opotiki, supported the British side by providing information on Māori attitudes and dispositions. Völkner paid for his indiscretion with his life. Selwyn and Morgan acted as chaplains to the British troops. The Wesleyans too were often strenuously pro-government and one of them, John Whiteley, was killed in 1869. The Catholics, who were mainly French, were suspected of spying for the Māori side, though unjustly so. Bishop Pompallier withdrew them from war-torn districts. Later, as the wars dragged on expensively, there was much criticism from the more remote European settlers, particularly South Islanders.

The wars brought unprecedented Māori unity but also new divisions. Māori clergy became divided in their loyalties. Some, like Hoane Wiremu Hipango of Wanganui, opted for the British side; others, like Henare Taratoa, acted as 'chaplains' for the Māori troops. Taratoa had been trained by Selwyn at St John's College and served as a teacher for Hadfield at Otaki, but joined in the Māori defence of Gate Pa, and drew up a Christian code of conduct which was found pinned to his body when he was killed at Te Ranga. The rise of Pai Marire and Te Kooti's Ringatu movement further emphasized the parting of Māori and Pākehā Christianity. On the battlefield there was often an impressive representation from outside tribes: troops from Waikato tribes fought in the first and second Taranaki wars; troops from Taranaki, upper Wanganui, Bay of Plenty, Urewera, and East Coast tribes fought in Waikato. Usually they were recruited on the basis of kinship connections; others, it would seem, fought from a sense of mission, to support the Māori King and nation, or merely for adventure, bravado, and mana.

But everywhere there were Māori who remained neutral or who supported the Pākehā side by fighting with the European troops, or acting as guides and advisers. As the wars dragged on and new divisions were caused by the Hauhau movement, the number of Māori allies or kūpapa gradually increased with tribes like Arawa, Ngāti Porou, Ngāti Kahungunu, and Wanganui supplying contingents under their own or European officers. Thus the wars offered a new opportunity to pay off old scores and to profit at the expense of traditional rivals. The rewards were seldom substantial. On the contrary, some of the Ngāti Kahungunu chiefs who fought against Te Kooti had to sell or mortgage land to meet their expenses; and some of the kūpapa of lower Waikato found their land wrongly included within the confiscation.[47] Nevertheless, the kūpapa had earned themselves a place in the post-war settlement. They could not be denied the rights and privileges that were accorded to faithful Pākehā subjects in the colony, and they continued to work with Government after the war.

Table 5: Land confiscated from Māori (in acres)

Locality	Area originally confiscated	Area purchased	Area returned	Area finally confiscated
Taranaki	1,275,000	557,000	256,000	462,000
Waikato	1,202,172		314,264	887,908
Tauranga	290,000	240,250		49,750
Opotiki	448,000	6,340	230,600	211,060

The Commission did not include the area of land that was in effect confiscated on the East Coast under the East Coast Lands Investigation Acts, 1866 and 1867. Nevertheless the total area finally confiscated appears to have been small — some 50,000 acres in Poverty Bay and a small area at Wairoa. See Report of the Native Land Claims Commission, *AJHR*, 1921–22, G–5, pp. 14–20.
Source: Royal Commission on Confiscated Lands, *AJHR*, 1928, G–7, pp. 6–22

Many rebels (and, as it turned out, many kūpapa) were penalized by the confiscation of their land under the New Zealand Settlements Act of 1863. Though Grey had wisely refused to confiscate land during Heke's war, he now accepted the policy so eagerly demanded by his responsible ministers. The Domett Ministry proposed to confiscate huge areas of land — including all of the Waikato north of a line drawn from Raglan to Tauranga — to locate military settlements on the frontiers and, from the sale of the remainder of the land, to defray the costs of the war. But neither the Domett Ministry nor the reconstructed Ministry under Fox and Whitaker could persuade Grey to sign the Proclamations that would give effect to the confiscation. It was not until a new 'Self-Reliant' Ministry came in under Weld in 1864 that Grey finally signed Proclamations providing for the confiscation of nearly 3¼ million acres in Waikato, Taranaki, and the Bay of Plenty, a smaller area than Domett and Fox had demanded.[48] Subsequently about half of the area was paid for or returned to Māori owners. (See Table 5.)

In the selection of the land for confiscation, fertility and the strategic location of land were more important than the owners' part in rebellion. Some tribes, like Ngāti Maniapoto, who were heavily engaged in the Taranaki and Waikato wars, got off scot-free; others, such as the central Waikato tribes, lost virtually all their lands. The plan to sell large areas of confiscated land at high prices was a dismal failure. Even the military settlements that were established on the Waikato frontier, at Taranaki, Tauranga, and Opotiki did not live up to expectations, since many of the settlers walked off to more attractive speculations like the Thames goldfield. In South Taranaki, Titokowaru's military victories in 1867–68 and Te Whiti's passive resistance campaign through the 1870s prevented the occupation of confiscated land. But in due course the confiscated land was occupied and the settlements thrived; war, confiscation, and military settlement had considerably expanded the European frontier.

After the wars, settlers moved further into the interior of the North Island, assisted by the operations of the Native Land Court, and protected, if need be, by the military settlers, the Armed Constabulary, and the police. The Court had been established under the Native Lands Act of 1865 which permitted settlers to lease or purchase land from Māori named in the Court's certificates of title. In Hawke's Bay in particular, European pastoralists acquired large areas of land by ruthlessly exploiting Māori cupidity, indebtedness, and legal inexperience.[49] In the 1870s government purchase of Māori land was resumed with money from the Vogel loans. Private and government purchase agents competed for favoured blocks, but, because the Government issued Proclamations prohibiting private purchase of the disputed blocks, this seldom resulted in better prices for Māori vendors.

The Native Land Court was an effective instrument in breaking communal resistance to land sales, especially the King's anti-land-selling league. When his supporters boycotted the Court they found that the land was awarded to land-sellers who attended the Court sittings. In the case of the Ngāti Hauā land, the Kingite section under Tana Tamihana, a son of Wiremu Tamihana, boycotted the Court and was left out of the Court's awards; the land-selling faction promptly leased and sold large areas of land to J. C. Firth and other Europeans. The same procedures were applied to other tribes with land bordering the King Country, and eventually to the King Country itself. Here, the leading Ngāti Maniapoto chiefs, Rewi and Wahanui, allowed the main trunk railway to enter the King Country and to put their lands before the Court — so that it could define the tribal boundaries. In fact the Court's award paved the way for government negotiations to purchase the land itself. The Court decided in the Rohepotae case in 1888 that the King and his Waikato tribe had no claim to land in the King Country since they had taken up occupation after 1840, the cut-off date which the Court applied for establishing title.[50] This finally destroyed the King's land league. Now only the remote Urewera remained to be opened for European settlement, and in 1892 the Tūhoe leaders allowed surveys for roads, if not yet for European settlement.

In fifty years the greater part of New Zealand had been purchased by the Crown or European settlers, much of it at nominal prices. By 1892 Māori retained 10,849,486 acres of land, mainly in the more remote part of the North Island, and 2,442,469 acres of this area was leased to Europeans.[51] But with the Māori population still declining there seemed to be no reason to halt the European acquisition of Māori land.

From the early 1870s Government had attempted to deal with remaining Māori resistance by diplomacy and conciliation rather than military action. Sir Donald McLean, Native Minister from 1869 until his death in 1876, applied this policy with some success. So did Grey during his short-lived premiership from 1877–79, and his Native Minister, John Sheehan, though they were less successful than McLean. Beneath the politicians was a network of Resident Magistrates and, in sensitive border areas, special agents, who tried to keep law and order, promote the activities of the Native Land Court, retain the loyalty of kūpapa chiefs, and conciliate rebel chiefs.[52] On the Māori side there was also a strong desire for peace, born of the futility of unequal warfare and the fear of further confiscation of land. It was manifest both in the King Country where Tawhiao, the second King, issued repeated calls to his followers to maintain peace; and in Taranaki where the prophet Te Whiti from his Parihaka settlement was developing a policy of passive resistance to the European occupation of the confiscated lands.

Confiscation — the raupatu — was the main barrier to reconciliation. As Tamati Ngapora, a younger brother of the first Māori King and chief adviser to the second, put it in 1872, 'If the blood of our people only had been spilled, and the land remained, then this trouble would have been over long ago.'[53] Māori did not resent their defeat in war; only the accompanying loss of land. McLean and then Grey repeatedly tried to persuade Tawhiao and his Waikato followers to return to reserves on the confiscated land on the west bank of the Waikato river. Each time Tawhiao refused to accept anything less than the return of all of the confiscated land in Waikato. To the Europeans this was an impossible demand. Finally, John Bryce, Native Minister in the Hall Government, ignored the King and negotiated directly with the Ngāti Maniapoto chiefs for the opening of the King Country to the railway and the Native Land Court. In 1884 the new Premier, Sir Robert Stout, turned the first sod on the King Country section of the main trunk railway. Although the King came out of the King Country and settled at Pukekawa in the lower Waikato, the running sore of the confiscation prevented reconciliation. Tawhiao took a petition to the Queen in 1884 pleading for Māori self-government but he was referred back to the New Zealand Government which rejected his plea. So the King movement set up its own parliament, a Kauhanganui, under a constitution promulgated in 1894. Though lacking the support it had commanded in the 1860s, the movement was still a force for Māori separation.

The other centre of resistance stemming from confiscation was in southern Taranaki. Here much of the confiscated land had remained in Māori occupation. In 1877 Grey tried to open the confiscated Waimate plain for European settlement but the survey was cut through Māori cultivations and was interrupted by followers of Te Whiti who announced that the resistance would continue until promised reserves were set aside.[54] A commission of inquiry was established and, on the basis of its report, some reserves were promised. The Government attempted to open the remainder of the land, including the Parihaka block, for settlement. Once more an attempt was made to cut through cultivations; this time Te Whiti's followers erected fences across the road. Hundreds of them were arrested and gaoled. Te Whiti was riding on the crest of a wave as Māori from all over the country flocked to his support. Te Whiti's mana had begun to exceed that of the Māori King. But the patience of the Pākehā had been tried to the limit. In October 1881 William Rolleston, a South Islander with a genuine sympathy for the plight of North Island Māori, was replaced as Native Minister by John Bryce, a Wanganui member who had served in the settler militia during the wars and who was prepared to use force. In November 1881 Bryce rode on Parihaka at the head of 1,500 Armed Constabulary and volunteer militia. There was no resistance. Te Whiti and his principal lieutenant, Tohu Kakahi, were arrested and transported to the South Island where they were kept without trial for nearly two years. The Parihaka residents were dispersed, and the Waimate plains opened for European settlement. It was a demonstration of military muscle — of the willingness of the Pākehā to use force to facilitate the colonization of the North Island.

This remedy was repeated on several lesser occasions. Te Whiti and his supporters were periodically arrested and gaoled for acts of defiance. In 1889 an armed force of settlers and Māori volunteers arrested a pardoned Te Kooti when he attempted to return to the Poverty Bay. In 1895 a detachment of troops went into the Urewera to overawe Māori who obstructed a survey. In 1898 the 120 men of the Permanent Force, armed with maxim guns, were sent to the tiny settlement of Waima on the Hokianga harbour to persuade Hone Toia and his followers to pay a dog tax. And as late as 1916 armed police entered the Urewera where they fought a gun battle and killed two followers of the prophet, Rua Kenana, in what has been called 'the last shooting in the Anglo-Māori wars'.[55]

A raw military edge to race relations thus persisted until the early twentieth century. In the circumstances, passive resistance was an inadequate tactic for Māori. But there were other ways in which some of them attempted to protect their interests in the post-war years. The kūpapa chiefs, for instance, usually worked within the Pākehā system. They took up the four seats allocated to Māori in the House of Representatives under an Act of 1867. And if at first they seemed little more than nominees of Native Minister McLean, they soon became bitter if unsuccessful opponents of the Māori land legislation of the time. In Hawke's Bay some of the kūpapa leaders, headed by Henare Matua and advised by sympathetic

Europeans, tested the legality of the land purchases in the courts, appealed to the Hawke's Bay Native Lands Alienation Commission of 1873, and worked through the Greyite opposition in Parliament. But this Repudiation movement, as it was called, was unsuccessful in upsetting the land transactions, and was in turn repudiated when Grey got into office.[56] Māori had to make their own way in Parliament. Later, better-educated members, like Hirini Taiwhanga and Hone Heke Rankin from Northern Maori, James Carroll and Wi Pere of Eastern Maori, and Tame Parata of Southern Maori gained seats in Parliament. Such men could give a good account of themselves: for instance, Taiwhanga initiated a determined 'stonewall' against the 1888 Native Land Bill.[57] Carroll became Minister for Native Affairs in Seddon's Government.

Nevertheless, the Pākehā Parliament in Wellington did not satisfy Māori political aspirations. There were several attempts to establish separate Māori parliaments, including the King movement's Kauhanganui. Rather more important was the rival Kotahitanga parliament, which emerged from numerous tribal gatherings in the 1880s.[58] Significantly, the chief promoters of Kotahitanga were the kūpapa leaders. But it was not until 1892 that such a parliament was formally constituted at Waitangi. Thereafter it continued to meet annually at different Māori centres around the North Island until 1902. In the 1890s the Māori member for Northern Māori, Hone Heke Rankin, made three attempts to get legislative sanction for the Māori parliament. But each time his Bill was dismissed; the Europeans had no intention of granting 'Home Rule' to the Māori.

In 1890 the fate of the Māori remained in balance. Their population was still declining. The Darwinian prognosis that 'native' races confronted with European colonization were doomed to extinction seemed to be confirmed: the Māori would share the fate of the Tasmanian Aborigine and, nearer to home, the Chatham Islands Moriori, now almost extinct. The best that could be hoped for was that a remnant of the Māori would, through miscegenation, survive in the 'blood' of many Pākehā New Zealanders.

Most Europeans accepted this prognosis with equanimity. Some saw a shred of hope in the assimilation policy. It was necessary, according to Henry Sewell, to bring about 'the detribalization of the Natives — to destroy, if it were possible, the principle of communism which ran through the whole of their institutions . . . and which stood as a barrier in the way of all attempts to amalgamate the Native race into our own social and political system'. Captain W. R. Russell went further and asserted that it was necessary to 'make the natives self-reliant, or you doom them inevitably to gradual extinction'.[59] But Russell's statement might well have been reversed. Forcing Māori to stand on their own feet in an unregulated exchange economy, with Māori land an item of exchange and a security for debt, threatened them with landlessness, possibly even extinction. Land became a bank that was soon mortgaged beyond redemption, the sale of land a substitute for work; and the Land Court hearings an opportunity for drunkenness and demoralization that helped to facilitate depopulation.[60] But a few Europeans were aware of the danger. Thus Sir Robert Stout told the Native Land Laws Commission in 1891: 'The Natives cannot equal the Europeans in buying, or selling, or in other things. They have not gone through that long process of evolution which the white race has gone through. . . . The Natives have not emerged from the communal system fifty years, and it is absurd to say that they can compete with Europeans. . . . I say, therefore, that the State . . . has, so far as the Maoris are concerned, to be a paternal State.' One member of the Commission, James Carroll, reiterated Stout's view with a rhetorical question: 'Is it not a somewhat melancholy reflection that, during all the years the New Zealand Parliament has been legislating upon Native-land matters, no single *bona fide* attempt has been made to induce the Natives to become thoroughly useful settlers in the true sense of the word? No attempt has been made to educate them in acquiring industrial knowledge or . . . industrial pursuits.'[61]

Nevertheless, there had been some attempts to promote Māori welfare and education. After the wars the missions tried to regather their dispersed Christian flocks, many of whom had become adherents of the Māori prophets, Te Ua Haumene, Te Kooti, Te Whiti, and Tawhiao. By the 1870s most of the pioneer European missionaries were dead or retired. Anglican mission work was carried out through ordinary parishes, by Māori clergy trained at Te Rau theological college, and church boarding-schools such as Te Aute, Hukarere, St Stephen's, and Queen Victoria. The Methodists followed a similar policy. The Catholics, after the withdrawal of the French Marists during the war, resumed mission activity in the 1880s when Mill Hill Fathers and the Society of Mary sent priests into Māori districts. In the 1880s a new organization, the Mormon Church, entered the Māori field. Christianity remained a force in Māori society, however divided it might have become between orthodox European churches and independent Māori faiths.

The earthly welfare of the Māori depended on secular agencies. With the collapse of the missions during the war, Government assumed the main responsibility for Māori education. A Native Schools Act of 1867 allowed the establishment of primary schools for Māori pupils, once the Māori parents had elected a management committee, provided a site, half the costs of construction and maintenance, one-quarter of the teacher's salary, and the cost of books. With such conditions and with war continuing in some districts, few schools came into existence — only thirteen by 1870. The financial conditions were eased in 1871 and thereafter many more schools were opened. By 1879, fifty-seven had been established. In 1880 James Pope was appointed Inspector of the Native Schools. He held the post for twenty-three years, regularly visited all the schools, and published an influential manual, *Health for the Maori* (1884). Te Popi, as he was affectionately known, set the Native Schools system on a viable and progressive path. Although separate educational systems had been created for Māori and Europeans, education was not completely segregated. An increasing number of Māori children attended state primary schools; a few

Pākehā children attended the Native schools where no other was available. The Native schools were staffed by European teachers, but sometimes Māori assistants were employed. Most of the members of the school committees were Māori. Thus in education, as in other spheres of social activity, there was a large measure of separation, but also a degree of social interaction for pupils and parents alike.

Other forms of social interaction also recognized the co-existence of two social systems. Traditional Māori social structures persisted despite modification through the century. So too did ceremonies like the hui (a political as well as a social gathering) and the tangihanga or funeral wake. Indeed it would seem that the intra-tribal hui, particularly those associated with the King movement and the prophet, Te Whiti, became larger, more frequent and of greater political significance as the tide of colonization threatened to engulf Māori districts. Europeans who attended these hui for personal or political reasons were invariably hospitably treated, more especially where they conducted themselves according to Māori etiquette. Political or diplomatic negotiations had to be carried on in the Māori style, and to respect the mana of important chiefs.

Likewise, Māori who attended European functions had to behave in the Pākehā way. It was not unusual for important Māori chiefs, particularly potential or actual allies, to be invited to levees or balls. In the 1880s when Rewi Maniapoto and King Tawhiao emerged from the King Country, they were accorded civic dinners by the Waikato towns, even, in Tawhiao's case, by the city of Auckland, though as S. von Sturmer observed, 'of course it is land and railways the Pakehas want.'[62] Māori entered with enthusiasm into numerous other activities. They attended and competed at European agricultural shows, race meetings, athletic events, rugby, and regattas. They indulged, frequently to excess, in smoking and drinking, and some were granted 'bush licences' to sell liquor in Māori districts under the Outlying Districts Sale of Spirits Act (1870). Later, when temperance organizations began to operate, some Māori, including Tawhiao, took the pledge, though the King himself was an erratic observer.[63]

Social contacts sometimes went beyond polite mixing. Intermarriage, which had continued through the war, gradually increased afterwards. In the 1891 census, 219 European men were recorded as married to Māori women; many more had de facto Māori wives.[64] So far marriage, like prostitution and concubinage, had been largely confined to Pākehā men and Māori women. But after the wars there were some marriages of Māori men to Pākehā women. Such marriages, though no doubt the subject of much veiled comment, do not appear to have caused much Pākehā male jealousy; certainly there was no attempt to legislate them out of existence, as happened in Britain's African colonies at this time. Though it was assumed by Europeans that the Māori spouses and children of Pākehā would become Europeanized, this did not invariably happen. Indeed, when records were first taken in the 1886 census, 1,958 half-castes were listed as 'living as Europeans' and 2,254 as 'living as Maoris'. In 1891 the figures were 2,184 and 2,661 respectively. The fact that rather more than half in each census were described as 'living as Maoris' is an important reminder that racial interaction was a two-way process.⁶⁵ Two societies continued to exist in New Zealand.

They did so, however, on an unequal basis. For the Māori, who were dominant in 1840, had been subordinated to the Europeans by 1890. In 1891 Māori constituted a mere 7 per cent of the population, and their number was declining while that of the Europeans increased. They were subjected to laws which they neither made, despite the plaintive voice of four representatives in a House of seventy-four, nor administered. The legislative, executive, and judicial arms of government combined to bring the Māori and their lands within the scope of those laws as rapidly as possible, a process that was accelerated from 1890 by the newly elected Liberal Government. By 1892 the Māori retained less than one-sixth of the country and most of that was remote, rugged, and bush-clad. The main agricultural producers of the 1840s and 1850s, they were now relegated to a precarious subsistence on the fringe of a rapidly expanding European agricultural economy. Māori grew scarcely enough crops for their own needs and relied increasingly on seasonal labour on European farms and public works. They were in danger of becoming, as they always feared they would become, hewers of wood and drawers of water for the Pākehā. They were neither peasants nor yet proletarians, but were suspended uneasily between the two. Their living conditions were appalling. Most of them lived in makeshift camps, without sanitation. They were afflicted by a host of infectious diseases and there was a very high rate of infant mortality. Traditional remedies were of no use for treating European diseases, which were frequently fatal. Māori received little medical aid other than periodic inoculations and handouts of medicines. They were seldom treated by doctors, let alone admitted to hospitals. For the most part they had to fend for themselves.⁶⁶

Yet at any one time there were considerable variations in the condition of different Māori communities. Those groups which shut themselves away from European contact, and more particularly from land dealing and all its repercussions, tended to be better off than those who became so involved. For instance, in the 1870s followers of the King in the King Country and of Te Whiti at Parihaka were noted for their extensive cultivations, their social cohesion and purpose, and the absence of drunkenness and demoralization that characterized neighbouring groups who were involved in land selling and in contact with European settlements.⁶⁷ The same could be said for the even more isolated Tūhoe people. As the *New Zealand Herald* reported following a visit of the Governor to the Urewera country in 1891: 'It is said that the tribe is not by any means dying out. This is no doubt due to their healthy life, and their avoidance of the pakeha. When their silly prejudices against European civilization get broken down, and they have learnt to appreciate the joys of the whisky bottle, and have acquired other pakeha vices, they will no doubt diminish in numbers as rapidly as other tribes are doing.'[68] It was much the same with another remote tribe, the Ngāti Porou of East Coast, although they had been more in contact with Europeans. They had shrewdly retained the best of their lands and were, by the 1890s, embarked on successful ventures in pastoral farming under the leadership of Ropata Wahawaha and Paratene Ngata. Moreover, there were now signs of recovery in the population in some districts like Northland where Māori had been longest in contact with Europeans and had developed better resistance to disease. And in districts where the wave of land selling had passed and Māori communities still retained some land, there were usually one or two progressive leaders who farmed successfully or organized other enterprises, who built adequate weatherboard houses, supported the village schools, chaired the school committees, and were respected notables capable of dealing with Pākehā officials and settlers. And beneath them by the 1890s a new generation of Māori was emerging from the village schools — some of the more gifted of them to enter Te Aute or St Stephen's — who would in due course take over the leadership of Māori communities: a new net to go fishing.

It seemed that at least a significant number of Māori were responding to European culture, becoming, for better or for worse, 'civilized'. But this is an unduly Eurocentric view. Māori often took up European things with enthusiasm, but having experimented, just as quickly dropped them. Other aspects of European culture were incorporated into Māori culture, into a surviving, and in some respects expanding, social system. Despite all the forms of social interaction that occurred, the most significant development in race relations in the second half of the nineteenth century was the survival of the Māori as a distinct ethnic and social group in New Zealand, co-existing with, but not rigidly segregated from, the Europeans. Sometimes Māori and Pākehā lay in the same bed; more often they were in separate beds within the same house. But the Pākehā had got hold of the house.

CHAPTER 7

The Challenge to Mana Māori

Ann Parsonson

In 1840 chiefs throughout Aotearoa recorded their assent to Te Tiriti o Waitangi, the treaty drawn up by British representatives who sought a peaceful acquisition of sovereignty over these islands.[1] Many of the chiefs, even then, had misgivings about the increasing numbers of Pākehā arriving in their country, and they were ready to listen to the assurances of the Treaty-bearers that the Queen wished to protect them by sending a Governor. It was possible that a Governor might be useful. But if the Governor was visible, the machinery of government that accompanied him was not. Māori had no experience of the sort of power that might be assumed over them not only by governors, but by government officials, government commissioners, common law courts and — before long — by settler parliaments and their ministries. How could Māori have foreseen the challenge to their political and cultural autonomy which would follow the establishment of a new state by the British?[2] In the lifetime of one generation, the political, social, and economic landscape of Aotearoa was to alter dramatically, and communities throughout the islands had to make decisions about how to survive in a country increasingly run by Pākehā.[3]

That there should have been a clash of interests between the Māori, long established in Te Ika-a-Maui (the North Island) and Te Waipounamu (the South Island), and the new settlers who arrived from Britain in increasing numbers after 1840, was inevitable. Māori and British had different world views, different concepts of their relationship with the land, different ideas as to how communities should be organized and authority exercised in them, and different expectations of what the coming of British government would mean. The British settlers — part of a great emigration from a homeland in which there had been a dramatic population increase since the beginning of the century — had come to make new lives in a 'new' country. They expected to find Māori, even to meet certain humanitarian obligations to them, but they did not expect them to play much of a role in the development of New Zealand. If initially many settlers only survived with Māori assistance, they saw this as a temporary phase. Once they had got on their feet, they expected Māori to move aside so that British capital and British labour could work together to make the land productive, and profitable. The role of the state would be to facilitate this process, by ensuring that sufficient land was available for the settlers' needs, and by extending English law so that settlement could proceed safely. Thus the British, firmly convinced of the superiority of their own culture and institutions — like imperialists of every age — contemplated the extension of their control over the indigenous people of New Zealand.

If British settlers had a clear view of their role in building a new colony, what of the British Government? The fate of the Māori, should colonization take place, had been the subject of much discussion in the late 1830s, and there was a strong view in the Colonial Office that Māori should be protected from it. When the decision to proceed with annexation was finally taken, the Crown instructed its representative that he must gain Māori consent first. The drawing-up of a Treaty has often been cited as evidence of the humanitarian spirit of the age. But did it really signal an intent to recognize and safeguard the rights of the Māori? It has recently been argued that, whatever the humanitarian forces at work, there were legal reasons why annexation would not have been contemplated without Māori consent. By the early nineteenth century certain principles were well established in British practice: the Crown recognized the sovereignty of those non-Christian societies which could be identified as having some form of social organization and leadership, and recognized too that it was legally necessary to gain the agreement of the rulers of such societies before encroaching on that sovereignty, either by establishing complete power over their region (territorial sovereignty), or a more limited jurisdiction over British subjects within that region. British practice had thus changed since the earlier foundation of settlements on tribal lands in North America, when Indian consent to European declarations of sovereignty had not been sought. On the other hand the Crown — and later the United States Government — had recognized the existence of Indian land rights and entered into 'treaties' for the purchase of Indian land.[4]

By the early nineteenth century, then, the British were accustomed to drawing up agreements to put before other peoples for their assent. In this period governors in West Africa were making treaties with local rulers with wording similar to that of the Treaty of Waitangi, accepting cessions of sovereignty to the Crown while offering the people a guarantee of 'undisturbed possession' of their lands, British protection, and the grant of the rights and privileges of British subjects. The British, it appears, had devised a formula for securing cessions of sovereignty from tribal societies, and it was a formula which was varied at their discretion to suit local circumstances.[5] The British control of written agreements underlines imperial domination of dealings with indigenous peoples. It was the British who decided, as the extent of the New Zealand Company colonization schemes became evident, that sovereignty was to be proclaimed not over limited pockets of New Zealand, but over the whole country. It was the British who decided against offering the chiefs the retention of some legal sovereignty — or a status like that of American Indian tribes, defined in the

United States as 'domestic dependent nations'. The British also drew up the Treaty of Waitangi, securing (in the English version) the agreement of the chiefs to cede sovereignty to the Queen, and to sell such land as they wished to alienate only to the Queen, and guaranteeing to the 'Chiefs and Tribes . . . the full exclusive and undisturbed possession of their Lands and Estates Forests Fisheries and other properties' as long as they wished to retain them. In addition, Māori were promised the Queen's protection, and the rights and privileges of British subjects. The chiefs, however, put their names to a rather differently worded Treaty in the Māori language after lengthy discussions and explanations which were also all in Māori — ceding not 'sovereignty' but 'kāwanatanga' (governance), and in return receiving a guarantee not just of 'possession' but of 'te tino rangatiratanga' (the unqualified exercise of their chieftainship) over their lands, villages, and treasures.[6] The fact that the Treaty was written in two languages, not just one, clearly indicates that the British did attempt to ensure that Māori gave their 'free and intelligent consent' to the annexation of their country, as the Government had instructed. But was this all the British attempted? The final test of the sincerity of the Crown must surely be whether, having secured both sovereignty and the exclusive right of pre-emption over land, it took active steps subsequently to ensure that its Treaty guarantees to the chiefs were honoured. Even in English, the guarantees were powerful. In their own language, however, as some influential colonists soon came to appreciate, Māori were assured that their authority over their lands would be protected.[7] The very language of the two Treaty texts thus encapsulates the different understandings of chiefs and the Crown of the agreement that had been made. The English text, it has been suggested, is about 'a transfer of power'; the Māori text 'predicates a sharing of power and authority in the governance of the country between Crown and Maori'.[8] And Māori had little reason, in 1840, to fear that the arrival of the Governor would herald the rapid erosion of their control over their lives and resources.

At the time of annexation, there were many autonomous Māori communities. The population is not considered to have been large. Introduced diseases such as dysentery, influenza, tuberculosis, and measles had resulted in high levels of mortality since the late eighteenth century, and the most recent estimate of the 1840 population is 70,000–90,000.[9] But the people were widely dispersed throughout both islands, and they were also mobile within their respective hapū or iwi territories. They established their pā and their villages at places which offered good access to a wide range of resources, and ready means of communication with other communities. Some villages were quite small, with only thirty people, or fewer; but in more populous areas like the Bay of Plenty there were 100–200 people at even the smaller villages, and a few reached over 1,000.[10] People's way of life was shaped by the resources of the land, the sea and the coasts, and by the changing seasons. In different parts of the country people timed their movements according to the rich variety of local foods and to local conditions. In Te Waipounamu, for instance, Ngāi Tahu communities worked their mahinga kai (traditional food resources) over much of the island — but the exact timing of movements in each area varied. What was important was the management and conservation of each resource: plants were harvested at their peak, and great care was taken to preserve the adult breeding stock of birds and fish. In May, late autumn, and into winter, many family groups travelled to the back country to catch weka while they were fat, for fat was crucial for the storage process. The kiore (Māori rat) was also hunted at this time, when its meat was sweet from a diet of berries. During the period from July to October (depending on the area) kanakana and matamata, the young of īnanga, were taken as they swarmed up the rivers from the sea; from October to November the tī (cabbage trees) were harvested and kāuru, a food rich in sugars, was extracted. The forest birds kererū, kākā, and tūī were caught from December to July; young ducks in early summer when they were moulting and could be taken easily. Berries of many forest trees were gathered in summer; aruhe (fernroot) was dug from March to October. Eels were caught in large numbers at the lagoons as they migrated back to the sea from February to April, and preserved. From March to May was the tītī (muttonbird) season, when the young birds were taken on the Tītī Islands (off Stewart Island).[11] Kūmara could be grown as far south as Taumutu on the southern shores of Te Waihora (Lake Ellesmere), so that in the northern part of the region people also had gardens to attend to. And, like coastal peoples throughout the country, Ngāi Tahu depended heavily on kai moana, catching numbers of different species of fish both inshore and miles offshore. By the mid-nineteenth century the potato was widely grown in both islands, and wild pig had already become a useful addition to people's diet. But traditional foods remained of great importance, both to provide hospitality and pay respect to visitors, and for trade.

Each community had clearly established rights to resources within its rohe (region). Some rights — such as those to particular birding trees, or (as on the Tītī Islands) birding grounds (wakawaka) — descended within particular families; others (to resources which required substantial numbers of people to take and preserve the seasonal catch) within hapū. All such rights were carefully defended against trespass, since the strength and the standing of the various communities depended on their strength in resources. Trespass might be dealt with severely — depending, however, on the relationships between those involved, and the circumstances. Traditionally, those surprised in the act of emptying traps which were not theirs might be killed on the spot. People attempting to assert a new right might simply face a determined challenge from those who were not prepared to recognize such a right. If a new pā tuna was built, for instance, opponents might set fire to it. On other occasions, tensions might arise in the wake of intermarriage involving people from different hapū. Rights to a valued pā tuna — once exercised as a result of such a marriage — might not easily be given up by its descendants or their relatives.

In a society in which knowledge of people's rights was passed on orally, rather than recorded on paper, to maintain ahi kā (to keep one's rights 'warm') was of crucial importance. Families and communities worked their mahinga kai, moving within their rohe on foot or by canoe — or whaleboat, by the nineteenth century — depending on the time of year. As children grew up they learned their own hunting and gathering and fishing rights, and the basis of them. They learned the stories that recorded how those rights had been defended by tūpuna, or recognized by others down the generations. They learned the significance of certain names of places or of taonga — for some names had been given to record receipt of a gift from others, made in return for a gift of birds or eels. Only those whose rights to take those foods were recognized by their neighbours, could safely take possession of a gift given in return for them.

Traditions were crucial, too, in strengthening a community's sense of identity — with people, and with place. Everywhere, place names marked the links of tūpuna with the land; everywhere there were wāhi tapu, places where tūpuna had distinguished themselves or had done everyday things that were remembered, the urupā where their bones were finally laid to rest, the tūāhu where tohunga went to pray, the canoe landing and resting places. People's history was recorded all around them in the land. It was recorded also in whakapapa, the great nets of relationships which have been described as the backbone of iwi histories.[12] In some (but not all) iwi women played a crucial role in preserving and passing on knowledge of whakapapa, and their waiata and oriori and laments were often also composed to help children understand their ancestry, the circumstances of important historical events, and the links between people involved in them.

The identity of a community was bound up in its history, in its songs and taonga, in its land — and in the person of its chief. Compared with chiefs in some other Polynesian societies, Māori chiefs appeared less autocratic to outsiders. And it is true that Māori communities, formed in an environment whose resources required considerable mobility and considerable effort from everybody to gather and to process, were not as stratified as those in some Polynesian islands. But if chiefs lived and worked in the midst of communities of their relatives, and looked for guidance to them, the widely acknowledged leaders among them were men — or women — of great mana.[13]

Rangatira embodied the prestigious and spiritual powers of their ancestors. They were well born; but to attain leadership, ability in politics, in diplomacy, in war, in organization, and provision of hospitality had also to be evident. Above all, chiefs must be recognized by the people. In the words of one greatly respected authority, 'rangatira was people bestowed.' Chiefly authority was not exercised over people, but was exercised with their advice and support. A chief was 'a trustee for his people, an entrepreneur in all their enterprises'.[14]

Within the iwi, each community guarded its autonomy carefully. But a community did not simply comprise people of one hapū; nor did one family necessarily identify themselves always as belonging to any one hapū. There were hundreds of hapū names: some hapū — large social groups which functioned independently — were of major importance; others were much smaller, and a cluster of them, closely related by descent and intermarriage, might comprise a community, though they did not necessarily occupy a single village. People might identify themselves by descent from different tūpuna (and thus by a different hapū name) depending on where they lived, or claimed resources, or happened to be at any given time.[15] Among Ngāi Tahu, whose major hapū had dispersed throughout their rohe, multi-hapū settlements were typical. A detailed study of Ngāi Tahu hapū affiliations in two settlement areas (Temuka and lower Waitaki) in the 1840s and 1850s has shown that people were flexible in hapū affiliation. Understanding the question, 'What is your hapū?' to mean something like, 'By what right are you in this place?', they gave different answers depending on whether they were at temporary summer camps or a major permanent winter camp. At the former, they may have stressed family names which reflected family rights to the surrounding land and resources; at the latter they responded with names expressing hapū or common ancestral affiliations.[16]

Pākehā, struggling to come to terms with Māori social and political organization, were always anxious to categorize people neatly, and it may be that their nineteenth century accounts of hapū names sometimes gave a tidy picture that did not reflect the realities of people's lives. Nor is it clear how far the great movements of people which took place in the years before 1840 — in the wake of the arrival of Pākehā and their trade goods — may have affected the make-up of many communities and the way in which people identified themselves. By 1840 Kaiapoi people, for instance, were to be found based at Moeraki; Te Āti Awa people from Taranaki in the Nelson, Wellington, and Waikanae areas; Ngāti Kahungunu on Te Mahia peninsula; Ngāti Toa on the Kapiti Coast and at Cloudy Bay; Ngāti Raukawa at Otaki and Manawatu; Arawa people at Maketu in the Bay of Plenty. The scale of these movements — some the result of battles, others simply of a decision to migrate to take advantage of new trading opportunities — was unusual. But movement of people into new areas or the establishment of new villages in settled areas, had taken place for generations, and it may be that people were quite accustomed to carrying a variety of hapū names with them.

The constants, however, were community identity based on whakapapa, occupation, and participation, and acknowledgement of the leadership of a rangatira. The community met together to discuss its affairs, to plan for the organization of general food-gathering expeditions and the reception of visitors. It also played a crucial role in traditional law in ensuring social stability, operating within the religious framework of everyday life. There were well-understood mechanisms for dealing with offences and with disputes. A rāhui (restriction), for instance, protected resources at crucial seasons because of people's respect for the power of the ancestors to punish trespassers. But outsiders who ignored a rāhui might well find that the injured community would send a taua to seek satisfaction — not from the individuals who had breached the sanctions, but from the community to whom those people were responsible.[17] Each community defended its interests, its resources, its dignity, and prestige as against others — though it might join with its neighbours to face a common enemy. The strength, the reputation, and standing of a community were evident in the strength of its leadership, its wealth in resources and in taonga, in its ability to manaaki manuhiri (provide hospitality to visitors), and in the way others spoke of the people and considered their reactions in any political decision they took. Political alliances were made and unmade, but political unity had never been necessary until foreigners arrived and established their government. And Māori leaders were soon to find that the British had no difficulty exploiting a fluid society like theirs, to further British interests.

At the outset, of course, Māori were assured that they need not fear exploitation. But when they welcomed the new Governor (Kāwana) in 1840, they clearly had no way of knowing what some of the immediate effects of their agreement to allow the Crown to exercise power in their country would be. Initially, New Zealand became a Crown Colony of the empire; in 1852, however, a Constitution Act provided for the establishment of a bi-cameral General Assembly, and for a Provincial Council and elected Superintendent in each of the six new provinces. In 1856 the settlers achieved responsible government, which gave them control over internal affairs in the colony, though the Governor retained control over Māori matters (including land purchase) and defence. Settler ministries, anxious to undermine the Governor's control of these crucial areas, were restrained only by the fear of having to pay for imperial troops (whose numbers in New Zealand increased rapidly from 1860, when war broke out). The British Government insisted on retaining 'reasonable control over . . . Native policy' while its troops were in New Zealand, but in fact relaxed its control considerably in the years after 1863. The last troops were withdrawn in 1870, and by then the Governor's authority in Māori matters had been superseded by that of settler governments.[18]

Within twenty-five years of annexation, then, there had been great constitutional changes in New Zealand. Māori had not been consulted in this process; they had been consigned to a role as bystanders as the settlers agitated for and achieved 'self government'. From the early 1860s the settlers were ready to embark on the dismantling, by statute, of the control of Māori communities over their land and their future. They were to find that the British Government, which had 'handed over responsibility for Māori affairs without really trusting those to whom it was handed over', put few obstacles in their way.[19]

The groundwork, indeed, had already been laid in the Crown Colony years. From the beginning, it was clear that humanitarian views, however sincerely held by some British policymakers and by individuals (both in London and in Auckland), would have little enough success in moderating the impact of British settlement. Perhaps this was not surprising. Humanitarians, too, were people of their time, who saw assimilation, 'amalgamation into our own social and political system', as offering Māori the only path to survival in a colony of British settlement. The Māori, it was envisaged, would learn the English language and useful trades, would live (under English law) on individualized lands so that they came to appreciate the value of property, and in general would become productive members of a new society. As superior indigenous people, Māori were considered capable of benefiting from 'civilization', and it was the duty of the British to allow the people that opportunity. Such ethnocentric aims were based on an understanding of British needs in a new colony, rather than of Māori needs. And as the process of British settlement gathered momentum, the Government's intention of protecting colonists as well as Māori soon became apparent. Where there was a clash of interests, those of Māori might sometimes be upheld by a Governor. More often, they were set aside.[20]

Government capitulation to the needs of the settlers was evident, first, in the way it handled the problem of the New Zealand Company. Unable to reach agreement with the British Government on its role in the colonization of New Zealand, the Company — anxious to get its schemes off the ground before the Crown thwarted them by introducing Crown pre-emption over land — sent off a land-purchase expedition to New Zealand in 1839. The British Government issued a belated warning that no promise could be given to recognize title to land purchased from the Māori; but at the crucial moment, after years of scrutiny of the colonizers' various schemes, did nothing more to protect Māori from the Company purchasers. In 1839–40 chiefs of coastal settlements in the central part of New Zealand thus put their names to various Company land deeds without hesitation. The deeds, lengthy technical documents in English, purported to convey millions of acres of land to the Company, totally extinguishing Māori rights to their lands, harbours, and inland waterways. They left Māori without any land of their own, dependent on the Company to select portions of land (in some cases specified as a tenth of that purchased) as 'Native Reserves' to be held in trust for their 'future benefit'. It was intended that 'tenths' sections would be taken up by the chiefly families, scattered among those of the settlers so as to hasten assimilation. The reserves, the value of which would rapidly increase in a Company settlement, were to constitute the real 'payment' to Māori for their lands. But it is obvious that the chiefs, lacking any knowledge of the plans of the Company for the 'systematic colonization' of their country, and unable to comprehend their allocation to 'tenths' — despite the efforts of Wakefield's interpreters — did not see the transactions as compromising their position in their own territories. Like Māori in other parts of the country who entered into written transactions in the years before 1840, they did not interpret them in the same way that Pākehā did. They did not see themselves as transferring exclusive possession to Pākehā. They put their marks to deeds because this was the part of the transaction that mattered to the Pākehā, who wanted a written record of the 'purchase' to protect their own interests. They took the trade goods that were offered — guns and powder, tomahawks, blankets, tobacco, and cloth — and were prepared in return to accommodate a small number of Pākehā who might wish to live among them, and to respect Pākehā rights of occupation. The chiefs who dealt with William Wakefield, the Company representative, could not have conceived that their actions would have the effect of making them guests in their own country, completely dependent on the goodwill of newly arrived Pākehā for their right to occupy any land at all. Wakefield posed no physical, military threat; therefore his paper deeds posed no threat at all.[21]

Yet the chiefs who put their names to Wakefield's deeds were unable to escape the consequences of them. Behind the purchasers came boatloads of settler families, intent on taking possession of the lands which they believed they had fairly purchased from the Company, and which Wakefield told the Company he had conclusively purchased from the chiefs (though he was aware he had not dealt with all the tribes who occupied territory he claimed). And in the wake of the settlers came a new government and its officials. By the end of 1840 the British Government and the Company had reached an agreement by which the Company was to give up its claim to the vast tracts described in its deeds in return for a Crown grant of a certain number of acres calculated on the basis of the amount it had spent on colonization, and a charter of incorporation authorizing it to colonize and sell lands in New Zealand. It was considered, however, that the Company should still demonstrate to the Land Claims Commission, newly set up under statute to investigate all private purchases and decide on their validity, that its initial purchases had 'fairly extinguished the Māori title'. The Commissioner who dealt with the Company claims (a British lawyer) and the Governor thus made decisions which were to affect the lives of many Māori communities. Their position, it must be admitted, was not an easy one. Conscious of the need to honour the Treaty, but conscious too of the fact that hundreds of settlers had already been unloaded by the Company on New Zealand shores, they were caught in a dilemma. But their decisions gave little joy to Māori. In Taranaki, for instance, the Commissioner — unable to view the transactions from any perspective other than a British one — ruled that 60,000 acres of land had been properly purchased by the Company. Governor FitzRoy, advised that Te Āti Awa anger at this decision was such that it would not be practicable to enforce it, overturned it. But he made it clear to Te Āti Awa that they would have to accommodate the settlers who had already founded New Plymouth, and provide some land accordingly. British settlers could not be displaced.[22]

The same was true at Wellington, where even the Commissioner thought the original purchase shoddily conducted. But Te Āti Awa, Taranaki, and Ngāti Ruanui hapū who lived around the harbour were not offered the option of reconsidering the deal: despite objections, they were simply informed that small sums of 'compensation' had been set aside for them.[23] The Government then turned its attention to the question of how to provide for the economic future of Māori in a New Zealand Company settlement, given the confusion that the Native Reserve scheme had produced, and the unsuitable land chosen for Māori in the 'Country' sections. In 1846–47 a settlement was reached whereby the Wellington hapū lost hundreds of acres of their best cultivation land (now discovered to

be on settler sections), to have it replaced by selections of land drawn from
the original Company Native Reserves, Government and Public reserves.
The remnant of the 'tenths' proper was passed to a government Board to be
administered on behalf of the Māori. Under this regime much of the
valuable town land comprised in the Reserves was alienated in the early
1850s for 'public purposes' such as the Wellington Hospital, and College
and Grammar School endowments.[24]

The Government's concern with the needs of British settlement was also
evident from the outset in its general land policies. In 1840, the British
Government had made certain assumptions about land in New Zealand. It
had assumed, for instance, that Māori 'territorial rights' did not extend over
the entire country; that they were finite and could be marked off and
defined on maps. Indeed, the first Governor was instructed that government officials should set aside 'inalienable tracts' for the Māori, for their
permanent 'use and occupation'. The Government further assumed that
once Māori lands had been defined, and the claims of pre-annexation
purchasers had been investigated and met by grants whose size was carefully
restricted, sufficient 'unappropriated' land would remain to constitute a
Crown demesne. These lands could be sold for settlement, and would
produce a government revenue. Meanwhile, the entire country was to be
divided into English administrative units — counties, hundreds, townships
— and surveyed accordingly.

As late as 1846 the Governor was still receiving official instructions that
he should, if possible, ascertain and record the limits of tribally held lands
(and also the ownership of other lands in the colony), with a view to
declaring all the rest the royal demesne. Māori, argued Earl Grey, Secretary
of State for the Colonies, did not occupy all the land of New Zealand, and
only occupation and the expenditure of labour on land — its cultivation —
could bestow a right of property. The people's right to shift their
cultivations, according to their established practice, must be recognized;
but beyond this they could have no right to lands which were 'waste'. By
this time, admittedly, the British Government had realized that there might
be practical difficulties in enforcing its land policies. In the wake of protests
from chiefs, missionary bodies, and leading Auckland colonists, Governor
Grey was able to convince the Colonial Office that it would not be politic
to define and register Māori lands; the chiefs might resist, so that the peace
of the colony would be endangered. But Grey was left in no doubt as to
what was expected of him: if he could not deliver a Crown demesne by
proclamation, he was somehow to ensure that there was plenty of Crown
land available for British settlement.[25] Quite cynically, therefore, Grey
declared his intention of acquiring the land by vigorous use of the Crown's
right of pre-emption, buying land well in advance of settlement so that he
would need to pay Māori 'a merely nominal consideration'. It was better,
he argued, to pay the chiefs the 'compliment . . . of requesting their
acquiescence' in British occupation of their lands than to try and impose on
them foreign ideas of property rights. The important thing was that Māori

should retain enough land for their own 'subsistence', and that they were offered Crown recognition of their right to occupy their reserves 'for ever'. The real payment they would receive for their 'waste lands' was security of title to the lands they kept, and the rising value of those lands as British settlers became established nearby.[26]

Grey thus ignored the concerns earlier expressed by the Chief Protector of Aborigines and by Governor FitzRoy, his own predecessor, that the Crown ought to distance itself from the process of land purchase. Māori were already beginning to look askance at the Government because they saw its involvement in land purchase as self-interested and motivated solely by a concern for profit. FitzRoy, aware of this (and in any case short of funds) had in 1844 proclaimed the Crown's readiness to waive its right of pre-emption in certain cases, upon application by a purchaser. The Crown's role would be confined to scrutinizing such transactions, and to issuing Crown grants and collecting fees from purchasers once they were completed. Moreover, no purchaser would be allowed to buy lands clearly occupied or used by Māori or of special significance to them; and provision was to be made for the future benefit of the sellers by setting aside one tenth of the land purchased to generate revenue which could be spent on (for instance) schools and hospitals and their staff.[27] But the waiver policy was short-lived. It failed to produce the benefits for Māori that FitzRoy had intended, partly because he did not ensure that the policy was properly administered, and partly because Grey decided subsequently not to proceed with FitzRoy's reserve scheme. Moreover, the British Government got cold feet about the policy when FitzRoy's second waiver proclamation of October 1844 dropped the fees payable by purchasers to one penny per acre, thus sacrificing the Government's revenue from land sales. The second proclamation was not approved, and Grey was instructed that only the Government should negotiate with Māori to buy their lands.[28]

FitzRoy in fact had thought more about Māori needs and wishes than Grey did. The waiver policy was an attempt to resolve the basic contradiction inherent in the Government's pre-emption policy: that the Government could both protect the interests of the Māori, and buy their land. The pre-emptive right was long-established in North American colonies, and was considered necessary because it allowed both for the establishment of an orderly system of land title, and for protection of indigenous peoples. The courts indeed stressed its protective character. In the important New Zealand case R v. Symonds (1847) in which Grey had sought a ruling on the legality of FitzRoy's proclamations purporting to waive the pre-emptive right, the Supreme Court held that the Crown had to impose a restriction on Māori rights of alienation lest the people be exposed to the 'evil consequences' of private purchase which might amount to 'confiscation' of their lands in a very short time.[29] Whatever the legal view, however, the political realities were rather different. In subsequent years, Grey's policies of land purchase — notably in the South Island — demonstrated that the Crown was capable of riding roughshod over the rights of Māori sellers.

By this time, it is true, Māori had a better idea than in pre-annexation years as to the Pākehā understanding of a land transaction. From the beginning of 1841 until 1844 British commissioners investigated private land purchases in hearings held in every part of New Zealand. As dozens of Māori witnesses were cross-examined before large audiences of their relatives, as missionaries and Protectors of Aborigines campaigned on their behalf, and as the commissioners decided whether to allow or disallow claims brought before them, Māori quickly became aware of the true construction which the British placed on deeds of land purchase. They realized the significance of the deed itself — the written document, rather than mere usage — in establishing British ownership.

Why, then, did Māori offer land for sale in the 1840s and 1850s? Clearly, Māori in both islands were conscious of the opening of a new era, as settlers arrived in ever-increasing numbers. They had seen from the beginning that settlers were a useful market, and developed their own agriculture to supply it. They wanted access to the skills and goods the Pākehā brought with them. If settlers were established on the land they would contribute further to the income of the various hapū, so that they could purchase ploughs and horses and schooners. Hence the advice of Ngāti Kahungunu kaumātua to their people: 'Should the Pākehā wish to purchase land here, encourage him; no matter how small the amount he may offer, take it without hesitation. It is the Pākehā we want here. The Pākehā himself will be ample payment for our land, because we can only expect to become prosperous through him.'[30] Te Hapuku and the high-ranking woman Hine-i-paketia were two Hawke's Bay leaders who decided — because introduced predators had destroyed the birds and rats and thus the traditional value of their forests — that the land should be put to a different use by settling it with Pākehā.[31] And if some communities were able to organize themselves to acquire Pākehā and stock and mills, it became difficult for others to stand aloof. To do so might be to make the wrong decision about their economic future.

But the amount of land offered for sale in the 1840s and 1850s cannot be explained in terms of these motives alone. The pressure of government land purchase agents and of settlers was often a crucial factor. In some areas, where the settler need for land was seen to be especially great, the pressure was unremitting, and kept Māori communities in a state of continual excitement. Newspaper articles (read aloud by individuals who understood English) and direct approaches made by settlers, kept people informed of Pākehā anxieties and belligerence, and they were well aware of the attention lavished by government officials on those chiefs who were deemed 'friendly' because they sold, or might sell land, as opposed to the lack of interest, or downright discourtesy, with which those labelled 'non-sellers' were treated. In such circumstances the outbreak of a dispute — whether about land, or any other matter — might prompt some leaders to make an offer, especially if they felt a counter-offer was imminent. There were considerations operating at this point which were purely Māori. Although people knew that when a land transaction was completed, they could no longer occupy the block themselves, they did not see their sale of land as severing their association with it overnight. The sale and taking of payment for the land were part of the history of the land, and of those communities which entered into transactions. It was important, therefore, to make the first offer of a tract of land, because to initiate proceedings to bring Pākehā into the area could be taken as a strong statement of superior rights to do so. Similarly it was very important to the various whānau that their rights to the land be recognized when the payment for it was finally given out. The ceremony of payment was generally public, and the distribution of it carefully arranged so that the only people who participated were those whom the communities considered entitled. Where land purchase agents departed from this practice, they caused great anger.

The significance of the distribution of payment was such that it sometimes overwhelmed any considerations of profit represented by the purchase price. This was the case, for instance, when land called Tarurutangi, between New Plymouth and Waitara, was sold to the Government by Te Āti Awa in 1859. Tensions among the Puketapu hapū, constantly fanned by land purchasers, had erupted several years before in armed confrontation between the two leaders Te Whaitere Katatore and Rawiri Waiaua, which left several men dead including Rawiri Waiaua himself. The various communities involved finally agreed on sale of the land in the wake of their peace-making, and their determination to turn over to the Pākehā land which had been the cause of such raruraru among themselves may have been the crucial factor in their joint offer. Thus when the payment was distributed, the people of Katatore's pā decided not to keep their share. They received it, so that everyone knew their rights had been recognized, and took it that same night to the relatives of Rawiri Waiaua because of his death at the time he was trying to sell the land. In the continuing history of the land and of its people, the recognition of obligations to the living and to those who had passed on might be of much greater importance than the investment value of a couple of hundred pounds meted out by the Government.

Such considerations are a reminder that even after 1840 Māori did not necessarily enter into land transactions on the same basis and with the same understandings as did Pākehā. This was one reason why their power to negotiate an agreement was often limited. Moreover, Grey's abolition of the Aborigines Protection Department in 1846 meant that subsequently there was no independent protector of Māori interests present when purchases were made. The government buyers controlled the transaction, and they, for their part, were operating under considerable pressure to complete purchases, and to do so as cheaply as possible and at the cost of minimal reserves. Ngāi Tahu, whom the Government considered vulnerable because of their comparatively small numbers, were to suffer the results of this policy over many generations. Crippling losses of land shattered their economic base. The largest of the purchases of their land, the Kemp Purchase of 1848, resulted in government acquisition of 20 million acres of the South Island. It was hastily completed by Kemp (who never even set foot on the block) with utter lack of concern for the interests of Ngāi Tahu. Ngāi Tahu, lacking the advice of a Protector, committed themselves to an agreement which they were afterwards to find did not represent their view of the transaction at all. Partly this was because the boundaries were poorly defined in the deed, and partly because there were differences in wording between the Māori deed, signed by the chiefs, and its English translation (thus the people's mahinga kai, food gathering places, were promised them in Māori, but not in English). But Ngāi Tahu were also to be gravely disadvantaged because they discovered, too late, that the Pākehā would interpret a key phrase in the deed about reserves to suit Pākehā interests, rather than to safeguard the people's. Ngāi Tahu had agreed to leave it to the Governor to make reserves for them when the block was surveyed. They saw that part of the agreement as the Governor's guarantee that their interests would be protected when the reserves were made. What other guarantee could be as powerful as that of the Queen's representative? But what Kemp had secured for Governor Grey was total control over the size and location of the reserves. Nor could Ngāi Tahu enjoy any right of appeal against government decisions — as they were very soon to find. A new government official, Walter Mantell, blatantly disregarded Ngāi Tahu wishes as to the lands they wished to keep, and assumed the right on behalf of the Government to impose his selections on the people. Ngāi Tahu, who had been willing to sell land on the basis that their own needs would be met, thus found themselves in the quite incredible and unforeseen position of having to justify their wishes to a very young Englishman, who ignored them. Out of that vast block, Mantell's reserves averaged just under ten acres per person — a total of 6,359 acres.[32]

In other respects, too, Ngāi Tahu rights under the Treaty were ignored. In 1849, when the Canterbury Association (under the aegis of the New Zealand Company) was about to establish a new settlement around Port Cooper (Lyttelton) on Banks Peninsula, Governor Grey was anxious to help it acquire the land it needed. Grey took the self-serving view that the wording of the Kemp purchase deed of 1848 meant that Ngāi Tahu rights to the whole Peninsula (some 250,000 acres) had been extinguished, except for 30,000 acres known as the 'French block' which the British Government had decided to award to the Nanto-Bordelaise Company because of the costs it had incurred sending some fifty settlers to Akaroa in 1840. Mantell was instructed that he was to pay Ngāi Tahu 'compensation' for the Peninsula and create 'native reserves' there, but he was not to regard himself as making a new purchase. Mantell became aware that Kemp had not bought Banks Peninsula, and that Ngāi Tahu did not think they had sold it to him. But he was instructed privately by the Government to 'carry matters with a high hand', and to impress on the people that the Government knew they had received payments from French purchasers in the past. Even though the French purchases amounted to only 3,000 acres or so out of the whole of Banks Peninsula, Mantell convinced the people at Port Cooper and Port Levy that the Government believed it already owned the land, and intimidated many of them into signing his two deeds of cession in return for very small payments offered 'as a matter of grace', and small reserves.[33] He was unable, however, to reach any agreement with the 'insolent and turbulent' people of Akaroa. Despite the Crown's failure to purchase Akaroa, the Imperial Parliament nevertheless passed the Canterbury Association Lands Settlement Act in 1850, which gave control over 2.5 million acres of Canterbury land, including all of Banks Peninsula, to the Canterbury Association. It was not until 1856 that the Government recognized that Ngāi Tahu rights at Akaroa had not been properly 'extinguished'. Even then, although Ngāi Tahu received a payment of £150 for a block of Akaroa land, they still were not paid (and never were paid subsequently) for most of the 30,000 acres in 'the French block'.[34]

The Crown completed its purchases of Ngāi Tahu land by 1864. Everywhere the prices paid were low, and the reserves made for the people were totally inadequate. On Banks Peninsula, for instance, where the Crown acquired 230,000 acres, only 3,540 acres were set aside for Ngāi Tahu; at Otakou 9,615 acres were retained by the people out of a tract believed to contain 400,000 acres; at Murihiku 4,875 acres were reserved (out of 7 million acquired); and in the North Canterbury Purchase no reserves were made at all. Ngāi Tahu often found their requests for reserves were not met: at Kaikoura the people demanded 100,000 acres of their own land, but were able to obtain only 5,558 acres.[35] Mantell, who played a key role in implementing the reserves policy, evidently believed that small reserves would assist the process of undermining the tribal economy, so that individual Māori would be free to participate in the new settler economy. But he overlooked the fact that Māori would need capital to succeed. 'In stripping Ngāi Tahu of all but a tiny fraction of their lands, Mantell was depriving them of the collateral required to participate effectively in the new world, while at the same time preventing them securing access to their traditional resources.' In the long run, many people were to be left in poverty.[36]

Ngāi Tahu thus came to understand the power of the new Government in the years after annexation; and found its determination to set their interests aside baffling. In the same period, North Island chiefs were also coming to terms with the Government's evident resolve to advance the settlers' economic future at the expense of their own. By the 1850s the pressure on North Island Māori land was beginning to accelerate. It was evident for instance in the Government decision to move into the Wairarapa to buy up the lands of Ngāti Kahungunu. Here Pākehā runholders had established themselves on Māori land from the mid-forties, paying rents to Ngāti Kahungunu in defiance of the law. For it had been another major decision of the newly established Government, taken without any consultation, that Māori should not be allowed to lease their lands directly to settlers. After an initial provision in the Land Claims Ordinance 1841 that direct leases from Māori were null and void, the Native Land Purchase Ordinance 1846 made it an offence to occupy or run stock on or cultivate lands which were not Crown-granted, and provided for the conviction and fining of offenders. The Constitution Act of 1852 also contained a section which made direct leases from Māori null and void. The reason for this decision is obvious enough. As McLean himself put it in 1854: 'This system of leasing lands from the Natives was threatening to entail a most serious evil on the prospects of the colony, as they would not of course alienate any of their lands to the Crown if such a system was permitted to exist . . . To put an end to this system . . . was an object of continual solicitude on the part of the Government . . .'[37] The Government, however, had turned a blind eye to the Wairarapa 'squatters' — until it was ready to buy the land. By then, Ngāti Kahungunu were collecting an annual income from the land of some £1,200, and the settlers were getting restive. They were concerned not only because they thought Māori unwillingness to sell was mounting as their rents grew, but also because they could not protect themselves from encroachment by fellow Pākehā. Governor Grey thus sent McLean in to buy; and McLean began his campaign in 1851 by touring through the district on his way to Hawke's Bay laden with bags of sovereigns which were to be paid for Hawke's Bay blocks. He also began to warn off potential runholders, and even to turn recent occupiers off Wairarapa land. The message to Ngāti Kahungunu was clear; the Government was now prepared to take steps to put an end to their income from rents. In 1853 McLean returned to the Wairarapa to begin his purchases, and over the next two years secured 1.5 million acres for approximately £18,000.[38]

The Government policy on direct leasing of Māori land was to have dramatic implications for the ability of Māori communities to control their land and thus for the future of their economies. Yet its introduction had been silent, unheralded; it had not been discussed with Māori. This unilateral development of policy exemplified British assumptions that it was their right and duty to chart a path for the social and economic development of the less sophisticated 'natives'. By the mid-1850s the Government was ready to embark on new land policy initiatives, based on a growing belief that it was time to tackle one of the basic 'problems' of Māori society — its social structure. The Government could not legislate chiefs out of existence; but it could weaken their influence by undermining the cohesion of communities, based on their joint control of land. Over the next ten years it devoted itself to achieving this goal, and did not shrink from using troops against North Island Māori in the process.

Donald McLean, by 1854 head of a new Native Land Purchase Department, began with a scheme to encourage Māori to 'buy back' sections for themselves when they sold land. Instead of holding large reserves in common, they would hold individual Crown-granted sections. One advantage of this, in McLean's cynical view, was that much of the Government purchase price would at once be spent by the people on the cost of their new sections. But the main point of the scheme was to destroy 'their present precarious and unsatisfactory tenure' in order that 'their present system of communism may be gradually dissolved'.[39]

Several years later, the Government was to tackle the 'problem' of Māori landholding head-on at Waitara, north of New Plymouth, when a small group of people whose spokesman was Te Teira offered for sale land that the settlers coveted at the mouth of the river. Such offers were not unusual; but the Government's reaction on this occasion was. Determined to break what it saw as a 'deadlock' in land purchase in Taranaki, it ignored the claim of Wiremu Kingi Te Rangitake, a Te Āti Awa leader of great status who was principal chief at Waitara, to speak for all those inter-related hapū comprising the Waitara community whose interests would be directly affected by the sale, and who opposed it. Instead, the Government tried to deal with the Waitara community as individuals. They were given to understand that they could not now stop the purchase from being con- cluded: the only option open was for each 'man' to save his own 'piece', defined as a strip of cultivation, from being included in it. If individuals — or chiefs — would not point out their 'portions', it must be assumed that they were not 'part-owners' of the land. Once the offer to sell had been made, and the Government had decided it was valid and made a payment, the land was Queen's land, and could be surveyed.[40]

This the people would not accept. Te Teira and his relatives might indeed have a grievance against Wiremu Kingi which had led them to offer the land in the first place; they might have every right to uphold the mana of their family, and to take steps to make life difficult for the rest of the Waitara people. But communities also had to be able to protect themselves in such situations. Kingi tried to explain to the Government that it could not properly assert any authority over the land when a sale had not been generally agreed on. The land was still customary land, and the people would not recognize the Government's right to demand that they 'prove their claims' to it. But the Government sent in its surveyors, and, when they were obstructed by unarmed people, published a proclamation of martial law which in the Māori language read like a declaration of war, and sent in troops to fortify the Waitara block. The first shots of the war were fired by the British on 17 March 1860.[41]

Wiremu Kingi was not alone in his fears about government policy. Māori disquiet had led to the growth of land protectionist movements in both Taranaki and the Waikato in the early 1850s. In South Taranaki a great new house was finished in 1854 for a hui to unite the people against land-selling. In the Waikato about the same time there was considerable opposition to the activities of land purchase agents, and a rāhui was laid over a large tract of land to try to protect it. The first national hui of Māori leaders was called in 1856 at Taupo to deal with the perceived danger of the growth in settler power and of uncontrolled land sales. Here the raising-up of a king for the Māori was discussed — an ariki whose mana might stand against that of the English Queen Victoria; a king for his own people. Were the Māori not entitled to their own ruler? asked Wiremu Tamihana of Ngāti Hauā, who threw his weight behind the search for a king. Were not other nations separate from one another ('wehe ana he iwi wehe ana he iwi')? Were not the Jews of the Old Testament commanded by God to raise up their own king? 'Thou shalt in any wise set him king over thee, whom the Lord thy God shall choose: one from among thy brethren shalt thou set king over thee: thou mayest not set a stranger over thee, which is not thy brother.' Yet it was not intended that British authority should no longer be recognized in New Zealand. 'I do not desire to cast the Queen from this island,' Tamihana wrote to the Governor, 'but, from my piece [of land].'[42]

The first King, the aged ariki Potatau Te Wherowhero, was anointed in the Waikato in 1858. Here the Kīngitanga took root, drawing on the strength of the Tainui people. It could not unite them all, for among the numerous communities within the region, opposing interests had inevitably emerged over time; nor could it draw together in a permanent political forum the far-flung iwi of the island. Until the establishment of a British state in their country, chiefs had not needed to contemplate supra-tribal political unity or institutions. But if many communities preferred not to commit themselves and their lands to the King, concerns about the nature of their relationship with the new state were widespread. They surfaced at once at the first 'conference' of chiefs called by a New Zealand governor in twenty years of British rule, at Kohimarama; and even then, called only when war had broken out and the Government sought support for its actions. The chiefs were well aware of the shift in power that had taken place since the constitution had been put into effect, and well aware that they had been left out: they were not represented in the General Assembly or the Provincial Councils. It is not clear whether they knew of the fears that had been expressed in the House of Representatives in 1858, that Māori men might be considered to meet the small property quali-fication outlined in the constitution on the basis of their use and occupation of tribal land, and thus be eligible to vote, or even to stand for election. At a time when the Pākehā population was only slightly larger than that of the Māori, there was real concern in the House about the effect of enfranch-ising 'a large body of men, who are destitute of political knowledge . . . mainly ignorant of the language in which our laws are written, and among whom respect for the law cannot as yet be enforced . . .' The matter was referred to the British Government in 1859, and the Law Officers of the Crown gave their opinion that Māori were not qualified to vote, as the terms defining the property qualification in the constitution were all terms of English law. Most Pākehā politicians were relieved. 'The natives have a natural right, not to vote, but to be *well governed* . . .' argued Hugh Carleton; in his view Māori were already represented in the House by certain Pākehā members who guarded their rights carefully. In the mean-time, the franchise might serve as a lure to encourage Māori to secure individual Crown grants, and acquire 'a stake in the general welfare of the community'.[43] British and Māori views of their future together remained poles apart. Māori wanted an immediate relationship on equal terms with the Pākehā Government — some through the new King, others through a permanent chiefly council meeting with the Governor (which they saw as having been instituted at Kohimarama).[44] But in the next few years they saw that hope disintegrate. The British troops marched first into Waitara — and then, when government preparations were complete, into the Waikato, against the King.

The Government fought the wars to try to destroy mana motuhake (Māori autonomy). It justified the use of troops by asserting the need to defeat the pernicious influence of Māori 'land leagues' which led 'non-owner' chiefs like Kingi to prohibit 'rightful owners' from selling their land.[45] But the Government could not recognize such rights in chiefs, it argued, or it would strengthen the King 'confederacy' which aimed to subvert the Queen's authority. Moreover, its policies of inducing Māori to give up tribal tenure in favour of individual Crown titles would fail. The Queen had promised in the Treaty to allow 'each man' to sell his land. British law was the strength of the weak man, and the Queen must uphold her promise that each could do as he wished with 'his own' land. Thus the Government turned the Treaty against Māori communities. In effect, the rights that were guaranteed in article three of the Treaty were deemed to be the important ones: Māori rights as British subjects; Māori rights as individuals.[46]

For their part, the communities which faced the invasion of their lands by British and colonial troops fought to maintain their authority over their lands and their homes. They fought much more successfully than the British had expected. Governor Gore Browne had hoped for a quick victory at Waitara, but it eluded his forces completely. A year later they were still in the field, and the Government was ready to sit down and draw up peace terms. The British had reckoned without the development of Māori tactics to deal with superior British numbers and firepower. Māori, for their part, had carefully assessed the odds they were up against and had adapted their pā accordingly, changing their location, their function, and design. 'Modern' pā were designed to deal with two main problems. To protect the garrison from heavy bombardment, Māori built pā which were remarkable trench and bunker systems. To repel enemy assaults, defenders relied on carefully sited firing positions, pekerangi (light outer fences) which delayed a storming-party, and traps such as hidden rifle trenches outside the pā (from which ambushes could be mounted). The pā could be thrown up quickly, and were expendable.[47]

The British had first been defeated at such pā in their war against Hone Heke in the Bay of Islands in 1845–46, but — unable to believe that 'uncivilized' Māori might outdo them in the higher arts of warfare — had not been able to recognize the Māori war effort for what it was. In Taranaki and the Waikato, similarly, they did not understand why it was that they could not inflict crushing military defeat. General Pratt finally resorted to sapping, digging trenches toward enemy lines and constructing protective redoubts as he went. He felt that he was making progress; but Taranaki Māori simply fell back behind the sap, building new fortifications as it proceeded. There was considerable British unease at the end of the 'first' war in Taranaki in 1861: not only was there no clear victory, but civilian casualties in overcrowded New Plymouth, from disease, had been high. Governor Gore Browne decided that the war must be carried to the place now identified as the 'heart' of the Māori resistance (the Kīngitanga lands) if 'rebellion' was ever to be 'put down'. Governor Grey, his successor, suspended the plan but, while he did not immediately abandon the possibility of coming to terms with the Kīngitanga, he also began marshalling his resources for a military invasion. Yet although the Waikato heartlands were occupied by thousands of British and colonial troops during 1863–64, they did not get as far south as the Government had wanted. Even at Orakau, the last battle fought in the Waikato in 1864, though the Māori defenders had eventually to evacuate through a cordon of British troops which completely surrounded the pā, the chief Rewi Maniapoto was not captured. General Cameron afterwards withdrew the core of his strike troops from the Waikato, feeling that he could not secure the sort of decisive victory the Government expected.[48] Indeed, at Tauranga, he subsequently suffered defeat at Gate Pā, a classic 'modern pā', which withstood a massive artillery barrage before the British charge was repulsed with heavy casualties.

Ultimately, however, overwhelming British numbers meant that Māori were unable to stave off British victory. From the beginning of 1864 Māori who had defended themselves against the British troops found themselves staring at the ultimate weapon the Government had designed against them: defeat by confiscation of land. The troops might not have performed as expected; but nevertheless they had secured over a million acres in the Waikato, and in Taranaki the process of military occupation continued for several years. For the settler Government the prize of the wars was gaining control of the land. After legal advice was taken, it had been decided in 1863 that the compulsory taking of Māori land should be accomplished not by executive action, but by the passing of a statute by Parliament. This would meet two possible objections. First, a statute would prevail over the guarantees in article two of the Treaty. Secondly, if Māori rights as British subjects were admitted, then their rights to private property (which were guaranteed by the law of England) could only be extinguished, if the 'public necessity' required it, by Parliament, the supreme law-making body.[49] One's land might only be taken legally by consent of representatives of 'the people'. Māori, unrepresented as they were in Parliament at this time, might have been surprised by this discussion, had they known of it. Such constitutional niceties would hardly have seemed relevant. When the New Zealand Settlements Bill was introduced into Parliament late in 1863, some Pākehā voices were raised in defence of Māori rights: disquiet was expressed about the trampling on the guarantees of the Treaty of Waitangi. Henry Sewell, who held office in various settler ministries during this period, published a pamphlet called *The New Zealand Native Rebellion* in which he attacked the Government's confiscation measures as 'panic-legislation', into which members of the House were hurried 'with very slight information as to facts, and without time for enquiry or thought'. The Governor, he alleged, had lost a splendid opportunity of coming to terms with the Kīngitanga at the beginning of the year, and had planned his own attack on the Waikato. How, then, could Māori be accused of 'treason' or 'rebellion'?[50] But the Government emphasized the need to punish 'rebels', as well as to defeat them, and to secure Māori obedience to the law. By taking land, it would be better able to ensure the peace and security of the country, both by introducing a settler population into 'disturbed districts' which could 'put down outbreaks', and by deterring other tribes from 'rebellion'.[51] The Governor postponed the operation of the act, but did not prevent it; and in London the Law Officers of the Crown swept aside the fears of the Colonial Office officials that the act might after all be unconstitutional, stating that 'the Laws of England have repeatedly recognized the necessity for exceptional legislation, to suppress a rebellion threatening the existence of the State.'[52]

Technically, then, Māori who had fought against the Crown were in 'rebellion', a label which caused anger ever after to their descendants. Pointing to the offensive actions of the British troops at the outset of the wars in Taranaki and Waikato, they asked how defence of their homes deserved such a label. But the definition stuck, and indeed it was central to the operation of The New Zealand Settlements Act. Where the Government was satisfied that a tribe or 'Section of a tribe or any considerable number thereof ' had been in rebellion against Her Majesty's authority, it might declare their lands subject to the Act, declaring them to be Crown lands and available for settlement. Military settlers were to be provided for first, then remaining lands could be surveyed and sold. Compensation courts were set up to determine which Māori were eligible to receive compensation in land or money for their lands thus taken. Thus power passed to a small group of Pākehā men appointed judges for the purpose, to determine which Māori were 'rebels' and which 'loyal'. Māori who hoped to salvage anything from the confiscation had to appear before these courts to justify their claims, and to find out how much land they might be awarded, in what areas. Whatever the Government's justifications for confiscation, the result of it was to break Māori authority over their lands in those central North Island areas where the Act was applied. Māori became supplicants in British courts for the right to take title — Crown title — to portions of their own lands.

Distress at confiscation and the long slow processes of its enforcement on the ground led to resistance and to further outbreaks of fighting. In the second phase of the North Island wars the Government was preoccupied with defeating the followers of the Hauhau faith, and those of Te Kooti (on the East Coast) and Titokowaru (on the West Coast). Te Ua Haumene (founder of the Hauhau faith), Te Kooti, and Titokowaru were all leaders who arose in the period of turmoil of the 1860s. Each of them came to be associated in the minds of Pākehā with bloody deeds and 'fanatical' religious practices; each seemed to provide strong justification for the continuation of the wars. Pākehā, fighting for control of their new country, were not in any mood to understand or accommodate leaders who were seen only as anti-Pākehā and anti-government, exercising an 'unwholesome' influence over large numbers of people.

Te Ua, it is true, was anti-missionary and anti-English; with God's help he hoped for deliverance for the Māori, and the establishment of a Māori state whose boundaries the Pākehā would not penetrate. But the guiding principle of his teachings, drawn from the Bible, was pai mārire, goodness and peace. Hauhau services, which aroused immediate Pākehā suspicion, were pentecostal, reflecting Te Ua's belief in Christ's promise to send the Holy Spirit to his disciples. But in a time of war, when the faith offered strength to those who fought the Government, it became associated with military resistance rather than with the peaceful and righteous society its founder had hoped for. The killing of the Opotiki missionary Völkner (who had unequivocally taken the part of the Government in the war) was not at all in accordance with Te Ua's instructions to his messengers who were sent to carry God's work across the island; but it set the seal on the Pākehā view of Hauhau as fanatics, who must be defeated.[53] Many Māori too, rejected the faith, for reasons which varied from fear of government retaliation, or fear that the independence of their own communities might be undermined, to a simple preference for more familiar 'missionary' religion.

Followers of Te Ua, and followers of Te Kooti and of Titokowaru too, thus found themselves facing Māori as well as Pākehā opponents in the field. Te Hura Te Taiwhakaripi led the Ngāti Awa defenders of their lands against much stronger colonial and Arawa forces sent to the Bay of Plenty after the killing of Völkner and of James Fulloon, who had been sent to apprehend those involved in Völkner's death.[54] Te Kooti in particular made himself powerful Māori enemies because of his attack in November 1868 on Poverty Bay, in which over fifty people were killed (more than twenty of them Māori) and some executed after capture. Yet he had not sought a fight with the Government. Unjustly imprisoned in 1866 in the wake of fighting in Poverty Bay, he devised a remarkable plan two years later for the escape by sea of nearly 300 men, women, and children held by the Government on the Chatham Islands, and returned to Poverty Bay. Unable to secure the consent of King Tawhiao for his passage inland to Waikato, however, Te Kooti then made his fateful decision to try to take Poverty Bay. Thereafter he faced constant pursuit, and only his skill as a guerilla fighter, and as a commander (whose authority was believed to come from God) saved him. Finally in 1872 he gained sanctuary in the King Country, and thereafter 'ceased strife', evolving from Scripture the rituals and teachings of the Ringatū Church.[55]

The people of Taranaki, too, had long been anxious for peace. In the wake of the 'paper' confiscation and of the spread of the Hauhau faith the Government had sent first imperial and then colonial troops to South Taranaki, to impress on the Māori the need to 'submit' and accept the loss of their land. In successive campaigns, the people's villages and cultivations were systematically destroyed. Titokowaru himself had begun a peace campaign in 1867 to try to placate the authorities. But as 'creeping confiscation' continued on the ground, fighting broke out again in 1868. During 1868–69 Titokowaru, a leader of military genius, caused the Government great anxiety, destroying one colonial force, and comprehensively defeating another; he appeared to offer a real threat to successful confiscation in Taranaki.[56] But early in 1869 he suddenly withdrew inland, for reasons which outsiders still debate. The people of Taranaki would not fight again. Nor would they cease to challenge the confiscation. When in 1877 the Government decided to enforce the confiscation of the Waimate Plains to 'open up' the land for settlement, a new leader, Te Whiti-o-Rongomai, guided the people in the peaceful assertion of their rights to the land; at first ploughing settler sections on land that had been taken, later erecting fences to prevent the new roads cutting through their cultivations. These were difficult tactics for a government to deal with; it worried that a court might not convict Māori who were arrested, and release them, and that infuriated settlers might then take matters into their own hands. The Government responded with a series of measures that did not escape censure in Parliament: acts with a limited life such as The Maori Prisoners' Trials Act 1879, which provided for the continuing imprisonment of arrested ploughmen until the Governor in Council should fix a date for their trial, and The Maori Prisoners Act 1880 which provided that all those awaiting trial or held in custody were deemed to have been lawfully arrested and to be in lawful custody until such time as the Governor in Council should issue an order for their release. The West Coast Settlement (North Island) Act 1880 included sections allowing any member of the Armed Constabulary, at any time over the next three years, to arrest without warrant anyone committing an offence — or who might 'reasonably be suspected' of being about to commit an offence — such as interfering with a survey, unlawfully ploughing or fencing or obstructing a road; if convicted by the Court such offenders could be imprisoned for up to two years, with or without hard labour. A number of members of Parliament were uneasy at legislating for such gross infringement of the rights of individuals in a British country. But the measures were passed, and several hundred men were arrested and detained in South Island gaols under them.

Meanwhile, the confusion resulting from the Government's piecemeal approach to enforcing the Taranaki confiscation over the previous fifteen years had been highlighted by the reports of the West Coast Commission, appointed by the Government to investigate Māori grievances relating to the confiscation. The Commission aimed (in its own words) both to 'do justice to the Natives' and to continue 'English settlement of the country'; it recommended that adequate reserves be marked off on both the Waimate Plains and at Parihaka for the Ngāti Ruanui and Taranaki peoples. But though the process of making reserves was begun in some areas alongside the survey of land for settlement, the Government had no great commitment to reaching a settlement with Te Whiti, to ensuring that he knew where the Parihaka reserves were actually to be, or to overcoming the people's mistrust of government intentions — the product of years of harsh experience. At the end of 1881, when the Government could wait no longer to 'deal with the problems' on the West Coast, a volunteer force was sent to Parihaka, the village was destroyed, its leaders arrested (and held without trial for sixteen months under further special legislation), and over 1,500 people dispersed under escort.[57] Subsequently, the people were allowed to return, and the allocation of the West Coast Settlement reserves was completed. But the reserves were made over by statute to the Public Trustee to administer. Though they were originally intended to be inalienable, and to provide a secure income from leases for the people, amending legislation progressively favoured the interests of the lessors over those of the lessees. By 1892 the Trustee had power to grant leases for twenty-one years with the right of perpetual renewal.[58] Such government acts left bitterness in their wake which has lasted till the present.

In some North Island areas, then, the Government took land by force and by confiscation. Elsewhere its weapon was a new institution called the Native Land Court, established in its lasting form (after a preliminary experiment under an act of 1862) in 1865. The Native Lands Act under which it was established was not at all reticent, on one level, about the function of the court: it was to ascertain the owners of land 'still subject to Maori proprietary customs . . . and to encourage the extinction of such proprietary customs and to provide for the conversion of such modes of ownership into titles derived from the Crown'. This was what the settler government had been aiming at before the wars; now it felt able to pass a statute which would ensure that customary title would be transmuted into negotiable paper titles. The purpose of these developments, as spelt out a few years later by Henry Sewell, was twofold: first, to enable the British to colonize the North Island — in other words, to make the land easier to buy because the Court would identify and record all the owners of any given block — and secondly, to 'detribalize' the Māori by destroying 'the principle of communism which ran through the whole of their institutions, upon which their social system was based'.[59] At the same time the Crown waived pre-emption and allowed settlers to purchase land directly. The Government, by now, was no longer concerned with upholding the guarantees of Māori rights (as Māori understood them) in article two of the Treaty of Waitangi. The Pākehā population far outstripped that of the Māori, troops were under arms in various parts of the North Island, and the Government took it upon itself to attempt to shatter the social and political organization of an indigenous society on the grounds that being like the British would be better for the people, and better for British settlement.

The work of the Land Court was to have dramatic implications for Māori communities. By setting up the Court the state finally gained control of Māori land outside the confiscation areas. Māori could not lease or sell their land unless its title had been decided by the Court; and the fact that its job was to give final judgments on the ownership of land also put great pressure on communities to bring their land into the Court, lest their claims be undermined, or might seem to the Court to be undermined, by the initiatives of others. Once any individual Māori had brought his or her claims before the Court, it had the power to determine the right of all 'claimants' to the land and then (under the 1865 Act) to issue certificates of title to no more than ten persons. The Governor might then cause a Crown grant to be made to the persons named in the deed or, alternatively, if the

Māori found to be entitled had already signed deeds of sale, to the Pākehā purchaser of the land.

From this time on, Māori land became enmeshed in the processes of the Land Court. A bewildering succession of amending statutes was passed: long complex documents, drafted in legal language which would make any layperson balk. As a result, claimants might not have been aware what their rights were at any given time when the Court was adjudicating on their land. Ngāti Whātua, for instance, were one iwi who were to find only much later that their last block of land at Orakei in the Auckland area had been awarded to thirteen men — not as tribal trustees for over 100 people (as could and should have been done under an amending Native Lands Act of 1867) — but as absolute owners to the exclusion of all others. This act of the Court was to make a mockery of the attempt of the chief Apihai Te Kawau to ensure that the land could never be alienated out of the possession of Ngāti Whātua. As a result of later decisions of the Court, and later statutes such as The Native Lands Act 1894 (which facilitated the making of orders partitioning the Orakei Block among the small number of 'owners'), the land was individualized and later purchased by the Crown.[60]

A major amendment to Māori land legislation was The Native Land Act 1873, which was later described by the Native Land Laws Commission of 1891 as carrying the system of individual ownership to its limits: 'the whole people of the tribe individually became the owners — not as a tribe, but as individuals.' The Act provided that every individual 'owner' should have his or her name registered on a list called a Memorial of Ownership, and required all of them to agree before the land could be sold. If only a majority agreed to sell or lease, however, the Court could partition the land in proportion to the 'shares' of sellers and non-sellers so that a transaction could take place. The Government's preoccupation with defining individual 'proportionate shares' to land was purely Pākehā. It led to the problem of fragmented ownership, which was to plague thousands of people over many generations. The Court — which had power to decide on succession to shares in cases where Māori died without making a will (as most did) — had decided at the outset that children might inherit in equal shares, land interests from both their parents in various blocks. Over the years the total number of shares in a block thus multiplied, while the proportion of land held by any one 'owner' in a single block diminished. The whole system underlined the lack of government interest in the ability of Māori to develop their own land. As later commissions were to point out, the costs of litigation, and of survey and partition of land were often prohibitive, and people were deterred from embarking on an expensive process in order to secure a legal interest in the land. How then could they raise loan finance for development?[61]

The whole Land Court process was in fact designed so that buyers could identify owners, and initiate transactions with them. And in the post-war years buyers were legion. The Crown re-entered the purchase business alongside private buyers in the 1870s, and many communities found themselves coping with both sorts of agents simultaneously. Lands of the

Te Roroa people of Ngāti Whātua, for instance (whose rohe extended south from Hokianga) were targeted by the Crown for land purchase operations from 1874 on. The competition for land between private and Crown agents led to practices which Te Roroa would later complain of — notably payment of tāmana, or advance payments for land before its title had been decided in the Land Court, taking advantage of the people's need for cash, binding them to sell (at low acreage rates) once the land was processed by the Court. Crown agents also conducted surveys with undue speed, to meet Court sitting dates. The unfinished plans of field surveyors who had consulted with both Māori and land purchase agents about boundaries, were replaced in Land Court records by plans compiled by draughtsmen who had not been on the ground. The result of this was that reserved areas previously agreed on with Te Roroa were lost to them, because they were not surveyed or properly marked on the plans.[62]

Some land legislation, it must be said, was designed to achieve reform of the Land Court and land purchase procedures. The Native Lands Frauds Prevention Act 1870 empowered the Governor to appoint Trust Commissioners to examine all alienations of Māori land to ensure that they were 'fair and equitable'. The 1873 Native Land Act contained a section providing that it was the duty of newly appointed District Officers to see that inalienable reserves were set aside in various blocks in the district, amounting altogether to at least fifty acres for every man, woman, and child. The Native Equitable Owners Act 1886 provided a mechanism for admitting to land titles people who had been shut out from them as a result of the operation of the 'ten-owner' section of the 1865 Act. Some members of Parliament (Sewell among them) felt strongly that it was their duty to identify and suppress abuses of the system they had established. Many of the controls they designed, however (as later commissions reported) were neglected or systematically eroded. But quite apart from this, the major problem was the system itself. W. L. Rees, a lawyer with wide interests in politics, colonization, and in Māori land management, pointed this out from 1884 in his cogent criticisms of the Government's Māori land legislation. The principal cause of the 'ridiculous' number of acts and their 'contradictory' nature, he alleged, was 'the efforts always made by their framers to deal with Maori tribes owning land as if they were Englishmen, owning in severalty under a title of freehold'. He slated the laws as having resulted in a system of land-transfer which was expensive, complicated, slow, and inefficient; nor did it even produce certainty of title. The interests of neither Māori nor Pākehā buyers had been protected. Parliament, he argued, must change the law and allow the people to act tribally in accordance with the 'genius of their customs'. It must give Māori the power to manage their own estates by committees, just as the properties of companies were managed by directors. It must forbid dealings with individual Māori and thus restore the people's confidence in their ability to control their lands as they wished to.[63] But the Government shrank from dismantling the Native Land Court.

If the Land Court offered little protection to Māori customary title, it is hardly surprising that Māori also failed to find protection for their rights in New Zealand courts. Yet this too was a post-war development. Earlier indications had been that common law protection would be available to Māori property rights, in line with precedents established elsewhere. Certain common law principles known as the doctrine of aboriginal title had been established over time in North American colonies, where the British had first contemplated the legal status of indigenous tribal societies. The doctrine of aboriginal title offered legal protection to indigenous land rights, because it allowed that pre-existing property rights under customary law legally survived the change of sovereignty. In other words, Māori might expect the courts to uphold their title, which could only be extinguished with their free consent. The judges in the New Zealand Supreme Court, in the early case *R v. Symonds* (1847), had clearly recognized the legal rights of Māori tribes to their ancestral lands, and it seemed that the doctrine of aboriginal title had been successfully transferred to New Zealand.[64]

Whether Māori would have appreciated the doctrine of aboriginal title, had it been explained to them at that time, is uncertain. It was an imported doctrine based on constitutional concepts which would have been quite foreign to Māori: that the Crown (according to ancient feudal theory) was technically the ultimate owner of all land in its territory, but that such ownership was subject to indigenous title. As it turned out, however, the doctrine of aboriginal title, even on its own terms, did not stand Māori in good stead in the courts. Judges are not always bound by precedent, and important judgments can chart new interpretations of the law. In 1877 the Chief Justice, Prendergast, ruled that the courts had no jurisdiction to entertain any claims based on a supposed aboriginal title. In his landmark judgment in *Wi Parata v. The Bishop of Wellington* (1877), influenced by a narrow group of contemporary English writers on international law who argued that tribal societies had no legal status whatsoever, Prendergast denied that native title had any basis in common law. The Treaty of Waitangi had no validity as an instrument of cession since Māori, as a tribal society, had no legal status, and no customary rights which the courts could enforce; therefore the Treaty could not transform the Māori right of occupation into a legal right. Secondly, he argued that Māori held rights to their lands, once the Crown declared sovereignty, only on sufferance. Ignoring the fact that Māori had long been considered British subjects, and that the Crown could not therefore make 'acts of state' against them, Prendergast argued that land transactions conducted by the Crown with Māori were 'acts of state', which could not therefore be examined by the courts.

The practical effects of this approach were to be far-reaching. Ngāti Toa (in *Wi Parata*) had sought the return of Porirua land gifted to Bishop Selwyn in 1848 but not used for the purpose stated (a school), on the grounds that a Crown grant for the land had subsequently been issued to the Bishop without their knowledge, and was therefore void. Chief Justice Prendergast dismissed the claim on the grounds that it had no legal basis.

The agreement between Ngāti Toa and the Bishop was a legal nullity. Only the Crown could extinguish native title, and once a Crown grant was issued it did not matter whether the native owners had agreed or not.

The courts, moreover, denied Māori any remedy for trespass on their land. Pākehā, evidently, might construct buildings and a railway for conveying logs on Māori land; but Māori could not sue them successfully in colonial courts because they did not hold their land on Crown titles. Even though they might hold a Memorial of Ownership from the Land Court, this was not a Crown-derived, freehold title.[65]

Fishing rights were also to be profoundly affected, well into the twentieth century, by the attitude of the courts to customary title. Yet Chief Judge Fenton had shown how fishing rights could have been safeguarded by the courts. In his famous *Kauwaeranga* Judgment delivered in the Native Land Court in 1870, he held that the Crown's right to the foreshore was subject to Māori customary usage. At the date of the Treaty of Waitangi, the land claimed was a 'native fishery'; therefore its exclusive and undisturbed possession was guaranteed Māori by article two. Fenton rejected the application before him by Hoterene Taipari and others of Ngāti Maru for a certificate of title to the land itself, tidal mudflats long used for fishing, but did issue an order which entitled the claimants to exclusive fishing rights between high water mark and low water mark.[66] Given the presence of gold beneath the mudflats, and the perceived necessity to protect the Crown's interest in the gold, this approach might well be seen as self-serving — and quite at odds with Māori views of their rights. But the Court did at least offer some protection of Māori fishing rights. The Native Lands Act 1909, however, shut out the Land Court from dealing with 'non-territorial' customary title. Thereafter fishing rights were dealt with in the common law courts, and Māori convicted of breaching various fishing regulations who tried to argue for the exercise of a customary fishing right (which appeared to be protected in fishing legislation) made no impression on the courts at all. The Treaty of Waitangi could not create legal rights, according to the courts: if Māori were to have special rights to fish in the sea or in tidal waters, Parliament must pass legislation conferring such rights.[67]

The fate of Māori fishing rights in legal terms highlights the inability of Māori to protect and to develop an essential part of their economy in a settler-dominated New Zealand. At the outset Parliament passed statutes which seemed to take no account at all of Māori fishing rights. Since title to the foreshore was vested in the Crown by a prerogative title at common law, Parliament gave the Governor power, in The Public Reserves Act 1854, to make grants to Superintendents or to 'other persons' of any land below high-water mark in harbours, navigable rivers, and on the sea coasts. This power was widely used to transfer acres of foreshore to provincial governments for such purposes as harbour development. The Harbours Act 1878 provided that tidal land could only be granted if Parliament passed special legislation; but land continued to be vested in harbour boards, and Māori interests were not protected.[68] As Pākehā interest in fisheries grew,

Parliament also began to pass fishing legislation. Underlying these laws were certain assumptions about the nature of Māori fishing interests which 'were to be so engrained in over a century of subsequent fishing laws as to make virtually incomprehensible any other view'.[69] The laws assumed that the Crown had an unrestricted right to dispose of the inshore and offshore fisheries; that the Treaty of Waitangi had no real bearing on the fisheries issue; that Māori fishing had had no commercial component (despite substantial evidence to the contrary); and that non-Māori interests could be licensed for commercial exploitation, while Māori interests could be provided for in non-commercial reserves near to their major villages.

By the end of the nineteenth century Māori fishing was already affected by the development of the Pākehā fishing industry. The Ngāi Tahu people of Otakou, for instance, were finding themselves squeezed out of their fishing trade by Pākehā operators. From the time of the foundation of Dunedin in 1848, they had supplied the settlement with fish. But by the mid-1860s a small Pākehā industry was established in Dunedin, employing some sixty people, and by 1872 three fishing companies were established there, which were trawling outside the Heads. By 1877 there were already signs of over-fishing in Otago Harbour — once famed for the quality and quantity of its fish — and before long fish would be described as 'less than scarce'. The new fishermen had not taken any steps to conserve the resource that their industry depended on.[70]

In this period, however, it was Māori fishing rights in inland waters that were worst affected by the spread of British settlement. Ngāi Tahu, despite the Crown undertaking recorded in the Kemp purchase deed of 1848 to protect their mahinga kai, found that the Government had little interest in upholding its promises. The Government official, Mantell, later described how he had dealt with requests from Ngāi Tahu to protect their all-important eeling rights, at the time when he laid out the reserves in Canterbury: 'At almost every reserve the right to maintain the old and to make new eel-weirs was claimed, but I knew these weirs to be so great an impediment to the drainage of the country that in no case would I give way upon this point . . .'[71] When British and Māori economic interests came into conflict, the British assumption was that Māori interests must give way. This explains the fate of Te Waihora (later called Lake Ellesmere), described as 'one of Ngāi Tahu's most precious taonga', 'teeming with millions of eels, flounders, herrings, cockles, pipis, and waterfowl' — over which no reserves of any kind were created to protect its use by Ngāi Tahu.[72] By 1880 settler drainage of the lake, and pollution of many of the streams feeding the lake, were having a dramatic effect on the eel fisheries.[73]

In the North Island, too, Māori fisheries were increasingly being trespassed on in the post-war years. Ngāi Te Rangi watched with concern as Pākehā blundered into their own carefully-apportioned fishing grounds both inside and outside the Tauranga heads; Ngāti Pāoa saw their flounder and pipi being taken by outsiders; Ngāti Whātua wondered why Pākehā took their fish, shellfish, and oysters at Kaipara without asking permission; Ngāpuhi were distressed at the wholesale destruction of their oysters on the foreshore of the Bay of Islands.[74] And the British introduction of various species of trout resulted in the virtual extermination of indigenous lake and river fish which had been important foods for Māori in both islands: kōkopu, īnanga, kākahi, kōura, kōaro. The Arawa people of Rotorua were left very bitter at the fate of their fisheries, and at the imposition of licence fees if they wished to catch imported fish in their own streams.[75]

Loss of control over their fisheries and over their land became crucial issues for Māori leaders in the late nineteenth century: they appeared repeatedly in petitions, in representations made to ministers, in the speeches of Māori members of Parliament. Settler politicians could hardly have claimed that they were not aware of Māori concerns. Yet it was still easy for those concerns to be set aside. The creation of the four Māori parliamentary seats in 1867 (after the Pākehā population had outnumbered the Māori) did not result in any widespread Māori enthusiasm for the Pākehā political system. Little provision was made at first for Māori speakers to participate in an English-speaking assembly, which led to some sarcastic comments from Māori leaders on the tokenism of the new arrangements. On a population basis Māori should have had fourteen or fifteen seats.[76] What they wanted, however, and were never able to achieve, was tribal representation.

Yet Māori members were prepared to challenge government policies vigorously. Some fought lonely battles in the House — like the southern member Hori Kerei Taiaroa who went into Parliament determined to make Pākehā listen to Te Kerēme, the Claim of Ngāi Tahu against the Crown stemming from the broken promises made at the time of the major land transactions. Taiaroa believed that the only route to success was through Parliament; and his determination to convince his Pākehā colleagues of his commitment to legal process led him to painful meetings in the late 1870s with those Ngāi Tahu who sought to re-establish their rights to the central lands of the South Island by more direct means. Under the spiritual leadership of Te Maiharoa more than a hundred people embarked on a heke inland to Omarama in the winter of 1877 and built a village on land which was part of a vast Pākehā sheep station. But the Native Minister told them they had to go, and finally, early in 1879, Taiaroa visited the people to support the Government's message publicly. Only privately did he tell the Government what he felt he could not say aloud to the people: 'Sir . . . I felt I could never argue with them, or speak to them, on account of my certain belief that they are quite right.'[77] In August armed police escorted Ngāi Tahu off the land.

The feelings of failure among the Māori members of the House of Representatives were summarized in a letter they sent to the Aborigines Protection Society in London in 1883. They could not influence the Government, they complained, or prevent it from continually breaking the land guarantee of the Treaty.[78] During the 1880s two Māori delegations, one from Ngāpuhi, one led by King Tawhiao, visited England to appeal directly to the Crown: to 'the source and fountain of authority, to the place where the Queen lives, that she may redress the ills of the Maori race inflicted on them by the Government of New Zealand'.[79] Both took their stand on the Treaty of Waitangi; both sought the grant of a Māori parliament or government to make laws for their own people and lands. The British Secretary of State wondered, as he referred the petition back to the New Zealand Government for comment, if section 71 of the constitution might be applied so that native laws and customs might apply in 'native territory' rather than colonial laws. The local government was not at all anxious to co-operate; and if the British Government was displeased by the general tone of the reply from New Zealand, it also considered itself quite unable, constitutionally, to intervene in the affairs of a responsibly governed colony. In the course of a heated debate in the House of Commons, Lord Randolph Churchill protested vigorously at such a position. Could imperial obligations under treaties, he asked, be abandoned so easily? '. . . such a monstrous doctrine would lead to any amount of injustice and oppression in the treatment of Native Races.'[80]

But by the late nineteenth century the Treaty of Waitangi was important only to Māori. The New Zealand Government was unimpressed by the great hui which took place during the 1870s and 1880s at Orakei and in the Bay of Islands and elsewhere, seeking government recognition of Māori grievances — unimpressed even by the kotahitanga parliaments which began to meet from 1892. Yet the kotahitanga movement grew from the work of major chiefs throughout the North Island (many of them long considered loyal allies by the Government) who pledged themselves to union and to setting up a Māori government under the mana of the Treaty.[81] The chiefs did their utmost to show how parallel institutions might work in New Zealand: they set up a bi-cameral parliament based on that of the Pākehā; they tried to secure the passing of a Native Rights Act by the General Assembly which would grant a Constitution to all Māori, allowing them to pass laws in their own elected parliament to govern themselves and their lands. But the Liberal Government would not consider any initiative which might remove the control of Māori land, and its purchase, from settler hands: perhaps because Māori had made it clear that they wished to lease their lands, but not to sell them.[82] The kotahitanga leaders had eventually to accept the defeat of their bill — and, for the time being, of their vision of equal rights for Māori and Pākehā.

The immense strength of the late nineteenth century Māori political movements is evidence enough that Māori were not ready to withdraw into demoralized isolation. Though their population, by 1896, was at its lowest ebb since contact with Pākehā, they had resisted the first great push of the British to assimilate them. It was not that they rejected Western technology or trade, or new political and legal systems, or the Bible, or literacy or the English language. On the contrary, people had seized on all of them and wanted to find out how to make them useful for their own purposes. But Māori had never considered that the price of Pākehā knowledge was loss of autonomy. As it became obvious that Pākehā had a different view, and were not prepared to support their kaupapa, Māori had to settle instead for a long period of uncomfortable co-operation within

Pākehā political institutions. It would be another hundred years before a new Māori renaissance engendered a whole new range of iwi-based institutions — modern corporate rūnanga, iwi trusts, and the National Māori Congress — which would meet with a more positive response from the Government.

PART III

A Time of Transition

CHAPTER 8

Parties and Political Change

Len Richardson

In August 1890 New Zealand was plunged into its first crisis in the relations between labour and capital, a two-month-long strike which tied up the ports and involved some 8,000 unionists. A confrontation on the waterfront was not unexpected, but the scale and bitterness of the conflict surprised and alarmed most observers. Shipping and mining interests had developed close links and together they watched with some concern throughout the 1880s as unions in their industries grew in number and increased their organization. They viewed as deliberately provocative the combination of seamen, watersiders, and miners in the Maritime Council of 1889, a federation intended to incorporate unions drawn from a range of occupations.

Union officials saw their organization as defensive rather than aggressive, a retaliation against what they termed the growth of monopoly capitalism. They wanted the negotiating role of unions recognized by employers, and preference given to union members. The leaders of the Maritime Council, especially J. A. Millar, national secretary of the Seamen's Union from Port Chalmers, and John Lomas, a Methodist lay preacher and coalminer from the remote and forbidding Denniston plateau, saw unionism as the only means by which working men could improve their position in society. Thus, when Australian seamen went on strike early in 1890, protesting against their employers' refusal to acknowledge the right of marine officers to belong to a union, the Maritime Council instructed its members to stop work. The future of unionism was in the balance. Should the shipping companies break the waterfront unions in Australia, the struggle would, they believed, soon be transferred across the Tasman.[1]

Unlike New Zealand's subsequent waterfront confrontations of 1913 and 1951, the maritime strike was a bloodless affair. The outcome, the rout of the strikers, was never in doubt. Unemployment made labour easy to recruit, and union organization could not sustain a prolonged campaign. Defeat destroyed the Maritime Council and the unions supporting it almost disintegrated. But the heightened awareness engendered by the conflict among urban wage-earners carried the unionists further into the political arena. In the election of December 1890, five Labour members entered Parliament along with thirty-eight others endorsed by trade unions and labour bodies. Contemporaries were quick to acknowledge a connection between the strike, labour's involvement in politics, and the defeat of the Government led by Harry Atkinson. The victors celebrated the triumph of democracy: 'Beaten in one direction the Unions and the People have conquered in another.'[2] The vanquished attributed their defeat to the politics of class and party; labour, some feared, would 'be blatant' in the new Parliament.[3]

Political rhetoric exaggerated the gap between conservative and radical. Yet the maritime strike undoubtedly hastened the process whereby party and class replaced faction and locality as the major determinants of political loyalties. In a country where the dominant economic interests and aspirations long remained rural and where industry grew slowly, change was gradual. The years following the strike were marked still by consensus rather than conflict: parties remained unstable and class peripheral; organized labour co-operated with Liberal majorities, who introduced social, political, and industrial reforms, and sought thereby to balance above sectional interests. By the first two decades of the twentieth century the interests of property and labour had diverged to the point where consensus disintegrated. The rival sectional interests each produced a political party (Reform and Labour). Party organization, however, remained rudimentary, and the Liberals continued as the party of consensus, cutting across class lines. Finally, after 1920, Labour grew into a mass party. It became confident of its class base and began to reach out for the middle ground of politics. Labour's victory in 1935 put the two non-labour parties on the defensive and led them to combine and organize also along mass lines. With the formation of the National Party in 1936, nearly fifty years after the maritime strike, a class-based, two-party political system emerged.

The general election of 1890, immediately after the strike, exhibited little of the political polarization that was to follow. The Premier, Harry Atkinson, and his rival, John Ballance, led loosely organized teams, not parties, to the polls. When parliamentary candidates were nominated, they pledged their support to either the Ministry or the Opposition. Such support was always conditional upon the needs of the locality, and might well be limited to the endorsement of only some of a leader's proposals. Each leader issued a manifesto designed to encompass as wide a variety of supporters as possible. Thus the policies advanced by each group reflected the divergences of its members. The ideological gap between the Government and the Opposition was slight. Both advocated economy, protection for colonial industries, and land settlement. They differed principally over the question of taxation. Ballance proposed a graduated land tax as a means of persuading big landowners to trim their holdings to an economic level. This apparent threat to the colony's rural interests was coupled with promised tax exemptions for small and middling farmers. Atkinson proposed to retain the existing property tax which, because it fell upon improvements as well as land, was particularly onerous to the small and middling farmers.

Despite this minimal platform divergence, the election was fought with unusual intensity, especially in the cities. Urban voters particularly were critical of the Atkinson Ministry's handling of the maritime strike. At first Atkinson had allowed the strike to take its course, only belatedly calling a conference between employers and employees (which the employers boycotted). When the railwaymen joined the strikers, the Premier gave his full support to the commissioners who controlled the railways. This identification of the Ministry with the employers hardened the resolve of the defeated unionists to be represented politically by 'men of their class'.[4] Organized labour was firmly enlisted behind the Opposition.

Politicians on both sides were surprised by the extent of labour's political involvement, especially in the southern cities. In Dunedin in 1890 the unionists of the depressed industrial suburbs launched New Zealand's first labour party. The high degree of organization that this Dunedin party developed gave labour bargaining power. Labour leaders realized that their short-term interests were best served by aligning themselves with Opposition members who had put labour's case during the maritime strike and who needed the urban vote. The alliance was based on a history of co-operation. Middle-class radicals had strong links with the unions and had led the agitation which produced the Sweating Commission in 1890. Labour's election platform also stressed the need for reforms in working conditions, protection for manufacturing, land reforms as a means of solving urban problems, and opposition to immigration. Moderate though the programme was, it did not diminish labour's political fervour. Co-operation was necessary tactically, but to labour leaders the Opposition was merely a political party, whereas the labour party represented the Dunedin working class in action.[5]

Labour organization was more rudimentary in the other main centres, although in Christchurch a labour-based group, the People's Political Association, was formed for the election. Calls for an independent labour party were resisted mainly on pragmatic grounds; there was no time for the necessary organization.[6] But wage-earner enthusiasm was high, as the polls were to indicate. In Christchurch and Dunedin at least, the 1890 election became a struggle between the working class, with their middle-class allies, and the rest of urban society.

In rural electorates class attitudes remained subordinate to those of community or locality. Property-owners viewed the growing union activity with concern: some felt that the maritime strike presaged revolution, and they reacted almost hysterically. With more than a little annoyance a Canterbury runholder noted privately that the 'gentlemen shearers' had stopped work to vote.[7] But labour posed no real threat in country electorates, despite the fact that depression had undermined confidence in the propertied élite which dominated rural politics. Ballance's promises may have been attractive to many country people, but they did not rush to vote. Abstention was probably the decisive factor in rural electorates.[8]

Despite the euphoric pronouncement that the people had endorsed

'Liberal principles, Liberal measures and the Liberal party',[9] the outcome of the election was not immediately apparent. Most Government supporters conceded that Atkinson no longer possessed a mandate, but doubted Ballance's ability to put together a viable ministry. Some drew comforting parallels from the past, anticipating a return to the uncertainty of 1884 when ministries were made and broken almost overnight.[10] This analysis ignored the strength of the anti-Atkinson vote and the extent to which Ballance had attracted the support of the discontented in both town and country.

The new Parliament met in January 1891. In an early division Atkinson was defeated on a vote to elect the Speaker. He resigned, and Ballance was called upon to form a ministry. Many members had decided to support Ballance as a result of Atkinson's improper packing of the Legislative Council in an effort to counter his loss of support among the people by building up an unassailable majority in the Upper House. His action lent credibility to Ballance's claims that the election had been a battle between the 'champions of the people' and the 'champions of privilege', and allowed the new Ministry to discredit their opponents with the label 'conservative'.[11] The appointment of John Ballance as Premier on a liberal and reformist programme ushered in a period of Liberal administration that was to last until 1912, a period during which the Liberals evolved into New Zealand's first organized political party.

Between 1891 and 1893 the struggle within Parliament focused on land. Land reform was central to the radical ideology of the late 1880s and early 1890s, both as a solution to urban problems and as a social good in itself. In the election campaign Ballance and his followers, especially John McKenzie, had promised to 'burst up the big estates' and 'put the small man on the land', but these slogans were bound to cause a variety of expectations. The more radical land-reformers, influenced by the writings of J. S. Mill and Henry George, wanted land nationalized. They argued for a progressive land tax accompanied by state purchase of land at market value in cases where owners objected to the tax. Land thus obtained by the Crown could be leased, and rentals periodically revalued so that the community as a whole benefited from land-created wealth. Most Liberals, however, favoured taxation as a means of squeezing the speculator and persuading big land-holders to reduce their holdings, but were wary of altering forms of tenure. Ballance, who in the 1880s had promoted his own version of nationalization, moved cautiously. His Land and Income Assessment Act of 1891 imposed 1d. in the pound on the unimproved value of land valued at over £500. There was also to be a graduated tax starting at ⅛d. in the pound rising to 2d. on estates worth £5,000 or more. Absentee owners paid a further 20 per cent. The raising of the exemption figure to £5,000 and the complete exemption of Crown tenants in fact relieved some 10,000 odd property-holders of the burden of direct taxation.

Legislation to alter Crown land tenure set the fears of property-holders at rest. In 1892 John McKenzie, Minister of Lands and an ardent land reformer, introduced a new leasehold tenure. It was a skilful compromise between the demands of the radical land reformers and the more conservative instincts of small and middling farmers. McKenzie's lease-in-perpetuity offered Crown lessees a 999-year lease without revaluation and hence gave the rights of freehold in all but name. Moreover, as McKenzie constantly stressed, the new tenure was an optional one; selectors could choose to purchase Crown land outright or pay a higher rental and retain the right of purchase. The mixture of tenures reassured established farmers and fostered Liberal support in the countryside.[12]

The more radical Liberals found McKenzie's compromise distasteful, although they recognized its political value. Their influence was waning, however, and diminished further when the rough ex-goldfields publican, Richard John Seddon, became Premier. Early in 1893 Ballance's health deteriorated and Seddon was appointed Leader of the House. The appointment did not signify an automatic right of succession; Ballance, indeed, favoured Sir Robert Stout, the Dunedin radical. But Stout was not in the House, and before a seat could be found for him, Ballance died, leaving the radicals without a candidate capable of dislodging Seddon. Most Liberal members clearly preferred the prospect of limited reform under Seddon's leadership to any alternative the urban radicals might offer.[13]

Stout resisted Seddon's appointment, and sought the support of the prohibition movement in his struggle against the West Coaster. By the early 1890s prohibition had become a divisive social issue, cutting across party allegiances. Without warning, Stout appealed over his party's head to the electorate. He introduced a Bill early in the 1893 session to give a simple majority in each licensing district a direct veto and power to close all licensed premises in it without compensation. Seddon responded with a Government Bill that prohibitionists denounced as a victory for the brewers. A bare majority of prohibition votes could close the doors of every fourth pub; a two-thirds vote was needed before a district went dry, and half the enrolled voters were required to have voted before the poll was valid. Stout fought Seddon's Bill clause by clause, and, with the support of a vociferous temperance movement, led by the New Zealand Alliance and the Women's Christian Temperance Union, promoted himself as an alternative Liberal leader. He had greatly over-estimated the parliamentary support for prohibition, but the question was popular enough throughout the country to be a considerable electoral embarrassment to the Liberals.[14]

An alliance between the temperance and women's suffrage movements made Stout's activities all the more dangerous to the Liberals. Ballance had originally been sympathetic to the suffragists, but once in office his suspicion that women were a conservative influence in society made him less eager. Similar views about women led Opposition members to different conclusions. The conservative member Sir John Hall believed that giving women the vote would 'increase the influence of the *settler* and *family*-man, as against the loafing single men who had so great a voice in the last elections'.[15] When Seddon became Premier, the suffragists were downcast,

205

for they regarded him as their 'worst enemy in the Cabinet'.[16] But the new leader could not afford to antagonize the powerful alliance. When Sir John Hall proposed an amendment giving women the franchise to the Government's Electoral Bill of 1893, Seddon allowed it through the House, assuming that the Legislative Council would reject it. But by a narrow margin of two votes, New Zealand women were granted the right to vote. Despite the politicians' fears, their vote in the 1893 election had no discernible impact at the polls.[17]

The election of 1893 consolidated Seddon's position as leader. He required from candidates a pledge of support in return for official recognition. This practice, known as the 'hallmark', was widely condemned but extremely effective. After the election, the weakly led Opposition was unable to act with the cohesion that Seddon encouraged among Liberals by a combination of policy measures and public works benefits. Still, party organization remained slack within the House; Seddon had many unreliable members behind him, the Opposition was fragmented, and there were many independents. Outside Parliament, Liberal organizations remained a loose assemblage of electorate and regional associations, and the Opposition almost entirely lacked a structure. The so-called National Association, formed in 1891 to supply the deficiency, was without effect.

The election increased the parliamentary strength of the Liberals by thirteen to a total of fifty-one of the seventy-four European seats. The number of Liberal members from rural constituencies doubled. Small farmers, farm labourers, and those who expected to benefit from rural development had been won over by McKenzie's land legislation and by the 'purchase' of the Cheviot estate in 1892 and its subsequent division. Men hungry for land knew little of the manoeuvring by which Cheviot trustees foisted the land upon the Government; they envisaged a succession of Cheviots through the country and the settling of thousands of men upon the land. Their votes confirmed the Liberals as the party of 'the country' and provided McKenzie with the foundation for 'perhaps the strongest rural consensus in our history'.[18]

As they won support in the countryside, the Liberals began to lose it in the towns. Five of their city seats went to the Opposition in 1893. The trade unions were unable to continue organizing the labour vote as unemployment persisted and membership fell. The licensing question, so rashly raised by Stout, also cost the Liberals urban votes. These losses made it more difficult for the labour movement to offer support to the Liberals in return for concessions. The movement was fortunate, however, in having one outstanding advocate in Cabinet, William Pember Reeves, Minister of Labour from 1892 to 1896. Like many of his contemporaries, Reeves equated socialism with the democratic use of state power to regulate and ameliorate *laissez-faire* capitalism. The collective power of the community should be used to defend the weak and produce a more civilized society. Reeves gave expression to these ideas in a number of 'labour laws' culminating in the comprehensive Factories Act of 1894, which provided for the registration and inspection of factories and closely regulated the employment of women and children. It was this legislation that led Albert Métin, a young French radical visiting New Zealand in 1899, to describe it as the 'classical land of state socialism and labour legislation'.[19]

His most important piece of legislation was the Industrial Conciliation and Arbitration Act of 1894. The I.C. and A. Act was intended to provide a mechanism for peaceful settlement of industrial disputes and 'encourage the formation of industrial unions'. The country was divided into districts, each with a conciliation board upon which unions and employers were represented. Disputes came to these boards: where a decision was reached (and Reeves expected that in most cases it would be), it was set out in the form of an industrial agreement or referred to the central Arbitration Court so that the settlement could be incorporated into an award which would apply to all workers in the industry concerned. If the board failed to resolve a dispute, the case went on to the Court whose decision had the binding force of law. The right to strike was restricted while conciliation and arbitration procedures were in progress. Registration was voluntary and unions could opt to pursue instead the customary procedure of collective bargaining with their employers. Most did seek the recognition offered, and unions grew rapidly in size and number.

Unionists in New Zealand had traditionally been opposed to compulsory arbitration. Like their British and American counterparts, they believed that all governments would be biased against labour. The maritime strike and the subsequent collapse of the unions, however, compelled unionists to adopt a more pragmatic stance. They hoped the Act would force employers to recognize the negotiating role of unions. The employers were almost unanimously hostile to the legislation but were too weak politically to prevent it. Country interests, stronger in Parliament after the 1893 general election, were inclined to see the measure as a means of disciplining fractious city unionists. Reeves certainly encouraged the view that his Act would curb urban unrest.[20]

Within two years of his greatest legislative achievement Reeves was on his way to London. As Agent-General and then in 1905 New Zealand's first High Commissioner in Britain, he was to occupy a position of great prestige but little influence. His departure showed that neither the Liberals nor the country had room for a thoroughgoing radical. As one of Stout's supporters, Reeves had accepted Seddon only on the understanding that he had a free hand in the administration of labour affairs. But he persisted with labour legislation to the point where it threatened to disrupt the Liberal party. Country members came to suspect that Reeves was bent on building urban labour into a powerful political force that would endanger their interests. When in 1895 he introduced a round of new labour Bills, Seddon warned that the Government would not legislate only for one class;[21] Government members opposed the Bills in the House; and newspapers up and down the country accused Reeves of legislating ahead of the electorate's needs. His departure left the urban wage-earners without a voice in Government. Most Liberals did not sympathize with his vision of a country characterized by small industry, small unions, and small farms. The future lay with those who took a more dynamic view, led by Seddon, McKenzie, and J. G. Ward.

These men advocated an expansionist rural policy, closer land settlement, state loans for farmers, a renewed public works programme to service the rural economy, and an improvement in the standard of farming. The programme required a return to state borrowing, at first to finance loans to farmers and soon to finance public works. Borrowing was anathema to Reeves and to other urban radicals, who remembered the excesses of the Vogel era and the burden of debt it bequeathed. The new Liberal policies began to be implemented with the Advances to Settlers Act in 1894. Under the Act farmers could borrow from the state upon security at reasonable interest rates. The state, in its turn, raised the money by overseas loans. In 1895 Ward — ebullient as Colonial Treasurer and in private life a reckless financier not above using political power for personal advantage — negotiated overseas a 3 per cent loan. He came back to a hero's welcome. Politics had returned to the familiar path of borrowing for development. Loans to settlers, the acquisition of estates for closer settlement, a vigorous policy of Māori land purchase for sale and lease to settlers, and the construction of roads, bridges, and railways dominated the Liberal programmes. The towns were intended to benefit in their turn from this stimulated and expanding rural economy, and with the return of prosperity in the late 1890s they did. The Liberal policies also fostered private subdivision of land; this together with refrigeration (rather than direct state intervention) was responsible for the transformation of large parts of the North Island into small dairy farms. By such means the Liberal Party consolidated its rural support.

The strength of the Liberals also depended on the success of Seddon and McKenzie in establishing a firmer discipline, both in Parliament and throughout the extra-parliamentary organization. The victory of 1890 had been achieved by the activity of local Liberal groups, especially in the cities. Stout had built upon this in 1891 with a Dunedin-based National Liberal Association. Ballance's preoccupations, however, were parliamentary, and local organizations continued to take the initiative in areas of policy formation and candidate selection. Seddon adopted a new role, that of dictatorial party boss, in an attempt to unify the party. In 1894 he rejected a set of radical policy proposals put forward by the Auckland Liberal Association as a 'very nice little pill' but 'not one that he could swallow':[22] thereafter he imposed his will by reserving to himself the final voice in candidate selection. In 1899 he formed the Liberal and Labour Federation, a nation-wide political organization intended to systematize and centralize electoral management.

Seddon's dominance in the House was facilitated by an inept and leaderless Opposition. John Bryce, who headed the retrenchment and free-trade faction, replaced Atkinson as Opposition leader, but he resigned after four months. His successor, the aloof and ponderous Canterbury farmer William Rolleston, lost his seat in 1893. W. R. Russell, who reluctantly accepted the leadership in 1895, seriously promoted coalition so that 'prudent men acting at strategic moments'[23] might curb Liberal excesses. The emergence of Stout as the harshest critic of the Liberal Ministry raised the prospect of an anti-Seddon union under Stout's leadership, but, when this lapsed, personal abuse of the Premier and criticism of his administration took precedence over the creation of an alternative political programme. Although Seddon's methods were an affront to the social sensibilities of the old propertied élite, the legislation of his party did not seriously disturb them. The lease-in-perpetuity was an optional tenure and posed no threat to existing freehold; the chief beneficiaries of the Advances to Settlers Act were established farmers who were able to re-finance existing debt and improve their farms. Seddon was, on a realistic assessment, the most effective bulwark against radicalism that the Opposition possessed.

By the end of the century the Liberals had become, in comparison with any previous political grouping, a party with mass organization and a strong leadership. The Lib-Lab Federation united regional associations into a body with a national conference and a national council, and for the first time New Zealanders could become members of a political party by paying a subscription. Effective power still rested with local notables in the electorates and with Seddon at the centre, but a model for future party structure had been created.

The style of leadership also altered. Grey stumping the country in 1879 had been denounced by observers. But Seddon, beginning as Minister of Public Works in 1891, became a popular public figure. He was tall and stout; he had a powerful voice and an unending flow of words; he delighted to manipulate crowds and to endear himself to individuals. In and out of Parliament he was a full-time, professional politician, enjoying the exercise of power and using his popularity to maintain it. He dominated Parliament, the Liberal Party, and a sufficient majority in the country. Even so, by the time of his death in 1906, his and the Liberal hegemony were under serious threat.

Although the Liberal Government after 1900 was frequently embarrassed in Parliament by maverick independents and small groups of dissident radicals, the real threat to its stability came from the emergence of a powerful new pressure group in the electorate — the alliance of large and small rural property-holders. As they became more established, the small farmers, whether state leaseholders or freeholders, became less satisfied with the Government which had, in many cases, helped them to begin farming. There arose, in the early twentieth century, a chorus of rural complaint which combined demands for the freehold, free trade, free access to Māori lands, better and more roads, bridges, freedom from government inspectors, and security from the threat of trade unionists and socialists. In particular, the freehold became a rallying point for established and aspiring property-holders alike, both freeholders and leaseholders.

These grievances were given an organized form in 1899 when dairy farmers in Taranaki and the far north launched the New Zealand Farmers'

Union. It spread rapidly, especially in newly opened North Island districts where the lack of roads and of credit was most keenly felt. In some districts more established farmers assumed the leadership. Though the Farmers' Union claimed to be non-political, it quickly became politically effective. High office in the Union was a powerful advantage to rural candidates. Union branches more often endorsed the candidates of the governing Liberal Party than those of the Opposition until the 1908 election, after which it became clear that a Government deeply divided on the issue of the freehold could not satisfy rural demand, and Farmers' Union support swung to the Opposition. Within Parliament, Liberal advocates of the freehold and of the leasehold lived uneasily together. Seddon fully appreciated the political dangers of the alliance between large and small rural property, and tried in vain to head it off. Ward, Premier after Seddon's death in 1906, did as little as possible, but the striking Liberal victory in the 1908 election was more apparent than real and was followed by the accelerating disintegration of the Liberals. The Farmers' Union drew together the ranks of rural conservatism, which increasingly gave support to a new political grouping — the Reform Party led by W. F. Massey.[24]

In the first half-dozen years of the century Seddon faced urban as well as rural discontent. In 1902, heartened by the success of the Farmers' Union, employers formed a New Zealand Employers' Federation. Regional associations of employers had appeared during the maritime strike, and Reeves's I.C. and A. Act encouraged their formation. Opposed to the introduction of compulsory conciliation and arbitration, employers regarded subsequent factory legislation as 'most socialistic and ruinous'. They were especially critical of the 'meddlesome' influence of the Labour Department, which had been established in 1892. Its first Secretary, Edward Tregear, was held to be antagonistic towards all employers. He would not be satisfied, employers alleged, until there was 'one employer only and that employer was the state'.[25] Tregear's intentions were not so aggressive. He envisaged his Department as a 'benevolent bureaucracy' serving as a buttress between capital and labour.[26] But when he sponsored a move to extend the powers of search granted factory inspectors to inspectors of awards, employers responded by appointing a 'vigilance committee' to keep a watching brief on all industrial legislation. They felt too that they needed a permanent organization in Wellington to represent their interests within the arbitration system. The Farmers' Union was broadly sympathetic to an alliance with the Employers' Federation, but sectional differences in the end ruled out the merger. The distance between urban and rural propertied interests had, however, narrowed, adding to the support for Massey's Reform Party.

Disaffection from the Liberals amongst wage-earners, which had begun in the mid-1890s, continued, and in this the changing administration of the Arbitration Court had a part to play. After 1900, as the Court became both slower and more parsimonious in its deliberations, the wage-earners' share in mounting prosperity diminished. As real wages declined in the early years of the century, the Court became the chief target for the labour movement it had helped to fashion. The arbitration system also fostered the growth of small unions: by 1907 there were 290 registered unions with 45,614 members, but nearly half the unions had fewer than fifty members. This multiplication of unions was denounced by those union organizers who sought to direct the growing industrial force towards new and radical ends.

Union officials, nonetheless, soon learned to use the arbitration system to their advantage. They sought first to establish universal preference for unionists, thereby giving unions control over employment under each award and gaining some protection against competition from immigrant labourers. In the 1890s the Court granted preference in some cases, and the 'closed shop' was established to a degree. By the early twentieth century some unions were demanding wage increases to keep pace with a rising cost of living, and asking the Court, in setting wage levels, to introduce an element of profit-sharing. Unions objected to the Court's tendency to measure worker claims against both the ability of individual industries to pay (when their profitability was low) and the impact wage increases would have on the economy. The employers possessed superior technical competence in the presentation of evidence to the conciliation boards and the Arbitration Court: to minimize their disadvantage, union leaders sought to extend the Labour Department's authority to examine employers' records.[27]

The growing legalism and delays of the Court frustrated the labour movement, which began to question both arbitration and the political alliance that produced it. Union restlessness had led to talk in 1898 of an independent labour party; it was partly in response to this that Seddon had set up the Lib-Lab Federation. The Old Age Pensions Act of 1898 was to some extent intended to satisfy workers' demands. But although he was Minister of Labour after Reeves, Seddon paid little real attention to labour matters. The frequent amendments to the I.C. and A. Act were in general unfavourable to unions. By 1904 labour problems required more direct action and the Trades and Labour Councils set up the Political Labour League, which supported several Labour candidates in the 1905 and 1908 elections. Still, Seddon retained the loyalty of most wage-earners and his death in 1906 made it more difficult for the Liberals to retain this support. Labour leaders doubted Ward's ability to reform the arbitration system.[28]

Labour disenchantment provided fertile ground for the radical critics of the Liberals. In 1901 socialist groups joined to form the tiny New Zealand Socialist Party. They attacked the arbitration system, which they saw as a splendid capitalistic device for keeping the workers in subjection. They set out to destroy capitalism and chose the strike as their weapon. This required a reorganization of the entire labour movement. In place of the multiplicity of small unions, the socialists envisaged a federation of all workers organized according to industry rather than craft, an aim that had been foreshadowed in 1890 by the Maritime Council. Any dispute could then be transformed quickly into a general strike. There could be no more fundamental attack on liberalism; this was the language of class warfare.

The advocates of class made most headway in the raw and isolated coalmining communities of the West Coast. From the coalfields Patrick Hickey, a New Zealander with recent experience among American syndicalists, and two young Australian socialists, P. C. Webb and Robert Semple, led an assault on the arbitration system. In 1908 at the Blackball mine they successfully carried a strike in defiance of the courts. Victory encouraged the militants and in the same year they formed the Federation of Miners, which adopted almost entirely the syndicalist doctrine of the Western Federation of Miners of the United States. This stressed the efficacy of industrial rather than political activity and sought social revolution. In 1909 other unions joined with them in the national Federation of Labour, the so-called Red Federation, which urged member unions to opt out of the arbitration system. Registration under the 1878 Trade Union Act would allow them to strike with impunity. Most affiliating unions sympathized with the militants' strong anti-arbitration stand but did not share the revolutionary enthusiasms of the Red Fed leaders. The rank and file preferred the reform offered by the Arbitration Court, for they valued the protection of its awards. To employers, however, the radical rhetoric of the leaders seemed a direct menace.[29]

Despite the Red Feds' declared contempt for politics, they created an almost insoluble dilemma for the Liberals, and especially for the new Premier, J. G. Ward, who was already regarded with suspicion by conservative country backbenchers. It was largely to allay their fears that Ward proclaimed a 'legislative holiday' in 1908, trying to silence opposition by avoiding contentious issues. He could not afford, however, to alienate labour. His inability to take any firm line with the Red Feds left him open to taunts of being 'soft' on socialism, and a rejuvenated Opposition was thus provided with an election-winning formula.

Providing fuel for the mounting discontent with the Liberals was the expansion of the civil service in the early years of the twentieth century. Under the Liberal administration, twelve new departments had been created, the most important of which were the Departments of Agriculture and Labour. Work in fields such as health and education had also been extended, and the number of civil servants had dramatically increased. These departments interacted with local officials and interest groups to give considerable scope to 'men with programmes',[30] professional civil servants who shared, articulated, and sometimes transformed the intentions of their political masters. Remarkable among them was Edward Tregear, the first Secretary of Labour, who did not merely administer the Reevesian programme but moulded and extended it. He built up a detailed body of legislation and an efficient department which controlled three important areas — conditions of work, industrial relations, and employment. By 1908 the Labour Department, of which Tregear had been in 1891 the sole member, employed eighty-three full-time staff and used in addition a host of policemen as employment agents and factory inspectors. Reform in education led also to centralization and administrative growth. George

Hogben became Secretary of the Department of Education in 1899 and by the First World War had greatly improved the national primary school service by removing the power of appointment from local authorities. He also expanded the secondary system and introduced technical education.[31]

The extension of state regulation and its concomitant, an enlarged civil service, drew complaints that New Zealand was drifting towards government by bureaucracy. The Farmers' Union and the Employers' Federation both vigorously condemned the Labour Department. The Department's efforts to improve accommodation for shearers and its strict surveillance of factory legislation hit the employers' pockets directly. By contrast, the labour movement welcomed the extension of the Department's powers. The Farmers' Union, too, actively sought the assistance of the Department of Agriculture, although dairy farmers sometimes found inspectors irksome. Opposition members alleged that property-owners were disadvantaged by the growing dominance of the state in the economy. Wage-earners, they claimed, were taught 'to "stand in" with the Government if they wished to be remembered in the distribution of loaves and fishes'.[32] The Government was accused of stacking the civil service with 'temporary permanent clerks', especially in the Railways and the Post Office where entry was not governed by examination. With the Premier a Catholic, the question of political patronage was linked also with sectarianism.

The Opposition took full advantage of this dissatisfaction. Their leader from 1903 was William Massey, a small, 'almost suburban' farmer from Mangere, who had been involved in colonial politics since 1891. A staunch defender of *laissez-faire* capitalism, he had opposed Liberal legislation as unnecessary state interference and he was a leading figure in the ultra-conservative National Association. These attitudes placed him to the right of the new generation of small farmers who had begun by the late 1890s to move away from the Liberals. Massey read the signs of change less accurately than some of his colleagues but eventually abandoned his earlier positions. He came to adopt a prudent attitude to borrowing that in effect meant continuing the level established by Ward. By advocating an increase in the graduated land tax in 1907, he was seen to be discarding his old allies, the big landholders. His strong stand against the Blackball strikers allowed him to pose as a defender of 'true liberalism', holding the line against revolutionary socialists. Ward by his indecisiveness, said Massey, had betrayed the Liberal heritage.

The Opposition became more organized for the 1911 election. Massey was their first full-time politician. He stumped the country, fashioning a reputation as a credible alternative to Ward. Fear of the socialist menace united the Opposition and attracted the Liberal right-wing. He dropped the rural demand for free trade, and so drew the support of urban businessmen, many of whom were dependent on tariff protection. The link between rural and urban property was cemented in 1909 when Massey chose an urban title for his predominantly rural party. The label was borrowed from an independent Christchurch organization, the Political

Reform League, concerned primarily with such urban issues as purifying the civil service of Liberal nominees and its allegedly large Roman Catholic element. Massey as a Protestant Ulsterman needed no instruction on such views. Property had re-grouped under a leader who offered protection from socialists and a more efficient administration of the Liberal dispensation.

Despite Reform's improved prospects, the politics of the first decade of the twentieth century are better seen in terms of Liberal decline. Many farmers and residents of small country townships in districts opened up in the 1890s shifted allegiance to Opposition candidates as their districts became more established and as their demands and grievances grew. But they did not do so in sufficient numbers to cause any significant turnover of seats until the 1911 election. In the towns and mining districts, Labour presented another threat. The weakness of the Liberals' position was demonstrated by their introduction of the second ballot. Where no candidate secured an outright majority, there was to be a further contest between the two at the top of the first poll. Ward calculated that narrow Opposition wins, with Labour running third, would be turned into Liberal victories by re-routing Labour votes. This system, which was abolished in 1913, in fact worked against the Liberals more often than not.[33]

The 1911 general election produced a stalemate; neither Ward nor Massey gained a majority, though the Reform Party made considerable gains. Ward resigned, and when Parliament met in 1912, the conservative Thomas Mackenzie led the Liberal Government into defeat. On a motion of confidence Massey gained the support of enough right-wing and independent Liberals to defeat the Government. Among those who crossed the floor were the embittered J. A. Millar, the leader of the maritime strike in 1890 and a firmly anti-militant Minister of Labour under Ward, and a handful of country Liberal members who had committed themselves to the freehold cause. So ended twenty-two years of Liberal rule, in bitterness and division. The change was not much more than one of administration, which confirmed the conservatism of the electorate, the predominance of country interests, and the continuity in New Zealand politics.

The Government led by Massey reflected his party's reliance upon urban and rural property. The Cabinet was roughly divided between city and country members, chiefly urban professional men like the lawyers F. H. D. Bell and A. L. Herdman, and rural gentry like W. H. Herries and R. H. Rhodes. The country members were not new farmers from the backblocks but the 'old guard' who had resolutely opposed the Liberals throughout the 1890s. Outside Cabinet, Reform's parliamentary team was dominated by self-made men who wanted office and who, like Massey, had little sympathy for city unionists. The scene was set for a confrontation between the Government and the Red Feds. Urban wage-earner unrest was by now widespread. Rural settlement, which had been the mainstay of so much Liberal reform, had never been much more than a dream to city-dwellers. Increasing land-values, the freehold option, and speculation had removed the profitable farm from the reach of all but those with substantial private means. A new generation of wage-earners was growing up in the poorer suburbs and inner-city areas with political expectations that were essentially urban.

The violence with which conflict erupted nonetheless shocked all parties. In May 1912, just before Reform came to power, an industrial dispute had broken out at the Waihi gold-mine. The goldminers had affiliated to the Red Federation and Semple's advocacy had won wage increases and improved conditions. These successes convinced sufficient doubters within the union for its leaders to withdraw from registration under the I.C. and A. Act, thereby giving goldminers the freedom to strike. In protest, a group of some forty engine drivers within the industry formed their own union with the intention of registering under the Act. The Red Feds feared that the engine drivers would negotiate an award that, under the terms of an amendment to the Act, introduced by the Liberals, could be applied to all workers in the industry: the entire work-force could thus be driven back to arbitration. The miners threatened to strike unless the company dismissed the engine drivers. The employers refused, the miners struck, and when Reform came to power the dispute was unresolved.

Massey was determined to drive the strikers back to arbitration. The police took a 'particularly combative stance',[34] calculating that a sudden sharp clash between strikers and arbitrationists would produce a quick settlement. Shots were fired, a policeman injured, and a striker clubbed to death. H. E. Holland, an Australian socialist fresh from the industrial battlefields of Broken Hill, put the Red Fed reaction succinctly in *The Tragic Story of the Waihi Strike* in 1913: 'The outburst of outrage and lawlessness at Waihi was undeniably planned by the mine-owners, with the Government for aiders and abettors.'[35] His words enshrined the events of Waihi in labour mythology. The Red Feds also drew more practical conclusions from their defeat: a militant industrial strategy could be crushed between the sectional interests of craft unionists and a government determined to establish the Arbitration Court as a new province for law and order.

In 1913 the various segments of the labour and socialist movements began to draw together. The Red Feds summoned a 'unity conference' in July, from which emerged two new organizations, the Social Democratic Party and the United Federation of Labour. Together they were intended to unite the workers, the one in politics and the other in industry. The UFL was a less radical industrial organization than the earlier Federation of Labour. Gone was the objective taken over from the revolutionary American body, the Industrial Workers of the World, and in its place was a pledge to assist the overthrow of capitalism by strikes. Even this was too much for the more moderate unions, who withdrew. The new federation was hardly established before it was asked, in September, to assume control of a dispute between Wellington watersiders and their employers. The Red Fed leaders of the UFL preferred negotiation but the rank and file wanted action. Reluctantly the executive called a general strike. Seamen, watersiders, and coalminers struck. Massey treated this as a trial of strength. 'Massey's Cossacks', mounted police specially recruited from the farming districts, rode in thousands into Wellington to open the port and clear the strikers from the streets. There were ugly clashes and blood was shed. Drunken 'specials', it was alleged, ran amok in Post Office Square and Buckle Street, batonned bystanders, and recklessly discharged revolvers.[36] In December the unionists gave in. The Red Feds and their methods were discredited; 'law and order' was restored.

Massey followed up his victory in the streets with legislation. The Police Offences Amendment Act (1913) restricted picketing and the Labour Disputes Investigation Act (1913) was passed to prevent unions registered under the 1878 Trade Union Act from striking without penalty. Confronted by an apparently aggressive Government, the Red Feds quickly shed their professed contempt for politics. There was general support for greater labour involvement in politics, but considerable opposition to the Red Feds' leadership of the SDP. The Trades and Labour Councils, which had formed a New Zealand Labour Party in 1910 and successfully promoted two candidates in the 1911 general election, rejected the radicals. Despite the division, the SDP achieved some electoral success; Paddy Webb, ex-president of the Federation of Labour, won the Grey seat and the ardent prohibitionist, James McCombs, was elected for Lyttelton in by-elections during 1913. The SDP's fighting platform reflected its union origins and its awareness of the needs of wage-earners. Demands grew for the accurate measurement of the wages of labour and the cost of living, the provision of workers' homes, and a network of welfare legislation.[37] War brought more sharply into focus the social cost of government policies directed by men of property and provided the final impetus towards the formation of a working-class party.

The outbreak of war in August 1914 helped to embitter politics. The country went to the polls in December after a campaign in which personality and point-scoring were more conspicuous than policy. Reform set the tone with a 'khaki' campaign drawing on patriotic fervour. Ward, Massey said, was hand-in-glove with the Red Feds and needed the support of the Social Democrats to win office. He insinuated that the Liberals were disloyal, claiming that the headquarters of their Social Democrat allies was in Berlin. An informal election agreement between the Liberals and the SDP to prevent a split in the anti-Reform vote gave some weight to Massey's charge. Ward, who had resumed the Liberal leadership, countered by distinguishing between 'sane' and 'revolutionary' labour and announced a wide-ranging programme of reforms. Labour was divided between militant Social Democrats, the moderate United Labour Party, and various independent candidates. Memories of Waihi and 'Massey's Cossacks' produced acrimonious urban campaigns. In Ponsonby, Massey was greeted by a 'howling mob' who slashed the hood and tyres of his car. Mounted police were required to clear a path for his departure. The election result was virtual stalemate. It was six months before the state of the parties was clear. Finally, forty-one Reform members faced thirty-nine on the Opposition benches, including six Social Democrat and Labour members. The crushing of the 1912–13 strikes did Massey less harm than expected in the cities and he gained votes in the countryside by the granting of the freehold option to lease-in-perpetuity tenants and by his strike-breaking, which restored the shipping of primary exports.[38]

Ward was determined to take advantage of the confused political situation which followed the poll. He was encouraged by public demands for politicians to put aside party politics and, like Britain, form a national coalition. In August 1915, after several months of mean-spirited jockeying for party advantage, Ward and Massey reluctantly formed a joint war-time administration. It was a formula for frustration. Ward shared all but the title of Prime Minister yet retained his position as Leader of the Opposition. The decision to require unanimous Cabinet decisions hindered administration; contentious issues were shelved and necessary innovations were abandoned by default.

Throughout the war the National Government faced severe domestic problems. By 1919 real wages had reached their lowest point since the turn of the century. Farmers, however, profited from the commandeer system, under which the British Government purchased New Zealand's chief exports. Massey thought farmers were entitled to all they could get: 'to pay them less would be to confiscate part of their earnings.'[39] Ward, conscious of his need to retain urban support, did not regard profits as sacrosanct. As Minister of Finance, he brought down a Cost of Living Bill, which established a Board of Trade with powers to investigate and report on price movement but not to fix prices. Some Liberal MPs criticized the legislation and their complaints became more vocal as Government inaction further compromised their standing in the cities. They also denounced the 'utterly selfish and unpatriotic dairy farmers' and wanted the Government to commandeer the wheat crop. Dr H. T. J. Thacker, the outspoken and popular Liberal member for Christchurch East, publicly repudiated both his party and its leader. The unease of Liberal city members grew as labour activity intensified.

In the working-class suburbs of the main centres, labour groups campaigned against profiteering, against the rising cost of living, and against a system which allowed 'cockies and capitalists to prosper while others fought in their place'.[40] The process by which Labour emerged as the party of urban protest had begun. At first, protest was widely based. Clergymen, scandalized by rampant profiteering, joined trade unionists and Liberal and Labour politicians in demanding a more equitable sharing of the burden of war. The decision by Labour's parliamentary representatives to stand aloof from the Coalition and form themselves into an organized group furthered their claim to be the true parliamentary Opposition. The war, moreover, drove labour groups together: economic grievances made an alliance with radicals more acceptable to moderate labour. In July 1916 the New Zealand Labour Party was formed.

If any one single issue brought labour groups behind the party it was military conscription, which was introduced in 1916. Labour argued that confiscated war profits, if applied to improving soldiers' pay and conditions, would make conscription unnecessary. Reaction to Labour's campaign against conscription was almost hysterical. Conservatives branded all opposition to conscription, radical or mildly critical, as disloyal. It was but a short step to regard criticism of the Government as obstructing the war effort. In the furore, Liberal MPs drew back and Labour emerged as the party of urban protest. The election of Red Fed leaders Bob Semple and Peter Fraser to Wellington seats in by-elections late in 1918 confirmed Labour hopes and Liberal fears.[41]

While his party remained in coalition with Reform, Ward could do little about the Labour threat. When the war ended he quickly withdrew and offered the electorate a radical programme. Reform denounced Ward's opportunism and his failure to maintain a united front against the socialists. Massey put himself forward as the defender of the middle class — in his view almost everybody not in the ranks of organized labour — against the excesses of Labour or 'Wardism'.

The 1919 election was the most difficult Massey had to face. Of the three party leaders, he stood to suffer most from the shortcomings of the war-time administration. Party organization had atrophied and Reform went to the polls on its record as a loose confederation held together by Massey's personal prestige. War-time by-election successes, in contrast, had raised Labour's expectations. Harry Holland, now party leader, sought to drive the other two parties together. The real struggle, in his view, was between capitalism and socialism, but the socialist millennium could not be achieved overnight. As a beginning, Holland promised to 'secure every immediate improvement within the bounds of possibility'. Labour candidates stressed 'improvement' rather than 'transformation' in the campaigns. They were consciously establishing their claim to be legitimate heirs of Ballance and Seddon, especially where urban radicalism was entrenched. In Christchurch, Labour spokesmen had built their war-time urban campaign around a programme of municipal socialism. They promoted publicly owned trading schemes for bakeries and butcher shops as the soundest way of controlling the cost of living.[42]

It was five years since politicians had faced the electorate. The convergence of sectarianism and prohibition in the Protestant Political Association formed in July 1917 increased acrimony. Led by a fanatical prohibitionist Baptist minister, the Rev. Howard Elliott, the PPA was created to fight 'rum', 'Romanism', and 'rebellion'. Elliott assumed the existence of an alliance between the Labour Party and the Catholic Church and set out to destroy it. He alleged that while patriotic Protestants were doing their duty, Catholic 'shirkers' were organizing politically to control the country. Elliott expressed the growing resentment of a significant number of Protestants at what seemed to be growing Catholic assertiveness. The *Ne Temere* papal decree of 1908, which held that marriages involving a Roman Catholic were valid only if performed before a priest, produced bitter exchanges between Protestant and Catholic leaders. The rivalry between the Protestant Bible-in-Schools League and the Catholic hierarchy in their efforts to influence educational policy reached its peak in the pre-war years. The exemption of the Catholic clergy from conscription was a further grievance and there was the old allegation that Ward had stacked the civil service with Catholics. By 1919 the PPA claimed a membership of over 200,000 and Elliott boasted that it was the most powerful political party in the country. Whatever its numerical strength, Massey, who as an Ulsterman privately shared its views, was sufficiently impressed with its potential as a vote-winner to negotiate an informal alliance.[43]

The election was a resounding victory for Massey: Reform won forty-six seats, the Liberals twenty, and Labour eight. The mandate was, however, more qualified than it appeared. Reform won only 36 per cent of the votes, and although it remained the 'premier farmer's party' its percentage of rural votes fell. But the Liberals suffered most. Their radical programme alienated support in the countryside, where they lost ground to Reform, but came too late to arrest the drift to Labour in the cities. Only in the smaller towns, especially in the South Island, did the Liberals retain their support. Ward's defeat in Awarua left the party without effective leadership. The chief political beneficiary of the war was Labour, which trebled its 1914 vote and received 24 per cent of the Dominion total. Holland was nevertheless disappointed that the net return was a mere eight seats. He had predicted that Labour would emerge as the dominant party or at least hold the balance of power. Labour's support was too thinly spread in the countryside and too concentrated in working-class suburbs to be registered adequately in newly won seats. But Labour had arrived as the urban party of protest.

The next three elections followed the pattern established in 1919: the existence of three major parties and a considerable number of independent candidates, and a fairly high and fluctuating level of non-voting indicated a period of political uncertainty. In terms of seats won, the results were clear: Reform won in 1919, 1922, and 1925, and lost in 1928. Its representation in the House rose and fell, however, far more than its share of voter support, and the same is true of other parties. This disparity was caused by the participation of more than two major parties in an electoral system in which the leading candidate wins irrespective of his percentage of the vote. The Liberals too were in some disarray, campaigning as National in 1925 and merging into a more or less new party, United, in 1928. Nevertheless, the Liberals, as well as the better organized and more effectively led Reform and Labour Parties, had a considerable basis of support throughout the decade. A sectional analysis of voting shows the parties to be much more evenly balanced than the numbers of MPs each managed to have elected would suggest.[44] Reform was strong in city, town, and country, though always strongest in the country. The Liberals' strength in the towns and the country remained considerable; it fell away sharply in the cities, however, as Labour increased, until 1928, when its recovery there was at the expense

219

of Reform. Throughout the four elections Labour gained more support in the cities than any other party, and secured a respectable fifth of the voters in the towns. But it was weak in the country areas, except those districts with a mining or timber-milling population.

Though each party had a solid base of sectional support, there was still a good deal of instability at the electoral level. As the Liberals had largely abandoned their flirtation with radical reform, there were now two parties of the *status quo*, and voters moved in some numbers between them. Liberal and Reform kept a solid conservative majority of voters behind them throughout the decade, and, as the Coalition, maintained it in 1931. Both parties subscribed to conventional political wisdom and regarded farming as the central economic activity. If farmers were prosperous, other sections of New Zealand society would also be prosperous by 'spin-off'. This analysis ran counter to the facts of social change. It has been estimated that, between 1911 and 1926, 40 per cent of all New Zealanders changed their place of residence from rural to urban, by migrating to the cities or simply by living in a rapidly growing town. Nonetheless, large numbers of urban voters continued to think in terms of policies directed at the countryside.[45] During and after the war there were powerful electoral pressures to make the Dominion a land 'fit for heroes to live in'. Returned soldiers were to be put on the best farms the state could buy for them or on land they could buy for themselves with government loans. A few Labour voices questioned the assumptions behind this attempt to revive a Liberal ideal. James McCombs of the SDP pointed out that country workers were only 20 per cent of the Expeditionary Forces and wanted to know whether industrial workers or shop assistants would be set up in small businesses.[46]

The prosperity that sustained the rural policies of the Reform Government came to an abrupt end in 1921–22. Dairy farmers, especially those on recently acquired marginal pumice and bush land in the Auckland province, demanded cheaper credit, marketing controls, and reduction of mortgages. These demands were accompanied by attacks on urban middlemen allegedly manipulating Reform Party policy for their own ends. Some Auckland dairy farmers were sufficiently alienated to talk of a separate Country Party, and they threatened to co-operate electorally with Labour.

This agrarian radicalism was strongest among the dairy farmers of the far north and did not move far from its regional base. Beyond these limits the Country Party remained a threat rather than an active political organization: sectional interests among farmers were so distinct that they could not co-operate for long; rural activists had to contend with an ingrained regionalism; and all but the most ardent agrarian radicals were brought into line by reminders that independent Country Party candidates would dangerously split the anti-Labour vote. Nevertheless, Country Party candidates contested a handful of North Island seats at each election between 1925 and 1935. By virtue of an informal alliance with the Liberals, their leader Captain Henry Rushworth won the Bay of Islands seat in 1928. Despite limited electoral progress the Country Party was effective as a pressure and protest group.

The appearance of the Country Party compelled Massey to make a series of strategic concessions to his rural supporters. In 1921–22 he introduced the Meat Export Control Act which established a board to handle beef and mutton exports, and a further Act of 1923 to regulate the dairy export trade. He responded less quickly to demands that the state provide extensive cheap credit. It was his successor, J. G. Coates, who through the Rural Advances Act of 1926 created a new section of the State Advances Department with power to raise funds by the issue of bonds and to apply the money to rural loans on first mortgage. Coates also provided for limited short-term loans with the Rural Intermediate Credit Act of 1927. These measures did little for dairy farmers in trouble but they effectively neutralized the Country Party threat.[47]

The interests of urban wage-earners took second place to those of farmers in the 1920s. After the 1921–22 slump, the staff of the Public Service was trimmed and wages were cut by between 7 and 10 per cent. The I.C. and A. Act was altered to allow the Arbitration Court to take into account the 'economic conditions affecting any trade or industry'. In May 1922 the adjusted basic wage was reduced by 5s. per week. Faced with what many came to see as an act of aggression by a 'cockies' Government, urban wage-earners looked to Labour to protect their interests. The slump tended to polarize political opinion in the cities at the expense of the Liberals. In the 1922 general election Labour nearly doubled its city seats, which rose from seven to thirteen, and increased its parliamentary strength to seventeen. The Liberals, who campaigned badly, won twenty-four seats, but the Liberal Party was a shadow of its old self. A few of its members went over to Massey, giving him an overall majority. Politics, so Holland hoped, would soon be reduced to its essentials — a contest between the representatives of capital and those of labour. Reform suffered heavy losses, and with thirty-eight seats Massey was forced to rely upon wayward Liberals to remain in power. This made him receptive to the notion of an anti-Labour alliance; but it was to be another decade before Holland had the two-party contest he wanted.[48]

Despite an improved showing at the polls, formidable obstacles still barred Labour's way. The anti-conscription origins and militant past of the Labour Party's Red Fed leaders deterred those still attached to the Lib-Lab alliance. Moreover, just as one generation of militant unionists was accepting the need for political organization, another emerged determined to advance labour's cause by industrial means. The Alliance of Labour, led by James Roberts, which drew together coalminers, seamen, watersiders, and other transport workers, was formed in 1919. Its supporters hoped that the Alliance would ultimately encompass all unionists, organized into industrial departments. Militancy was to fade in the face of growing unemployment, but a lengthy coal strike in 1919 seemed to presage a return to industrial conflict.[49] The new wave of syndicalism also affected rural interests more directly than had the Red Feds. In 1917 agricultural and pastoral workers and freezing workers formed national unions. Recruiting drives by the

Alliance of Labour (aimed at bringing all country workers together in a single union) antagonized farmers. Unionists were seen as the vanguard of a party whose ultimate objective was to confiscate property.

The 1922 election had clearly demonstrated that without rural votes Labour could never hope to govern. The problem of finding an acceptable land policy haunted Labour leaders throughout the 1920s. Holland's world was urban and industrial and he displayed little interest in rural matters. He assumed that the socialization objective included land nationalization. In 1919 the Party had spelt out its attitude to land, to the confusion of its own candidates and the electorate. Land tenure was to be one of 'occupancy and use'. Whatever the difficulties of this phrase, the intention that land was only to be sold 'to or from the state' was clear enough: a Labour government would gradually nationalize all privately held land. This conviction was strengthened by the removal of the words 'or from' in 1924. To Labour candidates, the land programme was 'a hell of a grill to toast a candidate on when the audience is hostile'.[50] As in 1922, farmers generally rejected Labour in the 1925 general election. Reform increased its representation to fifty-six; Labour lost five seats, reducing its strength to twelve; and the Liberals, who faced the electors as the National Party, slumped to nine. The rebuff compelled Labour to look afresh at its rural policies.

Labour's efforts in early 1927 to 'support and defend the working farmer in his everyday grievances and disabilities' implied that the existing basis of land ownership and the concept of state assistance to farmers had been accepted. When Holland presented the new policy to North Island dairy farmers he linked it with an advocacy of dairy export control, which he alleged was being undermined by a government hostile to controls and acting in the interests of London speculators. Labour argued that the periodic slumps in prices for primary produce could only be banished when there was an assured market and prices were guaranteed. By 1928 Labour had begun to grapple with the real problems faced by struggling small farmers.[51]

The moderation of land policy was part of Labour's transformation from protest party to credible alternative government. The Labour Party that was to win office in 1935 was shaped by three men with few peers among New Zealand's political leaders — Harry Holland, Walter Nash, and Peter Fraser. Unschooled but widely read, they were, like most Labour politicians, immigrants. Holland's upbringing in the Salvation Army and an apprenticeship in the Sydney labour movement combined to produce an amalgam of idealism and mental rigour. As leader of a protest group, Holland was unequalled; his idealism and faith in Labour's cause were an inspiration. Nash, an English Christian Socialist with greater patience than Holland for the necessary tasks of organization, presided over the construction of what has been described as 'New Zealand's first modern political organisation'.[52] By the mid–1920s the quality of Labour organization far surpassed that of its opponents. Together with Fraser, a dour but politically shrewd Scot with an increasing interest in welfare policies, Nash greatly influenced the direction and pace of policy change.

Holland's role in policy formation was minimal, but his influence in shaping opinion in the electorate was considerable.[53]

Armed with its new rural policy Labour approached the 1928 general election expectantly. Many commentators predicted a straight battle between Labour and Reform: instead the rank outsider, United (a new party incorporating the Liberals), won more seats than any other party. Throughout the 1920s the Liberals had drifted aimlessly under a succession of ineffective leaders, including T. M. Wilford and G. W. Forbes. Only months before the election they turned to Sir Joseph Ward, now in his seventies and MP for Invercargill. In a fit of nostalgia, the electors opted for the most successful formula of the past: borrowing for development. Ward, his eyesight now badly failing, had misread his speech notes and promised to borrow £70 million immediately instead of over ten years. The error won the election.

United's victory was primarily a rejection of Reform, and especially of Gordon Coates, its leader. One of the generation of young farmers who had broken in farms in the far north, Coates had entered Parliament in 1911 as an Independent Liberal. With three other freehold colleagues he crossed the floor the following year and helped bring down the Liberal Government. A distinguished war record hastened his rise within the Reform Party. In the Massey Ministry of 1919 he held several portfolios, including that of Native Minister, and established a reputation as a vigorous and innovative Minister of Public Works and of Railways. Whereas Massey remained an essentially nineteenth-century politician firmly committed to free enterprise, Coates was prepared to use the power of the state. He brought in the first child allowance in 1926, providing state payments to low income families with more than two children.

But Coates was unable to satisfy both rural and urban supporters. In 1925 he had been advertised as a saviour by New Zealand's most unscrupulous electoral organizer, A. E. Davy: the voters were urged to get their 'Coats off with Coates', the man who gets things done. By 1928 disillusioned dairy farmers were claiming that Coates had failed to break the vicious circle of falling returns, fixed mortgage repayments, and increasing costs. Many rural voters considered that Reform had become a tool in the hands of its urban allies. Businessmen in turn resented promotion of state activity by a man who had promised 'more business in government and less government in business'. In 1928 Reform's business supporters began to move against Coates, and some turned to the new United Party, which sought to unite the Liberals and all elements of the anti-Coates protest under Ward. Active in the campaign was the ubiquitous Davy. Disillusioned by the growth of state power under Coates, he now used his talent as a political entrepreneur to promote another leader.[54]

Thus Coates lost the 1928 election. But by giving Ward thirty-four seats (including four independents) to Reform's twenty-nine and Labour's nineteen, the voters created a United government unlikely to prove stable. It soon became apparent, too, that the United Party had little to offer.

Unable to borrow and failing in health, Ward simply waited. His inaction alienated Labour members who held him in power, but they were reluctant to withdraw their support for fear that Reform would replace United and, under pressure from the Farmers' Union, attack wages. Labour withdrew its support for United soon after Ward resigned in May 1930. His successor, G. W. Forbes, has been castigated as New Zealand's least impressive twentieth-century prime minister. His rigidly orthodox policies made fusion between United and Reform more certain, and in 1931 these two parties formed the Coalition Government with Forbes as Prime Minister. The British example of a National Government created to deal with the Depression of the 1930s strengthened the argument that New Zealand was confronted by a national emergency as urgent as that of war, which had produced a coalition sixteen years before.

The alliance of the opposing parties brought little immediate advantage to the Labour Party. Holland feared that it might be thrust into power in circumstances that would make it impossible to implement Labour's policy. Party policy held that full employment could best be achieved by establishing a central bank, floating an internal loan, and fostering closer land settlement. There was a new emphasis on industrialization as a means of alleviating unemployment. Party members were, however, divided as to how these goals could be achieved. The Party 'presented a cacophony in all but its opposition to deflation'.[55] Some wanted increased taxation, a few like John A. Lee wanted a note issue, while official policy favoured internal development loans. Against this, the newly formed Coalition asked the electors in December 1931 for a blank cheque. Responsible men, they claimed, could not 'commit themselves in advance to details of policy'. Holland's refusal to join the Coalition was put forward as evidence of Labour's opportunism and continuing disloyalty. Despite the difficulties of apportioning some constituencies between Reform and United candidates and a rash of dissatisfied Independent Coalition candidates, Forbes and Coates won the 1931 election with fifty seats to Labour's twenty-four.

The Coalition victory was less convincing than it looked. Labour's gain in seats was accompanied by a sufficient increase in voters to give it greater popular support (though not in rural districts) than either the Reform or the United components of the Coalition. Further, non–voting increased considerably, and so did voting for independent and Country Party candidates. This fragmentation of the conservative vote offered clear warning to Forbes and Coates: unless they arrested the dissatisfaction among their supporters they could be destroyed by losses to both the right and the left.

The economic crisis deepened. So too did sectional animosities in Coalition ranks. The urban and rural wings clashed openly over the Government's decision to devalue. Farming interests had for some time advocated a higher exchange rate and they had considerable support within the Coalition, where country Reform members were the dominant group. Devaluation was resolutely opposed by the Minister of Finance, W. Downie Stewart, the sole urban voice in Cabinet. He took the view that interference with the exchange rate was improper and contrary to the spirit of the Ottawa Agreement reached by Commonwealth Governments in August 1932. Ultimately, however, the clamour for devaluation could not be resisted; in January 1933 New Zealand devalued and farmers were thereby awarded a notional bonus. Stewart, as he had earlier threatened, resigned; Chambers of Commerce up and down the country protested vehemently. Whatever its merits, devaluation provided a rallying point for disaffected Coalition supporters.

It was as a result of devaluation that the ultra-conservative group known as the New Zealand Legion emerged. The initial impetus for the Legion was provided by dissatisfied Reform Party men, many of them established sheep farmers opposed to state interference, who had been overlooked as Coalition candidates in 1931. They were joined in the early months of 1933 by businessmen and professionals. The Legionnaires advanced old-fashioned *laissez-faire* views. There was nothing new in their repetition of the old formula — more business in government and less government in business — and nothing more outdated than their desire to end state paternalism. New Zealand's difficulties were regarded as moral and political rather than economic. The Legion itself soon disintegrated, but in the 1935 general election at least six ex-Legionnaires stood as candidates for the ultra-conservative Democrat Party which, by splintering the conservative vote, increased the size of Labour's majority.[56]

There were other rifts appearing among Coalition supporters. The struggling dairy farmers who had flirted with the Country Party during the 1920s demanded more rather than less government action. For many of them the Coalition's attempts to aid farmers (devaluation, a series of mortgage adjustment Acts, lowered interest rates, and reduced freight rates) offered too little and came too late. The paradox of poverty in a land of plenty drew their attention as never before to the economic system. Experts and governments seemed as bankrupt of ideas as they were of money. Overnight every man became his own economic theorist and groups preaching monetary reform multiplied. The most popular and significant was the Douglas Credit movement. Its analysis of the economic catastrophe and the proffered cure were disarmingly simple. By the nature of things, according to Douglas Credit theory, the community's purchasing power always fell short of production costs. The gap was bridged by banks which charged excessive interest. The state itself should intervene and stop the profiteering by issuing free or cheap credit. An attractive theory, it appealed particularly in rural areas and country towns. The distribution of the movement's rural membership corresponded closely with the pattern of dairy-farming regions. In 1932 the Auckland Farmers' Union (which covered roughly the northern half of the North Island) adopted Douglas Credit as its official policy. The movement also struck a responsive chord in the less prosperous middle-class suburbs in the cities, and by 1935 there were 225 branches throughout the country.

Labour was to be the chief political beneficiary of the heightened interest in monetary reform. Since the late 1920s the Labour Party had been endeavouring to gain a foothold in the countryside by placing greater emphasis upon rural credit. The immediate reaction of the Party to the 'free credit' proposals was somewhat ambivalent. To orthodox socialists, monetary reform did no more than tinker with the capitalist system. To Nash, more informed on the realities of the New Zealand economy, the monetary reformers under-estimated the extent to which the country's fortunes depended upon the British market for primary produce. He favoured guaranteed prices for farmers and bilateral trade agreements with Britain as the basis for a mildly inflationary programme. But there was a strong group of credit reformers in the Party and they influenced official policy. After 1933 Labour emphasized monetary reform in terms scarcely distinguishable from Douglas Credit.[57]

If the Coalition's orthodox and somewhat dilatory response to the Depression worked to Labour's benefit in the countryside, it prepared the way for an electoral landslide in the cities. The defence of farmers' incomes was undeniably important to New Zealand, but the Coalition policy of giving it priority over even the minimum welfare of wage-earners, was an act of social aggression. Deflationary policies in an already contracted economy produced inevitably a further contraction of employment and income. By July 1933 an estimated 81,000 people, or 12 per cent of the work-force, were jobless.[58] As important as unemployment, and indeed partly a cause of it, was the Government's attack on wages. Early in 1931 Forbes cut civil service salaries by 10 per cent. He then introduced legislation empowering the Arbitration Court to amend any award before expiry if economic circumstances warranted. In June 1931 the Court reduced all wages by 10 per cent. The following year Forbes gave in to farmers' clamours for compulsory conciliation and voluntary arbitration so that wage rates could be adjusted. The I.C. and A. Amendment Act destroyed the myth that the Court was independent and aloof from political pressures. It was followed by wholesale wage cuts, for whenever conciliation proceedings broke down the Arbitration Court could only be approached with the consent of both parties. Without this consent, awards lapsed after one month and employers could impose wages and conditions as they liked. Civil service wages were again lowered on a graduated scale, although most fell by 10 per cent.

The combination of unemployment and Government intervention rendered trade unions almost powerless to defend the interests of their members. Radicals and communists denounced union officials for accepting too readily conditions imposed by their employers and by the state. But union leaders had to match words with deeds and most chose to keep their organizations intact. Those few who heeded radical counsel did so with limited success. The coalminers, who declared a national stoppage in 1932, limited wage reductions in their industry to 10.8 per cent; at the same time their union lost half its members and those who remained worked irregularly in the pits. Similarly, when freezing workers refused to accept substantially reduced rates (between 16 and 66 per cent) for the 1932–33 season, the unionists were vanquished. Their employers recruited non-union labour, established company unions, and introduced the American 'chain' system of slaughtering. Defeats such as these chastened the advocates of direct action and united trade unions more firmly behind the Labour Party.

The chief victims of conservative policies were the unemployed. The Coalition's treatment of the jobless alienated many of its supporters. Government policy on unemployment was dominated by Forbe's conviction that the 'dole' was demoralizing: the jobless should work for their benefits. The Unemployment Act of 1930 established a fund financed by a special tax of £3 per year on every male over twenty. Provided they had paid their levy, the jobless were to be given work on schemes organized by the Unemployment Board. Initially no sustenance money was paid to those for whom work could not be found. As the numbers of unemployed grew, it became more and more difficult to find suitable work. Under Scheme 5 the Unemployment Board paid the wages of men employed on special work carried out by local bodies who provided materials and transport. The scheme encouraged labour-intensive projects that were frequently little more than make-work. Wages were reduced, work was rationed, and camps for single men were established in country areas, but by 1932 the Government's unemployment programme was in tatters.

Nearly half the registered unemployed were in the four main centres. This poverty was more than local charitable relief agencies, both public and private, could handle. In desperation some unemployed took their grievances into the streets, where protest erupted into violent rioting on a scale unprecedented in New Zealand's history. In January 1932, after a deputation of women had been denied food, several hundred starving unemployed marched on Wardell's grocery store in Dunedin, smashed a window, wrecked a van, and dispersed only when promised food. Unrest reached its peak in Auckland. On 14 April an organized protest march, called to denounce wage cuts and the Government's treatment of the unemployed, ran amok. When the 20,000 strong body reached the town hall chaos developed; an unemployed leader, Jim Edwards, was injured by a policeman's baton, whereupon thousands careered down Queen Street smashing shop windows as they went. There were ugly clashes between the unemployed and 'specials', men hastily enrolled as constables to restore law and order. Similar, though less violent, outbursts followed in the other main centres: Wellington rioters smashed 160 windows along Lambton Quay; in Dunedin a tram was set alight; in Christchurch a tramway strike gave rise to attacks on property and person. Yet for all the bitterness of the clashes they were in essence spontaneous, shortlived, and confined to the main centres.[59]

Forbes denied that the riots were an expression of genuine unemployed protest, but held that they were the work of a 'lawless minority' or Communist agitators. He introduced legislation that increased the Government's power to deal with them. The Public Safety Conservation Act, rushed through Parliament immediately after the Auckland and

Wellington riots, empowered the Government to proclaim a national emergency when public safety and public order were, or were likely to be, imperilled. The Finance Act of 1932 included a section which enabled 'disloyal' public servants to be dismissed. Punitive action was also taken against unions, such as the Post and Telegraph Association, which had actively protested against public service wage cuts. The panic measures drew criticism from a variety of organizations and individuals, and confirmed many in the belief that Government inaction rather than Communist activism was the cause of social disorder.

Although Communists were active among the unemployed and relief workers, their influence was minimal. In 1931 they formed the National Unemployed Workers' Movement as a trade union for the jobless and an organ for political protest. It encouraged relief workers to strike and to take their grievances into the streets. As leaders of the jobless, however, the Communists were at a disadvantage. Formed in 1921 the Communist Party was a tiny, faction-ridden body. Its greatest strength had been in the remote coalfield communities of the West Coast, but even there it was on the wane. Communist support among the unemployed was most marked in the secondary centres and rural areas where the Labour Party was least organized and relief rates at their lowest. Despite the spontaneous nature of the 1932 riots, the violence and destruction was used by conservatives and Labour supporters alike to discredit the Communists. By 1934 the pro-Labour National Union of the Unemployed had gained control of the unemployed, at least in the four main centres.[60]

As the politicians prepared to face the electors in 1935, few envisaged a Coalition victory. Neither Reform nor United had kept an effective organization alive between elections. The Coalition, encouraged by the size of its combined vote in 1931, took no steps to weld together its two parties. The sectional divisions (especially the rivalry between town and country) evident in conservative ranks throughout the 1920s had been stretched to breaking point by the Depression. The electoral mistrust that had hindered Labour's progress meanwhile diminished. Labour extended its support away from its working-class base into the ranks of white-collar and previously sceptical middle-class voters and began to seek the public support of religious leaders. At first, most churchmen regarded the economy as outside their domain, separating moral and socio-economic questions. The riots brought this distinction into question, especially in Methodist and Catholic circles. Some condemned the Coalition's 'political ineptitude and indifference',[61] and thereby undermined its support. Labour welcomed such implicit support for the legitimacy it bestowed upon its programme. Many Labour supporters, indeed, believed that they were fighting a moral crusade. They saw their party as a political embodiment of practical Christianity.[62] The death of Harry Holland, the old socialist preacher, in 1933 and his replacement by Michael Joseph Savage opportunely confirmed this new image. The Government's jamming of C. G. Scrimgeour's radio gospel programme, 'The Friendly Road', signified to many the Coalition's moral bankruptcy. Compared with the Coalition and with the new Democrat Party, Labour was well organized, with numerous and active branches, electorate representation committees which included the trade unions, a programme of financial and welfare measures, and strong leaders. It possessed an enthusiasm that more than made up for its relative lack of funds, and an idealism which appealed to a wide range of public feeling and proved more than enough to counter the almost total hostility of the press. The party of the urban wage-earner stood ready to take office as a broad-based party of reform.

CHAPTER 9

Economic Transformation

Tom Brooking

In the mid-1890s New Zealand entered an era of prosperity that was to last until the beginning of the 1920s. As wool prices gradually rose and the expanding dairy and frozen meat industries began to profit from improved prices on the London market, business confidence and internal investment recovered. The Liberal Government took some steps to assist recovery: the rescuing of the Bank of New Zealand in 1894 helped to restore business confidence; overseas loans reactivated development projects and made cheap credit available; a certain amount of protectionism and a rural credit programme possibly helped to stimulate internal demand. But these policies were implemented against a background of rising prices on the international market. The Liberals fostered rather than created prosperity.[1]

By the end of the 1890s the full impact of refrigeration was beginning to be felt, and it produced significant changes in the economy. There were now three staples in the export sector — wool, meat, and dairy produce — instead of the single staple, wool. (See Graph 4.) As a result, small-scale stock farming assumed increasing importance. In many respects, farming enjoyed a 'golden age' from the recovery of the late 1890s to the depression of 1921. Popular mythology has it that the struggling pioneer farmer reigned supreme, but in reality it was the established and more substantial farmers who prospered most. These men were only 'small' farmers in comparison with the big pastoralists of the mid-nineteenth century; they dominated the export sector and wielded a disproportionate political influence. The power of these small farmers in politics was greater in the first two decades of the twentieth century than it ever had been or ever would be again.[2] Their horizon clouded briefly in 1907–8 and in 1912–13, but rapidly cleared again.

Prosperity in this era was, however, unevenly distributed. Wage-earners generally fell behind many farmers and self-employed businessmen, and unemployment ran at surprisingly high levels. Up to 10 per cent of the work-force was probably unemployed in an intermittent and seasonal manner in the years preceding the First World War. Although this figure is slight compared with the perennial third unemployed in Edwardian England, it reveals that not all New Zealanders benefited from the rising export receipts.[3] The industrial militancy of the years 1912–13 is to be understood in the context of significant unemployment and a growing gap between prices and wages.

Had it not been for the outbreak of war in 1914, New Zealanders might have been forced to modify their dependence on the British market and to diversify; for by then the British market offered little scope for expansion.[4] Instead, high prices and guaranteed sales induced by the commandeer system (guaranteed prices set at high levels by the British Government in return for a monopoly over all exports of New Zealand's primary products during and after the First World War) encouraged New Zealand to concentrate further on the three staples and the British market. (See Graph 5.) With the help of settlement schemes for returned soldiers, rural land values shot up, farmers' cheques suddenly enlarged, and the general atmosphere of prosperity during the war helped to consolidate the pattern of economic development that had emerged in the early 1900s.

When the boom came to an abrupt end in 1921, largely as a result of the commandeer system ending and the international economy adjusting to post-war conditions, shock rippled through New Zealand society. An entire generation had come to assume that improvement was inevitable. Now adversity made an unwelcome reappearance in 'God's own country' and hardship was real. Rehabilitation schemes for soldier-settlers were rudely interrupted and many of these new farmers were forced off their land. The number of bankruptcies increased dramatically and unemployment rose. People became suddenly aware that New Zealand, like Britain, was not 'a land fit for heroes'.[5] The 1920s were a time of widespread disillusionment and political instability as well as economic insecurity.

The depression of 1921 was the first in a series of recessions and recoveries that lasted until 1930. In response to the crisis, a reputedly conservative Government introduced schemes for marketing control. The Government's participation in export marketing, partial though it was, marked the beginning of a significant shift in the economic system. By 1923 the economy was improving, and some of the benefits of the American boom of the mid-1920s could be seen in the growing number of motorcars and consumer goods that found their way into the country. Land speculation revived, if less dramatically than during and immediately after the war, and the Coates Government of 1925–28 implemented a large public works programme, building roads, railways, and hydro-electric power stations. Agricultural production also increased considerably over the 1920s as farming became more mechanized and farmers applied improved techniques. Even so, by 1926 New Zealand's real economic plight was only disguised by an increase in borrowing that prevented recession from sliding into depression.[6]

The growth of farming early in the century was accompanied by a decline in the importance of the extractive industries within the economy. In some cases this decline was absolute as well as relative. Kāuri gum production reached a peak in 1903 and then declined steadily. Milled timber ceased to be an important export, but increased production was absorbed in the local building industry. Coalmining expanded chiefly to provide fuel for the growing railway system. As railway construction slowed down in the 1920s, and later, as the use of electric power grew, the industry lost its importance. Goldmining retained some of its significance as an export industry until the First World War. There were considerable technological innovations, notably the use of dredges on alluvial fields and chemical processes in the quartz mines. But supplies of mineable gold ran out. No other usable sources of metals were discovered; the lack of iron, in particular, precluded large-scale industrialization.[7]

The growth of the tertiary sector in the late 1920s gave New Zealand at least a superficial resemblance to other Western countries. In 1896 approximately 42 per cent of the work-force was engaged in the primary sector (agriculture, mining, forestry, fishing, quarrying), 22 per cent in the secondary sector (manufacturing, construction, processing, power supply), and 36 per cent in the tertiary sector (services, white-collar work). In contrast, the figures for these sectors in 1926 were 30 per cent, 25 per cent, and 45 per cent. While these figures have been disputed, the growth of the tertiary sector, at the expense of the primary, is clear.[8] Much of the activity in the tertiary sector was productive, but New Zealand continued to rely almost exclusively on agricultural products and on the British market for its overseas income. Even before the Depression of the 1930s, the character of New Zealand had assumed a definite form — a predominantly urban nation dependent upon farming for economic survival. New Zealand was still Britain's outlying farm, even though it exhibited many of the demographic and sociological characteristics of an industrialized society.

This continuing dependence upon agriculture made New Zealand extremely vulnerable to the drop in prices for primary produce in 1929 and 1930. Borrowing no longer offered a solution. Although depression did not arrive immediately after the Wall Street crash, New Zealand's geographic isolation could not protect the country for long. In 1930 the overseas deficit rose alarmingly and business confidence crumbled. Disillusionment spread rapidly as farmers' incomes continued to fall despite their spectacular increases in production. The Depression of the 1930s had a major impact on the country's development, both in the short and the long term. Many (but by no means all) New Zealanders suffered genuine hardship between 1930 and 1935, although their suffering was not as great as in some other Western countries. Such economic improvements as increased savings and a reduced external deficit from 1933 did not affect the everyday lives of New Zealanders until many years later, and the country expressed its deep-felt dissatisfaction at the ballot box in 1935. In fact, the Coalition's leaders, especially Gordon Coates, were not committed to a classical *laissez-faire* philosophy, and were prepared to use state machinery to assist recovery. But orthodoxy helped to offset their more positive actions, and their obvious reluctance to provide assistance proved electorally disastrous.

Fluctuation is the pattern of the economy's course in the first half of the century: repeated recovery and recession arising from the condition of the international market. But although prosperity came and went, primary production continued dominant throughout. Its importance diminished beside the expanding secondary and tertiary sectors, and methods of agriculture changed significantly, but the restructuring of the economy took place largely through innovation and alteration in primary production. The following discussion thus centres on farming, on land, and on associated policies: first, kinds of farming and of landholding; secondly, the impact of science and technology, and reforms in marketing and organization; thirdly, the provision of credit and the move toward closer land settlement. Although the state remains peripheral, its actions touch on every aspect of economic life, and here attention is given particularly to its role in the provision of transport and power, and to its fiscal policy. Finally, the growth of the secondary and tertiary sectors is covered. The Depression of the 1930s draws together threads from preceding decades and reveals the dominant trends of New Zealand's economic life over the period.

The years after 1900 were marked by the growth of dairying and of mixed wool and fat-lamb farming, and the comparative decline of specialist wool-growing. Successive censuses show the number of dairy farms and dairy farmers rising steadily. The number of dairy farmers in 1891 was minute, and they represented a tiny fraction of all farmers. By 1901 there were nearly 5,000 and the figure had trebled by 1911, when about a third of all farmers classified themselves as dairy farmers. The major growth occurred during the first decade of the century. Arable farming and mixed cropping became relatively less important, except in Canterbury and Otago, and in those provinces arable farming turned increasingly toward meeting internal demand rather than the export market. However, the shift to intensive farming was more marked than that towards specialist farming, and 'mixed farming' remained an important category until well into the twentieth century. It was a gradual shift; growing internal demand during the 1870s stimulated dairying and fat-lamb farming and the same decade saw large amounts of land subdivided into smaller units.[9] After 1900, the trend towards intensive farming was firmly established. Small-scale farming became commercially viable. Prior to the 1890s a man required many sheep or a sizeable herd of cattle to make a living;[10] by the turn of the century a surplus could be earned from a few hundred sheep or a handful of dairy cattle. Subsistence farming, which had been widespread, became less common.

These smaller units were predominantly family farms. The 1926 census showed that 60 per cent of New Zealand farmers hired no labour, and farmers outnumbered rural labourers. These farmers relied entirely on their own labour and that of their families and neighbours. Small wonder that rural fertility rates remained high until the 1930s, or that most farmers favoured mechanization.[11] 'Relatives assisting' remained an important category in the agricultural work-force throughout this period. Family farming fostered egalitarian attitudes and was one of the factors making New Zealand a more mobile society than Britain.

The rise of the small farmer did not, of course, mean the disappearance of the big pastoralists. The continuing importance of wool ensured their survival, and their place in the economy was secured by the fact that so much marginal high country could only be farmed in large units.[12] The pastoralists assumed a lower profile than in previous years, especially in national politics. They cut their holdings and flocks back to more manageable levels, cashed in on rising land values through voluntary subdivision, invested in urban real estate, and continued in considerable comfort even though the ostentation of their earlier lifestyle was reduced.[13] Their dominance in terms of ownership of the sheep flock was reduced only slightly and the Sheep Owners' Federation exerted great political influence. But despite their wealth and power, the New Zealand pastoralists differed from the English gentry in one important particular: their agricultural system was not based on leasing out land to tenant farmers. Like other new world élites, the New Zealand 'squattocracy' did not live amongst a subservient population of tenants and labourers whose deferential patterns of economic and social behaviour perpetuated old world aristocracies. Despite the political rhetoric of the 1880s, they never held a sufficient monopoly over freehold land to act as a true equivalent of the English squire.[14]

As stock farming was established, other possible forms of land use were neglected. Vast stands of timber were indiscriminately burnt off and no serious attempt was made at reafforestation until the 1920s.[15] Horticulture, which nineteenth-century visionaries such as Sir George Grey imagined would hold the key to New Zealand's future, was generally ignored. Along with other forms of highly intensive farming, such as viticulture and poultry raising, horticulture was only developed as the metropolitan centres grew. The majority of New Zealand farmers, with the exception of some in Canterbury, Otago, and Southland, chose to grow grass rather than trees, crops, or other plants until well after the Second World War. When the South Islanders grew grain and root crops it was as a rotational supplement to their stock–raising rather than as a specialization. Fish, New Zealand's other major source of animal protein, and much used by the Māori, was also ignored. As long as agricultural prices remained high, the harvesting of New Zealand's rich coastal waters was carried out on a small scale and in a haphazard fashion.

The growth of dairying accentuated the divergence between land–use systems in the North and South Islands, and between farming systems in lowland and highland areas. By 1900 the North Island had outstripped the South in economic growth and population. From the 1880s on, vast areas of the North Island were opened for settlement — Taranaki, Manawatu, Waikato, Bay of Plenty, Northland, and later the centre of the North Island. These new zones of settlement, which grew with the dairy industry, attracted the younger sons of South Island farmers. Migration from the South to the North Island became a constant feature of New Zealand life from the late nineteenth century.[16] As the land-hungry moved north, two distinct farming systems emerged. South Island farming continued on a larger scale and generally retained a more mixed character. South Island farms were also longer established, better drained and fenced, and, with the exception of a few bush clad areas such as the Catlins and the West Coast, clear of trees and scrub. Most North Island farmers had to burn off the bush before they could work the land. This often forced them to hold several part-time jobs, such as contracting, timber-felling, or road-building, until their farms became productive.[17] It was scarcely surprising that the two groups of farmers seldom saw eye to eye, even within such supposedly national organizations as the New Zealand Farmers' Union. Established North Island farmers, especially in the Manawatu, had much in common with their South Island counterparts. But this group was a minority; by 1926 one-third of New Zealand farmers, most of them small farmers, were to be found in the Auckland province.

Attitudes toward land tenure reflected differences between farmers. South Island farmers generally found the Liberals' lease-in-perpetuity tenure (or 999-year lease) satisfactory. Most of the expensive improvements had already been undertaken by the big runholders and the disparities between the original and improved values of their properties were not great. Low rentals (4½ per cent interest) instead of heavy mortgage commitments freed their capital for such purposes as buying more stock. In contrast, many North Island farmers wanted the right to purchase their leasehold properties at original valuation so that they could profit from their hard-earned improvements by selling at enhanced value. F. F. Hockley, a delegate to the 1911 Dominion Conference of the Farmers' Union, summed up their attitude when he said that any man who took up a lease-in-perpetuity section 'and put the best twenty years of his life on it . . . would feel that every penny of the increased value belonged to him'. So much sweat was expended in clearing the bush that the difference in the value between unimproved and improved land was considerable. As land values continued to rise, that difference widened, and substantial profits could be made by buying cheap and selling dear. There was, therefore, a strong economic incentive behind the agitation of North Island leaseholders for the right to purchase their leasehold properties at original valuation. The same motivation inspired many freeholders, especially in the North Island, who cast an envious eye on Crown and Māori lands adjacent to their own properties. If that land was made freehold, they could buy their way into it. But there was principle as well as profit behind the agitation for the freehold. Nearly every witness to the 1905 Land Commission made it clear that he or his father had come to New Zealand in order to own a piece of land and become his own master. They were also worried about the question of inheritance. Many felt that the leasehold without right of purchase would place their sons at a serious disadvantage in comparison with freeholders, for it was difficult for leaseholders to move onto more valuable property, and loans were hard to raise on land owned by the Crown.[18]

Yet despite the campaign of the North Island leaseholders and freeholders within the Farmers' Union, the response was lukewarm when in 1912 and 1913 Massey's administration offered farmers the right to freehold lease-in-perpetuity properties at almost original valuation. Only 559 out of a total of about 10,000 lease-in-perpetuity tenants, or 6 per cent, took up the freehold option immediately.[19] The tenurial controversy was principally related to a deep-seated fear of the land nationalization theories of urban radicals. Leasehold land, including pastoral lease of mountainous areas, in any case only constituted about a third of the total number of holdings. From the beginning of settlement the freehold had been the dominant tenure and this was confirmed with the reform of the tenurial system in 1913. The right of purchase provided farmers not only with the security of ownership but also with a guarantee that the land policies of urban radicals would not prevail.

The land speculation that had begun with the return of prosperity in the mid-1890s was further stimulated by the end of the leasehold. During the First World War the scale of speculation was such that it can only be described as gambling. Estimates indicate that half the rural land in New Zealand changed hands between 1916 and 1924, and in some areas matters may have been even worse.[20] The value of farm land became grossly inflated and new farmers, especially settlers on schemes for returned soldiers, were over-committed to massive mortgage repayments. They were safe as long as international markets remained buoyant; but the depressions of the 1920s and 1930s made them suffer for their own excesses and more especially for those of their predecessors.[21]

Behind the growth of small farming lay one of the most significant technological developments to affect the New Zealand economy — the development of refrigeration. A new era began in New Zealand farming when refrigeration enabled perishable foodstuffs to be delivered in good condition to distant markets. Introduced first in 1882 for the export of meat, by the 1890s it had also opened up the British market to New Zealand butter and cheese. And with refrigeration came mechanization, in the processing of farm products in freezing works and dairy factories, and eventually the mechanization of farming itself, especially dairying. The growth of dairying and fat-lamb farming, the triumph of the freehold, and the predominance of the family farm — all encouraged advances in farming technique. Mechanization of farming, which proceeded steadily from the later nineteenth century on, not only substituted capital for labour but also, with the help of new scientific procedures, increased productivity.[22]

The most significant reductions in agricultural labour were caused by the shift from cropping to stock raising, but from the late nineteenth century technological innovation began to lower labour requirements on New Zealand farms. In the 1870s the horse-drawn reaper and binder began to replace men at harvest time, and in the 1880s traction engines and mechanical threshing mills made an appearance. Both these machines were, however, fairly inefficient, and a greater contribution was probably made by local manufacturers of agricultural machinery in adapting less spectacular equipment, such as harrows and hay-making apparatus, to meet the particular needs of New Zealand farming. The introduction of mechanically powered shearing machines during the late 1880s meant that fewer shearers were required, while these smaller gangs could shear many more sheep than large gangs working with hand shears. The internal combustion engine made its impact only indirectly, as cars and trucks began to ease the isolation of farmers and provide fast transport for their produce. The tractor, apparently an instrument of change, was not used widely until after 1935: the 5,349 tractors of 1935 had more than doubled by 1940.[23]

Within the dairy industry the adoption of the hand-operated cream separator immediately before the First World War meant that far less time was required to convert milk into cream and allowed farmers to by-pass one entire phase in the production of butter. Instead of milk being sent to nearby skimming stations, cream could now be transported direct to the dairy factory, with a marked improvement in quality. Hand-separators also produced skim-milk, which enabled many farmers to supplement their income by raising pigs. Cheese production, because it depended upon supplies of whole milk, continued to be concentrated in small factories in districts served by good roads, such as South Taranaki.

The most significant advances in mechanization occurred in the 1920s with the advent of electricity in the countryside and the widespread adoption of the milking machine, driven by either electricity or petrol motors. The milking machine caused something of a revolution. Many more cows could now be milked by fewer people. Life became a little more comfortable for the farmer and his family, and productivity rose sharply. So that farms could carry a larger number of cows, pasture management had to improve. Farmers were encouraged to aggregate their properties into bigger units. It was the milking machine, in association with herd testing, that lay behind the spectacular increases in productivity of the 1920s.[24]

Providing both management and labour themselves, many farmers had little time for planning. The natural fertility of land which had never been farmed before initially kept productivity high and disguised haphazard management. By the late nineteenth century, advocates of scientific farming, such as James Wilson and members of the various Agricultural and Pastoral Associations, were aware that science could benefit more established areas, such as Canterbury or Manawatu.[25] The Department of Agriculture (set up by John McKenzie in 1891 to improve farming) worked closely with these associations. As time went on, the regulatory activities of the Department assumed increasing importance. Quality control was upgraded through the systematic grading and branding carried out at major ports. Growing numbers of farm inspectors were employed to ensure that cows were milked and milk stored hygienically so that it reached the factories in a good condition. The campaign against pest infestation and stock disease intensified and some attempt was made to protect the domestic consumer against diseased milk and meat. The test for tuberculosis in milk sold to the public was introduced in 1898, and in 1900 it became compulsory for all stock to be slaughtered in licensed abattoirs.[26] Beside these activities the Department's advisory services suffered. The major exception, however, was the *Journal of Agriculture*, founded in 1910 and thereafter very useful to the practising farmer. Under the Liberals, instructors were also appointed to the Dairy Division to hold short courses in the field, and demonstration farms were set up. But otherwise the Liberals' record in agricultural education was not impressive.

A fall in soil fertility in the 1920s required farmers to pay more attention to management and to seek scientific remedies. In particular, an outbreak of bush sickness in the central North Island made it clear that artificial fertilizers would have to be used scientifically and more attention paid to pasture management. For the first time, scientists in the Department of Agriculture and the Department of Scientific and Industrial Research (1926) began to work in continuous and systematic consultation with farmers. In the late 1920s Massey Agricultural College and the Dairy Research Institute were established to tackle agricultural problems scientifically. About the same time Canterbury's agricultural college at Lincoln (established in 1880) was upgraded. Individual scientists working in these three institutions helped farmers in their efforts to improve production. A young chemist in the Department of Agriculture, Bernard Aston, pioneered work on the pumice lands of the central North Island where bush sickness was rampant. His investigations opened the way for others to prove that it could be controlled by the application of cobalt fertilizers. The research of A. H. Cockayne and Bruce Levy, of the Grasslands Division of the DSIR, on nitrogenous clovers, pasture management, and the application of fertilizers continued the 'grasslands revolution' and enabled farmers to carry more stock. But the full benefit of their work was not realized until aerial top-dressing became standard practice in the 1950s. Scientists working for the Dairy Research Institute, in particular H. R. Whitehead and F. H. McDowall, also made advances in bacteriology relating to cheese production, which were of international significance. But once again the advantages of these discoveries were not fully realized until after the Second World War, when improved technology made their application widespread. Rising prices for exports at that time encouraged farmers to take more risks and try new techniques. At the same time more attention was directed to drainage and erosion and pest control.[27]

The first decades of the twentieth century failed to produce anything in the field of animal breeding as important as the dual-purpose sheep developed in the late nineteenth century. Both the Drysdale and the Perendale (named after F. W. Dry and Geoffrey Peren of Massey College) resulted from research in animal genetics started in the 1930s, but they were not commercially significant until after the Second World War. The dual-purpose Romney remained the dominant breed of sheep, and Jerseys became the most favoured breed of dairy cow. The older dual-purpose Shorthorn cattle largely disappeared and the proportion of the older and bigger breeds of sheep such as Border Leicesters, Lincolns, and Corriedales declined. Stock management and farming practices improved as the Department of Agriculture, the DSIR, and the agricultural colleges kept farmers abreast of discoveries in these fields, although the educational impact of these institutions was less than they would have liked.[28]

While more sophisticated farming techniques were improving production, the processing and marketing of agricultural goods also required a higher degree of organization in order to meet the demands of the market, both local and export. The control and operation of these branches of the industry changed significantly in the first half of the century. In general, small-scale, locally controlled, and relatively inefficient operations gave way to larger, more centralized, and efficiency-conscious enterprises that frequently employed overseas capital and expertise.

One of the notable features of New Zealand agriculture is the farmers' co-operative. This form of organization has been employed most frequently within the dairy industry, but there were also numerous attempts, most of them unsuccessful, to set up general farmers' co-operatives during the 1880s. (The two successful general co-operatives were the Timaru-based New Zealand Farmers' Co-operative Association and the Christchurch-based Canterbury Farmers' Co-operative Association.)[29] The work that these general co-operatives tried to do was normally discharged by the stock and station agencies or town-based middlemen: most, therefore, were superfluous. In contrast, by 1900 local control of the dairy industry rested firmly with the farmer-run co-operatives.

Many of the dairy co-operatives grew from enterprises begun by individuals with capital resources, such as Chew Chong, the famous Chinese pioneer of the Taranaki dairy industry. But individual was soon replaced by collective control as the industry continued to expand. Many small localities came to have their own dairy factory run by local farmers. These often started as little more than skimming stations supplying central factories, but as use of the hand-operated cream separator spread and transport improved, the scale of these enterprises grew and operations became more centralized.

By the early twentieth century a distinct regional pattern of financial control had emerged. In Taranaki proprietary or public companies, which were controlled by a mixed group of shareholders, predominated. Elsewhere, especially in Manawatu, Waikato, and Northland, marketing was in the hands of co-operatives which farmers controlled by holding the majority of shares. Divisions within the industry in the 1920s were due partly to this difference, but such distinctions were rapidly overtaken by another development — the growing power of monopolies. Despite their more democratic appearance, the co-operatives were even more prone to merger than the proprietary companies. Both companies and co-operatives amalgamated steadily after 1900, and by the early 1920s the Hamilton-based New Zealand Co-operative Dairy Company had developed into a giant. The company's managing director, William Goodfellow, could quite properly be described as a monopolist.[30]

In 1923 a national Dairy Board was set up to provide a co-ordinated marketing service for those farmers who chose to use it — although few did. The Board had also been given reserve powers of compulsion, and in 1926 it decided to use them. The suggestion that all producers should pool their produce for export and that the entire operation should be controlled by the Board incensed many proprietary companies. Several co-operatives also opposed compulsion, fearing further domination by the New Zealand Co-operative Dairy Company when Goodfellow was appointed to the Dairy Board. Demand and supply conditions further decreased the scheme's chance of success. When in 1927 individual New Zealand exporters and the anti-monopoly group on the Board reinforced the objection of English importers, merchants, and dairy companies to any interference, the Board backed down.[31] Opinion within the dairy industry was sharply divided: many farmers felt that the Board's failure confirmed the dominance of middlemen whom they considered to be parasitic upon the industry. New Zealand's first attempt at exercising greater control over the distribution of its dairy produce on the British market ended in failure. A decade later, in 1936, the first Labour Government implemented its scheme of state-controlled marketing and the guaranteed price. Pooling of produce was then revived, and local payouts were separated from overseas prices in an endeavour to insulate the dairy industry.[32] Several years of depression had persuaded dairy farmers that limited state interference was preferable to chronic instability of prices, and they responded favourably. As many were men of limited capital, stability of income would assist them in budgeting and future planning. The guaranteed price scheme offered some prospect of reliability even if it precluded large profits in the event of sudden prosperity.

In the meat industry, the early involvement of enterprising big businessmen and overseas investors created a different pattern for marketing and control. By the twentieth century, however, a growing number of freezing works were operated co-operatively by local farmers. Many of these enterprises were remarkably successful until the First World War, when shortages of shipping space brought problems. Under-capitalization also made it difficult for co-operatives to keep pace with technological innovations and to meet rising freight bills. As competition with the bigger public companies intensified, talk of the entry of overseas 'trusts' became alarmist. The Government itself was concerned about the adverse effect which trusts were supposed to be having on world trade and responded to the fears of the co-operative companies by setting up a parliamentary committee in 1917. This committee concluded, on the basis of slender evidence, that both the British firm Vestey Brothers and the American group Armour and Company were operating in New Zealand and engaging in unfair practices. No action was taken while the post-war boom continued, but once prices fell in 1921 both farmers and the Government found a ready scapegoat for their troubles — the 'Meat Trust'. New Zealand farmers seemed unaware that the large-scale investigations into the activities of these so-called trusts, both in America and in Britain, had produced little evidence of a sinister conspiracy to control the meat industry. The Meat Board was established in the midst of this outburst of anti-trust feeling and represented a move by many producers to have a greater control of their own destiny. Before it was established, the

Government implemented a Farmers' Union demand by denying Armours a meat-export licence. This action won Massey's administration much support from farmers, apart from the big pastoralists, many of whom were connected with overseas companies and wanted entry to the lucrative American market. In contrast to the Farmers' Union, the Sheep Owners' Federation supported the granting of the export licence to Armours and consistently opposed the introduction of producer boards.[33] Despite their powerful opposition, the Meat Board proved to be one of the successes of the 1920s, because it had the widespread support of producers and, unlike the Dairy Board, did not attempt to interfere with distribution inside Britain.

The big wool-growers, backed by the stock and station agencies and British wool-buyers, always dominated wool marketing. The notion of a wool board, introduced in 1921 by smaller farmers who were members of the Farmers' Union, was rejected, initially by the big wool-growers and later by Government.[34] Combined purchasing of wool for export has been proposed at various times since the beginning of sheep farming but each time it has been successfully opposed by the powerful producers represented first by the Sheep Owners' Federation and later by the Sheep and Cattlemen's Association. Regular cycles of prosperity and depression have continued to benefit them even though a greater degree of stability would have suited many smaller-scale wool producers.

Marketing reform, then, was most successful in the meat industry from the 1920s, and partially successful in the dairy industry in the 1920s, and only occurred in the wool industry at a much later date.

In applying science to farming and in setting up the marketing boards, the state played a considerable role in encouraging agriculture. It also acted more directly upon the economy through the promotion of closer land settlement and through the provision of credit.

Between 1893 and 1906, the period during which the state was most active, over 2 million acres of land were made available for closer settlement by voluntary subdivision, while only 1.3 million acres were made available through the lands for settlement policy. John McKenzie's victory over the runholders was political and symbolic rather than economic. His land tax scarcely hurt anyone, least of all the prospering pastoralists. Compulsory repurchase (from absentee landowners) was invoked only thirteen times between 1892 and 1910. Even then the full powers of compulsory purchase were employed only four times; on other occasions they were used as a threat. Many runholders sold up because it was to their advantage to do so. Banks, financial companies, and other absentee owners had generally come to regard their estates as liabilities by the late 1890s and were content to convert them into cash. As land prices continued to rise, more individual runholders decided to sell up. The shift from extensive to intensive farming was already underway, and the principal effect of McKenzie's legislation was to overcome inertia.[35]

The Liberals also transferred 3 million acres of Māori land to Pākehā

241

ownership in an effort to quench the insatiable thirst of North Island settlers. In 1893 McKenzie brought Māori land sales under government direction, partly in an attempt to end unscrupulous dealing. But in the long term, government monopoly hastened rather than slowed alienation. Māori land was bought at prices well below market value, and, as it was so cheap, many more settlers benefited from the acquisition of this land than from the break-up of the large estates. By 1929 the Reform administration had bought a further 3.5 million acres from Māori. Māori landowners rather than the 'squattocracy' were vanquished by the state's promotion of closer settlement. John McKenzie made a greater contribution to the development of New Zealand farming as Minister of Agriculture than as Minister of Lands.

Cheap credit for farmers was essential to closer settlement, and the Advances to Settlers programme of Sir Joseph Ward was intended as a corollary to McKenzie's land settlement policies. A settler needed capital resources to buy stock and improve his holding; farmers from humble backgrounds, once they had paid their rent, would have few resources until they established their farms, and the state was obliged to help by making cheap credit readily available. In practice neither the Liberal nor the Reform Government was as generous as they wished to be thought. Both administrations provided farmers with a large amount of money at low rates of interest (far too much, according to contemporary economists such as J. B. Condliffe and H. Belshaw). But credit was chiefly made available to well-established farmers and was frequently used for speculative purposes. Many witnesses to the 1905 Land Commission complained that loans were cheaper and more readily available from private lending agencies than from the Advances to Settlers Office. Lower-risk, established freeholders gained the much larger share of loans from the Office. Yet even they did not feel they were treated generously.[36]

The Reform Government (1912–28) made more elaborate provision for cheap credit. The Advances to Settlers Office was upgraded into the State Advances Department in 1913. During the 1920s more money was poured into the rural sector to pacify the growing demand for agricultural banks run as co-operatives. In 1922 the Rural Credit Associations Act was passed to allow small lending associations to be established. After a Royal Commission reported favourably on agricultural banks in 1926, the Government passed a Rural Advances Act in the following year to set up a new branch of the State Advances Department to make available funds for first mortgages. In 1927 the Rural Intermediate Credit Act provided more money for Co-operative Associations. A number of measures were passed in the 1920s to protect some farmers from foreclosure when unable to repay their mortgages. Yet farmers remained dissatisfied, and their dissatisfaction baffled a succession of politicians, for, as the 1925 Commission admitted, rural credit in New Zealand was cheap and abundant. However, the anxiety of farmers arose from their lack of control over the institutions providing credit, in a period in which costs were climbing. It seemed to them that banks, other financial agencies, and the

Government deliberately kept credit beyond their reach. Some of the more well-to-do as well as marginal farmers were susceptible to the propaganda of any party that promised cheap credit in times of depression.[37]

Cheap credit was, ironically, as much a cause of small, under-capitalized farmers' problems as it was a cure. Loans had to be repaid, even if they were obtained at low rates of interest. When export prices fell, many farmers were unable to meet their commitments. Speculation rather than improvement was too often encouraged amongst more established farmers, and struggling marginal farmers were too readily lured into debt. The state was prepared to help men onto the land, but if that land proved to be unfarmable or too far from markets to be economically viable, the farmer was generally left to his own devices. The pioneers were expected to suffer so that later generations should prosper. The apparent beneficence of successive governments was frequently tinged with an almost cynical disregard for economic reality.[38] Faith in the virtue of hard work usually prevented politicians and the public from considering whether a land-settlement programme or the release of more credit was practicable. The belief that hard work plus a little capital conquered any adversity was to lead many New Zealand farmers to the edge of disaster in the 1930s.

Many settlement schemes were inadequately served by roads and were too far from the railway to use it. The fate of entire districts depended on whether or not a road, railway, or bridge was built. Roads and bridges for rural districts thus tended to dominate local and national politics. After the 1870s the state came to accept most of the responsibility for providing this infrastructure. Public money spent on land settlement, the Department of Agriculture, or rural credit was insignificant compared with that directed towards the public works programme. Only the state could raise large overseas loans to cover the cost of road and rail construction. The state more than any other employer could provide the expertise and labour to implement public works programmes. The building of many railway lines and roads was let out to contractors but the state provided the money.[39]

The Liberal Government's first concern in transport was railway construction. Control of railways was centralized, and in 1893 they were removed from the control of commissioners (who also supervised the small number of private companies) and placed under ministerial direction. By 1896 the North and South Islands had between them 2,014 miles of line and by the First World War a further 969 miles. These lines opened up areas for settlement and created several new towns which, although often small and isolated, collectively made a significant contribution to the country's development. After the completion of the main trunk lines (in 1908 for the North Island and 1912 for the South Island) Government attention turned to roads. Railways were still built, and over 300 miles of line were brought into service during the 1920s.[40] But after the 1920s governments were more concerned with contraction than expansion in railway construction.

The growing importance of small farming and the increasing use of the internal combustion engine after the turn of the century made roads a priority. The Liberals were, however, slow in meeting the needs of many North Island bush settlers for roads. Numerous witnesses to the 1905 Land Commission complained of the appalling state of country roads, and Opposition MPs echoed the complaint. Much of Massey's political success was related to his promises to improve North Island roads. In office he tried to keep these, but despite his efforts many roads, especially in more isolated areas such as Northland, existed only in the imagination of departmental cartographers. New Zealand had 48,000 miles of formed roads by 1929, but too many of them were in the wrong places. In 1922 the Main Highways Board was set up by Gordon Coates in an effort, not at that time successful, to create an efficient national system of major roads. However, the counties, who were paid state subsidies in return for eliminating tolls, remained in charge and frustrated Coates by diverting funds away from major roads to purely country roads. Trucking and bus services remained principally in the hands of private companies although local authorities began to operate bus services to supplement municipal tram networks from the 1920s.[41]

Despite the improvement in roading, coastal shipping remained an important form of transport. Until the late 1920s it was still easier to travel from Auckland to Whangarei by boat than by car. Unlike land transport, both coastal and oceanic shipping was exclusively owned by private enterprise. As costs continued to rise, English, Scots, and Australian capital was brought in. During the First World War, English interests came to control two major New Zealand shipping companies, the Union Steamship Company and the New Zealand Shipping Company. Partly in response to this, the possibility of setting up a state shipping line was discussed during the difficult years that followed the First World War. Parliament agreed to appoint a committee to investigate the proposal when it was advocated by the Farmers' Union. But farmers lost interest once post-war shipping shortages ended, and the plan came to nothing. Foreign and private ownership continued to dominate this capital-intensive and very expensive form of transport.[42]

Air travel obviously had only a small part to play in transport during this period. Initiative was left to private companies, with the Government providing landing grounds at minimal cost. By 1939 there were nine commercial airlines, which carried a mere 60,000 passengers annually.[43] The advantages of air travel to an elongated group of islands were not fully realized until after the Second World War.

The efficient functioning of the economy required not only transport but also energy. In providing this part of the infrastructure the state again followed local initiatives. Gas production had been encouraged and controlled by local authorities since the 1860s; civic authorities in Wellington and Christchurch took over the generation of electricity in the 1880s, after a few enterprising firms had demonstrated its usefulness. By 1900 most of the main cities had electric street-lighting, and electric trams were rapidly replacing the older horse-drawn vehicles. Gradually hydro-electric plants came to supersede the older coal-fired stations and the Government took its first initiative in 1903 when it established monopoly over all future hydro-electric generation. Lake Coleridge, finished in 1911, was the first large-scale station to be completed. By 1915 it was supplying Christchurch. Electrification proceeded apace throughout the 1920s. The state built a chain of generating stations and the administration of power supply was placed in the hands of new power boards in areas that municipal authorities were unable to serve. Electric power supplied by the state was directed towards the area of greatest demand, the homes of New Zealanders. Manufacturing did not benefit to the same extent as it did in Australia. Indeed, some factories such as the Lower Hutt car-assembly plants chose to generate their own power. Some farmers also made a similar decision as the cost of electricity tended, as a result of transmission loss, to outweigh its advantages in more remote areas. By the end of the 1920s the use of electricity had spread much more widely in New Zealand than in most other countries. Both local and central government could take credit for this achievement, which made life easier for all New Zealanders, especially country dwellers. By the 1930s both the leisure activities and the domestic duties of urban and rural New Zealanders became more uniform.[44]

The state began to exert a more direct influence upon the economy as a whole in the 1930s under the stimulus of depression. Before 1933 governments did not pursue well defined fiscal policy and generally they followed developments in the trade cycle. Government expenditure and revenue none the less clearly made an impact, and occasionally even produced a counter-cyclic effect. The value of the New Zealand pound was always tied to sterling, but banks in New Zealand framed their credit policies, and thereby influenced import spending, on the basis of their funds in London rather than on their gold reserves. In response to the Depression in January 1933 the Coalition Government under the influence of Gordon Coates devalued the pound, altering the exchange rate to make £100 (sterling) worth £125 (New Zealand). By taking this step the Coalition established that the Government and not the banking system now had responsibility for changes in monetary policies.

Coates intended to increase farmers' incomes and thereby revitalize the whole economy. The Danes, however, interpreted the move as one designed to make New Zealand exports more competitive; they lowered their prices and increased their share of the British market. So New Zealand earnings from exports did not in fact significantly increase. Sheepfarmers benefited but dairy farmers did not. The consumer nevertheless suffered from the higher prices of imported goods. Coates had introduced devaluation against considerable opposition, and it certainly did not have the intended effect. The action had adverse political consequences for Coates and the Coalition, and its contribution to economic recovery is uncertain.[45]

The other major area of fiscal policy over which the state exercised control was taxation. Before the late 1920s income tax affected only a small number of New Zealanders and most taxation was indirect. The Liberals taxed only those on relatively high incomes. Similarly the Liberal land tax applied only to owners of properties valued at more than £500. Compared with their modern counterparts, taxpayers were few and got off lightly. Some changes were introduced during the First World War, including a super-tax on excess profits, embargoes on various exports, and, most significantly, a progressive income tax in lieu of the land and income tax. These additional burdens were deeply resented (especially by farmers who had to keep their own books) and most disappeared soon after the return of peace. The increased death-duties of war-time were retained, but did not reach a high level. The antiquated system of taxation lingered on, but it proved cumbersome and inadequate in the more complex post-war situation. In 1929 major reforms simplified the system and made it more comprehensive. Most wage-earners became liable to pay income tax, and the old land tax was replaced by tax that affected nearly all full-time farmers. The major exceptions were holders of small state-leasehold properties. Rates of company taxation were also raised and exemptions from company tax reduced.[46]

These changes, however, did not have a major effect upon the taxation system. Indirect taxes upon a wide range of articles in everyday use remained more important than direct taxes. Government revenue from both kinds of tax fell with the Depression. But once Labour came to power and expanded welfare services, taxation rates and revenue from tax rose dramatically. By 1938 the *per capita* rate was just over £23; in 1929 it had been a little over £12. Even allowing for improved wages, the increase was substantial. The new levels of expenditure on such capital-intensive social services as health and education committed the ordinary New Zealander to paying a much greater proportion of his earnings in tax. But in 1938 most were only too willing to undertake such a commitment in exchange for greater security.

Despite the state's intervention to rescue the Bank of New Zealand in 1894, banking remained largely free from state regulation until the Reserve Bank was established late in 1933. Banks were controlled by private enterprise, which was considerably influenced by overseas interests. Banking services were dominated, but by no means monopolized, by the six major trading banks. Ownership of these varied. The Bank of New Zealand was principally owned and controlled by New Zealanders, although London bankers had some influence. Australian interests were dominant in the Bank of New South Wales and the Commercial Bank of Australia (not set up in New Zealand until 1912). Both English and Australian investors held major interests in the Union Bank of Australia and the Bank of Australasia (which were to amalgamate as the Australia and New Zealand Bank after the Second World War). And the National Bank of New Zealand was essentially English with a substantial New Zealand shareholding. These banks issued their own notes and cheques, and from the early 1900s offered long-term as well as short-term loans. The Bank of

New Zealand was ahead of its rivals as it held all government accounts. The Bank of New South Wales was its most successful rival, followed by the National Bank. The other three trading banks were not particularly successful in New Zealand.[47]

While the trading banks offered the most comprehensive range of services and financed almost all imports, they were not without rivals in providing investment opportunities and loan facilities. Savings banks had been set up in the main centres as early as the trading banks; these made credit available and offered attractive terms of interest to their depositors. Their turnover was never spectacularly high but it was steady. The funds of the Post Office Savings Bank (established in 1867) in contrast were entirely at the disposal of the Government, so it could not lend on mortgages. Its government backing was considered, however, a good guarantee of security by many small-scale investors and its deposits rose steadily (apart from the worst years of the 1930s depression).[48]

In the rural sector the trading banks often took second place to the stock and station agencies, which not only provided short-term and long-term credit but also assisted farmers in marketing their produce overseas and in buying and selling stock, implements, and necessities. They sometimes played a more active role than banks as financial advisers and kept a close eye on the budgeting of individual farmers. After the Depression many farms were run by the agencies. Like the banks, they were by the 1920s more professional in their style of operation, offering technical advice in place of commonsense suggestions, using specialists instead of untrained members of family firms. Book-keeping, for example, was increasingly put in the hands of an accountant.[49] Some dairy co-operatives also carried out these functions of advice and assistance.

The other major source of credit was the insurance company. Both customers who paid premiums on their life insurance policies and general shareholders expected that their money would secure a high return, and from 1900 to 1930 this was provided by mortgage finance. Increasingly insurance companies invested in mortgages rather than government and local body securities. This shift was most pronounced in the case of the Government Life Insurance office (founded 1869), which, like the Bank of New Zealand in its field, came to claim the largest share of local life assurance business in the early twentieth century. After 1930 it moved its investment away from mortgage finance to local authority and private company loans. The other companies, like most of the banks, were dominated by Australian, Anglo-Australian, or English directors, and they also steadily increased their life assurance business. Much of the investment of these companies seemed to be directed towards building construction, although they provided a considerable amount of mortgage finance.[50] Friendly societies were a popular means of providing for retirement and they too provided a limited amount of private loan finance. (In 1937 there were 960 friendly societies and lodges in New Zealand, with some 112,880 members.)[51] The other major activity of insurance companies was the provision of fire, marine, and (after 1900) accident insurance. Once again the State Insurance Office, established in 1903, helped to foster competition and reduce premiums. All in all, New Zealanders were well provided with both life assurance and fire and accident insurance. They were among the most heavily insured people in the world by the 1920s.

Two other institutions within the private sector provided credit — building societies and chain stores. Building societies benefited from urbanization and the consequent increase in house building that began around the turn of the century and stepped up during the 1920s. Sometimes they were speculative and offered little security to either investors or borrowers. But the better-managed societies provided a useful alternative form of savings and supply of credit. They were, however, vulnerable to any decline in building and their members suffered in the early 1920s and the 1930s. By the 1920s, building societies were second only to the State Advances Department in supplying money for house construction and purchase.[52]

The local store had been a significant source of credit, especially in rural areas, from the beginning of European settlement. During the depression of the 1880s this role was reduced, and largely taken over by the stock and station agencies. But when the first chain stores were established in the early 1900s, a new source of credit became available in the towns and cities. Some of them began to offer hire-purchase and time-payment facilities. Although many New Zealanders brought up under orthodox Victorian morality remained wary, the marked increase in the purchase of consumer goods after the late 1890s was undoubtedly stimulated by the easing of purchase terms.[53] Private loans, especially from solicitors' funds and from relatives, have also been a constant source of credit, especially of bridging finance.

The exact relation of private to public supply of credit has not been calculated, but it is clear that the private sector provided more than the public, in both town and country. State provision of credit to farmers was constantly supplemented by advances from the trading banks and stock and station agencies, as well as from other private agencies.

While the state supplemented credit supply and banking and insurance services, it made little attempt to regulate commercial activity until 1930. The Depression, however, made it plain to even the most conservative politicians that stricter controls were necessary if the country was to reduce spending and lower its deficits, both internal and external. Treasury officials, the Government's adviser, Sir Otto Niemeyer, and most politicians agreed as early as 1931 that New Zealand required a central bank to act as the Government's banker and to separate the Australian and New Zealand economies. Both advisers and politicians felt that many London bankers associated New Zealand with Australia, an association disadvantageous for New Zealand in raising loans because of the mistrust of Australia among English financiers.

Although tradition claims that the Reserve Bank was created only after the progressive Coates had overcome the opposition of his more conservative colleagues, it had been contemplated since 1931. The Reserve

Bank was set up as a central bank overseeing the operations of the six trading banks, rather than as a state bank of the type demanded by both the Labour and Douglas Credit movements. It was little more than an ineffectual adviser to Governments until the first Labour Government nationalized the Bank in 1936, made it directly responsible to the Minister of Finance, and empowered it to vary reserve requirements. An Amending Act in 1939 further increased government control.[54]

The Labour Government extended its influence over the banking system to finance its recovery policies. These were aimed not just at the situation of the farmer but also at the needs of the great majority of New Zealanders engaged in secondary and tertiary occupations. These sectors had, since the later nineteenth century, made a growing contribution to the domestic economy and employed an ever-expanding proportion of the population. Although agricultural products dominated exports, the percentage of the work-force engaged in agriculture was surprisingly small: at most a third but more often only about a quarter, when persons employed in the transport and processing of agricultural goods are excluded. Activities such as mining, quarrying, forestry, and fishing inflated the proportion employed in the primary sector, for up to 1926 these employed around 15 per cent of the primary work-force. The growth of small farming around 1910 increased the numbers employed in agriculture, but they dropped again during the 1920s. By 1930 under a quarter of the work-force was engaged in agriculture.

The secondary sector (manufacturing, processing, construction, and power-related industries) more or less equalled agriculture as an employer around 1911; by 1926 it had not changed greatly and still employed just under a quarter of the work-force. Manufacturing (that is, secondary manufacturing, excluding the processing of agricultural products) employed a steady 20 per cent of the work-force between 1911 and 1926. Absolute numbers naturally increased but only at the same rate as in other sectors. Although manufacturing did not contribute more than 5 per cent of export earnings, it produced a surprisingly wide range of goods, from bricks to beer and sweets to soap. Some local industries converted imported raw materials into finished products: the Mataura Paper Mills, for example, processed imported pulp into paper. More often, factories finished semi-processed or intermediate imports, as in the case of the Lower Hutt car-assembly plants. A significant proportion of the value of manufactured products was made up of imported components; nevertheless, manu-facturing's contribution to the Gross Domestic Product was high. Factory production for the entire inter-war period is estimated at over 20 per cent of GDP. (See Graph 2.) And in 1921 secondary manufacture began to exceed primary manufacture significantly as an employer.

Most of the factories were small workshops; as late as 1929, only 6 per cent of factories employed over fifty persons, and less than 4 per cent employed over a hundred. Often the employer and his workers toiled side by side and the gap between management and personnel was insignificant.

A good many enterprises were family firms, like that of H. E. Shacklock, until the 1930s when the evident need for more professional management brought rationalization. The absence of industrial concentrations and heavy industry was directly related to the lack of iron-ore deposits and to the size of the country. Blackland landscape was hard to find even in the mid-twentieth century; more smoke could be seen belching from the bush than from factory chimneys. Both market and labour-force were too small to sustain heavy industry. Steel and finished goods could be imported at lower cost because of the relatively high wages, limited technology, and poor economies of scale in New Zealand. But a certain amount of heavy industry did exist, and some large-scale operations. One-third of the factories in fact employed 80 per cent of those engaged in manufacturing. Typical of these large-scale factories were the engineering works in Christchurch and Dunedin, and some freezing works and timber-mills. Here the gap between employer and employee was wider than in the small factories, and the attitudes of workers were often those of the British or Australian working class. Some of the same characteristics were to be found in the mining towns on the West Coast of the South Island and, to a lesser extent, those near Huntly and Waihi, where there was specialization and dependence on one industry, a high risk factor in the work, and a feeling of solidarity and a propensity toward militancy in the work-force. But such places were atypical. In general, New Zealand industry was mixed rather than concentrated, operated on a relatively small scale, and was organized in an unsophisticated manner. It had, even so, a significant place within the economy, indicated by the fact that manufacturing's share of employment remained constant at a time when agricultural exports were being rapidly expanded and by its remarkable contribution to GDP. The share of New Zealand's manufacturing sector in GDP was only slightly behind that of Australia and the USA in the 1920s, despite the absence of the protective barriers that helped Australian and American industry.[55]

As agriculture's need for labour declined and secondary industry failed to offer opportunities for the growing number leaving the countryside, the work-force moved to the tertiary sector. Tertiary occupations were generally white-collar and clerical, but such a description conceals a multifarious range of workers including truck-drivers, shop-assistants, domestic servants, the ever-growing number of government servants, and the rather more static group of professionals.[56] As the tertiary sector became the major employer its contribution to both GDP and Gross National Product grew. (See Graph 2.)

More and more New Zealanders were thus becoming wage and salary earners employed by private enterprise and by government. This pattern was typical of all Western economies from the turn of the century. At the same time, fewer New Zealanders were making a direct contribution to exports. The view expressed by many farmers' organizations that the majority of the population was becoming parasitic upon the agricultural sector was, of course, far from true.[57] The relationship between primary producers and the rest of the country was symbiotic. A growing army of people was required to service the agricultural industry if New Zealand was to cope with the increasing complexity of quality control and marketing demanded by a competitive international trading system. More, too, were required to service the secondary sector as it increased production and became more sophisticated.

Once under way, the growth of the tertiary sector had its own dynamic. Increasing regulation of economic activity and other spheres of life meant that more people were involved in administering and implementing controls. The Labour Government's welfare legislation and more direct economic management made further demands on the tertiary sector. Growth halted briefly during the Depression, when people left the towns and service activities for the land and subsistence farming. But in general urbanization stimulated the expansion of the service sector. Growing personal wealth and shifting aspirations in the twentieth century increased public demand for a greater range of services from both state and private organizations.

The Depression of the 1930s was an uneven experience which affected some groups far more adversely than others. Despite chronically high unemployment, for example, the demand for consumer goods continued unabated throughout the decade. Sales of electric stoves and water-heaters continued to increase even in the worst years of the Depression; car ownership, however, declined significantly, and home ownership became more difficult.[58]

In the 1930s, unlike the 1880s, experience of the Depression differed more between occupational groups than it did between regions. The big pastoralists fared relatively well because they were organized to take full advantage of boom years, thereby surviving more easily the lean years of the trade cycle. Some even had sufficient capital resources to buy up cheap stock and land and to make substantial improvements to their properties. They were sufficiently credit-worthy, too, to persuade stock and station agencies to protect them from the threat of liquidation. Smaller farmers, by contrast, especially if their farms were marginal and they were not credit-worthy, had little chance of coping with mounting debts. Significant numbers were forced to surrender their holdings, although thanks to further legislation protecting farmers against foreclosure, there were fewer bankruptcies than in the 1920s.[59] Some manufacturers and other large employers also benefited from devaluation, the low level of wages, and the competition for jobs. They were able to expand, and so to take advantage of increasing consumption and government assistance after 1935. Even while some New Zealanders were rioting, others drove to race meetings or exclusive clubs in the latest model cars, and dressed in the height of fashion. Others, especially more established members of the business community, maintained a reasonable degree of comfort, although they lived less ostentatiously than in better times. Government servants were subjected to salary cuts, but provided they held their jobs they usually managed to keep up a reasonable level of consumption. Worst off were the unemployed, the unskilled, financially over-committed small farmers, women, and most Māori. Estimates of unemployment in New Zealand range from 12 to 15 per cent.[60] The less fortunate certainly suffered real hardship. Probably most had enough to eat but there was some poverty and malnutrition. All but the most conservative members of the community were incensed when they saw people go hungry in a land of plenty. A significant section of the electorate was radicalized and in 1935 voted into power a government containing men who a few years before had been considered disreputable, common, and dangerous.

The extent of hardship in those years will always be debated but the causes of the Depression are easier to ascertain. The raising of large-scale loans on the London money market to provide infrastructure and cheap credit made New Zealand heavily dependent upon external sources of capital. The high consumption and low internal investment that followed stimulated further overseas borrowing. The productive return on imported capital was small and soon a significant proportion of export earnings was allotted to servicing international debts. When prices for primary products fell suddenly in 1929 the many structural weaknesses within the New Zealand economy were exposed.[61]

Six years later the first Labour Government was elected. They were able to begin implementing reflationary policies just as the international economy improved. The Coalition Government under Coates had done more to aid recovery than contemporaries realized, especially through increasing government control of financial operations, through devaluation and the Reserve Bank, and by reducing overseas debt. But the Coalition's efforts were too little and too late. In contrast to the Coalition, Labour related its policy to a vision of future development. Although many of Labour's actions were in fact more pragmatic than theoretical, the new Government stimulated the economy, attacked economic problems in a more concerted, rational, and planned manner, and made a real if not entirely successful attempt to diversify and insulate the economy. Unemployment remained relatively high until the Second World War but men on relief work were paid award rates and no longer treated as if they were responsible for their plight. Margaret Galt's research also suggests that Labour succeeded in redistributing income more evenly amongst New Zealand's citizens.[62] Recovery was not instantaneous, but the new administration restored that elusive quality — confidence in the economy. Labour considerably improved a moderately promising situation, and the 1935 election accelerated the transition from a pre- to a post-Keynesian economy.

The New Zealand economy showed a remarkable resilience in the period between the 1890s and 1940s. Farming became more efficient, and enabled New Zealanders to enjoy a high standard of living, in the face of considerable difficulties. Industrialized countries erected tariff barriers to protect their own farming, freight costs increased greatly, and invisible imports (caused by a distant market) were a constant problem. Still, New

Zealand maintained a comparative advantage in pastoral farming, through hard work, improvements in quality control, and a more scientific approach to production and marketing. In the light of New Zealand's limited resource base, small population, and limited markets, this was no slight achievement, and it outweighs the negative aspects of the period — an exploitative attitude to the land, the destruction of the forests, the neglect of such alternatives as fishing. There were problems left for the future — inflated land values, secondary growth, decimated forests, and a lack of diversification. Critics of the Left, particularly dependency theorists, have argued that the policies of the reforming Liberal and Labour governments were little more than tinkering which did not address the key problems of dependence upon a narrow range of export products and a single market.[63] Attitudes of mind that enshrined individualism and accepted colonial dependence limited New Zealand's capacity to cope with a rapidly changing world. Yet in the 1930s there was a beginning to the revolution in attitudes that would be found necessary for survival.

CHAPTER 10

Towards a New Society [1]

Erik Olssen

In 1921 the Board of Health authorized an investigation into the rapid spread of venereal diseases. The community was alarmed. Many witnesses blamed the relaxation of traditional standards of sexual behaviour, and they did not lack figures. About one-third of all babies born in the first year of marriage had been conceived before the wedding; the rate of illegitimacy had risen; and divorce had become more common. 'Sexually suggestive' dress, 'modern forms of dancing', and the cinema were generally held responsible. In accordance with the increasingly secular spirit of the age, the investigating committee singled out the erosion of parental control, the lack of sexual education, the existence of a sub-stratum of 'mentally defective or morally imbecile' girls, and over-crowded housing. Its report concentrated on specific problems,[2] but, like most of the witnesses it heard, the committee worked on the assumption that the recent past represented a golden age free from such ills. This utopia, they believed, had been disrupted by urbanization and the decline in religious observance. The statisticians of the state tried to comprehend these trends as they bemoaned them, but with limited success.[3]

The widespread fear of venereal diseases was symptomatic of unsettling social change. The adults of the 1920s, born in the nineteenth century, had seen their world transformed. New Zealand society was moving from pre-industrial to industrial, from pre-modern to modern, a shift dramatized by the recency of organized European settlement.[4] A new society was emerging from the colonial frontier, characterized by towns and cities, bureaucracy, specialization, and organization. The social structure became more complex, the division of labour more intricate, the distinction between urban and rural more obvious. Although these changes occurred at different speeds in different areas they converged to integrate the fragmented regions and localities of the 1870s into modern New Zealand by the end of the 1920s.

The concept of modernization is central to this chapter but it is not to be understood as a process, let alone some 'hidden hand', but as a useful way of analysing an interrelated series of changes which occurred in the period 1890–1940. There are disadvantages in using the concept of modernization; it has been used loosely in other contexts, suggesting that change was uniform and social equilibrium natural. It has also been used as a teleological model. Such disadvantages are not intrinsic to the concept, especially when used to analyse a brief period. The advantages outweigh the disadvantages, however, if modernization is taken to mean four testable propositions about change in this period which specify: the broad direction of change; changing patterns of social organization; possible inter-connections between changes in different areas of social life; and the categories appropriate to analysing the organization of society.[5] None of these propositions deny that some social groups will resist or adapt to social change let alone that people may feel ambivalent about the processes that dominate their lives. By the same token, however, for some social groups modernization constituted an imperative.[6]

The concept of modernization highlights social changes congruent with industrialization (a sustained period of economic growth in which real incomes per head rise, continuing technological innovation occurs, the factory mode of production becomes more important, and population shifts from rural to urban areas). At the most general level modernization meant the increasing importance of New Zealand-wide patterns, structures, and organizations, facilitated but not determined by increasingly rapid forms of communication.[7] In both public and private sectors, bureaucracy expands; the number of people employed in clerical, secretarial, and managerial roles increases while the unskilled shrink; people organize themselves into groups for specific purposes and organize themselves nationally; specialization and the division of labour become more complex; and people are recruited for specialized tasks on the basis of merit and training rather than kin, race, sex, parentage, or age. Values become universalized and the educational system assumes an increased importance.

These processes started before 1890 and have continued to the present day, but they occurred most obviously in the years 1890–1940. This chapter concentrates on this period, before examining the impact of war and depression on a society seeking to retain its belief in individualism in a world where individuals seemed increasingly impotent, a society, more-over, in which such words as city and class not only referred to reality but warned against Old World evils.

A demographic revolution in the European population coincided with and reinforced the transformation of New Zealand society that began at the end of the nineteenth century. The links between demographic structure and social structure are not very clear but the receding frontier, which possessed a distinctive demographic pattern, facilitated the major social changes of the period. The non-Māori population increased (from 626,658 in 1891 to 1,491,484 in 1936) and aged (the average moving from twenty-five in 1896 to thirty-two in 1936). The sex ratio became more evenly balanced, while fertility and mortality declined.

Age and sex structures had lost their frontier characteristics by the second decade of the twentieth century. In the 1870s the colonial population was young, males outnumbered females, and rates of fertility and mortality were

Table 6: Urbanization, 1891–1936 (European population only)[1]

	1896	1901	1911	1921	1926	1936
European population of						
Auckland	57,616	67,226	102,676	157,757	192,233	210,393
Wellington	41,758	49,344	70,729	107,488	121,527	149,382
Christchurch	51,330	57,041	80,193	105,670	118,501	132,282
Dunedin	47,280	52,390	64,237	72,255	85,095	81,848
European population of four main centres as percentage of total European population	28.15	29.25	31.52	36.36	38.48	39.48
European population of towns larger than 8,000 (other than four main centres) as a percentage of total European population	2.64	2.45	7.35	12.87	13.7	14.33

1. The population here designated as 'European' includes all non-Māori groups.
Source: Calculated from *NZ Census* for years given.

high. As early as the 1880s the sex ratio had begun to change: there was a small surplus of women between the ages of fifteen and thirty in Christchurch and Dunedin. By 1900 the male–female ratio had become normal in most urban areas and in the four main cities and in most suburbs females exceeded males. Except in inner-city Auckland, where the trend reversed between 1900 and 1911, the female excess continued to grow in urban areas. In rural areas of the South Island the strong male predominance weakened considerably during the final decades of the nineteenth century, although in frontier areas of the North Island the male bias remained strong well into the twentieth century. Even in 1936 males in all rural areas still outnumbered females, especially between the ages of eighteen and forty-five. The surplus of rural males exceeded the surplus of urban females throughout the period, but the passing years saw the overall sex ratio move from 88 women to 100 men in 1891 to 97 women to 100 men in 1936. As the ratio changed, an increasing proportion of the adult male population married and established families.[8]

As a result of the declining mortality rate and the reduced role of immigration as a source of population growth between 1881 and 1911, the age structure matured. The middle-aged and the old became a larger proportion of the population as the youthful immigrants of the 1860s and 1870s aged. Benevolent Institutions found themselves providing accommodation for the destitute elderly, in 1898 the Government introduced a means-tested old age pension, and after the First World War the churches began building homes for old people. The distribution of age-groups varied, especially between urban and rural areas, but by the 1901 census the age structures of urban and rural New Zealand had stabilized. In rural areas there was a surplus of males at all ages from fifteen years through to retirement, at which point the proportion of males fell below the national average. Small towns had an excess of young children, young adults, and old people. Young adults from these towns and young women from rural areas migrated to larger towns and cities throughout the period. Between the two wars the older age-groups increased proportionately, and by 1936, despite the growth in the population, there were 15,267 fewer children under five years of age than there had been in 1916. Children under 15 years of age had declined from 40 per cent of the population in 1891 to 25.5 per cent by 1936.[9]

Natural increase surpassed immigration as a source of population growth in the 1870s and remained more important thereafter. Immigration continued to influence the shape of the population, however, especially in the North Island. The gain in population from immigration during the years 1901 to 1928 was a little over 200,000.[10] Those arriving before the First World War (mostly from England and Australia) included more men than women, and reinforced the frontier character of the age–sex structure (especially in Auckland). In the 1920s, however, the Government's intervention successfully reduced the sexual imbalance amongst immigrants.

The rapid decline in mortality and fertility amongst Europeans which began in the late nineteenth century also affected the shape of the population. The sharp fall in infant mortality, well under way before the foundation of the Plunket Society in 1907, was largely a function of declining fertility. (As the risk of mortality increases quickly with each birth, a decline in fertility brings a sharp fall in infant mortality.) In the early 1890s, for instance, more than 80 infants under twelve months died for every 1,000 live births; in the late 1930s only 32 out of every 1,000 died. Maternal mortality also fell and life expectancy increased markedly. With death visiting less frequently, the family became more stable. In 1900 thousands of people spent their Sundays at cemeteries and tending graves; by 1926 the custom had almost ceased. Simultaneously, the growing number of women in the population meant that a larger proportion of all men married. According to the 1891 census, 21 per cent of all men over forty-five were 'unmarried'; by 1936 the percentage had shrunk to 14. In the same period the number of unmarried women older than forty-five had increased, reflecting the emergence of a surplus of women in larger towns and cities. Whereas large groups of unmarried adult males created a demand for prostitution and often proved a source of criminal behaviour, the unmarried adult females served as bulwarks of social order. They not only worked as teachers and nurses, but also served on countless voluntary organizations to promote social welfare and provided essential support for their own kin. The shift from a frontier demographic structure to a more balanced age–sex structure, the fall in rates of mortality and fertility, the increased popularity of marriage, and the greater stability of the family contributed to the social changes of the period.[11]

The most striking demographic change during the period was urbanization, a function of industrialization. Growing towns and cities presented New Zealand society with problems that required planning and expertise for their solution. A new generation of technocrats, imbued with a faith that science and rationality would solve society's problems, became influential in administration at the national level and in most urban areas. The people themselves now formed organizations to achieve their goals: voluntary societies and structured activities began to replace the informal and spontaneous interactions of nineteenth-century New Zealand. The features that marked pioneer-frontier society retained some vitality in rural areas well into the twentieth century, but rural life remained the lot of a declining proportion of the population and was increasingly modified by innovations originating in urban centres.

Between the 1890s and the 1920s towns and cities grew not only in size but also in number. In 1896 over a quarter of the population lived in the four main cities (Auckland, Wellington, Christchurch, and Dunedin) and only one other town exceeded 8,000 persons.[12] By 1926 over a third of the population lived in the four cities and nearly half lived in towns larger than 8,000 persons (see Table 6). Population growth transformed the towns. In the last decade of the nineteenth century they had been walking towns, dominated by pedestrians and horses. Market gardens and livestock were common within urban boundaries, independent boroughs proliferated, and many houses stood amid empty sections. Most people worked, played, and lived within the suburb or borough. By 1926 the cities and towns had become centralized and more densely peopled. Most of the farms and market gardens within urban boundaries had been subdivided for residential purposes and the suburbs, which expanded rapidly after the turn of the century, became more exclusively residential. The electric tram, found in all cities by 1905, facilitated suburbanization and the integration of the urban region. During the 1920s the car, the tram, and the truck became the major means of transport within the cities, and children were no longer safe using the streets as playgrounds.[13]

Between the mid-1890s and the 1920s many cities and towns absorbed adjacent boroughs, centralized the provision of services, and tried to render urban government more stable and efficient. During the First World War the four cities, for instance, abolished the ward system in an effort to diminish parochialism and improve the quality of city councillors. Problems of drainage and water-supply required comprehensive and long-term planning, and the engineer emerged as the technocrat of the city. Between 1900 and 1905 transport became a municipal function and the Dunedin City Council became the first to acquire and develop its own hydroelectric scheme. With varying degrees of reluctance city councils also responded to local pressure by establishing libraries, museums, public baths, parks, and recreation grounds.[14] Cries for town planning became more insistent, encouraged by local beautification and amenities societies. In 1911 the Auckland City Council took the initiative in proposing legislation because, said the Mayor, Sir Arthur Myers, 'the evils that arise through the growth of towns at haphazard, without any systematic plan, or any reasonable provision for the future, are too obvious. . . .'[15] By all accounts Auckland had become a 'conspicuous example' of 'rapid development, land speculation, and municipal failure'.[16] The Town Planning Conference of 1919 revealed a general ignorance of basic concepts and a preoccupation with overcrowded housing, but the demand for better planning led finally to the Town Planning Act of 1926 and to the establishment of the Town Planning Institute in 1930.

With planning came bureaucracy. The application of expertise required efficient organization and systematic procedures. Nowhere was it more evident than in the Public Service. Before the reform of 1912, most departments of state were personal in style and control. Seddon, for instance, when approached for a job by an old friend, told a head of department to find him one. When it was discovered that he could not read, 'The department head sent the premier an explanatory memorandum: "I cannot employ this man. He is unable to read." Back came Seddon's reply: "Learn him!" '[17] Competitive examinations were introduced in 1886, but until 1912 they were used to recruit only a small proportion of total appointments. Only the Post Office and the Railways classified jobs. Each minister retained control of his department, made most appointments, and tried to control day-to-day administration. Between 1890 and 1912 the Public Service grew rapidly, but could not cope with the increasing complexity of government, let alone control and co-ordinate its own activities. The key to the efficient operation of the system was appointment by merit, job classification, and the substitution of bureaucratic for personal control.[18]

In 1912 the Government appointed William D. Hunt, manager of the Invercargill branch of the stock and station agents Wright Stephenson, and chairman of its board of directors, to head a commission of inquiry. The Hunt Commission criticized departmental autonomy, the absence of standardized procedures, and political intervention. It called for increased efficiency by means of job classification, systematic inspection, and standardized procedures for appointment, promotion, transfers, tenure, and holidays. The Commission also stressed the importance of recruiting people with the requisite technical and educational skills. Changes along these lines were already in hand, but the Hunt Commission's report accelerated the development of bureaucratic forms and procedures. The Public Service Act (1912) completed the process.[19] The absence of quite elementary statistics, discovered in the same year by the Cost of Living Commission, strengthened the case for the systematic collection and analysis of statistical information.[20] Procedures for efficient government were slowly being established.

These changes had their counterpart in the private sector. Some firms were now large enough to require the bureaucratization of decision-making and administration. The speed with which large-scale organization emerged generally depended upon the capital requirements of the industry. In banking, insurance, shipping, mining, transport, the timber industry, and some forms of engineering and manufacturing, the trend toward concentration, widely denounced as 'monopoly', was clear by the 1890s. At about this time, too, refrigeration made its impact on farming, and this new technology required dairy farmers to regulate and organize their production according to the needs of the export market. By 1929 less than 3 per cent of the factories employed more than 50 per cent of the manufacturing work-force, while establishments employing fewer than ten persons comprised 67 per cent of the total but employed only 16 per cent of factory workers. By 1940 the same trends were evident in brewing, construction, entertainment, and some sectors of the retail trade. Although some family firms limited their growth in order to retain personal control, the future belonged to the modernizers. There was now a demand for those with specialized skills, such as accountants. In 1915 the University of New Zealand authorized courses in commerce and accountancy. Rationalization, specialization, and consolidation had become the techniques for promoting efficiency and profitability in the business world.[21]

The informality of pioneer-frontier society persisted in rural areas long after it had disappeared from the cities. Until the late 1930s almost half the population still lived in towns under 8,000 people or in the country. Parochial loyalties survived, and older patterns of deference proved resilient, with kin, age, sex, and religion providing the bonds within communities. Except in run-holding areas such as South Canterbury, country people shared the same aspirations, the same values, belonged to the same clubs, sent their children to the same schools, played the same games, and belonged to a church. Variations depended both on the local economy and on the community's stage of development. The established farming and pastoral regions were by the 1890s prosperous and stable, and produced for the market. In more isolated areas, especially where poor soil limited productivity, subsistence farmers struggled for a living and often joined the seasonal work-force when they needed cash. Large areas of the North Island, in the process of being reclaimed from the bush or acquired from the Māori, remained frontier regions, predominantly male, and socially undifferentiated. But the major change of the period in rural New Zealand was the rise of the family farm, aided by the subdivision or sale to the Government of many of the large estates.[22]

Their owners, the run-holders in long-settled districts such as Canterbury, Marlborough, Wairarapa, and Hawke's Bay, lost much of their social and economic power towards the end of the nineteenth century. They compensated by organizing effectively. They also continued to emulate the lifestyle of the English squire, despite their fundamentally different economic base. At the turn of the century they could still be found migrating between country house and town club, sending their sons to schools such as Christ's College or even to England for their education, amusing themselves with hunts and balls, and acting as local benefactors and patrons. Large-scale agriculture and pastoralism depended heavily upon transient labour — the 'swaggers' of legend — and they too helped make rural society distinctive. By 1914, however, the social system of the run-holders had become but one form of rural society among others. The 'swaggers', too, began to disappear.[23]

The triumph of the family farm between 1890 and 1914 largely reflected the new profitability of dairying. In this sector the family regained its importance as an economic unit and the values of economic and religious individualism flourished. Often intensely suspicious of strangers and of cities, these communities tended to be inward-looking, self-reliant, and church-centred. Particularistic values flourished. Indeed, between 1875 and 1914 men in Oamaru rarely took as wives any woman living more than sixteen miles away.[24] Communication was informal, by networks of neighbours or kin, and before the First World War males dominated social life. The major social division, as in small towns, was between the stable families and the footloose young men of the district. In agricultural regions with a demand for seasonal labour this division often became the source of significant social tensions. Despite such tensions and the strength of individualism, in part a reflection of growing hostility to Liberal leasehold, small farmers and those who lived in small towns maintained a vigorous tradition of mutual aid. Branches of the major friendly societies proliferated throughout rural areas, spearheaded by the Manchester Unity Oddfellows, and the co-operative movement gathered momentum. By 1918, for instance, 84 per cent of the country's butter and cheese factories were co-operatives.[25]

By 1890 people in urban areas already thought of themselves as members of groups and took action through their group institutions. Voluntary organizations proliferated. But the social systems of the country proved inhospitable to group activity of this kind. The family and institutions such as the church or the lodge dominated. Otherwise organization, like communication, remained spontaneous and informal. Even sectional groups, such as farmers, found it hard to create organizations. The Agricultural and Pastoral Associations were largely city-based, and attempts to form a farmers' union proved ineffective until 1901 (and grew slowly until after the Second World War). Increasingly, however, the growth of technology and knowledge, the expansion of the stock and station agencies, the growing urban market and the increased importance of the world market, and then the car and the radio, began to integrate farmers and the inhabitants of small towns into the modern world. The farmer, like the small-town businessman, had to deal with new institutions, new technologies, and a more complex world in which his own power declined.[26] He had to organize or perish.

The new spirit of organization pervaded all spheres of New Zealand life: public and private, business and leisure, family and club. To some extent the process fed on itself. 'Organisation can be met only by organisation', as William Scott, one of the architects of the New Zealand Employers' Federation remarked.[27] Not even the playing field was exempt. In the 1860s and 1870s sport had been sporadic, spontaneous, and informal. Inter-provincial competition had the same character. Even the rules were flexible. Any number of men could play football, teams varying from ten to fifty players each; playing fields varied in size; games lasted any period mutually agreed upon; the players interpreted the rules during the game; and men played according to rules from soccer, rugby, and Australian football. The rules for the three codes, not to mention the hybrids, also varied from one locality to another. But this engaging informality had gone by 1900. The formation of provincial rugby unions, based on cities and larger towns, created some order, and in 1892 they established the New Zealand Rugby Football Union (minus some recalcitrant South Island unions that affiliated before the decade ended). The Union rationalized and systematized rules, organized competition, and appointed referees armed with considerable authority. As a distinctive code, rugby had been fostered by the secondary schools during the 1870s, but in the space of thirty years it became the national game. The success of the 1905 All Blacks in Britain helped make the game a vehicle for colonial cockiness and national pride. Large crowds gathered outside Post Offices to hear the results. The All Blacks' success in adopting specialized positional play contributed greatly to their success. The sense of national pride which the All Blacks generated helped to legitimize national structures even as the way they organized to play both reflected and reinforced the belief that specialization enhanced efficiency.[28]

The changing structure and role of the family most vividly reveals the new and modern forms of social organization. Over the period households generally became smaller and less likely to contain either servants or lodgers; they surrendered many welfare responsibilities to various state and voluntary agencies (thus eroding the significance of the Destitute Persons' Act); and they focused more on the moral and physical well-being of their children. Some young people even talked of the emotional and sexual needs of husbands and wives. At the same time specialists such as Dr Frederick Truby King brought scientific procedure into the home and trained women to be expert mothers; many women found themselves in a new confinement.[29]

The spectacular decline in fertility and family size, which inspired Truby King's concern with child-rearing, can be seen as another sign of the desire to plan for and control the future. Women who married in the year 1880 averaged, when their families were complete, 6.5 live births; the 'marriage cohort' of 1923 averaged 2.4 live births. Old age pensions, compulsory education, and the falling rate of infant mortality, all lessened the incentive to have large families. Abortifacients had always been available but abortion became a minor trade; unmarried but pregnant women and married women who wanted no more children provided the major market. Improved contraceptives also became available and the Army finally trained thousands of men in their use. In urban areas expectations of increased living standards rose between the mid-1890s and the First World War, and each extra child reduced the family's status and comfort. Urban middle-class families responded first to these pressures, manual workers followed suit after the First World War, and rural couples, who limited their fertility least, did so last. Perhaps most important, although least studied, new and rising standards of motherhood made smaller families desirable. Whatever the reasons, however, by the late 1930s the fertility rates of different strata and of urban and rural areas were converging. Even ideals about family size gained more uniformity as the various ethnic and religious groups were integrated into society. The modern family began to plan and control the number of children, and even, by the 1930s, their spacing.

In small towns and rural areas the family usually retained its control of social and economic functions, but in the cities, with the separation of home and work, the family tended to become more private, a refuge from the world. The extent of the trend is not clear, however, for in the urban handicraft sector the family often remained an economic unit and it seems that many actively resisted the separation of home and work, a process which reduced the father's involvement with his children. For all that, new ideas gained ground. The conjugal family constituted a new ideal. For many people, especially those from white-collar and semi-professional backgrounds, the family became a key to survival and a focus for much of their activity (reflecting in part the diverse social origins of these strata). In the 1880s the evangelical Protestant churches began articulating a new ideal of marital and parental responsibilities, an ideal which legitimized smaller families, and by the war the ideal was widely accepted. Men and women no longer accepted reproduction as the only or principal purpose of marriage. Home replaced the workshop as the centre of the skilled workers' world.

Friendly societies, once based on pubs, built their own halls, admitted women to membership, and organized dances rather than exclusively male carousals. Young married couples expected more of each other than their parents had, especially companionship, and some said that marriages should dissolve when love departed. The increasing importance of children, more and more the focus of family life, contained any threat of marital anarchy. The gendered division of familial labour survived virtually unquestioned, however, but the young now rejected many aspects of Victorian patriarchy although few went as far as the young girl who declared, 'The idea of sitting and waiting for a husband is absolutely revolting. . .' Increasingly the conjugal family lived alone. Widows and private hotels took over the task of housing single, unskilled working men (a declining proportion of the population). Kinship links remained important, especially as the proportion of the New Zealand-born grew, but the conjugal family became more of a world unto itself. The piano, common even in the homes of labourers by 1914, became the focus for family leisure.[30]

Changes in the family meant major changes for New Zealand's women while women's quest for greater equality helped to reshape the family. In 1896, articulate, middle-class women, often single and professional, took the initiative in forming the National Council of Women. Vision outstripped reality. Women found they did not constitute a cohesive social group based on a shared moral sensibility. The fate of *Daybreak* in the 1890s illustrates the point. Begun by women as a journal 'to ventilate the evils and grievances . . . in our midst', it had to resort within a few months to fashion notes in a vain effort to survive. As the National Council of Women faltered, the ideology which had been used to enlarge the freedom of women became the source of new forms of social control. The medical profession, led by Truby King, elaborated a scientific justification for confining women to the home. In 1907 Truby King and his wife formed the Royal New Zealand Society for the Health of Women and Children (known as the Plunket Society), to disseminate scientific methods of feeding and training children so that 'the main supplies of population for our asylums, hospitals, benevolent institutions, gaols, and slums would be cut off at sources.'[31] Although the desirability of higher education for women was the subject of considerable dispute, the view that women ought to be trained for motherhood and home management gained ground. One of the first aims of the Society was 'to inculcate a lofty view of the responsibilities of maternity and the duty of every mother to fit herself for the perfect fulfilment of the natural calls of motherhood. . . .'[32] Feminists such as Ada Wells, of the progressive Canterbury Women's Institute, were equally active in establishing motherhood and home-making as the only career for women. In 1909, indeed, home science became a subject at the University of Otago, and in 1912, a degree. The fast-growing Plunket Society also trained women in household management and motherhood. The isolated conjugal family, organized and run by the wife-mother and centred on the proper care and training of children, had become the norm for much of society. During the First World War, the Department of

Education made home science compulsory for all girls in secondary school. The appointment of Truby King as Director of Child Welfare in 1921 cemented the alliance.[33]

The altered status of women was reflected in legislation and employment. The Married Women's Property Act (1884), women's franchise (1893), the Divorce Act (1898), the repeal in 1910 of the Contagious Diseases Act, and the enactment of a law allowing women to stand for Parliament (1919) removed the most blatant forms of legal discrimination. In the 1880s women, usually from middle-income homes, began to enter secondary schools and universities, and during the 1890s they won the right to enter the medical and legal professions. Large numbers also escaped domestic service and prostitution by working in factories or training as teachers and nurses. In the late 1890s and early twentieth century the Labour Department opened a number of women's employment branches. Between 1910 and 1920 thousands of young women entered lower-paid jobs in the clerical-secretarial sector, although they still expected to leave the work-force when they married. By 1921 women constituted some 24 per cent of the work-force. In that year, however, only 9 per cent of the female work-force was married, although 19 per cent were widows. Despite the fact that women increasingly limited their fertility, few returned to the work-force. Indeed, women in the 1920s were on average fifty-four years old when their last child left school. Many middle-class women used their increased leisure to participate in voluntary organizations. After the First World War organizations such as the Mothers' Union and the League of Mothers reaffirmed the cults of domesticity and motherhood. They stressed the spiritual but now assumed the importance of science and experts. But young girls possessed a freedom and autonomy that their mothers had not had. After the war adolescents and young women asserted themselves more, and those who had entered the work-force before marriage showed a marked tendency to limit their fertility. As Helen Wilson wrote, reviewing her first eighty years, 'Of all the changes that have taken place in my long life perhaps the most fundamental is the altered place occupied in the world by women.'[34]

The welfare of children, increasingly the focus of family life, also became of greater public concern. Legislation raised the age of consent (1896), provided better protection for the homeless (1896), prohibited children from smoking (1903), and attempted to create effective legal structures for dealing with juveniles (1906). Over the first two decades of the twentieth century the concept of child welfare as a function of the state crystallized. In 1917 the Government appointed the first juvenile probation officer (although individuals from some churches had been doing probation work in the courts for some ten years), established probation homes, and extended the practice of home supervision. The Child Welfare Act of 1925 created Children's Courts with a preventive rather than a punitive purpose, and the Child Welfare Branch staffed by child welfare officers. Although the desire to help had to battle against the desire to save money, the state began to recognize children as a social asset, a process greatly accelerated by the prospect and reality of war. It instituted a backblocks' nursing scheme in 1909, a school medical service in 1912, and began training school dental nurses in 1921. During the 1920s the churches also responded by building orphanages. Adults also moved to tame the playground and control children's games (outlawing the more violent and sadistic of them), while local bodies built playgrounds and parks. In the early years of the century a consensus emerged that neither the physical nor the moral welfare of children could be left to the street. In 1908 the Boy Scout movement began in New Zealand, followed by the Boys' Brigade and Girl Guides.[35]

Toward the end of the nineteenth century the family's role in the care of delinquent children was also reduced. The Government, acting under pressure from voluntary societies and its own departments, expressed growing concern for the welfare of orphans and delinquents. Industrial schools, set up in increasing numbers in the 1880s, housed these children. Neither state nor private industrial schools were effectively controlled before 1895. The use of brutal punishments at Stoke Orphanage in Nelson became a public scandal and prompted the Government to appoint a commission of inquiry in 1900. In 1902 new regulations designed to improve conditions were gazetted. Each child was to have its own clothing, its own bed, ample and nutritious food, and an education. Boys and girls had to be segregated, a record of all punishments had to be kept, and vicious or sadistic punishments were prohibited. Two married women had to be attached to the staff of each institution and the regulations provided for regular and systematic inspection. John Beck, the officer in charge of industrial schools from 1915 to 1924, favoured replacing industrial schools with more specialized institutions. He phased out four industrial schools by 1924 and encouraged home supervision, probation homes, and institutions to deal with 'mental defect'. Volunteers established private initiatives where the state moved too slowly. For instance, in 1919 Dr Elizabeth Gunn established the first health camp.[36]

Traditional welfare systems, based on the individual or the family, began to fragment as the family became smaller and the state more 'grandmotherly'. Old age pensions were introduced in 1898, and by 1904 some 27 per cent of those eligible received them; a widow's pension was added in 1911, a pension for miners' phthisis in 1915, one for the blind in 1924, and another for low-income parents of more than two children in 1926. Disabled veterans of the First World War received a wide range of pensions and welfare services. Individuals and families were still deemed largely responsible for their own welfare, but the gap between the ideal and reality grew. Although about 20 per cent of the adult male population belonged to a friendly society, a proportion that remained roughly constant from 1910 until 1940, voluntary welfare agencies multiplied and became more professional and specialized. In 1929 the Cancer Society was formed, and in 1935, after an emotive campaign by the Rotary Clubs, the Crippled Children Society. The Plunket Society grew, building antenatal clinics, mothercraft centres, Karitane homes, and Plunket rooms. In 1930

Parliament passed the Unemployment Act to provide relief for jobless men, financed by a special tax upon all earnings. A combination of state help and self-help created institutions to assist the disabled and the disadvantaged.[37]

The family also lost much of its responsibility for the health of its members and the care of the sick. State control and increased specialization accompanied medical progress. The bubonic plague scare of 1900 led to the establishment of the Department of Public Health, and health became a major public concern in the early twentieth century. Wellington Hospital, for instance, opened a ward for consumptives in 1906, a fever hospital in 1910, a children's hospital in 1912, a laboratory in 1913, and a hospital for those with ear, nose, and throat problems in 1915. The St Helen's maternity hospital had been established in Wellington in 1904. Public hospitals were initially founded by local communities for isolating contagious diseases and providing for the poor. As advances in medical technology made hospitalization increasingly attractive, the public hospital evolved from one designed primarily for the poor into an institution dealing with all classes. The trend began in country areas and spread to the cities. In 1909 the Government empowered hospital boards to contract with friendly societies to provide free hospitalization to their members, their wives and children. Before long the major societies were seeking hospitalization for maternity. The increasing cost of hospitals required ever larger public subsidies; as the Government's subsidy grew the Department of Public Health increased its control over the hospital boards. During the 1920s it came to be accepted that public hospitals were open to all on a fee-for-service basis, 'with the charges waived in cases of inability to pay'. Because the hospitals generally charged too low a fee, on average 9s. per day, and had trouble recovering fees from patients, the hospital boards began urging the need to introduce some form of contributory health insurance scheme. Developments in medical technology and science, together with the recognition that ill health anywhere threatened health everywhere, fostered a clumsy movement toward new forms of collectivism.[38]

The state's assumption of traditional family functions was accompanied by a changing attitude to those committed to institutions. Prisons, industrial schools, and mental asylums had mostly been established to protect society and punish those imprisoned. But by 1900 specialists considered rehabilitation an important goal. Even the insane, who had long evoked fearful disgust, came to be seen by some as a medical rather than a religious problem, their rehabilitation possible. At Seacliff Asylum, Truby King pioneered new forms of treatment with some success, and in 1911 the Mental Defectives Act, based on the recommendations of a British Royal Commission, instituted improved methods of classifying the mentally ill, new methods of treatment, and rejected the use of words such as 'lunatic' and 'insane'. As in other areas of welfare, parsimony hobbled generosity. Yet the changing treatment of the mentally ill clearly demonstrates the challenge to the moral-religious values of the nineteenth century posed by the rational scientific attitudes of the twentieth. Staff–patient ratios

improved and steps were taken to train staff, especially in the period 1880–
1911. Public attitudes, dominated by shame, pity, and ignorance, changed
little.[39]

Many colonists believed that the problems of the old world did not exist
in New Zealand. A deep reluctance to admit the existence of social
problems often inhibited reform. The crime rate better than anything else
measured the gap between the new world and the old, and the colonists
viewed it with obsessive interest. In comparison to other societies the
incidence of crime was low and falling (an international trend). Male
immigrants, especially unskilled Catholics and Wesleyans, were over-
represented among the criminal population. Men were ten times more
likely than women to be convicted. Most prosecutions were for offences
against public order or property. In 1911, for instance, there were 11,418
prosecutions for drunkenness, 2,347 for breaking prohibition orders, 4,907
for breaches of bylaws, 1,779 for theft and other forms of stealing, 1,822 for
failing to pay maintenance, 764 for obscene language, and 610 for indecent,
riotous, or offensive behaviour. In small towns the police identified with
their communities and used the law to control transients. Even in the cities
most arrests occurred in the central city area. Suburban drunkards were
more likely to receive assistance from the policeman in getting home. A
few women also figured as a danger to community morals. They were
usually persistent offenders, like Clara Dodsworth, who had thirty-eight
previous convictions, and had 'no home, no friends'. According to
contemporary criminologists these women lacked the maternal instinct.
Although women committed few offences against persons or property the
Government established a separate prison for them in 1913 in the belief that
their maternal instincts could be revived. Despite the growing
preoccupation with crime and criminals the per capita rate of convictions
fell across the period and fell sharply after 1918, probably reflecting
declining transience, the shrinkage of the unskilled stratum, and the falling
number of unmarried males.[40]

A conviction that urban growth had spawned most social problems, such as
delinquency and poverty, prompted many Christians to believe that a crisis
confronted their churches. Figures for church attendance compounded
their fears; the 1881 census revealed that more than 70 per cent of the
population did not attend church and that working men had defected in
droves. It seems that church attendance rose during the late nineteenth
century, then fell, and fell sharply in the four cities as 'The sense of duty
about being in church each Sunday largely disappeared.' After 1911 even
attendance at Sunday School began to decline. Christians believed that the
social crisis reflected the waning influence of the churches. The crisis they
marched forth to meet, however, was their own as well as society's.[41]

The Protestants in particular set out with vigour to improve standards of
worldly morality. In the 1890s two powerful movements with strong
Protestant backing gathered momentum, one dedicated to the prohibition
of alcohol, the other to the institution of Bible reading in schools. Smaller

groups worked to outlaw gambling, opium traffic, and prostitution. The prohibition movement, by far the largest of these moral crusades, recruited most of its leaders and support from 'middling' folk who often lived in socially-mixed urban areas or farming districts with high numbers of unskilled men. Prohibitionists believed that the reform would revitalize the traditional values of self-help and self-discipline, regenerate the family, cure most social ills, and thus create 'Christ's kingdom on earth'. Women, especially those in the Women's Christian Temperance Union, became active. In the 1880s support came mainly from rural and lower middle-class city areas in the South Island, particularly those with strong Protestant churches, but in the period 1890–1914 it spread into the North Island and even working-class areas, despite opposition from papers such as the *Otago Workman* (1887–1900) and *New Zealand Truth* (1905–). Although Methodists and Baptists continued to provide much of the momentum, increasingly they used scientific rather than moral arguments and stressed the havoc wrought by alcohol on family life. By 1911 such arguments had persuaded a majority of voters to demand a 'dry' New Zealand. They failed to get it, but many hotels were closed, the minimum drinking age was set at twenty-one, and in 1916 the Government banned women from hotels and outlawed 'treating'. The war made alcohol seem both wasteful and inefficient. In 1917, bowing to public pressure, the Government imposed six o'clock closing for the duration of the war. In 1918 the expedient experiment became permanent. One year later only the vote of the troops in Britain saved New Zealand from national prohibition. For all that, convictions for drunkenness declined considerably across the period and per capita consumption of alcohol fell.[42]

The last two decades of the nineteenth century also saw many churches attempting to supplement the assistance to the poor and destitute which the Hospital and Charitable Aid Boards tried to provide. Led by the Salvation Army and the Methodists, the churches grappled with specific urban problems by creating such organizations as city missions and Samaritan homes for unwed mothers. The Methodist city missions organized soup kitchens for the unemployed and distributed food, coal, and clothing to the destitute. While some churches tried to help only the 'deserving poor' or members of their own church, others sought a broader sense of mission. In the late 1890s a number of inner-city Presbyterian parishes appointed Deaconesses to undertake welfare work and between 1907 and 1913 the Presbyterians also established social service associations in the four main cities. These were run by professional welfare workers 'to rescue those Presbyterian children who were drifting beyond the care of the Church'. Religious orders, such as the Sisters of Mercy, spearheaded the Catholic effort while Anglicans, although preoccupied with the Melanesian Mission, also set up inner-city missions. Because of Catholic success in establishing their own schools by 1914 the larger Protestant churches were keenly following suit.[43]

Although the Presbyterians and smaller Protestant congregations were most active in moral and social crusades, Anglicans outnumbered them.

The numerical predominance of the Anglicans in part reflected the fact that most migrants from England declared themselves members even though they never went to church. Active membership was not much larger than that of the Presbyterian or the Catholic Church. Anglicanism also contained extraordinary variety, not only on matters of politics but on questions of faith and liturgy. As the church of the upper middle class — at least outside the Presbyterian south — the Anglicans acquired an image of being conservative, affluent, and 'snobbish'. Yet Christian Socialists, English Tories, fundamentalists, Anglo-Catholics, and many who believed in the church's social role rather than its doctrines, all worshipped within the Anglican fold. These divisions reduced the social impact of the Anglicans, except in the missionary field, yet gave the church a marked vitality. Few of the unskilled attended the Anglican Church but it did command the loyalty of a socially mixed flock, although individual parishes tended to be homogeneous. Smaller Protestant churches and sects often contained a social mix within one congregation. However, the sects and smaller denominations usually built their churches in the inner city or in poorer suburbs, while the Presbyterians and Anglicans expanded more quickly into the prosperous suburbs. Suburban churches of larger denominations took on the character of the suburb or catered to higher-status groups within it, while the inner-city churches came to be patronized by wealthy businessmen and professionals. Small-town churches and their congregations preserved a more thorough social mix.

The Presbyterians, numerically and socially dominant in Otago and Southland, were much stronger in New Zealand than elsewhere in Australasia. Throughout the period 1890–1940 some 23–25 per cent of the population were nominal Presbyterians. About 23 per cent of these (or 6 per cent of the total population) were 'adherents'. From 1890 on the Presbyterians gained slightly in numbers, partly at the expense of the smaller churches such as the Baptists and Congregationalists. More important, they achieved national unity under the shrewd and forceful leadership of James Gibb, and enjoyed a period of spectacular growth in the North Island (particularly in the Auckland province). By 1938 there were 250 Presbyterian parishes (of which only eighty-eight were in the four cities) and 109 home mission stations. The strength and wealth of the Presbyterian community enabled it to expand into rural New Zealand and the suburbs. The Presbyterians provided crucial support for prohibition and the Bible-in-Schools campaign, and by 1905 they had also helped make respect for the Sabbath 'more powerful than ever'.[44]

Throughout the period only 14 per cent of the total population professed to be Catholics, but they often constituted around 20 per cent of the population in the poorer suburbs and some small towns, and over 30 per cent on the West Coast. Most New Zealand Catholics were of Irish descent. Against a background of Protestant hostility and the religious conflict in Ireland, a high degree of solidarity developed amongst the country's Catholics during this period. The creation of their remarkably comprehensive school system both forged and reflected that cohesion.

Catholic values, and the dominance of unskilled Irish, made most Catholics unsympathetic if not opposed to the major moral crusades of the period. In 1913 the Catholics organized themselves nationally, and in 1917 the paranoia of many Protestants found expression in the Protestant Political Association. 'The beast of Protestant bigotry stalked the land', fuelled by Ireland's disloyalty to the Empire, forcing Catholics to close ranks behind a strategy of institutional separatism. The fury of sectarian conflict should not obscure the fact that Catholics continued to work for acceptance by the community, supported temperance, disagreed about how best to react to Protestant bigotry, and watched their New Zealand-born children become New Zealanders.[45]

Protestants, especially in smaller denominations such as the Baptists and Congregationalists, generally emphasized morally correct behaviour and individual salvation. These churches were democratic in organization and in the 1880s they began to permit women to play a much larger role in the government of the church. Within the Presbyterian and (especially) the Anglican Churches, however, the demand for more liturgical forms of worship became increasingly insistent in the twenty years before the First World War. The new enthusiasm for ritual and liturgy among 'moneyed' people and their retreat from the stress on strenuously righteous behaviour reflected the changing tastes and values of the established and educated upper-middle and middle strata. These forms of worship thus began to be a measure of social distance, and provided a refuge from the world rather than a preparation for its battles. Within both Presbyterian and Anglican Churches this development triggered an anxious response from more fundamentalist congregations. The forms in question — the use of vestments and ceremonial among Anglicans, of hymns and crosses among Presbyterians — may have reflected deeper divisions. Among Anglicans, for instance, a 'low-church' synod such as Nelson strongly supported the prohibition and Bible-in-Schools movements, whereas 'high-church' synods rejected political activism.[46]

Despite sectarian divisions and doctrinal debates the churches shared many social functions. Membership served as an outward sign of respectability and a source of moral strength in a disordered world. For many, especially the women who frequently formed the larger part of the congregation, the church also offered hope, comfort, friendship, and child care on Sundays. In frontier society the churches had, in an informal manner, assumed various social functions that they lost as society became more complex, although church attendance in rural areas scarcely declined at all in the period 1891–1926. In rural and small-town society, however, the church remained a community institution and the guardian of community values, the minister a source of authority and power. Despite this, gradual and cumulative changes occurred: Sunday observance declined, revivals became less common and less important, the line between members and non-members blurred, and dogma disintegrated. Some even concluded that Christianity could be divorced from the church. Yet while the Protestant churches lost authority, and parental authority declined in Protestant families, the churches, even in urban areas, continued to preach the relevance of inherited moral values and voiced ambivalence about modernity.[47]

Rapid social change also had major implications for the world of work. Occupations tended to be more sharply defined; jobs became vocations, specialization became more important than versatility, and occupation became a central principle of social organization. A person's job increasingly determined income, status, life chances, and lifestyles. The education system was directed to the inculcation of the skills required in more specialized occupations. In steps and stages, unions, professional associations, and white-collar guilds were established. Dentists, nurses, and teachers successfully organized themselves and tried to achieve the status of professions. Union membership soared from about 8,000 in 1896 to around 57,000 in 1910 and 100,000 in 1927. Even within unskilled occupations, such as wharf-labouring, precisely calculated pay for different work, overtime, and varying conditions became common. By 1926 occupation had, in urban areas, become a dimension of identity, a more important clue to social position than family or place of residence.[48]

By the 1890s stratification within New Zealand society was already well established. The uppermost stratum comprised the bankers, the wealthy merchants and manufacturers, run-holders, and larger farmers. These men formed the chambers of commerce, the Agricultural and Pastoral Associations, belonged to élite social clubs, and co-operated with British and Australian capitalists. They shared a common lifestyle based in large measure on conspicuous consumption.[49] Overlapping this stratum was another composed of less wealthy businessmen and merchants, manufacturers, lawyers, and doctors, who operated mainly in local or regional markets and depended on the first group for access to credit. Then came small businessmen such as grocers and self-employed tradesmen — the urban counterpart of the small farmer — who dominated many towns and independent boroughs within cities. These three strata formed an entrepreneurial class linked by shared aspirations, values, and interests. They also dominated all the churches. In some senses they constituted a middle class.

Entrepreneurs dominated the middle class until about 1900 but the dramatic growth of white-collar occupations and semi-professions then transformed it. While employers and professionals remained roughly constant as a proportion of the work-force, the semi-professional and white-collar occupations grew rapidly. The proliferation of clerical, secretarial, and sales positions (most rapid between 1901 and 1921) overshadowed the growth of skilled and semi-skilled positions while the unskilled shrank dramatically. Most of these new occupations required knowledge and 'refinement' as distinct from manual skill and physical strength. As the occupational structure was transformed the old professions, led by the lawyers and the 'scientific' doctors, increasingly substituted university training for on-the-job apprenticeship. The same process transformed the engineer, often a skilled worker in 1890, into a professional by 1936. The change in the composition of the middle class and the significance of its internal differentiation was most marked within the cities and larger towns. In country districts, even in the 1930s, the station-master and the teacher still represented the middle classes! By the First World War hostility to trade unions and especially the Red Feds unified the varied strata of the middle class, although they never hesitated to organize in defence of their sectional interests. Older professions, such as medicine and law, had organized themselves by 1890; dentistry, accountancy, and most white-collar groups followed between 1900 and 1930. Even small businessmen, especially when affected by the arrival of oligopolies, tried to bypass the centralizing tendencies of capital by forming associations or co-operatives such as the Four Square grocery chain.[50]

The expansion of the white-collar and semi-professional strata in general reflects the shift from an entrepreneurial to a salaried middle class. In the cities (but not the smaller towns) salaried workers increasingly defined the character of the middle class. They were, however, a stratum without a name, for the phrase 'white collar' was rarely used by contemporaries. Nor is it clear that the defining characteristics of this stratum in other societies — disdain for manual work and hostility to unions — were central here. Many, indeed, were recruited not only from the sons and daughters of manual workers but among manual workers. Although white-collar men sought safety and self-respect within their own homes, stressed respectability, adopted eagerly the new 'scientific' dogmas of domesticity and motherhood, and tried to insulate themselves and their children from vulgarity and dirt, they also mixed easily with the self-employed and the skilled in lodges, churches, and sports clubs. Their wives, one suspects, became expert at negotiating social distance. Yet between 1890 and 1940 the middle class was transformed, and many phenomena of the period — such as the rise of the Reform Party, the burgeoning of the tourist industry after 1895, the rapid growth of friendly societies, and the idealization of the suburban home and the 'new model' family — in part have their origins in this new, affluent, urban middle class.[51]

The working class has attracted more scholarly attention than any other occupational grouping although much of that attention has focused on its political activities and industrial unrest. Long-term social processes, such as unionization and the formation of predominantly working-class residential areas, have received less attention although both, together with the Maritime Strike, played an important part in the growth of class consciousness. While structural changes made class formation possible, however, the skilled workers played a key role as agents. They spearheaded the wave of unionization which culminated in the Maritime Strike of 1890, articulated the Liberal–Labour political strategy, and used their political influence to shape the 'social laboratory'. Following enactment of compulsory arbitration in 1894 they led the second wave of unionization. The threat of being displaced by less skilled and cheaper workers — boys, women, Chinese — made the skilled particularly active in articulating an ideology which stressed the dignity of labour and the need for solidarity. Fear of de-skilling mobilized not only those skilled workers employed in factories and foundries but even the men in the handicraft trades where mechanization had scarcely occurred. Key propositions in socialist discourse, notably that which linked progress to the growth of factories and both to de-skilling, helped mobilize skilled masters and journeymen. Not only socialists accepted this view. In 1908 John Barr, a most conservative union leader, remarked that 'There was a time when a few pounds would equip a bootmaker with a kit of tools, and he could set up on his own account. Today he could only start a little cobbling business. . . .' Ironically, however, the handicraft sector showed no sign of shrinking and within this sector class position was in some measure a function of age. The Arbitration Court itself assumed the validity of handicraft norms and gave them legal force.[52]

In the late-1890s skilled workers and their employers rarely quarrelled over wages or conditions. After 1900 those issues became increasingly contentious. So did the issue of authority. In 1904–5 the miners began arguing that their working day should include time spent travelling underground. Other groups began demanding that they should be paid for preparatory tasks and cleaning up. When the miners won their point and then struck successfully at Blackball in 1908 their example proved contagious. Watersiders, shearers, labourers, and other groups of 'unskilled' men began organizing into unions to demand better conditions and a 'living wage'. Even farm labourers tried to organize. Young men emerged to speak of the workers' rights and the 'Red Dawn' of a new and just socialist society. The contagion spread, spearheaded by the 'Red' Federation of Labour. A growing number of the 'unskilled' had little faith in arbitration or Liberal–Labour politics, however, and called for 'direct action' in the 'class war'. Success fed on itself and rising expectations. Success also fed unionization, encouraged strikes, and fostered a sense of class identity. When defeat came in 1912–13 it only strengthened that sense of class identity among unionized workers.[53]

The term 'unskilled' increasingly supplanted the older one of 'labour', just as 'tradesman' or 'skilled' replaced 'artisan' and 'journeyman'. Most of those described as 'unskilled' resented the label. Even when the Arbitration Court finally classified all manual occupations into the three modern categories of unskilled, semi-skilled, and skilled, it continued to distinguish different classes of unskilled work. Miners, shearers, and seamen, for example, could earn as much as skilled men. Even builders' labourers, quarrymen, and helpers in the metal trades continued to be awarded wages comparable to those commanded by skilled men. Visitors often declared themselves 'astonished at the independence, comfort and . . . privacy which New Zealand labourers enjoyed . . .'[54] The difference between the hourly rate for skilled and unskilled had always been smaller in New Zealand than in Britain but the least skilled were more vulnerable to accidents and unemployment, they earned less, and tended to own or rent lower-value housing than skilled workers or white-collar men. Such differences were a matter of degree. When the Department of Labour investigated the relationship between earnings and unemployment in 1911–12 it found that skilled workers lost about 10 per cent of their potential earnings because of short time or unemployment whereas the unskilled lost, on average, 15 per cent. Other evidence suggests that size of family, the age and earnings of the children, access to supplementary income, and the availability of gardens all mattered. Thrift and industry were warp and woof to self respect and modest comfort.

Unlike the skilled, who tended to remain in their skilled trades once they married, the unskilled were highly transient. Tom Marshall described a typical career: 'I . . . have toiled as a miner, mill-hand, brickmaker, sailor etc., in Wales; a carter and clerk in London; a brickmaker, coalminer, wharfer, tally-clerk, etc., for nearly five years in New Zealand, and am at present a coalminer . . .'[55] A remarkably high proportion of the unskilled were transient, both in good years and bad. Between 1900 and 1922, for instance, only about half of the miners and wharfies were ever listed in street directories, and, of the stable half, up to 70 per cent stayed put less than five years and as many as 50 per cent less than two years. Even though we lack enough systematic studies of transience, let alone a rigorous theory, it was sufficiently extensive to have implications for community, voluntary organizations, and social structure, although these implications remain unclear. What is clear, however, is that men were more transient than women and single men more transient than married men. Some occupations were also 'by nature' transient and transience aimless; in other occupations transience and 'upwards mobility' correlate. Before the First World War, the levels of transience sustained by the unskilled appear to have been common to all social strata other than the skilled.[56]

If the relationship between geographical and social mobility remains to be charted, changes in the occupational pattern, along with fertility differentials, created opportunities for intra-generational social mobility. The handful of studies of social mobility in this period indicate that the unskilled enjoyed higher prospects for improving their social status and pay than any other occupational group. The children of the skilled and unskilled enjoyed still larger opportunities. Even in a stable occupational structure the existence of a demographic vacuum, created by differences in fertility between occupations or classes, generates opportunities for upward mobility. Those opportunities are greater still when the proportion of unskilled is declining while white-collar and semi-professional occupations expand. In New Zealand both trends coincided. Between 1880 and 1920 those in the urban population with high income and status limited their fertility while manual workers continued to have large families. The sons of the unskilled born between 1860 and 1900 entered a labour market in which the demand for unskilled workers was shrinking while that for skills — manual, educational, and white-collar — was expanding. Immigrants from Australia and Britain undoubtedly took many of these positions, as did the sons and daughters of farmers, who sustained a high fertility rate, but many migrants also ended up in 'unskilled' occupations. Some leading 'Red

Feds', indeed, were worried by the relative absence of New Zealand-born workers in their ranks. The persistence of the handicraft sector also sustained high levels of opportunity for self-employment.

New Zealand's prosperity between 1896 and the late 1920s, free access to secondary education from 1902 onwards, and the Government's resolve to encourage family farming undoubtedly reduced inequality and fostered social mobility. Not that New Zealand's wealthiest had ever been wealthy by international standards. The country's small size, small population, and limited resources helped ensure that 'the top of the New Zealand wealth hierarchy was equivalent to the second rank in New South Wales, the third rank in Britain, and would not even have ranked as wealthy in the United States.' Yet the wealth of the wealthiest declined sharply across this period as the great estates gave way to family farms, the country enjoyed a sustained period of rising living standards, and large areas of the North Island boomed. Opportunity beckoned South Islanders north and attracted an influx of immigrants both before the First World War and in the 1920s.[57]

Education became the key to social mobility although, given basic literacy, it was not necessarily the key to accumulating wealth. Those with some secondary education had the best chance of obtaining white-collar and semi-professional jobs, while the prerequisite for admission to the professions was a university qualification. Prior to 1890, few occupations required school skills beyond literacy and basic arithmetic. Secondary education, although supported by public endowments, was largely the preserve of the wealthy. In 1901, for instance, less than 3 per cent of those between the ages of twelve and eighteen attended public secondary schools, with about 5 per cent in addition attending a district high school or a Standard 7 class. Educational opportunities expanded when in 1901 and 1902 district high schools and endowed secondary schools were encouraged by increased per capita grants to admit more pupils. The demand for secondary education, especially at the Form III and Form IV level, far exceeded the expectations of George Hogben, the architect of the reform, or the Liberal Government which authorized this quiet revolution. By 1921 almost 13 per cent of the twelve- to eighteen-year-olds attended some secondary institution, and by 1939 the figure had climbed to 25 per cent. A small but growing proportion of the eligible age-group proceeded to university, most of them to be trained as teachers, lawyers, doctors, and engineers. Between 1911 and 1926 the four university colleges grew rapidly.[58]

While most of those who entered secondary institutions wanted academic courses, increasing numbers preferred technical education. As the pre-industrial apprenticeship system became outmoded, voluntary groups tried to provide technical colleges. By 1895 the four cities and Wanganui had such institutions. In 1905 Hogben, whose attempts to persuade secondary schools to undertake technical education had failed, reluctantly authorized the first technical day-school. From the outset technical schools had inferior status, the prerequisite for admission being the Certificate of Competency (unlike the secondary schools which required the Certificate of Proficiency). Enrolments grew steadily, however, and by 1921 some 18 per cent of those proceeding to post-primary institutions attended technical schools. Until 1920 girls outnumbered boys at these schools, most of them taking commercial courses to equip themselves for the fast-growing secretarial sector. Privately owned colleges also proliferated to meet the demand for secretarial and commercial courses. Many conservative unionists considered these institutions as 'workers' universities'. The Apprentices Act of 1923 made it possible for employers to specify formal training as part of apprenticeship and in 1926 the Railways Department established its own training schools for boys apprenticed in the metal trades.[59]

Vocational training received more emphasis in the 1920s and 1930s. In 1927 the Department of Education, nudged by voluntary local vocational guidance groups, issued its first handbook on careers, and devoted three of the thirty pages to careers for girls. The Certificate of Proficiency became the major determinant of occupational opportunity. Most of the boys who failed to obtain Proficiency in 1920 went farming or labouring; most of the girls into domestic service. The majority of those successful at this level intended proceeding to the post-primary level, at least for two years. Some of the girls going beyond primary school intended staying at home and helping their mothers, but more wanted to take paid employment. The majority of those entering high school in the 1920s sought white-collar occupations — principally in teaching and clerical work. A small number hoped to enter the Public Service, by sitting the Junior Civil Service examinations, and a few wished to take up a profession or go to university. Although the New Zealand Educational Institute and the Post-Primary Teachers' Association urged the adoption of more child-centred methods and subjects in education, a cry taken up by the Atmore Committee in 1929, inertia prevailed; the school system remained authoritarian.[60]

Training children for roles in the work-force emerged as an important function of the educational system during the first decades of the twentieth century. The system was designed to produce not only economically useful skills, however, but also sound morals and loyalty to the British Empire. Education was seen as a method of socializing the young in order to produce good, productive, and efficient citizens. By doing this the schools would help to contain and eradicate problems such as larrikinism. They were to render the disadvantaged loyal to the social order by inculcating patriotism, fostering ambition, and socializing such children into hierarchically structured and time-dominated organizations. Uniforms and team sports may have been as important a form of education as formal instruction. The formulation of these goals coincided with the centraliz-ation of the education system under bureaucratic control. Education lost its decentralized character: schools were no longer community institutions where adults acquired skills of self-government and sought to acquire civilized values.[61] By the mid-twentieth century the schools had acquired the task of creating a stable and integrated community and equipping workers with skills essential to the economy.

War and depression disrupted the latter part of the period from 1890 to 1940 and called in question the ability of humans to control either their society or their destiny. The impact of the First World War on society is not entirely clear but the main trends continued: the power of the state grew; organization became even more important; fertility and mortality rates continued downwards; occupation became the key to living standards; and efficiency became a cult. War also intensified the belief that New Zealand was an ideal society, first among the troops and then at home, while quickening fears about its vulnerability. Even the mounting cynicism among the troops only strengthened their belief in 'God's Own'. At home men and women struggled and sacrificed to keep things the same. Despite the Efficiency Board's recommendation that women replace men in skilled manual jobs, for instance, in order to free more men for military service, no change occurred. The Government responded by instituting censorship of films and books, tighter controls over immigration, and inveighing against 'foreign' trusts. Although by international standards New Zealand enjoyed industrial peace in 1918–20, any small strike seemed fraught with enormous possibilities after the Bolshevik Revolution; although 'slums' were few, any 'slum' aroused intense concern that Old World evils had taken root. The speed with which New Zealanders blamed Massey and Ward for bringing the 1918 influenza pandemic here nicely illustrates both the consensus that 'disease', like disorder, was foreign, and that New Zealand, unless vigilant, was vulnerable to infection.

By removing some 120,000 young men for military service the war helped train them for industrial society. During 1914 and early 1915 most of the volunteers were young, single, and unskilled; quite a few were unemployed; and some took the chance to desert their wives. The Army finally agreed to issue camp passes to wives wishing to search for errant husbands. Initially the war acted as an 'agent of fusion'. *The Maoriland Worker* voiced the hope that 'our race' would 'emerge triumphant'; the Government released all those imprisoned during the 1913 waterfront strike; and the Prime Minister praised the fighting qualities of the Red Feds. The Army taught men obedience and gave them discipline. At home the war enlarged opportunities for women in white-collar occupations, increased the number of patriotic and welfare societies (such as the Red Cross), and fostered concern about the nation's health and family life. Venereal diseases became a national obsession and a fashionable topic of conversation. The demands of war — rationality, stability, predictability — strengthened the position of organized groups. Government departments, chambers of commerce, employers' associations, manufacturers' associations, the Farmers' Union, and the Sheep Owners' Federation became part of a governing consensus. The war also allowed the upper middle and middle classes to seize the initiative in social action. They organized the bazaars, patriotic societies, and knitting groups. As the casualty rate rose and the voluntary system of recruitment broke down, the Government assumed wider powers even to the point of forcing sports clubs to cancel games. With the National Register in 1915 and the introduction of conscription in 1916, a decisive step was taken in creating the modern state. Yet wartime organizations enabled New Zealand to respond quickly to its worst-ever disease-disaster, which coincided with the end of the war. Influenza paralysed the whole country in November 1918, killing 6,413 Pākehā and 2,160 Māori. One outcome of this unprecedented disaster was the new Health Act of 1920, which gave the Health Department its modern structure.[62]

After the first wave of pro-imperial nationalism passed, so too did the sense of unified purpose it had fostered. The prospect and then the reality of conscription (especially in 1917, when the Army took 76,000 men), intensified the strain of sacrifice.[63] Tensions flared into conflicts, although the issues usually involved equality of sacrifice. Xenophobia erupted sporadically to target 'Germans' and other 'aliens'. Sectarian conflict also became explosive, inflamed by the revolutionary situation in Ireland. The Protestant Political Association recruited thousands of members. In 1916 the formation of the Transport Workers' Alliance marked the resurgence of 'Red Fed' militancy. Strikes, large anti-conscription conferences, and inflation intensified the sense of class among urban and organized working men.[64] The increasing support for Labour amongst Irish working-class Catholics, although a source of anxiety to the Protestant middle strata, helped to defuse religious conflict and to institutionalize class conflict. In 1918 three ex-Red Feds won by-elections and the voice of protest erupted into Parliament. Some scoffed at Labour's political strategy, but industrial militancy proved futile in the economic climate of the 1920s.[65] Working men and their women (for they were strongly patriarchal) still suffered from unemployment, poor housing, inadequate medical care, and irregular wages. A disproportionate number of those in prisons, mental asylums, and industrial schools came from the homes of the unskilled. Yet these proportions declined and most working men were more concerned about their prospects of owning a home than they were about the jobless.[66] During the Depression of the 1930s, its unions shattered, the labour movement mounted a triumphant political offensive: the first Labour Government was elected in 1935 and contained four miners, two navvies, one shearer, two tradesmen, and a lawyer. The Prime Minister had been a barrel-washer. Four ministers had spent time in Industrial School.

During the 1920s and 1930s, however, industrial militancy and the vitality of the Labour Party seemed, to suburban, small-town, and rural New Zealand, a part of the disorder and anarchy of the modern world. In comparison with Australia and Britain, ironically, the union movement lost ground in the period 1921–31, few workers struck, and relatively few workdays were lost through strikes. The heightened sense of vulnerability made any evidence of conflict more momentous. A sputtering economy and political uncertainty, partly a function of the three-party system, quickened the sense of potential disorder. Moral conflicts, usually spearheaded by the young, provided potent symbols of the issues. People quarrelled over American films, women's fashions, cosmetics, and popular dances. Gay McInnes, who grew up near a small town in Central Otago, recalled how you could 'laugh yourself silly over Laurel and Hardy or sigh over Janet Gaynor or watch Fred Astaire flinging Ginger Rogers about in a world of floating gowns . . .'[67] Even in country districts the Military Two-step and the sensuous Fox-Trot now rivalled the Barn Dance. The values of consumption began to replace those of thrift and production, hire purchase spread like wild-fire, and advertising celebrated the arrival of the consumer society. The affluence of the growing middle strata and the introduction of the forty-four-hour working week encouraged the growth of amusement parks and spectator sports, and created opportunities for entertainment entrepreneurs. The first picture palaces were constructed in 1915, and by 1918 more New Zealanders probably attended the pictures each week than went to church.[68]

Demographic trends from the earlier period consolidated in the 1920s. The movement to the four main centres slowed but continued. Many ex-servicemen, having seen 'Paree', refused to return to farms and small towns. Thousands of the young followed their example and headed to the cities. Marriage remained popular. Men and women married younger (when they married for the first time), and men increasingly married women not much younger than themselves. Although the war legitimized the gendered division of labour, couples had fewer children. Companionship had largely replaced reproduction as the main goal of marriage. More couples used birth control (although abstinence probably remained more important than condoms). Following the amendment of the Divorce Act in 1920, more and more couples divorced. Only 33 divorces were granted in 1897; by 1926 the total had soared to 614. Pre-marital conception remained at about 30 per cent of all first births and illegitimacy rose. The war and the declining fertility rate undoubtedly disrupted the marriage markets of New Zealand, but the nature of these changes remains obscure.[69]

As the cities grew suburbanization continued. Defended as a solution to inner-city housing problems, suburbanization in the 1920s reflected, in Auckland at least, the activities of speculators and builders financed by the State Advances Department and the fast-growing building societies. Real-estate salesmen provided the ideology: the suburb meant better prospects for home ownership, no overcrowding, less disease, and a more natural environment. Municipal ownership of the tramways ended whatever relationship had existed between suburban speculators and transport entrepreneurs, but privately owned bus companies may well have been part of suburban promotion. Rising costs meant that the bungalow, a mixture of Californian and Australian influences, began to replace the villa as the typical suburban house. However, for many people the sputtering economy of the 1920s transmuted the popular dream of a suburban bungalow into a mirage. In Auckland's western suburbs, for instance, home ownership declined, the poor could not afford to move, and, as critics had warned, unplanned suburban sprawl had proved, by the end of the decade, as monotonous if not as shoddy as terrace houses.[70]

By the end of the 1920s rural society (outside Northland) had achieved greater demographic maturity and institutional stability than in the first decades of the twentieth century. By 1916 one of the last rural frontiers, the King Country, had churches of all major denominations in all the larger towns; most towns could boast one lodge or friendly society; and in some towns the Catholics had built their schools. During the 1920s the Plunket Society spawned branches throughout rural New Zealand. By 1920 the citizens of most small towns could visit the cinema once a week, buy phonographs and cosmetics, and dance the new dances. The automobile, the telephone, and the radio weakened localism, but did not destroy it. The social consequences of these changes, indeed, were controlled more effectively in rural and small-town society. Organizations such as the Country Women's Institute and Young Farmers' Clubs, both established in the 1920s, generally strengthened community cohesion. On family farms home and work remained undivided, thus evading a major consequence of industrialization, and social change only reinforced the role of the family. Rural families were still larger than in the cities, patriarchy more relevant, and the family remained a vigorous social and economic unit. Communication also continued to be informal, and newspapers local (although many dailies became weeklies); but urban journals, radio, rural postal delivery, developments in agricultural science, and such educational changes as the Correspondence School, prefigured the increasing tendency for knowledge and ideas to spread from urban to rural areas. During the 1920s small-town rural society became part of modern New Zealand, although in many respects it remained distinctive.[71]

The Depression, which started in the towns as early as 1926, altered some patterns for a few years. The drift to the cities stopped, illegitimacy fell, and abortion seems to have become quite common. Many couples postponed marriage, while the married postponed having children. Education and apprenticeship no longer guaranteed work. In occupations such as teaching, women came under pressure to surrender their jobs to men. After the riots of 1932 a nervous Government tried to force the unemployed to enter work camps in rural areas but no measure could disguise the extent of unemployment.[72] The magnitude of the 'Great Depression', denied at first by many but obvious to all by late 1931, led many men and women to reaffirm their traditional values of individualism and community cohesion. Crowds flocked to community sings, aviators such as Jean Batten became more popular than film stars, and many towns organized carnivals and festivals to boost confidence. The clergy of all denominations joined in this reaffirmation of traditional values, and gave it political significance in 1934–35 by attacking the Coalition Government. Unemployment, while considerably lower than in many societies, came to be seen as unacceptable. Even the Anglicans, never known for political radicalism, declared full employment the only basis for a Christian society.[73]

The Depression reveals some otherwise obscure dimensions of society. Unemployment itself, of course, had long been familiar to unskilled workers. The census indicates that the rate varied between about 9 per cent in 1896 and about 2 per cent, the figure for 1916, but official statistics almost certainly understate the problem. Each winter unemployment mounted as seasonal work declined. Bad weather compounded the problem. Particular industries, such as flax-milling, were very unstable in their demand for labour. But in a colonial economy the balance of payments largely determined employment levels. Local bodies traditionally attempted to give some relief by expanding their capital works programmes, and the churches still ran soup kitchens and provided some cheap accommodation, clothing, footwear, and fuel. The first study of the unemployed found that 54 per cent of those registered in October 1929 were unskilled, more than half had dependents, over half had been unemployed at least six weeks, a majority were born in New Zealand, and all but a small proportion of the immigrants had been in the country more than one year. As the Government retrenched vigorously in 1932–33, unemployment hit the semi-skilled, the skilled, and even white-collar workers. More and more older men with families found themselves jobless. Voluntary welfare organizations and even the Unemployment Board could not cope. In 1932 riots occurred in the four main cities, some sections of the jobless became organized, and by the winter of 1933 at least 12 per cent of the work-force were unemployed. By 1933 the jobless outnumbered paid-up members of trade unions.[74]

At the bottom of the social structure were the destitute and the criminal. Little is known about the antipodean *lumpenproletariat*, although police, prisons, and even industrial schools existed largely to contain and control this group. Mother Mary Aubert, who founded a home for incurables in 1900, a soup kitchen, a crêche, a kindergarten, and a home for unwanted children, probably knew more about those who lived beneath society than anybody else. She recognized the moral and social sources of destitution: 'So often it is old age, infirmity, sickness, accidents, the loss or the departure of the head and supporter of the family. . . .' Widows or deserted wives with children, the unskilled, and migrants from rural areas were vulnerable, the old and disabled most vulnerable. A commission which investigated the plight of disabled servicemen in 1930 found that most of them lived on the margins of destitution in good years, but downturns in the business cycle plunged them into dreadful misery and squalor. Others were doomed from birth, as the details about infants admitted to Mother Aubert's home for unwanted children show — 'rotten with syphilis', 'blind due to gonorrhoea'. The Red Cross Society, the Returned Servicemen's Association, and others such as the Society for the Protection of Women and Children tried to provide relief and help. The widespread belief that such problems could not exist in the new world made the task of such organizations doubly difficult.[75]

The destitute often lived in hovels and shacks in the overcrowded inner-city districts with small clusters of non-European immigrants such as the Chinese, Indians, and Lebanese. Local efforts to destroy slums had recurred since the bubonic plague scare of 1900, but were always sporadic and ineffectual. In 1905 the Liberals passed the Workers' Dwelling Act, but by

282

1919 only 648 houses had been built and the poor could not afford them. The Advances to Workers Act (1906) proved more effective. By 1919 the money lent under this scheme had helped build 9,675 houses. Fast-rising rents, especially in the cities during the First World War, worsened the problem. The influenza epidemic of 1918 focused attention on 'slum' housing and the Government responded by passing the Housing Act (1919) and, more importantly, by pumping more than £35 million through State Advances to workers and returned servicemen during the 1920s. The Railways Department undertook a limited experiment, building 300 houses of prefabricated materials in Lower Hutt, and a few local bodies responded with 'no great enthusiasm' (in 1924 the Dunedin City Council built seven cottages, for which there were 100 applicants). The major venture of the decade, undertaken by the Housing Department and the Auckland City Council, was based on R. B. Hammond's prize-winning design for a garden suburb in Orakei. This plan for workers' housing became one of Auckland's 'most expensive and exclusive residential areas'. The census continued to monitor the proportion of the population housed in flats and tenements, largely (it seems) because it took this to be a measure of overcrowding, but no marked changes occurred and the level of home ownership remained remarkably high.[76]

Although home ownership remained high, concern with inner-city housing mounted again in 1934–35. *Truth* reported that in Wellington's central area 7,000 families lived in 'rotten, decrepit, stinking, disease-pregnant, damp, and vermin-infested houses'. In Auckland 35 per cent of all inner-city housing was described by the City Engineer as totally unsatisfactory. A government housing survey in the late 1930s revealed 27,000 houses in urgent need of demolition and another 55,000 in urgent need of repair.[77] The Labour Government tackled the housing crisis with audacity and zest. A new Department of Housing Construction, initially in co-operation with Fletcher Construction, built 3,445 houses in three hectic years. More important, Labour set new standards in construction and design, experimented with area planning, built some impressive apartment buildings and democratized the bungalow. The State Advances Department (later Corporation) also introduced quality controls for all houses it helped to finance. The poorest and the most destitute still complained that they could not afford decent housing and the Government refused to authorize slum clearance.[78]

The Labour Government elected in 1935 removed many inequalities. The new Government believed that all New Zealanders were entitled to a job or an unemployment benefit, an income adequate for a family with three children, free hospitalization, free maternity care, heavily subsidized medical attention, and a free education to university level. The old, the poor, the unemployed, and children benefited. The state now provided welfare services appropriate to a modern, urban society. The bureaucracy enjoyed its second period of rapid expansion, and the scale of state and local body activity required unprecedented numbers of highly skilled technicians and professionals. Just as the Red Feds had unwittingly helped integrate the unskilled into a modernizing society, so the Labour Government, through its concern for human welfare, accelerated the process of modernization while guaranteeing the economic security of those most at risk. The working class, the Catholics, and indeed the Māori began to receive a fairer deal.[79] The demographic, institutional, and occupational structures which emerged between the 1880s and 1920s did not change greatly, but Labour's triumph, underpinned by rising export prices, helped persuade people that they had finally mastered their society and their destiny.

The power of the state had become awesome. As John A. Lee, the novelist and politician, said in *Civilian Into Soldier* (1937), the Army could do everything but make men pregnant. In that novel the Army was portrayed as a machine, the ultimate expression of industrial society. Some rituals, like those of Anzac Day, celebrated the value of human life within this increasingly impersonal world. The Labour Government restored a sense of human potency and purpose, at least briefly (for the Second World War began in 1939), but for thousands of New Zealanders the recurrent rituals of sport reaffirmed their belief that individual skill and character mattered — not only mattered but could also determine outcomes. The same rituals reassured the anxious that urbanization had not emasculated a society of pioneers. Ritual mattered more than result. New Zealand sent an indifferent team to Britain in 1935 and suffered defeat at Springbok hands in 1937, yet the game of rugby football enjoyed enormous popularity throughout the inter-war years. Boys played the game at all ages, inter-school competition became very important, and vigorous club competitions took place in the cities and the farming areas. Provincial matches attracted large crowds, often as many as a test match. The structure of the sport allowed ethnic, religious, and local loyalties to be expressed, yet transcended them; the game incarnated egalitarian values, team-work, and the conviction that individual strength and skills mattered. In an increasingly urban world of more rigid structures and impersonal forces, where the process of becoming more modern seemed to entail both a society and an economy less sensitive to human control, rugby reassured New Zealanders that man, if not woman, was still the master of his fate, the captain of his soul.

CHAPTER 11

Between Two Worlds

Michael King

New Zealanders in 1900 were in no sense the 'one people' ('he iwi tahi tātou') that Governor Hobson had proclaimed them to be at the signing of the Treaty of Waitangi in 1840. Nor could they be said to be the two peoples, Māori and Pākehā, that twentieth-century politicians became so fond of calling them. The European population still preserved local and group loyalties. Most of the Māori population saw itself not as Māori but as members of hapū (sub-tribes) or iwi (tribes).

Identity was expressed through descent lines and proverbs. In the waiata tangi (laments) and pātere (chants or songs of assertion) of the period, references to identity and loss are invariably tribal and regional, never 'Māori'. People living at Maungapohatu in the Urewera would, in place of a surname, recite their whakapapa back to Huti, progenitor of the hapū Tamakaimoana, and say at the same time, 'Tūhoe moumou kai, moumou taonga, moumou tangata ki te Pō' (Tūhoe extravagant with food, with heirlooms, and with human life).[1] They would regard themselves as being as far removed from Waikato Māori as from Europeans.

In the late nineteenth and early twentieth centuries isolation reinforced local and tribal identity. Most of the Māori population (some 45,000) was located in scattered rural communities; tribe lived apart from tribe and Māori from Pākehā. The major concentrations were north of Whangarei, in South Auckland, Waikato and the King Country, the Bay of Plenty and the East Coast, Rangitikei, Wanganui, and Taranaki. Families tended to live in kāinga or, in more isolated districts, in homes outlying from kāinga. Life for people in such settlements was oriented around family, community, and tribe. Where families were in stable home units, the community orientation was likely to be that of hapū. Sometimes it would be to a wider tribal unit, such as Tūhoe, or to a waka grouping such as Tainui or Mataatua.

Leaders were effectively the kaumātua (family heads). The hapū would be spoken for on community occasions by rangatira who usually had a hereditary claim to leadership but who also required the confidence of the kaumātua. The way was opening for men with acquired skills (vocational or literary), quick wits, and eloquence to bid for leadership positions against those whose claim was purely hereditary. In the North Island, community decision-making was still centred on consensus-forming discussion among family heads on local marae. South Island villages had established rūnanga in which whole communities were involved, and which were spoken for by upoko rūnanga (community heads). In rare cases ariki spoke for confederations of hapū or tribes, such as Waikato–Maniapoto and Ngāti Tūwharetoa; more often, as in the case of Ngāi Tahu, Arawa, or Ngāti Porou, spokesmen would be rangatira dominant at a particular time or nominated for a particular project. Within these structures communities would organize their hui, tangi, and church functions, arrange marriages to strengthen useful alliances, plan, construct and maintain communal facilities, deal with local conflict, discuss land grievances, land sales and land development, and prepare submissions to Parliament, to MPs, and visiting dignitaries.

Over the first half of the twentieth century these social institutions weakened, as a result of an earlier population decline and the continuing loss of land. Migration in search of seasonal work also dispersed some tribes. When people left their own communities they tended to settle in other rural Māori communities, adopting the identity and kawa of their hosts or the family into which they married. This practice initially mitigated detribalization, but by the 1920s with greatly increased mobility, its effects were becoming apparent. The Depression of the 1930s, the Second World War, and urbanization were to accelerate the growth of Māori identity over tribal identity.

This shift in emphasis was accompanied by a number of significant changes. Population decline gave way to recovery; health, education, and hygiene improved; styles of leadership changed and government co-operation increased; a rural people became predominantly city-dwellers; participation and conflict took the place of isolation. By the 1960s and 1970s the people as a whole had acquired a view of themselves as Māori, although a strong sense of tribal identity persisted. In this chapter, changes in social and economic conditions throughout the period are covered first; then political developments through the activities of both national and community leaders. The conclusion focuses on aspects of participation and reviews the situation of Māori within New Zealand society in the mid-twentieth century.

At the turn of the century there was a widespread belief among Europeans that the Māori race was doomed to extinction. This was based partly on declining Māori numbers and partly on European unawareness of the livelier manifestations of communal Māori life. In fact, the Māori population was increasing: from an estimated low point of 42,113 in 1896, to 45,549 in 1901, 56,987 in 1921, and 115,676 in 1951. A high level of infant mortality in the first quarter of the twentieth century kept the rate of increase low. In the next quarter a continuing high birth rate, with a decline in infant mortality, resulted in a more rapid increase of the Māori population. Further, because the Māori birth rate remained higher than that for Europeans, Māori began to increase as a proportion of the total population.

Between Two Worlds

The causes of this recovery were at work before they became apparent. The Māori birth rate in the late nineteenth century was increasing even when the population itself was decreasing (as it did in the decade before 1896). Life expectancy greatly increased because of a fall in the mortality rate, going from 22.5–25 years in 1890 to 32.5–35 in 1905 and 46 in 1925.[2] The increase was due largely to the growing immunity amongst Māori to introduced diseases. Māori who survived nineteenth-century epidemics of whooping cough and measles developed some immunity, and passed it to their descendants. Intermarriage also transmitted immunity.

Public health programmes were launched in the early twentieth century under the Maori Council Act of 1900. Apirana Ngata, a Ngāti Porou who had graduated in law and arts from Canterbury University College in the 1890s, was organizing secretary of the councils from 1902 to 1904. Two Māori doctors also stimulated the work of the councils — Maui Pomare who became the first Maori Health Officer in 1900 and Peter Buck (Te Rangi Hiroa)[3] who became his assistant in 1905. In the following year responsibility for Māori health was transferred to the Department of Public Health. Under the Councils Act, district health councils were formed to improve sanitation and living conditions through local committees and local Māori sanitary inspectors. Pomare reported that by 1908, 1,057 substandard whare had been destroyed and 1,183 new ones built, as well as 839 latrines. These programmes made some improvements in village sanitation, but the councils lapsed into relative inactivity within a few years. Population recovery early in the century owed less to reform than to the decline in epidemics, the acquisition of immunity, and the increase in the child-bearing age-group. The last major epidemic was the influenza pandemic of 1918, in which at least 2,160 Māori died, at seven times the European death rate.[4]

Reports on health and sanitation remained critical of conditions in most areas of Māori population well into the 1930s. Tuberculosis, typhoid fever, dysentery, and diarrhoeal and respiratory diseases persisted, and took a disproportionate toll. In 1938 the Māori death rate per 1,000 was 24.3; that for non-Māori 9.7; the Māori infant-mortality rate was 153.2 per 1,000 live births as against 36.6 for non-Māori.[5] Buck was appointed first Director of Maori Hygiene in 1920. He built up cadres of 'nurses to Maoris' in the field and tried to revive the local health councils. His measures were not conspicuously successful. The nurses had to deal with patients in their homes where satisfactory treatment was often impossible, as infected people could not be segregated in over-crowded and insanitary conditions. There were no opportunities for preventive medicine and health care of children. Seriously ill patients often could not be persuaded to enter hospital. Buck's interests were turning towards ethnology. In 1930 Māori health was transferred to the Health Department's district medical officers; this presented 'a direct challenge to bring the state of Maori health to a standard more comparable with that of Europeans'.[6]

Systematic reforms in the field of Māori health were instituted in the 1930s when Dr H. B. Turbott became Medical Officer, first on the East

Coast, then in South Auckland. He was later appointed Director of School Hygiene. Turbott began from a premise that 'the Maori child grows up with a bias of superiority in physique and nutrition but, taking toll from the second month of life, unfavourable environmental conditions counteract the inborn advantages. Over-crowding, bad housing, faulty sanitation, ill-balanced diets, ignorance of hygiene and healthy living, soon cause inferiority . . .'[7] He attacked these causes vigorously, in his own health districts and throughout the country. He lobbied Peter Fraser (as Minister of Health from 1935 and Prime Minister from 1939) for special appropriations. The Government began to provide septic tanks and privies for Māori homes. Under his guidance Māori began to seek treatment for tuberculosis, although this remained a scourge until antibiotic treatment became available in the 1950s.

The Government also turned its attention in the 1930s to Māori housing which, as Turbott observed, had severely detrimental effects on health. In 1940 he calculated that 57 per cent still lived in over-crowded conditions, with 'six to twelve or even more people' sleeping in small rooms, that 36 per cent lived in houses unfit by minimum Pākehā standards, that only half had safe water supplies, and that a minority broadcast rubbish, including faeces.[8]

As Māori were normally unable to obtain housing finance, except through land development schemes, the Coalition Government passed the Native Housing Act in 1935, and the Labour Government funded the measure in 1937. By 1940, 1,592 new houses had been provided under this legislation and under the land development schemes. Many of the dwellings were, however, little more than sheds, and scarcely anything was done for urban housing.[9] The housing programme was resumed at an accelerated rate after the Second World War. By 1951, 3,051 homes (16 per cent of Māori houses) had been built; the number of occupied huts and whare had dropped from 4,676 in 1936 to 2,275 in 1951; and the number of tents and camps from 1,528 to 568; shacks and over-crowded houses from 71 to 32 per cent of all Māori houses.[10] Although inadequate housing had not been eliminated, substantial progress had been made.

The combination of all these measures brought spectacular improvements in Māori health. The death rate from tuberculosis dropped from 37 per 10,000 in 1941–45 to 10.06 in 1951–55, and 3.82 in 1956–60. The incidence of typhoid dropped from 14.2 per 10,000 in 1932 to 2.6 in 1948. Infant-mortality rates fell. The life expectancy of Māori rose from 46.6 years for males and 44.7 for females in 1925–27 to 57 and 59 in 1956–57.[11]

While efforts were being made to improve material conditions, some attention was also directed toward education. Up to the mid-1930s, both denominational and government Native Schools reflected the prevailing belief that the future of the Māori was in rural areas. In accordance with this belief, the Director of Education said in 1931: 'we should provide fully a type of education that would lead the lad to become a good farmer and the girl to become a good farmer's wife.'[12] The curriculum in Māori schools emphasized agriculture and manual and vocational training for boys and domestic training for girls. Few Māori pupils moved beyond primary level (about 8.4 per cent of Māori aged thirteen to seventeen in 1935).[13] Most were defeated by the Proficiency examination, the need to pay fees, or the scarcity of Māori secondary schools such as the church boarding-schools of which Te Aute College in Hawke's Bay was the most celebrated.[14] In 1925 the Maori Purposes Fund Board was set up, and at first it was chiefly used to provide scholarships for secondary education.[15]

The Labour Government elected in 1935 increased expenditure on education, consolidated rural schools, organized transport, abolished the Proficiency examination, made secondary education free for every pupil, and raised the school-leaving age to fifteen. Māori children thus benefited from the general upgrading of the education system. Although Native Schools, directly administered by the Department of Education, were still numerous, more and more Māori children were enrolled in the public primary schools administered by education boards. By 1953, 60 per cent of Māori children attended these public primary schools. By this time the Government had decided that Māori schools should be brought under the control of education boards, but gradually and with the consent of local communities.[16] Rural secondary education was improved by the building of eight Māori district high schools between 1941 and 1951, with an emphasis upon vocational training, especially woodwork and metalwork. These efforts and the movement to towns and cities increased the number of Māori pupils at secondary schools to about 30 per cent of Māori aged thirteen to seventeen by 1951.[17] But there was insufficient training for skilled manual work, and a lack of emphasis on academic education and professional qualifications.

Through changes in health, housing, and, to a lesser extent, education, conditions for Māori altered markedly in the first half of the twentieth century. Reforms in these fields, however, were dwarfed by the joint impact of two other features of the period — population increase at the beginning of the century and urbanization some forty years later. The movement of Māori to urban areas began during the Second World War, when manpower regulations and the Maori War Effort Organization opened up a variety of manufacturing and labouring jobs to Māori men and women.[18] The recreational attractions of city life also created in some areas 'a sort of fantasy contagion' that drew people to the cities.[19] In 1936 only 11.2 per cent of the Māori population had lived in urban areas; by 1945 this had risen to 19 per cent. After the war the need for jobs took families first into the smaller towns and then into the cities, and the urban increase continued.[20] There were 1,766 Māori in Auckland in 1935, 4,903 by 1945, and 7,621 in 1951.[21] The process was to intensify until by the late 1960s the Māori had become a predominantly urban people.

The consequences of this relocation were economic as well as social and cultural. Over the first half-century Māori had largely lost their traditional means of earning a living: much more of their land passed into Pākehā hands, and what remained was less and less able to support the growing population. They turned instead to a different economic system in the predominantly Pākehā towns and cities. Subsistence farming and collective ownership gave way to regular hours of work, wages, and, frequently, inequality of opportunity. Ownership of the land and its use were thus central issues for both Māori and Pākehā leaders throughout the period, and often remained a burning question for Māori who had become city dwellers as well as for those in rural areas.

At the beginning of the twentieth century well over 90 per cent of Māori lived in rural communities. The majority eked out a living from subsistence farming and seasonal labour — fencing, drain-laying, shearing, flax-cutting and processing, scrub-cutting, felling timber, gum-digging, and public works.[22] It was common for whole families or hapū to make up gangs specializing in specific jobs. In many areas they worked for local bodies or nearby European farmers. The Māori work-force of those years was a rural proletariat, part of it land-owning but not land-using; part of it disinherited by the loss of land. Māori farming was efficient on the East Coast and in northern Hawke's Bay, in part because Europeans such as the Williams family had helped to finance it. Few Māori at this time were wealthy. Some possessed large tracts of land, but usually of second-class quality needing capital and skill for development. Others derived considerable income from rents and sales, but it was rapidly used up, often for the benefit of community and tribe. Aroha and mana were attached to distribution rather than accumulation.

Māori had lost land by confiscation (Waikato, Bay of Plenty, and Taranaki), by unfair purchase in the South Island, and by the equally improper pressures exerted through the Native Land Court throughout the North Island. Even where they had inherited interests in land, these were frequently uneconomic. The numerous individuals named in certificates of title were awarded small and scattered shares. The land was marginal; it could not become productive without capital investment; it was divided by multiple inheritance. Māori farmers could not in practice raise loans from the state or private institutions. Most Māori farming was subsistence farming.

This situation often exacerbated racial tension. Europeans coveted land suitable for dairying and mixed farming. When Māori blocks lay idle as a result of these difficulties or for other cultural reasons (being tapu or having other traditional significance), it was taken as evidence of Māori unworthiness to own land or of racial and cultural inferiority. Though a great deal of Māori land was leased by Pākehā, this, at a time when the right to the freehold was a passionate cry, did not satisfy the settler demand for ownership. Māori landlordism was widely denounced; there was 'no getting over that inherent detestation of the white races, and especially of British peoples, towards anything which savours of rule by coloured or native races'.[23] Hostility to Māori landowning was fed by the land's frequently deteriorated and infested condition and by the failure or inability of its owners to pay rates and so contribute to local amenities, especially roading.

In the opening years of the twentieth century Pākehā demands for land grew. James Carroll, a Māori and Minister of Native Affairs in the Liberal Government from 1899 to 1912, was attacked for his 'tai hoa' policy of delaying sales and encouraging leasing. The Government had, under the Maori Lands Administration Act of 1900, set up a system of Māori-dominated land councils to encourage leasing. By 1905 it was forced to yield to pressure. In that year a new Act replaced the land councils with boards, under much more rigorous European control and with greater powers. An increased volume of Māori land passed through the boards into Pākehā occupancy and use.

Concern at the resumption of European land purchases led to the appointment of the Commission on Native Lands and Native Land Tenure in 1907, presided over by Sir Robert Stout, Chief Justice and former Premier; this was greatly influenced by Apirana Ngata, who had been elected Liberal MP for Eastern Maori in 1905. The Stout–Ngata Commission (as it came to be called) was set up to devise ways of utilizing Māori land and (implicitly) to do this in a manner that would be advantageous to both Māori owners and Pākehā would-be owners or leaseholders. In fact, the Commission proved itself almost wholly sympathetic to the difficulties of Māori owners:

The necessity of assisting the Maori to settle his own lands was never properly recognised. . . . The spectacle is presented to us of a people starving in the midst of plenty. If it is difficult for the European settler to acquire Maori land . . . it is more difficult for the individual Maori owner to acquire his own land, be he ever so ambitious and capable of using it. His energy is dissipated in the Land Courts in a protracted struggle, first, to establish his own right to it, and, secondly, to detach himself from the numerous other owners to whom he is genealogically bound in the title. And when he has succeeded he is handicapped by want of capital, by lack of training — he is under the ban as one of a spendthrift, easy-going, improvident people.[24]

But though the Commission called for action, little was done. Instead, more land was sold to Pākehā. Between 1911 and 1920 Māori holdings were further reduced from 7,137,205 to 4,787,686 acres. And of this total, over three-quarters of a million acres were leased to Europeans and a further three-quarters of a million estimated as unsuitable for development.[25] The tempo increased under the Reform Government after 1912. The new Native Minister, William Herries, pursued a policy of 'hustle'; he was amenable to the pressure of land speculators in a time of steeply rising land values, and towards the end of the First World War wanted to find land to settle returned soldiers. Maui Pomare, an MP in 1912 and a minister from that time to 1928, supported Herries, in the belief that the Māori would survive best if forced to be as resourceful and acquisitive as the Pākehā.[26]

Until the 1920s, such improvement as there was in Māori farming came chiefly from communal initiative. Some advantage was taken of the legal provisions for uniting land-holdings by consolidation (the exchange of interests to group shares into economic holdings) or by incorporation (vesting control of jointly held blocks in a committee of management). Until the mid-1920s, these attempts were mainly made on the East Coast and in the Urewera, especially among Ngāti Porou, guided by Ngata. At that time Ngāti Porou owned nearly a million sheep, a dairy company, a finance company, and a co-operative store. All this was accomplished without any significant loss of traditional attitudes and lifestyle.[27] But, although some substantial farms were established by both individuals and incorporations where there was suitable land, most Māori farming in the twentieth century remained small scale.[28]

In 1920 loans from accumulated Māori funds were made available to individual farmers through the Maori Trustee, but this did not go far enough to meet the growing demands on Māori farming. During the 1920s it became apparent that Māori land could not support the steadily increasing population unless Māori farming could become more efficient. It was Apirana Ngata who, on becoming Native Minister in the United Government of 1928, was able to pass the first effective legislation to assist Māori farming. He worked now in a more receptive climate. Pākehā politicians had become aware of the need to provide support for the growing Māori population; with the onset of the Depression in the late 1920s, too, there was a fear that Māori would become a burden on the taxpayer.[29] The efforts of Māori MPs and the Māori contribution to the First World War had also contributed to Pākehā acceptance of Māori needs.

The first Act for which Ngata was responsible as Minister provided, in 1929, state credit for Māori farmers. The district land boards allocated the loans under the administrative control of the Department of Native Affairs. Quickly a large number of state development schemes, incorporating hundreds of individual farms, were implemented. By 1934, seventy-six schemes were in operation, embracing some 650,000 acres, most of them in the eastern and central parts of the North Island.[30] Although in some cases Europeans were involved in administration, both leadership and labour were usually Māori and local. As well as increasing income and food production, the schemes made their impact on cultural life. Ngata's legislation owed much to his belief in the virtues of a rural and communal way of life that continued Māori traditions. Community buildings — carved meeting-houses, dining-rooms, and ablution-blocks — were erected to provide a basis for Māori activities such as hui, tangihanga, church meetings: a local and visible manifestation of Māori culture. By 1937 some 750,000 acres were being developed, of which 177,000 were under cultivation. The schemes were supporting 26,872 dairy cows, 29,213 run cattle, and 278,688 sheep, and were providing a livelihood for some 18,000 people, most of whom lived and worked in revitalized communities located on or near the land they were developing.[31]

The schemes became a permanent feature of Māori rural life, but Māori farming in general remained in a difficult situation. Some of the schemes, particularly in Northland, were on poor land — steep, unstable, remote —

and could not sustain production at an economic level. Others were too small, and this was true of dairy farms particularly (both Māori and Pākehā) throughout the 1920s and 1930s. Workers on such farms found that they could earn more as casual labour on more efficient farms, usually Pākehā-owned.[32] In other cases, land returning to Māori owners after the expiry of leases was in a run-down condition.[33]

These difficulties were exacerbated by the Depression. This hit especially hard in areas without land development schemes, where Māori depended for work upon Pākehā farmers and local bodies. Māori were among the first laid off, and, it is estimated, made up some 40 per cent of the unemployed.[34] It was harder for unemployed Māori to qualify for relief and payments were made at a lower rate, on the argument (for which Ngata was responsible) that many were normally unemployed in any case and could 'live off the land'.[35] But by 1933 three-quarters of the adult male Māori population was registered as unemployed; most relief payments made to them were funnelled from the Unemployment Board through the Native Department to workers on the land development schemes.[36]

The situation improved after 1935. The Labour Government abolished unequal relief rates and raised them for all relief workers. General economic recovery helped the land scheme farms and so increased rural employment. The benefits brought in by the Social Security Act (1938) for sickness, old age, and disability, and the expansion in the 1940s of family benefits, greatly increased the spending power of larger families. Some of the fear of grinding poverty was relieved. At the same time health services improved and (to a lesser extent) housing.

The majority of the Māori people remained, nonetheless, dependent upon farming, which could not support them. Uneconomic farming sent workers into the towns and cities; rural communities thus became less viable and urban migration more attractive. Rural depopulation and urbanization together were to contribute to a subsequent deterioration in race relations.

As social and economic circumstances changed, so too did concepts and styles of leadership. In the second half of the nineteenth century, defeat in war and loss of land had reduced the authority and independence of Māori leaders, both those who had opposed and those who had supported the settlers and their government. Some leaders, traditional or prophetic, had pursued separatist goals. But by the early twentieth century the more effective leaders tended to be those who could work in association with the Pākehā system of government. Later, some Pākehā took on leadership functions in Māori situations. All these people helped to change and improve the situation of Māori in the first half of the century.

The lingering support for small groups of separatists disappeared soon after the turn of the century. The Kotahitanga parliament based at Papawai, which had met several times in the 1890s, stopped meeting in 1902. The Kīngitanga parliament (associated with the King movement) came together regularly until the 1920s to discuss land grievances, theoretical applications of the Treaty of Waitangi, mana motuhake (the separate identity and sovereignty of the Māori people), and competing claims for chiefly authority. It became increasingly, however, a forum for one man, the Kingmaker, Tupu Taingakawa; and it was supported largely by his Ngāti Hauā kinsmen. After 1900 organization tended to revert to consultation and formation of policy within and between individual tribes. The exceptions were occasional inter-tribal hui to discuss national Māori issues at places such as Parewanui and Waahi; and, for a time, conferences of the Māori councils set up by the Act of 1900, which often used the Kotahitanga facilities at Papawai.

Efforts to preserve independence continued on a local and tribal basis. The majority who refused to accept the Maori Councils Act included the Tainui tribes who supported the Kīngitanga. Their leader, King Mahuta, accepted appointment to the Legislative and Executive Councils in 1902. But by 1910 he had returned disillusioned to the Waikato, and his followers limited their efforts to the management of local affairs. Parihaka, the Māori community most determined in the late nineteenth century to be non-tribal and to regulate its own affairs, disintegrated after the deaths in 1907 of its leaders Te Whiti O Rongomai and Tohu Kakahi.

Only one group sought complete independence — nearly one thousand members of the Tūhoe, Ngāti Awa, and Whakatohea tribes who followed the messianic leader Rua Kenana and his Wairua Tapu religion. His pā at Maungapohatu in the Urewera was raided by the police in 1916, and although Rua Kenana was apprehended on charges relating to seditious language and sly-grogging, the judge made it clear that the real issue was one of authority:

Now you learn that the law has a long arm, and that it can reach you however far back into the recesses of the forest you travel, and that in every corner of the great Empire to which we belong the King's law can reach anyone who offends against it. That is the lesson which you and your people should learn from this trial. . . .[37]

There was no more serious talk from this time on of separate Māori government.

More acceptable to the Pākehā was the leadership proffered by a group who came to call themselves the Young Maori Party. These were young professional men, most of them from the East Coast but some from the Arawa and Āti Awa tribes, who had been educated at Te Aute College and who worked together following the formation of the Te Aute College Students' Association in 1897. Several entered politics, not as a distinct political party but as Liberal and Reform MPs. The College's first headmaster, John Thornton, taught that 'when a weaker nation was living side by side with a stronger, the one weaker, poorer, and more ignorant . . . with no fixed customs, laws and habits . . . would soon die out, if it did not emulate the stronger. . . .'[38] The group's most prominent members were Apirana Ngata, Peter Buck, Maui Pomare, Tutere Wi Repa, Reweti Kohere, Edward Pohua Ellison, and Frederick Bennett (who was not educated at Te Aute). With the exception of Ngata, this group was 'characterized by its wholesale adoption of Pākehā culture and its readiness to scrap the surviving elements of its own. To them Māori society was degraded, demoralized, irreligious, beset with antiquated, depressing, and pernicious customs. Their task . . . was to reconstruct this society to make the race clean, industrious, sober and virtuous'.[39]

Their approach to Māori–Pākehā relations was pioneered by their political mentor, James Carroll, whose father was Irish and mother Māori. He believed that Māori parliamentarians should compete with Pākehā on their own terms and, where possible, beat them. He himself represented a European seat from 1893 to 1919, after six years as MP for Eastern Maori. Believing that there was no separate future for the Māori, Carroll frequently subordinated traditional Māori views to the Liberal Party policies of land acquisition. When he spoke of Māori needs, it was usually to point out aspects that his Pākehā colleagues would have to consider for tactical reasons. For a time he delayed further large-scale acquisition by Pākehā of Māori land, and he was genuinely sensitive to the difficulties of Māori owners. But he agreed fundamentally with Liberal policies and thought that the opening up of Māori land to Pākehā leaseholders would work to the advantage of both lessor and lessee.

The Young Maori Party leaders initially modelled themselves on Carroll. Like him they had to become national figures at a time when, to most Pākehā, Māori stocks were low and when overt racism was rampant. To win acceptance for their people and for themselves as Māori they had first to win acceptance as individuals, and this meant acceptance as Pākehā. Pomare stated this baldly in 1906: 'There is no alternative but to become a pakeha.'[40] This appealed to liberal Pākehā opinion as it did not present the threatening prospect of having to deal with the Māori as Māori.

Maui Pomare and Peter Buck were missionaries for this ideology. They believed that the Pākehā and his Western culture were permanent features of New Zealand life and that the future of the Māori lay in adopting Western practices, institutions, and technology. They advocated health and hygiene measures to halt what they believed to be the decline in population, and they encouraged literacy and agricultural development. They also advocated individualism in Māori life and the adoption of the Protestant work ethic; they sought to abolish what Pomare referred to as the pernicious customs of tangihanga, the hui, and the practices of tohunga.

By the end of the 1890s the separatist Kotahitanga campaign was petering out. Ngata and other advocates of co-operation with the Government, such as the Northern Maori MP Hone Heke Rankin, took charge and formulated proposals that emerged in the two Acts of 1900, the Maori Lands Administration Act and the Maori Councils Act. Of these, the latter was the more successful. The land councils, transformed in 1905 into land boards, became bodies that wholly served European interests. The Councils Act, in providing for district councils to supervise Māori affairs with powers similar to those for local authorities, recognized that Māori organization took place at community level. Māori councils were set up in

Part III: A Time of Transition

nineteen tribal districts, and in some operated vigorously through tribal leaders and committees. General conferences were also held to bring together elected Māori representatives from all over the country. The Liberal Government, Carroll, and Ngata hoped thus to divert support from the Kotahitanga parliament; and they succeeded.[41] But the councils were seriously under-financed by Government, and some met with a lack of co-operation. Around 1910 there was a general decline in their effectiveness.[42]

The Young Maori Party MPs fulfilled a function in articulating some Māori needs to Pākehā audiences and institutions, but amongst Māori people generally they wielded little influence outside their own electorates, and even within them (with the exception of Ngata) they had a restricted role. Tribalism remained the reality in rural Māori life, and tribal and regional leaders — such as Eru Ihaka in the far north, Te Puea Herangi in the Waikato, Te Hurinui Apanui of Ngāti Awa, Taare Tikao on Banks Peninsula — drew on local genealogy, tradition, and protocol for their support. They exercised the most effective influence over Māori community life until the Second World War. They remained proudly tribal. They were able to represent local opinion accurately and to harness community effort. From the 1930s they formed mutually advantageous relationships with parliamentarians and public servants. The Māori in Parliament needed strong allies at hapū and kāinga level: they had been elected to deal with taha Pākehā (the Pākehā aspects of life) not taha Māori; frequently they found themselves opposed by community spokesmen in their own electorates (especially in the case of Pomare) and yet not necessarily being rejected. For their part, local leaders strengthened their own positions by tapping the resources that parliamentarians like Ngata were able to offer. In this way Te Puea, Whina Cooper of Hokianga, Hone Heke Rankin of Ngāpuhi, Taiporoutu Mitchell of Te Arawa, Rima Whakarua of Taranaki, Hoeroa Marumaru of Rangitikei and Te Kani Te Ua of Ngāti Porou increased their influence, supervised local land development and marae-building programmes, stimulated cultural activities, and raised standards of living and morale in their territories.

Of this group none acquired more stature than Te Puea (1883–1952). Born into the Waikato kāhui ariki (paramount family) she rose to prominence in the Kīngitanga when she led the campaign against the conscription of Waikato Māori in the First World War. Her hereditary claims to leadership were strengthened by a sharp intellect, quick wits, remarkable fluency in Māori, and a formidable determination. All these qualities were in evidence when she established her model pā, Turangawaewae Marae at Ngaruawahia, from 1921. From the end of the 1920s she was a national Māori figure. Turangawaewae began to take on the character of a national marae, and Te Puea had access to additional resources from Government to achieve her objectives and to heighten her mana. With an effective local leader, Ngata's land development schemes had every chance of success; through them Waikato communities could subsist on their own territory and preserve their traditional life. This, in association with Te Puea's development of a regular calendar of Kīngitanga

296

activities in the 1930s and 1940s, took the Waikato a good way toward being, in her words, 'a people once again'.[43]

Like other successful local leaders, Te Puea was an innovator who appealed to precedent. In seeking the support of her people for a new programme, she would always find justification in tradition most often in the sayings of her grandfather King Tawhiao. Even when she was clearly breaking with tradition — by being a woman who stood and spoke in public, for example — she always made it clear that her action should not be taken as a reason for discarding tradition. She established too her own traditions: the Mahinarangi hui of 1929 made the Turongo hui nine years later easier; the makeshift hospital shelters and primitive attempts to cope with smallpox and influenza at Mangatawhiri anticipated a fuller health programme in the 1930s and 1940s. Even Western education became acceptable when she advocated it. She was able to strengthen the base of Māori values and institutions by the controlled intake and accommodation of Pākehā elements. 'Possibly the most influential woman in our political history', Te Puea was by any standards a remarkable leader.[44]

Some Pākehā politicians developed strong Māori sympathies. Foremost amongst them was Gordon Coates, initially Native Minister in the Reform Government from 1921 to 1925 and then Prime Minister from 1925 to 1928. Coates's sympathy for Māori grievances and his empathy with Māori leaders made him the first Pākehā politician to become a leader on Māori issues. He had grown up close to Māori communities around the Kaipara and he enjoyed Māori company and Māori ceremonial occasions. He became close to Ngata, then on the Opposition benches. When he became Prime Minister on Massey's death, Coates retained his responsibility for Native Affairs. He was determined 'to remove the old grievances so that economic and social change could proceed', and to tackle Māori problems 'in a comprehensive way rather than by the piecemeal efforts of the past'.[45]

As Native Minister Coates had an impressive record. He settled Arawa, Tūwharetoa, and Tūhoe land claims. He set an important precedent by establishing the Arawa Trust Board to dispense annual grants for economic and social development. He established the Sim Commission to inquire into confiscations of Waikato and Taranaki land, and its findings largely upheld Māori grievances. With Ngata advising him, he created the Maori Purposes Fund (from unclaimed interest earned by Native Land Boards) to make grants for educational, social, and cultural activities, and he passed the Maori Arts and Crafts Act in 1926 to set up an inter-tribal carving school in Rotorua and to encourage Māori art.

When Ngata became Minister of Native Affairs, in the United Government of 1928 and the Coalition of 1931, reform continued with increased momentum. He made use of large hui, such as that for the opening of Mahinarangi meeting-house in Ngaruawahia in 1929, for inter-tribal discussions on such general questions as how Māori should best share the kinds of opportunities offered by European society, and such specific topics as social welfare, land development, and Māori language, arts, and crafts.

Later there were major hui at Otaki (1936), Waitara (1937), Ngaruawahia again in 1938, and Ruatoria in 1943. Government programmes began to take root. For the first time, the activities of a Māori MP affected Māori life at community level.

In the late 1920s the leadership of Coates and Ngata on Māori matters began to be challenged by the Rātana movement. Tahupotiki Wiremu Ratana had begun his spiritual mission in November 1918, during the influenza epidemic, when he was forty-five years old. He had been sitting on the verandah of his home south of Wanganui, smoking his pipe and looking towards the Tasman Sea. A small cloud arose from the water and moved towards the house. When it was above him, Ratana heard the voice of God calling him: 'I have travelled around the world to find the people upon whom I can stand. I have come back to Aotearoa to choose you, the Maori people. . . . Cleanse yourself. . . . Unite the Maori people, turning them to Jehovah of the Thousands. . . .'[46] In the wake of this vision Ratana did attempt to cleanse himself. He read the Bible intensively, and J. H. Pope's pamphlet *Health for the Maori*. He began to preach the unity of the Māori people as God's chosen race, and to practise faith healing in his own family and then among a wider following. People began to visit him from all over the country.

Unlike other Māori leaders, Ratana was not of rangatira status and he did not have a tribal community base; he was not well educated in the Western sense, nor especially charismatic. He was a man of ordinary appearance, driven by an extraordinary mission and message. His success related to the social climate in which he began his preaching. The Māori people were reeling from the effects of the 1918 influenza epidemic. Many Māori servicemen had returned from the First World War impatient with the conservatism, the inertia, and the primitive conditions in rural Māori communities. They looked for leadership that would point the way towards material progress.

Ratana offered an Old Testament explanation for the displacement and suffering of the Māori people — identifying them, as earlier prophets had, with the Israelites — and he promised deliverance. Although he was emphatically Māori in his use of language and metaphor, he rejected many traditional practices and values such as tribalism, tangihanga, tapu, carving, and 'tohungaism'. He showed a practical side by encouraging wheat farming. His faith-healing was so spectacular that a settlement grew around his house and came to be called Ratana Pa. Ratana, now called the Māngai (for 'mouthpiece of God') by his followers, carried his preaching and healing to all parts of the country. He had a special appeal to those he called the Mōrehu — the growing number of detribalized, non-chiefly common people, most of them workers in country towns or subsistence farmers. He too quoted the words of Tawhaio: 'My friends are the shoemaker, the blacksmith, the watchmaker, carpenters, orphans and widows.'[47] He opposed rangatiratanga — the hereditary chiefly authority that Ngata, Te Puea, and others respected and exploited. The vision of betterment that he offered ordinary folk, many of them illiterate, uprooted, and (from the late

1920s) unemployed, appealed to them more than the sophisticated leadership of Pomare and Ngata.

From 1922 the Rātana movement was preoccupied increasingly with politics. It circulated a national petition (which eventually collected over 30,000 signatures) calling for the ratification of the Treaty of Waitangi. When Ratana's eldest son Tokouru contested Western Maori in 1922 he astonished observers by coming within 800 votes of unseating Maui Pomare. Ratana and his followers now constituted a political as well as a spiritual force. In 1928 the Māngai declared the end of his spiritual mission and the beginning of his temporal one, and he vowed to place four chosen followers — the Four Quarters — in the Māori parliamentary seats.

While much support came from the appeal of the Māngai and his programme, some arose from the apparent inability of the ruling political parties to offer ordinary Māori employment, land development, or the settlement of outstanding confiscation claims. The spectre of a radical Rātana bid for power and the loss of support for Reform and United candidates gave a sense of urgency to their programmes. In a separate effort to halt the growth of the Rātana movement, after it had been organized as an independent church, Ngata persuaded the Anglican Church to establish a specifically Māori bishopric of Aotearoa in 1928. F. A. Bennett was appointed, even though Ngata had supported a less 'Westernized' candidate. The Bishop was given no territorial diocese and could only enter other dioceses to minister to Māori at the invitation of his fellow bishops. The Bishops of Auckland and Waikato, in whose dioceses most of the Māori population lived, did not approve of the appointment and did not issue invitations. This severely restricted the work Bennett was able to do and reduced his position to one that was largely honorary.

Ngata was forced from office in 1934. Both the amount of money granted for land development (£500,000 by 1934) and his methods of administration provoked virulent attacks in the press and from the Labour Opposition. In 1934 a commission investigated criticisms of his adminis-tration, allegations of unfair dismissal, and accusations that he had favoured parties with whom he shared a financial interest. By his own admission Ngata had little time for 'red tape', which he regarded as unsuited to Māori matters. The commission's report[48] was unsympathetic to the case for 'special Maori requirements'. It found the Minister guilty of disregarding accepted channels, of not adequately accounting for the expenditure of state funds, of supporting Te Puea 'right or wrong' in disagreements with a European supervisor, and of using state funds without authority in the interests of his own family and tribe. None of these were criminal matters, but, unsupported by his colleagues and under fierce attack from the Labour Opposition, Ngata was forced to resign. He never regained ministerial office, although, during the Second World War, he had considerable influence with the Labour Prime Minister, Peter Fraser.

The Rātana movement in contrast enjoyed its first political success in 1932, when Eruera Tirikatene took Southern Maori in a by-election. Ngata had given little time to Māori problems in the South Island. With the intensification of the Depression in the 1930s, the Rātana movement gathered momentum. Candidates made much of the discrimination against Māori unemployed. They used the Treaty of Waitangi as a symbol for Pākehā breach of faith and called for its re-enactment. Some members of the Labour Party, especially a former Western Maori candidate, Rangi Mawhete, became convinced that Labour needed Rātana support. He persuaded H. E. Holland, Walter Nash, and Peter Fraser to attend meetings at which Rātana policies and wider Māori issues were discussed. Not all Labour MPs were convinced, but the capacity of the movement to secure Māori votes was indisputable.

Holland struck an informal alliance with the Māngai for the 1931 election. Rātana candidates, nominally independent, would vote with Labour; Labour would not put up official candidates. In 1932, Rātana pledged to co-operate with Labour and instructed Tirikatene to vote with it on most issues. When Tirikatene took his seat in Parliament, he was escorted by the two Labour whips. After the 1935 election Tirikatene was joined by Tokouru Ratana in Western Maori. Labour, by winning with a landslide majority, had increased its appeal to the Rātana movement. The Māngai visited the Prime Minister, M. J. Savage, at Parliament to formalize the association.[49]

No written agreement was drawn up or signed. Rātana candidates retained the designation Independent Ratana. Electoral support for the movement increased. Paraire Paikea took Northern Maori in 1938; and in 1943 Tiaki Omana achieved the incredible, replacing Ngata in Eastern Maori. The Four Quarters held the Māori seats, the prophecy of the Māngai was fulfilled, and for the foreseeable future Labour could count on retaining the support of those seats.

Ratana himself died in 1939. By then the pact with Labour had become part of the traditions of both movements. It was cemented both by Labour policies and by the continuing success of Rātana candidates, which in part depended on those policies. Māori workers shared in the expansion of economic activity, benefiting more spectacularly than Pākehā because their previous plight had been more acute. Labour introduced the secret ballot for Māori electors, equalized unemployment benefits and opportunities for housing finance, raised expenditure on Māori health and education, provided social security and the first Māori welfare officers, and settled contentious land claims in the South Island and Waikato. Labour on one hand made special provision for Māori needs, and on the other it helped Māori through its efforts to improve the economy generally and through its welfare policies. Labour's activities were welcomed not simply as a matter of monetary gain; they were also, as Te Puea noted in the case of Waikato, a public acknowledgement that many Māori grievances had been justified.[50] Although Rātana MPs may have been less capable than some of their predecessors and political opponents, they were able to point to a body of legislation that had improved the material circumstances of the Māori people.[51] Rātana followers also enjoyed the advantage that their basis was religious and political rather than regional and tribal. Hence they were more able to control party machinery throughout their electorates. In the 1940s and 1950s their grip on Labour Māori electoral organizations remained unchallenged.

Though the Labour–Rātana alliance was a matter of convenience, giving the Rātana MPs a voice in the governing party and giving Labour a group of safe seats, it was also a matter of conviction. This was especially true for Peter Fraser, Prime Minister from 1940 to 1949 and Native Minister after 1946. He believed that Māori deserved far more generous attention. And he was received by Māori with an affection not accorded any Pākehā leader since Coates. Fraser had informed himself on Māori affairs more than other Pākehā Labour politicians and had attended major hui and discussions. While Fraser was known to some as a man of frightening calculation and expediency, this was rarely his approach to Māori matters. His secretary, Michael Rotohiko Jones, has said that in Māori affairs 'Fraser governed with his heart rather than his head. He had never forgotten the experience of the crofters in Scotland.'[52]

In symbolic terms, Fraser's most important measures were his appointment in 1948 of Tipi Ropiha as Under-Secretary of Maori Affairs and the substitution of 'Māori' for 'Native' in all official usage from 1947, to avoid connotations of racial inequality. The change reflected the degree to which New Zealanders of Polynesian descent now regarded themselves as 'Māori'; and it indicated official sympathy and understanding. Fraser was able to say without hypocrisy in his final report as Minister of Maori Affairs, that his goal had been 'an independent, self-reliant and satisfied Maori race working side by side with the pakeha and with equal incentives, advantages, and rewards for efforts in all walks of life'.[53]

The most substantial piece of post-war Māori legislation was the Maori Social and Economic Advancement Act of 1945. The Māori MPs had sought to continue with a form of national organization, on the model of the Maori War Effort Organization, under their own influence and independent of the Department of Maori Affairs. But the Act was drafted in the Department, and so did not establish the structure sought by Tirikatene and Mawhete. It set up tribal committees and executives, from the marae to the regional level, concerned especially with welfare and marae administration. Welfare officers were appointed to the Department, and Maori Wardens were given welfare functions under tribal committees. By 1949 there were sixty-three tribal executives and 381 committees. Most were in rural areas and this at first limited their usefulness to the increasingly urban Māori population. Further limiting the effectiveness of the structure was the absence of an all-embracing body at the top, which the Māori MPs had sought; such a body was not formed until the Maori Council of 1962. Fraser's attitude to the Act was ambiguous. He feared that such a nation-wide organization would encourage Māori nationalism, and he had doubts about a measure offering special assistance. But he believed that it would strengthen existing Māori authority, and so lead to the ultimate objective of equality.[54]

Though the Act fell short of the hopes of the Māori MPs, and did not seriously challenge the role of the Maori Affairs Department as they had intended, it had some beneficial consequences. Welfare officers and wardens were able to assist those coping with the problems of urban life. A national organization, the Maori Women's Welfare League, was established in 1951 to involve the local communities in welfare.[55] The altered situation of the Māori people in the 1950s, compared with that of the early twentieth century — a higher educational level, a greater awareness of needs, an appreciation of the problems of urbanization — gave these post-war institutions a more real function than the councils set up in 1900.

Much of the responsibility for the administration of this Act and later measures that extended it fell to a new group of Māori leaders. They had been in the Maori Battalion and their attitudes were formed by experience in the Second World War. Men such as Jim Henare, Arapeta Awatere, Rangi Royal, Charles Bennett, Bill Herewini, Fred Baker, Moana Raureti, and John Rangihau moved into posts related to Māori concerns in the Public Service. Many had completed university degrees with rehabilitation assistance. Some, such as Henare Ngata and Harry Dansey, stayed outside the Government and Public Service but dealt with both in tribal and incorporation administration. They accepted that Western education and administrative skills were necessary in order to function within the bureaucracy. But, unlike their Young Maori Party predecessors, they had seen the survival of Māori language, ritual, and values, and they were impatient with anything less than full equality. One of their number, Rangi Logan, voiced their feeling in the 1946 election campaign: 'We did more than our share at El Alamein and elsewhere . . . we shed our blood in two world wars.' If this had done nothing else, he declared, it had at least purchased the right to equality.[56]

These men brought about the repeal of legislation prohibiting Māori from buying liquor for home consumption. They spoke out against other instances of discrimination in employment and accommodation that occurred with increasing frequency as Māori moved into urban areas after the war. Under Tipi Ropiha's leadership, they administered welfare policies designed to ease the transition to urban life. They accepted the need for the Department of Maori Affairs and its hierarchical structure with largely Pākehā direction at district level. They accepted, too, the land development schemes, the incorporations, and the welfare services. They realized that to make an impact on the political parties and the Public Service they had to lobby as Māori stating Māori causes: a tribal approach would have had little influence. Their Maori Battalion background helped them to view Māori as a people, rather than as a group of competing tribal units.

They were to be challenged a generation later by a group of young and largely urban Māori dissidents, many of whom had tertiary education. These spoke out for Māori interests more emphatically and more abrasively, and they were to question whether the Public Service and local authority structure, with Pākehā in key positions, was the most appropriate for Māori needs and aspirations. But in the 1940s and 1950s the pre-eminence of the post-war leaders was unchallenged.

The changes in the first fifty years of the twentieth century increased Māori participation in New Zealand life. Urbanization reduced the physical separation of the two races; Māori leaders entered national politics to secure some protection and some advantages from a system dominated by Pākehā. The Māori contribution to the two world wars also significantly altered the standing of Māori in Pākehā opinion. By the 1950s participation in this and other national activities made the Māori presence more visible.

Māori society had always placed a high value on prowess in battle, and this tradition continued. James Carroll was keen to lead a force of Māori to Samoa in 1899, and in March 1900 a large Māori meeting in Wellington demanded the despatch of a Native Contingent to the Boer War. Until 1914, however, the British Government would not use non-whites against whites. In the First World War the recruitment of Māori was allowed first for garrison duties, and from the time of the Gallipoli campaign, for combat zones. To the Māori parliamentary leaders especially, it was essential that Māori show themselves to be the equals of Pākehā in recruitment, casualty rates, and fighting skills. They raised volunteers for the Pioneer Battalion (conscription was not at first applied to Māori); Peter Buck sailed with the first contingent to Egypt. The recruitment campaign was not, however, an unqualified success. Some 2,200 men volunteered (about 20 per cent of the eligible age-group), but it was difficult to maintain reinforcements. Some tribes — Arawa, Ngāti Porou, and Ngāi Tahu — contributed disproportionately; others like Taranaki hardly at all. In Pomare's own electorate, Tainui refused to enlist and were conscripted towards the end of the war as a punishment.[57] The Māori contribution to the war effort, especially in Gallipoli and France, had some of the effect sought by the Māori MPs. It became more difficult for Pākehā leaders to discriminate against Māori. But the hopes of returning Battalion members that the conditions of war-time equality with Pākehā soldiers would continue were not fulfilled. There was not even an adequate rehabilitation programme for Māori servicemen.

The Māori response to the Second World War was more whole-hearted. There was no organized opposition to recruitment, and even without conscription over 17,000 Māori enlisted and 11,500 took places in essential industries. The Maori Battalion distinguished itself as a combat unit, particularly in North Africa and Italy, and individual soldiers such as Moananui-a-Kiwa Ngarimu and Arapeta Awatere were regarded as heroes by all New Zealand troops. At home the Māori contribution was co-ordinated through the Maori War Effort Organization. Under the direction of Paraire Paikea, MP for Northern Maori and Minister in charge of the Maori War Effort, it appointed recruiting and liaison officers at tribal level, and set up 407 tribal committees and sixty executives. These encouraged enlistment, mobilized men and women for essential industries, directed the growing of crops needed for the war effort, raised funds for the Red Cross, and collected comfort items for Māori prisoners of war and troops.[58]

Māori consciousness and confidence grew as a result. Māori had contributed to a successful national effort as a recognizably separate ethnic group with distinctive ways of organizing and operating. Returning servicemen this time demanded equality more successfully. The land development schemes were expanded as a rehabilitation measure, and Māori received business loans, tools-of-trade loans, trade training, and other educational assistance. The Rehabilitation Department, which continued its work well into the 1950s, insisted upon equality of treatment for Māori servicemen.

One of the few other national activities in which Māori participated fully was rugby. The game fostered a sense of identity amongst Māori, and on the football field Pākehā could see Māori engage in an activity that they understood and appreciated. The first Māori to represent New Zealand overseas went to Britain and Australia in 1888–89 as the New Zealand Native Team. Other tours followed, beginning in 1910. Māori were also selected for the country's national team, the All Blacks. There was no reluctance to accept Māori talent, except in the case of tours of South Africa, when Māori players were stood down. The differences between the two great rugby-playing nations were highlighted in 1921, however, when a Māori team played the Springboks at Napier. The local *Daily Telegraph* published a report by a South African journalist, expressing outrage at the sight of Europeans supporting the Māori against the white South Africans.[59] In the ensuing controversy, Māori and Pākehā opinion was unequivocally opposed to the South African viewpoint; most New Zealanders, however, continued to tolerate South African dictation of the racial composition of All Black teams touring that country.

To a lesser extent, national events such as royal tours and exhibitions also afforded opportunity for participation. At the exhibitions held in Christchurch (1906) and Dunedin (1925), and at the Centennial Exhibition of 1940, Māori culture was strongly represented; but in focusing on carving, costume, and action song the exhibitions probably conveyed little of the strength of Māori values for those committed to them. Māori loyalty to the British Crown and its representatives was a constant theme of twentieth-century Māori–Pākehā relations. For royal visits Māori were assembled at Rotorua for a single national welcome. Most tribes were represented, although many were scornful of the Arawa hosts because of the attention they gave to the entertainment of tourists. Some, such as Kīngitanga leaders, boycotted the royal functions at Rotorua because they wanted to welcome the visitors on their own territory, as other New Zealanders did. The Kīngitanga fulfilled a long-standing ambition in 1953 by having Queen Elizabeth II meet King Koroki at Turangawaewae.[60]

As the Māori presence began to be felt, Pākehā attitudes altered: respect gradually grew, and with it a degree of acceptance of Māori values. In addition, the changing climate of international opinion had its impact. The New Zealand Government embraced the idea of self-determination for peoples under colonial rule, and the Second World War itself began the world-wide process of decolonization. Ideals of racial equality began to be asserted more emphatically at home and abroad.

By mid-century there was a strong feeling that one era of Māori development had finished and another was beginning. This was voiced at the round of hui marking the six-hundredth anniversary of the reputed arrival of the 'Great Fleet' of canoes. The most dominant of the earlier national leaders had died. The Labour Government had been defeated at the end of 1949 and National had come to power without a single Māori member and without any conspicuous expertise in or sympathy for Māori affairs.

Urbanization in particular demanded dramatic changes in the management of Māori affairs. It presented migrants with a set of Pākehā suburban *mores* not experienced in Māori communities. Salaried incomes, accommodation, hire purchase, and door-to-door salesmanship presented difficulties; there was discrimination in employment, accommodation, and hotel bars. Māori and Pākehā were interacting in a variety of situations for the first time.

Differences between Māori and Pākehā thus became more apparent. In 1951, 57 per cent of the Māori population of 115,676 was twenty years old and younger (as against 34.8 per cent of Pākehā). The Māori birth rate was still considerably higher than that for non-Māori: 43.6 per 1,000 in 1955 as against 25 for non-Māori. The majority of the Māori work-force was unskilled and earning low incomes, especially in agriculture and related industries (33 per cent in 1951), and manufacturing (23 per cent). Only 3.36 per cent of Māori workers earned £700 or more per year, compared with 18.6 per cent for non-Māori. In 1956 only 6.56 per cent of the Māori work-force held professional, managerial, and clerical positions as against 26.69 per cent for non-Māori. All these factors combined to make urban Māori more vulnerable than Pākehā to economic hardship. Lower standards of education, income, health, and housing, and higher rates of Māori crime, became problems in the 1950s but attempts to deal with them — such as trade training schemes and hostel accommodation in towns — were not made on a large scale until well into the 1960s.

Aspects of Māori social structure and behaviour — the function of the extended family in an urban context, the problem of holding hui in the city, the question of whether to take tūpāpaku (corpses) home or to conduct tangihanga and burials in the towns — needed to be redefined. People from differing tribal backgrounds had to learn to co-operate to solve shared problems. Differences of kawa had to be resolved, traditional suspicions and antagonisms discarded or submerged. People in areas absorbed by expanding cities were sometimes unwilling to let others use existing marae facilities. New urban marae were set up. Māori discovered that detribalization could lead to a shared sense of Māori identity.[61] The numerous body of Mormons (Latter Day Saints) centred their lives upon their place of worship and its facilities, and developed a sense of identity outside the tribe, yet not specifically Māori.[62]

Māori were now beginning to act with a growing consciousness of Māori rather than tribal identity. This had been fostered by service in the Pioneer and Maori Battalions, by inter-tribal hui, by the gradual acceptance of agencies such as the Maori Purposes Fund Board, by the popularity of haka and action-song competitions, by co-operation in the construction and decoration of meeting-houses, by the growth of Māori sport, by participation in the Māori sections of the Christian churches, and through supra-tribal organizations like the Maori Women's Welfare League, established in 1951. The Rātana movement also did much to extend this growing sense of non-tribal Māori identity. The day-to-day interaction in the towns and suburbs of Māori from different tribes and backgrounds added knowledge of Māori identity to that of tribe. The term Māoritanga now came into wider use. It had been coined originally by Carroll to emphasize what New Zealand Polynesians shared: their language, manners of greeting and farewell, ways of giving and receiving hospitality, ways of relating within extended families, ways of dealing with death.[63]

Thus the 'two peoples, one nation' theme enunciated by the Governor General Lord Bledisloe in 1934 began to have some validity.[64] The Europeans of New Zealand were confronted, as they had never expected to be at the turn of the century, by an articulate, identifiable minority. The concept was useful in persuading a European-dominated Parliament and Public Service that the indigenous inhabitants were as worthy of consideration as the European immigrants; and, ultimately, that they needed more-than-equal consideration in education and land development to bring about equality of opportunity. The Stout–Ngata Commission's recommendations on Māori farming could be overlooked in 1908; a generation later they would win official acceptance because of the growth in Māori population and the growth in Pākehā regard for Māori.

New Zealand did not achieve the tranquil and egalitarian ideal proposed by Bledisloe, but the 'two peoples, one nation' myth helped protect the country from some of the more extreme manifestations of prejudice. It provided a moral imperative to which at least lip-service was paid and against which the performance of governments and individuals could be evaluated. It was to become, in the 1960s and 1970s, an ideological basis for bending national institutions towards Māori needs.

Harmony was assisted at least as much, however, by the fact that the two races were largely insulated from each other between the wars of the nineteenth century and the urbanization of the mid-twentieth century. As urbanization increased, active discrimination and passive lack of equal opportunity, especially of an institutional kind, became more apparent. Māori were told they had to learn about the Pākehā way of life; there was no pressure on Pākehā to learn Māori language and customs. Māori values and institutions had a lower status than their Pākehā equivalents. Proposals for the teaching of Māori were subject to 'the Pākehā veto'.

As contact between the two races increased, the attitudes of Māori leaders to Māori culture changed. Initially Ngata, Buck, and Pomare had worked to incorporate Western elements into Māori life. They had not even advocated the retention of the language. By 1929, however, Ngata saw a greater value in traditional elements of Māori life. 'We have survived to maintain some of the old traditions', he wrote to Buck, 'chiefly because back of us in those days was a small remnant who prized the tribal traditions and folk-lore, kept up the interest in the whakapapa, performed some of the old time hakas and carried on many of the crafts. Can we in our turn supply that background . . ?'[65] Ngata came to recognize that Māori were to remain a separately identifiable section of the New Zealand population, that Māori cultural forms were to persist with this physical survival, and that 'nothing was worse than for one to be with Maori features but without his own language'.[66]

From this time there was an increasing recognition by national Māori leaders that Māori society and its values had a present and a future. Ngata in 1940 spoke of Māoritanga as 'an emphasis on the continuing individuality of the Maori people, the maintenance of such Maori characteristics and such features of Maori culture as present day circumstances will permit, the inculcation of pride in Maori history and traditions, the retention so far as possible of the old time ceremonial, the continuous attempt to interpret the Maori point of view to the *pakeha* in power'.[67] There was also a recognition that the survival of Māori language and culture required conscious efforts to promote them. This new awareness created pressure for Māori language, history, and customs to be taught in schools to all pupils, not only to Māori children in Māori homes. Te Puea Herangi took up this theme in 1949: 'The language, history, crafts and traditions of the Maoris should be an essential part of the curriculum throughout the country. . . . Unity of Maori and Pakeha can only grow from each sharing the worthwhile elements in the other's culture.'[68] It was the cry of the future. But it was not to be taken seriously by the country's legislators and educational authorities for another generation.

CHAPTER 12

The Climate of Opinion

P. J. Gibbons

The habits of mind of European New Zealanders in the 1890s were predominantly British, like the settlers themselves. With the exception of a radical tradition to be imported from Australia after the turn of the century, the stock of both people and ideas was fairly complete by the 1890s. The British immigrants who continued to arrive throughout the first quarter of the twentieth century (apart from the war years) became numerically less significant as the size of the society they joined steadily increased, and despite the valuable intellectual and artistic accomplishments of a few individuals, collectively these later immigrants added nothing new to the ideas already in place by the 1890s. To understand, organize, and express their relationships with each other and with the rest of the world over the next half-century, then, European New Zealanders, both immigrants and locally born, were equipped with a stock of nineteenth-century British ideas. Plucked from their dynamic original social context, many of these British social attitudes and cultural values atrophied in a colonial framework where the social and cultural challenges which caused change in the parent society were absent. But colonial culture was free from certain constraints that operated in the older society. British ideas were often developed by the colonists in new and peculiar ways, so that by 1940 many essentially nineteenth-century British ideas had come to be expressed in a distinctively New Zealand manner.

What had been brought to New Zealand was not the full range but a selection of British social attitudes and cultural values. This limited the development of variety in the colonial culture, but, in the last years of the nineteenth century, New Zealand society still showed some kinds of variation. Particular regions, for instance, were marked by the religious and cultural preferences of the founders: Otago and Southland were Scottish and Presbyterian, while Canterbury and Hawke's Bay remained vestigially Anglican. By 1940, the diversity of British immigrant traditions had been transformed into a broadly colonial culture in which religious, regional, and cultural variations had become insignificant, where they had not entirely disappeared. The immigrants had died and the locally born colonists, already in a numerical majority by the 1890s, became dominant. However, the creation of a single colonial culture was also a highly conscious process.

Those classes which had most power — the gentry, the urban *haute bourgeoisie*, and the lower middle class — established the hegemonic values for the whole society; that is to say, the ruling classes successfully projected their particular ideological views to the extent that the subordinate classes generally accepted them as the natural way of interpreting and ordering the world. In the formation of public values the rural and urban lower classes had little influence, Māori people none at all. Women were not encouraged to express their views, except in certain artistic activities. The climate of opinion was that created by British-descended white adult males of the colonial ruling classes. Nevertheless, hegemony by definition implies resistance, and working class people, and women, as groups and as individuals, continually contested the consensual values.

The cultural life of New Zealand between the 1890s and 1940s can be discussed in three periods which, whatever the continuities, appear reasonably distinct one from another. From the 1890s to the First World War the richness of colonial life was provided by immigrants. At the same time, the homogeneity of colonial values was being emphasized both through a concern with racial identity and by the rejection of an imported radical political tradition. In the period from the end of the war to the end of the 1920s immigrant vitality had largely been replaced by a narrow, stern, relatively barren colonial version of the old values, especially those of race and empire. In the 1930s the hegemonic structure was not destroyed but considerably transformed under the impact of the Depression: the decade was marked by diversity and dissent, although these were within the limits of what had by then become an identifiable colonial tradition.

European New Zealanders of the late nineteenth century were, with a few ethnic exceptions, proud to call themselves British. For the colonists this was not only a cultural definition but also a racial one. They knew that Edward Gibbon Wakefield, Julius Vogel, and other 'systematic' colonizers had advocated careful selection of immigrants, and they therefore assumed that most colonists were the pick of British stock, equal to the best of the British, better than the worst, and certainly clean of the convictism that tainted neighbouring Australians. From such a perspective New Zealanders could feel they had a special destiny in the vanguard of British civilization.

New Zealanders ranked others as well as themselves on racial grounds. The European 'races' were superior to the non-European; the British 'race' had created the finest of all civilizations. The colonists therefore regarded as both acceptable and inevitable the subjection of non-European peoples by the imperial agents of European states. But they also believed the British way of life ought to prevail and they were distressed to see Samoa divided in 1899 between two foreign powers, Germany and the United States. In 1900 New Zealand was allowed by Britain to take up the white man's burden in the Cook Islands. By then, several thousand volunteer troops from New Zealand were involved in the South African war. Though the Afrikaaners were white farmer-settlers too, they were reviled by New Zealanders. Antipathies may have been sharpened by geographical isolation, but close contact did not necessarily make colonists more tolerant: when several hundred Dalmatians (from modern Yugoslavia) settled in the North Auckland gumfields during the 1890s New Zealanders were fiercely antagonistic towards them.[1]

The most unrelenting racial hatred was directed against 'Asiatics', especially Chinese people. Legislation severely restricted Asian immigration. The small numbers of Chinese who arrived in New Zealand were hard-working and law-abiding, yet New Zealanders persuaded themselves that Chinese people were debauched and drug-ridden, inclined to the worst vices and perversions, a threat to white womanhood and the purity of the Anglo-Saxon race. They were afraid, too, of the 'Yellow Peril', the countless millions believed to be waiting to swarm down from Asia to the thinly populated lands of the South Pacific. Rhetorical threats sometimes degenerated into physical attacks upon 'Celestial' launderers and greengrocers, and in Wellington in 1905 an elderly Chinese man was murdered by a European wanting to draw attention to his anti-Asiatic crusade.[2]

Concern with racial purity was not only a factor of settlement and colonial isolation but also an echo of ideas from overseas. Efforts to strengthen the physical and moral qualities of the colonists were similar to movements in Britain. In New Zealand the school cadet system and conscription were both intended to improve the race as well as defend it. The late nineteenth-century British debate about charity, pauperization, and degeneracy surfaced in New Zealand too. 'Outdoor relief', wrote the Inspector-General of Hospitals and Charitable Aid, Duncan MacGregor, in 1897, 'is as catching as small-pox and just as deadly.'[3] Edward Tregear, Secretary of the Labour Department, had been dismayed in the 1890s by his inability to keep casual labourers and wandering swaggers in regular work and, with German examples in mind, he advocated compulsory work-camps for the lazy and shiftless.[4] The eugenics movement, strong in Britain, Germany, and the United States, aroused some interest in the colony, and W. A. Chapple's 'scientific' study of *The Fertility of the Unfit* (1903) was written and published in New Zealand. 'The unfit in the state include all those mental and moral defectives who are unable or unwilling to support themselves according to the recognised laws of human society.' Regretting the infecundity of the fittest, Chapple proposed compulsory sterilization of the unfit.[5]

Belief in the superiority of the British people and development of myths about the selection of the original immigrant stock provided most European New Zealanders with a collective identity, a broad definition of themselves and their place in the world. They further defined themselves, and distinguished between each other, in terms of cultural origins and class. There were two large groups for whom loyalties based upon cultural origins were important. In Otago and Southland the Presbyterian Scots-descended settlers continued to give cultural life a distinctively Scottish flavour even after most of the Scots-born settlers had died. Unlike the Scots, the Irish had no particular area to call their own but, like the Scots, the Catholic Irish kept a sense of identity through religious faith and clerical leadership. The recurrent crises in British domestic politics over Ireland were widely reported and keenly followed by the Irish in New Zealand, and well into the twentieth century the Anglo-Irish, the Scots-Irish, and the Catholic Irish viewed each other suspiciously through the kaleidoscope of Irish history.[6] No other major group maintained an identity based upon locality or region of origin in Britain. Moreover, the high rate of geographical and occupational mobility within the colony, especially in the generation before the First World War, worked against the formation of strong vertical ties within local communities. Social attitudes and cultural values for most colonists were based upon class loyalties.

In the earliest period of organized European settlement the public values, the social and ideological orthodoxy proclaimed most frequently by those who attempted to set standards for society as a whole, were those of the gentry. Some of this group were immigrant English gentry, others 'self-made'. Though several developed urban business interests, their wealth, like that of the English landed families upon whom they modelled themselves, was derived from extensive landholding. They believed that people of their social eminence had a duty to provide political and cultural leadership for the colonial community. During the 1890s the political power of the gentry at the highest level was circumscribed, though it never entirely disappeared; but they maintained their dominance in educational institutions (particularly in secondary schools and in the four colleges that made up the University of New Zealand), in the Anglican Church, and in 'high culture' — notably literature and the fine arts. Their influence was further assured through the deference paid them by other colonists, especially lower-middle-class people who admired and imitated as much as they ridiculed the gentry's cultural pretensions and social rituals.

The classic middle class, the urban capitalists or *haute bourgeoisie*, were to be found mainly in the four largest towns. These representatives of the *haute bourgeoisie* were perhaps most prominent in Auckland and Dunedin — men such as John Logan Campbell, Arthur Myers, James Parr, L. D. and Arthur Nathan, Ernest and Eliot Davis, Bendix Hallenstein, Willi Fels — who engaged in importing, in large-scale retailing, in manufacturing. Whereas the gentry tried to maintain the values and relationships of pre-industrial society, the *haute bourgeoisie* propounded in public and exemplified in their work the values of modern capitalism; they believed in private enterprise, individualism, competition, freedom from any kinds of controls or restraints that might reduce the reproduction of their invested capital. The tolerance, worldliness, and sophistication of the *haute bourgeoisie* set them apart from the rest of colonial society. They were, in the colonial context, cosmopolitan people, often well-travelled and wealthy. Their range of interests was broad: they liked making music and hearing it, enjoyed the theatre, owned racehorses, filled their homes with fine furniture and the best art they could find. Their patronage of the arts was as important as that of the gentry in the development of high culture.[7]

In a small colony, however, there were few such people. Most New Zealand merchants were simply storekeepers; and together with the clerks, minor professional people, and middling farmers, the storekeepers made up a numerous lower middle class. Lower-middle-class people (like their counterparts in Britain) believed in middle-class values but they were narrower and more rigid, less adaptable and less sophisticated in their beliefs than the *haute bourgeoisie*. Thus they believed that work produced profit and hard work produced greater profit. Conversely they held in contempt those who did not work hard or appeared not to work at all. By contrast with both the gentry and the *haute bourgeoisie*, they emphasized not the extended family but the nuclear family as the primary social environment: for the lower middle class, the front room was the ideal place of recreation.

The social attitudes of the lower middle class were closer to those of the gentry than the *haute bourgeoisie*. Lower-middle-class men believed in social order and the hierarchical organization of society: they knew their place and expected their wives, children, and employees to keep theirs. 'The notion of respectability', André Siegfried noted in 1904, 'which marks for the people the man adorned with the semblance of fortune, good form, and official virtue, is known and admitted by everyone.'[8] For the lower middle class, respectability was perhaps even more important than solvency; this respectability included sobriety, scrupulous honesty, a reserved if not grave demeanour, and the suppression of sexuality.

The lower middle class promoted their attitudes in a variety of institutions. Many served in Parliament, but the righteousness of some offended party interests and the most unyielding, like the prohibitionist T. E. Taylor, had only occasional electoral success.[9] In the Protestant churches, particularly the Presbyterian Church and those sects which had a background of dissent such as Methodist and Baptist, they mounted moral crusades to make rhetoric and reality converge in public behaviour. Sloth, larrikinism, and tobacco were all attacked but their greatest effort was against the demon drink. The prohibition movement, in its fight against alcohol, joined together those who worried about the fitness of the race, the saving grace of God, the safety of the streets, and the security of the family. Perhaps it was also a populist rising against the urban capitalists who ran the breweries and allegedly kept politicians in their pockets; and, alternatively, an attack on the lower-class Irish with their reputed proclivity for too much liquor. The 'wowsers' went far towards making drinking a disreputable activity (but then so did the drinkers). The strength of the lower middle class was, however, less in national crusades than in local activity. Small townships proliferated, and in most of them lower-middle-class people established the climate of opinion. In each town they formed and staffed a web of social, sectarian, cultural, and recreational organizations designed to promulgate their social attitudes.

In Britain the lower middle class had remained socially marginal, squeezed between the urban capitalists and a numerous working class with its own rich traditional culture.[10] In colonial New Zealand these other groups were weaker and the lower middle class became socially central, one of the ruling classes which generated the 'ruling ideas'. New Zealand had no coherent working class, but many working-class immigrants. Some artisans acquired lower-middle-class status by becoming entrepreneurs; and one of the most significant working-class institutions in Britain, the Methodist Chapel, was to some extent appropriated in New Zealand by the middle classes. Some trade unions and mechanics' institutes were founded but imported working-class cultural patterns and institutions survived only in attenuated forms: working-class children played truant from school; their fathers fell out of work; there was a considerable amount of recreational drinking; gambling was endemic; petty theft was widespread; there was some prostitution; every town had its larrikins. Many of these activities were doubtless expressions of dissent from the exaggerated high-mindedness of the gentry or the triviality of the lower middle class, but some were probably degraded survivals of regional and street cultures of the British working classes. The truants, unemployed, boozers, gamblers, thieves, prostitutes, and larrikins were subjected to the strenuous disapproval of middle-class reformers, even to legislative sanctions.

For a few residents there was, especially in the 1890s, a vibrant intellectual life. At Canterbury College A. W. Bickerton, professor of chemistry and physics, vigorously promoted his 'partial impact' theory of stellar creation and the professor of English, J. Macmillan Brown, moved from literature through satire to an anthropological interest in the place of the Pacific Islands and their peoples in Caucasian civilization. William Pember Reeves, by birth and education a New Zealander though he had spent periods in England, was a journalist and politician who composed vigorous verse and wrote articles on socialism.[11] In Wellington, where there was no university college until 1899, intellectuals worked in the government bureaucracy. Scientists of various kinds, especially zoologists, botanists and geologists, explored isolated areas, collected specimens, and published descriptive works: they were moved not merely by their own inquisitiveness but by their vital function as field workers for European scholars engaged upon the classification of phenomena. In emphasizing the uniqueness of the local flora and fauna, the scientists helped to make it emblematic of New Zealand. S. Percy Smith and Edward Tregear, former surveyors who had become senior civil servants, had wide literary interests and a great deal of ethnological curiosity about the Polynesians. In 1892 they founded the Polynesian Society and its *Journal*, which became a major repository of information and speculation about the indigenous peoples of the Pacific. They were concerned not only with elucidation of Māori origins but also with a racial justification for the assimilation of the Māori and therefore fashioned out of the flimsiest linguistic evidence a myth that the *Aryan Maori* (as Tregear called one of his works) descended from the same common stock as the Anglo-Saxon. Smith tidied up as well as collected Māori traditions and in his hands the prehistoric Māori acquired a chronology and a set of founding fathers. Elsdon Best, a colleague and contemporary of Tregear and Smith but unlike them born in New Zealand, did much more original work, recording in the field the lore of the Māori.[12]

An interest in the identity of New Zealand was not confined to intellectuals. In the late nineteenth century there were many New Zealanders, especially among the gentry, who still felt they lived in exile: the homestead may have been on the Canterbury plains but Home was Britain; passenger steamers were 'Home boats'. But although most colonists maintained the rhetoric of exile, they neither hoped nor expected to return whence they came. Some searched for the distinctiveness of the place: those who had known no other home and were not likely to in future ceased to pine for the woods and downs of England and turned with enthusiasm to the local landscape — not the 'little mean dwellings painted a chocolate brown' with gardens full of 'cabbage stalks, sick hens and tomato cans' which Katherine Mansfield in *The Garden Party* depicted as characteristic of the colonial towns,[13] but the mountains and the bush. Tourist guidebooks extolled natural glories; in 1898 such local scenes as Mount Cook and Lake Taupo replaced the face of Queen Victoria on postage stamps.

One definition of local identity was partly negative: New Zealanders were not Australians or even 'Australasians'. Australia was geographically closer than any other land, and there was between Australia and New Zealand much trade and some exchange of talent. A good number of New Zealanders subscribed to and wrote for the Sydney *Bulletin*. There were similarities in the recent experiences of the various colonies, set out by W. P. Reeves in his *State Experiments in Australia and New Zealand*. But Australia was also quite different: huge, less politically integrated, the population predominantly urban and less homogeneously British than that of New Zealand. In the 1880s and 1890s federation with the Australian colonies had been discussed by New Zealand politicians, without much enthusiasm. Their apathy reflected that of the New Zealand public.[14]

National identity did not displace a sense of imperial identity. While the leaders of other white settler colonies in the late nineteenth and early twentieth centuries sought a measure of practical independence from Britain, New Zealand politicians hoped for a greater say in imperial affairs. 'New Zealand', said André Siegfried in 1904, 'may with justice be regarded as the English Colony which is most faithful to the mother-country.' Nevertheless, there was room for pride in local achievement. Political innovations during the 1890s and considerable prosperity after 1896 tempted New Zealanders to think well of what they had accomplished, particularly when overseas visitors agreed and hailed New Zealand as a social laboratory. Ironically the accolade of visiting commentators was an essential part of the criterion of achievement. The vulgar presumption of the turn-of-the-century Premier, R. J. Seddon, was symptomatic of a general conceit: 'God's own country', Seddon called New Zealand. This was a view passed on through 'readers' and other school textbooks to several generations of New Zealanders.[15]

Out of this mood of colonial self-confidence came several significant literary monuments. T. M. Hocken published a standard *Bibliography of the Literature relating to New Zealand* in 1909, an immense work of 600 pages. He was a bibliophile as well as bibliographer; his huge personal collection of books and documents on New Zealand and the Pacific became the

Hocken Library of the University of Otago in 1910. Alexander Turnbull, a wealthy Wellington merchant, had similar interests; his 50,000 volumes on New Zealand, the Pacific, exploration, and English literature were eventually bequeathed to the nation.[16] A third collector, Robert McNab, searched for materials on early New Zealand history in Australia, the United States, Britain, and France. Besides several books which rescued the early sealers, whalers, and traders from near-oblivion, he also compiled, at the suggestion of Seddon, a two-volume *Historical Records of New Zealand* (before 1840), published in 1908 and 1914.

From his exile in England, William Pember Reeves gave European New Zealanders their first distinguished history, a truly popular one which breathed life into all the free-floating myths of the local past. In the *Long White Cloud* (1898) and in his more serious political apologia, *State Experiments in Australia and New Zealand* (1902), Reeves formulated a new political myth, a Whiggish version of later nineteenth-century New Zealand history in which he proclaimed the efficacious benevolence of the state in the hands of 'progressives'. This myth has ever since been plundered by populists, socialists, and historians. A stern contemporary critique of the Liberals, *State Socialism in New Zealand* (1910), written from a conservative viewpoint by J. D. Le Rossignol (an American) and W. Downie Stewart (a New Zealander), had less influence than Reeves's work; it also had less style.

In this period New Zealanders wrote their most worthwhile literature when they reflected on politics and history, when they wrote about what they were certain they had done well. In works of the creative imagination they were less successful. A great deal of poor verse was published: 'a yearly heavy burden', Hocken noted in his *Bibliography*.[17] There was little fiction: most novels were either light romances or reminiscences of colonial life cast into picaresque form. Julius Vogel and Edward Tregear each wrote a prophetic novel of no great merit. Vogel looked for, among other things, the equality of women; Tregear made tasteless fun of the women's movement.[18] Edith Searle Grossman, one of the earliest women graduates from the University of New Zealand, wrote four feminist novels which set out many details of male brutality towards women. Grossman was the first colonial novelist to write with a political purpose. Of all the fiction by men, only that by William Satchell has literary as well as historical importance. In middle age Satchell published four novels, two of them set in Northland, a third against the backdrop of Auckland province in the racial wars of the 1860s. They have involved plots and a multitude of characters and are pessimistic in tone, for Satchell's faith in civilization was tempered by his pictures of individual failure and racial tragedy in the harsh context of pioneer society. Some of his settlers win out; others go insane, or take to drink. Almost alone of his generation, Satchell was sympathetic to the Māori people (though his view of them was also very romantic). After his historical novel *The Greenstone Door* (1914) provided a poor return he wrote no more. A notable aspect of much writing, whether verse or prose, fiction or non-fiction, in the 1890s and early 1900s, was a kind of literary nationalism, in which writers tried to create an authentic New Zealand literature by using the flora and fauna, and the Māori, as subjects. But neither in aesthetic nor in commercial terms were these efforts successful.[19]

Most of what New Zealanders read was from Britain: each boat brought its quota of high culture and popular culture — books of verse, fiction and non-fiction, and the *Illustrated London News*. The boats from Sydney and Melbourne in their turn carried musicians and actors from Australia to enliven the larger New Zealand towns. Modern drama and opera were rarely staged but Australasian impresarios, notably J. C. Williamson, supplied townspeople with a rich diet of operetta and lighter theatre. In between times there was vaudeville and variety, including the new moving pictures. Churchmen were not always amused by these entertainments but few could object to Gilbert and Sullivan, or to Nellie Stewart, who made frequent visits and performed in thirty-two towns on one two-month tour.[20]

Most New Zealand communities could mount 'concerts', at which amateurs of little skill recited maudlin verse or sang trivial songs. Any tendency towards the bawdiness of British vaudeville was firmly quashed by the respectable. In the four main centres there was sufficient talent and skill, some of it belonging to the locally born, to support a great deal of high quality choral music, particularly in Wellington, where Robert Parker organized large choral productions, and in Christchurch.[21] The first sizeable orchestras were gathered at the Exhibitions of 1890 and 1906. The conductor of the 1906 orchestra was Alfred Hill who had returned from study in Leipzig in the 1880s to conduct and compose in New Zealand. Several of his works had Māori themes and titles — the cantatas *Hinemoa* (1894) and *Tapu* (1903), his First Symphony, subtitled *Maori* (1896). His greatest success was a song, 'Waiata Poi', which has been called Hill's 'Land of Hope and Glory'. Hill apart — and though his music was distinguished by instrumental clarity it was not experimental in style — modern works were rarely heard. The repertoire of serious musicians was nineteenth-century romantic and national music, especially symphonies and an abundance of shorter items by Beethoven, Haydn, Schubert, Brahms, Delibes, Gounod, and Sullivan: most particularly welcomed was music by Mendelssohn. Only C. N. Bayertz in his iconoclastic journal *The Triad* offered sufficiently critical reviews of performance standards.[22] The most popular colonial ensembles were the brass bands, which produced sounds of reasonable quality in nearly every town.

Though there were art societies and galleries in the largest towns, the fine arts in general received much less support than music. However, in Auckland a number of painters of little originality manufactured 'realistic' portraits and historical scenes to satisfy the growing interest in things New Zealand; and two professionals, G. Lindauer from the 1870s and C. F. Goldie from the early twentieth century, were able to survive on the proceeds of sales. Far more important were three who from the 1890s lived and worked in relative obscurity for little financial reward but who influenced other artists: Petrus van der Velden discovered in the landscape turbulent forces avoided or unnoticed by earlier painters; James Nairn displayed impressionist techniques; Girolami Nerli explored personality.[23]

Nerli, Nairn, and van der Velden were immigrants; so were nearly all those of any accomplishment in science, art, letters, or music. However much they enriched the culture milieu of colonial New Zealand, there were too few of them to help more than a very small number of locally born people to develop and mature. Apart from small schools of art in a number of centres, there were, before the First World War, few institutions at which talented colonists could receive training: education in the fine arts or in the performing arts was mostly through private tuition. The state education system was firmly in the hands of lower-middle-class people who preferred the inculcation of basic literacy and vocational skills to heightened aesthetic sensibility; the university colleges were tiny; the cultural homogeneity of New Zealand was dispiriting and dulling. So people of talent often left New Zealand. Alfred Hill settled in Australia before the First World War. David Low, the cartoonist, joined the Sydney *Bulletin* in 1911. Ernest Rutherford graduated from Canterbury College in the 1890s and then went to Cambridge University; in 1908 he received a Nobel Prize for his research in chemistry. Rosina Buckman developed her soprano voice in Australia and England and sang *La Bohème* at Covent Garden before the First World War. After training at the Canterbury School of Art, Sydney Lough Thompson divided a long artistic career almost equally between New Zealand and France. The Dunedin painter Frances Hodgkins had a lengthy, hard-working, and successful career in Europe, but after 1906 she returned to New Zealand for only one brief visit.[24]

The children of the colonial *haute bourgeoisie* in particular became expatriates. Katherine Mansfield, daughter of the Wellington importer and bank director Harold Beauchamp, never returned after her second leave-taking. She lived with much zest a bohemian existence in England and France, publishing a considerable number of short stories critically acclaimed then and since for their sensitive depiction of social relationships.[25] The raw material for many stories was childhood memories of family and community life in Wellington. *The Doll's House* is justly celebrated for its literary merit; like *The Garden Party*, it also provides an ironic commentary upon the much vaunted egalitarianism of Seddonian New Zealand.

For the fact was, the school the Burnell children went to was not at all the kind of place their parents would have chosen if there had been any choice. But there was none. It was the only school for miles. And the consequence was all the children of the neighbourhood, the Judge's little girls, the doctor's daughters, the store-keeper's children, the milkman's, were forced to mix together. Not to speak of there being an equal number of rude, rough little boys as well. But the line had to be drawn somewhere. It was drawn at the Kelveys. Many of the children, including the Burnells, were not allowed even to speak to them. They walked past the Kelveys with their heads in the air, and as they set the fashion in all matters of behaviour, the Kelveys were shunned by everybody. Even the teacher had a special voice for them, and a special smile for the other children when Lil Kelvey came up to her desk with a bunch of dreadfully common-looking flowers.[26]

'I am ashamed of young New Zealand', wrote Mansfield in 1907, 'but what is to be done. All the fat framework of their brains must be demolished before they can begin to learn. They want a purifying influence — a mad wave of pre-Raphaelitism, of super aestheticism should intoxicate the country.' She wanted 'two or three persons gathered together to discuss line and form and atmosphere and sit at the street corners, in the shops, in the houses, at the Teas'. She hoped in vain. She was one of several women novelists, including Louisa Baker, Ellen Ellis, and Constance Clyde, who wrote with a political as well as literary purpose, concerned to raise the educational, political, and legal status of women. Jessie Mackay (in verse) and B. E. Baughan (in verse and short stories) struggled for the same causes.[27] But although there was to be no 'purifying influence' in high culture during this period, New Zealanders did face a significant ideological challenge. This challenge came through a re-invigorated labour movement.

In the nineteenth century labour organization had been weak. The Trades and Labour Councils formed in the 1880s had little influence, and the militant rhetoric provided by the maritime strike in 1890 faded quickly. But in the early 1900s a new and militant union movement sprang up, led by Patrick Hickey, an Irish New Zealander with union experience among the miners of the American west coast, and by several immigrants from Australia, notably P. C. Webb, Robert Semple, H. E. Holland, M. J. Savage, and W. E. Parry. Many of these men were Marxists, who believed in the class struggle, the overthrow of the capitalist state, and the 'socialization of the means of production, distribution, and exchange'. The political thought of New Zealanders generally was enriched by this socialist challenge. Socialist ideas of international brotherhood and equality gained some currency; colonial racism was more firmly identified. Before the First World War the socialists turned a tiny pacifist group, begun by Baptists and Congregationalists, into a sizeable anti-militarist movement which promoted conscientious objection to compulsory military service.[28] To the Reevesian myth of the benevolent state the socialists were able to add the notion of social transformation through control of the state by a majority social reformist parliamentary party. Though when many of the early socialists eventually reached Cabinet rank in the late 1930s and the 1940s they proved to be efficient administrators of colonial capitalism, their earlier influence should not be underrated: they created a small store of alternative ideological traditions which could be constantly drawn upon by reformers and unionists, and when there was an economic crisis in the 1930s the existence of these alternatives was to prove important.

When Britain went to war with Germany in August 1914, New Zealanders automatically became foes of Germany. There was no separate declaration of war, no debate in or out of Parliament, no public dissent except from some socialists. Though William Massey and J. G. Ward, Coalition leaders from 1915, were pleased to be consulted by the Imperial Government, they interfered not at all with British and allied strategic decisions: New Zealand was placed at the disposal of the British authorities almost as if it were a part of the British Isles. The major New Zealand war effort was the supply of troops: 100,000 New Zealanders served outside the colony, many in Australian and British formations but most of them with New Zealand units. They fought well and therefore were often given difficult tasks. As a result they were slaughtered in great numbers: 16,781 died. Another 45,000 were wounded.

Colonial courage was tested early in the war, against the Turkish forces on Gallipoli peninsula, where troops of the Australian and New Zealand Army Corps landed on 25 April 1915. The invaders had to attack up steep, rocky hillsides; the Turks commanded the heights from which they were never dislodged. After nine months the force was evacuated. The experience might well have turned New Zealand soldiers against war; instead they were resolute under impossible conditions. In all subsequent actions the soldiers tried, usually successfully, to reach this earliest standard: pre-war militarism reached its apotheosis in an active military tradition.

Patriotism (or jingoism) was almost obligatory for New Zealanders. Civilians busied themselves with the preparation of parcels for the troops. A constant stream of concerts and gala days was organized at which good cash was paid for mediocre entertainment in support of the war. In every town and district there was a patriotic society which co-ordinated civilian efforts to raise money. The societies were usually run by community leaders, gentry, middle-class and lower-middle-class people who controlled the county councils, borough councils, and other local institutions.

The other side of jingo-patriotism was xenophobia. Residents of German extraction, even British citizens with German-sounding names, were harassed and attacked, their businesses boycotted, shops vandalized. Before Britain entered the war, the German-born, English-educated professor of modern languages at Victoria University College, von Zedlitz, had volunteered for service in the German Red Cross; in 1915 the Government responded to public uproar by removing him from his post. In Auckland Coburg Street was eventually renamed Kitchener Avenue; Jermyn Street became Anzac Avenue.[29]

Enemies could, however, appear in many disguises. Having suffered so much in one of imperialism's little wars, the Waikato Māori people were disinclined to support another, much larger struggle. Most Waikato men who were conscripted refused to serve and many were arrested. Towards the Māori people in the Waikato many Europeans expressed great hostility. Labour leaders who spoke against conscription were imprisoned for sedition.[30] The Catholic Irish were suspect, though their clergy had supported the 'just war'; even tiny groups of religious objectors, such as Quakers and Christadelphians were relentlessly pursued during the war. The earliest pacifists were forced into troop-ships, a few taken under cruel circumstances to the front line in France. Religious objection to the war was later permitted for members of sects the respectability of which the authorities felt compelled to recognize, but non-combatant service was expected: several Quakers, refusing uniform entirely, were jailed.[31]

The long-term effect of the war upon New Zealand's cultural life is difficult to discern. There was no new sense of autonomy: the mature voices, critical of imperialism and its wars, were predominantly those of socialists and they had said their piece before the war. In the 1890s, R. J. Seddon had occasionally lectured English statesmen on their imperial duties; now when opinions were sought by the British Government local leaders replied: 'New Zealand is content to be bound by the determination of His Majesty's Government in London', although in practice the loyalty was a little less unconditional on such an issue as the Singapore naval base.[32]

The immediate, local consequences of war were the continuance of jingo-patriotism and the establishment of the Anzac tradition. Long after the battles were over, teachers were required to take loyalty oaths and New Zealand children saluted their country's flag. When James Liston, a Roman Catholic bishop of Irish descent, felt moved to tell a St Patrick's Day crowd in 1922 that foreign troops were murdering Irish patriots, he was (unsuccessfully) prosecuted for sedition. Memories of war produced no local poetry, no music, no art, little significant prose fiction, only gaunt stone cenotaphs, rolls of honour, memorial windows, and Anzac Day dawn parades. ANZAC was an acronym from the Australian and New Zealand Army Corps; 25 April each year, the anniversary of the initial landing at Gallipoli, was set aside as a commemorative occasion, a day of wreaths, a day without work or play — even the hotel bars and race-courses were closed.[33]

In Europe this was the era of futuristic and surrealistic art, atonal music, James Joyce's *Ulysses* and T. S. Eliot's *Waste Land*: in New Zealand it was the age of the cow-cockies, the heavily mortgaged smallholder dairy farmers who saw themselves as yeomen and pioneers conquering the wilderness. Their struggles were certainly heroic (and so were those of their wives and children used as cheap labour) but they were often isolated from life in the cities and resented the civilized ways of urban people. Many New Zealanders, perhaps the great majority, believed that the rural way of life was morally superior to that of the towns:[34] it followed that the smallholder farmers' antagonism to urban sophistication had to be treated with respect. If the political influence of the cow-cockies was disproportionate to their numbers, so was their cultural influence, which was almost entirely negative. Several decades later Maurice Shadbolt epitomized the attitudes of the backblocks cow-cocky in his novel *Strangers and Journeys*. Young Tim Livingston, the son of a King Country pioneer farmer, had been given a small box of paints by a neighbour's wife, a former teacher.

'What is the idea, boy?' his father asked.
'To paint pictures,' he said, though it seemed obvious.
'That's all very well,' his father observed, 'for those who have the time. Life is not pretty pictures.'[35]

Even in the four largest cities, which had long passed out of their pioneering stage, there was a decline in cultural and intellectual vigour by contrast with the early years of the century. Instead there was the cinema or the spurious vitality of febrile nightlife: the elderly Edward Tregear complained to a reporter for the newspaper *Truth* that in Goring Street, Wellington, he and others had lived in 'respectable serenity' until a cabaret had been opened, whereafter jazzy music, the shouts of dancers, the popping of corks and the noise of motor cars created Bedlam into the small hours of the morning.[36] Tregear was one of those colonists who had provided much of the intellectual and cultural energy of pre-war New Zealand; now his contribution had come to an end and he escaped from Bedlam to the quiet backwaters of Picton township. Though a few of Tregear's contemporaries lingered on (for example, Robert Stout, who had become an educational and judicial reactionary), the majority of immigrants from the Victorian era had died, and with them went most of what intellectual and cultural robustness colonial New Zealand had once possessed. The state school system enshrined the values of the lower middle class, listing neatness, politeness, helpfulness, and obedience as virtues to be taught in the classroom.[37]

The 1920s was the last great decade of the English and Australian touring companies.[38] Their fare was entertaining rather than sophisticated. New Zealand audiences saw Shakespeare, Goldsmith, and Ibsen, but a good proportion of the plays presented were the 'hits' of recent mediocre English playwrights. The programmes of such visiting celebrities as the violinists Jascha Heifetz and Fritz Kreisler, the singer Galli-Curci and the dancer Anna Pavlova seem to have been arranged mostly for the display of technical virtuosity. In the early 1920s, radio and cinema began to push vaudeville aside (though Harry Lauder could still draw crowds); towards the end of the decade the 'talkies' arrived at the cinema. 'All over Australasia', recalled Ngaio Marsh, 'one seemed to hear the desolate slam of stage doors.'[39]

Though the stage doors were closing on the touring companies, an indigenous live theatre, if not a professional one, was promised by the growth of amateur repertory groups. In the cities and provincial centres such groups staged a wide variety of plays; in the smaller towns they often fell under the control of lower-middle-class enthusiasts, who produced only slight works with respectable themes.[40] Similarly operatic societies mounted British and American musical comedies with their simple-minded themes of romantic love and virtue rewarded. Serious contemporary European music was rarely performed at all.

Instrumentalists in small ensembles earned a few shillings playing in dance halls or in cinemas. The word theatre increasingly meant for most New Zealanders a 'picture theatre' or cinema showing American and British films. A considerable number of films were made in New Zealand in the 1920s: most were of good technical quality and several of artistic merit, especially those produced by Rudall Hayward. However, the resources of New Zealand film-makers were slender: they could not compete with the flood of American and British feature films and their 'stars', especially after the introduction of 'talkies' at the end of the 1920s, and most gave up the unequal fight. An even newer entertainment technology was the wireless,

321

its impact in the 1920s limited by short transmission hours and primitive crystal set receivers. Broadcasting, unlike the film industry, remained firmly in the hands of New Zealanders. Many early programmes were studio performances by local musicians or 'live' sports broadcasts. Nevertheless, when various technical and copyright problems had been overcome, an increasing proportion of broadcasting time was spent on transmitting popular music recorded overseas.[41]

The daily newspapers, full of cable news from Britain, national politics, and 'social news', gave little space to creative efforts and none to independent commentators. Especially influential in country districts and small towns were the weeklies, such as the *Free Lance* and the Auckland *Weekly News*, bland, inoffensive, inconsequential potpourris. They included extravagant pictorial sections full of landscape, sports, and imperial photographs. Newspapers, weeklies and dailies alike, gave excessive publicity to the British royal family. Infrequent royal visitors had always been much fêted in New Zealand. What had been at the turn of the century vigorous expressions of loyalty gradually gave way to a sickly sentimentality; royal life was made into a kind of fairy tale. The visits of the King's eldest son in 1920 and of his second son in 1927 were attended by vast crowds and, in the first instance, adulation close to hysteria. Between visits royal persons were forever 'news'. It was an unreasonably strong and rather irrational attachment; monarchy was mystical rather than political. But New Zealanders attributed to the royal family a perfect set of middle-class values, and their standards of family life became a model for aspiration. It is probable that in the abdication crisis of 1936 most New Zealanders who judged Edward Windsor unfavourably did so because he had offended against their moral standards, not because of the constitutional issues involved.

There were small numbers of New Zealanders who struggled against the cultural poverty of the time, who sought stimulation. Mostly they found it outside New Zealand. Some were inspired by the example of Katherine Mansfield. She had left the crude confines of colonial life, tasted the exciting literary worlds of Britain and Europe, and had won critical acclaim with her published stories. Then she died early in 1923 and became a kind of martyr for the expatriate cause. There were other aspects of the Mansfield experience which perhaps were not fully appreciated: that the Wellington she had left was probably more intellectually rich than the Wellington of the 1920s; that she possessed surpassing genius; that she had often lived in hard, unpleasant conditions; that her father had provided an allowance. The outflow of expatriates was well under way before Mansfield had expired and before the legend was fully established, but she became a symbol of the promise which could be fulfilled in the old world.[42]

Expatriate academics and professional people slipped easily and completely into English life, partly prepared through graduation from the local university colleges which had retained English styles and manners; they felt, for the most, no exile in England. Among them were Ronald Syme, classical historian; A. C. Aitken, mathematician; Raymond Firth, anthropologist. Aspiring writers, artists, actors, singers, and dancers had a rather different experience. Their backgrounds were more varied, fewer had completed a formal tertiary education. They entered the competitive cultural world of London where creativity rather than social status ranked people. Bohemianism meant poverty, poverty bred feelings of alienation and sometimes a new sense of exile. Many did well: for example, Hector Bolitho, journalist and biographer, and David Low, the cartoonist. Not all expatriates travelled to London: Rewi Alley went to China; Te Rangi Hiroa (Peter Buck) continued his career as an anthropologist in Hawaii; Tom Heeney, the boxer, went to America and fought Gene Tunney for the world heavyweight championship in 1928. To leave New Zealand for other places was so much a standard occurrence of this period that when the *Encyclopedia of New Zealand* was prepared in the early 1960s by people of that generation a special and lengthy entry on 'Expatriates' was included.

The most peripatetic were the painters. The arts societies were well supported in the main centres and there was in the 1920s a growing interest in and encouragement of art education through schools of art. Nevertheless, the better painters, mainly women, acquired most of their technical maturity overseas. They included Dorothy K. Richmond, Olivia Spencer Bower, Edith Collier, Mabel Hill, Rhona Haszard, Ida Carey, Mina Arndt and Flora Scales, Raymond McIntyre and John Weeks. Many of these travellers returned and went on to paint and to teach.[43] In addition several English painters and art teachers were established in New Zealand in the 1920s: Roland Hopkins, R. N. Field, Robert Dunn, W. H. Allen, and Christopher Perkins by their works and their teaching significantly fertilized the fine arts, though their accomplishments and those of their colleagues and pupils were provincial rather than international in character. Outside the universities, no other area of high culture enjoyed a similar accretion of strength from migrants. Local confidence in the fine arts was signalled by a quarterly *Art in New Zealand*, with illustrations both in black and white and colour, which was first published in 1928.

A few writers of fiction managed to squeeze inspiration out of the social deprivations of pioneering life. Jane Mander, daughter of a Northland sawmiller, left New Zealand for the United States in 1912. *The Story of a New Zealand River* appeared in America in 1920, the first of four novels set in the gumfields and timber settlements of the north. Mander was the first to typify adequately in prose the sights, sounds, and smells of a New Zealand settlement landscape.[44] She also attempted to deal realistically with sexual relationships. In *Allen Adair*, the Oxford-educated pioneer, at odds with his wife, returns from Auckland with the silver tea-service she has craved for so long: 'At last she went into the front room, but when she heard Allen go into the back, where his cot had been all the winter, she sat down in her chair and wept, and forgot the silver tea service.'[45] Overseas reviewers were kind, but New Zealand was too full of passionate puritans who were hostile to her marital truths. Mander dealt no more with New Zealand in her work.

Frank S. Anthony, also New Zealand-born, spent eight years on the

high seas in peace and war before taking up a farm section in Taranaki in
1919. His bitter pioneer experiences he turned into stories, a few of which
were published in weeklies early in the 1920s. He began a novel, went to
England to develop his writing career, and died there in 1927. The
collected stories were published in 1938 but he did not become well
known until they were reworked in a jocular vein by another writer in the
1950s. In the original material, Anthony successfully pictured the
inarticulate, emotionally immature post-war peasant farmer. Mossy Road
'shouted its poverty to the most casual observer. Fences, houses,
outbuildings, and even the clothes of the inhabitants told the one tale,
shortage of cash, and hopelessness.' The women proved as fruitless as the
land: 'Gus was in the throes of another violent love affair, and there was
only one thing to be done. That was to leave him to it and hope for the
best. He'd come back to normal again, after being put in his place and
snubbed, and given the cold shoulder for a week or two.'[46] Anthony
captured, before anyone else, the speech of New Zealand males, and their
attitude to women; he was New Zealand's first comic writer.

There were other competent writers in the 1920s; several, such as Nelle
Scanlan, P. A. Lawlor, and Alan Mulgan, had learned as journalists how to
fashion good clear prose and they produced satisfactory if uninspired works
of fiction, travel, reminiscence. The least conventional novelist of the time
was perhaps Jean Devanney. She came from a working-class family and
claimed to be a Marxist. Like Mander, Devanney understood the central
importance of sexuality; like E. S. Grossman of the pre-war period, she was
a feminist who used the novel form for preaching social change: *The Butcher
Shop* (1926) with its images of violence and its socialist sympathies
scandalized many New Zealanders.

The period also saw the emergence from the large ruck of mediocre
versifiers of a handful who deserved the title poet. Eileen Duggan, devout
and intensely personal, produced two volumes of poems in the 1920s;
Ursula Bethell, after spending many years in England, returned to New
Zealand and published *From a Garden in the Antipodes* in 1929; a year later
He Shall Not Rise by A. R. D. Fairburn appeared. Fairburn shared with his
friend Geoffrey de Montalk and his contemporary D'Arcy Cresswell the
hope that a vigorous Antipodean poetry would regenerate the effete culture
of the metropolis, a view which prefigured a change in the emotional
relationship of colonists with Britain.[47] Greater than all these poets and
locally quite unrecognized in the 1920s except by a few friends (including
Fairburn) was R. A. K. Mason. His poems of the 1920s (first published in
The Beggar, 1924) may be classified as Georgian and in that context of
English literature he remains a minor but successful poet. In the New
Zealand context he was without peer, a strong voice of genius. He had a
fine sense of line and metre, in part absorbed from a good knowledge of
Latin verse. Mason did not share the prevailing colonial values: he was an
agnostic, an internationalist, he disliked war. While most New Zealanders
used their Anzac rituals to avoid confrontation with death, Mason
constantly recurred to the reality of loss.

We are they who are doomed to raise up no monuments
to outlast brass:
for even as quickly as our bodies' passing hence
our work shall pass
of us shall be no more memory left to any sense
than dew leaves upon grass. . . .[48]

Overseas his verse was praised; in New Zealand it was ignored and there are stories that Mason dumped many unsold copies of *The Beggar* in the Waitemata harbour.[49]

Several significant non-fiction works appeared in the 1920s. James Cowan, who had written books sympathetic to the Māori and also tourist guidebooks before the war, published his two-volume compilation *The New Zealand Wars* in 1922–23. Like certain American historians, his heroes were the frontiersmen and pioneers. In *The New Zealand Wars* Cowan commended the 'friendly' Maori forces, romanticized the defenders of Rangiriri and Orakau, and denigrated Te Kooti and the adherents of Pai Marire and Ringatu: the colonial troops were accorded an importance somewhat at variance with their actual performance, and the British army correspondingly received less than its due. Elsdon Best's bulkiest volumes also appeared in the 1920s, notably his standard ethnography *The Maori* (1924). There is a great contrast between the works of Cowan and Best, on the one hand, and J. B. Condliffe's *New Zealand in the Making* (an economic history with a cultural critique as a coda) and Raymond Firth's *Primitive Economics of the New Zealand Maori* (1929), a work of social anthropology, on the other. Cowan and Best lacked the academic training and overseas study which informed the crisp, orderly, theoretically informed works of Condliffe and Firth. This contrast is not quite so visible in two 'scientific' books, in which both authors combined enthusiasm and scholarship. Leonard Cockayne's *New Zealand Plants and their Story*, which first appeared in 1910, was virtually a new work in its revised 1919 edition. Cockayne introduced New Zealanders to an ecological appreciation of their flora, which fitted neatly into a small but growing conservation movement. Herbert Guthrie-Smith, a Scot by birth and educated in England, was not only a keen naturalist, but had literary ambitions as well: these were fulfilled by *Tutira* (1921), an ecological account of his Hawke's Bay sheep station. By implication *Tutira* has two other dimensions: it is the story of how a European migrant became a New Zealander through his accommodation with the landscape; it is also a critique of the ravages of Europeans, their despoliation of the land in contrast to the natural balance which had been maintained by the Māori.

Though the beauties of the scenic landscape were praised in school textbooks, so too were the 'pioneers' who had built farms and towns. Māori people who resisted the settlers were not at all well-regarded in textbooks such as *The Young Dominion* and *Our Nation's Story*. Thus Te Rauparaha led a 'wicked life' and Te Kooti's followers were 'savages', but 'the two races fought side by side as comrades in the greatest war in history' and 'the bond between the white New Zealander and the brown is a very strong one'. The New Zealand story was situated firmly in the framework of British political experience. 'In the first place', pupils in Standard 6 were able to read, the good citizen 'is proud to be a citizen of the British Empire, and in the second he is proud to be a citizen of New Zealand.'[50] To this emphasis on race, blood, and empire in schools was added 'civics', an uncritical course in political socialization, close to indoctrination. One civics textbook, *The New Zealand Citizen*, claimed that 'the first duty of the citizen' was 'to obey the laws of his government'; it was his duty not only to assist the police 'actively' whenever they required help but also 'always to treat them with respect'. While empire was extensively praised, *The New Zealand Citizen* had a single brief reference to the League of Nations.[51] Nevertheless, race and empire were supplemented, in a minor way, by expressions of faith in internationalism and the League of Nations in some school textbooks and the *School Journal* from the middle 1920s. J. B. Condliffe's *Short History of New Zealand* ended with a peroration in favour of the League, though it was a League which would derive strength from behaving like the British Commonwealth.[52] The growth of anti-war sentiment can also be discerned in the 1920s, especially in the League of Nations Union.

The most bitter commentary on New Zealand chauvinism was offered by the inhabitants of Western Samoa. These islands were administered by New Zealand under a League of Nations mandate. Officials from New Zealand had the opportunity to practise the paternalism developed with Māori people over the years on another Polynesian people. However, there was also a group of Europeans and mixed-race traders unwilling to endure political powerlessness and outraged by the imposition of such laws as liquor prohibition. One of the latter, O. F. Nelson, founded the Mau movement, and, though he was deported, the Mau organized pickets against the purchase of goods. New Zealand, in true imperial fashion, sent warships and 400 troops to Apia. On Black Saturday, 28 December 1929, a Mau welcome to a leader returned from exile became a mêlée in which twelve men died. More than a thousand Mau took to the bush, assisted with food and shelter by the majority of the population and pursued by police and marines with fixed bayonets. The League of Nations Permanent Mandates Commission at Geneva was naturally concerned by these events: had Government measures been preceded by 'study of the traditions, customs and psychology of the Native People', it asked.[53] The Samoan fiasco caused humiliation in New Zealand rather than understanding. As one civics textbook said, the English possessed 'a special talent for governing', including 'an unrivalled ability to govern subject races'.[54]

At the end of the 1920s the hegemonic structure was intact, entrenched in the civil and political order against the mad dreams of anarchists and artists. Outside the sway of the ruling classes there were only two large groups, the Māori people and some of the urban lower class. The Māori people had retained their own cultural system, but Europeans held them in subjection in various ways, denying them access to economic resources, especially capital, and constantly denigrating their *mores*. The urban lower class, however, had a greater struggle to maintain ideologies at variance with those of the ruling classes. Sports clubs, churches, schools, local government bodies, public libraries, newspapers, pubs: all these places of recreation, entertainment, and instruction were firmly in the hands of the ruling classes and mediated their values. Against such an array of institutions working people had only trade unions, with their annual picnics, a few working-men's clubs with small libraries for self-education, and local branches of the Labour Party.

This situation was altered by the onset of depression in the early 1930s. The crisis in Western capitalism shook the colonial economy: when the economic base was dislocated, the hegemonic superstructure was consequently transformed. New Zealanders were still drawing on the basic stock of ideas imported in the nineteenth century. But when it became clear under the impact of depression that the usual economic and political responses were inadequate, the colonial experience was ransacked. Many progressive ideas and policies which had been opposed and discarded by the ruling classes in earlier periods were rehabilitated. The alteration of opinion may be indicated, though not precisely measured, in the electoral support offered the Labour Party: in 1928 it received a quarter of the popular vote, a decade later more than half the votes cast were for the Labour Party.

It took time for misery and misgovernment to shake people out of their accustomed patterns of thought and action. There had been depressions before; this one would go, as slumps in the 1920s had gone. Moral arguments were used: people had enjoyed too much luxury; now, providentially, they must be thrifty and frugal. The middle classes added to their list of commitments service in organizations to collect blankets and food for the destitute and the hungry. They held 'cheer up' days, when the main streets of town were decorated and floats and bands paraded down them and people sang 'Happy Days are Here Again'.[55] Men were placed on relief work. It was a hard and sometimes sad time but it would pass.

As the prospect of good times receded people became angry. Yet it was not simply or even primarily misery that angered and ultimately radicalized so many people as the way the ruling classes institutionalized misery. As the Government cut wages and salaries, reduced expenditure on education and public works, and packed the unemployed off to work-camps often located in isolated places, the numbers of those who suffered greatly increased and their political consciousness correspondingly intensified. In work-camps or in road-gangs relief workers met men advocating a range of panaceas and thus many acquired new political ideas in novel circumstances; among the activists were Communists who helped form the Unemployed Workers Movement in many areas. Inhabitants of the work-camps learned to hate the governing classes who sentenced them to such misery.

A good proportion of those in work-camps and road-gangs were from the rural and urban lower classes. A sizeable minority of smallholder dairy farmers, struggling on overvalued land to pay mortgages which became even more crippling as export returns diminished, were also radicalized. The Depression hurt many lower-middle-class people. In earlier years they had exercised financial and social restraint: now many were in reduced circumstances, their wages and salaries cut or their trade diminished, their children facing unemployment, their small savings and insurances used to pay the mortgage. They were dismayed, some of them, by government retrenchment in the civil service and the state education system because these were lower-middle-class avenues of advancement. Many became bitter and critical.

The climate of opinion changed also within the churches and the universities. The churches had traditionally been agencies of social control, preaching obedience and promising rewards in a later life, but dissent became more pressing as the distressed sought comfort. The social gospel was proclaimed with a new urgency. A. H. Nordmeyer, a Presbyterian minister, became prominent in the Labour Party; Colin Scrimgeour, a former Methodist preacher, turned his religious programme on radio into a clamorous call for social justice.[56]

The four small New Zealand university colleges were not places where non-conformity was encouraged: indeed, Canterbury students helped to break a tramway strike, and when there were riots and rumours of riots in 1932 a number of Auckland students enlisted as special constables. But there were several people in the universities, both staff and students, who expressed objections to the established order. Most of them were cultural dissenters — that is, they disliked the colonial intolerance of creative experiments, the lack of artistic discrimination and aesthetic sensibility. A few were political rebels. These aspects of opposition were manifested in two *avant-garde* magazines: *Oriflamme*, produced at Canterbury College, and *Phoenix* from Auckland. *Oriflamme* was banned by university authorities after the first issue contained an article in favour of sexual emancipation.

Dissent in the churches and universities, normally institutions through which the power of the establishment was mediated, signified clearly the extent of opposition to the ruling classes. By 1932–33 a large proportion of New Zealanders were angry. There was little coherence in their anger, no ideological unity: it was, for the most part, an inchoate radicalism. The means of expressing this radical temper were limited by the narrowness of the colonial experience. In New Zealand almost all the disaffected eschewed rebellion or civil disorder. Some supported the right-wing New Zealand Legion, others the political and moral alternative of the Labour Party. The Labour Party became the receptacle, and the vehicle of expression, for a wide range of ideas now given the respectability of popular support under the impact of depression. The emphasis of Labour programmes reflected their clientele and was henceforth essentially populist. A significant portion of public opinion inclined towards ideas of an efficient and compassionate society built upon both Christian and humanist versions of human dignity and equality and the Labour Party subsumed these ideas in its rhetoric and in its programmes. After the Labour Party was elected to office in 1935, these ideas were given legislative sanction and were incorporated in the mainstream of colonial ideology.[57]

The Labour Party believed in using to the full the power of the state for change. This was a time-honoured tradition in New Zealand, but the Labour Party, partly because of its socialist roots, partly because of its massive electoral support, used state power more enthusiastically and extensively than any previous governing party. Hence much cultural innovation after 1935 was under the auspices of the state. By 1940 broadcasting was almost entirely in the hands of the Government. Professor James Shelley was made director of National Broadcasting; commercial radio was controlled by Colin Scrimgeour. The liberal academic who wanted to make New Zealand radio an educational vehicle (as Reith had done for the BBC) and 'Uncle Scrim' had no great regard for each other. Nevertheless, both men tried hard to influence the community and to use local people in programmes; each succeeded to a limited degree.[58]

The greatest state-sponsored cultural innovations in the later 1930s were in education. Many reforms had been discussed and even planned during the 1920s but they had either offended educational and social reactionaries or had been pushed aside in the massive retrenchment of the early 1930s.[59] A 'new freedom' was now introduced to primary schools: there was an attempt to diminish formal instruction in the elementary years and replace it by experiential learning. In 1938 the Proficiency examination was abolished to allow all pupils to proceed to full secondary schooling; in consequence the academic content of the secondary curriculum, which was dominated by the universities through the University Entrance examination, had to be reduced. In 1944 the Thomas Committee proposed a general education in 'core' subjects and the institution of a new School Certificate examination.[60] Government subsidies for the Workers' Educational Association were resumed in 1936, although the element of working-class participation of the 1920s and early 1930s had largely vanished by 1940. A Country Library Service began to move books regularly around the country districts and the small towns.

Possibly the most interesting of all the educational innovations was the Feilding Community Centre. H. C. D. Somerset and Gwen Somerset, teachers at Oxford District High School in Canterbury, had developed in association with the WEA in the 1920s a community education programme for the Oxford district. L. J. Wild, the headmaster of Feilding Agricultural High School, had similar interests and persuaded Peter Fraser to provide the necessary money and space for a Community Centre, to which the Somersets were appointed in 1938. The range of activities at the Centre was wide — forums on international issues, discussions on new and progressive educational ideas and practices, classes in parent education, in child development, courses on courtship and marriage, a club for adolescents, a film club, classes in prose writing, in art appreciation, a theatre group (the Feilding Community Players staged or read plays by Shakespeare, Shaw, Synge, Ibsen, O'Neill, Lillian Hellman).[61]

The Somersets, progressive liberals who were interested in world affairs, human relationships, and the arts, could not have mounted such a programme under the auspices of the state in the 1920s: the Feilding Community Centre experiment is indicative of the ideological shift in New Zealand during the 1930s. Society had become more open; there were new opportunities for individual and social growth; it was possible to discuss topics which were previously regarded as taboo. But the Feilding experiment also illustrated the limitations of ideological change: the scheme was not extended to other New Zealand communities. It could be said that the innovative temper of the 1930s allowed a left-liberal critique of society to emerge, to be seen as legitimate, even to be institutionalized in a small way, but not to prevail.

The achievements of local creative artists of almost all kinds in the 1930s were of a much higher level than previously. There were many reasons for this. There were more painters and writers in New Zealand, they often had contact with each other, they drew strength and inspiration from each other's work and from the accumulated advances in techniques, especially in poetry and painting. Returning expatriates contributed fresh perspectives and tested skills. M. H. Holcroft, novelist and journalist, travelled to England whence he returned 'with a new feeling' about his 'native country' which he expressed in *The Deepening Stream* (1940), an attempt to explore 'the nature of creative problems in New Zealand'.[62] The composer Douglas Lilburn completed his musical education in England and returned to New Zealand: by the 1940s his work was known both in London and in New Zealand.

The fine arts developed from the technical and institutional advances of the 1920s. R. N. Field and Christopher Perkins in particular were liberating influences: two artists inspired by the teaching and sense of artistic vocation of the former were M. T. Woollaston (who had also been influenced by Flora Scales) and Colin McCahon. Perkins portrayed not the virgin bush and mountains but the landscape which had suffered visitations from European hands. His successful evocation of matters peculiar to New Zealand helped make serious art more popular at a time when New Zealanders were grappling with a sense of place. So did the compositions of Russell Clark, and of Evelyn Page and Rita Angus, the best known of 'The Group', an informal group exhibiting annually in Christchurch during the 1930s. Nevertheless, many painters continued to tour the world.[63]

Yet the achievements of high culture were not simply a result of gradual colonial enrichment: they were also related to the Depression and its intellectual consequences. The more critical, open society which was brought into being in the 1930s suited iconoclastic artists. For many of them the political struggle paralleled their struggle for freedom of expression, for experimentation and innovation. Sometimes the links between cultural expression and increased political consciousness were quite clear and direct. R. A. K. Mason and Ronald Meek, both socialists, inaugurated the People's Theatre in the late 1930s. Several writers had been closely concerned with the political activities of the 1930s; those associated with *Phoenix* and *Oriflamme* had not only learned of the power of print to alarm the authorities but also recognized the creative freedom they could obtain by printing and publishing works themselves: no longer would local writers be caught between the unwillingness of local publishers to print new material and the editorial prejudices of British publishing. In the middle and later 1930s a great deal of distinguished New Zealand writing, verse in particular, was published by Robert Lowry in Auckland, and by Denis Glover and Leo Bensemann (using the imprint Caxton Press) in Christchurch: in their hands typography and book design was raised to the level of a fine art. In addition there appeared two radical journals of a kind not previously seen in New Zealand except for *Phoenix*. *Woman Today* (1937–39) was a feminist magazine; *Tomorrow*, the creation of Kennaway Henderson assisted by, among others, H. Winston Rhodes and Denis Glover, was a weekly (later fortnightly) of vigorous, often polemical comment on political and cultural affairs.

One of the first local works to be produced by the new presses was R. A. K. Mason's *No New Thing*, which Robert Lowry published after overseas editors had turned down the manuscript. The poems were dated 1924–29 but Mason's personal conflicts encapsulated general concerns of the 1930s and at last he had a ready if slight audience.

> For my bitter verses are
> sponges steeped in vinegar
> useless to the happy-eyed
> but handy for the crucified.[64]

Fairburn's long poem *Dominion,* published by the Caxton Press in 1938, tackled the experience of the Depression directly in poetry both lyrical and polemical.

> Consider the curious fate
> of the English immigrant:
> his wages were taken from him
> and exported to the colonies;
> sated with abstinence, gorged on deprivation,
> he followed them: to be confronted on arrival
> with the ghost of his back wages, a load of debt;
> the bond of kinship, the heritage of Empire.[65]

Fairburn's talents were expressed in all manner of forms, including political satire: *The Sky is a Limpet* was a dazzling display of puns upon the rhetoric of M. J. Savage, the Labour Prime Minister. Savage was at the time mortally ill, though this was not generally known; after his death Peter Fraser held it against Fairburn as a piece of callousness.

Allen Curnow, the most accomplished of those who wrote their first poetry in the 1930s, spun a New Zealand poetic myth out of the threads of the local past — the intersecting worlds of Europe and Polynesia, the tensions between people and land. Curnow observed 'The skeleton of the moa on iron crutches' in the Canterbury Museum and concluded, 'Not I, some child, born in a marvellous year,/Will learn the trick of standing upright here'. Yet he seemed to some contemporaries to have done just that, and to have discovered New Zealand in time and place.

> The pilgrim dream pricked by a cold dawn died
> Among the chemical farmers, the fresh towns; among
> Miners, not husbandmen, who piercing the side
> Let the land's life, found like all who had so long
>   Bloodily or tenderly striven
>   To rearrange the given,
>   It was something different, something
>   Nobody counted on.[66]

A small number of prose writers in the 1930s matched the achievements of the best poets. Archibald Baxter wrote a memoir of his treatment as a conscientious objector in the First World War. *We Will Not Cease* (1939) was composed in England in 1937: it is about the courage of ordinary New Zealand men, both soldiers and objectors, and the horror of war; but it is also the story of pathological cruelty, of the underside of the forces of law and order, of gaols and gaolers, military police, torture. John A. Lee, by contrast, lost an arm and won a medal in the war: he had a police record before the war, and a political one, as Labour MP, after the war. His novels, *Children of the Poor* (1934) and *The Hunted* (1936), both at least partly autobiographical, were crusades against injustice. Lee was from the working-class, out of 'the gutter'; in vigorous prose he impaled the hypocritical wowsers and righteous authorities who made life a misery for those of lower social status.

Under the pseudonym Robin Hyde, Iris Wilkinson was, in all senses of the term, New Zealand's most considerable novelist of the 1930s. She supported herself by journalism as she struggled against poor health and financial difficulties to develop her writing skills. In *The Godwits Fly* (1938) she explored the problems of cultural dependence and colonial identity which had troubled so many writers and artists. The godwits, marsh birds, migrate each autumn from New Zealand: 'They fly to Siberia. But to a child in this book, it was all more simple. A long way was a long way. North was mostly England, or a detour to England.' Colonials, she recognized, felt this same compulsion, suffered from 'England-hunger'.[67] The lower-middle-class heroine of *The Godwits Fly* resists the compulsion, stays in New Zealand; Robin Hyde herself finally left, spending some months in China where she wrote in an article: 'in our generation, and of our initiative, we loved England still, but we ceased to be "for ever England". We became, for as long as we have a country, New Zealand'.[68] Though Robin Hyde's resolution of the issues of cultural identity was noted and applauded in 1940 and later, recent critics have emphasized that she had more significant concerns. Phillida Bunkle, Linda Hardy, and Jacqueline Mathews, for example, claim that 'For Robin Hyde, the central problem of a colonial society was racial, sexual and economic conflict in a society whose very foundations were the expropriation and exploitation of land.' In seven major works, Hyde set down in prose an immense range of experiences and displayed the many contradictions which she recognized. Her last book was a report of her visit to China, *Dragon Rampant* (1939); her first was another non-fiction work, *Journalese* (1934). Beside *Godwits* there were four other novels: *Check to Your King* (1936), an historical novel based on the documentary materials left by the 1830s adventurer Charles de Thierry; the fantasy *Wednesday's Children* (1937); and *Passport to Hell* (1936) and *Nor the Years Condemn* (1938), which follow 'Starkie' and his contemporaries through the misfortunes of the Great War and postwar New Zealand. Hyde finally reached England in 1938, and died there, by her own hand, in 1939. She was then aged thirty-three. Several decades were to elapse before the depth and coherence as well as the breadth and variety of her work achieved full recognition.

Frank Sargeson came from a quintessentially lower-middle-class background. He was brought up in a small town, Hamilton, where his father was town clerk: both parents were puritanical and 'religious'. He made a journey to England, returned quickly, read voraciously the great literary works. He chose the New Zealand, or at least North Island, patois, and the short story form. His first story, 'Conversation with my Uncle', appeared in *Tomorrow* in 1935, and a small collection of such 'sketches' appeared the following year. In 1940 E. H. McCormick judged that there was in Sargeson's 'Kens, Toms and Neds and in their outlook something that is rooted in this country. . . . Frank Sargeson . . . is the exponent of a local tradition that has hitherto been inarticulate.'[69]

John Mulgan's background was more socially distinguished. His grandfather had been an inspector of schools, his father a man of letters with a high local reputation in the 1920s: father and grandfather had combined to write the civics textbook, *The New Zealand Citizen*. John Mulgan, a special constable in the riots of 1932, had found it difficult to attain his ambition of a Rhodes scholarship but he eventually arrived at Oxford, where he wrote *Man Alone*, published in London in 1939.[70] Like Sargeson, Lee and Archibald Baxter, and several of the poets, Mulgan identified with the oppressed, the victims of the social and political system. His anti-hero Johnson, is laconic, rootless, drifts from job to job, avoiding marriage, escapes from the riots to work for a farmer in the King Country: 'Sundays were the worst days on the farm. Even Stenning did not work then except to milk, and there was nothing to do for the three of them, Rua and Stenning and Johnson, but to sit about and wait for it to be Monday again.'[71] Johnson and Stenning fight over Rua, Stenning is killed in the scuffle, Johnson is pursued as a criminal, is smuggled out of New Zealand and eventually goes to Spain to fight for the Republicans against fascism.

'You ought to think a bit more about yourself', Petersen said. 'A fellow like you could have a place and settle down and do some decent steady work. You could have a good place on a ship if you cared to. If you get back to England now, you better try something like that. The world's full of too many fellows like you not knowing what to do with themselves and wandering round and agitating for more pay and getting into trouble of all kinds. I seen it happening the last thirty years. It was the war did it or what, I don't know.'

'I've worked hard all my life,' Johnson said, 'and been paid damn all. If fellows like me make more trouble now than they used to it's because they've got more sense.'[72]

In 1940 European New Zealanders celebrated their centenary, that is to say, the centenary of the arrival of William Hobson and the signing of the Treaty of Waitangi. There were, Denis Glover wrote tartly, 'fireworks and decorated cars/And pungas drooping from the verandahs',[73] but Joseph Heenan, Under-Secretary of the Internal Affairs Department, was determined to create cultural monuments through state sponsorship. There was a Centennial Exhibition, a showplace of local accomplishment, including some commissioned statuary of little distinction and, gathered from various galleries and private collections, an art exhibition of more merit: nearly all the exhibited painters had been born and educated overseas or had travelled outside New Zealand.[74] *Making New Zealand* was the first pictorial record of past and present; an historical atlas was planned, though not completed. There were prizes for orchestral and choral music (Douglas Lilburn won both), poetry, novels, short stories (Sargeson was first equal), essays (M. H. Holcroft for *The Deepening Stream*); no first prize was awarded for drama.

The most enduring commemoration was a series of volumes on New Zealand life, carefully designed by J. C. Beaglehole. In general the authors of these 'Centennial Surveys' — on discovery, exploration, women, education, science, literature and fine arts, pioneering, government, farming, external affairs, social life — were good-humoured, sometimes mildly critical but certain that there was a unique place called New Zealand inhabited by people quite distinctively New Zealanders who had built and were continuing to build a good society. The volume on 'Social Services' did not appear. W. B. Sutch's first version was returned for rewriting, and his second attempt was vetoed by the Prime Minister, Peter Fraser, who apparently feared that criticism of farmers would not help the war effort. But Sutch's reluctance to celebrate achievements and his emphasis on the limitations of the Welfare State were also disqualifications. The kind of New Zealand that most people wanted to read about was set out in Oliver Duff's *New Zealand Now*: male-dominated, and not greatly concerned about class, privilege or poverty. Probably the most influential of these works was E. H. McCormick's historical survey of *Letters and Art in New Zealand*; while he somewhat obliquely suggested that New Zealand writers during the 1930s had not added 'anything great and distinctive to the tradition of European civilisation', he set out very clearly how considerable the sum of their achievement was by contrast with earlier efforts.[75]

But achievements in high culture, though considerable, were limited: some New Zealanders had simply learnt local ways of expressing the stock of nineteenth-century British ideas and attitudes contained within the colonial culture. What had evolved can be dignified at most by the label provincial culture. A few people, it should be noted, were not content with New Zealandisms. Duff himself was none too happy about the unintellectual aspect of New Zealand's cultural landscape. One of the reasons R. A. K. Mason gave up writing poetry was to bring his 'artistic feelings into line with [his] intellectual knowledge'. He had become a Marxist and hoped to publish in the future 'some reasonably decent proletarian stuff'.[76] Frank Sargeson later accepted a Civil List pension yet felt it necessary to escape the constrictions of New Zealand society not as an expatriate but through an unconventional lifestyle. Such people were exceptions, oddities. The society in which they attempted to work was not passing beyond its pioneer origins to a new sophistication; in fact the pioneer achievement was being articulated more firmly than ever before.

The limits of change in the climate of opinion within New Zealand were mirrored in the attitudes New Zealanders held towards the outside world. London was still the centre of the world for European New Zealanders; there were few contacts with other than British people. Despite the popularity of American films and recorded music, and the relative geographic closeness of that English-speaking nation by contrast with Britain, no ties were developed with Americans. Even more remarkable — considering the nearness of Australia, the trade and migration both ways across the Tasman, and the fact that the Prime Minister and four others in the Labour Cabinet of 1935 were former Australians — cultural and political relationships with Australia and Australians were diminishing rather than deepening in the 1930s.

In 1926 the Balfour Report for the first time defined what had been evident for many years: that 'the dominions' — Australia, New Zealand, South Africa, Canada, Ireland — were *de facto* independent states. The Balfour Report was formally enshrined in an Act of the Imperial Parliament, the Statute of Westminster, passed in 1931. New Zealand politicians had not sought this measure; it was not adopted by the New Zealand Parliament until 1947. Perhaps this dilatoriness was only to be expected while the Government was led by Gordon Coates and George Forbes, heirs of Massey and Seddon. But in the later 1930s the Labour Government did not trouble to give legislative effect to the Statute of Westminster either: Labour leaders, like their predecessors, accepted some autonomy but felt no need to proclaim it. Although in 1936 and 1937 a good deal of emphasis was placed upon the League of Nations and collective security, the relationship with Britain remained at the heart of Labour's external policies. M. J. Savage wanted a foreign policy for the Commonwealth as a whole; he complained when there was inadequate consultation with 'the Dominions'. Nevertheless, he and other Labour ministers agreed that if Britain were involved in a war, New Zealand would fight too.[77] When war broke out in September 1939, the New Zealand Cabinet made a separate formal declaration of war, in contrast to what had occurred in 1914. The accompanying rhetoric was ambivalent, with references to New Zealand as a nation alongside declarations of great loyalty to Britain.[78]

In May 1940, the second large contingent of volunteer soldiers embarked on ships bound for overseas battlefields; in the same month the radical journal *Tomorrow* ceased publication because the editors had provided space for pacifists to make a case and the police informed the printers 'that no guarantee could be given that they were not to be prosecuted if they continued to print' such items.[79] These more or less simultaneous incidents perhaps epitomize the climate of opinion: on the one hand the existence of a tiny minority who held values opposed to those which generally prevailed, who were willing to express their opinions, and who had access to a forum in which they could be expressed; on the other hand the intolerance of dissent, even by a Labour Government whose members had once been feared as disloyal socialists, and the willingness of large numbers of New Zealanders to fight for race and empire.

CHAPTER 13

Imperialism and Nationalism

W. David McIntyre

When and how their country gained its independence is not a question New Zealanders ask themselves. If they did, few would have an answer. Unlike Americans, with the Declaration of Independence, or Indians with the 'transfer of power', New Zealand was a British colony which became an independent nation very gradually. There was no sudden cutting of the painter, such as is celebrated in most ex-colonial States. Nor was the birth of the modern State signalled in any great upheaval like the French or Russian revolutions. New Zealand became a sovereign independent state, a member of the community of nations, and at times achieved a reputation out of all proportion to its size, by a long, peaceful, and often subtle process. The landmarks are not dramatic and the process is suffused with paradox and ambiguity.

Until the early years of the twentieth century the overriding reality of New Zealand's place in the world was that it was a small, remote, British colony. Its political institutions were subordinate institutions. From 1840 sovereignty resided in the British Crown. Politics, law, economic activity, and social and cultural life derived largely from British roots and for long retained sustaining links with them. Yet, from the early days of colonization, distinctions had to be made. A sense of new identity began to belie formal constitutional status. There were distinctions between internal and external affairs. Sentiments of imperialism became mingled with a growing nationalism. There was much overlapping, parallel development, and sometimes regression from growing autonomy to greater dependency. Things would sometimes seem to be moving in opposite directions at the same time.

In his pioneering book on New Zealand nationalism, *A Destiny Apart*, Keith Sinclair has a chapter on 'Home' and 'Homies' in which he suggests that it is impossible to do justice to the complexity of New Zealand feelings about Motherland, Empire, and Commonwealth. He admits that 'those relationships were debated at least as obsessively as the idea of a new nation'.[1] Thus, for every nationalist manifestation, there was, for many years, a balancing imperialist counterpoint. The study of New Zealand's place in the world, its evolving defence and foreign policies, and people's perception of their own identity, is, therefore, a complex and subtle one.

As a colony, under the British Crown, from 1840 to 1907, New Zealand advanced rapidly to self-government. The beginning of parliamentary institutions in 1854 and responsible government two years later meant that the Crown, represented by the Governor, acted on the advice of ministers, who were in turn responsible to elected representatives. The Governor, though a key figure in the nineteenth century, became a mixture of constitutional head of state and imperial vice-regent. Governor Browne, who inaugurated the system in 1856, spelt out the practice. In all matters under the control of the colonial parliament (the General Assembly) he would act on the advice of ministers, whether he agreed or not. He would be a constitutional sovereign. In matters 'affecting the Queen's prerogative and Imperial Interests generally' he would receive advice but exercise his discretion. And among imperial interests (which meant external affairs) he included one important internal matter, Māori affairs, because he was responsible for security in the colony which he felt might be endangered by frequent changes of adviser in this matter.[2]

The distinction between internal and external affairs became marked. For most internal affairs, except the exercise of the royal prerogative and relations with the Māori, the colony became self-governing. In defence and foreign affairs it remained part of the British Empire where control was exercised from London. But even in these 'reserved' subjects, separate New Zealand aspirations and a sense of identity soon emerged. The Governor's prerogative powers were, in theory, formidable. In relation to bills before Parliament, choosing premiers, the term of ministers, appointments to the upper house, the granting of mercy, and being the channel of communication with the British Government he had to retain an active political role. Yet, in spite of these formal restraints on the colony's autonomy, most of these powers had been whittled away, with the consent of the Colonial Office, by the 1890s. The colony became virtually fully self-governing in internal affairs.[3]

In the case of Māori affairs, however, this was not achieved without the major upheaval known as the 'garrisons crisis' of 1870. Māori affairs had been reserved because of implications for the 'tranquillity' of the colony. With the outbreak of war in 1860 the matter appeared in more urgent light. Whose war was this — Britain's or the colony's? Who would fight; who would pay? The British Government became progressively unwilling to pay for settler land-grabbing and was eager to hand over Māori affairs. On the other hand the colony was not able to fight its own war; it needed the help of imperial troops. The British were not willing to hand over the control of their regiments. Thus, throughout the 1860s, there was ambiguity — 'double government' as it was called — which only ended in much recrimination during the crisis of 1870.

There were four phases in the build-up. First, in 1861 a resolution of the House of Representatives provided that the 'ordinary business' of Māori affairs would be handed over to the ministry. The Governor agreed to consult and take advice. Secondly, the British decided to reduce their military assistance. This was part of an empire-wide policy to reduce expenditure and force self-governing colonies to attend to their own internal security. Although New Zealand was exempt for a few years because of the war, and imperial troops reached a peak of 18,000 in 1864, thereafter they were withdrawn. One regiment only would be left, provided the Government spent £50,000 a year for Māori purposes. Additional units would have to be paid for by the colony. This continual British interference led to the third phase, the policy of 'self-reliance', adopted by the Weld Government in 1864. The British troops could go; the colony would raise its own Defence Force, and take full charge of Māori affairs. The trouble was, the colony needed to borrow to raise adequate forces. Although the Stafford Government (1865–69) adhered to the rhetoric of self-reliance it could not afford it. It gambled on delaying the British withdrawal, by haggling over finance, until the danger passed. The crunch came at a moment of great danger. The so-called Poverty Bay massacre (November 1868) and White Cliffs massacre, in Taranaki, (February 1869) caused panic among the settlers. The fourth phase in the process came with the withdrawal of the last regiment. Although a new government in June 1869 abandoned the pretence of self-reliance and pleaded retention of the troops, Lord Granville, the Secretary of State, said in London: 'I think we must harden our hearts.' The British decided to withdraw their troops and cease interfering in the internal affairs of the colony. The last regiment sailed away in February 1870.[4]

The incident caused the worst crisis in relations between New Zealand and Britain. There were cries that the mother country was 'cutting the painter'. Motions of censure were passed in both houses of the General Assembly. The Government made direct contact with the US Consul in Dunedin about improving trade with the USA. There was even wild journalistic talk of New Zealand becoming a State of the American Union, where the 'Indians' were being put in their place.[5] The crisis soon blew over and was followed by the euphoric splurge of borrowing in London to pay for the public works and immigration programme. What emerged from all the parliamentary wound-licking were some significant questions about New Zealand's place in the world. How would the colony be defended from external attack now that the garrison had gone? How far would New Zealand be involved in Britain's wars, or could the colony remain neutral? What voice might New Zealand receive in foreign policy which affected the colony? How would the colony stand in relation to the Pacific Islands?

New Zealand's security problem arose because a British dispute with another power might expose the colony to attack. Indeed, the garrisons crisis coincided with the Franco-Prussian war in Europe, which gave Russia the opportunity to renounce restrictions on the movements of its navy imposed after the Crimean War. During a period of diplomatic tension there were rumours that a Russian ship was in the South Pacific for the purpose of intercepting mails in the event of war. In December 1870 the Premier, William Fox, asked the Colonial Office how the colony would be defended now that the British garrison had gone, or whether it could become a neutral in war. In his reply, the Secretary of State turned the question back; he asked whether such neutrality would be honoured by an enemy and whether Britain would stick to its obligations to the colony.[6] New Zealand's security was firmly tied to Britain. Yet, by the 1880s, new modes of consultation and co-operation were evolved by which New Zealand was able to participate in international affairs. This involved three major developments: defence contributions, a voice in foreign policy, and regional initiatives.

New Zealand's contributions to the defence of the empire were made in the context of a strategic rationale known as the 'Blue water school' or 'Jervois doctrine', after Sir William Jervois, who was later Governor (1882–89). The key to the doctrine was seapower supremacy by the Royal Navy. This constituted the 'deterrent' to any attack on the empire. As the only possible threat would be sea-borne, this narrowed it to a European naval power. To pose a threat such a power would have to weaken its fleet in Europe to threaten a colony. Britain would, therefore, have to detach part of its fleet to either deter or destroy that threat. The essential condition was the maintenance of naval supremacy and the availability of defended bases in the colonies.[7] In theory the doctrine was water-tight, but in practice New Zealand felt isolated and vulnerable. Britain, for its part, found naval supremacy costly and it had many colonial defence commitments around the globe which were burdensome. Thus in the 1880s a system of mutual support was evolved. Britain supplied the deterrent — the fleet. Colonies gave support by creating defended naval bases, offering expeditionary forces to help in Britain's wars, and by voting subsidies to provide local units of the Royal Navy. An unwritten alliance, known as 'imperial defence' was forged.

New Zealand purchased coastal defence guns to protect the main ports. In 1882 four rather useless Thorneycroft spar torpedo boats were also purchased. In 1888 the Calliope dock was opened by the Auckland Harbour Board at Devonport with an Admiralty subsidy in return for naval priority rights for docking. In 1885 crises in Africa and Central Asia raised the question of sending an expeditionary force. For the campaign down the Nile to rescue General Gordon from Khartoum, New South Wales sent a Volunteer Battalion. In New Zealand there were numerous offers from volunteers all over the country, though the Government did not take them up. Later in 1885, however, during the Penjdeh crisis, when Russia appeared to threaten Afghanistan, and Britain stood poised to resist, the Cabinet offered a battalion of a thousand men (a quarter to be Māori) for service in Afghanistan or any part of the globe.[8] Although the crisis was short-lived and the offer was not actually sent to London until the need had passed, the colony had begun a tradition which continued until the Vietnam War of the 1960s. Two years later the first naval subsidy was voted. After several years of discussion, the Australian colonies and New Zealand persuaded the British Government to station an auxiliary squadron of five cruisers and two ocean-going torpedo boats in southern waters in peacetime. By the Australasian Naval Agreement of 1887 the colonies granted a contribution towards the cost. New Zealand contributed £20,000 per year on condition that two vessels were stationed in New Zealand waters as their headquarters in peacetime. The subsidy was renewed and raised to £40,000 in 1903 and £100,000 in 1908.[9]

As well as paying considerable sums for defence the colony also gained a small voice in foreign policy. From 1871 an Agent-General had been appointed in London, who was something in the nature of a 'resident minister' in the imperial capital. Although not the official channel of communication, which was still the Governor, the Agent-General (termed High Commissioner from 1905) was 'the eyes, the ears and voice of the New Zealand Government in Great Britain'.[10] Unlike ambassadors from foreign powers, who could knock only at the door of the Foreign Office, the High Commissioner had access to the other British departments of state. Another mode of consultation was the Colonial Conference. This was an indirect by-product of the garrisons crisis of 1870, when a demand went up for periodic meetings of representatives from the self-governing colonies. Two unofficial meetings held in 1869–70 and 1871 were not recognized by the British Government.[11] But in 1887 the opportunity was taken for calling a conference of colonial representatives at the time of Queen Victoria's golden jubilee. Here there was a lively exchange of views on a diversity of topics, especially empire trade, communications, and defence.[12] The British retained their control of policy, but colonial voices were heard. In the same year another avenue opened up when the Agent-General wanted to visit Paris to persuade the French Government to reduce its tariff on New Zealand's promising new export of frozen meat. The British insisted that their ambassador should conduct the negotiations — thus maintaining the diplomatic unity of the empire — but Sir Francis Dillon Bell, the Agent-General, went to Paris as adviser to the ambassador.[13]

By the 1890s the development of these modes of co-operation, combined with Britain's growing fear of industrial rivals, such as Germany and the United States, and its colonial rivals, France, Germany, and Russia, led on to talk of the federation or union of the empire. At the second Colonial Conference, during the Queen's diamond jubilee in 1897, the arch-imperialist Secretary of State, Joseph Chamberlain, made a tentative suggestion of a 'Great Council of the Empire'. Nothing came of the proposal. Most of the colonial premiers were satisfied with the recent consultations, but Seddon was one of two who favoured the idea.[14] In general, voluntary co-operation rather than any scheme of organic unity was preferred. There was, however, one significant area, where the British played a more passive role. In the matter of relations among the Australasian colonies and with the Pacific Islands there was considerable local initiative. In the Pacific region the British presence and role was there, but more distant and muted.

Between 1867 and 1883 nine inter-colonial conferences were held in Melbourne or Sydney. New Zealand attended in 1867, 1870, 1873, and 1877. Improved trade and communications were the main subjects for discussion and the British Government was persuaded in 1873 to permit a breach in their traditional policy of free trade by allowing reciprocal tariff preferences between the Australasian colonies. New Zealand did not, however, join the Federal Council for Australasia, a co-ordinating body created in 1883, mainly because of apathy, nor did it join the Australian federation in 1901. Although New Zealand representatives went to federal conferences in 1890 and 1891, they were absent from subsequent meetings.[15] When federation was debated in Parliament in 1890 Joseph Grimmond declared:

New Zealand should be a country for New Zealanders. With the wings of Great Britain over us we need to look to no other country or colony for protection . . . We are here the pioneers of a great nation, and shall, no doubt, have a glorious history . . . with a nationality of our own. . . . we ought to be a people by ourselves and keep New Zealand for the New Zealanders.[16]

Above all, New Zealanders did not feel 'Australian'. This glorious history referred to, also envisaged New Zealand as a colonial power in its own right in the Pacific. In 1873 Vogel proposed a Polynesian Company with the intention of gathering many Pacific islands into a dominion, with New Zealand as the seat of government, like the Dominion of Canada.[17] Britain annexed Fiji, reluctantly, in 1874. By the 1880s the white settlers there were asking for federation with New Zealand. Vogel was also eager to keep the French out of the New Hebrides, the Germans out of Tonga and Samoa, and to acquire the Cook Islands. In 1883 the Confederation and Annexation Bill gave authority for the Government to link up with any Pacific Island group not under the protection of another power. Very little came of this wave of colonial 'sub-imperialism'. The British made the Cook Islands a protectorate in 1888, which in 1901 was transferred to New Zealand. The island of Niue was added in 1905 and together they became New Zealand's first island territories.[18]

By the turn of the century imperialism — both in the sense of sentimental and military support for empire and territorial expansion in the islands — was playing a major role in the emergence of a New Zealand nationalism. While this might appear paradoxical to later generations, in the early twentieth century it made sense. New Zealand's adherence to its great power protector and mother country could be seen as fostering the 'national interest'. Imperialism was, as Sinclair suggests, a form of nationalism.[19] A further dimension of the paradox is evident when we realize that, in the very act of demonstrating solidarity with Britain, New Zealand could be found asserting its individual identity in various ways.

A vivid example occurred when the first expeditionary force went overseas to fight in the South African War between 1899 and 1902. Roughly 6,500 volunteers served in South Africa, in ten contingents, which each numbered between five hundred and a thousand men. Seventy lost their lives in combat or died of wounds. Rather more, 158, died of disease or accident. Although the contingents were small they achieved a high reputation. One of the British histories of the war called them the 'best mounted troops' in South Africa. General Sir Ian Hamilton said, 'I have never in my life met men I would sooner soldier with than the New Zealanders.'[20] Their identity was expressed in sobriquets such as 'Kiwi' and 'Maorilander' and in the fern leaf badge they sported. Sinclair has suggested that the 'first unmistakeable New Zealand voices which we can hear as a group come to us from the soldiers in South Africa'.[21] War — even an imperial war — became a major crucible of nationalism.

In the aftermath of the war there was soul-searching around the empire about military preparedness and a panic about 'race degeneracy'. Some comfort was derived by the British élite from the emerging identity, combined with imperial solidarity, of colonies like New Zealand. At the 1902 Colonial Conference, held at the time of the coronation of Edward VII, the idea of federation was again rejected, but voluntary co-operation continued. Seddon even suggested that the colonies should designate part of their armies for an 'Imperial Reserve Force' and that New Zealand would do this.[22] Faith in the British 'race' was also enhanced in 1905 by the triumphant rugby football tour of Britain by the pioneer 'All Blacks'. They won every game, except a poorly refereed one against Wales at Cardiff. The success of this disciplined squad (in numbered positions for the first time), captained by a veteran of the South African war, seemed to suggest that a new virile breed of men was developing in a pioneer land.[23]

Yet, while their separate sense of identity was enhanced, support for empire was undiminished. At the 1907 Colonial Conference it was agreed that the self-governing colonies should be distinguished from other dependencies by the style 'Dominion'. Thus the 'Dominion of New Zealand' came into being on 26 September 1907. Little changed; the Governor became Governor-General and his instructions were loosened, but it was largely a change of title.[24] The 'new nation' continued along the path of imperialism. The naval subsidy was increased in 1908. In the following year New Zealand even contributed to the Anglo–German battleship building race by offering to pay for one or two battleships for the Royal Navy. HMS *New Zealand*, a battle-cruiser, was launched in 1911.[25] Although intended as flagship of the China–Pacific Squadron it was, with the approval of the Dominion Government, stationed in British waters.

The Dominion also developed its own armed forces. Compulsory military training was brought in by the 1909 Defence Act, which provided for a universal obligation of training for cadets aged between 12 and 18 years and young men aged 18 to 21. The Permanent Force (regular army) was created for service at home and 'beyond the limits of New Zealand'. The large Territorial Force of 30,000 was for home service but men could volunteer for 'Special Service' overseas. The new army first went into camp during the summer of 1911–12.[26] In 1913 there was a move towards a local naval force. The British agreed to station two cruisers in New Zealand, lent a Captain as the Government's Naval Adviser, and lent an old cruiser, HMS *Philomel*, as a training vessel for a future New Zealand Division of the Royal Navy. The first training cruise began in 1914.[27] After these developments, the Dominion was comparatively well-prepared for war when it came.

The Great War (1914–18) accentuated the trends of imperialism and nationalism. New Zealand went to war, with great eagerness, upon a British declaration, without consultation. By the end of the war, the Prime Minister, Bill Massey, had spent many months away in London at consultations during the Imperial War Cabinets of 1917 and 1918. At the peace conference in Versailles, New Zealand, though still not a sovereign nation, received recognition as a 'State' by its separate representation. More significantly, participation in imperial campaigns created a much greater sense of New Zealand identity than the more modest excursion to South Africa at the turn of the century. Looking back on the war the Rev. Ormond Burton, an ex-soldier turned pacifist historian, could write: 'There was no longer any question but that New Zealanders had commenced to realise themselves as a nation.'[28]

The Dominion sent four expeditionary forces away to the war. First, only forty-eight hours after war was declared in 1914, the British called on New Zealand to occupy Western Samoa, site of a German radio station. A force of 1,413 men was ready in five days. Escorted by six cruisers including HMS *Philomel*, three companies of infantry and an artillery battery took Apia, the Samoan capital, unopposed on 30 August 1914 in very nearly the first allied 'victory' of the war.[29] The second force went to the Middle East. Three days after war broke out the Government offered a division of two brigades which was ready within the month. The New Zealanders arrived in Alexandria, Egypt, on 3 December 1914 and, with the addition of two Australian brigades, constituted the New Zealand and Australian Division. In January–February 1915 it assisted in the defence of the Suez Canal against the Turks.

The first major campaign in which the Division took part was the notorious and ill-fated assault of the Mediterranean Expeditionary Force on the Gallipoli peninsula in an effort to dislodge the Turkish hold on the Dardanelles. For this operation the New Zealand and Australian Division was paired with the 1st Australian Division to form the Australian and New Zealand Army Corps. From the idea of a New Zealand sergeant in the HQ postal office the acronym ANZAC was adopted — which identified the troops and their landing cove. It would soon become the permanent symbol of trans-Tasman co-operation. The assault, on a narrow beach, up steep, rugged hills, which began on 25 April 1915 and lasted till the evacuation on 19 December, was a fearful disaster, which failed in its objective. Of the 8,500 New Zealanders who fought, 2,700 were killed. But in the battle for Chunuk Bair the Wellington battalion briefly got as high into the Turkish position as any of the attackers. Fred Waite, the official historian of Gallipoli, later wrote: 'Before the war we were an untried and insular people; after Anzac we were tried and trusted.'[30]

The third contribution to the war, and by far the largest, was at full divisional strength on the Western Front in France and Belgium. Commanded by Major-General Andrew Russell, a Sandhurst-trained Hawke's Bay farmer, the New Zealand Division, which was built up to three four-battalion brigades, was one of the strongest on the allied side. From mid-1916 up to the armistice in November 1918 it took part in some of the tragic engagements of the Somme, Passchendaele, Ypres and Messines. Over 13,000 were killed and about 35,000 wounded. Ormond Burton wrote: 'Somewhere between the Landing at Anzac and the Battle of the Somme' New Zealand nationalism was born.[31] The fourth contribution was that of the Mounted Rifles Brigade which remained in the Middle East. After skirmishes with Senussi tribesmen to the west of Egypt in 1915–16, it joined the 3rd Australian Light-Horse Brigade to form the Australian and New Zealand Mounted Division (or Anzac Mounted Division) in the Palestine campaign of 1916–18. Major-General Edward Chayter at one time commanded the Division. The brigade took part in the advance on Damascus and lost 500 killed and 1,200 wounded.[32]

The personnel contribution of New Zealand between 1914 and 1918 stood high for so small a country. Over 100,000 soldiers and nurses formed the New Zealand Expeditionary Force. In addition some 3,000 served with British and Australian forces. Nearly 10 per cent of the total population of little more than a million served overseas. The number who were killed or died of wounds totalled 16,781. This represented 15 per 1,000 of the population, second only to Britain in the empire, though considerably less than some of the other belligerents — Serbia (57), France (34), Rumania (33), and Germany (30).[33] Volunteering failed to maintain the flow of re-enforcements, therefore conscription was adopted in 1916. By the end of the war 39,000 had been enlisted in this way. This in turn led to the political upheaval which saw the founding of the Labour Party; it also led to passive resistance from Māori in Taranaki, Waikato, and the Ureweras. By the end of the war the jingoism of 1914 had been succeeded by a sombre realization of the horrors, death, and mutilation encountered in far-off lands. While there was pride in New Zealand's exploits, there had been costs few families in the land did not pay.

There is no doubt that New Zealand emerged from the Great War with an enhanced identity and a new status. It signed the peace treaty and joined the League of Nations in 1920. Its role as a colonial power expanded when the mandate for Western Samoa and a joint mandate (with Britain and Australia) over Nauru were conferred by the League. Over the next decade the formal constitutional status of New Zealand as part of the newly styled 'British Commonwealth of Nations' was rapidly enhanced. But, true to the 'imperialist' nature of New Zealand's 'nationalism', there was a reluctance about adopting the new status and a continued identification with imperial causes.

In 1923 the right to sign separate treaties was acquired, but was not exercised for some years. The Balfour declaration on inter-imperial relations in 1926 was phrased in a way which suited either imperialist or national tastes. The mutual relation between Britain and the Dominion was defined:

They are autonomous Communities within the British Empire, equal in status, in no way subordinate one to another in any aspect of their domestic or external affairs, though united by a common allegiance to the Crown, and freely associated as members of the British Commonwealth of Nations.

It was agreed, at the same time, that governors–general would cease to represent the British Government, only the Crown, but New Zealand did not make the change until 1939. When the Statute of Westminster gave legal embodiment, in 1931, to these doctrines of autonomy, equality, common allegiance, and free association, by ending the sovereignty of the Westminster Parliament over the Dominions, New Zealand insisted that the application of the law should be optional. Canada, South Africa, and the Irish Free State became sovereign independent states in 1931. New Zealand did not 'adopt' the Statute for sixteen years.[34]

New Zealand was content to remain a 'Dominion'. When it finally acquired a navy in 1921, by taking on loan one, then two, British cruisers, it was designated the 'New Zealand Division of the Royal Navy'. In 1922, during the Chanak crisis, when it appeared Britain might fight the Turks over a small town beside the Dardanelles, memories of Gallipoli were invoked and New Zealand offered, without question, another expeditionary force. Over 14,000 men volunteered in less than a fortnight, but were not required as the crisis subsided.[35] The naval subsidy policy reached a new dimension in 1923 when the British sought help in building their great naval base at Singapore to service the 'main fleet' for operations in the Indian Ocean and Pacific in the event of war. New Zealand immediately offered £100,000. This was not used as the British suspended their project briefly, but in 1927, when work resumed, New Zealand gave £1 million over eight years.[36] In the depths of the Depression, when Japan struck first at Manchuria (1931) then at Shanghai (1932) at a time when the Singapore base had hardly begun, the Dominion Government felt a need for re-armament. Thus in 1933 a Six Year Plan (which included the building of a stronger air force) was commenced. When Italy attacked Ethiopia, in 1935, the Dominion was asked for help with one of the cruisers in the Indian Ocean, and readily obliged.[37]

New Zealand remained a loyal outpost of empire. More and more of the country's exports went to Britain in the 1920s. Content to be Britain's outlying farm, New Zealand eschewed the trappings of nationhood. It was perhaps appropriate that at the 1936 Olympic Games in Berlin as Jack Lovelock, a New Zealand medical student at Oxford, took the lead dramatically in the fifteen hundred metres, the English radio commentator Harold Abrahams threw BBC impartiality to the winds and, in one of the most famous sports broadcasts ever, cried out over the air: 'Come on Jack . . . Come on Jack . . . Jack. He's won — hurray!' Britain failed to win a single gold medal in Berlin. Lovelock in black shorts and singlet, sporting the silver fern leaf, had, nevertheless, provided a 'British' victory. The strains of 'God Save the King' were heard over the Nazi stadium. It symbolized well New Zealand's place in the world. In the same year, however, under the first Labour Government, New Zealand began to make a mark in the League of Nations quite distinct from the mother country.

PART IV

Precarious Maturity

CHAPTER 14

From Labour to National

Robert Chapman

Labour did more in 1935 than win an election triumphantly. The victory of 1935 and its popular confirmation in 1938 allowed the leaders of the Labour Party to shift the emphasis of the economy and amend its control, alter the balance of society and state, transform the prospects of the average family, and enlarge the education and hopes of young people. The patterns and institutions thereby established long outlasted the Party's own period in power. Like the Liberals after their victory in 1890, Labour after 1935 was able to set the terms of political debate and action for the next forty years. Like the Liberal Government, too, Labour in power became increasingly occupied with conserving the *status quo* it had established; and both governments were replaced in this task by a conservative party of administration.

The readiness to turn from one era to the next in 1935 came primarily from the breadth of feeling that it was no longer possible to go on in the old way. Likewise, the drive to change governments came not only from the persuasiveness and strength of the Labour Party but also from the bankruptcy and division of the previous order. For five years the country had been racked by depression, and criticism of the Coalition formed to face the crisis was wellnigh universal. Dissent on the right found a voice in the hurriedly formed Democrat Party,[1] which was intended to meet the dismay and bewilderment of respectable, conservative-voting folk in towns and city suburbs in the face of their own Government's failure. The Democrat programme, a paradoxical combination of promised austerity and generosity, was, however, reminiscent of other vanished hopes. Like their United predecessors, the Democrats were keen to lower taxes yet ready to borrow; hostile to the necessities of government yet prepared to offer self-contradictory terms in order that they personally might govern. None of the fifty-four Democrats found for the eighty seats[2] was elected, although their share of the vote was sufficient to divide conservatism in the face of the Labour challenge.

Division and disarray were exacerbated by a horde of Independents and mini-party candidates. Forty-four Independent, Country, and Liberal contestants also aimed for conservative support. (By contrast, Labour strongholds were threatened only by four Communist candidates, who were easily crushed; the four Māori seats were left to sympathetic Rātana

Party members; and six difficult constituencies were passed to Labour-inclined Independent or Country candidates.) To confront the competition for its share of the vote the Government had little to offer. The Government MPs reproduced in political organization the temporary common front represented by the Coalition Ministry. In May 1935 the National Political Federation was formed to support all Government candidates as 'Nationalists'.[3] The old party realities did not vanish, but conservative contestants endeavoured to co-operate locally while at the centre there was a common Federation organizer, an appointed executive, and funds from a few large contributors. Sitting members were endorsed by the Coalition leaders, G. W. Forbes and J. G. Coates, and policy came from the same source. When the National manifesto appeared in October, the Government cautiously tried to claim a reward for austere restraint while gesturing towards schemes for a milder future.[4] But the document was conspicuous for its vagueness about possible plans for when times had improved. If the schemes had been precise and definitely promised, they would have alarmed the very groups whose support was held by the Coalition's cost-cutting and budget-balancing. So National's candidates had to run on the Coalition's four-year record of administering the Depression, scarcely softened by qualified assurances of eventual change.

The Coalition record presented the broadest of targets, which Labour had been attacking for years. The Labour Party possessed a long-established and widely spread branch membership with a separate pyramid of elected party institutions to back up their parliamentarians and candidates. The public was already familiar with Labour's criticisms and alternatives, so their campaign had only to summarize, not establish, their case for ousting the Government. Their platform was a commitment to institutional change — change aimed at 'restoring a decent living standard to those who have been deprived of essentials for the past five years'.[5] The system would be altered, and made to work in new ways, but it would not be replaced. Socialism in the form of 'the public ownership of the means of production, distribution and exchange' was neither at hand nor contemplated. Rather, the Party aimed 'to organize an internal economy that will distribute the production and services in a way that will guarantee to every person able and willing to work an income sufficient to provide him and his dependants with everything necessary to make a "home" and "home life" in the best sense of the meaning of those terms'. It was an absolute rejection of the experiences of the Depression and a promise to reverse them.

Three kinds of pledge were given, aimed at economic restoration, direction, and welfare. To restore the economy and expand production Labour proposed that, in its first year of office, guaranteed prices would be paid for all primary production. All wage and salary cuts would be restored and relief pay increased 'immediately'. Labour would enact a statutory minimum wage and salary payment for all workers. Direction would be provided by 'putting our own production and marketing system in order'. Elements of insulation — controlled exports, overseas funds, and imports — can be glimpsed in Labour's policies. The Reserve Bank would become completely state owned and govern 'the flow of credit, the general price level, and the regulation of foreign exchange operations'. Coates's Mortgage Corporation would revert to the lines of the one-time State Advances Department, while 'the people's savings' were to be safeguarded by extending the facilities and deposit limits of the Post Office Savings Bank. Labour's election policy went on to present programmes for health, education, pensions, and superannuation which transcended any previous provisions. The education system was to be expanded at all levels. Age and dependence were to be fully provided for. The commitments were unhesitating, clear, and confident. They admitted no doubt that the resources would be there to accomplish them.

Despite all that National and the press could do to discredit the practicability of Labour's programme, enough voters were convinced that it could be done or must be tried to give Labour a victory comparable only with the triumph of the Liberals in 1890. National, Democrat, and Independent candidates were put to rout not just in the cities and towns but in the countryside as well. The National Political Federation went into the battle holding forty-six seats. It emerged with nineteen. Before the election Labour had twenty-four MPs: afterwards it numbered fifty-three, with six allies in addition.

An analysis of the 1935 election results is significant not only for revealing the force behind this upheaval but also because the new landscape of sectional allegiances that was created retained many of its major features, however eroded or built upon, until the 1970s.[6] In the 1920s Labour was primarily a city party, and, within the cities, the party of the poorer city electorates. In 1931 it held all fourteen such seats, so no further captures were to be made there.[7] Nevertheless, in 1935 the Labour vote rose in these electorates by 11.72 percentage points to reach 60.71 per cent of all those qualified to vote, while National dropped to 21.70 per cent. It was a lasting judgement and for forty years, until Dunedin North changed hands in 1975, Labour could count on all the poorer, inner-city electorates. Conversely, until the East Coast Bays by-election of 1980, National could rely absolutely on its few, richer city constituencies. There were only three of these in 1935 and, though all returned National members, the tide of conversion swept into these seats also and Labour's share of the vote swelled by 11.28 points. National's reduction in its richer city strongholds paid reluctant tribute to the lingering homogeneity of New Zealand's little cities and to the relative equality of New Zealand society which in some ways had been reinforced by the common misfortunes of the Depression.

The nine mixed and middling electorates, mostly suburbs resulting from the spread of tramcar lines and the motorbus, made up the third section of the cities. They were full of clerks, small business people, and skilled tradesmen — neither well-to-do nor poor in normal times, but further exposed, threatened, and reduced with every year of depression. In 1935 they turned to Labour with a decisiveness that pushed its share of the vote up by 12.37 points and gave the Party eight instead of the previous four mixed city seats. With Labour already established in its traditional strongholds, the greatest gains were to be made in the burgeoning suburbs. But all the city and town seats totalled less than half the House of Representatives (thirty-six out of eighty). Voters in the four Māori electorates remained overwhelmingly country people, and an artificial weighting supplied by the 'country quota' produced eight more country seats than would otherwise have existed.[8] Labour could not have become the Government without securing some corresponding measure of support from rural New Zealand. In fact the movement towards Labour was far greater outside the cities and towns than within them. As the thirty-five Coalition country representatives were winnowed down to fifteen National members, the number of country Labour MPs shot from three to twenty-three. The Coalition's four auxiliaries of 1931 became one Independent friend for National in 1935, while Labour found itself with five instead of two helpers. The biggest rise in votes for Labour candidates came in the seventeen seats dominated by farmers. There the gain was a massive 24.2 per cent of all qualified to vote. In the seventeen rural seats with sizeable populations in small towns Labour jumped by 17.1, and in the six special country electorates where mining or timber was significant the upward movement was 15.1. Labour dominated the mining and timber electorates; it scraped a half point lead over National in the rural seats; and ran only fourteen points behind National in the farmer constituencies.

In 1935 a whole succession of governments, summed up in a coalition of their remnants, had come to judgement. An economic system had faltered through a decade of disappointment to tragic collapse in the 1930s. Tutored by such a prolonged and savage lesson, New Zealanders were ready even in their most conservative strongholds to accept change and try a new direction. Labour had won a majority of seats and votes over National in every class of electorate except the richer city electorates and pure farmer seats, and stood as the victorious party in both city and countryside: it had achieved the consensual basis necessary for reshaping society and the economy.

This reshaping was ultimately the work of tens of thousands. At the centre, however, was Labour's Cabinet of thirteen whose nucleus was the triumvirate of Michael Joseph Savage, Peter Fraser, and Walter Nash. All three were born and raised in societies other than the New Zealand they changed.[9] Their families all hovered between insecurity and poverty, and each son grasped at education, loved books all his life, and had to leave school for work too early to measure himself scholastically. In their countries of origin, their class, and their hard experience of living, the three men symbolized the stock that had colonized New Zealand.

Life in New Zealand has a way of gradually extracting the political sting from its immigrants but these three continued to work at politics as they had in their homelands. Their socialism was more an attitude of mind — a hopeful faith in the possibilities of man — than a set of specific beliefs. The reading they quoted ranged from Bellamy, Hobson, and Blatchford to Henry George, John Stuart Mill, and Bernard Shaw. Their most frequent source was certainly the Bible. They represented different strands of the Labour movement — Fraser and Savage were early members of the Socialist Party and Nash was associated with the more moderate United Labour Party — but their attitudes were tempered by successive defeats and all converged together in the Labour Party.

Savage's prime ministership was settled as early as 1923 when he defeated Daniel Sullivan in an election for the new deputy chairmanship of the Parliamentary Labour Party. The balance of power in the caucus changed little during the 1920s and Savage was re-elected triennially as deputy to Harry Holland until the latter's death in October 1933. Peter Fraser, the only figure of almost equal prominence to Savage, nominated his old friend and senior to an unopposed succession as leader of the Labour Party, becoming his deputy. At the same time Nash earned his place in the triumvirate as the indefatigable national secretary from 1922 to 1932 and as theoretician and propagandist.[10] On entering Parliament in 1929, he became spokesman on financial matters.

The victory of 1935 more than doubled the size of caucus, and the addition of twenty-eight MPs entirely new to Parliament provoked a breach of the Parliamentary Labour Party's pattern for election to offices. The veteran Rex Mason moved that the leader be asked to select the members of the Cabinet.[11] In an unprecedented situation not covered by written rules, the jubilant caucus turned to its elected and triumphant leader. In a Cabinet of thirteen there was room for only half of those with reputation and experience. Ten came from Labour's strongholds in the four main centres, and the remaining three were from country districts. Problems with balanced representation led to the exclusion of a fourth Aucklander, John A. Lee, whose disappointed ambition was to cost the Party dearly.

There were no doubts in that first year, 1936, as to the speed, scope, and confidence of Cabinet's activity. They were putting a decent New Zealand back together again. The unemployed were helped first, with a Christmas bonus of a week's pay; in February higher rates for sustenance and relief work were announced, and those engaged in public works on relief were raised to standard pay. Then in May, Bob Semple laid before the House a three-year programme for £17.5 million to be spent on development works. The basic rate of £4 for a forty-hour week did no more than recover earlier conditions but it was a recovery enjoyed by 19,000 at the year's end. By December 1937 only 8,367 were left on increased sustenance and relief.[12] The attainment of absolutely full employment — a condition never previously achieved — had to wait on the Second World War.

Employed people were assisted by Nash's Finance Act (1936) which restored all award rates completely and eliminated all depression cuts to wages and salaries, while the Factories Amendment Act (1936) reduced the manufacturing week to forty hours. The Shops and Offices Amendment Act of the same year affected banks and insurance as well, regulated their hours of closing, and specified a maximum of forty-four hours. These two

Acts set the same minimum pay of £2 a week for established employees. The vast majority found their hours improved, their conditions brightened, and security slid in like a girder beneath them.[13]

The restored awards and new minimum scales immediately raised the purchasing power of wage and salary earners to the benefit of business and manufacturing. Improved and extended pensions had the same effect. Shorter hours also meant some sharing out of existing jobs to additional employees and, consequently, more consumers. The housing programme and subsequent reactivation of the building industry likewise worked to revive and restore what had been a grossly deflated economy while guaranteed prices meant a return of confidence among farmers. Labour was applying a complex of stimuli to the economy, each of which reinforced the others.

In 1936 the craft union stalwarts of the Party came into their kingdom. The Industrial Conciliation and Arbitration Amendment Act (1936) not only restored full jurisdiction to the Arbitration Court, but also required the Court to make general orders fixing basic wages both for men and for women which would apply to all awards and agreements in force. A social component was specified for the first time in that the male adult wage was to be based upon the needs of a man, wife, and three children. The Act also made union membership compulsory for all workers subject to any award or industrial agreement. Union membership soared from 81,000 in 1935 to 249,000 in 1938,[14] and awards and unions spread rapidly to fresh sectors of the economy.

Restored protection plus compulsory membership under the amended Act were ambiguous gifts for the remaining militants. For them the right to strike was a high price to pay for I.C. and A. protection, and the increase in membership was offset by the preference of most new members for Court awards over industrial action. But the general welcome the Act received was a sign that the powerlessness of unprotected unionism and the superiority of political action had been recognized. The politicians behind the legislation had themselves been unionists and often militants, but they had long grasped the axiom that in New Zealand a broad advance for working people would either arrive through the ballot box or it would not come at all. The strength of Labour's system, and the reason for its longevity, lay in the fact that the new Government was building on what the majority already believed.

In the more uncertain region of financial direction, Labour modified existing institutions where possible and then showed caution in using the powers it took. By the Reserve Bank Amendment Act (1936)[15] the Bank's private shareholding of £500,000 was bought out. It was important for Labour to be seen to be taking legally conclusive powers to direct this central institution of finance, so opening the way for the use of 'the people's credit' — that phrase of a thousand meanings and hopes.[16] As a state-owned, central bank, the Reserve Bank's general function was 'to give effect as far as may be to the monetary policy of the Government as communicated to it from time to time by the Minister of Finance'; and in addition to 'regulate and control credit and currency in New Zealand, the transfer . . . and the disposal of moneys that are derived from the sale of any New Zealand products and for the time being are held overseas'. Here as promised was the possibility of low interest or even no interest loans for public purposes on the credit of the country, and Nash was to use it in due time for financing the Dairy Account and for state housing. Wider use of low interest credit later became part of an argument within the Party about the pace of change, but the Act's powers initially satisfied popular expectations, while also making provisions for guaranteed prices and exchange control.

Labour used the promised guaranteed prices to assist the dairy industry, while the sheep farmers, who had suffered less and recovered earlier, opted to remain in the free market. Guaranteed prices did much for the recovery of farming and also led to a lasting reorganization of overseas marketing and to internal rationalization. An advisory committee devised a scheme whereby the state, since it was to guarantee prices, should buy all dairy produce at the wharfside, finance and insure it, negotiate its transport and storage, and then sell through selected British firms. This would cut out speculation by agents and several costly links in the chain to British wholesalers, besides providing a far more even flow on to the market. When the Primary Products Marketing Act was passed in 1936, farmers were not so much concerned with the structure of marketing as with the immediate and future levels of the guaranteed price. The final prices fixed for butter and cheese proved higher than either the eight- or the ten-year average which had been considered. For fixing future prices, however, the Act set out several possibly incompatible criteria, which concluded with the declaration that the price should assure any 'efficient producer . . . a sufficient net return from his business to enable him to maintain himself and his family in a reasonable standard of comfort'. Such a generous but indefinite aim mixed social equity with economics, and promised dissatisfaction and complaint once dairying had passed out of depression and the guarantee scheme had assisted farmers onto their feet.[17]

This took some time, however, and meanwhile thousands of farmers remained mired in mortgage debt. Help was given by the passage of the Mortgagors and Lessees Rehabilitation Act (1936).[18] The purpose was to keep farmers on the land as efficient producers and at the same time assure them of a 'reasonable standard of comfort' while likewise keeping urban householders in their homes. In replacing Coates's Mortgage Corporation of 1935 with the State Advances Corporation by an Act in 1936,[19] Nash drew on the reassurance conferred by long-established names. In fact the nostalgic name deflected attention from new powers of financial control and a considerable extension of activities. The Mortgage Corporation's private shareholders were bought out, and the Board of Directors was to have regard to the Minister's advice on policy. His direction, if given in writing, was binding. Besides providing cheap, long-term, rural and urban financing on first mortgage, the Corporation was also given power to lend to local authorities for construction of workers' housing and power to make advances for developing existing industries or for establishing new ones. The old Department and Coates's private Corporation had thus emerged combined and revitalized by the wily Minister into a public, all-purpose, long and intermediate-term lending institution, ready to play a full state part in advancing the mixed economy. While the farmer and his family stood to gain from all these credit and price guarantee measures, the dairy factory employees and contract and seasonal workers too were assisted by legislation and revived awards. The rural labourer had always been unprotected; now the Agricultural Workers Act (1936) set a minimum rate of pay and required a decent level of living conditions. Both pay and conditions were spartan but such an improvement that farmers immediately complained about rising costs of labour.[20]

The 1934 Labour Party Conference had proposed to the National Executive a housing construction scheme 'for all classes', rentals in accord with earnings, and fair rents legislation. The responsibility for action fell to Nash. James Fletcher, head of a large construction firm, offered his assistance because, though a Reform supporter, he believed in large-scale planning and in the inter-dependence of government and business. Nash also enlisted John A. Lee by asking him to prepare a report. Lee, although Under-Secretary and present at Cabinet, had been given neither a role nor perquisites by Savage. After handing in his resignation, he was quietened by being appointed 'Parliamentary Under-Secretary to the Minister of Finance (for Housing)'. Once given the task, Lee worked with verve, rapidity, and insight to get the massive project moving and to publicize its quality. His own vision was of a scheme 'socialistic in finance, construction and ownership'.[21]

State housing was indeed socially motivated and it was undoubtedly socially significant in its effects. But the state chose to act as a capitalist entrepreneur employing private firms to build a collective asset. Rents were aimed to cover the costs of construction and full maintenance, and thus permit the initial capital to be recycled into further building. To benefit from the economies of mass production, the Housing Department offered large contracts. Fletchers built most of the early Hutt, Miramar, and Orakei state houses but they bid so low, and wage and material costs rose so promptly, that the company only made a profit after years of loss. Increasingly contracts were broken down into units which smaller builders could bid for with their straitened resources.

State housing was therefore neither socialist in construction nor open-handedly Douglasite in financing, but it did remain state-owned. Leading Nationalists attacked the scheme and said it had 'knocked over private enterprise' and promoted tenancy instead of ownership; they urged that tenants should be able 'to acquire the houses for themselves'.[22] Labour replied that selling these houses would delay the time when low-cost rental housing needs were met and increase the average cost and therefore rental of the remaining houses. The Act remodelling and restoring State Advances had also permitted the Corporation to make loans on other houses up to 85 per cent of valuation. Nash intended to begin with state rental housing for the poorer groups and for families, and then provide State Advances assistance for lower to middling income groups to build and buy directly. State houses for renting and State Advances for owning were thus to be complementary schemes and represented successive phases for the individual family establishing a home of its own. If houses built for the first renting phase were to be sold, the vital first step for subsequent families would be eliminated.

Labour attempted to build enough houses to meet the needs inherited from the past and to stem present discontents. Over Labour's thirteen years of construction, the average number built per year was 2,475, precisely one-quarter of the total residential building permits issued. State Advances mortgages financed a further 16 per cent of all dwellings built over the same period, and the two schemes together gave state assistance to two in every five houses.[23] A whole generation of poorer families were thus able to establish themselves in reasonable comfort and security. The social effect was a levelling upwards which counteracted divisions exacerbated by the Depression. Equality in New Zealand life came to be symbolized by the spreading state house suburbs with their narrow range of incomes and their uniformities of occupation, age level, and style of life. But state housing provided an equalizing pause, not a self-enclosed, self-sustaining condition nor the seed-bed of equalitarian conviction. For thousands it meant more hope and opportunity, not less, of escaping outwards and upwards towards their own private future, a National-voting future.

Labour's policy had declared that 'when a nation through parsimony and false economy neglects the education of its children it not only deprives them of natural rights, but it creates a financial and social debt which can never be redeemed'.[24] Peter Fraser opened another door by setting the education system on the track toward rapid growth. He reopened the two teachers' training colleges remaining closed after the Depression and lowered the school entry age from six to five. The abolition of the Proficiency examination widened entry to secondary education and gave greater flexibility to the primary curriculum. Cuts in the teachers' salaries were restored and unemployed teachers moved back into teaching so that class sizes could fall. He restored grants to kindergartens and adult education while increasing funds for school maintenance, materials, crafts, libraries, Māori education, the correspondence system, the dental service, and bus transport for isolated pupils. Funds for constructing new schools and refurbishing old ones were more than doubled in one year.

Jobs, housing, and education — the basic elements underpinning family life and individual advancement — were thus being tackled. But what of the inevitable casualties of ill-health and old age? In February 1936 W. E. Parry, the Minister of Pensions, proposed that 30s. be fixed as the pension for all men at sixty and women at fifty-eight and suggested several new categories of pension.[25] Treasury told Cabinet that the pensions bill would go up two-and-a-half times and even a much lower increase would still have unbalanced the budget. After several stormy caucus meetings, the Pensions Amendment Act of September raised the old-age pension to

22*s*.6d. and in addition improved rates for widows and the blind, liberalized qualifications, and introduced pensions for deserted wives and invalids.

In July 1936 Peter Fraser set up a caucus committee to plan a health scheme under the chairmanship of Dr D. G. McMillan. The main problem encountered by the Health Committee was not financial but professional — the unremitting resistance of the New Zealand branch of the British Medical Association.[26] Its secretary, Dr J. P. S. Jamieson, proposed that only 'old-age pensioners, unemployed and unemployable, part-time and casual workers' should enjoy completely free medical service. For the rest of the population the BMA plan prescribed a mixture of compulsory insurance and private provision according to wealth.[27] The Health Committee's main report to Cabinet in September 1937 reaffirmed McMillan's plan for wide-ranging free services. Eventually Cabinet realized that any further steps toward implementing their election pledge of universal free health care would have to be taken without the support of the BMA.

The pensions proposals, too, were called into question. In London in 1937 Nash had encountered a chilly reception from Conservative ministers, officials, and bankers. It appeared that guaranteed prices would not be anchored by bilateral trading arrangements. Reductions in quotas were possible and any fall in prices would certainly bring exchange problems.[28] Nash, acutely aware of the likely expense of the pensions scheme as proposed by an inter-departmental committee, was bound to attend to suggestions for reducing the strain upon the budget. These he received from a British actuarial expert, G. H. Maddex, who returned to New Zealand with Nash and joined other key advisers in planning a funded superannuation scheme. Fraser as Minister of Health was also ready for retreat in the face of financial problems and an intransigent BMA. Finally, in February 1938, the ministers faced an unprepared and startled caucus with proposals for a limited free medical service, and a traditional insurance-style contributory scheme to meet general health, superannu-ation, and unemployment needs. It was a programme bound to provoke if not positively invite a successful backbench rebellion. Labour backbenchers were entirely unconvinced of the need for retreat and the caucus majority were ready to rally again to hold their leaders to party policy. The principles at stake were those espoused by the leaders themselves with emotional force on every previous occasion. The normal majority in the Labour caucus and Cabinet rapidly reasserted itself and against it the Nash–Fraser proposals stood little chance.

Fraser gave in gracefully, saying that he 'would accept it as the mind of caucus that the health scheme would be universal in its scope'.[29] Nash was more reluctant to relinquish his scheme. Caucus resolved that an alternative scheme should come before it in March. The Prime Minister unwisely attempted to short-circuit this by announcing to the press that there would be an all-party select committee to examine proposals for superannuation and health insurance. This move infuriated and united the Labour caucus, and gave hostages to further criticism from the BMA, the Opposition, and the newspapers. Caucus quickly formed a committee to formulate

Government policy. Back came a plan for universal free health provisions, wide-ranging and increased benefits, and an old-age pension at 30s. for men and women at sixty. This one comprehensive social security system was to be paid for half from general revenue and half from specific levies. At the end of March the system was confirmed as Government policy, to constitute the structure of the final Act. The backbench rebellion had succeeded despite financial anxieties because it reasserted a consensus few Labour MPs had ever doubted and because it returned to the long-held humanitarian hopes of the leaders themselves.

The last big Bill of the session, the Social Security Bill, was the most significant measure to come before what had already proved to be a transforming Parliament.[30] At the last moment Nash had added a provision for a truly universal superannuation payment at sixty-five of £10 per year which was to rise annually by £2 10s until it reached parity with the means-tested age benefit. The Opposition was in a difficult situation. They claimed that social security would ruin the friendly societies and penalize thrift; they forecast financial disaster and eventual failure to pay benefits; they predicted socialization of the medical profession and complete socialism in the country; and since the Prime Minister had repeated a clergyman's judgement that the scheme represented 'applied Christianity', National's next leader, Sidney Holland, called the whole basis of social security 'applied lunacy'.[31] National offered instead the kind of health proposals that the BMA had advocated, and suggested a superannuation scheme for the unprovided that left insurance-style provisions carrying most of that burden.

By the time Parliament concluded, it was obvious that Labour's Social Security Act would be the centrepiece of the election. National was confident, in the words of their leader, that 'the profession does not want it; most of the people do not want it. It is just a political stunt — merely the socialization of the doctors'. Labour was equally sure with Walter Nash that social security would 'confer more benefits on the people than any measure which has ever been enacted'.[32] Accordingly they set the election date for 15 October and the four-week campaign began.

The Opposition forces that faced Labour in 1938 were no longer the sad and disconcerted remnants of the old Reform and Liberal Parties that had dominated New Zealand parliaments for the first third of the century. It had been a small and weary band that faced Labour's legislative onslaught after the 1935 election. In weakness and defeat it had had to overcome its own divisions, find an attractive leadership, and discover some effective form of party organization. Although the prospect had been daunting, nevertheless between 1935 and 1938 a modern mass-based party did emerge; the anti-Labour forces were effectively unified; the problem of leadership was certainly tackled if not solved; and only the overall objective of electoral success remained to be tested.

The initiative was essentially non-parliamentary. In February 1936 Forbes and Coates met the Executive of the National Political Federation and a representative collection of Reform and United notables. At the founding conference in May 1936 the Executive of the National Political Federation, the nineteen National MPs, and 233 delegates from all over the country resolved to found a party open 'to all those people who put their faith in a policy based on sound finance and private enterprise'.[33] The party was to halt 'socialism' by gathering in the anti-Labour voters so divided by party and personal loyalties at the recent election.

The constitution was intended to contrast with those of the Reform and United Parties. The new, inclusive party was to be supported by a numerous membership paying subscriptions, drawn together in branches by social and political activities between elections and by working together during the election campaigns. Above this was a tightly structured system of representation, which co-ordinated electorate, divisional, and national organization and decision-making. Thus continuous activity was to replace triennial spurts; election was to supplant appointment, personal links, favours, and cliques; above all there was to be a party separate from the parliamentary party, with its own elected president and its own yearly conference. Although the new model bore a resemblance to the Conservative Party in Britain and the United Australia Party, it was designed to be like the proven Labour structure which National hoped to overcome.

The New Zealand National Party's greatest power was its members' right to select their own candidates. An anti-Labour candidate could now seek selection by exhaustive ballot from a carefully constituted and fully representative meeting, providing he was ready to sign a pledge to abide by the choice of the meeting, to support the chosen candidate, and to refuse, if unsuccessful, further nomination for that election. If successful, the chosen candidate could expect the support of the full party structure. The number of candidates on the anti-Labour side dropped from 177 in 1935 to 92 in 1938 while the number of straight fights — one Labour against one anti-Labour candidate — sprang from 15 to 68. Labour's twenty-year advantage in unity and organization had at last been matched.

Once the party structure had been established, the question of policy control and leadership remained. Here the parliamentary members of the party retained what was vital to them. The MPs of the National Political Federation kept their support and places in Parliament, the right of the parliamentary team to pick its leader, and their joint power to determine party policy. These parliamentarians passed on to the new party their own sense of past authority and future entitlement to govern, tactical knowledge of battle in the House and, above all, an unshakeable belief in New Zealand as an individualistic, farming economy of which they were the true representatives. They were intensely loyal to their own vision of New Zealand and to the Crown, eager to follow Britain's lead in matters economic and international yet otherwise little occupied with the outside world. They mistrusted the size and expense of the state while standing ready to use its powers and credit to promote primary industry and the development of communications and export facilities. They saw themselves as protecting and, where possible, advancing a pleasant if beleaguered land of family farms now threatened in their view by socialism, state control, protected unionism, and governmental extravagance. As Adam Hamilton put it in the House: 'It is not the job of the Government to try and break down everything that has been done in the past; not the Government's duty to revolutionise things and start off on some new and uncharted sea that might cause a wreck later.' Instead he looked 'to the people who have risen by some ability and some experience to a responsible position in society — those are the people to govern. What we want is a combination of the sound business element and the farming community. . . .'[34] It was thus a heritage of economic and social attitudes they transmitted rather than a body of polished doctrines linked into a philosophy. Nor had the Depression left them much by way of specific policies to bequeath.

The legacy of the Depression also deprived both Coates and Forbes of the leadership. Forbes as outgoing Prime Minister assumed leadership of the Opposition but he was not leader of the Party, which by August was pressing for a new joint leader of both Party and Opposition. The two principal contestants were Adam Hamilton, supported largely by ex-Reformers, and the Independent C. A. Wilkinson, who was put forward by the ex-United faction after he had joined the Opposition. Caucus narrowly chose Hamilton whereupon the Party's Dominion Council was informed and endorsed the choice.[35] The National Party was now complete, still together, and headed by one leader of the Opposition and the Party.

Policy was essentially in the hands of the MPs and their leader, providing they attended to Council's advice and took note of signals arising from the annual Conference. The 'Objects' of the Party were highly general and included loyalty to the King, efficient defence, and the pursuit of 'a policy of progressive social and humanitarian legislation'. At the next level the Party Conference was given the right 'to consider policy proposals'[36] but it was the Dominion Council which stated general policy after consulting from time to time with its parliamentary representatives through a standing committee on policy of three members from the Council and three MPs nominated by the leader of the Party. The leader's trio were thus in a position to check any Council tendency to move from broad if influential resolutions to unduly specific interference. Lastly, the critical business of the 'fighting policy' or election manifesto was to be the concern of the leader to formulate and announce after consulting Council. Agreement between MPs and party workers was so close as to the merits of private enterprise, the traditional elements of society they were bound to defend, and the need to oppose and resist Labour that there was no difficulty in framing the policy with which to fight the coming election.

By 1937 recruiting was in full swing. Party reports told of 405 branches, and by election year there were over 1,000 with an estimated membership of 100,000 which was growing fastest in country districts. The manifesto declared that the National Party represented all sections of society and stood for the small man, whether trader, farmer, manufacturer, or shopkeeper, aiming to protect them from 'ministerial dictatorship and interference'. Primary production was entitled 'to a standard of reward comparable with other industries' and there would be a vigorous land settlement policy. Tenants would be allowed to purchase state houses and, though the Social Security Act would not be operated by National, there would be a 'full and complete health service without charge to that section of the community that is unable to provide such service for itself'. At the same time, where possible, taxes would be reduced. In short, the newly active state with its social security and state tenants was to be turned back with the help of the voters because, as Hamilton said, 'we are convinced that no people of British stock are prepared to throw away their birthright of democracy for the rigid fetters of the Socialist State. . . .'[37]

The 1938 election was a heavy blow to those hoping to restore the power of government to the principles of the old regime. Labour MPs continued to outnumber National MPs by more than two to one, Labour representation standing at fifty-three to National's twenty-five. In votes, moreover, Labour and its allies reached a fresh peak of 52.3 per cent of those qualified to vote, a level not attained again by either party in the decades since. Yet there were compensating features for Nationalists within the general repulse they had suffered. The National Parliamentary Party had grown, with allies, from twenty-one to twenty-six while their vote had risen to reach 38.8 per cent. With only two Independent MPs left, each treated as quasi-members of one of the major parties, the armies of electors were now starkly defined as for and against the Government, Labour or National. National's limited advance in seats and Labour's superior gain in votes indicated that National had a long struggle ahead. It was to be another eleven years before a National Government came to power.

The victory of 1938 marked the peak of achievement for the New Zealand Labour Party in the twentieth century. This time Labour's support reached historic levels against an organized, united Opposition, and the verdict of the people was based on direct experience of Labour's policies in action. The increased vote encouraged those who hoped with the Prime Minister that New Zealand was indeed 'a social laboratory' with a progressive people willing and ready to push 'onward and upward'.[38] But instead of the years of development it had looked forward to, the Government immediately encountered the limitations of a small, dependent trading economy. A deliberate withdrawal of private capital exacerbated by the cost of overseas machinery and supplies had dangerously run down New Zealand's sterling balances from £29 million to £8 million in six months. Cabinet was compelled to introduce exchange controls in December 1938.

Nash was despatched to Britain and spent months in stubborn negotiation with the Conservative Government, the Bank of England, and British manufacturers and exporters. He had to pledge that import licensing would be re-examined and not used to foster 'uneconomic' industries and, in exchange, he got a small loan for defence, minor credits to buy British exports, and enough to roll over an expiring loan providing it was all repaid in five years — harsh terms which promised economic contraction in New Zealand. But only a month after Nash left England these bleak prospects were transformed by the outbreak of war. The British Government cabled offers to buy all New Zealand's exportable surplus of meat and dairy products and then wool. At a stroke Nash was presented with his long-sought government-to-government agreement for an expanding British market. Now New Zealand's credit in London and its sterling balances would rise simultaneously. The demands of war on British production and on vessels to carry it would also force New Zealand to manufacture as much as possible from its own resources while ensuring the strictest control over and selection of scarce imports.[39]

At home the Prime Minister and caucus were confronted with three problems summed up in one man, John A. Lee. For himself Lee sought preferment and power; for the Party and the country he envisaged transformation by the use of Reserve Bank credit at low or no interest. Convinced that his own and allied cases would be served by caucus control of Cabinet selection, Lee tried to strip the Prime Minister of his power to choose Cabinet. But Savage, aware of his own political value to the Party, simply ignored a narrow vote for preferential election by caucus and stretched out instead to the Central Executive of the Party, and eventually to the 1939 Conference, for fresh support. Lee was censured for his 'Lee Letter' which accused Nash of 'stupidity' and 'drift', and a complex arrangement for selection of Cabinet was confirmed which left the final choice in Savage's hands.[40]

Impatient at this check, Lee renewed his offensive. In another loose and hurtful article in July he attacked all three of Labour's leaders. The Prime Minister was struggling through the session ill with cancer, Nash was away negotiating, while Fraser, the deputy leader, was preoccupied with the forthcoming war. At Savage's last caucus in November 1939 Lee told the Prime Minister that he was 'someone made mentally sick by physical illness'.[41] The objective of the contest was changing from a matter of one or two Cabinet posts into the major question of who would succeed the Prime Minister, when, and with what kind of policy and colleagues. Instead of focusing on his ultimate rival, Fraser, Lee now felt compelled to strike straight at the Party's greatest strength, the figure and reputation of the Prime Minister himself. Lee published a signed article on physically and mentally sick leaders; his prescription was 'to cut off the diseased limb'. In response, the Cabinet dismissed Lee from his position as Under-Secretary. The Party's National Executive tried to hold Lee but he was beyond their control. In March 1940 the Annual Conference heard a statement written by Savage the previous month which denounced Lee's attempts to 'destroy me as a political force' and said that 'for about two years my life has been a living hell'. The Conference was told that Savage was near death and a relapse in January had been connected with the publication of Lee's article in December. Not even six hours of debate could save Lee once his expulsion was moved. Despite widespread aversion to so final a breach, expulsion was eventually carried 546 to 344, and Lee departed, leaving behind him the looming question of how many MPs and branch members might follow.[42]

Two days later the Prime Minister died and was mourned as deeply and widely as any man in the country's history. The people's judgement was clear: Joe Savage had been their leader as well as being, in a remarkably personal way, a friend to tens of thousands who had only glimpsed or heard him. His successor, Fraser, had little of the encompassing appeal of Savage but he had less need of it because for the next six years the demands and loyalties of war would bind New Zealanders and their society. Fraser used his strength in caucus to win the leadership with ease and have the existing Cabinet confirmed as well. Being a shrewd tactician who sensed when to yield, Fraser then changed sides on selection procedures and announced a caucus preferential ballot to fill the Cabinet position left vacant by Savage's death. Dr McMillan won his way in and Fraser's control was rivetted home.[43] Walter Nash was unanimously elected deputy leader.

Only one MP, W. E. Barnard, the Speaker of the House, followed Lee out of the Labour Party. Outside Parliament, Lee set up his own Democratic Labour Party and, though crowds flocked to hear his case and branches appeared all over the country, Lee so dominated the organization and policy-making that Barnard dropped out and membership dwindled.[44] War also quietened the erstwhile creditist faction within the Parliamentary Labour Party. With its economy insulated by the demands and stringencies of global war, New Zealand was hardly receptive to arguments seeking Reserve Bank credit to finance more jobs. Such unemployment as remained was rapidly turning into a scarcity of labour.

During the eight months before Hitler stormed westward in mid-1940, volunteering brought in all the fighting men necessary. With the Nazis in Norway and the Low Countries, however, a sudden clamour for drastic action arose from emotional public meetings held up and down New Zealand. Fraser promised compulsion and conscription along with a representative war council. In this war Labour intended to avoid conflict about equality of sacrifice, so powers to conscript wealth were to equal those to conscript men. But the proposed war council was rejected by National which wanted an end to Labour legislation and a two-party Cabinet. Dunkirk and the fall of France brought compromise and on 16 July 1940 Hamilton and Coates became members of a War Cabinet of six which would take the major decisions while Labour's regular Cabinet continued its largely domestic business. As a solution which worked well under great strains for over five years, the tandem Cabinets represented pragmatic politics at their most inventive.[45]

The discontented in National's caucus and party saw the War Cabinet as proof that Adam Hamilton had failed to obtain the right terms, just as he had failed to win the election. They put forward Sidney Holland, the managing director of an engineering company, who by buying a stockbreeding farm had also associated himself with National's rural interests. An aggressive debater, Holland had taken over his family's former seat in 1935 and therefore, unlike Hamilton, had no depression record to dog him. Elected at a meeting of the Parliamentary Party on 26 November

1940, he was confirmed by Dominion Council as leader of the National Party and led vigorously for over sixteen years.[46] Holland remained outside the War Cabinet and mounted an attack on domestic issues, claiming that there was a second war on the home front where the Government was implementing socialism.

The Government had been working not towards socialism but to achieve stabilization. Nash aimed to divert unsatisfied demand for goods into savings, increased taxation, and internal loans to finance the war. Everyone had less cash, but the lowest-income earners were dismayed to find that they too were targets for tax gathering. The Price Tribunal endeavoured to match internal price rises to costs and the Arbitration Court brought wages up 5 per cent, an amount roughly equivalent to price increases.[47] The wage-lag, although very minor, was felt keenly by Labour's supporters who could see the rest of the economy prospering.

The heroic disasters of Greece and Crete unrolled, Russia was invaded and sent reeling, and war in the Pacific became imminent. Fraser offered to 'reduce legislation on purely party lines to a minimum' and Parliament postponed the election due in 1941.[48] Once Singapore and the Indies fell, with the Japanese driving south-east through the Solomons, the war was felt as a direct and personal threat. Again the Prime Minister sought a wider participation by both parties. By June 1942 a War Administration had been formed which included seven Labour and six National Ministers while the War Cabinet was enlarged by the addition of Holland as the deputy chairman. The domestic Cabinet remained as before. For a brief time the arrangement worked well enough but trouble arose over the Huntly coal dispute. Holland objected to the Government obtaining a return to work by suspending miners' sentences, taking over the mines, and allowing the regular tribunal to settle the dispute — against the miners as it happened. The National caucus withdrew its six members from both War Administration and Cabinet so, when Coates and Hamilton rejoined the War Cabinet, they thereby estranged themselves from their Party. From October 1942, the war and the country were once again directed by tandem Cabinets.[49]

The dispute armed National for the resumption of party warfare with an issue — softness towards strikers — far more biting than unspecified charges of socialism. In its defence Labour could point to the restoration of industrial peace and the maintenance of production as well as to the full implementation of the social security scheme in 1941, after the final settlement with the medical practitioners. Labour also stabilized wages, costs, and prices. In the midst of inevitable scarcities, Labour hobbled inflation, caught up with it by wage orders, and finally stabilized it entirely.[50] Not all the effects of stability were, however, either wanted or intended. The worker's job was secure but with fixed wages, direction of labour, and pressure against strikes, there was no advantage to be had from the strong demand for labour. Meanwhile, businessmen and manufacturers had guaranteed markets, sure sales, a disciplined labour force with set wages and conditions, and price margins which provided uninterrupted profitability, capital growth, and resources for further investment. Marginal ventures became solid establishments while medium firms grew large. Stabilization froze the employed sector while freeing the employer sector for guaranteed expansion.

Farmers reacted more sharply to another kind of stabilization. In preparation for the servicemen who would soon return wanting houses and farms, the Servicemen's Settlement and Land Sales Act (1943) gave the Government power to acquire land suitable for subdivision and to control prices in all land sales.[51] New Zealand farmers had always expected to garner any long-term gain in land values. War had increased the value of land and now Labour was proposing to prevent the harvest or at least to pass part of it on to returned servicemen. National spokesmen accused Labour of using the resettlement of servicemen as a cloak for socialization. The Government responded by recalling that many hundreds of ex-soldiers had been forced to walk off their over-priced land in the 1920s and stressed that land sales control would preclude any repetition.

When the election was held in September 1943, the Government retained the Treasury benches securely enough but was nevertheless severely shaken. Opinion moved strongly against Labour (-8.74 per cent) and very weakly towards National (+1.27 per cent). The party to gain most was Lee's Democratic Soldier Labour Party (+4.34 per cent). This was an election of distractions: Labour's losses were virtually doubled by the Lee diversion while three right-wing splinter parties and a scattering of Independents (+2.03 per cent) drew off voters whom National might otherwise have captured. Assisted by DSL vote splitting, National took two city and two town constituencies while Labour retrieved the seats of Lee and Barnard. Where National truly prospered was in the countryside. Dissatisfaction amongst farmers about the level of guaranteed prices and land sales control cleared Labour from its last farmer seat and decisively swung the balance of rural electorates by presenting three more to National. But Labour still held all the special occupation country electorates, all the poorer city seats, four-fifths of both the town and mixed city constituencies, and at this election Labour not only captured Eastern Maori, the last of the four Māori seats, but registered increased support among all Māori voters. Labour ended with a majority of twelve — an ample margin but a dismaying decrease on the twenty-eight of five years before.

The 1943 election had come after four years of war — years of dislocation, anxiety, and frequently of personal tragedy. Peace was still two years off and community spirit was beginning to sag under the weight of controls, constrictions, shortages, and rationing. For some, personal savings climbed, farm mortgages were paid off, and war contracts compensated for regulated profits, but the average wage-earner had only overtime to offset wages which had been static since December 1942. There were gains — full employment and a good and varied diet in spite of rationing, the extension of the family benefit and of medical benefits to include family visits, and a guarantee of two weeks' paid holiday for all. But they soon merged into the prevailing sense of stabilized endurance in day-to-day life.[52]

The nationalization of the Bank of New Zealand held out a ray of hope to the radicals and the creditists when it was carried at the 1944 Labour Conference and enacted the following year. It proved not to affect the way the Bank did its business, however, and the Act left the other trading banks untouched. The New Zealand National Airways Act (1945)[53] brought internal airways into public ownership in line with previous government participation in the overseas Tasman Empire Airways and, less profitably, coal-mines passed one by one from thankful proprietors to public ownership. In the year the war ended, wage rates were edged upwards despite continuing price index stability. Parliamentarians first raised their own pay in December 1944. Agitation amongst lower paid workers led to a 5 per cent increase for all wage earners and later, in December 1945, a new Minimum Wage Act set £5 5s. for men and £3 3s. for women as the base for adult rates. The Government did not intend to abandon stabilization but to ease the policy's rigour in order to prolong it.[54] Whether they had eased it enough to prolong their own term in office at the next year's election remained to be seen.

Rehabilitation was the Government's showpiece for the 1946 election. Legislation in 1941 and 1943 had already prepared the way for assistance to men and women returning from service. From 1942 onwards servicemen came back eager to resume the better life they had fought for and, as their high Labour vote overseas in 1943 seemed to show, ready for changes. 'Rehab' absorbed them with minimal disturbance and impressive speed, backed up as it was by full employment, a cushion of savings, guaranteed markets, and continuing prosperity. Whatever ex-service people had intended, their rapid and successful reintegration worked to reinforce the existing situation.

In 1946 New Zealand prepared to contest its first 'one vote, one value' election. From 1881 there had been a 'country quota' and, from 1889, 28 per cent of imaginary extra population had been added to the real number of people living outside cities and towns. By the 1930s this equalled eight extra country seats. Rural areas contained a higher number of children so their inclusion in electoral redistributions also added to the number of country electorates. In 1945 Labour disposed of both distortions and incidentally assisted its own survival by eliminating a traditional conservative advantage.[55] National later put the total population back into the count, but the larger distortion of the 'country quota' did not return.

In the 1946 campaign National's hope was that widespread weariness with years of stabilization and restriction would finally bring them victory, whereas Labour supporters felt not only that their government might be needed to cope with another post-war depression, but also that theirs was the party for peace-time reconstruction. Voters rewarded both with added support when National rose by 4.7 per cent and Labour by 3.8 per cent. Every other cause either fell or disappeared. Labour's New Zealand-wide majority of support over National had shrunk only slightly but redistribution and many close contests had upset enough seats to leave the final balance at forty-two Labour to thirty-eight National.

The National Party stood baulked after two elections fought under Holland and eleven years of Labour rule. The surge in the number of National MPs had satisfied a somewhat chastened Party in 1943. After 1946 the leader's credibility was strained. Yet National had taken great strides under his leadership. Whereas in the 1920s the rural constituencies had been notoriously unstable, now National had engrossed all but one and advanced also into the new urban battlegrounds. Holland had assessed their marginal town and city targets shrewdly. Reversing tack in time for the 1943 election, the leader and his advisers accepted social security as a *fait accompli*. The 1943 manifesto also endeavoured to associate National with full employment.[56] Holland had grasped what Hamilton missed: that the unremitting advance of urbanization was putting the margin of election victory into the mixed town and city seats, where voters would demand established levels of welfare and employment.

Holland clearly understood the spectre in the party background which had to be banished when he claimed that 'We will never allow another 1930–35 slump to happen in this country — that is definite and positive.'[57] Once a post-war slump had failed to materialize, however, every year increased belief that National, like Labour, would prevent depression, preserve full employment, and maintain social welfare. National's other offerings also dated back to the 1943 manifesto and were repeated until they conferred victory in 1949. To everyone National offered 'competitive free enterprise', freedom from 'bureaucratic dictation', and an easing in the burden of taxation. For the townsman there was stress on home ownership, more house construction, sales to state tenants and 90 per cent loans for the freehold; the farmer and orchardist could expect abolition of the Internal Marketing Department, farmer control of production and marketing in co-operation with the government, plus guaranteed minimum prices and ceiling prices fixed by the producers themselves. The manufacturer would be given preference and protection. In short, Holland would retain key Labour gains; give National help as well; yet simultaneously confer lowered taxes and freedom from state interference.

Labour's leaders were left with small room for manoeuvre between the 1946 and 1949 elections. Their four-seat majority was workable but narrow. If Labour was still a party of change, it stood surrounded and perhaps trapped by the changes it had made. If it was a social democratic party, then it was committed by democracy to the economic system which the overwhelming majority continued to prefer, however frequently they called for its social impact to be modified. Moreover, New Zealanders themselves had changed because of the war and the opportunities opened up by economic and social security. There was a drive to enjoy the peace, to take Labour's achievements for granted as the basis for getting on with private life.

Fraser and Nash had been changed too, not simply by having achieved their main goals and by the pressure of defending them through six years of war and scarcity, but also by the enlargement of their own experience of power.[58] They focused as much on international politics and economics as on domestic affairs. The United Nations, in their view, embodied collective security for small nations like New Zealand. In the era of decolonization, New Zealand helped design and monitor trusteeship while taking steps toward Samoan independence.[59] Most of all, Labour's leaders worked to strengthen the progressive centre in international politics, the Commonwealth. At its core was Britain, now a Labour Britain and New Zealand's market, which needed New Zealand's food and help as it built social welfare at home and strove for stability in Europe. This wider view reinforced the leaders' conviction that they must go on as before, struggling to stabilize the gains in welfare, security, and potential prosperity which the progressive centre had won at home and abroad.

But continued stabilization and Labour's electoral recovery proved difficult to combine. The political costs of restraining suppressed inflation, of maintaining supplies to Britain so that rationing had to continue, and of controlling against a surge of expensive imports rose with every pledge the Opposition made. In 1947 Labour vainly attempted to win the countryside back by giving dairy farmers a joint industry and government Marketing Commission with an independent chairman and power to fix the guaranteed price and control their own marketing overseas.[60] The door stood ajar for further rises in farm incomes and local farm product prices. They did rise when some subsidies came off and, before the 1949 election, retail prices generally climbed while imports and consumer goods remained in short supply. In a racing economy, marriage and birth rates proceeded to outstrip house-building, electricity was restricted, rationing lingered, and the Government passed the Economic Stabilization Act to put stabilization on a permanent basis.[61] New Zealand voters, finding that reality fell well below their high peace-time hopes, decided the Government was to blame.

Labour had effected sweeping changes and, to consolidate them, needed to reach out and educate its public. The family benefit had been made universal, superannuation was still rising, and in 1947 increases in war pensions and all social security rates were enacted.[62] Benefits in the national income leapt from 6 to 11 per cent and, most vital of all, hourly wage rates beat price rises by 21 to 14 per cent from 1945 to 1949.[63] Labour, however, lacked a Savage to take people behind the ration coupons and the price changes and demonstrate the real gains. Instead of leading the politics of reconstruction, the attention of Labour's ageing, thinning team of oligarchs and administrators was fixed on the coming of the Cold War overseas and the spectacle of militant strikers at home.

The militancy that appeared in the middle of the war was confined to very few unions. The waterside workers and coal-miners between them accounted for three-quarters of all working days lost during the war,[64] and the watersiders in particular incurred the wrath of the public and the press. The watersiders dismissed stabilization and arbitration and trusted in their own strength, wage bargaining, and direct action. Their leader, Harold Barnes, saw himself as a socialist and believed, like other militants, that there was a radical option in both domestic and foreign policy. The Government conceded, cajoled, threatened, and denounced the watersiders through four disputes and achieved some success without, however, being able to put an end to the debilitating contest.

The Government refrained from using its real power until the Auckland carpenters' dispute in 1949. The carpenters began with a go-slow, were dismissed by their employers, and, when they refused to hand over the dispute to the Federation of Labour, were deregistered under the Arbitration Act. A new regional Carpenters' Union was formed by the moderates and, after half the Auckland members of the old union had joined, Angus McLagan, Minister of Labour and an ex-President of the FOL, registered them under the Act, and Auckland's building industry 'slowly returned to normal'.[65] Had the Government dealt as swiftly and conclusively with the watersiders, then the public impression of Labour's post-war industrial record would have been entirely different and decidedly more favourable.

While reluctant to discipline unionists who were against arbitration and stabilization, the Cabinet accepted the riskier task of reversing a Labour policy older than the Party itself — opposition to peace-time conscription. That such a measure was suggested early in 1949 reflected the dangerous tensions of the Cold War as well as the Prime Minister's personal commitment to the views of Attlee, Bevin, Truman, and their advisers. Fraser returned from a Commonwealth Conference and military briefings in London convinced that New Zealanders should be trained and ready for conflict.[66] He carried Cabinet and caucus and got qualified acceptance from the Party Conference. The Government rushed through an Act to hold a referendum and mounted a massive 'Yes' campaign of advertising, meetings, and radio speeches. Both major parties supported the campaign, which preoccupied them and the news media in what would otherwise have been the run-up to the general election. Most of the active resistance came from the Prime Minister's own party supporters and the result (49.1 per cent for, 13.9 per cent against, 37.0 per cent non-vote), while carrying peace-time conscription, suggested that apathy and disbelief were the Prime Minister's most widespread opponents.[67]

It was an encouraging prelude to National's electoral effort. The National Party's extensive advertising campaign was built round the slogan 'Make the £ Go Further', which exactly hit the popular sensitivity to scarcities and prices. National speeches dwelt on industrial unrest, the communist menace among militants and a promise of secret ballots to decide on voluntary or compulsory unionism. The sale of state houses to tenants was given greater prominence. The overriding promise was of freedom; freedom from restrictions, regulations, bureaucracy, and state interference, and the whole irksome burden of a war and its demands dragging so irritatingly into peace. The rest of the sectional appeals and welfare pledges were still reassuringly there in the manifesto. The campaign gave a gloss Labour could not counter.[68] The Government stood there, waving back at its record, and the crowd moved on.

In 1949 the Labour Government went out because its support shrank (-3.74 per cent), while National took power with a slightly more moderate rise (+3.28 per cent). The sectional structure of New Zealand's electoral politics had not altered, but the balance within it had been shifting steadily. National's substantial victory was the capture of four mixed city and two town seats thus giving it for the first time the preponderance in both classes. All four city marginals were in Auckland, the exuberantly growing commercial and manufacturing centre. The town seats of New Plymouth and Palmerston North were vigorous conversions and they made seven North Island seats out of the eight electorates taken by National. As Labour might gloomily have observed from the past history of New Zealand parties, the South Island is where parties retire when they either weaken or die.

The 1949 National Government did not bring a sharp change to the country. National had already accepted Labour's social welfare legislation and was increasingly realizing that full employment, like the adequate access to overseas markets conferred by war, was fundamental to the socio-economic system. Its ranks were full of people whose life-chances Labour had restored or launched. National's initial preoccupation was with discharging promises and altering the balance of beneficiaries under the system rather than with transforming the system itself.

The new National Cabinet began by making a dash for freedom. They ended rationing on petrol and butter and removed quantitative controls from many imports. State tenants were able to buy their houses on cheap mortgage. The Tenancy Act was eased for landlords and for farmers, land sales were to go back to market value, and the Servicemen's Settlement Act was to expire in 1952.[69] But state houses were still built, price control was maintained, the basis of import licensing survived, fair rents continued, and only farmers could point to a decisive advance.

Overseas events soon taught the new Government a lesson on inflation. The Korean War which began with the 1950 invasion of South Korea by the Communist regime in the north created a demand for clothing and blankets and, in turn, meant a boom for New Zealand wool producers. Though part of the proceeds from growers' sales was set aside by Act for payment later,[70] nevertheless the rural boom sucked in decontrolled imports, especially in 1951. Coming in at high overseas prices, these imports combined with domestic increases to produce unprecedented inflation. The Government was quickly brought to realize that decontrol might mean vulnerability, and that bonanzas for some could bring inflation for all. National was prepared to teach lessons, however, as well as to learn them.

National had long been waiting to complete what Labour had begun by deregistering the Carpenters' Union. The struggle began slowly with an exploratory period of six months during which the watersiders and their allies left the FOL and formed a rival Trade Union Congress committed to 'practical militancy'.[71] When National lifted food subsidies in May 1950, the old round of waterside wage claims, tribunals, temporary settlements, and stoppages revived. By September they had provoked the Government into declaring a state of emergency, but even then direct bargaining was allowed and a Royal Commission set up. It was not the Government but the employers and the unionists who by October had readied themselves to go over the brink. But when negotiations between watersiders and their employers broke down over a wage rise and the waterfront halted in February 1951, the Government was prepared.

Cabinet insisted on arbitration, which the unionists had earlier agreed to, and the employers demanded that overtime be accepted along with regular work. The union rejected the Cabinet ultimatum. The men continued to report for work while refusing to accept the employers' conditions, so no work was given. The Government saw it as a strike in defiance of the principle of arbitration: to the men it was a lockout by employers.[72] The struggle escalated rapidly. The Government again declared a state of emergency under the Public Safety Conservation Act (1932) and issued regulations which gave wide powers for dealing with a strike defined to include the refusal of overtime. Servicemen came on to the wharves to move perishables and, on 28 February, the Waterside Workers' Union was deregistered.

The conflict widened; grew embittered and at times violent on both sides; acquired passionate overtones with accusations of communism and treachery and muffled replies of union-smashing. Miners, freezing workers, harbour-board employees, seamen, and some hydro-construction workers came out. Railwaymen and most drivers only refused to handle goods unloaded by non-union labour. It was far from a general strike and in effect split the union movement into a mass and a minority. The FOL under its Vice-President, F. P. Walsh, made some attempts to secure conciliation and arbitration but, when these were rebuffed, turned to help the Government against its competitor, the TUC.

The Government set out to replace the waterfront union with a series of independent arbitrationist unions, one in each port. As each was formed it was registered and received an award binding on that port. The Government hoped not only to eliminate the watersiders' union but also to end the TUC and break the spirit of militancy in general.[73] Backed by a monopoly of opinion in the press and on the radio, it would earn recognition as the party of law and order, property, anti-communism, arbitration, and social peace.

The future of the Labour Party proved to be the largest victim of the conflict. Entering 1951 with the hope that rocketing prices would recall stabilization and restore it to power, the Party emerged with its post-war reputation reinforced as the party of indecision and temporizing in the face of the militant enemies of arbitration. Yet Walter Nash, elected Leader after Fraser's death in December 1950, was a devout believer in arbitration and the Party was committed to the principle. At the end of February Nash called for a compulsory conference. In April he offered to help achieve a settlement but rebuked the Government for unnecessarily infringing civil liberties and for letting the dispute drift on. He persuaded Barnes to accept arbitration and the Government's seven general points of settlement and wanted the Government to re-register the union. Holland refused, to applause from the press. At a meeting in the Auckland Domain on 13 May Nash set out Labour's position: he wanted the watersiders to return to work without victimization, wages settled by independent tribunal, harbour boards as the employers, and settlement by compulsory conference. He then added: 'We are not for the watersiders nor are we against them. . . .'[74] The phrase was seized on with relish by his opponents and dogged Nash and the Party thenceforth.

The Labour caucus itself was showing signs of strain. Some, like Semple, wanted total alignment with the FOL; others took Nash's position or showed a degree of sympathy with the desperate straits of the strikers. Walsh and the FOL were cool towards Nash; the days of Fraserian unity were gone. When Parliament was finally summoned on 26 June, Nash raised his points of settlement and Labour challenged the Government. On 11 July Holland abruptly announced a dissolution and a snap election. The people's verdict would decide on the Government's conduct and on Labour's response. The Waterside Workers' strike collapsed a month later, after five months and at a cost to the country of £40 million.[75]

The verdict of the 1951 election was straightforward. Non-voting moved powerfully up (+4.83 per cent) and everything else moved down, Labour losing most (-3.33 per cent) but the Government also showing a minor decline (-0.50 per cent). This loss may well have reflected voter opinion about inflation which, without the distraction provided by industrial turmoil, could have threatened National's tenure in office. As for Labour, it was hit in all types of seats except the Māori constituencies. However, the realities of the election were concealed from the public by the attention paid to seats and majorities. Four marginal seats passed from Labour to National, and the newspapers hailed this as a deserved triumph for Holland and his crushing of the militants. His majority had gone up from twelve to twenty and the future of his Government looked secure. In the waterfront crisis, National had carved out a special function for itself and dug a gulf between the two major parties in the popular consciousness. The Government's crusade against the militants locked in core support for National around such perennial and popular themes as law and order, anti-Communism, and curbing the unions. An underlying shift had occurred, which was eventually to transfer the role of being the normal party of government from Labour to National.

The National Government hastened to introduce legislation in October 1951 to check the militants. The I.C. and A. Amendment Act (1951) ensured secret ballots were taken on strikes and other major matters for union decision. To keep the port unions from uniting, the Act provided that the consent of the Minister of Labour was necessary for one union to include workers in another. The issue of voluntary unionism was dropped, however, because employers, farmers, and the FOL preferred existing controls while the Government could see the risk of smaller, voluntary memberships marching back to activism and militancy. The definition of a strike was widened to include any reduction of normal output or rate of work and heavy penalties for striking without a ballot were enacted. Those charged had to prove themselves innocent to go free.[76]

It was the Government's second measure, the Police Offences Amendment Bill, which roused widespread press and professional concern. Extensively amended after public submissions and passed in December, the Act was still a potentially devastating weapon in a democracy. Statements with a 'seditious intention', defined loosely to include exciting 'such hostility or ill-will between different classes of persons as may endanger the public safety', became illegal. The restricted penalties meant that, instead of a jury, a magistrate might deal summarily with this indefinite charge or the related offences of possessing 'seditious' literature or the printing press used to produce it. Again the onus of proof was on the defendant. Accompanying an unballoted strike with picketing, processions, demonstrations, or posters was also illegal. Until Labour repealed these provisions in 1959, they went virtually unused because the ostensible targets of the Act had already been defeated and dispersed. But the Act achieved its symbolic and psychological function of linking militant unionism with sedition. New Zealand's customary low level of industrial disputes and passive arbitration unionism was resumed and prevailed far into the 1960s, dominated until 1963 by the figure of the FOL President, F. P. Walsh.

The Government now turned its attention to recovering control of the economy. This necessity coincided with Commonwealth calls to cut imports since the entire sterling area found itself facing the fourth and most serious sterling-dollar crisis since the war.[77] The Government had freed four-fifths of the old import schedule, and trading bank credit had soared while private imports jumped by two-thirds in one year. The result had been a large payments deficit. In a dramatic turnabout all licences for American, Canadian, and Japanese imports were cancelled, and very few new ones issued. Exchange allocations for imports were cut drastically during 1952 and especially in 1953, and then eased in 1954, an election year. But exchange control remained a sharp contrast to the sense of release felt in National's first year.

By these measures the overall balance of payments was restored to credit. Yet it had only been done by compelling New Zealanders to return to minor shortages and major controls which proved no less irritating when imposed by bankers and National than when applied by public servants and Labour. Everybody including the Government was competing to build capital goods from housing to pulp mills, so capital issues control was imposed on the large borrower and credit was tight for the small.[78] To the disillusioned and discontented it was time for an untried option, for a third party, for some way of restoring hope that their unsatisfied post-war expectations might yet be met. The New Zealand Social Credit Political League endeavoured to provide that third option for the 1954 general election. The League had been created the previous year out of the scattered following of a propagandist body, the Social Credit Association, which had long put forward the doctrines of C. H. Douglas in the hope that an existing party would adopt and apply them. Neither party had done so, and now National's credit squeeze provided the right impetus for Social Crediters to form a party of their own.[79]

The League won a surprisingly large measure of support (+10.05 per cent), but failed to elect even one MP of its own. And rather than ousting the Government, Social Credit helped to preserve National for a further term. The Holland Government had stood on its record and the voters responded by decisively moving away (-7.62 per cent), but not towards its Labour alternative. The two main parties emerged separated by only one-tenth of one per cent of the qualified vote, but the National Government carried on with a substantial majority of ten seats, thanks to Social Credit's intervention and with the help of a skewed redistribution of electorates accentuated by the inclusion of the total population in boundary assessment and by the doubled allowable difference in electorate populations.[80]

Not that Labour had offered anything fresh by way of programmes or leadership for the election. Its policies were still those with which it had lost in 1949. There were energetic, capable men in the caucus like A. H. Nordmeyer, C. F. Skinner, and Frederick Hackett, but they were much outnumbered by constituency members going about their rounds and burnishing their union contacts. The ablest of them all, Nash, was into his seventies. He represented the great past of real change and high international drama. He stood also for electoral failure and there was even a feeble attempt to turn him out of the leadership in favour of Nordmeyer, the President of the Party.[81] So Nash remained, for the time being unable to lift his Party out of its over-dependence on the shrinking forces of the blue-collar unions.

Out of power, Labour had to work out its role for the future. It had to decide between the phase when it had grown as the working-man's party and the era when it had won, governed, and planned on a broad national basis. Labour's problem was to recognize the society it had shaped and understand the political consequences for a social democratic party bent on lasting revival. But the year 1954 was to mark something of a new beginning. In a caucus of thirty-five, a clear majority had won their way in at post-war elections. Moreover, 1954 was the year in which the natural marginals began to shift back to Labour when four North Island towns were taken.

National faced the reverse problem of watching its marginals beginning to shake loose and realizing from the steep drops in National's voting support and the ominously corresponding rises for Social Credit that this was principally a defection of the right and came especially from their preserves in the countryside. After five years National had not yet found a set of policies to keep them securely in power; on the contrary, their lead in votes was only just preserved by altering the balance of beneficiaries from the system and by taking emergency measures as well. The Government's major pre-election measure had been to relax allowable import allocations for 1954, then to announce in the July Budget that import control by exchange allocation would cease at the end of the year. The orders went in and the import rush was on, but not enough had arrived in New Zealand shops by election day to expunge past scarcities from the public mind. With allocation ended, however, the serious consequences for the country's balance of payments extended well into the Government's next term of office and had to be dealt with by renewing unpopular pressures. J. T. Watts, the new Minister of Finance, put his emphasis heavily on monetary policies.[82] The level of bank advances was pulled down by 13 per cent in fifteen months while Government cut its own programmes, capital issues, and hire purchase. Only interest rates moved up. Freezing companies and wool-buyers were given access to finance, but farmers, retailers, and ordinary private individuals found themselves under inescapable constraints at a time of prosperity and growth.

The demands of growth were pressing on every resource. Pushed along by handsome prices for primary products, farm production set new records, group-housing suburbs of young families called for schools and telephones and streets, factories spread, dams rose, trees fell, and over a quarter of the entire national product was thrust into capital formation. Though they had unevenly curbed and indulged the voters, the National Government had run the economy hard and could look back on their share of the 1950s as a decade of productive investment which would provide the 1960s with increased leisure and ease.[83]

Open access to markets in Britain underpinned the system. Labour's renegotiated bulk contract of 1948 had guaranteed markets at what proved progressively rising prices until 1955, but by agreement with Churchill's Conservative Government bulk contracts ended a year early. Access remained open, indeed it was separately guaranteed for meat and subsequently for dairy produce until 1967, but prices now took their chance on a free market. Large fluctuations and falls in butter and cheese prices in 1956–57 reintroduced farmers to the experience of British prices going down as well as up. This made the New Zealand guaranteed price for dairy products, backed by the dairy reserves and ultimately by the Government, all the more valuable, especially when an Act of 1956 gave producers a larger majority on their Marketing Commission, an Authority of their own to fix the price, and a limit on price drops of 5 per cent per year.[84] The various elements of Nash's vision — the inter-governmental bulk contracts, the Marketing Department, stabilization and control of land prices, price-fixing by the Minister — had all vanished like the Cheshire cat, leaving behind only the grin of the guaranteed price itself.

The 1956 Act also ensured undisputed succession to its author, K. J. Holyoake, who had been since 1947 the deputy leader. The blandness of Keith Holyoake's pronouncements concealed energy, deftness at parliamentary and caucus manoeuvre, a sixth sense for finding consensus and a Baldwinesque relish in riding the trends of the times in whatever direction they led. He had pacified the farmers in a Cabinet post more notable in the past for unseating the Minister than for raising him higher, and now the restive New Zealand electorate appeared to require a similar kind of coaxing. Holland was most reluctant to retire, but senior Cabinet colleagues eventually persuaded him to step down. Holyoake's first Ministry took office on 20 September, with just ten weeks to prepare for the election.

As in 1954, a great surge of imports swelled rapidly just before the election. Since the process started this time from an even lower level of overseas funds, the consequences of the rush were to prove even more damaging to the country, especially because in 1957 the prices for butter, cheese, and wool were collapsing. When F. P. Walsh warned of a crisis early in November, the Prime Minister denied there was room for more than concern and took no action.[85] National's surprising serenity in the face of calamity contrasted with the late-flowering invigoration of the seventy-five-year-old Labour leader. Walter Nash in 1957 represented both a resounding echo of humanitarian change and the possibility of restoring vanished stability. All suggested policy went to Nash and the announced platform came entirely from him. The family benefit for each child was to be raised from 10s. to 15s. weekly and was directed equally at all families while being most help to the poorest who were worst hit by inflation. It was 1935 and 1946 all over again. There was a scheme for free textbooks and the demand of new families for housing within their reach was to be met, first by renewing the 1954 offer of loans for new houses at 3 per cent with priorities fixed by need and, secondly, by a fresh proposal to permit the capitalization for housing of future family benefits up to a limit of £1,000. Nash aimed to increase equality of opportunity and welfare by redistributive methods, yet the whole Labour programme should involve little call on scarce overseas funds.

Labour like National had to face the problems of shifting from taxation on past incomes to taxation on present ones with the introduction of Holland's scheme, PAYE (Pay As You Earn). One year's tax would be due in February 1958, one month before the PAYE deductions would commence. Nash proposed rebating the first £100 of tax due in February. 'Walter's hundred quid', as its enemies and friends nicknamed it, was a nice round sum, easily remembered even when one's own tax might not reach the total to be rebated. National offered a complicated scheme 'built into the PAYE tables' to rebate 25 per cent on all incomes up to a limit of £75, though there was confusion about its continuation and effects.[86]

The 1957 result was a triumph for the simplicity and universal appeal of the Nash rebate and the wide attractiveness of the family benefit proposals. Labour's support rose in every kind of seat. In the mixed city constituencies the particular relevance of Labour's housing capitalization and 3 per cent interest schemes for the needs of the spreading white-collar suburbs lent extra strength to the Party. Five out of the six electorates which Labour captured and required to take power contained large areas of precisely this kind. A sound majority in votes (3.78 per cent) for the new Government gave only the thinnest of margins in the House; Labour led by only two seats and its working majority became one after the election of the Speaker. This was in strong contrast to National's previous majority of ten, based on a lead of 0.12 per cent.

The second Labour Government was driven to recapitulate in the course of just three years all the main phases of the fourteen years of the initial Labour Government. First it had to cope with an inherited crisis while at the same time implementing a whole programme of social and housing benefits. Then followed a period of austerity while the domestic economy was steered back towards health and as overseas prices gradually recovered. Finally the cycle ended with an easing of curbs and the upsurge of a growing and somewhat redesigned economy. The emotions these phases evoked were also familiar: enthusiasm for the benefits, irritation at import selection, followed by discontent at taxation and doing without. Instead of the mood lifting with recovery, that discontent lingered and was turned by the Opposition into impatience with the steering mechanism of the economy itself, so that remaining controls became an offence, the Government's capacity was resentfully distrusted, and even the clear evidence of a returned prosperity was disbelieved. For years afterwards the Nash Government's real if limited achievements were forgotten. The views of its opponents prevailed, and its record of social concern and hard-fought recovery was buried beneath the campaign set off by the 1958 'Black Budget', as Keith Holyoake dubbed it.

In many ways Labour invited its fate. Nash, instead of spacing out his welfare and housing pledges, hurried his programme through in the first year. Voters were left with nothing to look forward to. Moreover, Labour's changes were soon absorbed into normality and were crowded out of the news by more dramatic, less acceptable events. Nash and Nordmeyer, his Minister of Finance, were quick to grasp the dimensions of the import flood and to realize in addition they had been greeted with the worst collapse in the terms of trade since the days of the Depression.

To restore the economy they turned to import selection as being more speedy, discriminating, and capable of producing positive as well as negative effects than either exchange allocation or a credit squeeze. What they overlooked was the rush of unhappy memories they would provoke. The country had no wish to return to planned austerity. The Government could have controlled loosely and borrowed heavily overseas because New Zealand's credit was good. But Nash, having paid off much British-held debt during the war, preferred the Government to meet the shortfall in produce receipts by borrowing moderately and clearing the debt rapidly within the one parliamentary term.

Nordmeyer still had to reduce the excess purchasing power in the community, preferably without harming full employment or recovery. His Budget raising taxes on petrol, tobacco, and beer was praised by economists, but F. P. Walsh's FOL raged about the pockets of the workers being rifled and Labour branch members resigned in droves. The Opposition leader was quick to see that the Government, in mopping up the consequences of National's policies, had delivered itself into his hands.

Viewed in the light of later and far heavier taxation on the same items by subsequent governments, Nordmeyer's imposts may look minor, but for the remaining two-and-a-half years of that Parliament, Holyoake made the Chamber and the town halls boom with denunciations of the 'Black Budget'. The taxation was presented as though it were to pay for the Nash rebate and borrower-serviced housing loans, rather than as a measure to deal with the consequences of the plunge in overseas receipts, past expansion, and the imports crisis. Labour was charged with both bribing the electors and not keeping its promises; whereas it had in fact implemented pledges too quickly. It had no more on offer for the 1960 election.[87]

By the time November 1960 rolled round, the Leader of the Opposition had completed his work. He had known since April 1959 from a private poll that the country had swung heavily away from Labour. So he was careful to promise nothing of consequence himself in order to leave his hands free on financial matters and the public's expectations at a minimum. The election result duly demonstrated that National had no need to attract voters to win. Labour certainly lost the 1960 election (-5.87 per cent) rather than National doing much to win it (+1.64 per cent). The major destination of the departing thousands was into non-voting (+3.08 per cent) while Social Credit picked up a net gain of one-third as many (+1.03 per cent). National under Holyoake achieved a slightly smaller majority of the qualified vote (3.73 per cent) than Nash had won in 1957, but Keith Holyoake's majority was not two but twelve, and that looked far more convincing.

As he proved at three subsequent elections, Holyoake's majority was indeed strong enough to afford all the whittling away a broken Opposition could manage. Holyoake's greatest feat as a Prime Minister was the slowing down of every process which, if speedily dealt with, might have represented change and political harm. A master of consensus-making, Holyoake happily ran a Cabinet where he listened, quizzed and quietly commanded for eleven years. Defeat and three years in Opposition had cleared away nearly half his first Cabinet, allowing him to make the core of his new 1960 Ministry from four relatively young men. J. R. Marshall, J. R. Hanan, T. P. Shand, and J. K. McAlpine had all been tested in office by Holland and now proved their administrative ability.

Two problems in this Parliament and their solutions show the Holyoake style at work. There had long been ideological pressure from the party membership for an end to compulsory unionism, and campaigning against the Labour Government had heated the issue. Hearings on an amending Bill introduced in 1961 showed that employers', manufacturers', and farmers' organizations, as well as the unions, were still against change. The I.C. and A. Amendment Act[88] which emerged had provisions for either qualified or unqualified preference being given to unionists, so, though formally compulsion was gone, in practice it continued and union membership was maintained undisturbed. A far greater threat appeared in mid-term when overseas prices for produce plunged again. The Prime

Minister, who operated at all key points as his own Minister of Finance, was confronted with the kind of situation which had led to the 'Black Budget'. Treasury advised action of the same sort as it had urged on Nordmeyer, but this time the Government did nothing spectacular and, to the relief of the Prime Minister, prices rebounded, justifying his taking the risk. Indeed, he was able to make his principal theme for the 1963 election the fact that each year the rates of taxation had been lowered. 'Steady Does It' was the slogan adopted, and steady did it.

The result was the 'no change' election of 1963.[89] The outcome confirmed the political balance established by the 1960 election, this time with non-voting and Labour rising faintly, Social Credit and National falling slightly, and the new fringe, ultra-conservative Liberal Party (+0.77 per cent) being the minor gainer from a static situation. By making a late change of leader from Nash to Nordmeyer in 1963, Labour had helped the Prime Minister to still the swings of the 1950s and start the stasis of the 1960s; Nordmeyer's harsh reputation as an author of budgets hung strong in the air.

The underlying changes in the golden 1960s were social rather than political, technological rather than legislative, individual rather than public. If they took a mass form they did so as protest movements, confronting or, at the most, working alongside the party structures. The tertiary education boom, television, and the contraceptive pill were transforming family and personal relationships as well as the method by which politics were perceived. Government expenditure underwrote the surging development of health and education just as it provided roading for second cars and guarantees for group-housing suburbs. The Government tried clumsily and at first effectively to control political debate and controversy on radio and television, and prevent the appearance of private radio stations. The Government maintained the system, but the changes in society did not yet fully impinge on politics because full employment and prosperity provided a separate sphere for the elaboration and alterations going on in private life.

Prosperity was unevenly distributed both geographically and by occupational group and it was uneven through time. Prices wavered and farmers, beset by rising costs, were in a mood to strike at the Government in 1966.[90] The Vietnam conflict was said by the Government to involve New Zealand's treaty obligations under the South-East Asia Treaty Organization (1954) and a contingent was despatched to assist South Vietnam. Characteristically the Prime Minister kept the commitment small and avoided the conscription undertaken in Australia. But there was much high feeling both against and for New Zealand's participation, and Labour ranged itself uncertainly against New Zealand's presence in the conflict. The Opposition was now led by Norman Kirk, who had defeated Nordmeyer in the mid-term selection of leader. Kirk was not widely known outside his party, and to begin with he campaigned awkwardly in an election which demanded assurance about economics, a quality the ousted Nordmeyer had genuinely possessed. So the scene was set for

Holyoake to defeat Labour once more in 1966 but with a diminished majority.

Both major parties lost support (National -4.59 per cent; Labour -3.51 per cent) and the beneficiaries of this 'protest election' were Social Credit (+5.31 per cent) and non-voting (+3.57 per cent). The third party had in Vernon Cracknell a leader who had appeared on television and who now won Social Credit's first seat. As the parallel rise in abstention showed, however, it was not support for Douglas doctrine which was showing itself but discontent with the alternatives presented by the major parties. National lost two seats and Labour one, so the Government's majority became either eight or ten depending on which way Cracknell chose to vote. Nevertheless, for all the activity, this was another *status quo* election.

It was ironical that at this point the system began to show cracks. After the election the Prime Minister was injudicious enough to muse to journalists that he might consider retiring. 'When?' became an increasingly frequent question. Holyoake brought five new men into the Cabinet, including R. D. Muldoon who had been Under-Secretary for Finance. Unexpectedly the Minister of Finance died in February 1967 and in March, Muldoon, still ranked at number eighteen, succeeded to the position. From his initial Budget it was obvious that Muldoon was in charge at Treasury. He developed the practice of adjusting the economy by 'mini-budgets' which kept him not only on top of fluctuating conditions but also in front of Parliament and the television cameras. Muldoon was in fact New Zealand's first television politician, calculatedly at ease in the studio, aggressively clear and direct in his answers, and the master of a medium which at once lifted him into the public picture of the Government as constituted by the Prime Minister, his deputy John Marshall, and the Minister of Finance.

New Zealand was running into a recession which was sharp enough to cause noticeable unemployment and a net outflow of migrants, both considered extraordinary phenomena at the time. There was some recovery by election year, 1969, but there was considerable industrial tension which had been exacerbated by the Arbitration Court's 'nil' decision on an application for a general rise in wages. When a minor rise was secured by agreement between employers and trade unions, Muldoon denounced the 'unholy alliance' as he termed it, and the basic institution and practice of arbitration unionism entered a troubled time. The Finance Minister was in search of efficiency and control, but he was as yet no dogmatist of the classical private enterprise or Friedman persuasion. He changed the incidence of the tax structure by sharply lowering its highest rate. But he went on gathering rising revenues, thanks to fiscal drag, while continuing to adjust rates downwards in accord with the Holyoake formula for electoral appeals.

In the 1969 election[91] the formula barely worked and the Government's majority came down to six seats and 0.92 per cent. Social Credit and non-voting dropped together as political decisions became serious. This allowed both Labour (+3.52 per cent) and National (+2.56 per cent) to recover at different rates. The results revealed a different kind of judgement in the three main cities on the one hand, and in the rest of New Zealand on the other. The South Island, the towns, and the countryside felt left out of development and regarded themselves as the victims of recession. Labour's doctrine of regionalism and assistance with everything from freight rates to community colleges presented these areas with a hope of holding their place in a shifting, disturbing world, so they favoured Labour as against National.

Keith Holyoake had now to meet increased pressures without the aid of Ralph Hanan, his innovative Minister of Justice, and Thomas Shand, his guardian of order in the Department of Labour. They were dead, and his Cabinet faltered as it endeavoured to cope with the results of Britain's entry into the Common Market, with inflation, and with farmer discontent. Like Holland before him, Holyoake was loath to go. When he finally did so and his deputy became Prime Minister in February 1972, John Marshall had little prospect of reversing the downward political impetus in the ten months remaining before the election. He reshuffled his Cabinet fiercely but it was all to no avail. After twelve years National stood exhausted and half prepared for defeat.

CHAPTER 15

The Politics of Volatility, 1972–1991

Alan McRobie

In November 1972 the National Party, which had governed New Zealand for twenty of the previous twenty-three years, was defeated by a revitalized Labour Party. Although Labour's win did not surprise, the magnitude of its victory did. The Holyoake Government's consensus approach to decision-making throughout the 1960s, with its 'steady state' economic policies, had minimized the Government's decline in electoral support; the 1963, 1966, and 1969 elections all recorded two-party swings[1] well below 1 per cent and few seats changed party allegiance. What was remarkable about the Holyoake era was not the Government's comprehensive defeat in 1972 but National's ability to minimize electoral attrition, especially after the economic downturn which began in 1967.

With the benefit of hindsight, 1972 was very much a watershed election. The seven elections between 1950 and 1970 had resulted in only two changes of government; the seven elections since then have produced four changes. Three Prime Ministers and three Leaders of the Opposition strode the electoral stage between 1950 and the beginning of 1972; between 1972 and the end of 1990 the country had eight Prime Ministers (four of them between July 1989 and the end of 1990) and seven Leaders of the Opposition. In the 1950s and 1960s only twenty-nine electorates changed party allegiance; since then, however, incumbents have been defeated in no fewer than eighty-six seats. By-elections show a similar pattern: in the twenty years prior to 1970 only one government-held seat was won by an opposition candidate but, since 1970, government candidates have been defeated in no fewer than four out of a total of five by-election contests. Beginning about 1970 the politics of stability and consensus gave way to the politics of volatility and increasing political polarization as the two-party system that had dominated New Zealand's politics for nearly forty years came under increasing pressure.

Throughout the 1970s and 1980s three themes stand out. First, the steadily rising prosperity enjoyed during the 1950s and 1960s gave way to economic instability characterized by high and persistent inflation, generally declining terms of trade, and growing unemployment. Nevertheless, the long-standing policies of economic protectionism and insulation remained, at least until 1984, as successive governments endeavoured to preserve high levels of economic and social security.² Secondly, the failure of these policies engendered an increasing lack of electoral confidence in both Labour and National. As the electorate's cynicism grew, it responded by voting governments out of, rather than into, office, and also accorded increasing support to an expanding number of minor political parties. Finally, as governments changed, emphasis in foreign relations veered between the historical British and Western European orientation and the Asia-Pacific arena. Of particular significance were the renewed attempts by Labour governments to carve out a more independent, 'moral' path — for example, opposition to nuclear testing and South Africa's apartheid policies — and the equal determination of National governments to maintain New Zealand's traditional associations. New Zealand was a very different country in 1990 compared with only twenty years earlier.

Between 1969 and 1972 the National Government's political dominance finally crumbled. Although it retained office in 1969 with an increased share of the valid vote its parliamentary majority dropped from eight to six. Despite the country's obvious economic difficulties, notably the steep decline in returns for wool and dairy products and the renewed threat of Great Britain's entry into the European Economic Community, complacency remained the dominant electoral characteristic. Although bitterly disappointed with the 1969 election result Labour pressed on with its programme of rejuvenation begun after Norman Kirk took over as leader in December 1965. Then, it was still very much the party of the working class, the welfare state, the protector of society's poor, the friend of trade unions, and the party of state control as its core supporters continued to recall the poverty and unemployment of the Great Depression.³ It was a party that was still politically weak and badly organized, with many of its leading activists faithful adherents of a bygone age. During the later 1960s and early 1970s, however, the predominantly conservative trade unionists and supporters of the Government elected under Savage's leadership in 1935 were joined by a growing number of younger, well-educated liberals and radicals attracted to the Party largely because of its increasingly vocal opposition to the Vietnam war.⁴ Labour began to select younger candidates who were more closely in tune with the electorate's prevailing mood. They, in turn, helped the Party to broaden its support base further as Labour came to be accepted as a credible alternative government.

In part, too, Labour's developing political attraction stemmed from National's inability to persuade the electorate that it still had a sense of purpose and direction. Since 1949 National had evolved into a highly organized but totally pragmatic party whose main concern was to retain political power through more competent administration of the economy and the Labour-initiated social welfare infrastructure. After 1969 it began to lose its way as the consensus that had characterized the Holyoake years began to disintegrate, and as a number of diverse grievances — for example, increased use of economic controls, the recently introduced payroll tax, growing environmental concerns (the most prominent of which was the

'Save Manapouri' campaign), French atmospheric nuclear testing on the Pacific Island atoll of Mururoa, and the Springbok rugby tour of New Zealand scheduled for 1973 — accumulated. The electorate's growing anger was first felt three months after the 1969 election when the Government lost its traditionally safe Marlborough electorate in a by-election following the death of T. P. Shand, one of the leading members of the Holyoake administration. By the early 1970s National's image was that of an exhausted party and government.[5] Although rumours of the Prime Minister's impending retirement surfaced many times after 1966, Sir Keith Holyoake did not finally step aside until February 1972, a delay that did nothing to assist his party's electoral fortunes. Even then, the transfer of the leader's mantle did not pass smoothly as Jack Marshall, Holyoake's loyal deputy for the previous fifteen years, was challenged by the openly ambitious Robert Muldoon, Minister of Finance since 1967.[6] Although a majority of the National caucus supported Marshall, Muldoon was elected as deputy leader in an attempt to create a 'team' image.[7]

Under Marshall, National sought to project an image of a progressive and liberal party, one experienced in government. His leadership did not, however, inspire and, apart from a minor reshuffle induced largely by the impending retirement of a number of ministers, his cabinet appeared little different from that of his predecessor. Marshall also vacillated on a number of policy questions (for example, on whether the scheduled South African rugby tour should take place[8]) and — despite considerable evidence of the Government's growing unpopularity[9] — he ignored the enmity welling up across the country, particularly in Otago and Southland. The Government's obvious tiredness, coupled with the economically debilitating recession of the previous five years had taken its toll.[10]

A record 449 candidates contested the 1972 election. Since 1954, when Social Credit first emerged as a political party, general elections had been essentially three-party contests. In 1972, however, two new parties, the New Democrat Party (with 86 candidates) and Values (with 42), joined Labour, National, and Social Credit in the electoral arena. Another minor, essentially blackmail party, Liberal Reform, also contested twenty-six seats. Values, the world's first 'green' party, emerged — almost overnight — in mid-1972. A liberal-radical party, it lay beyond the stream of consciousness of most New Zealanders until a mere five weeks before the election when a television current affairs programme catapulted it into national prominence.[11] Its emphasis on a 'steady state' economy and environmental protection struck a responsive chord among a large segment of the electorate. The New Democrats on the other hand emerged in very different circumstances. After the momentum generated during the mid-1960s, and in the wake of the loss of its only parliamentary seat (Hobson in the far north of the country) in 1969, Social Crediters engaged in a fierce internal ideological debate on the Party's future direction. Antagonisms between feuding factions peaked at the Party's 1972 conference when the fundamentalist wing led by J. B. O'Brien (who had replaced Vernon Cracknell as leader in 1970) walked out of the conference and formed the

New Democrat Party which, O'Brien claimed, was the true heir to the Social Credit tradition.

The Government's election strategy emphasized its claim that it was both liberal and progressive. It also stressed repeatedly that, after five years of recession, economic expansion was again under way. As is common for a party seeking power, Labour promised a number of enhancements to the social welfare system, particularly in the areas of universal superannuation and no-fault accident compensation, and it was more attuned to demands of environmental lobby groups. Like the first Labour Government in 1935 it promised to stimulate the economy by ensuring that finance and resources would be matched. The electorate responded positively to Labour's slogan, 'It's Time — For Labour', and to Kirk's new assertiveness and outward confidence, by electing the Party to govern for the first time in five elections. Its overall majority of twenty-three seats was larger than any government since 1938, and many believed it to be sufficiently large to ensure that it would occupy the Treasury benches for a lengthy period.

In 1972 Labour's share of the total vote rose by 4.2 per cent to 48.4 per cent and the two-party swing of 4.4 per cent resulted in it increasing its parliamentary representation by fifteen seats, eleven of which were provincial city or mixed electorates where modern New Zealand elections are won and lost. Although support for National declined by 3.7 per cent to 41.5 per cent and the Party lost a total of twelve seats, including seven incumbent MPs, it still won more than 40 per cent of the total vote. With a competent party organizational structure still in existence its mass support base remained largely intact. None of the minor parties polled particularly well although Values, with only forty-two candidates, managed to win a creditable 2.1 per cent of the total vote. Social Credit, its pragmatic wing now led by a young and publicly attractive teachers' college lecturer, Bruce Beetham, survived the trauma of schism to capture 6.7 per cent of the vote. Although this was its lowest ever share of the total valid vote it was sufficient to ensure Social Credit's continued presence on the New Zealand political scene. Its fundamentalist adversary, the New Democrats, however, captured only 0.7 per cent of the total vote and promptly disappeared into political oblivion.

With only one member (Deputy Prime Minister Hugh Watt) previously having held ministerial rank, the new Government lacked experience. Nevertheless, within days of taking office Labour announced a number of decisions that underlined the fact that a new government with a different perspective was now in power. In his role as Minister of Foreign Affairs Kirk signalled a substantial shift in New Zealand's foreign policy perspective when he announced New Zealand's recognition of the Communist Chinese Government and the withdrawal of New Zealand troops from Vietnam.[12] In domestic policy a clear signal that the new Government was directly descended from the first Labour Government came when it announced that a 'Christmas bonus' — an extra benefit payment — would be paid to all means-tested beneficiaries.[13]

Inexperience in government, however, contributed to a number of economic policy decisions which were politically damaging in the longer term. Wage and price controls instituted by the previous Government were abolished with wages being left to find their own level through free collective bargaining. Price increases followed as manufacturers and retailers applied a 'cost-plus' principle. Inflation escalated with the rapid expansion of the money supply, and a more relaxed immigration policy resulting in a net influx of more than 100,000 immigrants between 1973 and 1975 fuelled demands for housing, education, health, and social welfare services. Government expenditure increased sharply in response to these demands and from the introduction of innovative social welfare programmes such as a domestic purposes benefit and the expansion of Accident Compensation benefits, both promised during the election campaign. At the same time, Government revenue was restricted through the implementation of a number of other election campaign pledges, notably the freezing of Post Office, railway, and electricity charges for three years. Intended as a curb on inflationary pressures, these decisions ultimately induced long-term economic dislocation.[14]

When Labour assumed office New Zealand's foreign exchange reserves were at record levels, the result of an export-led boom which saw the trade-price index increase by nearly 35 per cent between 1972 and 1974.[15] By the middle of 1973, however, inflationary pressures had grown to the point where the Government was forced to introduce regulations to freeze all awards and agreements for a period of ten months. On his return from an overseas trip in the middle of August Kirk announced that New Zealanders would have to 'quickly insulate' themselves from the world depression.[16] Two months later the first oil crisis sent shock waves throughout the Western industrial world and was followed shortly afterwards by a massive collapse in the prices New Zealand received for its wool. Insulation of the New Zealand economy from external pressures once again dominated the political agenda as the Government responded by borrowing overseas to offset the expected economic contraction and to spread the adjustment over several years. While fully consistent with the Keynesian policies followed by the first Labour Government, the huge fall in the terms of trade — 43 per cent in a little more than a year — was altogether too great for such measures to cushion New Zealand from the effects of the downturn.[17] Certainly, the Government could have lessened the impact by reneging on its election promises to freeze postal, electricity, and rail charges; it chose not to do so and entered the 1975 election campaign with a substantial millstone around its neck.

The Government also angered a large segment of the electorate in April 1973 when it compelled the New Zealand Rugby Football Union to call off a tour of New Zealand by the South African Springboks. Before the election Kirk had avoided committing himself on the propriety of the proposed tour although he did promise that a Labour Government would not interfere with arrangements already in place. His subsequent instruction to the Rugby Union returned to haunt the Labour Government throughout the remainder of its term in office and its credibility with the sporting public was further undermined during the 1975 election campaign when it stated that it would not prevent an All Black team from touring South Africa in 1976.[18] Both Opposition parties retorted that the Government could not be trusted since it had reneged on its 1972 election promise not to interfere with the 1973 tour.

Labour did, however, win plaudits for its unequivocal and persistent opposition to French atmospheric nuclear testing in the South Pacific. In June 1973 the Government reinforced its repeated public protests to the French Government by dispatching a frigate (whose crew included a Cabinet minister) to stand 'in silent witness' just beyond Mururoa's twelve-mile territorial limit in an attempt to shame France into ending its atmospheric testing programme. The following year it successfully challenged the moral legality of France's nuclear testing programme in the International Court of Justice. France refused to acknowledge the judgment or agree to abide by it, but, shortly afterwards, re-located its testing programme underground.[19]

In August 1974 Norman Kirk died after a short illness. In the context of the politics of the 1970s Kirk strode the political stage like a colossus, a man who had grown in stature over time as he had become accustomed to the trials and tribulations of leadership. By now a commanding and aggressive orator, he had dominated the political scene from before the 1972 election campaign until his death barely two years later. He was not, as one commentator has noted, 'a radical capable of transforming society. His ambition was, rather, to improve the existing order for the ordinary New Zealander'.[20] But he had inspired confidence. In his place the Labour caucus elected the mild-mannered Minister of Finance, W. E. Rowling, to leadership of the Government and the country. Whereas Kirk clearly belonged to and identified with the working class, under Rowling's leadership the Party moved further away from its working class roots.

As the 1975 election approached it became clear that the Government was in considerable difficulty as its political credibility was called increasingly into question. The buoyant economy of 1972–73 had deteriorated sharply: a balance of payments surplus of $1,000 million inherited from the second National Government had turned around to become a deficit of more than $1,000 million while unemployment, which had dropped spectacularly during the Government's first year in office, again rose above 5,000 as the Government's policy of borrowing to stave off an economic collapse failed.[21] Inflation trebled to 15 per cent despite Kirk's 1972 promise to 'knock inflation for six'. The arrest and subsequent trial of Dr W. B. Sutch, a former permanent head of the Industries and Commerce Department, also proved extremely embarrassing when it was revealed that Kirk had authorized Gerald O'Brien, a Labour MP and Vice-President of the Party, to seek monetary and economic advice which was independent of the Treasury, Reserve Bank, and the Government's own Minister of Finance. Nor was the Government's performance enhanced by a very public clash between its second- and third-ranked ministers over petrol rationing, or the spectacle of a minister who, within minutes, both denied and then confirmed that she had been followed by persons unknown.[22]

Throughout 1973 and much of 1974 the political impact of the National Opposition was minimal. Increasingly, criticism of its lacklustre performance in Parliament focused on its leader, Jack Marshall. He had failed to reinvigorate the Party in government in 1972 and he never adjusted to the role of Opposition leader, proving incapable of matching Kirk in their verbal clashes either inside or outside the House of Representatives. Eventually, a majority of the caucus were convinced that Marshall would have to go if the Party was to have any chance of winning in 1975. In July 1974, shortly before its annual conference, Marshall resigned and was replaced by the Party's aggressive and pugnacious deputy leader, Robert Muldoon.[23] Although initial reactions of rank-and-file members of the National Party to his elevation were at best lukewarm, Muldoon's dominant personality, his repeated and scathing attacks on the Government's credibility, his nationwide barnstorming tours, and the revamping of the Party's administration all helped it re-establish a large electoral support base. By the time its membership had reached 200,000 in mid-1975, it had largely regained credibility as an alternative government. Muldoon may not have been universally liked or respected but he was seen as the leader who was best equipped to lead New Zealand out of its economic difficulties. Ultimately, the 'Muldoon phenomenon' reached well beyond party cleavages to tap uncommitted voters and those who responded positively to plain and simple language no matter how bad the message. More than any other single person, Robert Muldoon can take credit for National's victory in 1975.

Seven themes, each of which focused on the Labour Government's alleged deficiencies and inadequacies, highlighted National's 1975 election campaign.[24] At its core were pledges to 'restore New Zealand's shattered economy'[25] and to ensure that citizens' freedoms were protected, but its election slogan, 'New Zealand the Way *You* Want It', encouraged each voter to interpret its policy proposals as he or she chose. One issue above all others dominated the campaign and played a critical role in the election result. As part of its 1972 campaign Labour — the so-called socialist party — promised that it would establish a compulsory contributory superannuation scheme. The New Zealand Superannuation Corporation was established in August 1974 and shortly afterwards National — the so-called free enterprise party — pledged to repeal Labour's contributory scheme and replace it with an alternative scheme to be fully funded out of taxation and apply to all citizens, not just those in the paid work-force. This was, without doubt, the biggest election bribe ever made in New Zealand politics and a blatant appeal to voters' greed. Not only did National promise to include those who were not part of the paid work-force (a sector not included in Labour's legislation) but, by proposing a reduction in the qualifying age from sixty-five to sixty years, the pool of eligible recipients was increased by over 30 per cent.[26] The potential difficulties this proposal posed to a brittle economy were of no consequence to voters; the problems arising therefrom were to be left to another generation to try to resolve. The campaign focused largely on the issue of leadership, especially Robert Muldoon's. From his assumption of his party's leadership he had engaged in a campaign of personal denigration directed at members of the Labour Cabinet and Rowling in particular.[27] In an ineffectual attempt to counter these attacks a group of well-known citizens spoke out, ostensibly in support of Rowling as Prime Minister but, in reality, in opposition to Muldoon.[28] But, after its initial impact, the 'Citizens for Rowling' campaign proved counter-productive as charges of character assassination were made by groups variously calling themselves, for example, 'Citizens for Muldoon' and 'Rugby Men for Rob'. Group by group they joined 'Rob's Mob' in public demonstrations of support for National's leader.

Although the public opinion polls throughout the second half of Labour's term in office indicated strengthening support for Muldoon and the National Party, few expected the Government to be defeated. Labour's twenty-three seat parliamentary majority had created an illusion of substantial and solid support, and the Party was convinced that this would cushion it against the inevitable electoral decline. Its complacency was, however, rudely shattered on election night when National swept back into power with a two-party swing of 8.4 per cent. The Government lost twenty-three of its fifty-five seats, including five seats held by ministers, and for the first time in forty years, a major political party had won less than 40 per cent of the total valid vote. The result represented an emphatic rejection of the Government: Labour's share of the vote declined by 8.8 per cent while National's rose by 6.1 per cent. Although Social Credit increased its vote share by 0.7 per cent to 7.4 per cent and Values (which contested all eighty-seven electorates in 1975) more than doubled its electoral support to 5.2 per cent, the substantially direct transfer of support between the major parties effectively shut out the smaller players. The electorate had passed judgement on Labour's stewardship during its term in office and found it woefully deficient.[29]

Political stability in democratic states is normally maintained by newly elected governments accepting most of the legislation passed by the previous government. This convention was strained between 1975 and 1977 as the National Government systematically dismantled many of Labour's legislative innovations. For example, only three days after he had been sworn in as Prime Minister, Muldoon unilaterally and without legislative authority announced the abandonment of the New Zealand Superannuation Fund.[30] During the course of the next year a number of other Labour Government initiatives were repealed or radically amended. These included the dissolution of the Local Government Commission (the fifth since 1945) appointed to implement Labour's local government restructuring proposals and its replacement by a new commission empowered to implement its reforms only where majority support of all affected electors was confirmed, a further reorganization of public broadcasting, and the abandonment of economic regulations introduced to control inflation.[31]

New Zealand governments have almost invariably shown a marked tendency to introduce election year budgets containing at least some expansionary elements, and Labour's 1975 Budget was no exception. Equally commonplace is the propensity of newly elected governments to move swiftly to discourage demand and restrain economic expansion. In 1976 charges for government services frozen by the Labour Government were substantially increased: postal charges doubled, electricity and rail transport charges were raised by 50 per cent, and subsidies on the basic commodities of bread and milk were substantially reduced (thus increasing the price to the consumer). In addition, transport and freight charges were increased indirectly through an increase in the price for petrol of 22 per cent. At the same time a general wage increase sought by the trade union movement was limited to just over 3 per cent. The consequence of these decisions was two-fold: by December 1976 inflation rose to 16.9 per cent[32] and economic activity contracted sharply. Although Muldoon in his role as Minister of Finance maintained the Government's internal and external borrowing programme at unprecedented levels, unemployment continued to grow rapidly to reach 22,300 by the end of 1978, despite the large-scale emigration accompanying the economic downturn. The Government's economic policies had failed to restore the shattered economy as promised; economic stagnation persisted, bringing with it increasing social friction and disharmony as different groups fought to secure for themselves a larger share of a shrinking economic cake.[33] Admittedly, some tentative steps were taken towards deregulating the country's financial markets. In March 1976 controls on interest rates were repealed, a decision that meant that the Government, too, was required to pay market rates for the money it borrowed. This, along with the introduction of National Superannuation in 1977, contributed substantially to the significant increase in government expenditure over the next decade and also maintained direct taxation at levels well above those the electorate regarded as acceptable.[34]

Muldoon, a conservative on economic matters, was reluctant to make major changes to the macroeconomic environment. His prescription for a return to economic prosperity was to fine-tune the interventionist policies of the previous forty years, and his later statement that 'any country which today allowed its economy to run completely free would get the worst of all worlds and go downhill very rapidly' succinctly encapsulated his economic philosophy.[35] As Minister of Finance between 1967 and 1972, and as both Prime Minister and Minister of Finance for nearly nine years between 1975 and 1984, his impact on the country's economy was much greater than any of his predecessors. His policies were, however, directed almost totally to commanding the electoral middle ground by preserving the economic security that electors had become dependent upon through reinforcing the state's role as provider of support. Inevitably, this took him along a socialist path signposted by universal superannuation and other generous social welfare policies, subsidies to exporters, and tariff walls to protect inefficient local industries. Voters supported him because he offered them the prospect of individual economic security.[36]

In foreign affairs National retreated from the previous Government's independent and 'moral' foreign policy stance and Pacific orientation. Labour's vehement opposition to nuclear weapons was modified as the National Government once again permitted British and American nuclear-powered warships and submarines to visit New Zealand's ports, despite growing public protests, as it sought to re-emphasize New Zealand's traditional links with the English-speaking and Western European world. Sporting contacts with South Africa were also resumed in the winter of 1976 when the All Blacks rugby team toured that country amidst protests from thousands of New Zealanders. Black Africa's response was a mass boycott of the Montreal Olympic Games by more than thirty black African states.[37] Sustained pressure on New Zealand to adhere to the international sporting boycott of South Africa followed until a declaration committing all Commonwealth governments to take 'every practical step to discourage contact or competition by their nationals with sporting organisations, teams or sportsmen from South Africa or from any other country where sports are organised on the basis of race, colour or ethnic origin'[38] was approved by the 1977 Commonwealth Prime Ministers' Conference. It was left to individual governments to decide how best to implement the obligation entered into at Gleneagles. Despite National's 1975 election campaign promise, public opinion — both internal and foreign — had forced the Government to change its policy stance to avert sanctions being imposed on New Zealand sportsmen and women.[39]

After 1975 Labour was a demoralized and dispirited party. Its grassroots organization had been largely undermined by the Party's performance in government and its few remaining energies were concentrated on rebuilding its shattered organizational structure. In its first year in opposition its parliamentary performance was lacklustre, and 1976 ended badly when Colin Moyle, one of its few experienced members, was forced to resign after misleading Parliament following allegations by Muldoon, under cover of parliamentary privilege, that Moyle had been apprehended by the police for alleged homosexual activities.

The unexpected death of Rangitikei MP and Speaker, Sir Roy Jack, in December 1977 created difficulties for National in one of its very safe electorates. Jack had already announced his retirement from politics, effective from the end of the Parliament, and National had selected Les Gandar (MP for the neighbouring Ruahine electorate which was to disappear at the next election as a consequence of the five-yearly revision of electoral boundaries) to succeed him. Jack's death forced National to nominate a stand-in candidate for the by-election and, in an upset result, Social Credit's leader, Bruce Beetham, won the seat by more than 1,300 votes.[40] His victory gave Social Credit a parliamentary platform for the first time in nine years and once again focused news media attention on the Party. Public support for Social Credit rose dramatically. With the National Government under considerable pressure for failing to produce policies that would turn the economy around, and with the Labour Party not shaping up in the public's estimation as a credible alternative government, the opportunity existed for Social Credit to become, at last, a significant force in New Zealand politics.

Despite the upsurge in popular support for Social Credit, however, the peculiarities of the first-past-the-post electoral system saw National returned to power in 1978 with a comfortable though much reduced parliamentary majority, even though its total vote plummeted by 7.8 per cent to only 39.8 per cent. Labour marginally increased its share of the vote to 40.4 per cent and, overall, aggregated over 10,000 more votes than the Government, but it still fell seven seats short of winning the Treasury Benches. And, despite Social Credit's high hopes of winning substantial parliamentary representation, the Party was effectively excluded from participation in the parliamentary process, even though it captured 16.1 per cent of the total valid vote, comfortably retained Rangitikei, and came second in ten other, mainly rural, electorates. Values' share of the total vote, however, declined dramatically to a mere 2.4 per cent. National's comfortable twelve-seat majority was the product of tactical voting resulting in a nationwide swing to Social Credit rather than an electoral endorsement of the Government. While not prepared to elect Labour to office electors severely chastised the National Government for failing to deliver on a number of key 1975 promises such as revitalizing the economy, reducing unemployment, and introducing voluntary trade unionism.[41]

Despite an expansionary election year Budget in 1978 New Zealand's economic woes persisted. The stagflation of the previous five years continued unabated as the economic problems identified by Muldoon in March 1976[42] — high inflation, a large balance of payments deficit, an unacceptably large Budget deficit, low levels of savings, and rising unemployment — remained. When the world's second oil crisis struck in mid-1979 New Zealand was, once again, subjected to further economic restraint by Government decree. This approach, a characteristic of post-election years, was maintained and reinforced in July 1979 with the passage of a Remuneration Act which provided a mechanism for government intervention in the area of industrial relations and wage fixing.[43]

In his 1979 Budget Muldoon proposed some modest restructuring of the New Zealand economy: controls on overseas investment were to be liberalized and new, fast-track procedures for government consents instituted for new industrial, advanced technology projects, particularly where these would utilize the country's as yet undeveloped energy resources. The Government's response to the second oil crisis was to seek to insulate New Zealand from the vagaries of the world economy by making it at least 60 per cent self-sufficient in energy through the development of its natural gas and abundant hydro-electricity energy potential. The objective was to provide a platform for the development of a more extensive and sophisticated heavy industrial and manufacturing base.

This growth strategy, dubbed 'Think Big' by its architects, became the cornerstone of National's 1981 election policy which promised to create 410,000 jobs during the 1980s.[44]

Even after New Zealand's endorsement of the Gleneagles Agreement, sporting events continued to impact on foreign policy. Following the Soviet Union's invasion of Afghanistan in 1979 the President of the United States urged all countries to boycott the 1980 Moscow Olympic Games in protest. In the face of mounting pressure from the Government, news media, and the general public, most of New Zealand's sporting bodies complied. In 1981 sporting contacts with South Africa resurfaced, this time through the scheduled visit to New Zealand by a Springbok Rugby Union football team. Despite rather half-hearted pleas from the Government, which was openly divided on the issue,[45] to call the tour off, the Rugby Union persisted with its plans and, for two months between late July and September 1981, New Zealand experienced levels of violence and disorder not seen for fifty years. As the tour progressed and opposition to it escalated, the issue shifted from the rights of sportspeople to play with whomever they wished to a question of law and order as opposed to mob rule. Police squads appeared in the streets in full riot gear, including long batons, to confront demonstrators, both passive and violent, whose objective was to force the authorities to abandon the tour. Although the Government and the Rugby Union were the focal points of much of the anger, both Opposition parties found themselves in political difficulties: a clear, uncompromising anti-tour position may well have won them electoral support in the main cities but was likely to prove equally costly in the smaller provincial city and rural electorates.

Between 1978 and 1981 National MPs and Party members became increasingly uncomfortable with Muldoon's leadership style. It was a style which engendered unease, fear, and — among some segments of the community — hatred, all of which compounded existing social strains.[46] Discontent reached a climax after the Government lost the hitherto fairly safe East Coast Bays (Auckland) electorate to Social Credit in an unnecessary by-election — precipitated by the Prime Minister when he appointed his Minister of Defence, Frank Gill, as Ambassador to the United States — in September 1980. This unexpected result generated a wave of anger among Party members. By the time Muldoon returned from India in mid-October, four leading (though not necessarily senior) members of his Cabinet, Derek Quigley (Minister of Housing), George Gair (Minister of Health), Jim Bolger (Minister of Labour) and Jim McLay (Minister of Justice), were plotting to overthrow him. The 'Colonel's Coup' as it became known failed, partly because Deputy Prime Minister, Brian Talboys, was away from New Zealand at the time and would not commit himself unequivocally to accepting nomination for the position; partly because Muldoon, in an interview on prime-time television, appealed over the heads of his caucus and the Party at large to 'Rob's Mob' throughout the country; and partly because Bolger changed sides. The struggle for the free enterprise soul of the Party had failed.[47] Muldoon's position as Prime

Minister was further entrenched but at the ultimate cost of a massive loss of support among rank-and-file Party members.

The Government was also embarrassed in 1980 when the Minister of Agriculture and one of the Prime Minister's close personal friends, Duncan MacIntyre, became involved in the Marginal Lands Board Loans affair. Allegations of preferential treatment favouring MacIntyre's daughter and son-in-law were made when it became known that they had been granted a loan from the Marginal Lands Board to develop a rural property near Wellington. At one stage when the application was being considered by the Board, MacIntyre was Acting-Minister of Lands. The subsequent Commission of Inquiry considered MacIntyre's evidence unconvincing; although there was no evidence of impropriety it concluded that his actions had demonstrated 'questionable judgement' and those of his colleague, the Minister of Lands (Venn Young), had been 'unwise'.[48] Though neither minister resigned — MacIntyre even became his Party's deputy leader in February 1981 — the incident provided Labour with an unmatched opportunity to mount a sustained attack on the Government's credibility.

Throughout 1981 the Government confronted a number of seemingly intractable problems. Inflation had climbed to a record 15.4 per cent and showed no sign of abating, unemployment had risen above 70,000, interest rates were rising rapidly (Muldoon's response was to impose controls on the maximum interest rates that could be offered to investors), the projected 1981–82 Budget deficit exceeded $2 billion, and economic growth was negligible. Politically, the loss of the East Coast Bays by-election and the subsequent challenge to Muldoon's leadership, the Marginal Lands Board affair, and outspoken support for the Springbok rugby tour by the Minister of Police (Ben Couch) all contributed to the impression of a government under severe pressure.

Labour in Opposition, however, evinced even greater disarray. Following the 1978 election Rowling took the unusual step (for New Zealand) of establishing a shadow cabinet. The experiment failed: one MP (Richard Prebble) refused to accept appointment, another (Roger Douglas) was dismissed after a short period for publishing an 'alternative budget'.[49] Labour's caucus was effectively divided into inner and outer groups.[50] The resultant tensions were highlighted in November 1979 when Northern Maori MP, Matiu Rata, resigned from the Party and, six months later, from his parliamentary seat, and stood, unsuccessfully, as candidate for the fledgling Mana Motuhake Party.[51] A few months later Nelson MP, Mel Courtney, also resigned from the Labour Party after continuing disagreements with his electorate organization. At the same time Labour's own leadership problems resurfaced. In November 1979 David Lange, who had been elected to Parliament in March 1977 to fill the vacancy created by Colin Moyle's resignation, replaced Bob Tizard as the Party's deputy leader.[52] Rowling's continued inability to enthuse the electorate was reflected in his Party's declining support in the public opinion polls and also in the increasing unrest within the caucus. Tensions were particularly acute during the final months of 1980, especially after Social Credit's success in the East Coast Bays by-election, and culminated in a direct challenge to Rowling's leadership in December. Rowling retained the leadership by one vote — his own.[53]

Between the beginning of 1979 and September 1980 successive public opinion polls showed that the major parties had nearly the same level of popular support but, following the East Coast Bays by-election, endorsement for Labour plummeted to an historic low just above 30 per cent as support for Social Credit surged upwards to virtual equality. Although Social Credit's popularity then declined gradually throughout 1981 to 20.7 per cent in the 1981 election it had, mainly through the efforts of its leader, largely succeeded in distancing itself from the economic theories of Major C. H. Douglas and in shedding its long-standing image as a party of well-meaning but naïve eccentrics. For many electors Social Credit appeared as a credible alternative to both major parties even though it offered an essentially negative route to change. The choice facing electors was simplified by the virtual collapse of Values as a viable political organization; after the 1978 election debacle, internecine warfare raged within the ranks of that Party and culminated in a major split at the 1979 conference. Thereafter Values ceased to be a significant electoral force.[54]

National was re-elected in 1981 with the narrowest of parliamentary majorities; after the Speaker had been chosen, the Government had a majority of one over all other parties. For the second consecutive election the Government had won fewer votes overall than Labour and, for the first time since 1928, neither major party won 40 per cent of the votes cast. National's vote share declined by 1.0 per cent to 38.8 per cent while Labour's dropped by 1.4 per cent to 39.0 per cent. But, while National suffered a nett loss of three seats, there was a two-party swing *to* the Government of 0.2 per cent. Labour failed to regain the Treasury benches for a number of reasons. First, it built up huge majorities in its own safe seats (where it did not matter) while losing narrowly in many others. Although Labour attracted greatly increased support in the main urban centres, notably Wellington and Christchurch, National was able to maintain its dominance in the smaller provincial city, mixed, and rural electorates. The explanation for this cleavage lies principally in the differential impact of the Springbok rugby tour. While not regarded as a major factor at the time of the election, the tour clearly had helped mould attitudes towards the Government, especially in centres where games were played and demonstrations occurred. It was a decisive factor in National's retention of power because it helped the Party to retain a number of provincial city and mixed electorates won narrowly in 1978.[55] Secondly, Muldoon's greater appeal to the electorate was significant if not crucial: fourteen times as many electors voted for National because they supported Muldoon as voted for Labour because they supported Rowling. Thirdly, Social Credit significantly increased its share of the valid vote, the only party to do so, but while it won 20.7 per cent of the votes cast and its candidates came second in eighteen electorates, it failed to enlarge its parliamentary representation above the two seats already held. Much of its electoral support was negative in character with over half coming from voters who were dissatisfied with the promises and performance of both Labour and National rather than any positive attraction to Social Credit. Despite the progress made, Social Credit's electoral underbelly was still very soft. Fourthly, Mana Motuhake, which contested all four Māori seats for the first time and came second in each one, drew votes mainly from the Labour Party which had dominated Māori politics for nearly forty years and now appeared to be in danger of losing the loyalty it had come to take for granted.[56] In the final analysis National won the election because it successfully fought a two-front war as it beat off Labour's attack in traditional marginal seats and held back a rampant Social Credit onslaught in a number of traditional National strongholds.

Even though National's effective parliamentary majority was only one seat Muldoon continued to govern as though he had a substantial majority, but the methods he used to manage his Government became increasingly authoritarian and overbearing. In June 1982 he introduced regulations under the 1948 Economic Stabilisation Act to impose a twelve-month wage and price freeze in a draconian attempt to bring rampant inflation, then running at an annual rate of 17.6 per cent, under control. In June 1983, shortly before they were due to expire, the regulations were extended for a further eight months. And, when price controls were finally lifted in February 1984 — after inflation had dropped to 4.7 per cent on an annual basis — the wage freeze was kept in place until tripartite wage talks between the Government, employers, and trade unions had reached a satisfactory conclusion. When interest rates failed to match the fall in inflation, Muldoon threatened, and then intervened directly, to regulate the level of interest rates for home mortgages. By May 1984 the infrastructure of economic controls was clearly disintegrating; they had produced serious economic distortions which were compounded because the Government failed to find a way of detaching itself from the web of regulatory controls without causing a huge and unacceptable surge in hyperinflation. Although Government intervention dominated policy-making between 1981 and 1984 National did take some tentative steps, consistent with its free enterprise philosophy, to free up the economy. For example, shop trading hours legislation was amended to permit Saturday shopping, the transport and freezing industries were delicensed to promote greater freedom, competition, and efficiency, movie film distribution was deregulated and, after numerous promises made over many years, voluntary trade unionism was finally written into law.[57]

Muldoon's increasingly arrogant demeanour repelled an increasing number of liberal middle-class voters including many National Party activists. After the move to replace him as leader failed in 1980 public criticism of his political manner and style grew more frequent. When he effectively sacked his *bête noir*, the Minister of Works and Development, Derek Quigley, in June 1982 for publicly criticizing the Government's economic direction he demonstrated all too clearly that he could not, and would not, tolerate any contrary view. But while dissatisfaction and public criticism of his leadership grew, no obvious successor existed, because Muldoon had ensured that anyone who threatened his pre-eminent position was rendered ineffective.[58]

Leadership problems also continued to divide the Labour Party after the 1981 election. Rowling, whose political credibility had been almost totally destroyed by Muldoon's attacks prior to the 1975 election, had now led the Party to three successive election defeats and continued to demonstrate his inability to maintain the undivided support and loyalty of either his parliamentary colleagues or the Party conference where he suffered a major defeat at the hands of the president in 1982.[59] Under his leadership the Party appeared to lack any coherent sense of purpose or direction. When, in December 1982, he finally announced his decision to stand down from the leadership David Lange was elected in his place and former law professor, Geoffrey Palmer, was elevated to the position of deputy leader ahead of populist candidate, Mike Moore.[60]

Throughout 1982 public support for both major parties had been evenly divided but it swung strongly towards the Labour Opposition in the six months following Lange's elevation. It then declined equally sharply as the Party again became embroiled in intra-party squabbles over candidate selections.[61] Coincidentally a new political party, founded by property magnate Robert Jones, emerged to challenge the Muldoon hegemony. The New Zealand Party's main, indeed sole, objective was to force National to return to its basic principles, if necessary by undermining its natural constituency and throwing the 1984 election to Labour. Its detailed policies closely resembled traditional National Party policy with the notable exception of its advocacy of unarmed neutrality and a nuclear-free New Zealand.[62] As a classic blackmail party the New Zealand Party attracted substantial support from most segments of an electorate fast becoming totally disenchanted with the style of the Muldoon Government.

As the New Zealand Party prospered, support for Social Credit declined. After 1981 its problems centred on maintaining its identity and credibility, and sustaining its earlier momentum with only two MPs. Social Credit's self-imposed 'balance of responsibility' principle was sorely tested in the early days of the 1982 parliamentary session when it acquiesced in the Government's legislation overturning the Planning Tribunal's refusal to grant a water right to allow the construction of the Clyde Dam to proceed.[63] An already cynical electorate concluded that Social Credit had abandoned its belief in political integrity and principle the first time it had been put to the test. Thereafter Social Credit's public support ebbed away to reach 6 per cent early in 1984, its credibility seriously undermined and the vacuum it left filled by the New Zealand Party.[64]

The electorate's disenchantment with the two major parties continued until the election. Three months before the election the combined support for parties *other* than Labour or National had risen above 20 per cent. By mid-1984 it was apparent that New Zealand's exchange rate was clearly overvalued while, politically, Government unity was disintegrating as resistance to its policies continued to grow within its ranks. In July 1983 a National MP, Marilyn Waring, had made public her opposition to the Government's nuclear warships policy[65]; in June 1984, with her colleague, Mike Minogue, she supported the introduction of Richard Prebble's New Zealand Nuclear-free Bill. The next day Waring resigned from the National caucus and, a few hours later Muldoon announced that the general election would be held on 14 July 1984, four-and-a-half months before the parliamentary term was scheduled to expire.

For Muldoon the central issue of the 1984 election campaign was leadership — his experience compared with Labour's inexperience.[66] This strategy undermined any possibility of National focusing on other key issues such as the economy, industrial relations, ANZUS, and the anti-nuclear question. Social Credit and the New Zealand Party, both of whom supported Labour's anti-nuclear stance, made Labour's task of spelling out its alternative policies (on health, housing, employment, education, the economy, and overseas debt) much easier by repeatedly attacking Muldoon and his leadership style. As the campaign advanced Muldoon looked increasingly tired and out of touch while Lange appeared assured, relaxed, and confident.

The electorate comprehensively repudiated the National Government in 1984. Although its share of the total vote slipped by only 2.9 percentage points to 35.9 per cent, it lost eleven seats, seven of them held by senior members of the Party. Nevertheless, although Labour won a comfortable parliamentary majority of seventeen seats over all other parties it failed to win strong electoral endorsement: its vote share rose by only 4 percentage points to 43.0 per cent. Social Credit's share of the vote slumped 13.1 percentage points to 7.6 per cent but, although Beetham lost the Rangitikei seat to National, the Party did manage to retain East Coast Bays and win Pakuranga from National. The New Zealand Party, however, failed to win any seats despite winning 12.3 per cent of the total vote. Although most observers believed that the New Zealand Party's presence had considerably boosted Labour's eventual parliamentary majority, a detailed analysis of data derived from a survey conducted immediately after the election suggests strongly that its overall impact was minimal with perhaps only one seat (the Auckland electorate of Pakuranga) being lost by National as a direct consequence of its intervention.[67] As in 1981 votes cast for minor parties were primarily protest votes directed more against the National Government than for another party, and in 1984 the New Zealand Party was seen as the more attractive alternative. With more than one in five electors casting votes for a party or candidate other than Labour or National, it is clear that the electorate's disenchantment with the two major parties was still very great.[68] Overall, while the result was a clear rejection of the National Government the electorate was not at all sure whether it wanted Labour to govern.[69]

The defeat of the third National Government marked the end of an era in New Zealand politics. For seventeen years Robert Muldoon had dominated the political stage, mesmerizing the electorate and exerting greater power and authority than any previous Prime Minister since Richard John Seddon. Frequently he had demonstrated an unerring ability to communicate with voters but, in 1984, he misread the temper of the country and, in so doing, failed to fulfil his objective — expressed in a television interview in July 1975 — of leaving New Zealand 'at least as good as when I took it over'.[70] The real significance of the 1984 election result lay not in the defeat of the third National Government and its replacement by the fourth Labour Government but in the generational change that had taken place. A government (like all others over the previous forty years) whose basic attitudes and values had been moulded by the trauma of the Great Depression and the Second World War, had been replaced by one whose attitudes and values had been moulded by the events of the 1950s and 1960s, notably economic prosperity and anti-war sentiment. Few members of Labour's caucus were able to recall at first hand the seminal experiences of depression and war that had dominated and directed New Zealand politics for nearly two generations. The average age of the new Government's eight Front Bench members was 41.6 years and none was yet fifty; the Prime Minister and his deputy were both aged forty-one years when they were sworn into office and neither had been an MP during Labour's previous administration. Nor was it constrained by the baggage of past Labour Governments, for the circumstances of the snap election meant that it owed few debts to the country's interest groups. Thus, it had a unique opportunity to institute a sharp change in policy direction.[71]

Even before it formally assumed office the fourth Labour Government was confronted with a major fiscal crisis. In the month between the dissolution of Parliament and election day the economy went into a tailspin as the Reserve Bank was forced to borrow $1,700 million overseas to protect the value of the $NZ. A devaluation was widely expected and, on the Monday after the election Lange requested the outgoing Government to devalue the $NZ by 20 per cent. At first Muldoon refused to adhere to the convention that an outgoing government acts on the advice of its successor prior to the formal transfer of power but, after pressure from a number of his own ministerial colleagues, he announced a devaluation and a three-month wage freeze, and the removal of controls on interest rates.[72]

The new Government's earliest decisions were to set the pattern for the next three years. The key minister was Roger Douglas, son and grandson of former Labour MPs, whom Lange had appointed Minister of Finance. During the late 1970s and early 1980s Douglas had become increasingly disenchanted with New Zealand's abysmal economic performance — in 1980 he published a slim book, *There's Got to be a Better Way: a Practical ABC to Solving New Zealand's Major Problems*,[73] which outlined his solutions to the country's economic malaise — and the Finance portfolio provided him with a unique opportunity to leave his mark on the country and its society. The economic policy changes he initiated were aimed at dismantling the infrastructure of economic regulations and restrictions that had been built up by successive governments over fifty years. The devaluation of the $NZ was soon matched by an end to interest rate controls, state-led investment strategies, negotiated wages policies, commitment to tariff protection, state assistance to agriculture and industry and, in March 1985, the managed exchange rate. This economic policy, labelled 'Rogernomics' by its critics, was driven by a market-liberal philosophy involving a mix of monetarist and supply-side economics.[74]

Other major structural changes soon followed including a decision that the state should disengage itself from all economic services that could just as easily be supplied by private enterprise. The Public Service Act passed in 1912 had established a politically neutral career-orientated public service, characterized by security of position tenure in return for loyalty to the government of the day. Successive Labour governments had shown their distrust of advice given by senior public servants, and the decision to end the state's domination of economic activity provided an opportunity for the Government to radically restructure the Public Service. In what turned out to be the first stage of a two-pronged attack, a number of long-established commercial-cum-social service departments (among them the Post Office, Ministry of Works, Forestry, and Railways) were abolished and replaced by stand-alone State-owned Enterprises (SOEs) charged with operating on a commercial basis, while the true costs of many other services provided by the state were to be recovered from users.[75] After the 1987 election, a number of SOEs — Telecom, Air New Zealand, the Government Printing Office, Postbank (the former Post Office Savings Bank), and the State Insurance Office — were sold to private enterprise with the receipts from the sales earmarked to help reduce the country's crippling overseas debt. The core Public Service was also restructured after the Government had forced the State Sector Act through Parliament. This new legislation included provisions replacing the well-established, politically neutral appointments system for top public servants with one which allowed the Government to become directly involved in the appointment of departmental chief executives.[76]

In its relationships with its traditional allies the Government also broke new ground. Labour had long opposed nuclear weapons and the use of nuclear energy for peaceful purposes, and during the previous eight-and-a-half years many Party members had been in the forefront of public opposition to the presence of nuclear-propelled ships and vessels capable of carrying nuclear weapons in New Zealand waters. Soon after he became leader in February 1983 Lange attempted, without success, to persuade the Labour Party to modify its anti-nuclear policy by distinguishing between nuclear propulsion and nuclear armaments.[77] Throughout the early 1980s public opinion moved, almost inexorably, towards the position held by Labour's extra-parliamentary party and, by August 1984, support and opposition was virtually equally divided on this issue.[78] Labour's anti-nuclear policy was immediately thrown into stark relief because the annual ANZUS Council meeting was scheduled to be held in Wellington on the Monday following the election. Although not yet sworn in as Prime

Minister, Lange met with the United States Secretary of State, George Schultz, and the Australian Foreign Minister, Bill Hayden, both of whom expressed uncompromising opposition to Labour's anti-nuclear policy. Schultz made it abundantly clear that continued access to New Zealand ports by United States naval vessels was critical to the maintenance of the ANZUS Treaty relationship.[79] The following February, however, the Government refused entry to a conventionally powered and almost certainly non-nuclear-armed warship, the USS *Buchanan*, because the United States Government would neither confirm nor deny that the vessel was carrying nuclear weapons. In the face of the Reagan administration's subsequent hostile reaction, relations between the two countries deteriorated and New Zealand's participation as a member of the ANZUS pact was effectively at an end.[80] Public support for Labour's anti-nuclear stance was reinforced from an unexpected quarter in July 1985 when the *Rainbow Warrior*, flagship of the Greenpeace movement, was bombed and sank in Auckland Harbour where it was being prepared to sail to the French Pacific island of Mururoa to protest against the French underground nuclear testing programme. Soon after, two French secret service agents were arrested and charged with the murder of a crew member who died in the attack.[81] This incident rallied the New Zealand electorate behind its government and strengthened its resolve to maintain its anti-nuclear position. For most of the period between 1984 and 1987 the National Opposition maintained its support for the ANZUS alliance. Eventually, however, it was forced to acknowledge the overwhelming strength of public anti-nuclear feeling and, five weeks before the 1987 election, Bolger announced that while a future National Government would continue to accept the United States' and Great Britain's 'neither confirm nor deny' policies it would make it clear that it did not welcome nuclear weapons in or near New Zealand ports. National's changed policy position meant, in effect, that it would allow naval vessels from these two countries to visit New Zealand ports 'on trust'.[82]

The constitutional crisis immediately following the 1984 election convinced Labour's deputy Prime Minister and Minister of Justice, Geoffrey Palmer, that New Zealand's loose and fragmentary constitutional structure needed to be tidied up. In 1986 Parliament passed The Constitution Act, an ordinary statute which made provision for the rapid transfer of power to a new government where the election night result was beyond doubt.[83] Palmer also introduced a number of other constitution-building measures. In 1985 he honoured Labour's election promise, made in response to rising demands for a fairer electoral system, to establish a Royal Commission to examine and report on the electoral system. The Commission reported in December 1986 and recommended that New Zealand should adopt a Mixed Member proportional electoral system similar to that used in West Germany. In 1986 he introduced a Bill of Rights to codify the basic rights of New Zealand citizens; a truncated and unentrenched statute was eventually passed in 1990.

Labour's break with its traditional economic and social policy perspectives led to growing disenchantment with the Party among many of its traditional activists and supporters. During the 1970s the Party had developed as the main political vehicle for an educated and articulate upwardly mobile middle class. At the same time its relationship with its traditional social base, the blue-collar trade unionists, became more and more strained, and although the Party had rejected a proposal to dissolve its formal ties with the trade union movement in 1982, the psychological ties between the two became increasingly frayed as the Government's *laissez-faire* economic policies took hold. On the other hand, business and financial leaders were generally extremely supportive of the radical overhaul of the economic infrastructure. As long-standing economic controls were swept away and as subsidies and other economic support mechanisms were abandoned the economy, especially the financial sector, boomed. But as the social costs of the policies pursued were reflected in rapidly rising inflation (peaking at 19 per cent in June 1987) and burgeoning unemployment, Labour supporters' antagonism towards 'their' Government grew apace. Its anti-nuclear stance was the only policy area where it had kept faith with its traditional constituency.[84]

These policy changes clearly harboured the potential for undermining the Government's electoral support but, in 1987, Labour finally buried the one-term jinx that had haunted it since 1949. It retained power with 48 per cent of the valid vote and fifty-seven parliamentary seats to National's 44 per cent of the vote and forty seats. Support for the Democratic Party (formerly Social Credit) declined still further to 5.7 per cent of the valid vote and it lost both its seats to National. No other party won more than 0.5 per cent of the total valid vote although Mana Motuhake did capture 17.2 per cent of the votes cast in the four Māori electorates. Despite an overall two-party swing against the Government of 2.4 per cent Labour boosted its parliamentary majority by two seats to become the first governing party since 1951 actually to increase its parliamentary representation in a general election. Labour's electoral strategy had been simple: its campaign focused almost exclusively on a small number of critical marginal electorates that it *had* to win in order to retain power while the remaining seats were largely ignored. Traditional Labour supporters, dissatisfied with the Government's political direction, were left free to express their opposition by voting against the Government — provided that this occurred in a 'safe' seat, regardless of whether it was held by Labour or National. Consequently, the two-party swing was uneven; the Government lost ground in most rural electorates, and also in its traditional heartland, but significantly increased its support in the wealthier metropolitan electorates including the traditionally National 'blue-ribbon' seats of Remuera (Auckland) and Fendalton (Christchurch).

Between 1984 and 1987 National had been openly and bitterly divided over leadership and a number of policy issues, and had turned inwards upon itself.[85] Historically, the Party has not been kind to its failed leaders and the 1984 election was no exception. But while the election debacle threatened Sir Robert Muldoon's leadership, he undermined his own position further

405

by initially refusing to implement the incoming Government's advice to devalue the $NZ. Thereafter support for him crumbled and in November 1984 he was replaced by his deputy of eight months, Jim McLay. Muldoon did not accept his demotion lightly and spent much of the next two years in a successful bid to undermine his Party's parliamentary and extra-parliamentary leadership. McLay was deposed by Bolger in April 1986 and, before the 1987 general election campaign commenced, both the Party president and general director had resigned. Labour's victory may be attributed, in part at least, to the belief of a large section of the electorate that National was not a credible alternative government. It had also succeeded in bringing together a new constituency comprising higher income, professional, and managerial people, most of whom had traditionally supported National. When coupled with the National Party's obvious disarray, this new coalition of support for Labour provided many voters with a clear-cut choice between the two major parties for the first time since 1975.[86] The Government was also assisted by the virtual disintegration of the New Zealand Party after the 1984 election, and by Social Credit's internal feuding over both its name change to the New Zealand Democratic Party in 1985 and a leadership struggle which saw Beetham ousted in 1986 after fourteen years at the helm. Thus, any serious alternative to the two major parties was effectively eliminated.[87]

Labour's victory euphoria was, however, shortlived. In October 1987 the world's stock markets slumped, the economy went into a tailspin and the New Zealand share market index plummeted 59 per cent in four months. During the next two-and-a-half years unemployment rose from just over 6 per cent to nearly 9 per cent, the Reserve Bank's pursuit of a 0–2 per cent annual inflation target sustained high interest rates, while an uncomfortably large balance of payments deficit added to the economic woes. The only tangible benefit was a drop in inflation from 19 per cent in June 1987 to 5 per cent just over three years later. The Government responded to the share market crash by announcing on 17 December a new, integrated economic and social policy package which included extensive tariff cuts, a flat rate of income tax, a guaranteed minimum family income, the privatization of a number of State-owned Enterprises, and the radical reform of local government.[88] Six weeks later, however, the Prime Minister effectively undermined this programme by unilaterally announcing that the flat tax and guaranteed minimum family income proposals would not proceed. Douglas cut short an overseas trip in a largely futile bid to preserve the main elements of the original announcement. His only success was to reach agreement on a compromise two-tier taxation structure, the main beneficiaries of which were people in the upper income groups.

During Labour's 1987 election campaign Lange had repeatedly emphasized that his Government's focus during its second term would be on social policy with education and health, in particular, being targeted for reform. Subsequent policy initiatives in these and other areas brought increased upheaval and uncertainty and further alienated many of the

Government's traditional supporters. In April 1989, Jim Anderton, the Party's president between 1979 and 1984 and MP for the safe Labour seat of Sydenham in Christchurch since 1984, resigned in protest at Labour's repeated deviations from its manifesto promises. Along with a number of members who resigned at the same time, he formed the NewLabour Party whose objective was to promote a managed economy, insulate it from external economic pressures and adopt a Keynesian approach to encouraging economic growth. About the same time business leaders began to upbraid the Government for its economic policies and performance because they believed that controls of the money supply had become too stringent. Public servants, too, were alienated from the Government by the impact of the State Sector Act, and supporters of the Government's anti-nuclear position were upset by its decision to participate in the construction and purchase of new Australian-built frigates.[89]

The greater part of Labour's second term was dominated by rapidly escalating internal political friction. The seeds of discontent had been sown as early as April 1987 as the hitherto close liaison and friendship between Lange and Douglas began to fray. After the election the relationship disintegrated completely as internecine warfare raged following the scuttling of the 17 December economic and social package. Factions within the Government's caucus were exposed as renewed emphasis on social policy highlighted the conflict between the supporters and opponents of Douglas's prescription for economic recovery. As the factions strove for supremacy the prospect of a challenge to Lange's leadership steadily increased. In November 1988 Richard Prebble, Minister in charge of State-owned Enterprises, questioned the Prime Minister's fitness to govern; Lange dismissed him from the Cabinet. Shortly before Christmas, Douglas signified that he would no longer serve in the Cabinet if Lange was re-elected as leader of the Labour Party the following February; Lange accepted Douglas's communication as a letter of resignation. During the first six months of 1989 Douglas, Prebble, and Trevor de Cleene (Minister of Revenue who had resigned his ministerial post in sympathy after Douglas was sacked) engaged in an orchestrated and very public campaign to undermine Lange's leadership.[90] At the height of this destabilization campaign Lange's position was further undermined by three separate incidents, one of which was largely of his own making. In a speech delivered at Harvard University in the United States towards the end of April 1989 Lange suggested that New Zealand might give formal notice of its withdrawal from the ANZUS alliance since it had been effectively excluded from any participation in its activities since 1985.[91] Although this matter had previously been raised at Cabinet level there is considerable doubt whether Lange's view had been endorsed by Cabinet. Anderton's resignation and a very public and physical clash between factions at the Party's Auckland regional conference also contributed to the public perception of a hopelessly divided party. Two months later, the divisions between the Party's left and right wings erupted into an open challenge to Lange's leadership. Although his support in caucus was still sufficient for him to withstand the challenge, Lange was forced to bow to caucus pressure and agree to fill the two Cabinet positions left vacant since the dismissals of Prebble and Douglas. When caucus elected Douglas to one of the vacant positions, Lange resigned as Prime Minister. He was succeeded by Geoffrey Palmer, an earnest but cautious and circumspect politician, a person whose loyalty could be depended upon and who had hitherto shown an ability to maintain reasonable harmony between the different factions in caucus. Palmer, however, was unable to provide the positive and dynamic leadership the Labour Party and the country were seeking and he failed to re-establish the Government's sense of purpose or policy direction. After thirteen months as Prime Minister, and only fifty-three days before the date scheduled for the election, a 'palace putsch' replaced him with third-ranked minister, Mike Moore. The Government's disarray and public humiliation were complete.

Rumblings of dissatisfaction following the National Party's 1987 defeat led directly to the replacement of its deputy leader, George Gair, by defence spokesperson, Don McKinnon. By early 1988, however, the economic downturn and disarray within the Government's ranks enabled National to surge ahead in public support and maintain its dominance until the 1990 election. Nevertheless, divisions similar to those afflicting the Government were present within National's caucus, especially on economic issues where the 'free marketeers' led by Ruth Richardson, the Party's spokesperson on finance, and Simon Upton were often in open conflict with the 'interventionists' headed by Winston Peters and Sir Robert Muldoon. At times Bolger's leadership appeared threatened, especially after public support for Peters surpassed that of his leader, but no formal challenge was ever mounted because no potential challenger, from either left or right, could garner sufficient support within caucus to topple him. National's massive lead in the public opinion polls also insulated him from potential challengers.

The 1990 election was fought mainly in the nation's living rooms through the medium of television. Inevitably, the Government was on the defensive although Moore strove valiantly to create the impression that his was a new government. He attempted to capture some of the initiative by reaching an accord with the Council of Trade Unions to limit wage increases for the next twelve months to a maximum of 2 per cent. As the party seeking to become the Government, National made a number of unequivocal promises — for example, that the superannuation surcharge imposed by the Labour Government in its 1984 Budget would be removed, that there would be no tax increases, that Labour's tertiary education tuition fee would be repealed, and that the number of police would be increased by 900. These were to create difficulties once it assumed office.

The election resulted in the worst defeat for an incumbent government since 1935. With the benefit of a massive two-party swing of 9.8 per cent, National captured twenty-seven seats from the Government, almost half of them provincial city and mixed electorates. Overall, National won sixty-seven of the ninety-seven parliamentary seats, Labour retained twenty-nine, and NewLabour, the only successful minor party, won one seat. This result was much more a condemnation of the performance of the Labour Government than any endorsement of National's policies for, although Labour's share of the valid vote declined by a massive 12.9 percentage points to 35.1 per cent, National's share rose only 3.8 percentage points to 47.8 per cent. The cynicism of the previous three years also manifested itself in a significant decline in the number of registered electors who voted, from 87.3 per cent to 83.4 per cent.[92] Another indicator of dissatisfaction with the major parties was the doubling of support for minor parties and independent candidates to 17.1 per cent when compared with 1987. Although it failed to win a seat the Green Party was the most successful of the minor parties; it contested seventy-one seats, came third in sixty and captured 6.8 per cent of the total valid vote. NewLabour took 5.2 per cent of the valid vote and won one seat when Anderton retained the Sydenham (Christchurch) electorate. This was the first time since the emergence of two-party politics that an MP had resigned the Party whip and been returned to Parliament in the subsequent election. New Zealand's perennial minor party, the Democrats, was all but annihilated as its support withered to a minuscule 1.7 per cent after another serious internal split. Of the remaining parties and candidates only Mana Motuhake made any substantial progress towards its goal. In the four Māori electorates, the only seats it contested, it won 22.4 per cent of the votes cast. But although its leader, former Labour Minister Matiu Rata, came within 1,000 votes of winning Northern Maori, the Party's other candidates made little or no impression on Labour's monopoly of the Māori seats. Māori disenchantment with mainstream politics appeared to be growing apace: turnout in the four Māori electorates declined by a massive 11.7 per cent to 59.4 per cent, an all-time low despite an increase of nearly 7 per cent in Māori electoral enrolments.

Although the 1990 election was unquestionably a comprehensive defeat for the Labour Government rather than a landslide victory for the parliamentary opposition, the new Government interpreted its huge parliamentary majority as a clear mandate to press ahead with economic reforms designed to reduce the role of the state in the lives of its citizens. The new Prime Minister, Jim Bolger, was very much a pragmatist in the mould of many former National Prime Ministers but he appeared to have been captured by the economic purists of the 'new-right'. Confirmation of this came with the appointment of Ruth Richardson as Minister of Finance and Jenny Shipley as Minister of Social Welfare. These two ministers, in particular, became very influential in the key economic and social policy-making areas. Ironically, Richardson's policies emphasized the purification and completion of the economic reform programme begun by Douglas during his first term as Minister of Finance, which had been comprehensively rejected by the electorate in October 1990.

Confronted by a large and burgeoning deficit the new Government announced its first major policy initiatives on 19 December, less than two months after it had taken office. Government spending was slashed as changes to the social welfare benefits structure were introduced, including substantial reductions in a range of social welfare monetary benefits affecting mainly lower income groups. These changes were accompanied by increased medical fees (through a reduction and, in some instances, elimination of state subsidies) and pharmaceutical prescription charges.[93] In May 1991 the Employment Contracts Act, designed to restructure labour relations in favour of employers by abolishing compulsory unionism, removing the rights of trade unions to insist on collective bargaining agreements and restricting their rights to take industrial action, was enacted. Richardson's first Budget, delivered at the end of July 1991, foreshadowed further major cuts to the long-established infrastructure of the welfare state. If implemented as announced, the top one-third of income earners would be required to make substantial contributions to their health costs. Proposed amendments to the Accident Compensation scheme aimed at transferring the costs of non-work accidents from employers to employees through a levy on incomes. The existing guaranteed retirement income provisions were to be replaced with new arrangements aimed at reducing the overall costs by changing the minimum qualifying age to sixty-five over a ten-year period, and although Labour's guaranteed retirement income surtax was to be abolished an even more stringent means-testing of other income was to be introduced in its stead. Students in tertiary institutions faced the prospect of lower levels of bursary support as parental means-testing was extended to students under the age of twenty-five. The entire thrust of the Budget was to minimize welfare dependency by targeting need, replacing the universal benefit structure which had been in place for more than fifty years with a safety-net approach to support for the community's less well-off citizens.[94] But, despite this harsh economic medicine and an annual inflation rate dropping below 3 per cent, the economy remained in deep recession — even bordering on depression — as real interest rates remained stubbornly high and businesses continued to shed workers.

A rising groundswell of disenchantment with National's policies was soon plainly evident. Denunciations, not only from those directly affected by the economic and social changes but also from within the National Party's caucus, began to be heard before the Government had been in office two months and reached crisis point following the Budget's presentation. A number of National MPs opposed to the emasculation of the welfare state — mainly but not exclusively persons elected for the first time in October 1990 — voiced their displeasure through public criticisms of the Government's policies and by crossing the floor of the House to vote against specific legislative proposals. Shortly after the 1991 Budget had been presented, two first-term National MPs, Gilbert Myles and Hamish MacIntyre, resigned from the Party. While their resignations were greeted with relief by the Party's hierarchy and most of its MPs, they attracted considerable sympathy and support among electors for their stand. For

410

National, worse was to come when two public opinion polls taken near the end of August 1991 revealed that support for the Government had dropped to an all-time low of around 20 per cent of the total electorate. But despite the torrent of criticism and clear public opposition to their policies, the two key ministers remained unmoved and claimed that any return to the policies of previous governments would spell disaster for the country in the long term.

The early 1990s, then, were characterized by deep disenchantment with both major parties. Political theory suggests that, in an overwhelmingly two-party system such as New Zealand has had over the past half century, the policies of the two parties will tend to converge.[95] In their efforts to win and retain the support of electors both Labour and National have modified their ideologies over time. The end result has been a marked coalescence on many policy issues, particularly economic, to the point where significant differences are to be found within rather than between them and electors have been left with no clear choice. An alliance comprising a number of smaller political parties emerged towards the end of 1991 but the fundamental philosophical differences of each of the partners must raise doubts about its long-term viability. Even if the present unity is preserved New Zealand's first-past-the-post electoral system may prove to be too great a hurdle for the coalition to win substantial electoral support. As the elections of 1893, 1938, 1975, and 1987 showed, the first election after a change of government is often more important than the election where a change of government occurs. It is possible, as the 1975 election showed, to reverse a government's policy decisions provided they have not already become embedded in the polity's economic and social fabric. By contrast, the elections of 1893, 1938, and 1987 confirmed the electorate's broad acceptance of the policy changes introduced by governments which were first elected at the previous election. The 1993 election could well prove to be crucially important in determining whether New Zealand will continue along the path of the 'enterprise state' or whether it will return to its traditional values of security and equality that have been the country's hallmark for the past century.

CHAPTER 16

Economic Trends and Economic Policy, 1938–1992

Gary Hawke

As incomes in New Zealand recovered from depression levels, the country's demand for imports rose. In December 1938, faced with a balance of payments crisis, the Labour Government introduced import and exchange controls. Unwilling to restrain imports by deliberately cutting incomes, the Government attempted instead to protect overseas reserves by licensing commodity imports and instituting exchange controls for other items involving overseas payments.[1]

Import and exchange controls varied in severity from time to time and gradually declined in importance before their abolition in 1984. They survived largely because of the protection they afforded particular industries. Although they were introduced mainly because of a balance of payments crisis, their protective implications were understood in the 1930s. Politicians, including Prime Minister Savage, who was typically vague on the subject, were apt to defend them in terms of their ability to promote industrial growth, even though they were well aware that New Zealand's real income was reduced if local industry grew only because cheaper imports were excluded. The profits and jobs of many firms did indeed come to depend on the shelter afforded by import controls, and the fear that they might be jeopardized made it politically difficult to manipulate the controls to contain foreign exchange payments within the limit of export earnings. And yet the workers in protected firms might have contributed more income in other occupations. In retrospect, the 1938 measures can be seen as a crucial component of the post-depression policy of insulating the New Zealand economy from overseas influences. As such they marked a significant discontinuity in the country's economic history.

Their significance was initially obscured. The Second World War dominated the New Zealand economy as it did other parts of New Zealand life. It was only in the early 1950s that the significance of the 1938 decisions became apparent. The New Zealand economy was then very much the product of its history. There were two principal elements in that. From the introduction of refrigeration in the 1890s, New Zealand had specialized in the provision of a small range of commodities, concentrating to a large extent on the British market, not because of any political considerations but because the British market was open and remunerative. In the early 1950s, more than 90 per cent of New Zealand's exports consisted of meat, wool, and dairy produce, and nearly two-thirds of them went to the United Kingdom. (This owes something to the high commodity prices of the early 1950s, and to the continued routing of trade through Britain, but it is nevertheless true that New Zealand in the early 1950s was closely tied economically to Britain.)

The second element which remained very strong was the reaction to the Depression, especially a continued emphasis on avoiding unemployment. Many countries experienced an expansion of social welfare programmes after the Second World War; New Zealand was unusual only in that its 'Welfare State' was related more to the first Labour Government elected in 1935 than to the experience of war (and even that characteristic was shared to a large extent with the United States). But in response to a foreign exchange crisis in 1938, the Government had declined to risk any repetition of the unemployment of the earlier 1930s and used direct controls rather than deflation. Import licensing and exchange controls were therefore regarded not as a wartime expedient, as was true of most countries, but as part of 'insulation', a policy to ensure New Zealand's control of its own destiny.

New Zealand experienced economic change and growth in the 1950s and 1960s. There was, however, a substantial element of continuity. An unusually low level of unemployment was preserved, but there was always a fear that the community would seek to buy more imports than could be financed from export receipts. 'Diversification' of exports loomed large in policy discussion. The 1970s saw not a release from the unwelcome 'foreign exchange constraint', but a markedly more adverse international environment. In retrospect, the 1970s look like an attempt to prolong the strategy of the 1950s and 1960s — to maintain a longstanding structure, merely modifying it when necessary. Change occurred in the 1980s with a new determination in economic policy to seek better use of New Zealand's own resources.

Normal international economic relations were interrupted by the Second World War.[2] Whether or not the controls adopted in 1938 would have prevented overseas reserves from being exhausted was still uncertain when the war intervened to alter the balance of overseas receipts and payments. Imports were reduced as European production was cut off or diverted to war uses. Exports, however, found a ready market as the British Government, learning from the experience of the First World War, speedily concluded an agreement to purchase the most important commodities in bulk. Prices were set at levels favourable to New Zealand, and although wartime inflation in Britain gradually reduced this advantage by raising the cost of imports, New Zealand found itself, in place of the exchange crisis of 1938, with an accumulation of overseas assets, even after some earlier loans were repaid.

The effects of the war went far beyond the balance of payments. People were diverted from production to the armed services, but New Zealand's major contribution to the war effort was food, mostly for Britain but later for the Pacific war zone as well. The British Government initially asked for cheese to meet its protein ration but subsequently gave priority to fats, and the dairy industry was asked to concentrate on butter. The industry responded well. Wartime patriotism encouraged producers to put Britain's need before private profit, but there were other stimuli as well. Priorities were determined by factory managers, far fewer in number than individual farmers, and therefore easier to convince and more accessible to legislative control. Sheep farmers were less subject to such pressures. Although Britain needed meat, the prices of the bulk purchase agreements were more favourable to wool, and farmers preferred to build up their flocks rather than to increase the proportion of lambs killed for meat. Other sectors of the economy were affected too. Manufacturing was promoted directly through the local production of war supplies such as radio equipment and small boats, and indirectly even more assisted as local goods were sought to replace unavailable imports. The construction industry, too, was fostered by requirements such as housing for American troops stationed in New Zealand.

While incomes were maintained, a substantial fraction of output was used for war rather than made available for purchase. There was, therefore, a potential for inflation. Insulating the economy became less urgent than restraining price rises. The Government was vigorous. It espoused the view that the war should be financed internally rather than by overseas borrowing, and persuaded the population that higher taxation was tolerable, even desirable. It borrowed within New Zealand, using titles such as 'Victory Bonds' and 'Liberty Loans' to encourage the belief that contributions helped to buy guns and tanks while the real objective was to reduce spending power. Bank lending and the raising of business finance were subjected to official controls. Prices and wages were subject to a stabilization scheme whereby subsidies were used to control certain key prices and wages were linked to a wartime price index. Some other incomes were controlled too, notably farm incomes, because a share of export proceeds was held back in reserve accounts. All of these policies (which were sometimes regarded with nostalgia when viewed from the experience of inflation in the 1970s or from the consequences of other means of controlling inflation in the late 1980s and early 1990s) were acceptable as part of the community's commitment to war. By and large they were successful. The wartime prices index understated the inflation experienced, as prices rose more rapidly for commodities which were not subject to controls or which were not included in the index. Nevertheless, conventional price indices, compiled but not published during the war, suggest that inflation was less in New Zealand than in most countries.

The structure set up to mediate the influence of the international economy on New Zealand could not long outlast the war. Some of the restraints had already broken down as particular groups became less convinced of the equity with which wages and other incomes were stabilized. But the end of the war inevitably threatened the export markets made so secure by bulk purchase agreements, and allowed imports to flow once again from Europe. None of this happened immediately, but people's plans and expectations were soon attuned to likely change.

Export markets in fact remained buoyant. It suited Britain to continue bulk purchase of meat until 1954. Worries about wool disappeared as the wartime stockpile was quickly disposed of and the price of wool was carried to a new record level by the Korean war. Dairy products too found a ready market. Despite this, exchange controls remained necessary because there was a shortage of American dollars. New Zealand belonged to the 'sterling area', a group of countries which settled their overseas debts mainly through London. Jointly they bought more from the USA than they sold there. Payments outside the sterling area were therefore subjected to controls administered mainly by the Bank of England, with which New Zealand's own system was readily co-ordinated. Restrictions on payments in US dollars were an irritant to many people, especially those whose daughters had married American military personnel, but New Zealand could not afford to be expelled from the sterling area. Furthermore, the Government and officials thought that New Zealand should be prepared to contribute to the common pool of US dollars from which it had benefited. Even when the boom in wool turned the country into a substantial net earner of US dollars, the rules of the sterling areas were observed.

Before the 'dollar scarcity' was resolved, New Zealand's exports generally justified some relaxation of restraint on overseas payments. But the newly elected National Government of the early 1950s went too far. Imports from the reviving industries of Europe flooded in beyond a level that could be financed, and the familiar controls were reimposed. For purely political reasons, they were initially disguised as 'exchange allocation', but the old foreign exchange constraint was soon recognized.[3]

From the mid-1950s to the late 1960s the ratio of imports and exports to national income declined, giving a false impression that international trade was becoming less important. But the relationship between the volume of trade and the volume of local production had not changed. The prices of exports and imports were not rising as fast as the prices of other goods, so that although exports took about the same proportion of total production and imports too continued to be about the same proportion in physical terms, the value of foreign trade declined as a fraction of Gross National Product (GNP).[4]

Neither the experience nor the explanation for it was unique to New Zealand. In general, productivity was increasing faster in the production of goods than of services; the prices of services therefore rose relative to those of goods. Services were more likely than goods to be produced and consumed within one country although some, such as insurance, were traded between countries. Goods therefore composed a larger proportion of international trade than they did of total production. It follows that the prices of goods and services traded between countries rose less than the prices of all goods and services. This basic explanation can be embellished in a variety of ways. For example, prices are assumed here to be tied closely to costs of production so that productivity trends are reflected immediately in prices. This is more true of competitive markets than those where inefficient producers could charge higher prices. But international markets were open to more traders and were therefore likely to be more competitive than national markets. For this reason too, the prices of goods and services traded internationally were always more restrained than those of goods and services produced and consumed within a particular country. In this respect too, New Zealand simply shared an international experience.[5]

It did not, however, share in the growth of the volume of trade relative to physical production which was a feature of the international economy in the 1950s and 1960s. When many restrictions on trade in manufactured goods in Europe and North America were relaxed from the 1950s onwards, countries were able to benefit from specialization within fine categories of products. Chemicals, for example, flowed both ways between pairs of countries as their industries concentrated on different kinds of chemicals. But New Zealand's exports, remaining firmly agricultural, did not share in this development.

The three traditional export categories, wool, meat, and dairy produce, were joined after the war by a fourth, forestry products. They varied in relative importance according to changes in overseas demand, and within the categories different products became prominent at different times (see Graphs 4 and 5). As sales of butter and cheese to Britain were limited by the slow growth of British demand and increasing restrictions by the British Government, other dairy products known as 'solid-non-fat products' began to be exported. For some of the 1960s, the beef market in the USA seemed to rival the sale of lamb to Britain, and mutton was exported to Japan in growing quantities. Diversification within the traditional exports was much more significant than the growth of manufactured exports until the late 1960s. (Even then the latter were dominated by aluminium, the receipts from which were nearly matched by the cost of imported raw material.)[5] Growth of manufactured exports was to be a feature of the 1970s and later.

Imports were always more varied than exports, as they must be for any country with an advantage in producing agricultural goods but a consumption pattern resembling that of countries combining similar income levels with an advantage in industrial goods. An increasing proportion of goods imported consisted of materials or capital goods for local production rather than finished goods for immediate consumption. This is a long-standing, although not uninterrupted, trend in New Zealand's economic history,[6] but before 1938 it resulted from private decisions that goods could be obtained more economically by importing materials and components for assembly in New Zealand. After 1938, it was fostered by import licensing. When the licensing system was adapted to protect local production, materials and equipment used in New Zealand industry were granted licences more readily than finished goods. (The increased proportion of materials rather than finished goods in imports probably contributed to the slower increase of import prices than average prices within New Zealand. The effects of licensing were much less simple than often imagined and originally intended.)

Changes in the composition of international trade in the 1950s and 1960s were more than matched by shifts in the relative importance of trading partners. In the 1930s, New Zealand's trade was increasingly concentrated on Britain, which erected fewer barriers against imports than most countries. Politicians such as Walter Nash hoped that import licensing would reinforce this trend, but from the 1950s the opposite was clearly apparent. Britain's economic growth was slower than that of many countries, British governments became more concerned with their own farmers, and from the early 1960s there was some likelihood that Britain would join the European Economic Community and adopt its protectionist agricultural policy. Accordingly, exports were gradually diversified away from Britain.[7] So were imports. There were a few bilateral agreements directly linking export markets and import sources, but most changes in imports came from the realization by private firms in New Zealand that Britain's slow growth had made goods from other countries cheaper. Thus motorbikes were obtained from Japan rather than Britain, and car-assembly firms sought supplies from Japan, Germany, and Italy as well as Britain. It may be, however, that New Zealand businesses and officials searching for new export markets increased awareness of cheaper alternatives to British imports (see Graph 6).

Many people would have liked these changes in international trade to be accelerated. Towards the end of the 1960s their hopes seemed to be fulfilled. It became easier to sell a wider variety of goods to a number of countries as a result of shifts in the relative values of various currencies, the most significant of which was the British Government's devaluation of sterling in 1967. In responding, the New Zealand Government took the opportunity to remove the premium which the New Zealand unit of currency had had over its Australian counterpart since 1948. Individual exporters then received more in New Zealand currency from sales in Australia and there was a surge of manufactured exports across the Tasman. Some other countries, especially those around the Pacific, were affected similarly and New Zealand seemed, at last, to be breaking out of the constrictions imposed on agricultural exports. Indeed, as traditional exports found a ready sale too, there seemed grounds for hope that at last exports might be able to finance the desired level of imports.

Euphoria did not last long. Agricultural exports rose partly because farmers expected the greater receipts they got after devaluation to be balanced before long by higher costs. They therefore sought a quick return, instead of building up their livestock so that more meat, wool, and dairy produce could be produced in the future. By the early 1970s the supplies of the traditional exports were less than buyers wanted. Furthermore, in 1973, oil producers increased their share of world income, and markets for manufactured exports contracted as incomes fell in overseas countries and governments acted to protect their own producers.

In the 1970s, New Zealand found that despite the diversification of exports which had resulted from government policies and the countless decisions of individual exporters and importers after 1938, it remained heavily dependent on the international economy. New Zealand had come to participate in international markets for a wider range of goods, and there was less concentration on Britain, but the importance of international trade in general had not lessened.[8]

International economic developments usually affect New Zealand's agricultural sector first. Until the oil crisis of the 1970s, fluctuations in the economy originated in exports rather than imports; not only did the agricultural sector provide most exports, but overseas markets also took most agricultural production. Farm products were processed to some extent through local industries and services, but exporting was generally direct enough to ensure that overseas conditions soon affected farm incomes. About two-thirds of the income of all farmers came from exports, and this fraction declined only slightly in the years after 1938.

'Insulationism' was built around agricultural exports and farm incomes. The guaranteed price scheme of the first Labour Government was intended to separate the incomes of dairy farmers from overseas sales of butter and cheese, although it was soon clear that the separation could not be complete. Other products were brought under marketing authorities which were eventually constituted as producer boards, with control shared between farmers and government.

The form these took varied from time to time. The Dairy Board was founded in the 1920s but on the introduction of the guaranteed price scheme in 1936 its marketing functions were taken over by a government department. This change was shortlived. In the post-war years, producer (marketing) boards were used rather than government departments. Their appearance was more consistent with the private enterprise stance of the National Party, and the Labour Government had already found that it was unwise for the Government to be responsible directly for the prices paid for farmers' produce. A semi-independent Dairy Products Marketing Commission was established in 1948, although the Government retained a strong influence over the crucial price decisions (and strengthened it in the 1950s). In 1961, the Commission and the Dairy Board were amalgamated. The Meat Board too was established in the 1920s but control over marketing was brought within the stabilization programme in the Second World War. When the wartime arrangements for meat marketing were finally terminated in 1954, a system of 'deficiency payments' was added to the functions of the Meat Board. This was a variant on guaranteed prices, the Board merely undertaking to supplement the prices paid for meat when they fell below certain levels. Deficiency payments were first made in 1959. In 1971, the Meat Board's powers were widened; it bought lamb and mutton in competition with private traders and began to market meat in Britain. (It had operated in 'non-traditional' markets throughout the

1960s.) The Wool Board was set up in 1944 and it co-operated with similar institutions in other countries, especially Australia, to sell the stockpile accumulated during the war. In 1952, a separate Wool Commission was established to set floor prices for wool. (If private trade resulted in lower prices, the Commission acquired the wool and marketed it.) In the 1963–64 season, wool prices were high and the Wool Commission added a ceiling; receipts above this were channelled into 'retention accounts' to be released when prices were low. By these means wool had something very like the guaranteed price scheme. The Commission bought a great deal of wool when prices fell in 1967 but gradually sold it in the following seasons. In 1972, the Commission was replaced by a Wool Marketing Corporation intended to be more positive in its operations, but farmer opposition denied it the power to acquire all the wool produced. The Corporation led the way with new marketing techniques such as selling by sample and offering wool of particular qualities whether from one grower or several. In 1978 it was combined with the Wool Board, which had retained traditional non-marketing activities. Other producer boards such as the Apple and Pear Board and the Honey Authority also grew out of wartime stabilization and a deliberate effort in the early 1950s to establish authorities for controlling and marketing nearly all products.

The naming and structure of particular boards was often at the centre of political debate, but more important than their form and organization was the very fact of their existence. Their function was to subject market receipts to some modifications and provide a means through which farmers could co-operate with the Government in negotiating access to overseas markets.[9] Major exporters could never be insulated entirely. Prices could be smoothed, but farmers were quick to resent any retention of part of 'their' earnings, and it was not possible to remove low prices leaving high ones unaffected. Furthermore, relative prices signal the activities which should be encouraged and while official intervention might be intended merely to smooth out overseas fluctuations, it usually involves misleading people who have to choose to produce one commodity rather than another. Even in the case of dairy prices where controversy was less than for most farm products, the failure of pay-out prices to signal the relative worth to the community of butter and cheese (and later other dairy products) was a source of dissatisfaction among dairy farmers and concerned those anxious that the economy should use its resources efficiently. Producer boards therefore gave most attention to defending and expanding their markets rather than to 'insulation' of their industries.

Farmers certainly responded to prices. The relative profitability to farmers of different products often determined their priorities, and thus affected the composition of overall farm output. So, when beef gave a better return than wool and lamb in the mid-1960s, cattle began to appear on what had long been exclusively sheep country in areas such as Hawke's Bay. For similar reasons, farmers in the dairying country of the Waikato started growing more grains, and those in Canterbury, lucerne. Studies of peasant agriculture around the world usually show strong responsiveness to relative prices, but New Zealand agriculture had been directed to international commerce from the mid-nineteenth century. Some changes were promoted by the Government; in the late 1960s, for example, government subsidies were introduced to encourage dairy farmers to produce beef. But such incentives were always secondary to relative market prices (and sometimes ill-timed).

New Zealand is often regarded as an agricultural country, especially by people abroad judging from its exports. Within the country, agriculture does not justify such prominence. It employs about the same share of the labour force as it does in several Western European countries and very much less than in the poorer countries of the world. But in New Zealand the notion of farmers as the 'backbone of the country' dies hard. It is at least vastly exaggerated; in the economic structure of the 1950s and 1960s, any special importance of agriculture was only that the level of imports desired tended to be greater than could be financed from exports, most of which were provided by agriculture. More recently, the best description is the even more orthodox 'comparative advantage' argument — that New Zealand agriculture provided the best opportunities for favourable participation in international markets.

The fraction of the labour force employed in agriculture fell from about one-third in 1938 to about one-eighth in the early 1970s after which it stabilized. The fraction of GNP derived directly from agriculture also fell in that period, mostly because the prices of farm products did not rise as rapidly as those of other goods (compare Graph 2). Such a movement away from agriculture was common in the richer countries in the world, and is mostly to be explained by the declining share of food in consumers' expenditure as incomes rise. New Zealand's agriculture was unusual in that its output per employee was higher than the average of all sectors, unlike most rich countries where agriculture is less efficient than manufacturing and many services.

Agricultural productivity grew substantially in the forty years after 1938. The increase in output per employee was dramatic, as output rose while the number of people employed (not only the fraction of the labour force but also the absolute number) declined until the late 1960s. The amount of land used by farmers remained much the same, as new areas brought into cultivation were balanced by farms lost to suburban development. The rise in output per employee was partly the result of substitution of machines and other capital equipment for labour. That the tractor stock of 1938 was only about one-tenth as big as the more powerful and versatile stock of the 1970s highlights the mechanization of farming, and the use of aircraft to spread fertilizers dramatizes it. Popular impressions of farming often exaggerate machinery, and much of the increase in agricultural capital took the form of buildings and improvements such as drainage and irrigation schemes. These too increased the area of land and the total output which could be managed by one farmer.

Substitution of capital for labour increased the complexity of the farmer's task. Greater mechanical expertise was required, and perhaps even more demanding were the difficult decisions to be made about financing capital improvements. But mere substitution of capital for labour does not increase the ratio of output to inputs, and it is higher productivity in this sense that makes a society richer. In post-war New Zealand, until the end of the 1960s, agricultural productivity rose at an average annual rate of about 1 per cent. Farm management in all its aspects — crop and animal husbandry, wise application of fertilizer, adjustment of the mix of products to market trends — was responsible for this. Some other agricultural systems, more able to take advantage of the hybrid crops resulting from research in botanical genetics, achieved greater increases, but given the high level of productivity which New Zealand farming had already reached in 1938 and the scientific difficulty of animal improvement, it was a creditable record.

Farming became much less simple, but it retained many attractions. Only ill-informed town-dwellers thought of farming as a life of luxury, but it always offered a way of living with a good deal of individual control over work. Time spent at a mid-week rugby match or on a journey to a chamber music concert (if one were accessible) had to be made up later, but at least there was no remote boss to be persuaded that it would be made up. As farmers dispensed with hired labour, replacing it more economically with buildings, machinery, and their own labour (often a different, more cerebral kind), the advantages of farm life became available to fewer people, and especially to fewer of those less well endowed with intelligence and education. Also, the economics of farming made it more difficult for people to obtain the way of life agriculture offers unless they inherited a farm.[10]

People therefore had to accept urban life, and most preferred it. Much of the new urban employment was provided by manufacturing, and its growth was closely connected with changes in import composition. The principal role of industry was to provide employment. Import licensing had initially been introduced in order to provide a direct control of imports and so resolve a balance of payments problem. They were used again for that purpose in both the early and the late 1950s, but their longer-term effect was to provide protection to New Zealand industry. It was difficult to use import licences to restrict total imports (as is necessary if the objective is balance of payments equilibrium) since refusing authority to import materials or equipment could cause unemployment — or, more immediately, political difficulty about the likelihood of unemployment. Consequently, import licensing was used to give preference for imports of equipment and raw material over imports of finished commodities which competed directly with the products of New Zealand industry. Local industry was protected so that manufacturers were confident that governments would maintain high levels of demand for their products. They were therefore willing to invest freely.

This combination of private and government decisions spread industrial growth over a wide variety of products and a large number of manufacturing units. The phrase 'hot-house growth of manufacturing' is justly applied to the activity fostered by import shortages during the Second World War.

While overall production rose, and the number of manufacturing establishments grew, their average size probably fell. This was reversed by the early 1950s but even so, most workers remained in establishments that would have been regarded as small in industrialized countries overseas, and which conducted only the finishing operations of manufacturing. The motor vehicle industry exemplified much of the character of local industry. New Zealand factories assembled a wide range of car models from c.k.d. (completely knocked down) packs — boxes of car parts like a model kitset; they did not press steel into appropriate shapes or use heavy tools to make engines — the key processes of the vehicle industries of Europe, Japan, and Australia. The technology of the New Zealand industry advanced, more components such as batteries and tyres were made locally, and the factories got bigger, but the nature of their operation remained much the same and the employees of individual works were still numbered in hundreds rather than thousands.

Not all industry was of that kind. From the 1890s manufacturing encompassed some export activity, mostly related to the local processing of refrigerated products. 'Primary produce processing' remained a significant part of manufacturing after 1938. Dairy factories were among the largest manufacturing units and grew substantially in size and complexity as tankers collected milk from a greater area for each factory and as more complex technology permitted a wider range of products to be made more quickly. Many freezing works were owned overseas and their directors were less sympathetic to experiments with expensive equipment than were their counterparts in the dairy industry. Changes were nevertheless forced on them as overseas markets set new requirements, partly because of rising standards of food preparation and partly because 'hygiene requirements' conveniently disguised import restrictions. Wool processing developed too. Until the 1950s, New Zealand wool was usually mixed with that of other countries so that there was little advantage in processing it locally. But new techniques for making carpets from local fibres without large-scale weaving allowed a New Zealand carpet industry to develop, led by firms such as Feltex and Kensington Carpets.

New export commodities required some local processing too. From the early 1950s the exotic forests planted before the Second World War provided not only trees for export in a raw state, but also the material for pulp, newsprint, and other paper products. Tasman Pulp and Paper and New Zealand Forest Products grew to be among the largest companies in New Zealand, supplying the local market and, in the case of the former, exporting a large proportion of its output. Processed horticultural products developed in a similar manner, although fewer were exported. Factory-made sauces were long familiar, but the processing of vegetables (especially peas) first by canning and then by freezing became a major industry only after the Second World War. Watties was the leader of several firms active in this field. Although most processing of local products concerned agriculture or forestry, there were some other resources that could be profitably exploited. New Zealand Steel, for instance, succeeded in making some simple steel products from the iron-sands of the west coast in the North Island.

Most manufacturing, however, continued to process imports. The range of goods produced expanded as ingenuity throughout the world created new products and brought new machines into use. Lists of principal products manufactured in New Zealand for 1976 added considerably to those of comparable 1951–52 lists: radios were joined by radiograms and television sets (including colour sets); refrigerator-freezers were replaced by more sophisticated devices; washing machines became fully automatic, and tumbler-driers were added.[11] Not all changes were visible to the consumer. Motorists saw little difference in their petrol, but from 1964 it was made from imported crude oil at the Whangarei refinery. Screws and nails looked the same, but were increasingly manufactured in New Zealand, as were many other metal and plastic products.

Contrary to many allegations, New Zealand's average level of protection was not high in an international perspective. But New Zealand was unusual among the relatively rich countries of the world in protecting industry rather than agriculture. Furthermore, New Zealand relied on import licensing rather than tariffs, and the distribution of protection among individual industries, products, and firms was haphazard. The co-ordination of tariffs is difficult enough since the protection accorded an industry depends on the import duties on components and the ratio of cost of materials to its selling price as well as on the duties levied on imported goods which compete with its product. But the calculations required in the case of licensing are more complex, and the limited inquiries which have been possible show wide and inexplicable differences. In comparisons among industries, it is difficult to see why those with high rates of protection were favoured more than those with low rates. Within industries, some firms were more efficient than others but the licensing system gave them no encouragement. Firms were rewarded for their skill in securing import licences rather than for their efficiency in using resources to make products which consumers wanted.

The two main advantages claimed for licensing over tariffs were a lesser inflationary effect and a greater role for social purpose — both were substantially misconceived. Tariffs raise prices more directly, but they also provide government revenue, thus lessening the need for taxes. And import licences confer on their holders an ability to raise prices. The premiums paid for companies with an entitlement to import licences indicate that the ability was used. Nor is there much evidence that import licensing gave social purpose priority over private profit, still less that this could not have been achieved in some other way. Governments certainly used the licensing system to promote particular industries. The resource processing industries, especially, were fostered, but it is doubtful whether profitability and social desirability really diverged in those cases. In others, such as the attempt of the second Labour Government to establish a cotton mill in Nelson in 1960, the wisdom of the 'social choice' is questionable. In any case, there was little effort to use import licensing to substitute a political or social notion of what is essential for the market criterion of what is profitable; most importing decisions continued to be private, guided by governments only to a preference for industrial inputs over finished goods. This could have been done equally well by differential tariffs (as indeed could further assistance to specific enterprises).

Most manufacturing was directed towards the local market, but there were links to the international economy through overseas investment. The control of foreigners over New Zealand industry was resented out of simple pride or a distaste for remitting profits to overseas owners. But foreigners wanted to begin or develop operations in New Zealand so that they could sell materials and components in place of excluded finished imports. Any protection of local industry would have had the same effect, but licensing made it especially important for foreign manufacturers to have close relations with the holders of import licences. It is ironic that the critics of foreign investment were often also the advocates of import licensing rather than tariffs.

In the 1950s and 1960s foreign investment came increasingly from America and Australia rather than Britain, paralleling the shift in the origin of imports. Differences between industries which were and were not substantially owned overseas are difficult to discern. Despite a continuing intermittent debate about foreign investment, there was never any serious question of New Zealand making do with less capital, and the country merely paid a market rate for resources owned overseas while local labour and capital received the same return as they earned in wholly New Zealand-owned enterprises.

Manufacturing was increasingly concentrated in the Auckland and South Auckland regions. Most decisions on industrial location were made by private entrepreneurs. With wages much the same throughout the country, they made most profit by locating industries so as to minimize the transport costs involved in collecting the materials and distributing the product. For much industry this required a location near a port (the source of imported materials), while Auckland provided the largest consumer market for most industrial products. Hence, businesses favoured Auckland. Furthermore, the trend to Auckland fed on itself. The relative size of the Auckland market grew as people migrated to the city from overseas or from within New Zealand because of the opportunities for industrial employment. While motor-vehicle assembly firms were likely to favour the Hutt Valley as much as Auckland in the 1930s — both were close to ports and the transport costs of delivering cars to customers were small when they were driven individually — by the 1960s Auckland was preferred unless special incentives were given to locate elsewhere. The pattern was typical of consumer-oriented industries.

The Bay of Plenty and South Auckland regions were also preferred as locations for the forest-based industries, since the central North Island forests were more accessible from those areas. Other industries processing agricultural produce stayed near their raw materials — food processing in Hawke's Bay and Canterbury, for example — and their geographic distribution became less like that of industry in general. New Zealand Steel, however, chose a location as close to the Auckland market as its raw material permitted.

By the late 1960s there was widespread unease about the dominance of Auckland. This concern had little economic justification. Society in general as well as individual businesses benefited from the minimization of transport costs: private location decisions diverge from what is desirable for the whole economy only if businesses are misled as to the relative costs of two sites. By the 1970s the real costs in Auckland of water supplies, sewerage, and social services such as law enforcement may have been greater than the prices charged businesses through rates and taxes, but, as Auckland is still a small city on a world scale, the divergence is unlikely to have been great. Government's intervention through regional development schemes was properly directed to the social life of the South Island and smaller North Island centres rather than to any economic distortion.

Social and economic concerns merge, and the development of industry in New Zealand owed much to the former.[12] Industry was protected to provide jobs, to give New Zealanders opportunities to develop and use a wider range of skills, and to absorb Māori and Pacific Island people into a bicultural and multicultural society. Ironically, the success with which full employment was pursued until the late 1960s led to frequent claims that labour was in short supply so that more migrants were desirable. The output of an individual industrialist might indeed have been constrained by the unavailability of labour so that more migrants would have been beneficial to the firm, especially if the costs of migration could be shifted to taxpayers generally through government subsidies. But migrants also demanded goods and services, especially if they arrived in family groups or formed households soon after arrival and so required housing and social services such as schools and health services. The economy as a whole then remained just as 'short of labour' after their arrival.

The connection of industry with migration was just one facet of the broad issue of economic policy as to how industry could provide jobs with minimum cost to the economy's productivity. That issue extended beyond industry to other sectors of the economy: construction, transport, energy, and services.

Both before and after 1938 big construction contracts caught the public eye. Railway construction became less important than it had been, although it continued after the Second World War with, for example, new rail links to the North Island forests in the 1950s and the Kaimai tunnel in the 1970s. Road and power schemes gained increasing prominence. Motorways in Auckland and Wellington were the most visible roading developments although New Zealanders returning after a lengthy absence might have found improvements in secondary routes and country roads more striking. The inclination to spread novelties among the regions sometimes led to the labelling of these improved roads in places such as Napier and Hastings as 'motorways'.

Hydro-electric power developments continued at a faster pace after the

Second World War. The Waikato River was transformed into a chain of lakes governed by dams generating electricity. Similar stations were built in the southern lakes and the Waitaki valley. A cable link between the North and South Islands, itself an expensive investment, enabled southern power to be used in the north. Construction also moved on to other North Island rivers. Electricity generation was not confined to waterworks; by the 1960s electricity could be obtained economically from oil and coal, and large investments were made in electricity schemes at Meremere, New Plymouth, and Huntly. The exploitation of Kapuni and Maui gas in Taranaki and the search for oil also called for much construction work.

Despite their prominence, such large projects probably never claimed more than half the total resources devoted to buildings of various kinds. For the 1960s and 1970s, quinquennial censuses of building and construction showed that buildings were about two-thirds of total output in 1963–64 and 1968–69 and about three-quarters in 1973–74. There is less direct evidence for the 1950s, but the pattern is likely to have been much the same. A large number of small buildings use more labour and capital in total than a small number of newsworthy engineering projects.

Houses and flats took more resources than any other kind of building, although their fraction of the total declined. In the early 1950s, there was still a legacy of inadequate housebuilding in the 1930s and war years to be made good. By the mid-1960s, builders were fully occupied keeping abreast of population growth, although it was local rather than national growth that was relevant to a particular group of builders as the demand for houses was governed by population redistribution within New Zealand and by the destinations of immigrants as well as by the population of the country as a whole. The building supplies industry also benefited from the gradual spread of more amenities among the housing stock; electric or gas stoves and flush lavatories became almost universal in the 1950s and 1960s. Although rural houses were at the end of the process, Māori housing was included in the general improvement.

In the early 1970s housebuilders were again under pressure as people born in the post-war rise in fertility formed families and tried to secure houses at the same time as another wave of immigrants arrived. The total demand could not be satisfied even when many prospective owners lowered their sights from detached houses to flats and apartments. (These nevertheless comprised only about one-sixth of dwellings built.) But the phase was temporary: as immigration gave way to emigration, and fertility declined sharply again, the ability to finance housebuilding rather than the physical capacity of builders once again determined the number built.

Although building trends in the 1960s have been described as a move away from 'social' towards 'productive' investment,[13] the allocation of items between social and productive uses is dubious. Commercial buildings were always rationalized as making head office functions more efficient, but they were at least partly a form of fringe benefit for executives and white-collar workers. Similarly, road improvements made business transport more efficient, but they also made social life more convenient for car owners.

Indeed, motorways may well have been built primarily because senior engineers wanted to play with the same toys as their overseas colleagues. A harsh verdict perhaps, but it is clear that while buildings and constructions of all kind took a large share of total investment throughout the years following the Second World War, early hopes of a consequential rapid growth of income were not fulfilled.

Much construction was concerned with energy, and trends in the use of energy are clearer. Coal became a more expensive source, and its share of total energy supply dropped from about 45 per cent in the war years to less than 20 per cent in the early 1970s. Transport and industrial users switched mainly to petroleum and householders to electricity. For most of the 1950s and 1960s, oil provided energy more cheaply than coal; so coal-burning railway equipment was replaced by diesel-using, and with road transport. The social impact of the decline of coal on the West Coast was enormous, as politicians were well aware, but in other parts of New Zealand cheap and efficient electricity was attractive and the West Coast was far away. By the end of the 1960s, however, there was reason to think that the price of oil would rise. The increase came in 1973, rather sooner and more sharply than expected, and the country did not adjust to it easily.

There were changes in the relative use of different modes of transport too. After the Second World War, passenger traffic moved away from railways, which by the 1970s were providing about half as many passenger-miles as they did during the war. People preferred to travel by air or car. The relative cost of air travel was declining all over the world, but the geography of New Zealand intensified the use of aircraft for internal travel. Crossing Cook Strait was easier and quicker by plane than by inter-island ferry; mountain terrain and the narrow gauge of the railways, together with the relatively long distances between major centres of population and the fact that airports could be located close to city centres, all combined to make air transport attractive. By the early 1970s, it dominated long-distance personal travel. With the availability of air travel, the tourist industry grew, retaining its emphasis on natural scenery. Many New Zealanders were disturbed by the provision of facilities for rich foreigners but others earned incomes from them and the receipts were a useful offset to the foreign exchange costs associated with New Zealanders travelling abroad. Real integration with an international market for tourism came gradually.

Shorter journeys were increasingly made by private car. Once a car had been bought for the sake of convenience, many of the annual costs were unavoidable, and only the small additional cost per kilometre had to be compared with the price of public transport. Public transport by road as well as by rail therefore declined. The trends of the 1960s and 1970s left commuters of the 1980s facing a sudden rise in the cost of petrol and frequently with little or no public transport.

Railways retained a larger share of goods transportation. They gained all but some specialized traffic from coastal shipping, especially when the North and South Islands were linked by rail ferries from 1963. And railways were protected from competition by road transport. Except for particular

427

goods such as livestock, or on certain routes where no rail service existed, road haulage firms were restricted to carrying goods only up to a certain distance. The limit was set at 30 miles (48 km) in the 1930s, increased to 40 miles (64 km) in 1961, and to 150 km in 1976. This restriction was almost the entire content of Government's policy, promulgated in 1931 and constantly reiterated, that transport systems should be 'co-ordinated'. It was a blunderbuss approach since an arbitrary distance limit did not match services to the most economic mode of transport. Nevertheless, because road transport firms did not have to pay the real social costs of building and maintaining roads, the limit may well have made some contributions towards an efficient use of the available transport systems.[14] It was only in the 1980s that a new approach was taken, focusing on transport as an economic system.

Aircraft had less impact on the movement of goods than of people, both within the country and internationally. Goods which were not bulky or heavy and for which speed was important were increasingly sent by air, but they remained a small fraction of the total. Railways and road haulage therefore remained pre-eminent internally, and shipping carried most exports and imports. International shipping services changed with the relative importance of trading partners and with improvements in shipping technology. The main example of the latter was containerization. It made the handling of goods more economical in places such as Europe and North America and even though the limitations of internal transport restricted the gains to New Zealand, overseas technical requirements simply had to be accepted. It was another example of expensive capital works not providing any great increase in local incomes.

Construction, transport, and energy all involve some physical equipment but their importance comes from the services they provide. Other services, such as those of shop assistants and public servants, are even more remote from any tangible output. As the proportion of the labour force employed by services increased, there were suggestions that an unproductive superstructure was being built on the backs of the real workers. There was no substance to such allegations. An economy exists to satisfy wants, and people were wanting services more than goods. Many services were involved in getting goods from the makers to those who wanted them: goods would simply pile up in factories but for the distribution system. But even services less directly involved with goods, such as education and travel agencies, provide satisfaction to their consumers.

The relative growth of services probably retarded growth in the overall productivity of the economy. This is partly a comment on the greater progress achieved in the production of goods than of services, and partly a statistical point, an implication of the conventions by which productivity is measured. The output of many services is usually measured by the wages and salaries paid to people employed in them; thus there cannot be an increase in output relative to labour costs. Better measurements of output are hard to find. The number of clients a social worker has, for example, is no surer guide to the quality of advice and help dispensed. Some overseas studies suggest that improvements in services which are neglected in conventional measurements of their output and productivity can be substantial, and this is likely to be true of New Zealand.

However, even after allowing for measurement problems, the growth of productivity in services was probably lower than in agriculture and industry. Services remained, on the whole, labour intensive and their efficiency could not readily be improved by substituting capital for labour. Some such substitution occurred; computers replaced clerks, machines took over some packaging tasks, and calculators permitted some reduction in the number of shop assistants. (Self-service in supermarkets differed from these in substituting the customer's unpaid labour for that of employees.) But capital could not be introduced as readily as it could in agriculture or manufacturing.

Because the productivity of services could not be improved as much as the productivity of processes making goods, the relative prices of services in New Zealand rose, as they did elsewhere. Resistance to price rises caused personal services to decline while more professional services survived and grew. Personal services were often replaced by home labour with the aid of household durables such as electric razors. Some professional services, notably teaching and medicine, were protected against rising labour costs by the willingness of governments (presumably at least bound if not guided by community wishes) to tolerate increased numbers and higher salaries. Other professional services which were sheltered from the scrutiny of final consumers were those purchased by manufacturers and incorporated in the cost of their products, such as accounting and legal advice. The passing of cheap personal services, such as that of barbers, was sometimes regretted, but the loss was simply part of economic growth. Surviving services had to provide incomes equal to those available in other occupations; few personal services could do so.

At the same time, the growing size of the economy permitted more specialization, especially within those services supplying businesses rather than individuals. An early development was 'instalment credit' or a hire purchase firm which provided finance so that a seller was paid immediately while purchasers spread their payments over a period of time. Other services such as guaranteeing mortgages in return for a small commission were added and through the 1950s, 1960s, and 1970s names like Broadlands, General Finance, and Marac became household terms as did American Express and Diners Club. What was sometimes seen as an unsavoury growth of city money-power was simply the reflection in the financial sector of the increased sophistication of economic institutions.

Not all the developments were well based. Some failures of judgement became only too obvious in crashes such as those of the Cornish Group, the JBL empire, and the Circuit companies in the early 1970s. Nor was all the growth of non-bank financial institutions due to their greater efficiency. The older trading banks were more directly restrained by governments' efforts to combat inflation by limiting the availability of finance and this restricted their ability to compete with newer institutions. The banks indeed complained that their relative decline in the financial system was entirely due to unfair discrimination by official controls, and their share of financial assets did increase again when government policies were changed in the 1970s to improve their competitive position while maintaining government influence over monetary trends. But a careful comparison with overseas trends suggests that the non-bank financial intermediaries gained more from specialization than from a privileged position in relation to controls.

The new financial institutions did not engulf those of longer standing. Like the trading banks, life insurance companies continued to be of major importance. Their business had an essential continuity; they accepted deposits from the public usually in the form of a regular premium, invested profitably, and returned the proceeds to the public in the form of annuities or a lump sum. But they did experience change. The profitable use of premiums changed with the development of industry and services within the economy. Mortgages of farmland became less dominant, and while the limited development of the stock exchange in New Zealand prevented as much movement into company shares as was common in other countries, investment in industrial and commercial building was significant and visible. The large urban buildings owned by insurance companies in the 1960s were the annuities of a large number of savers, not the embodiment of the power of a small élite. The insurance companies were sometimes criticized for not investing more in housing but they had to balance the interests of policy holders wanting housing loans against those concerned that their annuities should be as large as possible. Investment policies were influenced by governments too; as official controls spread beyond the trading banks, insurance companies were required to hold minimum amounts of government stocks which bore low interest rates. Taxpayers benefited at the expense, not of the large and powerful companies, but of all who owned life insurance policies (although there were some compensating tax concessions on insurance premiums).

It was not only in the more or less intended effects of government policy that local control of the financial sector was increased after 1938. Control of most of the trading banks had always been divided between local management and an overseas board of directors, but since the 1930s it has been tilted in favour of the former. The Reserve Bank insisted on dealing almost exclusively with the 'chief officer in New Zealand' for any individual trading bank; it was more convenient and the Reserve Bank did not wish to cause any conflicts with central banks overseas. The mere existence of the Reserve Bank itself increased the power of the New Zealand Government, but its effects went further. Local chief managers for any trading bank found support for their own position in any conflict with their overseas directors by referring to the expressed (and sometimes unexpressed) views of the local central bankers, and by what the chief trading bankers agreed amongst themselves, locally, before meeting the central bank. Directors retained control of such company affairs as dividend policy and senior appointments, but more and more banking decisions were made locally. Nationalism was expressed most elegantly in literature and the arts, but it existed in many other ways too.[15]

In the 1950s and 1960s, an attractively simple analysis of the New Zealand economy was accepted by most commentators. Governments spent more than they received in taxation, and the resulting deficit sustained a high level of demand within New Zealand. This was prevented from inducing more imports and a consequential balance of payments crisis by import licensing except for years such as 1957 and 1967 when a shortfall in exports upset the precarious balance. (In those years, balance of payments crises were actually precipitated by additional importing in anticipation of intensified direct controls.) The general effect was therefore that the budget preserved full employment at the expense of more inflation. Parts of this analysis were always suspect. Import licensing in fact affected the composition of imports more than their total, and until the 1970s inflation in New Zealand was more or less in line with that of its trading partners. The really cogent criticism of the analysis follows from a systematic distinction between government spending and receipts within New Zealand and its drawing on overseas earnings. This shows that the Government was not spending more in New Zealand than it took in such ways as taxation. There was not the net injection of spending on which the analysis depends.[16]

New Zealand did maintain very low levels of unemployment during the 1950s and 1960s.[17] Government spending made only a small net demand on resources within New Zealand, and imported consumer goods were restricted by licensing. Private business therefore had confidence in the ability of market demand to justify investment. The Government's impact was greatest through its influence on the expectations of a large number of individual businesses. While the growth of income seemed secure, the returns to investment would at worst be delayed and there was therefore no reason not to employ any resources available. That widespread confidence was severely shaken in 1967–68 and has not been re-established.

Economic trends after 1938 were, as before, determined by the countless decisions of consumers and producers. The economy remained decentralized and the notion of any politician 'running it' was as ludicrous as ever. Yet the influence of government was pervasive. In farming, semi-governmental boards controlled marketing; government research and advisory services facilitated productivity growth; subsidies assuaged short-term problems. Manufacturing grew under the shelter of import licensing. In construction, government organizations working on large contracts and private builders working on houses were both manipulated by governments in order to balance the availability of goods against demand. The transport industry had to respond to what government called 'co-ordination'. Monetary policy influenced the expansion of specific institutions. And at all times some pressure group was dissatisfied with government actions affecting it.

The aim of many government interventions was to avoid a long-term foreign exchange constraint by insulating the economy from overseas trends. Following a much older tradition, the government apparatus was also used as a convenient instrument for whatever governments and officials thought desirable.[18] The development policy characteristic of the half-century from the 1870s to the Depression of the 1930s simply acquired new forms and nuances. But the direction of the economy, none the less, lay firmly in the hands of the community; government planning never usurped the role of the many private decisions spread throughout the population.

The direct economic significance of government did not change markedly in the years after 1938. The proportion of the labour force employed by government and its share of the goods and services produced remained fairly constant. Government's share of total capital formation fluctuated but if anything declined rather than increased. The ever-popular myth of an inexorably advancing government had no foundation. Indeed, New Zealand was perhaps unusual in the comparative lack of growth in the Government's direct share of economic activities. New Zealand probably started the period since 1938 at a higher level than most countries, but even more important in explaining the relative constancy of the Government's share after the Second World War was the much smaller growth of defence spending than was experienced by most other countries. Growth of taxation (and government expenditure) relative to national income was a feature of the 1970s more than of the whole post-war economy.[19]

Government spending grew fastest in the fields of education and health, and in transfer payments within the welfare system. The community, in its political processes, decided that education and health care should be provided by government rather than by private enterprise. Private medical insurance schemes did grow in the 1960s as government facilities, despite their rising share of government spending, were unable to cope with the demands of patients and medical practitioners. Private schools, however, were unable to recoup rising costs and had to depend more and more on government aid. The rising costs of services severely affected education and health, and by the mid-1970s many people were asking whether they were not absorbing too much of the economy's income.

Transfer payments were the means whereby taxpayers provided groups such as the aged, the sick, and solo parents with a share of goods and services even if the recipients did not contribute to their production. The direct effect was to redistribute output without changing its total. The indirect effects were more subtle. When the spending patterns of recipients of welfare payments differed from those of taxpayers, there was a differential effect on producers of various goods. Throughout the 1950s and 1960s, food producers and makers of children's clothes probably gained most, at the expense of the producers of other goods within the much wider range purchased by taxpayers in general. With the introduction of national superannuation in the mid-1970s, many older people were better off and more overseas travel was probably purchased, again at the expense of other goods and services. The indirect effects of transfer payments may also have affected the total of output as well as its composition, if the level of taxes induced people to reduce the time they spent at work. Pronouncements on this 'disincentive' effect of taxes were legion from the 1930s to the 1970s, but its importance is simply unknown. Nor for that matter is it easy to assess the extent to which governments' actions changed the composition of output. Other things also promoted some goods and services at the expense of others: changes in the average age of the population, and the introduction of immigrant groups with distinctive expenditure patterns such as the Dutch in the late 1940s and the Polynesians in the 1970s were influential, but more important were technical change and the invention of new goods. It is difficult to separate out the effects of government.

From the 1930s governments accepted a much wider responsibility for regulating private enterprises. Earlier government agencies such as the Government Life Insurance Office and the State Coal Mines were established to check private enterprises by competing with them. Newer controls ranged from minutiae to general policies. Examples of the former can be found in many industries. Whether or not a licensing trust (itself a semi-governmental body) could borrow funds to establish a bottle store was a matter for ministerial decision. Political rhetoric against socialistic restrictions recurred constantly, but new regulations were needed to plug loopholes in earlier ones. Governments were no different from other rule-making bodies except that they were bigger and affected more people.

Only a little less detailed in their application were policies concerned with regional development and wage rates. Governments were persuaded, with varying degrees of conviction, that they should do something to help the 'regions' but did not provide anything more generalized than *ad hoc* transport subsidies. Wage negotiations were usually left to the Arbitration Court and to unions and employers until 1968, when the Court declined an application for a general wage order. It had always previously compromised between what unions sought and what employers conceded to be practicable, and the apparently surprised employers and unions were soon able to substitute their own agreement. It is doubtful whether the 'nil order' itself was very significant; inflation rates were rising and the intricate legal machinery of the Court could probably not have coped with the speed of change required in the late 1960s and early 1970s. But wage negotiations then moved away from traditional methods and successive governments intervened with detailed regulations in an endeavour to retard the price-wage-price spiral. The purpose of intervention was economic stability in general, but the regulations necessarily had to deal with innumerable specific situations.[20]

The most important government influence on the economy as a whole was fiscal policy. The idea that the Budget should be concerned not only with government housekeeping but with balancing aggregate demand with the goods and services available gained currency overseas only in the 1930s. It was readily accepted by such officials as Sir Bernard Ashwin, Secretary to the Treasury from 1939 to 1955, and was understood, at least in part, by

433

leading politicians from Nash to the present day. Throughout the period from 1938, the Government used its annual Budget to promote the 'stability' of the whole country. Individual taxes and subsidies and expenditure programmes affected some parts of the community more than others, whether intentionally as with taxes on cigarettes and subsidies on milk, or unintentionally with taxes intended only to raise revenue but necessarily affecting particular prices. Similarly, the funding of such projects as housing assistance was governed by the desirable level of total government spending, but none the less had an impact on both the profits of builders and the aspirations of home-seekers.

An influence on the economy even more diffuse than fiscal policy was the exchange rate. The value of New Zealand's currency relative to those of other countries was seldom changed. The devaluation of 1933 was reversed in 1948. In 1949 New Zealand matched the devaluation of sterling to maintain the same value relative to sterling (but a lower one to, for example, the American dollar). Another sterling devaluation in 1967 provided the occasion for the New Zealand Government to devalue even more so as to achieve parity with the Australian dollar. Later changes were more frequent. International developments put too great a strain on the system of fixed exchange rates established at the end of the Second World War and more flexibility was introduced. New Zealand governments responded cautiously with minor adjustments from time to time.

In overseas discussions of the matter, the exchange rate was usually considered to be connected directly with the balance of payments. It was held that devaluation could be expected, in most circumstances, to foster exports and discourage imports by making them more expensive. Thus it was an instrument for removing a balance of payments deficit at the cost of raising inflation. Revaluation could be expected to have the opposite effect. This theory had some influence in New Zealand. The 1948 revaluation was sometimes presented as taking advantage of a balance of payments surplus to restrain inflation. The 1967 devaluation was treated as an opportunity to break out of a balance of payments problem found to be increasingly constrictive.

The New Zealand approach, however, has placed much more weight on the effect of exchange rate changes on the distribution of income. Devaluation favoured exporters at the expense of consumers of finished goods and in 1933 and 1967 this was thought to be desirable; the revaluation of 1948 was intended to favour wage and salary earners buying imported goods at the expense of the relatively prosperous farmers. But the occasions for such deliberate intervention were few, while the traditional emphasis on income distribution made governments reluctant to use devaluation to counter balance of payments deficits. (They were also concerned that devaluation was often seen as a blow to national, or at least governmental, pride, and there was some doubt that devaluation would provide more than a brief respite in the balance of payments before being counteracted by the Arbitration Court adjusting wage rates in line with inflation.)

Governments affected income distribution in other ways too, notably through progressivity in the tax system (that is, taking in tax a greater fraction of higher than of lower incomes). The tax system probably became more progressive in the course of the Second World War, partly because of the attitudes of members of the Labour Government but more probably because it was easier to raise income taxes than indirect taxes. (The former are more likely to be progressive than the latter.) In the course of the war, income taxes came to be about two-thirds of the total taxation, reversing the ratio of indirect to direct taxes that prevailed in 1938. Thereafter the degree of progressivity changed little for twenty years, while tax avoidance ensured that its effects were no more than mild. That probably accorded with community wishes since most people thought that progressivity should really begin to bite at a level of income a little above their own. In the 1970s, changes were even less intentional than those during the war. As inflation carried incomes into higher tax brackets, income tax moved towards being proportional rather than progressive. The redistributive effect of government depends on the composition of its expenditure as well as on tax scales, and increased social security benefits for lower income earners, the aged, and, to a lesser extent, those with young families may well have come to be more important than income taxes. The net effect of changes in government expenditure and in the form and level of taxes since about 1970 is unclear. Furthermore, they are intermingled with other economic changes. Māori incomes, for example, have probably benefited more from urbanization than from any government policy, but even that is not certain (mainly because of the general government influence on the growth of industrial jobs).

Governments also affected income distribution through their own salary policies, especially for groups such as doctors. But the main influences remained the relative profitability of various kinds of private business, community notions of fair rewards, and the institutional arrangements by which those notions were made effectual. Analysis of these begins with overseas markets for agricultural products and their effect on farm incomes. An increase in farm incomes stimulated a greater demand for those industries which processed imports into farm requisites, while bigger export receipts fostered a more relaxed attitude towards the importing of materials and capital equipment generally. All industrialists could then expect employment to expand (through extended hours and more part-time workers) so that they could plan to sell more of their products. Importing profits, business profits, and wages in expanding industries rose. The Arbitration Court then took these movements into account in raising wage rates for those who had missed the direct impact. A decline in exports would be diffused in a reverse direction, although wages would stand still rather than decline. New Zealand operated an incomes policy before that term was recognized, let alone fashionable.[21]

Satisfaction with that policy diminished. It took almost a decade for the community to restore relative income levels after the Korean war boosted the incomes of sheep farmers, but only a few years to catch up to the muted boom in wool prices in 1963–64. Then, after the temporary collapse of the Arbitration Court in 1968, the community sought to keep pace instantaneously with export receipts, so destroying any chance of moderating the effects of overseas inflation. Furthermore, professional incomes were sustained while those of farmers declined between booms, so upsetting the customary pattern. And, of course, there were wide divergences within the categories discussed here; some lawyers earned much more than others, the net incomes of farmers depended on whether their farms were mortgaged, and while the experience of 'salary and wage earners' was about average, that group encompasses many more people than belong to trade unions. Present understanding of how income distribution changed is limited, and still more limited is any understanding of whether that change accorded with community preferences.[22]

Income is not the only reward of economic activity. Many people derive satisfaction from their employment in interesting intellectual or manual tasks, as well as from weekend activities. Such satisfactions were no doubt correlated with incomes but they could be catered for by an expansion of the economy without any change in average incomes. Opportunities for promotion were created by the increased scale of the economy irrespective of any change in overall productivity, and dwindled in the mid-1970s as the rate of growth of population declined. Even those who were convinced by the (cogent) arguments that population growth was not, in general, conducive to improvements in real incomes[23] found that many issues were more pressing when growth was absent. The general well-being of New Zealanders depended not only on per capita income but on the whole range of economic developments.

By the end of the 1960s, it was clear to some senior officials and informed commentators, but not to most of the public, that the economic structures which had evolved since the Second World War, very much influenced by the decisions of 1938 and the experiences of wartime, were not going to satisfy New Zealanders' aspirations for all time. Other countries were experiencing faster economic growth, and New Zealanders would not be content with living standards lower than those available elsewhere.

One reaction was to intensify the existing principal strategy. Export promotion received a very powerful external thrust. Britain had made its first moves towards joining the European Community (EC) in the early 1960s, but they were renewed in the late 1960s and were thereafter continual until its eventual entry in 1973. Unlike Australia, which had already seen that the importance of agricultural exports to Europe would decline while mineral exports to Japan could be increased, the New Zealand Government thought that it had little option but to seek to maintain traditional markets. A great deal of effort in succeeding years went into negotiations about access for lamb and dairy products to Britain and the European Community.

New Zealand's case to the EC met with some sympathy (assisted by a more or less explicit agreement that it would be presented with quiet reason while the Australians would make noisy protests, expecting nothing except less likelihood of being called on to support the New Zealand economy!).[24] But sympathy was always mixed with suggestions that New Zealand should do more to develop alternative markets. In any case, it had become apparent that the economic growth of Britain was relatively slow, and that Britain's domestic policies of protection for its own farmers were inevitably going to limit the possible expansion of New Zealand's traditional export markets.

Diversification of markets, however, was not enough. The principal engine of economic growth in the international economy was widely seen to be international trade in manufactured goods. There was little chance of the European Community or other countries opening themselves to agricultural goods. Therefore the appropriate strategy for New Zealand was to join in international trade in manufactured goods. An early response was the New Zealand–Australia Free Trade Agreement, NAFTA, a limited step towards freer trade with Australia. Devaluation to parity with Australia in 1967 was a stronger spur towards exporting manufactures to Australia. (The timing of devaluation was eventually determined by Britain's decisions about sterling, but it had been under active consideration in New Zealand for some time.) Another effort in the same direction was the National Development Conference of 1969, an attempt to get compatible objectives among different industries, and to shift towards an exporting industrial sector while preserving consensus on income distribution. These general measures were supported by the use of 'export incentives', tax concessions related to success in exporting non-traditional products or to new markets.

This exercise was first knocked off course by the boom of the early 1970s. Buoyant export receipts appeared to remove the perennial shortage of foreign exchange. There seemed to be no reason to worry about consistency and optimality of sectoral developments when imports could readily be financed. But that was a temporary phase. A more serious blow to the strategy of the National Development Conference was the oil crisis of 1973–74. It became much more difficult for New Zealand to grow through exports when a large slice of world income was transferred from the markets for New Zealand exports to oil-producing countries. Diversification is no protection when all export markets contract together.

New Zealand's response was to seek to spread the needed adjustment over several years by borrowing. This was in line with international recommendations to 'recycle petrodollars', and it was probably unavoidable in 1974–75 since it is very hard to turn around an economy and a public sector from a situation where there seemed to be no cash constraint to one where real average incomes were markedly reduced. But the strategy was persisted in for too long. The external environment was far from congenial. The Government responded with the 'growth projects', especially after a further rise in the relative price of oil in 1979. It was sensible to seek to use New Zealand's hydrocarbon resources which had become more valuable in line with the world price of oil. It is understandable but regrettable that this was presented in the readily understood but misleading rhetoric of

437

increasing New Zealand's self-sufficiency rather than as an element in a positive adaptation to a changed world economy. The real key was the competitiveness, in the light of international prices, of New Zealand's industries whether they were growth projects, suppliers to growth projects, or only indirectly linked with the growth projects.

At the same time, reduced real incomes intensified sectional conflict and fed inflation within New Zealand. Borrowing continued, defended as a sensible way to develop New Zealand's resources but in fact supporting domestic consumption at a level above that justified by production. Assistance to exporters was extended to agriculture with the result that producers were given no incentive to look at trends in world markets, while much of the support was captured by urban suppliers of inputs to farmers. Some farmers gained, less by increasing output of marketable produce than by selling farms at prices which included capitalization of government support.

There were achievements during the 1970s. Exports of manufactured goods, to Australia and other markets, did grow. Some of the agricultural sector developed markets in horticultural products and kiwifruit. The transport sector was significantly rationalized. A Closer Economic Relations (CER) agreement with Australia greatly extended NAFTA and provided exciting new opportunities for manufacturing. But by 1984, it was clear that existing policies were leading New Zealand into increased overseas debt while not removing the disparity of incomes compared with other countries. The mechanisms which had produced full employment in the 1950s and 1960s had been lost; the fundamental problems remained. The need for change was widely recognized. Most important, it was apparent to leading official economists. The election of a new government in July 1984, especially one which resulted from a snap election and had therefore given few hostages to particular interest groups, provided an opportunity for an unusually sharp change of direction.[25]

Economic policy, both macroeconomic and microeconomic, was focused on efficiency and equity. In the early 1980s, when official economists had time for some academic thinking because they were allowed little influence on immediate decisions, they reconsidered the traditional statement of the objectives of economic policy in terms of income growth, income distribution, minimization of inflation, balance of payments equilibrium, and full employment, and distinguished more clearly between those which were fundamental objectives and those which were means to those ends. Emphasis on efficiency and equity was the result. It was expressed very clearly in the Treasury briefing papers to the incoming Government in both 1984 and 1987, and although in neither case were all Treasury recommendations accepted, the basic goal of efficiency and equity was adopted.

Both of its components attracted debate. It might seem that efficiency is a more 'technical' and therefore less controversial topic, but before it can be determined whether maximum output is being secured from given resources, it is necessary to be sure of what is being produced. If broadcasting is simple provision of entertainment, then an efficient organization of it is very different from what is needed if 'public broadcasting' is distinct from 'commercial broadcasting' and is concerned with nation-building as well as entertainment. One must also know the market for which output is being produced. Whether or not a producer or marketing board is to be preferred to competitive marketing on efficiency grounds depends critically on the nature of the market being served. There are therefore debates within the meaning of efficiency, even when one puts aside simple misunderstandings which result when people interpret efficiency as concerned with cost-minimization rather than with the ratio of benefits to costs. But there is no doubt that passions are higher when the meaning of equity is debated. In particular, as more weight was given to achieving incomes comparable to those available overseas, less was given to securing full employment. The combination of protection and investment in low-yielding projects which had been used in earlier years was no longer acceptable, but no alternative was found. As the Government put more emphasis on social policy after it was re-elected in 1987, divisions within its ranks became deeper, culminating in December 1988 in the departure from Cabinet of the Minister of Finance who had directed the change in economic policy from 1984. Yet, throughout, efficiency and equity considerations were closely intertwined.

From 1984, New Zealand's economic strategy acquired a new coherence. It built on some earlier changes, especially the CER agreement with Australia, but there was a change of emphasis of a magnitude not seen since 1938. The essential change was towards a determination to make the best possible use of New Zealand resources so as to minimize the difference in living standards available in New Zealand and in those countries with which comparisons are usually made. This had two major aspects: improving the Government's own economic performance, and allowing other decision-makers more discretion within a general framework designed to encourage responsiveness to international price signals.

Determination to tackle the Government's own use of resources was shown most clearly in a process of public sector reorganization.[26] Key components of this were reform of state-owned enterprises, and the financial management reform process within the core public service. Reorganization of the 'Think Big' projects of the previous government, which included acknowledging the uneconomic use of resources which had resulted and providing a commercial basis for future operations, can be seen as a component of the former.

When a government department was invited to pursue both social and commercial objectives, it could arrange things to suit its own convenience, claiming that commercial objectives had to be tempered by social considerations and that social objectives had to be sacrificed to commercial pressures. The Government tried to separate state commercial activities and organize them as state-owned enterprises with clear commercial objectives. The essence of the SOE reorganization was to facilitate monitoring of efficient use of assets which are owned by the public, entrusting commercial objectives to management while reserving social considerations for the Government which can contract with an SOE where social and commercial considerations conflict. This had the additional advantage of making 'transparent' the use of public funds for particular purposes; it became easier to distinguish considered responses to social needs from compromises with special interests. In practice, there were few government subsidies and this engendered criticism from those who formerly benefited from concealed subsidization. Furthermore, the corporatization process left enterprises with managements which were not subject to normal financial monitoring through the stock exchange; the threat of takeovers is a powerful incentive to effective management, and there was therefore always doubt over whether maximum efficiency was being achieved. The Government concluded that it could sell several of its commercial operations for more than the net value of the income stream it could expect from them if they were maintained as SOEs. This was a highly controversial decision. On the one hand, it was argued that what was important was New Zealand control of important national interests and that this did not require ownership of commercial activities; it was therefore sensible to put those activities into a form where they made the best possible use of the resources they used. On the other hand, it was argued that the gains to local control which had been achieved since 1938 were being sacrificed. Most economists endorse the former argument, while being critical of some of the detailed judgements about appropriate sale prices. (Much public discussion was in terms of the sale of public assets to reduce government debt levels; 'selling the family silver'. Yet the key issue was not the Government's (notional) balance sheet but the use of resources by society as a whole.)

A similar verdict can be offered on the more general process of public sector reform. Departments were reorganized, with permanent heads (renamed chief executives) given more autonomy and responsibility for managing the resources at their disposal. The relationship between government and departments was changed from funding programmes to purchasing defined outputs. In essence, private sector management practices were introduced where possible. There was inevitably a great deal of concern about their future by existing public servants. There was a clear thrust in the State Services Commission towards finding appropriate places in the Government's organizations for all its staff, enabling managers to transfer staff to where they could best contribute to the Government's objectives. Nevertheless, many people lost their jobs, and expensive redundancy packages did not always seem adequate to them. There were also wider questions which still need reflection and innovative thinking. The relationship between the accountability of public servants to ministers and the accountability of the Executive to Parliament is one of the most important ones. Questions about how departments co-operate to give primacy to the interests of the Government as a whole remain problematical. Nevertheless, as was shown in a review of 1991, few people would reverse the fundamental changes which were achieved by the State

Sector Act (1988) and the Public Finance Act (1989).

The importance attached to providing an environment in which other decisionmakers were induced to respond to market signals is shown most clearly in the removal of producer subsidies and the reduction of protection. The former was carried out quickly; the latter was where the CER agreement was most important — it had already provided a timetable and this required only some acceleration. Ironically, the reduction of both subsidies and tariffs meant that the net effect on producers was much less than often thought (although individual producers had highly variable experiences).[27] What was most important in this process was that producers ceased to think that any action on their part required ministerial approval. New Zealand industrialists and managers were encouraged to develop the skills required to manage international businesses rather than cultivate their political lobbying abilities.

Encouraging decision-makers to respond to opportunities necessarily promoted efforts to remove barriers in the way of their doing so, and the Government therefore implemented a process of regulatory reform.[28] The intention was to remove inappropriate regulations, not all regulation. However, as the process started from a position where official controls were excessively detailed, it was not easy to maintain that distinction in popular discussion. Regulatory reform in the financial sector consisted of sweeping away a great many controls that had little economic support, and which were administratively impracticable in the face of changing technology. In other areas, there has been debate about whether only appropriate regulations are maintained.

The argument for 'transparency' — that if there are reasons for government to facilitate the operations of some group in society, they should be exposed for public scrutiny and debate — was applied not only to SOEs and the general area of regulatory activity, but also to industry assistance. The Government generally won high praise for its 'micro-economic' policy, by which is meant its actions on protection and assistance to individual industries. Naturally, even here, the verdict was far from unanimous. Farming interests believed that the removal of assistance was not even-handed, and those formerly employed in industries adversely affected by the removal of protection tended to believe that the Government made a wrong judgement about the social value of their activities.

Much more controversial, however, was macroeconomic policy. The Government's policy was to encourage the best use of New Zealand's resources in relation to world markets. It wanted to encourage what became known as 'restructuring', a reorientation of New Zealand firms and enterprises towards being international businesses rather than providers to a protected domestic market. But it also had to manage its own revenue and expenditure, and it was not easy to reconcile its fiscal position so as to support the 'restructuring' it wished to promote. Its problems and actions are conveniently discussed in terms of two components, tax policy and the combination of monetary policy, fiscal policy, and the exchange rate. But high-level policy discussion always saw the components as closely interrelated, and also interrelated with microeconomic policy.

On tax policy,[29] the key actions were to implement a switch from direct to indirect tax (recommended by various bodies since at least 1967)[30] and broadening the tax base so as to obtain a given total revenue from a lower average tax rate. The switch to indirect tax was achieved through a wide-ranging goods and services tax (GST), a value-added tax implemented with unusually few exemptions and now widely recognized internationally as a model. The administrative difficulties of GST were immense, but so was the determination to deal with them, and the introduction was extra-ordinarily smooth. On its own, the introduction of GST would have had undesired implications for income distribution but GST was not introduced on its own. The accompanying changes to social security benefits provided compensating changes in income distribution, although whether they were entirely adequate remains a matter of dispute.

Tax policy changes involved much more than GST. The basic thrust was to extend the tax base and reduce rates of tax and opportunities for avoidance. The process is a continuing one. The intellectual problems of dealing fairly and effectively with income derived from overseas are far from solved. So are those concerned with income which can be taken in the form of capital gains. Equally contentious is the appropriate treatment of savings, especially those in the form of superannuation contributions.

Issues of tax policy have been approached with a genuine attempt to promote efficiency and equity. Furthermore, they were approached at a high level of intellectual commitment, too much so for some practitioners who complained about the complexity and speed with which change was effected. Policymakers attempted to look beyond the superficial first effects of any particular measure and to include in their analysis the ultimate effects on the way in which resources in New Zealand would be used (thus con-fronting the fundamental issue of incomes in New Zealand relative to those available elsewhere) and on the distribution of income, not only through the initial impact but after allowing for reactions to government initiatives.

Tax policy was controversial enough, but it was the general stance of fiscal policy which attracted most dissent. The Government chose to withdraw from dealing in foreign currency and to allow the exchange rate to be determined in a free market. It gave up direct controls on wages, prices, and interest rates, but made a determined assault on inflation. To do so, it refused to use its power to create money, insisting on 'fully funding' any deficit between its revenue and its expenditure. That is, it borrowed from the public to cover its deficit so ensuring that there was no injection to the domestic economy. (Although largely forgotten now, 'fully funding' was a major item of debate in the mid-1980s.) Eventually, it greatly enhanced the autonomy of the Reserve Bank, and set it in a legislative framework which required it to focus its efforts on securing price stability. Such changes were radical, and far from understood. Nor did the Government secure immediately the outcomes it wanted. The Government's need to borrow required it to offer attractive interest rates, and these attracted investors from overseas as well as from within New

Zealand. As investment funds flowed into a free foreign exchange market, the exchange rate rose, and exporters, both agricultural and otherwise, found their returns from overseas sales worth less in New Zealand currency. Consumers gained from cheaper imports, but the loss of jobs from industry was more visible and painful. While there were some apparent countervailing gains by 1987, the international stock market crash of that year impacted heavily, revealing the unstable nature of some companies which had seemed to prosper in the new environment. Even by the middle of 1992, many thought that any gains from the change in policy were illusory. It therefore needs some care to spell out the nature of the policy and its effects. The background to all fiscal policy decisions was a level of overseas debt that was regarded as undesirable.[31] There was never any prospect (after the election campaign of 1984) that New Zealand would not be able to meet its obligations, but the level of overseas public debt was high. It was expensive to service, and would become more so if international rating agencies decided that the riskiness of existing instruments had increased. Interest payments, on the total debt and not only on the overseas portion, constituted a significant fraction of total government spending, and reduced the Government's freedom of manoeuvre. The lessons of the 1930s had not been forgotten, but Government's management of its own affairs had become markedly more important than it was in the 1950s and 1960s. There was therefore always concern with the level and nature of its expenditure. But that expenditure was critical to activities which were seen by many as essential to the social life of New Zealand (although criticized by others).

In its first term from 1984–87, the fourth Labour Government concentrated on getting in place a change of economic policy. Because of the joint objectives of efficiency and equity, that inevitably provoked debate over social policy; in areas such as tax policy, regulatory reform, and state sector reorganization, pressures which are often described as 'social' were central to defining the economic problems facing New Zealand and to the Government's response to them. It was, however, always clear that a more concentrated reformulation of particular aspects of social policy was on the agenda following immediate economic issues. After a great deal of hesitation, the personnel of a Royal Commission on Social Policy was appointed in 1986 and it reported in April, 1988.[32] There was a consensus on the general desirability of a wide-ranging review of the social policy which had developed from the Social Security Act of 1938, but no agreement on how it should proceed. The Commission adopted the approach of gathering a very wide range of opinion. It compiled a very long document which will be a source for academic study for many years. But it did not develop a sharp analysis of where social policy should be directed now. Popular opinion is naturally conservative — people tend to be satisfied except for their particular concerns — and to be divided. Thus people could readily agree that social and economic policy should be integrated, but they did not recognize how integrated they have always been, and where there were sharp differences of opinion, the Government was given little guidance on which option it should take.

The thrust of government policy was towards securing 'quality' of government expenditure, ensuring that public assets and public funds were used as well as possible for the objectives towards which they were directed. And those objectives still reflected the overriding aims of efficiency and equity. It was, however, difficult to persuade people that that is different from reducing government expenditure for its own sake. People tend to think that fiscal pressures can easily be resolved by reducing spending which is other than that which supports their particular interests. The intellectual and political difficulties are great. Economists think naturally of income maximization, not because they are materialists but because incomes provide people with choices. Even for policy objectives which are usually expressed in terms like 'participation in society' and which are therefore thought of as 'social' rather than 'economic', the experience of most people depends on their ability to make decisions about the disposition of household incomes. This is especially true of incomes earned in the labour market, which is a principal reason why employment levels have such social significance. But participation in society extends to collective activity, to the sense of belonging or social cohesion which follows from sharing in joint endeavours. Society may want to allocate some goods or services according to 'need' rather than according to income. It then has to find some means of judging 'need' and some process for ensuring that responsible institutions satisfy their mandate rather than use resources for their own purposes. It is not enough to say 'collective action' and rule out further debate about appropriate policies. Costs have to be allocated. Cosy collective arrangements do not always benefit the relatively powerless in society.

Between 1987 and 1990, the Labour Government was not able to resolve these dilemmas. It introduced changes in the education and health services which were designed to locate decision-making with those who were most likely to use resources wisely. But it failed to persuade opinion leaders, its own supporters, or the electorate that it was implementing a social policy which reconciled efficiency and equity. The National Government elected in 1990 initially seemed to have a simpler task. It had become concerned about 'welfare dependency' and it was less committed to maintaining the social services which had been built up after 1938. It was able to argue that 'self reliance' should be pursued in the social field as it had been in economic affairs. It therefore reduced a number of social welfare benefits as well as pursuing and extending the changes which had been made in education and health. Despite its advantages, it found that political pressures gave it difficulties just as they had its predecessor. In particular, it could not reduce the level of old age pensions as much as it intended (partly at least because of unwise commitments made in the course of the 1990 election).

The National Government found it easier to make changes in the labour market. Throughout the 1950s and 1960s, New Zealand rested heavily on collective wage bargaining. Indeed, the key instrument was often the General Wage Order of the Arbitration Court, which, in effect, adjusted all wage rates simultaneously. That system could not cope with the high rates of inflation which were experienced in the 1970s, but much of the basic system survived. There were strong links between key elements of the framework of the labour market: a registration system reserved coverage of employees in particular occupations to individual unions, 'blanket coverage' extended the wage rates of awards to employers not directly involved in their negotiation, and compulsory conciliation and arbitration provided that an outside authority resolved disputes so that employers and employees were not forced to find mutual agreement. Furthermore, because wage rates were imposed from outside, employers and employees did not have an incentive to find an accommodation of their distinct interests which served the wider social issues of making good use of all resources. International thinking was putting more and more emphasis on management within the firm as the source of productivity advance, which is in turn the source of increased incomes. ('Management' here is to be understood very widely to include communication and co-operation at all levels of employment.) The interrelationship between the elements of the labour market made it difficult to effect change in any one while leaving the others unchanged, but the labour market involves many people, including many not easily able to adapt to radical change. The Labour Government also had links to the trade union movement, but this was probably a minor element in its decision to use a slow pace of change. Compulsory arbitration was abandoned, but the strategy adopted was to widen the possibilities for negotiation between employers and employees, leaving them both to discover how a less constrained environment could work to their mutual interest.

The Labour Relations Act (1987) was much criticized by both employers and trade unions. It had the potential to stimulate desirable change. But at the time of the election of the National Government, it was unclear whether that change was occurring as fast as was desirable. In any case, the new Government adopted a quite different strategy. The Employment Contracts Act (1991) swept away most of the inherited structures. Its impact is still far from clear. Fears of immediate exploitation were not realized except in a few cases which probably owed little to the specific legislation. Employers and employees used their new freedom; outdated provisions were revised, as was the case with penal rates for weekend and evening work which reflected a social climate of an earlier era. Some employees lost, but others gained and so did consumers. The net balance in that case was probably in favour of the Act, but deeper implications in areas such as the relations between employers and employees in smaller and provincial concerns remain uncertain, as does the whole issue of whether the gains were not realizable under the 1987 legislation.

There were many calls between 1990 and 1992, as there had been between 1987 and 1990, for integration of social and economic policy.

They were mostly disguised demands for a different set of government policies; economic and social policies were integrated. From 1985, monetary policy was used to gain control of inflation and by 1991, for the first time for many years, it was less than that experienced by New Zealand's trading partners. The cost was heavy because high interest rates discouraged investment and employment. They also attracted an inflow of foreign funds and its effect of raising the New Zealand exchange rate strengthened pressure on producers of tradeable goods. But this could have been avoided only by a faster diminution of the Budget deficit. The essential policy decision was one with as many social as economic dimensions: the relative share of adjustment costs to be borne by those dependent for employment and incomes on the tradeables sector and those similarly dependent on government expenditure. Most social of all was the judgement that existing New Zealanders should rely less on forcing succeeding generations to finance current consumption. Discussion of the Budget deficit and the general strategy of fiscal policy is often regarded as technically demanding and of interest only to economists, but it is at the core of a social strategy.

Indeed, while successive governments have been criticized for adopting an 'inflation first' strategy, their overall policy has not had any single objective. 'Efficiency and equity' have been taken seriously. Macro-economic policy has been guided by a desire to improve the Government's use of the resources under its direct control and to guide private decisions towards a sensible use of resources relative to the international economy. Within that, monetary policy has been directed to controlling inflation, and in order to strengthen control of monetary trends, the exchange rate was allowed to float from March 1985. (It is difficult for people to believe that when the monetary authorities refrain from fixing the exchange rate, social control may be increased, but that is in fact the case.)

The whole structure of policy was aimed at satisfying community aspirations, social and economic. But those community aspirations are diverse and inconsistent so that no government can ever be entirely successful. And criticism of the Government grew as unemployment levels climbed. New Zealand was not an attractive place for investment. The sharemarket crash of 1987 had a deep impact, especially in the property sector, and the climate of opinion, most obviously in Auckland, remained pessimistic. While a careful review of the evidence shows that experience is highly variable within all sectors of the economy, with firms which were able to adapt to changed circumstances finding areas of expansion, the news media remained dominated by the negative aspects of economic restructuring.[33]

It is conventional now to say that after 1984, the Government took the right actions but in the wrong sequence, that it should have moved first on labour and goods markets and only later deregulated the financial markets.[34] There are obvious intellectual attractions in timing policy interventions according to the relative responsiveness of private sector participants, but such a choice was never available to policymakers. Exchange controls were breaking down anyway in 1984 as they were widely seen to be both ineffective and inappropriate in the face of technical change in communications. In a particular example, officials were well aware that there were dangers in floating the exchange rate when the Budget deficit was high. They recommended reducing the deficit as much as possible, and then faced the question — given that political judgement set a limit to how rapidly the deficit could be reduced — was it wise to float the exchange rate in order to gain monetary control? Advising them that it would have been even better to first further reduce the deficit is hardly helpful.

The policies which were adopted owed a great deal to analyses of New Zealand's own position, but they clearly related to an international climate of ideas and to policy changes in other countries. They are sometimes described as 'Reaganite' but more often as 'Thatcherite'. There are both differences and similarities between the policies which have been followed in New Zealand and those pursued in other countries. In some countries, such as the UK and the USA, a policy thrust towards economic efficiency was accompanied by a conservative political trend which favoured measures to revive traditional values and wished to promote individual reliance over collective activity. The link was not universal; it was not present in Australia, a number of European countries or Japan. In the latter country, indeed, there was a broader movement towards raising the emphasis on 'quality of life', and of promoting the 'consumer society' against a traditional emphasis on savings and family-based security, almost the reverse of the social context in Britain and the USA. In New Zealand, some people had a political desire to reduce public activity relative to private, and other commentators asked whether increased reliance on decentralized decision-making is necessarily accompanied by a decline of compassion relative to self-interest, but these are issues to be debated, not necessary concomitants of the economic policies which were followed. Simply characterizing those policies as 'Rogernomics', and assuming that they have all the same connotations as 'Reaganomics' and 'Thatcherism', is based on far too narrow a range of international comparisons.

In 1938, thoughtful commentators argued about 'insulationism' as a policy prescription for local circumstances. Political debate, however, proceeded much more in terms such as 'socialism' and 'nationalization' which were imported from abroad. In the 1980s, while there has been a great deal of informed debate about the future of the New Zealand economy, much political discussion has used rhetoric such as 'New Right' which has also been imported uncritically. It is now more likely to come from the USA than from the UK, but it is no more guaranteed to be appropriate to New Zealand's real issues than was the case with earlier imports.

Until the mid-1970s, each generation of New Zealanders had access to more goods and services than its predecessors. The national income statistics in Graph 1 show this clearly. So too do the visible improvements in housing, especially the layout of sections and the availability of household durables, and the increased mobility afforded by cars and roads. It can also be deduced from the way in which a richer society could support such specialized activities as full-time writers, artists, and potters. The post-1938 economy produced more growth of income per capita than any previous period of more than a few years. Indeed, for a while in the early 1970s, the 'problems of affluence' gained prominence; until the 1970s 'development' and the distribution of rewards were the dominant issues for New Zealand economists and politicians. In the change of policy direction from 1984, it proved more difficult than expected to reallocate resources among economic activities, and there was a lack of economic growth. Demographic trends also resulted in a higher ratio of people in the labour force. Wage levels increased even less than household incomes.

Even earlier, the rate of growth varied from time to time. Comparisons of the country's rate of growth with those of other countries need to be treated with care because the choice of time period can make a significant difference, and because the exchange rates used in many comparisons may not measure accurately the relative prices which determine the levels of goods and services available. New Zealand became wealthier during the Second World War although the creation of income was not then a primary objective. The recovery of Europe and the stockpiling that preceded and accompanied the Korean war provided markets for New Zealand goods and gave a pronounced boost to average incomes. Because a high level was reached in the early 1950s, the rate of growth over that decade as a whole was low. Studies made at the end of the 1950s were unduly pessimistic because the distorting effect of the Korean war was underrated.[35] Acceleration in the 1960s was sharply interrupted in 1967–68; the last years of that decade and the first years of the next were a muted repetition of the early 1950s as export prices rose dramatically. The international oil crisis of the early 1970s, and its repetition at the end of the decade had the effect of reducing New Zealand's income although consumption was maintained through overseas borrowing. The adjustment process undertaken in the 1980s included reductions in income to, in effect, pay for some of the earlier consumption financed by borrowing and also to achieve a reallocation of resources. The overriding observation is that New Zealand's income growth, through the 1960s as well as more recently, was lower than that achieved in many other countries.

The New Zealand Government of the early 1950s presided over a community which was essentially complacent about its expectations of economic growth and higher living standards. It is quite possible that New Zealand once did have the highest level of real per capita income in the world[36] but that had been a long time earlier and by the 1950s any simplistic economic interpretation of phrases such as 'God's Own Country' was strained. It was nevertheless not uncommon. There had been a distressing interruption in the Depression of the 1930s, and a further disruption during the Second World War, but the world was surely returning to normal in the 1950s?

The general impression towards the end of the 1980s is very different.

After some years of low rates of economic growth, and in the face of unfavourable levels of indicators such as unemployment, the prevailing belief is that New Zealand has experienced no growth and has become a poor country. That impression is no better substantiated than the earlier complacency. While 'real income' is usually understood as a technical and reasonably precise term, 'standards of living' is subject to more varying interpretations. It would therefore be possible to find several senses in which it could be said that standards of living had declined since the early 1950s. But there is one overwhelming reason for the change from complacency to excessive pessimism about New Zealand's economic standing, and it does not depend on the distinction between real incomes and standards of living.

It is simply that levels of incomes in New Zealand have declined relative to those of other countries. New Zealanders are accustomed to making international comparisons with the relatively rich countries of the world, especially those which belong to the OECD. International comparisons of income levels are notoriously treacherous. But the general picture is quite clear.[37] Throughout the period since 1960, and probably in the 1950s too, other countries were growing more rapidly than New Zealand. At first, it seemed simply that countries were recovering from the Second World War, but differential growth rates continued long after such a 'rebound' provided an explanation. Japan seemed to be an exceptional case, as indeed it was, but other countries were emulating it while New Zealand was not.

Towards the end of the 1980s, New Zealand's real income and standards of living were lower than those of the countries with which comparisons are normally made — Australia, Western Europe, and Japan. That was the fundamental reason for a reappraisal of economic strategy and a change of policy by the Government elected in 1984. At the same time, New Zealand remains a relatively wealthy country in a wider international perspective; statements about its relative position in a small subset of the world's economies were wrongly translated into belief that levels of income and standards of living were low and declining.

In the thirty years after 1938, local control became stronger, increasing the amount, complexity, and interest of local decision-making. Inter-dependence with the international economy remained important but a less direct determinant of fortunes. Income growth came from the more efficient use of resources in all sectors but agriculture retained special importance because of its close link with the foreign exchange constraint. That was as true in 1970 as it had been earlier, although the link had become much more complex. Most industry then remained an employment sponge rather than an engine of growth, although less so, and it did adopt more modern technology, use more varied skills, and offer different immediate challenges. Government came to carry out a wider range of functions within the economy, but decentralization of decision-making to individual firms and households remained a basic characteristic.

The 1970s brought new challenges, and mere modification of the existing structures proved unable to counter New Zealand's relative, but not absolute, decline in living standards. The 1980s brought a strong response in the sphere of policy formulation, but not in implementation and economic response. The challenge of preserving a unique New Zealand culture, participating in the international economy so as to satisfy New Zealanders' aspirations about relative living standards, remains for the 1990s. The first test will be whether an appropriate provision of collective goods can be combined with such an economy. The assumptions of the 1960s that social services need be only a supplement to a system of full employment cannot be sustained. This is not to say that unemployment needs to be tolerated but that the means by which full employment was achieved in earlier times are no longer available.

CHAPTER 17

The Social Pattern

Graeme Dunstall

For the period 1940–80, the pattern of New Zealand society is not simply defined. Forty years saw marked changes in the context of material life: war, prosperity and complacency, recession and uncertainty. War, bringing both austerity and full employment, was a hinge between periods of depression and affluence. Unsurpassed prosperity and social tranquillity characterized the two decades from 1945. From the late 1950s there were signs of rebellion among adolescents; by the early 1960s youth culture had been commercialized; from the mid-1960s it was politicized as counter culture. The late 1960s brought recession and participation in the Vietnam war; new forms of urban protest sprang up, the most enduring of which in the 1970s were a Māori cultural resurgence and a new feminist movement. Optimists saw in the growing diversity of lifestyle a new social pattern emerging. Yet in the social fabric, elements of continuity were as pervasive in the 1970s as they were in the 1940s.

The Second World War, at the beginning of the period, had few long-term effects in demographic and material terms. It claimed the lives of 11,625 New Zealanders, and a further 17,000 were wounded, but civilian life and property were largely unharmed. Over 150,000 men were in the armed forces at their peak in September 1942, and the civilian population came to know blackouts, sirens, fire watching, army parades, and fund-raising campaigns.[1] But the basic social pattern was disrupted only temporarily. In many respects the war merely accentuated the uniformity and drabness of life inherited from the depression of the 1930s.

From the 1940s, however, a number of long-established processes accelerated. Population growth, fertility transition, urbanization, and the development of a white-collar society helped to bring a new distinctiveness and complexity to New Zealand society. The social pattern developed an indigenous flavour. As M. K. Joseph observed:

> Consider now the nature of distilled
> Water which has boiled and left behind
> In the retort rewarding sediment
> Of salts and toxins. Chemically pure of course
> (No foreign bodies here) but to the taste
> Tasteless and flat. Let it spill on the ground,

Leach out its salts, accumulate its algae,
Be living: the savour's in impurity.
Is that what we are? something that boiled away
In the steaming flask of nineteenth century Europe?
Innocuous until now, or just beginning
To make its own impression on the tongue.[2]

Post-war New Zealand still lived on the intellectual and social capital produced in North America and Europe, yet the salts of a distinctive culture had begun to accumulate. In the minutiae of life, differences from the parent culture were already apparent. The European colonists like the Māori before them were fashioning a material culture to fit local needs. Social change in the twentieth century was only marginally influenced (before the 1960s) by the presence of the Māori, but it was continuously modified by successive waves of British immigrants and a world shrunk by ever-improving communications. Repeated infusions of distilled water kept the local sediment diluted. The mid-1970s saw the end of the great European migration; at the same time a Māori cultural resurgence gathered momentum in the cities. A distinctively New Zealand society had begun to emerge.

The new complexity of post-war society was wrought not only by changes in population and material life but also by shifts in opinion and belief that began in the 1930s and early 1940s. These were the years in which the dream of a material utopia was refurbished: New Zealand was to become, without class war, a 'country where the plenty of the machine age shall assure to all the rich life in goods and leisure that the genius and natural resources of our country make possible'.[3] Labour rejuvenated the egalitarian tradition in all its ambiguity: equality of condition and equality of opportunity for all. War heightened expectations of reconstruction and reform, and economic aspirations rose as a result of full employment. To a degree they were to be fulfilled: full employment continued for twenty years after the war, underpinning ever-increasing affluence. In this most sustained period of prosperity of the twentieth century the state took on new dimensions — maintaining affluence, tempering inequalities, ensuring security, and helping to maintain the high degree of uniformity in New Zealand life. To the comfortable and the complacent, the ethos of equality had been realized in the social pattern.

Yet the material utopia remained beyond grasp. Expectations rose continually in the acquisitive society. And the demands of materialism proved insatiable, as politicians found to their cost. The welfare state bred new problems: inflation, and with it new inequalities and new anxieties. The state might have 'civilized capitalism' but it had not stifled competitive individualism. During the late 1960s a range of youthful voices articulated the problems of the spirit in a materialistic culture. 'New Zealand is in the grip of a new depression', declared the manifesto of the newly formed Values Party in 1972. 'It is a depression which arises not from a lack of affluence but almost from too much of it. It is a depression in human values. . . .'[4] The years of full employment ended in 1967. From the late

1960s the economy took a turn for the worse, a decline broken only briefly by the export boom of 1973–74. For many the promise of affluence became uncertain. A further dimension was added to the doubts and divisions in society.[5]

The impact of all these developments on New Zealand's social structure is difficult to assess. For, despite recent research, the pattern of stratification 'has yet to be described in a way that is at all convincing'. It has perhaps been obscured most of all by the persistence of the concept of equality: the ruling idea of post-war society was that 'everybody acts the same, receives the same amount of the world's goods, everyone moves in the same direction'.[6] The ethos of equality sapped the consciousness of class. National and Labour politicians alike denied the existence of class war: for J. R. Marshall in 1947 New Zealand had 'no class distinctions to justify the theory of the class war'; for A. H. Nordmeyer in 1963 there was 'no place today for what used to be known as the class struggle'. Despite a growing tension from the late 1960s between the ideal of equality and the facts of material life, categories employed in the political rhetoric continued to be broad and all embracing: Norman Kirk talked of the 'little man', R. D. Muldoon of the 'ordinary bloke'.[7] Even so, politicians knew where to find their voters, and New Zealand politics remained class-based.[8] Many people still retained a general awareness of their position in a broad social layer, although they did not necessarily have a sense of class solidarity. In New Zealand, as in other advanced industrial societies, class awareness remained while class consciousness waned. A vaguely felt sense of class was fragmented in ways that blurred the contours of the evolving social structure. Consciousness of race, sex, and age increasingly cut across the broad layers of class. Patterns of consumption and leisure also began to suggest a more subtle social hierarchy. The continuing process of occupational change led to greater social differentiation in the urban world.

Occupational mobility contributed to the general feeling of fluidity in the social structure, but this was largely a product of population growth and change. This chapter, in examining facets of the social structure — housing, occupations, education, the distribution of income, social welfare, and patterns of consumption and leisure — looks first at demographic change in post-war New Zealand.

Attitudes and assumptions regarding population altered radically in the forty years following 1940. From the 1880s the Pākehā birth rate had followed the British trend — falling steeply until by the mid-1930s the population was barely replacing itself by natural increase. By contrast the Māori population started to grow rapidly in the inter-war years. In the late 1930s and early 1940s concern mounted in both Britain and New Zealand at the apparent imminence of a stationary European population. Fears were accentuated by the war. Remedial measures such as family and marriage allowances, cheaper housing, and the education of 'our young citizens' in the 'great creative function of reproduction and parenthood' were advocated.[9] In this light, Labour's welfare policies had a pro-natalist edge.

But fears were misplaced. The years 1945–75 saw the most sustained period of population growth this century — from 1.7 million to just over 3 million people. Indeed, the rate of growth at over 2 per cent per annum until the mid-1960s was high in comparison with most other countries of predominantly European population, and higher than the most optimistic forecast in 1946.[10] Both immigration and natural increase contributed to growth. Net immigration to New Zealand between 1947 and 1968 was 225,000. About 17 per cent of the immigrants were assisted by the Government. But only a third of the total population increase over this period came from new settlers and their children. The role of natural increase was more significant than ever before.[11]

Both Pākehā and Māori populations expanded rapidly, but the two peoples continued to have separate demographic histories. For Pākehā there was a 'baby boom'. From the low point of just over 16 per 1,000 in 1935–36, the European birth rate rose to over 26 per 1,000 by the late 1940s, a level maintained until 1961. The reversal was due in part to marriages and births delayed during the depression and war years being made up in the late 1940s. But there were more fundamental reasons for the change. The post-war years saw the end of the West European marriage pattern — the centuries-old pattern distinguished by high age at marriage and a high proportion of people who never married. Marriage became virtually universal and occurred at an earlier age. Such a trend was encouraged by full employment and the introduction of social security, the increasing participation of married women in the work-force (allowing marriages to be established on the basis of two incomes), and an improvement of birth control within marriage. Parenthood was still, however, a cultural imperative, and during the 'baby boom' children quickly followed marriage. The proportion of couples with two to four children was larger than that prevailing in the inter-war years, but there was no return to the large families of a century earlier. Prosperity enabled more couples to achieve their ideal of a small family more quickly. By contrast Māori families were larger. The birth rate remained high, and population growth came from a fall in mortality, especially infant mortality and mortality from tuberculosis. Further, a general improvement in living conditions followed from urbanization. But the gap between Māori and Pākehā health standards pointed to continuing inequalities.

With the 1960s came a new phase of population growth. From 1962 there was a sharp fall in European fertility, and by 1978 it had dropped almost to replacement level. Marriage at an early age continued, but families became smaller. The number of childless couples grew. A revolution in contraceptive methods (epitomized by 'the pill') gave a new freedom to women, heightening aspirations for self-fulfilment beyond the family. The fall in fertility was masked by the maturing of the 'boom' babies, who formed families in the late 1960s and early 1970s. And the rate of ex-nuptial births grew by a third in the period 1962–73, hinting at further changes in the marriage pattern. The Māori population continued to grow rapidly, reaching 270,000 in 1976. Mortality still fell, gradually approaching the Pākehā level (although a differential persisted). But a substantial decline in infant mortality triggered a sharp fall in Māori fertility from the mid-1960s. The approach of Māori fertility to Pākehā norms by the late 1970s was symptomatic of the transformation in Māori life since the war.

The late 1960s saw also a change in the balance of migration. For the first time since the depression, New Zealand began to lose population by migration. The balance was reversed spectacularly but briefly in the early 1970s when there was a net gain of some 108,000. But in 1976 large-scale emigration resumed, and in 1978–79, for the first time in New Zealand's history, the net loss of population by migration (mainly to Australia) exceeded the gain from natural increase. A stationary population had suddenly arrived. Yet the fears of the 1940s did not reappear. From the late 1960s there had been a profound shift in attitudes to population size and growth. Concern for the environment now loomed large.[12] Immigrants went out of favour for other reasons (particularly in Auckland, where the majority arrived): 'poms' from Britain competed for housing and jobs and Pacific Islanders (growing from 26,271 to 61,354 between 1966 and 1976) brought out latent feelings of racism.

The structure of the population altered significantly in the years after 1945, when 27 per cent of New Zealanders were under the age of fifteen. As a result of high fertility, this proportion had risen to 34 per cent by 1961. The Māori population was even more youthful: 50 per cent of Māori were under fifteen years in 1966. The governments of the 1950s were forced to meet the consequences of natural increase, in the provision of health care, education, employment, and housing. And the pressures on social policies continued in the 1960s as the 'baby boom' generation came of age. By 1976, for example, those in their twenties numbered half a million, an increase of two-thirds in fifteen years. Such was the demographic context for the soaring crime rates of the 1960s. However, falling fertility was to bring another kind of change: an ageing population. The growing numbers and proportion of those over the age of sixty placed increasing demands on community resources. Superannuation became a political issue in the 1970s.

By the late 1960s attitudes to population growth were influenced by the intensification of other demographic trends: patterns of redistribution within the country.[13] The rural world, shrinking since the turn of the century, grew smaller more rapidly after the Second World War. In 1936 a third of the population was rural, by 1976 the proportion was one-sixth. Urbanization was fuelled both by demographic and economic growth, and particularly by the effects of technological change in the countryside. In 'Littledene' (Oxford), H. C. D. Somerset's archetype of Canterbury rural life, there were about forty tractors in 1938; by 1955 there were 200 and haymaking had become 'a one-man process all through'.[14] Though declining in relative terms, the rural population continued to grow, as a result of both rising fertility and the subdivision and resettlement of land, especially in the Taupo and Bay of Plenty regions. By the end of the 1960s, however, the rural world was shrinking absolutely as well as relatively, almost all of the strictly rural areas registering declining populations.

The second main pattern of redistribution was the shifting regional balance. The North Island's share of the population rose from 67 per cent in 1945 to 73 per cent in 1976. But there was no absolute decline of the South Island population — it increased by some 305,000. The northerly drift altered the distribution within both islands, particularly in the North Island. The population of the King Country, West Coast, and hinterland of Dunedin, for instance, fell in the post-war period, while the Hawke's Bay, Manawatu, Nelson, and Southland regions grew substantially. Most growth occurred where the northernizing, urbanizing tendencies coincided — in the Auckland, South Auckland, and Bay of Plenty regions.

The third pattern was the changing distribution of population within the urbanizing world. Even in the Auckland region, sizeable towns such as Huntly, Te Aroha, and Morrinsville lost people in the late 1960s. The main centres were growing disproportionately, and Auckland above all. This divergence had already been established by the First World War; it increased markedly after the Second. At the end of the war just over half the population was already in the fourteen largest centres (defined statistically as 'urban areas'). By 1976, four more centres had joined the ranks of the urban areas, which now contained over two-thirds of the population. In 1945 Auckland had less population than Wellington and Christchurch together; thirty years later it had as many people (some 743,000) as the next three biggest centres combined. By the mid-1970s Auckland had a quarter of the country's population, and a third of those employed in manufacturing. Climate, jobs, and the 'contagion of numbers' drew migrants; its market and labour were magnets for entrepreneurs. Auckland grew inexorably, becoming the focus of prosperity, inequality, and anxiety.

Within the cities, most people lived in suburbia. The most spectacular example of the suburbanizing process was Auckland. Of its four statistical urban areas the central area (roughly the isthmus) was by the end of the war already a series of suburbs 'tied together by a sewerage system', encompassing the bulk of Auckland's population.[15] The proportion had dropped to two-fifths by 1976, by which time the population on the isthmus had virtually stopped growing. Spatially, Auckland had become vast on an international scale: stretching some 40 km south from Torbay to Papakura, some 25 km east from Massey to Howick. Availability of land and the universality of the motor-car since the war rapidly obliterated any sense of Auckland as a whole. But its constituent parts came to develop lives of their own: whorls and undulations of lawn bedecked bungalows slowly meshing into subtle patterns of community and class.

A drift to the north and to the towns was compounded by natural increase within the cities. The largest centres were reproducing themselves more than ever before. In the years 1966–75, an estimated 47 per cent of Auckland's growth came from its own natural increase. A further 23 per cent came from net migration to the metropolis directly from overseas.

Where Canterbury and Otago had secured a lion's share of the Vogel immigrants, Auckland and Wellington gained most from the new arrivals of the 1950s and 1960s. The remainder of Auckland's growth in 1966–75 came from internal migration. Only a fraction of these migrants came directly from the rural areas and small towns. As the 1971 census indicated, the basic pattern of internal migration was from the rural areas to the small towns, then to larger towns and thence to cities. This census also revealed a large part of society to be very mobile: almost four in every ten New Zealanders had moved house at least once during the preceding five years. White-collar workers (part of the expanding bureaucracies, both public and private) moved further and more frequently than blue-collar workers.[16] And the greatest mobility of population was found in Auckland and Wellington. In the post-war period, migration also occurred within the largest cities: between suburbs, from the centre to the perimeter, and increasingly in the 1960s an offsetting movement back into the centre.

The post-war patterns of migration were thrown into sharp relief by the urbanization of Māori and Pacific Islanders.[17] At the end of the war, three-quarters of the Māori population still lived in the country, in areas where there were relatively few Pākehā. By the mid-1970s, three-quarters of the Māori population was urban, over a fifth living in Auckland. In the 1950s a majority of migrants from Northland went directly to Auckland. Elsewhere the patterns of movement were more complex: first to adjacent rural areas or small towns, then to the city; first young single people, then families; first to inner Auckland, then to the suburbs; East Coast Māori to Wellington and Christchurch, Taranaki and Wanganui people to the towns of the central North Island before moving to Wellington or Auckland. The movement was impelled by population pressure in the countryside and encouraged by government policy. Thousands of villagers from the Pacific Islands also came to the cities, often by a process of chain-migration, looking for jobs, education, prestige, or earnings to support families back in Samoa, Tonga, or the Cook Islands. Herein lay an important difference between the Māori and Pacific Island migrant. Through inclination (and New Zealand government policy in the case of those from Samoa and Tonga) most Pacific Island migrants were initially not settlers but visitors — 'guestworkers' or sojourners looking to return home eventually. Samoan migrants, for example, brought their 'aiga (extended family) and their church. Like the Chinese and the Indians before them, they resisted assimilation. To some Europeans and Māori they became the new aliens.

So the growth and spatial change of the population helped to bring a new complexity to the social pattern. Differences between regional rates of economic growth increased. Anxieties about regional development emerged in the 1960s, and provincialism was rekindled (most strongly in the South Island), fuelled by resentments of Auckland's prosperity and Wellington's bureaucracy. Within the large towns and cities too there was growing residential differentiation. In the 1950s and 1960s, social differentiation became more finely and clearly graded in the burgeoning suburbs. Again the concept of equality appeared to be challenged. Housing, it seemed, reflected a growing divergence of life chances.[18]

Housing in suburbia is a central motif in the post-war social pattern. Vast tracts of suburban two- to three-bedroomed bungalows resulted partly from the trend to earlier and universal marriage but they also expressed the ruling ideas about family life and child-rearing, the need for privacy and space. Housing patterns summed up the Pākehā ethos of possessive individualism, equality, cultural homogeneity, and integration in race relations.

Home-ownership lay at the heart of the prevailing ethos, reflecting aspirations for security, independence, and respectability. Ownership also brought capital gains and enhanced social status. Decent cheap rental housing might have better suited the needs of mobile families, but in post-war New Zealand there was little available.[19] True, in 1937 the Labour Government embarked on a vigorous policy of building state houses for rental to people in the medium and lower income groups. Houses were to be allocated according to the merits of each case; there was no formal income bar. Until 1945, nearly half the housing permits issued were for state dwellings, although Labour also increased state finance for private housing. By 1949, nearly 29,000 state houses had been built. However, Labour's policy was redirected by the new National Government which promoted home-ownership. From 1950 eligibility for a state house was limited to those on low incomes, and tenants were given the opportunity to purchase. Moreover, National placed greater emphasis on private building by introducing its Group Building Scheme in 1953 and easing the conditions for State Advances loans. The second Labour Government accepted the changed direction: 3 per cent building loans and capitalization of the family benefit were introduced in 1958.

Private enterprise, nurtured by the state, thus became the means of meeting a housing shortage. At the end of the war there were 47,000 'unsatisfied applications' for state houses. The pressures were symbolized in Auckland in the late 1940s by overcrowding in Freeman's Bay slums and by transit camps in Victoria Park and the Domain. Depression and war had created a backlog made worse by a rapidly growing population. Demand appeared to ease by the early 1960s, though a disparity between Māori and Pākehā housing standards remained.[20] Pressures built up again during the 1960s as many already housed sought to improve their status, and as the post-war generation married. The growing numbers of flats for renting and for ownership mirrored other aspects of social change in the 1960s and early 1970s: the changing marriage patterns, a growing segment of footloose city youth, an ageing population, and the existence of a tenant class unable to afford a mortgage.

As a result of housing policies, state housing areas changed in character, and 'low cost' suburbs grew. Housing patterns mirrored a pervasive prosperity, symbolized by the overall improvement in Māori housing during the 1950s and 1960s. The proportion of houses owned (with or without a mortgage) rose in the 1950s from 61 to 69 per cent. The basic style of the suburban bungalow was generally uniform: an uneasy marriage of the competing ethics of individualism and equality. Even in rural 'Littledene', the new post-war housing was 'suburban rather than rural' in style.[21] Above all, the suburban house was the focus of the consumer society with an ever-rising standard of living, measured in terms of a car (or two), a lawnmower, and a broadening range of household gadgetry. Amenities such as an electric range, washing-machine, and refrigerator which were to be found in little more than half the houses in the late 1940s were well nigh universal by the mid-1960s. New Zealanders became steadily more comfortable than ever before.

Yet some were more comfortable than others. The state, in promoting home-ownership, also increased the financial burden for the home-owner. With inflation in land and property prices (particularly in the early 1970s), new mortgagors faced increasing pressure on income. The level of home-ownership did not rise much above the proportion reached by the beginning of the 1960s and the proportion of tenants grew slightly in the late 1960s. The condition of Māori is again indicative. Migration to the city had brought an improvement in Māori housing, but most Māori could not afford to live outside areas of cheap housing.[22] Porirua and Otara became symbols of the disadvantages of race and class.

So the changing housing patterns provide clues as to the evolution of the urban social structure since the war. The housing market reflected a social gradient. By the 1940s the ends of the gradient were to be found in areas such as Parnell and Freeman's Bay in Auckland, Karori and Newtown in Wellington, Merivale and Addington in Christchurch, all of which were established before the war. Others were post-war, for example, Pakuranga and Otara, Tawa and Porirua, Burnside and Bromley. These extremities, often associated with different altitudes in the city topography, also coincided with the foci of opposing political allegiances. In the traditional National and Labour suburbs there is evidence of continuing class awareness. Typical of post-war social structure, however, was the development of broadening zones of mixed social and political character.[23] In a situation where almost every new household 'gave birth to a new house in a new suburb',[24] these neighbourhoods were demographically homogeneous; their inhabitants tended to be at a similar stage in life cycle but represented many different occupations. But there is no clear evidence that these middling neighbourhoods contained coherent self-conscious classes. The nuances of the residential patterns showed consciousness of individual status rather than of group solidarity.

Housing patterns suggest, then, that the urban social structure became increasingly complex after 1945. Perceptions of social rank became even more ambiguous, unable to be explained in simple class terms. The possibility that class consciousness diminished during the 1950s and 1960s does not, however, imply that social inequalities (or social strata) were not present in post-war New Zealand.[25] Rather the general absence of a language of class suggests that until the late 1960s there was a prevailing belief in social mobility, in a society of 'fair shares', and in a common mean in lifestyles. The nature of the post-war social structure will be examined in terms of the change in occupations and education; the distribution of income and social welfare; and the evolving patterns of consumption and leisure.

In New Zealand, as in North America, occupation, income, and lifestyle have long been the key determinants of social position, and occupation perhaps the most important. The pattern of occupations has been a concomitant of urbanization. From the early decades of the twentieth century the fastest-growing occupations were those that processed farm produce for export and serviced the needs of the farmers and the expanding ranks of town dwellers. From the 1940s the rapid growth of the welfare state and in manufacturing brought ever-increasing numbers of workers into white-collar and blue-collar occupations. As a result the social structure came closer to the pattern in North America and north-west Europe.

By the 1960s the USA had become a white-collar society; by the 1970s New Zealand had become one also — with 41 per cent of occupations white collar in 1971, 38 per cent in manual labour, and 12 per cent engaged in farming. In the trend away from farming (and possibly from urban manual labour) towards white-collar occupations, New Zealand showed signs of becoming a post-industrial society, characterized by a service economy, by the pre-eminence of a professional and technical class, and by 'the centrality of theoretical knowledge as the source of innovation and of policy formulation for the society'.[26] But the significance of these features may be overstated. Much of the movement to white-collar employment reflected increased female participation in the work-force — the proportion rising from a quarter of all women over fifteen years of age in 1951 to a third in 1971.[27] In 1971, two-thirds of the female labour force had white-collar jobs in New Zealand; only a third of the male workers, whose jobs were likely to determine family status, were white collar. (See Tables 7 and 8.)

Nor should the trend to white-collar occupations deflect attention from the continuing importance of farming — especially when compared with Australia or the USA.[28] The years from the mid-1940s to the mid-1960s were the heyday of the family farm. The number of farm holdings rose from 86,239 in 1946 to a peak of 92,395 in 1955. In these years the new farmers were mainly ex-servicemen with farming experience, 12,236 being settled by 1955 under various rehabilitation schemes. The ranks of the working farmer continued to turn over: between 1959 and 1971, 111,218 properties changed hands. New farmers were recruited largely from within rural society, among farmers' sons and sharemilkers. In post-war society farmers continued to comprise the largest single occupation: in 1972 working owners, leaseholders, and sharemilkers totalled some 67,191.

They also comprised the most coherent and self-conscious community of interests in the 1950s and 1960s. Within this, various strata could be identified, often reflecting different stages in the careers of farming families. Basic distinctions could be drawn, for example, between the grazier who employed labour, the dairy farmer who relied on his family's labour, the farm managers and sharemilkers who worked for rentiers, and farm labourers who comprised 41 per cent of the farming labour force in 1971. Different interests persisted within rural society, their concerns institutionalized by the producer boards and the produce sections of Federated Farmers. Even so in comparison with the urban dweller, the farmers remained a self-conscious social group, united by a distinctive form of production and by an entrepreneurial ethic of personal profit and independence.

Table 7: Percentage distribution of male employment by major occupational group, 1951–71

| | 1951 | | 1966 | | 1971[1] | |
	Total	Māori	Total	Māori	Total	Māori
Professional and technical	4.9	1.2	7.8	1.8	10.4	2.3
Administrative and managerial	2.8	0.1	7.1	0.6	3.5	0.3
Clerical	9.6	1.8	8.0	2.0	8.9	3.0
Sales workers	7.6	0.7	6.9	1.1	9.8	1.3
Total white collar	24.9	3.8	29.8	5.5	32.6	6.9
Service workers	5.0	2.4	4.7	3.5	5.4	4.0
Agricultural, forestry, and fishermen	22.7	39.6	16.2	20.1	14.3	15.6
Production workers, transport equipment operators, labourers	47.0	52.5	49.0	69.6	46.6	69.8
Not classifiable	0.4	1.7	0.4	1.3	1.1	3.5

1. Because of a re-classification of occupations in 1971, the 1971 percentages are not entirely comparable with those of preceding censuses.
Source: Social Trends in New Zealand (NZ Dept. of Statistics, Wellington, 1977), pp. 173–4

From the mid-1950s the farming community began to shrink, absolutely as well as relatively. By 1972 the number of farm holdings had fallen by nearly a third. The most dramatic decline was in the number of dairy farmers from nearly 40,000 in 1950 to just over 17,000 in 1976. This reflected not just changes in types of farming, but also an exodus from the ranks of the small farmer. The size of an economic unit rose progressively and land prices rose, doubling in the 1950s, and again in the 1960s, before rising steeply in the early 1970s. But recruitment did not stop (indeed the numbers of sharemilkers increased by two-fifths in 1966–70). None the less, by the early 1970s, farming had become a means of social mobility for a diminishing number.

Table 8: Percentage distribution of female employment by major occupational groups, 1951–71

	1951		1966		1971[1]	
	Total	Māori	Total	Māori	Total	Māori
Professional and						
technical	14.5	8.8	16.5	8.8	17.2	7.4
Administrative and						
managerial	0.3	0.1	2.6	0.5	0.3	0.1
Clerical	27.1	7.7	29.1	8.1	33.1	14.6
Sales workers	12.5	2.0	11.9	3.6	11.6	3.8
Total white collar	54.4	18.6	60.1	21.0	62.2	25.9
Service workers	18.7	42.0	14.5	27.9	13.7	23.0
Agricultural workers	5.2	13.7	4.9	8.8	5.2	7.5
Production workers,						
transport operators,						
and labourers	20.9	23.8	19.8	38.4	17.4	36.0
Not classifiable	0.7	1.9	0.7	3.9	1.6	7.5

1. Because of a re-classification of occupations in 1971, the 1971 percentages are not entirely comparable with those of preceding censuses.

Source: *Social Trends in New Zealand*, pp. 173–4

While the farming community shrank, the ranks of the male blue-collar workers grew spectacularly, particularly in the building, transport, and manufacturing industries.[29] By 1976 blue-collar workers totalled over 400,000 or nearly 47 per cent of the male work-force — a proportion, however, that had scarcely changed since 1951. (See Table 7.) There is little firm evidence as to the sources of the expanding work-force. Where they did not follow their fathers, farmers' sons seem to have chosen blue-collar jobs. Similarly rural Māori youth migrating to the towns contributed; by 1966, 70 per cent of Māori males were blue-collar workers; Polynesian immigrants almost completely so. As with recent migrants to American and

British cities, Māori and Pacific Islanders in Auckland and Wellington were by the late 1960s forming a new 'under-class' — a stratum characterized by poorly paid employment, little job security, and small prospects of career advancement. But direct migration from the countryside accounted for only a small part of the growth of the largest towns. A sizeable proportion (two-fifths to a half) of the sons of businessmen and clerical workers also appear to have entered blue-collar occupations. Most of all, however, the urban working class probably grew by inheritance — by recruitment from the sons of blue-collar families and from working-class immigrants from Britain.

Despite their substantial growth in numbers, and a high degree of class inheritance, the blue-collar workers did not develop a more coherent class consciousness. If anything the reverse was true, in part because the industrial labour force was still dispersed, and worked mainly in small units of production. Although there was a clear tendency towards concentration, by 1969–70 only 43 per cent of the factory workers were employed in plants with more than 100 workers. Over half the factories still employed fewer than ten workers. Labour turnover also was high. During the 1960s there were only two years when the labour turnover of the whole male work-force fell below 20 per cent. Such high turnover was a product of virtually full employment, and it inhibited the building of strong group loyalties. Those industries with the greatest turnover often also had long records of industrial peace.

Changing jobs meant not just a search for better pay and conditions, but often a search for a different kind of work. Vocational mobility, together with a significant degree of geographic mobility, were long-established characteristics of the New Zealand work-force. Social mobility is less easy to establish. One study found that between 1956 and 1966 a general upward movement can be discerned with a bunching in the middle socio-economic categories.[30] However, the bottom three levels in the study all encompass blue-collar workers, and so any movement upwards (or downwards) within these groups may not mean any change in class awareness. Moreover, this approach provides no clear evidence as to individual career mobility. Broad shifts in socio-economic levels may merely reflect the continuing growth of white-collar jobs to which recruits came not so much from blue-collar workers as from newcomers to the labour force. Studies of occupational change between father and son suggest, however, that there has been a considerable amount of inter-generational mobility, both upwards and downwards.[31] So far research has left unresolved a number of questions about the extent of career mobility and how it may be perceived. It is, for instance, hard to define the status (and class) of the son of a Raglan fisherman who began as a car mechanic in the early 1960s, became a fruit-shop proprietor, sold up to become a salaried car-salesman in the mid-1970s, and then in the late 1970s became 'his own boss' again, as an insurance agent working on commission.

Unusual though this non-fictional case may be, the aspirations it embodies were widespread. Untold numbers of wage and salary earners sought to be their 'own boss', to be 'independent' tradesmen, professionals, and proprietors. This made their class position ambiguous. Many workers identified politically with small proprietors rather than with their fellow work-mates. Newcomers to the ranks of the small urban businessman are hard to estimate, as they have continually turned over. In the thirty years after the war the numbers of proprietors seem to have fluctuated with the economic fortunes of the country, growing during the early years of the 1950s, 1960s, and 1970s, declining in the latter years of each decade. Overall, the period 1951–71 saw the long-term decline of the small proprietor, falling by some 8,000 to 140,000 in 1971, and as a proportion of the work-force from a fifth to an eighth. The trend reversed sharply in the early 1970s.

In the towns during the 1950s and early 1960s, small retailers, manufacturers, and building contractors proliferated, fostered by the economic and social policies of the welfare state.[32] The number of retail stores in the four main centres grew by two-thirds in the twenty years to 1973 — keeping pace with population growth. Here the archetype was the family business of the dairy-grocer, following the population to the suburbs. Others with entrepreneurial drive and with technical skills and ingenuity sought a niche in manufacturing. Here typically was the mechanic, who with a little capital teamed up with another to start a small workshop. In the twenty-five years after the war the number of factories grew by two-thirds, of which those with less than ten employees grew by nearly a half. In the building industry the number of working proprietors virtually doubled between 1953 and 1964. By becoming small proprietors, many wage-earners achieved a measure of independence. But their relationship to work did not change. For most, entrepreneurial initiative was combined with manual labour, their income was low and often precarious, their status insecure.

Many returned to the ranks of the wage and salary earners. The building industry in particular was sensitive to economic fluctuations, the number of contractors declining by more than a fifth between 1964 and 1968. In retailing also, competition intensified with the growth of chain-stores and the appearance of shopping malls. Increasingly, buyers of corner dairies found they had paid several thousand dollars for the goodwill of a shop which produced a profit less than the adult minimum wage.[33] The number of dairy-groceries fell by 557 (or 10 per cent) between 1968 and 1973. The advent of a consumer society shifted the area of opportunity. The proportion of food retailers declined in the 1960s and 1970s, while clothing, hardware, electrical, and sporting goods stores, car sales and service firms grew in number and in size. In retailing as in farming, small proprietors came to require more technical skill and capital; and family labour was often insufficient to produce a good return. But capable workers were expensive and not easily found. As with farming, small businesses were subject to a mesh of health and other regulations that became steadily more stringent. And so many small proprietors felt a growing pressure from bureaucrats, bigger rivals, and seemingly 'bolshie' unions. In both town and countryside, the degree of support which Social Credit received from small proprietors in the 1960s and 1970s is perhaps indicative of resentments at their precarious status.[34] Such resentments were heightened as technical skill and salaried employment rather than capital and private enterprise increasingly offered the surest means of a secure income, social mobility, and prestige.

Where the male work-force as a whole grew by just under a fifth in the decade 1956–66, the numbers of professional and technical workers grew by more than two-fifths, administrative and managerial workers by more than a half, and clerical workers by a third. The number of salesmen of all kinds increased by little more than an eighth. The greatest expansion in the male white-collar work-force was amongst salaried workers: teachers, hospital staff, social workers, draughtsmen, engineering and science technicians, and the like. And where, in the retail and wholesale trade, working proprietors had roughly equalled the salaried managers in number in the mid-1950s, twenty years later managers outnumbered proprietors by two to one. The same trend towards a salariat can be observed in manufacturing, and in law and accountancy. These patterns were symptomatic of the continuing growth of public and private bureaucracies in post-war society. The public bureaucracy numbered some quarter of a million by 1970, having grown by nearly 100,000 in twenty years. However, as a proportion of the work-force (just over a fifth in 1949), it scarcely grew from the late 1940s. Equally significant was the growth of private bureaucracies which encompassed some 202,000 workers in the early 1970s.[35]

By this point then some two-fifths of the work-force belonged to bureaucracies — organizations with a specialization of jobs arranged in a hierarchical order of authority and governed by formal rules and regulations. The expanding bureaucracy conflicted with the pervasive entrepreneurial ethos of proprietorship, personal profit, and independence. In private and public institutions alike a salary implied security. And personal success was measured both in terms of promotion to positions of higher salary with 'perks' and of greater authority over subordinates. Recruitment and promotion were largely dependent upon expertise, training, and experience.[36] So the assumptions underpinning petty proprietorship were eroded. The jack-of-all-trades, who relied upon intuitive judgements and physical energy, gave way slowly to the expert with a formal qualification for a particular job — the technocrat.

This process accelerated markedly after the war. In 1971 more than a quarter of the male work-force aged forty-five or over had attended primary school only. By contrast, almost all under twenty had received a secondary education, and 16 per cent of the men aged twenty to twenty-four years had had at least a fleeting acquaintance with university.[37] Perhaps more significant was the expansion of vocational training, particularly for the public service, industry, and commerce. During the 1950s, university commerce, law, and engineering courses commanded the attention of a growing proportion of male students. From 1948 apprentices had to attend technical classes. By 1976 the Trades Certification Board had issued 43,356 trade certificates as well as 11,782 advanced certificates. From the 1950s the gap between the qualified tradesman and university graduate began to be filled by the certificated technician. In 1960 the Technicians Certification Authority was established; courses in the technical institutes proliferated. By 1972 the number of technical institutes had risen from two to twelve, and students in teachers' colleges doubled, reaching 10,693. By 1965 (according to one listing of 121 countries) New Zealand ranked second after the USA in the number of students in higher education per head of population. Increasingly education (or the acquisition of skills) rather than capital was seen as the means of self-advancement. The growing proportion of salary earners was gradually sorted into a finely graded hierarchy according to training and experience, upon which was based income and hence status. The pursuit of theoretical knowledge added a new dimension to social inequality.[38]

By 1971 one in three of the population was directly involved in the education system — as full-time student, teacher, or administrator. So the school like the suburban bungalow became a salient feature in the social pattern.[39] In education, unlike housing, the state system prevailed. Barely 12 per cent of primary pupils and 16 per cent of secondary pupils were in private schools in 1940; by 1975 the proportions were less than 10 per cent and 14.5 per cent respectively. State education was informed by the same ethos that infused official housing policies: the concepts of cultural uniformity, social integration, and, above all, equality. The credo of the system was enunciated by Peter Fraser as Minister of Education in 1939, in words written by C. E. Beeby, soon to be Director of Education and an imaginative leader of the state system for the next twenty years:

The Government's objective, broadly expressed, is that every person, whatever his level of academic ability, whether he be rich or poor, whether he live in town or country, has a right, as a citizen, to a free education of the kind for which he is best fitted, and to the fullest extent of his powers. . . . the present Government was the first to recognize explicitly that continued education is no longer a special privilege of the well-to-do or the academically able, but a right to be claimed by all who want it to the fullest extent that the State can provide. . . .[40]

Yet, in education as in housing, the concept of equality was ambiguous. It implied equality of access: none were to be denied education on the grounds of means, location, sex, race, or physical disability. It also implied equality of treatment, irrespective of ability and vocational aspirations. From 1877 there was a uniform syllabus in primary schools; from the 1930s the recognition of variation in ability and attainment led to 'social' promotion in primary schools on the basis of age rather than achievement; from 1945 there was a common core of subjects taken for the first two years in secondary schools. However, the Fraser–Beeby credo also insisted that schools 'that are to cater for the whole population must offer courses that are as rich and varied as are the needs and abilities of the children who enter them'.[41] Freed from the strait-jacket of the Proficiency examination in 1936, primary school teachers sought to tailor the national syllabus to the abilities of individual children, using a range of teaching methods. By contrast the secondary schools, swollen by the raising of the school-leaving age to fifteen in 1944, swapped one strait-jacket for another. In the same year 'Matric' (the university entrance examination which had dominated the narrowly academic syllabus of secondary schools) was abolished. In 1945 the recommendations of the Thomas Committee were adopted: in addition to a 'common core', pupils were to be provided with a wide selection of optional studies designed to suit individual needs and examined in an existing public examination, School Certificate. The concept of equality had another dimension — equality of opportunity. Whatever the intentions of the new syllabus, equality of educational opportunity continued to mean 'the opportunity to differentiate oneself from one's fellows, to win certificates of attainment that opened the way to more highly regarded vocational careers'. For some, school was a social equalizer, for most it was an arbiter of social position.[42]

From the differing connotations of equality stemmed many of the tensions in the education system in the post-war years. A sharp growth in numbers and a continuing relocation of the school population challenged the very notion of equality. Between 1945 and 1970 the primary school population doubled while the secondary school rolls increased nearly three-and-a-half-fold (a consequence not only of increased births but also of more pupils entering secondary school younger and staying longer). Spending on education rose from 6 to over 14 per cent of government expenditure, but pressure on facilities continued. 'Prefabs' proliferated in the suburban schools. And there was a shortage of well-qualified teachers, especially in the new suburban primary schools of the 1950s and the rural secondary schools of the 1960s. To some critics, maintaining equality of access had meant some inequality of treatment; quality was being threatened by quantity.

Such fears were heightened by other anxieties. In the 1950s there was mounting criticism of the aims and methods of primary education. Traditionalists accused 'Beebyism' — with its 'social' promotion, liberal curriculum, and flexible teaching methods (dubbed the play-way) — of lowering standards in the basic skills known as the three Rs, reading, writing, and arithmetic. But the Commission appointed by the second Labour Government in 1960 to assess the state system was 'satisfied that, underlying primary teaching method, there is now a body of educational theory that is firmly based and consistent'. The Commission had 'little sympathy' with those who wished to narrow schooling to the three Rs, nor did it support those who wished to extend the role of the school. 'Formation of character' may have been an important aim of the primary system in the 1880s and 1890s, but to the Commission in 1962 'the intellectual development of each pupil to his full capacity' was now the primary purpose of schools, an emphasis to be questioned by 'concerned parents' in the early 1970s.[43]

Herein lay the main criticism of secondary schools in the 1950s and 1960s. The curriculum changes of 1945 were intended to ensure (in the words of the Thomas Committee) 'that all post-primary pupils, irrespective of their varying abilities and their varying occupational ambitions, receive a generous and well balanced education'. A common curriculum helped to remove differences between the academic secondary and the technical high schools. Secondary schools became 'multi-lateral' or 'comprehensive', labels redolent of equality. In the view of the Commission on Education, School Certificate too had been 'a great leveller'. But this was only one perspective. For the Departmental examination took the place of 'Matric', quickly 'establishing itself with parents as a desired qualification for their children'. 'School Cert.' became the cultural norm that 'Proficiency' had been a generation earlier. So the intentions of the Thomas Committee were frustrated. Vocational courses dominated the curriculum. Streaming (on the basis of verbal ability and aspirations) in multi-lateral schools reinforced rather than eroded differences of social background and aspiration. The long-established single-sex state schools (such as Auckland Grammar and Christchurch Boys' High) maintained their pre-eminence in the pursuit of university scholarships. Equality of access to a 'comprehensive' school thus did not mean equality of opportunity.[44] But mounting public criticism focused not so much on the process of educational inequality as on the result: School Certificate. Its popularity was a source of frustration, especially as the Department of Education maintained a fixed percentage of passes (roughly 50 per cent) each year. Until the introduction of a new examination in 1969, the system offered no qualification to the large number who failed. By the beginning of the 1970s, 60 per cent of secondary school pupils left with some sort of qualification, double the proportion of ten years earlier.

Yet despite the apparent tendency towards a meritocracy, New Zealand could still be seen in 1960 as: 'a mediocracy — a society and economy conducted without a governing élite selected for high education and/or intelligence'. In the 1960s comparatively few executive-level public servants had high educational qualifications. Educationally, New Zealand was no more of a meritocracy than Britain or the USA. A study of school leavers and university entrants in 1961 concluded that 'there is still a considerable proportion of able children in the manual workers' group who are not going on to the University'. University student numbers doubled in the 1960s, the annual proportion of school leavers intending to go on to university more than doubled to about 12 per cent. Increasingly in the 1970s, public servants were recruited from the university and new politicians had university degrees. But there is little evidence that the educational under-achievement of children from blue-collar families diminished.[45]

As with class, so with sex: girls did not reap the full benefits of educational opportunity.[46] In the 1950s the proportion of girls leaving school with University Entrance sharply increased, approaching that of boys in 1960. But young women did not go on to university in the same proportion as men — a disparity that continued through the 1960s. And there was a considerable difference in the subjects taken, especially in the sixth form and at university. Even in co-educational schools, the sexes tended to be put in different streams and confirmed in the differences of role already implanted. Despite increasing educational attainment, women continued to be found mainly in short-term, semi-skilled jobs and in professions of low status.

Once again the condition of the Māori pointed up the post-war gap between the ethos and reality of equality. To Fraser in the 1940s, equality of educational opportunity was a means of bringing the Māori into the mainstream of social and economic life. Then only one in three Māori children proceeded to secondary school. With 'social' promotion, the majority did so by 1960. But on average they entered secondary school at a later age and left earlier with fewer qualifications than Pākehā children. In 1960, 70 per cent of non-Māori pupils left without School Certificate; 95 per cent of Māori pupils did so. Comparatively few Māori students entered the sixth form, and they were greatly under-represented at university. These disparities persisted into the 1960s and 1970s.[47] Education had not served to remove social inequality for Māori, any more than it had for some groups of Pākehā. Pākehā notions of educational equality for Māori in the 1940s were still circumscribed: an education for which Māori post-primary pupils were 'best fitted' meant an emphasis on training for manual labour. Although this was challenged late in the 1950s, Māori had still to make their way through a school system that was almost entirely monocultural. (Hillary College which opened in Otara in 1966 was a notable exception.) Educational under-achievement was both a consequence and a cause of lower occupational status. (See Tables 7 and 8.) The low educational attainment and the youthfulness of the increasingly blue-collar Māori worker meant that Māori incomes remained generally lower than those of the Pākehā.

To what extent then did a society of 'fair shares' — a more equitable distribution of income and wealth — develop in post-war New Zealand? Evidence is incomplete and difficult to interpret. Compared with the capitalist societies of North America and North-West Europe, New Zealand in the 1950s had a narrow range of incomes. Even so, inequality was probably greater than conventional wisdom allowed. Before the redistributive effects of tax and benefits, the ratio of low to high family incomes could have been as much as one to eight in the 1950s.[48] But what was the trend? Evidence about the movement of incomes and its effect upon equality points in two directions. One approach suggests that the distribution of 'employee income' was 'remarkably stable, showing little change over the thirty-five years from 1925–6 to 1960–1, except for some reduction in the proportion of very low incomes' after 1935. But this analysis goes on to argue that the distribution of 'employee income' widened during the 1950s, and that the 'incomes of people with low educational qualifications rose significantly less than the incomes of those with higher qualifications'. The same argument suggests that the distance between the highest and lowest incomes lengthened during the 1960s.[49] Another analysis, based upon a broader view of income and wealth, argues 'that at least until the early 1970's, the level of inequality was decreasing', and notes that while the richest 1 per cent of adults held 25 per cent of all wealth in 1956, they held only 18 per cent of it in 1966. So, too, in 1956 the top 20 per cent of the highest incomes received almost half of the 'recorded income'; by 1971 their share had decreased to 47 per cent. However, this argument also shows that images of increasing inequality were derived from the cities; while the population of Auckland rose by a third in the 1960s, its Māori population doubled and the number of Aucklanders on 'high incomes' increased by two-thirds.[50] It was in the cities that the social gradient lengthened, and social distance increased.

Table 9: Changing proportions of total private income by source of income, 1952–75

	1951–52 per cent	1959–60 per cent	1964–65 per cent	1969–70 per cent	1974–75 per cent
Salary and wage payments	48.6	51.8	53.3	57.4	64.7
Social security benefits & pensions	7.8	8.7	7.2	6.9	7.6
Farming	15.1	12.8	10.5	7.5	3.3
Business & investment	12.4	11.8	11.7	10.1	9.7
Company income (before distribution)	11.9	10.6	12.9	13.9	11.6
Other	4.3	4.2	4.3	4.1	3.1

Source: Derived from *Social Trends in New Zealand*, p. 184

There were other important changes in the distribution of income which help to account for the weakness and possible diminution of coherent class consciousness in the 1950s and 1960s. In the first place, wages grew as a proportion of total private income. (See Table 9.) This increase was apparently at the expense of profits, suggesting that workers may have been gaining at the expense of capitalists. But the statistics on this are ambiguous. Small proprietors, many of whom formed private companies and began to pay themselves, took a part of salary payments. Also, since the proportion of wage-earners rose, the workers' share per head did not necessarily increase much. During the Second World War workers' share of total private income was substantially eroded. This, together with the pressures of inflation, provided the context for heightened trade-union militancy in the late 1940s.[51] After the bitter 1951 waterfront dispute, the employees' share of private income seemed to increase. And the period 1952–64 was one of industrial peace in comparison with the years before and after. The full employment of the 1950s and early 1960s enabled individual workers to negotiate their own terms, weakened trade-union militancy, and sapped working-class consciousness. With the ending of full employment in 1967, the opposite became true. A rising rate of inflation, the sharply increasing tax burden of the average wage-earner, growing job insecurity, decreasing over-time, increasing difficulties in getting part-time work for working-class wives and husbands alike — together with the polarizing, hard-nosed rhetoric of the new National Party leader R. D. Muldoon — all served to enhance trade-union militancy. But militancy did not necessarily mean greater class consciousness. For wage-earners were also consumers and often ambivalent in their attitude to unionism. So unions (blue collar and white collar alike) were foci not so much of class as of occupational consciousness, as different groups of wage and salary workers jockeyed to maintain or improve their relative position.

Perhaps the gain of wage-earners relative to proprietors was less significant than the changes in the ranks of the high-income earners. Led by doctors, lawyers, accountants, company executives, and top public servants, professional and managerial men supplanted farmers as New Zealand's élite in terms of income, if not of wealth. An élite recruited increasingly on the basis of education, skill, and seniority — rather than of capital — served to dilute the traditional concepts of class.

Table 10: Married women in the labour force as a percentage of all married women in the same age group, 1936–76

Age (years)	1936	1945	1956	1966	1971	1976
16–19	5.7	18.2	18.5	23.5	30.3	40.3
20–24	4.3	17.4	19.4	26.7	34.3	44.0
25–29	3.7	10.3	11.7	15.8	20.7	28.8
30–34	3.6	8.0	11.3	16.4	24.3	31.5
35–39	3.6	8.4	13.9	21.8	31.8	41.7
40–44	3.9	8.7	16.6	26.9	35.3	46.3
45–49	4.4	7.8	17.5	27.2	35.9	44.2
50–54	4.2	6.1	15.5	25.2	30.7	37.8
55–59	4.2	4.6	10.8	18.5	22.0	25.4
60–64	2.8	2.5	5.2	9.5	11.2	11.4
65+	1.6	1.0	1.6	2.1	2.4	2.4
All ages 16+	3.7	7.7	12.9	19.9	26.1	32.6

Source: NZOYB, 1981, p. 801

Perceptions of class and of 'fair shares' were further complicated by another change in the distribution of income: the shifting pattern of household income.[52] Of great importance to household incomes was the growing participation of married women in the work-force. (See Table 10.) Post-war society saw an increasing disparity between one- and two-income families. By the mid-1970s this disparity had become a matter of social concern. But the pattern was complicated by child-rearing, which wrought a distinctive life cycle in female employment — and a further disparity between households with children and a growing number without. In 1971, for example, less than a fifth of women with pre-school children worked, while almost half of those with school-aged children did so. Withdrawal from and subsequent re-entry of wives into the work-force also made for sharp changes in the economic fortunes of the family. Economic inequalities derived as much from a person's stage in life as from occupation and sex.

The distribution of income has long been influenced by state activity. The pattern of social policies since 1940 owes much to the first Labour Government. These offered not so much a new direction as a reaffirmation and extension of notions of equality. In 1935 benefits were to be 'non-contributory, universal, comprehensive, and adequate'; medical care was to be provided on the same basis as education.[53] Traditions began earlier were to be extended.

However, just as Labour's credo of educational equality contained ambiguities, so the Government's early thinking on social policy produced tensions, both financial and ideological. The cold facts of finance, and the desire to give the needy generous treatment, cut across the equally strong desire to give universal benefits as a right. Thus the means test (and, at least in theory for some beneficiaries, a 'morality' test) continued. The aim became redistribution to bring about a greater equality of economic status rather than equality of access to benefits irrespective of income. The desire 'to provide a more equitable distribution of the national income'[54] while removing the taint of charity was reflected in the financing of the scheme from a social security tax on all incomes and a subsidy from the consolidated fund. Labour secured increased revenue in rough proportion to ability to pay, while conferring a sense of a right to a benefit. And, in aspiration at least, the Social Security Act of 1938 marked the transition from providing merely a subsistence income to an attempt to meet 'the normal needs' of beneficiaries.[55] This concept was left undefined until the early 1970s; the level of benefits set earlier probably did not amount to much more than subsistence for most.

But the Labour Government clung to the concept of the optimum in 'universal' medical care. Cost was a factor, but ultimately it was the doctors in 'the most powerful trade union in the country' who did most to puncture the dream of 1935 — even while becoming the chief beneficiaries of the welfare state.[56] The Government sought to end direct payment by patients; the doctors wanted to preserve the much vaunted doctor–patient relationship and the private enterprise character of their profession by continuing to receive fees. In 1941, both sides compromised: the general practitioners accepted a fee-for-service of 7s. 6d. which could be paid directly by the state; the Government accepted that doctors could ask their patients for a small additional fee for service. For the time being the Government had obtained substantially free general medical care without 'charity', while the doctors obtained (in John A. Lee's acid phrase) 'an extra thirty pieces of bronze'.[57] Between 1941 and 1947 (despite the financial exigencies of war) the Government broadened the scope of treatment; the cost rising to nearly 6 per cent of total government expenditure. Socially, a transformation had apparently occurred in health care.

Yet Labour in New Zealand failed to achieve what Labour in Britain was able to with the establishment of the National Health Service in 1948: a system of health care that was comprehensive and virtually free to the patient.[58] Major lacunae continued in the New Zealand system, such as universal dental and optical services, and general medical care became progressively less 'free' as doctors' fees soared. Above all, the Social Security Act failed to produce an integrated health service. It left administration largely in the hands of an out-moded system of hospital boards. A large proportion of health care remained in the hands of private practitioners and private hospitals.

So from the 1940s a dual system developed (in contrast to the erosion of private education). Inequalities of access and treatment grew in the 1960s and 1970s. Where schools followed the population, public hospitals remained *in situ*. Expensive buildings at the centre of cities were remote from the burgeoning suburbs. Total government expenditure on health as a proportion of Gross Domestic Product had risen from 1.21 per cent in 1938 to 3.51 per cent by 1949; but this level was barely maintained in the 1950s. Certainly, during the 1960s, the proportion crept up to 4.41 per cent by 1972 and from this point it rose sharply to 5.58 per cent in 1978. Yet, 'after allowing for cost increases and the growing population the real growth of health services was relatively small'.[59] Despite growth, the supply of public hospital beds and services did not keep up with demand. In the two decades 1951–71 the number of 'public' beds grew by less than a quarter, well below the rate of population growth. Hospital waiting-lists lengthened. The gap was partly made up by private hospital beds which grew by some 56 per cent in the same period.

The re-emergence of the private sector was encouraged by the National Government. National had accepted social security as a *fait accompli*; but was faced with an ever-increasing demand for medical services, and with sharply increasing costs. National readily fell in with the ethos of many doctors who preached self-help and were themselves responding to market forces. In the 1960s, specialists in private practice grew in number at the expense of general practitioners, who clustered in the wealthier suburbs rather than in the areas of greatest need such as Otara and Porirua. In promoting the Southern Cross Medical Care Society in 1961, doctors led the 'market's quiet counter-revolution' against the 1938 ideals.[60] Private insurance promised relief from doctors' bills and quick access to private hospitals. Growing numbers of the more affluent and healthy resorted to medical care societies which by the mid-1970s covered some 500,000 people. Such numbers were a measure of the degree of dissatisfaction with access to public hospital services. But there was little public outcry, even in Auckland where the deterioration of general hospital services was most visible. Medical insurance had irrevocably sapped political support for the principles of 1938. It had created in the 1960s and early 1970s a huge vested interest (of doctors, private hospitals, and the insured) which successfully resisted the third Labour Government's proposals to revitalize the public sector at the expense of the private.

The ideal of a universal health service which seemed to be firmly established by 1947 became less of a reality during National's reign. Such a retreat arose more from neglect than from policies of deliberate withdrawal — before 1976 at least. The same lack of commitment also undermined the level of social security benefits between the early 1950s and the early 1970s. At a time of economic growth and unprecedented prosperity, cash benefits as a proportion of Gross National Product fell away until 1972–73; except for the years of the short-lived second Labour Government. (See Table 11.)[61]

Table 11: Social security benefits as a percentage of GNP for selected years (ending 31 March) 1939–77

	Cash benefits	Health benefits	Total benefits
1939	4.78	–	4.78
1947	7.03	1.46	8.49
1956	5.72	1.58	7.30
1961	7.21	1.61	8.82
1966	5.77	1.06	6.83
1971	5.51	1.14	6.65
1973	6.00	1.03	7.03
1976	7.18	1.28	8.46
1977	7.42	1.26	8.68

Source: Report of the Royal Commission on Social Security in New Zealand, 1972, Appendix 11A; figures 1973–77 calculated from NZOYB, 1978, pp. 151 and 911

The age benefit was typical: in 1946 the benefit for a married couple had been 63 per cent of average weekly earnings, by 1970 it was less than 48 per cent. The family benefit, increased only once between 1946 and 1972, was eroded even further. In the 1960s, New Zealand and Australia were the only countries belonging to the Organization for Economic Co-operation and Development in which expenditure on income maintenance as a proportion of national income actually declined — despite the fact that New Zealand had a relatively high burden of dependency and its pensioner population was growing.[62] To some extent National's social policy shifted from income maintenance to dealing with individual situations through case work. Even so the ranks of government and local authority social workers grew fairly slowly before the 1960s.[63] Increasingly the Government sought to work through the growing number of voluntary organizations established to cover needs untouched by official social policy. Prime examples of voluntary organizations encouraged by Government were marriage guidance councils (first established in 1948) and the New Zealand Society for the Intellectually Handicapped founded in 1949.

Although wage-earners may have secured an increasing share of private income, this was not true of beneficiaries.[64] Poverty (defined in relative terms) was rediscovered in New Zealand at the end of the 1960s, just as it had been in Britain, USA, and Australia earlier in the decade.[65] During the inflation of the early 1950s the hardship of some beneficiaries had been highlighted. Though National believed the current level of benefits to be adequate, it introduced in 1952 'supplementary assistance' for needy beneficiaries — some 10 per cent of beneficiaries by 1971. By the early 1970s, however, the dimensions of poverty were perceived to be much broader than this. Almost by definition beneficiaries were poor — especially the aged. Thirty per cent of those on an age benefit were experiencing some degree of hardship, according to a government survey published in 1975. Families with dependent children were likely to be in poverty; in 1975 it was estimated that 18 per cent of the population (some 550,000) were in poverty.

The early 1970s marked a turning point in social policy.[66] In 1969 National appointed a Royal Commission to assess the principles of social security and the adequacy of benefits. Its report in 1972 was essentially conservative, endorsing the principles of 1938. However, in assessing the adequacy of benefits the Commission took up where the Social Security Act had left off, shifting from a concept of a subsistence income to one which would 'enable beneficiaries with small or no other resources to "participate in and belong to" the mainstream of their community'.[67] National accepted the Commission's report in principle and quickly implemented some of its recommendations — for example, doubling the family benefit, while ending the tax exemptions for children. But in the same year the National Government also enacted accident compensation. This marked a new departure in social policy, treating generously those (injured on the road or on the job) who had been only partially covered by social security. The Act (extended by Labour in 1973 to cover all non-earners) provided benefits which were earnings-related and not income-tested. The scheme was financed by the insurance principle with compulsory contributions from employers, the self-employed, and motor-vehicle owners. Accident compensation preserved inequality by seeking to maintain continuity of income.

Continuity of economic status was the essence of a new Labour Party

475

scheme for state superannuation enacted in 1974. Here was a further departure from the tradition begun in 1898: an earnings-related benefit from the New Zealand Superannuation Scheme was based on contributions. National, led by R. D. Muldoon, opposed Labour's scheme and presented an alternative for the 1975 election: universal superannuation from the age of sixty paid out of taxation. The aim of the first Labour Government seemed to be realized. Yet National went far beyond Labour's intentions in 1935 or the recommendations of the Royal Commission on Social Security. By promising a benefit for married couples at 80 per cent of the 'average ordinary-time working wage', it gave a generous benefit to many who did not need it. Furthermore, National was committed to an ever-rising expenditure on the aged at a time when economic growth had virtually ceased. The effects were quickly seen on social policy. To pay for national superannuation other categories of beneficiary and social service were disadvantaged. The priorities of 1938 had been reversed: major discrepancies now existed between the economic consequences of accidents and age on the one hand, and sickness, unemployment, and solo parenthood (for example) on the other. In the forty years from 1938, social policy had helped to reshape, but not to erode, the contours of inequality.

While inequalities in the distribution of income continued in post-war New Zealand, the badges of social position became more subtle. During two decades from the late 1940s, many of the visible differences in lifestyle between worker and boss lessened. The universality of both the suburban bungalow with its common trappings and the car gave a broad uniformity to the material culture. None the less, between the bungalows of, say, Remuera and Otara, great disparities continued. The better-off turned to an ever-widening range of goods and services: from Ford Customline to Jaguar and a second car, Hi-Fi and colour TV, pottery and Persian rugs, dishwasher and dining out, skiing and swimming pool, jet boat and holidays abroad. Conspicuous consumption served to underline social position. Yet the resentments latent in the relatively deprived were weakly expressed. Those nearer the bottom of the social gradient sought to emulate not those nearer the top, but rather their neighbours. Inequalities were perceived as removable, and the egalitarian myth maintained. Rising expectations were matched by a continuing increase in the discretionary income of the average New Zealander in the 1950s and early 1960s — more money to spend on cars, household goods, and leisure pursuits.[68] Even so the links between levels of income and patterns of consumption were not necessarily direct. Hire purchase allowed many to keep up with the Joneses nearby. Increasingly in the 1960s, the factory car park (for example) reflected the varieties of individual aspiration and the pecking order of company cars more than the broad contours of class. Lifestyles became more difficult to delineate in terms of class.

This was particularly true of leisure patterns, dominated as they were in the 1950s by the male stereotype of 'rugby, racing, and beer'.[69] The rugby club, the pub, the race course, and the TAB were institutions of social integration for males at least — though the private bar and the Members' Stand pointed to a continuing distinction between the respectable and the rough. Other distinctions were made mainly on the basis of prowess. The image of rugby as a 'great leveller' persisted into the 1970s although it was wearing thin from the 1950s. Māori were excluded from the 1949 and 1960 All Black tours of South Africa as they had been in 1928. Preparations for the 1960 tour were marked with a degree of protest from the churches, spokesmen of Māori communities, the trade unions and the universities, which ensured that Māori would be included in any future tours, as three were in 1970. But in the 1960s there were few Māori in test teams, in comparison to the growing proportion found in rugby league. Rugby became more exclusive at the representative level: the 1972 All Blacks were composed mainly of professional men and farmers, while the Kiwis (League) drew mainly from factory, sales, and clerical workers. In the summer sports too, softball was preferred by Māori and blue-collar workers, while cricket was traditionally the game of the better-off Pākehā. However, in most sports, occupation and income were probably less significant in patterns of participation and association than age, marriage, sex, and ethnicity.

The broad continuities in leisure patterns are easier to discern than the changes. Youth (especially young men) predominated in sport; marriage made leisure largely home-centred — especially for the women. Suburbanization produced uniformities: gardening and, from the 1960s, watching television being universal. Conversely, growing affluence, mobility, numbers, and ethnic variety (in Auckland and Wellington particularly) brought an increasing diversity of activity, from Ngāti Pōneke and urban marae to Pacific Island churches, from Downstage to discos, from surfing to saunas, from housie to hang-gliding, from continuing education to CARE (Citizens' Association for Racial Equality), from periodic detention to luxurious leisure at Pauanui, from marching girls to Mongrel Mobs.

Class was only one kind of fissure in post-war society. It was intersected by other lines of cleavage. In the urbanizing world other self-conscious groups existed or appeared, not based on occupation and income but on sex, age, and cultural origins and aspirations. Women, youth, Māori, and Pacific Island immigrants began to feel an identity of interest between themselves and against others.[70]

Māori self-consciousness had been present for generations, but intensified as the interaction between the races grew. Post-war urbanization reduced social separation. As the material conditions of Māori began to converge towards those of Pākehā, the quickening pace of social change heightened the awareness of disparities in housing, educational attainment, employment, and income. In the late 1950s the increasing appearance of Māori youth in city magistrate and children's courts seemed symptomatic of social dislocation. Culturally, questions of identity were raised anew. Few towns had 'the facilities and the environment for maintaining Maori cultural practices'.[71]

To these 'problems', Pākehā and Māori leadership had different answers. The 1961 report of J. K. Hunn pinpointed the material inequalities between Māori and Pākehā. Yet he was optimistic: 'evolution governs policy, not *vice versa*' and evolution was 'clearly integrating Maori and Pakeha'. The urban drift was welcomed, indeed it should be 'actively nurtured' as the 'quickest and surest way of integrating the two species of New Zealander' and preventing a 'colour problem from arising'. Integration was thus the goal of official policy and 'the problem for the Maori people' was 'not one of destination or route, but of pace'. Hunn defined integration as 'to combine (not fuse) the Maori and Pakeha elements to form one nation wherein Maori culture remains distinct'. But he displayed a shallow understanding of Māori culture, and added that the two races showed signs of passing through integration to assimilation.[72] Hunn had failed to perceive the strong Māori desire for a separate cultural identity, indeed for cultural renewal in the cities. Articulate Māori opinion rejected the official concept of integration.

None the less, the Hunn Report became the basis of National's policy in the 1960s.[73] In housing, the Government attempted to meet its statistical targets. As measured by the 1971 census, the gap between Māori and Pākehā housing conditions was small. The Department of Maori Affairs attempted to promote integration by 'pepper-potting' Māori houses amongst Pākehā ones in the towns. The State Advances Corporation, however, continued to house families on the basis of need and income. Thus the housing programme led not to integration but to concentrations of Māori in suburban tracts of state rental houses. And for many Māori the pressures of low income were reinforced by their own preferences: concentration was preferable to cultural isolation.

Acting on Hunn's suggestion to 'transform the scene' in education, the Government established the Maori Education Foundation in 1961. Māori aspirations and finance were stimulated by government support. By the early 1970s the Foundation had helped many Māori through secondary and tertiary education; but it did not close the qualification gap between Māori and Pākehā. In the early 1960s the Foundation promoted pre-school education, and by the early 1970s about one in four Māori children attended pre-school groups alongside Pākehā children. Yet 'broadly speaking, increasing Pakeha presence in community and pre-school resulted in the elimination of Maori practices and orientation in favour of Pakeha ones and decreasing participation by Maoris especially as leaders'.[74] Pre-school, like other institutions shared with the Pākehā, was not necessarily a vehicle for integration.

With land held on Māori title, National's policy did not follow Hunn so much as the 1965 Pritchard-Waetford Committee which recommended Crown purchase of uneconomic interests — ignoring the strong desire of Māori land owners for assistance to develop the land themselves.[75] Under the Maori Affairs Amendment Act (1967) Māori land held by not more than four joint owners was to be exempted from the jurisdiction of the Maori Land Court. To many Māori critics the Act opened the way for the more rapid alienation of Māori land. This traditional issue above all heightened Māori sense of identity in the 1960s and early 1970s. Urban immigrants and tangata whenua (the local people) alike looked for their tūrangawaewae ('a standing place' — a marae with which they could identify). Hence the drive to establish urban marae, and the continuing importance of ancestral land as a source of identity. Increasing anxieties at the continuing loss of land were given expression in the Maori Land March in 1975 and the Bastion Point issue.

But land was not the only issue. From the late 1960s there was an increasingly effective assertion of issues of cultural identity in an urban setting. Young Māori began to show 'a remarkable enthusiasm for coming to terms with their cultural heritage'.[76] New urban groups did not use traditional Māori means of protest: they demonstrated, distributed pamphlets, heckled Government spokesmen, marched on Parliament, 'sat in'. The novelty lay in adopting the tactics of Pākehā protest groups and in making skilful use of the news media, especially television. Nga Tamatoa, founded in Auckland in 1970, quickly became the largest of the protest groups. It was led mainly by university and teachers' college students, although it gained support from blue-collar Māori youth. It gave forceful expression to Māori grievances: the loss of land, the declining use of the Māori language, the continuance of discrimination, and the existence of what came to be termed 'institutional racism', especially in the Pākehā-dominated systems of education and justice. To Nga Tamatoa: 'There is no Maori problem, what we have is a problem with Pakehas.'[77] Together with other groups (notably Te Reo Maori and Te Roopu o te Matakite), Nga Tamatoa succeeded in focusing public attention on Māori issues and shifting the climate of influential opinion. Government departments and public agencies such as the Broadcasting Corporation were forced to re-examine their policies. In its legislation, particularly the Maori Affairs Amendment Act of 1974, the third Labour Government went some way to meet Māori criticisms. In policy as in popular parlance, the concept of a multicultural society replaced that of integration in the early 1970s. Māoritanga had a future in the urban world.

As with the fissure of race in the social structure, so with that of sex: radical feminists and Māori radicals alike articulated from the late 1960s a heightened sense of self-consciousness — a sense of grievance, anger, and oppression that challenged the dominant values of Pākehā masculine culture.[78] Yet such parallels should not be pushed too far. Māori shared certain beliefs and a sense of identity. Not so with women, most of whom were separated by their relationships with men from others of their sex. Their sense of group identity and solidarity remained weakly developed. On such issues as a mother's wage, extended child-care facilities, sex education in schools, and liberalized abortion policies, women (like men) were divided. None the less, for many women as for most Māori, changing material circumstances from the 1940s provided fuel for agitation against the *status quo* to be ignited by a current of ideas which began to flow strongly during the 1960s.

For women, increasing participation in the labour force was fundamental to their changing circumstances. Here the war marked a turning point. Certainly in the decade following 1945 the level of participation of married women aged sixteen to twenty-nine years barely increased. (See Table 10.) There was a 'baby boom'; the 'cult of domesticity' seemed resurgent. None the less, middle-aged married women re-entered the work-force in steadily increasing proportions from 1945. In this the anxious saw an explanation for increasing juvenile delinquency. But in the longer term engrained attitudes against working wives were slowly eroded. A continuing demand for female labour in the cities provided the opportunity for younger mothers to enter paid work, especially from the late 1960s. Rising living costs and standards of comfort impelled many into such jobs as came their way. More importantly, by the mid-1960s most mothers were completing their child-bearing before they were thirty, and all their children were at school before they became thirty-five. Paid employment offered the opportunity for a measure of adult companionship, personal autonomy, and (for some) achievement and a sense of self — an escape from suburban life which could be isolated, dreary, and unfulfilling.[79]

Greater participation in the economy did not bring with it greater social and economic equality. There was little change in the range of occupations undertaken by women. The distinction of 'woman's work', at lower rates of pay and with little chance for advancement, was maintained in the factory and the office as it was in the home. Inequalities of pay and prospects in the Public Service (where the proportion of female clerical workers had risen from 5 to 25 per cent between 1939 and 1947) provided the fuel for the first stirrings of a new campaign for sexual equality. From 1954 the Public Service Association campaigned for the immediate achievement of equal pay — a goal adopted by the second Labour Government. The Government Service Equal Pay Act of 1960 was followed by legislation in 1972 intended to introduce equal pay more generally. Yet the advent of equal pay did not bring with it equal opportunity, which required a more fundamental change in attitudes and institutions. Working mothers still bore the chief responsibility for maintaining the home. The lack of child-care centres reflected the continuing strength of the view that women with pre-school children should remain at home. Till the late 1960s at least, most women entered the work-force 'without altering either the assumptions about their "place" or the actual pattern of discrimination which kept them in sex-typed jobs'.[80] So the campaign for equal pay was overtaken in the late 1960s by a more profound challenge to prevailing concepts of equality: the movement for women's liberation.

For such a movement to gather strength, discontented women had to overcome their isolation, their tendency to view their problems as a product of their individual situation rather than of the social structure. They needed to realize as the American Betty Friedan declared in 1963, 'they all shared the same problem'.[81] A new women's movement grew on the basis of self-knowledge, a changing social climate, new organization and new issues — all profoundly influenced by the current of feminist ideas flowing in from America. 'Voice of America' lectures on 'The Potential of Women' broadcast in 1965 inspired local courses on 'The Changing Role of Women'. From such a Wellington course in 1966 the Society for Research on Women emerged, to map for the first time the social condition of New Zealand women. Greater pressure for change came from new feminist organizations, such as the National Organization for Women and Auckland Women's Liberation, formed in the early 1970s. From the latter group came *Broadsheet* (from 1972) and the main impetus for the first United Women's Convention in 1973. Such activism was part and parcel of the growth of political pressure groups from the late 1960s. More than this, the changing social climate especially amongst youth, emphasized greater personal freedom — 'doing your own thing'. Women's liberation sought freedom of choice along with equality of opportunity. In so doing it 'questioned *everything*' in a male-dominated society, particularly the traditional roles within marriage and the family.[82] During the 1970s various feminist critiques of society were elaborated: whether 'radical', 'socialist', or 'lesbian', all looked to a profound transformation in the social pattern. The small, often informal, groups of women that proliferated reflected the variety of concerns that recruited growing numbers into the ranks of feminists: Rape Crisis, Women's Refuge, Women's Resource Centres, Working Women's Alliance, Sisters Overseas Service (abortion referral), Sisters for Homophile Equality, study and 'consciousness raising' groups. True, in their social background the activists were probably not representative of all women, being relatively better off, well educated, generally in their late twenties or thirties and in professional occupations when working outside the home. And, in so far as 'abortion on demand' was a leading plank of women's liberation, the continuing strength of the Society for the Protection of the Unborn Child reflected a measure of anti-feminism in the community. So did the Save Our Homes Campaign in 1977. Even so the 'distortions as well as the justices of liberation crept even to the bastions of the suburbs, in [a] deep and undermining assault. . . .'[83]

Together Māori cultural resurgence and the women's liberation movement were the enduring elements of a 'new wave of protest' that brought a new hue to the social fabric from the late 1960s. Did they portend 'the radicalisation of increasing numbers of New Zealanders' that activists looked for in the early 1970s?[84] Clear tendencies to 'separatism' — to seek independence of Pākehā or male dominated institutions — underlined the challenge to the *status quo*. Changing relationships between Māori and Pākehā, women and men, suggested that in the future the texture of social life would be transformed. In fact the long-established contours of inequality (economic, racial, and sexual) remained, largely resistant to the pressures for change. In 1980 it was not clear that the social pattern of the next thirty years would differ profoundly from that of the past.

CHAPTER 18

A Revolution in Social Policy, 1981–1991

Geoffrey W. Rice

Definitions of social policy in the modern state vary from one academic discipline to another, and range from simple to complex, but the classic definition by Marshall is a useful starting point: 'The policy of governments having a direct impact on the welfare of citizens, by providing them with services or income.'[1] This definition sits at the narrow end of the range, and implies a predominantly institutional or administrative approach. Narrow definitions of social policy tend to be characterized by 'the view from the top' (or from the centre looking out to the periphery), and are often confined to the portfolios of health, education, and welfare. At the other extreme, holistic definitions of social policy seem to embrace virtually every government activity affecting the citizen's welfare, and may include economic policy, the tax system, housing, justice, immigration, and employment policies.[2] Such complex definitions may also include consideration of the delivery and receiving end of policies, rather than mere policy-making. In historians' parlance, this resembles the *Annales* approach of 'history from below', which adopts a holistic and even environmental approach to social change. But the broader a definition, the less useful it becomes as a tool of analysis, and in the case of social policy in New Zealand over the last decade, there is the additional difficulty that very recent policy changes may not have had sufficient time to produce clear results, let alone detailed studies of their impact at the receiving end.[3] The definition of social policy adopted in this chapter of necessity sits closer to the narrow end of the spectrum, as a record of policy changes rather than their delivery or reception, but it is a little broader than Marshall's classic dictum. Social policy is here taken to mean the traditional core of government decisions affecting health, education, social welfare services, and income support, with the addition of housing policy, since this has always been a central feature of the New Zealand welfare state.

Social policy in New Zealand is often simply equated with 'the welfare state'. This is a portmanteau term denoting the package of reforms enacted by the first Labour Government in the 1930s, in particular the 1938 Social Security Act which introduced medical and hospital benefits, sickness and unemployment benefits, and new provision for orphans and the elderly. Labour's concern for the citizen's welfare 'from the cradle to the grave' extended to education, which was to be universal, free, and secular in character, and to housing, which in the provision of low-interest mortgages through the State Advances Corporation enabled a whole generation of New Zealanders to become home-owners rather than tenants. The basic structure of the 1930s welfare state in New Zealand persisted into the 1980s, reflecting a broad-based consensus that the state should promote social harmony by taking a collective responsibility for the welfare of all its citizens, sharing resources through public funding of education, income support, health services, and housing, in order to protect the unfortunate and safeguard the nation's children.

The welfare state is not unique to New Zealand, for similar packages of social policies have characterized all the leading industrial nations of Europe and North America since the Second World War, usually proceeding hand in glove with Keynesian economic policies. Most social scientists agree that there are three distinct types of modern welfare state operating in the world today.[4] The first is usually described as a rights-based or social-citizenship model. This is based on the idea that a healthy democracy needs to ensure that all of its citizens can participate fully in community affairs and in the political process, and that social services should be available to maintain a person's membership of society, as of right, regardless of accidents or misfortunes such as sickness or unemployment, which are often beyond the individual's control. Scandinavian countries such as Sweden and Denmark offer the most successful and complete examples of the rights-based social citizenship model. These have also been described as 'social democratic welfare states'.

The second model is the insurance-based welfare state in which the size of an individual's previous contributions to a fund determines their level of support, rather than the person's actual need. This model originated in nineteenth century Germany, and still predominates there and in most European countries such as Austria, France, Italy, and the Netherlands, and in Japan. This type of welfare state favours those in paid employment, and discriminates against those who are not, such as women caring for children at home, so most modern states find it necessary to provide means-tested assistance for those unable to contribute to welfare or superannuation funds. In these 'conservative welfare states', economic and social policies are viewed as complementary, within a framework of strong social controls.

The third model is a residual or minimalist welfare system in which the state provides only a 'safety net' for the very poor and needy, and expects most citizens to provide for their own welfare needs in the marketplace or from charities. This is the classical liberal *laissez-faire* ideology of self-reliance and individual responsibility which characterized the English Poor Law from the sixteenth to the early twentieth century, and is today best exemplified by the USA. The residualist or 'safety net' doctrine has been revived in recent years by theorists of the New Right such as Hayek who criticize the rights-based welfare state for sapping individual initiative and distorting the free play of market forces in the economy. Such critics claim that the rights-based welfare state is too expensive and ultimately unsupportable in the post-Keynesian world economy.[5]

By the early 1980s New Zealand's welfare state still largely corresponded to the first of these models, but not as completely as Sweden or Denmark. Social policy was a mixed bag, or several bags, rather than a single suitcase. Health, education, and family income assistance were universal in both theory and practice, but some forms of assistance, notably in housing and invalid benefits, were targeted to those most in need by means-testing. However, the bulk of the state's social welfare spending (including family benefit) was not means-tested, and National Superannuation was paid to all citizens over sixty years of age regardless of other income. New Zealand governments have been wary of insurance-based schemes, so the second model of the welfare state has never taken root here, but means-testing for some benefits made the New Zealand system something of a hybrid, incorporating elements of the rights-based and residualist models. Voluntary agencies and church-based charities have always played a significant if little-recognized role in New Zealand society, and levels of welfare expenditure in relation to GDP were low by international standards, so that some observers would have placed New Zealand among the 'reluctant welfare states', along with Britain and Australia, even before the radical changes of 1990–91.[6] But on the whole, New Zealand was still a 'cradle to the grave' welfare state, in sharp contrast to the welfare system of the USA.

Social policy in the 1970s and early 1980s continued to be pragmatic and *ad hoc* rather than driven by any single ideology or political agenda. The basic principles of the 1930s welfare state had been accepted by both major political parties, and such changes as occurred were in close accord with these underlying principles, suggesting that they were axiomatic for most New Zealanders. Thus the 1970s had seen the addition of a Domestic Purposes Benefit (1973) for solo parents, and a no-fault earnings-related Accident Compensation Scheme (1973), which abolished overnight a whole field of litigation in the area of torts and negligence. A new disability allowance in 1975 and the National Superannuation scheme of 1976 were the only other notable changes of these years. By 1981 New Zealand had a social security system which looked like a form of community insurance, yet it was funded not on an insurance basis but from general taxation. (The old Social Security fund was abolished in 1964.) Eligibility was based on residence rather than tax or contributions, the family was assumed to be the basic social and economic unit, and the three major areas of family support, medical benefits, and superannuation were universally open to all citizens. As the *Yearbook* proudly claimed, year after year, New Zealand's welfare system reflected 'the traditional humanitarian, egalitarian and pragmatic approach' of most New Zealanders, and their acceptance of the principle of 'community responsibility for social welfare'.[7]

The central agency of social policy in New Zealand had become the Department of Social Welfare, which was formed in 1972 from the amalgamation of the Social Security Department and the Child Welfare

Division of the Department of Education. As well as administering the Social Welfare Act of 1971, and the 1964 Social Security Act, the Department was given responsibility for aspects of the Children and Young Persons Act (1974) and the Disabled Persons Welfare Act (1975), as well as older War Pensions and Rehabilitation legislation. Specific policy objectives, which still applied in the early 1980s, included safeguarding individuals against loss or reduction of income through age, incapacity, widowhood, orphanhood, unemployment or other circumstances, by providing 'income security at a level which will enable them to belong and participate in the community'. Cash benefits comprised the most visible part of income support by social welfare, but social services administered by the department included foster homes, institutional care for children at risk, preventive social work, general counselling services, home help, rest homes for the elderly, disability allowances, emergency benefits, allowances for parents of seriously handicapped children, and telephone rental concessions. There were 242,000 medical benefits paid in 1980, and $1.9 million in cash benefits. Total social welfare expenditure in 1980 was $2,164 million, or 10.3 per cent of GDP. This represented an annual expenditure of $692 per head of population.[8]

Up to the end of the Muldoon administration in 1984, social policy in New Zealand continued in its traditional path of *ad hoc* incrementalism, with no major policy changes or radical new departures. In April 1981 a Liable Parent Contribution Scheme was introduced in an attempt to claw back some of the soaring expenditure on Domestic Purposes Benefits (which had reached $252.6 million in 1982) but over the period 1986–89 the Liable Parent Contribution Scheme brought in barely 5 per cent of total DPB expenditure.[9] Though defaulters could have the contributions deducted from wages at source, the scheme was massively evaded, and some separated parents even absconded to Australia to avoid it. Further tinkering with benefits and income support in the early 1980s was avoided by Muldoon's wage and price freeze, imposed in 1982 (later extended for another year until 1984). In the Health portfolio, rationalization of hospital administration was signalled in the Area Health Boards Act of 1983, which proposed the restructuring of twenty-seven hospital boards, large and small, into fourteen Area Health Boards with a population-based funding formula. Despite loud protests from some regions, this reform proceeded over the next six years, and decentralized the public health activities which had hitherto been performed by the Department of Health.[10]

Economic and fiscal policies preoccupied the fourth Labour Government in its first term of office (1984–87), and social policy suffered from prevarication if not simple neglect. Ministers repeatedly promised that once the essential economic reforms were in place, Labour would devote a second term in office to social policy reforms in health, education, and welfare. The most significant developments of these years affecting the welfare of individual New Zealanders occurred in fiscal rather than social policy. Labour instituted a radical change in the nature of New Zealand's tax regime, with a reduction in personal tax scales to foster initiative and greater productivity, and the introduction of a Goods and Services Tax initially set at 10 per cent and later raised to 12.5 per cent. This major shift from direct to indirect taxation imposed a heavier burden on middle and lower income groups, whose members could not avoid paying more for essentials, while upper income groups enjoyed a greater disposable income thanks to the lower personal tax rates. In 1985 Labour also introduced a controversial taxation surcharge on other income for national superannuitants, despite pre-election promises to the contrary. Labour's other most significant social policy measures in its first term included the 1986 introduction of Family Support, an income-tested refundable tax credit replacing the previous child supplement and family care benefits, and a Guaranteed Minimum Family Income for low earners with children. These measures were (in part at least) moves to ameliorate the effects of economic and fiscal policies, rather than harbingers of any coherent set of social policy objectives. Indeed, some observers wondered if Labour in its first term even had a social policy.[11]

Policy was in the making, however, on a scale never before seen in New Zealand, and 1988 provided a rich harvest of advice in the form of no fewer than eight reports from a variety of working groups and 'Taskforces' set up by the Labour Government to review social policy. Most of these were the products of impatience, for the Government already had a Royal Commission on Social Policy working to a two-year timetable, which also reported (earlier than planned) in 1988. Few governments in any country can have had so much expert advice tendered on social policy in one year, or managed to ignore so much of it.

The Royal Commission on Social Policy was appointed in October 1986, under the leadership of Sir Ivor Richardson, a judge of the Court of Appeal, and with a budget of $5 million. The Commission then embarked on a remarkable exercise in public consultation which attracted some 6,000 submissions and drew as many more citizens to public meetings all over New Zealand. An attitudinal survey was also conducted amongst a carefully chosen cross-section of 1,792 people. The result was a massive five-volume report which not only comprised the survey and submission results but also included many commissioned reports by recognized experts on particular aspects of social policy.[12] Altogether *The April Report* is a remarkable snapshot of New Zealand society in the late twentieth century, with scarcely any significant areas of social policy overlooked. Unlike the narrow and hastily composed reports from Treasury and other review committees, the Royal Commission must be regarded as the authentic voice of the people of New Zealand.

The Royal Commission publicized its terms of reference in a booklet entitled *A Fair and Just Society*, published in July 1987. Four other booklets were also issued, one dealing with social policy implications of the Treaty of Waitangi, and another with the nature of work in New Zealand. The definition of social policy adopted by the Commission was 'all those things deliberately done by government to promote wellbeing and to limit the effects of misfortune, primarily in terms of material advantages and disadvantages'. The Commission's warrant laid great stress on the concept of a fair society, and whether or not New Zealand fell short of the standards of a fair society. These five standards were: (1) dignity and self-determination of individuals, families, and communities; (2) maintenance of a standard of living sufficient to ensure that everybody can participate in and have a sense of belonging to the community; (3) genuine opportunity for all people, of whatever age, race, gender, social and economic position or abilities to develop their own potential; (4) a fair distribution of the wealth and resources of New Zealand including access to the resources which contribute to social wellbeing; and (5) acceptance of the identity and cultures of different peoples within the community, and understanding and respect for cultural diversity. The scope of this Commission was much broader than any previous investigations of social policy; its aim was to identify the changes necessary 'to secure a more fair, humanitarian, consistent, efficient and economical social policy' to meet changing needs 'and achieve a more just society'.[13]

In its discussion of the terms of reference, the Commission observed that social policy involves a range of resources which are not limitless, and governments are entitled to place a high value on efficiency and economy in the use of such resources. But in other respects, it claimed, social policy involves a broader set of values which should not be dominated by considerations of fiscal efficiency only: 'A balance must be struck.' Greater fairness may in some cases be at the expense of some consistency in principle or practice; the larger emphasis must be on the active participation of all citizens in the enjoyment of the nation's resources. In its conclusions, the Commission emphasized three principles vital to the future social wellbeing of New Zealanders: the principle of voice (to be part of the decision-making process); the principle of choice (based on full information), and the principle of safe prospect (the ability to plan with reasonable confidence for the future).[14] The balance between individual freedoms and the responsibilities of group membership distinctive to New Zealand was held to reflect the principle of partnership embodied in the Treaty of Waitangi, and volume II of *The April Report* devoted considerable attention to Treaty issues.

The Commission found much to praise in the comprehensive nature of New Zealand's welfare state, but also saw plenty of room for improvement, especially in the areas of policy development and public consultation, co-ordination of social and economic policies, income support, and the delivery of social services. The Commission also identified key areas of concern: 'If we are to succeed as a society, New Zealand must do much better in two central areas. One is race relations and particularly the position of the Maori. The other is the role of women.'[15] One of the reasons identified for the success of the welfare state in New Zealand was the contribution of women as unpaid domestic workers and care-givers to children. Recognition of this contribution suggested that a carer's allowance might help to redress the imbalance between male and female roles in child-care. The Commission also recognized the principles of the

Treaty of Waitangi (partnership, protection, participation) as fundamental to the future growth of social harmony in New Zealand, and recommended that the Treaty be made part of the constitution.

In short, the 1988 Royal Commission on Social Policy provided the Government with a comprehensive and coherent framework for future policy development. But it did not say exactly what needed to be done next, and there were other sources of advice reaching ministerial eyes and ears which often directly contradicted the carefully considered judgements of the Royal Commission. Foremost among these other sources was the Treasury, which appeared to many of the general public as the guiding hand behind most of the Labour Government's economic and fiscal decisions in the 1980s. In its reports to the incoming Government after the elections of 1984 and 1987, it was clear that the younger generation of Treasury economists placed particular emphasis on principles of individual choice and free play of market forces.[16] 'Equity, efficiency and accountability' were the buzz-words which captured ministerial attention, along with clichés such as 'the level playing field', 'user-pays', and 'market forces'. The implications of such slogans for social policy were to emerge in the form of recommendations for less government interference, targeted assistance, and 'welfare pluralism', with the private sector supplying more of the services previously provided by central government. Tempted by the dangling carrot of fiscal savings, some elements within the Labour Government favoured radical social policy reforms consistent with a New Right conservative ideology, but they were strongly resisted by more traditional elements within the Government and the Labour Party, who were determined to preserve Labour's traditional social-democratic philosophy. The struggle between these competing ideologies did much to delay if not paralyse social policy reform in several key areas during Labour's second term of office.

Treasury advice could not be ignored, however, because the mounting cost of social services added a 'fiscal crisis' dimension to the ideological debates between user-pays and welfare-state advocates. By 1989 net expenditure on social welfare had reached $8,177 million annually, and no fewer than 1,190,736 cash benefits were being disbursed in a population of only 3.3 million. Unemployment benefits had soared from $2.1 million in 1968 to a staggering $987 million in 1989, with 8.4 per cent of the labour force out of work. Domestic Purposes Benefit payments had almost quadrupled from $252 million in 1982 to $962 million in 1989. But the most alarming statistic of all was that for National Superannuation, which had cost $114 million in 1977; by 1989 it was costing the country $4,314 million each year. Even allowing for inflation, such figures lent weight to the arguments of those who claimed that the welfare state was no longer supportable in its traditional form in a period of high unemployment.[17]

Apart from Treasury, the Government received a bumper crop of advice in 1988 from the various working parties and 'Taskforces' it had set up to review policy options for hospitals, education, housing, employment, and Māori affairs. Unlike the fat volumes of the Royal Commission on Social

Policy (which it was rumoured some MPs used as doorstops), these were mostly slim A4 size paperbacks of about 100 pages, studded with headings and flow-charts.[18] Some of these committees were headed by people from business or management backgrounds, so it was not surprising that their recommendations often echoed the Treasury line of improved efficiency, equity, economy, and market forces, with decentralization and devolution to reduce the role of government and remove the supposed 'dead hand' of bureaucracy. In some areas, though, the findings of the Royal Commission on Social Policy were confirmed, so it is difficult to generalize simply about the recommendations made by these various working parties. Nor did the Government always accept the recommendations in full; while some social services were to be contracted out, the state remained the principal funder and provider in the areas of education, health, and housing, despite advice to the contrary from Treasury. It may be clearer if we take each of these areas in turn and place these reports in context, before finally considering the sweeping changes made to social policy by the National Government in 1990 and 1991.

In the health sector, as we have seen, administrative rationalization into Area Health Boards was proceeding during the first term of the fourth Labour Government. Boards were given greater responsibility for the efficient use of their funds in terms of the actual needs of their regions. This reform was in line with Treasury thinking on decentralization and greater accountability, but access to primary health care appeared to be shrinking, as general practitioners' fees rose and people without private medical insurance increasingly turned to hospital emergency services for 'free' care. Hospital costs rose and waiting lists lengthened. The Government responded by setting up a Health Benefits Review Taskforce which reported in 1986. Among other things, this group examined the funding of primary health services, and suggested an enlarged role for private and voluntary agencies. Another taskforce on Hospitals and Related Services reported in 1988 (the Gibbs Report) and recommended sweeping structural changes to hospital management and administration. Though the Government decided not to adopt the major changes of either report, they had a significant indirect effect on hospital managers and Area Health Boards in the drawing up of spending priorities. In the meantime, the General Medical Services Benefit was increased (October 1988) and early in 1989 a new Minister of Health, Helen Clark, declared a strong commitment to public health, including the condemnation of tobacco smoking. The Health Department was restructured and 'streamlined', and a Health Charter was introduced requiring each Area Health Board to set 'health goals' and sign an accountability agreement with the minister. Though not achieved without some protest and resentment, the old tripartite system of hospital control by doctors, nurses, and administrators was replaced by a system of general management similar to that of the business sector. While health workers were heard to complain that there now seemed to be more administrators than doctors or nurses, gains in efficiency were becoming evident by the end of 1990, and total health expenditure was held steady over the decade 1980–90 at about 7 per cent of GDP, in contrast to the sharp rise of the previous decade.[19]

Another area in which Labour resisted the radical restructuring urged by Treasury (and such pressure groups as the Business Roundtable) was that of housing. The Housing Corporation was formed in 1974 from the amalgamation of the former State Advances Corporation and the Housing Division of the Ministry of Works. It also took over the state's provision of housing for the elderly from the Health Department. The Housing Corporation thus became a large enterprise by New Zealand standards; in March 1989 its rental housing stock was valued at $3.2 billion. Housing benefits had always been targeted towards society's least affluent members, with the provision of low-rental state-owned accommodation, subsidized first-home mortgages, and the accommodation benefit. Many of the Corporation's mortgage clients were people in serious need: 42 per cent were beneficiaries in 1989. Residential Tenancies legislation in 1986 and 1987 also enabled the Housing Corporation to collect bond money from tenants of private landlords, and to mediate in disputes between them, so that the Corporation grew into an untidy hybrid, combining social with commercial roles. This offended Treasury ideologues, who pressed for the dismantling of the Housing Corporation into two or more state-owned enterprises in the late 1980s. But, armed with the recommendations of the Royal Commission on Social Policy and the advice of the 1988 National Housing Commission, the Labour Government resisted Treasury pressure, and retained its pragmatic mixture of housing policy as a central pillar of New Zealand's welfare state.[20]

By contrast, the fourth Labour Government in its second term committed itself to drastic and rapid reforms in education. This proved to be 'a strategic sector in the political and ideological struggles over social policy during the late 1980s'.[21] Gerald Grace has argued that Treasury, aided by the Business Roundtable and *Metro* magazine, deliberately created a crisis of confidence in New Zealand's education system during the run-up to the 1987 election, on which the National Party capitalized in its manifesto, *A Nation at Risk*. In its briefing to the incoming Government in 1987, Treasury officials made a strong and unprecedented attempt to influence education policy, setting out an ideological agenda derived from New Right principles which ran directly counter to Peter Fraser's classic 1939 policy statement on education.[22] Treasury saw education not as a right or a public good but merely as another commodity in the market place, and saw the relationship between the education system and its participants as that of vendor and customer. The Labour Government recognized this as a major challenge which had to be addressed and met, lest the 1930s principles of a free, universal, and secular education for all were overturned by rampant private enterprise, user-pays, and free-market philosophies.[23]

David Lange took over the Education portfolio, in addition to his duties as Prime Minister — a clear indication of the importance which now attached to this key area of social policy — and promptly commissioned a series of special working parties on schools, universities, and early childhood care. These all reported during 1988. The Picot Report favoured a major restructuring of the Department of Education with the devolution of many of its functions to new Boards of Trustees, in which parents and local communities would assume considerable responsibilities for the financing, management, and maintenance of schools.[24] The Hawke Report on Post-Compulsory Education and Training proposed a radical restructuring of tertiary education, in which the usage and concepts of the business world were freely applied to polytechnics and universities. Principals and vice-chancellors were to become 'chief executives'. Each institution would be required to draw up a corporate plan and negotiate a charter with the minister incorporating such powerful lines of accountability to the minister that the New Zealand Vice-Chancellors' Committee saw the Hawke Report as a threat to university autonomy and academic freedom.[25] Other zealots for reform characterized staff as 'resources', and university graduates as 'product'. The user-pays principle pointed towards a removal of bursary allowances to students and a substantial rise in fees, for which a system of student loans was mooted; but the trading banks proved extremely reluctant to set up any such system. The only unqualified success for Labour's education policy came from the Meade Report on early childhood care and education, which accorded closely with the principles of the 1988 Royal Commission on Social Policy.[26] Many of its key proposals were readily endorsed and implemented by a government desperate for public approval in at least one area of its reforms.

The Picot and Hawke reports aroused such a storm of protest from the most articulate sectors of New Zealand society that the Government swiftly produced its own modified blueprint for education reform, entitled *Tomorrow's Schools* (August, 1988).[27] This document invited further public debate and consultation, and was followed early in 1989 by *Learning for Life*.[28] But by now the teachers' unions and university staff and students' associations had recognized even the modified proposals as a 'hostile agenda', threatening teachers' traditional claims to collective bargaining and national award coverage. The proposal to abolish the national system of teacher registration was seen as a potentially disastrous step towards a lowering of educational standards, in which private schools could hire unqualified staff at lower pay rates than state schools. Despite loud protests and contrary advice, the Labour Government pushed ahead with remarkable speed. The result was a complicated and often contradictory set of reforms for schools, and a Treasury triumph in tertiary education, involving major funding changes and a new fees structure. David Lange's resignation from the Cabinet in mid-1989 meant that the driver who had set this juggernaut careering downhill was no longer at the controls and much opprobrium fell on the head of his successor as Minister of Education, Phil Goff. Labour's education reforms undoubtedly contributed to the deep discontent and widespread mistrust of Labour which the electorate expressed at the 1990 election.

Taking the broadest possible definition of social policy, the 1980s had seen a great many changes in the nature and delivery of government activity in New Zealand. The fourth Labour Government had embarked on a fundamental reform of the Public Service, resulting in the dismantling of 'the long-established, unified, career-based' civil service, which had grown enormously within a framework essentially unchanged since 1912, and replaced it with 'a smaller output-oriented, departmentally based structure'. Under the State Sector Act (1988), Chief Executives were appointed on short-term contracts which placed great emphasis on accountability and managerial performance, and several government departments were massively restructured, while some commercial activities (such as the Government Printing Office) were sold off, and delivery functions were contracted out to the private sector.[29] Some National MPs may have felt they were taking over a rather different country from the one they last governed in 1984. At the receiving end of social policy, in its broadest sense, ordinary New Zealanders lamented the closure of many Post Offices and Post Office Savings Banks, especially in smaller towns and rural areas. Privatization of state-owned enterprises was accompanied by widespread redundancies in the public sector, adding to a sense of insecurity and unease, that the pace of reform and restructuring was being pushed too fast in Labour's second term of office.[30] Public confidence in one of the bastions of the welfare state, the hospitals (and hospital doctors), was seriously shaken by the revelations of the Cervical Cancer Inquiry in Auckland, which added weight to feminist arguments that women were the exploited under-class of a New Zealand which was still structurally a monocultural patriarchal society.[31] Though Labour had shown its commitment to a bicultural society by its support of the Treaty of Waitangi and the Waitangi Tribunal, and the devolution of Maori Affairs to local 'Iwi' Authorities, all the indicators of Māori achievement or welfare in the fields of health, education, and employment continued to be very bleak. By 1991, Māori unemployment had reached 27 per cent, compared with 7.7 per cent for the Pākehā workforce.[32] Restructuring of local government in New Zealand had been long overdue, but the scale of changes proposed and then implemented at great speed by the Local Government Commission under Brian Elwood left many communities dazed and bewildered. The principles invoked strongly resembled the state sector reforms, and the lack of consultation (or the lack of notice taken of local submissions) added further to a widespread sense that everything was in a state of flux and uncertainty.[33] By the end of the 1980s, many New Zealanders were suffering from that collective anxiety dubbed by Alvin Toffler as 'future shock'.

National's landslide election victory in 1990 had major implications for social policy, in view of the much-publicized admiration of the new Minister of Finance, Ruth Richardson, for the New Right ideology favoured by Treasury and National's traditional supporters in the Business Roundtable. National had promised substantial increases in spending on key areas of social policy, using proceeds from the sale of Telecom, but that surplus was quickly diverted to save the Bank of New Zealand from collapse, and the new National Government soon claimed that the fiscal crisis was much worse than it had thought. As with Labour in its 1984–87 term, social policy was once again to be fiscally driven. In its Economic and Social Initiative of December 1990, National announced a series of major benefit cuts which saw weekly incomes for some beneficiaries and low-income families slashed by almost a third. All benefits now had much tighter rules for eligibility, youth rates were extended from age 20 to 25, a longer stand-down period for those seeking the unemployment benefit was imposed, and user-pays part-charges were forecast for health services. The ostensible aim of this package was to reduce 'welfare dependency' and encourage the long-term unemployed to rejoin the work-force. But while the economy floundered in its deepest recession since the 1930s, there were few jobs to be had. Most people guessed that the real aim was simply fiscal, to balance the books by taking from the least powerful members of society: altogether, the December 1990 cuts were forecast to remove $1,275 billion from the social welfare budget. As Ruth Richardson put it: 'In general, those individuals and families with reasonable means should attend to their own needs. As a broad principle, the top third of all income earners can be expected to meet most of the cost of their social services.'[34] This statement sounded a clear warning that National was moving decisively away from the social-citizenship model of the welfare state towards the residual or minimalist model.

If this were not bad news enough, worse was to come in National's 1991 Budget. Ruth Richardson's Budget speech announced 'a fundamental change to the role of the state in New Zealand' which had major implications in all areas of social policy and welfare spending.[35] In the Health portfolio, the Area Health Boards (which had only just begun to show returns of greater economy and efficiency) were to be replaced by four regional authorities headed by government-appointed commissioners, who would contract for health services from public, private, and voluntary providers. This change had as its manifest aim the separation of funding from provision, to remove the state from the latter. Most large hospitals were to become Crown Health Enterprises with appointed boards of directors. Part-charges for hospital services were introduced on 1 February 1992, and a Community Services Card was issued to all beneficiaries and the chronically ill to establish their entitlement to the medical services subsidy. Everybody else now has to pay for a night spent in a public hospital, or new prescriptions from their doctor. Hospitals have suddenly had to be equipped with cash registers and credit card machines.

Treasury's user-pays agenda in social policy had prevailed in the Health portfolio, departing radically from the philosophy broadly accepted since the 1930s by both major political parties. These changes pulled New Zealand's health system much closer to the United States model, prompting further growth of private health insurance. Once again, a major change in social policy had been instituted without any trials or pilot schemes, in quite indecent haste, and almost total absence of consultation with the professionals who actually staffed the health system.

Before the 1990 election, one aspect of social policy which seemed to be fairly stable was the state old–age pension (National Superannuation) which had been renamed the Guaranteed Retirement Income (GRI) and adjusted in Labour's 1989 Budget to remain somewhere between 65 and 72 per cent of the average wage after tax. The surcharge on additional income was retained, and the age of entitlement was to be raised gradually from 60 to 65 years, from the year 2006. Though unusual by comparison with most OECD countries, New Zealand's superannuation system was projected to cost only 7.5 per cent of the total tax base, and it seemed a fair and simple way to give retired people the dignity of a universal pension paid as of right.[36]

National had pledged to abolish the surcharge if elected, but otherwise seemed committed to the principle of a universal tax-funded pension, and reiterated its promises on superannuation when it became the Government. But the benefit cuts announced in December 1990 contrasted so sharply with the generosity of the GRI that major changes were expected. The Government soon called for a bipartisan conference on superannuation. The Labour Opposition attended the first meeting, but then refused to be party to what it foresaw as a radical departure in social policy. Treasury provided the National Government with a variety of options, all designed to achieve short-term fiscal savings by setting the level of 'adequate income' far below that which had been accepted as the norm over the previous decade.

Among all the cuts and changes announced by Ruth Richardson in her 1991 Budget speech, none caused greater shock or outrage than the statement on the Guaranteed Retirement Income. Pre-election promises were broken at every turn. Though the surcharge was abolished, pensions were frozen until 1993, and a much harsher income test was to apply from 1992. Any income above $4,160 per annum would abate the pension by 90 cents in the dollar. For married couples under 70 years of age, their entire pension would be lost once joint income from other sources reached $23,740 and they would not be eligible for a Community Services Card to gain access to medical benefits. The effective marginal tax rate on each dollar earned over the exemption would be 92.8 per cent. The legislation for these changes was rushed through in a marathon 100-hour sitting of Parliament following the Budget, with no select committee scrutiny.

The Budget proposals aroused such a storm of protest and were so comprehensively condemned by all sectors of society that the Government had to back down, and in November 1991 declared a return to individual-based pensions and a surcharge through the tax system. Thus some of the harshest features of the Budget proposals were reversed, but the freeze and the rise in entitlement age remained. The Minister of Social Welfare, Jenny Shipley, attempted to explain the changes to social policy in a statement entitled, *Social Assistance: Welfare that Works* (1991), but this only revealed how central the pension plan had been to the whole range of welfare changes. In the minister's words, the state would provide no more than a 'safety net' for 'those who can demonstrate genuine need'.[37] This phrase more than any other clearly identified National's approach to social policy as that of the residual or minimalist model, and marked the abandonment of a 'cradle to grave' concept of the welfare state. Further refinements were promised, but when some of these were leaked to the media in September 1991, another wave of anger from the elderly and some backbenchers within the National Government provoked yet another back-down, and on 3 October Prime Minister Bolger announced a substantial reversal of the Budget proposals for GRI.

Though superannuitants were again made eligible for the Community Services Card, many more would be liable for some sort of tax surcharge on additional income, and elderly people with even a modest income were to face hospital and medical part-charges from September 1992. In short, National badly mishandled its social policy changes as they affected the elderly, and the future of GRI is still far from clear. But National's intention had been made nakedly obvious: to move decisively from a rights-based universal pension towards a residualist 'safety-net' pension scheme, in which pensioners were regarded as dependants. The state's role was reduced to preventing dire poverty in old age, but little more. Most pensioners were to be significantly worse off than under any previous form of National Superannuation.[38]

Just before the end of 1991, Housing Minister John Luxton announced major reforms in housing policy, which, when added to the benefit cuts previously announced, compounded the harshness of National's social policy changes. A new Housing Ministry was to take over the administration of residential rental property and all housing subsidies were to be delivered by the Social Welfare Department in a single Accommodation Supplement. A new state-owned enterprise would own and manage rental accommodation on a commercial basis, with rents set according to family size. Though the Government had backed away from setting rents at the full market rate, most state house tenants faced very substantial rent increases, and some immediately moved 'down-market' to cheaper (and often more crowded) accommodation. These changes were imposed with very little research or prior consultation, and once again appeared to be fiscally driven with scant concern for their feasibility or fairness.[39]

In tertiary education, the 1991 Budget changes were equally draconian and unpopular. The Study Right entitlement was reduced from five to three years, with substantial cuts in student allowances, which were now targeted on parental income until the student turned 24. Thresholds were set so low that most tertiary students found themselves ineligible for any sort of state assistance. A state-funded loans scheme was introduced which would reclaim the money through the tax system at ten cents for every dollar earned above $12,670 once the graduate was in paid employment, but the nominal 6 per cent interest rate was misleading, as repayment would greatly inflate a graduate's marginal tax rate. At first, the

Government declared that students would not be eligible for a Community Services Card, but later changed its mind on this point. Though the Budget increased the number of places in tertiary institutions, there was no adjustment for inflation, and the universities were faced with a massive 'capital charge' on their buildings and plant. Altogether, National's changes produced a very odd system, which contradicted its own policy of having a well-educated and flexible work-force; the effect of higher fees and lower allowances was to disadvantage all students, especially mature students and women. In one critic's words, the education reforms were 'discriminatory, inequitable, and inefficient.'[40] Added to the drastic changes announced in health, housing, and income support, National's social policies together constituted a firm if not arrogant rejection of the principles and recommendations of the 1988 Royal Commission on Social Policy. As that document warned, the most disadvantaged members of New Zealand society were Māori and women. National's policies seemed likely to worsen rather than improve their situation, and it was a bitter irony that the two ministers chiefly concerned were women, including the country's first-ever female Minister of Finance.

A major feature of the National Government's approach to social policy has been its move away from 'universalist' social assistance towards 'targeted' or 'means-tested' assistance. Arguments in support of the latter approach usually boil down to those of cost-effectiveness and equity, which dominated Treasury advice and government thinking across the 1980s. Housing is one area where such arguments carry some weight, but the longer-term consequences of a strongly targeted social policy appear likely to undermine yet further New Zealand's traditional welfare state. Means-tested social policies have a tendency to get meaner, while universalist programmes with a higher proportion of middle-class participants are politically much harder to cut. Heavy targeting of benefits tends in the long run to create 'poverty traps' and social inequality, and to diminish any sense of community or shared citizenship. Thus targeting and joint-income testing run counter to the values espoused by the 1988 Royal Commission on Social Policy, and in practical terms cost a great deal more to administer so that the original aims of equity and efficiency may not be fulfilled.[41]

At the time of writing it is difficult to predict the final shape of social policy in the aftermath of National's 1990–91 changes, but their broad implications are clear enough. In terms of the three models of the welfare state outlined at the start of this chapter, New Zealand no longer has the same sort of welfare state which it enjoyed from the 1930s to the 1980s. There has been a radical shift in the underlying philosophy of social policy, largely under pressure from short-term fiscal crises, away from the long-familiar 'cradle to the grave' rights-based welfare state towards the opposite extreme of a residualist 'safety-net' model. The picture is still very messy and uncertain because of the Bolger Government's remarkable capacity for sudden reversals and changes of policy, and some areas of social policy have been moved further along the spectrum than others, but the overall trend is unmistakeable. National's reforms constitute such a striking contrast with the settled pattern of the previous half-century that the term revolution is not inappropriate, especially in view of the speed of change, the lack of public consultation or mandate, and the ideological rationales offered by way of justification. Only time will tell if the electorate is content to accept such sweeping alterations to the welfare state; but, as historians well know, every revolution creates the possibility of a counter-revolution.

CHAPTER 19

Māori People since 1950

Ranginui J. Walker

In the pre-colonial period of New Zealand history, the Māori people were divided into forty-two distinct tribal groups. Some tribes in the populous central North Island formed confederations under ariki. These were the paramount chiefs whose lineages traced their descent from ancestors who arrived in New Zealand on one of the ocean-voyaging vessels of the fourteenth century. The signing of the Treaty of Waitangi in 1840 with the British Crown ushered in the historic process of colonization, alienation of land, and political subjection. When the General Assembly met for the first time in 1854, Māori people had no representation. They tried to counter their exclusion from government by electing a Māori King to hold the mana whenua, sovereignty over the land. Tribes that did not support the King attempted to pursue their political objectives through the unity movement of Kotahitanga. For two decades this movement held a series of inter-tribal meetings to discuss the protection of Māori land and resources under the Treaty of Waitangi. It culminated in the establishment of the Māori Parliament in 1892. The Governor waged war against the Māori King and confiscated three million acres of land under the New Zealand Settlements Act 1863. After the New Zealand Wars, the Māori still held the major portion of the North Island, sixteen million acres to the Crown's ten million acres. From 1867 to the turn of the century, this land was systematically alienated by legal artifice through the operations of the Native Land Court. The four Māori Members of Parliament, whose seats were established in 1867, were unable to protect Māori land from alienation. The Māori had only four seats in a House of seventy, when on the basis of population numbers (in 1867) they were entitled to twenty seats. In the 1890s, the Kauhanganui (King's Council) and Kotahitanga (Māori Parliament) tried to avert total dispossession of land by making representations to Parliament. They were ignored.[1] By 1900, introduced diseases, war, and loss of land had reduced the Māori population by half down to 45,549.[2] Interest in Kotahitanga and the Kauhanganui declined and the political initiative passed from chiefs to the educated élite.

Political subjection and dispossession of their resources defined the Māori as the brown underclass of New Zealand society. Institutions such as the education system served to maintain that structural inequality. The

Māori wanted access through schooling to knowledge which had made Europeans great. But they were thwarted by the underlying agenda of those who controlled the curriculum. Missionary policy restricted instruction in literacy to the Māori language. Students were given access to scriptural material only and kept away from secular knowledge.[3] With the establishment of the native schools in 1867, Māori was displaced entirely by English as the medium of instruction. But the policy of language displacement met resistance which slowed educational progress in the state schools. The one beacon of success was the Anglican Church school of Te Aute College. Its headmaster John Thornton prepared the brightest pupils for the matriculation exam to enable them to enter the professions. At the turn of the century, Te Aute College produced Apirana Ngata, Peter Buck, and Maui Pomare, the first Māori scholars to graduate from university. Although these men worked through mainstream politics to improve the lot of the Māori, they were a challenge to Pākehā dominance. Officials in the Education Department moved to stifle Māori education.[4]

After the turn of the century George Hogben, Director of Education, advocated the introduction of manual and technical instruction for Māori schools. The Department of Education put pressure on Te Aute College to replace its academic curriculum with agricultural training by threatening withdrawal of scholarships for its matriculation programme. William Bird, Inspector of Native Schools, argued before a Royal Commission that the aim of education was to train Māori for life among their own people and 'not to mingle with Europeans and compete with Europeans in trade and commerce'.[5] Even as late as 1931, T. B. Strong, Director of Education, contended that Māori schools should turn out boys to be good farmers and girls to be good farmers' wives. Strong went so far as to say he did not want white teachers to encourage pupils to take arithmetic beyond their present or even possible future needs.[6]

The two-tier system of education was extended into the Māori district high schools when they were established in the 1940s. The curriculum followed the existing policy of providing practical courses in metalwork, home management, cookery, and infant welfare.[7] School Certificate courses were not provided until 1945, when they were requested by Māori parents. This inferior education provision for Māori delayed the appearance of the second wave of Māori graduates for another fifty years.

The first Māori graduates, Ngata, Buck, and Pomare, entered Parliament to negotiate a more equitable share of the nation's resources for the Māori people. As the Māori population recovered to 63,670 over the first three decades of the century, Ngata fostered a revival of interest in Māori art, literature, action songs, and the building of carved houses. But on the fundamental issue of land, he was unable to prevent its alienation. By 1936, when the population had almost doubled to 82,326, the Māori land base was reduced to 4,992,013 acres. The major portion of these remnant lands, 3,103,182 acres, was leased by Pākehā.[8]

During the Depression of the 1930s, the people became disillusioned with the élite and turned to the prophet leader Ratana. He sought an accommodation with mainstream politics. Between 1932 and 1943 Ratana captured the four Māori seats and aligned them with the Labour Party. Nothing substantive accrued from that alliance to the Māori except the general benefits of the welfare state.[9]

The problem of a rising Māori population deriving a living from a diminishing land base was identified by Professor H. Belshaw in 1939 at the first national conference of young Māori leaders. Belshaw anticipated the Māori would have to migrate to towns and cities because the Māori land development schemes started by Ngata earlier in the decade would support only a quarter of the population.[10] Twenty years later, the Hunn Report made the same observation. If all remnant Māori lands were developed and settled, no more than 4,000 farms would be provided. By that time the Māori population would be half a million.[11]

In 1926, only 9 per cent of the Māori population lived in cities and boroughs.[12] By 1951, this had increased to 19 per cent. Awareness of this demographic shift of the population was reflected in the recommendations of the Young Maori Leaders Conference in 1939. These included proposals for the establishment of a social and cultural centre in Auckland, formation of Māori discussion groups, adult education for Māori, and the establishment of an urban marae.[13] The Second World War acted as a catalyst in stimulating the pace of the rural–urban shift of the Māori population. Under the Manpower Regulations, young Māori not eligible for military service were directed to contribute to the war effort by working in essential industries. Young women were put to work in factories, or on farms as land-girls. The men were put to work in the industrial areas of Penrose and Westfield. The social problems concerning the moral well-being of young people living away from home prompted the Department of Maori Affairs to appoint six Māori welfare officers in the main urban centres.

After the war, men of the 28 Maori Battalion sought equality by moving to cities in search of work. But the highest employment that the most able leaders of the Battalion could find was in the Department of Maori Affairs, or in teaching. These included three former commanders of the Battalion and several majors and lieutenants.[14] In 1956, only 3.43 per cent of the Māori work-force was in the professional, technical, and related fields. The dearth of Māori in the professions was the direct outcome of Education Department policy. The first wave of migrants were by design poorly educated. The Hunn Report (1961) brought the problem out into the public domain. The report identified a 'statistical blackout' of Māori at the higher levels of schooling. In secondary education, only 0.5 per cent of Māori students reached the sixth form compared to 3.8 per cent of Pākehā. At university Māori enrolment was only one-eighth of what it should have been.[15] Lack of educational qualifications meant that Māori migrants were concentrated in certain fields of employment such as freezing works, road maintenance, factories, transport, building trades,[16] farming, fishing, forestry, mining, transport, and labouring occupations.[17]

By 1956 urban-dwelling Māori had increased to 24 per cent.

Newspapers of the day commented on this development as a 'drift to the towns'. The negative connotation inherent in the word 'drift' was put into perspective by Hunn saying, 'It seems to be a case of Māoris on wheels heading fast for the towns. The so-called 'urban drift' is not so much a 'drift' as an irreversible migration in search of work.'[18] Anthropologist Joan Metge put the matter more succinctly by calling it 'A New Māori Migration' in search of 'the Big Three factors of work, money and pleasure.'[19]

The Department of Maori Affairs gave additional impetus to the urban migration by initiating a Māori urban relocation programme in 1960. Rural families living on seasonal work and the subsistence economy of gardening, hunting, and gathering seafood were encouraged to abandon the shellfish beds and move to towns where they could get work. By 1965 the scheme had relocated 399 families and assisted 485 other families to find work or accommodation.[20] One of the visible effects of the urban migration was the abandonment of small uneconomic farm units under Ngata's land development schemes. Of the 298 registered Māori incorporations, over 50 per cent were inoperative by 1961. There was a similar decline of Māori farmers down to 2,116.[21]

Metge's study of urbanization in Auckland revealed a complex pattern of migration. Half the sample in her study went directly from their tribal area to the city. One-third shifted from one rural area to another before heading for a major city. The rest went via small towns and cities to larger cities.[22] In the early stages of the migration, the preferred location for lodging was near the city centre, close to places of work and entertainment. In the case of Auckland, the migrants concentrated in the inner city areas of Freeman's Bay, Ponsonby, Herne Bay, and Grey Lynn. But as the migration gathered momentum, accommodation became overcrowded. To relieve the pressure, the Department of Maori Affairs aimed to expand its housing programme from 700 in 1960 to 2,000 by 1967.[23]

In major cities, the Department of Maori Affairs tried to follow a policy of 'pepper potting' Māori dwellings in new subdivisions in the interest of integrating the migrants into the host community. The ideal was to have only one Māori dwelling to a block of Pākehā houses. The policy was never fully implemented. In cities such as Rotorua, where land was at a premium, all-Māori settlements had to be built at Koutu and Ngapuna, otherwise no houses would have been built at all.[24]

The largest provider of houses was the State Advances Corporation. To relieve the housing shortage in Auckland, the Corporation, together with the Ministry of Works, planned whole new satellite housing estates in Otara, Mangere, and Te Atatu. Similar estates were built in the Wellington suburbs of Porirua, Hutt Valley, and Wainuiomata. The planning of new housing subdivisions provided for a one-third mix of private, state, and group houses.[25] Since the Maori Affairs housing programme was limited to the virtually destitute, the majority of Māori people obtained a home or rental accommodation through the State Advances Corporation. The Corporation did not have a 'pepper potting' policy; consequently there was a critical build-up in the density of Māori numbers to 10 per cent or more in some housing estates. In the satellite town of Otara, the Māori population comprised almost a third of the population of 20,955.[26] One street in Otara for instance had nine Māori houses in a contiguous row. This critical density had an important bearing on the adjustment of migrants to urban life. It allowed Māori to identify with each other and form voluntary associations to cope with the problems of urban life.

Rural Māori are located socially in the kinship networks of whānau (extended family), hapū (sub-tribe), and iwi (tribe). The focal point of community sentiment and group activities for these social units is the marae with its ancestral house.[27] The marae is the location for religious and secular activities including church services, meetings, twenty-first birthdays, weddings, official welcomes, headstone unveilings, and fund-raising. One of the basic functions of a marae is the conduct of tangihanga, the rituals associated with farewelling the dead. The rituals are usually conducted in the Māori language, despite its erosion among the young under Pākehā influence.

Within tribal communities was a well-defined system of rank and social control in the form of kaumātua (elders), kuia (female elder) pakeke (parents, uncles, and aunts), religious mentors, and Māori wardens. The most mobile of Māori migrants were young people, who, once beyond the constraints of their communities, relished the freedom of the cities. Many were not equipped for that freedom and soon fell into conflict with the law. The Māori male offending rate in 1958 was 5.3 per cent — almost three and a half times higher than that of the Pākehā (1.5 per cent).[28] Ten years later, the problem had increased. By the age of seventeen, 40.1 per cent of Māori boys had had at least one court appearance, compared to 10.3 per cent of non-Māori boys. For Māori girls the rate was 16.7 per cent, compared to 2.8 per cent for non-Māori.[29]

Besides trying to manage the young, adult migrants had a different set of problems to deal with. There were three developmental tasks that migrants had to undertake in adjusting to urban life. These included learning survival skills in the cash economy of the urban-industrial complex, transplantation of their culture into the urban milieu, and the development of political structures and strategies for dealing with metropolitan society.

The migrants had to function as members of the urban community. Adjustments included finding regular employment, and commitment to the cash nexus by meeting obligations on mortgages, rates, rent, power charges, hire-purchase, and taxes. Most people soon learned how to cope. But a minority who got into difficulties had to be assisted with budgeting by churches, welfare organizations, and the Department of Maori Affairs. Once committed to this system, the migrants were irrevocably integrated into the economic system of mainstream society. The practice in the rural areas of supplementary subsistence activities such as gardening, hunting, and foraging for kai moana (seafood) to supplement low cash income was no longer an option. Food was now a commodity purchased entirely in the marketplace. Foraging for seafood became merely an occasional recreational activity. Thus the universal culture of capitalism integrated the Māori into mainstream Pākehā society. Besides the workplace, other integrative mechanisms included church affiliations and sport. Māori women and men shared with their Pākehā associates a passion for competitive team sports, particularly basketball (now netball), rugby football, and rugby league.

The increase in Māori–Pākehā interaction in urban life was reflected by the incidence of intermarriage. In 1960, half the marriages contracted by Māori men and women were with Pākehā spouses.[30] Sexual congress between Māori and Pākehā began with the whalers, sealers, and traders early in the nineteenth century. By the end of the century, as the Pākehā population grew and the Māori declined, it was believed that amalgamation of the races would resolve the problem of the Māori maintaining their cultural identity and the challenge this posed to colonialism.[31] This view prevailed up to the time of the Hunn Report, which proclaimed that 'miscegenation is inexorably integrating, even assimilating, the two races'.[32]

Assimilation implied the complete loss of Māori culture — but that had not occurred. For this reason, the Hunn Report redefined official policy in terms of integration. The policy meant Māori and Pākehā combined into one nation but with Māori culture remaining distinct. The Report concluded that assimilation was inevitable, because intermarriage had reduced full-blooded Māori down to 20 per cent.[33] The authors of the Report had not taken into account the process of enculturation in the development of identity. Māori on the other hand saw integration as simply a new word for the old policy of assimilation. In cities where Pākehā dominated, and assimilation was a real possibility, the Māori had to take positive measures to maintain their culture and transplant it into the urban milieu. This was the second development task in the adjustment to urban life.

Voluntary associations were the key to the successful adjustment of the Māori to urban life. These associations were structured around Māori identity and the common goal of preserving Māori culture and spiritual values. They included Māori sections of the orthodox churches, the Māori protest churches of Ringatu and Rātana, culture clubs, sports clubs, family and tribal organizations, benevolent societies, Māori committees, Māori wardens, Māori councils, Maori Women's Welfare League, and Te Ropu Whakawhanaunga i nga Hahi (Maori Ecumenical Council of Churches).

In the alien and impersonal environment of cities, some people, with a sufficient number of kinsmen in the same city, formalized their kinship ties by establishing family clubs for the purpose of assisting each other financially in times of bereavement. The main cost was the return of deceased persons to their home marae for burial. Although in the early stages some clubs were unstable, others endured for long periods.[34] The most enduring were those that grew into hapū and tribal associations. Many of them built community centres or marae for their members.

The Māori missions of the Anglican, Roman Catholic, Presbyterian, Mormon, and Methodist churches, along with the Rātana and Ringatu churches, helped integrate migrants into urban life with both church and secular activities. The latter included fostering youth clubs, culture clubs, and sports teams. The experience in Auckland indicated that, away from tribal areas, church affiliation served as an integrative mechanism in place of kinship for people from different tribes.

Māori culture clubs were formed in the first decade of the urban migration to perpetuate interest in Māori singing, action songs, oratory, and arts and crafts. In Auckland, the Maranga Club founded by Arapeta Awatere taught traditions and marae protocol as well as singing and dancing. In 1962, Awatere taught a course in marae etiquette in the adult education programme of the Extension Department of Auckland University. In Wellington, the Ngāti Pōneke Club did the same. Wiremu Parker taught Māori language and culture courses in the Extension Department at Victoria University. The name Ngāti Pōneke symbolized emerging Māori consciousness of pan-tribalism as an ideology for the recruitment of membership. In Auckland, the term Ngāti Akarana[35] was coined to name pan-tribal groups mobilized in 1953 to ensure that urban Māori had a role in welcoming Queen Elizabeth II on her visit to New Zealand. The ideology of pan-tribalism is a direct outcome of urbanization. By the 1970s, when 75 per cent of the Māori population had become urbanized, there was an efflorescence of Māori culture clubs. Cultural competitions were organized at regional and national levels. In the same decade, teachers in Auckland secondary schools initiated Māori oratory competitions. Other regions did the same. Auckland Secondary Schools also formed Māori clubs to compete in the Māori and Pacific Island Cultural Festival. In 1991 over fifty schools were involved in the festival.

The desire expressed at the Young Maori Leaders Conference in 1939 for a marae in Auckland was partially met by the establishment of the Maori Community Centre in 1948. During the 1950s, the Maori Community Centre was the focal point for the entertainment of the young people in the city. But the centre was an incomplete substitute for a marae. When the influential Māori educator John Waititi died in 1965, special permission had to be obtained from the City Council for the tangi to be held there. In the 1950s, the Aotearoa Marae Society was the first pan-Māori group to try to build a marae in Auckland. Although carvings were produced, the marae was not built because of factional disputes.

The first urban marae built in Auckland was Te Puea, which was opened at Mangere in 1965. It is essentially a traditional kin-based institution belonging to the Tainui confederation of tribes. The marae is built on seven acres of Māori land excluded from confiscation by the Government and held by a Waikato family. When the Surplus Lands Commission made an *ex gratia* payment of £4,000 to King Koroki, he donated the money to start the marae project. Other tribes had a stake in the marae through donations and the fund-raising efforts of the Waitemata Executive. Māori committees at Onehunga, Mangere, and Ihumatao also raised funds for the project. Use of the marae was so heavy that it was clear many others would have to be built.

The other traditional tangata whenua marae in Auckland belonged to the Ngāti Whātua of Orakei at Okahu Bay. That marae was not able to fulfil its obligations to host migrant Māori because of its takeover and destruction by Government action in 1952. When the meeting house Te Puru o Tamaki was demolished, one of the elders burnt the timbers in situ to ensure that the ashes of the ancestor would remain where they were meant to be.[36]

In 1953 the Crown set aside a reserve for a new marae site on the high ground behind Kitemoana Street overlooking the old marae. Orakei Marae had a chequered career arising out of the Government gazetting it as a reserve for the use and benefit of Māori, meaning migrant Māori as well as tangata whenua. A composite multi-tribal trust board, including Pākehā, left the Ngāti Whātua of Orakei in the invidious position of not being in control of their own marae. The marae complex consisting of a playcentre, prefabricated meeting room, education and reception centre, and a finely carved ancestral house named Tumutumuwhenua, was twenty years in the making. The opening of the house was delayed pending the Government's implementation of the Waitangi Tribunal's recommendation that the land title be vested in the Ngāti Whātua of Orakei Maori Trust Board.[37] Before the order became effective, Tumutumuwhenua was destroyed by fire in January 1990. It has since been reconstructed.

A variation on the traditional marae is the kin-based community centre at Point Chevalier belonging to the Mahurehure migrants from the Hokianga. Although the land is not a marae reserve, ideologically the centre is treated as a marae. It is a place where members of the Mahurehure tribe can fulfil their social and cultural needs in an urban setting. The Tuhoe Benevolent Society, consisting of members of a tribe from the Bay of Plenty, wanted a facility of their own in Auckland. After first seeking permission from the tangata whenua, the society refurbished an existing building in Panmure and converted it into a full marae complex named Tira Hou. Similarly, the related Ngāti Awa people from the Bay of Plenty built the Mataatua Marae in Mangere.

Another alternative to traditional kin-based marae are community centres and full marae complexes built by Māori sections of various religious denominations. The Te Unga Waka centre opened in 1965 was the first of this kind built by the Māori Catholic community of Auckland. This was followed by the opening of Tatai Hono Marae by Kingi Ihaka of the Anglican Maori Mission in 1969. Both these facilities consist of refurbished buildings. Whaiora Marae was next to be opened in 1977 by the Māori Catholic community of Otara.[38] This marae has a fully carved house named Waiariki with an adjoining dining hall and ablution facilities.

With the relocation of migrant Māori in the 1960s from the decaying inner city areas to the new satellite housing estates on the periphery of Auckland, there was a need felt in the new communities for their own marae. Secular pan-tribal marae building associations were formed to raise funds for new marae projects. The John Waititi Memorial Marae at Te Atatu, which was opened in 1980, is the prototype of the modern urban marae that is not kin-based. Other marae of this type, either completed or in progress, are located at Otara, Papakura, Northcote, and Manurewa. The most recent innovation in marae development has been the establishment of marae facilities on the campuses of secondary schools, colleges of education, and universities. The facilities range from pre-fabricated classrooms decorated with carvings, to purpose-built, fully decorated meeting houses with ancillary facilities. The finest examples of this type of marae are Te Herenga Waka at Victoria University and Waipapa at the University of Auckland. The location of these marae are symbolic cultural statements of the ethos and dynamism of the Māori cultural renaissance.

The third adjustment migrants had to make to urban life was to develop political structures and strategies to deal with Pākehā domination. One of the consequences of urbanization is increased knowledge of the alienating culture. It is that knowledge which 'leads to transforming action resulting in a culture which is being freed from alienation'.[39] Migrants had to develop new systems of leadership and social organization to negotiate Pākehā accommodation to Māori cultural and political aspirations. The mechanism that evolved to achieve this was multi-level voluntary associations. The groups involved were tribal, parochial, pan-tribal, ad hoc activists, professional educators, and national associations.

The tribal enclaves at Orakei and Ihumatao which were engulfed by urban growth were overwhelmed by the physical transformation of their environment through the actions of Government and local bodies. The Ngāti Whātua at Orakei were systematically dispossessed of their inalienable 700 acre estate by the actions of the Crown and relocated from the papa kāinga (dwelling place) at Okahu Bay to Kitemoana Street.[40] There they were treated as wards of the state, and denied for twenty years even the fundamental right granted to their fellow citizens to purchase their own state houses.[41] In 1975 the Orakei Maori Action Committee was formed to initiate change.

The Māori community at Ihumatao suffered similar dispossession and alienation at the hands of local bodies. As the millennial kaitiaki (custodians) of the Manukau Harbour, they watched with impotence its progressive degradation by reclamations, enclosures, pollution from industrial development, and denial of access to their traditional sources of seafood by the building of the Mangere sewage treatment plant and Auckland International Airport. Their subjection as a powerless minority was epitomized by having to suffer the odoriferous presence of the sewage treatment plant while their village remained unconnected to it for twenty years. In the 1970s the community combined with Ngāti Te Ata of Waiuku to form Te Puaha Ki Manukau, the guardians of the Manukau. This group lodged the Manukau claim with the Waitangi Tribunal in 1984.

The tribal committees at Onehunga, Ihumatao, and Mangere involved in raising funds for the Mangere Marae operated under the statutory mandate of the Maori Social and Economic Advancement Act 1945. The committees were charged under the Act with promoting the social, cultural, educational, economic, and spiritual well-being of the Māori. Together, the tribal committees formed the Waitemata Tribal Executive, a pan-tribal body that acted officially on behalf of migrant Māori as well as the tangata whenua tribes of the Auckland isthmus. The Waitemata Executive ran the Maori Community Centre which played a prominent part in the recreational life of migrants during the 1950s.

As the migrant population increased, new opportunities for leadership developed. Women who had been members of Māori committees in the Country Women's Institute, or members of the Maori Health League, sought assistance from Major Rangi Royal in the Department of Maori Affairs to form the Maori Women's Welfare League. The first Dominion Council of the League was elected at a hui in Wellington in 1951 with Whina Cooper as its first Dominion President (until 1957). The formation of district councils and local branches followed. The first political success of the League derived from its survey of Māori housing needs in Auckland. It brought to the attention of the authorities the insanitary and overcrowded conditions in which migrant Māori were living. The report put pressure on the Department of Maori Affairs and the State Advances Corporation to expand their housing programme for needy families. For ten years the annual conferences of the Maori Women's League provided the only national platform for the articulation of Māori needs in education, health, child care, and housing.[42] At the parochial and national level, the League got involved with fund-raising for the Maori Education Foundation in 1962. It also put its weight behind the playcentre movement and was instrumental in the rapid spread of playcentres to rural as well as urban communities. The League produced several influential leaders and spokespersons for Māori people, such as Whina Cooper and the League's Dominion President in the late 1970s, Miraka Szászy (who went on to become director of Nga Tapuwae College).

Urbanization provided an opportunity for a meritocracy of educated leaders in the teaching profession to emerge and exercise a significant role in the mediation of cultural politics between Māori and Pākehā. In 1959 Maharaia Winiata and Matiu Te Hau, the Māori tutors in Adult Education at Auckland University, organized the second Young Maori Leaders Conference. As young men they had both attended the first conference organized by Ngata and Belshaw in 1939.[43] The conference provided an opportunity for twenty-seven elders and fifty young men and women to come together and discuss Māori concerns in education, health, housing, employment, and the development of land. The conference brought together the empirical knowledge of the people and the critical knowledge of the leaders, which became transformed into knowledge of the underlying causes of Māori subjection.[44]

The political consciousness forged by the Young Maori Leaders was reflected in the conference recommendations. They sought inclusion of Māori studies in the school curriculum, the appointment of lecturers in

Māori studies at teachers' colleges, the appointment of a Māori liaison officer to the Education Department, and rationalization of the award of educational grants and scholarships on the basis of merit and need.[45] These recommendations came to fruition in 1961 with the appointment of Harry Lambert to Auckland Teachers' College and John Waititi as Māori education adviser in the Auckland regional office of the Department of Education.

Subsequently regional conferences were held at Kaitaia, Ngaruawahia, Whakatane, and Gisborne in 1960. Over the next two years, regional conferences were held at Tauranga, Taupo, Rotorua, Ruatoria, and Wairoa. These conferences played an important part in raising political consciousness among widely separated Māori communities. They resulted in the formation of study groups at Rotorua, Taupo, Tauranga, Whakatane, and Opotiki to discuss the Hunn Report and the issues it had raised concerning land, education, health, and criminal offending.

In the 1960s Māori teachers began to influence education policy to accommodate Māori needs. In the vanguard was John Waititi who was appointed Advisor to the Officer for Maori Education. In 1962 he organized an extensive fund-raising campaign in Auckland for the Maori Education Foundation. He also persuaded a number of adult Māori to go back to night school to sit School Certificate. His Te Rangatahi text books encouraged the spread of the teaching of the Māori language in secondary schools and night classes. The most taxing part of Waititi's role as an educator was persuading his Pākehā colleagues in the Education Department to modify their educational provisions in the curriculum to meet Māori needs. Although Waititi's death at an early age in 1965 was a severe loss to Māori people, he at least had set the stage for the gains that were made in education in the next decade.

In 1967 the influence of Māori teachers on educational thinking was made manifest in the New Zealand Education Institute Report on Māori education. The report stated that

a modification of opinion and policy has slowly upgraded the opinion of Maoritanga in New Zealand society. This reversal has been brought about by Maoris themselves, but many present ills are the direct result of misguided past policies . . . It must be remembered that the Maori is both a New Zealander and a Maori. He has an inalienable right to be both.[46]

The Young Maori Leaders Conference 1970 at Auckland University added to the pressure for educational reform, by demanding the compulsory teaching of the Māori language in secondary schools. The young urban educated leaders at the conference knew intuitively that 'there is no transformation without action'.[47] To ensure that the resolution was followed up by ongoing action, they formed the activist Nga Tamatoa group. Tamatoa promulgated a nation-wide petition for the inclusion of Māori language in schools, initiated Māori Language Day, and petitioned the Minister of Education to establish a one-year teacher training course for native speakers of Māori.

In 1971 the National Advisory Committee on Maori Education

produced an influential report that spelt out clearly in a three-point plan the transformations Māori wanted in the education system: first, that cultural differences needed to be understood, accepted, and respected by children and teachers; secondly, that the school curriculum must find a place for the understanding of Māoritanga; and thirdly, that in order to achieve the goal of equality of opportunity, special measures needed to be taken.[48]

Special measures to improve Māori education included lowered pupil–teacher ratios, provisions for teacher aides, guidance counsellors, and other ancillary staff for schools with significant numbers of Māori students. Māori studies became a growth area in education. By the mid-1970s, all teacher training institutions had appointed lecturers in Māori studies. By 1976 there were 123 secondary schools teaching Māori to 11,000 pupils compared to only 10 schools previously. At the primary level there were 100 schools offering Māori studies programmes.[49] This remarkable turnaround from exclusion to inclusion was due to the efforts of Māori teachers to promote and maintain their distinct cultural identity within the education system.

During World War II, the Maori War Effort Organisation made use of tribal structures to establish committees to raise money for the War Effort. The tribal committees were so effective that they were given a mandate to continue functioning after the war under the Maori Social and Economic Advancement Act 1945. But as the Māori became increasingly urbanized, the tribal committees were redesignated Māori committees under the Maori Welfare Act 1962.

In the absence of traditional authority structures, Māori committees provided an outlet for legitimating leaders who wanted to take responsibility for dealing with delinquency, parental neglect of children, drunkenness, and indebtedness caused by overcommitment to hire-purchase and time-payment agreements. These problems were particularly manifested in the new housing estate of Otara in the late 1960s when hundreds of people at a time were relocated there as each new block of houses was opened up. The Otara Māori Committee, led by men and women who had experience in tribal committees, used the powers of the Maori Welfare Act as their mandate to deal with these issues. Upwards of forty Māori wardens were appointed to patrol the hotels in South Auckland and keep a watch over families in their neighbourhood.

The Otara Māori Committee operated a budgeting service for people facing judgment summons for indebtedness, launched the Otara Marae project, and instituted Māori courts to deal with petty offenders. The Committee also functioned as a conduit between its constituents and local authorities. It became adept at negotiating budgetary deals on behalf of its clients with business houses. When the Manukau City Council offered the Committee a room above the shopping centre for a marae it declined. The officers of the City Council had to be instructed on the functions of a marae, the symbolism of the buildings, and their disposition according to the laws of tapu. Thus, the cultural transactions became two-way. Once it was sensitized to Māori needs, the Manukau City Council became very supportive of its Māori constituents and their marae projects. The Otara Māori Committee was an example of what could be done under the Maori Welfare Act at the parochial level. Committees in Auckland and other parts of the country carried out similar functions in varying degrees.

In the 1970s there were more than thirty-six marae and Māori committees in the Auckland region. Collectively they constituted the Auckland District Maori Council. This body used its statutory standing to negotiate Māori social and cultural aspirations with local bodies and government. It began by getting a Māori section written into the planning scheme of the Auckland Regional Authority (ARA). It then opened up the ARA to Māori representation by gaining access to the planning committee of the authority. The Council made extensive submissions to local bodies, the Waitangi Tribunal, ministers, and committees of inquiry on wide-ranging issues such as the Maori Land Court, mining of urupā, pollution of the Manukau Harbour, Bastion Point electoral reform, and deaths of patients in custody at Oakley Hospital.

The top tier of the Māori committee and district council structure is the New Zealand Maori Council. It was initially comprised of seven district councils based on the Maori Land Court boundaries of Taitokerau, Waikato, Waiariki, Aotea, Tairawhiti, Ikaroa, and Te Waipounamu. As the largest centre of the migrant Māori population, Auckland was given district council status. A decade later Wellington City also became a district council. Subsequently four tribally based councils were established for Takitimu, Raukawa, Maniapoto, and Hauraki.

The Maori Council took up a wide range of social issues including the problems of prostitution, delinquency, rising Māori crime, and the appointment of Māori representatives to government bodies. The Council responded to bills referred to it by government for comment. Most of these were uncontested. But when it came to the Maori Affairs Amendment Bill 1967, the Council dug in. The major concern of rural-dominated district councils was land — particularly its retention and development. The Council opposed the compulsory purchase of uneconomic Māori land and the change in status of Māori land owned by fewer than three persons to general land. Although the Council succeeded in pegging the defined value of uneconomic land at $50.00 per hectare, it was not happy with the Bill when it was enacted.[50] One junior member of the Council labelled it the 'last land-grab'.

In the 1970s the Maori Council made wide-ranging submissions to ministers and select committees on various issues and bills in an attempt to ensure Māori concerns were addressed. They ranged from education to fisheries, land, the Race Relations Bill, housing, Maori Affairs Act, the Treaty of Waitangi, and the Town and Country Planning Act. The effect of the Council's submissions on the last three were particularly far-reaching in the Māori quest for justice and inclusion in the decision-making processes of the country. A leading figure in many of these discussions has been the President of the Maori Council since 1972, Sir Graham Latimer, who was a former chairman of the Taitokerau District Maori Council.

Frequently consulted by Government and the media on issues affecting Māori interests, he has often been called upon to fill the role of national spokesperson for Māori people.

The Council's efforts to amend the Town and Country Planning Act culminated in the inclusion of section 3(1)(g), which stated that the planning and administration of district and maritime schemes would take cognizance of matters of national importance. The relationship of the Māori people and their culture and traditions with their ancestral land was deemed to be one of those matters that local bodies now had to take into consideration. Apart from the recognition of traditional Māori fishing rights in the Fish Protection Act 1877, this was the first time that a general statute had made provision for the inclusion of Māori culture.

The Public Works Act, with its power to take Māori land compulsorily for public purposes, was one statute that irked Māori people as it incessantly chipped away at their diminishing land base. The Maori Council sought a return of land, taken under the Act, which was no longer being used for the purpose for which it was taken. To this end the Council succeeded in having section 436(1) of the Maori Affairs Act 1953 amended in 1975. It was another step in gaining relief from oppressive laws.

In 1971 Nga Tamatoa demonstrated against the Government-sponsored Treaty of Waitangi Day celebrations. The demonstration, together with Tamatoa's proclamation of a day of mourning for the loss of 63 million acres of Māori land, was an embarrassment to the Government. It referred the matter to the Maori Council for advice. The Council responded with a submission citing fourteen statutes that contradicted the Treaty of Waitangi. They ranged from the Public Works Act, through to the Mining Act, Petroleum Act, Rating Act, and the Town and Country Planning Act.[51]

Before the National Government could respond to the challenge posed by the Maori Council's submission, it lost office at the 1972 election, and the incoming Labour Government had to deal with it. The time had come for the Hon. Matiu Rata, Minister of Maori Affairs, to cement his place in history. He steered the Treaty of Waitangi Act 1975 through Parliament before the Government fell at the end of the year. That Act established the Waitangi Tribunal in 1976 as a mechanism to hear Māori grievances under the Treaty. Rata had hoped to make the Tribunal retrospective to 1900 but could not get approval from his caucus colleagues. Thus, the Tribunal was limited to hearing only those cases that arose after the Act came into force. Despite that limitation, a mechanism was in place that would evolve as time went on into something more potent than was envisaged by the Government.

A number of highly motivated political activists emerged from the urban experience of the 1970s. With no traditional mandate other than their sense of identity as Māori, they established their own groups to take up the Māori cause against government oppression. The leaders of these groups were young, and street-wise; some were well educated and some had experience in the trade union movement.

One of the first portents of modern Māori activism was *Te Hokioi*, an underground newspaper which appeared in 1968. The paper characterized itself as a taiaha (weapon) of truth for the Māori nation. The proponents of the paper knew instinctively the Freire dictum that to speak a true word is to transform the world.[52] Raising the political consciousness of Māori people to their oppression involved informing them of a wide range of issues. They ranged from the need to increase Māori representation in Parliament from four to seven members, to the expropriation of Māori land by local bodies under the Public Works Act.[53] The fourth issue of *Te Hokioi* published the Treaty of Waitangi as the mandate for its campaign on Māori rights. The first 800 copies of *Te Hokioi* were circulated among Māori patrons of taverns around Wellington. Enquiries from all parts of the North Island led to a wider circulation.

Out of *Te Hokioi* emerged the Maori Organisation on Human Rights (MOOHR). It too used the Treaty of Waitangi as its mandate.[54] MOOHR accused the education system of 'cultural murder' of the Māori language. It also advocated the recovery of Māori assets such as the South Island 'tenths' and Māori lands under perpetual lease, so that Māori would not be dependent on government welfare.[55]

While *Te Hokioi* and MOOHR were consciousness-raising devices, Nga Tamatoa became their action-oriented public face. Tamatoa sought ratification of the Treaty of Waitangi, equal Māori representation in Parliament, inclusion of Māori language in schools, return of confiscated Māori land (or compensation for it), correction of the Pākehā bias in history books, and Pākehā respect for Māori culture.[56] The strategies adopted by Tamatoa ranged from a nationwide petition to have Māori language taught in primary as well as secondary schools, through to making submissions on the Race Relations Bill, and mounting protest demonstrations as they did at Waitangi in 1971. Tamatoa had to bear the criticism from the Minister of Maori Affairs, Duncan MacIntyre, that they were 'not the true voice of the Maori people'. Even the Dominion President of the Maori Women's Welfare League criticized Tamatoa's actions at Waitangi as being too Pākehā and not true Māori.[57] Despite the criticism, Tamatoa's activism triggered the events that culminated in the establishment of the Waitangi Tribunal.

The ferment of political activism fostered by *Te Hokioi*, MOOHR, and Nga Tamatoa in the early 1970s coalesced into a Māori land rights movement. Land became the symbol of Māori alienation and political subjection to the will of the Pākehā majority. Māori anger over land was triggered by three statutes: the 1967 Maori Affairs Amendment Act, with its power to compulsorily alienate uneconomic Māori land; the Rating Act 1967, with its power to compel sale of land to recover unpaid rates; and the Town and Country Planning Act 1953, with its power to restrict use of Māori land by zoning laws.

Early in 1975 representatives of tribes with parochial land grievances against the Government or local bodies attended a hui at Mangere Marae, convened by former president of the Maori Women's Welfare League, Whina Cooper. This assembly launched Te Rōpu o Matakite which promoted the Māori Land March from Te Hapua, in the north, to the capital in Wellington. The march stayed at twenty-five marae *en route* down the centre of the North Island, politicizing people as it went. The march, under the slogan of 'not one more acre of Maori land' to be alienated, reached its climax on 13 October when thousands of people assembled in front of Parliament Buildings. There the Memorial of Rights was presented to the Prime Minister, Bill Rowling, seeking entrenchment of remaining Māori land from statutes with power to alienate, designate, or confiscate Māori land. The political effect of the Māori Land March made the subject of Māori land a sensitive issue in central government.

When the Land March ended it broke up into splinter groups. The main group, Matakite o Aotearoa, took up the cause of the Tainui Awhiro people at Raglan for the return of the Te Kopua block. This land was compulsorily taken in 1941 for an aerodrome under the War Emergency Regulations. It was subsequently vested in the Raglan County Council which let it to the local golf club. In April 1976 Matakite demonstrated on the golf course, focusing on a sacred burial site which had been converted into a bunker. Subsequently Matakite wrote to the Minister of Maori Affairs requesting that the land be revested in the Tainui Awhiro.[58] The Minister agreed to revest the land in the tribe under section 436(1) of the Maori Affairs Act 1953. This success was another example of the complementary nature of radical and conservative Māori politics. The activists did the protesting while the Maori Council got the legislative changes to achieve the common goal.

One of the most dramatic actions of the radical politics of the Māori land rights movement of the 1970s was the 506-day occupation of Bastion Point by the Orakei Maori Action Committee led by Joe Hawke. At issue was the systematic dispossession of Ngāti Whātua of Orakei by the Crown of their 700-acre estate set aside as a reserve for the tribe by the Native Land Court in 1869. Despite the Stout–Ngata Commission declaration in 1907 that the partition of the Orakei Block by the Native Land Court in 1898 was illegal and void,[59] the Crown proceeded to buy up Orakei in 1913. In a long-running battle against the state, Ngāti Whātua took eight actions to the Maori Land Court, four in the Supreme Court, two in the Court of Appeal, two in the Compensation Court, six appearances before Commissions or Committees of Inquiry, and made fifteen parliamentary petitions.[60] It was an unequal contest. In 1951 the Crown evicted Ngāti Whātua as squatters from their papa kāinga at Okahu Bay and moved the people into state houses in Kitemoana Street.

When the Government moved to subdivide sixty acres of Crown land on Bastion Point early in 1977, the Orakei Maori Action Committee occupied the land and demanded its return to Ngāti Whātua. The Government got an injunction in the High Court ruling that the occupation of Bastion Point was illegal.[61] On 28 May 1978, 600 policemen cleared Bastion Point of protesters and demolished their buildings. For the time being, state power had prevailed once more over a powerless minority.

The thrust of radical Māori politics culminated at the end of 1979 in the resignation of Matiu Rata, the Member for Northern Maori, from the Labour Party. In 1980 Rata resigned from Parliament and formed the Mana Motuhake Party to contest the by-election for the seat he had vacated. His resignation ended the forty-year Rātana liaison with the Labour Party. Although Rata lost the by-election, he took 38 per cent of the vote. In the 1981 election, Mana Motuhake fielded four candidates for the Māori seats. Although none was successful, the Mana Motuhake candidates displaced the National Party from second place in all four seats. Consequently, Labour could no longer take the Māori seats for granted.

In the 1980s the radical cutting edge of Māori politics was the Waitangi Action Committee (WAC). WAC took over from the moribund Tamatoa the role of mounting protest activity against the Waitangi celebrations. As the police response to the demonstrations became increasingly heavy-handed, WAC altered its strategy and mounted Te Hikoi ki Waitangi, the peaceful march in 1984 to stop the celebrations. The churches and Pākehā activist groups swelled the Hikoi to 3,000 people. The Hikoi demonstrated Māori solidarity to the Government by bringing together representatives of the two oldest Māori political movements, Kotahitanga and the King Movement. In the face of that solidarity, the Governor-General Sir David Beattie expressed a willingness to talk to a deputation from the Hikoi. Although the meeting was prevented by police action, it was an historic departure by Sir David Beattie to go against the advice of the Prime Minister.

The Hikoi was followed up in September by a hui at Turangawaewae Marae convened by Te Runanga Whakawhanaunga i nga Hahi to discuss the Treaty of Waitangi. The hui, attended by a thousand people, called on the Government to make the Waitangi Tribunal retrospective to 1840.[62] The Labour Government, mindful of the political threat from Mana Motuhake, responded by passing the Treaty of Waitangi Amendment Act 1985 to make the Waitangi Tribunal retrospective to 1840.

In the 1980s the Department of Maori Affairs initiated a new community development programme based on the philosophy of 'Tu Tangata', standing tall like a man to shape the 'stance of the people'.[63] The Secretary of Maori Affairs, Kara Puketapu, held three annual Hui Whakatauira, assemblies of a hundred Māori leaders in Wellington. The assemblies endorsed the programmes followed by the Department in the years leading up to its dissolution in 1988. These included a job-search programme for the unemployed, women's workshops, business workshops, job skills training, and Matua Whangai. The latter was a foster-parenting programme designed to take juveniles out of social welfare care and place them with their own tribal groups.[64] The Matua Whangai programme was so successful that social welfare homes were virtually emptied of their Māori inmates.

The most dynamic programme initiated by the Department of Maori Affairs was the Kōhanga Reo ('language nest'). Although the Māori language had been incorporated into the education system in the 1970s, research by Benton for the New Zealand Council for Educational Research indicated that the Māori language was dying out.[65] The elders at the 1981 Hui Whakatauira proposed the kōhanga reo, the pre-school language nest, to rescue the language from extinction. Within three years there were 188 kōhanga reo established around the country. kōhanga reo became the fastest growing political movement in the country as parents grappled with bureaucracy for resources to do the job. Symptomatic of this politicization was the attendance of over 1,000 people at the first kōhanga reo conference at Turangawaewae Marae in January 1984. By 1990 there were more than 550 kōhanga reo in operation.

In 1984 delegates at the Maori Educational Development Conference held at Ngaruawahia expressed concern over the need for Māori language continuity between kōhanga reo and primary school.[66] State schools offering bilingual programmes were thought to be second best to schools providing total immersion in the Māori language. Two Kura Kaupapa Māori schools were established in West Auckland after the conference. The purpose of these schools was to extend kōhanga reo Māori language education into primary schooling. The long-term aim was to secure survival of the Māori language into the twenty-first century and beyond. The basic characteristic of Kura Kaupapa Māori is a Māori-speaking environment in the playground as well as the classroom.[67] In 1987 Te Komiti o Nga Kura Kaupapa Māori o Tamaki Makaurau was formed to promote the establishment of Kura Kaupapa Māori on a national basis. This group persuaded the Minister of Education to establish a Kura Kaupapa Māori Working Party. Subsequently, Kura Kaupapa were officially recognized in the category for designated character schools.[68] The outcome was the full funding by the Ministry of Education of six Kura Kaupapa Māori in 1990 as a pilot scheme. Another five were funded in 1991, and twenty-three other groups expressed interest in joining the programme. In addition there are six privately funded Kura Kaupapa. Kura Kaupapa Māori have in effect

decoded the ideological interests of dominant Pakeha society which have imbued the structures of schooling, such as pedagogy, curriculum and evaluation . . . Kaupapa Maori schooling takes the validity and legitimacy of Maori knowledge for granted. It is this counter-logic which underpins the radical pedagogy of such schools.[69]

Although tribal incorporations such as Puketapu, Morikaunui, Mawhera, Mangatu, and Parinihi-ki-Waitotara are multi-million-dollar enterprises, they serve the interests of only those people who are shareholders in the land. People who are landless and have migrated to cities have sought to establish their own economic base that would operate in a pan-tribal manner in the open market.

The first pan-Māori corporate economic venture outside pastoral land use was Maori International Limited (MIL), launched in 1983. Although MIL's share issue realized only $75,000, it began trading by marketing high quality Māori craft work and conducting tourist visits to marae. Within the first three years MIL liquidated its establishment costs. MIL's conservative business strategy enabled it to survive the sharemarket crash in 1987. Two years later it was able to declare a profit of $77,873.

In 1984 the Hui Taumata, the Maori Economic Summit Development Conference, recommended the establishment of a Maori Economic Development Commission. The Maori Development Commission (MDC) was established in July 1987 with a capital base of $26 million. The bulk of the money came from government sources. Fletcher Challenge, Brierley Investments Limited, and the Development Finance Corporation put in $2 million each. In 1988 MDC refinanced the ailing Aokawa Bay Lake Resort at Rotoiti and injected finance into Te Awanui Huka Pak, a kiwifruit coolstore facility at Mt Maunganui. Its most promising recent investment is in Power Beat International, a company promoting a new twelve-volt battery into the international market place.

Within months of the Waitangi Tribunal being made retrospective to 1840, huge land claims were lodged by the Ngāi Tahu, Te Āti Awa, and Tainui tribes. The claims quickly rose to 150. From the defeat at Bastion Point, Joe Hawke came back to reclaim the land at Orakei. The Waitangi Tribunal ruled in 1987 that the Crown purchase of the Orakei Block breached its obligations under the Treaty of Waitangi to ensure that Ngāti Whātua at Orakei had a sufficient endowment for their needs. The Tribunal recommended vesting 67.25 ha of Crown land held as public parks and reserves in the Ngāti Whātua as Orakei Maori Trust Board. The parks were to be administered by a new Reserves Board comprised of Ngāti Whātua and the Auckland City Council. The Trust Board would receive an additional 3 ha for its own use and a cash settlement of $3 million for a rehabilitation programme for the tribe.[70]

Ngāti Whātua's success gave hope for other tribal land claims against the Crown. But when the State-Owned Enterprises Act 1986 came into force, the tribes became agitated when they realized the Crown was divesting itself of its land holdings and handing them over to the state-owned enterprises (SOEs) in May 1987. Once the SOEs onsold the land to a third party, the latter would be possessed of an estate in fee simple. The land would then be beyond the reach of potential claimants. Fortunately for the claimants, section 9 of the State-Owned Enterprises Act stated that nothing in the Act should permit the Crown to act in a manner that was inconsistent with the principles of the Treaty of Waitangi. Armed with section 9, the Maori Council filed an injunction in the High Court against the Crown to safeguard Māori land claims pending their hearing by the Waitangi Tribunal. The Court delivered its verdict on 29 June. Five judges were unanimous that the Treaty of Waitangi, given effect by section 9 of the State-Owned Enterprises Act, prevented the Crown from transferring land to SOEs without making arrangements to protect Māori claims.[73]

Despite the Court's judgment that Māori land claims against the Crown should be protected, Coalcorp proceeded with the sale of its mining interests in the Waikato. In order to protect its claim on a million acres of confiscated land, pending a hearing by the Waitangi Tribunal, the Tainui Trust Board filed an injunction in the High Court against the Crown and its agent Coalcorp. In granting the injunction, the Court also ruled that the Treaty of Waitangi (State Enterprises Act) 1988 applied as well to interests in land represented by the coal-mining licenses in the Crown's agreement with Coalcorp issued in March 1988.[74]

Success in safeguarding land claims through the High Court was matched by a similar action in court to reclaim Māori fisheries. In 1987, the Muriwhenua tribes of the Far North brought a case before the Waitangi Tribunal against the Government's Fisheries Quota Management System. The tribe argued that the granting of Individual Transferable Quota (ITQ) to fishermen (to catch particular species of fish) effectively created a property right in the sea, from which they were excluded. That was a clear breach of Article Two of the Treaty of Waitangi which guaranteed 'tino rangatiratanga' (absolute chieftainship) over fisheries. After hearing evidence of traditional use of fisheries up to 32 kilometres out to sea, the Tribunal gave an interim ruling that the area of sea referred to in the Muriwhenua claim was owned as property in the same way that land was owned. If the Crown wanted to use the sea in a commercial way it had to acquire the right from the traditional user.

The Muriwhenua claimants and the Maori Council filed an injunction in the High Court against the Crown's granting of ITQs in Muriwhenua waters. In the High Court, Justice Greig agreed with the Tribunal's ruling and ordered an interim stop to the issue of quota in Muriwhenua waters until Muriwhenua rights and the Crown's obligations under the Treaty were resolved.[71]

In October the Maori Council, Tainui Trust Board, the Ngai Tahu Trust Board, and other tribes lodged an injunction in the High Court to suspend the ITQ regime over all tribal waters around New Zealand. The logic of the Muriwhenua claim indicated that the sea around New Zealand was divided into zones controlled by tribes around the coastline. Although those rights were subject to proof, Justice Greig ruled that the ITQ system breached Māori rights under section 88 of the Fisheries Act. He ordered an interim stop to the system until Māori rights to the fisheries were fully and finally resolved.[72]

In the latter half of 1988, the Minister of Fisheries (Mr Moyle) and the Minister of State-Owned Enterprises (Mr Prebble) negotiated directly with the four leaders in the Māori fisheries claim. The negotiations culminated in the Maori Fisheries Bill returning 50 per cent of the fisheries to Māori ownership over a twenty-year period at the rate of 2.5 per cent per annum. The Bill came under heavy fire from the Opposition and from powerful vested interests in the fishing industry. Fletcher Challenge threatened to withdraw from a $200 million investment in fishing.[73] Commercial fishermen threatened to withhold resource rentals and not fill in quota returns.[74] The Leader of the Opposition, Mr Bolger, threatened to repeal the Bill when National came to power.[75] The Government succumbed to pressure. It withdrew the Bill and replaced it with another.

The Maori Fisheries Act 1989 rolled the Māori fisheries claim back to 10 per cent and established a Maori Fisheries Commission with a grant of $10 million. The Act also established Aotearoa Fisheries Limited as the commercial arm of the Commission. Only three of the Māori negotiators in the original fisheries claim were appointed to the seven member Commission. They were effectively outnumbered by Government appointees. The commercial functions of Aotearoa Fisheries locked Māori into the capitalist, extractive mode in the development and use of fisheries. The goal of the original claim, to provide employment in tribal areas, was forgotten. Thus the Act determined that Māori participation in the fishing industry would be compatible with Government economic goals.

The initiative regained by the Government bore fruit when Aotearoa Fisheries, financed by the Maori Development Corporation, entered into a joint venture with Wilson Neill Limited. The joint venture bought the inshore fishing operation of Fletcher Fishing for $20 million. Less than a year later, the joint venture was dissolved and Wilson Neill sold 50 per cent of its share in Moana Pacific to its Māori partner Aotearoa Fisheries. Aotearoa Fisheries holds a 60 per cent share in Moana Pacific. The other 40 per cent is held by Te Kupenga, a Māori consortium of five tribes financed by the Maori Development Corporation.[76]

The success in the High Court of three injunctions brought by Māori leaders against the Crown was an embarrassment to the Government. It impeded the Government's sale of Crown land and other assets under the State-Owned Enterprises Act, and the issue of ITQ under the fisheries Quota Management System. Pressure from vested interests in the fishing industry, and Opposition criticism of the Government's actions, indicated that the Government's Treaty policy was a political liability for the elections in 1990.

The Government attempted to distance itself from its Treaty policy by turning away from the Treaty itself and redirecting the discourse to the so-called 'principles of the Treaty'. It then proceeded unilaterally to define the principles in a document entitled 'Principles for Crown Action on the Treaty of Waitangi'. Although five principles were identified, primacy was given to the principle of kāwanatanga (the right to govern), ceded in the first clause of the Treaty. It was effectively an assertion of sovereignty. It asserted the hegemony of the state over the principle of 'tino rangatiratanga', the absolute chieftainship over land and treasured possessions guaranteed by clause 2 of the Treaty. 'Tino rangatiratanga' was reduced to the principle of self-management, the right of a tribe to organize as a tribe and control their own resources.[77] The Hon. Richard Prebble, Minister for State-Owned Enterprises, served notice in Parliament that Māori claims would not in future impede the actions of Government: 'One of those sovereign rights is to be able to carry out its economic policy, and that policy is to improve the business activities of Government state trading enterprises.'[78]

The Prime Minister, Geoffrey Palmer, was even more succinct on asserting the power of the state. In a 'Four Corners' television documentary early in 1990 on the Treaty of Waitangi he said:

When it comes to the question of allocation of resources, that is a political question for the Government. It is not a legal question for the courts and it will not be decided by the courts in any authoritative way.

The battle in the courts against the State-Owned Enterprises Act, and for the recovery of fisheries, was led by the Maori Council and individual tribes. Tribes not party to these events felt there was a need for a more concerted approach. After a preliminary meeting in July 1989 convened by the paramount chief Sir Hepi Te Heuheu, the tribes met in congress on 7 July 1990 at Turangawaewae Marae. There the National Congress of Tribes was officially inaugurated. The Congress, comprised of thirty-seven tribes, aimed to be independent of Government by setting its affiliation fee at $5,000 per annum. The test for the Congress as a political force will rest on the willingness of the tribes to bear the costs of running an organization in the national arena of politics.

The most salient feature of the history of the Māori people since 1950 has been the migration of over 75 per cent of the population from their rural tribal areas to towns and cities. There they became integrated into the economic mainstream of capitalism, while at the same time maintaining their culture and transplanting it into the urban milieu. The symbol of that transplanted culture is the urban marae with its associated rituals and community activities. The proliferation of urban marae, combined with the dynamic variations in the organizational structures underpinning them, are testament to the adaptability of the Māori and the vigour of their cultural renaissance.

Urbanization brought increased knowledge of metropolitan society and its social and political mechanisms that dominated the lives of Māori people. A wide range of radical, activist, and conservative political movements emerged to pursue the common agenda of self-determination, equality, social justice, return of assets, and maintenance of culture. With the Māori population today at 404,185, the continuity of the Māori cultural renaissance into the twenty-first century is assured.

CHAPTER 20

From Dual Dependency to Nuclear Free

W. David McIntyre

From the earliest days of the first Labour Government in 1935 New Zealand began to assert an independent voice in international affairs and not simply in empire affairs. Although some of the trappings of British sovereignty had yet to be severed and dependence on great power protection continued for forty years, New Zealand expressed a new assertiveness and claimed a distinctive voice. This was marked by progressive symbolic and constitutional moves and by the creation of the appropriate institutional framework for the conduct of diplomacy. The country also made its mark in man-for-man encounters in the military and sporting fields.

An important symbolic change was the demise of the 'Dominion of New Zealand'. In 1945, during British Commonwealth ministerial meetings prior to the San Francisco Conference on United Nations Organization, Alister McIntosh, the Secretary for External Affairs, said that the country wished to be referred to as 'New Zealand'.[1] In the following year an instruction went to government departments that, as their stationery supplies were renewed, 'New Zealand' must appear on their letterheads with the New Zealand coat of arms in place of the royal coat of arms.[2] It took some years for the international yearbooks to catch up with this change and 'Dominion weather forecasts' and 'Dominion Trotting Championships' and the 'Dominion Art Gallery' were still evident twenty years later. The law caught up with the symbolism in 1947 when the Statute of Westminster was adopted and Parliament was also given, by a British Act, the full amending power for the 1852 Constitution Act.[3] 'New Zealand' appeared in the Royal Titles Act on the accession of Queen Elizabeth II in 1953. Twenty years later she became 'Queen of New Zealand', with Britain subsumed among her 'other realms'. It was not, however, until the 1986 Constitution Act that the last trappings of former imperial sovereignty were severed. Now for the first time, a New Zealand act became the authority for Parliament's existence in place of the Westminster Act of 1852.[4]

As well as the symbols and rights of sovereignty the machinery of diplomacy was evolved. Before the Second World War external affairs were handled by the Prime Minister's Department, where an Imperial

Affairs Officer, Carl Berendsen, had been appointed in 1926. Essentially he handled correspondence with the High Commissioner in London, who also doubled as representative at the League of Nations. During the war, Legations were opened in Washington (1941) and Moscow (1944) and High Commissions in Ottawa (1942) and Canberra (1943). More importantly the Department of External Affairs was created in 1943.[5] For over thirty years it was closely associated with the Prime Minister's Department. The permanent head of that department doubled as Secretary for External Affairs and the Prime Minister usually took the external affairs portfolio. From the 1940s a tradition of recruiting some of the brightest graduates from universities for the diplomatic service was developed. Though very small for many years, the department changed rapidly from the 1960s in response to the development of the European Community (EC) and decolonization in the Pacific. The name was changed to Ministry of Foreign Affairs in 1970. In 1975, when Robert Muldoon took the finance portfolio, the link with the Prime Minister's Department was ended and the ministry moved out of Parliament Buildings. In 1988 it merged with the trade relations branch of the Department of Trade and Industry and became the Ministry of External Relations and Trade (MERT). Its 'corporate plan' focused on six programmes: security, economic growth, international order, New Zealand's image abroad, New Zealanders overseas, and agency services.[6]

The spread of diplomatic representation reflected New Zealand's evolving links with various regions and, sometimes, the ideological predilections of the ruling party. Thus the Moscow Legation was closed in 1950 by the first National Government and not re-opened until 1973 by the third Labour Government. Tokyo saw the first new Embassy after the war in 1947. National opened Embassies in Paris and The Hague in 1950. A move into South-East Asia began with a Commissioner based in Singapore in 1955. Embassies followed in Bangkok and Jakarta in 1957 and High Commissions in Kuala Lumpur (1957) and Hong Kong (1960). During the 1960s Embassies were opened in four EC capitals, Brussels, Rome, Athens, and Bonn. From the 1970s priority was given to the Pacific Basin, with new High Commissions in six Commonwealth countries, Embassies in South Korea, the Peoples Republic of China, the Philippines, and two Latin-American countries (later reduced to one). A growing trade with the Middle East led to Embassies in Iran and Iraq in 1975. Belated recognition of the importance of independent Africa led to the establishment of a High Commission in Harare, Zimbabwe, in 1988, whence the High Commissioner was later accredited to Mozambique and Tanzania. By 1990 New Zealand had posts in 45 countries, and 81 countries were represented in New Zealand.[7]

The first Labour Government, which started the move to an independent foreign policy, was faced in 1935 with a conflict between ideology and the needs of security. During its years of opposition the Labour Party had been anti-imperialist, anti-militarist, and wedded to socialist internationalism. It opposed compulsory military training, the acquisition of cruisers, and contributions to the Singapore base. At first it was hostile to the League of Nations. Its 1919 manifesto on the peace settlement declared that the world could never be made safe for humanity while 'Capitalism, with its adjuncts of Imperialism and militarism, remains'. It wanted workers in all countries to unite 'for the purpose of superseding Capitalism with industrial democracy, which is Socialism, and forming not a league of nations, but a league of peoples . . .'[8] But gradually Labour's stance on the League changed. During the Chanak crisis in 1922 it argued that the dispute should be referred to the League. By the 1930s, with the advance of Japanese militarism and the rise of fascism in Italy, Germany, and Spain, Labour looked to the League as an instrument for arbitration, the protection of small nations, and collective security in general.[9]

Prior to the first Labour Government New Zealand had made little mark at the League. Sir James Allen, who represented the Dominion from 1920 to 1926, wore grey not black suits to demonstrate a democratic outlook, and he demanded frugality in the League's budget. He became known as a stickler for financial cheeseparing and wished to disfranchise states which defaulted on their dues.[10] After 1935 New Zealand stood out, and achieved some notoriety, in opposition to Britain on four issues — Ethiopia, reform of the Covenant, Spain, and China.[11] Taking office only two months after the Italian invasion of Ethiopia the Labour Government was confronted with the first of these issues within a week of taking office. It came in the shape of an Anglo–French plan to divide up Ethiopia to buy off Italy and end the war. Savage replied that his Government were 'quite unable to associate themselves' with the proposal.[12] The disagreement was in secret, and the plan was anyway soon repudiated, but the differences became public on the second matter, which concerned the reform of the League. Ethiopia was conquered in May 1936 and, in view of the failure of sanctions to stop the Italians, all members were invited to submit proposals as to how the League might be strengthened. The British declined and urged the Dominions to refrain. But New Zealand went ahead with twenty-one proposals to strengthen the League and give it power to apply tough sanctions against aggressors. New Zealand was prepared to take its 'collective share' in economic sanctions and the 'collective application of force'. It wanted such sanctions to be 'immediate and automatic'. It called for a 'collective peace system' which would be universal in application. Although the Dominion Government realized the ideal of universal collective security was not practicable in the short run, it went ahead and lodged its proposals with the Secretary-General with the caveat that it would 'not demur to consideration of progress by stages or to alternative proposals'.[13]

Presentation of the reform proposals was the first task performed at Geneva by Bill Jordan, Labour's High Commissioner in London. He also stood forth against the British on the third matter, the Spanish civil war, in 1936. Because of Italian and German assistance to the military rebels under Colonel Franco and Russian support for the Popular Front Government, the civil war became a symbolic contest between Fascism and Communism. Thousands of volunteers formed international brigades to assist the Popular Front, including eleven men from New Zealand. In addition an ambulance with three nurses was sent by the left-wing Spanish Medical Aid Society.[14] When the Spanish Government appealed to the League, Britain and France insisted on non-intervention. Jordan, in some notable speeches, called on the League to at least investigate the issues, but the only other support for the Popular Front came from the Soviet Union. After Italy prevailed in Ethiopia and Franco took over Spain, the British accorded recognition to the new regimes. New Zealand declined to be associated with the British moves. The fourth issue was the Japanese invasion of China in 1937. China's appeal to the League met only innocuous resolutions about not bombing civilians and furnishing medical aid. Jordan moved amendments to condemn Japan and give positive support to China but, again, the only support came from the Soviet Union. By the end of 1938 Jordan had to report to Wellington that the cause of collective security through the League was doomed.[15]

New Zealand's outspoken stance at Geneva in the years 1936, 1937, and 1938 won recognition as an assertion of the 'alternative' view to that of prevailing balance-of-power diplomacy. It has been called the statement of a 'moral foreign policy', but it failed.[16] It is important to remember, however, that the Labour Government was not pacifist. It hedged its bets on defence and adopted a 'belt and braces' approach. While trying, through the League, the new alternative of universal collective security, it did not neglect conventional national security.

Because Labour's predilections in Opposition were anti-imperialist and anti-militarist, it reviewed defence expenditure when it took office and was inclined, at first, to build up the air force (as a demonstrably defensive arm), cut out the cruisers, and stop planning for an expeditionary force (which were both viewed as imperialist). In the event, Labour *did* create a separate air force, which by 1939 was the most costly of the armed forces. But it also accepted the more up-to-date cruisers, *Achilles* and *Leander*, and enlarged the Devonport dockyard to take them. It treated the army as the Cinderella of the services, but it began belatedly, in 1938, to encourage recruiting for the Territorial Force, and (without Government sanction) the recruiting officers asked men if they would be willing to serve overseas. As compared with the depression days of the early 1930s the first Labour Government fostered a modest re-armament programme, which was nearing completion when war broke out in 1939.[17]

The Second World War (1939–45) underlined the established themes of New Zealand's external relations but added important new ones. The imperial theme was still foremost. The main wartime contribution in personnel was alongside the British. Labour's recent espousal of collective security was revived during the creation of the United Nations. Anzac links were formalized in the Canberra Pact of 1944. The big change brought on by the war, however, was the need to turn to the United States as the main protector in the Pacific. At the same time the Government was anxious that New Zealand should represent a 'British' presence in this theatre.

When war with Germany broke out in 1939 the Cabinet made its own independent decision, shortly before midnight on 3 September, to associate itself with Britain's declaration of war. Two days later Savage broadcast the country's loyalty to Britain: 'Where she goes, we go, where she stands, we stand.'[18] The infant navy was placed under Admiralty control; an air force team, which was in Britain to take over thirty Wellington bombers, became the nucleus of the first Commonwealth squadron in the RAF, and an army expeditionary force of divisional strength was offered on 13 September 1939.[19] Thus, in the war with Germany, instinctive traditional support for the mother country was forthcoming. New Zealand pilots fought in the Battle of Britain (June–September 1940). While the army's 2 Division was sent to Egypt to complete training and relieve British units, one brigade was diverted to Britain and became part of the defences of south-east England after Dunkirk. HMS *Achilles* went to blockade German shipping off South America, and in December 1940 played a notable part in the action against the pocket battleship *Graf Spee* in the Battle of the River Plate.[20]

Italy's entry into the war and the fall of France, in June 1940, induced the first of three major landmarks for New Zealand during the war. It meant that the British navy now had to face the combined strength of the German and Italian navies without the help of the French navy. Thus on 13 June 1940 the New Zealand and Australian governments were informed that, if Japan took advantage of Britain's embarrassment in Europe to strike in the Pacific, the plan to send the main fleet to Singapore could not be implemented at once and the Dominions would have to rely on the United States for protection. Faced with this major turning point in the balance-of-power Peter Fraser's Government did not panic. It told the British that the situation was not unexpected; it sought a review of strategic priorities and also planned for diplomatic representation in Washington. Walter Nash, the Minister of Finance, went as New Zealand Minister to the USA in 1942.[21] The phase of 'dual dependency' had begun.

Meanwhile 2 Division fought in the Commonwealth armies against the Italians and Germans in North Africa. Divisional Signals, the Engineers' railway and water-supply companies, and the Service Corps' transport units all took part in the successful desert campaign in Libya from December 1940 to January 1941. The Division was finally brought together in March 1941 under the command of Major-General Bernard Freyberg V.C. It was thoroughly blooded in costly disasters in Greece (April 1941), Crete (May 1941), and the attempt to relieve Tobruk (November 1941 to January 1942) during which it incurred 10,000 casualties. During the battles to hold Egypt in mid-1942 the Division's strength was reduced from 20,000 to 13,000 in a month. Then, from the battle of El Alamein in October 1942 to the capture of Tunis seven months later, 2 Division played its part in the ejection of the Germans and Italians from North Africa.[22]

Japan's dramatic entry into the war in December 1941 led to the second great landmark. A decision had to be made on whether to continue in the war against Italy and Germany in the Mediterranean or to concentrate against Japan in the Pacific. Responsibility had already been assumed for the defence of some British colonies in the Pacific. An infantry company had been sent in 1939 to Fanning Island (a cable station half-way between Hawaii and the Cook Islands). A brigade was sent to Fiji in 1940.[23] The outbreak of war in the Pacific, with simultaneous Japanese attacks on Malaya, Pearl Harbor, and the Philippines on the night of 7–8 December 1941, was soon followed by the shock of the sinking of HMS *Prince of Wales* and HMS *Repulse* off the coast of Malaya two days later. The fall of Singapore on 15 February left New Zealand feeling more vulnerable to invasion than at any time in its history.

A second brigade was sent to Fiji and the force there was designated 3 Division from May 1942. Growing fears in the Pacific led Fraser to warn Freyberg early in 1942 that 2 Division might have to follow the Australians and return to the Pacific. A decision was delayed. The USA took responsibility for Fanning and Fiji, and 3 Division was brought home. American forces would also help New Zealand. The US Commander-in-Chief South Pacific set up his headquarters in Auckland and the First US Marine Division arrived in 1942. For two years there were 20,000 American troops in the country while 50,000 New Zealanders served overseas.[24]

After the Battle of El Alamein and the Anglo-American landings in North Africa, Fraser did ask, in November 1942, for the return of 2 Division. He was persuaded by Churchill and Roosevelt that it would be too disruptive to shipping. But in April 1943, when the British wanted to train 2 Division for the invasion of Sicily, Fraser withheld consent until the future of the expeditionary forces was discussed in a secret session of Parliament in May 1943. Here the second great landmark was encountered — the most agonizing decision of the war.[25] Pacific or Mediterranean — where should New Zealanders serve? It was agreed to try both for a time — 2 Division to stay in the Mediterranean and a reduced 3 Division to stay in the Pacific. Thus 2 Division fought in the Italian campaign from October 1943 until the occupation of Trieste in May 1945.[26] 3 Division joined the Americans in the Solomons Campaign and took part in three island landings (September–October 1943 and February 1944). At this point, the Dominion having reached the limit of its manpower resources, 3 Division was withdrawn and disbanded.[27] However, the navy and air force stayed on in the Pacific. Both cruisers were badly damaged off the Solomons and a minesweeper was sunk. Seven air squadrons and radar units helped garrison Guadalcanal, the New Hebrides, Fiji, and Norfolk Island. A five squadron task force operated from a ring of bases around Rabaul early in 1945. Two cruisers and a corvette joined the British Commonwealth Pacific Fleet in operations off Japan in 1945, when a quarter of the pilots on the British carriers were New Zealanders.[28] New Zealand was represented at the signing of the Japanese surrender in Tokyo Bay on 3 September 1945.

If the war underlined traditional ties with Britain and led to the forging of new ones with the United States, it also caused a formalizing of trans-

Tasman relations. In spite of the Anzac spirit dating from Gallipoli, Australia and New Zealand had remained rivals in trade and sport. Their defence relations with Britain were likened to the spokes of a wheel. They communicated via London, the hub; but little contact was maintained around the rim. Thus, in spite of a pledge in 1938 to work together in defence, decisions were made without consultation. The New Zealand Expeditionary Force was offered unilaterally in 1939, even though the Australians had deliberately waited to consult New Zealand.[29] The decision to leave the Division in the Mediterranean in 1943 brought from the Australian Prime Minister the bitter comment: 'For every soldier New Zealand keeps away from the Pacific theatre either an Australian or American has to fill his place.'[30] Thus in 1944 there was a need to mend fences and present a united front to the big power protectors. The third landmark of the war, then, was the Australian–New Zealand Agreement (Canberra Pact) signed on 21 January 1944, which pledged both countries to work together in the post-war Pacific. They asserted a claim for consultation at the highest level in all armistice arrangements. They committed themselves to treat their security as a whole, within any post-war scheme of collective security, in a 'regional zone of defence' stretching from the islands northeast of Australia to Western Samoa and the Cook Islands.[31] Little was done immediately, but in the long run Anzac links were to become New Zealand's most enduring ties.

Universal collective security, however, remained an ideal for the first Labour Government. Peter Fraser played a significant role at the San Francisco Conference on the United Nations. New Zealand fought hard to amend the great power draft of the UN Charter, to give a greater role for small nations. It tried unsuccessfully to get four major amendments passed. On the purposes of the UN it wanted a commitment to the preservation of 'territorial integrity' and 'political independence' of all members. Under principles it wanted a pledge to the collective resistance of aggression. It tried to give the General Assembly greater powers, and it strongly opposed the great power unanimity rule (the veto) in the Security Council. It tried, in fact, to implement in San Francisco the spirit of the twenty-one points submitted to the League of Nations in 1936. All this failed, but New Zealand delegates did secure an amendment making the Economic and Social Council a principal organ of the UN; they secured another ensuring the 'exclusively international' character of the Secretariat, and Fraser, as Chairman of the Trusteeship Committee, ensured the Trusteeship Council had adequate means to scrutinize the administration of the ex-League of Nation Mandates, which became UN Trust Territories.[32] The UN did not, however, create a satisfactory collective security system and New Zealand faced the post-war world in the situation of 'dual dependency' — reliance on Britain and the United States — which would continue in various forms for forty years.

In the immediate post-war years external affairs began to be more complex. The great hopes invested by Labour in the United Nations were soon dashed as the Cold War came to dominate international affairs. Close co-operation was maintained within the British Commonwealth — especially with Britain and Australia. The United States was the predominant power of the Pacific and, therefore, the ultimate backstop of New Zealand's security. But, whereas New Zealand had long had a voice in Common-wealth affairs, the United States was a more aloof and unpredictable ally. There emerged what F. L. W. Wood called 'The Anzac Dilemma'. How should a balance be maintained between relations with Britain, the traditional partner, but remote from the Pacific and in decline as a power, and relations with the USA, the stronger, but less intimate friend, who wielded the power in the Pacific?[33] The dilemma was never satisfactorily resolved, though in the decades after 1945 the system of 'dual dependency' continued. A series of alliance arrangements known as ANZAM, ANZUS, and SEATO was created, which provided the working framework for much of New Zealand's external affairs.

There was a brief moment in 1946, when the dilemma might have been resolved in a comprehensive pact embracing New Zealand, Australia, Britain, and the United States. This arose over an American desire to maintain certain bases which it had built in the Pacific Islands during the war. Initially conceived as a scheme for a world-wide chain of bases to serve an international security force, the proposal rapidly became one concerned with American national security. It involved New Zealand's island territory of Western Samoa, Australia's base at Manus in the Admiralty Islands, and the British territories of Fiji, the Solomons, Christmas Island, and the Ellice Islands. As the US Government made separate approaches to the three Commonwealth countries, the Australian Government suggested (and the other two agreed) that they should concert their approach to the matter. The Commonwealth countries would not agree to the American bases without an American guarantee of their security.[34] It was hoped that a 'BRITANZUS' arrangement might be possible. The Americans, however, did not want commitments; they sought only bases on a care and maintenance arrangement and, anyway, they soon reduced their needs. An American–Commonwealth Pacific pact never eventuated, but the desire for an American guarantee for New Zealand remained because of the lessons of the war.

Within the Commonwealth there was now an emphasis on regional responsibilities. Britain could no longer guarantee the security of the entire Commonwealth, though still felt an obligation to kith and kin in New Zealand and Australia. An example of the new regional emphasis was the supervision of the British Commonwealth Occupation Force in Japan. Instead of control from London, the Force came under a 'Joint Chiefs of Staff, Australia' organization in Melbourne and it was commanded by an Australian general.[35] Although the Melbourne organization was short-lived it was agreed that the Australian Chiefs of Staff machinery, with British and New Zealand representatives, should have overall planning control of the defences of the Australian, New Zealand, and Malayan area. This evolved into the ANZAM Committee — defined as a 'Planning machinery for co-ordinating the Planning of Australia, New Zealand and the Territories in South-East Asia where the U.K. has Responsibilities'.[36]

Co-operation with Britain, as in pre-war imperial defence, was also resumed when Britain faced up to burdensome Cold War problems. RNZAF aircrew went to assist in the Berlin airlift in 1948. Three frigates were offered in 1949 when it appeared that the new Peoples Republic of China would threaten Hong Kong. They were not required, but a flight of Dakota transport planes was sent to Singapore for ferry work to Hong Kong and they were later employed in the campaign against Communist guerillas in Malaya.[37]

The biggest post-war commitment was to contingency planning for reinforcements to the British in the Middle East. As they contemplated the possibility of a third world war the British Chiefs of Staff had identified the Soviet Union as the potential enemy and Western Europe or the Middle East as the most likely theatres of war. In Anglo-American global planning the Middle East was deemed a British responsibility and Commonwealth assistance was sought in 1948.[38] Peter Fraser for New Zealand gave the most positive response, even though peace-time conscription had to be resumed. This (though not the commitment) was put to the electorate in a referendum in 1949 and approved.[39] Military planning and training was based on the despatch of an expeditionary force of an infantry division and five air squadrons — a total force of some 35,000 — to the Middle East within three months of the outbreak of war. In 1951 a fighter/ground attack squadron was stationed in Cyprus. This Middle East commitment in a future war became an additional reason for wanting an American guarantee in the Pacific.

Talk of such a guarantee resumed after 1949, when the North Atlantic Treaty bound the USA and Canada to the defence of Western Europe. There were soon calls for a 'Pacific Pact' on similar lines, and New Zealand made it clear that it would welcome such a pact provided the United States and Britain were included.[40] Desire for a guarantee became even keener when the United States prepared a 'peace of reconciliation' with Japan. A peace treaty, designed to keep Japan out of Communist hands, would end control over Japan and even permit re-armament. New Zealand and Australia refused to support such a peace without an American guarantee.

Matters came to a head when the Korean war broke out in June 1950. Taking advantage of a Russian boycott of the United Nations, because of the refusal to admit the Peoples Republic of China, the United States secured UN condemnation of North Korean aggression and called for assistance. New Zealand immediately sent two frigates to assist UN forces, but the British, who also sent naval forces, urged that land forces should not be sent. They feared that this might disrupt their plans for the defence of the Middle East and, at the same time, tempt a Russian move into that quarter. When the British suddenly changed their mind, in July 1950, New Zealand followed suit and got in its announcement of land forces a few hours before the British and the Australians.[41] New Zealand's 'Kay force' consisted of an artillery regiment, with supply and transport troops, making a total of two thousand men. It eventually became part of a unique Commonwealth Division — a traditional linkage in a new-style UN operation.

The Korean war hastened American preparations for the Japanese peace treaty. Anzac willingness to help in Korea may have helped the Americans to come round to the desired security guarantee. President Truman sent John Foster Dulles to Tokyo to finalize the peace treaty in January 1951 and authorized him to visit Canberra and Wellington to discuss a guarantee. Dulles took with him a draft proposal for a Pacific pact in the form of a Presidential Declaration, to be made after ministerial agreement, which would apply to the 'island nations of the Pacific'.[42] The parties to this pact would be the United States, Australia, New Zealand, Japan, the Philippines, and possibly Indonesia. Britain was deliberately excluded, partly because Dulles had forgotten about its territories in North Borneo and also because the US did not want commitments to Hong Kong and wanted to avoid claims for inclusion from France, the Netherlands, and Portugal, which also had territories in the region. Although the British Chiefs of Staff welcomed a guarantee to Australia and New Zealand which would facilitate Anzac assistance in the Middle East, the British representative in Tokyo bluntly opposed British exclusion from the pact and put Dulles on the defensive.[43] Meanwhile, in Washington, another approach emerged in discussions with the New Zealand Prime Minister. Sidney Holland made a strong plea for guarantees to New Zealand in the Pacific because of the large commitment of up to 35,000 men for the Middle East in a war. Thus, Dean Rusk, the Assistant Secretary of State, suggested a tripartite treaty between Australia, New Zealand, and the United States, which was eagerly welcomed by Holland, who alerted Wellington and Canberra.[44] When Dulles went to Canberra in February 1951 the Australians, with New Zealand support, made it clear that they would not support the 'soft' Japanese peace treaty unless they had a guarantee. A tripartite treaty was, therefore, drafted in Canberra.[45] It was signed in San Francisco on 1 September 1951, a week before the Japanese peace treaty. The ANZUS alliance provided that any threat to the three parties would be regarded by each as threatening their own peace and security and they would consult. They also undertook 'separately and jointly' to 'maintain and develop their individual and collective capacity to resist armed attack'. An ANZUS Council was created for periodic consultations.[46] ANZUS would 'bolt the back door' as the Anzac partners helped Britain in the Middle East.

The British were upset by their exclusion from ANZUS, because they also were committed to help the Tasman neighbours. Although the Attlee Government gave formal encouragement to ANZUS because of the importance of the guarantee for the Middle East commitment, the Cabinet had been divided.[47] When the Conservatives returned to power in Britain two months after the signing of ANZUS, Winston Churchill put some forceful pressure on the New Zealand and Australian Prime Ministers to get Britain admitted to ANZUS Council meetings.[48] New Zealand had always wanted this, but the Americans were adamant that admission of Britain would raise the question of admitting countries like the Philippines or France. A way out was sought in a wider, more comprehensive, security pact.

The growing fear in the early 1950s was that the Peoples Republic of China, established by Mao Tse-tung in October 1949, would intervene in South-East Asia as it did in Korea in 1950. With the French fighting the Communist Viet Minh in Indo-China and the British at war with Communist guerrillas in Malaya, there were fears for the general security of South-East Asia, and joint British–French–American Staff talks began in 1951 with Australian and New Zealand observers. Two ideas emerged. First, that a strategic reserve should be built up in South-East Asia as a nucleus force to deter China, and, secondly, that a wider multi-lateral security alliance should be created.[49] This would have the incidental advantage for New Zealand of removing the objections to Britain's exclusion from ANZUS.

In 1953 a Five Power Staff Agency (United States, Britain, France, Australia, and New Zealand) came into being to study the problems of deterring or combatting a Chinese incursion into South-East Asia.[50] The British persuaded Australia and New Zealand to co-operate in a Common-wealth Far East strategic reserve in Malaya.[51] However, schemes for a wider security pact were delayed because of American reluctance until 1954, when the French garrison at Dien Bien Dhu was invested by the Viet Minh and the French appealed to the United States for help. Although the American Chiefs of Staff briefly toyed with the idea of sending bombers to try and relieve the French (and there was even consideration of using atomic bombs),[52] the Americans would not assist the French without allies and these were not forthcoming. In an abrupt about-turn Dulles, now Secretary of State, proposed an anti-Communist alliance in South-East Asia. The British, though keen on some arrangement, wanted a wider pact, to include, if possible, neutralist countries like Burma and Indonesia as well as the South Asian nations, especially India.[53] In the event, the South-East Asian Collective Defence Treaty (or Manila Pact) was signed on 8 September 1954, by the ANZUS partners, two colonial powers (Britain and France), and only three Asian members (Thailand, the Philippines, and Pakistan).

Like ANZUS the Manila Pact made provision for a Council, for separate and joint development of individual and collective capacities to resist attack, and each party recognized that aggression within the treaty area would endanger its own peace and safety. In a separate 'Understanding', however, the United States applied this only to 'Communist aggression'. All the parties agreed in an attached protocol to apply the treaty to former French Indo-China — the states of Cambodia, Laos, and Vietnam.[54] Unlike ANZUS there was provision for economic and technical assistance and in 1955 the South-East Asian Treaty Organisation came into being in Bangkok. It created a Military Liaison Group, a Military Planning Office, and also civil committees, one to combat subversion, one of economic experts, and another on cultural matters.[55] SEATO had the advantage for New Zealand of including Britain with the ANZUS partners; indeed, during the planning stages British 'informal observers' attended ANZUS deputies' meetings in Washington. At the same time the Commonwealth Far East Strategic Reserve was created in Malaya. Its prime role was a reserve to support SEATO and deter Chinese intervention; the secondary role was the external defence of Malaya, and it had an immediate role of assisting in the operations against the communist guerrillas in Malaya.[56] New Zealand contributed an SAS Squadron in 1956 followed by an infantry battalion in 1957. The fighter squadron was moved from Cyprus to Malaya. When Malaya gained its independence in 1957 external defence was covered by an Anglo-Malayan Defence Agreement (AMDA) with which New Zealand and Australia were associated.

ANZAM, ANZUS, SEATO, and AMDA all came to focus on the same region. The ending of the Middle East commitment was dramatically demonstrated in 1956 during the Suez Crisis, when Holland was, at first, willing for the cruiser *Royalist* to take part. But, on the advice of the officials, New Zealand held aloof at the last minute. The rationale of the growing New Zealand commitment in South-East Asia — quite different, but more active than the contingency plans for the Middle East — was the concept of 'forward defence'. China was seen as the protagonist and China was to be held, in the last resort, at the Songkla line, on the Thai-Malayan border. In support of this doctrine New Zealanders were involved in five deployments in the 1950s and 1960s.

First, there was the Emergency in Malaya, where the SAS squadron went on jungle patrols and the air force gave back-up.[57] Secondly, in 1962, after Communist Pathet Lao made incursions into North-East Thailand, thirty SAS men deployed along with British, Australian, and American troops on the Thai border. In 1964 thirty-three New Zealand army engineers helped build airfields in northern Thailand and two years later a specialist road-building team went under the Colombo Plan.[58] Thirdly, New Zealand transport aircraft helped ferry 2,000 men of the Strategic Reserve to Brunei in December 1962 to help suppress a pro-Indonesian revolt in the oil-rich Sultanate.[59] Fourthly, there was a major contribution during Indonesia's 'Confrontation' with Malaysia in 1962–66. In an attempt to prevent the creation of Malaysia (by the federation of Malaya and the North Borneo territories), Indonesia infiltrated across the Borneo borders and landed guerillas in southern Malaya. The New Zealand battalion was used in these operations, with the addition of a forty-man Ranger Squadron. The transport aircraft were also employed and a bomber squadron brought from New Zealand. A frigate joined the Far East fleet and some crew were provided for coastal mine-sweepers. Over a thousand New Zealanders were involved in combatting Confrontation, which proved to be their biggest South-East Asian contribution.[60] The longest, and most controversial, however, was the involvement in Vietnam.

The Vietnam war became New Zealand's longest war and represented a major turning point in external affairs. The United States, having failed to prevent a Communist state in North Vietnam in the 1950s, tried to support a non-Communist South Vietnam in the 1960s and sought allies in their effort. When Australia sent military advisers in 1962 New Zealand was slow to respond, and sent, instead, a five-man civilian surgical team. After further requests at a SEATO Council meeting in 1964 a twenty-five strong Engineers' detachment was sent for road and bridge building. By 1965, however, as the United States began to bomb North Vietnam and sent in combat troops to the South, there was further pressure on New Zealand for a contribution. The Government showed great reluctance, but after Australia made a commitment in 1965, and requests came from both the US and South Vietnamese Governments, the Holyoake Government agreed to send about 500 men. Forward defence, allied solidarity, and resistance to Communism were given as the reasons. New Zealand's 'front line' was seen to be in South-East Asia and Holyoake said, 'We must, I believe, range ourselves with our American and Australian allies.'[61]

Vietnam proved to be a major turning point for five reasons. It was the first time New Zealand had gone to war without Britain. Secondly, the commitment was small compared with all earlier wars — only 550 at the peak. The artillery battery, which served from July 1965 until May 1971 was the longest continuous deployment in action in the country's history.[62] In 1967 two infantry companies were contributed to an ANZAC battalion, and in 1968 an SAS troop joined an Australian squadron. Four helicopter pilots flew with the Australian Air Force. Thirdly, the absorption of the effort into the Australian Task Force became a problem. It was felt that not enough recognition was given to New Zealand's national identity. Fourthly, New Zealanders found themselves on the losing side for the first time. A non-Communist South Vietnam was not achieved. Finally, there was unprecedented domestic opposition to the war, part of a new interest in foreign affairs, which by the 1970s began to contribute new agendas in foreign policy.

Participation in the Cold War alliance system and the five deployments in South-East Asia in the 1960s were summed up in 1966 in a statement of national objectives which implied obligations of mutuality. The aim, as it had been for a century, was: 'to establish a claim upon our major allies for consultation, a voice in important decisions, and in the last resort, and most importantly, military assistance and protection in time of need. This requires New Zealand to demonstrate willingness to make an appropriate degree of national defensive effort, and willingness and ability to assist our allies in matters affecting *their* national interests.'[63] Here was the rationale for all the activity so far from New Zealand's shores. By the 1970s, however, the global scene and the alliance environment had changed dramatically. New Zealand began to concentrate on the South Pacific and to take a more consciously independent stance on many issues. This was, in the first instance, induced by the withdrawal from South-East Asia of the two allies of 'dual dependency' days. It was accentuated by Britain's entry into the EC in 1973.

The British announced their withdrawal from 'East of Suez' in 1966. They completed the move ten years later, leaving only a small garrison in Hong Kong. The Americans went more quickly. In 1968 President Johnson decided not to stand for a second term because of domestic divisions caused by the Vietnam war. His Republican successor announced the 'Nixon Doctrine' in 1969. The US would reduce its involvement and expect greater self-reliance in its allies. The last US combat troops left Vietnam in 1972 and the US Embassy was evacuated in 1975. The Americans retired from the Asian mainland to their 'off-shore' bases in the Philippines and Okinawa. Could New Zealand stay in South-East Asia outside great power arrangements?

In the case of Malaysia and Singapore the decision was made, in 1969, that New Zealand *would* stay behind, along with Australia, after the British withdrawal. In the event, that withdrawal had a brief stay of execution during the days of the Heath Conservative Government, 1970–74, when new Five Power Defence Arrangements involving Malaysia, Singapore, Britain, Australia, and New Zealand were negotiated. New Zealand agreed to participate in an ANZUK force.[64] In the case of Vietnam there could be no question of remaining. The combat troops were withdrawn in 1971, leaving only two twenty-five-man training teams to assist the South Vietnamese army. While demonstrating an interest in South-East Asian security by leaving the battalion and other forces in Singapore, New Zealand began, at last, to give priority to its own region, the South Pacific.

In 1971 Wellington played host to the first South Pacific Forum, a meeting of heads of government of the independent and self-governing South Pacific countries. The President of Nauru, the Prime Ministers of Fiji, Tonga, Western Samoa, and New Zealand, the Premier of the Cook Islands, and the Australian Minister of External Affairs attended. Over the next sixteen years the Forum grew to fifteen members, including two non-Commonwealth states. In 1972 the South Pacific Bureau for Economic Co-operation based in Fiji became the Forum's secretariat.[65] By the early 1970s both National and Labour leaders were adopting the rhetoric of 'independence' and 'self-reliance' in foreign affairs. With the election of the third Labour Government under Norman Kirk in 1972, New Zealand began to make a mark not unlike that of the first Labour Government in the 1930s.

Kirk asserted that a moral stance in world affairs was possible. He adopted one especially in relation to two items which loomed large on the 'new agenda' of the 1970s — nuclear weapons and sporting contacts with South Africa. Kirk had only twenty-one months in office, before his death in 1974, but in that time he made some dramatic initiatives in his foreign affairs portfolio which gained New Zealand new international prominence. The last New Zealanders were brought back from Vietnam by Christmas 1972. The Peoples Republic of China was recognized and a New Zealand Embassy established in Beijing. A Moscow Embassy was re-opened after over twenty years. On the sports issue a Springbok tour of New Zealand was prevented in 1973 for fear of jeopardizing the Tenth Commonwealth

Games, which were successfully (and profitably) held in Christchurch in the following year. To demonstrate opposition to French nuclear tests in the Pacific a frigate was sent into the test area with a Cabinet minister on board, which drew the attention of the world media. Along with Australia, a case to restrain the French was taken to the International Court. At the Commonwealth Heads of Government meeting in 1973 Kirk also secured a resolution opposing all nuclear testing, which was promulgated on Hiroshima Day. He gained African approval for the resolution by giving sympathetic support for African concerns relating to Southern Africa. After Kirk's death his successor, Bill Rowling, pressed ahead with the project for a nuclear-weapon-free zone in the South Pacific. He planned to withdraw the battalion from Singapore. He also looked to trade opportunities in Eastern Europe and the Middle East.[66]

Much (but not all) of this was reversed with the return to power of National in 1975 under Robert Muldoon. Plans for the nuclear-free zone lapsed. The new Government sought to 'resuscitate' ANZUS. It welcomed visits by US warships knowing they would 'neither confirm nor deny' whether they carried nuclear warheads. Progressively through the later 1970s and early 1980s, visiting American submarines and cruisers were greeted by large fleets of protest vessels. In the sporting arena, contacts with South Africa were resumed on the principle of 'keeping politics out of sport'. An All Black tour to South Africa went ahead in 1976 at the time of the Soweto riots. This led to an attempt to have New Zealand banned from the 1976 Olympic Games. It failed, but it led to an African boycott of the Games by all but two small non-Commonwealth countries. Nigeria also boycotted the Commonwealth Games in 1978. The Springbok tour of New Zealand in 1981 led to unprecedented civil strife and the cancellation of one game when demonstrators invaded the field. Scenes of police in riot gear confronting defiant demonstrators attracted as much attention in the world media as Labour's frigate at Mururoa.[67]

The new priority in foreign affairs in the Muldoon years was trade diversification. 'Our foreign policy is trade',[68] declared Muldoon, and in this respect there were major successes in new markets such as the Middle East and China. There was also a continuing security concentration on the South Pacific. Plans for a 'Ready Reaction Force' for deployment in the islands were made.[69] South-East Asia received less emphasis as SEATO was dismantled in 1977. However, the New Zealand Force in Singapore was still not brought home and the Government adhered to the Five Power Defence Arrangements. A growing interest in Africa was evident in the contingent which was offered for the Commonwealth Monitoring Force which supervised the Zimbabwe cease-fire in 1979 and a parliamentary team was sent to observe the ensuing elections.[70] By the 1980s, old Cold War antagonisms were being played down as Russia and China, the bogey-men of four decades, became considerable, if not always reliable, customers for New Zealand products. The military security aspect of foreign affairs gave way to trading, regional concerns and, later, environmental concerns. Of the latter, questions relating to nuclear weapons loomed large.

By the 1984 general election only the National Party still supported an ANZUS alliance which involved unconditional visits by US warships. The Labour Party, the Democrats, and the recently formed New Zealand Party were opposed to nuclear ship visits and advocated a revision of ANZUS. The fourth Labour Government of David Lange, after the landslide victory of 1984, hoped that an arrangement could be made with the United States whereby New Zealand could become nuclear free but remain in ANZUS. The Government urged the United States to test its policy by requesting a ship visit. But when application was made for a visit by the destroyer USS *Buchanan* in February 1985 Lange refused, since the ship was nuclear capable. The United States Government reacted sharply for fear that the anti-nuclear contagion would spread. It withdrew intelligence sharing and military co-operation. ANZUS was declared 'inoperative' in relation to New Zealand and in 1986 the guarantee under the treaty was suspended. The British also cancelled warship visits as they, too, applied the 'neither confirm nor deny' rule. It was the most dramatic turn-around in New Zealand's position in forty years. But the Lange Government was unrepentant and gained considerable popularity. It went on to sign the Treaty of Rarotonga on 8 August 1985, creating the South Pacific Nuclear Weapon Free Zone.[71]

A unique aspect of the fourth Labour Government's approach to defence and foreign policy was the appointment of the Defence Committee of Inquiry to consult public opinion before future policies were finalized. It was chaired by Frank Corner, a retired diplomat who had been one of the first of the young recruits to the Department of External Affairs, became ambassador in Washington and had been permanent head of the department under Kirk. The other members were Major-General Poananga, a former Chief of the General Staff, and two anti-nuclearists, Diane Hunt, a DSIR scientist, and Kevin Clements, a lecturer in sociology. The Committee received over 4,000 submissions, held public hearings in the main centres, and commissioned a detailed public opinion poll. The report *Defence and Security: What New Zealanders Want*, published in 1986, saw three main options for the country: collective security, non-nuclear armed defence or unarmed defence. Contrary to the findings of the questionnaire, the unconventional second and third options were given considerable space in the report. But the conclusion was that opinion around the country was 'deeply divided'.[72] It found that 73 per cent of the respondents wanted to be nuclear free but 72 per cent wanted to stay in alliances. A nuclear-free New Zealand inside ANZUS was the most favoured position: 44 per cent wanted to stay in ANZUS and ban nuclear ships; 37 per cent would stay in ANZUS and allow nuclear ships. When the 44 per cent were confronted with the impossibility of a nuclear-free New Zealand inside ANZUS and faced a choice between ANZUS or ship bans, 52 per cent would allow ships and stay in ANZUS, and 44 per cent would get out of ANZUS to avoid ship visits.[73] Because of the customary margin of error the poll indicated that no real consensus existed. With such a close result the Government was clearly disappointed and tried to discredit the report. It went ahead with its policies and legislated for a nuclear-free land. The United States demoted New Zealand from 'ally' to 'friendly country'.

In 1987 the Defence Review suggested that, for the first time, a logical and coherent strategy had been worked out to defend New Zealand interests against any credible threats that might be presented. Such threats did not include invasion, since the South Pacific was seen as a 'uniquely favourable strategic environment'.[74] More likely was terrorism, such as the French sinking of the Greenpeace ship *Rainbow Warrior* in 1985; violation of the Exclusive Economic Zone around the shores; natural disasters, or instability in the Pacific Island nations. The conclusion was that New Zealand needed to have, for the first time, a capability to operate independently though more probably with Australia. A management review of defence establishments by private consultants in 1988 also strayed into the strategic policy realm. To retain an ability to deal with terrorism and infringements to sovereignty over natural resources, and an ability to act independently (or alongside Australia) in the South Pacific, a maritime capability was essential. New Zealand had to demonstrate its willingness and ability to defend its sovereignty and that of its neighbours. 'Given the nature of its own defence resources, New Zealand is unable to do a great deal in the region without Australian support and (preferably) assistance.' The prime object of foreign policy was therefore seen as ensuring that Australia remained interested in New Zealand's security. Australia would want reciprocal help. New Zealand would need to demonstrate that it was a capable partner.[75] Thus priority was given in the late 1980s to trans-Tasman relations.

In place of an 'inoperative' ANZUS the bilateral link with Australia was strengthened. The provision, under the Closer Economic Relations Agreement of 1983, for the progressive development of free trade between the two countries by 1995, was brought forward to 1990. In the privatization of Air New Zealand political preference was given to a consortium including Qantas rather than to British Airways, the preferred partner of the management. In a controversial decision on replacement vessels for the navy, the Government entered an ANZAC frigate-building project jointly with Australia in 1989. Though off-the-shelf vessels from elsewhere might have been cheaper, the Government decided to purchase two ANZAC frigates, with an option of two more, on the condition that New Zealand firms had the right to contract for supply and construction work over the entire project. The political priority of close relations with Australia was deemed to be worth paying for in these ways.

New Zealand's external affairs since 1935 present a great paradox. The 'small power rampant'[76] of the 1930s and 1940s, which tried to achieve a system of universal collective security through the League and the UN was, in reality, still a dependency. Nuclear-free New Zealand, in the second half of the 1980s, won recognition as a small nation prepared to defy its super-power protector in a matter of principle. Yet the pretension of influencing global concerns had been abandoned in favour of a focus on the immediate

Pacific environment. Moreover, the dramatic political pendulum swings of the 1970s and 1980s indicated a country still uncertain of its place in the world. As Frank Corner suggested in the 1986 inquiry report, Britain's entry into the EC and its withdrawal from East of Suez had forced a military, political, economic, and cultural re-appraisal. 'No longer did New Zealanders know where they stood . . . To some it was as if New Zealand was being made afresh.'[77] Looking to the United States for protection since 1940 had not involved a transfer of sentiment. There was a gap between official and popular perceptions of America. Opinion was found to be deeply divided.

Solace could be found in two non-political developments. First, there was considerable success in trade diversification. At the end of the Second World War 70 per cent of the country's exports went to Britain, which still remained the largest market, taking a third of the exports, at the time it joined the EC in 1973. But the writing had long been on the wall. The British proportion continued to fall steadily until 1980, when, for the first time, Britain was not New Zealand's largest market. It was overtaken by the United States, which was in turn soon overtaken by Japan and Australia. In 1989 Japan, taking 18 per cent, was the largest market and Britain was fourth with only 7 per cent. Useful markets had also opened in Canada, China, South Korea, Russia, and Iran. Looked at regionally, the EC countries took 18 per cent; but the Pacific Basin accounted for 75 per cent.

The second source of solace came from the concept that man-for-man, woman-for-woman, New Zealanders were 'as good as the next person'. This had long been recognized in the military sphere beginning with South Africa and Gallipoli. It was attested to by Rommel in the Second World War. In 1986 the former commander of the SAS in Malaya wrote: 'Let's not be modest . . . man for man we are capable of producing the best troops in the business.'[78] Yet by the time of the Gulf War in 1991 a change was evident. Although the newly elected National Government sought to mend fences with the United States by sending a contribution to the multi-national coalition to fight Iraq, no combat troops were sent. New Zealand's contribution consisted of two RNZAF transport planes operating out of Riyadh with the RAF, and two medical teams serving in Bahrain with a US naval and a British air force hospital — a total of 114 personnel.[79] For the first time New Zealanders did not go to fight in a major war. Yet there was no public regret.

To many others unconcerned with national glory or the niceties of diplomacy, there was a passionate identification with the country's sporting successes. The All Blacks, who had been a major focus of national identity throughout the century, confirmed their primacy by winning the first World Cup Rugby contest in 1987 and remaining unbeaten for four years. But other sports also began to take the limelight. The hockey gold medal was won (against Australia) at the 1976 Olympic Games, and the All Whites soccer team reached the finals round of the World Cup in 1982. A New Zealand cricket team defeated England in 1977 (on the fortieth attempt!). A rowing eight and women's netball team became world champions, and New Zealand yachts won the Whitbread round-the-world race. A small country was seen to be capable of success in big-time sport. Indeed, an analysis of the medal winners in the 1984 Olympic Games devised a 'success ratio' based on total points (5 for gold, 3 for silver, and 1 for bronze) divided by total population in millions. New Zealand came out far ahead with 13.93 followed by Romania 7.32.[80] While such figures are hardly consistent with the Olympic ideal of 'individual' rather than 'national' achievement, they underline one of the most popular perceptions of New Zealand's place in the world. During the same Olympic Games, held only weeks after Labour's landslide win in the 1984 snap election, Auckland was awarded the 1990 Commonwealth Games. After years of controversy focusing on rugby contacts with South Africa, New Zealand, under the Lange Government, won support from African countries. At the previous Commonwealth Games in 1986 in Scotland more countries boycotted the events than competed. Such a spectre mitigated against full commercial sponsorship in Auckland. Yet one of the first events of the country's sesquicentennial commemorations in 1990 proved to be a great success. Fifty-five countries and 2,100 competitors made it the biggest Commonwealth Games to date; and it was unmarred by boycotts. The official report rhapsodized: 'We had given the country its greatest moment on the world stage . . .'[81] Nuclear-free New Zealand had become more concerned about its image than its security.

CHAPTER 21

The Awakening Imagination, 1940–1980

W. H. Oliver

The way had been prepared earlier, but the breakthrough came with the end of the Second World War. In less than twenty years the whole society had passed through a series of awakening experiences — depression, recovery, mobilization, the prospect of invasion, victory, peace, and the brief surge of hope it brought. These crowded years transformed a colonial society into an independent one; they shaped the literature and the art of the 1940s and 1950s; they underlay the more diverse developments of later years.

The centennial of 1940 had been planned as spirits lifted after the Depression; but at the same time peace was slipping away in Europe. It was celebrated by a people once again at war, whose history had been repeatedly affected by war at home and abroad, or by the fear of it. Nevertheless, the Centennial saluted the peaceful arts, the progress that had been made in agriculture, industry, democracy, racial harmony, and, more modestly, in culture. The ceremonial occasions, the displays of material advancement, the diversions of the amusement park were accompanied by music from a symphony orchestra, by an exhibition of paintings, by musical and literary competitions, and by a series of well-designed books, the Centennial surveys. With due restraint, cultural maturity was asserted and celebrated. To a degree, too, it was demonstrated. E. H. McCormick's *Letters and Art in New Zealand* (1940) and M. H. Holcroft's *The Deepening Stream* (1940) — a commissioned survey volume and a prize-winning essay — laid the foundations of a critical tradition and began a small but real intellectual revolution.

The Centennial celebrated a century of colonization; the remembered achievements were British. In the second year of the second Pākehā century the settlers faced their grimmest threat, that of a Japanese victory in the Pacific, and were taught that the British, in whom they had trusted for the first century, were no longer reliable. War provided danger and boredom, and both turned minds to culture. Though the danger was not in fact close it seemed to be, and the boredom, as the mild austerities of war stretched into the peace, was real enough. The cultural mood was optimistic and progressivist. The American presence widened horizons and prompted the writing of some useful books, most notably F. L. W. Wood's *This New Zealand* (1946). The alliance with Russia made radicalism respectable; it was possible to buy a Christmas card bearing the likenesses of Churchill, Roosevelt, and Stalin. Left-wing bookshops opened in the main centres; slender Faber volumes of verse looked down on pamphlets from the International Publishing House, Moscow. A Progressive Publishing Society set up in business and published some polemic, stories, and poems — a muted performance for a radical publisher. Its flimsy annual *New Zealand New Writing* was a pallid imitation of *Penguin New Writing*, even to the trademark kiwi on the cover. The Caxton Press was more successful. Its periodical *Book* had both style and substance. War-time New Zealanders read more, but they turned to the *Penguin* rather than the *New Zealand New Writing*, to the Faber rather than the Caxton poets.

Peace had a greater impact than war: it aroused a determination to recover the gains of the later 1930s, and to make fresh ones. Thousands of servicemen returned, many with their eyes opened by exotic experiences. Some had been encouraged to read, think, and write by the Army Education Welfare Service. In their hundreds they transformed the university colleges. Peaceful travellers departed again, many for postgraduate study. Earlier exiles returned, some to look and go away, some to stay. The small but culturally vigorous body of Jewish refugees increased. Overseas artists arrived and were greeted with enormous enthusiasm: the Boyd Neel String Orchestra in 1947 and the Old Vic Theatre Company in 1948. An international pianist, Lili Kraus, lived, played, and taught in New Zealand. Poets wrote verses for her, and there was a good literary journal to publish them. For among those returning was Charles Brasch, ready after a long exile to put into effect a plan he and Denis Glover had formed in war-time London. The outcome, in 1947, was *Landfall*.[1]

For the first time there existed a professional New Zealand journal of literature, of the arts, and (to a lesser extent) of affairs. It had a reliable publisher, the Caxton Press, and good printers, Denis Glover and Leo Bensemann. Of greater importance, it had a full-time editor with private means and a sense of mission. Brasch had been born into a Dunedin Jewish family from Germany; his upbringing had steeped his mind in European culture. Like many of his generation, he spent a long period out of New Zealand. He was drawn early to literature, became a poet, and published *The Land and the People* in 1939. He was also an evangelist, and *Landfall*, which he edited for twenty years, was his testament. Regularly, in each issue of the journal, he propounded a cultural ideology that was Eurocentric and élitist.[2] Otherwise *Landfall* was distinguished not by a pro- gramme but by a manner and a tone. It was a little too solemn, too devout even, for a culture in greater danger from high-mindedness than high spirits. Still, the journal and the decade suited each other. There was little in the literature and art of these years to suggest more than a wry smile. Before long *Landfall* was supported by public money, from the Literary Fund.

This Fund, established in 1946, was the creation of a public servant, Joseph Heenan, and a politician, Peter Fraser. The state had financed books, music, and painting during the Centennial without a continuing commitment to the arts. Now it moved permanently, if frugally, into patronage. Power and culture, each for its own ends, reached out to clasp hands, though they did not yet embrace. The Fund subsidized safe publications (not, probably, that there was much else available). In 1949 it sent its first writer, Allen Curnow, overseas. Its resources have grown with the years; its grants to writers have eased their lives; its subsidies have encouraged what was in the 1940s a minute publishing industry. With increasing frequency in the 1950s, state money found its way to the other arts, in a series of specific subsidies which were put on a regular and formal basis through the Arts Advisory Council in 1961, raised in status to the Queen Elizabeth II Arts Council two years later.[3]

The foundation of a symphony orchestra, again under the aegis of the state, was the third major initiative of the 1940s. 'A fresh sign of courage and faith' Charles Brasch called it before it had played a note. There was outraged hostility when Anderson Tyrer was appointed conductor, and a good deal of disappointment at its early performances. Hampered by the volume of work expected of it, the discontent of its players, and the dubious politics of its administration (Peter Fraser was said to take an interest in it), the orchestra had a slow start. But before the decade was out, the promise it was to fulfil had been heard under Eugene Goossens as guest conductor. In its second year the orchestra performed Douglas Lilburn's *Song of the Antipodes*, a work whose title (more than the music itself) invited a good deal of talk about landscape. Mountains and sea or not, a mature orchestral work had been written by a New Zealand composer and performed by a permanent New Zealand orchestra, and that had not happened before. It went on happening, especially after the appointment of James Robertson as conductor in 1954. Many believed that the works of New Zealand composers were not performed often enough or well enough, perhaps forgetting that earlier they had not even been written.[4]

These developments — a magazine, an orchestra, a small fund — are remarkable only in the context of the barrenness that preceded them. Within a few years they were taken for granted, their activities deplored or applauded, their successors and extensions in place. The growth of such institutions — through individual initiative, increasing public support, and government, corporate, and private patronage — continued uninterrupted to the late 1970s. In these thirty years New Zealand acquired a cultural infrastructure, a set of institutions to distribute resources to individuals and groups active in the arts, either as creators or as performers.[5] Though its essential function is supportive, the capacity of the infrastructure to give or to withhold enables its controllers to influence the course of cultural development and even to modify the character of creative activity.

This chapter turns first to that activity, to literature, the arts, and social criticism; then to the infrastructure by which they have been, in some measure, sustained; and finally to the relationship between the arts and society. These themes are explored chiefly as they are exemplified by the achievements of the 1940s and 1950s, decades of new and formative activity.

The Caxton Press anthology, *A Book of New Zealand Verse, 1923–1945*, for the first time gave poetry in New Zealand a look of competence and maturity. It was apparent that in twenty years a dozen or so people had written well. The writers had neither a style nor an ideology in common. In manner they were all some distance from modernist English and American verse; in matter many showed a concern with history, landscape, society, and human relationships. Most were deliberate explorers of the past and the present, looking around and behind them as if for the first time: they were, in fact, the first generation of poets to do so. They had left behind the imitativeness and the facile exploitation of local colour which vitiated so much recent and contemporary verse; they responded directly to their times and places.

This generalized sense of place, rather more than immediate recognizability, was the 'New Zealandness' that Curnow advocated in his introduction, a lengthy analysis which joined McCormick's survey and Holcroft's essay as a foundation document in literary criticism. Much that has been offered since about New Zealand poetry begins from this analysis, often by way of dissent and sometimes by way of misconstruction. Indeed, Curnow risked misunderstanding by too rigorous an insistence upon the need of the poet to 'seek forms as immediate in experience as the island soil under his feet'.[6] With this went a high view of poetry as both the consciousness and the conscience of society. Taken together, these suggestions gave the introduction the appearance of a manifesto for cultural nationalism.

The poems in the anthology showed a sharp improvement in quality rather than a revolution in sensibility. The only poet to give evidence of an innovative spirit was the anthology's editor. Curnow's *At Dead Low Water* (1949) showed an unusual intellectual restlessness and precision. His *Poems 1949–1957* demonstrated that these qualities were highly personal, sometimes intensely private. It is a paradox that in the 1940s and 1950s his prose earned him a reputation which his verse denied, that of being a dedicated poetical geographer. His 'themes' — voyaging, discovery, islands, settlements, ancestors, violence, death, and loss — are images of a mind in search of its own identity and only incidentally of society's. Precisely in the poem commissioned by the Government for the tercentenary of Tasman's discovery, 'Landfall in Unknown Seas', he anticipated those images of violence and death which recur in his more personal writing of the 1970s:

> Over the yellow sands and the clear
> Shallows, the dull filament
> Flickers, the blood of strangers:
> Death discovered the Sailor

O in a flash, in a flat calm,
A clash of boats in the bay
And the day marred with murder.[7]

If Curnow was the only truly modern poet of the 1940s, Charles Brasch reached a comparable individuality. He displayed no virtuosity, a lack that served him well. In *Disputed Ground* (1948) he showed a grim stiff-jointedness, and an inability to be glib, that heightened the power of his insight into the significance of the land and its past.

> The future and the past stand at our doors,
> Beggars who for one look of trust will open
> Worlds that can answer our unknown desires,
> Entering us like rain and sun to ripen.

Like Curnow, he lasted well, writing better as he grew older. The three volumes of poems written in the years before his death in 1973 were his best — deeply personal and intense.[8]

Most of James K. Baxter's work in the 1940s and 1950s shared the traditionalism of his older contemporaries. Within these limitations Baxter was extraordinarily versatile. The publication of *Beyond the Palisade* (1944) announced the presence of a striking young poet. By the later 1950s he had moved from bardic rapture through preaching to a much more personal anguish:

> But I too roast in the brass bull
> Of conscience, remembering at this autumn table
> Women ganched in cupboards of the mind or
> Geometrical on the black glaze of an urn. . . .

His output until his death in 1972 was prodigious; his public presence such that he was the only poet since Thomas Bracken to become a household name. His impact was great, but more upon lifestyle than the practice of poetry. The good poems are admirable; there are a great number of them and the best are of unforgettable power. Their range — from bawdy balladry to painful introspection — is wider than that of any other New Zealand poet. Nevertheless, he remains something of an anachronism; the direction of the future was set by less romantic and more inquisitive, if less powerful, minds.[9]

Often in the poetry of Ursula Bethell, J. R. Hervey, Denis Glover, and Charles Brasch, locality, landscape, and history were abstract symbolic presences. More typically, in the following years, the sense of place and past became concrete and particular. It lost none of its force in this transition, rather gaining in immediacy and impact. It gained, too, by being expressed less self-consciously. People and places became elements in an expanding range of experience. Within that range, the significance of personal relationships came to occupy a larger place. At the same time, literature itself and the intellectual traditions it conveys became more important.

There was, too, in the 1950s a new awareness that the individual vision did not simply reflect and express the commonly shared reality, but transformed it. Enough remained of the immediate and the indigenous to encourage the opinion that spiritual map-making was continuing. But it was a different cartography, closer to Curnow's example than to his precept.

Hubert Witheford and Charles Spear exemplify this new emphasis. Witheford's magnolia has roots that go deeper than the native clay:

> Forth from earth's opened side
> The slow, slow fountain plays,
> Its twisted streams of wood
> Flowing to the measure of a giant time
> To statelier music than our lives may know.[10]

Sometimes locality figures in Witheford's poems — a mountain range, a glimpse of a suburb, an earthquake — but it is reshaped into an interior landscape. The immediate environment has no echo at all in Charles Spear:

> The paladins played chess and did not care,
> The crocus pierced the turf with random dart.
> Then twanged a cord. Through space, from Oultremer,
> That other arrow veered towards your heart.[11]

His only volume, *Twopence Coloured* (1951), is an arresting collection of carefully wrought lyrics. They are mannered, but the mannerism is functional: it turns these mementos into bright images of a heritage too easily forgotten. Yet they are contemporary in their concern with war and desolation; they are relevant to a country whose history includes the Crusades, the wars of Europe, and London as the capital of a great empire. For this poet, literature is life.

It was so for many poets in the 1950s: they were discovering that the 'island soil' on which they stood was in fact a continent of ideas, values, and practices. M. K. Joseph's first two books of poems, *Imaginary Islands* (1950) and *The Living Countries* (1959), show a sensibility that is shaped by literature and learning.[12] Within this perspective the New Zealand locality is transformed and enriched. Kendrick Smithyman, one of the first New Zealand poets to absorb American influences, focused his attention on a precise locality — the Auckland region — but he sees it within a wider human context.

Other poets — Ruth Dallas, W. H. Oliver, Keith Sinclair, Alistair Campbell — stayed fairly close to the themes of the previous decade. Campbell's *Mine Eyes Dazzle* (1950) enjoyed an astonishing success. The eloquence and unabashed romanticism of these lyrics of love and death set in a familiar landscape of mountain, river, and sea touched a nerve in the experience of a great number of readers.[13] Unlike Campbell, Louis Johnson was self-consciously a poet of the small town and the city. Like many of the fiction writers of the decade, Johnson intently examined the damage people do to each other in intimate situations, in their suburban and small-town bungalows, in city streets and tenements. His example was important. Earlier poetry had tended to neglect the human detail of New Zealand life, the buildings that had been put up on the soil, and the lives that went on within them. With Johnson, that neglect ended.[14]

He was, as well as a poet, a crusader, in a cause never exactly defined. His older contemporaries, especially Curnow, Holcroft, and Brasch, were charged with embracing a South Island nature mysticism and of writing as if New Zealand lacked people. Social reality, the attack went, was urban; the task ahead was to populate the empty country, to move from 'the people' as an abstraction to people as individuals. The cultural reality, further, was international; locality was incidental.[15] But the argument raised more problems than it solved. Neither nationalism nor inter-nationalism could alone answer the questions posed by living, working, and writing in New Zealand, a country which has never fully satisfied the need for an identity. When they wrote poems, if not when they wrote polemic, the protagonists did not seek to escape from this dilemma. Curnow and Johnson, in different ways, were faithful both to the cultural inheritance and the environment in which they lived.

Two anthologies, the Oxford *Anthology of New Zealand Verse* (1956) and the *Penguin Book of New Zealand Verse* (1960), reinforced the impression of permanence gained in the 1950s. It was enhanced by the first collected poems (Ursula Bethell, Robin Hyde, and A. R. D. Fairburn) and substantial new volumes from Eileen Duggan, Baxter, Glover, Hervey, Brasch, and Curnow. New names kept appearing, in *Landfall* and *Poetry Yearbook*, names that were to mean a great deal in the 1960s and 1970s: Peter Bland, C. K. Stead, Hone Tuwhare, Vincent O'Sullivan, Michael Jackson, Gordon Challis, and Owen Leeming. A critical edge, too, had developed; lengthy articles greeted collected volumes, and new books were respectfully reviewed. And, sure sign of acceptance, the first postgraduate theses on New Zealand poetry appeared. It was, by the end of the 1950s, well established.[16]

So, too, was fiction. 'Five New Zealand novels in . . . a twelve month', Brasch exclaimed in 1958. Even at the beginning of the 1950s there was a solid body of work, most of which had been published since 1940.[17] Though some capable writers — such as G. R. Gilbert, A. P. Gaskell, and J. R. Cole — did not fulfil their early promise, three substantial reputations were established in the 1940s and grew over the following years, those of Frank Sargeson, Dan Davin, and James Courage.

Courage found in childhood, the family, and sexual relationships situations of stress and deprivation. Davin examined the disturbance of the talented young shifting from the crippling restraints of home, class, and locality to the wider horizons of adolescence and opportunity, at university, in the city, and 'overseas'. Each had a specific regional and social milieu: Courage the Canterbury pastoral gentry, Davin the small-farmer Catholic communities of Southland. For each the family is the place where alienation starts, a destructive but inescapable environment. Parent and child are enemies who cannot escape each other; sexuality is destructive — for Davin, religion as well. Both writers present an extreme indictment of basic social institutions.[18]

Sargeson was a greater artist; he was also given, or chose, a harder destiny. The strategy of secure expatriation — Davin in British publishing and Courage on a private income — was not available to the small-town solicitor's clerk of humble origins and no academic distinction. He survived arduously, setting up as a full-time creative writer with, at first, no greater support than a disability pension, the meagre rewards of publication, and a little market-gardening. The effort was heroic, and the results remarkable. He was more deliberately innovative than Davin or Courage, but his was a narrower vision. His protagonists are solitaries; at most they interact with one or two others and then only marginally. Society is a looming presence, diffuse and hostile.

In the 1940s his output was considerable: three collections of stories, and his first novel, *I Saw in My Dream* (1949). In the 1950s he turned, with less assurance, to the novella (*I For One*, 1954) and again to the novel (*Memoirs of a Peon*, 1965); the later 1960s and the 1970s were filled with more stories, more novels, plays, and three brief volumes of autobiography. The stories of the 1940s remain his highest achievement. They have a severe economy and a technical ingenuity which remained unique until well into the 1950s and have not been common since; and a habit of understatement and ellipsis that even he was not to maintain for long. No-one in New Zealand has controlled the 'I' of fiction with so much skill and purpose. The author carefully sustains a position of moral neutrality. But, simply in giving his protagonists the dual role of victim and witness, he makes an act of moral judgement, an implicit condemnation of society and of those who make their peace with it.

Sargeson used the conventions of social realism, especially a careful attention to the detail of circumstances and to the nuances of everyday speech. He created a poetic language of great subtlety from the clichés, the slang, and the understatements of barely articulate people. So, to his enthusiastic readers, these early stories were a revelation of the society they experienced day by day. But he was less of a social realist than other short-story writers in the 1940s, such as Cole and Gaskell. His social range is restricted; he has no room for — let alone sympathy with — the dominant New Zealand lower middle class, the milieu from which he sprang and which he repudiated.[19]

The output of the 1950s was considerable: four more novels from Courage and two from Davin, as well as many new writers. Of these, two stand out, Janet Frame and Maurice Duggan. A slender volume of stories appeared in 1951, *The Lagoon*. It was well, if tepidly, received: had not Janet Frame followed it with a striking first novel in 1957, *Owls Do Cry*, she would have become another of the many half-forgotten names. With his first collection of stories, *Immanuel's Land* (1956), Maurice Duggan made an irresistible claim upon attention. In many ways they are dissimilar — Duggan was often the self-conscious craftsman, while Frame allowed no notions of discipline and form to constrain her. But they are alike in the exuberance of their prose, their rejection of the conventions of social realism, their readiness to run the risks of over-writing, and their steady attention to interior states of mind.

It is easier to locate Duggan in the history of New Zealand fiction; he shares with Davin a painful response to a Catholic childhood, and he sharply delineates social institutions and relationships. All his stories, put together, would come to little more than 400 pages, but it is a dense and compact body of work. Both the stories of adolescent despair in *Immanuel's Land* and the painful analyses of mature failure in *O'Leary's Orchard* (1970) exhibit a fertile interaction between private vision and public experience. Both are sombrely depicted, but illuminated by more wit and irony than most New Zealand writers have been able to command.[20]

Janet Frame went on with undiminished vigour through the 1970s. *Owls Do Cry* set a pattern of theme, imagery, and outlook from which she has seldom departed. Language itself is often her subject as well as her method, language as the means by which a better world is constructed from within, and the hostile world either transformed or denied. Typically, children and isolates rely upon the light of 'the inward sun' to create a bearable environment. The towns and suburbs are either transfigured into symbols of deprivation or reduced to drab ordinariness to provide a counterpoint to inner reality. Her prose ranges between careful reportage and surreal prose poetry; the shifts in style and viewpoint are abrupt and often disconcerting. The power is undeniable, but there has been less development than is to be found in Duggan's slighter corpus. *Owls Do Cry* will remain a landmark; the rest must be held, at the very least, in great respect.[21] Similar, though less spectacular, is the record of Sylvia Ashton-Warner, whose first novel, *Spinster* (1958), achieved instant acclaim. She, too, has written a great deal since, but later novels have added little to the originality of *Spinster*.

The most substantial novel written in the 1950s was not published until 1963. An extract from a work in progress by 'Chris Bell' appeared in *Landfall* in 1951. The author was in fact Bill Pearson, and the work was *Coal Flat* (1963). Its flaws are obvious enough: the prose is uneventful, the plot predictable, the well-to-do wicked, the poor deprived, and the Māori romantic. But none of that matters much: the 'hero' is the community, not any of the individuals who make it up; the heart of the book is social analysis. A reader might be hard put to recall any particular person in it, but the Westland mining community is indelibly impressed.[22]

Something of the same broad social intention was announced, ambitiously, by Maurice Shadbolt when he called his book of stories *The New Zealanders* (1959) — a striking contrast with Pearson's carefully limited title. Pearson's novel has been his only one; Shadbolt's book the prelude to several best-sellers. *Strangers and Journeys* (1972) is a brave attempt at a portrait of society. It ranges over several generations, spans the hemispheres, incorporates a total social spectrum, and traces the fortunes of its characters through bush-farming, urban violence, revolutionary politics, and artistic creation. The wide canvas and the broad strokes did not prove easy to master. More manageable, and more fashionable, has been the smaller scale of stories and novels written by O. E. Middleton, Phillip Wilson, Maurice Gee, Helen Shaw, Ian Cross, Ruth France, M. K. Joseph, and Marilyn Duckworth during the 1950s.[23]

By the close of the decade the writing of fiction had become a cottage industry; its practitioners were often professional writers, at least in aspiration. Their achievements were considerable in bulk and often impressive in quality. Almost uniformly, they reiterated the earlier unfavourable verdict upon society and its impact upon the individual, and reviewers have constantly lamented the disinclination of fiction writers to attend to the positive and purposeful aspects of life in New Zealand. Certainly there is rather more exuberance in the poetry and more yet in the painting of the same period. However, it is significant that New Zealand fiction constantly sounds a 'sour discordant ground-tone'[24] — an almost unrelieved dissent from the conventional and consensual values of unity, harmony, and progress.

Painters, though they worked under more difficult conditions than writers, produced a great deal of new and exciting work in the 1940s. While books flowed into the country, paintings stayed overseas and good reproductions were scarce. Writers were assisted by a generation of creative printer-publishers — R. S. Lowry and R. N. Holloway in Auckland as well as Glover and Bensemann in Christchurch[25] — and the adventurous publishing house of Blackwood and Janet Paul. New painters had no such welcome. The numerous art societies were dominated by conservatives and hobbyists. When, in 1955, the Auckland City Art Gallery mounted a retrospective exhibition of the mildly modernist painter, John Weeks, it was also his first one-man show. Although T. A. McCormack had been painting well since the late 1920s, only three of the paintings hung at his 1959 retrospective were from public galleries.[26] The instances are extreme, but they illustrate the predicament of the painter: conservative art societies; a lack of dealer galleries; public galleries with fixed permanent displays, few exhibitions of current work, little money and less inclination to buy local works.

But there were other and better features. The Christchurch Group, founded in the late 1920s, held annual exhibitions and gave many new painters an opportunity. Public libraries and coffee houses began to hold exhibitions; Helen Hitchings, in Wellington, opened the first dealer gallery in 1948. It did not last long, but at the same time the Wellington Architectural Centre, which held many important exhibitions, was started by young architects with a keen interest in the visual arts. The schools of art at Auckland and Christchurch were reformed and became university faculties in 1950. Two years later Eric Westbrook was appointed to the Auckland City Art Gallery. He was New Zealand's first full-time professional director of a public gallery. It was not until the 1960s that this example was widely followed. This was the decade, too, in which the dealer galleries multiplied and the Arts Council began to operate with greater effect as a patron.[27]

In the visual arts the shift in sensibility that took place in the 1940s was more radical than the literary developments of the same decade. Three events at its close point to the shape of the new departures: the combined Woollaston–McCahon exhibition at the Helen Hitchings Gallery in Wellington, Milan Mrkusich's first one-man show at the Auckland School of Architecture, and Gordon Walters' at the Wellington Public Library. McCahon's quest for archetypical symbols, Woollaston's delight in colour and form, Mrkusich's movement into pure abstraction, and Walters' surrealism with its hints of his later abstract manner, all indicated that the modernist revolution in New Zealand had at last begun. The four artists were home-grown and largely self-taught; they were neither overwhelmed by overseas example nor inhibited by local precept. Each was to go his own way deflected neither by fashion nor indifference. But each, eventually, was to achieve a reputation, a market, and professional security. The 1950s, and especially the two following decades, were to prove hospitable to adventure in the arts, to the speed with which New Zealand painting became contemporary, distinguished, and fashionable.

Though these were the pace-setters, they were not on their own. Older painters who had shaped their styles in the 1920s and the 1930s continued to paint well, often challenged and stimulated by their younger contemporaries. Women were eminent among the more modest participants in the revolution of the 1940s — Rita Angus, Doris Lusk, Evelyn Page, Olivia Spencer Bower, May Smith, and Louise Henderson.[28] They were cautious painters, attaining an authentic personal vision within a narrow compass, seldom departing far from 'subject'. They were all (like Frances Hodgkins earlier) beneficiaries of that colonial-genteel tradition that made it acceptable, even estimable, for middle-class girls to occupy themselves with paint, preferably watercolour. All transcended these limitations and sometimes incurred the wrath of family and society in doing so. But the ability to transcend fell short of the capacity to break new ground.

Most of these women were South Islanders; Angus, Page, Lusk, and Spencer Bower were closely associated in the Christchurch Group. The South Island environment — mountains, coastline, plains, and rivers, and also towns, buildings, and gardens — is prominent in their work. In her early landscapes (*Akaroa Harbour*, 1949, for example), Doris Lusk simplified her scenes into essentials of shape, colour, and line. They celebrate the basic structure of the land and the natural forces that have shaped it.[29] Rita Angus's Central Otago and Hawke's Bay landscapes are designed to typify a whole region by arranging a diversity of items in a manner that presents them on a single vertical plane. Her portraits, too, are carefully assembled; the *Portrait of Betty Curnow* (1942) sets a powerful woman in an environment of highly specific domestic, social, and natural detail. Evelyn Page, their slightly older contemporary, was absorbed in people and their surroundings. A railway station, a harbour, a city street, a holiday crowd — these are her characteristic subjects of the 1940s, colourful, bustling, alive. Louise Henderson, Paris-born and Christchurch-trained, painted in Wellington in the 1940s; again people and human places predominate. The work of all four women was to grow in scope and strength over the 1950s and 1960s.

Though it was not always their main purpose, many of the artists of the 1940s and 1950s had a documentary intention. The 1940s' concern with identity and locality encouraged them to set down what Brasch called 'the unambiguous lineaments of a land no longer innocent of us'.[30] There was a constant flow of landscapes, old houses, and Maori. The exemplars of this documentary romanticism were Russell Clark and Eric Lee-Johnson, both products of the art schools and of commercial art, and too often their victims.[31] Clark's *Late Night* (1940) has everything from the glowing shop-windows to the dark hills hemming in the little town, from the petrol-pump to the horse and cart. Lee-Johnson made old and decrepit houses his own, both the grand memorials of the past and the shacks and cottages of humbler people. May Smith's *Mansion House, Kawau* (1949) and Olivia Spencer Bower's *Shed at 'Enys'* (1952) are more realistically 'at home' in their locations.

The people in Lee-Johnson's paintings are frequently cut-out adjuncts to the romantic scenery. But Māori subjects sometimes took Clark to greater heights: especially the monumental *Old Keta* of 1949, and (in sculpture) the head *Tuhoe Maori* (1958). Many painters took to Māori studies in the 1940s and 1950s. All this was an improvement on the 'dying race' romanticism of the Goldie–Lindauer–Hodgkins past, but still close to the dangerous edge of cultural imperialism. Ralph Hotere grew up in Northland during these years: there is something appropriate in his later becoming one of New Zealand's foremost abstractionists.[32]

By the end of the 1940s the isolation of painters from each other was breaking down, and public support was growing. For seven years the *Arts Yearbook* (1945–51) published reproductions, as did *Landfall*. The number and variety of exhibitions increased. Collectors began to buy new paintings, and critics to champion them. There was still indifference and hostility in the newspapers and entrenched conservatism in the public galleries and art societies. Sometimes there was little comprehension, even in more informed circles. A. R. D Fairburn, painter as well as poet, thought (in 1947) Rita Angus 'sweet', Evelyn Page 'muscle-bound', and Colin McCahon's work 'pretentious'.[33] M. T. Woollaston, however, was found more acceptable.

In the 1940s Woollaston continued with the themes and style that he had worked out in the 1930s, exploring the landscape and the people close to him. Hills and buildings are submerged into masses of colour, light, and shadow. *The Artist's House at Mapua* (c.1939) and *Upper Moutere* (1946) are characteristic early landscapes, using a narrow range of sombre but rich colours, applied solidly to the canvas, and expressing a sense of essential structure. In the portraits a constant character is set by *Artist's Wife* (c.1937) — the faces and bodies are chunky and solid; asleep or deeply intent, they are as dense and monumental as the hills about them. Woollaston shows a deep love and reverence for people and country; his achievement is to combine that respect with a transforming inner vision.[34]

McCahon, too, begins with landscape and people, but with an overt mysticism, a drastic simplification of forms, and a readiness to take risks that turned his early close association with the older Woollaston into an agreement not to talk about art. Mysticism took him two ways — first, to a simple contrast between light and dark, not so much an allegory of good and evil as of order and chaos; and, second, to a search beyond contemporary art for models in traditional religious painting. The results did not seem traditional: from about 1946 to about 1952 the series of crucifixions, entombments, madonnas, annunciations, and holy families excited both enthusiasm and ridicule. The gaunt, suffering faces were those of people seen from day to day; the landscape that of Nelson, Otago, and Canterbury. Even so, these paintings are wholly symbolic. Quite without conventional reticence, they are generally didactic. *The Valley of Dry Bones* (1947) litters a stark New Zealand valley with realistic bones and, so that the message might not be ignored, it issues from the mouth of the prophet: 'Come from the four Winds, O Breath, and breathe upon these Slain, that they may live.'[35] It was too disturbing for some. 'The symbolism is there all right,' wrote J. C. Beaglehole, 'like a jolt on the chin, but really it is doubtful whether this sort of symbolism calls for jolts on the chin.'[36] But others praised, bought, and collected. By the early 1950s McCahon, like Woollaston a few years later, had 'succeeded'; they were established painters, well on the way to security and public esteem.

These two painters were then and have remained spiritual explorers, trying to discover 'something logical, orderly and beautiful belonging to the land and not yet to its people'.[37] The departures taken by Milan Mrkusich and Gordon Walters in the 1940s were more radical. Each absorbed surrealist influences and moved beyond them into abstraction. Walters was greeted with some hostility at first in spite of being more representational; Mrkusich, leaving all figurative elements behind, was well enough received, but the climate of opinion was not yet ready to welcome abstraction. Walters stayed close to indigenous symbols. At first Māori rock-drawings and skeletal trees provided a basis for surreal and semi-abstract images. By the mid-1950s he had settled upon the koru motif derived from Māori rafter-designs, and began to refine it into a simple combination of straight line and circle. This gave him, in the 1960s, a vocabulary of forms which retained a sense of their origin and proved capable of great refinement and strength.[38] Mrkusich used for some time a grid pattern to contain and control carefully placed geometrical elements and subtly graduated colours. In later developments he retained this combination of mathematical precision and of movement, depth and warmth. Intellect and a mild emotion co-exist in these abstractions; they have scarcely any figurative echoes, but a painting like *City Lights* (1955) evokes its 'subject' more compellingly than most literal representations.[39] Together these two painters anticipated at the close of the 1940s much that was to follow.

In the 1950s the centre of gravity had shifted north, from Christchurch to Auckland, and the character of painting became more individual, more

551

particularist, and less brooding.[40] The City Art Gallery under first Westbrook and then Peter Tomory attempted to become the art centre of the country as well as of the city, and dealer galleries began to grow up around it. The festival movement began there; in 1954 the organizers of the first Auckland Festival were persuaded to commission ten works of art. With E. H. McCormick's help, the City Gallery redeemed the earlier obtuseness of the southern galleries in rejecting Hodgkins' *The Pleasure Garden* by mounting a scholarly exhibition of 'Frances Hodgkins and her Circle' in 1954. This historical bent, a feeling that the local past was not to be forgotten in the flood of international example, was a characteristic Auckland note of the 1950s.[41]

At the same time, New Zealand painters, as their isolation from the art centres of the world diminished through better reproductions, touring exhibitions, and overseas travel, responded more immediately to international styles. The new works by Louise Henderson shown in 1953 were highly sophisticated and strongly influenced by cubism. Two years later the Auckland City Art Gallery assembled its first (perhaps the country's first) large exhibition of sculpture, including works by Molly Macalister, W. R. Allen, and Alan Ingham. In Auckland too the Henry Moore exhibition drew 50,000 people; in all other centres only 10,000. The 'British Abstract Painters' exhibition of 1958 was lovingly displayed in Auckland; in Wellington the National Gallery refused to show it. In 1961 the Auckland Gallery sought to discover wider regional affinities in contemporary paintings from Japan, the American west coast, Australia, and New Zealand; the quest was in vain, but the exhibition, 'Painting from the Pacific', was an exciting, outward-looking venture.[42]

In the 1950s developments were taking place all over New Zealand as painters caught up with half a century of European and American example, experienced directly and no longer filtered through British practice. John Drawbridge, Don Peebles, Patrick Hanly, Keith Patterson, Robert Ellis, Michael Illingworth, and Ralph Hotere were painting by the end of the 1950s. Many went overseas and returned; all established themselves as major talents in the 1960s. Auckland, with a more developed art market, drew many of them and their contemporaries. But Auckland did not drain the other regions. By the end of the 1960s the secondary as well as the main centres were sharing in the vigorous growth of the visual arts. New Zealand painting had reached a high standard, and remained faithful both to the century that shaped it and the country in which it occurred.

Every New Zealand child since the nineteenth century has had in school some experience of literature and, if not of art, then of drawing. Generation after generation, too, has encountered music through hundreds of piano-teachers, choirs, and bands. Likewise, theatre has permeated the country, through school and Sunday School, women's groups, and drama societies. However, in music and theatre these vast social energies were directed to performance and to providing an audience. Radio and cinema, beginning in the 1920s, may have drawn audiences away, but the performers persisted in their thousands, in houses, churches, schools, community halls, and band rotundas.

This large establishment was dominated by conventional repertoires and was, for the most part, unreceptive to local plays and music. The opportunities that did exist for playwrights drew them away from local experience, for the theatrical societies were habituated to the more brittle kinds of British drama.[43] This situation hampered the development of an indigenous music and theatre. The composer and the playwright lived in a discouraging environment and could not count on performance. Only late in the 1950s did the music and plays written by New Zealanders become a noticeable (though still very small) part of cultural life.[44]

Douglas Lilburn was the only significant composer of the 1940s, but only a small number of concert-goers would have heard the New Zealand Symphony Orchestra play his *Song of the Antipodes* and the touring Boyd Neel Orchestra his *Diversions for Strings* in 1947. His numerous works in the 1950s were performed — perhaps more readily than would have been the case had he been working in London or New York — but not often or well enough for those who looked for a new start in music. His three symphonies (1951, 1953, and 1961), his settings of poems (by Allen Curnow, Denis Glover, and Alistair Campbell), and his instrumental and chamber pieces make up a major body of work, shifting steadily away from an evocative romanticism to a more energetic and severe manner. This progression culminates in the powerful *Third Symphony*. In the 1960s, his attention turned to electronic music, with striking results. He, like Curnow in poetry, was in the 1970s as original, as contemporary, and as experimental as any of the younger composers.[45]

By the end of the 1950s, Lilburn had been joined by a number of capable younger composers — among them Edwin Carr, David Farquhar, Ronald Tremaine, Larry Pruden, and John Rimmer — who owed a good deal to his encouragement and example. A few of them showed that capacity to interest sponsors and patrons which painters and writers had acquired; three of Edwin Carr's works in the late 1950s were commissioned. No composer, however, caught the public imagination; they remained, even to the sizeable concert-going public, little known.

The liveliest theatre groups in the later 1940s were the Community Arts Service in the Auckland region, Ngaio Marsh's student company, the Canterbury Players, who were inspired by her to an astonishing maturity (touring Shakespeare and Pirandello to Australia), and the social realist, sometimes proletarian, Unity Theatre in Wellington. Only the last was a school for playwrights. Ngaio Marsh, however, with an arresting production of Curnow's verse play, *The Axe*, in 1948, offered a high point in New Zealand drama. And, close to the end of its active life, the Community Arts Service staged Curnow's second play, *Moon Section*, in 1959. In Wellington, Bruce Mason was the most fertile of a small group of playwrights whose works were staged by Unity Theatre; the close relationship between writer and company shown at Unity in these years later became a feature of New Zealand theatre.[46]

Mason, by the end of the 1950s, was on the way to becoming a public figure. Several of his plays had been produced, and he had even tried his hand at light opera. *The End of the Golden Weather* (1962) marked the arrival of New Zealand drama at the popular level. He solved the problems of cost by creating a one-man, set-less, touring theatre, and played on nearly every small and large stage in the country.[47] By the early 1960s locally written plays were performed regularly. Poets and novelists turned to theatre and found producers and players ready to guide them. Baxter's early plays were produced by Unity and by Richard Campion's New Zealand Theatre Company; later Baxter was to work closely with Patrick Carey at Dunedin's Globe Theatre. In Auckland the Workers' Educational Association and the New Independent Theatre produced plays by Frank Sargeson. About the same time specialist playwrights began to appear, continuing the tradition started by Mason — Joseph Musaphia, Alexander Guyan, and Campbell Caldwell — again closely associated with producers and players. Radio drama, too, began to draw in more local writers. The Broadcasting Corporation actively encouraged playwrights and produced an increasing number of their works.[48] Theatre, as well as music, developed a New Zealand dimension, by adding a handful of local works to the still overwhelmingly overseas and traditional repertoires. It was not yet a summer, but there were some swallows by the early 1960s.

Between them, the stories, poems, plays, and paintings of the 1940s and 1950s contained a considerable body of social comment — more, in fact, than was to be found in works of theory and analysis. Further, social commentary was more effective at a general than at a specific level. Attention was directed to exploring the overall character of New Zealand society, and to reflecting upon the bedevilling question of national identity, rather than to the analysis of particular social problems, even though those facing New Zealand after the war were real enough. Urban growth, the position of women, the welfare system, the nuclear peril, and race relations called for serious attention, but only race relations received it.

The Second World War focused attention upon 'the Māori situation'. Overseas the Maori Battalion became a source of national pride. At home the Māori population was increasing rapidly and becoming more and more urban, so more visible. The Labour–Rātana alliance was of great account politically. By the end of the 1940s, the climate of Pākehā opinion was changing. A few people, including the esteemed soldier Howard Kippenberger, were beginning to ask if it was right that Māori should be excluded from All Black teams touring South Africa. With the growing awareness came a good deal of research and reflection.[49]

A basic work published in 1940, *The Maori People Today*, was edited by a pioneer social scientist, I. L. G. Sutherland, and contained many articles by Apirana Ngata. The book was a review of the past and a stocktaking of the present, but it also put some vital questions to the future. Would the population outgrow the resources of Māori land and farming? Would the Māori find a place in urban society other than that of the casual labourer?

Would they be able to preserve their Māori character in changed circumstances?[50] Since 1940 the Māori have become an urban people, but the other two questions await an answer.

Most of the writing on Māori history and society in the 1940s and 1950s was by Pākehā. But it was Peter Buck who encouraged Ernest and Pearl Beaglehole in their work published as *Some Modern Maoris* (1946). This was an exhaustive investigation of Māori in a small mixed community and its findings were disquieting. Land-holdings were inadequate to support the owners, and most workers were in unskilled jobs. Housing was sub-standard and over-crowded; Māori and Pākehā alike were prejudiced against mixed marriages; education provided no skills for the market-place and, moreover, ran contrary to the ethos of the Māori home.[51] These findings have been endorsed by subsequent studies.

The Beagleholes' work rejected the prevailing optimism of most Pākehā, who felt that progress and harmony had been achieved for both races. A number of historical writings of the 1950s also tried to correct popularly received opinions and, by setting the record straight to help redress past and present injustices. Dick Scott's *The Parihaka Story* (1954), Keith Sinclair's *The Origins of the Maori Wars* (1957), and J. O. Miller's *Early Victorian New Zealand* (1958) found greed and oppression in Pākehā dealings with Māori. In fiction, too, Roderick Finlayson expressed admiration and anger about the situation of Māori.[52] An early feature film, *Broken Barriers* made by Pacific Films, explored the problems of a love affair between a Māori and a Pākehā. Late in the decade, *Landfall* published its first article on race relations. The author was an American, David P. Ausubel; his book *The Fern and the Tiki* (1960), which said some hard things about New Zealand and especially about its racial situation, was widely resented by Pākehā intellectuals.[53]

International affairs also drew scholarly attention in the 1940s and 1950s. The foundation was laid in 1940, this time by a volume in the Centennial series, F. L. W. Wood's *New Zealand in the World*. For Wood, the connection with Great Britain was central, as it was, too, for a collection of essays to which he contributed in 1944, *New Zealand and the Statute of Westminster*. But New Zealand's international position had shifted away from Britain and Europe with the fall of Singapore three years earlier. Politicians and public servants, chiefly Peter Fraser and Alister McIntosh, responded to this shift with the Canberra Pact, a post-British and anti-American agreement with the Australian Government in which the two countries staked out a claim to a place in the Pacific. There was a muted intellectual parallel to this change of focus: some polemic by H. Winston Rhodes and R. A. K. Mason, some ethnographic studies by Ernest Beaglehole, and an acute analysis of New Zealand's situation in the face of American power in the Pacific, Wood's widely read article, 'The Anzac Dilemma'.[54]

Writing about other aspects of New Zealand society was most successful when it was least specific, when it turned to broad questions and to social character and identity. M. H. Holcroft reflecting on the relationship between society and the arts in his prize-winning Centennial essay, *The Deepening Stream*, set the pattern, which continued with some of Curnow's poems and prose and many of Brasch's *Landfall* editorials. Early in the 1950s, in essays by James K. Baxter, Bill Pearson, and R. M. Chapman, the theme was elaborated into a secular social gospel. No one of these writers was ready to allow that the arts might have no social function; each assigned to them a reformist and almost a redemptive role. On the way, they paused long enough for some acute social analysis.

Holcroft's essays were an impressive, if from time to time vague and fragmentary, achievement. Though his chief concern was the problem of identity, he wrote perceptively on social topics: regional diversity in education, the dangers of consumerism, the prevalence of gambling, the risks of welfare. In broad strokes he depicted a small, easeful, careless society, educated rather than enlightened, with a good deal of mediocrity and an intolerance of criticism (but in great need of it). Criticism, evaluation, and self-realization — these are the tasks he assigned to literature, the arts, and philosophy. From this vantage point he evaluated, often perceptively, the work of a handful of the 'new' writers, Ursula Bethell, A. R. D. Fairburn, and D'Arcy Cresswell.[55]

The social critics of the early 1950s continued to identify public ills and prescribe a cultural remedy, but in a less temperate spirit. The decade began with more acrimony and anxiety: these were the years of the Cold War and the new National Government, of Korea and the waterfront dispute. Liberal men began to express their anger. In 1951 Baxter addressed a Writers' Conference (the first since the Authors' Week of 1936) on *Recent Trends in New Zealand Poetry*. Though the lecture contained much comment on poetry, it was acclaimed more for its social gospel than its literary perception. Baxter summoned society to find its redemption in the truth of poetry; he demanded that the poet should be 'a cell of good living in a corrupt society, and . . . by writing and example attempt to change it'.[56] Baxter was never to tire of uttering this message, nor his audiences of hearing it.

In the following year Bill Pearson's essay 'Fretful Sleepers' appeared, written looking homeward in anger from London. It was a fine piece of polemic and a penetrating if wholly impressionistic social analysis.

Walk into a Saturday-afternoon bar and hear the noise: do you get the impression of *stalling*? The tobacco-smoke is dense with small-talk: a huddle of urgent men proofing the void with the saga of Highland Prince, greasing the unknown with a bookie's pencil.

The writer, says Pearson, is hardly better off than the citizenry he should redeem; he is tempted into mere denunciation, over-refinement, and emigration. But his true task is a noble and arduous one.

Our job is to penetrate the torpor and out of meaninglessness make a pattern that means something. . . . I mean living not only among but as one of the people and feeling your way into their problems, their hopes, their gripes and their gropings, without like them trying to sleep them off.[57]

Robert Chapman, writing at much the same time, wore a scholar's gown over the preacher's bands. In 'Fiction and the Social Pattern', he identified three strands in New Zealand life. First, an inherited pattern of mean-spirited behaviour which he called puritanism; second, a liberal humanitarian tradition which had been less dominant than some New Zealanders supposed; and third, an environment that made a puritanical life unnecessary — 'a land of milk and honey, a lucky historical accident'. Society adhered obsessively to its inherited restraints; the writers drew upon the liberal tradition to persuade men that they could enjoy freedom in abundance.

. . . the attitude which the New Zealand writer takes to his society, and which informs his work, will continue to be based on the possibility here of a truly human ease and depth of living and on an attack on the distortions produced by an irrelevant puritanism of misplaced demands and guilts. The artist must sound his trumpet of insight until the walls of Jericho — the pattern as it is — fall down.[58]

Over the next few decades behaviour was to become more free and social attitudes were to relax, but the walls of Jericho were not going to fall down. The gain from this development of literary criticism was intellectual. It lifted social commentary to a new level.

Pearson, Chapman, and Baxter wisely left alone one question that had fascinated writers in the 1940s, that of national identity. Curnow, in his introduction to the Caxton anthology, had speculated upon it; so had Holcroft, at greater length, in his essays, wondering hesitantly if there was a 'national soul' or if one would appear. No one could be quite sure what they had in mind; the language they used was mystical and elusive. It is, however, understandable that thoughtful people should, around the time of the collapse of British power and the weakening of the imperial sense of identity, wonder if New Zealand did not possess a set of common characteristics like, say, Ireland or Poland. As neither a separate culture nor the oppressive presence of a master-race was observable, the quest proved fruitless. But it did draw attention to the fact of experiences shared by all New Zealanders, in particular the immigrant voyage and the adaptation of inherited values and habits to a new environment. These are experiences of the descendants of the Māori voyagers, of the successive waves of British immigrants, of the Dalmatian, Scandinavian, and Chinese immigrants, and, in more recent times, of Dutch, British, Islander, and Asian settlers. Social historians and social scientists have still not gone far enough in the direction in which Holcroft, Chapman, and Pearson pointed.[59]

Even by the end of the 1950s historians were still more concerned with generalities than specific analysis of New Zealand society: Keith Sinclair (*A History of New Zealand*, 1959) looked for identity in the imposed necessities of the Pacific environment; W. H. Oliver (*The Story of New Zealand*, 1960) in the determining strength of British inheritance. Neither approach encouraged too close a look at the changing forms of behaviour and organization through which a society expresses its character. They remain only lightly explored. So, too, do many of the specific fields of social research; here the harvest of the 1960s and 1970s has not been as abundant as in the arts.

The upsurge in the arts of the 1940s and 1950s was accompanied by rapid growth in the institutions supporting them. By the early 1960s the main elements of the infrastructure were in place.[60] Most of it had been built by the state, formally by subsidy and patronage, and informally through the provision of jobs (chiefly at the universities) which enabled their occupants to write, compose, paint, and perform. More generally still, the state encouraged the arts (and all forms of recreation), by reducing the working week, raising the level of incomes, and enlarging the scope and scale of education. At the same time, private initiative, local body support, and corporate patronage increased. Beneath it all lay a shift in the pattern of consumption, a shift towards the arts, encouraged by a level of affluence sufficient to sustain the new appetite for paintings, books, and performances.

Foremost of the state agencies was the broadcasting system. Radio had been hiring performers since the 1920s. In the late 1930s, its function as a cultural service industry began to expand, especially in music and drama. Broadcasting fees became a regular part of the income of musicians and actors. When in 1946 the state orchestra had to be found a state home, the most obvious, if not the most welcome, location was the New Zealand Broadcasting Service.[61]

Perhaps by accident, the NZBS became the publisher of the country's only cultural and intellectual weekly. The *Radio Record* became the *New Zealand Listener* in 1939; the paper carried all the radio programmes for the week, and so it sold. Oliver Duff, the first editor, turned its opening pages into a magazine within a magazine. Editorials and correspondence columns became notable for seriousness, controversy, and sometimes for wit. Single-handed, Gordon Mirams created film reviewing. Book reviewing became a weekly feature, for the first time, in a paper that covered the whole country. M. H. Holcroft, editor from 1949 to 1967, increased the publication of stories and poems. By the early 1950s more money was passing from the state to writers through the *Listener* than through the Literary Fund. Moreover, though there has often been the threat and sometimes the reality of political intimidation, the journal has always been ready to encourage controversy.[62]

The post-war period saw other developments. The School Publications Branch (of the Department of Education), founded before the war, expanded and produced a notable series of bulletins and journals and an influential periodical, *Education*.[63] The National Library Service was set up in 1945, incorporating the Country Library Service which Fraser, prompted by G. T. Alley, had established before the war. Alley, appropriately, became National Librarian in 1964, and began the arduous process of integrating the three state libraries (General Assembly, National Library Service, and — to the alarm of its devoted Friends — the Alexander

Turnbull). Alley, who had learned his trade in the Canterbury Workers' Educational Association, also had a hand in the reconstruction of adult education under university control in 1947.[64] Within a decade this system of university adult education began to move away from the grassroots intentions of its originators; it was as well that in some places the less élitist WEA stayed in existence.

The most striking development in adult education occurred in the Auckland region in the late 1940s, where the Community Arts Service, inspired by Laurence Baigent and Owen Jensen, took drama, music, and paintings to the remotest corners of their province. Its annual Music School at Cambridge, with such tutors as Douglas Lilburn and Lili Kraus, laid some of the foundations for professional training; its small touring group of professional actors enlisted an astonishing amount of community support and participation, especially in small centres.[65] Some thought that it might become a constituent part of a national theatre, a goal zealously but vainly pursued during the 1940s. A national theatre, a national opera, and a national ballet, it was hoped, would emerge from under the wing of the maternal state, as had the orchestra.

These hopes proved vain but the Government did establish the film industry. The National Film Unit had been set up in 1941 for propaganda purposes; after the war it turned to tourist promotion. Its *Weekly Review* was the first local newsreel and accustomed the still massive cinema audiences to the sight of their own people and places on the screen. Its documentaries, many directed by John Feeney, reached a high standard; the most notable were *Legend of the Wanganui River* and *Pumicelands*. Brian Brake, later a renowned photographer, was one of the unit's cameramen, and filmed the lyrical *Snows of Aorangi*, with a commentary made up from the poems of James K. Baxter. Writers and composers were hired from time to time. Again, the state provided artists with opportunities and some money.[66]

These direct interventions were the work of the first Labour Government, which fell in 1949. Its National successor did not at first display the same alliance of politicians and administrators sympathetic to the life of the mind and the spirit.[67] But though little was dismantled, the 1950s were the years of private not state initiative in the arts. The state settled down to the role of paymaster, rewarding enterprises that had already demonstrated a measure of success.

Typically, under the new dispensation, a start was made by an enthusiast with a hard core of supporters. Once a degree of public acceptance was shown, the support of the state was enlisted. Local resources also were tapped, especially in Auckland, where the City Council began to spend considerable sums on its art gallery. Business joined in: New Zealand breweries sponsored an opera production in 1959. In that year a private endowment enabled Otago University to set up the Burns Fellowship for creative writers. Local and corporate patronage, through prizes, competitions, bursaries and fellowships, and art gallery finance, expanded during the 1960s and 1970s. But the great provider remained the state. It became the main support of the enterprises privately launched in the 1950s; the Arts Council rose to a position in which it could determine the more expensive developments.

Among the casualties of Labour's dismissal was the confidently expected national theatre: in 1949 Peter Fraser endorsed the proposal but lost the election. Instead, Richard and Edith Campion devoted their artistic and financial resources to the New Zealand Players, a touring professional company who recreated the rather precious high standards of the Old Vic. 'They have', a friendly critic wrote in 1954, 'done it extremely well; as well, for all practical purposes, as the original; which is why one may legitimately implore them to stop, before . . . they have embalmed their talents and our tastes in the amber of unalterable artificiality.'[68] Stop they did, not for these reasons, but because they ran out of money in an attempt to be 'national' in a long, narrow country with a dispersed population. When professional theatre re-emerged in the 1960s, it was firmly rooted in the experience of amateurs, the devotion of small companies, local enthusiasm, and state subsidy.

Chamber music, opera, and ballet were also launched by private enterprise and then supported by public money. The Wellington Chamber Music Society (1945) owed a good deal to the stimulus of European, often Jewish, immigrants; chamber music societies followed in other cities, and it became clear that multitudes of New Zealanders had a taste for this most refined of musical experiences. They formed the Federation of Chamber Music Societies in 1950 and worked out a cost-sharing arrangement with the NZBS by which overseas artists were brought to New Zealand and employment given to local performers. As the Music Federation since 1972, it has become a major cultural institution, organizing concert seasons in most towns.

A Danish immigrant, Poul Gnatt, formed the New Zealand Ballet Company in 1953, and a New Zealand singer, Donald Munro, the New Zealand Opera Company in the following year. Here the problems of scale were greater than with chamber music. Large popular works from the classical repertoire drew in crowds but multiplied costs. Neither company surmounted the problems of topography and cost, or managed to tread the invisible line between quality and popularity — the problems that had proved fatal to the New Zealand Players. But as local initiatives could not meet what was, somewhat grudgingly, accepted as a public need, the state undertook to support these two bodies. It also helped to maintain a number of small professional theatres and privately founded professional or semi-professional small orchestras such as the Alex Lindsay String Orchestra. Though often fragile and transitory, these groups have kept coming into existence. They have also kept asking for, and often getting, state, local, and corporate support. Music, theatre, opera, and ballet quickly came to absorb a major part of the Arts Council's resources, a development little to the taste of those concerned with the visual arts.

Though by the end of the 1950s the only regular channel of state subsidy was the Literary Fund, a good deal of money was passing through Internal

Affairs to finance specific cultural events and enterprises. A degree of co-ordination was required. In 1960 the level of funding was increased; a year later the Advisory Arts Council was set up; in 1963, a year in which the monarch toured the country, it became the Queen Elizabeth II Arts Council.

Not everyone welcomed the change. Brasch was suspicious and Fairburn, sturdy individualist, totally hostile:

. . . the practice and appreciation of the arts . . . has achieved such a vogue that a new industry is being built up — one that has, among its other aims, the enlargement of its empire among the white-collar classes, and the development of State patronage. As our leisure increases, it is possible that the various activities that go under the name of 'culture' may become a rival to sport as a palliative for suburban boredom.[69]

It was a prescient but a useless protest. The time of the do-it-yourself individualist had passed; both pioneer and proletarian virtue were at a discount. The era of the cultural bureaucrat, the patronized producer, and the subsidized consumer had arrived.

This infrastructure filled out in the 1960s and the 1970s. The Literary Fund and the Arts Council extended the range of their activities; corporate and private patronage grew. The only new state initiative was the formation of the National Film Commission in 1978, to help finance the growing number of private film-makers. A number of feature films were produced in the 1970s; some, such as *Sleeping Dogs, Solo,* and *Skindeep,* succeeded on the commercial circuit. More than a dozen professional theatres came into existence, following the example set by Downstage in Wellington in 1964. Prompted by the Literary Fund Committee, most universities set up writing fellowships; Otago, first in the field, added music and visual arts fellowships. Businesses, also at the instance of this Committee, set up writing fellowships; others have sponsored painting competitions. Firms, government departments, and local authorities commissioned murals and statuary to adorn their buildings and parks. Most sizeable towns acquired professionally directed galleries; dealer galleries multiplied. By the end of the 1970s, the infrastructure was beginning to reflect the diversity of New Zealand society.

It was also beginning to reflect that society's deepening inequalities. The egalitarian hopes of the founders of state patronage, the Labour politicians and their public servant allies, have not been fulfilled. The system rewards talent, and talent depends upon prior social and economic advantages; it has come to nourish a cultural élite with a fast track to resources, one confirmed in its placidity by its growing dependence. This may change, for though the flow of public and private money has increased, it has not done so at a rate sufficient to keep pace with inflation.[70] Nevertheless, neither inflation nor the break in affluence which began in the late 1960s has as yet destroyed either the public or the private sectors of the infrastructure. The persistent appetite for expensive pictures, books, and performances, the constant capacity of cultural entrepreneurs to secure subsidies and make profits, the increasing body of professional writers, painters, and performers, confirm the impression that the growth of a cultural élite is part of a wider erosion of social equality.

Apart from the fact that television was introduced in 1960, it is impossible to separate the next twenty years from the twenty that came before. And though the social effects of television are pervasive, they are also uneven. Documentary film and drama have been stimulated, with sometimes admirable and sometimes lamentable results. Literature, the visual arts, and music have not been changed; at most, cultural programmes have been useful public relations exercises. Television's first twenty years only marginally touched the cultural life of New Zealand, which retained the basic character it acquired in the 1940s and 1950s. Within this continuity the variety of emphases and directions grew; the development of all the arts gathered momentum.

The earlier quest for 'national identity' reflected the need of individuals to feel that their poetry, prose, or painting deepened their knowledge of their country. The need was still felt: critics and producers alike looked to the arts to satisfy a need for self-awareness; literature and the arts show a close relationship with the locality. There was a massive inflow of international influences, and in some ways — abstract painting, for example — this diminished the sense of locality. But that sense proved very resilient, and some of the influences from overseas in fact strengthened it.

Architecture demonstrates some of this interplay between the international and the local. Exiles from Europe, such as E. A. Plishke, brought the Bauhaus influence with them, and it was constantly reinforced by postgraduate study abroad. The stress that the great French architect Le Corbusier placed upon respect for local material, traditions, and environment encouraged the search for an indigenous style. In the 1940s and 1950s, inspired by Vernon Brown at the Auckland School of Architecture, there was a new drive towards high standards of design, respect for the environment, and harmony with the landscape. This coincided with an awakening of interest in the colonial past; the National Historic Places Trust was set up in 1954 to record and preserve historic sites and buildings. Architects began to look back to the unpretentiousness of early colonial buildings and their easy affinity with the landscape. Christchurch has a fine inheritance of colonial houses and public buildings; there the work of Miles Warren recaptured that tradition. Good building in the 1960s and 1970s demonstrated its firm adherence to international standards, to the immediate environment, and to earlier achievements.[71]

In painting and literature, too, overseas models were heeded, sometimes with unprofitable alacrity. Still, the level of abstraction reached by Don Peebles in painting and Bill Manhire in poetry remained exceptional. More typically the imagination was anchored to a place and to a time, in a way that was modified by a broadening of experience and interest over these two decades. Since the 1950s, the relevance of the local and particular was no longer so strenuously defended. The sense of cultural fragility diminished.

Maurice Gee exemplifies this new sense of assurance. His locations are the recurrent ones of New Zealand social life — football field, racetrack, pub, small town, and farm. His earlier novels and stories are much concerned with violence, violence that typically occurs in sport and in families — in itself a sharp-edged comment upon New Zealand society. *Plumb* (1978) was his crowning early achievement, and there the social dimension extends to include a long period of history and a broad range of activities, from parliamentary politics to a communal farm.[72] Gee is as intensely individual in vision as Janet Frame, but his vision does not come close, as hers does, to obliterating the environment. Maurice Shadbolt's two epics, *Strangers and Journeys* (1972) and *The Lovelock Version* (1980), and C. K. Stead's political fable, *Smith's Dream* (1971), retain elements of an earlier self-consciousness, but nevertheless deal effectively with basic issues in New Zealand history and contemporary life. In his one New Zealand novel — the ambitious *MacKenzie* (1970) — James McNeish also handles a wide social and political scene, that of colonial Canterbury. These novelists, Stead, Shadbolt, Frame, Gee, and McNeish, responded effectively to large and complex social situations with a breadth of purpose which only John Mulgan and Bill Pearson achieved earlier.

The most characteristic poetry of the 1960s and 1970s, like the novels, is faithful to a diversity of experience.[73] Kendrick Smithyman, a prolific poet during this period, provides the best example. Unlike many poets, both earlier and contemporary, he does not write only from high points of intense feeling, but also tries to convey his total consciousness, public and private, local and external, past and present. The effect is like that of abstract painting — a grid of intellect that contains and comments upon a fluid field of emotion and experience. And in this field there is a place for his times of boredom as well as of rejoicing, his private interests as well as his public positions. No person's world is in itself uninteresting: the problem is whether the guide talks interestingly about it. Smithyman usually does.

So, in the multitude of verses that poured from him, did James K. Baxter in the last few years of his life, as he struggled out of the straitjacket of rhetoric and virtuosity into plain, direct speech. Only then did he manage an intimate voice unimpeded by attitudes too easily struck and too carefully sustained. Individual poems, in great number, stand out from the earlier output. The later period brought whole sequences of moving talk, still passionate but newly wry and humorous.

Ian Wedde, another who tries to bring to the reader a diverse assemblage of personal experiences, has an arresting though a less consistently convincing voice. His field is that of the everyday life of New Zealanders, past and present: a house, a woman, a child, a circle of friends, a garden, a city, a history. The work of Vincent O'Sullivan, perhaps the most satisfying of the poets who rose to prominence in the 1960s, has greater depth. His voice is more various, more argumentative, more subtle. Though the achievement is uneven, the slope of the graph is steeply upwards. The experience behind the poems is wide in space and deep in time. It is closer to public experience than most recent poetry in New Zealand; hardly anyone else, in the 1970s, has been capable of a political poem. O'Sullivan, like only Glover before him, created a persona to epitomize a central aspect of New Zealand life. But Glover's 'Harry' stays in the hills, a loner and a recluse; O'Sullivan's 'Butcher' is a richer and more various archetype. He does not brood; he talks sharply and sometimes savagely; he is busy with women and customers and acquaintances in a lightly sketched but authentic social setting.

But the greater successor, and surpasser, of Harry (and of Sargeson's sufferers and Mulgan's loner) is Maurice Gee's George Plumb. An authority figure and a rebel, a thinker and an activist, a domestic tyrant and a social reformer, a free spirit and a sexually inhibited man — here is a figure whose affirmations, negations, and contradictions go a long way to expressing the essence of the New Zealand human environment. The private, the intimate, and the public intersect and clash. Plumb is a deaf old man who persists in using an inefficient ear-trumpet to preserve the sanctity of his inner world, but is devastated when it is destroyed. The equal and conflicting necessity of both inner and outer worlds are held in a balance that does violence to neither. In poetry, this high point of justice to both realities was achieved at nearly the same time by Allen Curnow in *An Incorrigible Music* (1979): the blood and violence of the fish on the hook and under the gutting knife, and the terrorist killing of Aldo Moro, a private perception and a public disorder, live together in a depiction of the universality of violence and death.

Gee's fiction and Curnow's poetry merge the universal and the particular. This is the case, too, with later painting and sculpture. Most artists have not left the world 'out there' far behind: it is a vividly realized and readily recognized environment of familiar places and people. In sculpture Greer Twiss found some of his aptest subjects in athletes; the figures were a long way from realism but close to social reality.[74] Not only people and landscape, but words and messages were a major element in painting. McCahon made whole paintings from letters, numbers, and words; many have followed his example by integrating speech into pictures. Ralph Hotere's abstracts suggest hardly anything that is figurative or even symbolic, but titles like *Sangro, Polaris, Algérie* suggest a message which is, however, withheld.

By the early 1960s New Zealand was becoming crowded with younger painters.[75] They had behind them the examples of McCahon and Mrkusich, an art-school training that had become contemporary, a reasonable prospect of early overseas travel, and the beginnings of an 'art scene' and an art market. Their elders — W. A. Sutton, Rita Angus, Doris Lusk, and Louise Henderson — joined the search for modernity. It was a various and an undogmatic renaissance, with room for the hyper-realism of Michael Smither, the abstraction of Ray Thorburn, and the social commentary of Garth Tapper. The lineaments of locality, no longer as unambiguous as Brasch had found them, were there more often than not.

Patrick Hanly, in several series of paintings in the 1960s, set out to realize in colour, light, and form the qualities of a Pacific habitat. His shift to the near-domestic series *'Inside' the Garden* (1968) indicated one aspect of the altered character of the 1970s — a turning inwards to the private, the secluded, the self-contained.[76] In the 1960s, Robert Ellis began to depict the city in semi-abstract patterns of roads, lights, and dark masses which could be the places where people live. Michael Illingworth started to people the suburban scene, only half-affectionately, with small, painted half-men and half-women; Don Binney overwhelmed coastline and buildings with huge birds, bland but ominous messengers. This diversity increased in the following decade. Many made beginnings that appeared likely to lead into a future full of achievement: Brent Wong's precise landscapes and buildings with their arbitrary but curiously apt surrealist constructions, effortlessly airborne over the too-heavy land; Tony Fomison's powerful brooding heads, heavy and Polynesian, perhaps presences of a past the careful present cannot dispel; Phillip Clairmont's never quite disintegrating dissections of the everyday contents of everyday houses. Both Fomison and Clairmont responded violently to New Zealand's major shared experience of the 1960s — the trauma of Vietnam.[77]

As public receptivity to art increased, the isolation and insecurity of the artist grew less. There were more painters and sculptors, writers, and composers; they were more concentrated in cities; they lived in a society that could afford to reward them and often did; they were supported by an infrastructure that had not even a shadowy existence when the Second World War ended. Most important, the pluralist society in which they lived had yet to demonstrate that the trend towards greater tolerance over the last forty years would be reversed. Significant as these developments were, their continuance could not be taken for granted. Economic recession could yet reach the relatively well-to-do who support the arts; the state could run down the infrastructure more rapidly than it built it up; the polarization which goes with a pluralist society could well breed an intolerance of sub-cultural values and behaviour. The arts are as accessible to the penalties of social change as to its benefits. They are part of the pattern of society.

The arts and society have a complex relationship, one that contains both affinity and disharmony. When the images presented by literature, painting, or theatre arise from matters of broad social concern, they show the affinity between the two. When they arise from viewpoints at odds with dominant values, they illustrate both the disharmony between the arts and society and the disharmony within society itself.

Social disharmony was vigorously expressed over thirty years in agitation and protest. A succession of protest movements through the 1950s and 1960s focused on such broad issues as race relations, international affairs, nuclear warfare, and civil liberties. The 1970s brought two significant changes. First, more intimate issues became dominant; abortion, for instance, was the rallying point for the most vehement agitation. Second, broader agitations concentrated more on specific issues: thus the movement to 'ban the bomb' began to devote its attention more to specific campaigns, such as that for a nuclear-free zone in the Pacific. The spread, over much the same period, of the communes underlines the new prominence of the intimate environment. So, too, did arguments for an economic policy favouring small production units. The craft movement and the shift of townspeople to small rural farms pointed the same way. In art galleries, professional theatres, publishing, and film-making there was an increase of small-scale enterprises.[78]

In parallel, one of the features of the 1970s was a deepening concern for the condition of personal and intimate relationships. Domesticity was a recurrent theme in painting — Smither's immediate family, Illingworth's pathetic couples, David Armitage's erotic celebrations, and Clairmont's tormented interiors. In writing, it was present in Baxter's prayers for his communal family, Wedde's poems for his son, and Lauris Edmond's exploration of mother–daughter relationships. Domesticity, further, was central to many acute current issues — abortion, censorship, sexual education, women's rights, and (in the renewed stress upon hapū and marae) Māori identity. Each side of such issues exhibited a preoccupation with the most intimate, the most public, and the most strained social institution, the family.

These shifts in values and behaviour took place against a background of general change which challenged more confident earlier assumptions. Recent history is not a tale of upheavals, but of slowly waxing and waning confidence. By the mid-1950s there was relief that the threatening post-war decade had at least been survived. The balance of terror was an answer, of sorts, to international disorder. Industrial strife had receded; with the other nagging domestic anxiety, inflation, it seemed to have been smoothed away by affluence. A mild optimism persisted into the middle 1960s; hope was not dispelled even by the Vietnam war. This, in New Zealand, was the Holyoake era; the prospect of disaster could not be taken too seriously when it had so benign and awkward an appearance. The tide, in the 1960s, seemed to be flowing in a liberal direction.

The Vietnam protest and the anti-apartheid movement grew greatly in that decade; they were sustaining to their participants; they were socially unifying in recruiting minority support from a wide spectrum; briefly, in the early 1970s, they seemed to have succeeded.[79] The anti-apartheid movement confidently shifted its focus to racial discrimination at home; a heightened demand for rights and recognition arose from some Māori; civil rights were jealously defended; a radical feminist movement emerged; censorship became more liberal; the anti-nuclear movement broadened its support by concentrating upon testing in the Pacific. Total success could never, at least in cooler moments, be entertained; but total failure seemed as far away. It is not surprising that a decade so marked by confidence, action, and affluence experienced growth and diversity, both in movements of opinion and in the arts.

The habit of protest and the consolidation of the arts lasted into the 1970s, a decade in which the problems intensified and took on every appearance of being both permanent and without solution.[80] The tide turned towards reaction. After the last vain spurt of social democracy, Norman Kirk's brief rule, the country fell into the hands of harder men, whose way with problems and distress was less caring and no more successful. The arts continued to flourish under these changed circumstances. As public problems became less soluble, food, drink, music, plays, poems, novels, and pictures answered a demand for the quiet and for the manageable. This narrowing of horizons, this inward shift of vision, was a source of strength to the arts, both to their quantity and to their marketability. Protest, in altered ways, flourished too. Groups, often violently opposed to each other, cherished the values which gave them cohesion and which they believed to be endangered.

The 1970s' heightened intensity of social concern brought with it an abundance of prophets: agitators and officials, private citizens and public spokesmen, poets and political scientists. The reports of the Planning Council and the Commission for the Future, both official bodies, were as anxious and apprehensive behind their statistical façades as the novels of Maurice Gee, the poems of James K. Baxter, and the paintings of Michael Illingworth. The movements of opinion on either side of urgent public issues exhibited the same moral concern and purpose, the same sense of unease. Social scientists, artists, and citizens displayed the perplexity of individuals trying to understand ambiguous bodies of data, and the passionate need of alarmed people to convert others to their convictions.[81]

This temper of mind informed such diverse movements as the pro- and anti-abortion groups, the liberals and 'back to basics' advocates in education, the defenders of the environment and the prophets of growth, the campaigners for open government and the apologists for official secrecy, the opponents of apartheid and the defenders of 'no politics in sport'. It was present in the two movements examined here as instances of the correlation between the arts and other affirmations of opinion and values — the movements for women's rights and for Māori rights. Each movement exhibited great energy, diversity, and internal discord; each had excited antipathy among the very people whose cause it sought to advance; each worked close to the heart of traditional values and assumptions. And in each the complex relationship between art and society may be exemplified.

The movement of women into the work-force, into public life, and into situations of greater personal independence, though far from complete, had accelerated since the Second World War. Though the possibility of achieving personal satisfaction through economic independence had increased, in other respects the gains of women were limited. At the higher levels of power and participation they remained seriously under-represented, even in such occupations as teaching and the health services, where they were very numerous. They were, in fact, most often employed in those occupations which are extensions of traditionally ascribed female roles, calling for those capacities — solicitude for children and for the sick, the preparation of food, and manual dexterity — which were held to be typically feminine. In most occupations women met the rigidities of institutional structures and the still formidable weight of male prejudice. Literature and the arts in contrast are relatively open; they are, as professions, simple in structure and loosely organized — and they may be less marked by prejudice. This social situation allowed women considerable scope for success in cultural activities. Constraints remained; they may even have been increased by the growth of the infrastructure which brought about a degree of institutionalization. However, the passage of talent to the top is freer than in most other activities.

Women and the arts have been close since the colonial foundation. Although some writers were involved in the early phases of the women's movement, typically their efforts were absorbed in safeguarding their individual capacities against the expectation that art was a suitable accomplishment rather than an absorbing career. The change in the position of women which began during the Second World War was followed by change in their artistic and political roles. The restrictions that qualified earlier achievement were no longer so marked. In fiction, Janet Frame and Sylvia Ashton-Warner, in music Jenny McLeod, in sculpture Molly Macalister, in painting Gretchen Albrecht encompassed a wide spectrum of social, intellectual, and emotional experience. There is nothing, in the limited sense of the word, feminine about them. Further, radical feminism began to make an impact in a handful of novels, stories, poems, and paintings, and in the beginnings of feminist satire, polemic, and criticism.[82]

Many remained self-committed to the art of the miniature and the domestic interior. This is both understandable and highly traditional. What was less traditional, but equally understandable, was the sharp edge of criticism which informs the domestic interiors of, say, Jacqueline Fahey and Glenda Randerson. And if much in the anthology of women's poetry, *Private Gardens* (1977), deserved that unfortunate title, much did not — for example, the poems of Elizabeth Smither, Jan Kemp, Ruth Dallas, and Mary Stanley. Nor do the poems of Janet Frame, who did not consent to be included in it. The private garden was on the way to becoming a public arena in fiction as well — in the writings of Margaret Sutherland, Joy Cowley, and Fiona Kidman. There was a new sexual consciousness, a more aggressive spirit and a heightened awareness of the hostility of a male cultural environment.

Assertiveness was not limited to the arts; it was socially pervasive, from a determined defence of home and family to an equally energetic vindication of sexual freedom. Feminist goals were far from attainment; the economic situation of women, both in the work-place and in the home, deteriorated in the 1970s; the anxiety and activism of conservative women in defence of threatened values deepened. The social situation, the rhetoric, and the capacity existed to turn feminism into a new cultural radicalism. The other insurgency of the 1970s, the assertion of Māori rights, exhibited precisely the same features.

Again the Second World War laid the foundations. The anti-apartheid movement, decolonization, and the American civil rights movement combined to deepen Māori awareness of deprivation and distinctiveness, and to awaken Pākehā guilt. Māoritanga, however understood, became a vantage point from which polemicists on either side of the ethnic divide mounted a criticism of mainstream society. The sudden visibility of the Māori was a multiple and self-contradictory development. The koru became the symbol of Air New Zealand, the motif of Gordon Walters' abstracts, and the title of a Māori journal of the arts. The Howard Morrison quartet rose to the top of popular music as Hone Tuwhare, Witi Ihimaera, and Ralph Hotere became prominent in the arts. Politicians, publicity agents, and media people fell over their feet trying to incorporate Māori elements while James K. Baxter offered aroha to decadent Pākehā and Colin McCahon celebrated the memory of Te Whiti and Rua Kenana. Radio and television started Māori programmes. Māori painters and writers became prominent, and Māori studies spread in the schools, teachers' colleges, and universities. The Maori Artists and Writers Society held a series of annual conferences; Pacific (that is, Polynesian, Melanesian, and Aborigine) arts festivals were launched; the Arts Council acquired a Maori and South Pacific subsidiary. Kiri Te Kanawa became an international star; Māori activists began to use the language of resistance, separatism, and revolt.

These manifestations ranged from attempts to incorporate Māori elements into expressions of national unity and harmonious pluralism to revolutionary defiance and vehement reverse-racism. On the Māori side, the response extended from the conformism of those who have succeeded in mainstream society to the chauvinism of those who see such conformity as a betrayal; and on the Pākehā side, from hostility at this disturbance of a comfortable myth to the uncritical elevation of an imaginary Māori social ideal. The cultural manifestations covered most of this range.

By the mid-1960s Māori literature in English consisted of little more than a volume of poems by Hone Tuwhare and a handful of short stories.[83] After some fifteen years, Tuwhare had published several volumes and become a public figure; the novels and stories of Ihimaera had been enthusiastically received and the author recruited into the Foreign Affairs Ministry; Patricia Grace's novels had quietly but profoundly explored the perplexities of a mixed inheritance; a New Zealand-educated Samoan, Albert Wendt, had begun a career in New Zealand that took him to international eminence; anthologies were regularly appearing, and publishers were scrambling to make their lists look Māori.

The visual artists were as numerous and as prolific. Rei Hamon, an untaught mystical pointilliste, became a celebrity and the Prime Minister gave one of his paintings to the Queen. Selwyn Muru, Para Matchett, and Muru Walters set out to recover traditional motifs and to adapt them to European conventions. Younger artists were emerging from the art schools, and finding (sometimes) a happy marriage between the conventions of contemporary art and traditional carving and painting.

The tone and the manner of this work is varied; overall, it is less than violent and radical. Hone Tuwhare is more elegiac and humorous than satirical and savage. Ihimaera explored the anguish of the urban Māori young in the hands of hostile white police and officials, but the anger was balanced by a wistfulness for an irrecoverable rural childhood. Patricia Grace, for all her quietness of voice, was more disturbing in her exploration of loss and her quest for the recovery of tradition. Nor was there much ferocity in the painting. The mood was nostalgic and celebratory — ominous and brooding at times — but no more than in the writing was there an anticipation of 'the fire next time'. It is too early to draw any conclusion other than that an awakening has occurred, of ambiguous character so far; that it will continue; that politics and economics may turn it into an instance of art in the service of revolution.

Colonial artists, taking their social function seriously, felt called upon to express the aspirations of their community, especially to assert that these men (seldom these women) were fit instruments of a secular providence. William Fox placed figures in his landscapes, small but not intimidated, often with an arm raised in a gesture that set back the crowding hills and aspired to the empty, glowing sky. The land was yielding to man, the subduer, the maker. Now that the re-making is over, there is less confidence, but more art. The hills, in Colin McCahon's early landscapes, have been stripped bare and populated by prophetic figures issuing a summons to moral and spiritual enlightenment. Brent Wong's hills are pocked with erosion and scuffed with scrubby growth; there are no people, but sometimes the houses they have left derelict. Fox's sky is high, bright, friendly. McCahon's is written over with promises yet to be fulfilled. Wong's sky is visited by remote and powerful presences, elaborate baroque assemblages, threatening and removed. The earthly paradise has given way to prophecy, and, when prophecy failed, to apprehension.

CHAPTER 22

The Recognition of Difference

Peter Simpson

The comprehensive social, economic, and political changes which occurred in New Zealand in the 1980s had the magnitude of what an observer of natural cataclysms might call a fifty- or even a hundred-year event. Within a few years the country was transformed from the seemingly prosperous, cohesive, and homogeneous society of the post-war decades to the much more unstable and divided (though also more various and dynamic) society of the 1990s. Inevitably such changes registered on the sensitive recording instruments of literature and the performing and visual arts — the particular forms of cultural expression which are the focus of this chapter.

From one point of view, of course, everything which happens in a society constitutes its culture: what people eat and drink, what they wear, the sort of houses they live in, what sort of work they do, how they educate their children, how they occupy their leisure time, what kind of videos they watch, and so on. In this broad sense of culture a survey of New Zealand since 1980 would need to consider phenomena as diverse as fast-foods, ethnic cuisines, telethons, one-day cricket, gangs, yuppies, food banks, street kids, corporate yachts, and much more besides.

The relationship between political, economic, and social developments on the one hand and cultural expression (in the more limited and exclusive sense surveyed here) on the other is seldom explicit or direct. Of course there were some paintings, songs, films, plays, photographs, and carvings which referred directly to momentous events of the time — the Springbok Tour protests of 1981, the sinking of the Rainbow Warrior, the boom and bust of the stockmarket, the debate about the Treaty of Waitangi, the threatened melt-down of the welfare state — but most artists favoured more oblique ways of registering their time and place. All the same, there were big changes in every field of cultural expression which in part reflected forces active in other spheres of the national life.

A helpful lever in distinguishing these changes is the concept of 'difference', a key word in the lexicon of the era which is capable of two distinct and even conflicting readings. In one reading 'difference' is related to cultural nationalism or 'the search for a national identity'[1] which was ubiquitous in the post-war decades. A classic specimen is the statement in the introduction to Allen Curnow's *Penguin Book of New Zealand Verse* (1960) that New Zealand poets 'at their best see differently, and see different things, from others' because of 'peculiar pressures' exerted on poets (and by implication on all New Zealanders) by 'the isolation of the country, its physical character, and its history'.[2] In the 1980s cultural nationalism remained a live issue for both advocates and detractors in every sphere of cultural expression.

To its detractors cultural nationalism was anachronistic, regressive, hostile to innovation, and in general a balefully prescriptive and exclusive cultural programme.[3] Some argued that it grossly underestimated the importance of influences from abroad, and masked the ideological privileging of a specific set of values and a particular structure of power. Opposition to cultural nationalism came from advocates of internationalism or from groups or individuals who felt excluded from its prescriptions by gender, ethnic background, class, politics or philosophy. In other words it was resisted by those whose own sense of 'difference' was not defined in 'national' terms.

This second usage of 'difference', then, was contradictory to, or at least in dynamic tension with, the first. If the first usage suggested an equivalence between 'difference' and 'identity', the second implied that 'national identity' excludes or denies 'difference'. In New Zealand terms the identity usually defined as 'true' or 'real' was perceived as liable to be Pākehā, male, heterosexual, and middle class.

Recognition of difference in this second sense was a powerful force in the 1980s, involving movements such as feminism, Māori sovereignty, and gay liberation, while the diversifying impact of Pacific and Asian immigrants, and the irrigating influence of the philosophies of post-structuralism (to which the concept of 'difference' is fundamental) also contributed to breaking down a monolithic myth of 'national identity'. Acceptance of difference led to eclecticism and pluralism in cultural expression, the recognition of diverse influences, and a multiplication of valid directions.

Cultural nationalism, however, had by the 1980s evolved from the forms it had taken in the past, in accordance with shifts in the relationships between the former colony and its source culture (New Zealand and Britain) on the one hand, and between the 'colonizers' (European settlers and their descendants) and the 'colonized' (the Māori inhabitants and their descendants) on the other. Earlier, cultural nationalism tended to be colonizer-dominated and fixated on the relationship between 'here' and 'there', New Zealand and Europe. A more independent line in international affairs, epitomized by the Lange government's anti-nuclear policies, contributed to the breakdown of this attitude, as did the diversification of trade consequent upon Britain's entry to the European Economic Community in 1973.

De-emphasizing the European connection caused the pendulum to swing away from history (Britain and Europe) towards geography (the Pacific) as the major determinant in cultural affairs. Pākehā New Zealanders tended to move from seeing themselves as 'colonized' (in relation to the British) to a perception of themselves as 'colonizers' in relation to the Māori. Paradoxically, it was only as Pākehā collectively came to terms with their relationship to Europe that the question of the relationship of the two cultures within the country came more fully into focus. This process was hastened by the increasing assertiveness of Māori consciousness, especially after the Land March on Parliament in 1975. The cultural nationalism advocated in the 1980s increasingly took a bi-cultural, 'post-colonial' form.[4]

New Zealand culture in the 1980s and 1990s presents, then, a paradoxical profile. On the one hand it was increasingly liberated from the 'cultural cringe' associated with a colonial or provincial mind-set, more confidently centred in its outlook, more accepting of the given conditions of location and cultural context, more 'different' from other Western countries. On the other hand, as Mark Williams has pointed out, 'the process by which New Zealand society became assimilated into the prevailing forms, cultural as well as economic, of Western capitalism was accelerated';[5] the culture became less different from other places, but simultaneously more sensitive to differences, especially of gender and ethnicity, within the society. It is in relation to this dynamic structure of paradoxes that the various forms of cultural expression and the myriad individual practices within them can be located.

The Penguin Book of New Zealand Verse (1985), edited by Ian Wedde and Harvey McQueen — like its identically named predecessor twenty-five years earlier — epitomized the context for poetry of its time. Wedde's introduction ambitiously sought a synthesis of the contradictory 'nationalist' and 'internationalist' approaches which had dominated earlier discussion by emphasizing not the content of poetry but its medium — language — which (in the case of New Zealand English) is both local and international at the same time.[6] New Zealand poets are different (he implied) because they *say* differently, and *say* different things from poets elsewhere. In their selections the editors gave expanded attention to women writers, were less hierarchical in the allocation of space, and took an inclusive approach to the pluralism of contemporary poetry. More controversial was their idealistically bicultural inclusion of substantial quantities of poetry in Māori (with translations in English).[7]

But poetry in the 1980s was too various to be contained with any one critical formulation, as several anthologists noted.[8] Murray Edmond and Mary Paul, for instance, with reference to emergent poets of the 1980s (though their remarks could be applied more generally), noted changes in 'style, theory, politics and publishing strategies . . . accompanied by an intense debate about the nature and function of poetry' and identified five distinct if overlapping categories of poet: those following a 'high internationalist legacy' (for example, Leigh Davis, Michele Leggott), those extending the mainstream New Zealand tradition of poet as seer and sayer (for example, John Newton, Gregory O'Brien), those using poetry to express Māori consciousness (for example, Keri Hulme, Apirana Taylor), those writing out of the theory and practice of feminism (for example, Heather McPherson, Joanna Paul), and those aiming to extend the audience for poetry through oral performance (for example, David Eggleton, Cilla McQueen).[9]

Within this context of debate, diversity, and difference poets of many different backgrounds, generations, and persuasions were active. During the 1980s and early 1990s many of the poets who had become established earlier consolidated their positions by publishing collected editions or substantial selections of their poems in addition to new work. These included Fleur Adcock, Peter Bland, Alan Brunton, Alistair Campbell, Allen Curnow, Ruth Dallas, Lauris Edmond, Sam Hunt, Kevin Ireland, Michael Jackson, Fiona Kidman, Rachel McAlpine, Bill Manhire, Vincent O'Sullivan, Kendrick Smithyman, C. K. Stead, Hone Tuwhare, and Ian Wedde.

Two of these volumes, Lauris Edmond's *Selected Poems* (1984) — formally conservative but eloquent and well-managed poems — and Allen Curnow's *Continuum: New and Later Poems, 1972–88* (1988) won the Commonwealth Poetry Prize. Curnow was also awarded the Queen's Medal for Poetry, a fitting recognition for a poet whose sixty-year career showed no sign of flagging as he continued into the 1990s to scrutinize both word and world in poems of great force and precision, many of the more recent focusing with resonance and clarity on scenes of distant childhood. Kendrick Smithyman was another senior poet who went from strength to strength.

Of poets in mid-career among the most consistent performers were Murray Edmond (*End Wall* (1981), *Letters and Paragraphs* (1987), *From the Word Go* (1992)), Bill Manhire (*Zoetropes: Poems 1972–82* (1984), *Milky Way Bar* (1991)), Elizabeth Smither (*Casanova's Ankle* (1981), *Professor Musgrove's Canary* (1986), *A Pattern of Marching* (1989)), and Ian Wedde (*Driving Into the Storm: Selected Poems* (1987), *Tendering*, (1988)). While quite dissimilar to each other in many respects they each manifested an alert responsiveness to how words mesh with experience, so that their poems refresh the reader's sense of the possibilities of both language and life.

In prose fiction the death in 1982 of Frank Sargeson marked the end of an era, for, by the end of the decade, the Sargeson tradition of story writing founded on a style of chastened realism using local idiom had been fragmented and deconstructed, and the domination of fiction by the viewpoint of a Pākehā-male-outsider at odds with the social order had ended. Furthermore, the novel had taken over from the short story as the fictional medium preferred by writers, publishers, and readers due to a combination of the more expansive confidence among writers, the growth of an audience for local fiction beyond the minority audience of literary journals such as *Landfall* and *Islands* to which the short story was suited, and the needs of an expanding local publishing industry for which novels were a more easily marketable product. By the 1990s the once irregular trickle of novels had become a reliably steady stream.

Some writers, such as Owen Marshall, Vincent O'Sullivan, Michael Gifkins, and Fiona Farrell Poole continued practising the short story as their preferred medium, and the cutting edge of experimentation was generally found in the shorter form, as demonstrated, for instance, by Russell Haley, Damien Wilkins, and Anne Kennedy.[10] The majority of fiction writers published both short stories and novels. A potent symbol of the changed profile of fiction was Keri Hulme's *The Bone People* (1983). Her rapid rise from obscurity to national and international success (including the Booker Prize) through this large, idiosyncratic novel represented the triumph of the marginal, itself a major theme of the 1980s. The broad appeal of the novel had less to do with the painful realism of its central sequences than with the regenerative romance of its ending which did not so much reject the 'I'-centred Pākehā tradition (of man or woman alone) as subsume it into the 'we'-consciousness of Māori communalism. It was seemingly to this optimistic if hazy vision of bi-cultural fusion that many readers responded enthusiastically. *The Bone People* fitted its time perfectly and its popularity was a stimulus to both writers and publishers.

According to Mark Williams, 'at no time since the 1930s has fiction in this country been so directly involved with crucial and unresolved questions of national self-definition and evaluation as was the case in the late 1980s.'[11] Both Māori and Pākehā writers contributed to this environment of post-colonial self-scrutiny, either by directly addressing the contemporary scene — as in novels such as Sue McCauley's *Other Halves* (1982), Marilyn Duckworth's *Disorderly Conduct* (1984), Patricia Grace's *Potiki* (1986), Janet Frame's *The Carpathians* (1988), Alan Duff's *Once Were Warriors* (1990), and Albert Wendt's *Ola* (1991) — or through imaginatively reconstructing the past, whether in family, tribal, or national terms.

The technically demanding task of finding narrative means of embodying both the pastness of the past and its continuing presence was attempted in two major efforts at a sort of 'national epic', Witi Ihimaera's *The Matriarch* and Ian Wedde's *Symmes Hole* (both 1986). Both employed contemporary narrators obsessed with recovering the past, both incorporated historical characters (Te Kooti, James 'Worser' Heberley), and both appropriated historical art works (Verdi's operas, Melville's *Moby Dick*) in fictions of audacious 'bricolage', in the sense of making something new out of heterogeneous borrowings.[12]

A fuller account of this historicizing impulse would need to consider also Maurice Gee's trilogy *Plumb* (1978), *Meg* (1981), and *Sole Survivor* (1983) — a remarkable reconstruction of intergenerational family life and an apotheosis of the tradition of critical realism — and Maurice Shadbolt's historical trio, *The Lovelock Version* (1980), *Season of the Jew* (1986) — a Pākehā version, in striking contrast to Ihimaera's, of Te Kooti's rebellion — and *Monday's Warriors* (1990). C. K. Stead's *All Visitors Ashore* (1984), Fiona Kidman's *The Book of Secrets* (1987), and Stevan Eldred-Grigg's *Oracles and Miracles* (1987) were other noteworthy fictional reconstructions of portions of the writers' personal and the country's collective past, while

Mike Johnson's *Lear* (1986) convincingly projected a nightmare vision of the future. Other interesting new fiction writers to emerge during the period were Elizabeth Knox, Peter Wells, Lloyd Jones, and Barbara Anderson.

Personal or collective history also dominated non-fictional prose in the 1980s. Prior to Sargeson's masterly autobiography in three volumes — published separately during the 1970s and brought together as *Sargeson* (1981) — literary autobiography had seldom been practised in New Zealand. Subsequently there were numerous other autobiographers including Sylvia Ashton-Warner, M. H. Holcroft, Toss Woollaston (the painter), Ruth Dallas, Lauris Edmond, and Alistair Campbell. But the work which most deserved to stand beside Sargeson's for its artistry and its intriguing blend of disclosure and reticence was Janet Frame's trilogy, *To the Is-land* (1982), *An Angel at My Table* (1984) and *The Envoy from Mirror City* (1985).[13]

As Lawrence Jones has said, all these autobiographies were 'telling basically one story of a struggle against an aesthetically hostile environment, puritanical, materialist, conformist'.[14] Paradoxically, such articulations of the provincial past were themselves a major sign of entry to a post-provincial condition both by the individuals concerned and to some extent by the society itself, as art moved from the margins towards the mainstream.[15]

Michael King's *Being Pakeha: An Encounter with New Zealand and the Maori Renaissance* (1985) brought to the autobiographical mode the post-provincial/post-colonial perspective of a writer who had empathetically immersed himself in Māori culture and who addressed the growing sensitivity of Māori to having their culture interpreted and in a sense appropriated by Pākehā writers. The contribution of Māori writers to interpreting their own history and culture was, therefore, of growing importance, as in such books as Donna Awatere's polemical *Maori Sovereignty* (1984), Buddy Mikaere's *Te Maiharoa and the Promised Land* (1988), and Ranginui Walker's *Struggle Without End: Ka Whawhai Tonu Matou* (1990).

The preoccupation with history from a post-colonial perspective so dominant in the fiction of the period was not surprisingly also evident in historical writing itself. Three important examples were James Belich's revisionist study, *The New Zealand Wars* (1986), Claudia Orange's *The Treaty of Waitangi* (1987) — the most comprehensive of several studies of the Treaty as the sesquicentennial approached in 1990 — and Anne Salmond's *Two Worlds* (1992), an account from both sides of the fence of the first contacts between Māori and European.

Among the more lasting achievements of the 1990 sesquicentennial were significant works of scholarship timed to coincide with that date, notably *The Dictionary of New Zealand Biography* (Volume 1, 1990), edited by W. H. Oliver, which strove to move beyond traditional élites in giving expanded attention to both Māori and women subjects (including publication in the Māori language), and *The Oxford History of New Zealand*

Literature in English (1991), edited by Terry Sturm, also consciously non-élitist in including chapters on children's literature, non-fiction, and popular fiction alongside the more traditional literary genres.

Writing for children and young adults in New Zealand underwent, in Betty Gilderdale's words, a 'spectacular transformation in both the quantity and quality',[16] with more titles published since 1980 than in the entire previous history.[17] Some leading writers for adults also wrote for children, such as Joy Cowley, Patricia Grace, and Maurice Gee, but many specialist children's writers also emerged, including both those who wrote picture books for young readers — such as Lynley Dodd and Gavin Bishop — and those who wrote fiction for older children — such as Joan de Hamel, Caroline Macdonald, Joanna Orwin, and Tessa Duder. Exceptional in every respect was the prolific Margaret Mahy. Published in the United Kingdom, she won international awards for *The Haunting* (1982) and *The Changeover* (1984), and succeeded equally with titles aimed at teenage readers — *The Catalogue of the Universe* (1985) and *Memory* (1987) are other notable achievements — and with illustrated story books for younger children.

Funds from lottery profits considerably expanded the public funding for literature and the other arts during the 1980s, though this levelled off or declined after the 1991 Budget. The Literary Fund became part of the Queen Elizabeth II Arts Council. Establishment of a Ministry of Cultural Affairs in 1991 led to a major review of the activities of the Arts Council, including the Maori and South Pacific Arts Council.

The setting up of professional community theatres in the 1970s (partially subsidized by the Arts Council) was the crucial precondition for the belated emergence of significant local drama. Its progress was far from smooth. There was always a tension between the commercial realism of the theatres, with their need to put 'bums on seats', and the nationalism of writers determined to put New Zealand stories on the stage. Doubts about the availability of plays of sufficient quality and whether audiences would turn out for New Zealand plays tended to diminish after the outstanding commercial success of Roger Hall's comedies *Glide Time* and *Middle Age Spread* in the late 1970s, though larger venues such as Auckland's Mercury Theatre (which closed because of debt in 1992) found new local plays less commercially feasible than smaller theatres such as Theatre Corporate (Auckland), Circa (Wellington), Downstage (Wellington), The Court (Christchurch), or The Fortune (Dunedin).

The activities of Playmarket from the mid-1970s were important as an intermediary between playwrights and theatres, providing script advice, publication, a writers' agency, and (from 1980) a biennial playwright's workshop. Several of the most substantial plays of the period emerged from Playmarket workshops, including Greg McGee's *Foreskin's Lament* (1980), a trenchant analysis of society through the metaphor of rugby, Hilary Beaton's *Outside In* (1983), a powerful naturalistic study of a group of women prisoners, Renée's *Wednesday to Come* (1984), first of a trilogy exploring, from a feminist perspective, key historical events in the different generations of a family, and Stuart Hoar's *Squatter* (1986), a highly allusive, non-naturalistic analysis of the politics of colonization — all plays which engaged with what McGee's *Foreskin* called 'the heart and bowels of this country'.[18] Mervyn Thompson, a passionate advocate for New Zealand drama (*Songs to the Judges* (1980), *Coaltown Blues* (1984), *Passing Through* (1991)) and Vincent O'Sullivan (*Shuriken* (1982), *Jones & Jones* (1988), *Billy* (1989)) were other writers to make telling theatre out of reclamation of the past with one eye on the conflicts of the present.

A more populist approach was successful with *Footrot Flats* (1984), a musical version of Murray Ball's cartoons written by Roger Hall (book), Philip Norman (music), and A. K. Grant (lyrics) and with *Ladies' Night* (1989) by Stephen Sinclair and Anthony McCarten, a theatrical male strip-show. A vigorous alternative group theatre movement in the 1970s (Theatre Action, Amamus)[19] mostly failed to survive the economic recession of the 1980s, an exception being the radically eclectic Red Mole (*Comrade Savage* (1990), *The Book of Life* (1991)), who spent most of the 1980s overseas. Feminist and Māori groups, both with an extra-theatrical agenda, provided perhaps the most energetic alternative to mainstream amateur and professional theatre from the late 1980s, especially at the Depot in Wellington. *Hens' Teeth*, a group-scripted feminist cabaret, combined the talents of many women writers and performers. In the decade following *Maranga Mai* (1980), also group-written and performed, more than forty plays by Māori playwrights had productions, mostly 'directed towards the reclamation of culture and the re-establishment of cultural identity'.[20]

Prior to 1978 only a handful of feature films had been made in New Zealand; during the next decade the development was spectacular, with over sixty films released, though the growth rate fell off sharply after Budget changes in 1982 removed incentives which had attracted much private investment. The decisive impact of economic factors on film-making is evident from comparing 1983–84 (the last two years before the tax changes took effect) when thirty-one films were made, with 1985–86 when only six films were made.[21] More than half the films got financial support from the New Zealand Film Commission, established in 1978, which also assisted with promotion and distribution. New Zealand films were often critically successful abroad as well as at home, with special seasons being held in London, Paris, New York, and Sydney, but did not match the commercial success of Australian films such as *Crocodile Dundee* or *My Brilliant Career*.

Initially most New Zealand films were well-made action movies in the Hollywood manner, with much violence and humour and a strongly masculine outlook. Typical examples were Roger Donaldson's *Sleeping Dogs* (1977) and *Smash Palace* (1981), Geoff Murphy's *Goodbye Pork Pie* (1981) and *Utu* (1983), Sam Pillsbury's *The Scarecrow* (1982), and Ian Mune's *Came a Hot Friday* (1984). As Roger Horrocks has remarked, the ambience of this period is aptly caught in the title of Geoff Stevens's 1991 documentary, *Cowboys of Culture*.[22] Later the films became more various in style with female and Māori perspectives more prominent. Among the more notable film makers were Vincent Ward (*Vigil* (1984), *The Navigator* (1987)), Gaylene Preston (*Mr Wrong* (1984), *Ruby and Rata* (1990)), Merata Mita (*Patu* (1983), *Mauri* (1987)), Melanie Read (*Trial Run* (1983), *Send a Gorilla* (1988), Barry Barclay (*Ngati* (1986)), Leon Narbey (*Illustrious Energy* (1987)), and Jane Campion (*An Angel at My Table* (1990)). Vincent Ward brought a remarkable visual poetry to the screen; Merata Mita's films were notable for their emotional intensity; Jane Campion's luminous adaptation of Janet Frame's autobiographies, initially made for television, won several international awards. Peter Wells, Lisa Reihana, and Alison Maclean, among others, made successful short experimental films. The New Zealand Film Archive, dedicated to the collection and preservation of film and television materials, was established in 1981.

The average New Zealander watches more than twenty hours of television each week, and the steady decline in cinema attendance and the demise of evening newspapers is an indication of the growing cultural influence of the medium. A large proportion of the programming on New Zealand television comes from overseas. In fact, a smaller proportion (roughly a quarter) of television content is locally sourced in New Zealand than is locally sourced in most other countries. With the proliferation of channels and with increasing commercialization and deregulation of the medium (including, from 1991, the possibility of 100 per cent foreign ownership) this fraction is likely to get smaller. Sport and news made up by far the largest part of local content with drama and comedy, contributing, for example, a derisory 1.3 per cent in 1990. The high cost of local production as compared to buying programmes from the United States, Britain or Australia meant that commercial logic pointed in only one direction. Nevertheless, good quality television programmes were made in New Zealand in the 1980s in such genres as documentary (for example, *Landmarks* and *Wild South*), drama (for example, *Gloss* and *Shark in the Park*), entertainment (for example, *McPhail and Gadsby* and *The Billy T. James Show*) and children's programmes (for example, *Wild Track* and *Fireraiser*). Primarily television contributed to the homogenization of culture rather than to fostering either a sense of difference among minority subcultures or a sense of national difference. However, it does have the capacity for cultural integration through popular sporting fixtures (especially rugby and cricket) and through one-off events such as telethons or the Commonwealth Games held in Auckland in 1990. Ironically, nationalism is often appealed to directly by advertisements promoting the products of multinational companies such as Toyota.

In music also (as to varying degrees in all the arts) New Zealand performers and composers must co-exist with what is imported. An attempt in 1990 to redress the balance somewhat by legislating for a compulsory local quota on radio was swamped by the strong tide running towards the free market.[23] Whether the proliferation of radio and television stations in the wake of the radical deregulation of broadcasting after 1988 would have any positive spin-offs for New Zealand artists was still unclear by the early

1990s, though the signs were not initially auspicious.

The New Zealand Symphony Orchestra survived repeated bureaucratic and administrative upheavals, and, under a succession of guest conductors, maintained a demanding concert and recording schedule. Regional orchestras became well-established in the main centres and, similarly, regional opera companies gained sufficient foothold to induce the country's international stars (Kiri Te Kanawa, Malvina Major, Donald McIntyre) to perform here. The Schola Musica, a professional training orchestra for young musicians, unfortunately failed to survive restructuring, but the establishment of The New Zealand String Quartet in 1987 was a compensating event. The Music Federation continued to operate a national circuit for chamber-music performers both from New Zealand and overseas. The Royal New Zealand Ballet Company made successful visits to Australia in 1981 and China in 1985. In dance, similar problems of striking an appropriate balance between performing the inherited tradition and creating new works were experienced. The choreographers Mary-Jane O'Reilly (associated with a successful modern dance group, Limbs), Michael Parmenter, and Douglas Wright made perhaps the greatest contributions to an indigenous dance tradition.

New Zealand-based composers increasingly drew on the Asian/Pacific environment for inspiration, examples being Ross Harris' collaboration with Witi Ihimaera in the opera *Waituhi* (1984), the Indonesian-influenced scores of Jack Body, and the eclectic sources of the innovative percussion group, From Scratch. The example of Douglas Lilburn in working with natural sounds of wind, water, and birdsong was followed by several other composers working in a variety of modes including the electro-acoustic mode, some of them expatriates who maintained connections with their birthplace such as Lyell Cresswell, Annea Lockwood, and Gillian White-head. Among resident composers who made distinctive contributions were John Rimmer, Dorothy Buchanan, Jenny McLeod, and John Cousins.

In popular music the lively lyrics, rhythms, and stage act of the rock group Split Enz achieved a deserved measure of international success, while the Polynesian group Herbs created a popular and engaging style of Pacific reggae. The record label Flying Nun established an impressive catalogue of alternative rock music, much of it originating in the South Island, from groups such as The Chills and Straitjacket Fits. New Zealand musicians struggled to achieve exposure on ratings-driven commercial radio, though university stations were more supportive of the local product. Live performances whether in pubs, clubs or on campus remained an important part of youth culture. John Dix's *Stranded in Paradise: New Zealand Rock'n'roll, 1955–88* (1988) recorded the constantly changing history of a vital scene.

Ho toi whakairo he mana tangata.
Where there is artistic excellence there is human dignity.

Artistic excellence and human dignity — transcending cultural boundaries

— were paramount in three events which, taken together, provide a matrix for considering the visual arts. These were *Te Maori* — the superb collection of Māori carvings which toured the main centres in 1986–87 after returning home from its success in the United States — and the outstanding posthumous retrospective exhibitions of Rita Angus (National Gallery, 1982) and Colin McCahon (Auckland City Art Gallery, 1988), both revered ancestor-figures in New Zealand art.

The most comprehensive attempt at a panoramic snapshot, across several media, of the visual-arts scene in the 1980s was *Content/Context: A Survey of New Zealand Art*, a two-part exhibition curated for the National Gallery by Luit Bieringa in 1986–87. Some sixty artists, working in painting, sculpture, photography, and video, were included, ranging from senior figures such as Toss Woollaston and Gordon Walters (representing previously ascendant styles of expressive realism and modernist abstraction), to the emergent artists of the eclectic 1980s.[24] According to Bieringa, 'there is no single thing called New Zealand art. There is Maori art, there is women's art, there is art made in and of New Zealand.'[25] The exhibition affirmed both the plurality of artistic perspectives and the importance of locality and context without chasing the chimera of a singular 'national' identity in art.

The immense mana of *Te Maori* boosted the already strongly emergent Māori visual arts movement, both traditional and modern. The exclusion of women's arts such as weaving from *Te Maori* provided a spur for exhibitions like *Karanga, Karanga* (1986) which punctured the outworn Pākehā distinction between art and craft. Also in 1986 *Te Ao Marama: Seven Maori Artists* toured Australia, and *Haongia Te Taonga* (Waikato Museum) brought together four kaumātua of Māori art — Ralph Hotere, Selwyn Muru, Paratene Matchitt, and Arnold Wilson. Also included in this exhibition was Kura Te Waru-Rewiri, one of a strong group of younger women artists (Robin Kahukiwa, Shona Rapira Davies, and Emare Karaka) who made use of Western/Pākehā art conventions and models to make strongly Māori visual statements. *Kohia ko Taikaka*, a Māori-curated, multi-generational and multi-tribal exhibition mounted by the National Gallery in 1990, successfully brought contemporary Māori art into the Pākehā context of an art museum without losing touch with its roots in the marae-based culture of Māoritanga. Also in 1990 more than twenty waka (canoes) were assembled at Waitangi for the sesquicentennial commemorations, an event which inspired Māori and Pākehā alike.

Individual women artists (Rita Angus, Doris Lusk, Louise Henderson) have always been prominent in New Zealand art, but 'women's art' as such grew out of feminism in the 1970s. Early initiatives in Christchurch eventually led to the establishment of The Women's Gallery in Wellington (1979–83), dedicated to 'breaking out of the images men have presented to us and exploring our exclusively female experience'.[26] Exhibitions, books, and special issues of art magazines devoted to women artists also helped correct a perceived gender imbalance.

In the later 1980s a discernible shift occurred in women's art. French feminists (Julia Kristeva, Luce Irigaray) tended to replace Americans (Judy Chicago, Lucy Lippard) as primary influences among younger artists. As Lita Barrie argued, the quest for the 'feminine' was not to be confused with either biological gender, nor with women as culturally constructed in male-dominated society, but entailed seeking expression for a feminine 'unconscious' uncontaminated by male coding.[27] There was a movement away from traditional media and materials towards forms like photography, installation, and mixed media construction for questioning and challenging 'patriarchal' structures and expressing feminine difference. Pauline Rhodes, Ruth Watson, Megan Jenkinson, Fiona Pardington, Merylyn Tweedie, and Alexis Hunter illustrate, with great diversity of media and style, this development.

The infusion from both Māori and women's perspectives of a more political or critical element into art chimed with international developments in art theory and practice such as postmodernism and poststructuralism which became influential among artists and curators and in journals such as *Parallax* (1982–83), *And* (1983–85), and *Antic* (1986–91). Absorption of such tendencies had speeded up markedly with developments in technology and New Zealand's more direct involvement in the global economy. Thematically centred exhibitions with strong curatorial input such as *Sex & Sign* (curated by Wystan Curnow for Artspace, 1988), *Now See Hear!* (Gregory Burke and Ian Wedde for Wellington City Art Gallery, 1990), and *Signatures of Place* (Francis Pound for Govett-Brewster Gallery, 1991) were influential conduits for new ideas. The exhibitions *Headlands: Thinking Through New Zealand Art, Distance Looks Our Way*, and *Pacific Parallels: Artists and the Landscape in New Zealand* projected three contemporary perspectives on New Zealand art into Australia, Spain, and the United States respectively in 1992.

In painting, established modes such as various forms of realism (Grahame Sydney, Glenda Randerson, Michael Stevenson), expressionism (Philip Clairmont, Bill Hammond, Jeffrey Harris, Tony Fomison), and abstraction (Milan Mrkusich, Don Peebles, Max Gimblett, Gretchen Albrecht, Stephen Bambury) continued in use while some artists (Richard Killeen, Ian Scott) moved successively from realism through abstraction to postmodern figuration. The Auckland City Art Gallery's three *Aspects of New Zealand Art* exhibitions (*The Grid, Anxious Images,* and *New Image,* which dealt respectively with abstraction, expressionism, and postmodernism) addressed several of these tendencies.

The return to landscape and figuration often involved a critique of representation itself rather than the naïve imitation of past art styles. Deliberate appropriations from other artists and allusions to art historical motifs reflected postmodern scepticism about the possibility of originality or 'making it new' in the modernist sense. Artists such as Gavin Chilcott and Julia Morison were characteristically allusive and self-conscious in manipulating artistic signs and conventions. The ideational content of art (as distinct from the purely aesthetic) increased as the modernist ideal of aesthetic contemplation gave way to a concern with the cultural and political positioning of art.

Changes related to those which occurred in painting also affected sculpture, photography, and other media. Auckland City Art Gallery's two-part *Aspects of New Zealand Sculpture* (1985–86), for example, demonstrated a wide range of possible idioms from Neil Dawson's witty high-tech illusionism to Jacqueline Fraser's improvisational, non-monumental, environment-specific installations. A shared concern with 'this land, its Pacific-ness and the indigenous cultures of the region'[28] linked sculptors as various as Chris Booth, Christine Hellyer, and Warren Viscoe. Performance and installation works predominated in occasional ANZART symposia which sustained a useful trans-Tasman traffic in sculptural ideas.

Photography gained added status through carefully curated survey shows such as *Views/Exposures* (National Gallery, 1982) and *Imposing Narratives: Beyond the Documentary in Recent New Zealand Photography* (Wellington City Gallery, 1990), exhibitions which charted a progressive movement away from the previously dominant documentary tradition towards alternative strategies, especially those which challenged and subverted photography's supposed truth-telling capacities. The diversity represented by Laurence Abehart, Bruce Foster, Fiona Clark, Peter Hannken, Peter Black, Anne Noble, Glenn Busch, Peter Peryer, Margaret Dawson, Robin Morrison, Christine Webster, and Marie Shannon makes significant generalization difficult, beyond demonstrating photography's vitality and strength.

Printmaking in the 1980s lacked the opportunities for national exposure of other media, reflecting perhaps a comparative lack of interest within public galleries. The Govett-Brewster's *Directions in New Zealand Print Making* (1980) and the Wellington City Gallery's *Print Series* (1987) were important initiatives which showed that printmakers themselves were far from dormant. While many different print methods had talented exponents, screen-printing was very popular with the public because of its capacity for exciting use of colour, and lithography became steadily more prominent with the expansion of print workshops, such as the Muka Gallery in Auckland and The Limeworks in Christchurch. Barry Cleavin, Kate Coolahan, Pat Hanly, Rodney Fumpston, and Denys Watkins were printmakers who achieved wider exposure through retrospective and/or touring exhibitions.

The distinction between art and craft — irrelevant in Māori culture but fundamental in European-derived Pākehā culture — became ever more difficult to sustain as craft itself progressively moved away from the strictly functional towards work which gave priority to making an expressive statement. It became increasingly evident that there was a continuum rather than an absolute distinction between art and craft and that the categorizing of particular objects depended more on context than on inherent attributes. Such a recognition was inherent in the decision of the Dowse Art Museum to change its name (from Art Gallery) in order to help break down anachronistic distinctions between art and craft and between Pākehā and

Polynesian craftspeople (through exhibitions such as *Pacific Adornment*, 1984–85). Pacific Island crafts and performance greatly enriched the cultural mix across the spectrum from weaving to dance, a multicultural perspective highlighted, for instance, at South Pacific Arts Festivals and at the spectacular opening ceremony of the Commonwealth Games in 1990.

Craft in New Zealand has been described as 'dynamic, evolving and eclectic'[29] and this description applies whether the material used is wood, clay, stone, shell, bone, fibre, or glass. Pottery is probably the area of craft which has most practitioners, most support from the public, and the greatest recognition for its accomplishments both within New Zealand and overseas. Great diversification of style and technique from the mid-1970s onwards was apparent, for instance, among winners of the annual Fletcher Brownbuilt Pottery Award (later the Fletcher Challenge Ceramics Award) who included Rick Rudd, Debbie Pointon, Beverly Luxton, Chester Nealie, Ray Rogers, Merilyn Wiseman, and Steve Fullmer, each radically different in their approach to clay. Ceramics were appropriately chosen to represent New Zealand craft at the World Expo in Seville in 1992.

In all the visual arts the growth in the number of practitioners was matched by a corresponding increase in the size of the audience for art. By the early 1990s there were more than 20 dealer galleries in Auckland and more than 10 in both Wellington and Christchurch, reflecting the expanding number of both private and corporate collectors. Prices rose rapidly (a Colin McCahon from the early 1950s sold for $160,000 in 1987) and the purchase of art for investment or speculation increased, though the post-1987 recession brought a decline. Public galleries attracted large crowds, especially for highly promoted 'blockbuster' shows like *Te Maori* or *America and Europe: A Century of Modern Masters: the Thyssen-Bornemisza Collection*. Corporate sponsorship of exhibitions (such as Mobil's involvement in *Te Maori*) became important as rising prices (and user-pays economics) put pressure on public-gallery budgets. Nevertheless, increasing professionalism in public institutions was evident, including those in provincial centres such as Wanganui and New Plymouth which often had innovative programmes. Better catalogues, books, and magazines (such as the quarterly *Art New Zealand*, published from 1976) reflected a big growth in art writing, a process stimulated by a world-wide intensification of art discourse. Visiting international shows of German, British, Australian, and American art, together with increased travel and overseas exhibition by New Zealand artists, and frequent return visits by expatriates, also increased the inwards and outwards flow of art information.

In Janet Frame's *The Carpathians* (1988) a Māori woman, Hene Hunuere, says: 'There was a time, you see, when this country and both Maori and Pakeha and others were nothing because we thought we were so far away — far away from the rulers, the seat of Empire; but now we're ourselves, and we can't be ignored or made nothing and no-one, because the distance has gone.'[30] And in 1990 the visual artist Julian Dashper wrote: 'It is an irony of our time that New Zealand's Pacific distance is an advantage to us.

That very distance whose obstacle shaped our past will continue to affect us by placing us in a fresh context. Distance is no longer an excuse, but has instead become an introduction.'[31] The juxtaposition of these utterances captures some of the paradoxes of New Zealand's cultural condition in the 1990s. The old New Zealand, buttressed by isolation and the protection of a colonial economy had gone, and with it full employment and the security provided by the welfare state. But gone also was monocultural myopia and the paralysing sense of provincial disability. The new conditions were harsher, more exposed to the world and the world's ill but also to its stimulus and opportunities, encouraging fresh perspectives for New Zealanders on who they are and where they live. The cultural ferment of the 1980s and 1990s, as many groups and individuals sought expression for their sense of difference, suggests that there was gain as well as loss in the transformation.

> Ka pū te rūhā; ka hao te rangatahi.
> The old net is cast aside; the new net goes fishing.

Glossary of Māori Terms*

ariki   *paramount chief*
aroha   *regard, love, compassion*
atua   *god, or spirit*
haka   *chants of defiance accompanied by a stylized dance*
hapū   *sub-tribe, or clan*
heke   *migration*
hui   *gathering (often for political as well as social purposes)*
īnanga   *whitebait*
iwi   *tribe*
kai moana   *seafood*
kāinga   *village, usually of a single hapū*
karakia   *incantation, prayer*
kauhanganui   *parliament*
kaumātua   *elder, family head*
kaupapa   *ideas*
kāuri   (Agathis australis) *forest tree valued for timber and resinous gum*
kawa   *etiquette relating to marae activities*
kiekie   (Freycinetia banksii) *a climbing plant*
koru   (Pratia physaloides) *fern frond*
kotahitanga   *unity*
kūmara   (Ipomoea batatas) *sweet potato*
kūpapa   *neutral (often applied to pro-Government Māori)*
mākutu   *sorcery*
mana   *spiritual power, authority, prestige*
marae   *open space in front of a meeting-house, place of assembly*
moa   *large flightless bird of the order Dinornithiformes, now extinct*
moko   *tattoo*
muru   *plunder*
oriori   *sleep-time chant*
pā   *fortified place*
pā tuna   *eel-weir*
Pākehā   *person of non-Māori descent (usually European)*
poi   *a dance performed with poi (light balls on string)*
rangatira   *chief*
raupō   (Typha augustifolia) *bulrush*
rūnanga   *group of elders, or a descent group as a political entity*
tangi   *death ceremonial, cry of lament*
tangihanga   *funeral wake*
taniwha   *water-dwelling spirit or monster*
taonga   *sacred treasure, cultural heritage*
tapu   *under spiritual restriction; sacred*

*See note on Māori usage, p. xvi

586

taua   *war-party*
tiki   *stylized human image made from wood or stone*
toetoe   *various species of long grass with tall, feathery flower-heads*
tohunga   *expert or specialist, often in religious matters*
tūahu   *shrine, sacred place*
tūpuna   *ancestors*
urupā   *burial ground*
utu   *satisfaction*
waiata   *song*
waka   *a group of tribes based on common descent from occupants of an early migratory canoe*
whakapapa   *genealogy*
whānau   *extended family*
whare   *house*
wharepuni   *well-built sleeping house*

MAP 2: Māori Tribal Locations

SOUTH ISLAND

In the South Island, the Ngāi Tahu Whānui comprises three founding tribes;
Waitaha, Ngāti Māmoe and Ngāi Tahu (or Kāi Tahu, in southern dialect).
Collectively they are known as Ngāi Tahu.

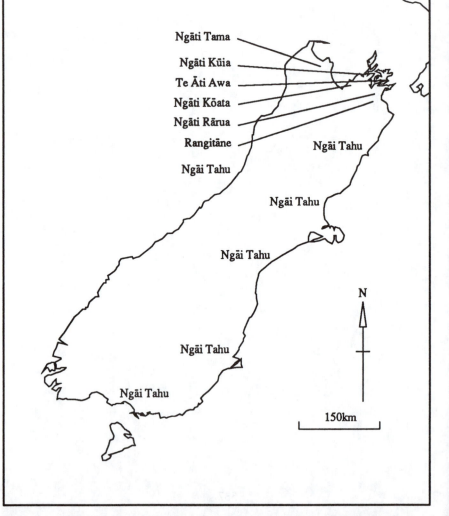

NORTH ISLAND

The following broad regional descriptions may also be encountered:
Te Taitokerau (Northern Tribes)
Tainui (Central North Island)
Te Taihauāuru (West Coast)
Te Tairāwhiti (East Coast)
Te Ūpoko o Te Ika (Head of the Fish Tribes: Lower North Island)

18. Ngāti Whanaunga
19. Ngāti Maru
20. Ngāti Tamaterā
21. Ngāti Ranginui
22. Ngāi Te Rangi
23. Te Arawa
24. Ngāti Awa
25. Tūhoe
26. Te Whakatōhea
27. Ngāi Tai
28. Whānau-a-Apanui
29. Ngāti Porou
30. Te Aitanga-a-Hauiti
31. Te Aitanga-a-Māhaki
32. Ngāti Ruapani
33. Rongowhakaata
34. Ngai Tamanuhiri

1. Te Aupōuri
2. Te Rārawa
3. Ngāti Kahu
4. Ngāti Hine
5. Ngāpuhi
6. Ngāti Wai
7. Uriohau
8. Ngāti Whātua
9. Ngāti Mahuta
10. Ngāti Whātua ki Tāmaki
11. Ngāti Pāoa
12. Ngāti Te Ata
13. Waikato
14. Ngāti Mahuta
15. Ngāti Raukawa
16. Ngāti Toa
17. Ngāti Maniapoto

38. Ngāti Tūwharetoa
39. Ngāti Tama
40. Ngāti Mutunga
41. Te Āti Awa
42. Taranaki
43. Ngā Ruahine
44. Ngāti Ruanui
45. Ngā Rauru
46. Te Āti Hau
47. Ngāti Apa
48. Muaūpoko
49. Rangitāne

N

150km

35. Ngāti Kahungunu ki Te Wairoa
36. Ngāti Kahungunu ki Te Heretaunga
37. Ngāti Kahungunu ki Te Wairarapa

Map 3: Principal towns, cities, and regions

Significant places named in text are shown as well as main towns and cities.
Names of districts in common use are also given.

Provincial boundaries at 1876 (Southland 1871)

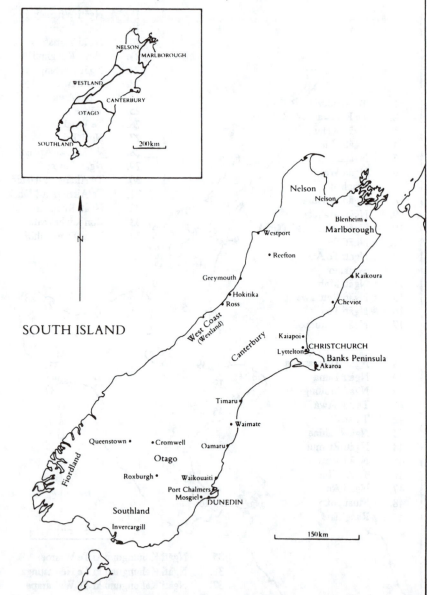

NELSON
MARLBOROUGH
WESTLAND
CANTERBURY
OTAGO
SOUTHLAND

200 km

N

SOUTH ISLAND

Nelson
Nelson

Blenheim
Marlborough

Westport

Reefton

Greymouth

Kaikoura

Hokitika
Ross

Cheviot

West Coast (Westland)

Canterbury

Kaiapoi
CHRISTCHURCH
Lyttelton
Banks Peninsula
Akaroa

Timaru

Waimate

Queenstown   Cromwell
Otago   Oamaru

Fiordland

Roxburgh
Waikouaiti
Port Chalmers
Mosgiel
DUNEDIN

Southland

Invercargill

150 km

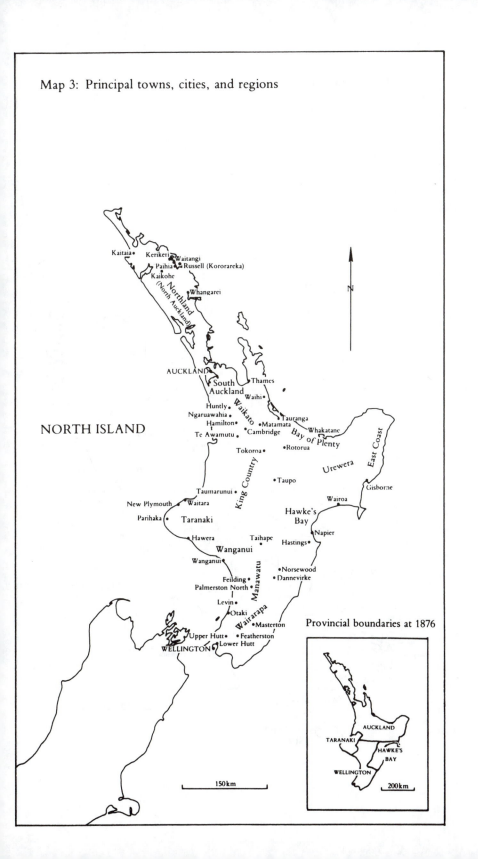

Map 3: Principal towns, cities, and regions

N

Kaitaia
Kerikeri
Waitangi
Paihia
Russell (Kororareka)
Kaikohe
Whangarei
Northland
(North Auckland)

AUCKLAND
South
Auckland
Thames
Waihi
Huntly
Ngaruawahia
Hamilton
Waikato
Tauranga
Matamata
Te Awamutu
Cambridge
Bay of Plenty
Whakatane
Rotorua

NORTH ISLAND

Tokoroa
East Coast
Urewera
King Country
Taupo
Gisborne

Taumarunui
New Plymouth
Waitara
Wairoa
Parihaka
Taranaki
Hawke's
Bay
Napier
Hawera
Taihape
Hastings
Wanganui
Wanganui
Manawatu
Norsewood
Dannevirke
Feilding
Palmerston North
Levin
Otaki
Wairarapa
Masterton
Upper Hutt
Featherston
WELLINGTON
Lower Hutt

Provincial boundaries at 1876

AUCKLAND
TARANAKI
HAWKE'S
BAY
WELLINGTON

150 km

200 km

Map 4: Physical features

Cape Farewell

Golden Bay

D'Urville I

Pelorus Sound

Queen Charlotte Sound

Tasman Bay

Tasman Mts

COOK STRAIT

Buller R

Cape Foulwind

Wairau R

Kaikoura Ra

Lewis Pass

Taramakau R

Arthur's Pass

L Coleridge

Pegasus Bay

Waimakariri R

Mt Cook ▲

Southern Alps

L Tekapo

Banks Peninsula

L Pukaki

Rakaia R

L Ohau

Rangitata R

L Wanaka

L Hawea

Milford Sound

Haast Pass

SOUTH ISLAND

L Wakatipu

Waitaki R

Doubtful Sound

L Te Anau

L Manapouri

Resolution I

Dusky Sound

Otago Peninsula

Preservation Inlet

Taieri R

Clutha R

FOVEAUX STRAIT

150 km

STEWART ISLAND

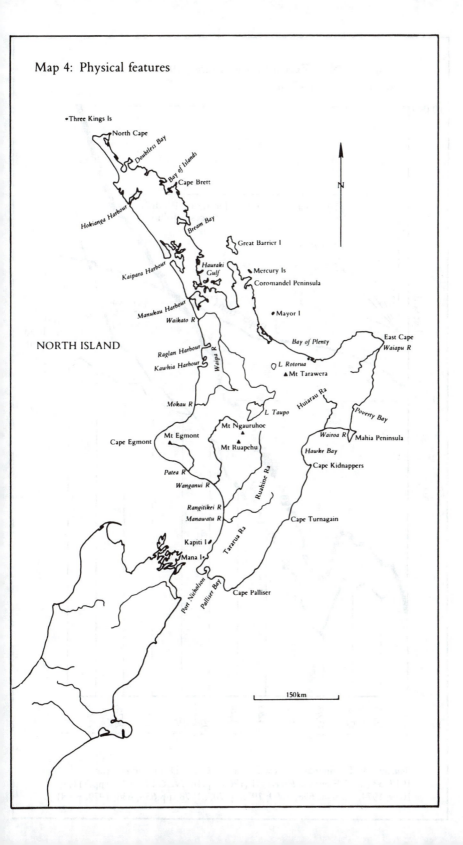

Map 4: Physical features

•Three Kings Is
North Cape
Doubtless Bay
Bay of Islands
Cape Brett
Hokianga Harbour
Bream Bay
Great Barrier I
N
Kaipara Harbour
Hauraki Gulf
Mercury Is
Coromandel Peninsula
Manukau Harbour
Waikato R
Mayor I
NORTH ISLAND
Bay of Plenty
East Cape
Waiapu R
Raglan Harbour
Kawhia Harbour
Waipa R
L. Rotorua
▲Mt Tarawera
Mokau R
L. Taupo
Huiarau Ra
Poverty Bay
Mt Ngauruhoe
Cape Egmont
Mt Egmont
Mt Ruapehu
Wairoa R
Mahia Peninsula
Hawke Bay
Cape Kidnappers
Patea R
Wanganui R
Ruahine Ra
Rangitikei R
Manawatu R
Cape Turnagain
Kapiti I
Tararua Ra
Mana I
Port Nicholson
Palliser Bay
Cape Palliser

150 km

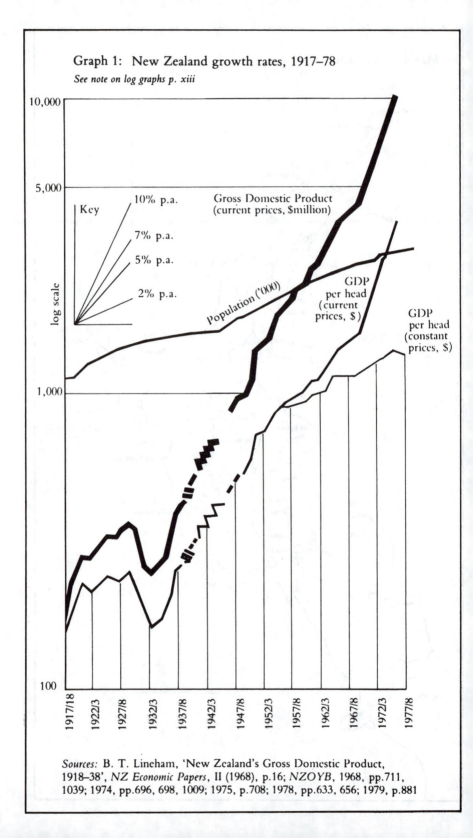

Graph 1: New Zealand growth rates, 1917–78

See note on log graphs p. xiii

Key

10% p.a.

7% p.a.

5% p.a.

2% p.a.

log scale

Gross Domestic Product
(current prices, $million)

Population ('000)

GDP
per head
(current
prices, $)

GDP
per head
(constant
prices, $)

10,000

5,000

1,000

100

1917/18
1922/3
1927/8
1932/3
1937/8
1942/3
1947/8
1952/3
1957/8
1962/3
1967/8
1972/3
1977/8

Sources: B. T. Lineham, 'New Zealand's Gross Domestic Product,
1918–38', *NZ Economic Papers*, II (1968), p.16; *NZOYB*, 1968, pp.711,
1039; 1974, pp.696, 698, 1009; 1975, p.708; 1978, pp.633, 656; 1979, p.881

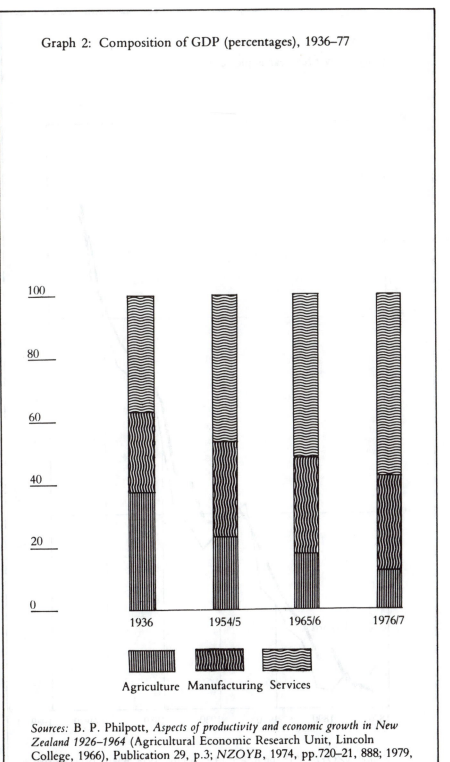

Graph 2: Composition of GDP (percentages), 1936–77

Agriculture Manufacturing Services

Sources: B. P. Philpott, *Aspects of productivity and economic growth in New Zealand 1926–1964* (Agricultural Economic Research Unit, Lincoln College, 1966), Publication 29, p.3; *NZOYB*, 1974, pp.720–21, 888; 1979, p.624

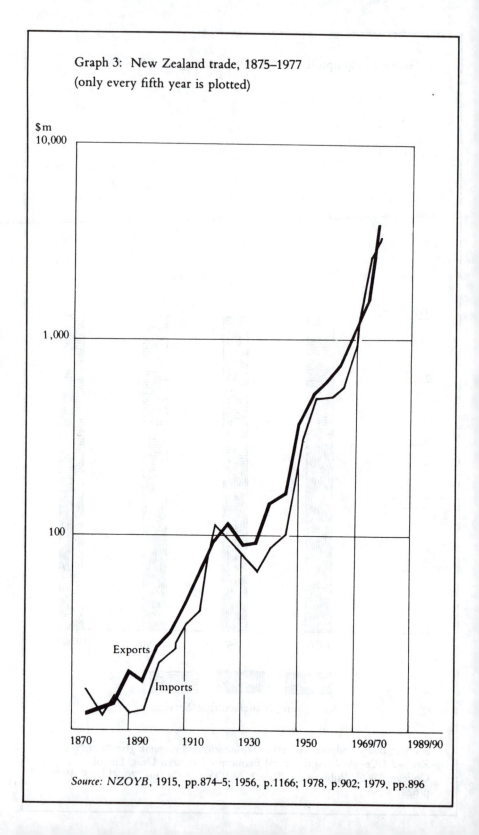

Graph 3: New Zealand trade, 1875–1977
(only every fifth year is plotted)

$m

10,000

1,000

100

Exports

Imports

1870   1890   1910   1930   1950   1969/70   1989/90

Source: NZOYB, 1915, pp.874–5; 1956, p.1166; 1978, p.902; 1979, pp.896

Graph 4: Composition of exports, 1861–1976 (by value)

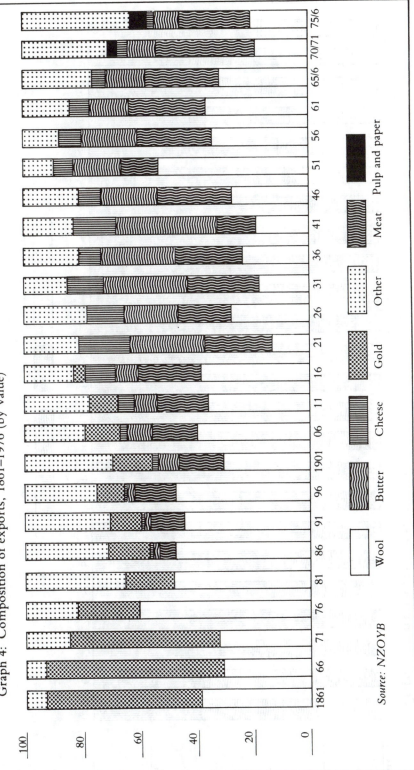

Source: *NZOYB*

Wool   Butter   Cheese   Gold   Other   Meat   Pulp and paper

Graph 5: Direction of exports, 1861–1976

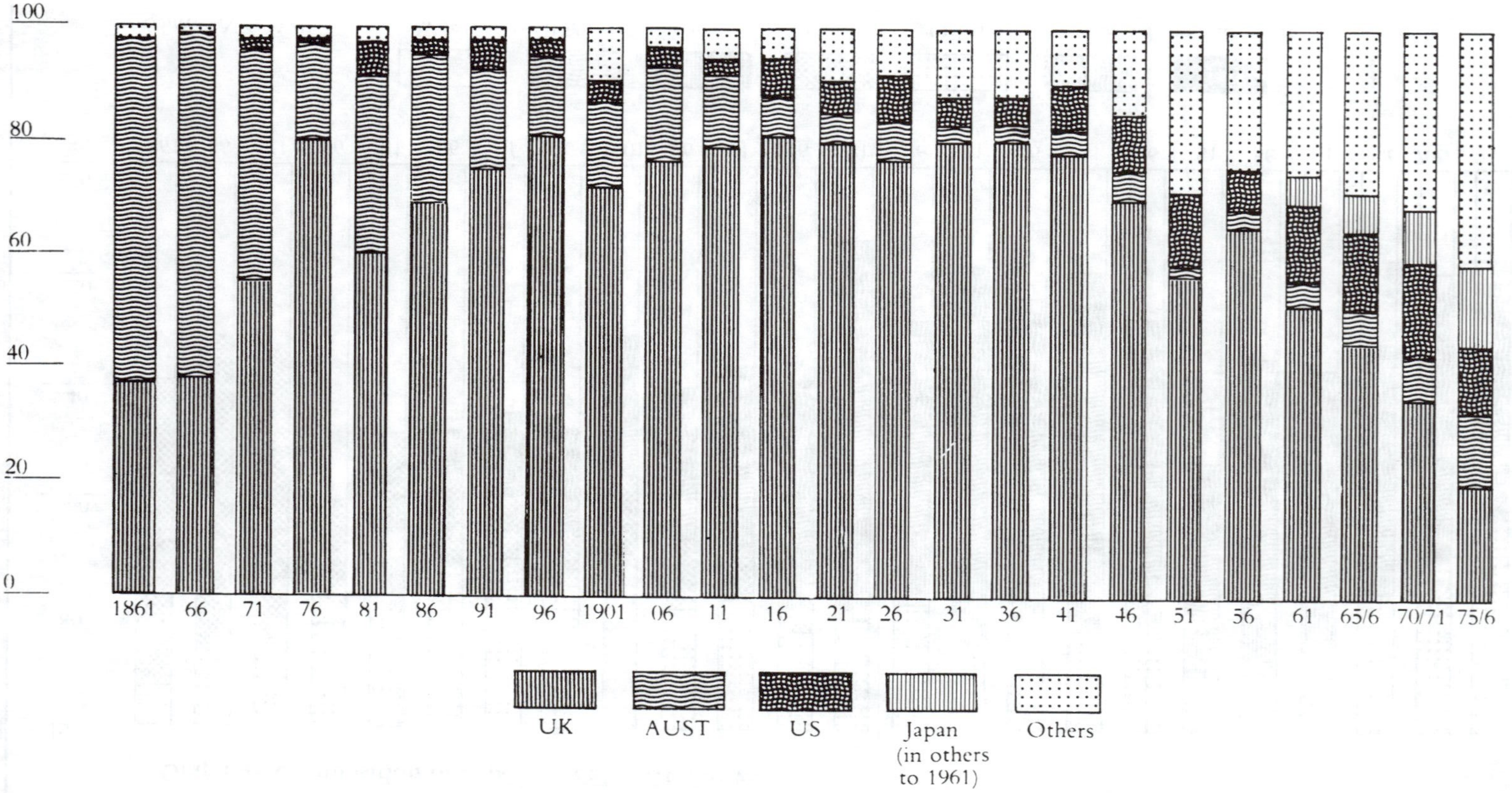

Graph 6: Direction of imports, 1861-1976

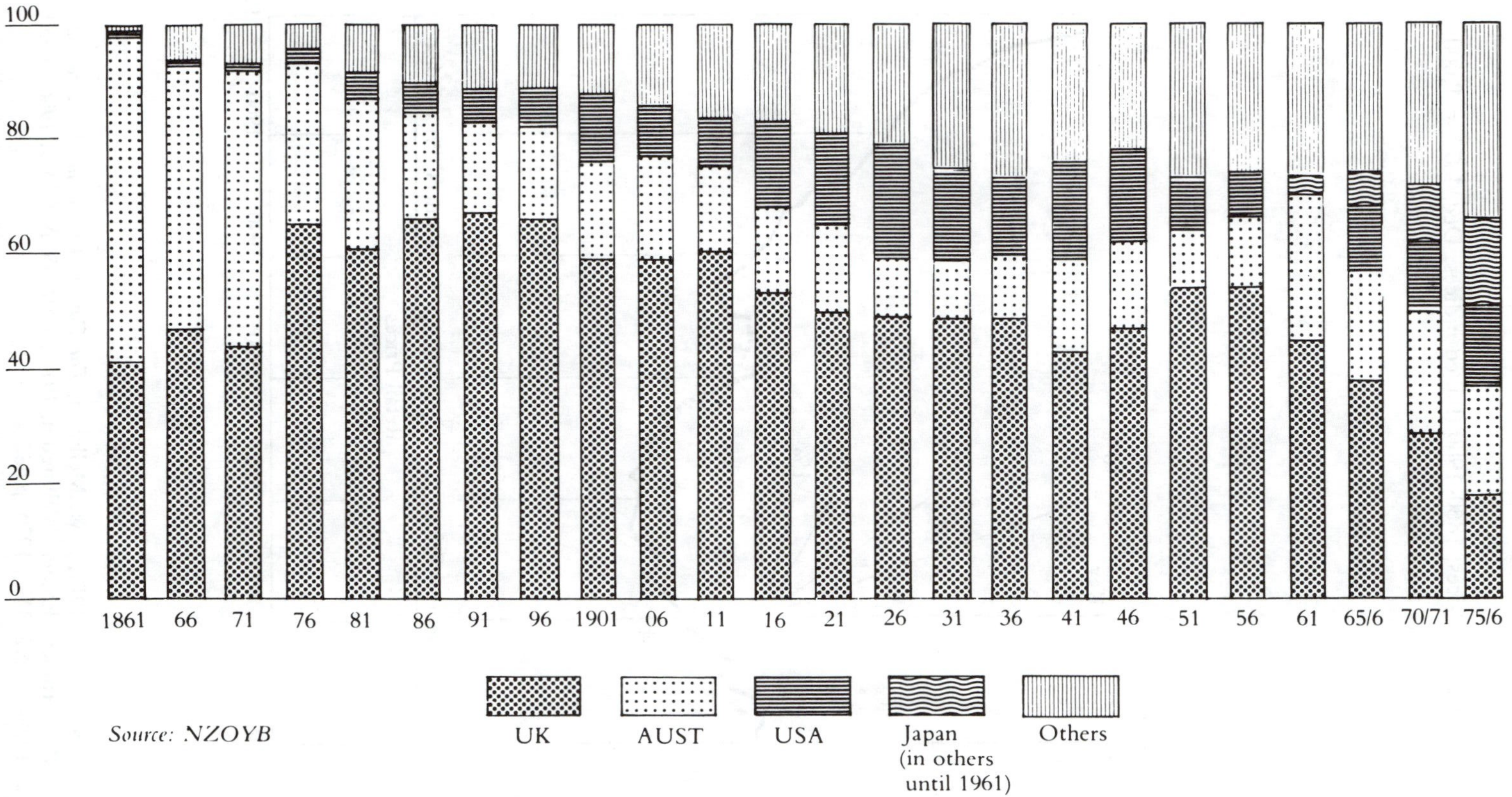

Source: *NZOYB*

UK   AUST   USA   Japan (in others until 1961)   Others

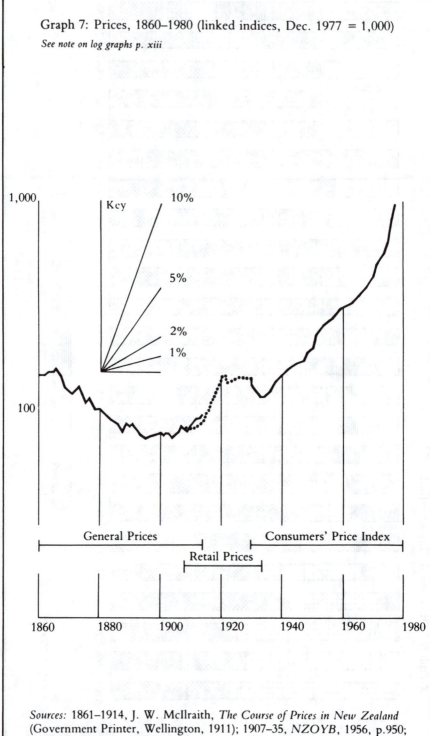

Graph 7: Prices, 1860–1980 (linked indices, Dec. 1977 = 1,000)
See note on log graphs p. xiii

Key
10%
5%
2%
1%

1,000

100

General Prices   Consumers' Price Index

Retail Prices

1860   1880   1900   1920   1940   1960   1980

Sources: 1861–1914, J. W. McIlraith, *The Course of Prices in New Zealand* (Government Printer, Wellington, 1911); 1907–35, *NZOYB*, 1956, p.950; 1929–78, *NZOYB*, 1979, p.887

Graph 8: Enumerated population at five-yearly censuses

Number (Million)

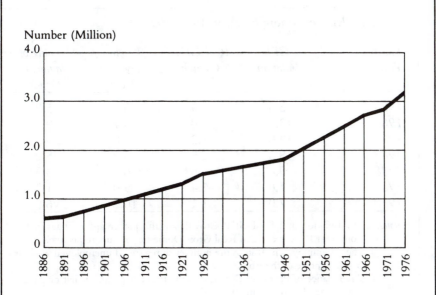

Note: No censuses were taken in 1931 and 1941.

Source: NZOYB, 1980, p. 56

Statistical Appendix

Table 1: Macroeconomic policy, 1984–1990

March Year	CPI Inflation	Real GDP Growth	Unem- ployment Rate	Balance of Payments Deficit
1984	3.5	2.9	5.7	5.8
1985	13.2	5.0	4.7	9.2
1986	13.0	1.2	3.8	9.4
1987	18.3	2.5	5.2	5.2
1988	9.0	0.5	6.3	3.3
1989	4.0	-1.4	9.0	1.3
1990	7.0	1.1	10.2	6.0

Notes: CPI Inflation and Real GDP Growth are the percentage changes in the Consumer Price Index and Real Gross Domestic Product respectively.
The Unemployment Rate is the number of registered unemployed workers as a percentage of the labour force.
The Balance of Payments Deficit is the Current Account Deficit given as a percentage of Gross Domestic Product.

Source: Dalziel and Lattimore (1991)

Table 2: Composition of GDP

	1983/84	1988/89
Primary	9.6	10.7
Secondary	31.6	25.6
Tertiary	58.9	63.8

Source: Department of Statistics. This table is analogous to Graph 2, but the underlying statistical concepts and measurements have been modified over time.

Table 3:   Composition of exports (%)

	1982-83	*1986-88*	*1990-91*
Dairy products	18.4	12.4	14.2
Meat products	30.4	27.4	23.6
Wool	13.5	13.8	7.0
Horticultural products	3.0	6.4	7.7
Fish	4.1	6.4	5.2
Other food	3.2	3.2	2.6
Textiles	2.8	3.4	2.0
Wood & products	2.3	2.2	5.0
Paper & products	5.1	5.2	5.3
Energy	0.4	1.1	4.6
Mining products	0.6	0.4	0.3
Chemicals	5.0	5.4	5.7
Ceramics	0.6	0.4	0.2
Basic metals	6.2	7.1	8.7
Machinery & metal products	3.4	3.8	4.6
Other manufactured products	1.1	1.4	3.3
Total goods exports	100	100	100

Source: NZ Planning Council, National Sectoral Programme. Note in comparison to Graph 4, the wider range of goods; this would be accentuated if exports of services were also considered.

Table 4:   Direction of exports (%)

	1970	*1990*
UK	36.0	7.3
Other EC	13.0	11.8
Japan	9.7	17.0
Other Asia	11.1	30.0
Australia	7.6	18.8
USA	15.5	13.1
Other	7.1	2.0
Total	100	100

Source: Ministry of External Relations and Trade: *New Zealand's External Trade Statistics* (1991)

Table 5: Direction of imports (%)

	1976	1981	1986	1991
UK	19.4	12.9	8.8	7.2
Japan	14.0	13.3	14.5	16.3
Australia	12.6	13.8	17.3	19.5
USA	11.9	13.5	15.6	13.3
Other	42.1	46.6	43.8	43.8
Total	100	100	100	100

Source: *New Zealand Official Yearbook*

Table 6: Enumerated population at five-yearly censuses

1976	3,129,383
1981	3,175,737
1986	3,397,084
1991	3,439,950

Sources: *New Zealand Official Yearbook*, 1990, p. 129; *Key Statistics* (Department of Statistics, 1991)

Abbreviations

ACAG	Auckland City Art Gallery
AEHR	*Australian Economic History Review*
AJHR	*Appendices to the Journal of the House of Representatives*
ANU	Australian National University
ANZHES	Australian and New Zealand History of Education Society
ANZJS	*Australian and New Zealand Journal of Sociology*
ANZUS	Australia, New Zealand, United States Pact
ATL	Alexander Turnbull Library
Auckland Museum	Auckland Institute and Museum
AUP	Auckland Unversity Press
CER	Closer Economic Relations, Australia–New Zealand
CTU	Council of Trade Unions
DPB	Domestic Purposes Benefit
DSIR	Department of Scientific and Industrial Research
FOL	Federation of Labour
GDP	Gross Domestic Product
GNP	Gross National Product
GST	Goods and Services Tax
HSANZ	*Historical Studies of Australia and New Zealand*
IUP/BPP	Irish University Press Series/British Parliamentary Papers
JPS	*Journal of the Polynesian Society*
MERT	Ministry of External Relations and Trade
NAFTA	New Zealand–Australia Free Trade Agreement
NZBR	New Zealand Business Roundtable
NZCER	New Zealand Council for Educational Research
NZG	*New Zealand Geographer*
NZJES	*New Zealand Journal for Educational Studies*
NZJH	*New Zealand Journal of History*
NZOYB	*New Zealand Official Yearbook*
OECD	Organization for Economic Cooperation and Development
OUP	Oxford University Press
PNP	Port Nicholson Press
PS	*Pacific Studies*
SAS	Special Air Services
SEATO	South East Asian Treaty Organization
SOE	State-Owned Enterprise
TAB	Totalisator Agency Board
TUC	Trades Union Congress
VUP	Victoria University of Wellington Press

For theses and research essays only, the following abbreviations have been used:

Auckland	University of Auckland
Canterbury	University of Canterbury, Christchurch
Massey	Massey University, Palmerston North
Otago	University of Otago, Dunedin
Victoria	Victoria University of Wellington
Waikato	University of Waikato, Hamilton

References*

CHAPTER 1: THE POLYNESIAN FOUNDATION

1. Kirch and Hunt, 'The spatial and temporal boundaries of Lapita', in Kirch and Hunt (eds.), *Archaeology of the Lapita Cultural Complex*, pp. 9–17.
2. Houghton, 'Watom: the people'; Pietrusewsky, 'A study of skeletal and dental remains from Watom Island and comparisons with other Lapita people'; Green, 'Location of the Polynesian homeland'; Kirch, *The Evolution of the Polynesian Chiefdoms*, pp. 41–69.
3. Kirch, 'Rethinking East Polynesian prehistory'; Irwin, 'Against, across and down the wind'; Kirch, 'Problems and issues in Lapita archaeology', in Kirch and Hunt (eds.), *Archaeology of the Lapita Cultural Complex*, pp. 158–9.
4. Sharp, *Ancient Voyagers in the Pacific*; Lewis, *We, the Navigators*; Levison et al., *The Settlement of Polynesia*; Irwin, 'Against, across and down the wind'; Finney et al., 'Wait for the west wind'; Irwin, *The Prehistoric Exploration and Colonisation of the Pacific*.
5. Green, 'Adaptation and change in Maori culture', pp. 621, 624; Davidson, 'Maori prehistory: the state of the art', pp. 292–3; Sutton, 'A paradigmatic shift in Polynesian prehistory'; Anderson, 'The Last Archipelago'; Anderson and McGovern-Wilson, 'The pattern of prehistoric colonisation'; Anderson, 'The chronology of colonization in New Zealand'.
6. Simmons, *The Great New Zealand Myth*, pp. 316–21.
7. Golson, 'Culture change in prehistoric New Zealand', p. 36; Green, 'Adaptation and change', pp. 618–19; Davidson, *The Prehistory of New Zealand*, ch. 5.
8. McGlone, 'Polynesian deforestation of New Zealand'; McKelvey, 'Forest recolonization after recent volcanicity at west Taupo'; Anderson and McGlone, 'Living on the edge'.
9. H. M. Leach and B. F. Leach, 'Environmental change in Palliser Bay', in Leach and Leach (eds.), *Prehistoric Man in Palliser Bay*, p. 231; Davidson, *The Prehistory of New Zealand*, pp. 35–38. For an indication of the difficulties involved in the study of past climatic variations see Burrows, 'On New Zealand climate within the last 1000 years'.
10. B. F. Leach and H. M. Leach, 'Prehistoric communities in eastern Palliser Bay', in Leach and Leach (eds.), *Prehistoric Man in Palliser Bay*, pp. 254–5.
11. Unless specific reference is given, material in this section is based on Houghton, *The First New Zealanders*. For quotations see Beaglehole (ed.), *The Voyage of the Endeavour*, p. 278, and *The Endeavour Journal of Joseph Banks*, II, p. 11.
12. Houghton, 'The people of Wairau Bar', p. 232; D. G. Sutton, 'The prehistoric people of eastern Palliser Bay', in Leach and Leach (eds.), *Prehistoric Man in Palliser Bay*, pp. 188, 199; Phillipps, 'An estimation of fertility in prehistoric New Zealanders'; Brewis, 'Assessing infant mortality in prehistoric New Zealand'.
13. Sutton, 'Prehistoric people', p. 200.
14. B. F. Leach, 'Prehistoric communities in Palliser Bay', and 'The prehistory of the southern Wairarapa'.
15. H. M. Leach, 'Pre-European (1); the first 500 years', p. 118; Leach and Leach, 'Environmental change', p. 238.
16. Such classic works as Elsdon Best, *The Maori*, and Firth, *Primitive Economics of the New Zealand Maori*, draw heavily on nineteenth-century ethnographic accounts and present a composite picture of the Maori that is generalized in both space and time. See also Anne Salmond, 'Traditional Maori society revisited. A reconstruction based on James Cook's first voyage to New Zealand October 6 1769–March 31 1770' (paper presented at NZ Archaeological Association Annual Conference in Auckland, May 1979).

* See note on p. xvi

17. See Simmons, *The Great New Zealand Myth*, for extended scholarly discussion of Maori oral traditions; Simmons, 'A New Zealand myth', for a succinct summary of the arguments presented in the major work.
18. Beaglehole (ed.), *The Endeavour Journal*, I, p. 445; Salmond, 'Traditional Maori society revisited'.
19. H. M. Leach, 'Horticulture in prehistoric New Zealand', p. 182. These figures compare favourably with calculations based on midden analysis in Anderson, 'Archaeology and behaviour', p. 127, and Leach and Leach, 'Prehistoric communities', p. 266. See also Fox, 'Pa and people in New Zealand'; Jones and Law, 'Prehistoric population estimates for the Tolaga Bay vicinity'.
20. Davidson, *The Prehistory of New Zealand*, pp. 56–9; Pool, *Te Iwi Maori*, pp. 29–58.
21. Beaglehole (ed.), *The Voyage of the* Endeavour, pp. cli–cliv.
22. Beaglehole (ed.), *The Endeavour Journal*, II, p. 32; *The Voyage of the* Endeavour, pp. 582–3; *The Endeavour Journal*, I, pp. 415, 417; *The Voyage of the* Endeavour, pp. 188–191, 191 n.1; *The Endeavour Journal*, I, p. 432; *The Voyage of the* Endeavour, p. 584. See Jones and Law, 'Prehistoric population estimates' and Jones, ' "In much greater affluence" ', for discussion of the Anaura Bay case.
23. Davidson, 'The prehistory of Motutapu Island, New Zealand'.
24. Firth, *Primitive Economics*, pp. 96–102.
25. Anderson, 'Towards an explanation of protohistoric social organisation and settlement patterns amongst the southern Ngai Tahu'; Gaela Mair, 'Maori occupation of Palliser Bay during the protohistoric period', in Leach and Leach (eds.), *Prehistoric Man in Palliser Bay*; Salmond, 'Traditional Maori society revisited', p. 43; Sahlins, *Social Stratification in Polynesia*, pp. 139–80.
26. Firth, *We, the Tikopia*, pp. 344–72; Beaglehole (ed.), *The Endeavour Journal*, I, p. 454.
27. Groube, 'Models in prehistory', pp. 18–19; Kathleen Shawcross, 'The influence of politics on northern Maori settlement patterns' (paper presented at NZ Archaeological Association Conference, May 1971); Fenton, *Important Judgements, 1866–79*, pp. 57–79.
28. Beaglehole (ed.), *The Endeavour Journal*, I, p. 463.
29. Ibid., II, pp. 17–18.
30. N. J. Prickett, 'Prehistoric occupation in the Moikau Valley, Palliser Bay', in Leach and Leach (eds.), *Prehistoric Man in Palliser Bay*, pp. 34–6, 41–6; B. F. Leach, 'Excavations in the Washpool Valley, Palliser Bay', in Leach and Leach (eds.), *Prehistoric Man in Palliser Bay*, pp. 122–5; N. J. Prickett, 'An archaeologists' guide to the Maori dwelling'.
31. Beaglehole (ed.), *The Endeavour Journal*, II, p. 18; Davidson, *The Prehistory of New Zealand*, pp. 157–8; Leahy, 'Pa and external terraces with structures at Poor Hill'.
32. Sutton (ed.), *The Archaeology of the Kaainga*; Foster and Sewell, 'An open settlement in Tamaki'; Anderson, ' "Makeshift structures of little importance" '.
33. Leach and Leach, 'Prehistoric communities', p. 264; H. M. Leach, *Subsistence Patterns in Prehistoric New Zealand*, p. 72; Anderson, 'A review of economic patterns during the Archaic Phase in southern New Zealand'.
34. Emory, 'A re-examination of East Polynesian marae'; Bellwood, 'Dispersal centers in East Polynesia', pp. 100–2.
35. Oppenheim, *Maori Death Customs*, pp. 15–19.
36. Wilfred Shawcross, 'Kauri Point swamp'; Law, 'A Maori ritual site'; B. F. Leach, 'Excavations in the Washpool Valley', p. 124; B. F. Leach and H. M. Leach, 'Burial positions and orientations in Palliser Bay', in Leach and Leach (eds.), *Prehistoric Man in Palliser Bay*, p. 210.
37. Duff, *The Moa-hunter Period of Maori Culture*, pp. 32–66; Leach and Leach, 'Burial positions and orientations', pp. 210–12.
38. Elsdon Best, 'Maori eschatology'; Oppenheim, *Maori Death Customs*.
39. B. F. Leach, 'Sex and funebrial offerings at Wairau Bar'.
40. Beaglehole (ed.), *The Voyage of the* Endeavour, p. 242.
41. Translation by Oppenheim in *Maori Death Customs*, p. 51, original in A. T. Ngata (coll.), *Nga Moteatea (the Songs); A Selection of Annotated Tribal Songs of the Maori with English Translations. Part I* (Polynesian Society, Wellington, 1959), p. 148.

References

42. Fox, *Carved Maori Burial Chests*.
43. K. E. Prickett, 'The stone resources of early communities in Palliser Bay', in Leach and Leach (eds.), *Prehistoric Man in Palliser Bay*; B. F. Leach, 'Four centuries of community interaction and trade in Cook Strait, New Zealand'; Seelenfreund-Hirsch, 'The exploitation of Mayor Island obsidian'; S. B. Best, 'Adzes, rocks and men'; Mair, 'The protohistoric period of Wairarapa culture history', pp. 209ff.; Shortland, 'General condition of the natives of the Middle Island', p. 125.
44. Beaglehole (ed.), *The Endeavour Journal*, I, p. 438.
45. Beaglehole (ed.), *The Voyage of the Endeavour*, p. 250.
46. Sinoto and McCoy, 'Report on the preliminary excavation of an early habitation site on Huahine, Society Islands', pp. 167–8, plate 4.
47. Fox, *Prehistoric Maori Fortifications in the North Island of New Zealand*; Davidson, 'The *Paa Maaori* revisited'; Irwin, *Land, Pā and Polity*; Jones, 'Horticulture and settlement chronology of the Waipaoa River Catchment'.
48. Beaglehole (ed.), *The Voyage of the Endeavour*, p. 200.
49. Duff, 'The evolution of Maori warfare in New Zealand', p. 115; Vayda, *Maori Warfare*; R. G. Law, 'Bracken fern and kumara in Maori settlement' (paper presented at NZ Archaeological Association Conference, Dunedin, 1969).
50. Urlich, 'Migrations of the North Island Maoris 1800–1840'; Duff, 'The evolution of Maori warfare', p. 124; Simmons, 'Suggested periods in South Island prehistory', p. 55; B. F. Leach, 'The Ngai-Tahu migration'.
51. Duff, *Moa-hunter Period*, pp. 1–21; Cumberland, 'Moas and men: New Zealand about A.D. 1250', p. 166.
52. H. M. Leach, 'Horticulture in prehistoric New Zealand'; and *1,000 Years of Gardening in New Zealand*; Anderson, *When All the Moa-ovens Grew Cold*; Davidson, 'Auckland prehistory', p. 10; H. M. Leach, *Subsistence Patterns*, pp. 58–73; Davidson, *The Prehistory of New Zealand*, ch. 6.
53. Smith, 'Maori impact on the marine megafauna'.
54. Sewell, 'The fishhook assemblage from the Cross Creek Site'; Leach and Anderson, 'The role of labrid fish in prehistoric economics in New Zealand'; Crosby, 'Maori fishing gear'; Hjarno, 'Maori fishhooks in southern New Zealand'; Leahy, 'Whakamoenga Cave, Taupo', pp. 55–6, 58.
55. H. M. Leach, *1,000 Years of Gardening*, pp. 37–43, and 'Evidence of prehistoric gardens in eastern Palliser Bay', in Leach and Leach (eds.), *Prehistoric Man in Palliser Bay*.
56. Beaglehole (ed.), *The Voyage of the Endeavour*, pp. 583–4.
57. Fox, 'Prehistoric Maori storage pits'; Davidson, 'The excavation of Skipper's Ridge'; Harsant, 'Archaic storage pits at N44/97, Hahei'; Lawlor, 'Rua kuumara o Kawerau'; H. M. Leach, *1,000 Years of Gardening*, pp. 58–61.
58. Yen, *The Sweet Potato and Oceania*, p. 305.
59. Leach and Leach, 'Prehistoric communities', p. 263; H. M. Leach, 'The significance of early horticulture in Palliser Bay for New Zealand prehistory', in Leach and Leach (eds.), *Prehistoric Man in Palliser Bay*, p. 247; Wilson (ed.), *From the Beginning*, p. 90.
60. Fankhauser, 'Archaeometric studies of *Cordyline (ti)*'; Anderson and Ritchie, 'Pavements, pounamu and ti'; B. F. Leach, 'Excavations in the Washpool Valley', p. 124; Kathleen Shawcross, 'Fern-root, and the total scheme of 18th century Maori food production in agricultural areas'; Bellwood, 'Fortifications and economy in prehistoric New Zealand', p. 71.
61. Golson, 'Culture change'; Groube, 'From Archaic to Classic Maori'.
62. S. B. Best, 'The Maori adze', p. 334.
63. Moore, 'The Tahanga basalt'; Keyes, 'The D'Urville Island-Nelson metasomatised rocks and their significance in New Zealand prehistory'; N. J. Prickett, 'Adzes of Nelson argillite from the far north of New Zealand'; H. M. Leach and B. F. Leach, 'The Riverton site'.
64. Wilfred Shawcross, 'Stone flake industries in New Zealand'; B. F. Leach, 'The concept of similarity in prehistoric studies'; Jones, 'Skill with stone and wood', in Wilson (ed.), *From the Beginning*.

65. Hjarno, 'Maori fishhooks'; Davidson, *The Prehistory of New Zealand*, pp. 62–71.
66. Orchiston, 'Maori neck and ear ornaments of the 1770s'; B. F. Leach, 'Dentalium shell in New Zealand archaeological sites'; Skinner, 'Maori amulets'.
67. Duff, *Moa-hunter Period*, pp. 84–104; Leahy, 'Excavations at Hot Water Beach', p. 40.
68. Davidson, *The Prehistory of New Zealand*, pp. 90–1; Simmons, *Ta Moko*, p. 48.
69. Beaglehole (ed.), *The Endeavour Journal*, II, pp. 15, 16.
70. Mead, *Traditional Maori Clothing*, pp. 44–70. This is largely a study of change in Māori clothing since 1769.
71. Beaglehole (ed.), *The Endeavour Journal*, II, p. 16.
72. Buck, *The Evolution of Maori Clothing*; Simmons, 'The Lake Hauroko burial and the evolution of Maori clothing'.
73. Cassels, 'Early prehistoric wooden artefacts from the Waitore site'; Lawlor, 'Stylistic affinities of the Waitore site (N136/16) assemblage'. On the development of Māori art see also Mead, 'Ka tupu te toi whakairo ki Aotearoa', in Mead (ed.), *Te Maori*.
74. Golson, 'Culture change', p. 47.
75. Harlow, 'Regional variation in Maori'.
76. Beaglehole (ed.), *The Endeavour Journal*, I, p. 457.
77. Davidson, 'The prehistory of Motutapu Island'.
78. Leach and Leach, 'Prehistoric communities', p. 255; Mair, 'Maori occupation', p. 11; B. F. Leach, 'The prehistory of the southern Wairarapa'.

CHAPTER 2: NEW ZEALAND BEFORE ANNEXATION

1. *Abel Janszoon Tasman's Journal*, p. 20. For the name 'New Zealand', see Hooker, 'New light on the mapping and naming of New Zealand'; Stokes, 'The naming of New Zealand'.
2. McNab, *Historical Records of New Zealand*, II, pp. 4–13.
3. Beaglehole (ed.), *The Journals of Captain James Cook*, I, pp. 514–19.
4. Ibid, I, p. 281; II, p. 294.
5. Ibid, II, p. 171.
6. Beaglehole, *The Life of Captain James Cook*, p. 207.
7. *Crozet's Voyages to Tasmania, New Zealand, the Ladrone Islands, and the Philippines in the Years 1771–1772*, trs. H. Ling Roth (Truslove and Shirley; London, 1891).
8. Firth, *Economics of the New Zealand Maori*, p. 446.
9. McNab, *Historical Records*, I, p. 239. See also pp. 224–5.
10. McLintock, *The History of Otago*, pp. 58–9; McNab, *Murihiku and the Southern Islands*, p. 90; Tapp, *Early New Zealand*, p. 14; Howard, *Rakiura*, ch. 3.
11. Little, 'The sealing and whaling industry in Australia before 1850'.
12. Quoted in McNab, *Murihiku*, p. 86.
13. Straubel (ed.), *The Whaling Journal of Captain W. B. Rhodes*, pp. xxiii–xxiv.
14. Little, 'Sealing and whaling', p. 120.
15. *Sydney Gazette*, 23 July 1839; Entwisle, *The Otago Peninsula*, p. 22.
16. Ernst Dieffenbach, *Travels in New Zealand*, 2 vols. (John Murray, London, 1843), I, pp. 21–55; Wakefield, *Adventure in New Zealand*, I, p. 314–41.
17. Dieffenbach, *Travels*, I, pp. 52–5.
18. Figures drawing on different sources are to be found in Adams, *Fatal Necessity*, p. 249; Harrison Wright, *New Zealand, 1769–1840*, pp. 28–9; Tapp, *Early New Zealand*, p. 178; R. A. A. Sherrin and J. H. Wallace, *Early History of New Zealand* (Brett's Historical Series, Auckland, 1890), p. 215; Davidson, 'European penetration of the South Pacific', p. 394.
19. J. S. Polack, *New Zealand . . .*, 2 vols. (Richard Bentley, London, 1938), II, pp. 194–8.
20. Quoted in Owens, 'Missionary medicine and Maori health', p. 429.
21. Adams, *Fatal Necessity*, pp. 249, 29; Dieffenbach, *Travels*, I, pp. 227–8.
22. Hargreaves, 'Changing Maori agriculture in pre-Waitangi New Zealand'.

23. Varying views are taken by Harrison Wright, *New Zealand*, ch. 8; Owens, 'Christianity and the Maoris to 1840'; Binney, 'Christianity and the Maoris to 1840, a comment'; Howe, 'The Maori response to Christianity in the Thames–Waikato area'; Judith Binney, *NZJH*, x.1 (1976), pp. 75–9.

24. Alison Begg, 'The conversion to Christianity of the South Island Maori'; Howe, 'Maori response'; Oliver and Thomson, *Challenge and Response*, ch. 4; J. M. R. Owens, 'Early history of the Manawatu', in B. G. R. Saunders (ed.), *The Geography of the Manawatu* (Massey University, Palmerston North, 1972), pp. 1–24; Owens, 'The Wesleyan Mission to New Zealand'; Clover, 'Christianity among the South Taranaki Maoris'.

25. Ramsden, *Marsden and the Missions, Prelude to Waitangi*, ch. 8; Wilson, 'Papahurihia, first Maori prophet'; Phillips, 'The cult of Nakahi', p. 107; Binney, 'Papahurihia: some thoughts on interpretation'; Parr, 'Before the Pai Marire'.

26. Parsonson, 'The literate revolution in Polynesia'.

27. Hargreaves, *From Beads to Banknotes*, p. 22; Allan Sutherland, *Numismatic History of New Zealand: History Reflected in Money and Medals* (Royal Numismatic Society of New Zealand, Wellington, 1941).

28. Firth, *Economics*, pp. 110–16.

29. Oliver and Thomson, *Challenge and Response*; Urlich, 'The distribution and migrations of North Island Maori population about 1800–1840'; Firth, *Economics*, pp. 440–5.

30. *Church Missionary Record*, April 1838, p. 117; Polack, *New Zealand*, ii, pp. 431–7; Adams, *Fatal Necessity*, p. 88. The despatch is reprinted in the *Irish University Press Series of British Parliamentary Papers, Colonies, New Zealand* (Shannon, 1970), iii, pp. 60–6.

31. McLintock, *Crown Colony Government in New Zealand*, p. 22.

32. On the issue of whether the Governors had been authorized to include New Zealand in their jurisdiction, compare McLintock, *Crown Colony Government*, pp. 9–10 with Adams, *Fatal Necessity*, p. 52.

33. See McLintock, *Crown Colony Government*, p. 12, and Adams, *Fatal Necessity*, pp. 52–3.

34. John O'C. Ross, 'Busby and the declaration of independence'.

35. *Irish University Press Series of British Parliamentary Papers, Colonies, New Zealand* (Shannon, 1970), iii, pp. 9–19; William Barrett Marshall, *A Personal Narrative of Two Visits to New Zealand . . .* (James Nisbet, London, 1836); McNab, *The Old Whaling Days*, ch. 15; McNab, *Historical Records*, ii, pp. 604–22.

36. J. L. Nicholas, *Narrative of a Voyage to New Zealand . . .*, 2 vols. (J. Black, London, 1817), i, pp. 333–7; Elder (ed.), *The Letters and Journals of Samuel Marsden*, pp. 96–9.

37. Smith, *Maori Wars of the Nineteenth Century*; Hugh Carleton, *The Life of Henry Williams, Archdeacon of Waimate*, 2 vols. (Upton, Auckland, 1874), i, pp. 61–5; W. T. L. Travers, *The Stirring Times of Te Rauparaha* (Whitcombe and Tombs, Christchurch, 1906); Edward Shortland, *Traditions and Superstitions of the New Zealanders*, 2nd edn. (Longman, Brown, London, 1856), pp. 253–61; Melvin, 'Te Waharoa of the Ngatihaua'.

38. Andrew Vayda, *War in Ecological Perspective* (Plenum Press, New York, 1976), ch. 4; Urlich, 'Migrations of the North Island Maoris, 1800–1840', p. 23; Binney, 'Christianity and the Maoris', pp. 149–50.

39. Ballara, 'The role of warfare in Maori society in the early contact period'.

40. *Irish University Press Series of British Parliamentary Papers, Colonies, New Zealand* (Shannon, 1968), i (680), pp. 85–6; William Williams, 29 November 1830, in *Church Missionary Record*, September 1831, p. 206; evidence of Rev. William Yate in *Report from the Select Committee on Aborigines, Irish University Press Series of British Parliamentary Papers, Anthropology* (Shannon, 1968), i (538), p. 196; Polack, *New Zealand*, ii, pp. 35–6.

41. Elder (ed.), *Samuel Marsden*, p. 118; Shortland, *Traditions and Superstitions*, p. 227.

42. F. E. Maning, *Old New Zealand*; J. L. Craik, *The Library of Entertaining Knowledge — The New Zealanders* (Charles Knight, London, 1830), which contains John Rutherford's journal; Barnet Burns, *A Brief Narrative of a New Zealand Chief* (R. and D.

References

Read, Belfast, 1844). The reminiscences of John Marmon were published in various versions in the *NZ Herald*, 9 October–11 December 1880; the *Auckland Star*, 21 November 1881–25 March 1882; the *Otago Witness*, 26 November 1881–15 April 1882.

43. *Sydney Gazette*, 18 August 1838; see also 16 October 1838.
44. R. G. Jameson, *New Zealand, South Australia and New South Wales* . . . (Smith Elder, London 1842), pp. 187–91.
45. Shortland, *Traditions and Superstitions*, p. 234.
46. Letter written in 1839 quoted in Cheyne, 'Search for a Constitution', p. 146.
47. *Irish University Press Series of British Parliamentary Papers, Colonies, New Zealand* (Shannon, 1968), I (680), p. 164.
48. Quoted and discussed in Adams, *Fatal Necessity*, pp. 88–9.
49. Cumberland, 'Aotearoa Maori'; Pool, *The Maori Population of New Zealand, 1769–1971*. Convenient summaries of contemporary estimates of population are to be found in Pool, *Maori Population*, pp. 234–6, and Lewthwaite, 'The population of Aotearoa', p. 37. Skinner, 'The Maoris', p. 19, considered that Cook, 'who saw little of the South Island, and only the thickly populated districts of the north', over-estimated the Māori population.
50. *Church Missionary Record*, April 1838, pp. 110–11; May 1839, pp. 101–2; December 1839, pp. 286–7; Lewthwaite, 'The population of Aotearoa', pp. 45–8; Adams, *Fatal Necessity*, pp. 40–41; Harrison Wright, *New Zealand*, p. 64. A few years later, the missionary James Hamlin reported: 'From 1835 to 1838 it was considered that the population decreased; but that from 1838 to 1841 it has increased' — 'On the mythology of the New Zealanders', *The Tasmanian Journal of Natural Sciences, Agriculture, and Statistics, etc.*, I (Government Printer, Hobart, 1842), p. 355.
51. Pool, *Maori Population*, pp. 19, 109. Measles and scarlet fever do not appear to have reached the North Island in this period; Harrison Wright, *New Zealand*, p. 64. For details of epidemics, see Pool, *Maori Population*, ch. 5; Harrison Wright, *New Zealand*, ch. 4; Adams, *Fatal Necessity*, pp. 39–45; Gluckman, *Tangiwai*, pp. 161–72. For venereal disease and its effect on fertility, see Pool, *Maori Population*, pp. 93–7; Gluckman, *Tangiwai*, pp. 191–5; Harrison Wright, *New Zealand*, pp. 63, 124; Shawcross, 'Maoris of the Bay of Islands', pp. 35–43, 368–70.
52. Pool, *Maori Population*, pp. 76, 137–40; Gluckman, *Tangiwai*, p. 178; Harrison Wright, *New Zealand*, pp. 57, 72–5; Shawcross, 'Maoris of the Bay of Islands', pp. 369–70.
53. Skinner, 'The Maoris', p. 19; Durward, 'The Maori population of Otago'; Dieffenbach, *Travels*, II, pp. 22, 72–83; Lewthwaite, 'Population of Aotearoa', p. 51; Hargreaves, 'Changing Maori agriculture'; Howe, 'Maori response'; Porter (ed.), *The Turanga Journals*, p. 53; Owens, 'Missionary medicine'.
54. Groube, 'The origin and development of earthwork fortifications in the Pacific', p. 133; Green, 'Adaptation and change in Maori culture', pp. 625–9; Cumberland, 'Aotearoa Maori', p. 416; Norma McArthur, 'The demography of primitive populations', *Science*, vol. 167, no. 3921 (1970), pp. 1097–1101; Pool, *Maori Population*, p. 50. For a general criticism of claims of depopulation, see Edward Shortland, *The Southern Districts of New Zealand* (Longman, Brown, London, 1851), ch. 3. For further sources, see Hargreaves and Heenan, *An Annotated Bibliography of New Zealand Population*.
55. Adams, *Fatal Necessity*, pp. 25–8.
56. Ibid., p. 49.
57. *Sydney Gazette*, 28 February 1839; Davidson, 'European penetration', pp. 271–4; Campbell, *Poenamo*, pp. 44–5.
58. J. S. Marais, *The Colonisation of New Zealand* (OUP, London, 1927), p. 97.
59. Diary notebook of Edward Betts Hopper, 1832–9, MS Papers 535, ATL, referring to a meeting in Hampstead, 20 March 1838; Turnbull, *The New Zealand Bubble*, pp. 20–36.
60. W. D. McIntyre and W. J. Gardner (eds.), *Speeches and Documents on New Zealand History* (Clarendon Press, Oxford, 1971), pp. 10–18.

61. Ruth Ross in *The Treaty of Waitangi, Its Origins and Significance* (Victoria University Extension, Wellington, 1972), Publication 7, p. 30; Ruth Ross, 'Te Tiriti o Waitangi, texts and translations'. See also Claudia Orange, *The Treaty of Waitangi* (Wellington, 1987).
62. W. Colenso, *The Authentic and Genuine History of the Signing of the Treaty of Waitangi* . . . (Government Printer, Wellington, 1890); W. Colenso to Secretary, Church Missionary Society, 24 January 1840, W. Colenso, Letters November 1834–February 1849 MS 63A, Hocken Library; Correspondence relating to New Zealand, *Irish University Press Series of British Parliamentary Papers, Colonies, New Zealand* (Shannon, 1970), III (311), pp. 8–9; Journal of the Rev. Richard Taylor, vol.II, typescript, qMS 1833–73P, pp. 187–9, ATL; Carleton, *Henry Williams*, II, pp. 11–15.
63. *Southern Cross*, 23 July 1861, quoted in Ruth Ross, *The Treaty of Waitangi, Its Origins and Significance*, p. 33.
64. Texts and translations have been taken from A. H. McLintock (ed.), *An Encyclopaedia of New Zealand*, 3 vols. (Government Printer, Wellington, 1966), III, pp. 526–8.

CHAPTER 3: A COLONIAL ECONOMY

1. Economic developments affecting Māori within their own or European society are not directly treated in this survey. See chs. 6 and 7.
2. Simkin, *The Instability of a Dependent Economy*.
3. Adams, *Fatal Necessity*, Part 1.
4. Edward Gibbon Wakefield, evidence before the Parliamentary Select Committee on the Disposal of Land in Colonies, 27 June 1836, in W. D. McIntyre and W. J. Gardner (eds.), *Speeches and Documents on New Zealand History* (Clarendon Press, Oxford, 1971), p. 3.
5. Rutherford, *Sir George Grey*, p. 76.
6. Turnbull, *The New Zealand Bubble*, pp. 17–19, 29–31.
7. Miller, *Early Victorian New Zealand*, pp. 45–6.
8. Ibid., pp. 119–28.
9. Lloyd Prichard, *An Economic History of New Zealand to 1939*, Table 7, p. 40.
10. Ibid., Table 5, p. 38.
11. Rutherford, *Grey*, p. 187.
12. McLintock, *The History of Otago*, ch. 4; George Rennie, 'Address to Scotch farmers', 1843, in McIntyre and Gardner (eds.), *Speeches and Documents*, pp. 23–4.
13. Hight and Straubel (eds), *A History of Canterbury*, I, Section 3.
14. Bagnall, *Wairarapa*, ch. 8.
15. Sir George Grey to Earl Grey, 15 March 1849, *Irish University Press Series of British Parliamentary Papers, Colonies, New Zealand* (Shannon, 1969), VI [1136], p. 56.
16. Tritt, 'Sir George Grey's Land Settlement Policy'.
17. Gardner (ed.), *A History of Canterbury*, II, ch. 8.
18. Gardner, *The Amuri*, pp. 168, 171.
19. Cumming, 'The compact and financial settlement of 1856'.
20. Dalton, *War and Politics in New Zealand, 1855–1870*, pp. 180–2.
21. Sinclair and Mandle, *Open Account*, p. 17.
22. Angus, 'City and country: change and continuity', pp. 110–20.
23. Philip Ross May, 'Gold on the coast (1)', *New Zealand's Heritage*, III.31 (Hamlyn, Wellington, 1972), pp. 841–6; May, *The West Coast Gold Rushes*.
24. *Statistics of NZ*, 1866–70, Table 20 in each year, with reallocation of returns from south-west Nelson.
25. Salmon, *A History of Goldmining in New Zealand*, ch. 10 and Appendix, p. 289.
26. Chappell, *New Zealand Banker's Hundred*, ch. 1.
27. See letter of John McMullen to J. C. Raymond (1861), quoted in Butlin, *Australia and New Zealand Bank, the Bank of Australasia and the Union Bank of Australia Limited, 1828–1951*, p. 163.

28. Extracts from 1861 prospectus quoted in Moore and Barton, *Banking in New Zealand,* pp. 28–31.

29. Calculations based on table in Butlin, *Australia and New Zealand Bank,* p. 188.

30. G. R. Hawke, 'Towards a re-appraisal of the "Long Depression" in New Zealand, 1879–1895' (unpublished paper, Victoria University of Wellington, 1975), pp. 30–4.

31. Stone, *Makers of Fortune,* pp. 20, 22, 171–3; Dunstall, 'Colonial merchant', pp. 64–5, 71, 77.

32. Hanham, 'New Zealand promoters and British investors', p. 59, and Table, pp. 60–1.

33. This phrase was coined by G. M. Miller, formerly of the Economics Department, University of Canterbury.

34. Gardner (ed.), *A History of Canterbury,* II, p. 202.

35. Saul, *Studies in British Overseas Trade, 1870–1914,* pp. 67, Figure 4, p. 96, and ch. 8.

36. Sir Julius Vogel, *The Official Handbook of New Zealand . . .* (Wyman for NZ Government, London, 1875), pp. 14, 112, 119–21.

37. Dowie, 'Business politicians in action', p. 39; on government-bank co-operation see G. R. Hawke, 'A monetary approach to a reassessment of the "Vogel boom" in New Zealand in the 1870s' (address to Economic History Society of Australia and New Zealand, 1974), pp. 2, 25–7.

38. Estimates from Dowie, 'The course and character of capital formation in New Zealand, 1871–1900', Tables 2 and 3, pp. 54–5.

39. Estimates from Dowie, 'Studies in New Zealand investment, 1871–1900', Tables R–13, R–15, pp. 31–2.

40. Stone, *Makers of Fortune,* ch. 8.

41. Dowie, 'New Zealand investment', pp. 61–71.

42. Hawke, 'Disaggregation of the New Zealand labour force, 1871–1936', Table 6, p. 24, and Table 8, p. 28.

43. Hawke, 'A reassessment of the "Vogel boom" ', p. 25.

44. Arnold, 'The opening of the Great Bush', ch. 3, pp. 83 ff.; Petersen, *Forest Homes.*

45. W. B. Sutch, 'The Long Depression, 1865–95', in Sutch, *Colony or Nation,* p. 9.

46. Brian Easton, 'Recalculation of New Zealand terms of trade, 1862–1914' (unpublished paper, University of Canterbury, 1979).

47. Sinclair and Mandle, *Open Account,* p. 87.

48. Sutch dated his 'Long Depression' from 1865, possibly following J. W. McIlraith's 'New Zealand prices — annual average' graph (reproduced in Lloyd Prichard, *An Economic History,* following p. 182). It seems more realistic to view the gold-riches of the early 1860s as a brief acceleration in the difficult long-term process of a new colony establishing itself, and to link New Zealand movements more directly to British fluctuations. Hawke retains the term for the period 1879–95, in spite of misgivings (a) about its general applicability, and (b) about the term 'Great Depression' as applied to Great Britain, 1873–95 ('The "Long Depression" ', pp. 1–4).

49. This section is based on Hawke, 'Income estimates from monetary data', pp. 301–7, and other information supplied by the same author.

50. Hawke, 'The "Long Depression" ', p. 38.

51. Rosenberg, 'Capital imports and growth, the case of New Zealand', pp. 91–4, 109.

52. Simkin, *The Instability of a Dependent Economy,* pp. 83–4.

53. Hawke, 'The "Long Depression" ', p. 19.

54. *The Advertiser* (Adelaide), 1 September 1890.

55. Sir William F. D. Jervois to Baron Knutsford (confidential), 16 May 1888, CO 209/248, in McIntyre and Gardner (eds.), *Speeches and Documents,* p. 191.

56. Hawke, 'The "Long Depression" ', p. 21.

57. A. R. Hall, 'Capital imports and the composition of investments in a borrowing country', in Hall (ed.), *The Export of Capital from Britain,* pp. 143–52.

58. Stone, *Makers of Fortune,* ch. 7 and pp. 149, 164.

59. Eldred-Grigg, 'Whatever happened to the gentry?', pp. 11–15; Mackie, 'Prosperity in depression'.

60. Horsfield, 'The struggle for economic viability', pp. 98–9.

61. Gould, *The Grass Roots of New Zealand History*, p. 3 and *passim*; Gould, 'Pasture formation and improvement in New Zealand 1871–1911'.
62. Arnold, 'The virgin forest harvest and the development of colonial New Zealand', p. 105.
63. Reeves, *State Experiments in Australia and New Zealand*, i, p. 270.
64. Eldred-Grigg, 'Whatever happened to the gentry?', pp. 7–8.
65. Palmer, 'William Soltau Davidson'; Loach, *A History of the New Zealand Refrigerating Company*, pp. 28–32.
66. Horsfield, 'The struggle for economic viability', pp. 236–43; Scotter, *A History of Canterbury*, iii, ch. 8.
67. Sinclair and Mandle, *Open Account*, p. 115.
68. Stone, *Makers of Fortune*, p. 95.
69. *NZ Census*, 1896, Appendix A, Table ii, p. viii. This shows an increase of only 1,756 in the 'Number of hands employed' in 'Manufactories, works, etc.' between 1891 and 1896. Hawke, 'Disaggregation of the New Zealand labour force', Table 6 and 8, shows a much larger increase by using revised criteria.
70. Hawke, 'The "Long Depression" ', Table 7, p. 27.
71. Hawke, 'Disaggregation of the New Zealand labour force', Addendum, Table 4, p.4.
72. Campbell, ' "The black 'eighties" ', pp. 69–71.
73. Gould, 'The occupation of farm land in New Zealand', Table 1, p. 139.
74. Gould, 'The twilight of the estates'; Gardner, *The Amuri*, pp. 294–5.
75. Hanham, 'New Zealand promoters and British investors', pp. 74–7.
76. R. T. Shannon, 'The fall of Reeves, 1893–1896', in R. M. Chapman and Keith Sinclair (eds.), *Studies of a Small Democracy: Essays in Honour of Willis Airey* (Paul for University of Auckland, 1963), p. 143.
77. Gould, *Grass Roots*, p. 3.

CHAPTER 4: THE POLITICS OF SETTLEMENT

1. *Weekly Chronicle* (London), 22 September 1839.
2. See John Ward, Secretary of the New Zealand Land Company to Lord John Russell, 23 November 1839, *Irish University Press Series of British Parliamentary Papers, Colonies, New Zealand* (Shannon, 1970), iii, pp. 107–8.
3. Lord Normanby, Secretary of State for the Colonies to Captain Hobson, 14 August 1839, Colonial Office 209/4, pp. 251–81, Public Record Office, London.
4. Adams, *Fatal Necessity*, pp. 151–2.
5. McLintock, *Crown Colony Government in New Zealand*, pp. 99–105.
6. Rutherford (ed.), *The Founding of New Zealand*, pp. 22–3.
7. Allan, *Nelson*, p. 93.
8. Stone, 'Auckland's political opposition in the Crown Colony period, 1841–53'.
9. Miller, *Early Victorian New Zealand*, p. 148.
10. Rutherford, *Sir George Grey*, Part I.
11. William Fox, *How New Zealand Got its Constitution* (Wilson and Horton, Auckland, 1890).
12. Governor Grey to Earl Grey, Secretary of State for the Colonies, 3 May 1847, Colonial Office 209/52, pp. 247–63, Public Record Office, London.
13. Fox, *Constitution*; McLintock, *Crown Colony Government*, pp. 294–326; Miller, *Early Victorian New Zealand*, pp. 150–60.
14. Herron, 'The circumstances and effects of Sir George Grey's delay in summoning the first New Zealand General Assembly'.
15. Stuart, *Edward Gibbon Wakefield in New Zealand*, pp. 103–31.
16. Herron, 'Provincialism and centralism, 1853–1858', pp. 10–12.
17. *NZPD*, 1858–60, p. 11.
18. Arthur Samuel Atkinson Diary, entry for 18 July 1865, MS 1865–6P, ATL.
19. Herron, 'The structure and course of New Zealand politics, 1853–1858', pp. 100–1, 149.

References

20. Angus, 'City and country: change and continuity', pp. 192–9.
21. Herron, 'The franchise and New Zealand politics, 1853–8', p. 43.
22. Edward Jollie, 'Reminiscences 1841–65', p. 47, qMS 1870–80P, ATL.
23. Lipson, *The Politics of Equality*, p. 25.
24. *Otago Daily Times*, 4 September 1863.
25. Hanham, 'The political structure of Auckland, 1853–76', pp. 109–15; Stuart, *Wakefield*, pp. 111–12; for Robinson, see G. H. Scholefield (ed.), *A Dictionary of New Zealand Biography*, 2 vols. (NZ Dept. of Internal Affairs, Wellington, 1940), II, p. 248.
26. Jackson, *The New Zealand Legislative Council*, pp. 25–42, 47, 95.
27. *NZPD*, 1868, 3, p. 64.
28. Herron, 'Provincialism and centralism'.
29. Browne to Secretary of State for the Colonies, 12 March 1856, Colonial Office 209/135, pp. 256–8, Public Record Office, London; Keith Sinclair, *The Origins of the Maori Wars* (NZ University Press, Wellington, 1957), pp. 85–109; Dalton, *War and Politics in New Zealand, 1855–1870*, pp. 27–32.
30. Edward Wakefield, *Sir Edward William Stafford, G.C.M.G., A Memoir* (Walbrook and Co., London, 1922), pp. 7–10; Poff, 'William Fox', pp. 40–50.
31. Weld to Grey, Grey to Weld, 22 November 1864, *AJHR*, 1864, A–2; Williams, 'Frederick Weld', I, pp. 165–70.
32. *NZPD*, 1870, 7, 8, *passim*.
33. *NZPD*, 1870, 7, pp. 95–118.
34. J. C. Richmond to H. A. Atkinson, 4 October 1870, J. C. Richmond to H. R. Richmond, 18 January 1871, in G. H. Scholefield (ed.), *The Richmond-Atkinson Papers*, 2 vols. (Government Printer, Wellington, 1960), II, pp. 310–11, 314.
35. F. A. Weld, *Notes on New Zealand Affairs* (Edward Stanford, London, 1869), pp. 64–5.
36. Montgomery to Rolleston, 27 June 1870, Rolleston family, MS Papers 446/42, ATL.
37. Ewing, 'Public Service reform in New Zealand, 1866–1912', p. 11.
38. Reeves, *The Long White Cloud*, pp. 335–6.
39. This view is put forward by Armstrong, 'The politics of development'.
40. Hamer, 'The Agricultural Company and New Zealand politics, 1877–1886', pp. 141–64.
41. R. C. J. Stone, *Makers of Fortune: A Colonial Business Community and its Fall* (AUP/OUP, Auckland, 1973), pp. 177–80.
42. Reeves, *The Long White Cloud*, pp. 339–40; Wilson, *The Grey Government, 1877–9*.
43. Bohan, 'The General Election of 1879 in Canterbury'.
44. Bassett, *Sir Harry Atkinson*, pp. 72–4.
45. Stone, 'The Maori lands question and the fall of the Grey Government, 1879', pp. 66–70.
46. Seddon family, Papers 1850–1971, MS Papers 1619/41, ATL.
47. *NZPD*, 1882, 42, p. 515.
48. Bassett, *Atkinson*, pp. 110–13.
49. Ibid., pp. 92–106.
50. Millar, 'The General Election of 1884 in Canterbury', pp. 90–100; Rosanowski, 'The West Coast railways and New Zealand politics, 1878–1888', pp. 34–53; Stone, 'The Thames Valley and Rotorua Railway Company Limited, 1882–9', pp. 22–43.
51. Hamer, 'The Agricultural Company' pp. 154–5.
52. Ross, *New Zealand Aspirations in the Pacific in the Nineteenth Century*, pp. 106–218.
53. Grimshaw, *Women's Suffrage in New Zealand*.
54. Angus, 'City and country', pp. 432–91; Sinclair, 'The significance of the "Scarecrow Ministry", 1887–1891'; Whitehead, 'The 1887 General Election in Canterbury'.

CHAPTER 5: SETTLER SOCIETY

1. James Williamson, Recollections, MS 337, typescript, pp. 1–3, Auckland Museum.

References

2. Olson family, Letters, 1858–1889, MS 229, typescript, pp. 1–2, 12–13, 23–4, Auckland Museum; Catharine Ralfe, Life in New Zealand, 1866–1896, MS Papers 1129, ATL.
3. J. W. C. Galbraith, Letters 1880–1881, MS 110, typescript, p. 3, Auckland Museum: Frederick Weld to Charles Weld, 24 May 1855, Weld Papers, Box I, no. 12, National Archives; William Miles Maskell, Journal of Events from May 5th 1860 to May 10th 1861, 18 October 1860, MS MAS 1860–1863, ATL.
4. Charles Hursthouse, *New Zealand, The 'Britain of the South'*, 2nd edn. (Edward Stanford, London, 1861), pp. 398–400; *The New Zealand Year-Book, 1886–87* (Sampson Low, Marston, London), p. 270.
5. Sir Julius Vogel (ed.), *The Official Handbook of New Zealand . . .* (Wyman for the NZ Government, London, 1875), pp. 78–9.
6. Ibid., pp. 141, 171, 237–8, 119, 120–21.
7. Ralph Pickmere, Letters to his parents, 1860–1877, 26 May 1860, MS 815, typescript, pp. 23–4, Auckland Museum.
8. Samuel Stephens, Diaries, 1844–1854, 1 August 1844, Misc MS S5, Folder 1A, ATL; Hamilton, 'William Swainson', pp. 3–6.
9. Dr A. C. Barker's Journal, 20 September 1850, in MS BAR 1850–60, typescript, p. 4, ATL; W. Downie Stewart (ed.), *The Journal of George Hepburn on his Voyage from Scotland to Otago in 1850* (Coulls Somerville Wilkie, Dunedin, 1934), p. 48.
10. Fell, *A Colonist's Voyage to New Zealand*, pp. 36, 71, 51, 27–8; *The Maraval Jackdaw*, 1879–1880, MS, Taranaki Museum.
11. Extracts from J—'s Letter to a Friend, 23 April 1849, Dunedin, in *Emigrants' Letters: Being a Collection of Recent Communications from Settlers in the British Colonies* (Trelawney Saunders, London, 1850), p. 89.
12. Lady Eliza Grey, Letters, 1845–1850, 10 February 1850, MS Papers 860, typescript, p. 3, ATL; F. A. Weld to E. Stafford, 25–26 May 1854, E. W. Stafford, MS Papers 28 no. 47, ATL.
13. Curson, 'Auckland in 1842'.
14. W. G. Cowie, *Our Last Year in New Zealand, 1887* (Kegan Paul, London, 1888), p. 10.
15. G. B. Earp, *Hand-book for Intending Immigrants to the Southern Settlements of New Zealand* (W. S. Orr, London, 1849), pp. 38–44; Mrs J. MacDonald, *Thames Reminiscences* (Observer Printing, Auckland, 1926), p. 10.
16. Sarah Harris, Letters to her family, 1841–1847, undated letter *c.* May 1841, MS, typescript, pp. 4–5, Taranaki Museum; Emily Cumming Harris, Journal 1885–1890, August 1889, MS, 1979 typescript, p. 18, Taranaki Museum.
17. J. & J. Rust, Copies of business letters sent to merchants in Scotland and Sydney, 1852–1854, MS 664, typescript, pp. 40, 46, Auckland Museum.
18. Drummond (ed.), *The Auckland Journals of Vicesimus Lush*, p. 47; The Homeyer Journal: the narrative of a voyage in an emigrant ship from London to New Zealand in 1849, MS, typescript, pp. 70, 86, Taranaki Museum.
19. Drummond (ed.), *The Thames Journals of Vicesimus Lush*, p. 109.
20. Enid Evans (ed.), *Reminiscences by Mrs S. H. Selwyn, 1809–1867*, typescript, p. 19, Auckland Museum; Mrs E. P. Caldwell, Diary 1850–1860, MS 91, typescript, p. 21, Auckland Museum; Letter from New Plymouth, 19 November 1849, in *Emigrants' Letters*, p. 102; F. A. Weld, Journal 1844–46, 17–26 December 1844, Weld Papers, Box IV; Letter from New Plymouth, 19 November 1849, in *Emigrants' Letters*, p. 102: Ellen Fox, Journal and Letters, 1869–1876, 14 December 1869, MS in private collection.
21. Cowie, *Our Last Year*, pp. 136–7.
22. Stacpoole, *Colonial Architecture in New Zealand*, chs. 7, 10, 11; NZ Historic Places Trust, *Historic Buildings of New Zealand: North Island*, pp. 98–100.
23. Major James Pirie, Diary 1878–79, 9 March 1879, MS 427, Auckland Public Library.
24. Stacpoole, *Colonial Architecture*, pp. 8–9.
25. Hursthouse, *New Zealand*, p. 397; William Morgan, Journal 1852–1870, 24 April 1860, Micro MS 469, ATL; Samuel Stephens, Diaries 1844–1854, 12 June 1844; Robert Petch, Papers 1876–1882, 14 July 1877, 20 December 1880, Micro MS 349, ATL.

26. Mrs E. P. Caldwell, Diary 1850–1860, p. 9; Stewart, *My Simple Life in New Zealand*, pp. 65–7.
27. Dalziel, 'The colonial helpmeet', pp. 112–13.
28. Cowie, *Our Last Year*, p. 211.
29. Patrick Moran, Lenten Pastoral [13 January 1873], in Scholefield (ed.), *The Richmond-Atkinson Papers*, II, p. 338.
30. Harper, *Letters from New Zealand*, pp. 62–3; Cooper, *A Digger's Diary at the Thames, 1867*, p. 7; F. A. Weld to Humphrey Weld, 17 September 1845, Weld Papers, Box 1; Mrs E. P. Caldwell, Diary 1850–1860, p. 21; Drummond (ed.), *The Thames Journals*, p. 156.
31. Cooper, *A Digger's Diary*, p. 18; Cowie, *Our Last Year*, p. 45; Drummond (ed.), *The Thames Journals*, pp. 109, 115.
32. Powell, 'The church in Auckland society, 1880–1886'.
33. Mrs A. C. Barker's Journal, 3 January 1851, p. 22; W. M. Runciman, Diary of a voyage to New Zealand on the ship 'Hermione' 1881, 26 June 1881, MS papers 1414, typescript, p. 16, ATL.
34. Allen Curnow (ed.), *The Penguin Book of New Zealand Verse* (Penguin, Harmondsworth, 1960).
35. Evans (ed.), *Reminiscences by Mrs S. H. Selwyn*, p. 24.
36. Gillespie-Needham, 'The colonial and his books', chs. 16–21, pp. 238–459, discusses reading interests decade by decade.
37. Ibid., p. 311.
38. Emily Cumming Harris, Journal 1885–1890, 11 September 1889, p. 20.
39. A. H. McLintock (ed.), *An Encyclopaedia of New Zealand*, 3 vols. (Government Printer, Wellington, 1966), I, pp. 84–5.
40. Harris, Journal 1885–1890, 30 November 1890, p. 80.
41. John Logan Campbell, 30 November 1841, cited in Gillespie-Needham, 'The colonial and his books', p. 61; Arthur Clayden, 'New Zealand in 1884', *Royal Colonial Institute Reports and Proceedings*, XVI (1884–5), pp. 159–61.
42. Gillespie-Needham, 'The colonial and his books', p. 158.
43. Cumming and Cumming, *History of State Education in New Zealand, 1840–1975*, pp. 32, 78.
44. Towgood, 'Truancy in New Zealand'; *NZ Census*, 1891, Part VI, Table I, p. 227; *NZOYB*, 1893, p. 148.
45. Gardner, *Colonial Cap and Gown*, pp. 39, 26–34, 40–42, 59–67.
46. Margaret Richmond to C. W. Richmond, 10 July 1871, Scholefield (ed.), *The Richmond-Atkinson Papers*, II, p. 319; Harper, *Letters*, pp. 143–4.
47. Ibid., pp. 146–7.
48. Eldred-Grigg, 'The landed gentry of lowlands Ashburton County, 1890–96'; Campbell, 'The evolution of Hawke's Bay landed society'.
49. Maskell, Journal, 18 October 1860; Ellen Fox, Journal and Letters 1869–1876, 14 December 1869.
50. Mary Taylor to Ellen Nussey, 11 March 1851, cited in Gillespie-Needham, 'The colonial and his books', p. 29; Lady Eliza Grey, Letters 1845–1850, 10 February 1850; F. D. Bell, Reports and notes upon the Nelson settlement for 1849, Micro MS 531, p. 30, ATL; Mrs E. P.Caldwell, Diary 1850–1860, p. 11; Mrs E. C. Chamberlin, Letters 1869–1888, MS 178, 21 August [1878], typescript, p. 2, Auckland Museum.
51. Maskell, Journal, 18 October 1860.
52. Morgan, Journal, 24 April 1860.
53. Ralph Pickmere, Letters to his parents 1860–1877, 9 April 1877, p. 83.
54. James Edward FitzGerald, Letter to the *Lyttelton Times*, August 1852, cited in P. Clennell Fenwick, *The Christchurch Hospital: Historical and Descriptive Sketch* (Andrews, Baty, Christchurch, 1926), p. 34.
55. Whelan, 'The care of destitute, neglected and criminal children in New Zealand, 1840–1900'; Beagle, 'Children of the state'; *AJHR*, 1883, H–3A.
56. Chilton, 'The genesis of the welfare state'.

57. Drummond (ed.), *The Thames Journals*, p. 24; Ralfe, [Life in New Zealand], pp. 112–13; Chilton, 'The genesis of the welfare state', pp. 52–3.
58. Primrose, 'Society and the insane'; Gee, *The Devil's Own Brigade*.
59. *Statistics of NZ*, 1890, p. 68.
60. C. W. Richmond to Alice Blake, 9 August 1893, Scholefield (ed.), *The Richmond-Atkinson Papers*, II, p. 590.
61. Jane Maria Atkinson to Emily E. Richmond, 22 November 1878, J. C. Richmond to Emily Richmond, 12 May 1878, Scholefield (ed.), *The Richmond-Atkinson Papers*, II, pp. 459, 448; Cowie, *Our Last Year*, p. 280; R. D. Dansey, Reminiscences 1841–65, MS Papers 1138, ATL: Gregory, 'Saving the children in New Zealand'; Hoare, ' "Our comrades beyond the seas" ', pp. 77–9; McKimmey, 'The Temperance Movement in New Zealand'; Grimshaw, *Women's Suffrage in New Zealand*.

CHAPTER 6: MĀORI AND PĀKEHĀ

1. Parsonson, 'He whenua te utu', chs. 7, 8.
2. Wakefield, *Adventure in New Zealand*, I, pp. 202–3.
3. Rowley, *The Destruction of Aboriginal Society*, I, p. 15.
4. Sorrenson, 'How to civilize savages'.
5. Thomson, *The Story of New Zealand*, I, p. 301.
6. See for instance, 'A Friend of the Maoris', *Southern Cross*, 18 May 1860, and Gorst, *The Maori King*, pp. 77–8.
7. Ibid., p. 361; *Southern Cross*, 24 April, 19 May 1863.
8. Wakefield and Ward, *The British Colonisation of New Zealand*, p. 29.
9. Barrington and Beaglehole, *Maori Schools in a Changing Society*, pp. 33–70.
10. Ibid., p. 28.
11. Wright, *New Zealand, 1769–1840*, pp. 141–83; Owens, 'Christianity and the Maoris to 1840'; Binney, 'Christianity and the Maoris to 1840, a comment'.
12. Sinclair, 'Maori nationalism and the European economy, 1850–1860'.
13. Parsonson, 'He whenua te utu', pp. 189–98, 209–10, 230–1.
14. Rutherford, *Sir George Grey*, pp. 75, 102; Parsonson, 'He whenua te utu', pp. 202–9, 216, 234–42.
15. Grey to Earl Grey, 25 June 1846, cited Rutherford, *Grey*, p. 119. For an examination of the pre-1840 land claims controversy, see Rutherford, *Grey*, pp. 119–41.
16. Report of the Royal Commission . . . on . . . surplus lands, *AJHR*, 1948, G–8, pp. 1–78.
17. Adams, *Fatal Necessity*, pp. 167–72.
18. Sorrenson, 'The Maori people and the city of Auckland', pp. 8–9. The deed is in Turton (ed.), *Maori Deeds of Land Purchases*, I, pp. 268–9.
19. Sorrenson, 'The Maori people and the city of Auckland', p. 9.
20. Fargher, 'Donald McLean, Chief Land Purchase Agent (1846–1861) and Native Secretary (1856–1861)', pp. 20–21.
21. Rutherford, *Grey*, p. 185.
22. Ibid, pp. 181–5; Report of the Native Land Claims Commission, *AJHR*, 1921–2, G–5, pp. 27–40.
23. Sorrenson, 'The Maori King movement, 1858–1885', pp. 33–7.
24. For instance, J. G. A. Pocock, 'Introduction', and J. McLeod Henderson, 'The Ratana Movement', in Pocock (ed.), *The Maori and New Zealand Politics*, pp. 3, 63–6.
25. Ward, 'The origins of the Anglo-Maori wars'.
26. Wake, 'George Clarke and the government of the Maoris: 1840–1845', pp. 351–6.
27. Ward, *A Show of Justice*, pp. 66–8, 107, 126.
28. Allan, *Nelson*, pp. 241–63; Parsonson, 'He whenua te utu', pp. 217–24.
29. Wards, *The Shadow of the Land*, pp. 95–213.
30. Ibid., pp. 44–52, 266–351; Rutherford, *Grey*, pp. 99–118.

31. Grey to Earl Grey, 7 February 1852, cited Sinclair, *The Origins of the Maori Wars*, p. 42.
32. Sinclair, *Maori Wars*, pp. 1–11.
33. Sorrenson, 'The Maori King movement', pp. 44–5; for the traditional Waikato version of the selection of the King, see Maharaia Winiata, *History of the King Movement* (Ngaruawahia, 1958), and Hurinui, *King Potatau*, pp. 183–226.
34. 'Curiosus', in the *New Zealander*, 3 July 1858.
35. Ward, 'The Anglo-Maori wars', p. 165.
36. Sinclair, *Maori Wars*, pp. 110–225; Parsonson, 'He whenua te utu', pp. 230–303.
37. So far as the campaigns are concerned, now see Belich, *The New Zealand Wars* . . . (1986).
38. Grey's speech at Taupiri, 1 December 1861, cited Rutherford, *Grey*, p. 462.
39. Grey's speech at Taupiri, 1 January 1863, cited Gorst, *The Maori King*, p. 324.
40. Gorst, *The Maori King*, p. 380. Gorst wrongly dates the Koheroa engagement at 15 July.
41. This is the version reported by W. G. Mair, the interpreter who made the surrender offer on Cameron's behalf. The Māori who delivered the reply was probably Hauraki Tonganui of Taupo, not Rewi Maniapoto, as had commonly been supposed, though Hauraki was possibly acting as mouthpiece for Rewi. Cowan, *The New Zealand Wars*, I, pp. 390–94.
42. Ward, *A Show of Justice*, p. 194.
43. These are Cowan's figures (*The New Zealand Wars*, II, p. 268). Ward (*A Show of Justice*, p. 226) says that sixty Māori and thirty-four settlers were killed by Te Kooti's forces.
44. Belich, 'Titokowaru's war and its place in New Zealand history'. There is no satisfactory study of Te Kooti's campaigns.
45. Cowan, *The New Zealand Wars*, II, p. 553. These estimates are based on official figures and include about a hundred on each side for the wars of the 1840s. The actual number of deaths must have been considerably higher since Māori commonly carried off their dead, some European civilian casualties were not listed, and a good many who were listed as wounded must have subsequently died.
46. Martin, *The Taranaki Question*; Hadfield, *One of England's Little Wars; A Sequel to 'One of England's Little Wars'*, and *The New Zealand War*.
47. Sorrenson, 'The purchase of Maori Lands, 1865–1892', pp. 48–9, 51; Parsonson, 'Te mana o te Kingitanga Maori', p. 164.
48. Rutherford, *Grey*, pp. 491–520.
49. Sorrenson, 'The purchase of Maori Lands', pp. 44–51.
50. Ibid., pp. 71–113. For an alternative explanation of the opening of the King Country, which places more emphasis on rivalry between Ngāti Maniapoto leaders and the Waikato King, see Parsonson, 'Te mana o te Kingitanga Maori', *passim*.
51. *AJHR*, 1892, G–10, pp. 7–33.
52. Ward, *A Show of Justice*, pp. 228–50.
53. Quoted by 'An occasional correspondent' in the *Southern Cross*, 29 March 1872.
54. McMaster, 'Te Whiti and the Parihaka incident'.
55. Ward, 'The Anglo-Maori wars', p. 167.
56. Sorrenson, 'The purchase of Maori Lands', pp. 224–7; Ward, *A Show of Justice*, pp. 272–3, 277.
57. *NZPD*, 1888, 63, pp. 448–50 (Taiwhanga).
58. Williams, *Politics of the New Zealand Maori*, pp. 40–67.
59. *NZPD*, 1870, 9, p. 361; 1886, 55, p. 285.
60. Sorrenson, 'Land purchase methods', pp. 183–99.
61. Native Land Laws Commission, Evidence. *AJHR*, 1891, G–1, pp. 168, xxx.
62. S. von Sturmer to J. Webster, 25 January 1882, von Sturmer autograph letters, Auckland Public Library. See also Parsonson, 'Te mana o te Kingitangi Maori', pp. 73–5, 91–4, 100–4.
63. Ward, *A Show of Justice*, p. 249.
64. Ibid., p. 351.
65. Pool, *The Maori Population*, pp. 42–4, 237.
66. Lange, 'The revival of a dying race', pp. 16–70.

67. Sorrenson, 'Land purchase methods', pp. 192 ff.
68. *NZ Herald*, 28 March 1891.

CHAPTER 7: THE CHALLENGE TO MANA MĀORI

1. I wish to acknowledge helpful comments made on a draft of this chapter by Professor Alan Ward, Dr Chris Connolly, Dr Tipene O'Regan, Dr Maarire Goodall, Professor David McIntyre, Professor Keith Sorrenson, and Professor Gordon Orr.

2. The phrase "Māori political and cultural autonomy" is expressed in the title of this chapter as "mana Māori". This phrase has connotations of the distinctiveness and authority of Māori culture and institutions, and of Māori pride. It dates from a period when a new understanding of identity was emerging in response to the pressures of Pākehā power and culture, alongside older concepts of identity in terms of kinship and community.

3. Aotearoa has recently gained general acceptance as the Māori name for the whole of New Zealand, although it was in use with this meaning in the nineteenth century. The loan-word 'Nui' or later 'Niu Tīreni' was often used last century, especially in official translations.

4. McHugh, *The Maori Magna Carta: New Zealand Law and the Treaty of Waitangi*, pp. 21–30.

5. M. P. K. Sorrenson, 'Treaties in British colonial policy: precedents for Waitangi', in Renwick (ed.), *Sovereignty and Indigenous Rights: The Treaty of Waitangi in International Contexts*, pp. 16–20.

6. Translation of the Māori text of the Treaty by Professor I. H. Kawharu, in Kawharu (ed.), *Waitangi: Maori and Pakeha Perspectives of the Treaty of Waitangi*, pp. 319–20.

7. Bruce Biggs, 'Humpty-Dumpty and the Treaty of Waitangi', ibid., pp. 309–10.

8. Williams, David V. 'Te Tiriti o Waitangi — unique relationship between Crown and tangata whenua?', in Kawharu (ed.), *Waitangi: Maori and Pakeha Perspectives of the Treaty of Waitangi*, pp. 79–80.

9. Pool, *Te Iwi Maori: A New Zealand Population Past, Present and Projected*, pp. 42–58. The Māori population may have reached 100,000 at the time of European contact.

10. Church Register of Native Population 1846, MS 63, Auckland Institute and Museum; J. Irwin, 'John Alexander Wilson: first resident missionary in Opotiki-Whakatane, 1840–1851', *Historical Review (Journal of the Whakatane and District Historical Society)*, vol. 15, no. 3 (1967), p. 163.

11. Dacker, *The People of the Place: Mahika Kai*, pp. 8–13.

12. T. O'Regan, *Ka Korero o Mua o Kaitahu Whanui*, Evidence given before the Waitangi Tribunal in respect of the Ngāi Tahu claim (Wai 27), no. A27 (1987) p. 12; O'Regan, 'Te Kupenga o Nga Tupuna', in Wilson (ed.), *From the Beginning*, pp. 22–4.

13. Api Mahuika, 'Leadership: inherited and achieved', in King (ed.), *Te Ao Hurihuri: The World Moves On*, pp. 86–113.

14. The authorities cited here are the late John Rangihau of Tūhoe, and Professor I. H. Kawharu of Ngāti Whātua. See *Report of the Waitangi Tribunal on the Orakei Claim* (Wai 9), pp. 131–3.

15. *The Te Roroa Report 1992*, Waitangi Tribunal report (Wai 38), p. 7; Ballara, 'The origins of Ngāti Kahungunu', pp. 18–21.

16. Anderson, 'Towards an explanation of protohistoric social organisation and settlement patterns amongst the southern Ngāi Tahu', pp. 3–23.

17. Jackson, *The Maori and the Criminal Justice System: A New Perspective: He Whaipaanga Hou*, Part 2, pp. 33–44.

18. Dalton, *War and Politics in New Zealand, 1855–1870*, p. 242; McIntyre, *The Commonwealth of Nations: Origins and Impact, 1869–1971*, p. 58.

19. Morrell, *British Colonial Policy in the Mid-Victorian Age*, p. 374.

20. Adams, *Fatal Necessity*, pp. 210–13, 236–45; Ward, *A Show of Justice*, pp. 34–9. The explanation of 'amalgamation' is Henry Sewell's, in *NZPD*, 29 August 1870, p. 361.

21. Ann Parsonson, *Nga Whenua Tautohetohe o Taranaki: Land and Conflict in Taranaki, 1839–59*, Revision of Report no. 1 to the Waitangi Tribunal (Wai 143), no. A1a (1991) pp. 14–28; Ward, *A Report on the Historical Evidence: The Ngai Tahu Claim, Wai 27*, p. 75.

22. Parsonson, *Nga Whenua Tautohetohe o Taranaki*, pp. 46–66, 209–10; Tonk, 'The first New Zealand land commissions, 1840–1845', pp. 130, 172–3.

23. Ibid., pp. 222–37.

24. Evidence of Neville Gilmore, Wellington Tenths claim before the Waitangi Tribunal (Wai 145), no. A 11 (1991), pp. 52–9.

25. Parsonson, *Nga Whenua Tautohetohe o Taranaki*, pp. 184–93.

26. *The Ngai Tahu Report, 1991*, Waitangi Tribunal Report (Wai 27), pp. 257–61.

27. Clause 5 of the March 1844 proclamation stated that the purchaser should convey one tenth of the land purchased to the Crown 'for public purposes, especially the future benefit of the aborigines'. In his public statements, however, FitzRoy made it clear that he intended the 'tenth' to be managed by Trustees, for the benefit of Māori. *New Zealand Government Gazette*, 26 March 1844. See also Ann Parsonson, *Further Evidence in Respect of the Otakou Tenths*, Ngāi Tahu claim before the Waitangi Tribunal (Wai 27), no. R35 (1989), pp. 15–17.

28. Grey to Grey, 19 June 1847, IUP/BPP, vol. 5, pp. 663–5.

29. McHugh, *The Maori Magna Carta: New Zealand Law and the Treaty of Waitangi*, pp. 97–112. The Court found, predictably, that a Governor could not waive the Crown's right of pre-emption by proclamation.

30. *Lyttelton Times*, 4 November 1857.

31. Angela Ballara, 'Hine-i-paketia' and 'Te Hapuku', in *The Dictionary of New Zealand Biography*, vol. 1, pp. 190, 444.

32. *The Ngai Tahu Report, 1991*, Waitangi Tribunal Report, pp. 51–76.

33. In 1843 the Land Claims Commissioner estimated that Ngāi Tahu had sold only a few hundred acres at Port Akaroa to the French in 1840, as well as land at Port Levy, Port Cooper, and Pigeon Bay. The Waitangi Tribunal recently re-estimated the extent of the purchases at nearer 3,000 acres in total. Ibid., pp. 540–1.

34. Ibid., pp. 83–99, and ch. 9.

35. Ibid., pp. 42, 98–9, 114, 118–19, 827.

36. Ward, *A Report on the Historical Evidence: The Ngai Tahu Claim, Wai 27*, pp. 242–4.

37. Parsonson, *Nga Whenua Tautohetohe o Taranaki*, pp. 194–5.

38. Bagnall, *Wairarapa*, pp. 84–105.

39. McLean to Parris, 26 August 1857, *AJHR*, 1861, C–1, pp. 211–3.

40. See for instance the Government's Manifesto, *AJHR*, 1860, E–3, pp. 21–2; also ibid. (1861), C–1, pp. 224–5.

41. Ann Parsonson, 'Wiremu Kingi Te Rangitake', in *The Dictionary of New Zealand Biography*, vol. 1, pp. 499–502.

42. Wi Tamihana to the Governor of Auckland, 7 June 1861, *AJHR*, 1861, E–1B, pp. 18–19. See also statement of Tamihana, ibid., pp. 13–17 and Deuteronomy 17.15, a favourite text of Tamihana.

43. Papers relative to the right of aboriginal natives to the elective franchise, *AJHR*, 1860, E–7.

44. Gore Browne promised to reconvene the assembly the following year, but it never was reconvened by the Government. See Orange, 'The Covenant of Kohimarama', p. 76.

45. These were government labels. Kingi was classified as a 'non-owner' on the grounds that he had not pointed out his claims and invited investigation of them.

46. The right of an individual to sell land was also justified by the Government on the basis of a specious discussion of the wording of the pre-emption clause in the Māori language version of the Treaty. See [F. D. Bell, Frederick Whitaker and T. G. Browne], *Notes on Sir William Martin's Pamphlet Entitled the Taranaki Question*, published for the New Zealand Government, Auckland (1861) (Hocken Library facsimile edition, Dunedin, 1968). See also Gore Browne to Secretary of State, 4 December 1860, IUP/BPP, vol. 12, p. 196.

47. Belich, *The New Zealand Wars*, pp. 291–8.
48. Ibid., ch. 6–7 and pp. 166–176.
49. Grey to Newcastle, 24 February 1863, and enclosures, *AJHR*, 1863, E–3, pp. 12–16.
50. Sewell, *The New Zealand Native Rebellion*, pp. 2, 15–19.
51. Frederick Whitaker, Memorandum to the Governor, 4 January 1864, *AJHR*, 1864, A–1, pp. 3–4.
52. Law Officers to Cardwell, 14 May 1864, CO 209/186, p. 219.
53. Head, 'The gospel of Te Ua Haumene', pp. 7–44; Lyndsay Head, 'Te Ua Haumene', in *The Dictionary of New Zealand Biography*, vol. 1, pp. 511–13.
54. S. M. Mead and Miria Simpson, 'Te Hura Te Taiwhakaripi', ibid., pp. 453–4.
55. Judith Binney, 'Te Kooti Arikirangi Te Turuki', ibid., pp. 462–6.
56. James Belich, 'Riwha Titokowaru', ibid., pp. 541–5; Belich, *The New Zealand Wars*, ch. 12.
57. Riseborough, *Days of Darkness*, ch. 3–6.
58. Hazel Riseborough, *Background Papers for the Taranaki Raupatu Claim* (prepared for the Waitangi Tribunal) (Wai 143), no. A2, 1989, ch. 4.
59. *NZPD*, 1870, p. 361, cited in *Report of the Waitangi Tribunal on the Orakei Claim* (Wai 9), p. 30.
60. *Report of the Waitangi Tribunal on the Orakei Claim* (Wai 9), pp. 32–62, 151–9.
61. Ward, *A Show of Justice*, pp. 186–7; *AJHR*, 1891, Sess. 2, G–1; *AJHR*, 1907, G–1c, p. 8. See also Asher and Naulls, *Maori Land*, pp. 57–62.
62. *The Te Roroa Report, 1992*, Waitangi Tribunal Report, pp. 39–81.
63. *AJHR*, 1884, Sess. 2, G–2, pp. 1–5.
64. McHugh, *The Maori Magna Carta: New Zealand Law and the Treaty of Waitangi*, pp. 97–112.
65. *Mangakahia and Another v The New Zealand Timber Company, Limited* (1881–82), 2 NZLR (SC) 345.
66. See 'Kauwaeranga Judgment', edited by Alex Frame, published in *Victoria University of Wellington Law Review*, 14:3 (July 1984), pp. 227–45.
67. See *Waipapakura v Hempton* (1914), 33 NZLR 1065, cited in *The Treaty of Waitangi and Maori Fisheries: Mataitai: Nga Tikanga Maori me Te Tiriti o Waitangi*, pp. 127–8.
68. *The Treaty of Waitangi and Maori Fisheries*, pp. 160–1.
69. *Report of the Waitangi Tribunal on the Muriwhenua Fishing Claim* (Wai 22), p. 81.
70. Tony Walzl, 'Ngai Tahu Fishing; 1840–1908', Crown evidence presented before the Waitangi Tribunal in respect of the Ngāi Tahu claim, (Wai 27), no. S7, pp. 13–16, 42–5, 73–4.
71. *The Ngai Tahu Report, 1991*, Waitangi Tribunal Report, p. 497.
72. Ibid., pp. 863, 867; see also 'The Mahinga Kai Claim', in Evison (ed.), *The Treaty of Waitangi and the Ngai Tahu Claim: A Summary*, p. 43.
73. Evidence of Walzl, 'Ngai Tahu Fishing, 1840–1908', p. 87.
74. *The Treaty of Waitangi and Maori Fisheries*, pp. 147–53.
75. See ibid., p. 165; John Te H. Grace, *Tuwharetoa: The History of the Maori People of the Taupo District*, pp. 509–515; *AJHR*, 1908, G–1e, p. 5.
76. Sinclair, *Kinds of Peace*, p. 91.
77. Mikaere, *Te Maiharoa and the Promised Land*, p. 106.
78. Orange, *Treaty of Waitangi*, pp. 210–11.
79. Memorial of the Māori Chiefs Tawhiao, Wiremu Te Wheoro, Patara Te Tuhi, Topia Turoa, and Hori Ropihana, 15 July 1884, [C–4413], IUP/BPP, vol. 17, pp. 109–12.
80. 4 June 1885, Hansard's Parliamentary Debates, 3rd Series, vol. CCXCVIII (Cornelius Buck, London, 1885), col. 1257.
81. Orange, *The Treaty of Waitangi*, pp. 219–25.
82. See The Native Rights Act 1894 in New Zealand Parliament, *Bills Thrown Out: 1894* (Government Printer, Wellington, 1894); The Native Rights Act 1895, *Bills Thrown Out: 1895* (Government Printer, Wellington, 1895); and The Native Rights Act 1896, *Bills Thrown Out: 1896* (Government Printer, Wellington, 1896).

CHAPTER 8: PARTIES AND POLITICAL CHANGE

1. Merrett, 'A reappraisal of the 1890 maritime strike in New Zealand'; H. O. Roth, *Trade Unions in New Zealand, Past and Present* (Reed, Wellington, 1973), pp. 13–16.
2. *Lyttelton Times*, 6 December 1890.
3. W. J. Gardner, 'Colonial conservatism: the New Zealand experience, 1890–1912' (paper presented to the 38th ANZAAS Congress, Hobart, 1965), p. 4.
4. For a discussion of these themes and their application to Australia, see J. D. Rickard, *Class and Politics: New South Wales, Victoria and the Early Commonwealth, 1890–1910* (ANU, Canberra, 1976). See also Robinson, 'Class voting in New Zealand'.
5. This paragraph is based on Angus, 'City and country: change and continuity', pp. 492–563. The relevance of class attitudes in 1890 is much debated. See Oliver, 'Reeves, Sinclair and the social pattern'; Olssen, 'The "working class" in New Zealand'; W. H. Oliver, 'Class in New Zealand', *NZJH*, VIII. 2 (1974), pp. 182–3; C. Campbell, 'The working class and the Liberal Party in 1890'.
6. *Lyttelton Times*, 13 November 1890; Sinclair, *William Pember Reeves*, p. 114.
7. Francis Hayter Diaries, 1843–1891, 5 December 1890, Micro MS 244, ATL.
8. For a discussion of the election in the countryside, see Angus, 'City and country', pp. 535–56; Scotter, *A History of Canterbury*, III, pp. 186–90.
9. *Lyttelton Times*, 6 December 1890.
10. Gardner, 'Colonial conservatism', p. 4.
11. Sinclair, *Reeves,* pp. 127–93; Bassett, *Sir Harry Atkinson*, pp. 163–72; William Pember Reeves, *The Long White Cloud* (George Allen and Unwin, London, 1950), pp. 285–6.
12. Gardner, 'Colonial conservatism'; Sinclair, *Reeves*, pp. 149–50; McDonald, 'New Zealand land legislation'.
13. Shannon, 'The Liberal succession crisis in New Zealand, 1893'; Sinclair, *Reeves*, pp. 165–76; Reeves, *Long White Cloud*, pp. 295–7.
14. D. A. Hamer, 'Sir Robert Stout and the Labour question, 1870–1893', in Chapman and Sinclair (eds.), *Studies of a Small Democracy*; Sinclair, *Reeves*, pp. 177–93; Pearson, 'The political labour movement in Dunedin, 1890–1896'; Angus, 'City and country', pp. 572–99.
15. W. D. McIntyre and W. J. Gardner (eds.), *Speeches and Documents on New Zealand History* (Clarendon Press, Oxford, 1971), p. 204.
16. Grimshaw, *Women's Suffrage in New Zealand*, p. 89.
17. Ibid., pp. 74–123; Sinclair, *Reeves*, pp. 179–81.
18. Gardner, *The Farmer Politician in New Zealand History*, p. 5. On the 1893 general election see: Sinclair, *Reeves*, pp. 186–93; Angus, 'City and country', pp. 564–630; Downey, 'The 1893 general election in Canterbury'; R. T. Shannon, 'The fall of Reeves, 1893–1896', in Chapman and Sinclair (eds.), *Studies of a Small Democracy*, pp. 130–1.
19. Albert Métin, *Socialism Without Doctrine*, trs. Russel Ward (Alternative Publishing Co-operative, Sydney, 1977), p. 71.
20. Shannon, 'The fall of Reeves', pp. 127–52; Sinclair, *Reeves*, pp. 182–213; Oliver, 'Reeves, Sinclair and the social pattern', pp. 163–78. For the origins of the I. C. and A. Act, see Sinclair, *Reeves*, pp. 105–6, 110–12, 151–53; Holt, 'The political origins of compulsory arbitration in New Zealand'.
21. Sinclair, *Reeves*, p. 217.
22. Burdon, *King Dick*, p. 132.
23. Gardner, 'Colonial conservatism', p. 11.
24. Cleveland, 'An early New Zealand farmers' pressure group', pp. 69–82; Duncan, 'The New Zealand Farmers' Union as a political pressure group, 1900–1912', pp. 1–14; Brooking, 'Agrarian businessmen organise', pp. 320–64.
25. Cited by Rudman, 'Employer organisations', pp. 58, 64.
26. Gibbons, ' "Turning tramps into taxpayers" '.
27. Rosenberg, 'An early view of the New Zealand system of industrial conciliation and

arbitration'; Henry Broadhead, *State Regulation of Labour and Labour Disputes in New Zealand: A Description and a Criticism* . . . (Whitcombe and Tombs, Christchurch, 1908); Woods, *Industrial Conciliation and Arbitration in New Zealand*, pp. 48–80; Williams, 'Industrial militancy in New Zealand'.

28. See, for example, *Trades and Labour Councils of New Zealand. Report of Annual Conference held at Dunedin, March–April 1907* (Marriner and Spencer, Christchurch, 1907), p. 5.
29. O'Farrell, 'The 1908 Blackball strike', and 'The Blackball coal strike'; P. J. O'Farrell, 'Politics and Coal', in May (ed.), *Miners and Militants*. See also Roth, *Trade Unions,* pp. 27–30; R. C. J. Stone, 'The unions and the arbitration system, 1900–1937', in Chapman and Sinclair (eds.), *Studies of a Small Democracy*; P. H. Hickey, *'Red' Fed. Memoirs* (NZ Worker Print, Wellington, 1925).
30. Gibbons, ' "Turning tramps into taxpayers" ', p. 101.
31. Roth, *George Hogben*.
32. J. E. Le Rossignol and W. Downie Stewart, *State Socialism in New Zealand* (Harrap, London, 1910).
33. R. M. Chapman, 'The decline of the Liberals', in Chapman (ed.), *Ends and Means in New Zealand Politics*.
34. R. J. Campbell, 'The role of the police in the Waihi strike', p. 40.
35. H. E. Holland, 'Ballot Box', and R. S. Ross, *The Tragic Story of the Waihi Strike* ('Worker' Printery, Wellington, 1913; Hocken Library, Dunedin, 1975), p. 191; Erik Olssen, 'Trouble in Waihi', *New Zealand's Heritage*, x. 72 (Hamlyn, Wellington, 1971), pp. 1989–92. See also Roche, *The Red and the Gold* (1982).
36. *NZPD*, 1913, 167, pp. 275–7.
37. McIntyre and Gardner (eds.), *Speeches and Documents*, p. 229.
38. Wood, 'The origins of the first National Government', p. 93.
39. Gardner, *William Massey*, p. 21.
40. Plumridge, 'Labour in Christchurch', pp. 72–121.
41. Gustafson, *Labour's Path to Political Independence*; Plumridge, 'Labour in Christchurch'. See also O'Farrell, 'The formation of the New Zealand Labour Party', pp. 190–201.
42. Plumridge, 'Labour in Christchurch'.
43. Moores, 'The rise of the Protestant Political Association'; P. S. O'Connor, 'Sectarian conflict in New Zealand, 1911–1920', *PS*, xix.1 (1967), pp. 3–16, and 'Storm over the clergy — New Zealand, 1916–1917', *Journal of Religious History*, iv.2 (1966), pp. 129–48.
44. Chapman, *The Political Scene, 1919–1931*.
45. P. B. Hurricks, 'Reactions to urbanisation in New Zealand during the Nineteen Twenties', MA thesis, Canterbury (1975), especially pp. 49–89.
46. *NZPD*, 1915, 174, p. 226. For land speculation see Waterson, 'The Matamata Estate, 1904–1959'; J. B. Condliffe, *New Zealand in the Making: A Study of Economic and Social Development*, 2nd edn. (Allen and Unwin, London, 1959), pp. 273–9.
47. B. D. Graham, 'The Country Party idea in New Zealand politics, 1901–1935', in Chapman and Sinclair (eds.), *Studies of a Small Democracy*, pp. 175–220.
48. Brown, *The Rise of New Zealand Labour*; Burdon, *The New Dominion*; Chapman, *The Political Scene*; O'Farrell, *Harry Holland, Militant Socialist*.
49. Roth, *Trade Unions*, pp. 43–8; Stone, 'The unions and the arbitration system', pp. 207–14; Bollinger, *Against the Wind*, pp. 125–98.
50. Cited by Sinclair, *Walter Nash*, p. 74.
51. Brown, *New Zealand Labour*, pp. 78–96; Sinclair, *Nash*, pp. 72–8; Olssen, *John A. Lee*, pp. 32–5, 37–9.
52. Chapman, *The Political Scene*, p. 40.
53. O'Farrell, *Holland*; Sinclair, *Nash*; Thorn, *Peter Fraser*.
54. Farland, *Gordon Coates*; Chapman, *The Political Scene*, pp. 61–5; Burdon, *The New Dominion*, pp. 136–8.
55. Olssen, *Lee*, p. 54.
56. Pugh, 'The New Zealand Legion, 1932–1935', pp. 49–69.

57. Clifton, 'Douglas Credit and Labour'.
58. John Macrae and Keith Sinclair, 'Unemployment in New Zealand during the depression of the late 1920s and early 1930s', *AEHR*, xv.1 (1975), pp. 35–44.
59. Noonan, 'The riots of 1932'; Edwards, *Riot 1932*; M. B. Graham, 'The Christchurch tramway strike'; R. T. Robertson, 'The tyranny of circumstances: responses to unemployment in New Zealand, 1929–1935, with particular reference to Dunedin', PhD thesis, Otago (1978).
60. Powell, 'The history of a working class party, 1918–40'; Harris, 'The New Zealand Unemployed Workers Movement, 1931–39', pp. 130–47; Robertson, 'Isolation, ideology and impotence', pp. 149–64.
61. Clements, 'The churches and social policy', p. 201.
62. Reid, 'Church and state in New Zealand', p. 136.

CHAPTER 9: ECONOMIC TRANSFORMATION

1. G. R. Hawke, *The Making of New Zealand: An Economic History* (Cambridge University Press, 1985).
2. Gardner, *The Farmer Politician in New Zealand History*; Brooking, 'Agrarian businessmen organise', pp. 83–97.
3. Campbell, 'Unemployment in New Zealand'; Paul Thompson, *The Edwardians: The Remaking of British Society* (Paladin, London, 1977), pp. 21–42, 52–4.
4. William Ashworth, *An Economic History of England, 1870–1939*, 2nd edn. (Methuen, London, 1972); Donald N. McCloskey (ed.), *Essays on a Mature Economy: Britain After 1840* (Methuen, London, 1971).
5. George, 'The depression of 1921–22'.
6. Brian Easton, 'Three New Zealand depressions', in W. E. Willmott (ed.), *New Zealand and the World: Essays in Honour of Wolfgang Rosenberg* (W. E. Willmott, Christchurch, 1980).
7. The information in this paragraph is derived from Muriel F. Lloyd Prichard, *An Economic History of New Zealand to 1939* (Collins, Auckland, 1970), *passim*; Redmond, 'The rise of the Grey Valley coal industry'; Angus, *Papermaking Pioneers*; Williams, *Economic Geology of New Zealand*.
8. Meuli, 'Occupational change and bourgeois proliferation', is the source of these figures; G. R. Hawke, 'Disaggregation of the New Zealand labour force, 1871–1936' (Victoria University Working Papers in Economic History, 79/1, January, 1979), challenges and modifies them by claiming that the tertiary sector was less significant and the primary and secondary sectors larger and slower to decline. See also Hawke, *The Making of New Zealand*.
9. See Copland, 'Refrigeration'; Gould, 'The occupation of farm land'; Hargreaves, 'Speed the plough'; Hearn, 'South Canterbury'.
10. I. W. Horsfield, 'The struggle for economic viability', MA thesis, Victoria (1960) p. 98, estimated that 4,000 sheep were required, but his figures have subsequently been subjected to serious question.
11. See Heenan, 'The urbanisation of New Zealand's population: demographic patterns in the South Island, 1881–1961', in R. J. Johnston (ed.), *Urbanisation in New Zealand: Geographical Essays* (Reed, Wellington, 1974), pp. 108–31; H. C. D. Somerset, *Littledene: Patterns of Change* (Whitcoulls, Christchurch, 1974); Alley and Hall, *The Farmer in New Zealand*, pp. 87–120.
12. Gould, 'The twilight of the estates'.
13. Eldred-Grigg, 'Whatever happened to the gentry?'
14. Brooking, 'Agrarian businessmen organise', pp. 379–82, 244–9.
15. Poole, 'Return of the forests'.
16. Rollo Arnold, 'The opening of the Great Bush, 1869–1881: a social history of the bush settlements of Taranaki, Hawke's Bay and Wellington', PhD thesis, Victoria (1971).
17. Schaffer, 'Woodville'.

18. F. F. Hockley, *Farmers' Union Advocate*, Special supplement (5 August 1911), p. 6; Report of the Royal Commission on Land Settlement and Tenure, *AJHR*, 1905, C–4, C–4A, C–4B.

19. *AJHR*, 1914, C–1, p. iii.

20. Ibid., p. 275–6; Belshaw et al., *Agricultural Organization*, pp. 28–9, 433–4; Waterson, 'The Matamata Estate'.

21. George, 'The depression of 1921–22', Appendix D, pp. 227–9.

22. B. P. Philpott et al., *Estimates of Farm Income*.

23. *NZOYB*, 1935, p. 320, and 1941, p. 349; Evans, *A History of Farm Implements and Implement Firms in New Zealand*.

24. H. G. Philpott, *A History of the New Zealand Dairy Industry*, pp. 295–303; O'Connor, *The Growth of New Zealand Farming*, pp. 13–15; Warr, 'A changing dairy industry'.

25. Brooking, *Massey, Its Early Years*, pp. 13–27; Wild, *The Development of Agricultural Education*.

26. Brooking, 'Sir John McKenzie'; Rowe, 'The growth of agricultural administration'; Gibbons, 'Milk quality control'.

27. Malone, 'The grassland revolution'; Searell, 'Pioneering the pumice'; Smallfield, *The Grasslands Revolution in New Zealand*; Brooking, *Massey*, pp. 91–2; Lister, 'The eroding land'.

28. Brooking, *Massey*, pp. 80–103; Hamilton, *The Dairy Industry in New Zealand*.

29. Frequent reference was made to these two general co-operatives in the *NZ Farmer*, an agricultural weekly published in Auckland from 1885.

30. Warr, 'The beginnings of the dairy industry'; Lyon, 'Chew Chong and the butter trade'; Hill, 'The quest for control', pp. viii–6.

31. Brooking, 'Agrarian businessmen organise', pp. 373–4; Hill, 'Quest for control', pp. 7–15; Gaudin, 'The Coates Government', pp. 38, 44–8, 61, 80–88.

32. Hill, 'Quest for control'; Keith Sinclair, *Walter Nash* (AUP/OUP, Auckland, 1976), pp. 127–30, 168–9.

33. Report of the Meat Export Trade Committee, *AJHR*, 1917, 1–7; O'Connor, *Mr Massey and the American Meat Trust*; Bremer, 'The New Zealand Farmers' Union as an interest group', pp. 62–73.

34. Brooking, 'Agrarian businessmen organise', p. 381.

35. Duncan, 'The land for the people'; Eldred-Grigg, 'Whatever happened to the gentry?'; W. J. Gardner, *A Pastoral Kingdom Divided: Cheviot, 1889–94* (Bridget Williams Books, Wellington, 1992); McDonald, 'New Zealand land legislation'.

36. Condliffe, *New Zealand in the Making*, pp. 278–84; George, 'The depression of 1921–22', pp. 12–19; Bremer, 'The New Zealand Farmers' Union', pp. 154–60; Stenson, 'Origins of the Government Advances to Settlers Act, 1894'.

37. Graham, 'The Country Party idea in New Zealand politics'. For a revision of his ideas see Brooking, 'Agrarian businessmen organise', pp. 392–7, and Bremer, 'The New Zealand Farmers' Union', pp. 159–90.

38. Downes, 'Lands for the people', pp. 95–100; Muirhead, 'Heathfield and Waipati'; Orlowski, 'The subdivision and closer settlement of the Merrivale, Otahu and Beaumont Estates'.

39. Gibbons, 'Some New Zealand navvies'; Gibbons, ' "Turning tramps into taxpayers" '.

40. Lloyd Prichard, *Economic History*, p. 435; Chapman and Malone, *New Zealand in the Twenties*, pp. 18–19.

41. A. H. McLintock (ed.), *An Encyclopaedia of New Zealand*, 3 vols. (Government Printer, Wellington, 1966), III, pp. 106–7; Burdon, *The New Dominion*, pp. 104–7; Chapman and Malone, *The Twenties*, pp. 17–18; Bush, *Decently and In Order*, pp. 225 and 228–41; Hoy, 'Iron wheels in the streets'.

42. Arbon, *A History of the Union Steamship Co.*; I. J. Farquhar, *Union Fleet* (New Zealand Ship and Marine Society, Wellington, 1968), pp. 47–52; Holman, *In the Wake of Endeavour*, pp. 77–8. See also Gavin McLean, *The Southern Octopus* (1990).

43. Burdon, *New Dominion*, pp. 328–9.

44. Chapman and Malone, *The Twenties*, pp. 14–15; Searight, 'A bright new world'. For electricity's impact on rural life, see Somerset, *Littledene*, and Hawke, 'Economic decisions and political ossification'.
45. Hawke, *The Evolution of the New Zealand Economy*, pp. 20–1; Hawke, 'The Government and the depression of the 1930s'; Sinclair, *Nash*, pp. 100–1.
46. Condliffe, *New Zealand in the Making*, pp. 197–9, 265; Hawke, *Evolution*, p. 35, estimates that approximately two-thirds of taxation was indirect and one-third direct prior to the Second World War. After the war those percentages were reversed.
47. Hawke, *Evolution*, p. 18; Chappell, *New Zealand Banker's Hundred*; Sinclair and Mandle, *Open Account*; Butlin, *Australia and New Zealand Bank*.
48. *Auckland Savings Bank Centenary, 1847–1947* (Whitcombe and Tombs, Auckland, 1947); H. E. Carey, *New Plymouth Savings Bank Centenary, 1850–1950* (Taranaki Daily News, New Plymouth, 1950); *Dunedin Savings Bank Centenary, 1864–1964* (Whitcombe and Tombs, Dunedin, 1964); Robinson, *A History of the Post Office in New Zealand*, pp. 260–62.
49. Somerset, *Littledene*, pp. 16–20; Angus, *Donald Reid Otago Farmers' Limited*, pp. 71–7, 95; Parry, *N.M.A.*, pp. 161–9; Irving, *A Century's Challenge*, pp. 149–51.
50. On insurance companies see, for example, Vennell, *Tower of Strength*, pp. 76, 144–5; Vennell, *Risks and Rewards*.
51. *NZOYB*, 1939, p. 625.
52. Rogerson, ' "Cosy homes multiply" ', Appendix B.
53. See, for example, Brasch and Nicolson, *Hallensteins — The First Century*.
54. Hawke, *Between Governments and Banks*; Sinclair, *Nash*, pp. 101–7, 243–4.
55. On secondary industries and manufacturing, see Angus, *Papermaking Pioneers* and *The Ironmasters*; Blyth, 'The industrialisation of New Zealand'; Castle, *A Study of New Zealand Manufacturing*; Hawke, 'Disaggregation of the New Zealand labour force' and 'Long-term trends in New Zealand imports'; Lineham, 'New Zealand's Gross Domestic Product'; B. P. Philpott, *Aspects of Productivity and Economic Growth in New Zealand*.
56. By 1926, 12.7 per cent of the work-force was employed by the central government. Leslie Lipson, *The Politics of Equality: New Zealand's Adventures in Democracy* (University of Chicago Press, 1947), p. 369.
57. Graham, 'The Country Party idea'; Brooking, 'Agrarian businessmen organise', pp. 300–91, 398–400.
58. Hawke, 'Economic decisions', p. 232; Rogerson, ' "Cosy homes multiply" ', p. 179.
59. Report of the Dairy Industry Commission, *AJHR*, 1934, H–30; Condliffe, *Welfare State*; B. P. Philpott et al., *Estimates of Farm Income and Productivity in New Zealand*.
60. Robertson, 'The tyranny of circumstances', pp. 275–325, on the forgotten unemployed, boys, women, and Māori, and Appendix IV, pp. 465–9. Robertson argues for 15 per cent; Macrae and Sinclair, 'Unemployment in New Zealand', prefer 12 per cent.
61. Condliffe, *New Zealand in the Making*, pp. 44–9, 276–84. See also C. B. Schedvin, 'The long and the short of depression origins', in Robert Cooksey (ed.), *The Great Depression in Australia* (ANU, Canberra, 1970), pp. 418–19
62. Margaret Galt, 'Wealth and income in New Zealand, c. 1870 to c. 1939,' PhD thesis, Victoria (1985)
63. See, for example, Warwick Armstrong, 'New Zealand: imperialism, class and uneven development', *ANZJS*, xiv.3 (1978), pp. 297–303; Donald Denoon, *Settler Capitalism: The Dynamics of Dependent Development in the Southern Hemisphere* (OUP, 1983), and W. B. Sutch, *Colony or Nation? Economic Crises in New Zealand from the 1860s to the 1960s: addresses and papers*, ed. Michael Turnbull, 2nd. ed. (Sydney University Press, 1968).

CHAPTER 10: TOWARDS A NEW SOCIETY

1. I am grateful to the University of Otago for a Summer Research Fellowship which

allowed me to recruit the assistance of Stephen Clarke. He has helped me to update the notes and bibliography.

2. Report of the Committee of the Board of Health to Study Venereal Diseases, *AJHR*, 1922, H–31A, pp. 11–12; Philip Fleming, 'Fighting the "red plague": observations on the response to venereal disease in New Zealand, 1910–1945', *NZJH*, xxii.1 (1988), pp. 56–64.

3. Hurricks, 'Reactions to urbanisation in New Zealand during the 1920s'.

4. Marion J. Levy, Jr., *Modernization and the Structure of Societies* (Princeton University Press, 1966); E. A. Wrigley, 'The process of modernization and the industrial revolution in England', *Journal of Interdisciplinary History*, iii.2 (1972), pp. 225–9; Talcott Parsons, *The Social System* (The Free Press, Glencoe, Ill., 1951), pp. 58–67.

5. See especially the essays by Ian Weinberg and Charles Tilly in Edward B. Harvey, *Perspectives on Modernization: Essays in Memory of Ian Weinberg* (University of Toronto Press, Toronto, 1972).

6. In New Zealand, as in other societies, the word 'efficiency' denoted the imperative but that concept is not pursued here because of the editorial decision made in 1978 to separate social structure from culture.

7. I am indebted to Harvey, *Perspectives on Modernization*; Raymond Grew, 'More on modernization', *Journal of Social History* xiv.2 (1980), pp. 179–88; Peter Stearns, 'Modernization and social history: some suggestions, and a muted cheer', ibid., pp. 189–210; and Tamara Hareven, *Transitions: The Family and the Life Course in Historical Perspective* (Academic Press, New York, 1978).

8. Heenan, 'The urbanisation of New Zealand's population', pp. 116–21, and Olssen, 'Women, work, and society, 1880–1926', in Phillida Bunkle and Beryl Hughes, *Women in New Zealand Society* (Allen and Unwin, Wellington, 1981), pp. 159–83.

9. Heenan, 'Urbanisation', pp. 121–4; Heenan and Trlin, 'Population, society and economy'.

10. M. F. Lloyd Prichard, *An Economic History of New Zealand to 1939* (Collins, Auckland, 1939), p. 269.

11. Gilson, 'The changing New Zealand family'; Olssen and Levesque, 'Towards a history of the European family in New Zealand', p. 2; Phillipa Mein Smith, *Maternity in Dispute. New Zealand, 1920–1939* (Allen and Unwin, Wellington, 1986); for a general discussion, see Tamara K. Hareven, 'Modernization and family history; perspectives on social change', *Signs: Journal of Women in Culture and Society*, ii.1 (1976), pp. 190–206.

12. The figure of 8,000 was selected because the available evidence suggests that, as a rule, only in towns of that size or larger did class generate political alignments; see John R. Barnett, 'The evolution of the urban political structure of the North Island, 1945–1966', MA thesis, Otago (1968).

13. Clark, 'Dunedin at the turn of the century'; Armstrong, 'Auckland by gaslight'; Pownall, 'Metropolitan Auckland'; Stedman, 'The South Dunedin Flat'.

14. McDonald, *City of Dunedin*, chs. 7–9; Bush, *Decently and In Order*, chs. 3–8.

15. Arthur Myers, *Proposed Town Planning Bill . . .* (Brett Printing, Auckland, 1911).

16. Charles Reade, 'Town planning in Australasia; problems and progress in the South Pacific', *Town Planning Review*, iii.1, (1912), pp. 2–10; Richard Mabon, 'Vision and process: the genesis of town-planning in New Zealand, 1840–1926', research essay, Otago (1991).

17. Leslie Lipson, *The Politics of Equality: New Zealand's Adventures in Democracy* (University of Chicago Press, 1948), p. 423.

18. Gibbons, ' "Turning tramps into taxpayers" '; T. W. H. Brooking, 'Sir John McKenzie and the origins and growth of the Department of Agriculture, 1891–1900', MA thesis, Massey (1972); Lipson, *The Politics of Equality*, chs. 13, 14.

19. Public service of New Zealand, *AJHR*, 1912, H–34; Ewing, 'Public Service reform in New Zealand'; Alan Henderson, *The Quest for Efficiency: The Origins of the State Services Commission* (The Commission, Wellington, 1990).

20. 'Cost of living in New Zealand: report and evidence', *AJHR*, 1912, H–18.

21. Neil Robinson, *James Fletcher: Builder* (Hodder and Stoughton, London and Auckland, 1970); John Angus, *Papermaking Pioneers: A History of New Zealand Paper Mills Limited and its Predecessors* (New Zealand Paper Mills, Mataura, 1976), chs. 5–6, and *Donald Reid Otago Farmers' Limited: The Centennial History* (Donald Reid Otago Farmers, Dunedin, 1978), ch. 7; Harrison, 'The motion picture industry in New Zealand, 1896–1930', and N. Elliott, 'Anzac, Hollywood and home: cinemas and filmgoing in Auckland, 1909–1939', MA thesis, Auckland (1989).

22. Olssen, 'Social class in nineteenth century New Zealand', pp. 34–9.

23. J. D. Gould, 'The occupation of farm land in New Zealand, 1874–1911: a preliminary survey', *Business Archives and History*, v.2 (1965), pp. 123–41, and 'The twilight of the estates, 1891–1910'; *AEHR*, x.1 (1970), pp. 1–26; J. S. Duncan, 'The land for the people: settlement and rural population movements, 1886–1906', in Murray McCaskill (ed.), *Land and Livelihood: Geographical Essays in Honour of George Jobberns* (NZ Geographical Society, Christchurch, 1961); Powell, 'White collars and moleskin trousers'; and Graeme Steven, 'Swaggers and society: a New Zealand experience', research essay, Otago (1979).

24. Perry, 'Marriage-distance relationships in North Otago, 1875–1914' and Olssen, *A History of Otago* (John McIndoe, Dunedin, 1984), ch. 10.

25. Olssen, 'God's own country', in Judith Binney, Judith Bassett and Erik Olssen, *The People and the Land: Te Tangata me te Whenua: An Illustrated History of New Zealand, 1820–1920* (Allen and Unwin, Wellington, 1990), pp. 266–8 and Olssen, 'The Friendly Societies', forthcoming.

26. W. H. Oliver, 'New Zealand about 1890' (Macmillan Brown lectures, 1972), p. 17; Brooking, 'Agrarian businessmen organise', Part 3; Franklin, 'The village and the bush'; B. L. Evans, *A History of Agricultural Production and Marketing in New Zealand* (Keeling and Mundy, Palmerston North, [n.d]), Pt. II.

27. Scott to Manager Nightcaps Coal Co., 9 November 1909, Otago Employers' Association MSS, Hocken Library.

28. J. R. Barclay, 'An analysis of trends in New Zealand sport from 1840 to 1900', research essay, Massey (1977), pp. 141–5; Winston McCarthy, *Haka! The All Blacks Story* (Pelham Books, London, 1968), p. 58; Swindells, 'Social aspects of rugby in the Manawatu from 1878 to 1910'; Len Richardson, 'Race, rugby and empire', *Historical News*, December 1983; J. O. C. Phillips, 'Rugby, war and the mythology of the New Zealand male', *NZJH*, xviii.2 (1984), pp. 83–103; F. Hall, ' "The greater game": sport and society in World War One New Zealand', MA thesis, Canterbury (1989).

29. Olssen, 'Truby King and the Plunket Society: an analysis of a prescriptive ideology', *NZJH*, xv.1 (1981), pp. 3–23.

30. For these two paragraphs see Jacoby, 'A fertility analysis of New Zealand marriage cohorts'; Gilson-Vosburgh, *The New Zealand Family and Social Change*, chs. 3–4; Olssen and Levesque, 'European family', p. 16; Heenan, 'Urbanisation', pp. 111–16; A. R. Grigg, 'Prohibition and women: the preservation of an ideal and a myth', *NZJH*, xvii.2 (1983), pp. 144–65; David Pearson, 'Marriage and mobility in Wellington, 1881–1950', *NZJH*, xxii.2 (1988), pp. 135–51; Barbara Brookes, 'Housewives' depression', *NZJH*, xv.2 (1981), pp. 115–34; Christopher Pugsley, *On the Fringe of Hell: New Zealanders and Military Discipline in the First World War* (Hodder and Stoughton, Auckland, 1991), pp. 154–64; Olssen, 'Friendly Societies'; and for the quotation, Vincent O'Sullivan and Margaret Scott (eds.), *The Collected Letters of Katherine Mansfield, 1903–1917* (Clarendon Press, Oxford, 1984), p. 18.

31. King constantly repeated this promise; see F. Truby King, *Feeding and Care of Baby* (Macmillan, London, 1913), pp. 151–2.

32. Mary King, *Truby King the Man: A Biography* (Allen and Unwin, London, 1948), p. 154.

33. Tennant, 'Matrons with a mission'; Connell, 'Women in politics', pp. 51–6; Burdon, 'Sir Truby King'; Milne, 'The Plunket Society'; Strong, *Development of University Education in Home Science*; Tennant, 'Natural directions'; Susan Patullo, 'The cramming controversy in Otago, 1880–1908', research essay, Otago (1983); and S. Griffiths,

'Feminism and the ideology of motherhood in New Zealand, 1896–1930', MA thesis, Otago (1984).

34. Patricia Grimshaw, *Women's Suffrage in New Zealand* (AUP/OUP, Auckland, 1972), ch. 11; Gardner, *Colonial Cap and Gown*, chs. 3, 4; Tennant, 'Mrs Grace Neill in the Department of Asylums, Hospitals and Charitable Institutions' and 'Maternity and morality: homes for single mothers 1890–1930', *Womens Studies Journal*, II.1 (1985), pp. 28–49; McLeod, 'Activities of New Zealand Women during World War 1'; Griffiths, 'Feminism and the ideology of motherhood', chs. 4–6; Carol Brown, 'Ethel Benjamin — New Zealand's first woman lawyer', research essay, Otago (1985); Michael Belgrave, 'A subtle containment: women in New Zealand medicine, 1893–1941', *NZJH*, XXII.1 (1988), pp. 44–55; and Wilson, *My First Eighty Years* (Blackwood and Janet Paul, Hamilton, 1950), p. 180.

35. Tennant, 'Matrons with a mission'; Olssen and Levesque, 'European family', pp. 11–12; Gregory, 'Saving the children of New Zealand'; Sutton-Smith, *The Folk Games of Children*, pp. 10–13, 44–5, 215–21.

36. See Alan Somerville, 'Moominpappa got away: the state and child welfare in New Zealand, 1925–1930', research essay, Otago (1982); Bronwyn Dalley, 'From demi-mondes to slavery: a study of the Te Oranga Reformatory for Delinquent Women, 1900–1918', MA thesis, Massey (1987); Stephen Robertson, 'Production not reproduction: the problem of mental defect in New Zealand, 1900–1939', research essay, Otago (1989); and S. Bardsley, 'The functions of an institution: the Otekaieke Special School for Boys, 1908–1950', research essay, Otago (1991); Tennant, 'Missionaries of Health . . . ', in Linda Bryder, *A Healthy Country: Essays on the Social History of Medicine in New Zealand* (Bridget Williams Books, Wellington, 1991).

37. Oliver, 'The origins and growth of the welfare state', pp. 14–15; Mayhew, 'The Returned Servicemen's Association, 1916–1943'; Smith, 'The social history of community care of the disabled'; Royal New Zealand Society for the Health of Women and Children, *Annual Reports: Central Council and Dunedin Branch, November 1930* (Dunedin, 1930): Unemployment, *AJHR*, 1929, H–11B and 1930, H–11B; Robertson, 'The tyranny of circumstances', chs. 1–2; Tennant, *Paupers and Providers: Charitable Aid in New Zealand* (AUP/OUP, Auckland, 1989), chs. 6–10; Olssen, 'Friendly Societies'.

38. Hannah, 'The plague scare, 1900'; Smith, 'Community care of the disabled', p. 21; Lovell-Smith, *The New Zealand Doctor and the Welfare State*, ch. 3; Maclean, *Challenge for Health*; Barber and Towers, *Wellington Hospital, 1847–1976*; Michael Belgrave, ' "Medical men" and "lady doctors": the making of a New Zealand profession, 1867–1941', PhD thesis, Victoria (1986), ch. 6; G. W. Rice, 'The making of New Zealand's 1920 Health Act', *NZJH*, XXII.1 (1988), pp. 3–22; and Linda Bryder (ed.), *A Healthy Country*.

39. Stenson, 'Social legislation in New Zealand'; Beagle, 'Children of the state'; Beck, 'The development of child welfare'; Primrose, 'Society and the insane'; Hubbard, 'Lunatic asylums in Otago'; Cheryl Caldwell, 'Truby King and Seacliff Asylum, 1889–1907', research essay, Otago (1984); B. J. Labrum, 'Gender and lunacy: a study of women patients in the Auckland Lunatic Asylum, 1870–1910', MA thesis, Massey (1990).

40. *Statistics of NZ, 1911*, pp. 414–19; Higgins, 'The Prohibition Movement in Oamaru', pp. 10–19, *Evening Star* (Dunedin), 13 May 1909; Macdonald, 'Women and crime'; Miles Fairburn and Stephen Haslett, 'Violent crime in old and new societies: a case study based on New Zealand, 1850–1940', *Journal of Social History*, XX.1 (1986), pp. 90–126; and Bronwyn Dalley, 'Women's imprisonment in New Zealand, 1880–1920', PhD thesis, Otago (1992).

41. Hugh Jackson, *Churches and People in Australia and New Zealand, 1860–1930* (Allen and Unwin, Wellington, 1987), pp. 115–19 and p. 117 for the quotation.

42. For these two paragraphs see Powell, 'The church in Auckland society, 1880–1886'; Breward, *Godless Schools?* ; Grigg, 'Attack on the citadels'; Barber, 'The social crusader'; and Jackson, *Churches and People.*

43. Elder, *A History of the Presbyterian Church*, pp. 334–43, 346–57; Morrell, *The Anglican Church in New Zealand*, pp. 116–17, 126–30, 171–2; Mol, *Western Religion*, p. 356–79; Rafter, *Never Let Go!*; Waite, *Dear Mr Booth!*; Farrell, 'The Presbyterian Church and Social Welfare'; Roper, 'History of the social services of the Anglican Church in Canterbury'; Simon Rae, *From Relief to Social Service: A History of the Presbyterian Social Service Association, Otago, 1906–1981* (The Association, Dunedin, 1981).

44. André Siegfried, *Democracy in New Zealand*, trs. E. V. Burns (G. Bell, London, 1914), p. 322. See also for these two paragraphs, Elder, *Presbyterian Church*, ch. 10; Breward, *Godless Schools?*; Keith Furniss, 'The Moray Place Congregational Church, Dunedin: a social history', research essay, Otago (1975); Jane Teal, 'The social composition of Anglicans in Caversham, South Dunedin, St Kilda and St Clair in the Nineteenth Century', research essay, Otago (1978); Higgins, 'The Prohibition Movement', p. 85 and Table VI; Dennis McEldowney (ed.), *Presbyterians in Aotearoa, 1840–1990*, (Presbyterian Church of NZ, Wellington, 1990).

45. Moores, 'The rise of the Protestant Political Association'; R. P. Davis, *Irish Issues in New Zealand Politics, 1868–1922* (University of Otago Press, Dunedin, 1974); O'Connor, 'Sectarian conflict in New Zealand', and 'Protestants, Catholics, and the New Zealand Government'; Miles Fairburn, 'The farmers take over', in Keith Sinclair (ed.), *The Oxford Illustrated History of New Zealand* (OUP, Auckland, 1990), pp. 191–5; and P. J. O'Farrell, *Vanished Kingdoms: Irish in Australia and New Zealand. A Personal Excursion* (New South Wales University Press, Sydney, 1990), ch. 7.

46. Siegfried, *Democracy*, pp. 315–16; Barber, 'The Church Defence Society of Otago and Southland'.

47. Jackson, *Churches and People*, pp. 167–8.

48. J. W. Collins, *Inquiry into Cost of Living, 1910–1911* (Department of Labour, Wellington, 1912), p. 13; Gilson-Vosburgh, *New Zealand Family*, pp. 76–9; Roth, *Trade Unions in New Zealand*, Meuli, 'Occupational change and bourgeois proliferation'; Olssen, 'The origins of the Labour Party: a reconsideration', *NZJH*, XXI.1 (1987), pp. 79–96.

49. R. C. J. Stone, *Makers of Fortune: A Colonial Business Community and its Fall* (AUP/OUP, Auckland, 1973), chs. 8–10; Armstrong, 'New Zealand: imperialism, class and uneven development'; John Angus, 'City and country: change and continuity . . . Otago, 1877–1893', PhD thesis, Otago (1976), chs. 1–2.

50. Hughes, 'Nursing education: the collapse of the Diploma of Nursing at the University of Otago'; Cullen, *Lawfully Occupied*; T. W. H. Brooking, *A History of Dentistry in New Zealand* (NZ Dental Association, Dunedin, 1980); Jocelyn Ward, ' "For reasons of their own": a study of the Otago Employers' Association, 1901–1915', research essay, Otago (1984).

51. Many of these observations are based on my work on the social structure of Caversham; see 'The Friendly Societies', 'Social mobility in Caversham', and *The Skilled Workers of Caversham*, forthcoming ; David Pearson, *Johnsonville: Continuity and Change in a New Zealand Township* (Allen and Unwin, Sydney, 1980) and, for the concept of refinement, Elvin Hatch, *Respectable Lives: Social Standing in Rural New Zealand* (University of California Press, Berkeley, 1992).

52. For Barr, *NZPD* 1908, 143, p. 270. See also Olssen, *Otago*, ch. 8; Judi Boyd and Erik Olssen, 'The skilled workers: journeymen and masters in Caversham, 1880–1914', *NZJH*, XXII.2 (1988), pp. 118–34. For efforts to exclude 'minorities' from the labour force, see Stephen Robertson, 'Women workers and the New Zealand Court of Arbitration, 1894–1920', in Raelene Frances and Bruce Scates (eds.), *Women, Work and the Labour Movement in Australia and Aotearoa/New Zealand* (Australian Society for Labour History, Sydney, 1991), pp. 30–41 and Olssen, 'Racism and the New Zealand Labour Movement', forthcoming.

53. James Holt, *Compulsory Arbitration in New Zealand: The First Forty Years* (AUP, Auckland, 1987), pp. 37–8; B. J. G. Thompson, 'The Canterbury farm labourers' dispute: a study of the first attempt by a union of New Zealand farm labourers to come under the New Zealand arbitration system', MA thesis, Canterbury (1967); Erik

Olssen, *The Red Feds: Revolutionary Industrial Unionism and the New Zealand Federation of Labour, 1908–1914* (OUP, Auckland, 1988), chs. 1–8.

54. For example, Robert H. Hutchinson, *The 'Socialism' of New Zealand* (New Review Publishing Association, New York, 1916), p. 125.

55. John Child, 'Wages policy and wages movements in New Zealand, 1914–1923', *Journal of Industrial Relations*, XIII.2 (1971), pp. 164–76; *AJHR*, 1911, H–11; Olssen, *Red Feds*, pp. 97–100; and for Marshall see *Maoriland Worker*, 30 August 1912, p. 7.

56. Olssen and T. W. H. Brooking, 'Transience and mobility in Caversham', forthcoming; Willis, 'Defence not defiance', pp. 6–9; David Pearson, *Johnsonville*; Miles Fairburn, 'Why did the New Zealand Labour Party fail to win office until 1935?', *Political Science*, XXXVII.2 (1985), pp. 114–15; Caroline Daley, 'Taradale meets the ideal society and its enemies', *NZJH*, xxv.2 (1991), pp. 129–46.

57. Margaret Galt, 'Wealth and income in New Zealand, c.1870–c.1939', PhD thesis, Victoria (1985), p. 182. See also James Watson, 'Crisis and change: economic crisis and technological change in New Zealand between the wars', PhD thesis, University of Canterbury (1984); Peter Brosnan, 'Net interprovincial migration, 1886–1966', unpublished paper.

58. *Apprenticeship Question (New Zealand), 1923* . . . (W. A. G. Skinner, Government Printer, Wellington, 1923); McLaren, 'Education and politics . . ., parts I and 2'; Murdoch, *The High Schools of New Zealand*; Roth, *George Hogben*, pp. 99–100, 110–16; Beaglehole, *The University of New Zealand* and *Victoria University College*; Morrell, *The University of Otago*; Gardner et al., *A History of the University of Canterbury*; Gardner and Winterbourn, 'Education, 1877–1950'; Lucy Duncan, ' "What Katy Did in School": a study of curriculum development in Dunedin girls' secondary schools, 1900–1920', research essay, Otago (1982); Keith Sinclair, *A History of the University of Auckland, 1883–1983* (AUP/OUP, Auckland, 1983); Ruth Fry, *It's Different for Daughters: A History of the Curriculum for Girls in New Zealand Schools, 1900–1975* (NZ Council for Educational Research, Wellington, 1985); D. McKenzie, 'The growth of school credentialling, 1878–1900', in R. Openshaw and D. McKenzie (eds.), *Reinterpreting the Educational Past* (NZCER, Wellington, 1987), pp. 82–106.

59. Mutch, 'Aspects of the social and economic history of Auckland', pp. 297–300; Roth, *Hogben*, pp. 81, 91–3, 126–7; Nicol, *The Technical Schools of New Zealand*, p. 77; and *Apprenticeship Question*.

60. *Vocational Guidance: Post-primary Education and the Choice of a Career* . . . (Government Printer, Wellington, 1927, 1928, 1929); Report: Educational reorganisation in New Zealand, *AJHR*, 1930, 1 8A; D. McKenzie, 'The growth of school credentialling, 1878–1900'.

61. Ewing, *The Development of the New Zealand Primary School Curriculum*; Malone, 'The New Zealand School Journal and imperial ideology', McGeorge 'Military training in New Zealand primary schools'; Arnold, 'The village and the globe' and 'The Wellington Education Board'; McKenzie, 'The changing concept of equality in New Zealand education'.

62. Olssen, 'New Zealand and the war', unpublished paper; Paul Baker, *King and Country Call: New Zealanders, Conscription and the Great War* (AUP/OUP, Auckland, 1988), pp. 132–3, 245; Geoffrey Rice, *Black November: The 1918 Influenza Epidemic in New Zealand* (Allen and Unwin, Wellington, 1988); and Graham, 'The voluntary system', pp. 15, 30–1, 62–9.

63. Baker, *King and Country Call*, p. 245.

64. Graham, 'The voluntary system', pp. 126–7; Moores, 'Protestant Political Association', chs. 3–7; Stone, 'A history of trade unionism in New Zealand', and 'The unions and the arbitration system'; Richardson, 'Politics and war: coal miners and conscription'; Roth, *Trade Unions*, pp. 41–4.

65. Davis, 'The New Zealand Labour Party's "Irish campaign" '; Roth, *Trade Unions*, pp. 45–56; Michelle Slade, 'Industrial unionism in New Zealand, 1916–1925 . . . ', MA thesis, Auckland (1983).

66. Beagle, 'Children of the State', Table 5.8, p. 193; Primrose, 'Society and the insane',

pp. 205, 211–20; Miles Fairburn, 'Why did the New Zealand Labour Party fail to win office until 1935?', pp. 119–24; James Watson, 'An independent working class?', in John E. Martin and Kerry Taylor (eds.), *Culture and the Labour Movement* (Dunmore Press, Palmerston North, 1991), pp. 184–96.

67. For the evidence on unions and strikes see Fairburn, ibid., pp. 108–14; McInnes, *Castle on the Run* (Pegasus Press, Christchurch, 1969), p. 43, J. C. Beaglehole, *Victoria University College. An Essay Towards a History* (NZUP Press, Wellington, 1949); Sam Elworthy, *Ritual Song of Defiance: A Social History of Students at the University of Otago* (Otago University Students Association, Dunedin, 1990), ch. 2.
68. Harrison, 'The motion picture industry', p. 66.
69. Gilson-Vosburgh, *New Zealand Family*, pp. 32a, 55a, 87a, 133a; Brookes, 'The Committee of Inquiry into Abortion in New Zealand, 1936–37'; Rod Phillips, *Divorce in New Zealand: A Social History* (OUP, Auckland, 1981).
70. Rogerson, 'Cosy homes multiply', pp. 129, 137–80.
71. Burdon, *The New Dominion*; Somerset, *Littledene*; Duff, *New Zealand Now* ; Olssen, *Otago*, ch. 10; Hatch, *Respectable Lives*.
72. Robertson, 'Tyranny of circumstances', pp. 225–43, 283–6, 292–306; Gilson-Vosburgh, *New Zealand Family*, pp. 62–3; Brookes, 'The Committee of Inquiry into Abortion, 1936–37'.
73. Reid, 'Church and State in New Zealand'; Clements, 'The churches and social policy'; Francis Lavelle, 'The response of the churches in Dunedin to the depression, 1931–1936', research essay, Otago (1978).
74. Rosenberg, 'Full employment', p. 47; Campbell, 'Unemployment in New Zealand'; Tennant, *Paupers and Providers*, ch. 5; Unemployment, *AJHR*, 1929 and 1930, H–11B; Burdon, *The New Dominion*, ch. 10; Robertson, 'Tyranny of circumstances', chs. 3–5, 13, especially Table 13; Paul Harris, 'The New Zealand Unemployed Workers Movement, 1931–1939: Gisborne and the reliefworkers' strike', *NZJH*, x.2 (1976), pp. 130–42; Robertson, 'Isolation, ideology and impotence' and 'Government responses to unemployment in New Zealand, 1929–1935', *NZJH*, xvi.1 (1982), pp. 21–38; Morris, 'Unemployed organisations in New Zealand, 1926–1939'.
75. Tennant, *Paupers and Providers*, chs. 6–8; Rafter, *Never Let Go!*, pp. 87, 102; Ex-Soldiers Rehabilitation Commission, *AJHR*, 1930, H–39.
76. Clark, 'The slums of Dunedin'; Kennedy, 'Really concerned men', pp. 45–54; Millar, *Once Upon a Village*, p. 141, K. C. McDonald, *Dunedin*, p. 316, Bush, *Decently and In Order*, pp. 215, 287–9; Metge, 'The house that Jack built'; Lee, *Socialism in New Zealand*, pp. 60–7, Rogerson, 'Cosy homes multiply', p. 42; *AJHR*, 1927, C–1, p. 5, and 1928, C–1, p. 9.
77. *Truth*, 19 August 1936, p. 11; *NZ Herald*, 28 September 1937 and 23 November 1937; Olssen, *Lee*, p. 93.
78. Bland, *The Slums of Auckland*; Firth, *State Housing in New Zealand*; Metge, 'The house that Jack built'; Olssen, *Lee*, ch. 8.
79. Oliver, 'The origins and growth of the welfare state', pp. 19–24; Burdon, *The New Dominion*, chs. 15–20.

CHAPTER 11: BETWEEN TWO WORLDS

1. Sam Karetu, 'Language and protocol of the marae', in Michael King (ed.), *Te Ao Hurihuri*, p. 41.
2. Pool, *The Maori Population of New Zealand* , p. 143. See also Pearce, 'The size and location of the Maori population, 1857–96'.
3. Cody, *Man of Two Worlds*; Condliffe, *Te Rangi Hiroa*.
4. Pool, *Maori Population*, p. 110. See also R. T. Lange, 'The revival of a dying race'. On the Māori in the 1918 influenza pandemic, see Rice, *Black November*, ch. 6.
5. H. B. Turbott, 'Health and social welfare', in Sutherland (ed.), *The Maori People Today*, pp. 230–1.

6. Maclean, *Challenge for Health*, p. 204.
7. Turbott, 'Health and social welfare', p. 235.
8. Ibid., pp. 238–9. The statistics may be over-precise, but they convey a reliable general picture.
9. Orange, 'A kind of equality', p. 94.
10. Butterworth, 'A rural Maori renaissance?', p. 181.
11. Maclean, *Challenge for Health*, pp. 213, 215; Butterworth, 'Maori renaissance', p. 184.
12. Barrington and Beaglehole, *Maori Schools in a Changing Society*, pp. 209–10.
13. Butterworth, 'Maori renaissance', p. 185.
14. G. King, 'Aspects of secondary education in Maori denominational boarding schools'.
15. Butterworth, 'Maori renaissance', pp. 172–3.
16. Metge, *A New Maori Migration*, pp. 16–17; Metge, *The Maoris of New Zealand*, p. 56.
17. Butterworth, 'Maori renaissance', p. 185.
18. Metge, *Maori Migration*.
19. Ernest and Pearl Beaglehole, *Some Modern Maoris*, p. 35.
20. Butterworth, *The Maori in the New Zealand Economy*, p. 19. Other figures vary according to definitions of 'urban area'. See also J. R. McCreary, 'Population growth and urbanization', in Schwimmer (ed.), *The Maori People in the Nineteen-Sixties*.
21. Metge, *Maori Migration*, p. 111.
22. Michael King, *Te Puea*, p. 33; Binney et al., *Mihaia*, p. 21.
23. *NZ Herald*, 29 August 1905, quoted in Williams, *Politics of the New Zealand Maori*, pp. 123–4.
24. *AJHR*, 1907, G–1c, p. 15.
25. *AJHR*, 1920, G–9, pp. 2–3.
26. Butterworth, 'The politics of adaptation', ch. 4.
27. Worger, 'Te Puea, the Kingitanga, and Waikato', p. 102–3. See also Butterworth, 'Politics of adaptation'; for the largest incorporation, Mangatu, see Ward, 'The history of the East Coast Maori Trust'.
28. Martin, 'Aspects of Maori affairs in the Liberal period', pp. 138–59, and Appendix IIIc.
29. Butterworth, 'Maori renaissance', pp. 168; Worger, 'Te Puea', p. 116.
30. *AJHR*, 1934, G–11, Appendix I.
31. Butterworth, 'Maori renaissance', pp. 178–9; Michael King, *Te Puea*, p. 158.
32. Macrae, 'A study in the application of economic analysis to social issues', p. 179.
33. Oliver and Thomson, *Challenge and Response*, p. 237.
34. Orange, 'A kind of equality', p. 64.
35. Butterworth, 'Maori renaissance', p. 178.
36. *AJHR*, 1934, G–10, p. 1.
37. *NZ Herald*, 4 August 1916. See also Webster, *Rua and the Maori Millennium*, chs. 7–9, and Binney et al., *Mihaia*.
38. Fitzgerald, *Education and Identity*, p. 26.
39. R. J. Martin, quoted by Fitzgerald, *Education and Identity*, pp. 29–30.
40. *AJHR*, 1906, H–31, p. 67.
41. Williams, *Politics*, pp. 107–11.
42. R. T. Lange, 'Revival', pp. 302–7.
43. Michael King, *Te Puea*, p. 259.
44. Introduction in Pocock (ed.), *The Maori and New Zealand Politics*, p. 8.
45. Worger, 'Te Puea', p. 64. See also B. H. Farland, 'The political career of J. G. Coates', MA thesis, Victoria (1956), ch. 3.
46. Henderson, *Ratana*, pp. 25 ff.
47. Ibid., p. 57.
48. *AJHR*, 1934, G–11.
49. J. McLeod Henderson, 'The Ratana Movement', in Pocock (ed.), *The Maori and New Zealand Politics*, p. 71.
50. Michael King, *Te Puea*, p. 225.
51. Moana Raureti, 'The origins of the Ratana Movement', in Michael King (ed.), *Tihe Mauri Ora*, p. 59.

52. Michael King, *Te Puea*, pp. 202–3.
53. *AJHR*, 1949, G–9, p. 2.
54. Orange, 'A kind of equality', pp. 126–59; Butterworth, 'Maori renaissance', p. 189.
55. James, 'The Maori Women's Welfare League'; Winiata, *The Changing Role of the Leader in Maori Society*, pp. 165–70.
56. Undated clipping, 1946 election campaign, Elizabeth Ramsden Papers (private collection).
57. Cowan, *The Maoris in the Great War*; O'Connor, 'The recruitment of Maori soldiers'; Michael King, *Te Puea*, pp. 79–92.
58. Orange, 'A kind of equality', pp. 128–34, 142–56; Michael King, *Te Puea*, pp. 206–11.
59. Gordon Slatter, *On the Ball: The Centennial Book of New Zealand Rugby* (Whitcombe and Tombs, Christchurch, 1970), p. 162.
60. A. H. McLintock (ed.), *An Encyclopaedia of New Zealand*, 3 vols. (Government Printer, Wellington, 1966), III, p. 130.
61. Ranginui Walker, 'Marae: a place to stand', in Michael King (ed.), *Te Ao Hurihuri*, p. 27.
62. Barker, 'The connexion'.
63. Parker, 'The substance that remains', p. 190.
64. C. B. Bledisloe, *Ideals of Nationhood*, arr. T. Lindsay Buick (Thomas Avery, New Plymouth, 1935).
65. Apirana Ngata to Peter Buck, 5 January 1929, G. E. O. Ramsden, Papers 1813–1961, MS Papers 196/304, ATL.
66. Barrington and Beaglehole, *Maori Schools*, p. 207.
67. Apirana Ngata, 'Maori land settlement', in Sutherland (ed.), *The Maori People Today*, pp. 176–7.
68. Michael King, *Te Puea*, p. 249.

CHAPTER 12: THE CLIMATE OF OPINION

1. Ross, *New Zealand Aspirations in the Pacific in the Nineteenth Century*, pp. 234–70; Dunstall, 'Public attitudes and responses in New Zealand to the beginning of the Boer War'; Trlin, *Now Respected, Once Despised*, pp. 69–78; Mary Boyd, 'Racial attitudes of New Zealand officials in Western Samoa', *NZJH*, XXI.2 (1987), pp.139–55.
2. Fong, *The Chinese in New Zealand*, pp. 14–30; O'Connor, 'Keeping New Zealand white'. See also Jacqueline Leckie in *NZJH*, XIX.2 (1985), pp.103–29.
3. Quoted by Margaret Tennant, 'Mrs Grace Neill in the Department of Asylums, Hospitals and Charitable Institutions', *NZJH*, XII.1 (1978) p. 6.
4. Gibbons, ' "Turning tramps into taxpayers" ', pp. 80–89.
5. W. A. Chapple, *The Fertility of the Unfit* (Whitcombe and Tombs, Melbourne, 1903), pp. xv–xvi, 118–23.
6. R. P. Davis, *Irish Issues in New Zealand Politics*. See also D. H. Akenson, *Half the World from Home. Perspectives on the Irish in New Zealand, 1860–1950* (VUP, Wellington, 1990).
7. Portraits of this group are given by its members in Eliot R. Davis, *A Link with the Past* (Oswald-Sealy, Auckland, 1949) and Brasch, *Indirections*.
8. Siegfried, *Democracy in New Zealand*, p. 273.
9. MacLeod, *The Fighting Man*, pp. 33 ff.
10. G. Crossick, 'The emergence of the lower middle class in Britain: a discussion', in G. Crossick (ed.), *The Lower Middle Class in Britain, 1870–1914* (Croom Helm, London, 1977), pp. 11–60.
11. Burdon, *Scholar-Errant*, pp. 53–94; W. J. Gardner, 'Part I: the formative years, 1873–1918', in Gardner et al., *A History of the University of Canterbury*, pp. 101–12; Sinclair, *William Pember Reeves*, pp. 96–104.
12. M. P. K. Sorrenson, *Maori Origins and Migrations: The Genesis of Some Pakeha Myths and Legends* (AUP/OUP, Auckland, 1979), pp. 17–30, 45–7, 83; D. R. Simmons, *The*

Great New Zealand Myth (Reed, Wellington, 1976), pp. 58–9, 103–8, 315–16; Craig, *Man of the Mist*, pp. 57–133.

13. Katherine Mansfield, 'The garden party', in Ian A Gordon (ed.), *Undiscovered Country: The New Zealand Stories of Katherine Mansfield* (Longman Paul, Auckland, 1974), p. 221.

14. Arnold, 'The Australasian peoples and their world, 1888–1915', in Sinclair (ed.), *Tasman Relations*, pp. 52–70; K. Sinclair, *A Destiny Apart. New Zealand's Search for National Identity* (Allen and Unwin, Wellington, 1990).

15. Siegfried, *Democracy*, p. 357; Colin McGeorge, 'Learning about God's Own Country', *NZJES*, 18.1 (1983), pp. 3–12. See also McGeorge, 'Hear Our Voices We Entreat', *NZJH*, XVIII.1 (1984), pp. 3–18.

16. McCormick, *The Fascinating Folly*, pp. 32–47; McCormick, *Alexander Turnbull*; Bagnall, 'A troubled childhood'.

17. T. M. Hocken, *A Bibliography of the Literature Relating to New Zealand* (Government Printer, Wellington, 1909), p. vi.

18. Sir Julius Vogel, *Anno Domini 2000; Or Woman's Destiny* (Hutchinson, London, 1889); Edward Tregear, *Hedged with Divinities* (R. Coupland Harding, Wellington, 1895).

19. Wilson, *William Satchell*; Sinclair, *A Destiny Apart*.

20. Downes, *Shadows on the Stage*, pp. 89–157; H. McNaughton, 'Drama', in Sturm (ed.), *Oxford History of New Zealand Literature*.

21. *Cyclopedia of New Zealand*, 6 vols. (Cyclopedia Company Ltd., Wellington and Christchurch, 1897–1908), I, pp. 445–6; Margaret Campbell, *Music in Dunedin*, pp. 42–7, 50–3; Pritchard, 'Music in Canterbury', pp. 440–58.

22. Alan Mulgan, *Great Days in New Zealand Writing*, pp. 122–8; J. M. Thomson, *A Distant Music* ; Thomson, *The Oxford History of New Zealand Music*.

23. Docking, *Two Hundred Years of New Zealand Painting*, pp. 70–80; Brown and Keith, *An Introduction to New Zealand Painting*, pp. 49–96; Gordon H. Brown, *New Zealand Painting, 1900–1920*, pp. 30–2; Dunn, *Concise History of New Zealand Painting* (1991).

24. McCormick, *The Expatriate*, pp. 147–60, 191–205; McCormick, 'Frances Hodgkins'; Julie King, *Sydney Lough Thompson: at home and abroad* (1990).

25. See Stead (ed.), *The Letters and Journals of Katherine Mansfield*; O'Sullivan, *Katherine Mansfield's New Zealand*; Alpers, *The Life of Katherine Mansfield* (1989).

26. Katherine Mansfield, 'The doll's house', in Gordon, *Undiscovered Country*, p. 75.

27. Quoted by Berkman, *Katherine Mansfield*, pp. 24–5; Heather Roberts, *Where Did She Come From?* (1989).

28. Weitzel, 'Pacifists and anti-militarists in New Zealand'; Erik Olssen, *The Red Feds*.

29. Paul Baker, *King and Country Call*; Jock Phillips, *A Man's Country*; Beaglehole, *Victoria University College*, pp. 162–72; G. W. A. Bush, *Decently and In Order: The Government of the City of Auckland, 1840–1971* (Collins for the Auckland City Council, 1971), p. 113.

30. O'Connor, 'The recruitment of Maori soldiers'; Michael King, *Te Puea: A Biography* (Hodder and Stoughton, Auckland, 1977), pp. 79–97; P. J. O'Farrell, *Harry Holland, Militant Socialist* (ANU, Canberra, 1964), pp. 72–84.

31. O'Connor, 'The awkward ones — dealing with conscience'.

32. Wood, *The New Zealand People at War*, pp. 13–18.

33. Openshaw, 'Patriotism and the New Zealand Primary School', pp. 31–122; R. P. Davis, *Irish Issues*, p. 205; *NZ Statutes*, 1920, p. 57; C. Maclean and Jock Phillips, *The Sorrow and the Pride*; Maureen Sharp, 'Anzac Day in New Zealand, 1916–1939', *NZJH*, XV.2 (1981), pp. 97–114.

34. Fairburn, *The Ideal Society and its Enemies* (1989).

35. Maurice Shadbolt, *Strangers and Journeys* (London, 1971), p. 246.

36. Lawlor, *Confessions of a Journalist*, pp. 87–8, 252.

37. *NZ Gazette*, 1919, vol. 3, pp. 2897–8. The 1919 syllabus was a revision of the 1913 syllabus, the latter based on that of 1904: *NZ Gazette*, 1913, vol. 2, pp. 3699–700; *NZ Gazette*, 1904, vol. 1, p. 1085.

38. Harcourt, *A Dramatic Appearance*, p. 14; Hurst, *Music and the Stage in New Zealand*, pp. 62–77; McNaughton, 'Drama', in Sturm (ed.), *Oxford History of New Zealand Literature*.

39. Marsh, 'Theatre', p. 37. See also Margaret Lewis, *Ngaio Marsh, A Life* (Bridget Williams Books, Wellington, 1991).
40. Harcourt, *A Dramatic Appearance*, pp. 49–72; Mason, 'Theatre' pp. 242–3.
41. Denis and Bieringa (eds.), *Film in Aotearoa/New Zealand* (VUP, Wellington, 1992); Collins, *Broadcasting Grave and Gay*, pp. 13–45; Downes and Harcourt, *Voices in the Air*, pp. 10–52; Burdon, *The New Dominion*, pp. 91–6, 305–9.
42. Alan Mulgan, *New Zealand Writing*, pp. 65–8.
43. Brown and Keith, *Introduction*, pp. 97–106; Gordon H. Brown, *New Zealand Painting, 1900–1920*, pp. 20–22, 47; Gordon H. Brown, *New Zealand Painting, 1920–1940*, pp. 6–24, 36–41, 50, 72–3.
44. See, for example, Jane Mander, *Allen Adair*, ed. Dorothea Turner (AUP/OUP, Auckland, 1971), pp. 42–3.
45. Ibid., p. 156.
46. Frank S. Anthony, *Gus Tomlins: Together with the Original Stories of 'Me and Gus'*, ed. Terry Sturm (AUP/OUP, Auckland, 1977), pp. 89, 63.
47. Broughton, 'Problems and responses of three New Zealand poets in the 1920s', pp. 1–15.
48. R. A. K. Mason, *Collected Poems*, 3rd edn. (Pegasus, Christchurch, 1971), p. 30.
49. Weir, *R. A. K. Mason*, p. 22.
50. *Our Nation's Story: A Course of British History* . . . (Whitcombe and Tombs, Auckland, n.d.): *Standard IV*, pp. 52, 54; *Standard V*, p. 40; *Standard VI*, pp. 257–8.
51. E. K. Mulgan and Alan E. Mulgan, *The New Zealand Citizen*, 4th edn. (Whitcombe and Tombs, Auckland, 1925), pp. 69, 132–4.
52. The *School Journal* was issued free to pupils in state primary schools from 1907. See Jenkins, *Social Attitudes in the New Zealand School Journal*; Malone, 'The New Zealand School Journal and the imperial ideology'; J. B. Condliffe, *A Short History of New Zealand* (L. M. Isitt, Christchurch, 1925), p. 195.
53. Boyd, 'The record in Western Samoa to 1945'; Field, *Mau: Samoa's Struggle* . . . (1984).
54. Mulgan and Mulgan, *New Zealand Citizen*, pp. 35–6.
55. John Mulgan, *Man Alone*, 2nd edn. (Paul, Hamilton, 1949), pp. 41–2.
56. Edwards, *Scrim*, pp. 9–83.
57. Tony Simpson, 'Huey Long's other island: style in New Zealand politics', in Stephen Levine (ed.), *New Zealand Politics: A Reader* (Cheshire, Melbourne, 1975); J. Vowles, 'Ideology and the formation of the New Zealand Labour Party', *NZJH* XVI.1 (1982), pp. 39–55.
58. Downes and Harcourt, *Voices*, pp. 100–09.
59. Cumming and Cumming, *History of State Education in New Zealand*, pp. 233–4, 236–41, 247–51; C. E. Beeby, *The Biography of an Idea* (1992).
60. NZ Consultative Committee . . . [Thomas Committee], *The Post-Primary School Curriculum. Report* . . . (Government Printer, Wellington, 1944), pp. 4–9.
61. A. E. Campbell, *The Feilding Community Centre*, pp. 22–45; Somerset, *Two Experiments in Community Education*.
62. Holcroft, *Discovered Isles*, p. 12.
63. Dunn, 'Robert Field'; Brown and Keith, *Introduction*, pp. 106–28; Gordon H. Brown, *New Zealand Painting, 1920–1940*, pp. 60–61, 63–9; Docking, *Two Hundred Years*, pp. 124–30, 156–60, 184–6; Rachel Barrowman, *A Popular Vision*; Janet Paul and Neil Roberts, *Evelyn Page: Seven Decades* (1986).
64. Mason, *Collected Poems*, p. 53.
65. A. R. D. Fairburn, *Collected Poems* (Pegasus, Christchurch, 1966), p. 23.
66. Allen Curnow, *Collected Poems, 1933–1973* (Reed, Wellington, 1974), pp. 142, 80.
67. Robin Hyde, *The Godwits Fly*, ed. Gloria Rawlinson (AUP/OUP, Auckland, 1970), pp. xx, xiv.
68. Quoted by McCormick, *Letters and Art in New Zealand*, p. 178; Gillian Boddy and Jacqueline Matthews (eds.), *Disputed Ground: Robin Hyde, Journalist*; Phillida Bunkle, Linda Hardy, Jacqueline Matthews, 'Introduction', in Robin Hyde, *Nor the Years Condemn* (Auckland, 1982).

69. *The Stories of Frank Sargeson*, 2nd edn. (Longman Paul, Auckland, 1973), pp. 9–10; McCormick, *Letters and Art* (1940), pp. 181–2; see also K. Jensen, in *Landfall*, 44.1 (1990), pp. 32–44.
70. Day, *John Mulgan*, pp. 3–25.
71. John Mulgan, *Man Alone*, p. 92.
72. Ibid., pp. 181–2.
73. Denis Glover, *The Wind and the Sand: Poems, 1934–44* (Caxton, Christchurch, 1945), p. 44.
74. A. H. McLintock, *National Centennial Exhibition of New Zealand Art: Catalogue* (NZ Dept. of Internal Affairs, Wellington, 1940), pp. 17–18.
75. McCormick, *Letters and Art*, p. 195.
76. Quoted in Weir, *Mason*, p. 52.
77. Peters, 'New Zealand's attitudes to the reform of the League of Nations'; Wood, *New Zealand People at War*, pp. 7–12, 32–56.
78. Wood, *New Zealand People at War*, p. 11.
79. Denis Glover, *Hot Water Sailor* (Reed, Wellington, 1962), p. 110; A. Cutler, '*Tomorrow* magazine and New Zealand Politics, 1934–1940; *NZJH*, 24.1 (1990), pp. 22–44.

CHAPTER 13: IMPERIALISM AND NATIONALISM

1. K. Sinclair, *A Destiny Apart: New Zealand's Search for National Identity*, p. 94.
2. Browne's minute, 15 April 1856. W. David McIntyre and W. J. Gardner, (eds.), *Speeches and Documents on New Zealand History*, pp. 92–3.
3. D. K. Fieldhouse, 'Autochthonous elements in the evolution of dominion status: the case of New Zealand', *Journal of Commonwealth Political Studies*, 1962, 1(2), pp. 85–111.
4. W. P. Morrell, *British Colonial Policy in the Mid-Victorian Age*, pp. 244–376; B. J. Dalton, *War and Politics in New Zealand, 1855–1870* (University Press, Sydney, 1967), pp. 260–80.
5. G. C. Hensley, 'The withdrawal of the British troops from New Zealand', MA thesis, Canterbury (1957), pp. 220–2.
6. G. Barratt, *Russophobia in New Zealand, 1838–1908*, pp. 40–6; *Speeches and Documents on New Zealand History*, pp. 236–8; I. C. McGibbon, *The Path to Gallipoli: Defending New Zealand, 1840–1915*, pp. 20–2.
7. *Speeches and Documents on New Zealand History*, pp. 235–48; P. H. Scratchley, 'Defences of New Zealand', *AJHR*, 1880, A–4, p. 5; McGibbon, *The Path to Gallipoli*, pp. 31–4, 37–9.
8. *Speeches and Documents on New Zealand History*, p. 250; McGibbon, *The Path to Gallipoli*, p. 49.
9. *Speeches and Documents on New Zealand History*, pp. 252–5; D. C. Gordon, *The Dominion Partnership in Imperial Defense, 1870–1914*, pp. 78–93; McGibbon, *The Path to Gallipoli*, pp. 54–67, 137–48.
10. R. M. Dalziel, *The Origins of New Zealand Diplomacy: The Agent-General in London, 1870–1905*, p. 167.
11. C. C. Eldridge, *England's Mission: The Imperial Idea in the Age of Gladstone and Disraeli, 1868–1880* (Macmillan, London, 1973) pp. 104–10, 114–15.
12. J. E. Kendle, *The Colonial and Imperial Conferences, 1887–1911*, pp. 7–13.
13. *Speeches and Documents on New Zealand History*, pp. 250–2.
14. Kendle, *The Colonial and Imperial Conferences*, pp. 23–30; K. Sinclair, *Imperial Federation*, pp. 26–9; McGibbon, *The Path to Gallipoli*, p. 128.
15. R. M. Dalziel, *Julius Vogel: Business Politician*, pp. 131–3; K. Sinclair, 'Australasian inter-government negotiations, 1865–80', *AJPH*, 16:2 (1970), pp. 151–76; E. J. Tapp, 'New Zealand and Australian Federation', *HSANZ*, 5:19 (1952), pp. 244–57; F. L. W. Wood, 'Why did New Zealand not join the Australian Commonwealth in 1900–1901?' *NZJH* 2:2 (1968) 115–29; M. Fairburn, 'New Zealand and Australasian Federation, 1883–1901: another view', *NZJH*, 4:2 (1970), pp. 138–59.

16. *NZPD*, 1890, 69, p. 787; K. Sinclair, *Imperial Federation*, pp. 23–4; K. Sinclair, 'Why New Zealanders are not Australians: New Zealand and the Australian Federal Movement, 1881–1901', in *Tasman Relations*, pp. 90–103.
17. A. Ross, *New Zealand Aspirations in the Pacific in the Nineteenth Century*, pp. 115–24.
18. Ibid., 131–280; Dalziel, *Julius Vogel*, pp. 182–95; S. D. Wilson, 'The record in the Cook Islands and Niue, 1901–45', in A. Ross (ed.), *New Zealand's Record in the Pacific Islands in the Twentieth Century*, pp. 24–59.
19. Sinclair, *Imperial Federation*, pp. 12, 24; see also K. Sinclair, *The Native Born: The Origins of New Zealand Nationalism*.
20. D. O. W. Hall, *The New Zealanders in South Africa, 1899–1902*, pp. 11, 88, 97.
21. Sinclair, *A Destiny Apart*, p. 126 and *The Native Born*, pp. 3–4.
22. D. C. Gordon, *Dominion Partnership*, p. 162; McGibbon, *The Path to Gallipoli*, pp. 131–5.
23. J. O. C. Phillips, *A Man's Country: The Image of the Pakeha Male*, pp. 141–53 and 'Rugby, war and the mythology of the New Zealand male', *NZJH*, 18:2 (1984), pp. 83–103.
24. J. E. Kendle, *The Colonial and Imperial Conferences*, pp. 83–106; *Speeches and Documents on New Zealand History*, pp. 269–70.
25. Ibid., pp. 272–3.
26. W. David McIntyre, *New Zealand Prepares for War, 1919–1939*, pp. 21–2; D. K. Skow, 'The 1909 Defence Act: a case study in militarism in New Zealand'; McGibbon, *The Path to Gallipoli*, pp. 181–93.
27. I. C. McGibbon, *Blue-water Rationale: The Naval Defence of New Zealand*, pp. 13–17; T. G. Weir, 'New Zealand's naval policy, 1909–1914'; McGibbon, *The Path to Gallipoli*, pp. 210–32.
28. O. E. Burton, *The Silent Division: New Zealanders at the Front, 1914–1919*, p. 122; see also pp. 46–7, 123–4, 179.
29. S. J. Smith, 'The seizure and occupation of Samoa', in H. T. B. Drew (ed.), *The War Effort of New Zealand* (Whitcombe and Tombs, Auckland, 1923), pp. 23–41.
30. F. Waite, *The New Zealanders at Gallipoli*, p. 299; see also J. O. C. Philips, '75 Years since Gallipoli', in A. Anderson et. al., *Towards 1990*.
31. K. Sinclair, *A Destiny Apart*, p. 171; H. Stewart, *The New Zealand Division, 1916–1919* (Whitcombe and Tombs, Auckland, 1921).
32. C. G. Powles (ed.), *The History of the Canterbury Mounted Rifles, 1914–1919*, pp. 92–241.
33. J. M. Winter, *The Great War and the British People* (Macmillan, London, 1980), p. 75.
34. *Speeches and Documents on New Zealand History*, pp. 276–8, 286–94.
35. W. David McIntyre, *New Zealand Prepares for War*, pp. 72–5; A. Ross, 'Chanak', in *New Zealand's Heritage*, 6 (1973), pp. 2152–6.
36. W. David McIntyre, *The Rise and Fall of the Singapore Naval Base*, pp. 56, 64–6.
37. W. David McIntyre, *New Zealand Prepares for War*, pp. 128–31.

CHAPTER 14: FROM LABOUR TO NATIONAL

1. Wigglesworth, 'The Depression and the election of 1935', pp. 145–9.
2. Election results throughout are from the *Return* relative to each general election and included in *AJHR* as paper H–33 or 33A until 1969, and E.9 thereafter. Party affiliations derive from nomination and election lists, advertisements, and reports in the eight metropolitan daily newspapers.
3. Robinson, 'The rise of the New Zealand National Party, 1936–1949', p. 14.
4. *NZ Herald*, 30 October 1935, and Wigglesworth, 'The Depression and the election of 1935', pp. 141–2.
5. Paul, *Humanism in Politics*, Appendix C, 'Labour's election policy, 1935', pp. 164–74, for the material in this and the next paragraph.
6. Chapman, *Marginals '72*, pp. 1–8.

7. Chapman, *The Political Scene*, pp. 64–5.

8. Ibid., pp. 66–8.

9. Gustafson, *Michael Joseph Savage*, p. 6 and *passim*; Thorn, *Peter Fraser*, p. 13 and *passim*; Sinclair, *Walter Nash*, p. 1 and *passim*.

10. Gustafson, *Savage*, p. 14; Brown, *The Rise of New Zealand Labour*, pp. 37 and 76–7.

11. McLeay, 'Parliamentary careers in a two-party system', pp. 218–21.

12. *NZPD*, 1936, 244, pp. 450–1; *NZOYB*, 1937, pp. 700, 688; ibid., 1938, p. 744.

13. *NZ Statutes*, 1936, pp. 176–201, 90–99, 121–31.

14. Ibid., pp. 74–89; Hare, *Report on Industrial Relations in New Zealand*, p. 179.

15. Reserve Bank of New Zealand Amendment Act 1936, *NZ Statutes*, 1936, pp. 3–13.

16. *NZPD*, 1936, 244, p. 153 (Coates), '. . . I am prepared to agree that the credit of the people belongs to the people. . . .', and p. 159 (Savage), 'The public credit is pledged, and the productive power of the people must be the foundation of it in the long-run.'

17. For the Act see *NZ Statutes*, 1936, pp. 59–73; see also Hill, 'The quest for control,' pp. 309–19, 388–91.

18. *NZ Statutes*, 1936, pp. 289–341.

19. Ibid., pp. 132–53.

20. Ibid., pp. 262–72; Hill, 'The quest for control', p. 389.

21. Metge, ' "The house that Jack built" ', p. 16 and *passim*; Scholefield (ed.), *New Zealand Parliamentary Record 1840–1949*, p. 49; Lee, *Socialism in New Zealand*, p. 182.

22. *NZPD*, 1937, 249, pp. 1217–19 (Holyoake), and pp. 1188–9 (Ransom).

23. Peter Keeble, 'The first Labour Government's housing policies' (unpublished paper, Dept. of Political Studies, University of Auckland, 1979), p. 5, Table 1, and *passim*.

24. Paul, *Humanism in Politics*, p. 168. See also Ian Cumming and Alan Cumming, *History of State Education in New Zealand, 1840–1975* (Pitman, Wellington, 1978), pp. 254–68, and Thorn, *Fraser*, pp. 124, 132–4, 143–51.

25. Hanson, 'The social security story', pp. 55–7. See also Hanson, *The Politics of Social Security, passim*, and Lee, *Simple on a Soap-box*, pp. 82, 97–106.

26. Hanson, 'The social security story', pp. 59, 77–100. See also Lovell-Smith, *The New Zealand Doctor and the Welfare State*.

27. Hanson, *The Politics of Social Security*, pp. 60–2.

28. Sinclair, *Nash*, pp. 133–49, 160–67.

29. Hanson, 'The social security story', p. 112.

30. Social Security Act 1938, *NZ Statutes*, 1938, pp. 62–146.

31. *NZPD*, 1938, 252, p. 423 (Savage), p. 556 (Holland), cited Hanson, 'The social security story', pp. 142–3.

32. *NZPD*, 1938, 252, p. 341 (Hamilton), 253, p. 181 (Nash).

33. Robinson, 'New Zealand National Party', pp. 19, 17–51.

34. *NZPD*, 1938, 252, p. 338; *Auckland Star*, 11 March 1937; cited Robinson, 'New Zealand National Party', pp. 75, 74.

35. Milne, *Political Parties in New Zealand*, pp. 146–7; Robinson, 'New Zealand National Party', pp. 55–63.

36. Ibid., pp. 39, 21–2, 46–8.

37. 'Election Manifesto', New Zealand National Party, 1938, cited Robinson, 'New Zealand National Party', pp. 77–83; *Dominion*, 30 September 1938, cited Robinson, 'New Zealand National Party', p. 84.

38. *NZPD*, 1936, 244, p. 159.

39. Sinclair, *Nash*, pp. 170–89; Sutch, *The Quest for Security*, pp. 217–35.

40. Olssen, *John A. Lee*, pp. 133–40; Lee, *Simple on a Soap-box, passim*.

41. Ibid., p. 159, and for 'Psychopathology in politics', ibid., pp. 165–71.

42. Olssen, *Lee*, pp. 146–60; Lee, *Simple on a Soap-box*, pp. 178–207; Sinclair, *Nash*, pp. 190–7.

43. McLeay, 'Parliamentary careers', pp. 227–9. Cf. Milne, *Political Parties in New Zealand*, p. 145.

44. Olssen, *Lee*, pp. 161–73; Lee, *Simple on a Soap-box*, pp. 208–14.

45. Wood, *The New Zealand People at War*, pp. 131–42.

46. Robinson, 'New Zealand National Party', pp. 103–9; Milne, *Political Parties*, pp. 147–9; Frank Simpson (ed.), *Who's Who in New Zealand*, 6th edn. (Reed, Wellington, 1956), p. 123.
47. Baker, *The New Zealand People at War: War Economy*, pp. 278–81.
48. Prolongation of Parliament Act 1941, *NZ Statutes*, 1941, p. 306.
49. Wood, *People at War*, pp. 167–72, 228–39; Robinson, 'New Zealand National Party', pp. 127–44.
50. Baker, *War Economy*, pp. 298–317.
51. *NZ Statutes* 1943, pp. 85–116. Cf. Rehabilitation Act 1941 in *NZ Statutes*, 1941, pp. 307–19.
52. Sutch, *The Quest for Security*, pp. 299–303; Baker, *War Economy*, pp. 443–80.
53. Bank of New Zealand Act 1945, New Zealand National Airways Act 1945, *NZ Statutes*, 1945, pp. 121–30, 191–205.
54. Baker, *War Economy*, pp. 317–23, and on rehabilitation, pp. 502–19.
55. Electoral Amendment Act 1945, *NZ Statutes*, 1945, pp. 54–61.
56. 'Election Manifesto', New Zealand National Party, 1943, cited Robinson, 'New Zealand National Party', pp. 152–8.
57. S. G. Holland, *Passwords to Progress* (New Zealand National Party pamphlet, 1943), p. 21, cited Robinson, 'New Zealand National Party', p. 153. Cf. S. G. Holland, *Talking Things Over: Profit Sharing, Increased Production, Lower Prices, What They Mean to You!* (New Zealand National Party householder, *c.*1945).
58. Nash, *New Zealand, A Working Democracy*, pp. 193–313; Sinclair, *Nash*, pp. 210–55; Thorn, *Fraser*, pp. 231–40.
59. Samoa Amendment Act 1947, *NZ Statutes*, 1947, pp. 425–40.
60. Dairy Products Marketing Commission Act 1947, ibid., pp. 6–28.
61. *NZ Statutes*, 1948, pp. 347–55; Baker, *War Economy*, pp. 532–73.
62. Social Security Amendment Act 1947, *NZ Statutes*, 1947, pp. 225–32; War Pensions Amendment Act 1947, ibid., pp. 219–22.
63. Baker, *War Economy*, p. 545, Chart 82; ibid., p. 632; NZOYB, 1950, p. 716.
64. Baker, *War Economy*, p. 459.
65. Bassett, *Confrontation '51*, p. 30, pp. 13–33.
66. Sinclair, *Nash*, p. 274; Sutch, *The Quest for Security*, pp. 349–54.
67. NZOYB, 1950, p. 896.
68. Robinson, 'New Zealand National Party', pp. 180–6.
69. Tenancy Amendment Act 1950, *NZ Statutes,* 1950, pp. 86–94; Servicemen's Settlement Act 1950, ibid., pp. 494–523.
70. Wool Proceeds Retention Act 1950, ibid., pp. 1115–18; *New Zealand Economic Survey 1952* (Government Printer, Wellington, 1952), p. 58, Table 10.
71. Bassett, *Confrontation '51*, p. 48 and *passim*; Dick Scott, *151 Days*.
72. Bassett, *Confrontation '51*, pp. 97–9.
73. Ibid., pp. 113–14.
74. *NZ Herald*, 14 May 1951, cited Bassett, *Confrontation '51*, p. 174.
75. Ibid., p. 190.
76. Industrial Conciliation and Arbitration Amendment Act 1951, *NZ Statutes*, 1951, pp. 340–70; Police Offences Amendment Act 1951, ibid., pp. 391–407.
77. *New Zealand Economic Survey 1952* (Government Printer, Wellington, 1952), p. 23 and *passim*.
78. *Economic Survey of New Zealand 1954* (Government Printer, Wellington, 1954), pp. 17–22.
79. Colechin, 'The campaign of the Social Credit Political League'; Penfield, 'The New Zealand Social Credit Political League', pp. 33–7.
80. Electoral Amendment Act 1950, *NZ Statutes*, 1950, pp. 107–8.
81. Sinclair, *Nash*, pp. 292–4; McLeay, 'Parliamentary careers', pp. 233–4.
82. *New Zealand Economic Survey 1955* (Government Printer, Wellington, 1955), pp. 19–30.
83. *New Zealand Economic Survey 1956* (Government Printer, Wellington, 1956); *Economic Survey 1957* (Government Printer, Wellington, 1957).

84. Dairy Products Marketing Commission Amendment Act 1956, *NZ Statutes*, 1956, pp. 438–52.
85. Chapman et al., *New Zealand Politics in Action*, pp. 33–48.
86. Ibid., pp. 30–32.
87. Ibid., pp. 58–67.
88. Industrial Conciliation and Arbitration Amendment Act 1961, *NZ Statutes*, 1961, pp. 1809–17.
89. R. M. Chapman, 'The "no change" election', *Comment*, v.2 (1964), pp. 8–10.
90. A. V. Mitchell, 'Sotto voce: the voice of the people: elections — 1966 style', *Comment*, VIII.1 (1966), pp. 1–4.
91. R. M. Chapman, 'The 1969 election', *Comment*, x.4 (1970), pp. 14–18.

CHAPTER 15: THE POLITICS OF VOLATILITY

1. Two-party swing is defined as the *net* percentage change in support for the two main parties contesting an election.
2. In 1960 W. H. Oliver referred to these values as 'national obsessions'. See *The Story of New Zealand* (Faber and Faber, London, 1960), p. 278.
3. The Labour Party was still substantially the political wing of the working class and, as such, continued to be labelled as a 'socialist' party by its opponents. Ian Templeton and Keith Eunson, *Election '69* (Reed, Wellington, 1969).
4. See Templeton and Eunson, op. cit.; John Roberts 'Who won, who lost', in Brian Edwards (ed.), *Right Out* (Reed, Wellington, 1973), pp. 241–4.
5. See J. R. Marshall, 'And that was it', in Edwards, op. cit., pp. 40–2; John Roberts, op. cit., 244–8.
6. See Nigel S. Roberts, 'The New Zealand General Election of 1972', in Stephen Levine (ed.), *New Zealand Politics: A Reader* (Cheshire, Melbourne, 1975), p. 101.
7. See Warren Page and Brian Lockstone, *Landslide '72* (John McIndoe Ltd, Dunedin, 1973); Keith Jackson, 'Political leadership and succession in the New Zealand National Party', in Stephen Levine (ed.), *Politics in New Zealand: A Reader* (Allen and Unwin, Sydney, 1978), pp. 165–6.
8. Tony Brunt, 'In search of values', in Edwards, op. cit., p. 81.
9. Gordon Parry, 'How the South went sour', in Edwards, op. cit., pp. 223–37.
10. John Gould, *The Rake's Progress: The New Zealand Economy since 1945* (Hodder and Stoughton, Auckland, 1982), pp. 120–6.
11. Brunt, op. cit., pp. 79–92; Colin James, *The Quiet Revolution* (Allen and Unwin, Wellington, 1986), p. 34.
12. *The Press* (Christchurch), 23 December 1972.
13. The first Labour Government had made special grants to unemployed persons as the Christmas bonus shortly after taking office. See W. B. Sutch, *The Quest for Security in New Zealand* (OUP, Wellington, 1966), p. 198.
14. Gould, op. cit.; Howard R. Penniman (ed.) *New Zealand at the Polls: The General Election of 1978* (American Enterprise Institute, Washington, 1980), pp. 18–20.
15. Gould, op. cit., pp. 128–9.
16. *The Press* (Christchurch), 17 August 1973.
17. Gary R. Hawke, 'The New Zealand economy in 1990'. Paper presented to the International Workshop on 1991 Economic Outlook for Asian Economies, Tokyo, February 1991, p. 6; Gould, op. cit., pp. 130–3.
18. Nigel S. Roberts, 'The New Zealand General Election of 1975', *The Australian Quarterly*, March 1976, p. 108.
19. *AJHR*, 1974, A.1, 'Report of the Ministry of Foreign Affairs for the year ended 31 March 1974', pp. 30–2 and ibid., 1975, A.1, 'Report of the Ministry of Foreign Affairs for the year ended 31 March 1975', p. 25.
20. James, op. cit., p. 22.
21. Penniman, op. cit., pp. 21–2.

22. Nigel S. Roberts, 'The New Zealand General Election of 1975', pp. 98–9; G. A. Wood, *Why National Won* (John McIndoe, Dunedin, 1975), p. 16, n. 1.
23. See Jackson, op. cit. pp. 166–79.
24. The seven themes were: *Superannuation, Women's Rights, Housing, Freedoms, Industrial Relations, Immigration,* and *The Cities.* The full texts of the first four listed here were published as advertisements in daily newspapers in the week before the election (see *The Press,* 27 November 1972). Each television advertisement included a cartoon segment prepared by the American animation company, Hanna-Barbera. See Chris Wilkes, 'The great New Zealand melodrama: television and the 1975 general election' in Stephen Levine (ed.), *Politics in New Zealand,* pp. 207–21, for a fuller account of the impact of television advertising in the 1975 election.
25. *1975 National Party Manifesto: A Guide to What the Next National Government Will Do for New Zealand* (condensed version of party manifesto), New Zealand National Party, Wellington, 1975.
26. Keith Sinclair, *The Oxford Illustrated History of New Zealand* (OUP, Auckland, 1990), p. 355 described it as 'the most expensive electoral bribe in the country's history, and the most successful.' See *1976 Census of Population and Dwellings, Volume 2: Ages and Marital Status,* Department of Statistics, Wellington, 1979, p. 15, Table 5.
27. See Robert Chapman, 'The principal reasons we voted the way we did on November 29, 1975', *National Business Review,* 22 September 1976.
28. See David Excel (ed.), *Rowling: Citizens for Rowling* (Citizens for Rowling Campaign, Auckland, October 1975).
29. Alan McRobie and Nigel S. Roberts, *Election '78: The 1977 Electoral Redistribution and the 1978 General Election in New Zealand* (McIndoe, Dunedin, 1978) pp. 15–19.
30. Six months later the Chief Justice ruled that Muldoon's announcement was *ultra vires.* See Geoffrey Palmer, *Unbridled Power,* 2nd edn. (OUP, Auckland, 1987), pp. 186–8.
31. Penniman, op. cit., p. 25.
32. Nigel S. Roberts, 'The New Zealand General Election of 1975', p. 112; Stephen Levine and Juliet Lodge, *The New Zealand General Election of 1975* (Price Milburn/ NZUP, Wellington, 1976), p. 29; *New Zealand Official Yearbook 1990* (Department of Statistics, Wellington, 1990), p. 614.
33. Gould, op. cit., p. 149.
34. Gould, ibid., pp. 145–6; Hawke, *The Making of New Zealand: An Economic History* (Cambridge University Press, Cambridge, 1985), p. 330.
35. R. D. Muldoon, 'Preface', in *The New Zealand Economy: A Personal View* (Endeavour Press, Auckland, 1985).
36. James, op. cit., pp. 92–3.
37. *The Press* (Christchurch), 28 July 1976.
38. Luke Trainor, 'The primacy of internal policy: National, sport and external relations, 1975–78', *Political Science,* 30:2 (December 1978). The full text of the Gleneagles Agreement is included as an appendix to this article.
39. In 1975 National promised that it would not interfere with the freedom of New Zealanders 'to have contact or play sport with, or not have contact or play sport with, anyone in the world. It is the individual's own decision. Thus, if the Rugby Union wishes to invite the Springboks to New Zealand next winter, we will make them welcome.' See National's *1975 Manifesto* (condensed version).
40. Penniman, op. cit., p. 82, n. 22.
41. Ibid., p. 247.
42. Reserve Bank of New Zealand, *Bulletin,* March 1976, pp. 47–9.
43. Gould, op. cit., p. 149.
44. New Zealand National Party, 1981 Manifesto, *This is Your Future: Policies for the Decade of the 80's,* (New Zealand National Party, Wellington, 1981). In 1979 the Government had passed the National Development Act to minimize legal impediments and planning delays for proposed development projects. It was designed to partly or wholly override twenty-three existing statutes. In 1981 an amendment allowed projects designated as being of 'national importance' to proceed even more rapidly.

45. The Government's official policy was that it was adhering to the letter of the Gleneagles Agreement (i.e. to take 'every practical step to *discourage* contact . . .') but M. B. R. Couch, Minister of Maori Affairs and Minister of Police, openly supported the proposed tour.
46. James, op. cit., pp. 68–9.
47. Ibid., pp. 98–100.
48. *AJHR*, 1980, H.5, 'The report of the Commission of Inquiry into allegations of impropriety in respect of approval by the Marginal Lands Board of an application by James Maurice Fitzgerald and Audrey Fitzgerald', November 1980, pp. 108–12.
49. See *Christchurch Star*, 15 December 1979 and *The Star* (Christchurch), 27 June 1980.
50. See *The Press* (Christchurch), 2 November 1979 and John Henderson, *Rowling: The Man and the Myth* (ANZ and Fraser Books, 1981), pp. 24–8.
51. At the Labour Party's 1977 conference Rata had publicly warned delegates that the Party could no longer afford to ignore Māori aspirations and demands. In his 'Report of the Maori Policy Committee' (of which he was then chairperson) he noted: 'The Maori people entered a commitment with the Labour movement over 40 years ago and if the rate of our progress does not match our needs then we could be forced to look elsewhere and by any means we can muster to achieve our rights.'
52. There had been an attempt to install Lange as deputy leader in May 1978, only thirteen months after he had entered Parliament. See Henderson, op. cit., pp. 174–5.
53. Henderson, op. cit., pp. 24–5.
54. Penniman, op. cit., pp. 163–7.
55. Ninety per cent of electorates where support for the tour exceeded opposition swung *to* National but, with two exceptions, centres where a majority of electors were opposed to the tour recorded swings *against* the Government.
56. Mana Motuhake won 15.1 per cent of the votes cast in the four Māori electorates.
57. James, op. cit., pp. 96–7.
58. *The Press* (Christchurch), 15 June 1982 and *The Star* (Christchurch), 21 June 1982. For comment on the contrast between Quigley's dismissal and Couch's retention as a minister see John Roberts, *Politicians, Public Servants and Public Enterprise* (Institute of Policy Studies, Wellington, 1987), pp. 51–2.
59. *The Star* (Christchurch), 20 and 27 February 1982, and 4 and 15 March 1982; *The Press* Christchurch, 11 May 1982.
60. Moore, who was defeated by one vote, was the Lange faction's preferred choice as deputy leader.
61. See *The Press* (Christchurch) 6, 24, 26 and 27 September 1983, 3 October 1983, 2 and 4 May 1984; McRobie, *New Zealand Electoral Atlas*, (GP Books, Wellington, 1989), pp. 21–2 and p. 26, n. 35.
62. New Zealand Party, *A Manifesto of Recovery*, New Zealand Party, Wellington, 1984.
63. *The Statutes of New Zealand*, 1982, No. 20 (Clutha Valley (Clyde Dam) Empowering Act); *The Press* (Christchurch) 19 July 1982.
64. Raymond Miller, 'The Democratic Party', in Hyam Gold (ed.) *New Zealand Politics in Perspective*, (Longman Paul, Auckland, 1989), pp. 255–6.
65. *Otago Daily Times* (Dunedin), 1 August 1983.
66. 'You can have me and my people again or you can take your chance on the other lot' — Muldoon, special television announcement, TVNZ, 15 June 1984.
67. See *National Business Review–Heylen Poll*, October 1984; Alan McRobie, 'End of an era', unpublished paper, 1985, pp. 28–9; and Jack Vowles, 'People's choice', *Listener TV and Radio Times*, 24 December 1990, p. 22.
68. In the 1984 election minor party and independent candidates took 21.1 per cent of the total vote.
69. Keith Jackson, 'The New Zealand General Election of 1984', *Electoral Studies*, 4:1 (1985), pp. 75–9.
70. See Exel (ed.), op. cit., p. 16.
71. Hawke, 'The New Zealand economy in 1990', pp. 8–9; see also Jonathan Boston and Martin Holland, *The Fourth Labour Government: Radical Politics in New Zealand* (OUP,

Auckland, 1987), especially ch. 1; Roger Douglas and Louise Callan, *Towards Prosperity*, (David Bateman, Auckland, 1987); Margaret Wilson, *Labour in Government* (Allen and Unwin/PNP, Wellington, 1989).

72. See Douglas and Callan, op. cit., pp. 51–9.

73. Fourth Estate Books, Wellington, 1980.

74. Jonathan Boston and Keith Jackson, 'The New Zealand General Election of 1987', *Electoral Studies*, 7:2 (1988), pp. 70–1.

75. The objective of the reforms was to make management of the state's economic activities more flexible, efficient, and accountable.

76. *Statutes of New Zealand 1988*, No. 20 (State Sector Act).

77. *The Press* (Christchurch), 2 May and 6 September 1983. See also, Stuart McMillan, *Neither Confirm Nor Deny* (Allen and Unwin/PNP, Wellington, 1987).

78. McMillan, op. cit., pp. 30–5.

79. Keith Sinclair, *A History of New Zealand*, revised edn. (Penguin Books, Auckland, 1988), p. 321.

80. See Roderic Alley, 'ANZUS and the nuclear issue' in Jonathan Boston and Martin Holland (eds.), *The Fourth Labour Government* (OUP, Auckland, 1987), pp. 198–213; Margaret Wilson, *Labour in Government, 1984–1987* (Allen and Unwin/PNP, Wellington, 1989), ch. 4.

81. Alain Marfart and Dominique Prieur subsequently pleaded guilty to manslaughter and were sentenced to ten years' imprisonment. In 1986 the United Nations Secretary General mediated an agreement between the New Zealand and French Governments following which Marfart and Prieur were released into French custody on the understanding that they would be confined to Hao atoll until at least three years had elapsed from the date of their conviction. Both were subsequently returned to France before the three-year period had elapsed without New Zealand's permission or agreement first having been obtained. See David Lange, *Nuclear Free — The New Zealand Way* (Penguin Books, Auckland, 1990), ch. 9; McMillan, op. cit., pp. 37–8.

82. *New Zealand National Party, Manifesto '87: Let's Get New Zealand Right* (New Zealand National Party, Wellington, 1987), pp. 74–5; *The Press* (Christchurch), 10 July 1987. Six months before the 1990 election National unequivocally accepted the anti-nuclear legislation passed by the Labour Government in 1985. See *New Zealand National Party Manifesto, 1990* 'New Zealand in the world', (New Zealand National Party, Wellington, 1990), p. 1; *The Press* (Christchurch), 9 March 1990.

83. Under New Zealand law the formal declaration of an election result cannot take place until at least ten days have elapsed following the closing of the poll. The purpose of this provision is to allow time for special votes (cast outside the electorate or overseas) to be received and validated by the Returning Officer before the official count takes place.

84. Margaret Clark (ed.), *The 1987 Election: What Happened* (Social Sciences Research Fund Committee, Wellington, 1988), pp. 10–36.

85. Boston and Jackson, op. cit., p. 71.

86. Boston and Jackson, op. cit., pp. 70–1.

87. Ibid.

88. New Zealand Government, *Government Economic Statement*, 17 December 1987.

89. Ruth Dyson, 'The 1984–1990 Labour Government: what happened and why', in Elizabeth McLeay (ed.), *The 1990 General Election: Perspectives on Political Change in New Zealand* (Department of Politics, Wellington, Occasional publication) no. 3, pp. 9–16.

90. See Hawke, 'The New Zealand economy in 1990', p. 10.

91. Lange, op. cit., pp. 199–207. The contents of this speech were reported in New Zealand on the morning of 25 April, ANZAC day.

92. These data are based on the number of *valid* votes cast to the total number of registered electors. (The official election statistics (*AJHR*, E.9) include votes cast by persons who are *not* registered as electors — whose votes are, therefore, disallowed — in the total number of votes cast thus inflating the percentage turnout.)

93. New Zealand Government, *Economic and Social Initiative*, 19 December 1990.

94. *AJHR*, 1991, B.6, 'Budget 1991'.

95. Anthony Downs, *An Economic Theory of Democracy*, (Harper and Row, New York, 1957), ch. 4.

CHAPTER 16: ECONOMIC TRENDS AND ECONOMIC POLICY

1. Hawke, *Between Governments and Banks*, pp. 102–8.
2. Baker, *War Economy*; Simkin, 'Wartime changes in the New Zealand economy'; Wood, *The New Zealand People at War*.
3. Hawke, *Between Governments and Banks*, pp. 113–17.
4. Rowe, 'Import reliance 1950–65'; Brownlie, 'New Zealand's import function'; Eyre, 'Real imports and import ratios'; Tho, 'Implicit indices of export and import prices'.
5. These changes can best be traced in successive issues of *NZOYB* and *Reserve Bank Bulletin*.
6. Hawke, 'Long–term trends in New Zealand imports'.
7. Hawke, 'Diversification of New Zealand exports', *VUW Working Papers in Economic History*, 79/2 (Victoria University of Wellington, 1979). See P. Nicholl and A. Boaden, 'New Zealand: international economic trends', in Richard W. Baker and Gary R. Hawke (eds.), *ANZUS Economics* (Praeger, New York, forthcoming). See also J. D. Gould, *The Rake's Progress* (Hodder and Stoughton, Auckland, 1982); *The Muldoon Years* (Hodder and Stoughton, Auckland, 1985).
8. The best contemporary analysis of the mid-1970s is NZ Task Force, *New Zealand at the Turning Point*. For a different view of the 1967 devaluation, see Buckle, 'The response of New Zealand's pastoral exports to the 1967 devaluation'.
9. A. H. Ward, *A Command of Co-operatives*; Greensmith, *The New Zealand Wool Commission*; Evans, *A History of Agricultural Production and Marketing in New Zealand*. See also Hawke, *Making of New Zealand*, pp. 244–5.
10. The economic history of farming has to be put together from a wide variety of sources, notably again *NZOYB*. See also O'Malley et al., *Farming and Inflation*; Zanetti et al., *Report of the Farm Incomes Advisory Committee*; Philpott et al., *Estimates of Farm Income and Productivity in New Zealand*.
11. Cf. *NZOYB*, 1956, p. 616 and 1977, pp. 461–2. The annual reports of the Department of Industries and Commerce in *AJHR* frequently reported new products made by local industry, often exaggerating them into new industries.
12. Industrial history too has to be reconstructed from a wide variety of sources among which *NZOYB* is most important. See also Castle, *A Study of New Zealand Manufacturing*; Turkington, *Industrial Conflict*; Deane, *Foreign Investment in New Zealand Manufacturing*; Rose, *Development Options in the New Zealand Motor Car Assembly Industry*; Elley, 'Effective protection in selected New Zealand manufacturing industries in 1972–3'; Lloyd, *New Zealand Manufacturing Production and Trade with Australia*; Lloyd, *Economic Relationships between Australia and New Zealand*; McDonald, *Regional Development in New Zealand*; Franklin, *Trade, Growth and Anxiety*. For a different view of import licensing, see Rosenberg, *A Guidebook to New Zealand's Future*.
13. B. P. Philpott, 'Productivity, economic growth and the N.D.C.', Paper for Economic Society of Australia and New Zealand (October, 1971).
14. Young, 'The New Zealand transport policy study'; Hawke, 'The transport policy study'. On coastal shipping, see Rimmer, 'The changing status of New Zealand seaports' and 'Coastal shipping's changing role in New Zealand's space economy'. On building and construction, energy and transport generally, *NZOYB* is the most useful reference. See also A. J. Ward, 'Aspects of New Zealand housing', and on tourism, Lloyd, 'The economic development of the tourist industry in New Zealand'.
15. Analysis of services in general requires a combination of local sources such as Philpott, *Aspects of Productivity and Economic Growth in New Zealand*, and Tho and Philpott, 'Sectoral trends in gross output, factor inputs and labour productivity', with overseas research such as V. R. Fuchs, *The Service Economy* (National Bureau of Economic

Research, New York, 1968). On financial services see Hawke, *Between Governments and Banks*, ch. 8, and Bayliss, 'Money supply and selected liquid assets'.

16. The orthodox account underlay many 'establishment' reviews of the New Zealand economy such as the periodic reports of the NZ Monetary and Economic Council. It was also endorsed by many private commentators; early statements are H. G. Lang, 'Price and wage policy' in R. S. Parker (ed.), *Economic Stability in New Zealand* (NZ Institute of Public Administration, Wellington, 1953) and W. B. Sutch, *Problems of Prosperity* (Price Milburn, Wellington, 1962). The crucial criticism of the assumed role of fiscal policy is best expounded in M. J. Pope, 'The conceptual bases and interpretation of data for stabilisation purposes', *NZ Economic Papers*, V (1971), pp. 18–64.

17. Hawke, *Making of New Zealand*, pp. 190–7, 322–7.

18. Hawke, 'Acquisitiveness and equality in New Zealand's economic development'.

19. Pope, 'The public sector overload — is there any?'.

20. Blyth, *Inflation in New Zealand*, Appendix A; Woods, *The Industrial Relations Act, 1973*, and *The Industrial Relations Amending Legislation of 1976*; Seidman, *The Industrial Relations Systems of the United States and New Zealand*.

21. Blyth, 'The special case'; Blyth, 'The industrialization of New Zealand'.

22. Hawke, 'Inflation in New Zealand'.

23. Belshaw, *Immigration, Problems and Policies*; Gould, 'Some economic consequences of rapid population growth in New Zealand'; NZ Monetary and Economic Council, Report 12: *Increased Immigration and the New Zealand Economy* (November 1966).

24. It would be difficult to document any such understanding, but Sir Alan Westerman had no doubt that it was implicitly understood in Canberra.

25. For alternative accounts of the Labour Government elected in 1984, see J. Boston and M. Holland (eds.), *The Fourth Labour Government* (OUP, Auckland, 1987, revised edition 1990) and R. Rabel, 'New Zealand', in R. Baker and C. Morrison (eds.), *Australia, New Zealand and the United States: National Evolution and Alliance Relations* (Praeger, New York, 1991).

26. John Roberts, *Politicians, Public Servants & Public Enterprise* (VUP for Institute of Policy Studies, Wellington, 1987); Peter McKinlay, *Corporatisation: The Solution for State Owned Enterprise?* (VUP for Institute of Policy Studies, Wellington, 1987); G. W. Jones, *Privatisation: Reflections on the British Experience* (VUP for Institute of Policy Studies, Wellington, 1987); Greg Parston, *The Evolution of General Management in the National Health Service* (VUP for Institute of Policy Studies, Wellington, 1988); *The Producer Board Seminar Papers* (VUP for Institute of Policy Studies, Wellington, 1988), John Martin, *A Profession of Statecraft* (VUP for Institute of Policy Studies, Wellington, 1988) and *State Owned Enterprises: Privatisation and Regulation — Issues and Options* (VUP for Institute of Policy Studies, Wellington, 1988); Stephen Jennings and Susan Begg, *State Owned Enterprise Policy: Issues in Ownership and Regulation* (New Zealand Business Roundtable, Wellington, April 1988); R. S. Deane, 'Corporatisation and Privatisation: A Discussion of the Issues', speech to the Napier Chamber of Commerce, 31 May 1989, distributed by Electricorp; Lee McCabe, *Privatising State Owned Enterprises* (Economic Development Commission, Wellington, July 1989).

27. Alfred Y-T Wong, 'New Zealand's true rate of protection', *Reserve Bank Discussion Papers* G 89/4 (June, 1989).

28. An early stimulant of policy discussion was *The Regulated Economy: Report No 5 of the Economic Monitoring Group* (NZ Planning Council, Wellington, September 1985) but much of the public discussion was led by the Economic Development Commission. See, for example, David Haarmeyer *Competition Policy and Government Regulatory Intervention* (Economic Development Commission, Wellington, October 1988); *A Generic Approach to the Reform of Occupational Regulation* (Economic Development Commission, Wellington, December 1988). The Law Commission was also a prolific contributor.

29. The debate about tax policy can be followed in Alex Texeira, Claudia Scott and Martin Devlin, *Inside GST: The Development of the Goods and Services Tax* (VUP for Institute of Policy Studies, Wellington, 1986), John Prebble, *The Taxation of Controlled Foreign*

Corporations (VUP for Institute of Policy Studies, Wellington, 1987), Richard J. Vann, *Trans-Tasman Taxation of Equity Investment* (VUP for Institute of Policy Studies, Wellington, 1988), Cedric Sandford, *Taxing Wealth in New Zealand* (VUP for Institute of Policy Studies, Wellington, 1987), Gordon Bale, *Wealth Transfer Taxation* (VUP for Institute of Policy Studies, Wellington, 1989), Toni Ashton and Susan St John, *Superannuation in New Zealand: Averting the Crisis* (VUP for Institute of Policy Studies, Wellington, 1988) and the references given therein.

30. Ross Committee, 1967; McCaw Committee, 1981.
31. The best discussion remains: Economic Monitoring Group, *Foreign Exchange Constraints, Export Growth and Overseas Debt* (NZ Planning Council, Wellington, 1983). Subsequent Planning Council publications trace the policy debate through the 1980s. The best critical study is Paul Dalziel, 'National's macroeconomic policy', in Jonathan Boston and Paul Dalziel (eds.), *The Decent Society? Essays in Response to National's Economic and Social Policies* (OUP, Auckland, 1991), pp. 19–38.
32. Royal Commission on Social Policy, *The April Report*, 5 volumes, (Wellington, 1988). The Royal Commission also published many supporting papers, most notably *Working Papers on Income Maintenance and Taxation* (March, 1988) and *The Role of the State: Five Perspectives* (March, 1988).
33. *The Economy in Transition: Restructuring to 1989* (New Zealand Planning Council, Report of the Economic Monitoring Group, Wellington, July 1989).
34. *The Economist* 311(7607) (24 June 1989), pp. 17–18; A. Bollard and R. Buckle (eds.), *Economic Liberalization in New Zealand* (Allen and Unwin, Wellington, 1987).
35. Blyth, *Economic Growth, 1950–1960* ; NZ Monetary and Economic Report No. 2: *Economic Growth in New Zealand* (May 1962).
36. J. A. Dowie, 'A century-old estimate of the national income of New Zealand', *Business Archives & History*, VI (1966), pp. 117–31.
37. Hawke, *The Making of New Zealand: An Economic History* (Cambridge University Press, Cambridge, 1985), p. 329; A. C. Rayner et al. *The Economy in Transition: Restructuring to 1989* (New Zealand Planning Council, Economic Monitoring Group Report No 9, Wellington, July 1989), pp. 7–8.

CHAPTER 17: THE SOCIAL PATTERN

1. Baker, *The New Zealand People at War: War Economy*, pp. 445, 589, 591; Gerard, 'Christchurch, 1942', p. 43. See also Nancy Taylor, *The New Zealand People at War: The Home Front*, 2 vols., (Historical Publications Branch, Wellington, 1986).
2. M. K. Joseph, *Inscription on a Paper Dart: Selected Poems, 1945–72* (AUP/OUP, Auckland, 1974), p. 23.
3. 'The Labour Party Manifesto, 1935', in W. David McIntyre and W. J. Gardner (eds.), *Speeches and Documents on New Zealand History* (Clarendon Press, Oxford, 1971), p. 318.
4. 'Choices and echoes: excerpts from party programmes', in Stephen Levine (ed.), *New Zealand Politics: A Reader* (Cheshire, Melbourne, 1975), p. 125.
5. For views of the anxieties by the mid-1970s see: NZ Task Force, *New Zealand at the Turning Point*; Franklin, *Trade, Growth and Anxiety*, especially chs. 1, 9, and 10; W. H. Oliver, 'An uneasy retrospect', in Wards (ed.), *Thirteen Facets*; Donnelly, *Big Boys Don't Cry*, especially ch. 2.
6. Thompson, *Retreat from Apartheid*, p. 3; Bill Pearson, 'Fretful sleepers', *Landfall*, VI.3 (1952), p. 218.
7. J. R. Marshall, 'The philosophy of the National Party', in Levine (ed.), *New Zealand Politics*, p. 147; Nordmeyer in R. S. Milne, *Political Parties in New Zealand* (Clarendon Press, Oxford, 1966), p. 110; for Kirk see *Towards Nationhood: Selected Extracts from the Speeches of Norman Kirk, M.P.* (NZ Books, Palmerston North, 1969), and Norman Kirk, 'The philosophy of the Labour Party', in Levine (ed.), *New Zealand Politics*, pp. 142–6; for Muldoon see John T. Henderson, 'The "operational code" of Robert

David Muldoon', in Stephen Levine (ed.), *Politics in New Zealand: A Reader* (Allen and Unwin, Sydney, 1978).

8. Levine, *The New Zealand Political System*, ch. 5.
9. H. I. Sinclair, *Population: New Zealand's Problem*; Hercus, *Women and National Survival*, p. 20. For further references and commentary see Hargreaves and Heenan, *An Annotated Bibliography of New Zealand Population*; Franklin, 'New Zealand's population in the welfare era'.
10. Calvert, *The Future Population of New Zealand*, pp. 13, 65, 69–73.
11. This paragraph and the next four are based on the following sources: *Social Trends in New Zealand*, ch. 1; Hargreaves and Heenan, *New Zealand Population*, pp. 70, 136–7; *NZOYB*, 1978, Sections 3 and 4; Borrie, 'Recent and potential demographic dynamics of Australasia'; Miriam Gilson, 'Population growth in post-war New Zealand', in Forster (ed.), *Social Process in New Zealand*; E. M. K. Douglas, 'Recent changes in the population of New Zealand', in Webb and Collette (eds.), *New Zealand Society*; Gilson-Vosburgh, *The New Zealand Family and Social Change*; Pool, *The Maori Population of New Zealand*; Koopman-Boyden (ed.), *Families in New Zealand Society*; Franklin, *Trade, Growth and Anxiety*, pp. 8–20, 32–40; Neville and O'Neill (eds.), *The Population of New Zealand*.
12. See the party manifestos in 1972, Levine (ed.), *New Zealand Politics*, pp. 135–6.
13. This paragraph and the next six are based mainly on the following sources: *Social Trends*, pp. 7–9; *NZOYB*, 1972 and 1978, Section 3; Franklin, *Trade, Growth and Anxiety*, pp. 20–31, 49–57, and ch. 8; Gibson, 'Urbanization in New Zealand'; Thomson and Trlin (eds.), *Contemporary New Zealand*, chs. 6–8; Johnston (ed.), *Urbanisation in New Zealand*; Bush and Scott (eds.), *Auckland at Full Stretch*; Hearn and Slater (eds.), *North Otago Region and Development*, chs. 1–3; Hamer, 'A decade of regional imbalance in New Zealand'.
14. Somerset, *Littledene*, pp. 136–7.
15. Ibid., p. 107; K. B. Cumberland, 'The essential nature of Auckland', in Bush and Scott (eds.), *Auckland*, p. 23.
16. Keown, 'The career cycle and the stepwise migration process'.
17. For this paragraph see J. R. McCreary, 'Population growth and urbanisation', in Schwimmer (ed.), *The Maori People in the Nineteen-sixties*; Pool, *Maori Population*, pp. 198–210, 214, 219–20; David Boardman, 'Polynesian immigrants: migrating process and distribution in New Zealand', in Webb and Collette (eds.), *New Zealand Society*; Pitt and Macpherson, *Emerging Pluralism: The Samoan Community in New Zealand*, chs. 2 and 8.
18. NZ Task Force, *Turning Point*, pp. 152–3; T. G. McGee, 'The social ecology of New Zealand cities; a preliminary investigation', in Forster (ed.), *Social Process*, p. 156; Scott, *Regional Development Objectives and Policies*.
19. This paragraph and the next four have been based on 'Building, construction and housing' in *NZOYB*, 1946, 1956, 1959, and 1978; Erik Olssen, *John A. Lee* (University of Otago Press, Dunedin, 1977), ch. 8; R. T. Metge, ' "The house that Jack built": The origins of Labour state housing, 1935–1938', MA thesis, Auckland (1972); A. D. Trlin, 'State housing: shelter and welfare in suburbia', in Trlin (ed.), *Social Welfare and New Zealand Society*; G. W. A. Bush, *Decently and In Order: The Government of the City of Auckland* (Collins, Auckland, 1971), pp. 375–82; *Housing in New Zealand*; Kilmartin and Thorns, *Cities Unlimited*, especially ch. 7; Bush and Scott (eds.), *Auckland*, Part 2.
20. Hunn, 'Report on the Department of Maori Affairs', pp. 36–8, 125–7.
21. Somerset, *Littledene*, p. 106.
22. Rowland, 'Processes of Maori urbanisation', p. 20.
23. Pool, 'A method for the social grading of areas'; McGee, 'The social ecology of New Zealand cities'; Duncan Timms, *The Urban Mosaic* (Cambridge University Press, 1971), chs. 2, 4, and 5: R. J. Johnston, 'Neighbourhood patterns within urban areas', and James Forrest, 'Residential patterns in smaller towns', in R. J. Johnston (ed.), *Urbanisation*; Franklin, *Trade, Growth and Anxiety*, ch. 9; David Thorns, 'Urbanisation,

suburbanisation, and social class in New Zealand', in Pitt (ed.), *Social Class in New Zealand*; David Pearson, *Johnsonville*, especially chs. 4, 7.

24. Ian Reynolds, 'Housing in Auckland — fits and misfits', in Bush and Scott (eds.), *Auckland*, p. 83.

25. Cora Vellekoop, 'Social strata in New Zealand', in Forster (ed.), *Social Process*; John Collette, 'Social stratification in New Zealand', in Webb and Collete (eds.), *New Zealand Society*; Cora Vellekoop Baldock, 'Stratification and social welfare', in Trlin (ed.), *Social Welfare*; David Pitt, 'Are there social classes in New Zealand?' in Pitt (ed.), *Social Class*; Steven, 'Towards a class analysis of New Zealand'; Bedggood, *Rich and Poor in New Zealand*.

26. Daniel Bell, *The Coming of Post-industrial Society: A Venture in Social Forecasting* (Basic Books, New York, 1973), pp. 12–26. Cf. Anthony Giddens, *The Class Structure of the Advanced Societies* (Hutchinson, London, 1973), pp. 255–64; and Jonathan Gershuny, *After Industrial Society? The Emerging Self-service Economy* (Macmillan, London, 1978), especially chs. 4–6.

27. Hyman, 'Women in the New Zealand labour force'.

28. Material for this paragraph and the next two has been drawn mainly from: the sections on land tenure, farming, and employment in *NZOYB*, 1956, 1972, 1978; Franklin, *Trade, Growth and Anxiety*, ch. 6; Ward, 'The agricultural sector'; Ensor, 'The agricultural sector in action'; NZ Task Force, *Turning Point*, pp. 281–9.

29. Material for this paragraph and the next three has been mainly drawn from: the sections on manufacturing and employment in the *NZOYB*, 1972 and 1978; *Social Trends*, ch. 8; Lane, 'Growth and change'; Cora Vellekoop Baldock, 'Occupational choice and social class in New Zealand', and Cluny Macpherson, 'Polynesians in New Zealand: an emerging eth-class?', in Pitt (ed.), *Social Class*; J. H. Robb and Jonathan Cloud, 'Occupational mobility in a New Zealand provincial borough', P. A. Lane, 'Immigration and economics', and John Forster, 'Social development and labour force participation: the case of the Maori', in Webb and College (eds.), *New Zealand Society*; Franklin, *Trade, Growth and Anxiety*, chs. 3 and 7; Howells et al. (eds.), *Labour and Industrial Relations in New Zealand*, especially chs. 8, 11, 14; Wolfgang Rosenberg, 'The functions of full employment', in Thomson and Trlin (eds.), *Contemporary New Zealand*.

30. Franklin, *Trade, Growth and Anxiety*, pp. 73–6, using the data of Elley and Irving, 'Revised socio-economic index for New Zealand'.

31. Vellekoop Baldock, 'Occupational choice and social class', pp. 94–5; Pearson, *Johnsonville*, pp. 106–13.

32. Material for this paragraph and the next two comes mainly from the sections on distribution, manufacturing, building, and employment in *NZOYB* 1956, 1972, and 1978. See also James Forrest, 'Urbanisation and the retail trading system', in Johnston (ed.), *Urbanisation*; and NZ Task Force, *Turning Point*, pp. 317–19.

33. *The Press* (Christchurch), 6 December 1978, p. 16, 'The corner-dairy myth'.

34. Mitchell, *Politics and People in New Zealand*, p. 213.

35. Smith, *The New Zealand Bureaucrat*, p. 30; for local authority employees see *NZOYB*, 1956, p. 1061, 1972, p. 848; Franklin, *Trade, Growth and Anxiety*, pp. 79–80.

36. Smith, *The New Zealand Bureaucrat*, pp. 2–4 and ch. 9.

37. *NZ Census*, 1971, vol. 6, p. 13, Table 1. Statistics in this paragraph and the next eight have also been drawn from *Social Trends*, ch. 3; *NZOYB*, 1978, pp. 174–204; M. J. Cullen, *Lawfully Occupied: The Centennial History of the Otago District Law Society* (Otago District Law Society, Dunedin, 1979), pp. 136–44.

38. Charles Lewis Taylor and Michael C. Hudson, *World Handbook of Political and Social Indicators*, 2nd edn. (Yale University Press, New Haven, 1972), p. 229; Levett and Braithwaite, 'The growth of knowledge and inequality in New Zealand society'.

39. Ewing, *Development of the New Zealand Primary School Curriculum*; Dakin, *Education in New Zealand*; McLaren, *Education in a Small Democracy*; Cumming and Cumming, *History of State Education in New Zealand*; I. A. McLaren, 'Education', in Wards (ed.) *Thirteen Facets*.

40. *AJHR*, 1939, E. 1, pp. 2–3.
41. Ibid., p. 3.
42. Whitehead, 'The Thomas Report — a study in educational reform'; McKenzie, 'The changing concept of equality in New Zealand education', p. 100.
43. *Report of the Commission on Education in New Zealand*, pp. 21, 27, 32; McGeorge, 'Some old wine and some new bottles'.
44. Whitehead, 'The Thomas Report', pp. 55, 58; *Report of the Commission on Education*, pp. 42–3, 384; Harker, 'Social class factors in a New Zealand comprehensive school'; Vellekoop, 'Streaming and social class'.
45. Pocock, 'Meritocracy and mediocracy', p. 16; Smith, *The New Zealand Bureaucrat*, pp. 41–3; Bell, *Post-industrial Society*, p. 450; A. H. Halsey (ed.), *Trends in British Society since 1900* (Macmillan, London, 1972), p. 13; Giddens, *Class Structure*, p. 263; Parkyn, *Success and Failure at the University*, II, pp. 107–8.
46. *Report of the Commission on Education*, pp. 62–6, 315–16, 394; Society for Research on Women, *Urban Women*, chs. 6 and 8; *The Role of Women in New Zealand Society*, chs. 2, 4; National Council of Women in New Zealand, *What Price Equality?*
47. *Report of the Commission on Education*, ch. 8; John Forster and Peter Ramsay, 'Migration, education and occupation', in Forster (ed.), *Social Process*; Metge, *The Maoris of New Zealand*, ch. 12; Douglas Bray and Clement Hill (eds.), *Polynesian and Pakeha in New Zealand Education*, 2 vols. (Heinemann, Auckland, 1973 and 1974).
48. Harold Lydall, *The Structure of Earnings* (Clarendon Press, Oxford, 1968), pp. 156–8, 235; Robert W. Jackman, *Politics and Social Equality: A Comparative Analysis* (John Wiley, New York, 1975), pp. 210–11; C. Westrate, *Portrait of a Modern Mixed Economy, New Zealand*, 2nd edn. (Sweet and Maxwell, Wellington, 1966), p. 94.
49. Lydall, *The Structure of Earnings*, pp. 194, 252; see also Jackman, *Politics and Social Equality*, p. 198; Levett and Braithwaite, 'The growth of knowledge and inequality', pp. 56–8; John Macrae, 'Income distribution and poverty in New Zealand', in Pitt (ed.) *Social Class*; Vellekoop Baldock, 'Stratification and social welfare', pp. 136–7.
50. Brian Easton, 'Of dairy farmers and Auckland', *Comment*, NS, 5 (November 1978), p. 17; Brian Easton, *Social Policy and the Welfare State in New Zealand* (Allen and Unwin, Auckland, 1980), ch. 2.
51. For this paragraph see: *Social Trends*, pp. 178–9; Michael Bassett, *Confrontation '51: The 1951 Waterfront Dispute* (Reed, Wellington, 1972); H. O. Roth, *Trade Unions in New Zealand, Past and Present* (Reed, Wellington, 1973); Howells, et al. (eds.), *Labour and Industrial Relations*.
52. NZ Social Development Council, *Family Finances; New Zealand Household Survey Report, 1976–77* (NZ Dept. of Statistics, Wellington, 1977); Easton, 'Women and the personal income distribution'; Claire Hadfield, 'Whatever happened to the 40-hour week?', *Comment*, NS, 4 (August 1978), pp. 19–23.
53. Hanson, *The Politics of Social Security*, p. 39. For this and the next two paragraphs see also: Asa Briggs, 'The welfare state in historical perspective', *European Journal of Sociology*, II. 2 (1961), pp. 221–58; W. H. Oliver, 'The origins and growth of the welfare state', in Trlin (ed.), *Social Welfare*; Sutch, *The Responsible Society in New Zealand; Social Security in New Zealand*.
54. Report of Select Committee on National Health and Superannuation (1938) in McIntyre and Gardner (eds.), *Speeches and Documents*, p. 333.
55. Ibid., p. 332; see also *Social Security in New Zealand*, pp. 108–9.
56. Keith Sinclair, *Walter Nash* (AUP/OUP, Auckland, 1976), p. 210. For an account more sympathetic to the doctors see Lovell-Smith, *The New Zealand Doctor and the Welfare State*.
57. Cited Lovell-Smith, *The New Zealand Doctor*, p. 148.
58. For a comparative context see Kaim-Caudle, *Comparative Social Policy and Social Security*. For developments since 1945 see P. Avery Jack and J. H. Robb, 'Social welfare policies: development and patterns since 1945', in Trlin (ed.), *Social Welfare; A Health Service for New Zealand*, especially chs. 6–8.

59. Smith and Tatchell, *Health Expenditure in New Zealand*, p. 35. For statistics cited in this paragraph see also *Social Trends*, ch. 4.
60. Fougere, 'Medical insurance', pp. 86–90; Michael French, 'Public or private: a dilemma for health', in Palmer (ed.), *The Welfare State Today*.
61. Although the broad trends are similar these figures differ from those in NZ Planning Council, *The Welfare State? Social Policy in the 1980's*, p. 78, Table 16.
62. A. B. Atkinson, 'Social security: the future', *New Society*, XXXVII.722 (1976), p. 279; Kaim-Caudle, *Comparative Social Policy*, p. 19, and ch. 3.
63. For a critical view see Shirley, *Planning for Community*.
64. *Social Security in New Zealand*, p. 90.
65. Peter Townsend, 'Poverty as relative deprivation: resources and style of living' in Dorothy Wedderburn (ed.), *Poverty, Inequality and Class Structure* (Cambridge University Press, 1974), ch. 1; P. Avery Jack, 'Poverty and social security', in Webb and Collette (eds.), *New Zealand Society; Survey of Persons Aged 65 Years and Over* (Government Printer, Wellington, 1975); Easton, 'Poverty in New Zealand'; Bryant (ed.), *The Widening Gap*; Bedggood, *Rich and Poor*, ch. 7.
66. For this and the next paragraph see the essays in Palmer, *The Welfare State Today*; NZ Planning Council, *The Welfare State?*; Palmer, *Compensation for Incapacity*.
67. *Social Security in New Zealand*, p. 128.
68. Easton, *Consumption in New Zealand*, pp. 12–15.
69. For this and the next paragraph see David Pitt, 'The joiners: associations and leisure in New Zealand', and John Harré, 'Mixing and meeting', in Webb and Collette (eds.), *New Zealand Society*; Chapple, *Tokoroa: Creating a Community*, especially ch. 4; *Social Trends*, ch. 7; Cant (ed.), *Canterbury at Leisure*; Robb and Howorth, *New Zealand Recreation Survey*; John Hinchliff (ed.), *The Nature and Meaning of Sport in New Zealand* (Centre for Continuing Education, University of Auckland, 1978); Thompson, *Retreat from Apartheid*; M. N. Pearson, 'Heads in the sand: the 1956 Springbok tour to New Zealand in perspective'; David Pearson, *Johnsonville*, pp. 44–8, 161–2.
70. See the definition of class by E. P. Thompson, *The Making of the English Working Class* (Penguin, Harmondsworth, 1968), p. 9.
71. Hohepa, 'Maori and Pakeha: the one-people myth', p. 104; Schwimmer (ed.), *The Maori People*.
72. Hunn, 'Report', pp. 14–16; Biggs, 'Maori affairs and the Hunn Report'.
73. For this paragraph and the next see: Metge, *Maoris*, pp. 88–90 and ch. 12; *Housing in New Zealand*, ch. 9; Colgan, 'The Maori: integration or subjugation?'; Walsh, 'Developments since the Hunn Report and their bearing on education'.
74. Metge, *Maoris*, p. 162; McDonald, 'Pre-school education and Maori communities'.
75. Kawharu, *Maori Land Tenure*, chs. 6, 7; Douglas Sinclair, 'Land since the Treaty'.
76. I. H. Kawharu, 'Urban immigrants and *tangata whenua*', in Schwimmer (ed.), *The Maori People*, p. 181; Metge, *Maoris*, pp. 177–9, 238–45. This and the next paragraph are also based on comment in *Te Maori* (Journal of the NZ Maori Council, Wellington) I–VII (1969–75).
77. Cited Hohepa, 'Maori and Pakeha', p. 109.
78. Material for the next four paragraphs has been drawn from Joyce Herd, 'On women', in Wards (ed.), *Thirteen Facets*; Levine and Robinson, *The New Zealand Voter*, ch. 3; Baker, *People at War*, pp. 90–93, 437; Rosemary Seymour (ed.), *Research Papers '78: Women's Studies* (Women's Studies Association, Hamilton, 1978); Miriam Gilson, 'Women in employment', in Forster (ed.), *Social Process*; Society for Research on Women, *Urban Women*; National Council of Women, *What Price Equality?*; NZ Federation of University Women, *Women at Home; The Role of Women in New Zealand Society; Moral Delinquency in Children and Adolescents* (Report of the Special Committee, *AJHR*, 1954, H–47) ch. 10; Auckland Women's Liberation, 'Women's liberation', and Alan Levett, Graeme Sargent, and Margaret Shields, 'Society for Research on Women: political action and social research', in Levine (ed.), *New Zealand Politics*, pp. 239–48; Sandra Coney (ed.), *United Women's Convention — 1973 Report* (United Women's

Convention, Auckland, 1973); Joy Browne (ed.), *Changes, Chances, Choices — A Report on the United Women's Convention 1977* (United Women's Convention, Christchurch, 1978); Novitz, 'Marital and familial roles in New Zealand'; Keir, 'Women and political action'.

79. Images of young suburban housewives can be found in Margaret Sutherland, *The Love Contract* (William Heinemann, Auckland, 1976), and Fiona Kidman, *A Breed of Women* (Harper and Row, Sydney, 1979), chs. 10 and 12.
80. William H. Chafe, *Women and Equality: Changing Patterns in American Culture* (OUP, New York, 1978), p. 95.
81. Betty Friedan, *The Feminine Mystique* (Penguin, Harmondsworth, 1965), p. 17.
82. Christine Dann, 'Will the real women's liberation movement please stand up', *Broadsheet*, 53 (October 1977), p. 14.
83. Sutherland, *The Love Contract*, p. 108.
84. *The New Wave of Protest — A Socialist Strategy for New Zealand* (Socialist Books, Wellington, 1973), p. 5.

CHAPTER 18: A REVOLUTION IN SOCIAL POLICY

1. T. H. Marshall, *Social Policy*, 3rd edn. (Hutchinson, London, 1970), p. 7. See also R. M. Titmuss, *Social Policy, An Introduction* (Allen and Unwin, London, 1974).
2. See, for example, F. Williams, *Social Policy, A Critical Introduction: Issues of Race, Gender and Class* (Polity, Oxford, 1989); P. Townsend, *Sociology and Social Policy* (Penguin, Harmondsworth, 1975); G. Pascal, *Social Policy; A Feminist Analysis* (Tavistock, London, 1986).
3. Most recently see C. Waldegrave and P. Frater, *The National Government Budget Cuts of the First Year in Office: A Social Assessment* (Family Centre and Business and Economic Research, Wellington, 1991); P. Shannon, *Social Policy* (OUP, Auckland, 1991); and G. R. Hawke (ed.), *A Modest Safety Net? The Future of the Welfare State* (Institute of Policy Studies, Wellington, 1991).
4. A. Ware and R. Goodwin (eds.), *Needs and Welfare* (Sage, London, 1990), pp. 5–8. But note that one Treasury official dismisses this typology as mere 'classroom concepts', which he claims are 'irrelevant and unhelpful to understanding actual policy decisions'. N. Prebble, 'Critical new elements in government thinking', in Hawke (ed), *A Modest Safety Net?* (1991), pp. 203.
5. I. Shirley, 'Social policy', in P. Spoonley, D. Pearson and I. Shirley (eds.), *New Zealand Society* (Dunmore, Palmerston North, 1990), pp. 132–47.
6. Ibid., pp. 141–2.
7. *NZOYB*, 1981, p. 149.
8. Ibid., pp. 151–2.
9. *NZOYB*, 1990, p. 208. See also R. Stephens, 'Social policy reform: in retrospect and prospect', in A. Bollard and R. Buckle (eds.), *Economic Liberalisation in New Zealand* (Allen and Unwin, Wellington, 1987), pp. 299–329.
10. T. Ashton, 'Reform of the health services', in J. Boston and P. Dalziel (eds.), *The Decent Society?* (OUP, Auckland, 1992), pp. 146–68.
11. P. Koopman-Boyden, 'Social policy: has there been one?' in M. Holland and J. Boston (eds.), *The Fourth Labour Government*, 2nd edn., (OUP, Auckland, 1990), pp. 213–31.
12. Royal Commission on Social Policy, *The April Report*, 4 vols. in 5 (Government Printer, Wellington, 1988).
13. Ibid., vol. I, p. v.
14. P. Koopman-Boyden, 'Social policy: has there been one?', op. cit., p. 222.
15. Royal Commission on Social Policy, *Towards a Fair and Just Society* (Government Printer, Wellington, 1988), p. 2.
16. The Treasury, *Economic Management* (Wellington, 1984); The Treasury, *Government Management* (Wellington, 1987).
17. *NZOYB*, 1990, p. 203. An alternative view, frequently expressed by Brian Easton in

his *Listener* articles, was that monetarist policies had made unemployment much worse than it needed to be, reducing tax revenue and increasing welfare spending.

18. A. Gibbs, *Unshackling the Hospitals: Report of the Hospital and Related Services Taskforce* (Government Printer, Wellington, 1988); G. R. Hawke, *Report of the Working Group on Post-Compulsory Education and Training* (Government Printer, Wellington, 1988); B. Picot, *Administering for Excellence: Report of the Taskforce to Review Education Administration* (Government Printer, Wellington, 1988); E. Meade, *Education to be More: Report of the Early Childhood Care and Education Group* (Office of the Minister of Education, Wellington, 1988); M. Wilson, *Towards Employment Equity: Report of the Working Group on Equal Employment Opportunities and Equal Pay* (Government Printer, Wellington, 1988); K. T. Wetere, *Partnership Perspectives: A Discussion Paper of the Minister of Maori Affairs* (Government Printer, Wellington, 1988).
19. T. Ashton, 'Reform of the health services', op. cit., pp. 148–51.
20. E. McLeay, 'Housing policy', in J. Boston and P. Dalziel (eds.) *The Decent Society?* (OUP, Auckland, 1992) pp. 169–85.
21. G. Grace, 'Labour and education: the crisis and settlements of education policy', in *The Fourth Labour Government*, 2nd edn. (OUP, Auckland, 1990), pp. 177–8.
22. H. Lauder, 'The New Right and educational policy in New Zealand', *NZ Journal of Education Studies*, 22 (1987), pp. 3–23.
23. Grace, op. cit., pp. 171–2.
24. B. Picot, *Administering for Excellence*, pp. 45–50.
25. *New Zealand Vice-Chancellors' Committee Newsletter*, August 1989, p. 2. See also R. L. Watts, *New Zealand's Universities: Partners in National Development*, Report of the Universities Review Committee (Wellington, 1987).
26. E. Meade, *Education to be More*, Office of the Minister of Education (Government Printer, Wellington, 1988).
27. *Tomorrow's Schools: The Reform of Education Administration in New Zealand* (Government Printer, Wellington, 1988).
28. *Learning for Life: Education and Training Beyond the Age of Fifteen*, Office of the Minister of Education (Government Printer, Wellington, February 1989); *Learning for Life: Two: Policy Decisions* (Government Printer, Wellington, August 1989).
29. J. Martin, 'Rethinking the state services', in M. Holland and J. Boston (eds.), *The Fourth Labour Government* (OUP, Auckland, 1990), pp. 123–39.
30. M. Williams, 'The political economy of privatization', in M. Holland and J. Boston (eds.), *The Fourth Labour Government* (OUP, Auckland, 1990), pp. 140–64.
31. S. Cartwright, *The Report of the Committee of the Cervical Cancer Inquiry* (Government Printer, Auckland, 1988); S. Coney, *The Unfortunate Experiment* (Penguin, Auckland, 1988).
32. P. Dalziel, 'Politics for a decent society', in *The Decent Society*, ed. J. Boston and P. Dalziel (OUP, Auckland, 1992), pp. 208–223. See also A. Sharp, 'The problem of Maori Affairs, 1984–1989', in *The Fourth Labour Government*, 2nd edn. (1990), pp. 251–69.
33. G. Bush, 'The historic reorganization of local government', in *The Fourth Labour Government*, 2nd edn. (1990), pp. 232–50.
34. R. Richardson, 'Statement by the Minister of Finance', in *Economic and Social Initiative, December 1990; Statements to the House of Representatives* (Wellington, 1990), p. 20.
35. R. Richardson, *Budget B6* (GP Print, Wellington, 1991); C. Rudd, 'Controlling and restructuring public expenditure', in *The Decent Society?* (1992), pp. 39–58.
36. S. St John, 'National superannuation: or how not to make policy', in *The Decent Society?* (1992), pp. 126–45.
37. J. Shipley, with S. Upton, L. Smith and J. Luxton, *Social Assistance: Welfare that Works: A Statement of Government Policy on Social Assistance* (GP Print, Wellington, 1991), pp. 3–4, 13.
38. So too were unskilled and lower-paid workers, under the controversial Employment Contracts Act (1991) which made radical changes to the rules governing wage-bargaining, aimed at breaking the power of trade unions. See P. Walsh, 'The Employment Contracts Act', in *The Decent Society?* (1992), pp. 59–76.

39. J. Luxton, *Housing and Accommodation: Accommodation Assistance* (GP Print, Wellington, 1991).
40. J. Boston, 'The funding of tertiary education: rights and wrongs', in *The Decent Society*, (1992), p. 191.
41. J. Shipley, *Social Assistance: Welfare that Works*, p. 3; B. Barry, 'The welfare state versus the relief of poverty', in A. Ware and R. E. Goodwin (eds.), *Needs and Welfare* (Sage, London, 1990), pp. 73–103; J. Boston, 'Targeting: social assistance for all or just for the poor?' in *The Decent Society?* (1992), pp. 77–99.

CHAPTER 19: MĀORI PEOPLE SINCE 1950

1. R. Walker, *Ka Whawhai Tonu Matou: Struggle Without End* (1990), pp. 105–172.
2. *NZOYB*, 1963, p. 73.
3. Bronwyn Elsmore, *Like Them That Dream* (1985), p. 24.
4. R. J. Walker, 'Liberating Maori from Educational Subjection', President's address, Maori University Teachers' Association Annual Conference, Christchurch (1991), p. 6.
5. *AJHR*, 1906, G–5, p. 96.
6. Judith Simon, 'The place of schooling in Maori-Pakeha relations', p. 110.
7. *AJHR*, 1941, E–3, p. 3.
8. H. Belshaw, 'Preface', Young Maori Conference Report (1939), p. 1.
9. Walker, op. cit., p. 195.
10. Belshaw , op. cit., p. 11.
11. J. K. Hunn, 'Report on the Department of Maori Affairs', p. 29.
12. Hunn, 'Report', p. 19.
13. Young Maori Conference Report (1939), p. 46.
14. Walker, op. cit., p. 197.
15. Hunn, 'Report', pp. 24–5.
16. Joan Metge, *A New Maori Migration* (1964), p. 135.
17. Hunn, 'Report', p. 29.
18. Hunn, loc. cit.
19. Joan Metge, *A New Maori Migration* (1964), p. 128.
20. W. D. Rose, *The Maori in the New Zealand Economy*, (1967), p. 38.
21. Joan Metge, *The Maoris of New Zealand*, pp. 93–4.
22. Joan Metge, op. cit., pp. 131–2.
23. Hunn, 'Report', p. 7.
24. Hunn, 'Report', p. 41.
25. R. J. Walker, 'Maoris in a Metropolis' , p. 40.
26. R. J. Walker, 'Urbanism and cultural continuity', in P. Baxter and B. Sansom (eds.), *Race* (1972), p. 400.
27. R. J. Walker, 'Marae: a place to stand', in Michael King (ed.), *Te Ao Hurihuri*, pp. 21–6.
28. Hunn, 'Report', p. 32.
29. *Juvenile Crime in New Zealand*, Department of Social Welfare (1973), p. 16.
30. J. Harre, *Maori and Pakeha* (1966), p. 143.
31. Angela Ballara, *Proud to be White* (1982), pp. 88–9.
32. Hunn, 'Report', p. 18.
33. Hunn, loc. cit.
34. Metge, *The Maoris of New Zealand*, p. 171.
35. Metge, *The Maoris of New Zealand*, p. 212.
36. *Orakei Claim*, Waitangi Tribunal (1987), p. 88.
37. Ibid, p. 195.
38. *Whaiora Marae, Te Waiariki Meeting House* (1977), p. 1.
39. Paulo Freire, *Pedagogy of the Oppressed* (1972), p. 148.
40. *Orakei Claim*, Waitangi Tribunal (1987), pp. 1–86.
41. *The Social Welfare Needs of Maoris and Pacific Islanders in Auckland*, Report to the Minister

of Maori Affairs (1975), pp. 1–10.

42. Walker, *Ka Whawhai Tonu Matou* (1990), pp. 202–3.
43. R. J. Walker, 'Maori adult education', in R. Boshier (ed.), *Towards a Learning Society* (1980), p. 110.
44. Freire, op. cit., p. 104.
45. *Report of Young Maori Leaders Conference 1959*, p. 52.
46. *Report on Maori Education*, NZEI (1967), p. 26.
47. Freire, op. cit., p. 61.
48. *Maori Education, Report of the National Advisory Committee on Maori Education* (1971), p. 3.
49. R. J. Walker, 'Educational replanning for a multicultural society', in G. H. Robinson and B. T. O'Rourke, *Schools in New Zealand Society* (1980), p. 235.
50. Walker, *Ka Whawhai Tonu Matou* (1990), pp. 205–7.
51. H. K. Ngata, 'The Treaty of Waitangi and land: parts of the current law in contravention of the Treaty', in *The Treaty of Waitangi* (Victoria University, 1972), pp. 49–57.
52. Freire, op. cit, p. 60.
53. *Te Hokioi*, issue 2, pp. 2–3.
54. *Te Hokioi*, issue 3, pp. 5–6.
55. R. Walker, *Ka Whawhai Tonu Matou* (1990), p. 210.
56. 'The resurrection of Maori identity' (1971), unpublished paper submitted to the *New Zealand Listener*, reprinted and circulated by MOOHR.
57. *New Zealand Herald* (10 February 1971).
58. Te Matakite o Aotearoa, News Bulletin (May 1976).
59. Robert Stout and A. T. Ngata, 'Commission of Inquiry into Native Lands' *AJHR*, vol. IV G–1P, (1908), p. 5.
60. Waitangi Tribunal, *Orakei Report* (1987), p. 4.
61. *Bastion Point Judgment* (1978), p. 25.
62. Arapera Blank, Haare Williams and Manuka Henare, *He Korero mo Waitangi* (1985), p. 4.
63. Kara Puketapu, *Reform from Within* (1982), p. 4.
64. Department of Maori Affairs, *Annual Report* (1983), p. 6.
65. Richard Benton, *Who Speaks Maori in New Zealand?* pp. 22–3.
66. R. J. Walker, *Nga Tumanako* (1984), p. 16.
67. Elizabeth Rata, 'Kura kaupapa Maori', *PPTA Journal*, (1989), pp. 30–2.
68. Rata, loc. cit.
69. G. Smith, 'Kura kaupapa Maori', unpublished paper (1988), p. 18.
70. *Orakei Report*, Waitangi Tribunal (1987), p. 195.
71. *Muriwhenua Fishing Report*, Waitangi Tribunal (1988), pp. 307–14.
72. *Reasons for the Order of Justice Greig*, (NZMC papers 1987 with Luckie Hain Kennard & Slater, Wellington), pp. 2–8.
73. *Auckland Star* (14 July 1988).
74. *New Zealand Herald* (5 October 1988).
75. Ibid. (23 September 1988).
76. Ibid. (21 June 1991).
77. *Principles for Crown action on the Treaty of Waitangi* (1989), p. 7.
78. Jane Kelsey, *A Question of Honour? Labour and the Treaty, 1984–1989* (1990), p. 219.

CHAPTER 20: FROM DUAL DEPENDENCY TO NUCLEAR FREE

1. BCM (45) 19, Meeting of Officials, 12 April 1945. National Archives EA1, PM 111/1/13, Pt. 1.
2. G. A. Wood, 'The former "Dominion" of New Zealand', *Political Science*, 26 : 1 (1974), pp. 2–10.
3. W. David McIntyre and W. J. Gardner (eds.), *Speeches and Documents on New Zealand History* (Clarendon Press, Oxford, 1971), pp. 286–94.

4. K. J. Keith, 'Constitutional change', in I. Wards (ed.), *Thirteen Facets*, pp. 3–4; The Constitution Act, 1986, *New Zealand Statutes*, No. 114, 1986, vol. 2, pp. 989–1000.
5. A. McIntosh, 'Origins of the Department of External Affairs and the formulation of an independent foreign policy', in *New Zealand in World Affairs*, vol. 1 (NZIIA, Wellington, 1977), pp. 11–35.
6. *External Relations and Trade: A Guide* (Ministry of External Relations and Trade, Wellington, 1990), pp. 7–9; S. Hoadley, *The New Zealand Foreign Affairs Handbook* (OUP, Auckland, 1989), pp. 141–3.
7. Ibid., pp. 28–31.
8. *Speeches and Documents on New Zealand History*, pp. 354–5.
9. Ibid., pp. 356–8.
10. G. Chaudron, 'New Zealand and the League of Nations', PhD thesis, Canterbury, (1989), pp. 49–55.
11. Brief survey by a contemporary observer, J. V. Wilson, 'New Zealand's participation in international organisations' in T. C. Larkin (ed.) *New Zealand's External Relations*, pp. 61–71; see also W. David McIntyre, *New Zealand Prepares for War*, pp. 141–68.
12. Ibid., p. 146.
13. *Speeches and Documents on New Zealand History*, pp. 358–61.
14. See S. Skudder, ' "Bringing it home": New Zealand responses to the Spanish Civil War, 1936–1939', PhD thesis, Waikato (1986).
15. W. David McIntyre, *New Zealand Prepares for War*, pp. 167–8.
16. B. S. Bennett, *New Zealand's Moral Foreign Policy 1935–1939: The Promotion of Collective Security through the League of Nations* (NZIIA, Wellington, 1988); for a different view see Chaudron, *New Zealand and the League of Nations*, pp. 429–36.
17. W. David McIntyre, *New Zealand Prepares for War*, p. 187.
18. *Official History of New Zealand in the Second World War*: F. L. Wood, *The New Zealand People at War: Political and External Affairs* (Department of Internal Affairs, Wellington, 1958), p. 11. Subsequent works in the *Official History* will be prefaced by *OH* and cite author, volume, title, and date.
19. *OH: Documents Relating to New Zealand's Participation in the Second World War*, vol. 1 (1949), p. 21; Wood, *The People at War*, p. 98–101.
20. *OH*: S. D. Waters, *The Royal New Zealand Navy* (1950), pp. 28–74.
21. K. Sinclair, *Walter Nash* (OUP/AUP, Auckland, 1976), pp. 211–16.
22. *OH*: W. G. McClymont, *To Greece* (1959), D. M. Davin, *Crete* (1953), W. F. Murphy, *The Relief of Tobruk* (1961), J. L. Scoullar, *Battle for Egypt* (1955); R. Walker, *Alam Halfa to Alamein* (1967), W. G. Stevens, *Bardia to Enfidaville* (1962).
23. *OH*: O. Gillespie, *The Pacific* (1952), pp. 19–56.
24. *OH*: N. M. Taylor, *The Home Front* (1986), vol. 1, ch. 14.
25. A. McIntosh, 'Working with Peter Fraser in wartime: personal reminiscences', *NZJH*, x.1 (1976), p. 12.
26. *OH*: N. C. Phillips, *Italy*, vol. 1, *The Sangro to Cassino* (1957); R. Kay, *Italy*, vol. 2, *From Cassino to Trieste* (1967).
27. *OH: Documents Relating to New Zealand's Participation in the Second World War*, vol. III, p. 456.
28. J. Winton, *The Forgotten Fleet* (Michael Joseph, London, 1969), pp. 61, 284.
29. *Documents on New Zealand's External Relations* [*DNZER*], vol. 1, R. Kay (ed.), *The Australian-New Zealand Agreement 1944*, p. 5.
30. Ibid., p. 37.
31. Ibid., p. 142.
32. *Speeches and Documents on New Zealand History*, pp. 380–5.
33. F. L. W. Wood, 'The Anzac dilemma', *International Affairs*, vol. 29, no. 2 (1953), pp. 184–92.
34. J. F. Schnabel, *The History of the Joint Chiefs of Staff: The Joint Chiefs of Staff and National Policy*, vol. 1, *1945–1947* (Michael Glazier, Wilmington, 1979), pp. 299–346; PMM 46 (6), 23 April 1946 and PMM (46) 5th mtg., 26 April 1946. National Archives, Wellington, EA1, PM 153/23/3, Part 1.

35. *DNZER*, II, pp. 1294, 1318.
36. JP (49) 159 (Final), 22 December 1949. Public Record Office, London, DEFE 6/11.
37. R. M. Mullins, 'New Zealand's defence policy', *New Zealand External Affairs Review* XXII.7 (1972), p. 11; *NZPD*, 286 (1949), p. 1381.
38. Middle East Defence. UK Chiefs of Staff Committee. JP (48) 118 (5) (T. of R.) 4 November 1948. DEFE 6/7.
39. Fraser at UK Chiefs of Staff Committee, 1948, 179th mtg., 15 December 1948. EA1 PM 85/1/1 Pt. 3; *Speeches and Documents on New Zealand History*, pp. 424–5; Mullins, 'Defence policy', p. 10.
40. *DNZER*, III, p. 478.
41. I. C. McGibbon, 'New Zealand's intervention in the Korean War, June–July 1950', *International History Review*, vol. 11, no. 2 (1989), pp. 272–90; R. O'Neil, *Australia and the Korean War, 1950–53*, vol. 1, *Strategy and Diplomacy* (Australian War memorial, Canberra, 1981), pp. 75–6.
42. *Foreign Relations of the United States [FRUS]*, VI.1 (1951), pp. 132–47.
43. *FRUS*, VI.1 (1951), pp. 143–4.
44. Ibid., pp. 147–51; *DNZER*, III, pp. 583–4.
45. *FRUS*, VI.1 (1951), pp. 155–5; *DNZER*, III, pp. 593–614, 625–50; Notes kept by Brig. H. R. Rourke, Australian Archives, CRS A5954, Box 1819; See also P. Spender, *Exercises in Diplomacy: The ANZUS Treaty and the Colombo Plan* (University Press, Sydney, 1969), Part 1.
46. Text in *Speeches and Documents on New Zealand History*, pp. 386–8.
47. CM(51) 16th Conclusion, 1 March 1951; 19th Conclusion, 12 March 1951. Public Record Office, London, CAB 128/19.
48. Cables, Churchill to Holland, 26 September 1952 and to Menzies, 30 September 1952. Public Record Office, London, DO 35/5968; Notes of mtg. at 10 Downing Street, 12 December 1952. DO 35/5970.
49. Report to British Chiefs of Staff, JP (51) 114 (Final), 27 August 1951. DEFE 6/17.
50. Australian Defence Committee, 3 September 1953, Australian Archives, CRS A 2031, vol. 40.
51. Ibid., Australian Defence Committee, 13 August 1953, considering UK request of 29 June 1953; Report of Melbourne Conference, October 1953: British COS (54) 1st mtg. 5 January 1954. DEFE 4/68.
52. P. B. Davidson, *Vietnam at War: The History, 1946–1975* (Presidio, Ca.: Novata Press, 1988), p. 263.
53. M. Pearson, *Paper Tiger: New Zealand's Part in SEATO, 1954–1977*, p. 28.
54. *Speeches and Documents on New Zealand History*, p. 392.
55. Pearson, *Paper Tiger*, pp. 40, 45.
56. Annex B to JP (55) 38 (Final), 23 May 1955. Public Record Office, London, DEFE 7/20.
57. F. Rennie, *Regular Soldier: A Life in the New Zealand Army*, pp. 142–228.
58. Pearson, *Paper Tiger*, pp. 92–3; *AJHR*, 1964, H–19, p. 3; H–37, p. 4.
59. Ibid., loc. cit.
60. *AJHR*, 1966, H–4, pp. 6, 23–4.
61. *Speeches and Documents on New Zealand History*, pp. 398–401. See also D. McCraw, 'Reluctant ally', *NZJH*, XV.1 (1981), pp. 49–60; R. G. Glover, *New Zealand in Vietnam* (Dunmore Press, Palmerston North, 1986).
62. S. D. Newman, *Vietnam Gunners: 161 Battery RNZA, South Vietnam, 1965–71* (Moana Press, Tauranga, 1988).
63. *Speeches and Documents on New Zealand History*, p. 402.
64. Ibid., pp. 405–8.
65. S. Hoadley, *New Zealand Foreign Affairs Handbook*, pp. 46–7.
66. *AJHR*, 1974, A–1, and 1975, A–1.
67. See R. Thompson, 'Sporting contacts: an unhealed wound', *New Zealand International Review*, VIII.4 (1983), pp. 2–5.
68. Interview in ibid., V.I (1980), p. 3.

69. *AJHR*, 1983, G.4A, p. 28.
70. J. Crawford, 'Truce supervision: the Zimbabwe model', *New Zealand Foreign Affairs Review*, XIV.5 (1989), pp. 12–15 and 'A job well done: the New Zealand Army truce monitoring contingent, Rhodesia 1979–80' (Ministry of Defence typescript, Wellington, 1989).
71. S. McMillan, *Neither Confirm Nor Deny: The Nuclear Ships Dispute between New Zealand and the United States* (Allen and Unwin, Wellington, 1987); K. Clements, *Back from the Brink: The Creation of a Nuclear-free New Zealand* (Allen and Unwin, Wellington, 1988); J. Bercovitch (ed.), *ANZUS in Crisis: Alliance Management in International Affairs* (University of Canterbury Press, Christchurch, 1988); M. C. Pugh, *The ANZUS Crisis, Nuclear Visiting and Deterrence* (University Press, Cambridge, 1988); D. Lange, *Nuclear Free – The New Zealand Way* (Penguin, Auckland, 1990).
72. *Defence and Security: What New Zealanders Want. Report of the Defence Committee of Enquiry* (1988), p. 73.
73. Ibid., pp. 43–4.
74. *AJHR*, 1987, G.4A, p. 9.
75. *New Zealand Defence: Resource Management Review, 1988* (Strategos, Wellington, 1988), pp. 50–1.
76. F. L. Wood, *The New Zealand People at War: Political and External Affairs*, p. 370.
77. *Report of the Defence Committee of Enquiry* (1986), p. 11.
78. F. Rennie, *Regular Soldier: A Life in the New Zealand Army*, p. 306.
79. *New Zealand External Relations Review*, XLI.2 (1991), p. 49.
80. R. Scott, *Sport on the Move: The Report of the Sports Development Inquiry* (1985), pp. 128–9.
81. D. Bindoff and R. Palenski, *XIVth Commonwealth Games: The Official History, Auckland, 1990* (Moa Publications, Auckland, 1990), p. 11.

CHAPTER 21: THE AWAKENING IMAGINATION

1. Charles Brasch, *Indirections: A Memoir, 1909–1947* (OUP, Wellington, 1980), pp. 387–91.
2. Brasch (ed.), *Landfall Country*, pp. 430–59, reprints a selection of his editorials.
3. J. C. Beaglehole, 'Politics and culture', pp. 145–6; Simpson, *A Survey of the Arts in New Zealand*, pp. 88–91; NZ Dept. of Internal Affairs, *The New Zealand Literary Fund*.
4. Charles Brasch, *Landfall*, I.2 (1947), p. 82; J. C. Beaglehole, 'The National Orchestra'; Turner, 'The National Orchestra'.
5. Wystan Curnow, 'High culture in a small province', argues for the inevitable inadequacy of the infrastructure in New Zealand.
6. Allen Curnow (ed.), *A Book of New Zealand Verse*, p. 17.
7. Allen Curnow, *Collected Poems* (Reed, Wellington, 1974), pp. 137–8. See also Stead, 'Allen Curnow's poetry'; Sturm, 'Allen Curnow'.
8. Charles Brasch, *Disputed Ground* (Caxton, Christchurch, 1948), p. 13. See also Bertram, *Charles Brasch*; O'Sullivan, 'Brief permitted morning'; Dudding (ed.), 'Charles Brasch: tributes and memories'.
9. James K. Baxter, *In Fires of No Return* (OUP, London, 1958), p. 66. See also O'Sullivan, *James K. Baxter*; Owen Leeming, 'And the clay man?', *Landfall*, XXV.1 (1971), pp. 9–19; Stead, 'Towards Jerusalem: the later poetry of James K. Baxter'; McNaughton, 'Baxter as dramatist'; W. H. Oliver, *James K. Baxter, A Portrait* (PNP, Wellington, 1983).
10. Hubert Witheford, *The Falcon Mask* (Pegasus, Christchurch, 1951), p. 17.
11. Charles Spear, *Twopence Coloured* (Caxton, Christchurch, 1951), p. 16.
12. K. O. Arvidson, 'Lightning or Music', *Islands*, III.4 (1974), pp. 442–5.
13. David Gunby, 'Looking at Kapiti', *Islands*, I.2 (1972), pp. 178–80.
14. Smithyman, 'Wellington and the fifties', pp. 33–6.

15. Schwimmer, 'Commentary'; Johnson, 'Introduction'.
16. For selections from the poets noted here see O'Sullivan (ed.), *An Anthology of Twentieth Century New Zealand Poetry*.
17. Charles Brasch, *Landfall*, XII.4 (1958), p. 299; Chapman, 'Fiction and the social pattern'.
18. Copland, 'The New Zealand novels of James Courage'; Jones, 'The persistence of realism'.
19. Copland, *Frank Sargeson*; Rhodes, 'The moral climate of Sargeson's stories'; Horsman, 'The art of Frank Sargeson'; Dudding (ed.), 'In celebration, for Frank Sargeson'; McEldowney, *Frank Sargeson in His Time*.
20. Sturm, 'The short stories of Maurice Duggan'.
21. Evans, *Janet Frame*; Jones, 'No cowslip's bell in Waimaru'; Rhodes, 'Preludes and parables'; Alcock, 'Frame's binomial fall'.
22. Allen Curnow, '*Coal Flat* revisited'.
23. For a discussion of these writers see Rhodes, *New Zealand Fiction Since 1945*.
24. Chapman, 'Fiction and the social pattern', p. 53.
25. Holloway, 'Remembering Bob Lowry'; Milner, 'Denis Glover and the Caxton Club'.
26. M. K. Joseph, 'John Weeks', *Landfall*, IX.2 (1955), pp. 148–51; David Hall, 'T. A. McCormack', *Landfall*, XIII.2 (1959), pp. 168–9.
27. For a survey see Brown and Keith, *An Introduction to New Zealand Painting*. For discussion see Tomory, 'Looking at art in New Zealand' and 'Imaginary reefs and floating islands'.
28. Frederick Page, 'Rita Angus', *Landfall*, XV.3 (1961), pp. 204–5; Millar, *Doris Lusk Retrospective*; Paul, 'The Evelyn Page retrospective exhibition'; Mitchell, 'Olivia Spencer Bower'; E. H. McCormick, 'The Louise Henderson exhibition'; *Landfall*, VII.1 (1954), pp. 54–5; Janet Paul and Neil Roberts, *Evelyn Page: Seven Decades* (Robert McDougall Art Gallery, Christchurch/Allen and Unwin, Wellington, 1986).
29. John Summers, 'The Group show', *Landfall*, III.1 (1949), p. 63.
30. Brasch, *Disputed Ground*, p. 14.
31. Dunn, 'Russell Clark'; McCormick, 'Eric Lee-Johnson'; Dunn, 'Frozen flame and slain tree'.
32. Smith, *Ralph Hotere: A Survey, 1963–73*.
33. A. R. D. Fairburn, 'Art in Canterbury', *Landfall*, II.1 (1948), pp. 46–50.
34. Beiringa, 'M. T. Woollaston'; Summers, 'The Woollaston country'; Woollaston, 'The value of locality in art' and *The Far-Away Hills*.
35. O'Reilly, 'Introduction'; Beiringa, *McCahon: 'Religious' Works, 1946–1952*.
36. J. C. Beaglehole, 'Note on a collection of paintings', *Landfall*, V.3 (1951), p. 229.
37. Quoted in O'Reilly, 'Introduction', p. 8.
38. Hutchings, 'The hard-edge abstractions of Gordon Walters'; Dunn, 'The enigma of Gordon Walters' art'.
39. Wystan Curnow, 'Milan Mrkusich', *Landfall*, XV.2 (1961), pp. 171–3; Dunn and Vuletic, 'Essay on development'.
40. For a different view of Auckland painting see I. V. Porsolt's reviews in *Landfall*, XIII.4 (1959), pp. 364–7; XV.1 (1961), pp. 80–3; XVI.3 (1962), pp. 295–7.
41. Charles Brasch, 'Frances Hodgkins in Auckland', *Landfall*, VIII.3 (1954), pp. 209–12; Scott, 'The Frances Hodgkins controversy' and 'The pleasure garden'.
42. Michael Nicholson, 'Sculpture in Auckland', *Landfall*, IX.3 (1955), pp. 245–7; Wystan Curnow, 'Painting from the Pacific', *Landfall*, XV.3 (1961) pp. 259–62.
43. Mason, 'The plays of Claude Evans'.
44. Ritchie, 'Music'; Page, 'Music'; Harcourt, *A Dramatic Appearance*.
45. Mason, 'Douglas Lilburn's symphonies'.
46. J. G. A. Pocock, 'Two New Zealand plays', *Landfall*, VIII.1 (1954), pp. 52–4; Bruce Mason, 'Wellington's Unity Theatre', *Landfall*, IX.2 (1955), pp. 153–9.
47. McNaughton, 'The plays of Bruce Mason'.
48. Downes and Harcourt, *Voices in the Air*, pp. 158–63.

49. Thompson, *Race Relations in New Zealand*; Pearson, 'The Maori people'.
50. Sutherland (ed.), *The Maori People Today*, pp. 424–8.
51. Peter H. Buck (Te Rangi Hiroa), 'Foreword', in Ernest and Pearl Beaglehole, *Some Modern Maoris*, pp. ix–xv.
52. Pearson, 'Introduction'; McEldowney, 'Introduction'.
53. Ausubel, 'Race relations in New Zealand'.
54. E.g. R. A. K. Mason, *Frontier Forsaken: An Outline History of the Cook Islands* (Challenge, Auckland, 1947); H. Winston Rhodes, *War Over the Pacific* (Co-operative Book Society, Christchurch, 1941); Ernest Beaglehole, *Islands of Danger* (Progressive Publishing Society, Wellington, 1944); Wood, 'The Anzac dilemma'.
55. Holcroft, *The Deepening Stream, The Waiting Hills, Encircling Seas*, republished in one volume as *Discovered Isles*. See also Anderson, 'Mr Holcroft's islands'.
56. Baxter, *Recent Trends in New Zealand Poetry*, p. 18.
57. Pearson, 'Fretful sleepers', pp. 227–30.
58. Chapman, 'Fiction and the social pattern', p. 58.
59. Holcroft, *The Waiting Hills*, pp. 53–64; *Encircling Seas*, pp. 72–81.
60. Smyth, *The Role of Culture in Leisure-time in New Zealand*.
61. Downes and Harcourt, *Voices*, pp. 134–7; Mackay, *Broadcasting in New Zealand*, p. 93–7.
62. Holcroft, *Reluctant Editor*; John Roberts, 'Reluctant publisher', *Islands*, I.2 (1972), pp. 149–52.
63. H. M. Hallenan, 'The New Zealand School Publications Branch', *Educational Magazine*, xv.9 (1958), pp. 410–15.
64. Williams, *Structures and Attitudes in New Zealand Adult Education*.
65. O'Neill, 'The Community Arts Service drama'.
66. Allender, 'The National Film Unit' and 'Disordered cinema'; Downey, 'Documentary film in New Zealand'; Shadbolt, 'John Feeney and the National Film Unit'.
67. J. C. Beaglehole, 'Politics and culture', pp. 141–2.
68. J. G. A. Pocock, 'A producer's dream', *Landfall*, VIII.3 (September 1954), pp. 208–9.
69. Fairburn, 'The culture industry', p. 198.
70. Arts Council funding is analysed in *Action*, 15 (June/July 1980), pp. 1, 20.
71. Alington, 'Architecture'.
72. Roger Robinson, 'The resonance of myth', *Comment*, NS, 6 (February 1979), pp. 28–30; Bill Manhire, 'Growing points of truth', *Islands*, VII.3 (1979), pp. 300–7.
73. For a discussion of poetry see Stead, 'From Wystan to Carlos', and of literature, Jackson, 'Creative writing'.
74. Paul Beadle, 'Greer Twiss', *Landfall*, XIX.1 (1965), pp. 63–5; Barber, 'Completing the incomplete'.
75. Cape, *New Zealand Painting Since 1960*; Dunn, 'Present performance'; Brown, 'The visual arts'.
76. Brown, 'Patrick Hanly's Pacific Icons'.
77. Hutchings, 'Brent Wong'; Rowe, 'Brent Wong'; Fraser, 'Philip Clairmont'; Ross, 'A singular vision: the paintings of Tony Fomison'.
78. Tim Jones, *A Hard-won Freedom; Alternative Communities in New Zealand* (Hodder and Stoughton, Auckland, 1975); Murray Edmond, 'Group theatre'; Horrocks, 'Surviving in films' and 'Directed by Tony Williams'.
79. Thompson, *Retreat from Apartheid*, and Keenaway, *New Zealand Foreign Policy*, survey these issues.
80. Oliver, 'An uneasy retrospect'.
81. NZ Planning Council, *A Moment of Truth*, pp. 1–3, *The Welfare State?*, pp. 23–30; Zepke and Robinson, *Goals of New Zealanders*, pp. 7–18; NZ Task Force, *New Zealand at the Turning Point*, pp. 46–55.
82. Bill Manhire, 'Events as people', *Islands*, IV.1 (1977), pp. 44–9; Roberts, 'Where have all the fathers gone?' and 'Mother, wife and mistress'; Smart (ed.), 'Women on women'; Ensing (ed.), *Private Gardens*.

83. Pearson, 'The Maori and literature'; Mataira, 'Modern trends in Maori art forms'; Metge, *The Maoris of New Zealand*, ch. 17; Davis, *Contemporary Maori Art*; Grace and Ihimaera, 'The Maori in literature'; Alcock, 'Sons of the brave'.

CHAPTER 22: THE RECOGNITION OF DIFFERENCE

1. 'The search for a national identity' is the title of Chapter 8 in Gordon H. Brown and Hamish Keith, *An Introduction to New Zealand Painting, 1839–1967* (Collins, Auckland, 1968).
2. Allen Curnow, *Look Back Harder*, pp. 133, 134.
3. See for example, Francis Pound, 'The real and the unreal in New Zealand painting', *Art New Zealand*, 25 (1982), pp. 42–7.
4. See Simon During, 'Postmodernism or postcolonialism?' *Landfall*, 155 (September 1985), pp. 366–80.
5. Mark Williams, *Leaving the Highway*, p. 15.
6. '. . . the development of poetry in English in New Zealand is coeval with the developing growth of the language into its location, to the point where English as an international language can be felt to be original *where it is*.' Ian Wedde, 'Introduction' to *The Penguin Book of New Zealand Verse*, p. 23.
7. 'We found it impossible to envisage an anthology which could pretend there was only one language being cared for in the context of poetry here.' Ian Wedde, 'The Penguin: texts and contexts', *Span*, 18 (October 1984), p. 5. See also reviews by C. K. Stead and Keri Hulme in *Landfall*, 155 (September 1985), pp. 289–305, and by Peter Simpson and S. M. Mead in *Islands*, 36 (November 1985), pp. 155–63.
8. See editorial remarks by Mark Williams in *New Zealand Poetry, 1972–1987*, Vincent O'Sullivan in *An Anthology of Twentieth Century New Zealand Poetry*, and Harvey McQueen in *The Penguin Book of Contemporary New Zealand Poetry*.
9. Edmond and Paul in *The New Poets*, p. ix, xi–xiii.
10. Michael Morrissey (ed.), *The New Fiction*; Susan Davis and Russell Haley (eds.), *The Penguin Book of Contemporary New Zealand Short Stories*.
11. Williams, *Leaving the Highway*, p. 10.
12. Alex Calder, review of *The Matriarch*, in *Landfall*, 161 (March 1987), pp. 79–84.
13. Collected as *An Autobiography* (Random Century, Auckland, 1990).
14. Lawrence Jones, *Barbed Wire & Mirrors*, p. 341.
15. For the concept of the 'post-provincial', see 'Beyond the provincial' in Simpson, *Ronald Hugh Morrieson*, pp. 54–60.
16. Betty Gilderdale, 'Children's literature', in Sturm (ed.), *The Oxford History of New Zealand Literature in English*, p. 471.
17. Diane Hebley, 'Nightingales and tuis: a survey of New Zealand children's literature in the 1980s', *Landfall*, 171 (September 1989), p. 342.
18. Greg McGee, *Foreskin's Lament* (Price Milburn/VUP, Wellington, 1981) p. 68.
19. Paul Maunder's group Amamus became Theatre of the Eighth Day in the 1980s.
20. Roma Potiki in 'Introduction' to Simon Garrett (ed.), *He Rou Hou*, p. 10. See also the checklist 'First productions of stage plays by Maori playwrights' in the same volume.
21. Nicholas Reid, *A Decade of New Zealand Film*, pp. 13–14.
22. Roger Horrocks, 'Moving images in New Zealand' in Mary Barr (ed.), *Headlands*, p. 138. This article was also made use of in the comments about television.
23. Labour MP for Porirua, Graham Kelly, introduced a Private Member's Bill to Parliament for this purpose which lapsed after the 1990 General Election.
24. Retrospective exhibitions of Walters (Auckland City Art Gallery) and Woollaston (National Art Gallery) were mounted in 1983 and 1991 respectively.
25. Luit Bieringa, *Content/Context*, p. 11.
26. 'Why a women's gallery?' in *Mothers* (The Women's Gallery, Wellington, 1981), p. 31.

27. Lita Barrie, 'Jacqueline Fraser and feminine difference', *Art New Zealand*, 43 (Winter 1987), p. 50. See also her 'Remissions: towards a deconstruction of phallic univocality' in *Antic* 1, (June 1986), pp. 87–103.
28. Quoted in Gordon H. Brown, 'Aspects of recent New Zealand sculpture', *Art New Zealand*, 41 (Summer 1986–87), p. 53.
29. John Scott, 'Introduction' to *Mau Mahara: Our Stories in Craft* (Random Century, Auckland, 1990), p. 5.
30. Janet Frame, *The Carpathians* (Century Hutchinson, Auckland, 1988), p. 84.
31. Quoted in Francis Pound, 'Dashper and distance', in *Julian Dashper* (Sue Crockford Gallery, Auckland, n.d. [1991]).

Select Bibliographies[*]

CHAPTER 1: THE POLYNESIAN FOUNDATION

Anderson, Atholl J. 'Archaeology and behaviour', MA thesis, Otago (1973)
'A review of economic patterns during the Archaic Phase in southern New Zealand', *NZ Journal of Archaeology*, IV (1982), pp. 45–75
' "Makeshift structures of little importance": a reconsideration of Maori round huts', *JPS*, XCV.1 (1986), pp. 91–114
'The chronology of colonization in New Zealand', *Antiquity*, LXV (1991), pp. 767–95
'The last archipelago: 1000 years of Maori settlement in New Zealand' in *Towards 1990. Seven Leading Historians Examine Significant Aspects of New Zealand History* (Government Printer, Wellington, 1989)
'Towards an explanation of protohistoric social organisation and settlement patterns amongst the southern Ngai Tahu', *NZ Journal of Archaeology*, II (1980), pp. 3–23
When All the Moa-ovens Grew Cold (Otago Heritage Books, Dunedin, 1983)
Anderson, Atholl and McGlone, Matt. 'Living on the edge — prehistoric land and people in New Zealand', in J. Dodson (ed.), *The Naive Lands. Prehistory and Environmental Change in Australia and the Southwest Pacific* (Longman Cheshire, Melbourne, 1992)
Anderson, Atholl and McGovern-Wilson, Rick. 'The pattern of prehistoric colonisation of New Zealand', *Journal of the Royal Society of New Zealand*, XX.1 (1990), pp. 41–63
Anderson, Atholl and Ritchie, Neville. 'Pavements, pounamu and ti: the Dart Bridge site in Western Otago, New Zealand', *NZ Journal of Archaeology*, VIII (1986), pp. 115–141
Beaglehole, J. C. (ed.) *The Endeavour Journal of Joseph Banks, 1768–1771*, 2 vols. (Trustees of the Public Library of New South Wales in association with Angus and Robertson, Sydney, 1962)
The Journals of Captain James Cook on his Voyages of Discovery: The Voyage of the Endeavour 1768–1771, 2nd edn. (Cambridge University Press for the Hakluyt Society, 1968)
Bellwood, P. S. 'Dispersal centers in East Polynesia with special reference to the Society and Marquesas Islands' in R. C. Green and M. Kelly (eds.), *Studies in Oceanic Culture History*, I (Dept. of Anthropology, Bishop Museum, Honolulu, 1970)
'Fortifications and economy in prehistoric New Zealand', *Proceedings of the Prehistoric Society*, XXXVII (1971), pp. 56–95
Best, Elsdon. *The Maori*, 2 vols. (Polynesian Society, Wellington, 1924)
'Maori eschatology: the whare potae (house of mourning) and its lore; . . . ', *Transactions of the NZ Institute*, XXXVIII (1906), pp. 148–239.
Best, S. B. 'Adzes, rocks and men', MA research essay, Auckland (1975)
'The Maori adze: an explanation for change', *JPS*, LXXXVI.3 (1977), pp. 307–37
Brewis, Alexandra. 'Assessing infant mortality in prehistoric New Zealand: a life table approach', *NZ Journal of Archaeology*, X (1988), pp. 73–82
Buck, P. H. (Te Rangi Hiroa). *The Evolution of Maori Clothing* (Polynesian Society, Wellington, 1926)
Burrows, Colin. 'On New Zealand climate within the last 1000 years', *NZ Journal of Archaeology*, IV (1982), pp. 157–67
Cassels, Richard. 'Early prehistoric wooden artefacts from the Waitore site (N136/16), near Patea, Taranaki', *NZ Journal of Archaeology*, I (1979), pp. 85–108
Crosby, E. B. 'Maori fishing gear: A study of the development of Maori fishing gear, particularly in the North Island', MA thesis, Auckland (1966)
Cumberland, Kenneth B. 'Moas and men: New Zealand about A.D. 1250', *Geographical Review*, LII.2 (1962), pp. 151–73
Davidson, Janet. 'Auckland prehistory: a review', *Records of the Auckland Institute and Museum*, XV (1978), pp. 1–14
'Maori prehistory: the state of the art', *JPS*, XCII.3 (1983), pp. 291–307

[*] *See Abbreviations on pp. 605–6 and note on page xvii*

'The excavation of Skipper's Ridge (N40/7), Opito, Coromandel Peninsula, in 1959 and 1960', *Records of the Auckland Institute and Museum*, XII (1975), pp. 1–42

'The *Paa Maaori* revisited', *JPS*, XCVI.1 (1987), pp. 7–26

'The prehistory of Motutapu Island, New Zealand. Five centuries of Polynesian occupation in a changing landscape', *JPS*, LXXXVII.4 (1978), pp. 327–37

The Prehistory of New Zealand (Longman Paul, Auckland, 1984)

Duff, Roger. 'The evolution of Maori warfare in New Zealand', *NZ Archaeological Association Newsletter*, X.3 (1967), pp. 114–29

The Moa-hunter Period of Maori Culture, 2nd edn. (Government Printer, Wellington, 1956)

Emory, Kenneth. 'A re-examination of East Polynesian marae: many marae later', in R. C. Green and M. Kelly (eds.), *Studies in Oceanic Culture History*, I (Dept. of Anthropology, Bishop Museum, Honolulu, 1970)

Fankhauser, B. L. 'Archaeometric studies of *Cordyline (ti)* based on ethnobotanical and archaeological research', PhD thesis, Otago (1986)

Fenton, F. D. *Important Judgments Delivered in the Compensation Court and Native Land Court 1866–1879* (Native Land Court, Auckland, 1879)

Finney, Ben, Frost, Paul, Rhodes, Richard and Thompson, Nainoa. 'Wait for the west wind', *JPS*, XCVIII.3 (1989), pp. 261–302

Firth, Raymond. *Primitive Economics of the New Zealand Maori* (George Routledge, London, 1929)

We, The Tikopia (Allen and Unwin, London, 1936)

Foster, Russell and Sewell, Brenda. *An Open Settlement in Tamaki, Auckland, New Zealand. Excavation of Sites R11/887, R11/888 and R11/899* (Science and Research Directorate, Department of Conservation, Wellington, 1988)

Fox, Aileen. *Carved Maori Burial Chests. A Commentary and a Catalogue* (Auckland Institute and Museum, Auckland, 1983)

'Pa and people in New Zealand: an archaeological estimate of population', *NZ Journal of Archaeology*, V (1983), pp. 5–18

Prehistoric Maori Fortifications in the North Island of New Zealand (Longman Paul, Auckland, 1976)

'Prehistoric Maori storage pits: problems in interpretation', *JPS*, LXXXIII.2 (1974), pp. 141–54

Golson, Jack. 'Culture change in prehistoric New Zealand', in J. D. Freeman and W. R. Geddes (eds.), *Anthropology in the South Seas* (Thomas Avery, New Plymouth, 1959)

Green, R. C. 'Adaption and change in Maori culture', in G. Kuschel (ed.), *Biogeography and Ecology in New Zealand* (Dr W. Junk, The Hague, 1975)

'Location of the Polynesian homeland. A continuing problem', in Jim Hollyman and Andrew Pawley (eds.), *Studies in Pacific Languages & Cultures in Honour of Bruce Biggs* (Linguistic Society of New Zealand, Auckland, 1981)

Groube, L. M. 'From Archaic to Classic Maori', *Auckland Student Geographer*, VI (1969), pp. 1–11

'Models in prehistory: a consideration of the New Zealand evidence', *Archaeology and Physical Anthropology in Oceania*, II.1 (1967), pp. 1–27

Harlow, R. B. 'Regional variation in Maori', *NZ Journal of Archaeology*, I (1979), pp. 123–38

Harsant, Wendy J. 'Archaic storage pits at N44/97, Hahei, Coromandel Peninsula, New Zealand', *NZ Journal of Archaeology*, VI (1984), pp. 23–35

Hjarno, J. 'Maori fishhooks in southern New Zealand', *Records of the Otago Museum, Anthropology*, III (1967)

Houghton, Phillip. *The First New Zealanders* (Hodder and Stoughton, Auckland, 1980)

'The people of Wairau Bar', *Records of the Canterbury Museum*, IX.3 (1975), pp. 231–46

'Watom: the people', *Records of the Australian Museum*, XXXXI.3 (1989)

Irwin, Geoffrey. 'Against, across and down the wind: a case for the systematic exploration of the remote Pacific islands', *JPS*, XCVIII.2 (1989), pp. 167–206

Land, Pā and Polity. A Study Based on the Maori Fortifications of Pouto (New Zealand Archaeological Association, Auckland, 1985)

The Prehistoric Exploration and Colonisation of the Pacific (Cambridge University Press, 1992)

Jones, Kevin L. 'Horticulture and settlement chronology of the Waipaoa River catchment, East Coast, North Island, New Zealand', *NZ Journal of Archaeology*, x (1988), pp. 19–51

' "In much greater affluence": productivity and welfare in Maori gardening at Anaura Bay, October 1769', *JPS*, xcviii.1 (1989), pp. 49–75

Jones, Kevin L. and Law, R. Garry. 'Prehistoric population estimates for the Tolaga Bay vicinity, East Coast, North Island, New Zealand', *NZ Journal of Archaeology*, ix (1987), pp. 81–114

Keyes, I. W. 'The D'Urville Island–Nelson metasomatised rocks and their significance in New Zealand prehistory', *Historical Review (Journal of the Whakatane and District Historical Society)*, xxiii.1 (1975), pp. 1–17

Kirch, Patrick Vinton. *The Evolution of the Polynesian Chiefdoms* (Cambridge University Press, 1984)

'Rethinking East Polynesian prehistory', *JPS*, xcv.1 (1986), pp. 9–40

Kirch, Patrick V. and Hunt, Terry L. (eds.) *Archaeology of the Lapita Cultural Complex: A Critical Review* (Burke Museum, Seattle, 1988)

Law, R. G. 'A Maori ritual site', *JPS*, lxxv.4 (1966), pp. 502–3

Lawlor, Ian. 'Rua kuumara o Kawerau', in Susan Bulmer, Garry Law and Douglas Sutton (eds.), *A Lot of Spadework to be Done. Essays in Honour of Lady Aileen Fox* (New Zealand Archaeological Association, Auckland, 1983)

'Stylistic affinities of the Waitore site (N136/16) assemblage', *NZ Journal of Archaeology*, i (1979), pp. 109–14

Leach, B. F. *The Concept of Similarity in Prehistoric Studies* (Anthropology Department, University of Otago, Dunedin, 1969), Studies in Prehistoric Anthropology, I

'Dentalium shell in New Zealand archaeological sites', *Journal of the Royal Society of NZ*, vii.4 (1977), pp. 473–84

'Four centuries of community interaction and trade in Cook Strait, New Zealand', in Jim Specht and J. Peter White (eds.), *Trade and Exchange in Oceania and Australia* (Sydney University Press for the Australian Museum and the Anthropological Society of New South Wales, 1978)

'Prehistoric communities in Palliser Bay, New Zealand', PhD thesis, Otago (1976)

'Sex and funebrial offerings at Wairau Bar: a re-evaluation', *NZ Archaeological Association Newsletter*, xx.2 (1977), pp. 107–13

'The Ngai-Tahu migration: the "Norman Conquest" of the South Island', *NZ Archaeological Association Newsletter*, xxi.1 (1978), pp. 13–20

'The prehistory of the southern Wairarapa', *Journal of the Royal Society of NZ*, xi.1 (1981), pp. 11–33

Leach, B. F. and Anderson, A. J. 'The role of labrid fish in prehistoric economics in New Zealand', *Journal of Archaeological Science*, vi.1 (1979), pp. 1–15

Leach, B. F. and Leach, H. M. (eds.), *Prehistoric Man in Palliser Bay* (National Museum, Wellington, 1979)

Leach, H. M. 'Horticulture in prehistoric New Zealand', PhD thesis, Otago (1976)

'Pre-European (1): the first 500 years', *New Zealand's Nature Heritage*, i.5 (Hamlyn, Wellington, 1974), pp. 117–22

Subsistence Patterns in Prehistoric New Zealand (Anthropology Department, University of Otago, Dunedin, 1969) Studies in Prehistoric Anthropology, II

1000 Years of Gardening in New Zealand (Reed, Wellington, 1984)

Leach, H. M. and Leach, B. F. 'The Riverton site: an Archaic adze manufactory in western Southland, New Zealand', *NZ Journal of Archaeology*, ii (1980), pp. 99–140

Leahy, Anne. 'Excavations at Hot Water Beach (N44/69), Coromandel Peninsula', *Records of the Auckland Institute and Museum*, xi (1974), pp. 23–76

'Pa and external terraces with structures at Poor Hill (Site P5/227), Waimate North', *Records of the Auckland Institute and Museum*, xxv (1988), pp. 39–47

'Whakamoenga Cave, Taupo, N94/7, a report on the ecology, economy and stratigraphy', *Records of the Auckland Institute and Museum*, XIII (1976), pp. 29–75

Levison, Michael, Ward, R. Gerard and Webb, John W. *The Settlement of Polynesia: A Computer Simulation* (ANU Press, Canberra, 1973)

Lewis, David. *We, The Navigators: The Ancient Art of Landfinding in the Pacific* (ANU Press, Canberra, 1972)

McGlone, M. S. 'Polynesian deforestation of New Zealand: a preliminary synthesis', *Archaeology in Oceania*, XVIII.1 (1983), pp. 11–25

McKelvey, P. J. 'Forest recolonization after recent volcanicity at west Taupo', *NZ Journal of Forestry*, VI.5 (1953), pp. 435–48

Mair, Gaela. 'The Protohistoric Period of Wairarapa culture history', MA thesis, Otago (1972)

Mead, Sidney Moko. 'Ka tupu te toi whakairo ki Aotearoa. Becoming Maori art', in Sidney Moko Mead (ed.), *Te Maori. Maori Art from New Zealand Collections* (Heinemann in association with the American Federation of Arts, Auckland, 1984)

    Traditional Maori Clothing: A Study of Technological and Functional Change (Reed, Wellington, 1969)

Moore, P. R. 'The Tahanga basalt: an important resource in North Island prehistory', *Records of the Auckland Institute and Museum*, XIII (1976), pp. 77–93

Oppenheim, R. S. *Maori Death Customs* (Reed, Wellington, 1973)

Orchiston, D. Wayne. 'Maori neck and ear ornaments of the 1770s: a study in protohistoric ethno-archaeology', *Journal of the Royal Society of NZ*, II.1 (1972), pp. 91–107

Phillipps, M. A. L. 'An estimation of fertility in prehistoric New Zealanders', *NZ Journal of Archaeology*, II (1980), pp. 149–67

Pietrusewsky, M. 'A study of skeletal and dental remains from Watom Island and comparisons with other Lapita people', *Records of the Australian Museum*, XXXXI.3 (1989)

Pool, Ian. *Te Iwi Maori. A New Zealand Population Past, Present and Projected* (AUP, Auckland, 1991)

Prickett, Nigel. 'Adzes of Nelson argillite from the far north of New Zealand — the Auckland Museum collection', *Archaeology in New Zealand* XXXII.3 (1989), pp. 135–45

    'An archaeologists' guide to the Maori dwelling', *NZ Journal of Archaeology*, IV (1982), pp. 111–47

Sahlins, Marshall D. *Social Stratification in Polynesia* (University of Washington Press, Seattle, 1958)

Seelenfreund-Hirsch, Andrea C. 'The exploitation of Mayor Island obsidian in prehistoric New Zealand', PhD thesis, Otago (1985)

Sewell, Brenda. 'The fishhook assemblage from the Cross Creek Site (N40/260; T10/399), Sarah's Gully, Coromandel Peninsula, New Zealand', *NZ Journal of Archaeology*, X (1988), pp. 5–17

Sharp, Andrew. *Ancient Voyagers in the Pacific* (Penguin, Harmondsworth, 1957)

Shawcross, Kathleen. 'Fern-root, and the total scheme of 18th century Maori food production in agricultural areas', *JPS*, LXXVI.3 (1967), pp. 330–52

Shawcross, Wilfred. 'Kauri Point swamp: the ethnographic interpretation of a prehistoric site' in G. de G. Sieveking, I. H. Longworth and K. E. Wilson (eds.), *Problems in Economic and Social Archaeology* (Duckworth, London, 1976)

    'Stone flake industries in New Zealand', *JPS*, LXXIII.1 (1964), pp. 7–25

Shortland, Edward. 'General condition of the natives of the Middle Island', in Alexander Mackay, *A Compendium of Official Documents Relative to Native Affairs*, II (Luckie and Collins, Nelson, 1872)

Simmons, D. R. *The Great New Zealand Myth* (Reed, Wellington, 1976)

    'The Lake Hauroko burial and the evolution of Maori clothing', *Records of the Otago Museum, Anthropology*, V (1968), pp. 1–40

    'A New Zealand myth: Kupe, Toi and the "Fleet" ', *NZJH*, III.1 (1969), pp. 14–31

    'Suggested periods in South Island prehistory', *Records of the Auckland Institute and Museum*, X (1973), pp. 1–58

Ta Moko. The Art of Maori Tattoo (Reed Methuen, Auckland, 1986)

Sinoto, Y. H. and McCoy, P. C. 'Report on the preliminary excavation of an early habitation site on Huahine, Society Islands', *Journal de la Société des Océanistes*, XXXI.47 (1975), pp. 143–86

Skinner, H. D. 'Maori amulets', in H. D. Skinner, *Comparatively Speaking: Studies in Pacific Material Culture, 1921–1972* (University of Otago Press, Dunedin, 1974)

Smith, Ian W. G. 'Maori impact on the marine megafauna', in Douglas G. Sutton (ed.), *Saying So Doesn't Make it So. Essays in Honour of B. Foss Leach* (New Zealand Archaeological Association, Dunedin, 1989)

Sutton, Douglas G. 'A paradigmatic shift in Polynesian prehistory: implications for New Zealand', *NZ Journal of Archaeology*, IX (1987), pp. 135–55

Sutton, Douglas G. (ed.) *Archaeology of the Kaainga* (AUP, 1990)

Urlich, Dorothy. 'Migrations of the North Island Maoris, 1800–1840: a systems view of migration', *NZG*, XXVIII.1 (1972), pp. 23–35

Vayda, A. P. *Maori Warfare* (Polynesian Society, Wellington, 1960)

Wilson, John (ed.) *From the Beginning. The Archaeology of the Maori* (Penguin Books in association with the NZ Historic Places Trust, 1987)

Yen, D. E. *The Sweet Potato and Oceania: An Essay in Ethnobotany* (Bishop Museum, Honolulu, 1974)

CHAPTER 2: NEW ZEALAND BEFORE ANNEXATION

Abel Janszoon Tasman's Journal (Frederick Muller, Amsterdam, 1898)

Adams, Peter. *Fatal Necessity: British Intervention in New Zealand, 1830–1847* (AUP/OUP, Auckland, 1977)

Ballara, Angela. 'The role of warfare in Maori society in the early contact period', *JPS*, LXXXV.4 (1976), pp. 487–506

'Settlement patterns in the early European Maori phase of Maori society', *JPS*, LXXXVIII.2 (1979), pp. 199–213

Beaglehole, J. C. *The Life of Captain James Cook* (A. and C. Black, London, 1974)

Beaglehole, J. C. (ed.) *The Endeavour Journal of Joseph Banks, 1768–1771*, 2 vols. (Trustees of the Public Library of New South Wales in association with Angus and Robertson, Sydney, 1962)

The Journals of Captain James Cook on his Voyages of Discovery, 3 vols. in 4 and portfolio (Cambridge University Press for the Hakluyt Society, 1955–69)

Begg, Alison. 'The conversion to Christianity of the South Island Maori in the 1840s and 1850s', *Historical and Political Studies*, 3 (September 1972), pp. 11–17

Belich, James. [Review article] 'Hobson's choice', *NZJH*, XXIV. 2 (1990), pp. 200–7

Bell, Kenneth N. and Morrell, W. P. (eds.) *Select Documents on British Colonial Policy, 1830–1860* (Clarendon Press, Oxford, 1928)

Binney, Judith. 'Christianity and the Maoris to 1840, a comment', *NZJH*, III.2 (1969), pp. 143–65

'Maori oral narratives, Pakeha written texts: two forms of telling history', *NZJH*, XXI.1 (1987), pp. 16–28

'Papahurihia: some thoughts on interpretation', *JPH*, LXXV.3 (1966), pp. 321–31

The Legacy of Guilt: A Life of Thomas Kendall (OUP for University of Auckland, 1968)

Binney, Judith, Bassett, J. and Olssen, E. *The People and the Land: Te Tangata me Te Whenua: An Illustrated History of New Zealand, 1820–1920* (Allen and Unwin, Wellington, 1990)

Bowden, Ross. '*Tapu* and *Mana*: ritual authority and political power in traditional Maori society', *Journal of Pacific History*, XIV, Part 1 (1979), pp. 50–61

Burns, Patricia. *Te Rauparaha. A New Perspective* (Reed, Wellington, 1980)

Campbell, John Logan. *Poenamo: Sketches of the Early Days of New Zealand . . .* (Williams and Norgate, London, 1881; Wilson and Horton, Auckland 1970)

Cheyne, Sonia. 'Search for a constitution. People and politics in New Zealand's Crown colony years', PhD thesis, Otago (1975)

Churchward, L. G. 'Notes on American whaling activities in Australian waters, 1800–1850', *HSANZ*, iv.13 (1949), pp. 59–63

Clover, G. A. M. 'Christianity among the South Taranaki Maoris, 1840–53: A study of the Wesleyan Mission at Waimate South', MA thesis, Auckland (1973)

Coutts, Peter J. F. 'An approach to the investigation of colonial settlement patterns: whaling in southern New Zealand', *World Archaeology*, viii.3 (1976), pp. 291–305

'Merger or takeover? A survey of the effects of contact between European and Maori in the Foveaux Strait region', *JPS*, lxxviii.4 (1969), pp. 495–516

Cumberland, Kenneth B. 'Aotearoa Maori: New Zealand about 1870', *Geographical Review*, xxxix.3 (1949), pp. 401–24

Davidson, Allan K. and Lineham, Peter. *Transplanted Christianity. Documents Illustrating Aspects of New Zealand Church History* (College Communications, Auckland, 1987)

Davidson, J. W. 'European penetration of the South Pacific, 1779–1842', PhD thesis, Cambridge University (1942)

'New Zealand, 1820–1870: an essay in re-interpretation', *HSANZ*, v.20 (1953), pp. 349–60

Dreaver, A. J. *Horowhenua County and its People* (Dunmore Press, Levin, 1984)

Dunmore, John. *French Explorers in the Pacific*, 2 vols. (Clarendon Press, Oxford, 1965)

Durward, Elizabeth W. 'The Maori population of Otago', *JPS*, xlii.166 (1933), pp. 49–82

Earle, Augustus. *Narrative of a Residence in New Zealand. . .* , ed. E. H. McCormick (Clarendon Press, Oxford, 1966)

Elder, J. R. (ed.) *The Letters and Journals of Samuel Marsden, 1865–1838* (Coulls Somerville Wilkie, Dunedin, 1932)

Elsmore, Bronwyn. *Like Them That Dream: the Maori and the Old Testament* (The Tauranga Moana Press, Tauranga, 1985)

Mana from Heaven. A Century of Maori Prophets in New Zealand (Moana Press, Tauranga, 1989)

Entwisle, Peter. *The Otago Peninsula* (McIndoe, Dunedin, 1976)

Facsimiles of the Declaration of Independence and the Treaty of Waitangi (Government Printer, Wellington, 1960)

Firth, Raymond. *Economics of the New Zealand Maori* (Government Printer, Wellington, 1972)

Fisher, Robin. 'Henry Williams' leadership of the CMS mission to New Zealand', *NZJH*, ix.2 (1975), pp. 142–53

Forster, Honore. 'A Sydney whaler, 1829–32: the reminiscences of James Heberley', *Journal of Pacific History*, x.1–2 (1975), pp. 90–104

Garrett, Helen. *Te Manihera: The Life and Times of the Pioneer Missionary Robert Maunsell* (Reed, Auckland, 1991)

Gluckman, L. K. *Tangiwai: A Medical History of 19th Century New Zealand*, also known as *Medical History of New Zealand Prior to 1860* (Published by the author, Auckland, 1976)

Green, R. C. 'Adaptation and change in Maori culture', in G. Kuschel (ed.), *Biogeography and Ecology in New Zealand* (Dr W. Junk, The Hague, 1975)

Greenwood, Gordon. 'The contact of American whalers, sealers and adventurers with the New South Wales settlement', *Royal Australian Historical Society Journal and Proceedings*, xxix.3 (1943), pp. 133–56

Groube, L. M. 'The origin and development of earthwork fortifications in the Pacific', in R. C. Green and M. Kelly (eds.), *Studies in Oceanic Culture History*, i (Dept. of Anthropology, Bishop Museum, Honolulu, 1970)

Gunson, Walter Niel, *Messengers of Grace: Evangelical Missionaries in the South Seas, 1797–1860* (OUP, Melbourne, 1978)

Hamer, David and Nicholls, Roberta (eds.) *The Making of Wellington, 1800–1914* (VUP, Wellington, 1991)

Hamilton, Lila. 'Christianity among the Maoris. The Maoris and the Church Missionary Society's Mission, 1814–1868', PhD thesis, Otago (1970)

Hargreaves, R. P. 'Changing Maori agriculture in pre-Waitangi New Zealand', *JPS*, lxxii.2 (1963), pp. 101–17

From Beads to Banknotes, The Story of Money in New Zealand (McIndoe, Dunedin, 1972)

Hargreaves, R. P. and Heenan, L. D. B. *An Annotated Bibliography of New Zealand Population* (University of Otago Press, Dunedin, 1972)

Hooker, Brian. 'New light on the mapping and naming of New Zealand', *NZJH*, VI.2 (1972), pp. 158–67

Howard, Basil. *Rakiura, A History of Stewart Island, New Zealand* (Reed, Wellington, 1940)

Howe, K. R. 'The fate of the "savage" in Pacific historiography', *NZJH*, XI.2 (1977), pp. 137–54

'The Maori response to Christianity in the Thames–Waikato area, 1833–1840', *NZJH*, VII.1 (1973), pp. 28–46

Jackson, Michael. 'Literacy, communications and social change', in I. H. Kawharu (ed.), *Conflict and Compromise: Essays on the Maori Since Colonization* (Reed, Wellington, 1975)

Kawharu, I. H. (ed.) *Waitangi: Maori and Pakeha Perspectives of the Treaty of Waitangi* (OUP, Auckland, 1989)

Kenny, Robert W. 'Yankee whalers at the Bay of Islands', *American Neptune*, XII (January 1952), pp. 2–44

King, Michael. *Moriori: A People Rediscovered* (Viking, Auckland, 1989)

Lee, Jack. *'I Have Named it the Bay of Islands . . .'* (Hodder and Stoughton, Auckland, 1983)
Hokianga (Hodder and Stoughton, Auckland, 1987)

Lewthwaite, Gordon. 'The population of Aotearoa: its number and distribution', *NZG*, VI.1 (1950), pp. 35–52

Little, Barbara. 'The sealing and whaling industry in Australia before 1850', *AEHR*, IX.2 (1969), pp. 109–27

Low, Peter. 'Pompallier and the Treaty: a new discussion', *NZJH*, XXIV.2 (1990), pp. 190–99

McCay, S. J. D. 'Phormium Tenax in New Zealand History to 1872', MA thesis, Otago (1952)

Mackay, J. A. *Historic Poverty Bay and the East Coast, N.I., N.Z.* (J. G. Mackay, Gisborne, 1949)

McKeefry, Peter (ed.) *Fishers of Men* (Whitcombe and Tombs, Auckland, 1938)

McLintock, A. H. *The History of Otago. The Origins and Growth of a Wakefield Class Settlement* (Otago Centennial Publications, Dunedin, 1949)
Crown Colony Government in New Zealand (Government Printer, Wellington, 1958)

McNab, Robert. *From Tasman to Marsden: A History of Northern New Zealand from 1642 to 1818* (J. Wilkie, Dunedin, 1914)
Historical Records of New Zealand, 2 vols. (Government Printer, Wellington, 1908–1914; reprinted 1973)
Murihiku and the Southern Islands (William Smith, Invercargill, 1907; Wilson and Horton, Auckland, 1970)
The Old Whaling Days: A History of Southern New Zealand from 1830 to 1840 (Whitcombe and Tombs, Christchurch, 1913; Golden Press, Auckland, 1975)

Maning, F. E. *Old New Zealand: A Tale of the Good Old Times* (Smith, Elder, London, 1863; Golden Press, Auckland, in association with Whitcombe and Tombs, 1973)

Manning, Helen Taft. 'Lord Durham and the New Zealand Company', *NZJH*, VI.1 (1972) pp. 1–19
'Who ran the British Empire, 1830–1850?', *Journal of British Studies*, v.1 (1965), pp. 88–121

Markham, Edward. *New Zealand or Recollections of it*, ed. E. H. McCormick (Government Printer, Wellington, 1963)

Melvin, L. W. 'Te Waharoa of the Ngatihaua', *JPS*, LXXI.4 (1962), pp. 361–78

Millar, David. 'Whalers, flax traders and Maoris of the Cook Strait area', *Dominion Museum Records in Ethnology*, II.6 (1971), pp. 57–74

Morrell, W. P. *British Colonial Policy in the Age of Peel and Russell* (Clarendon Press, Oxford, 1930)

Morton, Albert Henry. 'Whaling in New Zealand waters in the first half of the nineteenth century', PhD thesis, Otago (1977)

Morton, Harry. *The Whale's Wake* (University of Otago Press, 1982)

Murray, Janet. 'A missionary in action', in Peter Munz (ed.), *The Feel of Truth: Essays in New Zealand and Pacific History* (Reed for Victoria University of Wellington, 1969), pp. 195–218

Oliver, W. H. and Thomson, Jane M. *Challenge and Response: A Study of the Development of the Gisborne East Coast Region* (East Coast Development Research Association, Gisborne, 1971)

Olssen, Erik. *A History of Otago* (John McIndoe, Dunedin, 1984)

Orange, Claudia. *The Treaty of Waitangi* (Allen and Unwin/PNP, Wellington, 1987)

Owens, J. M. R. 'Christianity and the Maoris to 1840', *NZJH*, II.1 (1968), pp. 18–40

    'Historians and the Treaty of Waitangi', *Archifacts, Bulletin of the Archives and Records Association of New Zealand* (April 1990), pp. 4–21

    'Missionary medicine and Maori health: the record of the Wesleyan mission to New Zealand before 1840', *JPS*, LXXXI.4 (1972), pp. 418–36

    Prophets in the Wilderness: The Wesleyan Mission to New Zealand, 1819–27 (AUP/OUP, Auckland, 1974)

    'The unexpected impact: missionaries and society in early 19th century New Zealand', in Christopher Nichol and James Veitch (eds.), *Religion in New Zealand* (Victoria University of Wellington, Wellington, 1980), pp. 13–52

    'Missionaries and the Treaty of Waitangi', *Wesley Historical Society Journal* (NZ), Proceedings, no. 49 (1986), pp. 17–40

    'The Wesleyan Mission to New Zealand, 1819–1840', PhD thesis, Victoria (1969)

Parr, C. J. 'Before the Pai Marire', *JPS*, LXXVI.1 (1967), pp. 35–46

    'Maori literacy, 1843–67', *JPS*, LXII.3 (1963), pp. 211–34

    'A missionary library. Printed attempts to instruct the Maori, 1815–1845', *JPS*, LXX.4 (1961), pp. 429–50

Parsonson, G. S. 'The literate revolution in Polynesia', *Journal of Pacific History*, II (1967), pp. 39–57

Phillips, W. J. 'The cult of Nakahi', *JPS*, LXXV.1 (1966), p. 107

Pool, D. Ian. *The Maori Population of New Zealand, 1769–1971* (AUP/OUP, Auckland, 1977)

Porter, Frances (ed.) *The Turanga Journals 1840–1850: Letters and Journals of William and Jane Williams, Missionaries to Poverty Bay* (Price Milburn for Victoria University Press, Wellington, 1974)

Rakena, Ruawai D. 'The Maori response to the gospel', *Proceedings of the Wesley Historical Society (New Zealand)*, XXV.1–4 (1971), pp. i–iv, 1–40

Ramsden, Eric. *Busby of Waitangi: H.M.'s Resident at New Zealand, 1833–1840* (Angus and Robertson, Sydney, 1942)

    Marsden and the Missions: Prelude to Waitangi (Reed, Dunedin, 1936)

Rickard, L. S. *The Whaling Trade in Old New Zealand* (Minerva, Auckland, 1965)

Rogers, Lawrence (ed.) *The Early Journals of Henry Williams, Senior Missionary in New Zealand of the Church Missionary Society, 1826–40* (Pegasus, Christchurch, 1961)

Ross, John O'C. 'Busby and the Declaration of Independence', *NZJH*, XIV.1 (1980) pp. 83–9

Ross, Ruth. 'Te Tiriti o Waitangi: texts and translations', *NZJH*, VI.2 (1972), pp. 129–57

Rutherford, J. *The Treaty of Waitangi and the Acquisition of British Sovereignty in New Zealand, 1840* (Auckland University College, 1949)

Shaw, A. G. L. 'British attitudes to the colonies, *ca* 1820–1850', *Journal of British Studies*, IX.1 (1969), pp. 71–95

Shawcross, Kathleen. 'Maoris of the Bay of Islands, 1769–1840: A study of changing Maori responses to European contact', MA thesis, Auckland (1967)

Shroff, G. W. 'George Clarke and the New Zealand Mission, 1824–1850', MA thesis, Auckland (1967)

Simpson, Miria. *Nga Tohu o Te Tiriti, Making a Mark. The Signatories to the Treaty of Waitangi* (National Library of New Zealand, Wellington, 1990)

Sinclair, Douglas. 'Land: Maori view and European response', in Michael King (ed.), *Te Ao Hurihuri, The World Moves On* (Hicks Smith, Wellington, 1975)

Sinclair, Keith. 'The Aborigines Protection Society and New Zealand — A study in Nineteenth Century opinion', MA thesis, Auckland (1946)

Sinclair, Keith (ed.) *The Oxford Illustrated History of New Zealand* (OUP, Auckland, 1990)

Sissons, Jeffrey, Wi Hongi, Wiremu and Hohepa, Pat. *The Pūriri Trees are Laughing. A Political History of Nga Puhi in the Inland Bay of Islands* (The Polynesian Society, Auckland, 1987)

Skinner, H. D. *Comparatively Speaking: Studies in Pacific Material Culture, 1921–72* (University of Otago Press, Dunedin, 1974)

'Culture areas in New Zealand', *JPS*, III.118 (1921), pp. 71–8

'The Maoris', in J. Holland et al. (eds.), *The Cambridge History of the British Empire*, VII, Pt. II (Cambridge University Press, 1933)

Smith, S. Percy. *Maori Wars of the Nineteenth Century: The Struggle of the Northern against the Southern Maori Tribes Prior to the Colonisation of New Zealand in 1840*, 2nd edn. (Whitcombe and Tombs, Christchurch, 1910)

Sorrenson, M. P. K. 'Towards a radical reinterpretation of New Zealand history; the role of the Waitangi Tribunal', *NZJH*, XXI.1 (April 1987), pp. 173–88

Sparrow, Christopher. 'The growth and status of the phormium tenax industry of New Zealand', *Economic Geography*, XLI.4 (1965), pp. 331–45

Starke, June. ' "Journal of a Rambler": John Boultbee in New Zealand, 1825–1828', *Turnbull Library Record*, IX.1 (1976), pp. 18–30

Starke, June (ed.) *Journal of a Rambler, The Journal of John Boultbee* (OUP, Auckland, 1986)

Stephens, P. R. 'Wheat-growing in New Zealand up to 1850', *NZ Wheat Review* (1953), pp. 11–16

Steven, Margaret. *Merchant Campbell, 1769–1846: A Study of Colonial Trade* (OUP in association with Australian National University, Melbourne, 1965)

Stokes, Evelyn. 'European discovery of New Zealand before 1642: a review of the evidence', *NZJH*, IV.1 (1970), pp. 3–19

'The naming of New Zealand', *NZG*, XXIV.2 (1968), pp. 201–4

Straubel, C. R. (ed.) *The Whaling Journal of Captain W. B. Rhodes*, (Whitcombe and Tombs, Christchurch, 1954)

Sutton, Douglas G. 'A culture history of the Chatham Islands', *JPS*, LXXXIX.1 (1980), pp. 67–93

'Maori demographic change, 1769–1840: the inner workings of "a picturesque but illogical simile" ', *JPS*, LXXXV.3 (1986), pp. 291–339

Tapp, E. J. *Early New Zealand, A Dependency of New South Wales, 1788–1841* (Melbourne University Press, 1958)

The Treaty of Waitangi. Its Origins and Significance (Victoria University of Wellington University Extension Publication no. 7, 1972)

The Dictionary of New Zealand Biography, Vol I, 1769–1869 (Allen and Unwin, Department of Internal Affairs, Wellington, 1990)

Thomson, Arthur. *The Story of New Zealand: Past and Present — Savage and Civilised*, 2 vols. (John Murray, London, 1859; Capper, Christchurch, 1974)

Thomson, Jane. 'Some reasons for the failure of the Roman Catholic mission to the Maoris, 1838–60', *NZJH*, III.2 (1969), pp. 166–74

'The Roman Catholic Mission in New Zealand, 1838–1870', MA thesis, Victoria (1966)

Turnbull, Michael. *The New Zealand Bubble: The Wakefield Theory in Practice* (Price Milburn, Wellington, 1959)

Urlich, Dorothy. 'The distributions and migrations of North Island Maori population about 1800–1840', MA thesis, Auckland (1969)

'The introduction and diffusion of firearms in New Zealand, 1800–1840', *JPS*, LXXIX.4 (1970), pp. 399–410

'Migrations of the North Island Maoris, 1800–1840: a systems view of migration', *NZG*, XXVIII.1 (1972), pp. 23–35

Vayda, A. P. 'Maori conquests in relation to the New Zealand environment', *JPS*, LXV.3 (1956), pp. 204–11

Maori Warfare (Polynesian Society, Wellington, 1960)

'Maoris and muskets in New Zealand: disruption of a war system', *Political Science Quarterly*, LXXXV.4 (1970), pp. 560–84

Wakefield, E. J. *Adventure in New Zealand, from 1839 to 1844; With Some Account of the Beginning of the British Colonization of the Islands*, 2 vols. (John Murray, London, 1845; Wilson and Horton, Auckland, 1970)

Ward, Alan. *A Show of Justice: Racial 'Amalgamation' in Nineteenth Century New Zealand* (AUP/OUP, Auckland, 1973)

Ward, John M. *British Policy in the South Pacific (1786–1893)* (Australasian Publishing Co., Sydney, 1948)

Wards, Ian. *The Shadow of the Land: A Study of British Policy and Racial Conflict in New Zealand, 1832–1852* (Government Printer, Wellington, 1968)

Wigglesworth, R. P. 'The myth and the reality: a study of the adaptation of John Marmon (1800?–1880)', research essay, Massey (1974)

'The New Zealand timber and flax trade, 1769–1840', PhD thesis, Massey (1981)

Willis, John Barnes. 'The Royal Navy in New Zealand, 1800–1850', MA thesis, Victoria (1959)

Wilson, Ormond. *From Hongi Hika to Hone Heke, a Quarter Century of Upheaval* (John McIndoe, Dunedin, 1985)

'John Rutherford', *Turnbull Library Record*, VII.1 (1974), pp. 15–27

Kororareka and Other Essays (John McIndoe, Dunedin, 1990)

'Papahurihia, first Maori Prophet', *JPS*, LXXIV.4 (1965) pp. 473–83

Wright, Harrison. *New Zealand, 1769–1840: Early Years of Western Contact* (Harvard University Press, Cambridge, Massachusetts, 1959)

Wright, Olive. *The Voyage of the Astrolabe from 1840: An English Rendering of the Journals of Dumont D'Urville and his Officers of their Visit to New Zealand in 1840 . . .* (Reed, Wellington, 1955)

Yarwood, A. T. *Samuel Marsden* (OUP, Melbourne, 1968)

Yen, D. E. 'The use of maize by the New Zealand Maoris', *Economic Botany*, XIII.4 (1959), pp. 319–27

Young, J. M. R. *Australia's Pacific Frontier: Economic and Cultural Expansion into the Pacific, 1795–1885* (Cassell Australia, Melbourne, 1967)

CHAPTER 3: A COLONIAL ECONOMY

Acland, L. G. D. *The Early Canterbury Runs*, 4th edn. revised by W. H. Scotter (Whitcoulls, Christchurch, 1975)

Adams, Jonathan. 'Governor FitzRoy's debentures and their role in his recall', *NZJH* XX.1 (1986), pp. 44–63

Adams, Peter. *Fatal Necessity: British Intervention in New Zealand, 1830–1847* (AUP/OUP, Auckland, 1977)

Angus, John. 'City and country: change and continuity. Electoral politics and society in Otago, 1877–1893', PhD thesis, Otago (1976)

Arnold, Rollo. 'English rural unionism and Taranaki immigration, 1871–1876', *NZJH*, VI.1 (1972), pp. 20–41

'The dynamics of quality of trans-Tasman migration, 1885–1910', *AEHR*, XXVI.1 (1986), pp. 1–20

'The opening of the Great Bush, 1869–1881: A social history of the bush settlements of Taranaki, Hawke's Bay and Wellington', PhD thesis, Victoria, (1971)

'The virgin forest harvest and the development of colonial New Zealand', *NZG*, XXXII.2 (1976), pp. 105–26

'Yeomen and nomads: New Zealand and the Australian shearing scene', *NZJH*, XVIII.2 (1984), pp. 117–42

Bagnall, A. G. *Wairarapa: An Historical Excursion* (Hedley's Bookshop for the Masterton Trust Lands Trust, 1976)

Blackstock, Raewyn. 'Sir Julius Vogel, 1876–1880: from politics to business', *NZJH*, v.2 (1971), pp. 150–70

Butlin, S. J. *Australia and New Zealand Bank; The Bank of Australasia and the Union Bank of Australia Limited, 1828–1951* (Longmans, London, 1961)

Campbell, R. J. ' "The black 'eighties": unemployment in New Zealand in the 1880s', *AEHR*, xvi.1 (1976), pp. 67–82

Chappell, N. M. *New Zealand Banker's Hundred: A History of the Bank of New Zealand, 1861–1961* (Bank of New Zealand, Wellington, 1961)

Condliffe, J. B. 'The external trade of New Zealand', *NZOYB*, 1915, pp. 858–962

New Zealand in the Making: A Study of Economic and Social Development, 2nd edn. (Allen and Unwin, London, 1959)

Cumming, J. P. 'The compact and financial settlement of 1856', MA thesis, Auckland (1963)

Dalton, B. J. *War and Politics in New Zealand, 1855–1870* (Sydney University Press, 1967)

Dalziel, Raewyn. *Julius Vogel: Business Politician* (AUP/OUP, Auckland, 1986)

Diamond, Marion. ' "Most injudicious . . . most injurious": the Royal Bank of Australia's loan to the New Zealand Government, 1842', *NZJH*, xx.1 (1986), pp. 64–72

Dowie, J. A. 'Business politicians in action: the New Zealand railway boom of the 1870s', *Business Archives and History*. v.1 (1965), pp. 32–56

'A century-old estimate of the national income of New Zealand', *Business Archives and History*, vi.2 (1966), pp. 117–31

'The course and character of capital formation in New Zealand, 1870–1900', *NZ Economic Papers*, i.1 (1966), pp. 38–58

'Inverse relations of the Australian and New Zealand economies, 1871–1900', *Australian Economic Papers*, ii.2 (1963), pp. 151–79

'Studies in New Zealand investment, 1871–1900', PhD thesis, ANU (1965)

Dunstall, G. C. 'Colonial merchant: J. T. MacKelvie, Brown Campbell and Co., and the business community of Auckland, 1865–71', MA thesis, Auckland, 1970

Easton, Brian. 'Three New Zealand depressions', in W. E. Willmott (ed.), *New Zealand and the World: Essays in Honour of Wolfgang Rosenberg* (W. E. Willmott, Christchurch, 1980)

Eldred-Grigg, Stevan. 'Whatever happened to the gentry? The large landowners of Ashburton County, 1890–1896', *NZJH*, xi.1 (1977), pp. 3–27

Fairburn, Miles. *The Ideal Society and its Enemies: The Foundations of Modern New Zealand Society, 1850–1900* (AUP, Auckland, 1989)

Gardner, W. J. *A Pastoral Kingdom Divided: Cheviot, 1889–94* (Bridget Williams Books, Wellington, 1992)

Gardner, W. J. *The Amuri: A County History*, rev. edn. (Amuri County Council, Culverden, 1983)

Gardner, W. J. (ed.) *A History of Canterbury, ii: General History 1854–76, and Cultural Aspects, 1850–1950* (Canterbury Centennial Historical and Literary Committee and Whitcombe and Tombs, Christchurch, 1971)

Gould, J. D. *The Grass Roots of New Zealand History: Pasture Formation and Improvement, 1871–1911* (Massey University, Palmerston North, 1974)

'The occupation of farm land in New Zealand, 1874–1911: a preliminary survey', *Business Archives and History*, v.2 (1965), pp. 123–41

'Pasture formation and improvement in New Zealand, 1871–1911', *AEHR*, xvi.1 (1976), pp. 1–22

'The twilight of the estates, 1891 to 1910', *AEHR*, x.1 (1970), pp. 1–26

Hall, A. R. (ed.) *The Export of Capital from Britain, 1870–1914* (Methuen, London, 1968)

Hanham, H. J. 'New Zealand promoters and British investors, 1860–1895', in R. M. Chapman and Keith Sinclair (eds.), *Studies of a Small Democracy: Essays in Honour of Willis Airey* (Paul for University of Auckland, 1963)

Harraway, H. C. 'John Roberts, man of business: (an account of John Roberts and the establishment of Murray, Roberts & Co. Ltd.)' MA thesis, Otago (1967)

Hawke, G. R. 'Disaggregation of the New Zealand labour force, 1871–1936' (Victoria University of Wellington Working Papers in Economic History, 79/1, January 1979)

'Income estimates from monetary data: further explorations', *Review of Income and Wealth*, xxi.3 (1975), pp. 301–7

'Long-term trends in New Zealand imports', *AEHR*, xviii.1 (1978), pp. 1–28

The Making of New Zealand: An Economic History (Cambridge University Press, Cambridge, 1985)

Hight, James and Straubel, C. R. (eds.) *A History of Canterbury*, i, *to 1854* (Canterbury Centennial Association, Christchurch, 1957)

Horsfield, I. W. 'The struggle for economic viability: a study in the development of the New Zealand economy in the nineteenth century', MA thesis, Victoria (1960)

Kearsley, G. W., Hearn, T. J. and Brooking, T. W. H. 'Land settlement and voting patterns in the Otago Provincial Council, 1863–1872', *NZJH*, xviii.1 (1984), pp. 19–33

Lloyd Prichard, Muriel F. *An Economic History of New Zealand to 1939* (Collins, Auckland, 1970)

Loach, A. C. *A History of the New Zealand Refrigerating Company* (Caxton for the New Zealand Refrigerating Company, Christchurch, 1970)

McIlraith, J. W. *The Course of Prices in New Zealand: An Inquiry into the Nature and Causes of the Variations in the Standard of Value in New Zealand* (Government Printer, Wellington, 1911)

Mackie, S. M. 'Prosperity in depression: the Chambers family — a case study of a landed family in Hawke's Bay during the depression, 1886–1896', research essay, Massey (1974)

McLintock, A. H. *The History of Otago: The Origins and Growth of a Wakefield Class Settlement* (Otago Centennial Historical Publications, Dunedin, 1949)

Martin, John. 'Whither the rural working class in nineteenth-century New Zealand?', *NZJH*, xvii.1 (1983), pp. 21–42

May, Philip Ross. *The West Coast Gold Rushes* (Pegasus, Christchurch, 1962)

Miller, John. *Early Victorian New Zealand: A Study of Racial Tension and Social Attitudes, 1839–1852* (OUP, London, 1958)

Moore, B. A. and Barton, J. S. *Banking in New Zealand* (New Zealand Bank Officers' Guild, Wellington, 1935)

Palmer, Mervyn. 'William Soltau Davidson: a pioneer of New Zealand estate management', *NZJH*, vii.2 (1973), pp. 148–64

Parry, Gordon. *N.M.A. The Story of the First Hundred Years: The National Mortgage and Agency Company of New Zealand Ltd., 1864–1964* (National Mortgage and Agency Co., Dunedin, 1964)

Petersen, G. C. *Forest Homes: The Story of the Scandinavian Settlements in the Forty Mile Bush, New Zealand* (Reed, Wellington, 1956)

Reeves, William Pember. *State Experiments in Australia and New Zealand*, 2 vols. (Grant Richards, London, 1902)

Rosenberg, Wolfgang. 'Capital imports and growth, the case of New Zealand: foreign investment in New Zealand, 1840–1958', *Economic Journal*, lxxi. 281 (1961), pp. 93–113

Rutherford, J. *Sir George Grey, K.C.B., 1812–1898: A Study in Colonial Government* (Cassell, London, 1961)

Salmon, J. H. M. *A History of Goldmining in New Zealand* (Government Printer, Wellington, 1963)

Saul, S. B. *Studies in British Overseas Trade, 1870–1914* (Liverpool University Press, 1967)

Scotter, W. H. *A History of Canterbury*, iii, *1876–1950* (Canterbury Historical and Literary Committee and Whitcombe and Tombs, Christchurch, 1965)

Simkin, C. G. F. 'Banking in New Zealand', in R. S. Sayers (ed.), *Banking in the British Commonwealth* (Clarendon Press, Oxford, 1962)

The Instability of a Dependent Economy: Economic Fluctuations in New Zealand, 1840–1914 (OUP, Oxford, 1951)

Sinclair, Keith and Mandle, W. F. *Open Account: A History of the Bank of New South Wales in New Zealand, 1861–1961* (Whitcombe and Tombs for the Bank of New South Wales, Wellington, 1961)

676

Stone, R. C. J. *Economic Development, 1870–1890: And the Social Consequences* (Heinemann, Auckland, 1967)

    Makers of Fortune: A Colonial Business Community and its Fall (AUP/OUP, Auckland, 1973)

    The Father and his Gift: John Logan Campbell's Later Years (AUP, Auckland, 1987)

    'The Thames Valley and Rotorua Railway Company Limited, 1882–9: a study of the relationship of business and government in nineteenth century New Zealand', *NZJH*, VIII.1 (1974), pp. 22–43

    Young Logan Campbell (AUP/OUP, Auckland, 1982)

Sutch, W. B. *Colony or Nation? Economic Crises in New Zealand from the 1860s to the 1960s: Addresses and Papers*, ed. Michael Turnbull, 2nd edn. (Sydney University Press, 1968)

Tritt, A. W. 'Sir George Grey's Land Settlement Policy, 1849–1854: a study of the background, nature and effects of the General Land Regulations, 4 March, 1853', MA thesis, Canterbury (1955)

Turnbull, Michael. *The New Zealand Bubble: The Wakefield Theory in Practice* (Price Milburn, Wellington, 1959)

CHAPTER 4: THE POLITICS OF SETTLEMENT

Adams, Peter. *Fatal Necessity: British Intervention in New Zealand, 1830–1847* (AUP/OUP, Auckland, 1977)

Allan, Ruth. *Nelson: A History of Early Settlement* (Reed, Wellington, 1965)

Angus, John. 'City and country: change and continuity. Electoral politics and society in Otago, 1877–1893', PhD thesis, Otago (1976)

Armstrong, Warwick. 'The politics of development: a study of the structure of politics from 1870 to 1890', MA thesis, Victoria (1960)

Bassett, Judith. *Sir Harry Atkinson, 1831–1892* (AUP/OUP, Auckland, 1975)

Bohan, Edmund. 'The 1879 general election in Canterbury', *PS*, XII.1 (1960) pp. 45–61

    'The General Election of 1879 in Canterbury', MA thesis, Canterbury (1958)

Burdon, R. M. *The Life and Times of Sir Julius Vogel* (Caxton, Christchurch, 1948)

Cheyne, Sonia. 'Search for a constitution. People and politics in New Zealand's Crown Colony years', PhD thesis, Otago (1975)

Cumming, J. P. 'The Compact and financial settlement of 1856', MA thesis, Auckland (1963)

Dalton, B. J. *War and Politics in New Zealand, 1855–1870* (Sydney University Press, 1967)

Dalziel, Raewyn. *Julius Vogel: Business Politician* (OUP, Auckland, 1986)

    'The "continuous ministry" revisited', *NZJH*, XXI.2 (1987), pp. 46–61

    The Origins of New Zealand Diplomacy: The Agent-General in London, 1870–1905 (Price Milburn for Victoria University Press, Wellington, 1975)

Evans, A. M. 'A study of Canterbury politics in the early 1880s with special reference to the General Election of 1881', MA thesis, Canterbury (1959)

Ewing, I. S. 'Public Service reform in New Zealand, 1866–1912', MA thesis, Auckland (1979)

Fieldhouse, D. K. 'Autochthonous elements in the evolution of dominion status: the case of New Zealand', *Journal of Commonwealth Political Studies*, I.2 (1962), pp. 85–111

Gisborne, William. *New Zealand Rulers and Statesman: From 1840 to 1897*, revised edn. (Sampson, Low, Marston, London, 1897)

Graham, Jeanine. *Frederick Weld* (AUP/OUP, Auckland, 1983)

Grimshaw, Patricia. *Women's Suffrage in New Zealand* (AUP/OUP, Auckland, 1972)

Hamer, D. A. 'The Agricultural Company and New Zealand politics, 1877–1886', *HSANZ*, X.38 (1962), pp. 141–64

    'The law and the prophet: a political biography of Sir Robert Stout (1844–1936)', MA thesis, Auckland (1960)

Hanham, H. J. 'The political structure of Auckland, 1853–76', MA thesis, Auckland (1950)

Herron, D. G. 'Alsatia or Utopia? New Zealand society and politics in the eighteen-fifties', *Landfall*, XIII.4 (1959), pp. 324–41

'The circumstances and effects of Sir George Grey's delay in summoning the first New Zealand General Assembly', *HSANZ*, VIII.32 (1959), pp. 364–82

'The franchise and New Zealand politics, 1853–8', *PS*, XII.1 (1960), pp. 28–44

'Provincialism and centralism, 1853–1858', in R. M. Chapman and Keith Sinclair (eds.), *Study of a Small Democracy: Essays in Honour of Willis Airey* (Paul for the University of Auckland, 1963)

'The structure and course of New Zealand politics, 1853–1858', PhD thesis, Otago (1959)

Hill, S. R. 'Local politics in the Auckland Province, 1867–71', MA thesis, Auckland (1958)

Hunt, J. L. 'The election of 1875–6 and the abolition of the provinces', MA thesis, Auckland (1961)

Jackson, W. K. *The New Zealand Legislative Council: A Study of the Establishment, Failure and Abolition of an Upper House* (University of Otago Press, Dunedin, 1972)

Kearsley, G. W., Hearn, T. J. and Brooking, T. W. H. 'Land settlement and voting patterns in the Otago Provincial Council, 1863–1872', *NZJH*, XVIII.1 (1984), pp. 19–33

Knaplund, Paul. *Gladstone and Britain's Imperial Policy* (Allen and Unwin, London, 1927)

Lewis, B. J. 'Politics of the Auckland Province, 1862–1867', MA thesis, Auckland (1957)

Lipson, Leslie. *The Politics of Equality: New Zealand's Adventures in Democracy* (University of Chicago Press, 1948)

McIntyre, W. David (ed.) *The Journal of Henry Sewell, 1853–7*, 2 vols. (Whitcoulls, Christchurch, 1980)

McLintock, A. H. *Crown Colony Government in New Zealand* (Government Printer, Wellington, 1958)

The History of Otago. The Origins and Growth of a Wakefield Class Settlement (Otago Centennial Historical Publications, Dunedin, 1949)

McLintock, A. H. and Wood, G. A. *The Upper House in Colonial New Zealand. A Study of the Legislative Council of New Zealand in the Period 1854–1887* (Wellington, 1989)

Millar, David. 'The General Election of 1884 in Canterbury, being a study of the structure of politics within the province of Canterbury, New Zealand', MA thesis, Canterbury (1960)

Miller, John. *Early Victorian New Zealand: A Study of Racial Tension and Social Attitudes, 1839–1852* (OUP, London, 1958)

Morrell, W. P. *British Colonial Policy in the Age of Peel and Russell* (Clarendon Press, Oxford, 1930)

British Colonial Policy in the Mid-Victorian Age: South Africa — New Zealand — the West Indies (Clarendon Press, Oxford, 1969)

The Provincial System in New Zealand, 1852–76 (Longmans Green for the Royal Empire Society, London, 1932)

Mullins, R. M. 'The division of power between the general and provincial governments, 1853–1867', MA thesis, Victoria (1953)

Poff, B. J. 'William Fox: early colonial years, 1842–1848', MA thesis, Canterbury (1969)

Polaschek, R. J. *Government Administration in New Zealand* (NZ Institute of Public Administration, Wellington, 1958)

Reeves, William Pember. *The Long White Cloud*, 2nd edn. (Horace Marshall, London, 1899)

Rosanowski, G. J. 'The West Coast railways and New Zealand politics, 1878–1888', *NZJH*, IV.1 (1970), pp. 34–53

Ross, Angus. *New Zealand Aspirations in the Pacific in the Nineteenth Century* (Clarendon Press, Oxford, 1964)

'The New Zealand Constitution Act of 1852: its authorship', *Historical and Political Studies*, I.1 (1969), pp. 61–7

Rutherford, J. *Sir George Grey, K.C.B., 1812–1898: A Study in Colonial Government* (Cassell, London, 1961)

Rutherford, J. (ed.) *The Founding of New Zealand: The Journals of Felton Mathew, First Surveyor-General of New Zealand, and his Wife, 1840–1847* (Reed for Auckland University College, 1940)

Bibliography

Saunders, Alfred. *History of New Zealand . . .*, 2 vols: I (Whitcombe and Tombs, Christchurch, 1896); II (Smith, Anthony, Sellars, Christchurch, 1899)
Scholefield, G. H. *Captain William Hobson, First Governor of New Zealand* (OUP, London, 1934)
Sinclair, Keith. 'The significance of "the Scarecrow Ministry", 1887–1891', in R. M. Chapman and Keith Sinclair (eds.), *Studies of a Small Democracy: Essays in Honour of Willis Airey* (Paul for the University of Auckland, 1963)
    William Pember Reeves: New Zealand Fabian (Clarendon Press, Oxford, 1965)
Stewart, William Downie. *William Rolleston, A New Zealand Statesman* (Whitcombe and Tombs, Christchurch, 1940)
Stone, R. C. J. 'Auckland's political opposition in the Crown Colony period, 1841–53', in L. E. Richardson and W. D. McIntyre (eds.), *Provincial Perspectives: Essays in Honour of W. J. Gardner* (University of Canterbury, Christchurch, 1980)
    'The Maori lands question and the fall of the Grey Government, 1879', *NZJH*, I.1 (1967), pp. 51–74
    'The Thames Valley and Rotorua Railway Company Limited, 1882–9: a study of the relationship of business and government in nineteenth century New Zealand', *NZJH*, VIII.1 (1974), pp. 22–43
Stuart, Peter. *Edward Gibbon Wakefield in New Zealand: His Political Career, 1853–4* (Price Milburn for Victoria University of Wellington, 1971)
Thompson, G. F. 'The politics of retrenchment: the origin and some aspects of the politics of the Hall Ministry, 1879–82', MA thesis, Victoria (1967)
Webb, Leicester. *Government in New Zealand* (NZ Dept. of Internal Affairs, Wellington, 1940)
Whitehead, C. 'The 1887 General Election in Canterbury', MA thesis, Canterbury (1961)
Williams, Jeanine. 'Frederick Weld: a political biography', PhD thesis, Auckland (1973)
    Frederick Weld (AUP/OUP, Auckland, 1983)
Wilson, T. G. *The Grey Government, 1877–9: An Episode in the Rise of Liberalism in New Zealand* (Auckland University College, 1954)
    The Rise of the New Zealand Liberal Party, 1880–90 (Auckland University College, 1956)
Wood, G. A. 'The 1878 Electoral Bill and franchise reform in nineteenth century New Zealand', *PS*, XXVIII.1 (1976), pp. 41–58
    'The political structure of New Zealand 1858 to 1861', PhD thesis, Otago (1965)
Wright-St. Clair, Rex. *Thoroughly a Man of the World: A Biography of Sir David Monro, M.D.* (Whitcombe and Tombs, Christchurch, 1971)
Young, John. 'The political conflict of 1875', *PS*, XIII.2 (1961), pp. 56–78
    'The politics of the Auckland province, 1872–1876' MA thesis, Auckland (1960)

CHAPTER 5: SETTLER SOCIETY

Allan, Ruth. *Nelson: A History of Early Settlement* (Reed, Wellington 1965)
Arnold, Rollo. 'English rural unionism and Taranaki immigration, 1871–1876', *NZJH*, VI.1 (1972), pp. 20–41
    The Farthest Promised Land: English Villagers, New Zealand Immigrants of the 1870s (VUP, Wellington, 1981)
Bagnall, A. G. *Wairarapa: An Historical Excursion* (Hedley's Bookshop for the Masterton Trust Lands Trust, 1976)
Barker, Mary Anne. *Station Amusements in New Zealand* (William Hunt, London, 1873; Wilson and Horton, Auckland, 1970)
    Station Life in New Zealand (Macmillan, London, 1883; Wilson and Horton, Auckland, 1970)
Bathgate, Alexander. *Colonial Experiences: Or Sketches of People and Places in the Province of Otago, New Zealand,* (James MacLehose, Glasgow, 1874; Capper, Christchurch, 1974)
Beagle, Jan. 'Children of the state: a study of the New Zealand industrial school system, 1880–1925', MA thesis, Auckland (1974)

679

Bloomfield, G. T. *New Zealand: A Handbook of Historical Statistics* (G. K. Hall, Boston, Mass., 1984)

Brookes, Barbara, Macdonald, Charlotte and Tennant, Margaret. *Women in History: Essays on European Women in New Zealand* (Allen and Unwin, Wellington, 1986)

Buick, Thomas Lindsay. *Old Manawatu: Or the Wild Days of the West* (Buick and Young, Palmerston North, 1903; Capper, Christchurch 1975)

Burnley, I. H. 'German immigration and settlement in New Zealand 1842–1914', *NZG*, XXIX.1 (1973), pp. 45–63

Burns, Patricia (ed. Henry Richardson) *Fatal Success: A History of the New Zealand Company* (Heinemann Reed, Auckland, 1989)

Butler, Peter. *Opium and Gold: A History of the Chinese Goldminers in New Zealand* (Alister Taylor, Martinborough, 1977)

Butler, Samuel. *A First Year in Canterbury Settlement* (Longman, Green, London, 1863)

Campbell, John Logan. *Poenamo: Sketches of the Early Days of New Zealand* . . . (Williams and Norgate, London, 1881; Wilson and Horton, Auckland, 1970)

Campbell, M. D. N. 'The evolution of Hawke's Bay landed society, 1850–1914', PhD thesis, Victoria (1972)

Chilton, M. F. 'The genesis of the welfare state: a study of hospitals and charitable aid in New Zealand, 1877–92', MA thesis, Canterbury (1968)

Cooper, Theophilus. *A Digger's Diary at the Thames, 1867*, Victorian New Zealand — a reprint series, 5 (Hocken Library, Dunedin, 1978)

Cumberland, Kenneth B. ' "Jimmy Grants" and "Mihaneres": New Zealand about 1853', *Economic Geography*, XXX.1 (1954), pp. 70–89

Cumberland, Kenneth B. and Hargreaves, R. P. 'Middle Island ascendant: New Zealand in 1881': Part 1, *NZG*, XI.2 (1955), pp. 95–118; Part 2, *NZG*, XII.1 (1956), pp. 51–74

Cumming, Ian and Cumming, Alan. *History of State Education in New Zealand, 1840–1975* (Pitman, Wellington, 1978)

Curson, P. H. 'Auckland in 1842', *NZG*, XXX.2 (1974), pp. 107–28

Dalziel, Raewyn. 'The colonial helpmeet: women's role and the vote in nineteenth century New Zealand', *NZJH*, XI.2 (1977), pp. 112–23

Deans, John (ed.) *Pioneers of Canterbury: Deans Letters, 1840–1854* (Reed, Dunedin and Wellington, 1937)

Docking, Gil. *Two Hundred Years of New Zealand Painting* (Reed, Wellington, 1971)

Downes, Peter. *Shadows on the Stage: Theatre in New Zealand: In the First Seventy Years* (McIndoe, Dunedin, 1975)

Drummond, Alison (ed.) *The Auckland Journals of Vicesimus Lush, 1850–63* (Pegasus, Christchurch, 1971)

Married and Gone to New Zealand . . . (Paul, Auckland and Hamilton, 1960)

The Thames Journals of Vicesimus Lush, 1868–82 (Pegasus, Christchurch, 1975)

Drummond, Alison and Drummond, L. R. *At Home in New Zealand: An Illustrated History of Everyday Things Before 1865* (Paul, Auckland, 1967)

Ebbett, Eve. *In True Colonial Fashion: A Lively Look at What Colonials Wore* (Reed, Wellington, 1977)

Elder, J. R. *The History of the Presbyterian Church of New Zealand, 1840–1940* (Presbyterian Bookroom, Christchurch, 1940)

Eldred-Grigg, Stevan. *A Southern Gentry: New Zealanders Who Inherited the Earth* (A. H. and A. W. Reed, Wellington, 1980)

Pleasures of the Flesh (A. H. and A. W. Reed, Wellington, 1984)

'The landed gentry of lowlands Ashburton County, 1890–96', MA thesis, Canterbury (1974)

Elphick, Judith. 'Auckland 1870–74: a social portrait', MA thesis, Auckland (1974)

'What's wrong with Emma? The feminist debate in colonial Auckland', *NZJH*, IX.2 (1975), pp. 126–41

Fairburn, Miles. 'Local community or atomized society?', *NZJH*, XVI.2 (1982), pp. 146–67

'Social mobility and opportunity in nineteenth-century New Zealand', *NZJH*, XIII.1 (1979), pp. 43–60

The Ideal Society and its Enemies (AUP, Auckland, 1989)

Fell, Alfred. *A Colonist's Voyage to New Zealand Under Sail in the Early 'Forties'* (Townsend, Exeter, 1926; Capper, Christchurch, 1973)

Forrest, James. 'Population and settlement on the Otago goldfields, 1861–1870', *NZG*, XVII.1 (1961), pp. 64–86

Fraser, Bryce, (ed.) *The New Zealand Book of Events* (Reed Methuen, Auckland, 1986)

Galbreath, Ross. *Walter Buller: The Reluctant Conservationist* (GP Books, Wellington, 1989)

Gardner, W. J. *Colonial Cap and Gown: Studies in the Mid-Victorian Universities of Australasia* (University of Canterbury, Christchurch, 1979)

Gardner, W. J. (ed.) *A History of Canterbury*, II: *General History, 1854–76, and Cultural Aspects, 1850–1950* (Canterbury Centennial Historical and Literary Committee and Whitcombe and Tombs, Christchurch, 1971)

Gee, David. *The Devil's Own Brigade: A History of the Lyttelton Gaol, 1860–1920* (Millwood Press, Wellington, 1975)

Gibson, C. J. 'A demographic history of New Zealand', PhD thesis, University of California, Berkeley, (1971)

Gillespie, Oliver. *South Canterbury: A Record of Settlement*, 2nd edn. (South Canterbury Centennial History Committee, Timaru, 1971)

Gillespie-Needham, D. 'The colonial and his books: a study of reading in nineteenth century New Zealand', PhD thesis, Victoria (1971)

Godley, John R. (ed.) *Letters from Early New Zealand by Charlotte Godley, 1850–1853* (Christchurch, Whitcombe and Tombs, 1951)

Gregory, P. A. 'Saving the children in New Zealand: a study of social attitudes towards larrikinism in the later 19th century', research essay, Massey (1975)

Grimshaw, Patricia. *Women's Suffrage in New Zealand* (AUP/OUP, Auckland, 1972)

Hale, Allen. *Pioneer Nurserymen of New Zealand* (Reed for the NZ Horticultural Trades Association, Wellington, 1955)

Hamer, D. A. 'Towns in nineteenth-century New Zealand', *NZJH*, XIII.1 (1979), pp. 5–20

Hamer, David and Nicholls, Roberta (eds.) *The Making of Wellington, 1800–1914* (VUP, Wellington, 1991)

Hamilton, S. P. 'William Swainson: Attorney General of New Zealand', MA thesis, University of New Zealand (1949)

Hargreaves, R. P. 'The golden age: New Zealand about 1867', *NZG*, XVI.1 (1960), pp. 1–32

Harper, Henry W. *Letters from New Zealand, 1857–1911: Being Some Account of Life and Work in the Province of Canterbury, South Island* (H. Rees, London, 1914)

Hawkins, D. N. *Beyond the Waimakariri: A Regional History* . . . (Whitcombe and Tombs, Christchurch, 1957)

   Rangiora: The Passing Years and People in a Canterbury Country Town (Rangiora Borough Council, Rangiora, 1983)

Herron, D. G. 'Alsatia or Utopia? New Zealand society and politics in the eighteen-fifties', *Landfall*, XIII.4 (1959), pp. 324–41

Hight, James and Straubel, C. R. (eds.) *A History of Canterbury*, I: *to 1854* (Canterbury Centennial Association and Whitcombe and Tombs, Christchurch, 1957)

Hill, Richard. *The History of Policing in New Zealand*: Part I, *Policing the Colonial Frontier* (Historical Publications Branch, Wellington, 1986)

Hoare, Michael. ' "Our comrades beyond the seas": colonial youth movements, 1880–1920', *Turnbull Library Record*, XII.2 (1979), pp. 73–94

Holcroft, M. H. *Old Invercargill* (McIndoe, Dunedin, 1976)

Hurst, Maurice. *Music and the Stage in New Zealand: A Century of Entertainment, 1840–1943* (Begg, Auckland, 1944)

Johnston, Judith. 'Information and emigration: the image making process', *NZG*, XXXIII.2 (1977), pp. 60–7

Limbrick, W. E. (ed.) *Bishop Selwyn in New Zealand, 1841–68* (Dunmore, Palmerston North, 1983)

McCormick, E. H. *Letters and Art in New Zealand* (NZ Dept. of Internal Affairs, Wellington, 1940)

Macdonald, Charlotte. *A Woman of Good Character: Single Women as Immigrant Settlers in Nineteenth Century New Zealand* (Allen and Unwin/Historical Branch, Wellington, 1990)

McGeorge, Colin. 'Hear Our Voices, We Entreat; schools and the "colonial twang", 1880–1930', *NZJH*, xviii.1 (1984), pp. 3–18

Macgregor, Miriam. *Petticoat Pioneers: North Island Women of the Colonial Era*, 2 vols. (Reed, Wellington, 1973, 1975)

Mackey, J. *The Making of a State Education System: The Passing of the New Zealand Act, 1877* (Geoffrey Chapman, London, 1967)

Maclean, F. S. *Challenge for Health: A History of Public Health in New Zealand* (Government Printer, Wellington, 1964)

McIntosh, A. D. (ed.) *Marlborough: A Provincial History* (Marlborough Provincial Historical Committee, Blenheim, 1940)

McKimmey, Paul. 'The temperance movement in New Zealand, 1835–1894', MA thesis, Auckland (1968)

McLaren, I. A. 'Education and politics: background to the Secondary Schools Act, 1903. Part I: secondary education for the privileged', *NZJES*, v.2 (1970), pp. 94–114

McLintock, A. H. *The History of Otago. The Origins and Growth of a Wakefield Class Settlement* (Otago Centennial Historical Publications, Dunedin, 1949)

May, Philip Ross. *The West Coast Gold Rushes*, 2nd edn. (Pegasus, Christchurch, 1967)

Miller, John. *Early Victorian New Zealand: A Study of Racial Tension and Social Attitudes, 1839–1852* (OUP, London, 1958)

Money, C. L. *Knocking About in New Zealand* (Samuel Mullen, Melbourne, 1871; Capper, Christchurch, 1972)

Morrell, W. P. *The Anglican Church in New Zealand: A History* (Anglican Church of the Province of New Zealand, Dunedin, 1973)

Neil, James. *New Zealand Family Herb Doctor* (Mills, Dick, Dunedin, 1889; Capper, Christchurch, 1980)

NZ Historic Places Trust. *Historic Buildings of New Zealand: North Island* (Cassell, Auckland, 1979)

Historic Buildings of New Zealand: South Island (Methuen, Auckland, 1983)

Oliver, W. H. 'Social policy in the Liberal period', *NZJH*, xiii.1 (1979), pp. 25–33

Platts, Una. *Nineteenth Century New Zealand Artists: A Guide and Handbook* (Avon Fine Prints, Christchurch, 1980)

Population of New Zealand, vol. I, ESCAP Country Monographs Series, no. 12 (United Nations, New York, 1985)

Porter, Frances. *Born to New Zealand: A Biography of Jane Maria Atkinson* (Allen and Unwin, Wellington, 1989)

Powell, M. J. 'The church in Auckland society, 1880–1886', MA thesis, Auckland (1970)

Pownall, L. L. 'The origins of towns in New Zealand', *NZG*, xii.2 (1956), pp. 173–188

Primrose, M. S. 'Society and the insane: a study of mental illness in New Zealand, 1867–1926, with special reference to the Auckland Mental Hospital', MA thesis, Auckland (1968)

Richardson, Len and McIntyre, W. David (eds.) *Provincial Perspectives: Essays in Honour of W. J. Gardner* (University of Canterbury Press, 1980)

Rutherford, J. and Skinner, W. H. *The Establishment of the New Plymouth Settlement in New Zealand, 1841–1843* (Thomas Avery, New Plymouth, 1940)

Scholefield, G. H. (ed.) *The Richmond-Atkinson Papers*, 2 vols. (Government Printer, Wellington, 1960)

Scotter, W. H. *A History of Canterbury: iii, 1876–1950* (Canterbury Centennial Historical and Literary Committee and Whitcombe and Tombs, Christchurch, 1965)

Sharp, C. Andrew (ed.) *The Dillon Letters: The Letters of the Hon. Constantine Dillon* (Reed, Wellington, 1964)

Simmons, E. R. *A Brief History of the Catholic Church in New Zealand* (Catholic Publications Centre, Auckland, 1978)

Simpson, Helen. *The Women of New Zealand* (NZ Dept. of Internal Affairs, Wellington, 1940)

Sinclair, Keith (ed.) *Tasman Relations* (AUP, Auckland, 1987)

Soper, Eileen. *The Otago of Our Mothers* (Otago Centennial Historical Publications, Dunedin, 1948; Capper, Christchurch, 1978)

Stacpoole, John. *Colonial Architecture in New Zealand* (Reed, Wellington, 1976)

Stewart, Adela. *My Simple Life in New Zealand* (Robert Banks, London, 1908; Wilson and Horton, Auckland, 1971)

Stokes, Evelyn. *A History of Tauranga County* (Dunmore, Palmerston North, 1980)

Swainson, William. *Auckland, The Capital of New Zealand, and the Country Adjacent . . .* (Smith, Elder, London, 1853; Wilson and Horton, Auckland, 1971)

Tennant, Margaret. 'Duncan MacGregor and charitable aid administration, 1886–1896', *NZJH*, xiii.1 (1979), pp. 33–40

The Dictionary of New Zealand Biography, Vol. I, 1769–1869 (Allen and Unwin, Wellington, 1990)

Thomson, W. L. (ed.) *Brett's Colonists' Guide and Cyclopaedia of Useful Knowledge* (Brett Printing, Auckland, 1883; Capper, Christchurch, 1980)

Towgood, H. 'Truancy in New Zealand in the later nineteenth century', research essay, Massey (1977)

Toynbee, Claire. 'Class and social structure in nineteenth-century New Zealand', *NZJH*, xiii.1 (1979), pp. 65–80

Tremewan, Peter. *French Akaroa: An Attempt to Colonise Southern New Zealand* (University of Canterbury, Christchurch, 1990)

Trollope, Anthony. *Australia and New Zealand*, 2 vols. (Chapman and Hall, London, 1873)

Turnbull, Michael. *The New Zealand Bubble: The Wakefield Theory in Practice* (Price Milburn, Wellington, 1959)

Wallace, Stuart. 'Town versus gown in Auckland, 1872–1919', *NZJH*, vii.2 (1973), pp. 165–85

Whelan, P. J. 'The care of destitute, neglected and criminal children in New Zealand, 1840–1900', MA thesis, Victoria (1956)

Wilson, T. Y. 'New Zealand prisons, 1880–1909: the administration of colonial Arthur Hume', MA thesis, Victoria (1970)

Woodhouse, A. E. (ed.) *Tales of Pioneer Women: Collected by the Womens Institutes of New Zealand* (Whitcombe and Tombs, Christchurch, 1940)

Wynn, Graeme. 'Conservation and society in late nineteenth-century New Zealand', *NZJH*, xi.2 (1977), pp. 124–36

CHAPTER 6: MĀORI AND PĀKEHĀ

Adams, Peter. *Fatal Necessity: British Intervention in New Zealand, 1830–1847* (AUP/OUP, Auckland, 1977)

Allan, Ruth. *Nelson: A History of Early Settlement* (Reed, Wellington, 1965)

Barrington, J. M. and Beaglehole, T. H. *Maori Schools in a Changing Society: An Historical Review* (NZCER, Wellington, 1974)

Belich, James. *'I Shall Not Die': Titokowaru's War: New Zealand, 1868–9* (Allen and Unwin/ PNP, Wellington, 1989)

  The New Zealand Wars and the Victorian Interpretation of Racial Conflict (AUP, Auckland, 1986)

  'Titokowaru's war and its place in New Zealand history', MA thesis, Victoria (1979)

Binney, Judith. 'Christianity and the Maoris to 1840, a comment', *NZJH*, iii.2 (1969), pp. 143–65

Cowan, James. *The New Zealand Wars: A History of the Maori Campaigns and the Pioneering Period*, 2 vols. (Government Printer, Wellington, 1922–23)

Fargher, R. W. S. 'Donald McLean, Chief Land Purchase Agent (1846–1861) and Native Secretary (1856–1861)', MA thesis, Auckland (1947)

Gorst, J. E. *The Maori King; Or, The Story of our Quarrel with the Natives of New Zealand* (Macmillan, London, 1864; Capper, Christchurch, 1974)

Hadfield, Octavius. *The New Zealand War: The Second Year of 'One of England's Little Wars'* (Williams and Norgate, London, 1861)

    One of England's Little Wars: A Letter to the Right Hon. the Duke of Newcastle, Secretary of State for the Colonies (Williams and Norgate, London, 1860)

    A Sequel to 'One of England's Little Wars': Being an Account of the Real Origin of the War in New Zealand (Williams and Norgate, London, 1861)

Hurinui (Jones), Pei Te. *King Potatau: An Account of the Life of Potatau Te Wherowhero, The First Maori King* (Polynesian Society, Wellington, 1960)

Lange, R. T. 'The revival of a dying race: a study of Maori health reform, 1900–1918, and its nineteenth century background', MA thesis, Auckland (1972)

McMaster, N. M. 'Te Whiti and the Parihaka incident', MA thesis, Victoria (1959)

Martin, William. *The Taranaki Question* (Melanesian Press, Auckland, 1860)

Mikaere, Buddy. *Te Maiharoa and the Promised Land* (Auckland, 1988)

Owens, J. M. R. 'Christianity and the Maoris to 1840', *NZJH*, ii.1 (1968), pp. 18–40

Parsonson, Ann. 'He whenua te utu (The payment will be land)', PhD thesis, Canterbury (1978)

    'Te mana o te Kingitanga Maori: A study of Waikato–Ngatimaniapoto relations during the struggle for the King Country, 1878–84', MA thesis, Canterbury (1972)

Pocock, J. G. A. (ed.) *The Maori and New Zealand Politics* (Paul, Auckland and Hamilton, 1965)

Pool, D. Ian. *The Maori Population of New Zealand, 1769–1971* (AUP/OUP, Auckland, 1977)

Riseborough, Hazel. *Days of Darkness. Taranaki, 1878–1884* (Allen and Unwin/Historical Branch, Wellington, 1988)

Ross, Ruth. 'Te Tiriti o Waitangi: texts and translations', *NZJH*, vi.2 (1972), pp. 129–57

Rowley, C. D. *The Destruction of Aboriginal Society*, 2nd edn., 3 vols. (Penguin, Harmondsworth, 1972)

Rutherford, J. *Sir George Grey K.C.B., 1812–1898: A Study in Colonial Government* (Cassell, London, 1961)

Sinclair, Keith. 'Maori nationalism and the European economy, 1850–1860', *HSANZ*, v.18 (1952), pp. 119–34

    The Origins of the Maori Wars (NZ University Press, Wellington, 1957)

Sorrenson, M. P. K. 'How to civilize savages: some "answers" from nineteenth century New Zealand', *NZJH*, ix.2 (1975), pp. 97–110

    'Land purchase methods and their effect on Maori population, 1865–1901', *JPS*, xiv.3 (1956), pp. 183–99

    'The Maori King movement, 1858–1885', in R. M. Chapman and Keith Sinclair (eds.), *Studies of a Small Democracy: Essays in Honour of Willis Airey* (Paul for University of Auckland, 1963)

    'The Maori people and the city of Auckland', *Te Ao Hou*, 27 (June 1959), pp. 8–13

    'The purchase of Maori lands, 1865–1892', MA thesis, Auckland (1955)

    'Towards a radical reinterpretation of New Zealand history: the role of the Waitangi Tribunal', *NZJH*, xxi.1 (1987), pp. 173–88

Thomson, Arthur. *The Story of New Zealand: Past and Present — Savage and Civilized*, 2 vols. (John Murray, London, 1859; Capper, Christchurch, 1974)

Turton, H. H. (ed.) *Maori Deeds of Land Purchases in the North Island of New Zealand*, 2 vols. (Government Printer, Wellington 1877, 1878)

Wake, C. H. 'George Clarke, and the government of the Maoris: 1840–45', *HSANZ*, x.39 (1962), pp. 339–56

Wakefield, E. G. and Ward, J. *The British Colonization of New Zealand* (J. W. Parker, London, 1837)

Wakefield, E. J. *Adventure in New Zealand from 1839 to 1844; With Some Account of the*

Beginning of the British Colonization of the Islands, 2 vols. (John Murray, London, 1845; Wilson and Horton, Auckland, 1971)

Ward, Alan. 'The origins of the Anglo-Maori wars: a reconsideration', *NZJH*, I.2 (1967), pp. 148–70

A Show of Justice: Racial 'Amalgamation' in Nineteenth Century New Zealand (ANU Press, Canberra, 1974)

Wards, Ian. *The Shadow of the Land: A Study of British Policy and Racial Conflict in New Zealand, 1832–1852* (Government Printer, Wellington, 1968)

Williams, John. *Politics of the New Zealand Maori: Protest and Co-operation, 1891–1909* (University of Washington Press, Seattle, 1969)

Wright, Harrison. *New Zealand, 1769–1840: Early Years of Western Contact* (Harvard University Press, Cambridge, Mass., 1967)

CHAPTER 7: THE CHALLENGE TO MANA MĀORI

Adams, Peter. *Fatal Necessity: British Intervention in New Zealand, 1830–1847* (AUP/OUP, Auckland, 1977)

Anderson, Atholl J. 'Towards an explanation of protohistoric social organisation and settlement patterns amongst the southern Ngai Tahu', *NZ Journal of Archaeology*, II (1980), pp. 3–23

Andrews, C. Lesley. 'Aspects of development, 1870–1890', in I. H. Kawharu (ed.), *Conflict and Compromise: Essays on the Maori since Colonisation* (Reed, Wellington, 1975)

Asher, George and Naulls, David. *Maori Land* (New Zealand Planning Council, Wellington, 1987)

Bagnall, A. G. *Wairarapa: An Historical Excursion* (Hedley's Bookshop for the Masterton Trust Lands Trust, Masterton, 1976)

Ballara, Angela. *Proud to be White? A Survey of Pakeha Prejudice in New Zealand* (Heinemann, Auckland, 1986)

'The pursuit of mana? A re-evaluation of the process of land alienation by Maoris, 1840–1890', *JPS*, 91.4 (1982), pp. 519–541

Ballara, Heather Angela. 'The origins of Ngāti Kahungunu', PhD thesis, Victoria University of Wellington (1991)

Barlow, Cleve. *Tikanga Whakaaro: Key Concepts in Maori Culture* (OUP, Auckland, 1991)

Belich, James. *'I Shall Not Die': Titokowaru's War: New Zealand, 1868–9* (Allen and Unwin/PNP, Wellington, 1989)

The New Zealand Wars and the Victorian Interpretation of Racial Conflict (AUP, Auckland, 1986)

Binney, Judith. 'Maori oral narratives, Pakeha written texts: two forms of telling history', *NZJH*, XXI.2 (1987), pp. 16–28

Binney, Judith and Chaplin, Gillian. *Nga Morehu: The Survivors* (OUP, Auckland, 1986)

Burns, Patricia (ed. Henry Richardson). *Fatal Success: A History of the New Zealand Company* (Heinemann Reed, Auckland, 1989)

Butterworth, G. V. and Young, H. R. *Maori Affairs/Nga Take Maori* (Iwi Transition Agency/GP Books, Wellington, 1990)

Cleave, Peter. 'Tribal and state-like political formations in New Zealand Maori society, 1750–1900', *JPS*, 92.1 (1983), pp. 51–92

Dacker, Bill. *The People of the Place: Mahika Kai* (Belonging Here/Toi Take-take), (New Zealand 1990 Commission, Wellington, 1990)

Dalton, B. J. *War and Politics in New Zealand, 1855–1870* (Sydney University Press, Sydney, 1967)

Eldridge, C. C. *Victorian Imperialism* (Hodder and Stoughton, London, 1978)

Elsmore, Bronwyn. *Mana from Heaven: A Century of Maori Prophets in New Zealand* (Moana Press, Tauranga, 1989)

Evison, Harry C. (ed.) *The Treaty of Waitangi & the Ngai Tahu Claim: A Summary* (Ngai Tahu Maori Trust Board, Christchurch, 1988)

Frame, Alex (ed.) 'Kauwaeranga judgment', *Victoria University of Wellington Law Review*, 14.3 (1984), pp. 227–45

Galbreath, Ross. *Walter Buller: The Reluctant Conservationist* (GP Books, Wellington, 1989)

Grace, John Te H. *Tuwharetoa: The History of the Maori People of the Taupo District* (Reed, Wellington, 1959, reprinted 1970)

Graham, Jeanine. *Frederick Weld* (AUP/OUP, Auckland, 1983)

Head, L. 'The gospel of Te Ua Haumene', *JPS*, 101.2 (1992), pp. 7–44

Hill, Richard S. *Policing the Colonial Frontier: The Theory and Practice of Coercive Social and Racial Control in New Zealand, 1767–1867*, Parts One and Two (Historical Publications Branch, Department of Internal Affairs, Wellington, 1986)

Hill, Richard S. *The Colonial Frontier Tamed: New Zealand Policing in Transition, 1867–1886* (Historical Branch, Department of Internal Affairs/GP Books, Wellington, 1989)

Howe, K. R. *Race Relations: Australia and New Zealand: A Comparative Survey, 1770's–1970's* (Methuen, Wellington, 1977)

Jackson, Moana. *The Maori and the Criminal Justice System: A New Perspective: He Whaipaanga Hou*, Part 2 (Department of Justice, Wellington, 1988)

Kawharu, I. H. *Maori Land Tenure: Studies of a Changing Institution* (Clarendon Press, Oxford, 1977)

Kawharu, I. H. (ed.) *Waitangi: Maori and Pakeha Perspectives of the Treaty of Waitangi* (OUP, Auckland, 1989)

King, Michael. *Maori: A Photographic and Social History* (Heinemann, Auckland, 1983)

King, Michael (ed.) *Te Ao Hurihuri: The World Moves On: Aspects of Maoritanga* (Hicks Smith and Sons, Wellington, 1975)

Lian, Kwen-fee. 'Interpreting Maori history: a case for a historical sociology', *JPS*, 96.4 (1987), pp. 445–71

Macdonald, Charlotte, Penfold, Merimeri and Williams, Bridget (eds.) *The Book of New Zealand Women: Ko kui ma te Kaupapa* (Bridget Williams Books, Wellington, 1991)

McHugh, Paul. 'The legal status of Maori fishing rights in tidal waters', *Victoria University of Wellington Law Review*, 14 (1984), pp. 247–73

The Maori Magna Carta: New Zealand Law and the Treaty of Waitangi (OUP, Auckland, 1991)

McIntyre, W. David. *The Commonwealth of Nations: Origins and Impact, 1869–1971* (University of Minnesota Press, Minneapolis, 1977)

McKenzie, D. F. *Oral Culture, Literacy and Print in Early New Zealand: The Treaty of Waitangi* (VUP/Alexander Turnbull Library Endowment Trust, Wellington, 1985)

Mahuta, R. T. 'Taawhiao's Dream', Macmillan Brown Lecture, University of Waikato (1990)

Mikaere, Buddy. *Te Maiharoa and the Promised Land* (Heinemann, Auckland, 1988)

Morrell, W. P. *British Colonial Policy in the Mid-Victorian Age: South Africa, New Zealand, The West Indies* (Clarendon Press, Oxford, 1969)

Nga Tangata Taumata Rau: 1769–1869 (Allen and Unwin/Te Tari Taiwhenua, Wellington, 1990) [Māori biographies from *The Dictionary of New Zealand Biography*, vol. 1 (in Māori)]

Oliver, W. H. and Thomson, Jane M. *Challenge and Response: A Study of the Development of the Gisborne East Coast Region* (East Coast Development Research Association, Gisborne, 1971)

O'Regan, Tipene. 'Te kupenga o nga tupuna', in John Wilson (ed.), *From the Beginning: The Archaeology of the Maori* (Penguin Books/New Zealand Historic Places Trust, Auckland, 1987)

Orange, Claudia. 'The covenant of Kohimarama: a ratification of the Treaty of Waitangi', *NZJH*, xiv.1 (1980), pp. 61–82

The Treaty of Waitangi (Allen and Unwin/PNP, Wellington, 1987)

Parsonson, Ann R. 'The expansion of a competitive society: a study in nineteenth century Maori history', *NZJH*, xiv.1 (1980), pp. 45–60

'The pursuit of mana', in W. H. Oliver with B. R. Williams (eds.) *The Oxford History of New Zealand* (Clarendon Press/OUP, Wellington, 1981), pp. 140–67

Pere, Joseph. 'Hitori Maori', in Colin Davis and Peter Lineham (eds.) *The Future of the Past: Themes in New Zealand History* (Department of History, Massey University, 1991)

Pool, Ian. *Te Iwi Maori: A New Zealand Population Past, Present and Projected* (AUP, Auckland, 1991)

Porter, Bernard. *The Lion's Share: A Short History of British Imperialism, 1850–1970* (Longman, London, 1975)

Renwick, William (ed.) *Sovereignty & Indigenous Rights: The Treaty of Waitangi in International Contexts* (VUP, Wellington, 1991)

Report of the Waitangi Tribunal on the Manukau Claim (Wai 8), (Waitangi Tribunal, Department of Justice, Wellington, 1985)

Report of the Waitangi Tribunal on the Muriwhenua Fishing Claim (Wai 22), (Waitangi Tribunal, Department of Justice, Wellington, 1988)

Report of the Waitangi Tribunal on the Orakei Claim (Wai 9), (Waitangi Tribunal, Department of Justice, Wellington, 1987)

Riseborough, Hazel. *Days of Darkness: Taranaki, 1878–1884* (Allen and Unwin/Historical Branch, Wellington, 1989)

Salmond, Anne. 'The study of traditional Maori society: the state of the art', *JPS*, 92.3 (1983), pp. 309–331

Sewell, Henry. *The New Zealand Native Rebellion: Letter to Lord Lyttleton*, (Auckland, 1864; Hocken Library, Dunedin, 1974)

Sinclair, Keith. *Kinds of Peace: Maori People After the Wars, 1870–85* (AUP, Auckland, 1991)
The Origins of the Maori Wars (NZ University Press, Wellington, 1957)

Sinclair, Keith (ed.) *The Oxford Illustrated History of New Zealand* (OUP, Auckland, 1990)

Sissons, Jeffrey. *Te Waimana: The Spring of Mana: Tuhoe History and the Colonial Encounter* (University of Otago Press, Dunedin, 1991)

Sorrenson, M. P. K. 'Giving better effect to the Treaty: some thoughts for 1990', *NZJH*, XXIV.2 (1990), pp. 135–49

Steven, Rob. 'Land and white settler colonialism: the case of Aotearoa', in David Novitz and Bill Willmott (eds.) *Culture and Identity in New Zealand* (GP Books, Wellington, 1989)

Stokes, Evelyn. *Te Raupatu o Tauranga Moana: The Confiscation of Tauranga Lands* (University of Waikato, Hamilton, 1989)

Tau, Rawiri Te Maire. 'Kurakura Ngai Tahu', MA thesis, Canterbury (1992)

Tau, Te Maire, Goodall, Anake, Palmer, David and Tau, Rakiihia. *Te Whakatau Kaupapa: Ngai Tahu Resource Management Strategy for the Canterbury Region* (Aoraki Press, Wellington, 1990)

Te Awekotuku, Ngahuia. *Mana Wahine Maori: Selected Writings on Maori Women's Art, Culture and Politics* (New Women's Press, Auckland, 1991)

The Dictionary of New Zealand Biography, Volume I: 1769–1869 (Allen and Unwin/ Department of Internal Affairs, Wellington, 1990)

The Ngai Tahu Report, 1991 (Wai 27), Waitangi Tribunal Report, 3 vols. (Brooker and Friend, Wellington, 1991)

The Ngati Rangiteaorere Claim Report, 1990 (Wai 32), Waitangi Tribunal Report (Brooker and Friend, Wellington, 1990)

The People of Many Peaks: The Maori Biographies from The Dictionary of New Zealand Biography, Volume I: 1769–1869 (Bridget Williams Books/Department of Internal Affairs, Wellington, 1990)

The Te Roroa Report, 1992 (Wai 38), Waitangi Tribunal Report (Brooker and Friend, Wellington, 1992)

The Treaty of Waitangi and Maori Fisheries: Mataitai: Nga Tikanga Maori me te Tiriti o Waitangi: A Background Paper (Law Commission, Wellington, 1989)

Tonk, Rosemarie V. 'The first New Zealand land commissions, 1840–1845', MA thesis, Canterbury (1986)

Tremewan, Peter. *French Akaroa: An Attempt to Colonise Southern New Zealand* (University of Canterbury Press, Christchurch, 1990)

Walker, Ranginui. *Ka Whawhai Tonu Matou: Struggle Without End* (Penguin, Auckland, 1990)

Ward, Alan. 'Commentary: the Treaty and the purchase of Maori land', *NZJH*, xxii.2 (1988), pp. 169–74

    A Report on the Historical Evidence: The Ngai Tahu Claim [before the Waitangi Tribunal], Wai 27, no. TI (1989)

    A Show of Justice: Racial 'Amalgamation' in Nineteenth Century New Zealand (AUP/OUP, Auckland, 1973)

Wards, Ian. *The Shadow of the Land: A Study of British Policy and Racial Conflict in New Zealand, 1832–1852* (Historical Publications, Department of Internal Affairs, Wellington, 1968)

Watson, M. K. and Patterson, B. R. 'The growth and subordination of the Maori economy in the Wellington region of New Zealand, 1840–52', *Pacific Viewpoint*, 26: 3 (1985), pp. 521–45

Williams, John A. *Politics of the New Zealand Maori: Protest and Cooperation, 1891–1909* (OUP for the University of Auckland, 1969)

Wyatt, Philippa. 'The old land claims and the concept of "sale": a case study', MA thesis, Auckland (1991)

CHAPTER 8: PARTIES AND POLITICAL CHANGE

Aimer, E. P. 'The politics of a city: a study in the Auckland urban area, 1899–1935', MA thesis, Auckland (1958)

Angus, John. 'City and country: change and continuity. Electoral politics and society in Otago, 1877–1893', PhD thesis, Otago (1976)

Ash. G. G. 'Ideas of society and state in the New Zealand of 1890, especially as seen in, and as influencing, the General Election in Canterbury', MA thesis, Canterbury (1962)

Bassett, Judith. *Sir Harry Atkinson, 1831–1892* (AUP/OUP, Auckland, 1975)

Bassett, Michael. 'In search of Sir Joseph Ward', *NZJH*, xxi.2 (1987), pp. 112–24

Bollinger, Conrad. *Against the Wind: The Story of the New Zealand Seamen's Union* (New Zealand Seamen's Union, Wellington, 1968)

Breen, Helen. 'Oamaru in the depression of the 1930s', MA thesis, Canterbury (1977)

Brooking, T. W. H. 'Agrarian businessmen organise: a comparative study of the origins and early phase of development of the National Farmers' Union of England and Wales and the New Zealand Farmers' Union, ca. 1900–1929', PhD thesis, Otago (1978)

    'Sir John McKenzie and the origins and growth of the Department of Agriculture, 1891–1900', MA thesis, Massey (1972)

Brown, Bruce. *The Rise of New Zealand Labour: A History of the New Zealand Labour Party from 1916 to 1940* (Price Milburn, Wellington, 1962)

Burdon, R. M. *King Dick: A Biography of Richard John Seddon* (Whitcombe and Tombs, Christchurch, 1955)

    The New Dominion: A Social and Political History of New Zealand, 1918–1939 (Reed, Wellington, 1965)

Campbell, C. 'The working class and the Liberal Party in 1890', *NZJH*, ix.1 (1975), pp. 41–51

Campbell, R. J. 'The role of the police in the Waihi strike: some new evidence', *PS*, xxvi.2 (1974), pp. 34–40

Chapman, R. M. *The Political Scene, 1919–1931* (Heinemann, Auckland, 1969)

    'The significance of the 1928 General Election', MA thesis, Auckland (1948)

Chapman, R. M. (ed.) *Ends and Means in New Zealand Politics* (University of Auckland, 1961)

Chapman, R. M. and Sinclair, Keith (eds.) *Studies of a Small Democracy: Essays in Honour of Willis Airey* (Paul for University of Auckland, Hamilton, 1963)

Clements, K. P. 'The churches and social policy: a study in the relationship of ideology to action', PhD thesis, Victoria (1970)

Cleveland, Les. 'An early New Zealand farmers' pressure group', in Les Cleveland (ed.), *The Anatomy of Influence: Pressure Groups and Politics in New Zealand* (Hicks Smith, Wellington, 1972)

Clifton, Robin. 'Douglas Credit and Labour', *Comment*, III.4 (1962), pp. 23–9

Connell, E. 'Women in politics, 1893–1896: a study of women's organisations and their interest in social and political reform', research essay, Otago (1975)

Crook, H. 'The significance of the 1890 election', MA thesis, Auckland (1953)

Dalziel, Raewyn. 'The colonial helpmeet: women's role and the vote in nineteenth-century New Zealand', *NZJH*, XI.2 (1977), pp. 112–23

Davis, R. P. *Irish Issues in New Zealand Politics, 1868–1922* (University of Otago Press, Dunedin, 1974)

Downey, P. H. 'The 1893 General Election in Canterbury', MA thesis, Canterbury (1966)

Duncan, R. J. 'The New Zealand Farmers' Union as a political pressure group, 1900–1912', MA thesis, Victoria (1965)

Edwards, James. *Riot 1932* (Whitcoulls, Christchurch, 1974)

Eldred-Grigg, Stevan. 'Whatever happened to the gentry? The large landowners of Ashburton County, 1890–1896', *NZJH*, XI.1 (1977), pp. 3–27

Ewing, I. S. 'Public Service reform in New Zealand, 1866–1912', MA thesis, Auckland (1978)

Farland, B. H. *Gordon Coates* (Reed, Wellington,1969)

'Political career of J. G. Coates', MA thesis, Victoria (1969)

Gager, O. J. 'The New Zealand Labour Movement and war, 1914–1918', MA thesis, Auckland (1962)

Gardner, W. J. *The Farmer Politician in New Zealand History* (Massey University, Palmerston North, 1970)

William Massey (Reed, Wellington, 1969)

Gaudin, J. H. 'The Coates Government, 1925–1928', MA thesis, Auckland (1971)

Gibbons, P. J. ' "Turning tramps into taxpayers": the Department of Labour and the casual labourer in the 1890s', MA thesis, Massey (1970)

Graham, C. 'Relief camps in the depression, 1931–5', research essay, Otago (1976)

Graham, M. B. 'The Christchurch tramway strike', research essay, Canterbury (1977)

Grimshaw, Patricia. *Women's Suffrage in New Zealand* (AUP/OUP, Auckland, 1972)

Gustafson, B. S. *Labour's Path to Political Independents: The Origins and Establishment of the New Zealand Labour Party, 1900–1919* (AUP/OUP, Auckland, 1980)

Habershon, R. G. 'A study in politics, 1929–31', MA thesis, Auckland (1958)

Hamer, David. *The New Zealand Liberals. The Years of Power, 1891–1912* (AUP, Auckland, 1988)

Harris, Paul. 'The New Zealand unemployed workers movement, 1931–1939: Gisborne and the relief workers' strike', *NZJH*, X.2 (1976), pp. 130–42

Hayburn, Ralph. 'William Pember Reeves, *The Times*, and New Zealand's Industrial Conciliation and Arbitration Act, 1900–1908', *NZJH*, XXI.2 (1988), pp. 251–69

Holt, James. *Compulsory Arbitration in New Zealand: The First Forty Years* (AUP, Auckland, 1987)

'The political origins of compulsory arbitration in New Zealand: a comparison with Great Britain', *NZJH*, X.2 (1976), pp. 99–111

Hunt, J. Y. 'The development of the Labour Party in New Zealand as a political organisation from 1913 to 1919', MA thesis, Auckland (1947)

Kelly, Daniel. *Peter Fraser* (Reed, Wellington, 1968)

Lipson, Leslie. *The Politics of Equality: New Zealand's Adventures in Democracy* (University of Chicago Press, 1948)

Logan, J. A. 'The Public Safety Conservation Act', research essay, Otago (1976)

McDonald, J. D. N. 'New Zealand land legislation', *HSANZ*, v.19 (1952), pp. 195–211

Malone, E. P. 'The rural vote: voting trends in the Waikato, 1922–1935', MA thesis, Auckland (1958)

May, Philip Ross (ed.) *Miners and Militants* (Whitcoulls for the University of Canterbury, Christchurch, 1975)

Merrett, Ian. 'A reappraisal of the 1890 maritime strike in New Zealand', MA thesis, Canterbury (1969)

Moores, H. S. 'The rise of the Protestant Political Association: sectarianism in New Zealand politics during World War I', MA thesis, Auckland (1966)

Bibliography

Newman, R. K. 'Liberal policy and the Left Wing, 1908–1911: a study of middle class radicalism in New Zealand', MA thesis, Auckland (1965)

Noonan, Rosslyn. 'The riots of 1932: a study of social unrest in Auckland, Wellington, Dunedin', MA thesis, Auckland (1969)

O'Connor, P. S. 'The awkward ones — dealing with conscience, 1916–1918', NZJH, VIII.2, pp. 118–36

O'Farrell, P. J. 'The Blackball coal strike', New Zealand's Heritage, v.68 (Hamlyn, Wellington, 1971), pp. 1888–94

'The formation of the New Zealand Labour Party', HS, VIII.38 (1962), pp. 190–201

Harry Holland, Militant Socialist (ANU, Canberra, 1964)

'The 1908 Blackball strike', PS, XI.1 (1959), pp. 53–64

'The Russian Revolution and the Labour movements of Australia and New Zealand, 1917–1922', International Review of Social History, VIII (1963), Part 2, pp. 177–97

Oliver, W. H. 'Reeves, Sinclair and the social pattern' in Peter Munz (ed.), The Feel of Truth: Essays in New Zealand and Pacific History (Reed for Victoria University of Wellington, 1969)

Olssen, Erik. John A. Lee (University of Otago Press, Dunedin, 1977)

The Red Feds: Revolutionary Industrial Unionism and the New Zealand Federation of Labour, 1908–1913 (OUP, Auckland, 1988)

'The Seamen's Union and industrial militancy, 1908–13', NZJH, XIX.1 (1985), pp. 14–37

'The "working class" in New Zealand', NZJH, VIII.1 (1974), pp. 44–60

'W. T. Mills, E. J. B. Allen, J. A. Lee and socialism in New Zealand', NZJH, X.2 (1976), pp. 112–29

Pearson, C. R. 'The political labour movement in Dunedin, 1890–1986', research essay, Otago (1974)

Pitt, David, (ed.) Social Class in New Zealand (Longman Paul, Auckland, 1977)

Plumridge, E. W. 'Labour in Christchurch: community and consciousness, 1914–1919', MA thesis, Canterbury (1979)

'The necessary but not sufficient condition: Christchurch labour and working class culture', NZJH, XIX.2 (1985), pp. 130–50

Powell, J. R. 'The history of a working class party, 1918–40', MA thesis, Victoria (1949)

Pugh, Michael. 'The New Zealand Legion, 1932–1935', NZJH, v.1 (1971), pp. 49–69

Reid, A. J. S. 'Church and state in New Zealand, 1930–35: a study of the social thought and influence of the Christian church in a period of economic crisis', MA thesis, Victoria (1961)

Robertson, R. T. 'Isolation, ideology and impotence. Organizations for the unemployed during the Great Depression, 1930–1935', NZJH, XIII.2 (1979), pp. 149–64

Robinson, Alan. 'Class voting in New Zealand: a comment on Alford's comparison of class voting, in the Anglo-American political systems', in Seymour M. Lipset and Stein Rokkan (eds.), Party Systems and Voter Alignments: Cross-National Perspectives (The Free Press, New York, 1967)

Roche, S. The Red and the Gold: An Informal Account of the Waihi Strike (OUP, Auckland, 1982)

Rosenberg, Wolfgang (ed.) 'An early view of the New Zealand system of industrial conciliation and arbitration: F. R. Chapman (1849–1936)', Labour History, XX.20 (May 1971), pp. 9–16

Roth, H. George Hogben: A Biography (NZCER, Wellington, 1952)

Rudman, R. S. 'Employer organisations: their development and role in industrial relations', in John Howells, Noel Woods, F. L. J. Young (eds.), Labour and Industrial Relations in New Zealand (Pitman, Melbourne, 1974)

Scotter, W. H. A History of Canterbury, III, 1876–1950 (Canterbury Centennial Historical and Literary Committee and Whitcombe and Tombs, Christchurch, 1965)

Shannon, R. T. 'The Liberal succession crisis in New Zealand, 1893', HSANZ, VIII.30 (1958), pp. 193–201

Sinclair, Keith. 'The Lee–Sutch syndrome: New Zealand Labour Party policies and politics, 1930–40' *NZJH*, VIII.2 (1974), pp. 95–117

Walter Nash (AUP/OUP, Auckland, 1976)

William Pember Reeves: New Zealand Fabian (Clarendon Press, Oxford, 1965)

Tait, P. S. 'The depression of the 1930s in Rangitikei', MA thesis, Massey (1978)

Thorn, James. *Peter Fraser, New Zealand's Wartime Prime Minister* (Oldhams Press, London, 1952)

Waterson, D. B. 'The Matamata Estate, 1904–1959: land transfers and subdivisions in the Waikato', *NZJH*, III.1 (1969), pp. 32–51

Whitcher, G. F. 'The new Liberal Party, 1905', MA thesis, Canterbury (1966)

Williams, A. 'Industrial militancy in New Zealand: the contributing influence of the Industrial Conciliation and Arbitration Act, and its administration, 1894–1908', PhD thesis, Massey (1977)

Wood, Anthony. 'The origins of the first National Government: a study in New Zealand wartime politics, 1914–15', MA thesis, Canterbury (1963)

Woods, N. S. *Industrial Conciliation and Arbitration in New Zealand* (Government Printer, Wellington, 1963)

CHAPTER 9: ECONOMIC TRANSFORMATION

Alley, G. T. and Hall, D. O. W. *The Farmer in New Zealand* (NZ Dept. of Internal Affairs, Wellington, 1941)

Angus, John. *Donald Reid Otago Farmers' Limited: A History of Service to the Farming Community of Otago* (Donald Reid Otago Farmers' Ltd., Dunedin, 1978)

The Ironmasters: The First Hundred Years of H. E. Shacklock Limited (Shacklock, Dunedin, 1973)

Papermaking Pioneers: A History of New Zealand Paper Mills Limited and its Predecessors, 1876–1976 (New Zealand Paper Mills, Mataura, 1976)

Arbon, A. L. *A History of the Union Steam Ship Co. of New Zealand, 1875–1971*, 2 vols. (R. H. Parsons, Lobethal, South Australia, 1973–74)

Belshaw, H., Stephens, F. B. and Williams, D. O. *Agricultural Organization in New Zealand: A Survey of Land Utilization, Farm Organization, Finance and Marketing* (Melbourne University Press/OUP, 1936)

Blyth, C. A. 'The industrialisation of New Zealand', *NZ Economic Papers*, VIII (1974), pp. 1–22

Brasch, Charles and Nicholson, C. R. *Hallensteins: The First Century, 1873–1973* (Hallenstein Bros., Dunedin, 1973)

Bremer, R. J. 'The New Zealand Farmers' Union as an interest group: some aspects of farm politics, 1918–1928', MA thesis, Victoria (1966)

Brooking, T. W. H. 'Agrarian businessmen organise: a comparative study of the origins and early phase of development of the National Farmers' Union of England and Wales and the New Zealand Farmers' Union, ca. 1900–1929', PhD thesis, Otago (1978)

Massey: Its Early Years: A History of the Development of Massey Agricultural College to 1943 (Massey Alumni Association, Palmerston North, 1977)

'Sir John McKenzie and the origins and growth of the Department of Agriculture, 1891–1900', MA thesis, Massey (1972)

Burdon, R. M. *The New Dominion: A Social and Political History of New Zealand, 1918–39* (Reed, Wellington, 1965)

Bush, G. W. A. *Decently and In Order: The Government of the City of Auckland, 1840–1971: The Centennial History of the Auckland City Council* (Collins for the Auckland City Council, 1971)

Butlin, S. J. *Australia and New Zealand Bank; The Bank of Australasia and the Union Bank of Australia Limited, 1828–1951* (Longmans, London, 1961)

Campbell, R. J. 'Unemployment in New Zealand, 1875–1914', MPhil thesis, Massey (1976)

Castle, L. V. *A Study of New Zealand Manufacturing* (Dept. of Economics, Victoria University of Wellington, 1966)

Castle, L. V., Gillion, C. and Ross, B. J. *Structure of the New Zealand Economy* (Heinemann, Auckland, 1977)

Chapman, R. M. and Malone, E. P. *New Zealand in the Twenties: Social Change and Material Progress* (Heinemann, Auckland, 1969)

Chappell, N. M. *New Zealand Banker's Hundred: A History of the Bank of New Zealand, 1861–1961* (Bank of New Zealand, Wellington, 1961)

Condliffe, J. B. *New Zealand in the Making: A Study of Economic and Social Development*, 2nd edn. (Allen and Unwin, London, 1959)

The Welfare State in New Zealand (Allen and Unwin, London, 1959)

Copland, M. J. 'Refrigeration: its impact upon New Zealand, 1882–86', research essay, Otago (1972)

Cuff, Martine. *Totara Estate: Centenary of the Frozen Meat Industry* (NZ Historic Places Trust, Wellington, 1982)

Downie, J. A. 'Studies in New Zealand investment, 1871–1900', PhD thesis, ANU (1965)

Downes, C. D. R. 'Lands for the people: the life and work of Sir John McKenzie (1838–1901), including a study of New Zealand land legislation (1882–1900)', MA thesis, Otago (1954)

Duncan, J. S. 'The land for the people: land settlement and rural population movements, 1886–1906', in Murray McCaskill (ed.), *Land and Livelihood: Geographical Essays in Honour of George Jobberns* (NZ Geographical Society, Christchurch, 1962)

Eldred-Grigg, Stevan. 'Whatever happened to the gentry? The large landowners of Ashburton County, 1890–1896', *NZJH*, XI.1 (1977), pp. 3–27

Evans, B. L. *A History of Agricultural Production and Marketing in New Zealand* (Keeling and Mundy, Palmerston North, 1969)

A History of Farm Implements and Implement Firms in New Zealand (Fisher Printing, Feilding, 1956)

Galt, Margaret. 'Wealth and income in New Zealand, c.1870–c.1939', PhD thesis, Victoria (1985)

Gardner, W. J. *The Farmer Politician in New Zealand History* (Massey University, Palmerston North, 1970)

A Pastoral Kingdom Divided: Cheviot, 1889–94 (Bridget Williams Books, Wellington, 1992)

Gaudin, J. A. 'The Coates Government, 1925–1928', MA thesis, Auckland (1971)

George, D. J. 'The depression of 1921–22 in New Zealand', MA thesis Auckland (1969)

Gibbons, P. J. 'Milk quality control: an example of bureaucratic growth', *NZ Journal of Public Administration*, XL.1 (1978), pp. 62–71

'Some New Zealand navvies. Co-operative workers, 1891–1912', *NZJH*, XL.1 (1977), pp. 54–75

' "Turning tramps into taxpayers": the Department of Labour and the casual labourer in the 1890s', MA thesis, Massey (1970)

Gould, J. D. 'The occupation of farm land in New Zealand, 1874–1911: a preliminary survey', *Business Archives and History*, v.2 (1965), pp. 123–41

'The twilight of the estates, 1891 to 1910', *AEHR*, x.1 (1970), pp. 1–26

Graham, B. D. 'The Country Party idea in New Zealand politics, 1901–1935', in R. M. Chapman and Keith Sinclair (eds.), *Studies of a Small Democracy: Essays in Honour of Willis Airey* (Paul for University of Auckland, 1963)

Hamilton, W. M. *The Dairy Industry in New Zealand* (Government Printer, Wellington, 1944)

Hargreaves, R. P. 'Speed the plough: an historical geography of New Zealand farming before the introduction of refrigeration', PhD thesis, Otago (1966)

Hawke, G. R. *Between Governments and Banks: A History of the Reserve Bank of New Zealand* (Government Printer, Wellington, 1973)

'Economic decisions and political ossification', in Peter Munz (ed.), *The Feel of Truth: Essays in New Zealand and Pacific History* (Reed for Victoria University of Wellington, 1969)

The Evolution of the New Zealand Economy (Heinemann, Auckland, 1977)

'The Government and the depression of the 1930s in New Zealand: an essay towards a revision', *AEHR*, XIII.1 (1973), pp. 72–95

'Long-term trends in New Zealand imports', *AEHR*, XVIII.1 (1978), pp. 1–28

The Making of New Zealand: An Economic History (Cambridge University Press, Cambridge, 1985)

Hearn, T. J. 'South Canterbury: some aspects of the historical geography of agriculture 1851–1901', MA thesis, Otago (1971)

Hill, R. J. M. 'The quest for control: the New Zealand Dairy Industry and the guaranteed price, 1921–36', MA thesis, Auckland (1974)

Holman, Gordon. *In the Wake of* Endeavour: *The History of the New Zealand Shipping Company and Federal Steam Navigation Company* (Charles Knight, London, 1973)

Hoy, D. G. 'Iron wheels in the streets', in N. L. McLeod and B. H. Farland (eds.), *Wellington Prospect: Survey of a City, 1840–1970* (Hicks Smith, Wellington, 1970)

Irving, J. C. *A Century's Challenge: Wright Stephenson and Company Limited, 1861–1961* (Wright Stephenson, Wellington, 1961)

Lineham, B. T. 'New Zealand's Gross Domestic Product, 1918/38', *NZ Economic Papers*, II.2 (1968), pp. 15–26

Lister, R. G. 'The eroding land', *New Zealand's Heritage*, v.72 (Hamlyn, Wellington, 1973), pp. 1993–8

Lyon, Rosemary. 'Chew Chong and the butter trade', *New Zealand's Heritage*, IV.51 (Hamlyn, Wellington, 1972), pp. 1416–18

Macdonald, B. and Thomson, D. 'Mortgage relief, farm finance and rural depression in New Zealand in the 1930s', *NZJH*, XXI.2 (1987), pp. 228–50

Macrae, John and Sinclair, Keith. 'Unemployment in New Zealand during the depression of the late 1920s and early 1930s', *AEHR*, XV.1 (1975), pp. 35–44

McDonald, J. N. D. 'New Zealand land legislation', *HSANZ*, v.19 (1952), pp. 195–211

McLean, Gavin. *The Southern Octopus. The Rise of a Shipping Empire* (Ship and Marine Society, Wellington, 1990)

Malone, E. P. 'The grassland revolution', *New Zealand's Heritage*, VI.78 (Hamlyn, Wellington, 1973), pp. 2157–63

Meuli, P. M. 'Occupational change and bourgeois proliferation: a study of new middle class expansion in New Zealand, 1896–1926', MA thesis, Victoria (1977)

Muirhead, J. G. 'Heathfield and Waipati: improved farm settlements 1893–1914', research essay, Otago (1978)

O'Connor, P. S. *The Growth of New Zealand Farming, 1890–1918* (Heinemann, Auckland, 1970)

Mr Massey and the American Meat Trust: Some Highlights on the Origins of the Meat Board (Massey University, Palmerston North, 1972)

Orlowski, K. D. 'The subdivision and closer settlement of the Merrivale, Otahu and Beaumont estates in the Southland land district, 1895–1912', MA thesis, Otago (1976)

Parry, Gordon. *N.M.A. The Story of the First Hundred Years: The National Mortgage and Agency Company of New Zealand Ltd., 1864–1964* (National Mortgage and Agency Co., Dunedin, 1964)

Underwriting Adventure: A Centennial History of the National Insurance Company of New Zealand Limited (National Insurance Company, Dunedin, 1973)

Philpott, B. P. *Aspects of Productivity and Economic Growth in New Zealand, 1926–1964* (Agricultural Economics Research Unit, Lincoln College, 1966), Publication 29

Philpott, B. P. et al. *Estimates of Farm Income and Productivity in New Zealand, 1921–1965* (Agricultural Economics Research Unit, Lincoln College, 1967), Publication 30

Philpott, H. G. *A History of the New Zealand Dairy Industry, 1840–1935* (Government Printer, Wellington, 1937), pp. 295–303

Poole, A. L. 'The return of the forests', *New Zealand's Heritage*, VI.84 (Hamlyn, Wellington, 1973), pp. 2342–7

Redmond, P. I. 'The rise of the Grey Valley coal industry, 1870–1880', MA thesis, Canterbury (1979)

Robertson, R. T. 'The tyranny of circumstances: responses to unemployment in New Zealand, 1929–1935, with particular reference to Dunedin', PhD thesis, Otago (1978)

Robinson, Howard. *A History of the Post Office in New Zealand* (Government Printer, Wellington, 1964)

Rogerson, E. W. ' "Cosy homes multiply": a study of suburban expansion in western Auckland, 1918–31', MA thesis, Auckland (1976)

Rowe, C. J. 'The growth of agricultural administration, 1880–1900: the dairy industry as a test case', MA thesis, Massey (1973)

Schaffer, R. J. 'Woodville: genesis of a bush frontier community, 1874–1887', MA thesis, Massey (1973)

Scott, D. F. 'The mechanisation of farming', *New Zealand's Heritage*, vi.82 (Hamlyn, Wellington, 1973), pp. 2292–6

Searell, Pamela. 'Pioneering the pumice', *New Zealand's Heritage*, v.72 (Hamlyn, Wellington, 1973), pp. 2012–16

Searight, Sarah. 'A bright new world', *New Zealand's Heritage*, iv.54 (Hamlyn, Wellington, 1972), pp. 1485–90

Sinclair, Keith and Mandle, W. F. *Open Account: A History of the Bank of New South Wales in New Zealand, 1861–1961* (Whitcombe and Tombs for the Bank of New South Wales, Wellington, 1961)

Smallfield, P. W. *The Grasslands Revolution in New Zealand* (Hodder and Stoughton, Auckland, 1970)

Stenson, M. R. 'The origins of the Government Advances to Settlers Act, 1894', MA thesis, Auckland (1962)

Stephens, P. R. 'Innovation on the farm', *New Zealand's Heritage*, vi.81 (Hamlyn, Wellington, 1973), pp. 2260–64

Stone, R. C. J. *Makers of Fortune: A Colonial Business Community and its Fall* (AUP/OUP, Auckland, 1973)

Vennell, C. W. *Risks and Rewards: A Policy of Enterprise, 1872–1972; A Centennial History of the South British Insurance Company Limited* (Wilson and Horton for South British Insurance, Auckland, 1972)

   Tower of Strength: A Centennial History of the New Zealand Government Life Insurance Office, 1869–1969 (Wilson and Horton, Auckland, 1969)

Warr, E. C. R. 'The beginnings of the dairy industry', *New Zealand's Heritage*, iv.51 (Hamlyn, Wellington, 1972), pp. 1407–13

   'A changing dairy industry', *New Zealand's Heritage*, vi.77 (Hamlyn, Wellington, 1973), pp. 2135–8

Waterson, D. B. 'The Matamata Estate, 1904–1959: land transfers and subdivision in the Waikato', *NZJH*, iii.1 (1969), pp. 32–51

Wild, L. J. *The Development of Agricultural Education in New Zealand*. The Macmillan Brown Lectures delivered at Canterbury University College, July 1952 (Whitcombe and Tombs, Christchurch, 1953)

   The Life and Times of Sir James Wilson of Bulls (Whitcombe and Tombs, Wellington, 1953)

Williams, G. J. *Economic Geology of New Zealand* (Australasian Institute of Mining and Metallurgy, Melbourne, 1965)

CHAPTER 10: TOWARDS A NEW SOCIETY

Armstrong, R. Warwick. 'Auckland by gaslight: an urban geography of 1896', *NZG*, xv.2 (1959), pp. 173–89

   'New Zealand: imperialism, class and uneven development', *ANZJS*, xiv.3 (1978), pp. 297–303

Arnold, Rollo. 'The village and the globe: aspects of the social origins of schooling in Victorian New Zealand', *ANZHES Journal*, v.2 (1976), pp. 1–12

'The Wellington Education Board, 1878–1901: grappling with educational backwardness and advancing settlement', *ANZHES Journal*, vi.2 (1977), pp. 43–55

Baker, Paul. *King and Country Call: New Zealanders, Conscription and the Great War* (AUP/ OUP, Auckland, 1988)

Barber, L. H. 'The Church Defence Society of Otago and Southland, 1897', MA thesis, Massey (1970)

'The social crusader: James Gibb at the Australasian pastoral frontier, 1882–1935', PhD thesis, Massey (1975)

Barber, L. H. and Towers, R. J. *Wellington Hospital, 1847–1976* (Wellington Hospital Board, 1976)

Bardsley, S. 'The functions of an institution: the Otekaieke special school for boys, 1908– 1950', research essay, Otago (1991)

Barnett, John R. 'The evolution of the urban political structure of the North Island, 1945– 1966', MA thesis, Otago (1968)

Beagle, Jan. 'Children of the state: a study of the New Zealand industrial school system, 1880–1925', MA thesis, Auckland (1974)

Beaglehole, J. C. *The University of New Zealand: An Historical Study* (NZCER, Wellington, 1937)

Victoria University College: An Essay Towards a History (NZ University Press, Wellington, 1949)

Beck, John. 'The development of child welfare', in I. Davey (ed.), *Fifty Years of National Eduation in New Zealand, 1878–1928* (Whitcombe and Tombs, Wellington, 1928)

Belgrave, Michael. 'A subtle containment: women in New Zealand medicine, 1893–1941', *NZJH*, xxii.1 (1988), pp. 44–55

' "Medical men" and "lady doctors": the making of a New Zealand profession, 1867– 1941', PhD thesis, Victoria (1986)

Binney, Judith, Bassett, Judith and Olssen, Erik. *The People and the Land: Te Tangata me te Whenua: An Illustrated History of New Zealand, 1820–1920* (Allen and Unwin, Wellington, 1990)

Bland, W. B. *Slums of Auckland* (Progressive Publishing Society, Auckland, 1942)

Boyd, Judi and Olssen, Erik. 'The skilled workers: journeymen and masters in Caversham, 1880–1914', *NZJH*, xxii.2 (1988), pp. 118–34

Breward, Ian. *Godless Schools? A Study in Protestant Reactions to the Education Act of 1877* (Presbyterian Bookroom, Christchurch, 1967)

Brookes, Barbara. 'Housewives' depression', *NZJH*, xv.2 (1981), pp. 115–34

Brooking, T. W. H. 'Agrarian businessmen organise: a comparative study of the origins and early phase of development of the National Farmers' Union of England and Wales and the New Zealand Farmers' Union, ca. 1900–1929', PhD thesis, Otago (1978)

A History of Dentistry in New Zealand (NZ Dental Association, Dunedin, 1980)

Brosnan, Peter. 'Net interprovinical migration, 1886–1966', unpublished paper

Brown, Carol. 'Ethel Benjamin — New Zealand's first woman lawyer', research essay, Otago (1985)

Bryder, Linda. ' "Lessons" of the 1918 influenza epidemic in Auckland', *NZJH*, xvi.2 (1982), pp. 97–121

Bryder, Linda (ed.) *A Healthy Country: Essays on the Social History of Medicine in New Zealand* (Bridget Williams Books, Wellington, 1991)

Burdon, R. M. 'Sir Truby King', in R. M. Burdon, *New Zealand Notables, Series Two* (Caxton, Christchurch, 1945)

The New Dominion: A Social and Political History of New Zealand, 1918–39 (Reed, Wellington, 1965)

Bush, G. W. A. *Decently and In Order: The Government of the City of Auckland, 1840–1971. The Centennial History of the Auckland City Council* (Collins for the Auckland City Council, 1971)

Caldwell, Cheryl. 'Truby King and Seacliff Asylum, 1889–1907', research essay, Otago (1984)

Campbell, R. J. 'Unemployment in New Zealand, 1875–1914', MPhil thesis, Massey (1976)

Child, John. 'Wages policy and wages movements in New Zealand, 1914–1923', *Journal of Industrial Relations*, XIII.2 (1971), pp. 164–76

Clark, W. A. V. 'Dunedin at the turn of the century', *NZG*, XVIII.1 (1962), pp. 93–115
   'The slums of Dunedin, 1900–1910', *NZ Geographers' Conference, Proceedings*, III (August 1961), pp. 85–92

Clements, K. P. 'The churches and social policy: a study in the relationship of ideology to action', PhD thesis, Victoria (1970)

Connell, E. C. 'Women in politics, 1893–1896: a study of women's organisations and their interest in social and political reform', research essay, Otago (1975)

Cullen, M. J. *Lawfully Occupied: The Centennial History of the Otago District Law Society* (Otago District Law Society, Dunedin, 1979)

Cumming, Ian and Cumming, Alan. *History of State Education in New Zealand, 1840–1975* (Pitman, Wellington, 1978)

Daley, Caroline. 'Taradale meets the ideal society and its enemies', *NZJH*, XXV.2 (1991), pp. 129–46

Dalley, Bronwyn. 'From demi-mondes to slavery: a study of the Te Oranga Reformatory for Delinquent Women, 1900–1918', MA thesis, Massey (1987)
   'Women's imprisonment in New Zealand, 1880–1920', PhD thesis, Otago (1992)

Davis, R. P. 'The New Zealand Labour Party's "Irish campaign", 1916–1921', *PS*, XIX.2 (1967), pp. 13–23

Donald, Jane. 'The man upon the land: the Land for Settlements Act in the Wellington Land District, 1897–1906', research essay, Massey (1976)

Duff, Oliver. *New Zealand Now . . .* (Department of Internal Affairs, Wellington, 1941)

Duncan, Lucy. ' "What Katy Did in School": a study of curriculum development in Dunedin girls' secondary schools, 1900–1920', research essay, Otago (1982)

Elder, J. R. *A History of the Presbyterian Church in New Zealand, 1840–1940* (Presbyterian Bookroom, Christchurch, 1940)

Eldred-Grigg, S. *A New History of Canterbury* (McIndoe, Dunedin, 1982)
   Pleasures of the Flesh: Sex and Drugs in Colonial New Zealand, 1840–1915 (Reed, Wellington, 1984)

Elliott, N. 'Anzac, Hollywood and home: cinemas and filmgoing in Auckland, 1909–1939', MA thesis, Auckland (1989)

Elworthy, Sam. *Ritual Song of Defiance: A Social History of Students at the University of Otago* (Otago University Students Association, Dunedin, 1990)

Ewing, I. S. 'Public Service reform in New Zealand, 1866–1912', MA thesis, Auckland (1979)

Ewing, J. L. *Development of the New Zealand Primary School Curriculum, 1877–1970* (NZCER, Wellington, 1970)

Fairburn, Miles. 'Social mobility and opportunity in nineteenth-century New Zealand', *NZJH*, XIII.1 (1979), pp. 43–60
   'The farmers take over (1912–1930)', in Keith Sinclair (ed.), *The Oxford Illustrated History of New Zealand* (OUP, Auckland, 1990)
   The Ideal Society and its Enemies. The Foundations of Modern New Zealand Society, 1850–1900 (AUP, Auckland, 1989)
   'The rural myth and the new urban frontier: an approach to New Zealand social history, 1870–1940', *NZJH*, IX.1 (1975), pp. 3–21
   'Why did the New Zealand Labour Party fail to win office until 1935?', *Political Science*, XXXVII.2 (1985), pp. 101–24

Fairburn, Miles and Haslett, Stephen. 'Violent crime in old and new societies: a case study based on New Zealand, 1850–1940', *Journal of Social History*, XX.1 (1986), pp. 90–126

Farrell, Jill. 'The Presbyterian Church and Social Welfare, 1900–1912', research essay, Otago (1979)

Firth, Cedric. *State Housing in New Zealand* (Ministry of Works, Wellington, 1949)

Fleming, Philip. 'Fighting the "red plague": observations on the response to venereal disease in New Zealand, 1910–1945', *NZJH*, XXII.1 (1988), pp. 56–64.

Franklin, S. H. 'New Zealand's population in the welfare era, 1901–1962', in R. F. Watters (ed.), *Land and Society in New Zealand: Essays in Historical Geography* (Reed, Wellington, 1965)

'The village and the bush', in John Forster (ed.), *Social Process in New Zealand: Readings in Sociology* (Longman Paul, Auckland, 1969)

Fry, Ruth. *It's Different for Daughters: A History of the Curriculum for Girls in New Zealand Schools, 1900–1975* (NZCER, Wellington, 1985)

Galt, Margaret. 'Wealth and income in New Zealand, c.1870–c.1939', PhD thesis, Victoria (1985)

Gardner, W. J. *Colonial Cap and Gown: Studies in the Mid-Victorian Universities of Australasia* (University of Canterbury, Christchurch, 1979)

Gardner, W. J., Beardsley, E. T. and Carter, T. E. *A History of the University of Canterbury, 1873–1973* (University of Canterbury, Christchurch, 1973)

Gardner, W. J. and Winterbourn, Ralph. 'Education, 1877–1950', in W. J. Gardner (ed.), *A History of Canterbury, II: General History, 1854–76, and Cultural Aspects, 1850–1950* (Canterbury Centennial Historical and Literary Committee and Whitcombe and Tombs, Christchurch, 1971)

Gibbons, P. J. ' "Turning tramps into taxpayers": the Department of Labour and the casual labourer in the 1890s', MA thesis, Massey (1970)

Gilson, Miriam. 'The changing New Zealand family: a demographic analysis', in H. Stewart Houston (ed.), *Marriage and the Family in New Zealand* (Sweet and Maxwell, Wellington, 1970)

'Women in employment', in John Forster (ed.), *Social Process in New Zealand* (Longman Paul, Auckland, 1969), pp. 29–48, 183–97

Gilson-Vosburgh, Miriam. *The New Zealand Family and Social Change: A Trend Analysis* (Victoria University of Wellington, 1978), Occasional papers in sociology and social welfare, 1

Graham, John. 'The voluntary system: recruiting, 1914–1916', MA thesis, Auckland (1971)

Gregory, P. A. 'Saving the children in New Zealand: a study of social attitudes towards larrikinism in the later nineteenth century', research essay, Massey (1975)

Grew, Raymond. 'More on modernization', *Journal of Social History*, XIV.2 (1980), pp. 179–88

Griffiths, S. 'Feminism and the ideology of motherhood in New Zealand, 1896–1930', MA thesis, Otago (1984)

Grigg, A. R. 'Prohibition and women: the preservation of an ideal and a myth', *NZJH*, XVII.2 (1983), pp. 144–65

'The attack on the citadels of liquordom: the Prohibition Movement in New Zealand, 1894–1914', PhD thesis, Otago (1978)

Hall, F. ' "The greater game": sport and society in World War One New Zealand', MA thesis, Canterbury (1989)

Hamer, David and Nicholls, Roberta (eds.) *The Making of Wellington, 1800–1914* (VUP, Wellington, 1991)

Hannah, Michael. 'The plague scare, 1900. Factors relating to the establishment of the Department of Public Health', research essay, Otago (1975)

Hareven, Tamara. *Transitions: The Family and Life Course in Historical Perspective* (Academic Press, New York, 1978)

Harrison, P. A. 'The motion picture industry in New Zealand, 1896–1930', MA thesis, Auckland (1974)

Harvey, Edward B. (ed.) *Perspectives on Modernization* (University of Toronto Press, Toronto, 1972)

Hatch, Elvin. *Respectable Lives: Social Standing in Rural New Zealand* (University of California Press, Berkeley, 1992)

Heenan, L. B. L. 'The urbanisation of New Zealand's population: demographic patterns in the South Island, 1881–1961', in R. J. Johnston (ed.), *Urbanisation in New Zealand: Geographical Essays* (Reed, Wellington, 1973)

697

Heenan, L. B. D. and Trlin, A. D. 'Population, society and economy', in R. J. Johnston (ed.), *Society and Environment in New Zealand* (Whitcombe and Tombs, Christchurch, 1974)

Henderson, Alan. *The Quest for Efficiency: The Origins of the State Services Commission* (The Commission, Wellington, 1990)

Higgins, Pamela. 'The Prohibition Movement in Oamaru, 1893–1905', research essay, Otago (1978)

Hill, Richard S. *The History of Policing in New Zealand: Vol. II, The Colonial Frontier Tamed. New Zealand Policing in Transition, 1867–1886* (Historical Publications Branch/GP Books, Wellington, 1989)

Holt, James. *Compulsory Arbitration in New Zealand: The First Forty Years* (AUP, Auckland, 1987)

Hoy, D. G. 'Iron wheels in the streets', in N. L. McLeod and B. H. Farland (eds.), *Wellington Prospect: Survey of a City, 1840–1970* (Hicks Smith, Wellington, 1970)

Hubbard, Caroline. 'Lunatic asylums in Otago, 1882–1911', research essay, Otago (1977)

Hughes, Beryl. 'Nursing education: the collapse of the Diploma of Nursing at the University of Otago, 1925–1926', *NZJH*, XII.1 (1978), pp. 17–33

Hurricks, P. B. 'Reactions to urbanisation in New Zealand during the 1920s', MA thesis, Canterbury (1975)

Hutchinson, Robert H. *The 'Socialism' of New Zealand* (New Review Publishing Association, New York, 1916), p. 125

Jackson, Hugh. *Churches and People in Australia and New Zealand, 1860–1930* (Allen and Unwin, Wellington, 1987)

Jacoby, E. G. 'A fertility analysis of New Zealand marriage cohorts', *Population Studies: A Journal of Demography*, XII.1 (1958), pp. 18–39

Kennedy, Stephen. ' "Really concerned men": a history of the Dunedin labourer and his union, 1905–1911', research essay, Otago (1978)

Labrum, B. J. 'Gender and lunacy: a study of women patients in the Auckland Lunatic Asylum, 1870–1910', MA thesis, Massey (1990)

Lee, John A. *Socialism in New Zealand* (Werner Laurie, London, 1938)

Lloyd, Jacky. 'Marital breakdown', in Peggy Koopman-Boyden (ed.), *Families in New Zealand Society* (Methuen, Wellington, 1978)

Lovell-Smith, J. B. *The New Zealand Doctor and the Welfare State* (Paul, Auckland, 1966)

Macdonald, Charlotte. 'Crime and punishment in New Zealand, 1840–1913: a gendered history', *NZJH*, XXIII.1 (1989), pp. 5–21

'Women and crime in New Zealand society, 1888–1910', research essay, Massey (1977)

Macdonald, Charlotte, Penfold, M. and Williams, B. (eds.) *The Book of New Zealand Women: Ka Kui Ma Te Kaupapa* (Bridget Williams Books, Wellington, 1991)

McDonald, K. C. *City of Dunedin: A Century of Civic Enterprise* (Dunedin City Corporation, 1965)

McEldowney, Dennis (ed.) *Presbyterians in Aotearoa, 1840–1990* (Presbyterian Church of NZ, Wellington, 1990)

McGeorge, C. M. 'Military training in New Zealand primary schools, 1900–1912', *ANZHES Journal*, III.2 (1974), pp. 1–10

McInnes, Gay. *Castle on the Run* (Pegasus Press, Christchurch, 1969)

McKenzie, D. 'The growth of school credentialling, 1878–1900', in R. Openshaw and D. McKenzie (eds.), *Reinterpreting the Educational Past* (NZCER, Wellington, 1987), pp. 82–106

McKenzie, J. D. S. 'The changing concept of equality in New Zealand education', *NZJES*, X.2 (1975), pp. 93–110

McKimmey Paul. 'The temperance movement in New Zealand, 1835–1894', MA thesis, Auckland (1968)

McLaren, I. A. 'Education and politics: background to the Secondary Schools Act, 1903. Part 1: secondary education for the privileged', *NZJES*, V.2 (1970), pp. 94–114

'Education and politics: background to the Secondary Schools Act, 1903. Part 2: secondary education for the deserving', *NZJES*, VI.1 (1971), pp. 1–23

Maclean, F. S. *Challenge for Health. A History of Public Health in New Zealand* (Government Printer, Wellington, 1964)

McLeod, J. C. 'Activities of New Zealand Women during World War 1', research essay, Otago (1978)

Mabon, Richard. 'Vision and process: the genesis of town-planning in New Zealand, 1840–1926', research essay, Otago (1991)

Malone, E. P. 'The New Zealand School Journal and the imperial ideology', *NZJH*, VII.1 (1973), pp. 12–27

Mayhew, W. R. 'The Returned Services Association, 1916–1943', MA thesis, Otago, (1943)

Mein Smith, Philippa. *Maternity in Dispute. New Zealand, 1920–1939* (Historical Publications Branch, Wellington, 1986)

Metge, R. T. ' "The house that Jack built": the origins of Labour state housing, 1935–8, with particular reference to the role of J. A. Lee', MA thesis, Auckland (1972)

Meuli, P. M. 'Occupational change and bourgeois proliferation: a study of new middle class expansion in New Zealand, 1896–1926', MA thesis, Victoria (1977)

Millar, David. *Once Upon a Village: A History of Lower Hutt, 1819–1965* (NZ University Press for Lower Hutt City Corporation, 1972)

Milne, Lynne. 'The Plunket Society: an experiment in infant welfare', research essay, Otago (1976)

Mol, J. J. *Western Religion: A Country by Country Sociological Inquiry* (Mouton, The Hague, 1972)

Moores, H. S. 'The rise of the Protestant Political Association: sectarianism in New Zealand politics during World War I', MA thesis, Auckland (1966)

Morrell, W. P. *The Anglican Church in New Zealand: A History* (McIndoe for the Anglican Church of the Province of New Zealand, Dunedin, 1973)

The University of Otago: A Centennial History (University of Otago Press, Dunedin, 1969)

Morris, P. G. 'Unemployed organizations in New Zealand, 1926–1939, with particular reference to Wellington', MA thesis, Victoria (1949)

Murdoch, John. *The High Schools of New Zealand: A Critical Survey* (NZCER, Wellington, 1943)

Mutch, Margaret. 'Aspects of the social and economic history of Auckland, 1890–1896', 2 vols., MA thesis, Auckland (1968)

Nicol, John. *The Technical Schools of New Zealand: An Historical Survey* (NZCER, Wellington, 1940)

O'Connor, P. S. ' "Protestants", Catholics and the New Zealand Government, 1916–18', in G. A. Wood and P. S. O'Connor (eds.), *W. P. Morrell: A Tribute* (University of Otago Press, Dunedin, 1973)

'Sectarian conflict in New Zealand, 1911–1920', *PS*, XIX.1 (1967), pp. 3–16

O'Farrell, P. J. *Vanished Kingdoms: Irish in Australia and New Zealand. A Personal Excursion* (NSW University Press, Sydney, 1990)

Oliver, W. H. 'Reeves, Sinclair and the social pattern', in Peter Munz (ed.), *The Feel of Truth: Essays in New Zealand and Pacific History* (Reed for Victoria University of Wellington, 1969)

'The origins and growth of the welfare state', in A. D. Trlin (ed.), *Social Welfare and New Zealand Society* (Methuen, Wellington, 1977)

Olssen, Erik. *A History of Otago* (John McIndoe, Dunedin, 1984)

'Historiography of the New Zealand Labour Movement, 1880–1916', *Historical News*, 37 (Aug. 1978), pp. 1–5

John A. Lee (University of Otago Press, Dunedin, 1977)

'Social class in nineteenth-century New Zealand', in David Pitt (ed.), *Social Class in New Zealand* (Longman Paul, Auckland, 1977)

'The origins of the Labour Party: a reconsideration', *NZJH*, XXI.1 (1987), pp. 79–96

The Red Feds: Revolutionary Industrial Unionism and the New Zealand Federation of Labour, 1908–1914 (OUP, Auckland, 1988)

'The "working class" in New Zealand', *NZJH*, VIII.1 (1974), pp. 44–60

'Truby King and the Plunket Society: an analysis of a prescriptive ideology', *NZJH*, xv.1 (1981), pp. 3–23

'Women, work, and society, 1880–1926', in Phillida Bunkle and Beryl Hughes, *Women in New Zealand Society* (Allen and Unwin, Wellington, 1981), pp. 159–83

Olssen, Erik and Lévesque, Andrée. 'Towards a history of the European family in New Zealand', in Peggy Koopman-Boyden, *Families in New Zealand Society* (Methuen, Wellington, 1978)

O'Sullivan, Vincent and Scott, Margaret (eds.) *The Collected Letters of Katherine Mansfield, 1903–1917* (Clarendon Press, Oxford, 1984)

Parsons, Talcott. *The Social System* (The Free Press, Glencoe, 1951), pp. 58–67

Patullo, Susan. 'The cramming controversy in Otago, 1880–1908', research essay, Otago (1983)

Peach, A. A. 'The social effects of the depression in Auckland, 1930–35', MA thesis, Auckland (1971)

Pearson, David. *Johnsonville: Continuity and Change in a New Zealand Township* (Allen and Unwin, Sydney, 1980)

'Marriage and mobility in Wellington, 1881–1980', *NZJH*, xxii.2 (1988), pp. 135–51

Peters, Marie. *Christchurch-St Michael's: A Study in Anglicanism in New Zealand, 1851–1972* (University of Canterbury, Christchurch, 1986)

Phillips, J. O. C. 'Rugby, war and the mythology of the New Zealand male', *NZJH*, xviii.2 (1984), pp. 83–103

Phillips, Rod. *Divorce in New Zealand: A Social History* (OUP, Auckland, 1981)

Plumridge, L. 'The necessary but not sufficient condition: Christchurch labour and working class culture', *NZJH*, xix.2 (1985), pp. 130–50

Powell, J. M. 'White collars and moleskin trousers: politicians, administrators, and settlers on the Cheviot Estate, 1893–1914', *NZG*, xxvii.2 (1971) pp. 151–74

Powell, M. J. 'The church in Auckland society, 1880–1886', MA thesis Auckland (1970)

Pownall, L. L. 'Metropolitan Auckland, 1740–1945: the historical geography of a New Zealand city', *NZG*, vi.2 (1950) pp. 107–24

Primrose, M. S. 'Society and the insane: a study of mental illness in New Zealand, 1867–1926, with special reference to the Auckland Mental Hospital', MA thesis, Auckland (1968)

Pugsley, Christopher. *On the Fringe of Hell: New Zealanders and Military Discipline in the First World War* (Hodder and Stoughton, Auckland, 1991)

Rafter, Pat. *Never Let Go! The Remarkable Story of Mother Aubert* (Reed, Wellington, 1972)

Rae, Simon. *From Relief to Social Service: A History of the Presbyterian Social Service Association, Otago, 1906–1981* (Presbyterian Social Service Association, Dunedin, 1981)

Reid, A. J. S. 'Church and state in New Zealand, 1930–35: a study of the social thought and influence of the Christian church in a period of economic crisis', MA thesis, Victoria (1961)

Rice, Geoffrey W. *Black November: The 1918 Influenza Epidemic in New Zealand* (Allen and Unwin, Wellington, 1988)

'The making of New Zealand's 1920 Health Act', *NZJH*, xxii.1 (1988), pp. 3–22

Richardson, L. E. 'Politics and war: coal miners and conscription', in Philip Ross May (ed.), *Miners and Militants: Politics in Westland 1865–1918* (Whitcoulls for the University of Canterbury, Christchurch, 1975)

'Race, rugby and empire', *Historical News*, Dec. 1983

Robertson, R. T. 'Isolation, ideology and impotence. Organisations for the unemployed during the Great Depression, 1930–1935', *NZJH*, xiii.2 (1979) pp. 149–64

'Government responses to unemployment in New Zealand, 1929–1935', *NZJH*, xvi.1 (1982), pp. 21–38

'The tyranny of circumstances: responses to unemployment in New Zealand, 1929–1935, with particular reference to Dunedin', PhD thesis, Otago (1978)

Robertson, Stephen. 'Production not reproduction: the problem of mental defects in New Zealand, 1900–1939', research essay, Otago (1989)

'Women workers and the New Zealand Court of Arbitration, 1894–1920', in Raelene

Frances and Bruce Scates (eds.), *Women, Work and the Labour Movement in Australia and Aotearoa/New Zealand* (Australian Society for Labour History, Sydney, 1991), pp. 30–41

Rogerson, E. W. ' "Cosy homes multiply": a study of suburban expansion in western Auckland, 1918–31', MA thesis, Auckland (1976)

Roper, M. L. 'History of the social services of the Anglican Church in Canterbury', MA thesis, Canterbury (1943)

Rosenberg, Wolfgang. 'Full employment: the fulcrum of social welfare', in A. D. Trlin (ed.), *Social Welfare and New Zealand Society* (Methuen, Wellington, 1977), pp. 45–60

Roth, H. O. *George Hogben: A Biography* (NZCER, Wellington, 1952)

Trade Unions in New Zealand, Past and Present (Reed, Wellington, 1973)

Scotter, W. H. *Run, Estate and Farm: A History of the Kakanui and the Waiareka Valleys, North Otago* (Otago Centennial Publications, Dunedin, 1948)

Sinclair, Keith. *A History of the University of Auckland, 1883–1983* (AUP/OUP, Auckland, 1983)

Smith, Valerie. 'The social history of community care of the disabled', in J. S. Dodge and J. M. Dodge (eds.), *The Community Care of the Disabled. Proceedings of a Seminar . . .* (Department of University Extension, Dunedin, 1979)

Somerset, H. C. D. *Littledene: Patterns of Change* (NZCER, Wellington, 1974)

Somerville, Alan. 'Moominpappa got away: the state and child welfare in New Zealand, 1925–1930', research essay, Otago (1982)

Stearns, Peter. 'Modernization and social history: some suggestions, and a muted cheer', *Journal of Social History*, xiv.2 (1980), pp. 189–210

Stedman, G. N. 'The South Dunedin Flat: a study in urbanisation, 1849–1965', MA thesis, Otago (1966)

Stenson, M. M. 'Social legislation in New Zealand, 1900–1930', MA thesis, Auckland (1962)

Steven, Graeme. 'Swaggers and society: a New Zealand experience', research essay, Otago (1979)

Stone, R. C. J. 'A history of trade unionism in New Zealand, 1913–37', MA thesis, Auckland (1948)

'The unions and the arbitration system', in R. M. Chapman and Keith Sinclair (eds.), *Studies of a Small Democracy: Essays in Honour of Willis Airey* (Paul for University of Auckland, 1963)

Strong, A. M. *History of the Development of University Education in Home Science in New Zealand, 1911–1936* (Otago University, Dunedin, 1937)

Sutton-Smith, Brian. *The Folkgames of Children* (University of Texas Press for the American Folklore Society, Austin, 1972)

Swindells, Neal. 'Social aspects of rugby football in Manawatu, from 1878 to 1910', research essay, Massey (1978)

Tennant, Margaret. 'Elderly indigents and old men's homes', *NZJH*, xvii.1 (1983), pp. 3–20

'Maternity and morality: homes for single mothers, 1890–1930', *Women's Studies Journal*, ii.1 (1985), pp. 28–49

'Matrons with a mission: women's organisations in New Zealand, 1893–1915', MA thesis, Massey (1976)

'Mrs Grace Neill in the Department of Asylums, Hospitals and Charitable Institutions', *NZJH*, xii.1 (1978), pp. 3–16

'Natural directions: the New Zealand movement for sexual differentiation in education during the early twentieth century', *NZJES*, xii.2 (1977), pp. 142–53

Paupers and Providers: Charitable Aid in New Zealand (AUP/OUP, Auckland, 1989)

Thompson, B. J. G. 'The Canterbury farm labourers' dispute: a study of the first attempt by a union of New Zealand farm labourers to come under the New Zealand arbitration system', MA thesis, Canterbury (1967)

Tiwari, K. N. (ed.) *Indians in New Zealand: Studies in a Sub-Culture* (Price Milburn, Wellington, 1980)

Waite, J. C. *Dear Mr Booth! Some Early Chapters of the History of the Salvation Army in New Zealand* (Salvation Army Territorial Headquarters, Wellington, 1964)

Ward, Jocelyn. ' "For reasons of their own": a study of the Otago Employers' Association, 1901–1915', research essay, Otago (1984)
Watson, James. 'Crisis and change: economic crisis and technological change in New Zealand between the wars', PhD thesis, Canterbury (1984)
Willis, Susan. ' "Defence not defiance": the Port Chalmers Marine Labourers Union, 1907 1912', research essay, Otago (1978)
Wilson, H. *My First Eighty Years* (Blackwood and Janet Paul, Hamilton, 1950)

CHAPTER 11: BETWEEN TWO WORLDS

Ballara, Angela. *Proud to be White? A Survey of Pakeha Prejudice in New Zealand* (Heinemann, Auckland, 1986)
Barker, I. R. 'The connexion: the Mormon Church and the Maori people', MA thesis, Victoria (1967)
Barrington, J. M. and Beaglehole, T. H. *Maori Schools in a Changing Society: An Historical Review* (NZCER, Wellington, 1974)
Beaglehole, Ernest and Pearl. *Some Modern Maoris* (NZCER, Wellington, 1946)
Binney, Judith. 'Maori oral narratives, Pakeha written texts; two forms of telling history', *NZJH*, xxi.1 (1987), pp. 16–28
Binney, Judith and Chaplin, Gillian. *Ngā Mōrehu: The Survivors* (AUP, Auckland, 1986)
Binney, Judith, Chaplin, Gillian and Wallace, Craig. *Mihaia: The Prophet Rua Kenana and his Community at Maungapohatu* (OUP, Wellington, 1979)
Butterworth, G. V. *The Maori in the New Zealand Economy* (NZ Dept. of Industries and Commerce, Wellington, 1967)
　　'The politics of adaptation: the career of Sir Apirana Ngata, 1874–1928', MA thesis, Victoria (1969)
　　'A rural Maori renaissance? Maori society and politics, 1920 to 1951', *JPS*, LXXXI.2 (1972), pp. 160–93
Cody, J. F. *Man of Two Worlds: Sir Maui Pomare* (Reed, Wellington, 1953)
Condliffe, J. B. *Te Rangi Hiroa: The Life of Sir Peter Buck* (Whitcombe and Tombs, Christchurch, 1971)
Cowan, James. *The Maoris in the Great War . . .* (Whitcombe and Tombs, Wellington, 1926)
Fitzgerald, Thomas K. *Education and Identity: A Study of the New Zealand Maori Graduate* (NZCER, Wellington, 1977)
Henderson, J. McLeod. *Ratana: The Man, the Church, the Political Movement* (Reed with the Polynesian Society, Wellington, 1972)
James, Beverley L. 'The Maori Women's Welfare League: from social movement to voluntary association', MSocSci thesis, Waikato (1977)
King, G. 'Aspects of secondary education in Maori denominational boarding schools, 1920–1940', MA thesis, Victoria (1979)
King, Michael. *Apirana Ngata, E Tipu e Rea* (Department of Education, Wellington, 1988)
　　Maori, A Photographic and Social History (Heinemann, Auckland, 1983)
　　Te Puea: A Biography (Hodder and Stoughton, Auckland, 1977)
　　Tihe Mauri Ora: Aspects of Maoritanga (Methuen, Wellington, 1978)
　　Whina, A Biography of Whina Cooper (Hodder and Stoughton, Auckland, 1983)
King, Michael (ed.) *Te Ao Hurihuri: The World Moves On* (Hicks Smith/Methuen, Wellington, 1977)
Kohere, Raweti. *The Autobiography of a Maori* (Reed, Wellington, 1951)
Lange, R. T. 'The revival of a dying race: a study of Maori health reform, 1900–1918, and its nineteenth century background', MA thesis, Auckland (1972)
Lange, S. 'A Maori "renaissance" in the twentieth century?', *Auckland University Historical Society Annual*, 1975, pp. 61–9
Maclean, F. S. *Challenge for Health: A History of Public Health in New Zealand* (Government Printer, Wellington, 1964)

Macrae, John. 'A study in the application of economic analysis to social issues: the Maori and the New Zealand economy', PhD thesis, Auckland (1975)

Martin, R. J. 'Aspects of Maori affairs in the Liberal period', MA thesis, Victoria (1956)

Metge, Joan. *A New Maori Migration: Rural and Urban Relations in Northern New Zealand* (Melbourne University Press, 1964)

The Maoris of New Zealand (Routledge and Kegan Paul, London, 1967)

O'Connor, P. S. 'The recruitment of Maori soldiers, 1914–1918', *PS*, XIX.2 (1967), pp. 48–83

Oliver, W. H. and Thomson, Jane M. *Challenge and Response: A Study of the Development of the Gisborne East Coast Region* (East Coast Development Research Association, Gisborne, 1971)

Orange, Claudia J. 'A kind of equality: Labour and the Maori people, 1935–1949', MA thesis, Auckland (1977)

Parker, Wiremu. 'The substance that remains', in Ian Wards (ed.), *Thirteen Facets: Essays to Commemorate the Silver Jubilee of Queen Elizabeth the Second, 1952–1977* (Government Printer, Wellington, 1978)

Pearce, N. G. 'The size and location of the Maori population, 1857–96 — a statistical study', MA thesis, Victoria (1952)

Pocock, J. G. A. (ed.), *The Maori and New Zealand Politics* (Paul, Auckland and Hamilton, 1965)

Pool, D. Ian. *Te Iwi Maori, A New Zealand Population Past, Present and Projected* (AUP, Auckland, 1991)

The Maori Population of New Zealand, 1769–1971 (AUP/OUP, Auckland, 1977)

Schwimmer, Erik (ed.) *The Maori People in the Nineteen-Sixties* (Paul, Auckland, 1968)

Sinclair, Keith (ed.) *The Oxford Illustrated History of New Zealand* (OUP, Auckland, 1990)

Sorrenson, M. P. K. *Integration or Identity? Cultural Interaction in New Zealand since 1911* (Heinemann, Auckland, 1971)

'Maori land development', *New Zealand's Heritage*, VI.83 (Hamlyn, Wellington, 1971), pp. 2309–15

'Modern Maori: The Young Maori Party to Mana Motuhake', in Keith Sinclair (ed.), *The Oxford Illustrated History of New Zealand* (OUP, Auckland, 1990)

Sorrenson, M. P. K. (ed.) *Na To Hoa Aroha: From Your Dear Friend. The Correspondence Between Sir Apirana Ngata and Sir Peter Buck, 1925–50*, 3 vols (AUP, Auckland, 1986–88)

Stirling, Amiria and Salmond, Anne. *Amiria: The Life Story of a Maori Woman* (Reed, Wellington, 1976)

Sutherland, I. L. G. *The Maori Situation* (Harry Tombs, Wellington, 1935)

Sutherland, I. L. G. (ed.) *The Maori People Today: A General Survey* (NZ Institute of International Affairs and NZCER, Wellington, 1940)

Walker, Ranginui. *Ka Whawhai Tonu Matou: Struggle Without End* (Penguin, Auckland, 1990)

Ward, Alan. 'The history of the East Coast Maori Trust', MA thesis, Victoria (1958)

Webster, Peter. *Rua and the Maori Millennium* (Price Milburn for Victoria University Press, Wellington, 1979)

Williams, John. *Politics of the New Zealand Maori: Protest and Co-operation, 1891–1909* (University of Washington Press, Seattle, 1969)

Winiata, Maharaia. *The Changing Role of the Leader in Maori Society: A Study in Social Change and Race Relations* (Paul, Auckland, 1967)

Worger, W. H. 'Te Puea, the Kingitanga, and Waikato', MA thesis, Auckland (1975)

CHAPTER 12: THE CLIMATE OF OPINION

Akenson, Donald Harman. *Half the World from Home: Perspectives on the Irish in New Zealand, 1860–1950* (VUP, Wellington, 1990)

Alpers, Antony. *The Life of Katherine Mansfield* (Jonathan Cape, London, 1980)

Arnold, Rollo. 'The Australasian Peoples and their World, 1888–1915', in Sinclair (ed.), *Tasman Relations*, pp. 52–70

Baker, Paul. *King and Country Call: New Zealanders, Conscription and the Great War* (AUP, Auckland, 1988)

Barrowman, Rachel. *A Popular Vision: The Arts and the Left in New Zealand, 1930–1950* (VUP, Wellington, 1991)

Bassett, Judith. ' "A Thousand Miles of Loyalty": The Royal Tour of 1901', *NZJH*, XXI.1 (1987), pp. 125–38

Batten, Juliet. 'Art and Identity', in Novitz and Willmott (eds.), *Culture and Identity in New Zealand*, pp. 212–36

Beaglehole, J. C. *Victoria University College: An Essay Towards A History* (NZ University Press, Wellington, 1949)

Beeby, C. E. *The Biography of an Idea: Beeby on Education*, ed. Paula Wagemaker (NZCER, Wellington, 1992)

Berkman, Sylvia. *Katherine Mansfield: A Critical Study* (Yale University Press, New Haven, 1951)

Boddy, Gillian and Mathews, Jacqueline (eds.) *Disputed Ground: Robin Hyde, Journalist* (VUP, Wellington, 1991)

Boyd, Mary. 'Racial attitudes of New Zealand officials in Western Samoa', *NZJH*, XXI.2 (1987), pp. 139–55

Brasch, Charles. *Indirections: A Memoir, 1909–1947* (OUP, Wellington, 1980)

Broughton, W. S. 'Problems and responses of three New Zealand poets in the 1920s', in Curnow (ed.), *Essays on New Zealand Literature* (Heinemann, Auckland, 1973)

Brown, Colin. 'Church, Culture and Identity', in Novitz and Willmott (eds.), *Culture and Identity in New Zealand*, pp. 237–59

Brown, Gordon H. *New Zealand Painting, 1900–1920: Traditions and Departures* (QEII Arts Council, Wellington, 1972)

    New Zealand Painting, 1920–1940: Adaptation and Nationalism (QEII Arts Council, Wellington, 1975)

Brown, Gordon H. and Keith, Hamish. *An Introduction to New Zealand Painting, 1839–1980*, rev. edn. (Collins, Auckland, 1982)

Bunkle, Phillida, Hardy, Linda, and Mathews, Jacqueline. 'Introduction', in Robin Hyde, *Nor The Years Condemn* (New Women's Press, Auckland, 1984)

Burdon, R. M. *The New Dominion: A Social and Political History of New Zealand, 1918–39* (Reed, Wellington, 1965)

    Scholar-Errant: A Biography of Professor A. W. Bickerton (Pegasus, Christchurch, 1956)

Campbell, A. E. *The Feilding Community Centre* (NZCER, Wellington, 1945)

Colless, Brian and Donovan, Peter (eds.) *Religion in New Zealand Society* (Palmerston North, 1980)

Collins, Ken G. *Broadcasting Grave and Gay* (Caxton, Christchurch, 1967)

Craig, E. W. G. *Man of the Mist: A Biography of Elsdon Best* (Reed, Wellington, 1964)

Cumming, Ian and Cumming, Alan. *History of State Education in New Zealand, 1840–1975* (Pitman, Wellington, 1978)

Cutler, Andrew. '*Tomorrow* magazine and New Zealand politics, 1934–1940', *NZJH*, XXIV.1 (1990), pp. 22–44

Cvitanovich, Lynley. *Breaking the Silence: An Analysis of the Selected Fiction of Two New Zealand Women Writers* (NZ Cultural Studies Working Group/Department of Sociology, Massey University, Palmerston North, 1985)

Davis, R. P. *Irish Issues in New Zealand Politics, 1868–1922* (University of Otago Press, Dunedin, 1974)

Day, Paul. *John Mulgan* (OUP, Wellington, 1977)

Dennis, Jonathan and Bieringa, Jan (eds.) *Film in Aotearoa/New Zealand* (VUP, Wellington, 1992)

Docking, Gil. *Two Hundred Years of New Zealand Painting* (Bateman, Auckland, 1990)

Downes, Peter. *Shadows on the Stage: Theatre in New Zealand: In the First Seventy Years* (McIndoe, Dunedin, 1975)

Downes, Peter and Harcourt, Peter. *Voices in the Air: Radio Broadcasting in New Zealand: A Documentary* (Methuen and Radio New Zealand, Wellington, 1976)

Dunn, Michael. *A Concise History of New Zealand Painting* (Bateman, Auckland, 1991)

Dunstall, Graeme. 'Public attitudes and responses in New Zealand to the beginning of the Boer War, 1899', *Auckland University Historical Society Annual*, I (1967), pp. 8–22

Edwards, Les. *Scrim: Radio Rebel in Retrospect* (Hodder and Stoughton, Auckland, 1971)

Eldred-Grigg, Stevan. 'A Bourgeois Blue? Nationalism and letters from the 1920s to the 1950s', *Landfall*, 41 (1987), pp. 293–311

Ewing, J. K. *Development of the New Zealand Primary School Curriculum, 1877–1970* (NZCER, Wellington, 1970)

Fairburn, Miles. *The Ideal Society and Its Enemies* (AUP, Auckland, 1989)

'The rural myth and the new urban frontier: an approach to New Zealand social history, 1870–1940', *NZJH*, IX.1 (1975), pp. 3–21

Fleming, C. A. *Science, Settlers and Scholars: The Centennial History of the Royal Society of New Zealand* (Wellington, 1987)

Fong, Ng Bickleen. *The Chinese in New Zealand: A Study in Assimilation* (Hong Kong University Press/OUP, 1959)

Galbreath, Ross A. 'Colonisation, science and conservation: the development of colonial attitudes towards the native life of New Zealand', DPhil thesis, Waikato (1989)

Walter Buller: The Reluctant Conservationist (GP Books, Wellington, 1989)

Gardner, W. J., Beardsley, E. T. and Carter, T. E. *A History of the University of Canterbury, 1873–1973* (University of Canterbury, Christchurch, 1973)

Garrett, Jane. *An Artist's Daughter: With Christopher Perkins in New Zealand, 1929–34* (Shoal Bay Press, Auckland, 1986)

Gibbons, P. J. 'A Note on writing, identity and colonisation in Aotearoa', *Sites*, 13 (1986), pp. 32–8

Harcourt, Peter. *A Dramatic Appearance: New Zealand Theatre, 1920–1970* (Methuen, Wellington, 1978)

Hoare, M. E. and Bell, L. G. (eds.) *In Search of New Zealand's Scientific Heritage*: selected papers from the *History of Science in New Zealand Conference . . . 1983* (Royal Society of New Zealand/ATL, Wellington, 1984)

Holcroft, M. H. *Discovered Isles: A Trilogy* (Caxton, Christchurch, 1950)

Howe, K. R. *Singer in a Songless Land: A Life of Edward Tregear* (AUP, Auckland, 1991)

Hurst, Maurice. *Music and the Stage in New Zealand: A Century of Entertainment, 1840–1943* (Begg, Auckland, 1944)

Jackson, Hugh. *Churches and People in Australia and New Zealand, 1860–1930* (Allen and Unwin, Wellington, 1987)

'Churchgoing in nineteenth century New Zealand', *NZJH*, XVII.1 (1983), pp. 43–59

Jackson, McD. P. 'Poetry: Beginnings to 1945', in Sturm (ed.), *Oxford History of New Zealand Literature*, pp. 335–84

Jensen, K. 'Holes, wholeness and holiness in Frank Sargeson's writing', *Landfall*, 44.1 (1990), pp. 32–44

Jones, Lawrence. 'Novel', in Sturm (ed.), *Oxford History of New Zealand Literature*, pp. 271–332

King, Julie. *Sydney Lough Thompson: at home and abroad* (Robert McDougall Gallery, Christchurch, 1990)

King, Michael. 'Introduction', in James Cowan, *The New Zealand Wars: A History of the Maori Campaigns and the Pioneering Period*, 3rd edn., 2 vols (Government Printer, Wellington, 1983), pp. v–xi

Lawlor, Pat. *Confessions of a Journalist* (Whitcombe and Tombs, Auckland, 1972)

Leckie, Jacqueline. 'In Defence of Race and Empire: the White New Zealand League at Pukekohe', *NZJH*, XIX.2 (1985), pp. 103–29

Lewis, Margaret. *Ngaio Marsh: A Life* (Bridget Williams Books, Wellington, 1991)

McCormick, E. H. *Alexander Turnbull: His Life, His Circle, His Collections* (ATL, Wellington, 1974)

The Expatriate: A Study of Frances Hodgkins (NZ University Press, Wellington, 1954)

The Fascinating Folly: Dr Hocken and his Fellow Collectors (University of Otago Press, Dunedin, 1961)

'Frances Hodgkins: a pictorial biography', *Ascent*, 5 (1969), pp. 8–29

Letters and Art in New Zealand (NZ Department of Internal Affairs, Wellington, 1940)

McEldowney, Dennis. *Frank Sargeson in His Time* (McIndoe, Dunedin, 1976)

McEldowney, Dennis (ed.) *Presbyterians in Aotearoa, 1840–1990* (Presbyterian Church of NZ, Wellington, 1990)

McGeorge, Colin. 'Learning about God's Own Country', *NZJES*, XVIII (1983), pp. 3–12

'Hear Our Voices We Entreat: Schools and the "Colonial Twang", 1880–1930', *NZJH*, XVIII.1 (1984), pp. 3–18

McNaughton, Howard. 'Drama', in Sturm (ed.), *Oxford History of New Zealand Literature*, pp. 271–332

Maclean, Chris and Phillips, Jock. *The Sorrow and the Pride: New Zealand War Memorials* (Historical Branch/GP Books, Wellington, 1990)

Macleod, Nellie F. H. *The Fighting Man* (Dunbar and Summers, Christchurch, 1964)

Malone, E. P. 'The New Zealand School Journal and the imperial ideology', *NZJH*, VII.1 (1973), pp. 12–27

Marsh, Ngaio. 'Theatre: a note on the status quo', *Landfall*, I.1 (1947), pp. 37–43

Matthews, Jacqueline. 'The Journalism of Robin Hyde', in Gillian Boddy and Jacqueline Matthews (eds.), *Disputed Ground: Robin Hyde, Journalist* (VUP, Wellington, 1991), pp. 83–141

Mulgan, Alan. *Great Days in New Zealand Writing* (Reed, Wellington, 1962)

Munz, Peter (ed.) *The Feel of Truth: Essays in New Zealand and Pacific History presented to F. L. Wood and J. C. Beaglehole* (Reed, Wellington, 1969)

Nichol, C. and Veitch, J. (eds.) *Religion in New Zealand* (VUP, Wellington, 1980)

Novitz, David and Willmott, Bill (eds.) *Culture and Identity in New Zealand* (GP Books, Wellington, 1989)

O'Connor, P. S. 'The awkward ones — dealing with conscience, 1916–18', *NZJH*, VIII.2 (1974), pp. 118–36

'Keeping New Zealand white, 1908–1920', *NZJH*, II.1 (1968), pp. 41–65

'Mr Massey and the P.P.A. — a suspicion confirmed', *NZ Journal of Public Administration*, 28:2 (1966), pp. 69–74

' "Protestants", Catholics and the New Zealand Government, 1916–18', in G. A. Wood and P. S. O'Connor (eds.), *W. P. Morrell: A Tribute* (University of Otago Press, Dunedin, 1973)

'The recruitment of Maori soldiers, 1914–1918', *PS*, XIX.2 (1967), p. 48–83

'Sectarian conflict in New Zealand, 1911–1920', *PS*, XIX.1 (1967), pp. 3–16

'Storm over the clergy — New Zealand, 1917', *Journal of Religious History*, IV.2 (1966), pp. 129–48

Olssen, Erik. *The Red Feds: Revolutionary Industrial Unionism and the New Zealand Federation of Labour, 1908–14* (OUP, Auckland, 1988)

'W. T. Mills, E. J. B. Allen, J. A. Lee and socialism in New Zealand', *NZJH*, X.2 (1976), pp. 112–29

Openshaw, Roger. 'Patriotism and the New Zealand primary school: the decisive years of the twenties', DPhil thesis, Waikato (1978)

O'Sullivan, Vincent. *Katherine Mansfield's New Zealand* (Golden Press, Auckland, 1974)

Paul, Janet and Roberts, Neil. *Evelyn Page: Seven Decades* (Robert McDougall Art Gallery/Allen and Unwin, Christchurch and Wellington, 1986)

Peters, Marie. *Christchurch — St Michael's: A Study in Anglicanism in New Zealand, 1851–1972* (University of Canterbury, Christchurch, 1986)

Phillips, J. O. C. *A Man's Country. The Image of the Pakeha Male. A History* (Penguin, Auckland, 1987)

'Musings in Maoriland — or was there a *Bulletin* school in New Zealand?', *Historical Studies*, 20 (1983), pp. 520–35

'Of verandahs and fish and chips and footie on Saturday afternoon', *NZJH*, XXIV.2 (1990), pp. 118–134

'Rugby, war and the mythology of the New Zealand male', *NZJH*, xviii.2 (1984), pp. 83–103

'War and National Identity', in Novitz and Willmott (eds.), *Culture and Identity in New Zealand*, pp. 91–109

Phillips, J. O. C. (ed.) *Te Whenua, Te Iwi: The Land and the People* (Allen and Unwin/PNP, Wellington, 1987)

Pound, Francis. 'The land, the light and nationalist myth in New Zealand art', in Phillips (ed.), *Te Whenua, Te Iwi*, pp. 48–60

Renwick, W. L. ' "Show us these islands and ourselves . . . give us a home in thought" ', *NZJH*, xxi (1987), pp. 197–214

Roberts, Heather. *Where Did She Come From? New Zealand Women Novelists, 1862–1987* (Allen and Unwin/PNP, Wellington, 1989)

Ross, Angus. *New Zealand Aspirations in the Pacific in the Nineteenth Century* (Clarendon Press, Oxford, 1964)

Scott, Dick. *Years of the Pooh-Bah: A Cook Islands History* (Cook Islands Trading Corp/ Hodder and Stoughton, Rarotonga, 1991)

Sharpe, Maureen. 'Anzac day in New Zealand, 1916–1939', *NZJH*, xv.2 (1981), pp. 97–114

Siegfried, André. *Democracy in New Zealand*, trans. E. V. Burns (G. Bell and Sons, London, 1914)

Simpson, Adrienne (ed.) *Opera in New Zealand: Aspects of History and Performance* (Witham Press, Wellington, 1990)

Simpson, Adrienne and Downes, Peter. *Southern Voices: International Opera Singers of New Zealand* (Reed, Auckland, 1992)

Sinclair, Keith. *A Destiny Apart: New Zealand's Search for National Identity* (Allen and Unwin/ PNP, Wellington, 1986)

'New Zealand literary history', *NZJH*, xii.1 (1978) pp. 69–74

'Why New Zealanders are not Australians: New Zealand and the Australian federal movement, 1881–1901', in Sinclair (ed.), *Tasman Relations*, pp. 90–103

William Pember Reeves: New Zealand Fabian (Clarendon Press, Oxford, 1965)

Sinclair, Keith (ed.) *Tasman Relations: New Zealand and Australia, 1788–1988* (AUP, Auckland, 1988)

Somerset, Gwendolen L. *Two Experiments in Community Education: Oxford and Feilding* (National Council of Adult Education, Wellington, 1972)

Sorrenson, M. P. K. *Manifest Duty: The Polynesian Society over a Hundred Years* (Polynesian Society, Auckland, 1992)

Stead, C. K. (ed.) *The Letters and Journals of Katherine Mansfield: A Selection* (Penguin, Harmondsworth, Middlesex, 1977)

Sturm, Terry (ed.) *The Oxford History of New Zealand Literature in English* (OUP, Auckland, 1991)

Thomson, A. D. *The Life and Correspondence of Leonard Cockayne* (Caxton, Christchurch, 1983)

Thomson, J. M. *A Distant Music: The Life and Times of Alfred Hill, 1870–1960* (OUP, Auckland, 1980)

The Oxford History of New Zealand Music (OUP, Auckland, 1991)

Trlin, A. D. *Now Respected, Once Despised: Yugoslavs in New Zealand* (Dunmore, Palmerston North, 1979)

Vowles, Jack. 'Ideology and the formation of the New Zealand Labour Party', *NZJH*, xvi.1 (1982), pp. 39–55

'Liberal democracy: Pakeha political ideology', *NZJH*, xxi.2 (1987), pp. 215–27

Weir, J. E. *R. A. K. Mason* (OUP, Wellington, 1977)

Weitzel, R. L. 'Pacifists and anti-militarists in New Zealand, 1909–1914', *NZJH*, viii.2 (1973), pp. 128–47

Wevers, Lydia. 'The Short Story', in Sturm (ed.), *Oxford History of New Zealand Literature*, pp. 203–68

Wilson, Phillip. *William Satchell* (Twayne, New York, 1968)

Wood, F. L. W. *The New Zealand People at War: Political and External Affairs* (NZ Department of Internal Affairs, Wellington, 1958)

CHAPTER 13: IMPERIALISM AND NATIONALISM

Allin, C. D. *Australasian Preferential Tariffs and Imperial Free Trade* (Minnesota University Press, Minneapolis, 1929)

Barratt, G. *Russophobia in New Zealand, 1838–1908* (Dunmore Press, Palmerston North, 1981)

Burton, O. E. *The Silent Division: New Zealanders at the Front, 1914–1919* (Angus and Robertson, Sydney, 1935)

Dalziel, R. *Julius Vogel: Business Politician* (AUP/OUP, Auckland, 1986)

Dalziel, R. M. *The Origins of New Zealand Diplomacy: The Agent-General in London, 1870–1905* (VUP, Wellington, 1973)

Fairburn, M. 'New Zealand and Australasian Federation, 1883–1901: another view', *NZJH*, IV.2 (1970), pp. 138–59

Field, Michael J. *Mau: Samoa's Struggle Against New Zealand Oppression* (Reed, Wellington, 1984)

Fieldhouse, D. K. 'Autochthonous elements in the evolution of Dominion status: the case of New Zealand', *Journal of Commonwealth Political Studies*, 1:2 (1962), pp. 85–111

Hall, D. O. W. *The New Zealanders in South Africa, 1899–1902* (Department of Internal Affairs, Wellington, 1949)

Hensley, G. C. 'The withdrawal of the British troops from New Zealand', MA thesis, Canterbury (1957)

Hunt, R. T. 'Independence agitation in New Zealand, 1869–1871', MA thesis, Otago (1950)

Kendle, J. E. *The Colonial and Imperial Conferences, 1887–1911* (Longmans, London, 1967)

Kendle, J. E. 'The Round Table Movement, New Zealand, and the Imperial Conference of 1911', *Journal of Commonwealth Political Studies*, 3:2 (1965), pp. 104–17

Knaplund, P. *Gladstone and Britain's Imperial Policy* (Allen and Unwin, London, 1927)

McGibbon, I. *The Path to Gallipoli: Defending New Zealand, 1840–1915* (GP Books, Wellington, 1991)

McGibbon, I. C. *Blue-water Rationale: The Naval Defence of New Zealand, 1914–1942* (Historical Publications Branch, Wellington, 1981)

McIntyre, W. David. *New Zealand Prepares for War: Defence Policy, 1919–1939* (University of Canterbury Press, Christchurch, 1988)

The Rise and Fall of the Singapore Naval Base, 1919–1942 (Macmillan, London, 1979)

McIntyre, W. David and Gardner, W. J. (eds). *Speeches and Documents on New Zealand History* (Clarendon Press, Oxford, 1971)

Morrell, W. P. *British Colonial Policy in the Mid-Victorian Age: South Africa, New Zealand, The West Indies* (Clarendon Press, Oxford, 1969)

Phillips, J. *A Man's Country. The Image of the Pakeha Male. A History* (Penguin Books, Auckland, 1987)

Phillips, J. O. C. 'Rugby, war and the mythology of the New Zealand male', *NZJH*, 18(2): (1984), pp. 83–103

'75 Years since Gallipoli', in Anderson, A. et al., *Towards 1990: Seven Leading Historians Examine Significant Aspects of New Zealand History* (GP Books, Wellington 1989)

Powles, C. G. (ed.). *The History of the Canterbury Mounted Rifles, 1914–1919* (Whitcombe and Tombs, Auckland, 1928)

Pugsley, C. *Gallipoli: The New Zealand Story* (Hodder and Stoughton, Auckland, 1984)

Ross, A. 'Chanak', in *New Zealand's Heritage*, 6 (Hamlyn, Wellington, 1971–73), pp. 2152–6

'New Zealand and the Statute of Westminster', *Journal of Imperial and Commonwealth History*, 8:1 (1979), pp. 136–58

New Zealand Aspirations in the Pacific in the Nineteenth Century (Clarendon Press, Oxford, 1964)

'Reluctant Dominion or dutiful daughter? New Zealand and the Commonwealth in the inter-war years', *Journal of Commonwealth Political Studies*, 10:1 (1972), pp. 28–44

Ross, A. (ed.) *New Zealand's Record in the Pacific Islands in the Twentieth Century* (Longman Paul, Auckland, 1969)

Shadbolt, M. *Voices of Gallipoli* (Hodder and Stoughton, Auckland, 1988)

Sinclair, K. *A Destiny Apart: New Zealand's Search for National Identity* (Unwin/PNP, Wellington, 1986)

'Australasian inter-government negotiations, 1865–80', *Australian Journal of Politics and History*, 16:2 (1970), pp. 151–76

Imperial Federation: A Study of New Zealand Policy and Opinion, 1880–1914 (Athlone Press, London, 1955)

The Native Born: The Origins of New Zealand Nationalism (Massey University, Palmerston North, 1986)

'Why New Zealanders are not Australians: New Zealand and the Australian Federal Movement, 1881–1901', in Sinclair (ed.), *Tasman Relations*, (AUP, Auckland, 1987), pp. 90–103

Skow, D. K. 'The 1909 Defence Act: a case study in militarism in New Zealand', research essay (Otago) 1981

Tapp, E. J. 'New Zealand and Australian Federation', *HSANZ*, 5:19 (1952), pp. 244–57

Waite, F. *The New Zealanders at Gallipoli* (Whitcombe and Tombs, Auckland, 1919)

Weir, T. G. 'New Zealand's naval policy, 1909–1914', MA thesis, Canterbury (1973)

Williams, P. 'New Zealand and the 1930 Imperial Conference', *NZJH*, v.1 (1971), pp. 31–48

Wood, F. L. W. *New Zealand in the World* (Department of Internal Affairs, Wellington, 1940)

'Why did New Zealand not join the Australian Commonwealth in 1900–1901?' *NZJH*, II.2 (1968), pp. 115–29

CHAPTER 14: FROM LABOUR TO NATIONAL

Baker, J. V. T. *The New Zealand People at War: War Economy* (NZ Dept. of Internal Affairs, Wellington, 1965)

Bassett, Michael. *Confrontation '51: The 1951 Waterfront Dispute* (Reed, Wellington, 1972)

The Third Labour Government: A Personal History (Dunmore, Palmerston North, 1976)

Beaglehole, J. C. 'New Zealand since the war, 4: politics and culture', *Landfall*, xv.2 (1961), pp. 138–52

Belshaw, Horace (ed.) *New Zealand* (University of California Press, Berkeley and Los Angeles, 1947)

Brown, Bruce. *The Rise of New Zealand Labour: A History of the New Zealand Labour Party from 1916 to 1940* (Price Milburn, Wellington, 1962)

Chapman, R. M. *Marginals '72: An Analysis of New Zealand's Marginal Electorates* (Heinemann, Auckland, 1972)

'New Zealand since the war, 8: politics and society', *Landfall*, xvi.3 (1962), pp. 252–76

The Political Scene, 1919–1931 (Heinemann, Auckland, 1969)

'The response to Labour and the question of parallelism of opinion, 1928–1960', in R. M. Chapman and Keith Sinclair (eds), *Studies of a Small Democracy: Essays in Honour of Willis Airey* (Paul for University of Auckland, 1963)

Chapman, R. M., Jackson, W. K and Mitchell, A. V. *New Zealand Politics in Action: The 1960 General Election* (OUP, London, 1962)

Clark, Helen. 'Political attitudes in the New Zealand countryside', MA thesis, Auckland (1974)

Colechin, J. E. 'The campaign of the Social Credit Political League', in *The New Zealand General Election of 1957* (Dept. of Political Science, Victoria University of Wellington, 1958)

Condliffe, J. B. *The Welfare State in New Zealand* (Allen and Unwin, London, 1959)

Easton, Brian. *Social Policy and the Welfare State in New Zealand* (Allen and Unwin, Auckland, 1980)

Franklin, S. H. *Trade, Growth and Anxiety: New Zealand Beyond the Welfare State* (Methuen, Wellington, 1978)

Goff, Philip. 'Labour and the unions: the politics of industrial relations under the third Labour Government', MA thesis, Auckland (1979)

Goldstein, Ray with Alley, Rod (eds.) *Labour in Power — Promise and Performance: Evaluations of the Work of the New Zealand Government from 1972 to 1975* (Price Milburn for NZ University Press, Wellington, 1975)

Gustafson, Barry. 'Continuing transformation: the structure, composition, and functioning of the New Zealand Labour Party in the Auckland region, 1949–70', PhD thesis, Auckland (1973)

 From the Cradle to the Grave: A Biography of Michael Joseph Savage (Reed Methuen, Auckland, 1986)

 Michael Joseph Savage (Reed, Wellington, 1968)

 Social Change and Party Organisation: The New Zealand Labour Party since 1945 (Sage Publications, London, 1976)

Hanson, Elizabeth. *The Politics of Social Security: The 1938 Act and some Later Developments* (AUP/OUP, Auckland, 1980)

 'The social security story: a study of the political origins of the 1938 Social Security Act', MA thesis, Auckland (1975)

Hare, A. E. C. *Report on Industrial Relations in New Zealand* (Victoria University College, Wellington, 1946)

Hawkins, Wayne. 'The Hon. Duncan MacIntyre as Minister of Maori Affairs', MA thesis, Auckland (1975)

Hill, R. J. M. 'The quest for control: the New Zealand dairy industry and the guaranteed price, 1921–1936', MA thesis, Auckland (1974)

Hume, K. T. 'Party servants: a study of senior and junior branch activists of the National Party', MA thesis, Auckland (1972)

Jackson, S. K. 'Politics in the Eastern Maori Electorate, 1928–1969: an enquiry into Maori politics as a unique system', MA thesis, Auckland (1977)

Jackson, W. K. *The New Zealand Legislative Council: A Study of the Establishment, Failure and Abolition of an Upper House* (University of Otago Press, Dunedin, 1972)

 New Zealand, Politics of Change (Reed, Wellington, 1973)

Keeble, Peter. 'National and Labour Government housing policies, 1969–75', MA thesis, Auckland (1976)

Levine, Stephen (ed.) *New Zealand Politics: A Reader* (Cheshire, Melbourne, 1975)

 Politics in New Zealand: A Reader (Allen and Unwin, Sydney, 1978)

Lee, John A. *Simple on a Soap-box* (Collins, Auckland, 1963)

 Socialism in New Zealand (Werner Laurie, London, 1938)

Lipson, Leslie. *The Politics of Equality: New Zealand's Adventures in Democracy* (University of Chicago Press, 1948)

Lovell-Smith, J. B. *The New Zealand Doctor and the Welfare State* (Paul, Auckland, 1966)

Macdonald, Gerard. 'The News Media Ownership Act of 1965: a case study in the relationship of press and polity', MA thesis, Auckland (1973)

McCracken, A. J. 'Maori voting and non-voting, 1928–1969: a study of changes in voting patterns preceding and accompanying urban migration', MA thesis, Auckland (1971)

McLeay, E. M. 'Parliamentary careers in a two-party system: Cabinet selection in New Zealand', PhD thesis, Auckland (1978)

Mendelsohn, Ronald. *Social Security in the British Commonwealth: Great Britain, Canada, Australia, New Zealand* (University of London, the Athlone Press, 1954)

Metge, R. T. ' "The house that Jack built": the origins of Labour housing, 1935–8 with particular reference to the role of J. A. Lee', MA thesis, Auckland, (1972)

Milne, R. S. *Political Parties in New Zealand* (Clarendon Press, Oxford, 1966)

Mitchell, A. V. *Government by Party; Parliament and Politics in New Zealand* (Whitcombe and Tombs, Christchurch, 1966)

 Politics and People in New Zealand (Whitcombe and Tombs, Christchurch, 1969)

Mulgan, Richard. *Democracy and Power in New Zealand. A Study of New Zealand Politics* (OUP, Auckland, 1984)

Nash, Walter. *New Zealand, A Working Democracy* (Duell, Sloan and Pearce, New York, 1943)

Northey, Richard. 'The annual conferences of the New Zealand Labour Party', MA thesis, Auckland (1973)

Olssen, Erik. *John A. Lee* (University of Otago Press, Dunedin, 1977)

Orbell, J. M. 'Politics of prosperity: a study of political opinion in Auckland city and surrounds, 1938–1957', 2 vols., MA thesis, Auckland (1960)

Parker, R. S. (ed.) *Economic Stability in New Zealand* (NZ Institute of Public Administration, Wellington, 1953)

Paul, J. T. *Humanism in Politics: New Zealand Labour Party Retrospect* (NZ Labour Party, Wellington, 1946)

Pearson, Bill. 'New Zealand since the war, 7: the Maori people', *Landfall*, xvi.2 (1962), pp. 148–80

Penfold, John. 'The New Zealand Social Credit Political League', *PS*, viii.1 (1955), pp. 33–7

Price, Macalister. 'The political vocation: a study of the recruitment and selection of parliamentary candidates in the New Zealand National Party', MA thesis, Auckland (1972)

Robinson, Alan. 'The rise of the New Zealand National Party, 1936–1949', MA thesis, Victoria, (1957)

Roth, H. *Trade Unions in New Zealand, Past and Present* (Reed, Wellington, 1973)

Scholefield, G. H. (ed.) *New Zealand Parliamentary Record, 1940–1949* (Government Printer, Wellington, 1950)

Scott, Dick. *151 Days: History of the Great Waterfront Lockout and Supporting Strikes, February 15–July 15, 1951* (NZ Waterside Workers' Union (Deregistered), Auckland, 1952)

Scott, K. J. *The New Zealand Constitution* (Clarendon Press, Oxford, 1962)

Scott, K. J. (ed.) *Welfare in New Zealand* (NZ Institute of Public Administration, Wellington, 1955)

Shorter, Colin. 'Political thought in New Zealand: the ideologies, the values, and beliefs of the New Zealand National and Labour parliamentary parties', MA thesis, Auckland, (1974)

Sinclair, Keith. *Walter Nash* (AUP/OUP, Auckland, 1976)

Stone, Raewyn, 'The political response to the question of abortion in New Zealand . . . 1970–1975', MA thesis, Auckland (1977)

Sutch, W. B. *The Quest for Security in New Zealand, 1840 to 1966* (OUP, Wellington, 1966)
    Colony or Nation: Economic Crises in New Zealand from the 1860s to the 1960s: Addresses and Papers, ed. Michael Turnbull (Sydney University Press, 1966)

Tabacoff, David. 'The role of the Maori M.P. in contemporary New Zealand politics', research essay, Auckland (1972)

Thorn, James. *Peter Fraser, New Zealand's Wartime Prime Minister* (Oldhams, London, 1952)

Vowles, Jack. 'Ideology and the formation of the New Zealand Labour Party', *NZJH*, xvi.1 (1982), pp. 39–55

Wards, Ian (ed.) *Thirteen Facets: Essays to Celebrate the Silver Jubilee of Queen Elizabeth the Second, 1952–1977* (Government Printer, Wellington, 1978)

Webb, Leicester. *Government in New Zealand* (NZ Dept. of Internal Affairs, Wellington, 1940)

Westrate, C. *Portrait of a Modern Mixed Economy: New Zealand* (NZ University Press, Wellington, 1959)

Wigglesworth, Sondra. 'The Depression and the election of 1935: a study of the Coalition's measures during the depression and the effect of these measures upon the election result of 1935', MA thesis, Auckland (1954)

Wilson, J. O. (ed.) *New Zealand Parliamentary Record, 1940–1949; Supplement, 1950–1969* (Government Printer, Wellington, 1969)

Wood, F. L. W. *The New Zealand People at War: Political and External Affairs* (NZ Dept. of Internal Affairs, Wellington, 1958)

CHAPTER 15: THE POLITICS OF VOLATILITY

Bassett, Michael. *The Third Labour Government* (Dunmore, Palmerston North, 1976)

Bean, Clive S. 'Leadership and voting in the 1978 New Zealand General Election', *Political Science*, 33:1 (1981), pp. 10–19

'Political leaders and voter perceptions: images of Muldoon and Rowling at the 1975 and 1978 New Zealand General Elections', *Political Science*, 32:1 (1980), pp. 55–75

Boston, Jonathan. 'By-elections in New Zealand', *Political Science*, 32:2 (1980), pp. 103–27

Boston, Jonathan and Holland, Martin (eds.) *The Fourth Labour Government: Radical Politics in New Zealand*, 1st edn. (OUP, Auckland, 1987)

Boston, Jonathan and Jackson, Keith. 'The New Zealand General Election of 1987', *Electoral Studies*, 7:2 (1988), pp. 70–5

Bryant, George. *Beetham* (Dunmore Press, Palmerston North, 1981)

Chapman, George. *The Years of Lightning* (Reed, Wellington, 1980)

Clark, Margaret (ed.) *The 1987 Election: What Happened?* (Social Sciences Research Fund Committee, Wellington, 1988)

Clements, Kevin P. 'The Citizens for Rowling Campaign: an insider's view', *Political Science*, 28:2 (1976), pp. 81–96

Douglas, Roger. *There's Got to be a Better Way: A Practical ABC to Solving New Zealand's Major Problems* (Fourth Estate, Wellington, 1980)

Douglas, Roger and Callan, Louise. *Towards Prosperity* (Bateman, Auckland, 1987)

Edwards, Brian (ed.) *Right Out* (Reed, Wellington, 1973)

Excel, David (ed.) *Rowling: Citizens for Rowling* (Citizens for Rowling Campaign, Auckland, 1975)

Garnier, Tony, Kohn, Bruce and Booth, Pat. *The Hunter and the Hill: New Zealand Politics in the Kirk Years* (Cassell New Zealand, Auckland, 1978)

Garnier, Tony and Levine, Stephen. *Election '81: An End to Muldoonism?* (Methuen, Auckland, 1981)

Gold, Hyam (ed.) *New Zealand Politics in Perspective* (Longman Paul, Auckland, 1st edn. 1985, 2nd edn. 1989, 3rd edn. 1992)

Goldstein, Ray and Alley, Roderic. *Labour in Power: Promise and Performance* (Price Milburn/NZ University Press, Wellington, 1975)

Gould, John. *The Rake's Progress: The New Zealand Economy Since 1945* (Hodder and Stoughton, Auckland, 1982)

Grierson, Josephine. *The Hell Of It: Early Days in the New Zealand Party* (Reed Methuen, Auckland, 1985)

Gustafson, Barry. *The First 50 Years: A History of the New Zealand National Party* (Reed Methuen, Auckland, 1986)

Hawke, G. R. *The Making of New Zealand: An Economic History* (Cambridge University Press, Cambridge, 1985)

'The New Zealand economy in 1990' (Paper presented to the International Workshop on 1991 Economic Outlook for Asian Economies, Tokyo, February 1991)

Hayward, Margaret. *Diary of the Kirk Years* (Cape Catley and Reed, Wellington, 1981)

Henderson, John. *Rowling: The Man and the Myth* (ANZ/Fraser, Auckland, 1981)

Holland, Martin and Boston, Jonathan (eds.) *The Fourth Labour Government: Politics and Policy in New Zealand*, rev. 2nd edn. (OUP, Auckland, 1990)

Jackson, Keith. 'The New Zealand General Election of 1984', *Electoral Studies*, 4:1 (1985), pp. 75–9

James, Colin. *The Quiet Revolution* (Allen and Unwin/PNP, Wellington, 1986)

James, Colin and McRobie, Alan. *Changes? The 1990 Election* (Allen and Unwin/PNP, Wellington, 1990)

Jones, Robert. *New Zealand the Way I Want It* (Whitcoulls, Christchurch, 1978)

The Permit (William Collins, Auckland, 1984)

Lange, David. *Nuclear Free — The New Zealand Way* (Penguin, Auckland, 1990)

Levine, Stephen (ed.) *New Zealand Politics: A Reader* (Cheshire, Melbourne, 1975)

Politics in New Zealand: A Reader (Allen and Unwin, Sydney, 1978)

Levine, Stephen and Lodge, Juliet. *The New Zealand General Election of 1975* (Price Milburn/NZ University Press, Wellington, 1976)

Levine, Stephen, Lodge, Juliet, and Roberts, Nigel S. 'The New Zealand General Election of 1990', *Political Science*, 43:1 (1991), pp. 1–19

McCraw, David. 'Social Credit's role in the New Zealand party system', *Political Science*, 31:1 (1979), pp. 54–60

McLeay, Elizabeth (ed.) *The 1990 General Election: Perspectives on Political Change in New Zealand* (Occasional paper no. 3, Department of Politics, Victoria University of Wellington, Wellington, 1991)

McMillan, Stuart. *Neither Confirm Nor Deny* (Allen and Unwin/PNP, Wellington, 1987)

McRobie, Alan. *Election '84* (MC Enterprises, Christchurch, 1984)

New Zealand Electoral Atlas (GP Books, Wellington, 1989)

'The New Zealand General Election of 1990', *Electoral Studies*, 10:2 (1991), pp. 158–71

McRobie, Alan and Roberts, Nigel S. *Election '78: The 1977 Electoral Redistribution and the 1978 General Election in New Zealand* (McIndoe, Dunedin, 1978)

Muldoon, Robert. *Muldoon* (Reed, Wellington, 1977)

My Way (Reed, Wellington, 1981)

The New Zealand Economy: A Personal View (Endeavour Press, Auckland, 1985)

The Rise and Fall of a Young Turk (Reed, Wellington, 1974)

Mulgan, Richard. *Democracy and Power in New Zealand* (OUP, Auckland, 1st edn. 1984, 2nd edn. 1989)

Oliver, W. H. *The Story of New Zealand* (Faber and Faber, London, 1960)

Page, Warren and Lockstone, Brian. *Landslide '72* (McIndoe, Dunedin, 1973)

Palmer, Geoffrey. *Unbridled Power* (OUP, Auckland, 1st edn. 1979, 2nd edn. 1987)

Penniman, Howard R. (ed.) *New Zealand at the Polls: The General Election of 1978* (American Enterprise Institute, Washington, D.C., 1980)

Roberts, John. *Politicians, Public Servants and Public Enterprise* (Institute of Policy Studies, Wellington, 1987)

Roberts, Nigel S. 'The New Zealand General Election of 1975', *Australian Quarterly*, March 1976, pp. 97–114

Sheppard, Michael. *Social Credit Inside and Out* (Caveman Press, Dunedin, 1981)

Sinclair, Keith. *A History of New Zealand*, rev. edn. (Penguin, Auckland, 1988)

Sinclair, Keith (ed.) *The Oxford Illustrated History of New Zealand* (OUP, Auckland, 1990)

Sutch, W. B. *The Quest for Security in New Zealand* (OUP, Wellington, 1966)

Templeton, Ian and Eunson, Keith. *Election '69* (Reed, Wellington, 1969)

Trainor, Luke. 'The primacy of internal policy: National, sport and external relations, 1975–78', *Political Science*, 30:2 (1978), pp. 63–78

Walker, Ranginui. *Ka Whawhai Tonu Matou: Struggle Without End* (Penguin, Auckland, 1990)

Wilson, Margaret. *Labour in Government* (Allen and Unwin/PNP, Wellington, 1989)

Wood, G. A. *Why National Won* (McIndoe, Dunedin, 1975)

Zavos, Spiro. *The Real Muldoon* (Fourth Estate, Wellington, 1978)

Crusade: Social Credit's Drive for Power (INL Print, Wellington, 1981)

CHAPTER 16: ECONOMIC TRENDS AND ECONOMIC POLICY

Ashton, Toni and St John, Susan. *Superannuation in New Zealand: Averting the Crisis* (VUP for Institute of Policy Studies, Wellington, 1988)

Baker, J. V. T. *The New Zealand People at War: War Economy* (NZ Dept. of Internal Affairs, Wellington, 1965)

Bale, Gordon. *Wealth Transfer Taxation* (VUP for Institute of Policy Studies, Wellington, 1989)

Bayliss, L. C. 'Money supply and selected liquid assets', *NZ Economic Papers*, x (1976), pp. 83–105

Belshaw, H. *Immigration, Problems and Policies* (Wright and Carman, Wellington, 1952)

Blyth, C. A. *Economic Growth, 1950–1960* (NZ Institute of Economic Research, Wellington, 1961), Research paper 1

  Inflation in New Zealand (Allen and Unwin, Sydney, and NZ Institute of Economic Research, Wellington, 1977)

  'The industrialization of New Zealand', *NZ Economic Papers*, VIII (1974), pp. 1–22

  'The special case: the political economy of New Zealand', *PS*, XVIII.1 (1966), pp. 38–51

Bollard, A. and Buckle, R. (eds.) *Economic Liberalization in New Zealand* (Allen and Unwin, Wellington, 1987)

Boston, Jonathan and Holland, Martin (eds.) *The Fourth Labour Government* (OUP, Auckland, 1987)

Brownlie, A. D. 'New Zealand's import function', *NZ Economic Papers*, I.2 (1967), pp. 16–20

Buckle, R. A. 'The response of New Zealand's pastoral exports to the 1967 revaluation', *NZ Economic Papers*, XI (1977), pp. 25–51

Castle, L. M. *A Study of New Zealand Manufacturing* (Victoria University of Wellington, 1966)

Dalziel, Paul. 'National's macroeconomic policy', in Jonathan Boston and Paul Dalziel (eds.), *The Decent Society? Essays in Response to National's Economic and Social Policies* (OUP, Auckland, 1991), pp. 19–38

Deane, R. S. 'Corporatisation and privatisation: a discussion of the issues', speech to the Napier Chamber of Commerce, 31 May 1989, distributed by the Electricity Corporation of New Zealand

  Foreign Investment in New Zealand Manufacturing (Sweet and Maxwell, Wellington, 1970)

Dowie, J. A. 'A century-old estimate of the national income of New Zealand', *Business Archives & History* VI (1966), pp. 117–31

Economic Development Commission. *A Generic Approach to the Reform of Occupational Regulation* (Economic Development Commission, Wellington, December 1988)

Economic Monitoring Group. *Foreign Exchange Constraints, Export Growth and Overseas Debt* (NZ Planning Council, Wellington, 1983)

Economic Monitoring Group. *The Economy in Transition: Restructuring to 1989* (New Zealand Planning Council, Wellington, 1989)

Economic Monitoring Group. *The Regulated Economy* (NZ Planning Council, Wellington, September 1985)

Elley, V. 'Effective protection in selected New Zealand manufacturing industries in 1972–3' (Victoria University of Wellington, 1976), Project on Economic Planning, Occasional paper 29

Evans, B. L. *A History of Agricultural Production and Marketing in New Zealand* (Keeling and Mundy, Palmerston North, 1969)

Eyre, D. L. 'Real imports and import ratios, 1954/5–1974/5' (Victoria University of Wellington, 1975), Project on Economic Planning, internal staff paper 8

Franklin, S. H. *Trade, Growth and Anxiety: New Zealand Beyond the Welfare State* (Methuen, Wellington, 1978)

Gould, J. D. 'Some economic consequences of rapid population growth in New Zealand', *Landfall*, XVIII.1 (1964), pp. 74–87

  The Muldoon Years (Hodder and Stoughton, Auckland, 1985)

  The Rake's Progress (Hodder and Stoughton, Auckland, 1982)

Greensmith, E. L. *The New Zealand Wool Commission* (NZ Wool Marketing Corporation, Wellington, 1976)

Haarmeyer, David. *Competition Policy and Government Regulatory Intervention* (Economic Development Commission, Wellington, October 1988)

Hawke, G. R. 'Acquisitiveness and equality in New Zealand's economic development', *Economic History Review*, 2nd series, XXXII.3 (August 1979), pp. 376–90

Between Governments and Banks: A History of the Reserve Bank of New Zealand (Government Printer, Wellington, 1973)

'Diversification of New Zealand exports', VUW working papers in Economic History, 79/2 (Victoria University of Wellington, 1979)

'Inflation in New Zealand', *NZ Economic Papers*, XI (1977), pp. 206–9

'Long-term trends in New Zealand imports', *AEHR*, XVIII.1 (1978), p. 1–28

The Making of New Zealand: An Economic History (Cambridge University Press, Cambridge, 1985)

'The transport policy study: an outsider's view', *NZ Economic Papers*, IX (1975), p. 22–32

Holland, Martin and Boston, Jonathan (eds.) *The Fourth Labour Government*, rev. 2nd edn. (OUP, Auckland, 1990)

Jennings, Stephen and Begg, Susan. *State Owned Enterprise Policy: Issues in Ownership and Regulation* (New Zealand Business Roundtable, Wellington, April 1988)

Jones, G. W. *Privatisation: Reflections on the British Experience* (VUP for Institute of Policy Studies, Wellington, 1987)

Lang, H. G. 'Price and wage policy', in R. S. Parker (ed.), *Economic Stability in New Zealand* (NZ Institute of Public Administration, Wellington, 1953)

Lloyd, P. J. *Economic Relationships between Australia and New Zealand* (ANU Press, Canberra, 1976)

New Zealand Manufacturing Production and Trade with Australia (NZ Institute of Economic Research, Wellington, 1971), Research paper 17

The Economic Development of the Tourist Industry in New Zealand (NZ Institute of Economic Research, Wellington, 1964), Research paper 6

Martin, John. *A Profession of Statecraft* (VUP for Institute of Policy Studies, Wellington, 1988)

McCabe, Lee. *Privatising State Owned Enterprises* (Economic Development Commission, Wellington, July 1989)

McDonald, T. K. *Regional Development in New Zealand* (NZ Institute of Economic Research Contract Research Unit, Wellington, 1969)

McKinlay, Peter. *Corporatisation: The Solution for State Owned Enterprise?* rev. edn. (VUP for Institute of Policy Studies, Wellington, 1987)

O'Malley, T. R., Gillion, C. and Rose, W. D. *Farming and Inflation: A Report to the New Zealand Dairy Board and the New Zealand Meat Producers' Board* (NZ Institute of Economic Research Contract Research Unit, 1973), Research paper 8

Parston, Greg. *The Evolution of General Management in the National Health Service* (VUP for Institute of Policy Studies, Wellington, 1988)

Philpott, B. P. et al. *Aspects of Productivity and Economic Growth in New Zealand, 1926–1964* (Agricultural Economics Research Unit, Lincoln College, 1966), Publication 29

Philpott, B. P. et al. *Estimates of Farm Income and Productivity in New Zealand, 1921–1965* (Agricultural Economics Research Unit, Lincoln College, 1967), Publication 30

Pope, M. J. 'The conceptual bases and interpretation of data for stabilisation purposes', *NZ Economic Papers*, V (1971), pp. 18–64

'The public sector overload — is there any?' (NZ Institute of Economic Research, Wellington, 1978), Occasional paper 5

Prebble, John. *The Taxation of Controlled Foreign Corporations* (VUP for Institute of Policy Studies, Wellington, 1987)

Rabel, R. 'New Zealand', in R. Baker and C. Morrison (eds.) *Australia, New Zealand and the United States: National Evolution and Alliance Relations* (Praeger, New York, 1991)

Rayner, A. C. et al. *The Economy in Transition: Restructuring to 1989* (New Zealand Planning Council, Economic Monitoring Group Report No. 9, Wellington, July 1989), pp. 7–8

Rimmer, P. J. 'The changing status of New Zealand seaports, 1853–1968' and 'Coastal shipping changing role in New Zealand's space economy', in R. J. Johnston (ed.), *Urbanisation in New Zealand: Geographical Essays* (Reed, Wellington, 1973)

Roberts, John. *Politicians, Public Servants & Public Enterprise* (VUP for Institute of Policy Studies, Wellington, 1987)

Rose, W. D. *Development Options in the New Zealand Motor Car Assembly Industry* (NZ Institute of Economic Research, Wellington, 1971), Research paper 16

Rosenberg, Wolfgang. *A Guidebook to New Zealand's Future* (Caxton, Christchurch, 1968)

Rowe, J. W. 'Import reliance, 1950–65', *NZ Economic Papers*, I.1 (1966), pp. 24–30

Royal Commission on Social Policy. *The April Report.* 5 volumes, (Wellington, 1988)

Royal Commission on Social Policy. *The Role of the State: Five Perspectives* (Wellington, 1988)

Royal Commission on Social Policy. *Working Papers on Income Maintenance and Taxation* (Wellington, 1988)

Sandford, Cedric. *Taxing Wealth in New Zealand* (VUP for Institute of Policy Studies, Wellington, 1987)

Seidman, J. *The Industrial Relations Systems of the United States and New Zealand: A Comparison* (Industrial Relations Centre, Victoria University of Wellington, 1975), Occasional paper 16

Simkin, C. G. F. 'Wartime changes in the New Zealand economy', *Economic Record*, XXIV.46 (1948), pp. 18–31

State Owned Enterprises: Privatisation and Regulation — Issues and Options (VUP for Institute of Policy Studies, Wellington, 1988)

Sutch, W. B. *Problems of Prosperity* (Price Milburn, Wellington, 1962)

Texeira, Alex, Scott, Claudia and Devlin, Martin. *Inside GST: The Development of the Goods and Services Tax* (VUP for Institute of Policy Studies, Wellington, 1986)

The Producer Board Seminar Papers (VUP for Institute of Policy Studies, Wellington, 1988)

Tho, N. D. 'Implicit indices of export and import prices' (Victoria University of Wellington, 1975), Project on Economic Planning, internal staff paper 9

Tho, N. D. and Philpott, B. P. 'Sectoral trends in gross output, factor inputs and labour productivity' (Victoria University of Wellington, 1976), Project on Economic Planning, Occasional paper 30

Turkington, D. J. *Industrial Conflict: A Study of Three New Zealand Industries* (Methuen and Industrial Relations Centre, Victoria University of Wellington, 1976)

Vann, Richard J. *Trans-Tasman Taxation of Equity Investment* (VUP for Institute of Policy Studies, Wellington, 1988)

Ward, A. H. *A Command of Co–operatives: The Development of Leadership, Marketing and Price Control in the Co-operative Dairy Industry of New Zealand* (NZ Dairy Board, Wellington, 1975)

Ward, A. J. 'Aspects of New Zealand housing', MA thesis, Victoria (1977)

Wood, F. L. W. *The New Zealand People at War: Political and External Affairs* (NZ Dept. of Internal Affairs, Wellington, 1958)

Woods, N. S. *The Industrial Relations Act, 1973* and *The Industrial Relations Amending Legislation of 1976* (Industrial Relations Centre, Victoria University of Wellington, 1974 and 1977), Occasional papers 11 and 21

Young, A. W. 'The New Zealand transport policy study', *NZ Economic Papers*, IX (1975), pp. 1–21

Zanetti, G. N. et al. *Report of the Farm Incomes Advisory Committee to the Minister of Agriculture and Fisheries* (Wellington, 1975)

CHAPTER 17: THE SOCIAL PATTERN

Baker, J. V. T. *The New Zealand People at War: War Economy* (NZ Dept. of Internal Affairs, Wellington, 1965)

Bedggood, David. *Rich and Poor in New Zealand* (Allen and Unwin, Auckland, 1980)

Biggs, Bruce. 'Maori Affairs and the Hunn Report', *JPS*, LXX.3 (1961), pp. 361–4

Borrie, W. D. 'Recent and potential demographic dynamics of Australasia', in K. W. Thomson and A. D. Trlin (eds.), *Contemporary New Zealand: Essays on the Human*

Resource, Urban Growth and Problems of Society (Hicks Smith, Wellington, 1973)

Bryant, George (ed.) *The Widening Gap: Poverty in New Zealand* (Cassell, Auckland, 1979)

Bunkle, Phillida and Hughes, Beryl (eds.) *Women in New Zealand Society* (Allen and Unwin, Auckland, 1980)

Bush, G. W. A. and Scott, Claudia (eds.) *Auckland at Full Stretch* (Auckland City Council and the Board of Urban Studies, University of Auckland, 1977)

Calvert, G. N. *The Future Population of New Zealand: A Statistical Analysis* (Treasury, Wellington, 1946)

Campbell, A. E., Parkyn, G. W. and Ewing, J. L. *Compulsory Education in New Zealand*, 2nd edn. (Unesco, Paris, 1972)

Cant, R. G. (ed.) *Canterbury at Leisure: Studies in Internal Tourism and Recreation* (Canterbury Branch, NZ Geographical Society, 1976)

Chapple, D. L. *Tokoroa: Creating a Community* (Longman Paul, Auckland, 1976)

Colgan, D. M. 'The Maori: integration or subjugation?', in Graham Vaughan (ed.), *Racial Issues in New Zealand* (Akarana Press, Auckland, 1972)

Cumming, Ian and Cumming, Alan. *History of State Education in New Zealand, 1840–1975* (Pitman, Wellington, 1978)

Dakin, J. C. *Education in New Zealand* (Leonard Fullerton, Auckland, 1973)

Donnelly, Felix. *Big Boys Don't Cry* (Cassell, Auckland, 1978)

Easton, Brian. *Consumption in New Zealand, 1954–5 to 1964–5* (NZ Institute of Economic Research, Wellington, 1967), Research paper 10

   'Poverty in New Zealand: estimates and reflections', *PS*, XXVIII.2 (1976) pp. 127–40

   'Women and the personal income distribution', in Rosemary Seymour (ed.), *Research Papers '78: Women's Studies* (Women's Studies Association, Hamilton, 1978)

Elley, W. B. and Irving, J. C. 'Revised socio-economic index for New Zealand', *NZJES*, XI.1 (1976), pp. 25–36

Ensor, Mary. 'The agricultural sector in action: the quest for wool marketing reform, 1964–1972' in Stephen Levine (ed.), *Politics in New Zealand: A Reader* (Allen and Unwin, Sydney, 1978)

Ewing, J. L. *Development of the New Zealand Primary School Curriculum, 1877–1970* (NZCER, Wellington, 1970)

Forster, John (ed.) *Social Process in New Zealand: Readings in Sociology* (Longman Paul, Auckland, 1969)

Fougere, G. M. 'Medical insurance: the market's quiet counter-revolution', in D. W. Beaven and Brian Easton (eds.), *The Future of New Zealand Medicine* (N. M. Peryer, Christchurch, 1974)

Franklin, S. H. 'New Zealand's population in the welfare era, 1901–61', in R. F. Watters (ed.), *Land and Society in New Zealand: Essays in Historical Geography* (Reed, Wellington, 1965)

   Trade, Growth and Anxiety: New Zealand Beyond the Welfare State (Methuen, Wellington, 1978)

Gerard, Jessica. 'Christchurch, 1942: a community at war', research essay, Canterbury (1976)

Gibson, C. J. 'Urbanization in New Zealand: a comparative analysis', *Demography*, X.1 (1973), pp. 71–84

Gilson-Vosburgh, Miriam. *The New Zealand Family and Social Change: A Trend Analysis* (Department of Sociology and Social Work, Victoria University of Wellington, 1978)

Grant, David. *Out in the Cold: Pacifists and Conscientious Objectors in New Zealand during World War Two* (Reed Methuen, Auckland, 1986)

Hamer, Paul. 'A decade of regional imbalance in New Zealand', in P. A. Lane and Paul Hamer (eds.), *Decade of Change: Economic Growth and Prospects in New Zealand, 1960–1970* (Reed, Wellington, 1973)

Hanson, Elizabeth. *The Politics of Social Security* (AUP/OUP, Auckland, 1980)

Hargreaves, R. P. and Heenan, L. D. B. *An Annotated Bibliography of New Zealand Population* (University of Otago Press, Dunedin, 1972)

717

Harker, R. K. 'Social class factors in a New Zealand comprehensive school', in
    G. H. Robinson and B. T. O'Rourke (eds.), *Schools in New Zealand Society: A Book of
    Readings* (John Wiley, Sydney, 1973)
    'A Health Service for New Zealand', *AJHR*, 1974, H.23
Hearn, T. J. and Slater, Frances A. (eds.) *North Otago Region and Development* (Department of
    University Extension, University of Otago, 1973)
Henderson, John. 'The "operational code" of Robert David Muldoon', in Stephen Levine
    (ed.) *Politics in New Zealand: A Reader* (Allen and Unwin, Sydney, 1978)
Hercus, C. E. *Women and National Survival* (Canterbury University College, Christchurch,
    1940)
Hohepa, Pat. 'Maori and Pakeha: the one-people myth', in Michael King (ed.), *Tihe Mauri
    Ora: Aspects of Maoritanga* (Methuen, Wellington, 1978)
Housing in New Zealand (Report of the Commission of Inquiry), *AJHR*, 1971, H.51
Howells, J. M., Woods, N. S. and Young, F. J. L. (eds.) *Labour and Industrial Relations in New
    Zealand* (Pitman, Carlton, Victoria, 1974)
Hunn, J. K. 'Report on Department of Maori Affairs with statistical supplement', *AJHR*,
    1961, G.10
Hyman, Prue. 'Women in the New Zealand labour force', in Rosemary Seymour (ed.),
    Research Papers '78: Women's Studies (Women's Studies Association, Hamilton, 1978),
    pp. 24–36
Johnston, R. J. (ed.) *Urbanisation in New Zealand: Geographical Essays* (Reed, Wellington,
    1973)
Kaim-Caudle, P. R. *Comparative Social Policy and Social Security: A Ten–country Study* (Martin
    Robertson, London, 1973)
Karetu, Sam. 'Kawa in crisis', in Michael King (ed.), *Tihe Mauri Ora: Aspects of Maoritanga*
    (Methuen, Wellington, 1978)
Kawharu, I. H. *Maori Land Tenure: Studies of a Changing Institution* (Clarendon Press, Oxford,
    1977)
Keir, Marie. 'Women and political action: the Women's Electoral Lobby, 1975', in Stephen
    Levine (ed.), *Politics in New Zealand: A Reader* (Allen and Unwin, Sydney, 1978)
Keown, P. A. 'The career cycle and the stepwise migration process (applied to western
    Southland)', *NZG*, xxvii.2 (1971), pp. 175–84
Kernot, Bernard. 'Maori strategies: ethnic politics in New Zealand', in Stephen Levine (ed.),
    New Zealand Politics: A Reader (Cheshire, Melbourne, 1975)
Kilmartin, Leslie and Thorns, David C. *Cities Unlimited: The Sociology of Urban Development
    in Australia and New Zealand* (Allen and Unwin, Sydney, 1978)
Koopman-Boyden, Peggy (ed.) *Families in New Zealand Society* (Methuen, Wellington,
    1978)
Lane, P. A. 'Growth and change', in P. A. Lane and Paul Hamer (eds.), *Decade of Change:
    Economic Growth and Prospects in New Zealand, 1960–1970* (Reed, Wellington, 1973)
Levett, Allan and Braithwaite, Eric. 'The growth of knowledge and inequality in New
    Zealand society', *New Zealand Libraries*, xxxviii.2 (1975), pp. 50–73
Levine, Stephen. *The New Zealand Political System: Politics in a Small Society* (Allen and
    Unwin, Sydney, 1979)
Levine, Stephen and Robinson, Alan. *The New Zealand Voter — A Survey of Public Opinion
    and Electoral Behaviour* (Price Milburn, Wellington, 1976)
Lovell-Smith, J. B. *The New Zealand Doctor and the Welfare State* (Paul, Auckland, 1966)
McDonald, Geraldine. 'Pre-school education and Maori communities: a matter of values',
    in Douglas Bray and Clement Hills (eds.), *Polynesian and Pakeha in New Zealand
    Education*, ii (Heinemann, Auckland, 1974)
McGeorge, Colin. 'Some old wine and some new bottles: religious and moral education in
    New Zealand', *Journal of Moral Education*, iv.3 (1975), pp. 215–33
McKenzie, J. D. S. 'The changing concept of equality in New Zealand education', *NZJES*,
    x.2 (1975), pp. 93–110
McLaren, I. A. *Education in a Small Democracy: New Zealand* (Routledge and Kegan Paul,
    London, 1974)

Metge, Joan. *The Maoris of New Zealand, Rautahi*, 2nd edn. (Routledge and Kegan Paul, London, 1976)

Mitchell, A. V. *Politics and People in New Zealand* (Whitcombe and Tombs, Christchurch, 1969)

National Council of Women in New Zealand. *What Price Equality? Women and Work in New Zealand* (National Council of Women, Dunedin, 1974)

NZ Federation of University Women. *Women at Home: A New Zealand Survey* (Federation of University Women, Wellington, 1976)

NZ Planning Council. *The Welfare State? Social Policy in the 1980's* (Planning Council, Wellington, 1979)

NZ Social Development Council. *Family Finances: Can the Community Do Better?* (Social Development Council, Wellington, 1977)

NZ Task Force on Economic and Social Planning. *New Zealand at the Turning Point* (Task Force, Wellington, 1976)

Neville, R. J. Warwick and O'Neill, C. James (eds.) *The Population of New Zealand: Interdisciplinary Perspectives* (Longman Paul, Auckland, 1979)

Novitz, Rosemary. 'Marital and familial roles in New Zealand: the challenge of the women's liberation movement', in Peggy Koopman-Boyden (ed.), *Families in New Zealand Society* (Methuen, Wellington, 1978)

Palmer, Geoffrey. *Compensation for Incapacity: A Study of Law and Social Change in New Zealand and Australia* (OUP, Wellington, 1979)

Palmer, Geoffrey (ed.) *The Welfare State Today* (Fourth Estate, Wellington, 1977)

Parkyn, G. W. *Success and Failure at the University*, 2 vols. (NZCER, Wellington, 1967)

Pearson, David. *Johnsonville: Continuity and Change in a New Zealand Township* (Allen and Unwin, Sydney, 1980)

Pearson, M. N. 'Heads in the sand: the 1956 Springbok tour to New Zealand in perspective', in Richard Cashman and Michael McKierman (eds.), *Sport in History: The Making of Modern Sporting History* (University of Queensland Press, 1979)

Pitt, David (ed.) *Social Class in New Zealand* (Longman Paul, Auckland, 1977)

Pitt, David and Macpherson, Cluny. *Emerging Pluralism: The Samoan Community in New Zealand* (Longman Paul, Auckland, 1974)

Pocock, J. G. A. 'Meritocracy and mediocracy', *Comment*, I.2 (1960), pp. 13–17

Pool, D. Ian. *The Maori Population of New Zealand, 1769–1971* (AUP/OUP, Auckland, 1977)

'A method for the social grading of areas', *Pacific Viewpoint*, I.2 (1960), pp. 225–34

Rangihau, John. 'Being Maori', in Michael King (ed.), *Te Ao Hurihuri: The World Moves On* (Hicks Smith, Wellington, 1975)

Report of the Commission on Education in New Zealand, *AJHR*, 1962, E.2

Robb, Murray and Howorth, Hilary. *New Zealand Recreation Survey: Preliminary Report* (NZ Council for Recreation and Sport, Wellington, 1977)

The Role of Women in New Zealand Society (Report of the Select Committee), *AJHR*, 1975, I.13

Rowland, D. T. 'Processes of Maori urbanisation', *NZG*, XXVIII.1 (1972), pp. 1–22

Schwimmer, Erik (ed.) *The Maori People in the Nineteen-sixties* (Longman Paul, Auckland, 1968)

Scott, Claudia. *Regional Development Objectives and Policies: An Appraisal* (NZ Planning Council, Wellington, 1980)

Shirley, Ian F. *Planning for Community: The Mythology of Community Development and Social Planning* (Dunmore, Palmerston North, 1979)

Sinclair, Douglas. 'Land since the Treaty: the nibble, the bite, the swallow', in Michael King (ed.), *Te Ao Hurihuri: The World Moves On* (Hicks Smith, Wellington, 1975)

Sinclair, H. I. *Population: New Zealand's Problem* (Gordon and Gotch, Dunedin, 1944)

Smith, A. G. and Tatchell, P. M. *Health Expenditure in New Zealand — Trends and Growth Patterns* (NZ Dept. of Health, Wellington, 1979)

Smith, Thomas B. *The New Zealand Bureaucrat* (Cheshire, Wellington, 1974)

Social Security in New Zealand (Report of the Royal Commission), *AJHR*, 1972, H.53

Social Trends in New Zealand (NZ Dept. of Statistics, Wellington, 1977)
Society for Research on Women in New Zealand, Urban Women (Society for Research on Women, Dunedin, 1972)
Somerset, H. C. D. Littledene: Patterns of Change (NZCER, Wellington, 1974)
Steven, Rob. 'Towards a class analysis of New Zealand', ANZJS, xiv.2 (1978), pp. 113–29
Sutch, W. B. The Responsible Society in New Zealand (Whitcombe and Tombs, Christchurch, 1971)
Taylor, Nancy M. The New Zealand People at War: The Home Front, 2 vols (Historical Publications Branch, Wellington, 1986)
Thompson, Richard. Retreat from Apartheid: New Zealand's Sporting Contacts with South Africa (OUP, Wellington, 1975)
Thomson, K. W. and Trlin, A. D. (eds.) Contemporary New Zealand: Essays on the Human Resource, Urban Growth and Problems of Society (Hicks Smith, Wellington, 1973)
Trlin, A. D. (ed.) Social Welfare and New Zealand Society (Methuen, Wellington, 1977)
Vellekoop, Cora. 'Streaming and social class', in G. H. Robinson and B. T. O'Rourke (eds.), Schools in New Zealand Society: A Book of Readings (John Wiley, Sydney, 1973)
Walsh, A. C. 'Developments since the Hunn Report and their bearing on education', in Douglas Bray and Clement Hill (eds.), Polynesian and Pakeha in New Zealand Education (Heinemann, Auckland, 1973)
Ward, A. B. 'The agricultural sector', in P. A. Lane and Paul Hamer (eds.), Decade of Change: Economic Growth and Prospects in New Zealand, 1960–1970 (Reed, Wellington, 1973)
Wards, Ian (ed.) Thirteen Facets: Essays to Celebrate the Silver Jubilee of Queen Elizabeth the Second, 1952–1977 (Government Printer, Wellington, 1978)
Webb, Stephen D. and Collette, John (eds.) New Zealand Society: Contemporary Perspectives (John Wiley, Sydney, 1973)
Whitehead, C. 'The Thomas Report — a study in educational reform', NZJES, ix.1 (1974), pp. 52–64

CHAPTER 18: A REVOLUTION IN SOCIAL POLICY

Bollard, Alan and Buckle, Robert. Economic Liberalisation in New Zealand (Allen and Unwin, Wellington, 1987)
Boston, Jonathan and Dalziel, Paul (eds.) The Decent Society? Essays in Response to National's Economic and Social Policies (OUP, Auckland, 1992)
Britton, Steve, Le Heron, Richard and Pawson, Eric (eds.) Changing Places in New Zealand: A Geography of Restructuring (NZ Geographical Society, Christchurch, 1992)
Building Economic Growth: Economic Strategy (GP Print, Wellington, 1990); 'Social Reform', pp. 69–104
Building Economic Growth: Social Policy: Welfare State Reform in the 1990 Budget (GP Print, Wellington, 1990)
Davis, Peter (ed.) For Health or Profit? Medicine, the Pharmaceutical Industry, and the State in New Zealand (OUP, Auckland, 1992)
Easton, Brian. Social Policy and the Welfare State in New Zealand (Allen and Unwin, Sydney, 1980)
Gibbs, Alan. Unshackling the Hospitals: Report of the Hospital and Related Services Taskforce (Government Printer, Wellington, 1988)
Glennerster, H. (ed.) The Future of the Welfare State (Heinemann, London, 1983)
Grace, Gerald. Education: Commodity or Public Good? (VUP, Wellington, 1988)
Hawke, Gary R. Report of the Working Group on Post-Compulsory Education and Training (Government Printer, Wellington, 1988)
Hawke, Gary (ed.) A Modest Safety Net? The Future of the Welfare State (Institute of Policy Studies, Wellington, 1991)
Hindess, B. Freedom, Equality and the Market: Arguments on Social Policy (Tavistock, London, 1987)

Holland, Martin and Boston, Jonathan (eds.) *The Fourth Labour Government: Politics and Policy in New Zealand*, 2nd edn. (OUP, Auckland, 1990)

Jesson, Bruce with Ryan, A. and Spoonley, P. *Revival of the Right: New Zealand Politics in the 1980s* (Heinemann Reed, Auckland, 1988)

Learning for Life; One: Education and Training Beyond the Age of Fifteen, Office of the Minister of Education (Government Printer, Wellington, 1989)

Learning for Life; Two: Policy Decisions, Office of the Minister of Education (Government Printer, Wellington, 1989)

Marshall, Thomas H. *Social Policy*, 3rd edn. (Hutchinson, London, 1970)

Meade, E. *Education to be More: Report of the Early Childhood Care and Education Group* (Government Printer, Wellington, 1988)

National Housing Commission. *Housing New Zealand: Provision and Policy at the Crossroads* (Government Printer, Wellington, 1988)

NZ Business Roundtable. *Reforming Tertiary Education in New Zealand* (NZBR, Wellington, 1988)

NZ Council for Educational Research. *How Fair is New Zealand Education?* (NZCER, Wellington, 1987)

Pascal, Gillian. *Social Policy: A Feminist Analysis* (Tavistock, London, 1986)

Prebble, Mark. *Report of the Change Team on Targeting Social Assistance* (GP Books, Wellington, 1991)

Renwick, W. L. (ed.) *Moving Targets: Six Essays on Educational Policy* (NZCER, Wellington, 1986)

Roper, Clinton. *The Report of a Ministerial Committee of Inquiry into Violence* (Government Printer, Wellington, 1987)

Roper, Clinton. *Te Ara Hou: The New Way. Report of the Ministerial Committee of Inquiry into the Prison System* (Government Printer, Wellington, 1989)

Royal Commission on Social Policy. *The April Report*, Volume I, 'New Zealand today'; Volume II, 'Future directions'; Volume III, Parts One and Two, 'Associated papers'; Volume IV, 'Social perspectives' (Government Printer, Wellington, 1988)

Royal Commission on Social Policy. *Towards a Fair and Just Society* (Government Printer, Wellington, 1988)

Scott, Claudia with Fougere, Geoff and Marwick, John. *Choices for Health Care. Report of the Health Benefits Review* (Government Printer, Wellington, 1986)

Shannon, Pat. *Social Policy* (OUP, Auckland, 1991)

Shipley, Jenny, with Upton, S., Smith, L. and Luxton, J. *Social Assistance: Welfare that Works. A Statement of Government Policy on Social Assistance, 30 July 1991* (GP Print, Wellington, 1991)

Spoonley, Paul with Pearson, D. and Shirley, I. *New Zealand Society: A Sociological Introduction* (Dunmore, Palmerston North, 1990)

Thomson, David. *Selfish Generations? The Ageing of New Zealand's Welfare State* (Bridget Williams, Wellington, 1991)

Titmuss, R. M. *Social Policy: An Introduction* (Allen and Unwin, London, 1974)

Tomorrow's Schools: The Reform of Education Administration in New Zealand. Office of the Minister of Education (Government Printer, Wellington, 1988)

Townsend, P. *Sociology and Social Policy* (Penguin, Harmondsworth, 1975)

The Treasury. *Economic Management* (Wellington, 1984); *Government Management* (Wellington, 1987)

Waldegrave, Charles and Frater, P. *The National Government Budget Cuts of the First Year in Office: A Social Assessment* (Family Centre and Business and Economic Research Limited, Wellington, 1991)

Ware, Alan and Goodin, Robert E. *Needs and Welfare* (Sage, London, 1990)

Waring, Marilyn. *Counting for Nothing* (Allen and Unwin, Sydney, 1988)

Watts, R. L. *New Zealand's Universities: Partners in National Development* (NZ Vice-Chancellors' Committee, Wellington, 1987)

Wetere, K. T. *Partnership Perspectives: A Discussion Paper of the Minister of Maori Affairs* (Government Printer, Wellington, 1988)

Williams, Fiona. *Social Policy: A Critical Introduction; Issues of Race, Gender and Class* (Polity, Oxford, 1989)

Wilson, Margaret. *Towards Employment Equity: Report of the Working Group on Equal Employment Opportunities and Equal Pay* (Government Printer, Wellington, 1988)

CHAPTER 19: MĀORI PEOPLE SINCE 1950

Ballara, Angela. *Proud to be White? A Survey of Pakeha Prejudice in New Zealand* (Heinemann, Auckland, 1986)

Bastion Point Judgment, the Judgment of Mr Justice Speight (Department of Lands and Survey, Auckland, 1978)

Baxter, P. and Sansom, B. (eds.) *Race and Social Difference* (Penguin, Harmondsworth, 1972)

Benton, R. *Who Speaks Maori in New Zealand?* (NZCER, Wellington, 1979)

Blank, A., Williams, H. and Henare, M. (eds.) *He Korero mo Waitangi* (Te Runanga Whaka-whanaunga i nga Haahi, Auckland, n.d.)

Boshier, R. *Towards a Learning Society* (Learning Press, Vancouver, 1980)

Elsmore, Bronwyn. *Like Them That Dream. The Maori and the Old Testament* (Tauranga Moana Press, Tauranga, 1985)

Freire, Paulo. *Pedagogy of the Oppressed* (Penguin, Harmondsworth, 1972)

Harre, J. *Maori and Pakeha* (A. H. and A. W. Reed, Auckland, 1966)

Harrison, P. *Whaiora Marae, Te Waiariki Meeting House* (Otara Maori Catholic Society, Otara, 1977)

Hunn, J. K. 'Report on the Department of Maori Affairs with Statistical Supplement', *AJHR*, 1961, G.10

Juvenile Crime in New Zealand (Department of Social Welfare, Wellington, 1973)

Kelsey, Jane. *A Question of Honour? Labour and the Treaty, 1984–1989* (Allen and Unwin, Wellington, 1990)

King, M. (ed.) *Te Ao Hurihuri: The World Moves On* (Hicks Smith/Methuen, Wellington, 1975)

Metge, J. *A New Maori Migration* (Athlone Press, London, 1964)

The Maoris of New Zealand (Routledge and Kegan Paul, London, 1967)

Report of the Waitangi Tribunal on the Muriwhenua Fishing Claim (Wai 22), (Waitangi Tribunal, Department of Justice, Wellington, 1988)

Report of the Waitangi Tribunal on the Orakei Claim (Wai 9) (Waitangi Tribunal, Department of Justice, Wellington, 1987)

Robinson, G. H. and O'Rourke, B. T. (eds.) *Schools in New Zealand Society* (Longman Paul, Auckland, 1980)

Principles for Crown Action on the Treaty of Waitangi (Department of Justice, Wellington, 1989)

Puketapu, K. *Reform from Within* (Department of Maori Affairs, Wellington, 1982)

Report on Maori Education (New Zealand Educational Institute, Wellington, 1967)

Report of the National Advisory Committee on Maori Education (Education Department, Wellington, 1971)

Report of Young Maori Conference (Adult Education Department, University of Auckland, 1939)

Rose, W. D. *The Maori in the New Zealand Economy* (Department of Industry and Commerce, Wellington, 1967)

Simon, Judith. 'The place of schooling in Maori–Pakeha relations', PhD thesis, Auckland (1990)

The Treaty of Waitangi, its Origins and Significance (Extension Department, Victoria University, Wellington, 1972)

Walker, R. *Ka Whawhai Tonu Matou, Struggle Without End* (Penguin, Auckland, 1990)

'Maoris in a metropolis', PhD thesis, Auckland (1970)

Nga Tumanako, Report of the Maori Educational Development Conference (Centre for Continuing Education, University of Auckland, 1984)

722

CHAPTER 20: FROM DUAL DEPENDENCY TO NUCLEAR FREE

Baker, J. V. T. *The New Zealand People at War: War Economy* (Department of Internal Affairs, Wellington, 1965)

Ball, D. (ed.) *The ANZAC Connection* (Allen and Unwin, Sydney, 1985)

Barber, L. H. *Red Coat to Jungle Green: New Zealand's Army in Peace and War* (INL Print, Lower Hutt, 1989)

Bennett, B. S. *New Zealand's Moral Foreign Policy, 1935–1939: The Promotion of Collective Security Through the League of Nations* (New Zealand Institute of International Affairs, Wellington, 1988)

Bentley, G. *RNZAF: A Short History* (Reed, Wellington, 1969)

Bercovitch, J. *ANZUS in Crisis: Alliance Management in International Affairs* (University of Canterbury Press, Christchurch, 1988)

Brown, B. *The Rise of New Zealand Labour: A History of the Labour Party from 1916 to 1940* (Price Milburn, Wellington, 1962)

Burnett, A. *The A-NZ-US Triangle* (ANU, Canberra, 1988)

Chaudron, G. 'New Zealand and the League of Nations', PhD thesis, Canterbury (1989)

Clements, K. *Back from the Brink: The Creation of a Nuclear-free New Zealand* (Allen and Unwin/PNP, 1988)

Day, D. 'Anzacs on the run: the view from Whitehall, 1941–42', *Journal of Imperial and Commonwealth History*, 14:3 (1986), pp. 187–202

Garnier, T. et al. *The Hunter and the Hill: New Zealand Politics in the Kirk Years* (Cassell, Auckland, 1978)

Gillespie, O. H. *The Pacific* (Department of Internal Affairs, Wellington, 1952)

Glover, R. G. *New Zealand in Vietnam: A Study of the Use of Force in International Law* (Dunmore, Palmerston North, 1986)

Gold, H. (ed.) *New Directions in New Zealand Foreign Policy* (Benton Ross, Auckland, 1985)

Gould, J. *The Muldoon Years: An Essay on New Zealand's Recent Economic Growth* (Hodder and Stoughton, Auckland, 1985)

Harker, J. *HMNZS Achilles* (Collins, London and Auckland, 1980)

Harland, W. B. 'New Zealand, the United States and Asia: the background to the ANZUS treaty', in Munz, P. (ed.), *The Feel of Truth: Essays in New Zealand and Pacific History Presented to F. L. W. Wood and J. C. Beaglehole* (Reed, Wellington, 1969)

Henderson, J. et al. *Beyond New Zealand: The Foreign Policy of a Small State* (Methuen, Auckland, 1980)

Hoadley, S. *The New Zealand Foreign Affairs Handbook* (OUP, Auckland, 1989)

Jackson, K. 'New Zealand and Southeast Asia', *Journal of Commonwealth Political Studies*, 9:1 (1971), pp. 3–18

Jennings, P. *The Armed Forces of New Zealand and the ANZUS Split: Costs and Consequences* (New Zealand Institute of International Affairs, Wellington, 1988)

Kay, R. (ed.) *Documents on New Zealand External Affairs*, vol. I, *The Australian-New Zealand Agreement, 1944* (Historical Publications Branch, Wellington, 1922)

    Documents on New Zealand External Relations, vol. II, *The Surrender and Occupation of Japan* (Historical Publications Branch, Wellington, 1982)

    Documents on New Zealand External Relations, vol. III, *The ANZUS Pact and the Treaty of Peace with Japan* (Historical Publications Branch, Wellington, 1985)

Keith, K. J. 'Constitutional change', in I. Wards (ed.), *Thirteen Facets: Essays to Celebrate the Silver Jubilee of Queen Elizabeth the Second, 1952–1977* (Government Printer, Wellington, 1978)

Kennaway, R. *New Zealand Foreign Policy, 1951–1971* (Hicks Smith, Wellington, 1972)

Kirk, N. *New Zealand in the World of the 1970s* (Ministry of Foreign Affairs, Wellington, 1973)

Lange, D. *Nuclear Free — The New Zealand Way* (Penguin, Auckland, 1990)

Larkin, T. C. (ed.) *New Zealand's External Relations* (New Zealand Institute of Public Administration, Wellington, 1962)

Lissington, M. P. *New Zealand and the United States, 1840–1949* (Government Printer, Wellington, 1972)

New Zealand and Japan, 1900–1941 (Government Printer, Wellington, 1972)

McCraw, D. 'Reluctant ally: New Zealand's entry into the Vietnam War', *NZJH*, xv.1 (1981), pp. 49–60

McGibbon, I. C. *Blue-water Rationale: The Naval Defence of New Zealand, 1914–1942* (Historical Publications Branch, Wellington, 1981)

McGibbon, I. C. 'New Zealand's intervention in the Korean War, June–July 1950', *International History Review*, 11:2 (1989), pp. 272–90

McKinnon, M. (ed.) *The American Connection: Essays from the Stout Centre Conference* (Allen and Unwin/PNP, Wellington, 1988)

McIntosh, A. et al. *New Zealand in World Affairs*, vol. I (New Zealand Institute of International Affairs, Wellington, 1977)

McIntyre, W. David. *New Zealand Prepares for War: Defence Policy, 1919–39* (University of Canterbury Press, Christchurch, 1988)

The Rise and Fall of the Singapore Naval Base, 1919–1942 (Macmillan, London, 1979)

McIntyre, W. David and Gardner, W. J. (eds.) *Speeches and Documents on New Zealand History* (Clarendon Press, Oxford, 1971)

McMillan, Stuart. *Neither Confirm nor Deny: The Nuclear Ships Dispute between New Zealand and the United States* (Allen and Unwin/PNP, Wellington, 1987)

Mullins, R. M. 'New Zealand's defence policy', *New Zealand Foreign Affairs Review*, 22:7 (1972), pp. 4–36

Pearson, M. *Paper Tiger: New Zealand's Part in SEATO, 1954–1977* (New Zealand Institute of International Affairs, Wellington, 1989)

Pugh, M. *The ANZUS Crisis, Nuclear Visiting and Deterrence* (Cambridge University Press, Cambridge, 1989)

Ross, A. (ed.) *New Zealand's Record in the Pacific Islands in the Twentieth Century* (Longman Paul, Auckland, 1969)

Ross, J. M. S. *Royal New Zealand Air Force* (Department of Internal Affairs, Wellington, 1955)

Roberts, N. *New Zealand and Nuclear Testing in the Pacific* (New Zealand Institute of International Affairs, Wellington, 1972)

Reese, T. R. *Australia, New Zealand and the United States: A Survey of International Relations* (OUP, London, 1969)

Sinclair, K. (ed.) *Tasman Relations: New Zealand and Australia, 1788–1988* (AUP, Auckland, 1988)

Skudder, S. ' "Bringing it home": New Zealand responses to the Spanish Civil War, 1936–1939', PhD thesis, Waikato (1986)

Taylor, N. M. *The New Zealand People at War: The Home Front*, 2 vols. (Historical Publications Branch, Wellington, 1986)

Templeton, M. *Top Hats Are Not Being Taken: A Short History of the New Zealand Legation in Moscow, 1944–1950* (New Zealand Institute of International Affairs, Wellington, 1989)

Trotter, A. *New Zealand and Japan, 1945–1952* (Athlone Press, London, 1990)

'New Zealanders and the international military tribunal in the Far East', *NZJH*, xxiii.2 (1989), pp. 142–56

'New Zealand in world affairs: Sir Carl Berendsen in Washington, 1944–1952', *International History Review*, 12:3 (1990), pp. 466–89

'Personality in foreign policy: Sir Carl Berendsen in Washington', *NZJH*, xx.2 (1986), pp. 167–80

Waters, S. D. *The Royal New Zealand Navy* (Department of Internal Affairs, Wellington, 1956)

Wood, G. A. 'The former Dominion of New Zealand', *Political Science*, 26:1 (1974), pp. 2–10

Wood, F. L. W. *New Zealand in the World* (Department of Internal Affairs, Wellington, 1940)

Wood, F. L. W. *The New Zealand People at War: Political and External Affairs* (Department of Internal Affairs, Wellington, 1958)

CHAPTER 21: THE AWAKENING IMAGINATION

Alcock, Peter. 'Frame's binomial fall, or fire and four in Waimaru', *Landfall*, xxix.3 (1975), pp. 179–87

'Sons of the brave: a conference of a different kind', *Landfall*, xxxii.4 (1978), pp. 308–14

Alington, William. 'Architecture', in Ian Wards (ed.), *Thirteen Facets: Essays to Celebrate the Silver Jubilee of Queen Elizabeth the Second, 1952–1977* (Government Printer, Wellington, 1978)

Allender, Robert. 'Disordered cinema', *Landfall*, v.4 (1951), pp. 296–304

'The National Film Unit', *Landfall*, ii.4 (1948), pp. 320–7

Anderson, D. M. 'Mr Holcroft's islands', *Landfall*, vi.1 (1952), pp. 5–20

Ausubel, David. 'Race relations in New Zealand', *Landfall*, xii.3 (1958), pp. 233–46

Barber, Bruce. 'Completing the incomplete: a survey of developments in the work of sculptor Greer Twiss', *Islands*, iv.4 (1975), pp. 405–40

Baxter, James K. *Recent Trends in New Zealand Poetry* (Caxton, Christchurch, 1951), reprinted in Frank McKay (ed.), *James K. Baxter as Critic: A Selection of his Literary Criticism* (Heinemann, Auckland, 1973)

Baysting, Arthur (ed.) *The Young New Zealand Poets* (Heinemann, Auckland, 1973)

Beaglehole, Ernest and Pearl. *Some Modern Maoris* (NZCER, Wellington, 1946)

Beaglehole, J. C. 'The National Orchestra', *Landfall*, ii.4 (1948), pp. 307–20

'New Zealand since the war, 4: politics and culture', *Landfall*, xv.2 (1961), pp. 138–52

Beaglehole, J. C. (ed.) *New Zealand and the Statute of Westminster* (Victoria University College, Wellington, 1944)

Beiringa, Luit. 'M. T. Woollaston', in *M. T. Woollaston: Works/1933–1973* (Manawatu Art Gallery, Palmerston North, 1973)

McCahon: 'Religious' Works, 1946–1952 (Manawatu Art Gallery, Palmerston North, 1975)

Bertram, James. *Charles Brasch* (OUP, Wellington, 1976)

Brasch, Charles (ed.) *Landfall Country: Work from* Landfall, *1947–61* (Caxton, Christchurch, 1962)

Brown, Gordon H. 'Patrick Hanly's Pacific Icons', *Ascent* i.1 (1967), pp. 16–23

'The visual arts', in Ian Wards (ed.), *Thirteen Facets: Essays to Celebrate the Silver Jubilee of Queen Elizabeth the Second, 1952–1977* (Government Printer, Wellington, 1978)

Brown, Gordon H. and Keith, Hamish. *An Introduction to New Zealand Painting, 1839–1967* (Collins, Auckland, 1969)

Cape, Peter. *New Zealand Painting since 1960: A Study in Themes and Developments* (Collins, Auckland 1979)

Chapman, R. M. 'Fiction and the social pattern', *Landfall*, vii.1 (1953), pp. 26–58, reprinted in Wystan Curnow (ed.), *Essays on New Zealand Literature*, pp. 71–98 (Heinemann, Auckland, 1973)

Chapman, R. M. and Bennett, Jonathan (eds.) *An Anthology of New Zealand Verse* (OUP, London and Wellington, 1956)

Copland, R. A. *Frank Sargeson* (OUP, Wellington, 1976)

'The New Zealand novels of James Courage', *Landfall*, xviii.3 (1964), pp. 235–49

Curnow, Allen, '*Coal Flat* revisited', in Cherry Hankin (ed.), *Critical Essays on the New Zealand Novel* (Heinemann, Auckland, 1976)

'New Zealand literature: the case for a working definition', in M. F. Lloyd Prichard (ed.), *The Future of New Zealand* (Whitcombe and Tombs, Christchurch, 1963), reprinted in Wystan Curnow (ed.) *Essays on New Zealand Literature* (Heinemann, Auckland, 1973)

Curnow, Allen (ed.) *A Book of New Zealand Verse, 1923–45* (Caxton, Christchurch, 1945; rev. edn., 1951)

The Penguin Book of New Zealand Verse (Penguin, Harmondsworth, 1960)

Curnow, Wystan. 'High culture in a small province', in Wystan Curnow (ed.), *Essays on New Zealand Literature* (Heinemann, Auckland, 1973)

Davis, Frank. *Contemporary Maori Art* (Waikato Art Museum, Hamilton, 1976)

Downes, Peter and Harcourt, Peter. *Voices in the Air: Radio Broadcasting in New Zealand: A Documentary* (Methuen and Radio New Zealand, Wellington, 1976)

Downey, P. J. 'Documentary film in New Zealand', *Landfall*, ix.4 (1955), pp. 343–8

Dudding, Robin (ed.) 'Charles Brasch: tributes and memories', *Islands* ii.3 (1973), pp. 233–62

'In celebration, for Frank Sargeson at 75', *Islands*, vi.3 (1978), pp. 212–360

Dunn, Michael. 'The enigma of Gordon Walters' art', *Art New Zealand*, 9 (1978), pp. 56–63

'Frozen flame and slain tree', *Art New Zealand*, 13 (1979), pp. 40–45

'Present performance: sculpture and painting', *Islands*, ii.4 (1973), pp. 369–80

'Russell Clark', in *Russell Clark: Retrospective Exhibition* (McDougall Art Gallery, Christchurch, 1975)

Dunn, Michael and Vuletic, Petar L. 'Essay on development', in *Milan Mrkusich: Paintings, 1946–1972* (ACAG, 1972)

Edmond, Murray. 'Group theatre', *Islands*, i.2 (1972), pp. 157–62

Ensing, Riemke (ed.) *Private Gardens: An Anthology of New Zealand Women Poets* (Caveman, Dunedin, 1977)

Evans, Patrick. *Janet Frame* (Twayne, Boston, 1977)

'Paradise or slaughterhouse: some aspects of New Zealand proletarian fiction', *Islands*, viii.1 (1980), pp. 71–85

'The provincial dilemma', *Landfall*, xxx.1 (1976), pp. 25–36; xxx.3 (1976), pp. 246–58; xxxi.1 (1977), pp. 9–22

Fairburn, A. R. D. 'The culture industry', *Landfall*, x.3 (1956), pp. 198–211

Fraser, Ross. 'Philip Clairmont: the anachronism of visionary perception', *Art New Zealand*, 1 (1976), pp. 18–20

Grace, Patricia and Ihimaera, Witi. 'The Maori in literature', in Michael King (ed.), *Tihe Mauri Ora* (Methuen, Wellington, 1978)

Hankin, Cherry. 'Language as theme in *Owls Do Cry*', in Cherry Hankin (ed.), *Critical Essays on the New Zealand Novel* (Heinemann, Auckland, 1976)

'Realism, nationalism and the double scale of values in the criticism of New Zealand fiction', *Landfall*, xxxii.4 (1978), pp. 293–303

Harcourt, Peter. *A Dramatic Appearance: New Zealand Theatre, 1920–1970* (Methuen, Wellington, 1978)

Holcroft, M. H. *The Deepening Stream: Cultural Influences in New Zealand* (Caxton, Christchurch, 1940)

Discovered Isles: A Trilogy (Caxton, Christchurch, 1950)

Encircling Seas: An Essay (Caxton, Christchurch, 1946)

Reluctant Editor: The 'Listener' Years, 1949–67 (Reed, Wellington, 1969)

The Waiting Hills (Progressive Publishing Society, Wellington, 1943)

Holloway, Ronald. 'Remembering Bob Lowry', *Landfall*, xviii.1 (1964), pp. 54–8

Horrocks, Roger. 'Directed by Tony Williams', *Islands*, vi.2 (1977), pp. 136–60

Horsman, E. A. 'The art of Frank Sargeson', *Landfall*, xix.2 (1965), pp. 129–34

Hutchings, P. AE. 'Brent Wong: surrealism in a bland landscape', *Islands*, i.2 (1972), pp. 117–36

'The hard-edge abstractions of Gordon Walters', *Ascent*, i.4 (1969), pp. 5–15

Jackson, MacD. P. 'Creative writing', in Ian Wards (ed.), *Thirteen Facets: Essays to Celebrate the Silver Jubilee of Queen Elizabeth the Second, 1952–1977* (Government Printer, Wellington, 1978)

Johnson, Louis. 'Introduction', in Louis Johnson (ed.), *New Zealand Poetry Yearbook*, ii (Reed, Wellington, 1952)

Jones, Lawrence. 'No cowslip's bell in Waimaru: the personal vision of "Owls do cry" ', *Landfall*, xxiv.3 (1970), pp. 280–96

'The persistence of realism: the stories of Dan Davin and Noel Hilliard', *Islands*, vi.2 (1977), pp. 182–200

Kennaway, Richard. *New Zealand Foreign Policy* (Hicks Smith, Wellington, 1972)

McCormick, E. H. 'Eric Lee-Johnson', in Janet Paul (ed.), *Eric Lee-Johnson* (Paul, Hamilton, 1956)

Letters and Art in New Zealand (NZ Dept. of Internal Affairs, Wellington, 1940)

New Zealand Literature: A Survey (OUP, London, 1959)

McEldowney, Dennis. *Frank Sargeson in his Time* (McIndoe, Dunedin, 1976)

'Introduction', in Dennis McEldowney (ed.), *Tidal Creek* (AUP/OUP, Auckland, 1979)

Mackay, Ian K. *Broadcasting in New Zealand* (Reed, Wellington, 1953)

McNaughton, Howard. 'Baxter as dramatist', *Islands*, ii.2 (1973), pp. 184–92

'The plays of Bruce Mason', *Landfall*, xxvii.2 (1973), pp. 102–38

Mason, Bruce. 'Douglas Lilburn's symphonies', *Landfall*, viii.2 (1954), pp. 124–7

'The plays of Claude Evans', *Landfall*, x.1 (1956), pp. 43–8

Mason, Bruce and Pocock, John. *Theatre in Danger: A Correspondence* (Paul, Hamilton, 1957)

Mataira, Katarina. 'Modern trends in Maori art forms', in Erik Schwimmer (ed.), *The Maori People in the Nineteen-sixties* (Paul, Auckland, 1968)

Metge, Joan. *The Maoris of New Zealand: Rautahi*, 2nd edn. (Routledge and Kegan Paul, London, 1976)

Millar, D. P. *Doris Lusk Retrospective* (Dowse Gallery, Lower Hutt, 1973)

Milner, Ian. 'Denis Glover and the Caxton Club', *Islands*, iv.3 (1975), pp. 265–70

Mitchell, Alison. 'Olivia Spencer Bower: biography', in *Retrospective: Olivia Spencer Bower* (Christchurch City Council, 1977)

NZ Department of Internal Affairs. *The New Zealand Literary Fund, 1946–70* (Government Printer, Wellington, 1970)

NZ Planning Council. *A Moment of Truth* (NZ Planning Council, Wellington, 1977)

The Welfare State? Social Policy in the 1980's (NZ Planning Council, Wellington, 1979)

NZ Task Force on Economic and Social Planning. *New Zealand at the Turning Point* (NZ Task Force, Wellington, 1976)

Oliver, W. H. 'An uneasy retrospect', in Ian Wards (ed.), *Thirteen Facets: Essays to Celebrate the Silver Jubilee of Queen Elizabeth the Second, 1952–1977* (Government Printer, Wellington, 1978)

O'Neill, Joseph. 'The Community Arts Service drama', *Landfall*, vii.2 (1953), pp. 133–7

O'Reilly, R. N. 'Introduction', in *Colin McCahon: A Survey Exhibition* (ACAG, 1972)

O'Sullivan, Vincent. ' "Brief permitted morning" — notes on the poetry of Charles Brasch', *Landfall*, xxiii.4 (1969), pp. 338–53

James K. Baxter (OUP, Wellington, 1976)

O'Sullivan, Vincent (ed.) *An Anthology of Twentieth Century New Zealand Poetry*, 2nd edn. (OUP, Wellington, 1976)

Page, Frederick. 'Music', in Ian Wards (ed.), *Thirteen Facets: Essays to Celebrate the Silver Jubilee of Queen Elizabeth the Second, 1952–1977* (Government Printer, Wellington, 1978)

Paul, Janet. 'The Evelyn Page retrospective exhibition', *Landfall*, xxv.1 (1971), pp. 84–9

Pearson, Bill. 'Fretful sleepers', *Landfall*, vi.3 (1952), pp. 201–30, reprinted in Bill Pearson, *Fretful Sleepers and Other Essays* (Heinemann, Auckland, 1973)

'Introduction', in Bill Pearson (ed.), *Brown Man's Burden and Later Stories* (AUP/OUP, Auckland, 1973)

'The Maori and literature 1938–65', in Erik Schwimmer (ed.), *The Maori People in the Nineteen-sixties* (Paul, Auckland, 1968)

'New Zealand since the war, 7: the Maori people', *Landfall*, xvi.2 (1972), pp. 148–80

Phillips, Peter. *A Question of Priorities: New Zealanders in Conversation about their Future* (NZ Commission for the Future, Wellington, 1979)

Rhodes, H. Winston. 'The moral climate of Sargeson's stories', *Landfall*, ix.1 (1955), pp. 25–41

New Zealand Fiction since 1945: A Critical Survey of Recent Novels and Short Stories (McIndoe, Dunedin, 1968)

'Preludes and parables', *Landfall*, xxvi.2 (1972), pp. 135–46

Ritchie, John A. 'Music', in A. L. McLeod (ed.), *The Pattern of New Zealand Culture* (Cornell University Press, Ithaca, 1968)

Roberts, Heather. 'Mother, wife and mistress: women characters in the New Zealand novel from 1920 to 1940', *Landfall*, xxix.3 (1975), pp. 233–47

'Where have all the fathers gone?', *Landfall*, xxxii.2 (1978), pp. 161–7

Ross, James. 'A singular vision: the paintings of Tony Fomison', *Art New Zealand*, 2 (1976), pp. 21–3

Rowe, Neil. 'Brent Wong', *Art New Zealand*, 12 (1978), pp. 42–9

Schwimmer, Erik. 'Commentary', in Louis Johnson (ed.), *New Zealand Poetry Yearbook*, I (Reed, Wellington, 1951), pp. 65–70

Scott, T. H. 'The Frances Hodgkins controversy', *Landfall*, iii.4 (1949), pp. 360–74

'The Pleasure Garden: a postscript', *Landfall*, v.4 (1951), pp. 311–13

Shadbolt, Maurice. 'John Feeney and the National Film Unit', *Landfall*, xii.3 (1958), pp. 226–32

Simpson, E. C. *A Survey of the Arts in New Zealand* (Wellington Chamber Music Society, 1961)

Smart, Peter (ed.) 'Women on women', *Landfall*, xxxiii.2 (1979)

Smith, Peter. *Ralph Hotere: A Survey, 1963–73* (Dunedin Public Art Gallery, 1974)

Smithyman, Kendrick. *A Way of Saying: A Study of New Zealand Poetry* (Collins, Auckland, 1965)

'Wellington and the fifties: the true voice of feeling', in Wystan Curnow (ed.), *Essays on New Zealand Literature* (Heinemann, Auckland, 1973)

Smyth, Bernard. *The Role of Culture in Leisure-time in New Zealand* (Unesco, Paris, 1973)

Stead, C. K. 'Allen Curnow's poetry: notes towards a criticism', *Landfall*, xvii.1 (1963), pp. 26–45, reprinted in Wystan Curnow (ed.), *Essays on New Zealand Literature* (Heinemann, Auckland, 1973)

'From Wystan to Carlos: modern and modernism in recent New Zealand poetry', *Islands*, vii.5 (1979), pp. 467–86

'Towards Jerusalem: the later poetry of James K. Baxter', *Islands*, ii.1 (1973), pp. 7–18

Sturm, Terry. 'Allen Curnow: forty years of poems', *Islands*, iv.1 (1975), pp. 50–71

'The short stories of Maurice Duggan', *Landfall*, xxv.1 (1971), pp. 50–71

Summers, John. 'The Woollaston country: a partisan review', *Ascent*, i.1 (1967), pp. 5–10

Sutherland, I. L. G. (ed.) *The Maori People Today: A General Survey* (NZ Institute of International Affairs and NZCER, Wellington, 1940)

Thompson, Richard. *Race Relations in New Zealand: A Review of the Literature* (National Council of Churches, Christchurch, 1963)

Retreat from Apartheid: New Zealand's Sporting Contacts with South Africa (OUP, Wellington, 1975)

Tomory, P. A. 'Imaginary reefs and floating islands', *Ascent*, i.2 (1968), pp. 5–20

'Looking at art in New Zealand', *Landfall*, xii.2 (1958), pp. 153–69

Turner, Dorothea. 'The National Orchestra', *Landfall*, x.4 (1956), pp. 340–4

Williams, Barry. *Structures and Attitudes in New Zealand Adult Education* (NZCER, Wellington, 1978)

Wilson, Rodney. 'Formal abstraction in post-war New Zealand painting', *Art New Zealand*, 2 (October/November 1976), pp. 13–20

Wood, F. L. W. 'The Anzac dilemma', *International Affairs*, xxix.2 (1953), pp. 184–92

This New Zealand (Paul, Hamilton, 1946)

Woollaston, M. T. *The Far-away Hills: A Meditation on the New Zealand Landscape* (Auckland Gallery Associates, 1962)

'The value of locality in art', *Landfall*, xv.1 (1961), pp, 73–6

Zepke, Nick and Robinson, John. *Goals of New Zealanders: A Discussion Paper* (NZ Commission for the Future, Wellington, 1979)

CHAPTER 22: THE RECOGNITION OF DIFFERENCE

A New Act for the Arts: Reviewing the Queen Elizabeth II Arts Council of New Zealand Act, 1974 (Ministry of Cultural Affairs, Wellington, 1992)

Alcock, Peter. 'Rites of passage: New Zealand poetry in transition, 1985–87', Part 1, *Journal of New Zealand Literature*, 5 (1987), pp. 29–44; Part 2, *Journal of New Zealand Literature*, 6 (1988), pp. 28–48

Alley, Elizabeth. 'An interview with Janet Frame', *Landfall*, 178 (June 1991), pp. 154–68

Arvidson, Ken. 'Curnow, Stead and O'Sullivan: major sensibilities in New Zealand poetry', *Journal of New Zealand Literature*, 1 (1983), pp. 31–48

Balme, Christopher. 'New Maori theatre in New Zealand', *Australasian Drama Studies*, 15/16 (October 1989/April 1990), pp. 149–66

Barnett, Gerald. *Toss Woollaston: An Illustrated Biography* (National Art Gallery, Wellington, 1991)

Barr, Jim and Mary (eds.) *Philip Clairmont* (Sarjeant Art Gallery, Wanganui, 1987)
    Neil Dawson: Site Works, 1981–89 (National Art Gallery, 1989)
    Peter Peryer: Photographs (Sarjeant Art Gallery, Wanganui, 1985)
    When Art Hits the Headlines (National Art Gallery, Wellington, 1987)

Barr, Mary (ed.) *Distance Looks our Way: 10 Artists from New Zealand* (Distance Looks Our Way Trust, Wellington, 1992)
    Headlands: Thinking Through New Zealand Art (Museum of Contemporary Art, Sydney, 1992)

Barrie, Lita. 'Beyond aesthetics: readings in cultural intervention', *Art New Zealand*, 46 (Autumn 1988), pp. 98–102
    'Further toward a deconstruction of phallic univocality: deferrals', *Antic*, 2 (March 1987), pp. 19–47
    'Remissions: toward a deconstruction of phallic univocality', *Antic*, 1 (June 1986), pp. 87–103

Barton, Christina (ed.) *After McCahon: Some Configurations, in Recent Art* (ACAG, Auckland, 1989)

Bassant, Bob. 'Casting off the cultural corset: interview with James Mack', *New Zealand Crafts*, 20 (Autumn 1987), pp. 7–9

Beatson, Peter. *The Healing Tongue: Themes in Contemporary Maori Literature* (Massey University, Palmerston North, 1989)

Bell, Leonard. *The Maori in European Art* (Reed, Wellington, 1980)

Bett, Elva. *New Zealand Art: A Modern Perspective* (Reed/Methuen, Auckland, 1986)

Bieringa, Luit (ed.) *Content/Context: A Survey of Recent New Zealand Art* (National Art Gallery, Wellington, 1986)

Black, Sebastian. 'New Zealand plays, playwrights and theatres: first productions, January–October 1982', *Journal of New Zealand Literature*, 1 (1983), pp. 5–16
    'Oh, to be in Russia: New Zealand playwrights and directors', *Act*, 9 (1984), pp. 62–4

Black, Sebastian (ed.) 'Theatre and drama in New Zealand', *Australasian Drama Studies*, 18 (April 1991)

Blackley, Roger. *Two Centuries of New Zealand Landscape Art* (ACAG, Auckland, 1990)

Blake, Christopher. 'The case for change: strategies for the performing arts', *Music in New Zealand*, 6 (Spring 1989), pp. 8–10

Blumhardt, Doreen and Brake, Brian. *Craft New Zealand: The Art of the Craftsman* (Reed, Wellington, 1981)

Body, Jack. 'A New Zealand composer in Asia', *Landfall*, 143 (September 1982), pp. 312–17
    'The characteristics of New Zealand music in aspects of New Zealand composition, 1950–80', *Canzona*, 4:12 (1982)

Bogle, Andrew. 'Some contemporary New Zealand printmakers and their processes of work', *Art New Zealand*, 14 (1980), pp. 36–43

Bogle, Andrew (ed.) *Rodney Fumpston: One Decade* (ACAG, Auckland, 1983)

Aspects of New Zealand Art: The Grid (ACAG, Auckland, 1983)

Boyd-Bell, Robert. *New Zealand Television: The First 25 Years* (Reed/Methuen, Auckland, 1985)

Brake, Brian, Simmons, David R. and Penfold, Merimeri, (eds.) *Te Maori: Te Hokinga Mai. The Return Home* (ACAG, Auckland, 1986)

Broughton, William. 'Short fiction 1985–87', *Journal of New Zealand Literature*, 6 (1988), pp. 81–95

Brown, Amy Mihi. 'Karanga, karanga', *New Zealand Crafts*, 18 (Spring 1986), pp. 4–6

Brown, Gordon H. 'Aspects of recent New Zealand sculpture', *Art New Zealand*, 41 (Summer 1986–87), pp. 52–5

Colin McCahon: Artist (Reed, Wellington, 1984)

Brown, Gordon H., Curnow, Wystan, Green, Tony and Johnston, Alexa M. (eds.) *Colin McCahon: Gates and Journeys* (ACAG, Auckland 1988)

Brown, Gordon H. and Keith, Hamish. *An Introduction to New Zealand Painting, 1839–1980*, rev. edn. (Collins, Auckland, 1982)

Brunton, Alan. 'A big one! The Penguin book of contemporary New Zealand poetry', *Sport*, 4 (Autumn 1990), pp. 145–58

A Red Mole Sketchbook (VUP, Wellington, 1989)

Burke, Gregory (ed.) *Drawing Analogies: Recent Dimensions in New Zealand Drawing* (Wellington City Art Gallery, Wellington, 1988)

Imposing Narratives: Beyond the Documentary in Recent New Zealand Photography (Wellington City Art Gallery, Wellington, 1990)

Caffin, Elizabeth. 'Ways of saying in recent New Zealand fiction', *Journal of New Zealand Literature*, 2 (1984), pp. 7–16

Carnegie, David. 'Recent New Zealand drama', *Journal of New Zealand Literature*, 3 (1985), pp. 7–16

Clark, Trish and Curnow, Wystan (eds.) *Pleasures and Dangers: Artists of the '90's* (Moet and Chandon NZ Art Foundation/Longman Paul, Auckland, 1992)

Cochrane, Grace. '2nd crafts biennale, Auckland, opening address', *New Zealand Crafts*, 30 (Summer 1989), p. 9–14

Cochrane, Kirsty. 'On the map: Vincent O'Sullivan, Fleur Adcock, Bill Manhire, Ian Wedde', *Journal of New Zealand Literature*, 2 (1984), pp. 59–74

Cooper, Ronda. 'Recent New Zealand poetry', *Journal of New Zealand Literature*, 2 (1984), pp. 23–43

Cooper, Wiremu et al. (eds.) *Taonga Maori: A Spiritual Journey Expressed through Maori Art* (National Museum, Wellington, 1989)

Curnow, Allen. *Look Back Harder: Critical Writings, 1935–1984* (AUP, Auckland, 1987)

Curnow, Allen, Ihimaera, Witi and Woollaston, Sir Tosswill. *New Zealand Through the Arts: Past and Present* (Friends of the Turnbull Library, Wellington, 1982)

Curnow, Wystan (ed.) *I Will Need Words: Colin McCahon's Word and Number Paintings* (National Art Gallery, Wellington, 1984)

'Postmodernism in poetry and the visual arts', *Parallax*, 1 (Spring 1982), pp. 7–28

Putting the Land on the Map: Art and Cartography in New Zealand since 1840 (Govett-Brewster Art Gallery, New Plymouth, 1989)

Sex & Sign, 1987–88 (Artspace, Auckland, 1987)

'Seven painters/the eighties: the politics of abstraction', *Art New Zealand*, 28 (1983), pp. 34–8

'Speech balloons and conversation bubbles', *And*, 4 (October 1985), pp. 125–48

Transformation: Recent Paintings by Max Gimblett (ACAG, Auckland, 1984)

Dale, Judith. 'Women's theatre and why', *Australasian Drama Studies*, 18 (April 1991), pp. 159–82

Dalziel, Margaret. *Janet Frame* (OUP, Wellington, 1980)

Davis, Leigh. 'Set up', *And*, 1 (October 1983), pp. 1–8

'Solo Curnow', *And*, 3 (October 1984), pp. 49–62

Davis, Susan and Haley, Russell (eds.) *The Penguin Book of Contemporary New Zealand Short Stories* (Penguin, Auckland, 1989)

Dennis, Jonathan and Bieringa, Jan (eds.) *Film in Aotearoa/New Zealand* (VUP, Wellington, 1992)

Dix, John. *Stranded in Paradise: New Zealand Rock'n'roll, 1955–88* (Paradise Publications, Wellington, 1988)

Docking, Gil. *Two Hundred Years of New Zealand Painting*, revised edition with additions by Michael Dunn (Reed/Methuen, Auckland, 1990)

Dowling, David. 'Craft interview with Ian Wedde', *Landfall*, 154 (June 1985), pp. 159–81

Dunn, Michael. *A Concise History of New Zealand Painting* (Bateman, Auckland, 1991)

'Content/context: a survey of recent contemporary art', *Art New Zealand*, 42 (Autumn 1987), pp. 40–5

Dunn, Michael (ed.) *Gordon Walters* (ACAG, Auckland, 1983)

Ian Scott Paintings, 1968–1982 (Lopdell Gallery, Waitakere City, 1991)

During, Simon. 'Postmodernism or postcolonialism? *Landfall*, 155 (September 1985), pp. 366–80

'Towards a revision of local critical habits', *And*, 1 (October 1983), pp. 75–92

'What was the west? Some relations between modernity, colonisation and writing', *Sport*, 4 (Autumn 1990), pp. 63–89

Eastmond, Elizabeth and Johnston, Alexa. *Alexis Hunter: Fears, Dreams, Desires* (ACAG, Auckland, 1989)

Eastmond, Elizabeth and Penfold, Merimeri. *Women and the Arts in New Zealand: Forty Works, 1936–86* (Penguin, Auckland, 1986)

Easton, Brian. 'Broadcasting, 1985–90: commercialism vs culture', *Landfall*, 175 (September 1990), pp. 276–90

Edgar, John (ed.) *Bone Stone Shell: New Jewellery New Zealand* (Ministry of Foreign Affairs, Wellington, 1988)

Edmond, Murray. 'Interview with Margaret Mahy', *Landfall*, 162 (June 1967), pp. 164–86

'Lighting out for paradise: New Zealand theatre and the "other" tradition', *Australasian Drama Studies*, 18 (April 1991), pp. 183–206

'Squatter and the making of New Zealand theatre', *Untold*, 9/10 (1988), pp. 16–24

Edmond, Murray and Paul, Mary (eds.) *The New Poets: Initiatives in New Zealand Poetry* (Allen and Unwin, Wellington, 1987)

Eldredge, Charles (ed.) *Pacific Parallels: Art and the Landscape in New Zealand* (NZ/US Art Foundation, Washington, DC, 1991)

Eldred–Grigg, Stevan. 'A bourgeois blue? Nationalism and letters from the 1920s to the 1950s', *Landfall*, 163 (September 1987), pp. 293–311

Evans, Marian, Lonie, Bridie and Lloyd, Tilly (eds.) *A Women's Picture Book* (Government Printer, Wellington, 1988)

Evans, Miriama. 'Politics and Maori literature', *Landfall*, 153 (March 1985), pp. 40–5

Evans, Miriama, McQueen, Harvey and Wedde, Ian (eds.) *The Penguin Book of Contemporary New Zealand Poetry* (Penguin, Auckland, 1989)

Evans, Patrick. 'The muse as rough beast; the autobiography of Janet Frame', *Untold*, 6 (Spring 1986), pp. 1–10

The Penguin History of New Zealand Literature (Penguin, Auckland, 1990)

Friedlander, Marti and Barr, Jim and Mary *Contemporary New Zealand Painters A–M* (Alister Taylor, Martinborough, 1980)

Garrett, Simon (ed.) *He Reo Hou: Five Plays by Maori Playwrights* (Playmarket, Wellington, 1991)

'The plays, playmakers and playhouses of recent New Zealand Theatre', *Australasian Drama Studies*, 18 (April 1991), pp. 30–46

Garrity, T. P. (ed.) *A Tribute to Colin McCahon, 1919–87* (Hocken Library, Dunedin, 1987)

Geraets, John. 'Literary biography in New Zealand', *Journal of New Zealand Literature*, 7 (1989), pp. 87–105

Gilderdale, Betty. *A Sea Change: 145 Years of New Zealand Junior Fiction* (Longman Paul, Auckland, 1982)

Gill, Linda and Pound, Francis (eds.) *After Nature: Gretchen Albrecht: A Survey — 23 Years* (Sarjeant Art Gallery, Wanganui, 1986)

Haley, Russell. *Hanly: A New Zealand Artist* (Hodder and Stoughton, Auckland, 1989)

Harris, Valerie and Norman, Philip (eds.) 'Douglas Lilburn: a festschrift for Douglas Lilburn on his retirement from Victoria University of Wellington', *Canzona*, 1:3 (January 1980)

Hebley, Diana. 'Nightingales and tuis: a survey of New Zealand children's literature in the 1980s', *Landfall*, 171 (September 1989), pp. 340–52

Horrocks, Roger. 'An essay about experimental films that ended up as an essay about New Zealand', *Parallax*, 1 (Spring 1982), pp. 78–89

'' "'Natural' as only you can be": some readings of contemporary New Zealand poetry', *And*, 4 (October 1985), pp. 101–23

New Zealand Film Makers at the Auckland City Art Gallery, 1984–85 (ACAG, Auckland, 1984–1985)

'No theory permitted on these premises', *And*, 2 (1984), pp. 119–37

'Off the map', *Parallax*, 2 (Winter 1983), pp. 247–55

'The invention of New Zealand', *And*, 1 (October 1983), pp. 9–30

'To postulate a ready and understanding reader', *And*, 3 (October 1984), pp. 120–30

Hubbard, George and Craw, Robin. 'Beyond kia ora: the paraesthetics of choice', *Antic*, 8 (December 1990), p. 28

Hulse, Michael. 'When God died: six contemporary poets', *Sport*, 8 (Autumn 1992), pp. 131–8

Ihimaera, Witi and Long, D. S. (eds.) *Into the World of Light: An Anthology of Maori Writing* (Heinemann, Auckland, 1982)

Ireland, Peter (ed.) *Views/Exposures: 10 Contemporary New Zealand Photographers* (National Art Gallery, Wellington, 1982)

Jackson, Mac. 'Interview with Kendrick Smithyman', *Landfall*, 168 (December 1988), pp. 403–20

Johnston, Alexa M. (ed.) *Aspects of New Zealand Art: Anxious Images* (ACAG, Auckland, 1984)

Johnston, Alexa, Wilson, T. L. Rodney and Pitts, Priscilla. *Sculpture, 1986* (ACAG, Auckland, 1986)

Jones, Lawrence. *Barbed Wire & Mirrors: Essays on New Zealand Prose*, 2nd edn. (University of Otago Press, Dunedin, 1990)

'Continuing accomplishment: novels in 1988', *Journal of New Zealand Literature*, 7 (1989), pp. 106–30

'Reflections on a bumper year in fiction', *Journal of New Zealand Literature*, 3 (1985), pp. 17–34

'The one story, two ways of telling, and three perspectives: recent New Zealand literary autobiography', *Ariel*, 16:4 (October 1985), pp. 127–50

Kedgley, Sue (ed.) *Our Own Country* (Penguin, Auckland, 1989)

King, Leo, 'Craft history and criticism', *New Zealand Crafts*, 34 (Summer 1990), pp. 33–8

Kirker, Anne. *New Zealand Women Artists* (Reed/Methuen, Auckland, 1986)

Kirker, Anne (ed.) *Denys Watkins: Printed Images* (National Art Gallery, Wellington, 1984)

Lamb, Jonathon. 'Problems of originality: or, beware pakeha baring guilts', *Landfall*, 159 (September 1986), pp. 352–8

'The uncanny in Auckland', *And*, 4 (October 1985), pp. 32–45

Lambert, Max (ed.) *The Fifth Air New Zealand Almanac, 1989* (New Zealand Press Association, Wellington, 1988)

Leek, Robert-H. 'Homegrown drama of the mid-eighties', *Journal of New Zealand Literature*, 5 (1987), pp. 2–13

'New drama 1986–87: various shades of laughter', *Journal of New Zealand Literature*, 5 (1988), pp. 3–27

Leonard, Robert (ed.) *Nobodies: Adventures of the Ageneric Figure* (National Art Gallery, Wellington, 1989)

Leonard, Robert and Ireland, Peter (eds.) *Nature Morte: 105 Photographs 1971–89 by Laurence Abehart* (National Art Gallery, Wellington, 1990)

Leonard, Robert and McKenzie, Stuart. 'Pathetic projections: wilfulness in the wilderness', *Antic*, 5 (June 1989), pp. 36–48

Loney, Alan (ed.) 'The state of the crafts', *New Zealand Crafts*, 28 (Winter Double Issue, 1989)

McEldowney, Dennis. 'Recent literary biography', *Journal of New Zealand Literature*, 2 (1984), pp. 47–58

McIntosh, Jill (ed.) *Contemporary New Zealand Prints* (Allen and Unwin/PNP, Wellington, 1989)

McKessar, Paul. 'Flying Nun Records', *Music in New Zealand*, 2 (Spring 1988), pp. 26–30

McLeod, Marian and Wevers, Lydia (eds.) *Women's Work: Contemporary Stories by New Zealand Women* (OUP, Auckland, 1985)

McNaughton, Howard. 'Historical elements in recent New Zealand drama', *Journal of New Zealand Literature*, 2 (1984), pp. 17–22

Mahy, Margaret. 'A dissolving ghost: possible operations of truth in children's books and the lives of children', *Sport*, 7 (Winter 1991), pp. 5–24

Manhire, Bill. 'Breaking the line: a view of American and New Zealand poetry', *Islands*, 38 (December 1987), pp. 142–54

Maurice Gee (OUP, Auckland, 1986)

Marquis, Claudia. 'Telling tales out of school: "young adult" fiction in New Zealand', *Landfall*, 179 (September 1991), pp. 329–50

Mataira, Katarina. *Maori Artists of the South Pacific* (Nga Puna Waihanga, Raglan, 1984)

Mead, Sidney Moko (ed.) *Te Maori: Maori Art from New Zealand Collections* (Heinemann, Auckland, 1984)

Morison, Julia. *Vademecum and Golem* (Artis Gallery, Auckland, 1986)

Morrissey, Michael (ed.) *The New Fiction* (Lindon, Auckland, 1985)

Nealie, Chester (ed.) *Ceramics '86: Contemporary Works in Clay* (Govett-Brewster Gallery, New Plymouth, 1986)

Needham, John. 'Recent poetry and Coleridgean principles', *Journal of New Zealand Literature*, 3 (1985), pp. 35–56

Nicholas, Darcy and Kaa, Keri. *Seven Maori Artists* (Government Printer, Wellington, 1986)

Norman, Philip (ed.) 'Aspects of New Zealand composition', *Canzona*, 3:10 (November 1981)

Novitz, David and Willmott, Bill. *Culture and Identity in New Zealand* (GP Books, Wellington, 1989)

O'Brien, Gregory and Cross, Robert. *Moments of Invention: Portraits of 21 New Zealand Writers* (Heinemann/Reed, Auckland, 1988)

O'Sullivan, Vincent (ed.) *An Anthology of Twentieth Century New Zealand Poetry*, 3rd edn. (OUP, Auckland, 1987)

Panoho, Rangihiroa. *W.A.R.: Whatu Aho Rua* (Sarjeant Gallery, Wanganui, 1989)

Paul, Janet et al. (eds.) *Rita Angus* (National Art Gallery, Wellington, 1982)

Parkinson, Cecilia and Parker, John. *Profiles: 24 New Zealand Potters* (Bateman, Auckland, 1988)

Pendergrast, Mick. *Feathers and Fibre: A Survey of Traditional and Contemporary Maori Craft* (Penguin, Auckland, 1984)

Perry, Nick. 'Common coinage — Telethon and cultural criticism in New Zealand', *Landfall*, 149 (March 1984), pp. 89–103

Pittway, Gail. 'Inscapes and escape: novels by New Zealand women, 1986–87', *Journal of New Zealand Literature*, 6 (1988), pp. 49–57

Potiki, Roma. 'A Maori point of view: the journey from anxiety to confidence', *Australasian Drama Studies*, 18 (April 1991), pp. 57–63

Pound, Francis (ed.) *Aspects of New Zealand Art: New Image* (ACAG, Auckland, 1983)

Forty Modern New Zealand Paintings (Penguin, Auckland, 1985)

Frames on the Land: Early Landscape Painting in New Zealand (Collins, Auckland, 1983)

'Harsh clarities: meteorological and geographical determinism in New Zealand art commentary refuted', *Parallax*, 2 (Winter 1983), pp. 263–9

'Nationalist antipathies: a compendium', *Antic*, 1 (June 1986), pp. 73–84

NZXI (ACAG, Auckland, 1988)

Richard Killeen: Two Signwriters, Two Fathers (Peter McLeavey Gallery, Wellington, 1991)

Signatures of Place: Paintings & Place-names (Govett-Brewster Art Gallery, New Plymouth, 1991)

'The real and the unreal in New Zealand painting', *Art New Zealand*, 25 (1982), pp. 42–7

Pound, Francis and Barr, Jim and Mary. *Julian Dashper* (Sue Crockford Gallery, Auckland, n.d. [1991])

Puketapu-Hetet, Erenora. *Maori Weaving* (Pitman, Auckland, 1989)

Ramsden, Irihapeti et al. (eds.) *Mana Tiriti: The Art of Protest and Partnership* (Brassell, Wellington, 1991)

Rees, Nonnita. ' "Getting New Zealand writing into theatres": the story of Playmarket', *Australasian Drama Studies*, 3:1 (October, 1984), pp. 23–30

Reid, Nicholas. *A Decade of New Zealand Film* (McIndoe, Dunedin, 1986)

Ricketts, Harry. *Talking About Ourselves: Twelve New Zealand Poets in Conversation* (Mallinson Rendel, Wellington, 1986)

Roberts, Heather. *Where Did She Come From? New Zealand Women Novelists, 1862–1987* (Allen and Unwin/PNP, Wellington, 1989)

Roberts, John. 'The new Museum of New Zealand: thoughts on museological strategies', *Art New Zealand*, 56 (Spring 1990), pp. 94–7

Roddick, Alan. *Allen Curnow* (OUP, Wellington, 1980)

Ross, J. C. 'Growth in all directions: novels by men, 1986–87', *Journal of New Zealand Literature*, 6 (1988), pp. 58–80

Ross, James and Simmons, Laurence (eds.) *Gordon Walters: Order and Intuition* (the editors, Auckland, 1989)

Rowe, Neil. *Hanly: The Painter as Printmaker* (Wairarapa Arts Centre, Masterton, 1981)

Schulz, Derek (ed.) *Seven Painters: The Eighties* (Sarjeant Art Gallery, Wanganui, 1982)

Simmons, Laurence. ' "Language is not neutral": Killeen's feminism', *Antic*, 7 (June 1990), pp. 75–94

Simpson, Peter. 'Allen Curnow talks to Peter Simpson', *Landfall*, 175 (September, 1990), pp. 296–313

'All in the family: continuum of discourse in recent New Zealand criticism', *Ariel*, vol. 16, no. 4 (October 1985), pp. 3–26

'Recent fiction and the Sargeson tradition', *Journal of New Zealand Literature*, 1 (1983), pp. 17–29

Ronald Hugh Morrieson (OUP, Auckland, 1982)

'What is it makes the stranger? Making it strange in some New Zealand texts', *Untold*, 6 (Spring 1986), pp. 38–43

Smart, Jonathan and Lauder, Hugh. 'Ideology and political art in New Zealand: a radical view', *Landfall*, 153 (March 1985), pp. 81–100

Smithyman, Kendrick. 'Singing to the ancestors: some aspects of recent poetry in New Zealand', *Journal of Commonwealth Literature*, 17 (1982), pp. 28–44

Standring, Douglas. 'Inside and out: recent short fiction', *Sport*, 3 (Spring 1989), pp. 139–48

Stead, C. K. *Answering to the Language: Essays on Modern Writers* (AUP, Auckland, 1989)

In the Glass Case: Essays on New Zealand Literature (AUP/OUP, Auckland, 1981)

Sturm, Terry (ed.) 'Guest editorial', *Australasian Drama Studies*, 3:1 (1984), pp. 3–4

The Oxford History of New Zealand Literature in English (OUP, Auckland, 1991)

Taylor, Apirana and Burke, Rod. 'Kohia ko taikaka anake at the National Art Gallery', *Art New Zealand*, 58 (Autumn 1991), pp. 58–64

Thomson, John. *New Zealand Drama, 1930–80: An Illustrated History* (OUP, Auckland, 1984)

Thomson, John Mansfield. *Biographical Dictionary of New Zealand Composers* (VUP, Wellington, 1990)

The Oxford History of New Zealand Music (OUP, Auckland, 1991)

Thompson, Mervyn. 'Promise and frustration: New Zealand playwrighting since 1975', *Australasian Drama Studies*, 3:1 (October, 1984), pp. 122–8

Singing the Blues (Blacktown, Christchurch, 1991)

Tonks, Joy. *The New Zealand Symphony Orchestra: The First Forty Years* (Reed/Methuen, Auckland, 1986)

Tweedie, Merylyn. *Six Women Photographers* (Photoforum, Auckland, 1987)

Watson, John. 'From Mansfield to Svensson: the female hero in recent short fiction by women writers', *Journal of New Zealand Literature*, 7 (1989), pp. 44–64

Watson, Ruth. 'Much ado about some bodies: adventures in the shed', *Antic*, 6 (November 1989), pp. 5–11

Wedde, Ian. 'The Penguin: texts and contexts', *Span*, 19 (October, 1984), pp. 46–63

Wedde, Ian and Burke, Gregory (eds.) *Now See Hear!: Art, Language and Translation* (VUP, Wellington, 1990)

Wedde, Ian and McQueen, Harvey (eds.) *The Penguin Book of New Zealand Verse* (Penguin, Auckland, 1985)

Wevers, Lydia (ed.) *New Zealand Short Stories: Fourth Series* (OUP, Auckland, 1984)

Yellow Pencils: Contemporary Poetry by New Zealand Women (OUP, Auckland, 1988)

Wilcox, Leonard. 'Postmodernism or antimodernism?', *Landfall*, 155 (September, 1985), pp. 344–64

Williams, Mark. 'An interview with Witi Ihimaera', *Landfall*, 179 (September, 1991), pp. 281–97

Leaving the Highway: Six New Zealand Novelists (AUP, Auckland, 1990)

'Literary recession: New Zealand fiction, 1985–86', *Journal of New Zealand Literature*, 5 (1987), pp. 14–28

'On the margins: New Zealand little magazines from *Freed* to *And* ', *Journal of New Zealand Literature*, 5 (1987), pp. 73–91

'Repetitious beginnings: literary history in the late 1980s', *Journal of New Zealand Literature*, 7 (1989), pp. 65–86

Williams, Mark (ed.) *The Caxton Press Anthology: New Zealand Poetry, 1972–1986* (Caxton, Christchurch, 1987)

Wilson, T. L. Rodney (ed.) *Ewe & Eye: Barry Cleavin, Prints and Drawings, 1966–81* (ACAG, Auckland, 1982)

Wilson, T. L. Rodney and Leech, Peter. *Milan Mrkusich: A Decade Further On, 1974–83* (ACAG, Auckland, 1985)

Zepke, Stephen. 'Difference without binary oppositions: a chance for a choice!', *Antic*, 8 (December 1990), p. 29

'Repetitions: towards a re-construction of phallic univocality', *Antic*, 7 (June 1990), pp. 41–56.

Index

Note: Writers and artists mentioned in the last two chapters are indexed only selectively. See also the relevant subject headings: Architecture; Art galleries; Arts; Autobiography; Ballet; Carving, Māori; Children's literature; Crafts; Exhibitions; Fiction; Films; Historiography; Music; Painting; Photography; Poetry; Print-making; Sculpture; Social and literary criticism; Theatre.

Doyle, Edward, 42
Dress: and social status, 121–2
Dry, F. W., 238
Duckworth, Marilyn, 547, 575
Duff, Oliver, 334, 558
Duggan, Eileen, 324, 545
Duggan, Maurice, 546–7
Dunedin, 80
Dunn, Robert, 323
Dutch immigration. *See* Immigration

Earle, Augustus, 131
East and West Coast Railway League, 108
Economy: (1840–90s), 57–85; (1890s–1920s), 230–44; (1930s), 245–53; (later 1930s–mid-50s), 412–15; (mid-1950s–1960s), 415–36; (1970s–1984), 436–8; (1984–90), 438–40; (1990–), 444–7. *See also* Depression; Exports; Farming; Finance; Imports; Industry
Economy, Māori: (–1769), 3, 9–10, 18, 20–22, 26; (1769–1840), 35–6, 39–40; (*c.* 1840–*c.* 1890), 145, 163; (*c.* 1890–) 289–93, 305
Edmond, Lauris, 566, 574, 576
Education: (1870s–90s), 132–3; (1890s–1930s), 276–7, 321, 325–6; (later 1930s–40s), 329–30, 359; (1950s–70s), 465–9; (1980s), 490–1; (1990s), 495–6. *See also* Schools
Education, Māori, 143–4, 163–4, 288–9, 469, 478–9, 507–9
Education, 558
Education Department. *See* Government departments
Elections: by-elections (1913) 216, (1918) 218, (1977) 394, (1980) 353, 396; 'country quota', 107, 354, 369; general elections (1853) 93, (1887) 109–10, (1890) 111, 202, 203–4, (1893) 206, (1911) 214, 216, (1914) 216, (1919) 218, (1922) 221, (1925) 222, (1928) 223, 327, (1931) 224, 300, (1935) 225, 279, 300, 352–4, (1938) 364, (1943) 368, (1946) 369–70, (1949) 372–3, (1951) 375, (1954) 376–7, (1957) 379, (1960) 381, (1963) 382, (1966) 382–3, (1969) 383–4, (1972) 384, 385–8; (1975) 391–2; (1978) 395; (1981) 398–9; (1984) 401–2, 438; (1987) 405–6; (1990) 408–9; procedures, 95–7; second ballot, 214; secret ballot, 95–6, 300. *See also* Franchise
Elizabeth, 42, 44
Elliott, Howard, 218–19
Ellison, Edward Pohua, 294
Elwood, Brian, 492
Emigration, 84, 113, 383, 455
Employers, regional associations of, 210, 278
Employers Federation, New Zealand, 210, 213
Employment, 212, 224, 356, 366–73 *passim*, 381–4 *passim*, 438, 450, 464, 471. *See also* Labour force; Occupational and social mobility
Encyclopedia of New Zealand, 323
Endeavour, 13, 18

English immigration. *See* Immigration, British
European Economic Community, 384, 386, 436–7, 521
Exchange control. *See* Finance
Exhibitions, 131, 304, 334, 548–52 *passim*, 581–3 *passim*
Exports: British market, 76, 230–1, 236, 378, 412–13, 416, 417, 436–7; bulk purchase, 414–15; commandeer system, 217, 231; dairy produce, 230, 236, 357, 412–20 *passim*, 422; diversification, 413, 416, 417, 437, 537; forestry products, 416, 422; gold, 66–7, 74; guaranteed price system, 222, 226, 240, 352, 357, 371, 378, 418, 419; manufactured goods, 416, 417; by Māori, 145; marketing, 222, 239–41, 357, 371, 378, 418–19, 439, 441; meat, 78, 80–1, 230, 236, 412–20 *passim*, 422; wheat, 79; wool, 70, 74, 78, 230, 241, 373, 412–20 *passim*, 435–6. *See also* Farming; Prices, export
Eyre, Edward (Lieutenant-Governor), 92

Fairburn, A. R. D., 324, 331, 545, 561
Family: Māori, 8, 305; nuclear, 263–4, 280, 312; role of, 472; rural, 263, 281; Samoan ('*aiga*), 457; size, 263, 265, 454. *See also* Benefits; Social structure, Māori; Women
Farmers' Union. *See* New Zealand Farmers' Union
Farming: arable, 233–4; capital development, 420–1; cattle, 419; dairy, 73, 82, 220–1, 223, 233–4, 236–7, 260, 261, 293, 320, 327–8, 358, 460–2, 419; family farms, 233–4, 236, 260, 261, 320, 460; intensive, 234; Māori, 35–6, 145, 152, 165–6, 290–3, 296–8 *passim*; management, 421; mechanization, 79, 236–7, 420–1, 455; number of holdings, 460, 461; productivity per man, 420; scientific development, 79, 236–9, 421; sheep, 62–4, 70, 80, 233, 236, 414; state activity in, 82, 222, 237–8, 242–3, 292, 358, 419, 431; subsistence, 61, 73–4, 78, 81–2, 165, 233, 251, 261, 290; wheat, 35–6, 79, 298, 419. *See also* Exports; Industry, primary; Labour force
'Fatal impact' theory. *See* Race relations
Featherston, Isaac, 92, 99, 100, 102
Federal Council for Australasia, 342
Federation of Labour ('Red Feds'). *See* Trade unions
Feilding Community Centre, 329–30
Fels, Willi, 311
Feltex New Zealand Ltd., 422
Fenton, F. D. (Chief Judge), 194
Fertility. *See* Births
Fiction, 315–18 *passim*, 323–4, 332–4, 545–8, 555, 563, 564, 574–6
Field, R. N., 323, 330
Fiji, 342
Films, 321, 555, 559, 561, 578–9
Finance: balance of payments, 74, 77–8, 282, 380, 412, 413, 421, 431, 434; capital

Radio, 321–2, 329, 382, 558, 579–80
Radio Record, 558
Raglan golf course, 513
Railways. *See* Public works programmes;
 Transport
Rainbow Warrior, 404, 536, 571
Raine, Thomas, 34
Ralfe, Catherine, 113
Ramsay, David, 34
Randerson, Glenda, 568, 582
Rangiaowhia, 156
Rangihau, John, 302
Rata, Matiu, 397, 409, 511, 514
Ratana, Tahupotiki Wiremu, 298–300
Ratana, Tokouru, 299, 300
Ratana Party, 299–301, 306, 351–2, 499–500,
 514
Raureti, Moana, 302
Read, Gabriel, 66
Recreation, 129–31, 262, 321, 476–7
Red Cross Society (International), 278, 282, 303
'Red Feds', 212, 215–16, 221, 273, 278, 279,
 283. *See also* Trade unions
Rees, W. L., 192
Reeves, William Pember, 80, 86, 110, 206–11
 passim, 313, 314, 315
Reform Associations, 110
Reform Government, 214, 219–20, 235, 242,
 291, 297
Reform Party, 202, 210–29 *passim*, 299, 361–3
 passim
Refrigeration, 78, 80, 230, 236, 260, 412
Regionalism: and the economy, 64–7, 75, 76,
 78, 425, 433; and provincial government,
 72, 74, 94, 99, 100–5; regional
 development, 73–4, 384, 424–5, 457–8; and
 settlement, 115–16, 119–20, 127, 221, 308
Regulations: land (1851) 63, (1853) 64;
 manpower (1940), 289, 500; waterfront
 strike emergency (1951), 374
Rehabilitation assistance: farming, 220, 231,
 291, 460; loans and education, 303–4, 369;
 and Māori, 302, 303, 303–4
Religion: in nineteenth century, 127–9;
 observance of, 122, 126–7, 144, 269–70;
 sectarianism, 213, 219, 271, 279, 312; in
 twentieth century, 268–72. *See also*
 Churches; Missionaries
Religion, Māori: pre-European, 16–17;
 nineteenth-century, 36–9, 143–5, 157, 163;
 twentieth-century, 294, 298–9. *See also*
 Missionaries; Pai Marire; Papahurihia;
 Ratana, Tahupotiki Wiremu; Te Whiti O
 Rongomai; Wairua Tapu
Repudiation movement, 162
Reserve Bank of New Zealand, 246, 248–9,
 252, 352–3, 356–7, 430, 442
Responsible government. *See* Government,
 responsible
Returned servicemen, 220, 231, 291, 298, 303–
 4, 368, 540. *See also* Rehabilitation
 assistance

Returned Servicemen's Association, 282
Rewi Maniopoto, 155, 156, 159, 164
Rhodes, H. Winston, 331, 556
Rhodes, R. H., 214
Rhodes, W. B., 35
Richardson, Sir Ivor, 486
Richardson, Ruth, 408, 409
Richmond, C. W., 101, 138
Richmond, Dorothy K., 323
Richmond, James C., 103, 131, 139
Richmond, Mathew, 90
Rimmer, John, 553, 580
Ringatū, 157, 188, 325
Ritchie, J. M., 69
Roads. *See* Public works programmes;
 Transport
Roberts, James, 221
Robinson, John, 97
Rolleston, William, 103, 107, 108, 161, 208
Roman Catholics. *See* Churches; Missionaries
Ropata Wahawaha, 156, 166
Ropiha, Tapi, 301, 302
Rowling, W. E., 390, 392, 397, 400, 513, 534
Royal, Rangi, 302, 507
Royal Society of New Zealand. *See* New
 Zealand Institute
Royal visits, 304, 504, 569
Royalist, 531
Rua Kenana, 161, 294
Ruatara, 35, 36
Rugby football, 262, 284, 304, 477. *See also* All
 Blacks; Springbok tours
Rugby League, 477
Rūnanga. *See* Maori councils
Runciman, William, 129
Rushworth, Henry, 220
Russell, Andrew (Major-General), 345
Russell, Lord John (Colonial Secretary), 146
Russell, Thomas, 65, 67, 68, 77, 78, 105
Russell, W. R., 162, 208–9
Rutherford, Duncan, 84
Rutherford, Ernest, 317
Rutherford, George, 64
Rutherford, John, 47

St Helen's Maternity Hospital, 267
St John's Theological College, 157
St Stephen's College, 144, 163, 166
Salaries. *See* Wages
Salmond, Anne, 576
Salvation Army. *See* Churches
Samoans. *See* Immigration, Pacific Islanders
Sargeson, Frank, 333–5 *passim*, 545–6, 554,
 574, 576
Satchell, William, 315
Savage, Michael Joseph, 228, 300, 318, 331,
 355, 365–6, 412, 522, 524
Scales, Flora, 323, 330
Scandinavians. *See* Immigration
Scanlan, Nelle, 324
'Scarecrow' Ministry, 110
Schola Musica, 580